Tolley's
Health and Safety
at Work
Handbook
2000

Tolley's Health and Safety at Work Handbook 2000

Twelfth Edition

Crown copyright material is reproduced with the permission
of the Controller of Her Majesty's Stationery Office.

Published by
Tolley
2 Addiscombe Road
Croydon Surrey CR9 5AF England
0181-686 9141

Typeset in Great Britain by
Letterpart Limited
Reigate, Surrey

Printed in Great Britain by
Rexam Digital Imaging Ltd,
Reading

ꝶ A member of the Reed Elsevier plc group

ISBN 0 75450 139-6

List of Contributors

Ron Akass, TD, MIOSH, RSP, Senior Partner, Lonsdale Safety & Business Consultants

Sally Andrews, LLB, LLM, Solicitor, Cartwrights

Mike Bateman, BSc, MIOSH, RSP, Independent Health and Safety Consultant

Janet Braune, LLB, Barrister

Alison Brown, LLB, MIOSH, Solicitor, Cameron McKenna

David Brown, BA, Solicitor, Partner, Nicholson Graham & Jones

Martin Bruffell, LLB, Partner, Berrymans Lace Mawer

Kitty Debenham, BA (Oxon), Solicitor, Simmons & Simmons

Malcolm Dewis, LLB (Lond), FIISRM, MIOSH, Independent Health and Safety Consultant

Christopher Eskell, TD, LLB, MIMgt, Partner, Cartwrights

Janet Gaymer, MA (Oxon), LLM (Lond), Partner, Simmons & Simmons

Andrew Gilbert, LLB, Partner, Kennedys

Dorothy Henderson, BA, Partner, Travers Smith Braithwaite

Rhiannon Hughes, BA, Solicitor, Cameron McKenna

Mariel Irvine, BA (Dubl), Dip Law, Solicitor, Kennedys

Ian Jerome, BSc, Senior Consultant, Education and Training, Loss Prevention Council

Andrew Leaitherland, LLM, Partner, Davies Wallis Foyster

Joanne Lunn, BA, MPhil, Solicitor, Senior Law Lecturer, Manchester Metropolitan University

Kate Murphy, M Env Law, Sustainability Advisory Services, KPMG

Peter Neild, LLB, Solicitor, Berrymans Lace Mawer

Samuel Nerdal, Civil Engineer, Amtri Veritas Ltd

Cathy Nolan, BSc, Grad Dip OH & S, Grad Dip Occ Hyg, MIOSH, MAIOH

Andrea Oates, BSc, Health and Safety Researcher, Labour Research Department

Fred Osliff, MIOSH, MISTC, Partner, Penmen & Co

George Pitblado, I Eng, MI Plant E, MIIRSM, MWM Soc, Partner, GMP Support Services Consultants

Laura Pitman, BA (Cantab), Solicitor, Travers Smith Braithwaite

Adrian Ramsey, Cert Ed, Partner, Immediate Response UK

Mary Spear, BA (Cantab), Solicitor, Cartwrights

Roger Tompsett, BSc(Eng), MIOA, Head of Acoustics, WS Atkins Noise & Vibration

Mark Tyler, MA, LLM, MIOSH, Partner, Cameron McKenna

George Ventris, formerly secretary of the HSC's Construction Industry Advisory Committee (CONIAC) and a leader of HSE's Construction National Interest Group

Jeffrey Wale, LLB, Partner, Berrymans Lace Mawer

Allan Weir, MA, C Eng, MIOSH, Health and Safety Consultant

Nigel Williams, MA (Cantab), Partner, Cartwrights

Contents

Contents

First-Aid

Health and Safety Commission and Executive

Joint Consultation – Safety Representatives and Safety Committees

Lifting Machinery and Equipment

List of Tables

List of Illustrations/Diagrams

Abbreviations and References

Many abbreviations occur only in one section of the book and are set out in full there. The following is a list of abbreviations used more frequently or throughout the book.

Organisations/Publications

ACAS	=	Advisory, Conciliation and Arbitration Service
ACOP	=	Approved Code of Practice
BS	=	British Standard
BSC	=	British Safety Council
CBI	=	Confederation of British Industry
Cmnd	=	Command Paper
COIT	=	Central Office of the Industrial Tribunals
CPS	=	Crown Prosecution Service
DSS	=	Department of Social Security
EU	=	European Union
HMIP	=	HM Inspectorate of Pollution (now part of the Environment Agency)
HSC	=	Health and Safety Commission
HSE	=	Health and Safety Executive
HMSO	=	Her Majesty's Stationery Office
HSIB	=	Health and Safety Information Bulletin
ILO	=	International Labour Office
IOSH	=	Institution of Occupational Safety and Health
JCT	=	Joint Contracts Tribunal
MoD	=	Ministry of Defence
RoSPA	=	Royal Society for the Prevention of Accidents
TUC	=	Trades Union Congress

Statutes/Statutory Instruments

CHIP	=	Chemicals (Hazard Information and Packaging for Supply) Regulations 1994 as amended
COSHH	=	Control of Substances Hazardous to Health Regulations 1994
CPA	=	Consumer Protection Act 1987
EA	=	Environment Act 1995
EPA 1990	=	Environmental Protection Act 1990
EPCA	=	Employment Protection (Consolidation) Act 1978
ERA	=	Employment Rights Act 1996
FA	=	Factories Act 1961
FSA 1990	=	Food Safety Act 1990
HSWA	=	Health and Safety at Work etc. Act 1974
OLA	=	Occupiers' Liability Act 1957
OSRPA	=	Offices, Shops and Railway Premises Act 1963
TURERA	=	Trade Union Reform and Employment Rights Act 1993
UCTA	=	Unfair Contract Terms Act 1977
Reg	=	Regulation (or Statutory Instrument)
SI	=	Statutory Instrument
SR&O	=	Statutory Rule and Order
Sch	=	Schedule
s or Sec	=	Section

Case citations

AC	=	Appeal Cases
AER	=	All England Reports
ALJR	=	Australian Law Journal Reports
Camp	=	Campbell Reports
CB, NS	=	Common Bench, New Series (ended 1865)
Ch	=	Chancery Reports
CL	=	Current Law
CLY	=	Current Law Year Book
CMLR	=	Community Law Reports
COD	=	Crown Office Digest
Con LR	=	Construction Law Reports
Cr App R	=	Criminal Appeal Reports
Crim LR	=	Criminal Law Review
East	=	East's Term Reports
EG	=	Estates Gazette
Env LR	=	Environmental Law Reports
Exch	=	Exchequer Reports
F & F	=	Foster & Finlayson (ended 1867)
H & C	=	Hurlstone & Norman
HSIB	=	Health and Safety Information Bulletin
ICR	=	Industrial Cases Reports
IRLR	=	Industrial Relations Law Reports
JP	=	Justice of the Peace and Local Government Review
KB/QB	=	Law Reports, King's (Queen's) Bench Division
KIR	=	Knight's Industrial Reports
LGR	=	Local Government Reports
LJKB	=	Law Journal Reports – New Series, Kings Bench
Lloyd's Rep	=	Lloyd's List Reports
M & W	=	Meeson & Welby
Med LR	=	Medical Law Reports
NLJ	=	New Law Journal
PIQR	=	Personal Injuries and Quantum Reports
RTR	=	Road Traffic Reports
SCCR	=	Scottish Criminal Case Reports
SJ	=	Solicitors' Journal
SLT/SLT (Notes)	=	Scots Law Times/(Notes)
Taunt	=	Taunton Reports
TLR	=	Times Law Reports
WLR	=	Weekly Law Reports

Legal terminology

ECJ	=	European Court of Justice
HL	=	House of Lords
CA	=	Court of Appeal
EAT	=	Employment Appeal Tribunal
IT	=	Industrial Tribunal
J	=	Mr Justice, a junior judge, normally sitting in a court of first instance
LJ	=	Lord Justice, a senior judge, normally sitting in a court of appeal
plaintiff	=	the person presenting a claim in a civil action
defendant	=	the person against whom a claim is brought in a civil action
appellant	=	the person bringing an appeal in a civil action
respondent	=	the person against whom an appeal is brought in a civil action

tort	=	a species of civil action for injury or damage where the remedy or redress is an award of unliquidated damages
volenti non fit injuria	=	'to one who is willing no harm is done'; a complete defence in a civil action
novus actus interveniens	=	supervening act of third party
obiter dicta	=	words said by the way
ratio decidendi	=	principle of a case
res ipsa loquitur	=	the event itself is evidence of negligence (a principle in the law of tort); the assertion can be rebutted by the defendant

Introduction

1.

This Introduction is in three main parts

— recent trends in UK health and safety law and its enforcement (this starts at paragraph 2);

— the structure of UK health and safety law (starting at paragraph 15);

— the management of health and safety at work (starting at paragraph 21).

Recent trends in UK health and safety law

The role of the European Union

2.

For the past decade the European Union (EU) has provided the principal motor for changes in UK health and safety legislation. Article 118A in the Treaty of Rome gives health and safety prominence in the objectives of the EU. The Social Charter also contains a declaration on health and safety, although this has no legal force. Whilst the EU can issue its own regulations, it mainly operates through directives requiring Member States to pass their own legislation. The 'Framework Directive' adopted in 1989 contained many broad duties, including the requirement to assess risks and introduce appropriate control measures. Other directives have since been adopted or proposed, including many relating to technical standards and safety requirements for specific products.

Implementation of EU Directives

3.

The UK, along with other Member States, must implement EU directives by designated dates. This is normally overseen by the Health and Safety Commission (HSC) which first circulates consultative documents incorporating the proposed regulations together with a related Approved Code of Practice (ACoP) and/or guidance to interested parties (trades unions, employers' organisations, professional bodies, local authorities etc.). Following the consultation process, the HSC submits a final version to the Secretary of State who then lays the regulations before Parliament. It is at this stage that a date for their coming into force is determined – usually that stipulated by the original EU directive.

The 'six pack' and beyond

4.

This process peaked on 1 January 1993 when six sets of regulations came into operation on the same day. These were:

● the *Management of Health and Safety at Work Regulations 1992 (SI 1992 No 2051)*;

● the *Provision and Use of Work Equipment Regulations 1992 (PUWER) (SI 1992 No 2932)*;

- the *Workplace (Health, Safety and Welfare) Regulations 1992 (SI 1992 No 3004)*;

- the *Personal Protective Equipment at Work Regulations 1992 (SI 1992 No 2966)*;

- the *Manual Handling Operations Regulations 1992 (SI 1992 No 2793)*; and

- the *Health and Safety (Display Screen Equipment) Regulations 1992 (SI 1992 No 2792)*.

Some of the requirements of these regulations are discussed later in this Introduction and many aspects of them are dealt with elsewhere in this publication.

5.   Although the pace has slackened since, new regulations and changed requirements continue to appear on a regular basis. These have included a new version of *PUWER*, the *Provision and Use of Work Equipment Regulations 1998 (SI 1998 No 2306)* and amendments to the *Management of Health and Safety at Work Regulations*. A summary of the more significant changes during the last couple of years is provided in paragraph 14. Application of the requirements of some of the more specific EU directives has resulted in some quite detailed regulations or ACoPs, which runs counter to the original objective-setting approach of the *Health and Safety at Work etc. Act 1974 (HSWA 1974)*. Concerns have been expressed (not least within the UK) in relation to the variable standards of implementation and enforcement within EU Member States. There have been moves recently to address these concerns and also to evaluate the impact of EU directives.

Deregulation

6.   The latter stages of the Conservative Government of 1979–1997 saw a drive towards deregulation because of the perceived burden of legislation on business and particularly on small employers. As part of this process the HSC was asked to review health and safety regulations and its report was published in May 1994. However, the scope of its recommendations was limited by the need to comply with EU directives and by the requirement contained in *HSWA 1974, s 1(2)* that any new regulations or orders must maintain or improve health and safety standards.

Consequently the report recommended no major changes; its main effect has been the repeal of some outdated legislation which had limited application anyway because alternative legislation already existed. Also the HSE was to attempt to make its Approved Codes of Practice and Guidance publications more 'user friendly'.

Many people, however – both inside and outside the HSC and HSE – were concerned that political pressure was being brought to bear on the enforcement of health and safety legislation. Criticisms particularly centred around the so-called 'minded to' procedure which required inspectors to advise employers in writing of their intention to issue an improvement notice.

The Labour Government

7.   The present Labour Government came to power in May 1997 and one of its early actions was to remove the 'minded to' procedure. Responsibility for the HSE passed to the newly created Department of Environment, Transport and the Regions (DETR) early in 1998 which announced an increase in HSE funding of £4.5 million. At the same time the DETR stated that ways of enforcing the law more effectively would be discussed and attention would be given to countering possible evasion by employers of their health and safety responsibilities, through their use of homeworkers and the 'apparently self-employed'. The Government also announced

that the HSE would be developing a long-term strategy for occupational health: asbestos, work-related stress, hand-arm vibration and solvents have all been mentioned as specific areas of interest.

8.   In 1999 the Minister responsible for health and safety announced that the Government would be marking the twenty-fifth anniversary of the *Health and Safety at Work etc. Act 1974* with a full review of the law relating to health and safety. Many observers expect this review to extend to the penalties available for breaches of the law, particularly in the light of several high profile prosecutions (see paragraph 10).

Manslaughter

9.   Although the highly publicised 'corporate manslaughter' prosecution following the *Herald of Free Enterprise* disaster was unsuccessful, both the company and a director involved in the subsequent Lyme Bay canoeing tragedy were convicted under manslaughter charges.

The Labour Government has clearly indicated its intention to move further down this path with the publication in 1998 of '*Work-related deaths – a protocol for liaison*'. The protocol involves the Crown Prosecution Service (CPS), the Health and Safety Executive (HSE) and the Association of Chief Police Officers (ACPO). Changes in the law – creating a new offence of 'corporate killing' – have been mooted which, if introduced, should make it easier to prosecute employers following workplace deaths.

Further evidence of this trend has been provided by the manslaughter prosecutions resulting from the Southall rail crash in September 1997 and the arrests early in 1999 of a site worker and a foreman on suspicion of manslaughter following a fatal accident on a Lancashire construction site.

High profile cases

10.   In some major cases, courts have shown an increasing willingness to impose significant fines.

In September 1994 six people were killed and seven seriously injured when a pedestrian walkway at the port of Ramsgate collapsed. After a twenty-five day trial early in 1997, two Swedish companies which had constructed and designed the walkway were fined £750,000 and £250,000 respectively, Lloyds Register of Shipping (which inspected the walkway) was fined £500,000 and Port Ramsgate, the client, was fined £200,000. With costs added to the total fines of £1.7 million, the bill to the defendants for the criminal proceedings alone came to a total of just under £2.5 million.

The collapse in October 1994 of a rail tunnel being constructed at Heathrow did not result in any injuries but was described in court as one of the 'biggest near misses' in years. When the prosecution came to court in 1999, Balfour Beatty Civil Engineering were fined £700,000 plus £100,000 costs, with the tunnelling sub-contractor, Geoconsult GES MBH, fined £500,000 plus £100,000 costs.

Both of these cases show how responsibilities for health and safety are often shared between companies, with the Ramsgate prosecution illustrating, in particular, the importance of exerting control throughout the 'supply chain'.

The sentences imposed on brothers Andrew and Neil Medley by Leeds Crown Court on 16 April 1999 provide something of a contrast. Eleven charges under the *Control of Asbestos at Work Regulations 1987*, the *Asbestos (Licensing) Regulations 1983* and the *Employment of Women, Young Persons and Children Act 1920* had been brought against the brothers and their thermal engineering company following a year-long investigation by the HSE after a tip-off that schoolboys had been used to remove asbestos-based ceiling tiles from a factory. During the course of their enquiries HSE inspectors uncovered evidence that health and safety requirements had been routinely and consistently ignored, and that employees and members of the public had been potentially put at risk for financial gain. One of the inspectors gave evidence to the Crown Court that 'in thirty years handling asbestos cases this is by far the most serious that I have dealt with'.

By the time of the court hearing, the company had gone into liquidation. Neil Medley was ordered to do 240 hours' community service (the maximum possible in the circumstances). The judge decided not to fine the defendants because they were of 'very limited means' and because he considered it more appropriate that they should pay some of the prosecution costs, which amounted to more than £70,000. In the event, Neil Medley was ordered to pay £4,000 in costs, Andrew £2,000. The judge observed that though that was 'perhaps pitifully inadequate', he had to be governed by their means as individuals, notwithstanding that he was 'not satisfied that those had been fully put before me'. No terms of imprisonment, actual or suspended, were imposed on the defendants. Nor did the judge follow the prosecution's suggestion that the Medleys should be disqualified from holding a directorship, utilising the powers available to the court under the *Company Directors Disqualification Act 1986*.

The sentences imposed in the *Medley* case would seem to sit rather uneasily with the guidelines on the appropriate level of penalty for serious breaches of health and safety legislation laid down by the Court of Appeal in *R v F Howe & Son (Engineering) Ltd [1999] 2 AER 249*, and endorsed by the same court in *R v Rollco Screw and Rivet Co Ltd [1999] IRLR 439* and, more specifically, sentences passed on defendants in recent, serious, asbestos cases which have invariably resulted in terms of imprisonment or suspended sentences, and swingeing fines. The first ever custodial sentence, one of three months, was imposed on Roy Hill by Bristol Crown Court in January 1996 following his conviction for breaches of the asbestos regulations. The second custodial sentence was handed down by Birmingham Crown Court in September 1998 to Paul Evans who received a nine-month term of imprisonment for carrying out work involving asbestos without the necessary licence.

Self-regulation

11.   The *Health and Safety at Work etc. Act 1974* was the result of a Parliamentary Commission chaired by Lord Alf Robens which reported in 1972. One of the key recommendations of the Robens Commission was that the emphasis of legislation should switch from prescriptive requirements (often relating to specific industries, equipment or processes) to more general obligations. This approach is typified by the all-embracing nature of *HSWA 1974, ss 2 and 3*, albeit qualified by the phrase 'so far as is reasonably practicable'.

It was felt that this would encourage much more 'self-regulation' by employers who would address all of the health and safety risks involved in their activities rather than just dealing with those for which there were specific legal provisions. Whilst this approach has been partially successful, there are always those employers who require an external stimulus to take appropriate action. In a tribute to the first Director General of the HSE, the late John Locke, it was said by the HSE's former Director of Field Operations, Jim Hammer, that 'John knew . . . that legislation without effective inspection is no more than an essay in ethics'.

Risk assessments

12.   Much recent UK legislation has included a requirement for some type of risk assessment. The concept was introduced in the early 1980s in regulations applying to asbestos and lead but it came to wider prominence as a core requirement of the *Control of Substances Hazardous to Health Regulations 1988 ('COSHH')*. The 'Six Pack' of regulations which came into force on 1 January 1993 (see paragraph 4. above) continued this trend with four sets of regulations requiring an assessment of one kind or another. The most important of these was the general requirement for risk assessment contained in *Regulation 3* of the *Management of Health and Safety at Work Regulations 1992* ('the *Management Regulations*'). Other important regulations requiring more specific types of risk assessment relate to noise, manual handling operations, personal protective equipment, display screen equipment and fire precautions.

In practice a less formal type of risk assessment was already required by health and safety legislation – an assessment of the level of risk, the adequacy of existing precautions and the costs of additional precautions was necessary in order to determine what was 'reasonably practicable'. Risk assessment takes the concept of self-regulation somewhat further – employers must be able to demonstrate that they have identified relevant risks together with appropriate precautions and in most cases must have records available to prove this. To make a rather paradoxical statement, this makes enforcement of self-regulation considerably easier.

Supply-chain regulation

13.   Since the introduction of *HSWA 1974*, many court decisions, most notably those involving Swan Hunter Shipbuilders and Associated Octel, have emphasised that employers often have responsibilities for the activities of employees of other organisations. The structure of *HSWA 1974* and much subsidiary legislation is such that responsibilities overlap between employers rather than being neatly apportioned between them. Employers must do more than simply not turn a blind eye to the obvious health and safety failings of those with whom they come into contact: they must often take a pro-active interest in the health and safety standards of others.

This principle is exemplified by the Ramsgate prosecution (see paragraph 10). Despite having engaged specialists to carry out the design, construction and checking of the passenger walkway, Port Ramsgate was still convicted of an offence. Mr Justice Clark stated that 'the jury has found, in my judgement correctly, that an owner and operator of a port cannot simply sit back and do nothing and rely on others, however expert'.

In recent years a growing number of larger companies, local authorities and other public bodies have had increasingly formalised procedures for checking the health and safety standards of contractors wishing to work for them. This process has been accelerated by the demands of the *Construction (Design and Management) Regulations 1994* ('*CDM*') which require clients to satisfy themselves (via their planning supervisors) that potential principal contractors are capable of dealing with the health and safety issues associated with projects. The regulations also place responsibilities on principal contractors in respect of sub-contractors. Consequently contractors are frequently required to provide details of their health and safety policies and generic risk assessments together with risk assessments and/or method statements for specific projects or activities. Many clients also take an extremely hands-on approach in policing the work of contractors on their premises. This regulation of health and safety through the supply chain seems likely to increase.

Recent changes in legislation

14.   Summarised below in alphabetical order are the more significant changes in health and safety legislation in recent years.

- *Confined Spaces Regulations 1997 (SI 1997 No 1713)*

  These provide a definition of 'confined space' in which various defined foreseeable 'specified risks' may arise. Entry into confined spaces must be avoided unless this is not reasonably practicable. Where entry is made, it must be in accordance with a safe system of work (arrived at through a process of risk assessment) and with suitable emergency arrangements in place. HSE booklet L101 '*Safe Work in Confined Spaces*' contains an Approved Code of Practice (ACoP) and much practical guidance.

- *Construction (Health, Safety and Welfare) Regulations 1996 (SI 1996 No 1592)*

  These consolidate, modernise and simplify most of the previous regulations relating to construction as well as introducing some new requirements resulting from an EC Directive. Although detailed in some areas, the Regulations adopt an objective-setting approach in others. They are supported by an HSE booklet, HS(G) 150 '*Health and Safety in Construction*' and several other HSE publications. Lifting operations in construction are now covered by the *Lifting Operations and Lifting Equipment Regulations 1998* (see below).

- *Control of Lead at Work Regulations 1998 (SI 1998 No 543)*

  These set stricter levels of lead in blood at which employers must remove employees from work. The HSE has published a revised edition of its ACoP – COP 2 '*Control of lead at work*'.

- *Control of Major Accident Hazards Regulations 1999 (COMAH 1999) (SI 1999 No 743)*

  COMAH 1999 replaces the *Control of Industrial Major Accident Hazard Regulations 1984 (CIMAH)*. The Regulations apply where specified quantities of dangerous substances are present, requiring the preparation of a Major Accident Prevention Policy (MAPP). Additional requirements are placed on 'top tier sites' where more dangerous substances are kept. Enforcement will be co-ordinated between the HSE and the Environment Agency, with the HSE for the first time having to charge companies for inspections. '*A Guide to the Control of Major Accident Hazard Regulations*' was published by the HSE in 1999.

- *Diving at Work Regulations 1997 (SI 1997 No 2776)*

  These replace and modernise previous requirements for commercial diving and also apply to the UK Continental Shelf. Some previously exempt groups (the media, researchers and recreational instructors) are now included. Practical information on compliance is provided in five ACoPs:

  — L103: Commercial diving projects offshore;

  — L104: Commercial diving projects inland / inshore;

  — L105: Recreational diving projects;

  — L106: Media diving projects;

  — L107: Scientific and archaeological diving projects.

- *Fire Precautions (Workplace) Regulations 1997 (SI 1997 No 1840)*

These came into force on 1 December 1997 after a long process of consultation and redrafting. They apply to workplaces not already holding a current fire certificate under the *Fire Precautions Act 1971* or sportsground legislation. Some workplaces, including ships, aircraft and means of transport are excluded. An assessment of fire risks must be carried out and appropriate precautions taken, e.g. for fire detection and warning, means of escape, fire fighting equipment, emergency planning. The Regulations are enforced by fire authorities (not the HSE), and the Home Office has published an advisory booklet '*Fire Precautions in the Workplace*'. Some amendments to the Regulations were expected early in 1999 and many observers anticipate an eventual consolidation of all workplace fire safety legislation.

- *Health and Safety (Young Persons) Regulations 1997 (SI 1997 No 135)*

These amended the *Management of Health and Safety at Work Regulations 1992*. They require employers to assess risks to young people (under 18s) before they start work, taking into account their inexperience, lack of awareness of existing and potential risks, and immaturity. The risk assessment may necessitate prohibiting the young person from certain work activities, except under close control. Parents of school-age children (e.g. on work experience programmes) must be provided with information about risks and control measures. HSE booklet, HS(G) 165 '*Young People at Work*', provides guidance on the Regulations.

- *Lifting Operations and Lifting Equipment Regulations 1998 (LOLER 1998) (SI 1998 No 2307)*

These replace most of the previous sector-based law relating to lifting equipment (including hoists and lifts). Employers now have a choice between ensuring thorough examinations of lifting equipment either at fixed intervals or in accordance with an examination scheme. A key requirement in *Regulation 8* is for lifting operations to be 'properly planned by a competent person; appropriately supervised; and carried out in a safe manner'.

HSE booklet L113 '*Safe Use of Lifting Equipment*' includes an ACoP and guidance.

- *Offshore Electricity and Noise Regulations 1997 (SI 1997 No 1993)*

The *Electricity at Work Regulations 1989* and *Noise at Work Regulations 1989* were amended so that they applied offshore from 21 February 1998.

- *Police Health and Safety Act 1997*

This Act came into force on 1 July 1998, bringing police officers within the scope of the *HSWA 1974*. A consultation process was underway early in 1999 to review the implications of introducing regulations to apply all the health and safety regulations in force prior to July 1998 to police officers.

- *Provision and Use of Work Equipment Regulations 1998 (PUWER 1998) (SI 1998 No 2306)*

These make some changes to the general requirements of *PUWER 1992* (which they replace) including requiring inspections of work equipment where relevant (*Reg 6*).

Specific sections concerning mobile work equipment (*Regs 25–30*) and power presses (*Regs 31–35*) have been added.

The remaining provisions of several old regulations have been revoked including those relating to unfenced machinery, power presses, abrasive wheels and woodworking machines. The HSE has published several booklets on the Regulations:

— L22: Safe use of work equipment (ACoP and guidance);

— L112: Safe use of power presses (ACoP and guidance);

— L114: Safe use of woodworking machinery (ACoP and guidance).

● *Railway Safety (Miscellaneous Provisions) Regulations 1997 (SI 1997 No 553)* and *Level Crossings Regulations 1997 (SI 1997 No 487)*

These two sets of regulations modernised and strengthened previous legislation, some of which was 150 years old. The HSE has published two related booklets:

— L97: A Guide to the Level Crossings Regulations;

— L98: Railway Safety Miscellaneous Provisions: Guidance on the Regulations.

● *Transport of Dangerous Goods (Safety Advisers) Regulations 1999 (SI 1999 No 257)*

Employers who are involved in the transport of dangerous goods by road or rail must appoint qualified safety advisers by 31 December 1999. The advisers must hold a relevant vocational training certificate, acquired by passing an examination based on a specified syllabus.

HSE has produced a series of booklets (HS(G) 160–164) on various aspects of transporting different types of dangerous goods by road or rail.

● *Working Time Regulations 1998 (SI 1998 No 1883)*

These implement the EC Working Time Directive and the working time provisions of the Young Workers Directive. They came into operation on 1 October 1998 and are enforced by the HSE in respect of weekly working time and night work, and by employment tribunals in relation to rest periods, breaks and annual leave. The DTI has published a free booklet, '*A Guide to Working Time Regulations*'.

Various minor amendments have also been made to existing regulations. These have involved:

● *Asbestos (Licensing) Regulations 1983 (SI 1983 No 1649)*

Work with asbestos insulation board has been brought into the scope of the Regulations from February 1999. Contractors will now need a licence from the HSE before working with this material.

● *Carriage of Dangerous Goods (Amendment) Regulations 1999 (SI 1999 No 303)*

These implemented various amendments resulting from changes to EC Directives. HSE leaflet IND(G) 234 summarises the present legislation governing carriage of dangerous goods.

● *Control of Asbestos at Work Regulations 1987 (SI 1987 No 2115)*

The Regulations now apply to all types of work which may lead to exposure. The exposure level has been lowered for white asbestos fibres, and asbestos-analysing laboratories must be accredited to EN 45001.

- *Control of Substances Hazardous to Health Regulations 1999 (COSHH 1999) (SI 1999 No 437)*

   Amendments coming into effect on 30 June 1998 (*Control of Substances Hazardous to Health (Amendment) Regulations 1998*) prohibited the supply of several chlorinated solvents for use in 'diffusive applications'. Several further amendments to the 1994 Regulations, introduced by these 1999 Regulations, came into force on 25 March 1999, including a redefinition of what constitutes suitable personal protective equipment. The schedule listing maximum exposure limits has been taken out of the Regulations, but the list will continue to be published annually in HSE's EH40 booklet. The 1999 Regulations together with a revised ACoP have been published in HSE booklet L5.

- *Chemicals (Hazard Information and Packaging for Supply) (Amendment) Regulations 1999 (CHIP 1999) (SI 1999 No 197)*

   The latest amendment to *CHIP 1994* came into operation on 1 March 1999. This introduced a supplement to the 4th edition of the Approved Supply List introduced by *CHIP 1998 (SI 1998 No 3106)*. Both the Approved Supply List and the supplement are available from HSE Books.

The structure of UK health and safety law

15.   Health and safety in the workplace involves two different branches of the law – criminal law (dealt with below) and civil law (referred to in paragraph 20).

Criminal law

16.   Criminal law is the process by which society, through the courts, punishes organisations or individuals for breaches of its rules. These rules, known as 'statutory duties', are comprised in Acts passed by Parliament (e.g. *Health and Safety at Work etc. Act 1974*) or regulations which are made by Government Ministers using powers given to them by virtue of Acts (e.g. the *Manual Handling Operations Regulations 1992*).

Cases involving breaches of criminal law may be brought before the courts by the enforcement authorities which, in the case of health and safety law, are the Health and Safety Executive (HSE) and local authorities via their environmental health departments (see ENFORCEMENT). Magistrates' courts hear the vast majority of health and safety prosecutions although more serious cases can be heard by the Crown Courts. The maximum fine which can be imposed by the magistrates' courts is currently £20,000 for breaches of certain sections of *HSWA 1974* and £5,000 for most other offences.

Where cases are heard by the Crown Court there is no limit on the fines which can be imposed. Paragraph 10 details some significant fines resulting from recent cases. There are also a limited number of health and safety offences which can result in prison sentences of up to two years. These include:

—   contravention of licensing requirements (e.g. for asbestos removal);

—   explosives-related offences;

—   contravention of an improvement or prohibition notice;

—   contravention of a court remedy order.

As in all criminal prosecutions the case must be proved 'beyond all reasonable doubt'. There is a right of appeal to the Court of Appeal (Criminal Division) and eventually to the House of Lords or even the European courts, although in practice very few health and safety cases go to appeal. A death involving work activities might result in manslaughter charges which could lead to more severe penalties – paragraph 9 considered the increasing likelihood of manslaughter cases.

The Health and Safety at Work etc. Act 1974 (HSWA 1974)

17. *HSWA 1974* is the most important Act of Parliament relating to health and safety. It applies to everyone 'at work' – employers, self-employed and employees (with the exception of domestic servants in private households). It also protects the general public who may be affected by work activities. HSE has published a booklet, '*A guide to the Health and Safety at Work etc. Act 1974*' (ref L1).

Some of the key sections of the Act are listed below.

Section 2 – Duties of employers

Section 2(1) is the catch-all provision: 'It shall be the duty of every employer to ensure, so far as is reasonably practicable, the health, safety and welfare at work of all his employees.' See below for further discussion of the term 'reasonably practicable'.

Section 2(2) goes on to detail more specific requirements relating to:

— the provision and maintenance of plant and systems of work;

— the use, handling, storage and transport of articles and substances;

— the provision of information, instruction, training and supervision;

— places of work and means of access and egress;

— the working environment, facilities and welfare arrangements.

These are also qualified by the term 'reasonably practicable'.

Section 2(3) provides that an employer with five or more employees must prepare a written health and safety policy statement, together with the organisation and arrangements for carrying it out, and bring this to the notice of employees (see paragraph 23).

Section 3 – Duties to others

Section 3(1) provides: 'It shall be the duty of every employer to conduct his undertaking in such a way as to ensure, so far as is reasonably practicable, that persons not in his employment who may be affected thereby are not exposed to risks to their health or safety.'

Employers thus have duties to contractors (and their employees), visitors, customers, members of the emergency services, neighbours, passers-by and the public at large. This may extend to include trespassers, particularly if it is 'reasonably foreseeable' that they could be endangered, for example where high-risk workplaces are left unfenced.

Individuals who are self-employed are placed under a similar duty and must also take care of themselves. (If they have employees, they must comply with *section 2*).

Section 4 – Duties relating to premises

Under this section persons in total or partial control of work premises (and plant or substances within them) must take 'reasonable' measures to ensure the health and safety of those who are not their employees. These responsibilities might be held by landlords or managing agents etc., even if they have no presence on the premises.

Section 6 – Duties of manufacturers, suppliers etc.

Those who design, manufacture, import, supply, erect or install any article, plant, machinery, equipment or appliances for use at work, or who manufacture, import or supply any substance for use at work, have duties under this section.

Section 7 – Duties of employees

'It shall be the duty of every employee while at work:

(a)   to take reasonable care for the health and safety of himself and of other persons who may be affected by his acts or omissions at work; and

(b)   as regards any duty or requirement imposed on his employer or any other person by or under any of the relevant statutory provisions, to co-operate with him so far as is necessary to enable that duty or requirement to be complied with.'

Consequently employees must not do, or fail to do, anything which could endanger themselves or others. It should be noted that managers and supervisors also hold these duties as employees.

Section 8 – Interference and misuse

'No person shall intentionally or recklessly interfere with or misuse anything provided in the interests of health, safety or welfare in pursuance of any of the relevant statutory provisions.'

Section 9 – Duty not to charge

'No employer shall levy or permit to be levied on any employee of his any charge in respect of anything done or provided in pursuance of any specific requirement of the relevant statutory provisions.'

Levels of duty

Health and safety law contains different levels of duty:

Absolute

Absolute requirements must be complied with whatever the practicalities of the situation or the economic burden.

Practicable

The term 'practicable' means that measures must be possible in the light of current knowledge and invention.

Reasonably practicable

This term is contained in the main sections of *HSWA 1974* and many important Regulations. It requires the risk to be weighed against the costs necessary to avert it (including time and trouble as well as financial cost). If, compared with the costs involved, the risk is small then the precautions need not be taken – it should be noted that such a comparison should be made before any incident has occurred. The burden of proof, however, rests on the person with the duty (usually the employer) – they must prove why something was not reasonably practicable at a particular point in time. The duty holder's ability to meet the cost is not a factor to be taken into account.

In effect, considering what is 'reasonably practicable' requires that a risk assessment be carried out. The existence of a well-documented and carefully considered risk assessment would go a long way towards supporting a case on what was or was not reasonably practicable. Neither risks nor costs remain the same for ever and what is practicable or reasonably practicable will change with time – hence the need to keep risk assessments up to date.

The 'six pack'

18.

The term 'six pack' is often used to describe the six Regulations which all came into operation on 1 January 1993 to implement EC Directives. They are:

Management of Health and Safety at Work Regulations 1992 (SI 1992 No 2051)

Employers and the self-employed are required to manage the health and safety aspects of their activities in a systematic and responsible way. The Regulations include requirements for risk assessment, the availability of competent health and safety advice and emergency procedures – several of these management issues are dealt with later in this Introduction (see paragraph 21 *et seq*).

Provision and Use of Work Equipment Regulations 1992 (PUWER 1992) (SI 1992 No 2932)

These Regulations, which have now been superseded by *PUWER 1998* (see paragraph 14), covered equipment safety, including the guarding of machinery. The definition of 'work equipment' also includes hand tools, vehicles, laboratory apparatus, lifting equipment, access equipment etc.

Workplace (Health, Safety and Welfare) Regulations 1992 (SI 1992 No 3004)

Physical working conditions, safe access for pedestrians and vehicles, and welfare provisions are covered by these Regulations.

Personal Protective Equipment at Work Regulations 1992 (SI 1992 No 2966)

Employers must assess the personal protective equipment (PPE) needs created by their work activities, provide the necessary PPE, and take reasonable steps to ensure its use.

Manual Handling Operations Regulations 1992 (SI 1992 No 2793)

Manual handling operations involving risk of injury must either be avoided or be assessed by the employer with steps taken to reduce the risk, so far as is reasonably practicable.

Health and Safety (Display Screen Equipment) Regulations 1992 (SI 1992 No 2792)

Where there is significant use of display screen equipment (DSE), employers must assess DSE workstations and offer 'users' eye and eyesight tests (which may necessitate provision of spectacles for DSE work).

Other important Regulations

19.   *Construction (Design and Management) Regulations 1994 (SI 1994 No 3140)*

The broad definition of 'construction work' used in the Regulations means that they apply to many medium-sized engineering and maintenance projects as well as to traditional construction activities and all demolition work. The Regulations provide for specific duties to be carried out by the 'client' (who must appoint a 'planning supervisor') and by the 'principal contractor' (who may in some cases also be the client). Key requirements of the Regulations are for the development and implementation of a formal 'health and safety plan' and the creation of a 'health and safety file' for the project.

Control of Substances Hazardous to Health Regulations 1999 (COSHH) (SI 1999 No 437)

These require an assessment to be made of all substances hazardous to health in order to identify means of preventing or controlling exposure. There are also requirements for the proper use and maintenance of control measures and for workplace monitoring and health surveillance in certain circumstances.

Electricity at Work Regulations 1989 (SI 1989 No 635)

These Regulations contain requirements relating to the construction and maintenance of all electrical systems and work activities on or near such systems. They apply to all electrical equipment, from a battery-operated torch to a high-voltage transmission line.

Health and Safety (Consultation with Employees) Regulations 1996 (SI 1996 No 1513)

These Regulations extended the previous requirements (contained in the *Safety Representatives and Safety Committees Regulations 1977*) so that employers must now also consult workers not covered by trade union safety representatives.

Health and Safety (First-Aid) Regulations 1981 (SI 1981 No 917)

Basic first-aid equipment controlled by an 'appointed person' must be provided for all workplaces. Higher risk activities or larger numbers of employees may require additional equipment and fully trained first-aiders.

Health and Safety (Safety Signs and Signals) Regulations 1996 (SI 1996 No 341)

These Regulations require safety signs to be provided, where appropriate, for risks which cannot adequately be controlled by other means. Signs must be of the prescribed design and colours.

Health and Safety (Training for Employment) Regulations 1990 (SI 1990 No 1380)

Those receiving 'relevant training' (through training for employment schemes or work experience programmes) are treated as being 'at work' for the purposes of health and safety law. The provider of the 'relevant training' is deemed to be their employer – youth trainees and students on work experience placements therefore have the status of employees and must be protected accordingly.

Noise at Work Regulations 1989 (SI 1989 No 1790)

Employers must carry out an assessment to determine the level of exposure to noise of their employees. The precautions required include noise reduction measures, provision of hearing protection and the establishment of hearing protection zones.

Reporting of Injuries, Diseases and Dangerous Occurrences Regulations 1995 (RIDDOR) (SI 1995 No 3163)

Fatal accidents, major injuries (as defined) and dangerous occurrences (as defined) must be reported immediately to the enforcing authority. Accidents involving four or more days' absence must be reported in writing within seven days.

Safety Representatives and Safety Committees Regulations 1977 (SI 1977 No 500)

Members of recognised trade unions may appoint safety representatives to represent them formally in consultations with their employer in respect of health and safety issues. The functions and rights of safety representatives are detailed in the Regulations. The employer must establish a safety committee if at least two representatives request this in writing.

Civil law

20.

A civil action can be initiated by an employee who has suffered injury or damage to health caused by their work. This may be based upon the law of negligence, i.e. where the employer has been in breach of the duty of care which he owes to the employee. Being part of the common law, the law of negligence has evolved, and continues to evolve, by virtue of decisions in the courts – Parliament has had virtually no role to play in its development.

Civil actions may also be brought on the grounds of breach of statutory duty – it should be noted, however, that *HSWA 1974* and most of the provisions in the *Management of Health and Safety at Work Regulations 1992* do not confer a right of civil action, although the statutory duties owed by employers to employees under *HSWA 1974* have their equivalent obligations at common law.

Duty of care

Every member of society is under a 'duty of care', i.e. to take reasonable care to avoid acts or omissions which they can reasonably foresee are likely to injure their neighbour (anyone who ought reasonably to have been kept in mind). What is 'reasonable' will depend upon the circumstances.

Employers owe a duty of care not only to employees but also to such people as contractors, visitors, customers, and people on neighbouring property. In the case of the duty of care owed by employers to employees, it includes the duty to provide:

— safe premises;

— a safe system of work;

— safe plant, equipment and tools; and

— safe fellow workers.

Occupiers of premises are under statutory duties comprised in the *Occupiers' Liability Acts* of 1957 and 1984 (see OCCUPIERS' LIABILITY), and those suffering injury because of a defect in a product may sue the producer or importer under the *Consumer Protection Act 1987* (see PRODUCT SAFETY).

Vicarious liability

Employers are liable to persons injured by the wrongful acts of their employees, if such acts are committed in the course of their employment. Thus if an employee's careless driving of a forklift truck injures another employee (or a contractor or customer), the employer is likely to be liable. There is no vicarious liability if the act is not committed in the course of employment – thus the employer is not likely to be held liable if one employee assaults another.

Civil procedure

Civil actions must commence within three years from the time of knowledge of the cause of action. In an action for negligence, this will be the date on which the plaintiff knew or should have known that there was a significant injury and that it was caused by the employer's negligence. The plaintiff must be prepared to prove his case in the courts, but in practice most cases are settled out of court following negotiations between the plaintiff's legal representatives and the employer's insurers or their representatives. The *Employers' Liability (Compulsory Insurance) Act 1969* requires employers to be insured against such actions (see EMPLOYERS' LIABILITY INSURANCE), although some public bodies, for example local authorities, are exempt from the provisions of this Act.

As the result of recommendations made by Lord Woolf in his '*Access to Justice*' report of 1996, the *Civil Procedure Rules 1998* introduced widespread changes to civil procedure on 26 April 1999, affecting the progress of civil claims from their commencement to their conclusion. The rules involve a 'pre-action protocol' and govern the conduct of litigation in a way that is intended to limit delay. In most cases a single expert, medical or non-medical, will be instructed rather than each party using separate experts. Even if the case goes to court, the expert's report will usually be in writing, with both parties able to ask written questions of the expert and to see the replies. The new arrangements include a fast track system for personal injury claims up to a value of £15,000.

Damages

Damages are assessed under a number of headings including:

—   loss of earnings (prior to trial);

—   damage to clothing, property etc.;

—   pain and suffering (before and after trial);

—   future loss of earnings;

—   disfigurement;

—   medical or nursing expenses; and

—   inability to pursue personal or social interests or activities.

Defences

The plaintiff must prove breach of a statutory duty or of the duty of care on a balance of probabilities. However, a number of defences are available to the employer, including:

● **contributory negligence**

The employer may claim that the injured person was careless or reckless – for example, that he ignored clear safety rules or disobeyed instructions. Accidental errors are distinguished from a failure to take reasonable care. Damages will be reduced by the percentage of contributory negligence established, which will vary with the facts of each case.

● **injuries not reasonably foreseeable**

The employer may claim that the injuries were beyond normal expectation or control (an act of God). In cases of noise-induced hearing damage, mesothelioma (an asbestos-related cancer) or vibration-induced white finger, the courts have established dates after which a reasonable employer should have been aware of the relevant risks and taken precautions.

● **voluntary assumption of risk**

If an employee consents to take risks as part of the job, the employer may escape liability. However, this defence (*volenti non fit injuria*) cannot be used for cases involving breach of statutory duty – no one can contract out of their statutory obligations or be deprived of statutory protection.

Other civil actions

Other health and safety related situations may result in civil actions by employees. Employment protection legislation has recently been strengthened in relation to dismissals or redundancies resulting from health and safety activities (including refusal to work in situations of serious and imminent danger). Suspension or dismissal on maternity or medical grounds may also give a right of action. See EMPLOYMENT PROTECTION.

Management of health and safety at work

21.   The Robens doctrine of self-regulation (see paragraph 11) has been developed considerably in recent years by the HSE as it has paid increasing attention to the way health and safety is managed. Its Accident Prevention Advisory Unit (APAU) worked with a number of large organisations from the late 1970s onwards, steadily

building up its expertise. This culminated in the publication by the HSE in 1991 of '*Successful Health and Safety Management*'. A revised edition of the booklet (reference HS(G) 65) was published in 1997.

'*Successful Health and Safety Management*' drew together much of what was already known about management techniques and the principles on which they are based. This included the earlier work of H L Heinrich and Frank Bird in the United States. The introduction to the booklet included the paragraph:

> 'Many of the features of effective health and safety management are indistinguishable from the sound management practices advocated by proponents of quality and business excellence. Indeed, commercially successful companies often also excel at health and safety management, precisely because they bring efficient business expertise to bear on health and safety as on all other aspects of their operations. The general principles of good management are therefore a sound basis for deciding how to bring about improved health and safety performance.'

However, the then Chief Inspector of Factories, Tony Linehan, stated in his Foreword:

> 'The path described is neither easy nor short. There are no short cuts to successful health and safety management. It cannot be sidelined. It must not be delegated out of sight. The clearest lesson from practical experience is that the starting point is the genuine and thoughtful commitment of top management. I believe firmly that such commitment is beneficial and worthwhile.'

Since the publication of '*Successful Health and Safety Management*', several of its principles have found their way into statutory obligations – particularly through the requirements for risk assessments included in a number of Regulations, and in *Regulation 4* of the *Management of Health and Safety at Work Regulations 1992* which requires the application of the 'management cycle' to health and safety precautions (see paragraph 24).

The costs of accidents

22.

Their own humanitarian attitudes together with social pressures and the possibility of legal sanctions have for many years acted as powerful motivational factors for employers to avoid accidents at work. '*Successful Health and Safety Management*' drew attention to the high costs to employers of failing to manage health and safety effectively. This theme was developed further by the publication by the HSE in 1993 of '*The Costs of Accidents at Work*'.

The APAU carried out five detailed case studies in different industrial sectors in order to determine the full cost of accidents. Employers often believe that most accident costs are covered by insurance but the studies demonstrated the opposite. The ratio between insured and uninsured costs varied from 1:8 to 1:36.

Whilst insurance is likely to cover employer's liability and public liability claims and major damage costs, together with major losses due to business interruption, there are a host of uninsured costs associated with accidents, many of which go unrecorded.

Employee sick pay can usually be quantified but the costs of minor accident repairs are often hidden within much larger maintenance figures, and loss or damage of product due to accidents is seldom separated out from other wastage statistics. Indirect losses due to the unavailability of staff or equipment while both are being 'repaired' are difficult to quantify as are other indirect costs such as the administrative time involved and the possible damage to the employer's image (to staff, customers or the wider public, including investors).

Statistical analysis has shown that for all businesses the number of serious accidents is small in relation to the number of minor accidents and damage incidents – although these latter types may not be fully recorded or investigated. Whilst minor accidents and damage incidents seldom result in insurance claims, their cumulative effects result in significant uninsured costs to the employer. Accidents were found to be costing one of the companies in the APAU study 37 per cent of its annual profits.

Health and safety policies

23.   *'Successful Health and Safety Management'* stated that 'accidents are caused by the absence of adequate management control' and stressed the importance of effective health and safety policies in establishing such control. *Section 2(3)* of the *Health and Safety at Work etc. Act 1974* requires employers to prepare in writing:

- a statement of their general policy with respect to the health and safety at work of their employees; and

- the organisation and arrangements for carrying out the policy.

It also requires the statement to be brought to the notice of all employees – employers with fewer than five employees are exempt from this requirement.

Policies are normally divided into three sections, to meet the three separate demands of *HSWA 1974*:

(i) The statement of intent

This involves a general statement of good intent, usually linked to a commitment to comply with relevant legislation. Many employers extend their policies so as to relate also to the health and safety of others affected by their activities. In order to demonstrate clearly that there is commitment at a high level, the statement should preferably be signed by the chairman, chief executive or someone in a similar position of seniority.

(ii) Organisational responsibilities

It is vitally important that the responsibilities for putting the good intentions into practice are clearly identified. In a small organisation this may be relatively simple but larger employers should identify the responsibilities held by those at different levels in the management structure. Whilst reference to employees' responsibilities may be included, it should be emphasised that the law requires the employer's organisation to be detailed in writing. Types of responsibilities to be covered in the policy might include:

- making adequate resources available to implement the policy;

- setting health and safety objectives;

- developing suitable procedures and safe systems;

- delegating specific responsibilities to others;

- monitoring the effectiveness of others in carrying out their responsibilities;

- monitoring standards within the workplace; and

- feeding concerns up through the organisation.

(iii) Arrangements

The policy need not contain all of the organisation's arrangements relating to health and safety but should contain information as to where they might be found, for example in a separate health and safety manual or within various procedural documents. Topics which may require detailed arrangements to be specified are:

— operational procedures relating to health and safety;

— training;

— personal protective equipment;

— health and safety inspection programmes;

— accident and incident investigation arrangements;

— fire and other emergency procedures;

— first aid;

— occupational health;

— control of contractors and visitors;

— consultation with employees; and

— audits of health and safety arrangements.

Employees must be aware of the policy and, in particular, must understand the arrangements which affect them and what their own responsibilities might be. They may be given their own copy (for example, within an employee handbook) or the policy might be displayed around the workplace. With regard to some arrangements detailed briefings may be necessary, for example as part of induction training.

Employers must revise their policies as often 'as may be appropriate'. Larger employers are likely to need to arrange for formal review and, where necessary, for revision to take place on a regular basis (e.g. by way of an ISO 9000 procedure). Dating of the policy document is an important part of this process.

Application of the 'management cycle'

24.

As stated in paragraph 12, a requirement for a risk assessment has been included in many recent health and safety regulations. Even where there is no explicit requirement, it is often implicit within the wording of regulations that compliance will involve a risk assessment process. This is frequently stated in the accompanying ACoP or guidance – the *Provision and Use of Work Equipment Regulations 1998*, the *Lifting Operations and Lifting Equipment Regulations 1998* and the *Confined Spaces Regulations 1997* all provide examples of this.

Whilst risk assessment involves the identification of risks and an assessment of their significance, its purpose is to identify the measures necessary to eliminate the risks or to control them to a satisfactory degree. There is, however, little point in going through the process of risk assessment if these precautions are not actually implemented in the workplace. The 'theory' of the risk assessment must become reality in a practical setting.

The importance of this is recognised by the juxtaposition in the *Management of Health and Safety at Work Regulations 1992* (the *Management Regulations*) of *Regulation 3* requiring 'risk assessment' and *Regulation 4* entitled 'Health and safety arrangements'. *Paragraph (1)* of *Regulation 4* states that:

'Every employer shall make and give effect to such arrangements as are appropriate, having regard to the nature of his activities and the size of his undertaking for the effective planning, organising, control, monitoring and review of the preventive and protective measures.'

Paragraph (2) of *Regulation 4* requires employers with five or more employees to record these arrangements.

Such a 'management cycle' has long been applied to other areas of business activity, such as finance, but relatively few employers have utilised it in relation to health and safety. Managers have often stated their good intentions but have not always set up the organisational structure and control to implement those intentions and have failed to monitor what is actually happening in the workplace.

The cycle can be applied to an employer's overall approach to health and safety:

Plan — through the statement of intent within the health and safety policy;

Organise — by allocating responsibilities for implementing the policy and making the necessary resources available;

Control — through application of relevant management systems and techniques and the use of performance standards;

Monitor— through health and safety audits and inspections;

Review— in health and safety committee and management meetings.

At a different level the cycle can be applied to management systems or procedures, such as those for carrying out health and safety inspections:

Plan — through a statement of intent to conduct regular inspections;

Organise — by having a formal procedure relating to inspections – where, who by, how often;

Control — by specifying arrangements for reporting on inspections and implementing remedial actions, and by providing training in inspection techniques;

Monitor — through checking that inspections are being carried out as scheduled, reviewing the quality of inspection reports and making sure that remedial action is being implemented;

Review — by investigating the reasons for any shortcomings in the system (and looping back to the start of the cycle to plan how to correct these).

British Standard 8800 '*Guide to Occupational Health and Safety Management Systems*' and many other commercially available management systems are based upon similar application of the management cycle. However, whether or not employers use such formal systems, the principles of the cycle should always be applied to all aspects of health and safety management. The *Management Regulations* have made this a statutory obligation.

Sources of health and safety advice

Within '*Successful Health and Safety Management*' the HSE emphasised the importance of establishing a positive health and safety culture within an organisation as a prerequisite of effective health and safety management. It referred to the 'four Cs' as key components in establishing such a culture: control, competence, communication and co-operation.

While competence in health and safety matters is relevant throughout any workforce, it is particularly important at management levels. The *Management Regula-*

tions have taken this concept further by requiring (in *Regulation 6*) every employer to appoint one or more competent persons to assist him in complying with the law. The ACoP accompanying the Regulations states that the size and type of resource required will be relative to the size of the organisation and the risks present in its activities. Full-time or part-time specialists may be appointed, or use may be made of external consultants. Smaller employers may appoint themselves, provided that they are competent – the ACoP refers to competence as comprising both the possession of theoretical knowledge and the capacity to put it into practice in the work situation. An awareness of the limits of one's own knowledge and capabilities is also important.

Health and safety training is available from many different sources. The following organisations either provide training themselves or oversee training through accredited training centres.

- National Examination Board in Occupational Safety and Health (NEBOSH)

  tel: 0116 288 8858

- Institution of Occupational Safety and Health (IOSH)

  tel: 0116 257 3100

- Chartered Institution of Environmental Health (CIEH)

  tel: 0171 928 6006

- Royal Society for the Prevention of Accidents (RoSPA)

  tel: 0121 248 2000

- British Safety Council (BSC)

  tel: 0181 741 1231

There are many independent consultants who can provide advice and assistance on health and safety matters. Consultants are listed in the Yellow Pages and the Institution of Occupational Safety and Health (see above) maintains a consultants' register. Employers planning to use consultants' services can obtain a copy of a free HSE leaflet, '*Selecting a Health and Safety Consultancy*' (IND(G) 33).

The HSE itself can also be a valuable source of information and advice:

- HSE Books tel: 01787 881165 fax: 01787 313995

  The HSE has a huge range of priced publications and free leaflets, some of which are referred to elsewhere in this Introduction. '*The Essentials of Health and Safety at Work*' is a useful starting point for the small employer.

- HSE Infoline tel: 0541 545500

  Open Monday to Friday 8.30am to 5pm to provide information on workplace health and safety.

- HSE Home Page on the Internet: http://www.open.gov.uk/hse/hsehome.htm

  An online enquiry service can be accessed from the home page.

- '*Escaping the Maze*'

  This video guide, designed to help companies through the maze of health and safety information and its different sources, is available from HSE Video (tel: 0845 741 9411)

Of course, within this issue of *Tolley's Health and Safety at Work* you will find it easy to access much valuable information and practical advice, designed to keep you up-to-date with the law and all recent and relevant developments.

Access, Traffic Routes and Vehicles

Introduction

With the regular daily flow of labour to and from the workplace and vehicles making deliveries and collecting items, access and egress points constitute potentially hazardous situations. For this reason there is a duty on employers and factory occupiers to 'provide and maintain' safe access to and egress from a place of work both under statute and at common law. As part and parcel of compliance with the *Building Regulations 1991 (SI 1991 No 2768)*, this includes access facilities for disabled workers and visitors (that is, persons who have difficulty walking or are in a wheelchair, or, alternatively, have a hearing problem or impaired vision) (see further W11028 WORKPLACES – HEALTH, SAFETY AND WELFARE), as well as proper precautions to effect entry or exit, to or from confined spaces, where a build-up of gas/combustible substances can be a real though not obvious danger (see A1022 below). Statutory requirements consist of general duties under *HSWA*, which apply to all employers, and the more specific duties of the *Workplace (Health, Safety and Welfare) Regulations 1992 (SI 1992 No 3004)*.

The term 'access' is a comprehensive one and refers to just about anything that can reasonably be regarded as means of entrance/exit to a workplace, even if it is not the usual method of access/egress. Unreasonable means of access/egress would not be included, such as a dangerous short-cut, particularly if management has drawn a worker's attention to the danger, though the fact that a worker is a trespasser has not prevented recovery of damages (*Westwood v The Post Office [1973] 3 AER 184*). Access to a fork lift truck qualified, for the purposes of *Sec 29(1)* of the *Factories Act 1961* (repealed as from 1 January 1996), the fork lift truck being a 'place' (*Gunnion v Roche Products Ltd, The Times, 4 November 1994*). The proper procedure is for the employer/factory occupier to designate points of access/egress for workers and see that they are safe, well-lit, maintained and (if necessary) manned and de-iced. Moreover, the statutory duties apply to access/egress points to any place where any employees have to work, and not merely their normal workplace.

This chapter summarises key statutory and common law duties in connection with:

(*a*)   access and egress;

(*b*)   vehicular traffic routes for internal traffic and deliveries;

(*c*)   work vehicles and delivery vehicles – with particular emphasis on potentially hazardous activities involving such vehicles; and

(*d*)   work in confined spaces, of necessity involving access and egress points.

Statutory duties concerning workplace access and egress – Workplace (Health, Safety and Welfare) Regulations 1992 (SI 1992 No 3004)

Statutory duties centre around:

> (*a*)   the organisation of safe workplace transport systems;
>
> (*b*)   the suitability of traffic routes for vehicles and pedestrians; and
>
> (*c*)   the need to keep vehicles and pedestrians separate.

Organisation of safe workplace transport systems

A1003   Every workplace must (so far as is reasonably practicable) be so organised that pedestrians and vehicles can circulate in a safe manner. [*Reg 17(1)*].

Suitability of traffic routes

A1004   Traffic routes in a workplace must be suitable for the persons or vehicles using them, sufficient in number, in suitable positions and of sufficient size. [*Reg 17(2)*].

More particularly:

> (*a*)   pedestrians or vehicles must be able to use traffic routes without endangering those at work;
>
> (*b*)   there must be sufficient separation of traffic routes from doors, gates and pedestrian traffic routes, in the case of vehicles;
>
> (*c*)   where vehicles and pedestrians use the same traffic routes, there must be sufficient space between them; and
>
> (*d*)   where necessary, all traffic routes must be suitably indicated.

[*Reg 17(3)(4)*].

Compliance with these statutory duties involves provision of safe access for:

> (i)   vehicles, with attention being paid to design and layout of road systems, loading bays and parking spaces for employees and visitors; and
>
> (ii)   pedestrians, so as to avoid their coming into contact with vehicles.

Traffic routes for vehicles

A1005   There should be sufficient traffic routes to allow vehicles to circulate safely and without difficulty. As for internal traffic, lines marked on roads/access routes in and between buildings should clearly indicate where vehicles are to pass e.g. fork lift trucks. Obstructions, such as limited headroom, are acceptable if clearly indicated. Temporary obstacles should be brought to the attention of drivers by warning signs or hazard cones or, alternatively, access prevented or restricted. Both internal and delivery traffic should be subject to sensible speed limits (e.g. 10 mph), which should be clearly displayed. Speed ramps (sleeping policemen), preceded by a warning sign or mark, are necessary, save for fork lift trucks, on workplace approaches. The traffic route should be wide enough to allow vehicles to pass and repass oncoming or parked traffic, and it may be advisable to introduce one way systems or parking restrictions. Traffic signs on roads, for example speed limit signs, must conform with those on public roads, whether or not the road is subject to the *Road Traffic Regulations Act 1984.*

Checklist – safe traffic routes

A1006   Safe traffic routes should:

> (*a*)   provide the safest route possible between places where vehicles have to call or deliver;

(*b*) be wide enough for the safe movement of the largest vehicle, including visiting vehicles (e.g. articulated lorries, ambulances etc.) and should allow vehicles to pass oncoming or parked vehicles safely. One way systems or parking restrictions are desirable;

(*c*) avoid vulnerable areas/items, such as fuel or chemical tanks or pipes, open or unprotected edges, and structures likely to collapse;

(*d*) incorporate safe areas for loading/unloading;

(*e*) avoid sharp or blind bends; if this is not possible, hazards should be indicated (e.g. blind corner);

(*f*) ensure that road/rail crossings are kept to a minimum and are clearly signed;

(*g*) ensure that entrances/gateways are wide enough; if necessary, to accommodate a second vehicle that may have stopped, without causing obstruction;

(*h*) set sensible speed limits, which are clearly signposted. Where necessary, ramps should be used to retard speed, and road humps or bollards to restrict the width of the road. These should be preceded by a warning sign or mark on the road. Fork lift trucks should not have to pass over road humps, unless of a type capable of doing so;

(*j*) give prominent warning of limited headroom, both in advance and at an obstruction. Overhead electric cables or pipes containing flammable/hazardous chemicals should be shielded, i.e. using goal posts, height gauge posts or barriers;

(*k*) ensure that routes on open manoeuvring areas/yards are marked and signposted, and banksmen are employed to supervise the safe movement of vehicles;

(*l*) ensure that people at risk from exhaust fumes or material falling from vehicles are screened or protected; and

(*m*) restrict vehicle access where high-risk substances are stored (e.g. LPG) and where refuelling takes place.

Traffic routes for pedestrians
Checklist – safe traffic routes

A1007 In the case of pedestrians, the main object of the traffic route is to prevent their coming into contact with vehicles. Safe traffic routes should:

(*a*) provide separate routes/pavements for pedestrians, to keep them away from vehicles;

(*b*) where necessary, provide suitable barriers/guard rails at entrances/exits and at the corners of buildings;

(*c*) where traffic routes are used by both pedestrians and vehicles, be wide enough to allow vehicles to pass pedestrians safely;

(*d*) where pedestrian and vehicle routes cross, provide appropriate crossing points, which should be used. These should be clearly marked and signposted. If necessary, barriers or rails should be provided to prevent pedestrians crossing at dangerous points and to direct them to designated crossing points. Where traffic volume is high, traffic lights, bridges or subways should feature;

(*e*)   where crowds use or are likely to use roadways, e.g. at the end of a shift, stop vehicles from using them at such times;

(*f*)   provide separate vehicle and pedestrian doors in premises, with vision panels on all doors;

(*g*)   provide high visibility clothing for people permitted in delivery areas (e.g. bright jackets/overalls);

(*h*)   where the public has access (e.g. at a farm or factory shop), public access points should be as near as possible to shops and separate from work activities.

(See also W11012 WORKPLACES.)

Vehicles

A1008   Vehicles account for a high percentage of deaths and injuries at work. In 1994 77 people were killed, including six members of the public; there were 1,363 major injuries and 4,698 workers had to take three or more days off work as a result of vehicle injury. Many of these casualties occur whilst vehicles are reversing, though activities such as loading and unloading, sheeting and unsheeting, as well as cleaning, can similarly lead to injuries, especially where employees are struck by a falling load or a fall from a height on, say, a tanker or HGV. So, too, climbing and descending ladders on tankers during delivery and 'dipping' at petrol forecourts can be hazardous, access onto vehicles and egress being as important as design and construction. Tipping, too, has its dangers, with tipping vehicles, tipping trailers and tankers overturning in considerable numbers. Also, sheeting and unsheeting operations have led to sheeters slipping or losing their grip or falling whilst walking on top of loads or in consequence of ropes breaking; absence of, or inadequate, training being an additional factor in injuries involving work vehicles. This part of the chapter considers the general statutory requirements relating to vehicles at work, precautions in connection with potentially hazardous operations involving vehicles, as well as providing a checklist for vehicle safety. Specific construction and use requirements are not considered.

General statutory requirements

A1009   Both work and private vehicles come within the parameters of health and safety at work. Regarding work vehicles, employers have the direct responsibilities of provision and maintenance generally under *HSWA s 2*, and, more specifically, under the *Provision and Use of Work Equipment Regulations 1998 (SI 1998 No 2306)* (*PUWER*), vehicles qualifying as 'work equipment'. Regarding private vehicles, employers have much less control – at least, as far as design, construction and use are concerned – but should, nevertheless, endeavour to ensure regulated use via:

(*a*)   restricted routes and access;

(*b*)   provision of clearly signposted parking areas away from hazardous activities and operations; and

(*c*)   enforcement of speed limits.

Work vehicles

A1010   Generally, work vehicles should be as safe, stable, efficient and roadworthy as private vehicles on public roads. As work equipment they are subject to the controls of *PUWER*, the latter specifying provision, maintenance and access requirements, whilst employers must also ensure that drivers are suitably trained in conformity with the requirements of the *Management of Health and Safety at Work Regulations 1992 (SI 1992 No 2051)*.

Provision

A1011   All employers must ensure that work equipment:

(*a*)   is so constructed and adapted as to be suitable for its purpose;

(*b*)   when selected, caters for risks to the health and safety of persons where the equipment is to be used; and

(*c*)   is only used for operations specified and under suitable conditions.

[*PUWER, Reg 4*].

Compliance with these requirements on the part of operators of HGVs, fork lift trucks, dump trucks and mobile cranes presupposes conformity with the following checklist, namely:

(i)   a high level of stability;

(ii)   safe means of access and egress to and from the cab;

(iii)   suitable and effective service and parking brakes;

(iv)   windscreens with wipers and external mirrors giving optimum all-round visibility;

(v)   a horn, vehicle lights, reflectors, reversing lights, reversing alarms;

(vi)   suitable painting/markings so as to be conspicuous;

(vii)   provision of a seat and seat belts;

(viii)   guards on dangerous parts (e.g. power take-offs);

(ix)   driver protection to prevent injury from overturning, and from falling objects or materials; and

(x)   driver protection from adverse weather.

Maintenance

A1012   All employers must ensure that work equipment is maintained in an efficient state, in efficient working order and in good repair. [*PUWER, Reg 5*]. This combines the need for basic daily safety checks by the driver before using the vehicle, as well as preventive inspections and services carried out at regular intervals of time and/or mileage. As regards basic daily safety checks, employers should provide drivers with the following list:

brakes, tyres, steering, mirrors, windscreen washers and wipers, warning signals and specific safety systems (e.g. control interlocks)

and see that drivers carry out the checks.

Training of drivers

A1013   All employers must:

(*a*)   in entrusting tasks to employees, take into account their capabilities as regards health and safety; and (*b*)   ensure that employees are provided with adequate health and safety training on recruitment and exposure to new or increased risks.

[*Management of Health and Safety at Work Regulations 1992, Reg 11*].

In order to conform with these requirements, employers should ensure that, for general purposes, drivers of work vehicles are over 17 and have passed their driving test or, in the case of drivers of HGVs, that they are over 21 and have passed the HGV test. Moreover, to ensure continued competence, or to accommodate new risks at work or a changing work environment, employers should provide safety updates on an on-going basis as well as refresher training, and require approved drivers to report any conviction for a driving offence, whether or not involving a company vehicle.

Contractors and subcontractors

A1014   Similar assurances (see A1013 above) should be obtained from drivers of contractors and subcontractors visiting an employer's workplace. If they are not forthcoming, permission to work on site or in-house should be refused until either the contractor's vehicles comply with statutory requirement and/or his drivers are adequately trained. Training of contractor's drivers would normally be undertaken by contractors themselves, though site or in-house hazards, routes to be used etc. should be communicated to contractors by employers or occupiers. Contractors should be left in no doubt of the penalties involved for failure to conform with safe working practices – a useful way of ensuring enforcement on the part of contractors and subcontractors is to issue a licence.

Access to vehicles

A1015   In addition to *Regulation 4* of *PUWER* (see A1011 above), employers (and others having control, to any extent, of workplaces (see OCCUPIERS' LIABILITY)), who operate/use vehicles, are subject to:

(*a*)   the fall prevention requirements of *Regulation 13* of the *Workplace (Health, Safety and Welfare) Regulations 1992* (see W9003 WORK AT HEIGHTS). As far as possible, compliance with this regulation would obviate the need for climbing on top of vehicles (by bottom-filling) and also require vehicle operators to ensure that loads are evenly distributed, packaged properly and secured in the interests of drivers going down slopes and up steep hills (see further A1018 below).

(*b*)   the co-operation requirements of *Regulation 9* of the *Management of Health and Safety at Work Regulations 1992*, specifying that where activities of different employers interact, different employers may need to co-operate with each other and co-ordinate preventive and protective measures. This regulation is particularly relevant to tanker deliveries and 'dipping' at petrol forecourts as well as loading and/or unloading operations. For 'dipping' purposes or gaining top access to tankers, access should be by a ladder at the front or rear, such ladders being properly constructed, maintained and securely fixed; ideally, they should incline inwards towards the top. Failing this, employers of tanker drivers and forecourt owners should liaise on potential risks involved in tanker deliveries, e.g. the provision of suitable step-ladders on the part of the latter. As for carriage of goods and loading/unloading operations, this regulation places a duty on consignors to ensure that goods are evenly distributed, properly packaged and secured.

Potentially hazardous operations

A1016   The following activities and operations are potentially hazardous in connection with vehicles.

Reversing

A1017   Approximately a quarter of all deaths at work are caused by reversing vehicles; in addition, negligent reversing can result in costly damage to premises, plant and goods. Where possible, workplace design should aspire to obviate the need for reversing by the incorporation of one-way traffic systems. Failing this, reversing areas should be clearly identified and marked, non-essential personnel excluded from the area, and, ideally, banksmen wearing high-visibility clothing should be in attendance to guide drivers through, and keep non-essential personnel and pedestrians away from, the reversing area. Vehicles should be fitted with external side-mounted and rear-view mirrors – as, indeed, many now are. Closed-circuit television systems are also advisable for enabling drivers to see round 'blind spots' and corners.

Loading and unloading

A1018   Because employees can be seriously injured by falling loads or overturning vehicles, loading/unloading should not be carried out:

(*a*)   near passing traffic, pedestrians and other employees;

(*b*)   where there is a possibility of contact with overhead electric cables;

(*c*)   on steep gradients;

(*d*)   unless the load is spread evenly (racking will assist load stability);

(*e*)   unless the vehicle has its brakes applied or is stabilised (similarly with trailers); or

(*f*)   with the driver in the cab.

(See also OFFICES AND SHOPS.)

Tipping

A1019   Overturning of lorries and trailers is the main hazard associated with tipping. In order to minimise the potential for injuries, tipping operations should only occur:

(*a*)   after drivers have consulted with site operators and checked that loads are evenly distributed;

(*b*)   when non-essential personnel are not present;

(*c*)   on level and stable ground away from power lines and pipework; and

(*d*)   with the driver in the cab and the cab door closed.

Moreover, after discharge, drivers should ensure that the body of the vehicle is completely empty and should not drive the vehicle in an endeavour to free a stuck load.

Giving unauthorised lifts

A1020   Giving unauthorised lifts in work vehicles is both a criminal offence and can lead to employers being involved in civil liability. Thus, 'every employer shall ensure that work equipment is used only for operations for which, and under conditions for which, it is suitable'. [*PUWER, Reg 4*].

Where a driver of a work vehicle gives employees and/or others unauthorised lifts, his employer could find himself prosecuted for breach of the above regulation, whilst the driver himself may be similarly prosecuted for breach of *Sec 7* of *HSWA*, as endangering co-employees and members of the public. In addition, although acting in an unauthorised manner and contrary to instructions, the employee may well involve his employer in vicarious liability for any subsequent injury to a co-employee and/or member of the public (see further *Rose v Plenty* at E11004 EMPLOYERS' DUTIES TO THEIR EMPLOYEES).

Where instructions to employees not to give unauthorised lifts are clearly displayed in a work vehicle, and an employee nevertheless gives an unauthorised lift and a co-employee or member of the public is injured or killed as a result of the employee's negligent driving, the plaintiff knowing that the driver should not give lifts, it can be argued that the employee has exceeded the scope of his employment and so the employer is absolved from liability. (In *Twine v Bean's Express [1946] 1 AER 202* a driver gave a lift to a third party who was killed in consequence of his negligent driving. There was a notice in the van prohibiting drivers from giving lifts. It was held that the employer was not liable, as the driver was acting outside the parameters of his employment when giving a lift.)

Conversely, courts have taken the view that such conduct, on the part of drivers, does not circumscribe the scope of employment but rather constitutes performance of work in an unauthorised manner, so leaving the employer liable as the employee is doing what he is employed to do but doing it wrongly (see further *Rose v Plenty* and *Century Insurance Co v Northern Ireland Road Transport Board* at E11004 EMPLOYERS' DUTIES TO THEIR EMPLOYEES). Yet again, if the passenger, having seen the prohibition on unauthorised lifts in the vehicle, nevertheless accepted a lift and was injured, arguably, if an adult rather than a minor, he has agreed to run the risk of negligent injury and so will forfeit the right to compensation.

Common law duty of care

A1021   At common law every employer owes all his employees a duty to provide and maintain safe means of access to and egress from places of work. Moreover, this duty extends to the workforce of another employer/contractor who happens to be working temporarily on the premises. Hence the common law duty covers all workplaces, out of doors as well as indoors, above ground or below, and extends to factories, mines, schools, universities, aircraft, ships, buses and even fire engines and appliances (*Cox v Angus [1981] ICR 683*, where a fireman injured in a cab was entitled to damages at common law).

Confined spaces

A1022   Accidents and fatalities (see, for instance, the case of *Baker v T E Hopkins & Son Ltd [1959] 3 AER 225* where a doctor was overcome by carbon monoxide fumes while going to rescue two workmen down a well – the defence of *volenti non fit injuria* jailed), such as drowning, poisoning by fumes or gassing, have happened as a result of working in confined spaces. Normal safe practice is a formalised permit to work system or checklist tailored to a particular task and requiring appropriate and sufficient personal protective equipment. Hazards typical of this sort of operation are:

(*a*)   atmospheric hazards – oxygen deficiency, enrichment, toxic gases (e.g. carbon monoxide), explosive atmospheres (e.g. methane in sewers);

(*b*)   physical hazards – low entry headroom or low working headroom, protruding pipes, wet surfaces underfoot as well as any electrical or mechanical hazards;

(*c*)   chemical hazards – concentration of toxic gas can quickly build up, where there is a combination of chemical cleaning substances and restricted air flow or movement.

In order to combat this variety of hazards peculiar to work in confined spaces, use of both gas detection equipment and suitable personal protective equipment are a prerequisite, since entry/exit paths are necessarily restricted.

Prior to entry, gas checks should test for (*a*) oxygen deficiency/enrichment, then (*b*) combustible gas and (*c*) toxic gas, by detection equipment being lowered into the space. This will determine the nature of personal protective equipment necessary. If gas is present in any quantity, the offending space should then be either naturally or mechanically ventilated. Where gas is present, entry should only take place in emergencies, subject to the correct respiratory protective equipment being worn. Assuming gas checks establish that there is no gaseous atmosphere, entry can then be made without use of respiratory equipment; any atmospheric change subsequently registering on the gas detection equipment.

Permits to work

Permits to work provide a formal safety control system against accidental injury to personnel, plant or products, when foreseeably hazardous work is undertaken. The permit to work, consisting of a document detailing the work to be done and precautions to be taken (see *fig. 1*), is a statement that all foreseeable hazards have been noted and precautions defined. It does not, in itself, make the job safe but relies for effectiveness on specified personnel implementing it conscientiously under supervision and control.

Requirements of permits to work

(1)   The permit must specify clearly who is to do the work, the time for which it is valid, the work to be done and the necessary precautions.

(2)   Until the permit is cancelled, it supersedes all other instructions.

(3)   During the currency of the permit, no person must work at any place or on any plant not earmarked as safe by the permit.

(4)   No person must carry out any work not covered in the permit. If there is a change in work rotation, the permit must be amended or cancelled. This latter can only be done by the originator of the permit.

(5)   Where another person takes over a permit, as, for instance, in an emergency, that person must assume full responsibility for the work, either until the work is complete or he has formally returned the permit to the originator.

(6)   There must be liaison with other work areas whose activities could be affected by permit work.

(7)   Where permit work is to be carried out on part of a site or on specific plant, the limits of the work area must be clearly marked.

(8)   Permits to work must take into account on-site contractors who should be briefed before commencement of work. Moreover, compliance with safety regulations and procedures, including permits to work, should be a condition of contract (see CONSTRUCTION AND BUILDING OPERATIONS).

Use of permits

Permits to work should be used for the following activities:

(*a*)   entry into confined spaces/closed vessels/vats;

(*b*)   work involving demolition of pipelines or opening of plant containing steam, ammonia, chlorine, hazardous chemicals, vapours, gases or liquids under pressure;

(*c*)   work in certain electrical systems;

(*d*)   welding and cutting work (other than in workshops);

(*e*)   work in isolated locations or where access is difficult, or at heights;

(*f*)   work near or requiring use of highly flammable/explosive/toxic substances;

(*g*)   work causing atmospheric pollution;

(*h*)   pressure testing;

(*j*)   fumigation operations using gases;

(*k*)   ionising radiations work; and

(*l*)   any of the above activities involving on-site contractors.

Cancellation of permit

Once scheduled work is complete, the permit to work certificate should be cancelled and returned to the originator, who should see that all permit work has been carried out satisfactorily. The originator should then sign the declaration to the effect that all personnel, equipment and plant have been removed from the area. The plant and equipment should then be returned to service and the person responsible for the plant should check that the permit has been properly cancelled and then make a final entry on the certificate, accepting responsibility for the plant.

Documentation

Permits should be printed in triplicate, self-carbonned and serial-numbered. The originator should distribute them as follows:

(*a*)   the original to the person undertaking the work (and possibly posted at place of work);

(*b*)   the first copy to be given to the person responsible for the area in which work is to be carried out; and

(*c*)   the second copy should be retained by the originator.

Competent / authorised persons

Not infrequently, health and safety legislation requires certain duties, normally involving a high degree of expertise, to be carried out only by 'competent' or, less often, 'authorised' or even 'qualified' personnel. Examples abound as follows:

(1)   *Electricity at Work Regulations 1989, Reg 16* – persons to be competent to prevent danger and injury.

(2)   *Abrasive Wheels Regulations 1970, Reg 9* – mounting of abrasive wheels.

(3)   *Power Presses Regulations 1965, Regs 4, 5* – carrying out inspections and testing safety devices.

(4)   *Factories Act 1961, s 22(2)* – examination of hoists/lifts.

(5)   *Offshore Installations and Pipeline Works (Management and Administration) Regulations 1995, Reg 6* – appointment of a competent installation manager and *Reg 13* – helideck operations.

(6)   *Offshore Installations (Operational Safety, Health and Welfare) Regulations 1976, Reg 6* – examination of lifting machinery.

(7)   *Management of Health and Safety at Work Regulations 1992, Reg 6* – all employers to appoint a 'competent' person to assist in health and safety compliance.

(8)   *Pressure Systems and Transportable Gas Containers Regulations 1989, Regs 8–10* – written scheme for periodic examination by a competent person, for users of installed, and owners of mobile systems.

(9)   *Gas Safety (Installation and Use) Regulations 1994, Reg 3* – competent gas fitters.

(10)   *Construction (Design and Management) Regulations 1994, Regs 6(6), 8(1)* – appointment of a competent person as a planning supervisor, and a competent contractor as principal contractor.

(11)   *Control of Asbestos at Work Regulations 1987, Reg 10* – control measures/protective equipment must be regularly examined and tested by a competent person.

(12)   *Diving Operations at Work Regulations 1981, Reg 5* – diving contractor must appoint a diving supervisor.

(13)   *Health and Safety (First-Aid) Regulations 1981, Reg 3* – appointment of an adequate number of suitably trained and qualified first-aiders.

(14)   *Ionising Radiations Regulations 1985, Reg 10* – appointment of radiation protection advisers.

(15)   *Construction (Health, Safety and Welfare) Regulations 1996*

    (a)   installation, erection, substantial addition or alteration of scaffolds and personal suspension equipment [*Reg 6(8)*];

    (b)   erection and dismantling of supporting buttresses [*Reg 9(3)*];

    (c)   planning and carrying out of demolition and dismantling [*Reg 10(2)*];

    (d)   installation, alteration or dismantling of equipment for supporting excavations [*Reg 12(5)*];

    (e)   construction, installation, alteration or dismantling of cofferdams and caissons [*Reg 13(2)*];

PERMIT TO WORK CERTIFICATE

LOCATION: **ORIGINATOR:**   **DATE:**

PART A
Valid from .... (time) to .... (time) on .... (date)
Issued by .... to ....
This permit is issued for the following work ....
in .... department/area/section.

PART B – PRECAUTIONS	YES/NO	N/A	SIGNATURE
1 The above plant has been removed from service and persons under my supervision have been informed.			
2 The above plant has been isolated from all sources of: (a) ingress of dangerous fumes, flammable and toxic substances (b) electrical and mechanical power; (c) heat, steam and/or hot water.			
3 The above plant has been freed of dangerous substances.			
4 Atmospheric tests have been carried out and the atmosphere is safe.			
5 The area is roped off or otherwise segregated from adjacent areas.			
6 The appropriate danger/caution notices have been displayed.			
7 The following additional safety precautions have been taken: (a) the use of safety belt and life line; (b) the use of goggles and/or gloves; (c) the use of flameproof lamps; (d) the use of fresh air/self-contained breathing apparatus; (e) prohibition on naked lights/sources of ignition; (f) .... (g) .... (h)			

Part C – DECLARATION
I hereby declare that the operations detailed in Parts A and B have been completed and that the above particulars are correct.
Signed .... Date .... Time ....

PART D – RECEIPT/ACCEPTANCE OF CERTIFICATE
I have read and understand this certificate and will undertake to work in accordance with the conditions in it.
Signed .... Date .... Time ....

PART E – COMPLETION OF WORK
The work has been completed and all persons under my supervision, materials and equipment have been withdrawn.
Signed .... Date .... Time ....

PART F – REQUEST FOR EXTENSION
The work has NOT been completed and permission to continue is requested.
Signed .... Date .... Time ....

PART G – EXTENSION
I have re-examined the plant detailed above and confirm that the certificate
may be extended to expire at .... (time).
Further precautions ....
Signed .... Date .... Time ....

PART H – CANCELLATION OF PERMIT
I hereby declare this Permit to Work cancelled and that all precautionary
measures specified have been withdrawn.
Signed.. Date .... Time ....

PART I – RETURN TO SERVICE
I accept the above plant back into service.
Signed .... Date .... Time ....

**PART J – REMARKS, SPECIAL CONDITIONS AND EXTRA
        INFORMATION**

> (f)   control of vessels for conveying construction workers over water [*Reg 14(3)*];
>
> (g)   inspection of places of work on construction sites [*Reg 29*].

(16)   *Work in Compressed Air Regulations 1996, Reg 5* – appointment of a compressed air contractor.

(17)   *Carriage of Dangerous Goods by Road Regulations 1996, Reg 24* – supervision of parked vehicles carrying dangerous goods.

(18)   *Carriage of Explosives by Road Regulations 1996, Reg 20* – attendance of parked vehicles carrying explosives.

It is, therefore, unfortunate that 'competence', obviously a key requirement, has generally not been defined either by statute or case law – an exception being the *Management of Health and Safety at Work Regulations 1992 (SI 1992 No 2051)*, which refer to a person as being 'competent' where he has sufficient training and experience or knowledge as to enable him to assist in securing compliance, on the part of the employer, with the necessary safety legislation and maintenance procedures. [*Regs 6(5), 7(3)*].

Statutory requirements

A1023   It should be noted that the *Confined Spaces Regulations 1997 (SI 1997 No 1713)* came into force on 28 January 1998. These repeal *Factories Act 1961, s 30*, and impose requirements and prohibitions with respect to the health and safety of persons carrying out work in confined spaces.

A 'confined space' is defined in *reg 1(2)* as 'any place, including any chamber, tank, vat, silo, pit, trench, pipe, sewer, flue, well or other similar space in which, by virtue of its enclosed nature, there arises a reasonably foreseeable specified risk'.

A 'specified risk' means a risk of:

(*a*)   serious injury to any person at work arising from a fire or explosion;

(*b*)   without prejudice to paragraph (*a*) –

   (i)   the loss of consciousness of any person at work arising from an increase in body temperature;

   (ii)   the loss of consciousness or asphyxiation of any person at work arising from gas, fume, vapour or the lack of oxygen;

(*c*)   the drowning of any person at work arising from an increase in the level of a liquid; or

(*d*)   the asphyxiation of any person at work arising from a free flowing solid or the inability to reach a respirable environment due to entrapment by a free flowing solid.

Regulation 4 prohibits a person from entering a confined space to carry out work for any purpose where it is reasonably practicable to carry out the work by other means.

If, however, a person is required to work in a confined space, a risk assessment must be undertaken to comply with the requirements of the *Management of Health and Safety at Work Regulations 1992, Reg 3*. The risk assessment must be undertaken by a competent person and the outcomes of the risk assessment process will then provide the basis for the development of a safe system of work (*Confined Spaces Regulations 1997, Reg 3*).

The risk assessment process should make use of all available information such as engineering drawings, working plans, soil or geological information and take into consideration factors such as the general condition of the confined space, work to be undertaken in the space to minimise hazards produced in the area, need for isolation of the space and the requirements for emergency rescue. In particular, information should be collected and assessed on the previous contents of the confined space, residues that still may be present, contamination that may arise from adjacent plant, processes, gas mains, surrounding soil, land or strata; oxygen level and physical dimensions of the space that may limit safe access and/or egress. The work to be undertaken should be assessed to determine if additional risks will be produced as a result of this work and systems developed to control these risks. All information collected should be recorded and a safe system of work developed for safe entry.

The main elements to consider when designing a safe system of work include the following:

(*a*)   supervision,

(*b*)   competence for confined spaces working,

(*c*)   communications,

(*d*)   testing/monitoring the atmosphere,

(*e*)   gas purging,

(*f*)   ventilation,

(*g*)   removal of residues,

(*h*)   isolation from gases, liquids and other flowing materials,

(*j*)   isolation from mechanical and electrical equipment,

(*k*)   selection and use of suitable equipment,

(*l*)   personal protective equipment (PPE) and respiratory protective equipment (RPE), (*m*)   portable gas cylinders and internal combustion engines,

(*n*)   gas supplied by pipes and hoses,

(*o*)   access and egress,

(*p*)   fire prevention,

(*q*)   lighting,

(*r*)   static electricity,

(*s*)   smoking,

(*t*)   emergencies and rescue,

(*u*)   limited working time.

[*Confined Spaces Regulations 1997, Reg 4*].

Regulation 6 provides for circumstances allowing the Health and Safety Executive to grant exemption certificates.

Accident Reporting

Introduction

A3001 Employers (both onshore and offshore [*Reporting of Injuries, Diseases and Dangerous Occurrences Regulations 1995 (RIDDOR) (SI 1995 No 3163), Reg 12*]) and other 'responsible persons' (see A3004 below) who have control over employees and work premises are required to notify and report to the relevant enforcing authority (see A3003 below) the following specified events occurring at work:

(a) accidents causing injuries, fatal and non-fatal, including:

(i) acts of non-consensual physical violence committed at work, and

(ii) acts of suicide occurring on, or in the course of, the operation of a railway, tramway, trolley or guided transport system

[*Reg 2(1)*];

(b) occupational diseases; and

(c) dangerous occurrences, even where no injury results.

The duty to report applies not only in the case of accidents to employees, but also to visitors, customers and members of the public killed or injured by work activities [*Reg 3(1)*].

Approximately 1.5 million work-related injuries happen in a given year, over a third of which are caught by *RIDDOR*. Around 60% are treated at hospital, with about 4% of casualties being detained for more than 24 hours. Work-related injuries and ill health are responsible for around 29 million days off work each year – that is just over one day for every worker. Over two-fifths of reported major injuries are attributable to falls from heights, and one-third of reported over-3-day injuries are caused by handling accidents.

Reporting of Injuries, Diseases and Dangerous Occurrences Regulations 1995 (RIDDOR) – (SI 1995 No 3163)

A3002 Coming into effect on 1 April 1996, these regulations cover:

(a) reportable work injuries (see A3006 below);

(b) reportable occupational diseases (see Appendix B at A3028 below) – now 47 in all;

(c) reportable dangerous occurrences (see A3008 and Appendix A at A3027 below) – now 83 in all;

(d) road accidents involving work (see A3018 below); and

(e) gas incidents (see A3019 below).

Records must be kept by employers and other 'responsible persons' (see A3004 below) of such injuries, diseases and dangerous occurrences for a minimum of three years from the date they were made. In addition, employers must also keep an Accident Book (BI 510). Absences from work over a three-day period, due to work injury, are reportable directly to the HSE (or other enforcing authority). Injuries and dangerous occurrences are reportable on Form F2508 and diseases on Form F2508A (see A3011 and Appendices C and D at A3029, A3030 below). As for notification of major accident hazards, see CONTROL OF MAJOR ACCIDENT HAZARDS.

Relevant enforcing authority

A3003

Health and safety law is separately enforced either by the Health and Safety Executive (HSE), or by local authorities, through their environmental health departments, depending on the nature of the business activity in question. Under *RIDDOR*, notifications and reports should be directed to the authority responsible for the premises where the reportable event occurs (or in connection with which the work causing the event is being carried out). Details of HSE offices are listed in Appendix E to this chapter.

Persons responsible for notification and reporting

A3004

The person generally responsible for reporting injury-causing accidents, deaths or diseases is the employer. Failing that, the person having control of the work premises or activity will be the responsible person. [*Reg 2(1)*]. In certain cases these normal rules are displaced and there are specifically designated 'responsible persons', e.g. in the case of mines, quarries, offshore installations, vehicles, diving operations and pipelines (see Table 1 below).

Table 1

Persons generally responsible for reporting accidents

Death, major injury, over-3-day injury or specified occupational disease:	of an employee at work	that person's employer
	of a person receiving training for employment	the person whose undertaking makes immediate provision of the training
	of a self-employed person at work in premises under the control of someone else	the person for the time being having control of the premises in connection with the carrying on by him of any trade, business or undertaking
Specified major injury or condition, or over-3-day injury:	of a self-employed person at work in premises under his control	the self-employed person or someone acting on his behalf

Death, or specified major injury or condition:	of a person who is not himself at work (but is affected by the work of someone else), e.g. a member of the public, a shop customer, a resident of a nursing home	the person for the time being having control of the premises in connection with the carrying on by him of any trade, business or undertaking at which, or in connection with the work at which, the accident causing the injury happened

[*Reg 2(1)(b)*].

Persons responsible for reporting accidents in specific locations

A mine	the mine manager
A quarry	the quarry owner
A closed tip	the owner of the mine or quarry with which the tip is associated
An offshore installation (except in the case of reportable diseases)	the duty holder
A dangerous occurrence at a pipeline	the owner of the pipeline
A dangerous occurrence at a well	the appointed person or, failing that, the concession owner
A diving operation (except in the case of reportable diseases)	the diving contractor
A vehicle	the vehicle operator

[*Reg 2(1)(a)*].

In situations where the responsible person is difficult to identify because of the shared control of a site or operations, arrangements should be made to determine who will deal with *RIDDOR* reporting in line with the duty to co-operate and co-ordinate under the *Management of Health and Safety at Work Regulations 1992, Reg 9*.

What is covered?

A3005　　Covered by these Regulations are events involving:

(a)　　employees;

(b)　　self-employed persons;

(c)　　trainees;

(d)　　a person, not an employee or trainee, on premises under the control of another, or who was otherwise involved in an accident (e.g. a visitor, customer, passenger or bystander).

Major injuries or conditions

A3006

Where any person dies or suffers a major injury as a result of, or in connection with, work, such an incident must be notified and reported. The person who dies or suffers injury need not be at work; it is enough if the death or injury arose from a work activity. For example, reporting requirements would apply to a shopper who fell and was injured on an escalator, so long as the injury was connected with the escalator; a member of the public overcome by fumes on a visit to a factory and who lost consciousness; a patient in a nursing home who fell over an electrical cable lying across the floor and was injured; or a pupil or student killed or injured in the course of his curricular work which was supervised by a lecturer or teacher.

Reportable major injuries and conditions are as follows:

(*a*)   any fracture (other than to fingers, thumbs or toes);

(*b*)   any amputation;

(*c*)   dislocation of shoulder, hip, knee or spine;

(*d*)   loss of sight (whether temporary or permanent);

(*e*)   a chemical or hot metal burn to the eye or any penetrating eye injury;

(*f*)   any injury resulting from an electric shock or electrical burn (including any electrical burn caused by arcing or arcing products) leading to unconsciousness or requiring resuscitation or admittance to hospital for more than 24 hours;

(*g*)   any other injury

(i)   leading to hypothermia, heat-induced illness or unconsciousness,

(ii)   requiring resuscitation, or

(iii)   requiring admittance to hospital for more than 24 hours;

(*h*)   loss of consciousness caused by asphyxia or by exposure to a harmful substance or biological agent;

(*j*)   either

(i)   acute illness requiring medical treatment, or

(ii)   loss of consciousness

resulting from the absorption of any substance by inhalation, ingestion or through the skin;

(*k*)   acute illness requiring medical treatment where there is reason to believe that this resulted from exposure to a biological agent or its toxins or infected material.

[*Reg 2(1), Sch 1*].

Injuries incapacitating for more than three consecutive days

A3007

Where a person at work is incapacitated for more than three consecutive days from carrying out his/her normal contractual work (excluding the day of the accident but including every day thereafter, whether or not such days would normally have been working days) owing to an injury resulting from an accident at work (other than an injury reportable as a major injury listed in A3006 above), a report of the accident in writing on Form F2508 must be sent to the enforcing authority as soon as is practicable and in any event within ten days of the accident. [*Reg 3(2)*].

It should be noted that in the event of a three-day injury, the employee may or may not be at work. The criterion is inability to carry out their normal work.

Specified dangerous occurrences

A3008   83 types of reportable dangerous occurrences are specified in *Schedule 2*, ranging from general dangerous occurrences (e.g. the collapse of a building or structure, the explosion of a pressure vessel, and accidental releases of significant quantities of dangerous substances) to more specific dangerous occurrences in mines, quarries, transport systems and offshore installations (see Appendix A at A3027 below).

Specified diseases

A3009   Where a worker suffers from an occupational disease related to a particular activity or process (as specified in *Schedule 3*), a report must be sent to the enforcing authority. [*Reg 5(1)*].

This duty arises only when an employer has received information in writing from a registered medical practitioner diagnosing one of the reportable diseases. (In the case of the self-employed, the duty is triggered regardless of whether or not the information is given to him in writing.) Many of these diseases are those for which disablement benefit is ordinarily prescribed. (In respect of offshore workers, such diseases tend to be communicable.)

Moreover, the *Industrial Diseases (Notification) Act 1981* and the *Registration of Births and Deaths Regulations 1987 (SI 1987 No 2088)* require that particulars are to be included on the death certificate as to whether death might have been due to, or contributed to by, the deceased's employment. Such particulars are to be supplied by the doctor who attended the deceased during the last illness. (The full list of specified diseases is contained in Appendix B at A3028 below.)

Duty to notify/report

Duty to notify

A3010   'Responsible persons' must notify enforcing authorities (see A3003 above) by the quickest means practicable (normally by telephone) of the following:

(*a*)   death as a result of an accident arising out of, or in connection with, work;

(*b*)   'major injury' (see A3006 above) of a person at work as a result of an accident arising out of, or in connection with, work;

(*c*)   injury suffered by a person not at work (e.g. a visitor, customer, client, passenger or bystander) as a result of an accident arising out of, or in connection with, work, where that person is taken from the accident site to a hospital for treatment;

(*d*)   major injury suffered by a person not at work, as a result of an accident arising out of, or in connection with, work at a hospital;

(*e*)   a dangerous occurrence (see A3008 above)

[*Reg 3(1)*];

(*f*)   road injuries or deaths [*Reg 10(2)*] (see A3018 below); and

(g)   gas incidents [*Reg 6(1)*] (see A3019 below).

Duty to report

A3011   Responsible persons must also formally report events causing death or major injury, dangerous occurrences and details associated with workers' occupational diseases. In cases of death, major injury and accidents leading to hospitalisation, the duty to report extends to visitors, bystanders and other non-employees. More particularly, within ten days of the incident, responsible persons must send a written report form to the relevant enforcing authority in relation to:

(a)   all events which require notification (listed in (a) to (g) at A3010 above);

(b)   the death of an employee if it occurs within a year following a reportable injury (whether or not reported under (a)) [*Reg 4*] (see A3017 below);

(c)   incapacitation for work of a person at work for more than three consecutive days as a result of an injury caused by an accident at work [*Reg 3(2)*] (see A3007 above);

(d)   specified occupational diseases relating to persons at work (see A3009 ABOVE AND APPENDIX B PART I AT A3028 below), and also specifically those suffered by workers on offshore installations (see Appendix B Part II at A3028 below) [*Reg 5(1)*], provided that, in both cases,

(i)   the responsible person has received a written statement by a doctor diagnosing the specified disease, in the case of an employee, or

(ii)   a self-employed person has been informed by a doctor that he is suffering from a specified disease.

[*Reg 5(2)*].

Exceptions to notification and reporting

A3012   There is no requirement to notify or report the injury or death of:

(a)   a patient undergoing treatment in a hospital or a doctor's or dentist's surgery [*Reg 10(1)*]; or

(b)   a member of the armed forces of the Crown [*Reg 10(3)*].

Duty to keep records

A3013   Records of injury-causing accidents, dangerous occurrences and specified diseases must be kept by responsible persons for at least three years. [*Reg 7*].

Injuries and dangerous occurrences

A3014   In the case of injuries and dangerous occurrences, such records must contain:

(a)   date and time of the accident or dangerous occurrence;

(b)   if an accident is suffered by a person at work –

(i)   full name,

(ii)   occupation, and

(iii)   nature of the injury;

(c)   in the event of an accident suffered by a person not at work –

   (i) full name,

   (ii) status (e.g. passenger, customer, visitor or bystander), and

   (iii) nature of injury;

(*d*) place where the accident or dangerous occurrence happened;

(*e*) a brief description of the circumstances;

(*f*) the date that the event was first reported to the enforcing authority;

(*g*) the method by which the event was reported.

[*Sch 4, Part I*].

Disease

A3015 In the case of specified diseases, such records must contain:

(*a*) date of diagnosis;

(*b*) name of the person affected;

(*c*) occupation of the person affected;

(*d*) name or nature of the disease;

(*e*) the date on which the disease was first reported to the enforcing authority; and

(*f*) the method by which disease was reported.

[*Sch 4, Part II*].

Action to be taken by employers and others when accidents occur at work

A3016   *fig. 1*

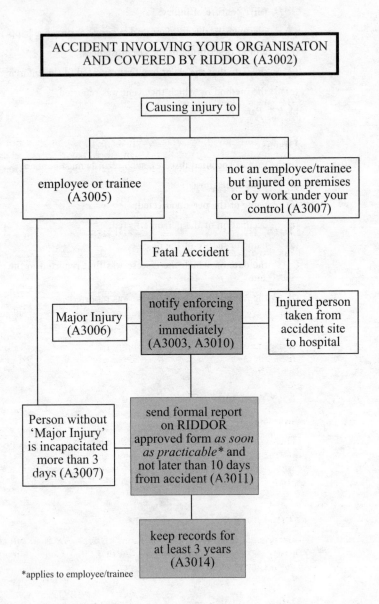

ACCIDENT INVOLVING YOUR ORGANISATON
AND COVERED BY RIDDOR (A3002)

Causing injury to

employee or trainee
(A3005)

not an employee/trainee
but injured on premises
or by work under your
control (A3007)

Fatal Accident

Major Injury
(A3006)

notify enforcing
authority
immediately
(A3003, A3010)

Injured person
taken from
accident site
to hospital

Person without
'Major Injury'
is incapacitated
more than 3
days (A3007)

send formal report
on RIDDOR
approved form *as soon
as practicable** and
not later than 10 days
from accident (A3011)

keep records for
at least 3 years
(A3014)

*applies to employee/trainee

Reporting the death of an employee

A3017   Where an employee, as a result of an accident at work, has suffered a reportable injury/condition which is the cause of his death within one year of the date of the accident, the employer must inform the enforcing authority in writing of the death as soon as it comes to his attention, whether or not the accident has been reported under *Regulation 3*. [*Reg 4*].

Road accidents

A3018 Road accident deaths and injuries are notifiable and reportable if the death or major injury is caused by or connected with:

(*a*) exposure to any substance conveyed by road;

(*b*) loading or unloading vehicles;

(*c*) construction, demolition, alteration or maintenance activities on public roads; or

(*d*) an accident involving a train.

[*Reg 10(2)*].

The person injured, whether fatally or not, may or may not be engaged in the above-mentioned activities. Thus, an employee struck by a passing vehicle or a motorist injured by falling scaffolding, are covered. In addition, certain dangerous occurrences on public highways and private roads are covered (see Appendix A at A3027 below).

Duty to report gas incidents

Gas suppliers

A3019 Where:

(*a*) a conveyor of flammable gas through a fixed pipe distribution system, or

(*b*) a filler, importer or supplier (not by way of the retail trade) of a refillable container containing liquefied petroleum gas

receives notification of any death, injury or condition (see A3010 above) which has arisen out of, or in connection with, the gas supplied, filled or imported, he must immediately notify the HSE and then send a report of the incident within 14 days. [*Reg 6(1)*].

Gas fitters

A3020 Where an employer or self-employed person who is an approved gas fitter has information that a gas fitting, flue or ventilation is, or is likely to cause, death or major injury, he is required to report that fact to the HSE on a prescribed form within 14 days. [*Reg 6(2)*].

Penalties

A3021 Contravention of any of the provisions of *RIDDOR* is an offence. The maximum penalty on summary conviction is a fine of £5,000. Conviction on indictment in the Crown Court carries an unlimited fine.

Defence in proceedings for breach of Regulations

A3022 It is a defence under the Regulations for a person to prove that:

(*a*) he was not aware of the event requiring him to notify or send a report to the enforcing authority; and

(*b*) he had taken all reasonable steps to have all such events brought to his notice.

[*Reg 11*].

Objectives of accident reporting

A3023

There should be an effective accident reporting and investigation system in all organisations. Accident reporting procedures should be clearly established in writing with individual reporting responsibilities specified. Staff should be trained in the system and disciplinary action may have to be taken where there is a failure to comply with it. Moreover, there is a case for all accidents, no matter how trivial they may seem, being reported through the internal reporting procedures.

The principal objectives of an accident reporting procedure are:

(*a*)   to ensure compliance with current legislation, e.g. *RIDDOR*;

(*b*)   to enable prompt remedial action to be taken;

(*c*)   to assist in monitoring the implementation of statements of health and safety policy (see further STATEMENTS OF HEALTH AND SAFETY POLICY);

(*d*)   to assist decision-making, planning and future resource allocation;

(*e*)   to provide feedback information which can be used in the development of future safety strategies and safe systems of work; and

(*f*)   to provide information to other interested parties.

Duty of disclosure of accident data

A3024

Employers are under a duty to disclose accident data to works safety representatives and, in the course of litigation, to legal representatives of persons claiming damages for death or personal injury.

Safety representatives

A3025

An employer must make available to safety representatives of both unionised and non-unionised workforces the information within the employer's knowledge necessary to enable them to fulfil their functions. [*Safety Representatives and Safety Committees Regulations 1977 (SI 1977 No 500), Reg 7(2)*; *Health and Safety (Consultation with Employees) Regulations 1996 (SI 1996 No 1513), Reg 5(1)*]. The Approved Code of Practice in association with these Regulations states that such information should include information which the employer keeps relating to the occurrence of any accident, dangerous occurrence or notifiable industrial disease and any associated statistical records. (Code of Practice: Safety Representatives and Safety Committees 1976, para 6(c)). See JOINT CONSULTATION – SAFETY REPRESENTATIVES AND SAFETY COMMITTEES.

Legal representatives

A3026

In the course of litigation (and sometimes before proceedings have actually begun) obligations may arise to give disclosure of relevant documents concerning an accident – even if they are confidential. Legal representatives of an injured party would expect reasonable access to *RIDDOR* information. The decision in *Waugh v British Railways Board [1979] 2 AER 1169* established that where an employer seeks to withhold on grounds of privilege a report made following an accident, he can only do so if its dominant purpose is related to actual or potential hostile legal proceedings. In *Waugh* a report was commissioned for two purposes following the death of an employee: (*a*) to recommend improvements in safety measures, and (*b*) to gather material for the employer's defence. It was held that the report was not privileged.

Employees who suffer an accident at work can also contact the Law Society's Accident Line on (0500) 192 939.

Appendix A

List of Reportable Dangerous Occurrences

A3027

PART I(A) – GENERAL

Lifting machinery, etc.

1.   The collapse of, the overturning of, or the failure of any load-bearing part of any –

    (a)   lift or hoist;

    (b)   crane or derrick;

    (c)   mobile powered access platform;

    (d)   access cradle or window-cleaning cradle;

    (e)   excavator;

    (f)   pile-driving frame or rig having an overall height, when operating, of more than 7 metres; or

    (g)   fork lift truck.

Pressure systems

2.   The failure of any closed vessel (including a boiler or boiler tube) or of any associated pipework, in which the internal pressure was above or below atmospheric pressure, where the failure has the potential to cause the death of any person.

Freight containers

3.   (1) The failure of any freight container in any of its load-bearing parts while it is being raised, lowered or suspended.

(2) In this paragraph, 'freight container' means a container as defined in regulation 2(1) of the Freight Containers (Safety Convention) Regulations 1984.

Overhead electric lines

4.   Any unintentional incident in which plant or equipment either –

    (a)   comes into contact with an uninsulated overhead electric line in which the voltage exceeds 200 volts; or

    (b)   causes an electrical discharge from such an electric line by coming into close proximity to it.

Electrical short circuit

5.   Electrical short circuit or overload attended by fire or explosion which results in the stoppage of the plant involved for more than 24 hours or which has the potential to cause the death of any person.

Explosives

6. (1) Any of the following incidents involving explosives –

(a)   the unintentional explosion or ignition of explosives other than one –

(i)   caused by the unintentional discharge of a weapon where, apart from that unintentional discharge, the weapon and explosives functioned as they were designed to do; or

(ii)   where a fail-safe device or safe system of work functioned so as to prevent any person from being injured in consequence of the explosion or ignition;

(b)   a misfire (other than one at a mine or quarry or inside a well or one involving a weapon) except where a fail-safe device or safe system of work functioned so as to prevent any person from being endangered in consequence of the misfire;

(c)   the failure of the shots in any demolition operation to cause the intended extent of collapse or direction of fall of a building or structure;

(d)   the projection of material (other than at a quarry) beyond the boundary of the site on which the explosives are being used or beyond the danger zone in circumstances such that any person was or might have been injured thereby;

(e)   any injury to a person (other than at a mine or quarry or one otherwise reportable under these Regulations) involving first-aid or medical treatment resulting from the explosion or discharge of any explosives or detonator.

(2) In this paragraph 'explosives' means any explosive of a type which would, were it being transported, be assigned to class 1 within the meaning of the Classification and Labelling of Explosives Regulations 1983 and 'danger zone' means the area from which persons have been excluded or forbidden to enter to avoid being endangered by any explosion or ignition of explosives.

Biological agents

7.   Any accident or incident which resulted or could have resulted in the release or escape of a biological agent likely to cause severe human infection or illness.

Malfunction of radiation generators, etc.

8.   (1) Any incident in which –

(a)   the malfunction of a radiation generator or its ancillary equipment used in fixed or mobile industrial radiography, the irradiation of food or the processing of products by irradiation, which causes it to fail to de-energise at the end of the intended exposure period; or

(b)   the malfunction of equipment used in fixed or mobile industrial radiography or gamma irradiation causes a radioactive source to fail to return to its safe position by the normal means at the end of the intended exposure period.

(2) In this paragraph 'radiation generator' has the same meaning as in regulation 2 of the Ionising Radiations Regulations 1985.

Breathing apparatus

9.   (1) Any incident in which breathing apparatus malfunctions –

(a)   while in use, or

(b)   during testing immediately prior to use in such a way that had the malfunction occurred while the apparatus was in use it would have posed a danger to the health or safety of the user.

(2) This paragraph shall not apply to breathing apparatus while it is being –

(a)   used in a mine; or

(b)   maintained or tested as part of a routine maintenance procedure.

Diving operations

10.   Any of the following incidents in relation to a diving project –

(a)   the failure or the endangering of –

(i)   any lifting equipment associated with the diving operation, or

(ii)   life support equipment, including control panels, hoses and breathing apparatus,

which puts a diver at risk;

(b)   any damage to, or endangering of, the dive platform, or any failure of the dive platform to remain on station, which puts a diver at risk;

(c)   the trapping of a diver;

(d)   any explosion in the vicinity of a diver; or

(e)   any uncontrolled ascent or any omitted decompression which puts a diver at risk.

Collapse of scaffolding

11.   The complete or partial collapse of –

(a)   any scaffold which is –

(i)   more than 5 metres in height which results in a substantial part of the scaffold falling or overturning; or

(ii)   erected over or adjacent to water in circumstances such that there would be a risk of drowning to a person falling from the scaffold into the water; or

(b)   the suspension arrangements (including any outrigger) of any slung or suspended scaffold which causes a working platform or cradle to fall.

Train collisions

12.   Any unintended collision of a train with any other train or vehicle, other than one reportable under Part IV of this Schedule, which caused, or might have caused, the death of, or major injury to, any person.

Wells

13.   Any of the following incidents in relation to a well (other than a well sunk for the purpose of the abstraction of water) –

(a)   a blow-out (that is to say an uncontrolled flow of well-fluids from a well);

(b)   the coming into operation of a blow-out prevention or diversion system to control a flow from a well where normal control procedures fail;

(c)   the detection of hydrogen sulphide in the course of operations at a well or in samples of well-fluids from a well where the presence of hydrogen sulphide in the reservoir being drawn on by the well was not anticipated by the responsible person before that detection;

(d)   the taking of precautionary measures additional to any contained in the original drilling programme following failure to maintain a planned minimum separation distance between wells drilled from a particular installation; or

(e)   the mechanical failure of any safety critical element of a well (and for this purpose the safety critical element of a well is any part of a well whose failure would cause or contribute to, or whose purpose is to prevent or limit the effect of, the unintentional release of fluids from a well or a reservoir being drawn on by a well).

Pipelines or pipeline works

14.   The following incidents in respect of a pipeline or pipeline works –

(a)   the uncontrolled or accidental escape of anything from, or inrush of anything into, a pipeline which has the potential to cause the death of, major injury or damage to the health of any person or which results in the pipeline being shut down for more than 24 hours;

(b)   the unintentional ignition of anything in a pipeline or of anything which, immediately before it was ignited, was in a pipeline;

(c)   any damage to any part of a pipeline which has the potential to cause the death of, major injury or damage to the health of any person or which results in the pipeline being shut down for more than 24 hours;

(d)   any substantial and unintentional change in the position of a pipeline requiring immediate attention to safeguard the integrity or safety of a pipeline;

(e)   any unintentional change in the subsoil or seabed in the vicinity of a pipeline which has the potential to affect the integrity or safety of a pipeline;

(f)   any failure of any pipeline isolation device, equipment or system which has the potential to cause the death of, major injury or damage to the health of any person or which results in the pipeline being shut down for more than 24 hours; or

(g)   any failure of equipment involved with pipeline works which has the potential to cause the death of, major injury or damage to the health of any person.

Fairground equipment

15.   The following incidents on fairground equipment in use or under test –

(a)   the failure of any load-bearing part;

(b)   the failure of any part designed to support or restrain passengers; or

(c)   the derailment or the unintended collision of cars or trains.

Carriage of dangerous substances by road

16.   (1) Any incident involving a road tanker or tank container used for the carriage dangerous goods in which –

(a)   the road tanker or vehicle carrying the tank container overturns (including turning onto its side);

(b)   the tank carrying the dangerous goods is seriously damaged;

(c)   there is an uncontrolled release or escape of the dangerous substance being carried; or

(d)   there is a fire involving the dangerous goods being carried.

17.   (1) Any incident involving a vehicle used for the carriage of dangerous goods, other than a vehicle to which paragraph 16 applies, where there is –

(a)   an uncontrolled release or escape of the dangerous goods being carried in such a quantity as to have the potential to cause the death of, or major injury to, any person; or

(b)   a fire which involves the dangerous goods being carried.

17A.   In paragraphs 16 and 17 above –

(a)   'road tanker' and 'tank container' have the same meanings as in regulation 2(1) of the Carriage of Dangerous Goods (Classification, Packaging and Labelling) and Use of Transportable Pressure Receptacles Regulations 1996 ('the 1996 Regulations');

(b)   'carriage' has the same meaning as in regulation 2(1) of the Carriage of Dangerous Goods by Road Regulations 1996; and

(c)   'dangerous goods' means any goods which fall within the definition of 'dangerous goods' on regulation 2(1) of the 1996 Regulations, other than –

(i)   explosives, or

(ii)   radioactive material (other than that which is being carried in accordance with the conditions specified in Schedules 1 to 4 of marginal 2704 to ADR),

and in this sub-paragraph 'ADR' has the meaning assigned to it by regulation 2(1) of the 1996 Regulations.

PART I(B) – DANGEROUS OCCURRENCES WHICH ARE REPORTABLE EXCEPT IN RELATION TO OFFSHORE WORKPLACES

Collapse of building or structure

18.   Any unintended collapse or partial collapse of –

(a)   any building or structure (whether above or below ground) under construction, reconstruction, alteration or demolition which involves a fall of more than 5 tonnes of material;

(b)   any floor or wall of any building (whether above or below ground) used as a place of work; or

(c)   any false-work.

Explosion or fire

19.   An explosion or fire occurring in any plant or premises which results in the stoppage of that plant or as the case may be the suspension of normal work in those premises for more than 24 hours, where the explosion or fire was due to the ignition of any material.

Escape of flammable substances

20.   (1) The sudden, uncontrolled release –

(a)   inside a building –

(i)   of 100 kilograms or more of a flammable liquid,

(ii)   of 10 kilograms or more of a flammable liquid at a temperature above its normal boiling point, or

(iii)   of 10 kilograms or more of a flammable gas; or

(b)   in the open air, of 500 kilograms or more of any of the substances referred to in sub-paragraph (a) above.

(2) In this paragraph, 'flammable liquid' and 'flammable gas' means respectively a liquid and a gas so classified in accordance with regulation 5(2), (3) or (5) of the Chemicals (Hazard Information and Packaging for Supply) Regulations 1994.

Escape of substances

21.   The accidental release or escape of any substance in a quantity sufficient to cause the death, major injury or any other damage to the health of any person.

PART II – DANGEROUS OCCURRENCES WHICH ARE REPORTABLE IN RELATION TO MINES

Fire or ignition of gas

22.   The ignition, below ground, of any gas (other than gas in a safety lamp) or of any dust.

23.   The accidental ignition of any gas in part of a firedamp drainage system on the surface or in an exhauster house.

24. The outbreak of any fire below ground.

25. An incident where any person in consequence of any smoke or any other indication that a fire may have broken out below ground has been caused to leave any place pursuant to either Regulation 11(1) of the Coal and Other Mines (Fire and Rescue) Regulations 1956 or section 79 of the Mines and Quarries Act 1954.

26. The outbreak of any fire on the surface which endangers the operation of any winding or haulage apparatus installed at a shaft or unwalkable outlet or of any mechanically operated apparatus for producing ventilation below ground.

Escape of gas

27. Any violent outburst of gas together with coal or other solid matter into the mine workings except when such outburst is caused intentionally.

Failure of plant or equipment

28. The breakage of any rope, chain, coupling, balance rope, guide rope, suspension gear or other gear used for or in connection with the carrying of persons through any shaft or staple shaft.

29. The breakage or unintentional uncoupling of any rope, chain, coupling, rope tensioning system or other gear used for or in connection with the transport of persons below ground, or breakage of any belt, rope or other gear used for or in connection with a belt conveyor designated by the mine manager as a man-riding conveyor.

30. An incident where any conveyance being used for the carriage of persons is overwound; or any conveyance not being so used is overwound and becomes detached from its winding rope; or any conveyance operated by means of the friction of a rope on a winding sheave is brought to rest by the apparatus provided in the headframe of the shaft or in the part of the shaft below the lowest landing for the time being in use, being apparatus provided for bringing the conveyance to rest in the event of its being overwound.

31. The stoppage of any ventilating apparatus (other than an auxiliary fan) which causes a substantial reduction in ventilation of the mine lasting for a period exceeding 30 minutes, except when for the purpose of planned maintenance.

32. The collapse of any headframe, winding engine house, fan house or storage bunker.

Breathing apparatus

33. At any mine an incident where –

    (a) breathing apparatus or a smoke helmet or other apparatus serving the same purpose or a self-rescuer, while being used, fails to function safely or develops a defect likely to affect its safe working; or

    (b) immediately after using and arising out of the use of breathing apparatus or a smoke helmet or other apparatus serving the same purpose or a self-rescuer, any person receives first-aid or medical treatment by reason of his unfitness or suspected unfitness at the mine.

Injury by explosion of blasting material etc.

34.   An incident in which any person suffers an injury (not being a major injury or one reportable under regulation 3(2)) which results from an explosion or discharge of any blasting material or device within the meaning of section 69(4) of the Mines and Quarries Act 1954 for which he receives first-aid or medical treatment at the mine.

Use of emergency escape apparatus

35.   An incident where any apparatus is used (other than for the purpose of training and practice) which has been provided at the mine in accordance with regulation 4 of the Mines (Safety of Exit) Regulations 1988 or where persons leave the mine when apparatus and equipment normally used by persons to leave the mine is unavailable.

Inrush of gas or water

36.   Any inrush of noxious or flammable gas from old workings.

37.   Any inrush of water or material which flows when wet from any source.

Insecure tip

38.   Any movement of material or any fire or any other event which indicates that a tip to which Part I of the Mines and Quarries (Tips) Act 1969 applies, is or is likely to become insecure.

Locomotives

39.   Any incident where an underground locomotive when not used for testing purposes is brought to rest by means other than its safety circuit protective devices or normal service brakes.

Falls of ground

40.   Any fall of ground, not being part of the normal operations at a mine, which results from a failure of an underground support system and prevents persons travelling through the area affected by the fall or which otherwise exposes them to danger.

PART III – DANGEROUS OCCURRENCES WHICH ARE REPORTABLE IN RELATION TO QUARRIES

Collapse of storage bunkers

41.   The collapse of any storage bunker.

Sinking of craft

42.   The sinking of any water-borne craft or hovercraft.

Injuries

43.   (1) An incident in which any person suffers an injury (not otherwise reportable under these Regulations) which results from an explosion or from the discharge of any explosives for which he receives first-aid or medical treatment at the quarry.

(2) In this paragraph, 'explosives' has the same meaning as in regulation 2(1) of the Quarries (Explosives) Regulations 1988.

Projection of substances outside quarry

44.   Any incident in which any substance is ascertained to have been projected beyond a quarry boundary as a result of blasting operations in circumstances in which any person was or might have been endangered.

Misfires

45.   Any misfire, as defined by regulation 2(1) of the Quarries (Explosives) Regulations 1988.

Insecure tips

46.   Any event (including any movement of material or any fire) which indicates that a tip, to which Part I of the Mines and Quarries (Tips) Act 1969 applies, is or is likely to become insecure.

Movement of slopes or faces

47.   Any movement or failure of an excavated slope or face which –

(a)   has the potential to cause the death of any person; or

(b)   adversely affects any building, contiguous land, transport system, footpath, public utility or service, watercourse, reservoir or area of public access.

Explosions or fires in vehicles or plant

48.   (1) Any explosion or fire occurring in any large vehicle or mobile plant which results in the stoppage of that vehicle or plant for more than 24 hours and which affects –

(a)   any place where persons normally work; or

(b)   the route of egress from such a place.

(2) In this paragraph, 'large vehicle or mobile plant' means –

(a)   a dump truck having a load capacity of at least 50 tonnes; or

(b)   an excavator having a bucket capacity of at least 5 cubic metres.

PART IV – DANGEROUS OCCURRENCES WHICH ARE REPORTABLE IN RESPECT OF RELEVANT TRANSPORT SYSTEMS

Accidents to passenger trains

49.   Any collision in which a passenger train collides with another train.

50.   Any case where a passenger train or any part of such a train unintentionally leaves the rails.

Accidents not involving passenger trains

51.   Any collision between trains, other than one between a passenger train and another train, on a running line where any train sustains damage as a result of the collision, and any such collision in a siding which results in a running line being obstructed.

52.   Any derailment, of a train other than a passenger train, on a running line, except a derailment which occurs during shunting operations and does not obstruct any other running line.

53.   Any derailment, of a train other than a passenger train, in a siding which results in a running line being obstructed.

Accidents involving any kind of train

54.   Any case of a train striking a buffer stop, other than in a siding, where damage is caused to the train.

55.   Any case of a train striking any cattle or horse, whether or not damage is caused to the train, or striking any other animal if, in consequence, damage (including damage to the windows of the driver's cab but excluding other damage consisting solely in the breakage of glass) is caused to the train necessitating immediate temporary or permanent repair.

56.   Any case of a train on a running line striking or being struck by any object which causes damage (including damage to the windows of the driver's cab but excluding other damage consisting solely in the breakage of glass) necessitating immediate temporary or permanent repair or which might have been liable to derail the train.

57.   Any case of a train, other than one on a railway, striking or being struck by a road vehicle.

58.   Any case of a passenger train, or any other train not fitted with continuous self-applying brakes, becoming unintentionally divided.

59.   (1) Any of the following classes of accident which occurs or is discovered whilst the train is on a running line –

(a)   the failure of an axle;

(b)   the failure of a wheel or tyre, including a tyre loose on its wheel;

(c)   the failure of a rope or the fastenings thereof or of the winding plant or equipment involved in working an incline;

(d)   any fire, severe electrical arcing or fusing in or on any part of a passenger train or a train carrying dangerous goods;

(e)   in the case of any train other than a passenger train, any severe electrical arcing or fusing, or any fire which was extinguished by a fire-fighting service; or

(f)   any other failure of any part of a train which is likely to cause an accident to that or any other train or to kill or injure any person.

(2)   In this paragraph 'dangerous goods' has the meaning applied to it in regulation 2(1) of the Carriage of Dangerous Goods (Classification, Packaging and Labelling) and the Use of Transportable Pressure Receptacles Regulations 1996.

Accidents and incidents at level crossings

60.   Any case of a train striking a road vehicle or gate at a level crossing.

61.   Any case of a train running onto a level crossing when not authorised to do so.

62.   A failure of the equipment at a level crossing which could endanger users of the road or path crossing the railway.

Accidents involving the permanent way and other works on or connected with a relevant transport system

63.   The failure of a rail in a running line or of a rack rail, which results in –

(a)   a complete fracture of the rail through its cross-section; or

(b)   in a piece becoming detached from the rail which necessitates an immediate stoppage of traffic or the immediate imposition of a speed restriction lower than that currently in force.

64.   A buckle of a running line which necessitates an immediate stoppage of traffic or the immediate imposition of a speed restriction lower than that currently in force.

65.   Any case of an aircraft or a vehicle of any kind landing on, running onto or coming to rest foul of the line, or damaging the line, which causes damage which obstructs the line or which damages any railway equipment at a level crossing.

66.   The runaway of an escalator, lift or passenger conveyor.

67.   Any fire or severe arcing or fusing which seriously affects the functioning of signalling equipment.

68.   Any fire affecting the permanent way or works of a relevant transport system which necessitates the suspension of services over any line, or the closure of any part of a station or signal box or other premises, for a period –

(a)   in the case of a fire affecting any part of a relevant transport system below ground, of more than 30 minutes, and

(b)   in any other case, of more than 1 hour.

69.   Any other fire which causes damage which has the potential to affect the running of a relevant transport system.

Accidents involving failure of the works on or connected with a relevant transport system

70.   (1) The following classes of accident where they are likely either to cause an accident to a train or to endanger any person –

(a)   the failure of a tunnel, bridge, viaduct, culvert, station, or other structure or any part thereof including the fixed electrical equipment of an electrified relevant transport system;

(b)   any failure in the signalling system which endangers or which has the potential to endanger the safe passage of trains other than a failure of a traffic light controlling the movement of vehicles on a road;

(c)   a slip of a cutting or of an embankment;

(d)   flooding of the permanent way;

(e)   the striking of a bridge by a vessel or by a road vehicle or its load; or

(f)   the failure of any other portion of the permanent way or works not specified above.

Incidents of serious congestion

71.   Any case where planned procedures or arrangements have been activated in order to control risks arising from an incident of undue passenger congestion at a station unless that congestion has been relieved within a period of time allowed for by those procedures or arrangements.

Incidents of signals passed without authority

72.   (1) Any case where a train, travelling on a running line or entering a running line from a siding, passes without authority a signal displaying a stop aspect unless –

(a)   the stop aspect was not displayed in sufficient time for the driver to stop safely at the signal; or

(b)   the line is equipped with automatic train protection equipment which is in operation.

(2) In this paragraph 'automatic train protection equipment' means equipment which automatically controls the speed of a train, either by bringing it to a halt or reducing its speed, in the event that the train passes a signal without authority or exceeds a prescribed speed limit.

PART V – DANGEROUS OCCURRENCES WHICH ARE REPORTABLE IN RESPECT OF AN OFFSHORE WORKPLACE

Release of petroleum hydrocarbon

73.   Any unintentional release of petroleum hydrocarbon on or from an offshore installation which –

(a)   results in –

      (i)   a fire or explosion; or

      (ii)   the taking of action to prevent or limit the consequences of a potential fire or explosion; or

(b)   has the potential to cause death or major injury to any person.

Fire or explosion

74.   Any fire or explosion at an offshore installation, other than one to which paragraph 73 above applies, which results in the stoppage of plant or the suspension of normal work.

Release or escape of dangerous substances

75.   The uncontrolled or unintentional release or escape of any substance (other than petroleum hydrocarbon) on or from an offshore installation which has the potential to cause the death of, major injury to or damage to the health of any person.

Collapses

76.   Any unintended collapse of any offshore installation or any unintended collapse of any part thereof or any plant thereon which jeopardises the overall structural integrity of the installation.

Dangerous occurrences

77.   Any of the following occurrences having the potential to cause death or major injury –

(a)   the failure of equipment required to maintain a floating offshore installation on station;

(b)   the dropping of any object on an offshore installation or on an attendant vessel or into the water adjacent to an installation or vessel; or

(c)   damage to or on an offshore installation caused by adverse weather conditions.

Collisions

78.   Any collision between a vessel or aircraft and an offshore installation which results in damage to the installation, the vessel or the aircraft.

79.   Any occurrence with the potential for a collision between a vessel and an offshore installation where, had a collision occurred, it would have been liable to jeopardise the overall structural integrity of the offshore installation.

Subsidence or collapse of seabed

80.   Any subsidence or local collapse of the seabed likely to affect the foundations of an offshore installation or the overall structural integrity of an offshore installation.

Loss of stability or buoyancy

81.   Any incident involving loss of stability or buoyancy of a floating offshore installation.

Evacuation

82.   Any evacuation (other than one arising out of an incident reportable under any other provision of these Regulations) of an offshore installation, in whole or part, in the interests of safety.

Falls into water

83. Any case of a person falling more than 2 metres into water (unless the fall results in death or injury required to be reported under sub-paragraphs (a)–(d) of regulation 3(1)).

[*The Reporting of Injuries, Diseases and Dangerous Occurrences Regulations 1995, Reg 2(1), Sch 2*].

Appendix B

List of Reportable Diseases

A3028   **PART I – OCCUPATIONAL DISEASES**

Column 1	Column 2
Diseases	**Activities**

Conditions due to physical agents and the physical demands of work

1.	Inflammation, ulceration or malignant disease of the skin due to ionising radiation.	
2.	Malignant disease of the bones due to ionising radiation.	Work with ionising radiation.
3.	Blood dyscrasia due to ionising radiation.	
4.	Cataract due to electromagnetic radiation.	Work involving exposure to electromagnetic radiation (including radiant heat).
5.	Decompression illness.	
6.	Barotrauma resulting in lung or other organ damage.	Work involving breathing gases at increased pressure (including diving).
7.	Dysbaric osteonecrosis.	
8.	Cramp of the hand or forearm due to repetitive movements.	Work involving prolonged periods of handwriting, typing or other repetitive movements of the fingers, hand or arm.
9.	Subcutaneous cellulitis of the hand (beat hand).	Physically demanding work causing severe or prolonged friction or pressure on the hand.
10.	Bursitis or subcutaneous cellulitis arising at or about the knee due to severe or prolonged external friction or pressure at or about the knee (beat knee).	Physically demanding work causing severe or prolonged friction or pressure at or about the knee.
11.	Bursitis or subcutaneous cellulitis arising at or about the elbow due to severe or prolonged external friction or pressure at or about the elbow (beat elbow).	Physically demanding work causing severe or prolonged friction or pressure at or about the elbow.
12.	Traumatic inflammation of the tendons of the hand or forearm or of the associated tendon sheaths.	Physically demanding work, frequent or repeated movements, constrained postures or extremes of extension or flexion of the hand or wrist.

Column 1	Column 2
Diseases	**Activities**
13. Carpal tunnel syndrome.	Work involving the use of hand-held vibrating tools.
14. Hand-arm vibration syndrome.	Work involving:
	(a) the use of chain saws, brush cutters or hand-held or hand-fed circular saws in forestry or wood-working;
	(b) the use of hand-held rotary tools in grinding material or in sanding or polishing metal;
	(c) the holding of material being ground or metal being sanded or polished by rotary tools;
	(d) the use of hand-held percussive metal-working tools or the holding of metal being worked upon by percussive tools in connection with riveting, caulking, chipping, hammering, fettling or swaging;
	(e) the use of hand-held powered percussive drills or hand-held powered percussive hammers in mining, quarrying or demolition, or on roads or footpaths (including road construction); or
	(f) the holding of material being worked upon by pounding machines in shoe manufacture.
Infections due to biological agents	
15. Anthrax.	(a) Work involving handling infected animals, their products or packaging containing infected material; or
	(b) work on infected sites.
16. Brucellosis.	Work involving contact with:

Column 1	Column 2
Diseases	**Activities**
	(a) animals or their carcasses (including any parts thereof) infected by brucella or the untreated products of same; or
	(b) laboratory specimens or vaccines of or containing brucella.
17. (a) Avian chlamydiosis.	Work involving contact with birds infected with chlamydia psittaci, or the remains or untreated products of such birds.
(b) Ovine chlamydiosis.	Work involving contact with sheep infected with chlamydia psittaci or the remains or untreated products of such sheep.
18. Hepatitis.	Work involving contact with:
	(a) human blood or human blood products; or
	(b) any source of viral hepatitis.
19. Legionellosis.	Work on or near cooling systems which are located in the workplace and use water; or work on hot water service systems located in the workplace which are likely to be a source of contamination.
20. Leptospirosis.	(a) Work in places which are or are liable to be infested by rats, fieldmice, voles or other small mammals;
	(b) work at dog kennels or involving the care or handling of dogs; or
	(c) work involving contact with bovine animals or their meat products or pigs or their meat products.
21. Lyme disease.	Work involving exposure to ticks (including in particular work by forestry workers, rangers, dairy farmers, game keepers and other persons engaged in countryside management).

Column 1	Column 2
Diseases	**Activities**
22. Q fever.	Work involving contact with animals, their remains or their untreated products.
23. Rabies.	Work involving handling or contact with infected animals.
24. *Streptococcus suis.*	Work involving contact with pigs infected with *Streptococcus suis*, or with the carcasses, products or residues of pigs so affected.
25. Tetanus.	Work involving contact with soil likely to be contaminated by animals.
26. Tuberculosis.	Work with persons, animals, human or animal remains or any other material which might be a source of infection.
27. Any infection reliably attributable to the performance of the work specified in the entry opposite hereto.	Work with micro-organisms; work with live or dead human beings in the course of providing any treatment or service or in conducting any investigation involving exposure to blood or body fluids; work with animals or any potentially infected material derived from any of the above.

Conditions due to substances

28.   Poisonings by any of the following: Any activity.

    (a)   acrylamide monomer;

    (b)   arsenic or one of its compounds;

    (c)   benzene or a homologue of benzene;

    (d)   beryllium or one of its compounds;

    (e)   cadmium or one of its compounds;

    (f)   carbon disulphide;

    (g)   diethylene dioxide (dioxan);

    (h)   ethylene oxide;

    (i)   lead or one of its compounds;

Column 1	Column 2
Diseases	**Activities**

    (j)   manganese or one of its compounds;

    (k)   mercury or one of its compounds;

    (l)   methyl bromide;

    (m)   nitrochlorobenzene, or a nitro–or amino–or chloro-derivative of benzene or of a homologue of benzene;

    (n)   oxides of nitrogen;

    (o)   phosphorus or one of its compounds.

29.   Cancer of a bronchus or lung.

    (a)   Work in or about a building where nickel is produced by decomposition of a gaseous nickel compound or where any industrial process which is ancillary or incidental to that process is carried on; or

    (b)   work involving exposure to bis(chloromethyl) ether or any electrolytic chromium processes (excluding passivation) which involve hexavalent chromium compounds, chromate production or zinc chromate pigment manufacture.

30.   Primary carcinoma of the lung where there is accompanying evidence of silicosis.

Any occupation in:

    (a)   glass manufacture;

    (b)   sandstone tunnelling or quarrying;

    (c)   the pottery industry;

    (d)   metal ore mining;

    (e)   slate quarrying or slate production;

    (f)   clay mining;

    (g)   the use of siliceous materials as abrasives;

    (h)   foundry work;

Column 1	Column 2
Diseases	**Activities**
	(i) granite tunnelling or quarrying; or
	(j) stone cutting or masonry.
31. Cancer of the urinary tract.	1. Work involving exposure to any of the following substances:
	(a) beta–naphthylamine or methylene–bis–orthochloroaniline;
	(b) diphenyl substituted by at least one nitro or primary amino group or by at least one nitro and primary amino group (including benzidine);
	(c) any of the substances mentioned in sub-paragraph (b) above if further ring substituted by halogeno, methyl or methoxy groups, but not by other groups; or
	(d) the salts of any of the substances mentioned in sub-paragraphs (a) to (c) above.
	2. The manufacture of auramine or magenta.
32. Bladder cancer.	Work involving exposure to aluminium smelting using the Soderberg process.
33. Angiosarcoma of the liver.	(a) Work in or about machinery or apparatus used for the polymerisation of vinyl chloride monomer, a process which, for the purposes of this sub-paragraph, comprises all operations up to and including the drying of the slurry produced by the polymerisation and the packaging of the dried product; or
	(b) work in a building or structure in which any part of the process referred to in the foregoing sub-paragraph takes place.

Column 1	Column 2
Diseases	**Activities**
34. Peripheral neuropathy.	Work involving the use or handling of or exposure to the fumes of or vapour containing n–hexane or methyl n–butyl ketone.
35. Chrome ulceration of: (a) the nose or throat; or (b) the skin of the hands or forearm.	Work involving exposure to chromic acid or to any other chromium compound.
36. Folliculitis. 37. Acne. 38. Skin cancer.	Work involving exposure to mineral oil, tar, pitch or arsenic.
39. Pneumoconiosis (excluding asbestosis).	1. (a) The mining, quarrying or working of silica rock or the working of dried quartzose sand, any dry deposit or residue of silica or any dry admixture containing such materials (including any activity in which any of the aforesaid operations are carried out incidentally to the mining or quarrying of other minerals or to the manufacture of articles containing crushed or ground silica rock); or (b) the handling of any of the materials specified in the foregoing sub-paragraph in or incidentally to any of the operations mentioned therein or substantial exposure to the dust arising from such operations.

Column 1	Column 2
Diseases	**Activities**

2. The breaking, crushing or grinding of flint, the working or handling of broken, crushed or ground flint or materials containing such flint or substantial exposure to the dust arising from any of such operations.

3. Sand blasting by means of compressed air with the use of quartzose sand or crushed silica rock or flint or substantial exposure to the dust arising from such sand blasting.

4. Work in a foundry or the performance of, or substantial exposure to the dust arising from, any of the following operations:

(a)   the freeing of steel castings from adherent siliceous substance or;

(b)   the freeing of metal castings from adherent siliceous substance:

  (i) by blasting with an abrasive propelled by compressed air, steam or a wheel, or

  (ii) by the use of power-driven tools.

5. The manufacture of china or earthenware (including sanitary earthenware, electrical earthenware and earthenware tiles) and any activity involving substantial exposure to the dust arising therefrom.

6. The grinding of mineral graphite or substantial exposure to the dust arising from such grinding.

7. The dressing of granite or any igneous rock by masons, the crushing of such materials or substantial exposure to the dust arising from such operations.

Column 1	Column 2
Diseases	**Activities**

8. The use or preparation for use of an abrasive wheel or substantial exposure to the dust arising therefrom.

9. (a) Work underground in any mine in which one of the objects of the mining operations is the getting of any material;

(b) the working or handling above ground at any coal or tin mine of any materials extracted therefrom or any operation incidental thereto;

(c) the trimming of coal in any ship, barge, lighter, dock or harbour or at any wharf or quay; or

(d) the sawing, splitting or dressing of slate or any operation incidental thereto.

10. The manufacture or work incidental to the manufacture of carbon electrodes by an industrial undertaking for use in the electrolytic extraction of aluminium from aluminium oxide and any activity involving substantial exposure to the dust therefrom.

11. Boiler scaling or substantial exposure to the dust arising therefrom.

40. Byssinosis.

The spinning or manipulation of raw or waste cotton or flax or the weaving of cotton or flax, carried out in each case in a room in a factory, together with any other work carried out in such a room.

Column 1	Column 2
Diseases	**Activities**
41. Mesothelioma.	(a) The working or handling of asbestos or any admixture of asbestos;
42. Lung cancer.	
43. Asbestosis.	(b) the manufacture or repair of asbestos textiles or other articles containing or composed of asbestos;
	(c) the cleaning of any machinery or plant used in any of the foregoing operations and of any chambers, fixtures and appliances for the collection of asbestos dust; or
	(d) substantial exposure to the dust arising from any of the foregoing operations.
44. Cancer of the nasal cavity or associated air sinuses.	1. (a) Work in or about a building where wooden furniture is manufactured;
	(b) work in a building used for the manufacture of footwear or components of footwear made wholly or partly of leather or fibre board; or
	(c) work at a place used wholly or mainly for the repair of footwear made wholly or partly of leather or fibre board.
	2. Work in or about a factory building where nickel is produced by decomposition of a gaseous nickel compound or in any process which is ancillary or incidental thereto.
45. Occupational dermatitis.	Work involving exposure to any of the following agents:
	(a) epoxy resin systems;
	(b) formaldehyde and its resins;
	(c) metalworking fluids;
	(d) chromate (hexavalent and derived from trivalent chromium);

Column 1	Column 2
Diseases	**Activities**
	(e) cement, plaster or concrete;
	(f) acrylates and methacrylates;
	(g) colophony (rosin) and its modified products;
	(h) glutaraldehyde;
	(i) mercaptobenzothiazole, thiurams, substituted paraphenylene-diamines and related rubber processing chemicals;
	(j) biocides, anti-bacterials, preservatives or disinfectants;
	(k) organic solvents;
	(l) antibiotics and other pharmaceuticals and therapeutic agents;
	(m) strong acids, strong alkalis, strong solutions (e.g. brine) and oxidising agents including domestic bleach or reducing agents;
	(n) hairdressing products including in particular dyes, shampoos, bleaches and permanent waving solutions;
	(o) soaps and detergents;
	(p) plants and plant-derived material including in particular the daffodil, tulip and chrysanthemum families, the parsley family (carrots, parsnips, parsley and celery), garlic and onion, hardwoods and the pine family;
	(q) fish, shell-fish or meat;
	(r) sugar or flour; or
	(s) any other known irritant or sensitising agent including in particular any chemical bearing the warning 'may cause sensitisation by skin contact' or 'irritating to the skin'.

Column 1	Column 2
Diseases	**Activities**

46. Extrinsic alveolitis (including farmer's lung).

Exposure to moulds, fungal spores or heterologous proteins during work in:

(a) agriculture, horticulture, forestry, cultivation of edible fungi or malt-working;

(b) loading, unloading or handling mouldy vegetable matter or edible fungi whilst same is being stored;

(c) caring for or handling birds; or

(d) handling bagasse.

47. Occupational asthma.

Work involving exposure to any of the following agents:

(a) isocyanates;

(b) platinum salts;

(c) fumes or dust arising from the manufacture, transport or use of hardening agents (including epoxy resin curing agents) based on phthalic anhydride, tetrachlorophthalic anhydride, trimellitic anhydride or triethylene-tetramine;

(d) fumes arising from the use of rosin as a soldering flux;

(e) proteolytic enzymes;

(f) animals including insects and other arthropods used for the purposes of research or education or in laboratories;

(g) dusts arising from the sowing, cultivation, harvesting, drying, handling, milling, transport or storage of barley, oats, rye, wheat or maize or the handling, milling, transport or storage of meal or flour made therefrom;

(h) antibiotics;

Column 1	Column 2
Diseases	**Activities**
	(i) cimetidine;
	(j) wood dust;
	(k) ispaghula;
	(l) castor bean dust;
	(m) ipecacuanha;
	(n) azodicarbonamide;
	(o) animals including insects and other arthropods (whether in their larval forms or not) used for the purposes of pest control or fruit cultivation or the larval forms of animals used for the purposes of research or education or in laboratories;
	(p) glutaraldehyde;
	(q) persulphate salts or henna;
	(r) crustaceans or fish or products arising from these in the food processing industry;
	(s) reactive dyes;
	(t) soya bean;
	(u) tea dust;
	(v) green coffee bean dust;
	(w) fumes from stainless steel welding;
	(x) any other sensitising agent, including in particular any chemical bearing the warning 'may cause sensitisation by inhalation'.

PART II – DISEASES ADDITIONALLY REPORTABLE IN RESPECT OF OFFSHORE WORKPLACES

48. Chickenpox.
49. Cholera.
50. Diphtheria.
51. Dysentery (amoebic or bacillary).
52. Acute encephalitis.
53. Erysipelas.
54. Food poisoning.

55.   Legionellosis.
56.   Malaria.
57.   Measles.
58.   Meningitis.
59.   Meningococcal septicaemia (without meningitis).
60.   Mumps.
61.   Paratyphoid fever.
62.   Plague.
63.   Acute poliomyelitis.
64.   Rabies.
65.   Rubella.
66.   Scarlet fever.
67.   Tetanus.
68.   Tuberculosis.
69.   Typhoid fever.
70.   Typhus.
71.   Viral haemorrhagic fevers.
72.   Viral hepatitis.

[*The Reporting of Injuries, Diseases and Dangerous Occurrences Regulations 1995, Reg 5(1)(2), Sch 3*].

Appendix C

Prescribed Form for Reporting an Injury or Dangerous Occurrence

A3029

HSE
Health & Safety
Executive

Health and Safety at Work etc Act 1974
The Reporting of Injuries, Diseases and Dangerous Occurrences Regulations 1995

Report of an injury or dangerous occurrence

Filling in this form
This form must be filled in by an employer or other responsible person.

Part A

About you

1 What is your full name?

2 What is your job title?

3 What is your telephone number?

About your organisation

4 What is the name of your organisation?

5 What is its address and postcode?

6 What type of work does the organisation do?

Part B

About the incident

1 On what date did the incident happen?

    /   /

2 At what time did the incident happen?
(Please use the 24-hour clock eg 0600)

3 Did the incident happen at the above address?

Yes ☐ Go to question 4

No ☐ Where did the incident happen?

    ☐ elsewhere in your organisation – give the name, address and postcode

    ☐ at someone else's premises – give the name, address and postcode

    ☐ in a public place – give details of where it happened

If you do not know the postcode, what is the name of the local authority?

4 In which department, or where on the premises, did the incident happen?

F2508 (01/96)

Part C

About the injured person

If you are reporting a dangerous occurrence, go to Part F.

If more than one person was injured in the same incident, please attach the details asked for in Part C and Part D for each injured person.

1 What is their full name?

2 What is their home address and postcode?

3 What is their home phone number?

4 How old are they?

5 Are they
    ☐ male?
    ☐ female?

6 What is their job title?

7 Was the injured person (tick only one box)
    ☐ one of your employees?
    ☐ on a training scheme? Give details:

    ☐ on work experience?
    ☐ employed by someone else? Give details of the employer:

    ☐ self-employed and at work?
    ☐ a member of the public?

Part D

About the injury

1 What was the injury? (eg fracture, laceration)

2 What part of the body was injured?

Continued overleaf

3 Was the injury (tick the one box that applies)

☐ a fatality?

☐ a major injury or condition? (see accompanying notes)

☐ an injury to an employee or self-employed person which prevented them doing their normal work for more than 3 days?

☐ an injury to a member of the public which meant they had to be taken from the scene of the accident to a hospital for treatment?

4 Did the injured person (tick all the boxes that apply)

☐ become unconscious?

☐ need resuscitation?

☐ remain in hospital for more than 24 hours?

☐ none of the above.

Part E

About the kind of accident

Please tick the one box that best describes what happened, then go to Part G.

☐ Contact with moving machinery or material being machined

☐ Hit by a moving, flying or falling object

☐ Hit by a moving vehicle

☐ Hit something fixed or stationary

☐ Injured while handling, lifting or carrying

☐ Slipped, tripped or fell on the same level

☐ Fell from a height

How high was the fall?

☐ metres

☐ Trapped by something collapsing

☐ Drowned or asphyxiated

☐ Exposed to, or in contact with, a harmful substance

☐ Exposed to fire

☐ Exposed to an explosion

☐ Contact with electricity or an electrical discharge

☐ Injured by an animal

☐ Physically assaulted by a person

☐ Another kind of accident (describe it in Part G)

Part F

Dangerous occurrences

Enter the number of the dangerous occurrence you are reporting. (The numbers are given in the Regulations and in the notes which accompany this form)

Part G

Describing what happened

Give as much detail as you can. For instance

- the name of any substance involved
- the name and type of any machine involved
- the events that led to the incident
- the part played by any people.

If it was a personal injury, give details of what the person was doing. Describe any action that has since been taken to prevent a similar incident. Use a separate piece of paper if you need to.

Part H

Your signature

Signature

Date

/ /

Where to send the form

Please send it to the Enforcing Authority for the place where it happened. If you do not know the Enforcing Authority, send it to the nearest HSE office.

For official use

Client number	Location number	Event number		
			☐ INV REP ☐ Y ☐ N	

Appendix D

Prescribed Form for Reporting a Case of Disease

A3030

Health and Safety at Work etc Act 1974
The Reporting of Injuries, Diseases and Dangerous Occurrences Regulations 1995

Report of a case of disease

Filling in this form
This form must be filled in by an employer or other responsible person.

Part A

About you

1 What is your full name?

2 What is your job title?

3 What is your telephone number?

About your organisation

4 What is the name of your organisation?

5 What is its address and postcode?

6 Does the affected person usually work at this address?
Yes ☐ Go to question 7
No ☐ Where do they normally work?

7 What type of work does the organisation do?

Part B

About the affected person

1 What is their full name?

2 What is their date of birth?
/ /

3 What is their job title?

4 Are they
☐ male?
☐ female?

5 Is the affected person (tick one box)
☐ one of your employees?
☐ on a training scheme? Give details:

☐ on work experience?
☐ employed by someone else? Give details:

☐ other? Give details:

F2508A (01/96)

Continued overleaf

Part C

The disease you are reporting

1 Please give:

- the name of the disease, and the type of work it is associated with; or

- the name and number of the disease *(from Schedule 3 of the Regulations – see the accompanying notes).*

2 What is the date of the statement of the doctor who first diagnosed or confirmed the disease?

    /   /

3 What is the name and address of the doctor?

Part D

Describing the work that led to the disease

Please describe any work done by the affected person which might have led to them getting the disease.

If the disease is thought to have been caused by exposure to an agent at work *(eg a specific chemical)* please say what that agent is.

Give any other information which is relevant.

Give your description here

Continue your description here

Part E

Your signature

Signature

Date

    /   /

Where to send the form

Please send it to the Enforcing Authority for the place where the affected person works. If you do not know the Enforcing Authority, send it to the nearest HSE office.

For official use

Client number

Location number

Event number

☐ INV REP ☐ Y ☐ N

Appendix E

Health and Safety Executive Regional Offices

A3031   **London and South East Region**

Covers the counties of Kent, Surrey, East Sussex and West Sussex, and all London Boroughs.

St Dunstans House
201–211 Borough High Street
London SE1 1GZ
Telephone: 0171 556 210
0*Fax*: 0171 556 2200

3 East Grinstead House
London Road
East Grinstead RH19 1RR
Telephone: 0181 235 8000
or: 01342 334 200
Fax: 0181 235 8001
or: 01342 334 222

Home Counties Region

Covers the counties of Bedfordshire, Berkshire, Buckinghamshire, Cambridgeshire, Dorset, Essex (except London Boroughs in Essex), Hampshire, Hertfordshire, Isle of Wight, Norfolk, Suffolk and Wiltshire.

14 Cardiff Road
Luton LU1 1PP
Telephone: 01582 444 200
Fax: 01582 444 320

Priestley House
Priestley Road
Basingstoke RG24 9NW
Telephone: 01256 404 000
Fax: 01256 404 100

39 Baddow Road
Chelmsford CM2 0HL
Telephone: 01245 706 200
Fax: 01245 706 222

Midlands Region

Covers the counties of West Midlands, Leicestershire, Northamptonshire, Oxfordshire, Warwickshire, Derbyshire, Lincolnshire and Nottinghamshire.

McLaren Building
35 Dale End
Birmingham B4 7NP
Telephone: 0121 607 6200
Fax: 0121 607 6349

Belgrave House
1 Greyfriars
Northampton NN1 2BS
Telephone: 01604 738 300
Fax: 01604 738 333

1st Floor
The Pearson Building
55 Upper Parliament Street
Nottingham NG1 6AU
Telephone: 01159 712 800
Fax: 01159 712 802

Yorkshire and North East Region

Covers the counties and unitary authorities of Hartlepool, Middlesbrough, Redcar and Cleveland, Stockton-on-Tees, Durham, Hull, North Lincolnshire, North East Lincolnshire, East Riding, York, North Yorkshire, Northumberland, West Yorkshire, Tyne and Wear and the Metropolitan Boroughs of Barnsley, Doncaster, Rotherham and Sheffield.

8 St Paul's Street
Leeds LS1 2LE
Telephone: 0113 283 4200
Fax: 0113 283 4296

Sovereign House
110 Queen Street
Sheffield S1 2ES
Telephone: 0114 291 2300
Fax: 0114 291 2379

Arden House
Regent Centre
Regent Farm Road
Gosforth
Newcastle upon Tyne NE3 3JN
Telephone: 0191 202 6200
Fax: 0191 202 6300

North West Region

Covers the counties of Cheshire, Cumbria, Greater Manchester, Lancashire and Merseyside.

Quay House
Quay Street
Manchester M3 3JB
Telephone: 0161 952 8200
Fax: 0161 952 8222

Victoria House
Ormskirk Road
Preston PR1 1HH
Telephone: 01772 836 200
Fax: 01772 836 222

The Triad
Stanley Road
Bootle
Merseyside L20 3PG
Telephone: 0151 479 2200
Fax: 0151 479 2201

Wales and West Region

Covers Wales, and the unitary authorities of Cornwall, Devon, Somerset, North West Somerset, Bath and North East Somerset, Bristol, South Gloucestershire, Gloucestershire, Hereford and Worcester, Shropshire and Staffordshire.

Brunel House
2 Fitzalan Road
Cardiff CF2 1SH
Telephone: 01222 263 000
Fax: 01222 263 120

Inter City House
Mitchell Lane
Victoria Street
Bristol BS1 6AN
Telephone: 0117 988 6000
Fax: 0117 926 2998

The Marches House
Midway
Newcastle-under-Lyme
Staffordshire ST5 1DT
Telephone: 01782 602 300
Fax: 01782 602 400

Scotland

Belford House
59 Belford Road
Edinburgh EH4 3UE
Telephone: 0131 247 2000
Fax: 0131 247 2121

375 West George Street
Glasgow G2 4LW
Telephone: 0141 275 3000
Fax: 0141 276 3100

Asbestos

Introduction

A5001   Asbestos (Greek meaning 'unburnable', 'unquenchable') is a naturally-occurring dangerous substance found throughout industry. It is a generic term for a variety of silicates of iron, magnesium, calcium, sodium and aluminium which naturally exist in fibrous form. Defined as 'any of the following minerals . . . crocidolite, amosite, chrysotile, fibrous actinolite, fibrous anthophyllite, fibrous tremolite and any mixture containing any of those minerals' (by the *Asbestos (Licensing) Regulations 1983 (SI 1983 No 1649)* as amended by the *Control of Asbestos at Work Regulations 1987 (SI 1987 No 2115)*), asbestos has emerged in the last decade as one of the most significant occupational health hazards worldwide.

Exposure to asbestos can lead to asbestosis or mesothelioma. Asbestosis is a widespread pneumoconiosis or fibrosis of the lungs, caused by inhalation of asbestos fibres deep into the lungs, thus impairing their capacity to absorb oxygen. As a result, victims become increasingly breathless and physical activity is curtailed. Asbestosis is exacerbated by tobacco smoking, particularly cigarettes. Mesothelioma is a tumour which attacks the pleura or the membrane covering both lungs and lining the inner wall of the chest cavity. It develops quickly and is normally fatal, as there is no cure.

Asbestosis together with mesothelioma accounted for 32 deaths in 1968, 74 in 1976 and 88 in 1983; and mesothelioma of the pleura accounted for 98 deaths in 1968, 198 in 1976, 400 in 1983 and 1,010 in 1991. More spectacularly, in North America the avalanche of product liability litigation involving asbestosis/mesothelioma resulted in America's biggest manufacturer of asbestos, Johns-Manville Corporation of Denver, filing for voluntary liquidation in the early eighties. As usual, developments have been more prosaic over here but asbestosis/mesothelioma claims, the flagship of 'long tail liability', have caused major headaches for liability insurance companies, including Lloyds and its 'names'.

Asbestos-related disease is currently responsible for about 3,000 deaths annually, and will probably increase to between 5,000 and 10,000 annually in the early 21st century – exposure to asbestos dust being the salient cause. For every death from mesothelioma, it is estimated that there is one from asbestos-related lung cancer. Although use of asbestos peaked in the 1970s, many buildings still contain asbestos materials, with the result that there may still be substantial exposure in building renovation/maintenance work, particularly amongst plumbers, gas fitters, carpenters and electricians.

The HSC has advised the Government to work towards an extension of the European asbestos ban. The EU already prohibits the use of blue asbestos (crocidolite) and brown asbestos (amosite) in manufactured products. The HSC wants this ban to include white asbestos (chrysotile), except for a limited number of essential uses where there are no satisfactory alternatives (see A5042 below). At present, white asbestos is still widely used in the construction industry in many parts of the world, accounting for 95 per cent of the world asbestos trade.

Pathological effects of exposure to asbestos

A5002   Health risks are associated with the inhalation of fibrous dust and its dispersion within the lungs and other parts of the body. Workers engaged in extracting the fibre and processing it, along with those manufacturing asbestos products, are particularly vulnerable. However, exposure to asbestos alone is uncommon; in practice other mineral dusts are normally inhaled along with asbestos and the effect of these and other pollutants, such as cigarette smoke, often combine to produce diseases such as asbestosis. Inhalation of asbestos can give rise to the following three medical conditions namely, asbestosis, cancer of the bronchial tubes and cancer of the pleural surface (see further A5031 below).

Asbestos social security awards peaked in 1986 at 329, whereas mesothelioma awards escalated from 93 in 1981 and 462 in 1990 to 1,010 in 1991.

Unlike many occupational diseases, asbestos-related diseases manifest themselves over an incubation period of anything from 20 to 30 years. In consequence, current incidence of asbestos-related disease is not a measure of the effects of present dust levels, but rather of past dust exposures, which were (obviously) too high. In addition, this 'long tail' liability has strained the application of the three year rule for personal injury claims operating under the *Limitation Act 1980* (see A5033 below and E11029 EMPLOYERS' DUTIES TO THEIR EMPLOYEES).

Control of exposure – control limits

A5003   Exposure to all forms of asbestos should be reduced to the minimum reasonably practicable (for the meaning of this expression, see E15017 ENFORCEMENT). Moreover, personal exposure should not exceed the *control limits* (formerly TLVs – threshold limit values). Control limits are the *upper* level of permitted exposure, for each species of asbestos. The following control limits apply (see also A5008 below):

(*a*)   for dust consisting of/containing chrysotile:
– 0.5 fibres per millilitre of air averaged over any continuous period of 4 hours,
– 1.5 fibres per millilitre of air averaged over any continuous period of 10 minutes;

(*b*)   for dust consisting of/containing any other form of asbestos, including mixtures of chrysotile and other asbestos:
– 0.2 fibres per millilitre of air averaged over any continuous period of 4 hours,
– 0.6 fibres per millilitre of air averaged over any continuous period of 10 minutes.

[*Reg 2 of the Control of Asbestos at Work Regulations 1987 (SI 1987 No 2115) as amended by the Control of Asbestos at Work (Amendment) Regulations 1992 (SI 1992 No 3068), Sch*].

(N.B. These measurements represent the concentration of fibres per millilitre of air sampled by routine atmospheric monitoring, e.g. by use of a static sampling device.)

For further excellent guidance on the measurement of airborne asbestos dust see the following HSE Guidance Notes, updated as of January 1996:

(i)   Asbestos: exposure limits and measurement of airborne dust concentrations (EH 10); and

(ii)   Asbestos fibres in air: sampling and evaluation by phase contrast microscopy (PCM) under the Control of Asbestos at Work Regulations 1987 (MDHS 39/4).

Control limits

A5004   Replacing TLVs, a control limit is the limit which is 'judged, after detailed consideration of the available evidence, to be "reasonably practicable" for the whole spectrum of work activities in Great Britain'. They are 'those exposure limits contained in regulations, approved codes of practice and EU Directives, or those agreed by the Health and Safety Commission'. Characteristically, they:

(a)   are set at a level which it would be reasonably practicable for relevant sectors of industry to achieve;

(b)   provide a clear indication of what the law requires as a maximum standard, so that when they are exceeded, employers know that they are in breach of *HSWA*; and

(c)   are based on a full review of medical/scientific evidence by the HSE and agreed by employers'/employees' organisations as acceptable.

A5005   Hence, as distinct from TLVs or recommended limits (which indicate the highest tolerable level of exposure), control limits represent the lowest exposure technically and economically possible. For this reason, control limits are not synonymous with safe levels of exposure which, once attained, make further improvements in dust control unnecessary. Rather they are gradually self-updating. Failure to comply with control limits, or to put it another way, reduce exposure to the minimum reasonably practicable, can result in prosecution or some other form of enforcement action (see ENFORCEMENT).

Statutory requirements governing exposure to asbestos

A5006   Compliance with control limits is only part of an employer's duty towards his employees under *HSWA* and the *Control of Asbestos at Work Regulations 1987*. The statutory requirements are as follows.

(a)   *General*. All employers must provide a safe working environment for their employees. [*HSWA s 2(2)(e)*]. This includes preventing the exposure of their employees to asbestos or, where it is not reasonably practicable to prevent such exposure, the provision of an environment in which exposure of employees to asbestos dust is reduced to the lowest levels reasonably practicable.

(b)   *Specific*. Specific statutory requirements relating to protection against exposure to asbestos are contained in the *Control of Asbestos at Work Regulations 1987 (SI 1987 No 2115)* as amended by the *Control of Asbestos at Work (Amendment) Regulations 1992 (SI 1992 No 3068)*, the *Asbestos (Licensing) Regulations 1983 (SI 1983 No 1649)* and the *Special Waste Regulations 1996 (SI 1996 No 972)*. Moreover, labelling of asbestos products used at work is required by the *Chemicals (Hazard Information and Packaging for Supply) Regulations 1994 (SI 1994 No 3247)* (CHIP 2), the *Carriage of Dangerous Goods by Road Regulations 1996 (SI 1996 No 2095)* and the *Carriage of Dangerous Goods (Classification, Packaging and Labelling) and Use of Transportable Pressure Receptacles Regulations 1996 (SI 1996 No 2092)*.

History of statute law on asbestos

A5007   The first regulations on asbestos, the *Asbestos Industry Regulations 1931*, were passed to control asbestosis in asbestos textile factories. These regulations were confined to asbestos factories handling and processing raw fibre. The purpose of these regulations was to prevent workers contracting asbestosis, since the dangers of lung cancer and mesothelioma were not then fully documented, nor were the varying levels of hazard associated with the three main species of asbestos, i.e. crocidolite, amosite and chrysotile – and so the regulations applied to all three species. The regulations protected workers in asbestos textile factories, manufacture of brake linings and asbestos cement works, usually against the least harmful species of asbestos, namely chrysotile. Significantly, however, workers in the thermal insulation industry exposed to the most harmful kind of asbestos, namely crocidolite, were not covered and their employers were under no statutory duties. Indeed, it was not until the *Asbestos Regulations 1969* were passed that these workers were covered for the first time.

Action levels and control limits

A5008   Being limited in operation to factories, the *Asbestos Regulations 1969* were replaced by the wider *Control of Asbestos at Work Regulations 1987*, extending to all workplaces where asbestos is made, used or handled. The basic duty of employers, whose employees are, or are liable to be exposed to above 'action level' asbestos, is to *prevent* the exposure of employees to asbestos. However, where *prevention* of exposure is not reasonably practicable in cost/benefit terms, employers must *reduce* exposure of their employees, by means other than use of respiratory protective equipment, to the lowest level reasonably practicable [*Reg 8(1)*]. 'Action level' refers to one of the following cumulative exposures to asbestos over a continuous twelve-week period, namely:

(*a*)   where exposure is solely to chrysotile (white asbestos), 96 fibre-hours per millilitre of air;

(*b*)   where exposure is to any other form of asbestos including crocidolite (blue asbestos) or amosite (brown asbestos) either alone or in conjunction with chrysotile (white asbestos), 48 fibre-hours per millilitre of air; or

(*c*)   where both types of exposure occur separately during the twelve-week period concerned, a proportionate number of fibre-hours per millilitre of air.

[*Control of Asbestos at Work Regulations 1992, Reg 2(1) as amended*].

However, where reduction of the exposure of employees below both the specified 'control limits' is not reasonably practicable in cost/benefit terms, employees must be supplied additionally with suitable and approved respiratory protective equipment in order to reduce the concentration of airborne asbestos inhaled by employees to a level below the specified 'control limit' [*Reg 8(2)*] (see A5003 above).

A5009   In addition, employers must designate asbestos areas (where exposure of employees might exceed the action level) and respirator zones (where concentrations of asbestos might exceed any control limit) [*Reg 14*], monitor the exposure of employees to asbestos [*Reg 15*], ensure that employees undergo regular periodic medical checks and keep health records for a minimum of forty years [*Reg 16*]. Breach of these regulations is an offence under the *Health and Safety at Work etc. Act 1974*, punishable by a maximum fine of £5,000 on summary conviction and an unlimited fine and/or up to two years' imprisonment on conviction on indictment. Moreover, many of the duties exist for the benefit not just of employees but also of other workers and the general public who may be affected by exposure to asbestos. The duties also apply to self-employed persons. [*Reg 3(2)*].

Control of Asbestos at Work Regulations 1987 (SI 1987 No 2115) (as amended)

Duty to assess risks

A5010   Contractors who undertake work on materials containing asbestos are on notice, as from 1988 at the latest, when these Regulations came into force, that there are serious health hazards connected with such work. In consequence, contractors are under a duty to find out about the risks associated with asbestos and take corresponding precautions. In *Barclays Bank plc v Fairclough Building Ltd (No 2) [1995] 1 AER 289*, BB contracted F to carry out maintenance work. F subcontracted the cleaning of corrugated asbestos roofs to C who, in turn, subcontracted it to T. Neither C nor T was experienced in cleaning asbestos roofs. T did the work using a high-pressure hose, which caused asbestos-contaminated slurry to enter buildings, leaving dangerous levels of asbestos dust and fibres. A prohibition notice required remedial work costing £4,000,000. BB obtained judgment against F; meanwhile C paid F £1,250,000. In C's action against T, the Court of Appeal overturned judgment given for T, holding that:

(*a*)   neither T nor C had exercised reasonable care and skill in the contractual chain for cleaning the asbestos roof, risks associated with asbestos being well publicised by the HSE and trade journals;

(*b*)   contractors cleaning asbestos roofs with high-pressure hoses undertake to do so safely and without causing extensive contamination of the surrounding area, therefore T was liable to C; *but*

(*c*)   because of (*a*) T's liability would be reduced by 50% to reflect the extent of C's contributory negligence.

Prohibitions on asbestos activities

A5011   No employer must carry out work which:

(*a*)   exposes, or

(*b*)   is liable to expose,

his employees to asbestos, unless first:

(i)   he has identified the type of asbestos involved in the work activity; or

(ii)   he has assumed that the asbestos is not chrysotile alone and treated it accordingly

[*Reg 4*];

(iii)   he has made and regularly reviewed an assessment of that exposure. Such assessment must:

(*a*)   identify the type of asbestos;

(*b*)   determine the nature and degree of exposure expected in the course of the work; and

(*c*)   specify the steps to be taken to prevent or to reduce exposure to the lowest level reasonably practicable. The assessment must be reviewed regularly and a new assessment substituted when there is reason to suspect that the existing assessment is no longer valid or there is a significant change in working conditions.

[Reg 5(4) as amended by Control of Asbestos at Work (Amendment) Regulations 1992, Sch];

(iv)   he has, if the work involves removal of asbestos from any building, prepared a written plan prior to the commencement of removal activities, a copy to be retained for at least two years following completion of the work *[Reg 5A as inserted by Control of Asbestos at Work (Amendment) Regulations 1992, Sch]* (see A5015, A5016 below);

(v)   he has notified the 'enforcing authority' (see E15003, E15004 ENFORCEMENT for the meaning of this expression) at least 14 days (amended from 28 days as from 1 February 1999) before commencing work, of:

(*a*)   his name, address and telephone number;

(*b*)   his usual place of business;

(*c*)   types of asbestos used or handled;

(*d*)   maximum quantity of asbestos on the premises (see A5015 below);

(*e*)   activities/processes involved on the premises;

(*f*)   products (if any) manufactured (see A5017 below);

(*g*)   date when work activity is to start.

Also any material change(s) in work activity involving asbestos must be notified. *[Reg 6, Sch 1]*.

Notification of work with asbestos: specimen form

A5012   To comply with *Regulation 6* of the *Control of Asbestos at Work Regulations 1987* the following particulars are to be sent to the relevant enforcing authority.

To comply with *Regulation 6* of the *Control of Asbestos at Work Regulations 1987* the following particulars are to be sent to the relevant Enforcing Authority.

Name ....

Company...

Usual place of business..

....

Telephone number ....

Brief description of work with asbestos

1 Type(s) of asbestos used or handled (crocidolite, amosite, chrysotile or other)

....

....

....

2 Maximum quantity of asbestos held on the premises at any one time

....

....

....

3 Activities or processes involved

....

....

....

4 Products manufactured

....

....

....

5 Date of commencement of work activity where work has yet to begin

....

....

....

fig. 1

Duties in connection with asbestos activities

Employers

A5013   All employers whose employees are, or are liable to be, exposed to asbestos (see A5008 above), must:

(*a*)   provide adequate information, instruction and training to such employees, so that they are aware of the risks and precautions to be taken (see A5021 below) [*Control of Asbestos at Work Regulations 1987, Reg 7*];

(*b*)   (i)   prevent exposure of employees to asbestos, but where prevention of exposure is not reasonably practicable, reduce exposure to the lowest level reasonably practicable by means other than use of respiratory protective equipment (that is, by substituting for asbestos a substance not creating a health risk or lesser health risk to employees) [*Reg 8(1A) as inserted by Control of Asbestos at Work (Amendment) Regulations 1992, Sch*],

          (ii)   where reduction to below both the applicable 'control limits' (see A5008 above) is not reasonably practicable, supply employees in addition with suitable and HSE-approved respiratory protective equipment in order to reduce the concentration of airborne asbestos inhaled by employees to a level below the specified 'control limit'

          [*Reg 8(2) and (3), as amended by Control of Asbestos at Work (Amendment) Regulations 1992, Sch*],

          (iii)   if an unforeseen event occurs, resulting in escape of asbestos into the workplace at a concentration that is liable to exceed any applicable control limit, ensure that only persons responsible for carrying out repairs are permitted in the affected area and are provided with respiratory protective equipment/clothing *and* that employees and other persons who may have been affected are notified immediately

          [*Reg 8(4) as amended by Control of Asbestos at Work (Amendment) Regulations 1992, Sch*];

(*c*)   ensure that personal protective equipment is properly used or applied [*Reg 9*];

(*d*)   and is maintained in a clean and efficient state and in good working order and is regularly examined/tested by a competent person. A record of such maintenance must be kept for at least five years [*Reg 10*];

(*e*)   provide adequate and suitable protective clothing and see that such clothing is disposed of as asbestos waste or, alternatively, cleaned at regular intervals. The clothing must first be packed in a suitable container labelled 'Warning. Contains asbestos. Breathing asbestos dust is dangerous to health. Follow safety instructions' [*Reg 11, Sch 2*];

(*f*)   prevent the spread of asbestos, but where prevention is not reasonably practicable, reduce its spread to the lowest level reasonably practicable [*Reg 12*] (see A5017 below);

(*g*)   keep work premises and plant clean and, in the case of new premises, ensure that they are:

          (i)   designed and constructed to facilitate cleaning, and

          (ii)   equipped with an adequate and suitable vacuum cleaning system which ideally should be a fixed system

[*Reg 13*].

(Under the previous *Asbestos Regulations 1969 (SI 1969 No 690)*, dry-sweeping asbestos dust qualified as a process, so that dust containing asbestos in excess of the threshold limit value was a breach of the regulations (*Edgson v Vickers plc, The Times, 8 April 1994*). It is likely that it would qualify as 'work' under the current regulations.)

Amendment regulations – the *Control of Asbestos at Work (Amendment) Regulations 1998 (SI 1998 No 3235)* – refocusing and tightening up the *Control of Asbestos at Work Regulations 1987 (CAW)* came into force on 1 February 1999. Specific changes to *CAW* include:

- reductions of the action level and control limit;

- clarification of the extent of the application of *CAW* to make it plain that all workers who are *liable* to be exposed to asbestos are covered;

- a requirement that respiratory protective equipment should be chosen to reduce exposure to a level that is as low as reasonably practicable;

- a requirement that employers keep a copy of their risk assessment and plan of work at the place to which they relate and while the work to which they relate is being carried out, and a requirement that employers ensure that, so far as is reasonably practicable, the work is carried out in accordance with the plan; and

- a reduction from 28 to 14 days of the period for advance notification to the enforcing authority of work with asbestos.

The amendments to *CAW* contain a requirement for laboratories which carry out asbestos-related analysis work to be accredited to the standard EN 45001.

Designated areas/air monitoring/health records

Designated asbestos areas/respirator zones

A5014   All employers must:

(a)   designate asbestos areas where exposure to asbestos of an employee exceeds, or is liable to exceed, the 'action level' (see A5008 above);

(b)   designate respirator zones where the concentration of asbestos exceeds, or is liable to exceed, any 'control limit' (see A5008 above);

(c)   ensure that employees (other than employees whose work so requires) do not either (i) enter or (ii) remain in any designated areas/zones;

(d)   ensure that employees do not eat/drink/smoke in designated areas/zones.

Both (a) asbestos areas and (b) respirator zones must be separately demarcated and identified by notices, and in the case of a respirator zone, the notice must require an employee entering the zone to wear respiratory protective equipment. [*Reg 14*].

Written assessments

A5015   Written assessments should specify:

(i)   type of work involved;

(ii)   reasons for not using a substitute material;

(iii)   type and quantity of asbestos and results of analysis;

(iv)   details of expected exposures – and, in particular,

(a)   likelihood of action level being exceeded (see A5008 above),

(b)   likelihood of control limit being exceeded (see A5008 above),

(c)   if above either relevant control limit, expected exposure, for selection of respiratory protective equipment,

(d)   frequency and duration of exposure,

(e)   expected exposure of non-employees,

(f)   air monitoring results,

(g)   measures to control exposure and release of asbestos to the environment,

(h)   procedures relating to provision and use of respiratory protective equipment and other protective equipment,

(j)   in case of demolition, procedures for asbestos to be removed before demolition begins,

(k)   procedures for dealing with emergencies,

(l)   procedures for removal of waste from the workplace.

(Approved Code of Practice to these Regulations).

Plan of work

A5016   An employer must not undertake any work involving the removal of asbestos from any building, structure, plant, installation or ship unless he has prepared a suitable written plan of work, giving details of:

(a)   nature/duration of work;

(b)   address/location of work;

(c)   methods for handling asbestos; and

(d)   equipment for protection and decontamination of employees, and protection of other persons on or near the worksite.

The plan, which must be submitted to the HSE on request, should indicate that, so far as reasonably practicable, asbestos/asbestos products have been removed prior to work commencement. [*Reg 5A*].

Reduction of exposure to asbestos

A5017   Exposure to asbestos can be reduced by technical measures (including local exhaust ventilation) and a suitable work system – the latter varying according to whether the working environment is construction or manufacturing.

In the case of *construction*, a suitable work system consists of:

(a)   removal of asbestos materials before other major work begins;

(b)   methods of work which minimise breakage, abrasion, machining or cutting of asbestos;

(c)   suppression of dust by wetting;

(d)   segregation of work with asbestos; and

(*e*)   prompt removal of off-cuts, waste and dust.

In the case of *manufacturing*, a suitable work system involves:

   (i) limiting quantity of asbestos used;

   (ii) limiting number of persons exposed;

   (iii) ensuring collection of waste and removal from work area as soon as possible in suitably labelled containers;

   (iv) ensuring that damaged containers of raw fibre or waste are repaired forthwith or placed inside another suitable container;

   (v) avoiding manual handling of raw fibre or intermediate products; and

   (vi) intermediate cleaning/sealing of all products containing asbestos.

[*Approved Code of Practice, paras 28, 29*].

Maintenance and inspection

A5018   Exhaust ventilation equipment should be:

(*a*)   inspected weekly, and

(*b*)   examined and tested by a competent person every six months.

[*Approved Code of Practice, para 38*].

Weekly inspections

A5019   Weekly inspections should include a check of position and condition of exhaust hoods and any visible signs of malfunction (e.g. dust deposits).

In particular,

(*a*)   if dust seems to be escaping, this should be checked using a dust lamp;

(*b*)   pressure drop across the filter should be checked in the case of manometers fitted to dust collectors;

(*c*)   filter hoppers/bins should be checked to ensure proper routine emptying;

(*d*)   records of weekly inspections should be kept and any faults logged; and

(*e*)   faults should be rectified quickly and a written note made of action taken.

[*Approved Code of Practice, para 40*].

Six-monthly examination and test

A5020   This should include:

(*a*)   *New equipment – Part I examination*

   (i) confirmation that system is satisfactorily controlling airborne asbestos;

   (ii) measurement of pressures and air velocities (including static and dynamic pressures, face and duct velocities as well as static pressure differences across fans and filters);

   (iii) checks on dust collection.

(*b*)   *Previously examined machinery – Part II examination*

   (i) visual check for deterioration/leakage;

(ii)   verification that method of use of system is satisfactory;

(iii)   check on dust collection;

(iv)   measurement of pressures/velocities.

This done, a report of the examination should be completed and signed within 14 days.

[*Approved Code of Practice, paras 41–47*].

Maintenance schedules

A5021   Maintenance procedures for all control measures and personal protective equipment should be drawn up including, as appropriate:

(*a*)   cleaning equipment – particularly vacuum cleaners (to BS 5145);

(*b*)   washing and changing facilities;

(*c*)   controls (including enclosures) to prevent contamination.

The maintenance schedule should specify:

(i)   what control measures require maintenance;

(ii)   when and how maintenance is to be carried out;

(iii) who is responsible for maintenance; and

(iv)   how defects are to be remedied.

[*Approved Code of Practice, paras 48, 49*].

Asbestos premises and hot work

A5022   Cleaning of asbestos-contaminated premises should be frequent, and for inside walls and ceilings at least once a year, though not by dry manual brushing or sweeping. Hosing is permissible if residues are suitably disposed of. Ideally, a fixed vacuum system should be installed, using high efficiency filters and venting (preferably) outside. Small amounts of asbestos dust can be removed with a well-dampened cloth.

Asbestos stripping should not be carried out on hot plant until absolutely necessary, and preferably on a scheduled basis during shutdowns or holidays, since the risk of heat stress is greater at such times, leading possibly to heat stroke which can be fatal. The main reason for this is that, as insulation material is progressively removed, heat input into the working area will increase; in addition, protective equipment is normally hooded with elasticated cuffs and ankles, restricting air movement over the body and minimising evaporation of sweat. Moreover, respiratory protective equipment often restricts breathing. Work in such high temperatures can cause burns, swelling of ankles and feet, fainting, muscle cramps, heat exhaustion, breathing difficulties and thirst; and so periodical break-offs are advisable as follows:

Work at 26.0°C – 27.5°C – 15 minutes rest after 45 minutes work

Work at 27.5°C – 29.0°C – 30 minutes rest after 30 minutes work

Work at 29.0°C – 31.0°C – 45 minutes rest after 15 minutes work.

Air monitoring

A5023   All employers must monitor the exposure of employees to asbestos and keep a record of such monitoring for:

(*a*)   forty years, if a health record (see A5024 below);

(*b*)   otherwise, five years.

[*Reg 15 as amended by Control of Asbestos at Work (Amendment) Regulations 1992, Sch*].

Health records/medical surveillance

A5024   All employers must:

(*a*)   keep health records of all employees exposed to asbestos exceeding 'action level' (see above) for at least forty years (the incubation period of many asbestos-related diseases) [*Reg 16(1) as amended by Control of Asbestos at Work (Amendment) Regulations 1992, Sch*];

(*b*)   require employees exposed to above 'action level' asbestos, to undergo a periodic medical examination at least every two years.

Employers must be issued with a certificate of examination and keep it for at least four years, giving a copy to the employee. Such medical examinations, carried out by Employment Medical Advisers (EMAs), during working hours and on work premises, are at the expense of the employer, who must provide suitable facilities. On being given reasonable notice, employers must allow employees access to health records. [*Reg 16*].

Washing facilities/storage/distribution/labelling etc.

A5025   All employers must:

(*a*)   provide employees exposed to asbestos with adequate and suitable facilities for

(i)   washing/changing,

(ii)   storage of protective clothing and personal clothing not worn during working hours, and

(iii)   separate storage of respiratory protective equipment

[*Reg 17*];

(*b*)   ensure that raw asbestos or waste containing asbestos is not

(i)   stored,

(ii)   received into or despatched from any place of work, or

(iii)   distributed (unless in a totally enclosed distribution system) within any place of work,

unless it is in a suitable and sealed container clearly labelled and marked [*Reg 18*].

Labelling/marking of raw asbestos, asbestos waste and asbestos products

A5026   (*a*)   Raw asbestos must be labelled in the prescribed form, using the words: 'Warning. Contains asbestos. Breathing asbestos dust is dangerous to health. Follow safety instructions'.

(*b*)   Waste containing asbestos must be labelled:

   (i)   in accordance with the *Chemicals (Hazard Information and Packaging for Supply) Regulations 1994 (SI 1994 No 3247) (CHIP 2)* or the *Carriage of Dangerous Goods (Classification, Packaging and Labelling) and Use of Transportable Pressure Receptacles Regulations 1996 (SI 1996 No 2092)* (see D1013–D1016 DANGEROUS SUBSTANCES I and D3006–D3014 DANGEROUS SUBSTANCES II);

   (ii)   if conveyed by road in a road tanker or tank container, in accordance with the *Carriage of Dangerous Goods by Road Regulations 1996 (SI 1996 No 2095)* (see D3018–D3034 DANGEROUS SUBSTANCES II).

(*c*)   Asbestos products must be labelled: 'Warning. Contains asbestos. Breathing asbestos dust is dangerous to health. Follow safety instructions'. [*Reg 19*]. If the product contains crocidolite, the words 'Contains asbestos' are replaced by 'Contains crocidolite/blue asbestos'.

(For the effect of 'warnings' on civil liability in connection with defective products, see P9033 PRODUCT SAFETY.)

Employees' duties

A5027   Every employee must:

(*a*)   make full and proper use of any control measures, personal protective equipment or other facility provided by the employer [*Reg 9(2)*];

(*b*)   report to the employer any defect in personal protective equipment or control measures [*Reg 9(2)*];

(*c*)   not enter/remain in (i) asbestos areas (ii) respirator zones (unless his work requires him to do so) [*Reg 14*]; and

(*d*)   when required by his employer, present himself during working hours for medical examination/checks [*Reg 16(4)*].

Prohibitions on the use of asbestos products – the Asbestos (Prohibitions) Regulations 1992 (SI 1992 No 3067)

(a) Amphibole asbestos

A5028   The *Asbestos (Prohibitions) Regulations 1992 (SI 1992 No 3067)* prohibit:

   (i)   importation into the United Kingdom of all forms of amphibole asbestos, namely crocidolite ('blue asbestos'), amosite ('brown asbestos'), fibrous actinolite, fibrous anthophyllite, fibrous tremolite and any mixture containing any of those minerals [*Reg 3*];

   (ii)   supply of amphibole asbestos or any product to which it has been added [*Reg 4*];

(iii) use of amphibole asbestos or any product to which it has been added, except products containing:

— crocidolite or amosite, which were in use before 1 January 1986; or

— other forms of amphibole asbestos, which were in use before 1 January 1993

[*Reg 5*];

(iv) asbestos spraying [*Reg 6*].

(b) Chrysotile asbestos

Supply and use of products containing chrysotile is prohibited as follows:

(i) materials/preparations for spraying;

(ii) paints/ varnishes;

(iii) filters for liquids;

(iv) road surfacing material with more than 2% fibre content;

(v) mortars, protective coatings, fillers, sealants, jointing compounds, mastics, glues, decorative products/finishes;

(vi) insulating or soundproofing materials with a low density;

(vii) air filters, filters used in transport and distribution of natural/town gas;

(viii) underlays for plastic floor/wall coverings;

(ix) textiles unless treated to avoid fibre release – diaphragms for electrolysis after 31 December 1998;

(x) roofing felt.

[*Reg 7(1), Sch*].

Working with asbestos insulation or asbestos coating – Asbestos (Licensing) Regulations 1983 (SI 1983 No 1649)

A5029   A system of licensing or advance notification applies to work with asbestos insulation or coating carried out by an employer or a self-employed person.

A licence is not necessary for such work where:

(*a*) (i) any person who carries out such work will not spend more than one hour on the work in seven consecutive days; and

(ii) the total time spent on the work by all persons involved in it does not exceed two hours; or

(*b*) (i) the employer or self-employed person is the occupier of the premises on which the work is carried out; and

(ii) he has given at least 14 days' notice (amended from 28 days as from 1 February 1999) to the HSE in advance, specifying the type of work to be carried out and the address of the premises at which it is to be done; or

(*c*) the work consists solely of air monitoring or collecting samples.

[*Reg 3*].

Even if a licence is not necessary, employers (or self-employed persons) must still comply with the *Control of Asbestos at Work Regulations 1987* and in particular, should:

(i) give to employees the necessary instruction and training;

(ii) provide adequate information to others (e.g. workforce of an outside contractor) who may be affected by the work;

(iii) achieve the lowest level of asbestos exposure reasonably practicable; and

(iv) ensure that employees are under medical surveillance.

The *Asbestos (Licensing) (Amendment) Regulations 1998 (SI 1998 No 3233)* came into force on 1 February 1999. They amend the definition in the 1983 Regulations of work with asbestos insulation and asbestos coating so as to cover only the work which consists of the removal, repair or disturbance of asbestos, and work which is ancillary to or supervising such work.

The main change to the 1983 Regulations is that an employer or self-employed person is now prohibited from carrying out work with asbestos insulating board without a licence. The 1998 Regulations require such work to be notified to the enforcing authority, and provide for exemption from such a prohibition and requirement to be granted by the Health and Safety Executive.

The period for notification to the enforcing authority of work with asbestos insulation, asbestos coating or asbestos insulating board is reduced from 28 to 14 days.

With the tightening up of asbestos legislation, the Health and Safety Executive (HSE) has produced two new Approved Codes of Practice (ACoPs) and published replacements for two widely used guidance publications.

The HSE has published two ACoPs to help employers understand their duties – '*Work with asbestos insulation, asbestos coating and asbestos insulating board*' (3rd edition) (L28) and '*The control of asbestos at work*' (3rd edition) (L27) – priced £6.75 each.

In addition two guidance notes, '*Controlled asbestos stripping techniques for work requiring a licence*' (HSG189/1) and '*Working with asbestos cement*' (HSG189/2), have been published.

HSG189/1 replaces HSE Guidance Note EH52, '*Removal techniques and associated waste handling for asbestos insulation, coatings and insulating board*', and provides practical advice on techniques for the safe removal of asbestos-containing materials covered by the *Asbestos (Licensing) Regulations 1983* (as amended).

The guidance is aimed at employers, contractors and self-employed people who require an asbestos licence from HSE's Asbestos Licensing Unit. The guidance takes into account research into wet and controlled dry stripping of asbestos and into the effectiveness of respiratory protective equipment.

HSG189/2 revises and replaces HSE Guidance Note EH71, '*Working with asbestos cement and asbestos insulating board*' (1996). The publication describes the properties of asbestos cement – often referred to as AC – and where the material can be found. It also gives practical advice on the necessary precautions to prevent exposure to asbestos fibres, or where this is not reasonably practicable, to reduce exposure to asbestos fibres. There are also examples of possible levels of exposure for typical work activities.

Employers and safety representatives are advised to ensure that out-of-date publications are removed and destroyed. Copies of all publications are available from HSE Books, PO Box 1999, Sudbury, Suffolk CO10 6FS.

The HSE has issued guidance to take account of the *Asbestos (Licensing) (Amendment) Regulations 1998 (SI 1998 No 3233)* which from 1 August 1999 require employers to hold a licence to carry out work with asbestos insulating board – this guidance reflects the tightening up of the 1983 Regulations as part of an ongoing campaign to reduce worker deaths from asbestos-related diseases.

'*A Guide to the Asbestos (Licensing) Regulations 1983 as amended*' explains how the Regulations work, how to apply for a licence and the other conditions HSE may impose on licence holders. It also explains the circumstances in which HSE may revoke a licence which have also recently been amended by the *Asbestos (Licensing) (Amendment) Regulations 1998*.

Copies of '*A guide to the Asbestos (Licensing) Regulations 1983 as amended*', price £6, are available from HSE Books.

The HSE has published some further guidance and information about working with asbestos to take into account recent changes in the law.

'*Selection of suitable respiratory protective equipment for work with asbestos*', IND(G)288, provides authoritative guidance for employers, the self-employed and safety representatives working in the construction and building maintenance industry, about choosing appropriate respiratory protective equipment (RPE).

Its easy to follow format includes control measures to apply before resorting to RPE, the need for equipment to support a CE marking and a number of worked examples to cover most situations working with asbestos-containing insulation materials. The booklet emphasises the need for consulting and training employees and some common misuses of RPE which will reduce its effectiveness.

'*Keep your mask on (asbestos dust kills)*' is a revision of an earlier document of the same name and it takes account of the recent amendments to the Approved Codes of Practice supporting the *Control of Asbestos at Work Regulations 1987*, which require employers to carry out tests to make sure that the RPE fits properly.

It is aimed mainly at workers involved in the asbestos stripping industry and explains the importance of wearing correctly selected and correctly fitting RPE. RPE that doesn't fit properly doesn't work properly! The leaflet stresses that workers must always wear their RPE in contaminated areas and warns them against adjusting or loosening it, to make it more comfortable.

'*Working with asbestos in buildings*', IND(G)289, is a new document which replaces two leaflets – '*Asbestos and you*' and '*Asbestos dust – the hidden killer*'. It is aimed at workers and self-employed contractors involved in building maintenance and repair work and service installations, e.g. plumbers, electricians, telecommunications engineers – anyone who might disturb asbestos during the course of their work.

The 15-page booklet explains what types of buildings are likely to contain asbestos and where it is likely to be found, including photographs of products which may contain asbestos. It also advises workers of the precautions they need to take to protect themselves.

'*Asbestos: Medical guidance note*', MS13, is primarily aimed at doctors, occupational health nurses and other healthcare professionals with responsibility for medical surveillance of employees exposed to asbestos. It includes information on asbestos-related diseases and guidance on the procedures to be followed when carrying out medical surveillance on workers exposed to asbestos. It is a revision of the previous edition of MS13 and takes account of recent amendments to the *Control of Asbestos at Work Regulations 1987.*

All publications are available from HSE Books, PO Box 1999, Sudbury, Suffolk CO10 6FS (tel: 01787 881165; fax: 01787 313995).

Issue of licence

A5030   Licence applications must be made to the HSE at least 28 days before the work is due to start [*Reg 4(1)*]. A fee is payable (currently £505.00 – *Health and Safety (Fees) Regulations 1999 (SI 1999 No 645), Reg 6, Sch 5*).

The HSE can:

(*a*)   impose a time limit on the period for which a licence is granted;

(*b*)   impose other conditions;

(*c*)   refuse to issue a licence;

(*d*)   vary conditions on a licence already granted; or

(*e*)   revoke a licence.

[*Reg 4(2)*].

There is an appeal to the Secretary of State under *HSWA s 44.*

Any conditions imposed will depend upon the applicant's previous track record with asbestos work; and companies with limited experience will receive more restrictive licences than companies with greater experience. In particular,

(i)   new applicants will receive a one year licence;

(ii)   renewal licensees will receive a licence for 30 months;

(iii)   licensees who have been the recipient of enforcement action but who are considered likely to improve, will be required to comply with an agreed method statement for each job;

(iv)   licensees with a poor first year record, but not bad enough for refusal, will receive a similar restrictive licence, but for one year.

For medical surveillance requirements, see A5024(*b*) above.

Occupational diseases associated with asbestos

A5031   There are three occupational diseases associated with working with asbestos, i.e.:

—   diffuse mesothelioma (D3);

—   primary carcinoma of the lung (D8); and

—   bilateral diffuse pleural thickening (D9).

The occupations for which these three conditions are prescribed are as follows:

(*a*)   working or handling asbestos, or any admixture of asbestos;

(*b*)   manufacture or repair of asbestos textiles or other articles containing or composed of asbestos;

(*c*)   cleaning of any machinery or plant used for (*a*) and (*b*), and of any chambers, fixtures and appliances for the collection of asbestos dust;

(*d*)   substantial exposure to dust arising from operations (*a*), (*b*) and (*c*).

[*Social Security (Industrial Injuries) (Prescribed Diseases) Regulations 1985 (SI 1985 No 967), Sch 1 as amended by the Social Security (Industrial Injuries) (Miscellaneous Amendments) Regulations 1997 (SI 1997 No 810)*].

Actions against the employer for asbestos-related diseases

A5032   In addition to being prescribed occupational diseases, asbestosis and mesothelioma may give rise to actions against the employer for breach of statutory duty and the common law duty of care (negligence) (*Bryce v Swan Hunter Group [1987] 2 Lloyd's Rep 426* concerning a painter, employed for most of his working life by various shipbuilding employers, who died, aged 60, from mesothelioma. The defendant employers were held liable for breach of statutory duty for failing to take all practical measures to reduce exposure of employees to asbestos dust (under the *Asbestos Regulations 1969*), but not for breach of duty at common law because, applying the standards of knowledge of the time (1947), it could not be suggested that the defendants had to prevent the employee from all exposure to dangerous quantities of asbestos dust).

Businesses carrying out operations involving asbestos may also be liable in negligence to members of the public who suffer foreseeable pulmonary injury, following exposure to airborne dust (*Margereson and Hancock v JW Roberts Ltd, The Times, 17 April 1996* where the defendant, a former factory owner, was held liable to two plaintiffs who contracted mesothelioma as a result of playing, when children, in a factory loading bay, where there were high concentrations of asbestos dust. As stated by Lord Lloyd in *Page v Smith, The Times, 12 May 1995*, 'the test in every case ought to be whether the defendant can reasonably foresee that his conduct will expose the plaintiff to the risk of personal injury'. On this basis, the defendant was liable if, as here, he should reasonably have foreseen the risk of some pulmonary injury, not necessarily mesothelioma).

Time limitation problems

A5033   Symptom manifestation can take anything from 20-30 years after exposure and consequently the possibility arises that actions for damages, being actions in respect of 'personal injuries', may become statute-barred.

The *Limitation Act 1980* states that the period for initiating action is three years from:

(*a*)   the date on which the cause of action accrued; or

(*b*)   the date of knowledge (if later) of the person injured.

[*Limitation Act 1980, s 11(4)*].

In *Central Asbestos Co Ltd v Dodd [1973] AC 518*, a workman was employed in a workshop where various processes connected with asbestos were carried out from 1952 to 1965. Throughout that period the employer was in breach of the *Asbestos Industry Regulations 1931* and, in consequence, the employee was exposed to asbestos dust and contracted asbestosis, leading eventually to his death. The employee's condition was diagnosed in January 1964, when he was advised by the

Pneumoconiosis Medical Panel not to carry on working with asbestos. Therefore, from that time he had actual knowledge that the disease had been caused by the inhalation of asbestos dust. He did not, however, feel ill then and so continued working for the company. In March 1964 he was awarded disability benefit based on 10 per cent disablement. In September 1965 he left the company on his doctor's advice. By then, he knew that (*a*) he was suffering from asbestosis, (*b*) the company had been convicted for breach of the *Asbestos Industry Regulations 1931* during all the period he had worked there, and (*c*) the nature of his condition meant that he had to stop working with asbestos. He did not, however, know he had a good cause of action against his employer, having been told by the works manager (who was also suffering from asbestosis) that if he received disability benefit he could not sue his employer. When he learned in April 1967 that a co-employee was suing the company, he also started legal action, in October 1967.

The employer argued that the claim was statute-barred under the *Limitation Act 1963* because the action had been begun more than three years from the date the employee had knowledge of the injury (January 1964). It was held (by the House of Lords) that the action was not statute-barred because the employee's ignorance of his legal rights was a 'material fact' of a 'decisive character'. Significantly, claims for asbestosis/mesothelioma cannot begin to run before a claimant has knowledge, both medical and legal, of his condition and liability for it.

Although employers can be sued for the death of employees caused by asbestos-related conditions, this does not necessarily extend to wives of asbestos workers (*Gunn v Wallsend Slipway and Engineering Co Ltd, The Times, 23 January 1989* where the wife of the plaintiff died as a result of mesothelioma caused by inhalation of asbestos from the plaintiff's working clothes, and it was held that the employers owed no duty of care to the deceased because in 1965 when the plaintiff ceased to be exposed to asbestos dust, medical knowledge did not extend to an appreciation that the condition could be contracted in that way, that is, by washing contaminated clothes).

Discretionary exclusion of time limits – asbestosis claims

A5034   Statutory time limits can be excluded if the court thinks it equitable to allow an action to proceed. [*Limitation Act 1980, s 33*].

Practical control measures

A5035   Asbestos has been the standard form of thermal insulation since the turn of the century and may be found in numerous locations in industrial, commercial and domestic premises. In its various forms, it may be present in lagging to pipework, tanks and boilers, or as a component of structural finishes, such as walls and ceilings. In most cases, the presence of asbestos is not considered until it is actually exposed through normal wear and tear on plant and structural finishes, through structural damage or during redevelopment work.

In order to prevent further exposure, a practical control system is necessary, which incorporates procedures for sampling, treatment or removal, and disposal of asbestos waste.

Asbestos has been used widely for the following industrial purposes:

(*a*)   as fire protection on structures, protected exits, doors and in fire breaks in service ducts;

(*b*)   in the construction of inner walls and partitions;

(c)   in switchgear areas;

(d)   in ceiling tiles and linings for semi-exposed areas e.g. loading bay canopies;

(e)   for thermal and acoustic insulation of buildings; and

(f)   for thermal insulation of cold stores.

It may be applied in several forms, namely:

—   *Sprayed asbestos coating.* The asbestos content is not normally less than 55%, and such coating usually contains amosite or crocidolite.

—   *Thermal insulation material.* Thermal insulation of services or process plant frequently consists of sectional insulation, such as asbestos insulation board, which may contain a considerable proportion of asbestos. In some cases asbestos may be a minor constituent of the mixture together with materials such as magnesia and diatomaceous earth. The asbestos content of insulation board is typically 16.25%, amosite being the most common form of asbestos used.

Sampling

A5036   An asbestos removal contractor should initially commence operation by taking a series of 10 gm samples in areas where asbestos is suspected. In large buildings this may entail taking several hundred samples for analysis. Once the results of these samples have been received a decision to remove or seal the asbestos must be taken. The actual sampling procedure needs a high degree of control in terms of site preparation for sampling, the use of personal protective equipment, the actual sampling process and despatch of samples. Specific provisions apply to those persons taking the sample, in exactly the same way as those engaged in removal or sealing of the asbestos.

Disposal of asbestos waste

A5037   Relevant to disposal of asbestos are:

(a)   the provision and use of suitable receptacles;

(b)   transfer procedures from surface to receptacles;

(c)   transfer procedures from working area to disposal point; and

(d)   action to be taken in the event of asbestos spillage.

Asbestos waste must be disposed of only at a suitably licensed disposal site and in accordance with specific requirements laid down by the waste regulation authority (in England and Wales, the Environment Agency; in Scotland, SEPA).

Transport of asbestos waste

A5038   Before transporting any asbestos waste, the haulier must ensure that, so far as is reasonably practicable:

(a)   suitable vehicles are available;

(b)   the release of asbestos dust is prevented;

(c)   effective arrangements exist for dealing with accidental spillage; and

(d)   effective arrangements exist for decontamination of the vehicle used for transport.

Such arrangements should ensure that asbestos dust is not released during decontamination.

Special Waste Regulations 1996 (SI 1996 No 972)

A5039   Duties under the *Special Waste Regulations 1996 (SI 1996 No 972)* are placed on:

(a)   persons who cause special waste (which includes asbestos) to be removed from premises ('consignors');

(b)   carriers; and

(c)   persons to whom such waste is delivered ('consignees').

The standard procedure is as follows:

(a)   the consignor must prepare five copies of a 'consignment note' (see A5043 below), complete Parts A and B of the note and enter a code, unique to that consignment, which has been obtained from the Environment Agency or SEPA. The consignor must send a copy of the note, as so completed, to the Agency for the place to which the consignment is to be transported (i.e. the Environment Agency for sites in England and Wales, and SEPA for sites in Scotland);

(b)   the carrier must complete Part C on each of the four remaining copies;

(c)   the consignor:

   (i)   must complete Part D on each of those copies;

   (ii)   must retain one copy (on which Parts A to D have been completed and the relevant unique code entered); and

   (iii)   must give the three remaining copies to the carrier;

(d)   the carrier must ensure that the copies which he has received:

   (i)   travel with the consignment; and

   (ii)   are given to the consignee on delivery of the consignment;

(e)   the consignee, on receiving the consignment, must:

   (i)   complete Part E on the three copies of the consignment note given to him;

   (ii)   retain one copy;

   (iii)   give one copy to the carrier; and

   (iv)   send one copy to the Agency for the place to which the consignment has been transported.

[*Reg 5*].

For at least three years consignors and carriers must keep a register containing copies of all consignment notes; a consignee must keep a register containing copies of all consignment notes until his waste management licence for the site is surrendered or revoked, when he must send the register to the Agency which must retain the register for at least three years [*Reg 15*].

Any person who deposits special waste on land must record the location of each deposit, keep such records until his waste management licence is surrendered or revoked and then send the records to the Agency [*Reg 16*].

Offences/penalties

A5040 Any consignor, carrier or consignee who fails to comply with the regulations is liable:

(*a*)   on summary conviction, to a fine of not more than £5,000; and

(*b*)   on conviction on indictment to an unlimited fine or imprisonment for up to two years, or both.

[*Reg 18*].

HSE Guidance Notes

A5041 A number of HSE Guidance Notes dealing with this subject are available and should be consulted, together with the Approved Codes of Practice which give practical guidance with regard to the *Asbestos (Licensing) Regulations 1983* and the *Control of Asbestos at Work Regulations 1987*, before any work involving asbestos is undertaken. These Guidance Notes are:

EH 10 – Asbestos: exposure limits and measurement of airborne dust concentrations. (1995)

EH 47 – The provision, use and maintenance of hygiene facilities for work with asbestos insulation and coatings. (1990)

EH 50 – Training operatives and supervisors for work with asbestos insulation and coatings. (1988)

EH 51 – Enclosures provided for work with asbestos insulation, coatings and insulation board. (1989)

EH 57 – The problems of asbestos removal at high temperatures. (1993)

HSG 189/1 – Controlled asbestos stripping techniques for work requiring a licence. (1999)

HSG 189/2 – Working with asbestos cement. (1999)

L 10 – A guide to the Control of Explosives Regulations 1983. (1991)

L 27 – The control of asbestos at work. Control of Asbestos at Work Regulations 1987 – approved code of practice. (1999)

L 28 – Work with asbestos insulation, asbestos coating and asbestos board. Control of Asbestos at Work Regulations 1987 – approved code of practice. (1999)

IND(G) 188P – Asbestos alert for building maintenance, repair and refurbishment workers. (1996)

IND(G) 288 – Selection of suitable respiratory protective equipment for work with asbestos. (1999)

IND(G) 289 – Working with asbestos in buildings. (1999)

Copies of these publications are available from HSE Books, PO Box 1999, Sudbury, Suffolk CO10 6FS (tel: 01787 881165; fax: 01787 313995).

HSC proposals for banning white asbestos

A5042 The HSC has decided to recommend a ban on the importation, supply and use of white asbestos, following consultation on proposals in 1998. The consultation exercise produced overwhelming support for regulations to introduce a ban – subject to derogations for safety-critical applications where no suitable substitutes are available.

HSC's decision follows a meeting on 4 May 1999 when member states of the European Community voted at a Technical Committee meeting for an amendment to the Marketing and Use Directive to ban white asbestos by 2005 throughout Europe. Subject to adoption by the EU Commission, this allows member states to introduce domestic bans before 2005.

HSC has asked the Health and Safety Executive to finish drafting regulations for a domestic ban, reflecting both HSC's discussions and points arising from the consultation.

It is not yet clear when the EU Commission will formally adopt the amendment to the Directive. Following adoption, the amended Directive only comes into force on the 20th day following its publication in the Official Journal. A period of 30 days between adoption and publication in the Official Journal can be expected.

Form for consignment note

A5043

CONSIGNMENT NOTE

SPECIAL WASTE REGULATIONS 1996	Consignment Note No _____
No of prenotice (*if different*) _____	Sheet of

A   CONSIGNMENT DETAILS   PLEASE TICK IF YOU ARE A TRANSFER STATION ☐

1. The waste described below is to be removed from (name, address and postcode)

2. The waste will be taken to (address & postcode)

3. The consignment(s) will be: one single ☐ a succession ☐ carrier's round ☐ other ☐

4. Expected removal date of first consignment: last consignment:

5. Name   On behalf of (company)

    Signature   Date

6. ☎   7.   The waste producer was (if different from 1)

B   DESCRIPTION OF THE WASTE   *No of additional sheet(s)* ☐

1. The waste is   2.   Classification

3. Physical Form: Liquid ☐ Powder ☐ Sludge ☐ Solid ☐ Mixed ☐   4.   Colour

5. Total quality for removal   quantity   units (eg kg/ltrs/tonnes)   Container type, number and size:

6. The chemical/biological components that make the waste special are:

Component	Concentration (% or mg/kg)	Component	Concentration (% or mg/kg)

7. The hazards are:

8. The process giving rise to waste is:

C   CARRIER'S CERTIFICATE   I certify that I today collected the consignment and that the details in A1, A2 and B1 above are correct. The Quantity collected in the load is:

    Name   On behalf of (company) (name & address)

    Signature   Date   at   hrs.

1. Carrier registration no/reason for exemption   2.   Vehicle registration no (or mode of transport, if not road)

D   CONSIGNOR'S CERTIFICATE

    I certify that the information in B and C above are correct, that the carrier is registered or exempt and was advised of the appropriate precautionary measures.

    Name   On behalf of (company)

    Signature   Date

E   CONSIGNEE'S CERTIFICATE

1. I received this waste on   at   hrs.   2.   Quantity received   quantity   units (eg kg/ltrs/tonnes)

3. Vehicle registration no   4.   Management Operation

I certify that waste management licence/authorisation/exemption no   authorises the management of the waste described in B

Name   On behalf of (company)

Signature   Date

FORM OF SCHEDULE

SPECIAL WASTE REGULATIONS 1996:   **Carrier Schedule:**   Consignment Note No _____

                                                    Sheet   of

---

Name and address of premises from which waste was removed	I certify that today I collected the quantity of waste shown from the address given here and will take it to the address given in A2 on the consignment note

	Quantity of waste removed	Carrier's signature and Date

I certify that the waste collected is as detailed above and conforms with the description given in B on the relevant consignment note

Name of Consignor	Signature and Date

Consignment Note No

Name and address of premises from which waste was removed	I certify that today I collected the quantity of waste shown from the address given here and will take it to the address given in A2 on the consignment note

Quantity of waste removed	Carrier's signature and Date

I certify that the waste collected is as detailed above and conforms with the description given in B on the relevant consignment note

Name of Consignor	Signature and Date

Consignment Note No

Name and address of premises from which waste was removed	I certify that today I collected the quantity of waste shown from the address given here and will take it to the address given in A2 on the consignment note

Quantity of waste removed	Carrier's signature and Date

I certify that the waste collected is as detailed above and conforms with the description given in B on the relevant consignment note

Name of Consignor	Signature and Date

Consignment Note No

Name and address of premises from which waste was removed	I certify that today I collected the quantity of waste shown from the address given here and will take it to the address given in A2 on the consignment note

Quantity of waste removed	Carrier's signature and Date

I certify that the waste collected is as detailed above and conforms with the description given in B on the relevant consignment note

Name of Consignor	Signature and Date

Consignment Note No

Name and address of premises from which waste was removed	I certify that today I collected the quantity of waste shown from the address given here and will take it to the address given in A2 on the consignment note

Quantity of waste removed	Carrier's signature and Date

I certify that the waste collected is as detailed above and conforms with the description given in B on the relevant consignment note

Name of Consignor	Signature and Date

Consignment Note No

Children and Young Persons

Introduction

C3001 Employment of children and young persons is restricted by statute. The law makes a distinction between children and young persons in the context of health and safety provisions.

Definition of 'child'

C3002 A child is a person under compulsory school-leaving age, i.e., at present, under 16. [*Education Act 1944, s 58(1); Education (School-Leaving Dates) Act 1976*].

Definition of 'young person'

C3003 A young person is a person who has ceased to be a child but who has not attained 18. [*Employment of Women, Young Persons and Children Act 1920, s 4; Factories Act 1961, s 176(1)*].

Prohibitions on the employment of children

C3004 No child under the age of 13 can be employed in any capacity, paid or otherwise as it is unlawful to employ children under the age of 13. There are also statutory restrictions in respect of young people between the age of 13-18.

It is forbidden to employ any child, whether paid or not, in any of the following circumstances:

(*a*)   where the child is under the age of 13;

(*b*)   before the end of school hours;

(*c*)   before 7 a.m. or after 7 p.m. on any day;

(*d*)   for more than two hours on any school day;

(*e*)   for more than two hours on Sunday.

[*Children and Young Persons Act 1933, s 18(1)(a)-(e)*].

The prohibitions set out above are general, applying to shops, offices and factories.

Information about health risks

C3005 Parents (or those *in loco parentis*) must be given comprehensible and relevant information about risks to health and safety and of measures taken to prevent or control them.

Management of Health and Safety at Work Regulations 1992 (SI 1992 No 2051) Reg 8(2) as amended by *Health and Safety (Young Persons) Regulations 1997 (SI 1997 No 135)*.

Industrial undertakings

C3006

In addition, there is the specific provision that no child can be employed in an industrial undertaking, i.e. mines, quarries, factories, building and works of engineering construction and transportation. Where young persons under sixteen years are employed in an industrial undertaking, a register of their names and dates of birth must be kept. [*Employment of Women, Young Persons and Children Act 1920, ss 1(1)–(4) and 4, Sch 1 Art 1*].

By-laws

C3007

Local authorities have the power to make by-laws relevant to the employment of children, although a similar power relating to young persons was revoked by the *Employment Act 1989*. [*Children and Young Persons Act 1933, s 18(2)*].

Offences

C3008

It is an offence for an employer to breach any of the general restrictions or by-laws. Any such breach makes the employer liable to a fine. [*Children and Young Persons Act 1933, s 21*].

Children (Protection at Work) Regulations 1998 (SI 1998 No 276)

C3009

As a result of EU Directive 94/33/EC on the protection of young people at work, the *Children (Protection at Work) Regulations 1998 (SI 1998 No 276)* came into effect on 4 August 1998.

These Regulations provide that only children of 14 years and above may be employed in any work (other than as employees of their parents or guardians on an occasional and short-term basis in family businesses) – work, however, must be *light* work.

Light work is defined as work which does not jeopardise a child's safety, health, development, attendance at school, participation in work experience or the capacity to benefit from instruction received.

The Regulations also provide for the employment of children over the age of 13 but only in *specific* categories of light work as prescribed by local authorities.

Children are not allowed to go abroad to work in terms of performing or taking part in sport or working as models where a payment is made, unless a licence is obtained.

In terms of permitted hours of work, the Regulations distinguish between children under and over 15 years of age.

Children under 15 years of age may work a maximum of:

- two hours per day; or
- 25 hours in any week.

For children over 15 years old, the maximum is:

- eight hours per day; or
- 35 hours in any week.

Daily hours relate to days when not required to attend school (excluding Sundays) and weekly hours relate to weeks when not attending school.

A rest period of one hour must be provided after four hours of work in any one day, and young persons must have at least two consecutive weeks free from any employment during school holidays.

Trainees

C3010   Trainees in receipt of 'relevant training' also receive the protection of the *Health and Safety at Work etc. Act 1974* and regulations made thereunder. 'Relevant employment' means work experience provided pursuant to a training course or programme, or training for employment or both, but not if the training is provided by an educational establishment, or if it is received under a contract of employment. This depends upon whichever government training schemes are running at the time. [*Health and Safety (Training for Employment) Regulations 1990 (SI 1990 No 1380)*]. Trainees who are employees are already covered under the general provisions of *HSWA*.

RIDDOR also applies to trainees and apprentices (see further ACCIDENT REPORTING).

Young persons

C3011   The approach, prior to the *Health and Safety (Young Persons) Regulations 1997 (SI 1997 No 135)*, to protecting young persons' health and safety at work focused on the type of work (e.g. working with machinery, power presses, circular saws) or particular processes (e.g. lead, enamelling) or industries (e.g. the pottery industry, offshore installations and agricultural activities).

The European Directive on the Protection of Young People at Work 94/33/EC initiated changes aimed at providing health and safety protection to young people whom it defined as 'any person under 18 years of age having an employment contract or an employment relationship defined by the law in force in a Member State and/or governed by the law in force in a Member State'. It considered that they form a particularly sensitive risk group and that they need to be specifically assessed and protected against particular risks arising from their lack of experience, absence of awareness of existing or potential risks and from their immaturity. *The Health and Safety (Young Persons) Regulations 1997 (SI 1997 No 135)* partially implemented the Directive by introducing new measures and revoking some of the previous legislation, in particular regarding machinery. It reflects the growing emphasis on risk assessment. These changes have been incorporated into UK law by amending the *Management of Health and Safety at Work Regulations 1992 (SI 1992 No 2051)* which now:

(a)   require employers to carry out a **risk assessment** before a young person begins work *(Reg 3(3A) of the 1992 Regulations)*;

(b)   specify that employers must take into consideration:

(i)   the inexperience, lack of awareness of risks and immaturity of young persons;

(ii)   the fitting-out and layout of the workplace and the workstation;

(iii)   the nature, degree and duration of exposure to physical, biological and chemical agents;

(iv)   the form, range and use of work equipment and the way in which it is handled;

(v)   the organisation of processes and activities;

(vi)   the extent of the health and safety training provided or to be provided to young persons; and

(vii)   risks from agents, processes and work listed in the Annex to the Directive.

[*Reg 3(3C)*].

The list in the Annex to Council Directive 94/33/EC is expressed to be non-exhaustive, and includes the following risks:

(1)   Physical agents:

(*a*)   ionising radiation;

(*b*)   work in a high-pressure atmosphere, e.g. pressurised containers, diving.

(2)   Specified biological agents.

(3)   Classified chemical agents being toxic, very toxic, corrosive or explosive, or

(*a*)   substances deemed harmful or irritant carrying one or more of the following risks:

—   irreversible effects;

—   sensitisation by inhalation and/or skin contact;

—   carcinogenics;

—   heritable genetic damage;

—   infertility or harm to unborn child;

(*b*)   lead or lead compounds absorbable by human contact;

(*c*)   asbestos.

(4)   Manufacturing and handling of fireworks and explosives.

(5)   Work with fierce or poisonous animals.

(6)   Industrial scale animal slaughter.

(7)   Work with or involving:

—   compressed, liquefied or dissolved gases;

—   vats, tanks, reservoirs or carboys containing chemical agents;

—   risk of structural collapse;

—   high-voltage electrical hazard;

—   pacing by machinery and paid by results.

Where an employer is employing a young person on 3 March 1997 there is an obligation on the employer to review the risks forthwith. [*Reg 3(3B)*].

Assessments and monitoring

C3012   Where the assessment shows that there is a risk to the safety, physical or mental health or development of a young person, a free assessment and monitoring of their health must be provided at regular intervals. [*Reg 5 of the 1992 Regulations*].

Information for employees

C3013 Every employer is under an obligation to provide his employee, including young people, with comprehensible and relevant information on:

(*a*) the risks to their health and safety identified by the assessment;

(*b*) the preventive and protective measures;

(*c*) procedures for serious and imminent danger and for dangerous areas;

(*d*) the identity of the persons nominated by the employer to implement evacuation procedures;

(*e*) the risks to other employees' health and safety that have been notified to the employer by other employers who share the workplace.

[*Reg 8* of the *1992 Regulations*].

Protection of young persons

C3014 Employers have a general duty to ensure that young persons employed by them are protected at work from any risks to their health or safety which are a consequence of their lack of experience, of absence of awareness of existing or potential risks or the fact that young persons are not yet fully mature.

There is also a general prohibition on the employment of young people for work —

(*a*) which is beyond their physical or psychological capacity;

(*b*) involving harmful exposure to toxic, carcinogenic or mutagenic agents which in any other way chronically affect human health;

(*c*) involving harmful exposure to radiation;

(*d*) involving the risk of accidents which it may reasonably be assumed cannot be recognised or avoided by young persons owing to their insufficient attention to safety or lack of experience or training; or

(*e*) in which there is a risk to health from extreme cold or heat or from noise or vibration.

This prohibition does not apply to young people who are no longer children if the work is necessary for their vocational training. However, such training must be under the supervision of a competent person, and any risk must be reduced to the lowest level that is reasonably practicable.

[*Reg 13D*].

Fitness for work in factories

C3015 Where a young person is employed to work in a factory the employer must send to the local careers office a written notice stating, *inter alia*, the work which the young person has been taken on to do, within seven days of their commencing work. The object of this duty is for the purposes of selective medical examinations where these may be of benefit. [*Factories Act 1961, s 119A; Employment Medical Advisory Service Act 1972, s 5*].

Where a factory inspector is of the opinion that the employment of a young person in a factory or particular process is either prejudicial to his health, or to the health of other persons, he may serve a notice on the factory occupier informing him accordingly, and recommending that the employment of the young person be discontinued after the period named in the notice. After the expiry of that period, the factory occupier must not employ the young person, unless either the factory doctor, or the employment medical adviser has personally examined the young person and certified him fit to work in the factory or at the process. [*Factories Act 1961, s 119*]. This section, in effect, empowers an inspector to require a fitness for work certificate.

The Working Time Directive and Regulations

C3016   The *Working Time Regulations 1998 (SI 1998 No 1833)* are the first significant piece of legislation to regulate working time in the UK (see WORKING TIME). They implement both the European Working Time Directive 93/104/EC and parts of the Protection of Young People at Work Directive 94/33/EC.

The provisions of the Regulations that are different to young workers (i.e. over 16 years old but under 18) as opposed to adults are those regarding rest entitlements and health and capacities assessments and the exclusions and exceptions from these provisions.

Whereas under *Reg 10(1)* an adult worker can only be asked to work a maximum thirteen-hour day, a young worker is entitled under *Reg 10(2)* to a slightly longer rest period and can only be asked to work a maximum twelve-hour day.

In addition to their daily rest periods, workers are entitled to a weekly uninterrupted rest period: for adult workers the weekly rest period must be not less than 24 hours in each seven-day period, whereas for young workers this period is increased to 48 hours in each seven-day period [*Reg 11(3)*].

In relation to young workers, the minimum 48 hour rest break in every seven-day period may be interrupted if the activities involve periods of work that are split up over the day or are of a short duration. They may also be reduced where this can be justified by the employer for technical or organisational reasons but cannot be reduced to a period of less than 36 consecutive hours.

Regulation 12(1) states that an adult worker who works for a daily working time of six hours or more is entitled to a rest break of at least twenty minutes. For young workers, *Regulation 12(4)* provides that this entitlement is to a rest break of 30 minutes where their daily working time is more than four-and-a-half hours.

In the case of young workers, in determining whether or not a young worker is entitled to a rest break, the employer must take into account any work performed by the young worker for any other employers on that day. The employer must then aggregate the number of hours worked both for him and for each additional employer [*Reg 11(8)*].

A duty to carry out a health assessment arises whenever a young worker is to be assigned to work during the period between 10.00 pm and 6.00 am [*Reg 7(2)*]. In addition, the assessment must cover not just the young worker's health but also his/her 'capacities' to take up the assignment. The DTI's *Guide to the Working Time Regulations* recommends that to deal with the added requirement for the health assessment to cover the capacities of the young worker, the assessment should also consider such issues as physique, maturity and experience and take into account competence to undertake the night work which has been assigned.

As already discussed at C3011 above, the *Management of Health and Safety at work Regulations 1992 (SI 1992 No 2051)* already require employers to assess the risk to the health and safety of employees and to take into account employees' capabilities as regards health and safety when entrusting tasks to them. However, the 1998 Regulations firm up those requirements. The purpose of the health assessment is to determine whether the worker is fit to carry out the night work to which he/she has been assigned, and to identify not only those whose health absolutely rules out night work altogether but also those who are suffering from a medical condition which may be exacerbated by working at night, such as diabetes.

There is no one particular way to carry out a health assessment. It does not appear that the health assessment must be a full medical carried out by a doctor. As a minimum, employers could construct a screening questionnaire for workers to complete before beginning night work.

Employers are not required to carry out a health assessment under *Reg 7(2)* in cases where the young worker is assigned to do work of an exceptional nature.

It is important to note that an employer's duty to carry out a health and capacities assessment in respect of young workers applies also to those young workers who are excepted from most of the provisions of the Regulations by virtue of being directly involved in an excluded sector or activity. These exclusions are set out in *Reg 18* as being:

— the following sectors of activity:

- air, rail, road, sea, inland waterway and lake transport;

- sea fishing;

- other workers at sea; or

— the activities of doctors in training; or

— where characteristics peculiar to certain specified services such as the armed forces or the police, or to certain specific activities in the civil protection services, inevitably conflict with the provisions of the Regulations.

Although it is not specifically stated that a worker cannot be assigned to night work if the health assessment reveals that the worker is suffering from a medical condition which is exacerbated by night work, such a conclusion may be deduced from *Reg 7(6)* which deals with the obligation to transfer night workers to day work on health grounds, where possible.

In addition, special provisions are made for young workers who are employed on ships [*Reg 26*]. Although those workers whose activities are in sea transport and other workers at sea are excluded from the provisions of the Regulations, this exclusion does not extend to young workers. *Regulation 26* disapplies the Regulations in relation to young workers whose employment is subject to Regulations under the *Merchant Shipping Act 1995, s 55(2)(b)*, in respect of:

- the duty to provide health assessments before being assigned to night work [*Reg 7(2)*];

- the twelve-hour daily rest entitlement [*Reg 10(2)*];

- the 48 hours' weekly rest [*Reg 11(3)*]; and

- the entitlement to a 30 minute rest break in work of four-and-a-half hours or more [*Reg 12(4)*].

Special provisions apply to young workers in a situation of *force majeure* [*Reg 27*] – this provision relates essentially to emergency situations or those that arise outside the normal course of events. Under *Reg 27*, where a young worker is required to undertake work for which no adult worker is available to perform, which is of a temporary nature and is required to be performed immediately where either:

- it is occasioned by an occurrence due to an unusual and unforeseeable circumstance beyond the employer's control; or

- there are exceptional events, the consequences of which could not have been avoided despite the exercise of all due care by the employer,

the Regulations will not apply to young workers in respect of:

- the extended right to a twelve-hour daily rest period [*Reg 10(2)*]; or

- the enhanced right to a 30 minute rest break in a working day of more than four-and-a-half hours [*Reg 12(4)*].

Where the Regulations are disapplied because of the operation of *Reg 27*, the young worker must be afforded compensatory rest within three weeks of the occurrence.

In relation to young workers serving as members of armed forces, the Regulations are disapplied in respect of the entitlements to:

- a twelve-hour daily rest period [*Reg 10(2)*]; and

- a 48 hour weekly rest period [*Reg 11(3)*].

Where a young worker is required to work during a period which would normally be the daily or weekly rest period in accordance with this exception, the individual must be allowed an appropriate period of compensatory rest.

Dangerous machines

C3017   With regard to dangerous machines in offices and shops, **all** employees, including young persons, must have received full instruction as to the dangers and precautions to be observed, and must also:

(*a*)   have received sufficient training in work at that machine; and

(*b*)   be under adequate supervision from a person with a thorough knowledge and experience of the machine.

[*Offices, Shops and Railway Premises Act 1963 s 19(1)*]. (Machines to which this section applies are prescribed in the *Prescribed Dangerous Machines Order 1964 (SI 1964 No 971)*.)

(See further OFFICES AND SHOPS.)

Machines for which training is specifically required

C3018   The *Dangerous Machines (Training of Young Persons) Order 1954 (SI 1954 No 921)* was revoked by the 1997 regulations with effect from 3 March 1997. As a consequence there is no longer a requirement for young people, *per se*, to have specific training for certain mechanically powered machines and other dangerous machines. It may of course be necessary as a result of the risk assessment or other provisions applying to all employees.

Prohibition on the use of power presses and circular saws

C3019   There is a general prohibition on the operation of power presses by young persons (under 18 years). [*Power Presses Regulations 1965 (SI 1965 No 1441), Reg 4(1)*]. Moreover, there is a similar prohibition on the operation of circular saws by young persons (under 18 years). [*Woodworking Machines Regulations 1974 (SI 1974 No 903), Reg 13(1)(3)*].

Maintenance operations

C3020   In all workplaces employers must ensure that:

(*a*)   all work equipment is constructed and adapted so that, so far as reasonably practicable, maintenance operations, involving risks to health and safety, can be carried out while work equipment is shut down; or

(*b*)   (i)   maintenance operations can be carried out without exposing the person carrying them out to danger, or

(ii)   appropriate measures can be taken to protect such person.

[*Provision and Use of Work Equipment Regulations 1998 (SI 1998 No 2306), Reg 22*]. (See further MACHINERY SAFETY.)

In practice, this means that maintenance work will be carried out whilst machinery is inactive. If, however, equipment has to be running or working during maintenance operations and this is attendant with risks, safeguards should be instituted, e.g. provision of temporary guards, limited movement controls, crawl speed operated by hold-to-run controls.

Restrictions on the employment of young persons – specific processes

C3021   Persons under 18 are prohibited from working in the following processes and occupations:

(*a*)   (i)   any lead process;

(ii)   work in any room where manipulation of raw oxide of lead or pasting is carried out;

[*Electric Accumulator Regulations 1925 (SR&O 1925 No 28), Reg 1*];

(*b*)   certain work in the pottery industry [*Pottery (Health and Welfare) Special Regulations 1950 (SI 1950 No 65), Reg 6, as amended by Employment Act 1989, Sch 8*];

(*c*)   work on offshore installations;

(*d*)   certain agricultural activities (see C3022 below);

(*e*)   painting any part of a factory building with lead paint [*Factories Act 1961, s 131*]. Supply and use of lead paint has been prohibited from 28 February 1992 except in connection with historic buildings and works of art [*Environmental Protection (Controls on Injurious Substances) Regulations 1992 (SI 1992 No 31)*] (see also DANGEROUS SUBSTANCES I).

Agriculture

C3022   Agriculture is the only major industry which has to take into account the constant presence of children and young persons. A considerable proportion of people killed in agricultural activities are children and young persons, particularly the former. Strict compliance with statutory requirements is, therefore, essential to combat this.

Main statutory prohibitions on jobs carried out by children and young persons

C3023   *Children*

(*a*)   *Children under 13 years.* A child under 13 must not:

(i)   drive or ride on a tractor when used in the course of agricultural operations [*Agriculture (Avoidance of Accidents to Children) Regulations 1958 (SI 1958 No 366), Regs 3, 4*];

(ii)   ride on agricultural implements, while they are being towed or propelled [*Reg 5*].

It is also an offence for a person to cause or permit a child under 13 to ride on or drive a tractor or machine, or to ride on an agricultural implement. [*Agriculture (Safety, Health and Welfare Provisions) Act 1956, s 7(3)*].

(*b*)   *Children under 16 years.* A child under 16 must not:

(i)   operate or assist at a circular saw [*Agriculture (Circular Saws) Regulations 1959 (SI 1959 No 427), Reg 2, Sch 2*]; and

(ii)   remove a guard from a field machine [*Agriculture (Field Machinery) Regulations 1962 (SI 1962 No 1472), Sch 1 Pt IV*].

(The *Agriculture (Safety, Health and Welfare Provisions) Act 1956*, the *Agriculture (Field Machinery) Regulations 1962* and the *Agriculture (Threshers and Balers) Regulations 1960* are currently under review.)

Young persons

A young person must not:

(*a*)   feed produce into a drum feeding mouth of a thresher [*Agriculture (Threshers and Balers) Regulations 1960 (SI 1960 No 1199), Sch Pt III*];

(*b*)   operate a circular saw, except under the supervision of a person over 18 with a thorough knowledge of its working [*Agriculture (Circular Saws) Regulations 1959, Reg 1, Sch 2*].

Compensation for Work Injuries/Diseases

Introduction

C6001 Compensation for work injuries, diseases and death is payable under two interrelated but nevertheless independent systems, namely, under the social security system and in the form of damages for civil wrongs (torts). The former is a form of public insurance, funded by employers/employees and taxpayers, and benefit is payable irrespective of liability on the part of an employer, i.e. 'no fault' – though connection with employment must be established. The social security system is bound by legislation, such as the various *Social Security Acts*, culminating in the present *Social Security Administration Act 1992* and the *Social Security (Contributions and Benefits) Act 1992 (SSCBA 1992)*, the *Statutory Sick Pay Act 1994*, the *Social Security (Incapacity for Work) Act 1994*, the *Social Security (Industrial Injuries) (Prescribed Diseases) Regulations 1985*, the *Social Security (Incapacity for Work) (General) Regulations 1995*, the *Social Security (Recoupment of Benefits) Act 1997*, and sundry other legislation.

The tort system relevant to personal injuries is a form of private insurance, funded by employers' liability insurance premiums (see EMPLOYERS' LIABILITY INSURANCE), and awards of damages in tort depend on proof of negligence against an employer. Current law relating to work injuries and diseases is to be found in a variety of Acts, such as the *Law Reform (Personal Injuries) Act 1948*, the *Employers' Liability (Compulsory Insurance) Act 1969*, the *Employers' Liability (Defective Equipment) Act 1969*, the *Damages Act 1996* and the common law of tort, particularly negligence. This section examines the two concurrent systems and interaction between them.

'*Guidelines for the Assessment of General Damages*', issued by the Judicial Studies Board, is a publication which aims to unify judicial approaches to awards of damages. These Guidelines are not a legal document, do not and are not expected to obviate the need for a full examination of the law applicable to each case.

A useful handbook, '*Industrial Injuries Handbook for Adjudicating Medical Officers*', was published in 1997. It sets out medical examination procedures, and points out that unlawful discrimination in the discharge of officers' duties must be avoided. It also offers guidance on the legislation, and discusses the effect of case law to help the reader with those matters which are not covered by the legislation. From the case law, for example, loss of faculty is described as a total loss of power or function of an organ of the body, including disfigurement.

Social security benefits

C6002 Changes were introduced by the provisions of the *Social Security (Incapacity for Work) Act 1994*, and regulations made under that Act, which came into force in April 1995, affected those on industrial injuries benefits. Sickness benefit and invalidity benefit were replaced by incapacity benefit which is payable at different rates, as before, but the higher rate is not be payable until after 364 days, instead of after 168 days.

The effect that this has had on industrial injuries benefits, including disablement benefit, is that industrial benefits continue to be payable after 90 days, but the benefits which are payable before and at the same time, that is, any national insurance benefits, are less for the relevant period. The higher adult dependant's allowance is delayed for 364 days when the long-term incapacity benefit increases begin. Claimants whose industrial injuries benefit is lower than the rate of incapacity for work benefit and who are thus entitled to claim this benefit are also affected. (See C6015–C6017 below for details of these changes.)

Entitlement to industrial injuries benefits now requires compliance with national insurance contribution conditions for incapacity benefit. The incapacity for work tests under the *Social Security (Incapacity for Work) Act 1994* and regulations do not apply to industrial disablement benefits. The medical adjudication procedures for these benefits continue with some modifications as before. The incapacity for work tests will apply to sufferers from industrial disablement if they apply for incapacity benefit before the ninety qualifying days for industrial disablement benefits begin, or if they do not qualify for industrial disablement benefit under the percentage or other rules, or if incapacity benefit is payable at a higher rate than industrial disablement pension rates and incapacity benefit is chosen by the claimant.

Under the rules for claimants for incapacity benefit, the employee has to supply information and evidence of sickness and be prepared to submit to a medical examination to decide the question of whether he is fit to work. If he has worked for more than eight weeks in the twenty-one weeks immediately preceding the first day of sickness, a test relevant to his incapacity to do work which he could reasonably be expected to do in the course of his occupation applies. This test criterion continues to the 197th day of incapacity. After that date, and for all claimants who do not qualify for the required period, an 'all work' test arises. Regulations provide for prescribed activities and a person's incapacity, by reason of a specific disease, or bodily or mental disablement, to perform these activities. These tests are detailed and are outside the scope of this book. [*SSCBA 1992, ss 171(A)-(G) as inserted by Social Security (Incapacity for Work) Act 1994, s 5*].

The *Social Security (Incapacity for Work) (General) Regulations 1995 (SI 1995 No 311)* as amended by the *Social Security (Incapacity for Work) (General) Regulations 1996 (SI 1996 No 484)*, provide that certain people are deemed to be incapable of work, including those suffering from a severe condition as defined in the regulations or those receiving certain regular treatment (such as chronic renal failure, hospital in-patients and those suffering from an infectious or contagious disease). A pregnant woman may also be deemed incapable of work if there is a serious risk to her health, or that of her unborn child, if she does not refrain from work, in the case of the 'own occupation' test; or in the case of the 'all work' test, if she does not refrain from work in any occupation. If she has no entitlement to maternity allowance or statutory maternity pay and the actual date of confinement has been certified, she is deemed to be incapable of work beginning with the first day of the sixth week before the expected week of confinement until the fourteenth day after the actual date of confinement and during this period she will therefore be entitled to claim incapacity benefit.

Whilst most actual work by a claimant disqualifies him from receiving this benefit on any day of such work, certain work does not stop benefit. [*Social Security (Incapacity for Work) Regulations, Reg 17*]. Earnings from such work must not exceed £58.00 per week (1999/2000) and in most cases must be for less than 16 hours per week. The exempt work is work done on the advice of a doctor which:

(*a*)   helps to improve, or to prevent or delay deterioration in the disease or bodily or mental disablement which causes that person's incapacity for work; or

(*b*)   is part of the treatment programme undertaken as a hospital in-patient or out-patient under medical supervision; or

(*c*)   is done when the claimant is attending a sheltered workshop for people with disabilities.

Voluntary work and duties as a member of a disability appeal tribunal or the Disability Living Allowance Advisory Board are also exempt work.

Under the *Social Security (Incapacity Benefit) (Transitional) Regulations 1995 (SI 1995 No 310)*, those who claimed and were in receipt of sickness benefit or invalidity benefit were automatically transferred to the new benefits without the need for a fresh claim, and a claim for industrial injuries was also transferred in the same way. These transitional regulations also preserved increases of allowances for those who were in receipt of the former benefits which will continue to be payable provided the spouse is residing with the beneficiary, or if the beneficiary is contributing to the maintenance of his spouse. Long-term incapacity benefit is paid to existing beneficiaries at the differential rates applicable to invalidity benefit before the changeover and adult dependency allowances will continue to be paid. Except in circumstances which are set out in the regulations, including assessment of industrial injuries, all of the transitional rights have been made subject to satisfaction of the stricter tests of incapacity for work.

Industrial injuries benefit

C6003   The benefits which are currently available to new claimants for industrial injuries benefits are industrial injuries disablement pension, constant attendance allowance and exceptionally severe disablement allowance. Disability working allowance may also be claimed in some circumstances (see C6016 below). Some older benefits continue to be payable to recipients who were receiving them when they were otherwise abolished, or whose entitlement arose before the relevant dates. Reduced earnings allowance was one of these benefits. (For details of these older benefits and more detailed social security benefits information, see *Tolley's Social Security and State Benefits Handbook*.)

Accident and personal injuries provisions

C6004   The employed earner must have suffered personal injury caused after 4 July 1948 by an accident arising out of and in the course of his employment, being employed earner's employment. [*SSCBA 1992, s 94*]. The *Reporting of Injuries, Diseases and Dangerous Occurrences Regulations 1995* require reports to be made on prescribed forms to the Health and Safety Executive forthwith after the occurrence of an accident or on receipt of a report from a registered medical practitioner of his diagnosis of a prescribed disease. A self-employed person may arrange for this report to be sent by someone else. Records must be kept for three years containing prescribed details of accidents, or the date of diagnosis of the disease, the occupation of the person affected and the nature of the disease. For more information on these regulations see ACCIDENT REPORTING.

Industrial accident and disease records may be kept for these three years on:

●   a B510 Accident Book;

- photocopies of completed form F2508; or

- computerised records.

Personal injury caused by accident

C6005   'Personal injury' includes physical and mental impairment, a hurt to body or mind, which includes nervous disorders or shocks (R(I) 22/52; R(I) 22/59). Damage to artificial limbs or appendages is not included unless the additional aid has become part of the body. Damage to a crutch, hearing aid, false teeth, a pair of glasses or an artificial leg is not included (R(I) 7/56).

The personal injury must have been caused by an accident. Although this is usually an unintended and unexpected occurrence, such as a fall, if a victim is injured by someone else, that may be an accident from the point of view of the victim (*Trim Joint District School Board v Kelly [1914] AC 667*). Where the employee injures himself, there is no need for there to have been any exceptional exertion on his part. For example, a labourer pushing a truck 'felt something go' and was incapable of work thereafter by reason of heart trouble. This counted as an industrial injury (C 27/49). The effect of the injury may be immediate or delayed if the full extent of the damage inflicted is not immediately apparent.

A relevant accident may still have occurred where a series of accidents without separate definite times cause personal injuries. An office worker was held to have suffered a series of accidents on each occasion she had been obliged to inhale her colleagues' tobacco smoke and this was held to have caused personal injuries. The fact that she was asthmatic did not debar benefit rights because of a pre-existing condition, or susceptibility in a victim does not affect benefits (R(I) 24/54; R(I) 43/55). However, where more than one accident gives rise to entitlement to industrial injuries benefit, the pensions will be aggregated so that the combined rate does not exceed the maximum rate. [*SSCBA 1992, s 107*]. (See Table 1 at C6017 below.)

'Accident' must be distinguished from 'process', that is, bodily or mental derangement not ascribable to a particular event. Injuries to health caused by processes are not industrial injuries, unless they lead to prescribed industrial diseases (see C6010 below). 'There must come a time when the indefinite number of so-called accidents and the length of time over which they occur, take away the name of accident and substitute that of process' (*Roberts v Dorothea Slate Quarries Co Ltd (No 1) [1948] 2 AER 201*).

Accident arising out of and in the course of employment

C6006   There is no need to show a cause for the relevant accident, such as a fall, provided that the employee was working in the employer's premises at the time of the accident. An accident arising in the course of employment is presumed to have arisen out of that employment, in the absence of any evidence to the contrary. What runs through all the case law is the common requirement giving rise to industrial injuries rights; namely, that the employee was doing something reasonably incidental to and within the scope of his employment, and this includes extra-mural activities which the employee has agreed to do (R(I) 39/56). A male nurse who was injured in a football match watched by patients in the hospital grounds succeeded in a claim for benefit as this was reasonably incidental to and within the scope of his employment (R(I) 3/57), but a policeman who was injured whilst playing football for his force was unable to recover benefit despite the fact that his employers had encouraged him to play in the game (*R v National Insurance Commissioner, ex parte Michael [1977] 2 AER 420*). Also, in *Faulkner v Chief Adjudication Officer, The*

Times, 8 April 1994; a police officer who was injured whilst playing for a police football team was not entitled to industrial injuries benefit despite the benefit to the community resulting from his participation. He was not on duty at the time. *Social Security Case 7/97/14111/96* concerned a clerical officer who was employed at the Benefits Agency. The officer correctly reported a neighbour for benefits fraud. This led to an assault by the neighbour on the officer. It was held that the officer was entitled to disablement benefit, since the assault was held to have occurred in the course of employment.

Whilst most claims will not cause much difficulty with respect to accidents arising out of and in the course of employment, a great deal of litigation has centred on cases where the employee is on the premises, but not working at his usual tasks, when he is injured. The effect of the case law concerning meal breaks, for example, shows that an accident during a meal break will be covered if the meal break is at a set time within a shift, and the employee is actually taking a meal; or if the employee has a set duty, such as keeping an eye on a vehicle during a meal break, and is carrying out this duty at the time of the accident.

Supplementary rules

C6007

Five statutory provisions establish rules under which the employee is deemed to be acting in the course of his employment duties. If the occurrence falls within these rules, the employee will be covered by industrial injuries benefit. These provisions are as follows:

(*a*)   Illegal employment – if the employee was not lawfully employed, or his employment was actually void because of some contravention of employment legislation. [*SSCBA 1992, s 97*].

(*b*)   Acting in breach of regulations, or orders of the employer – if the employee is not acting outside his authority under his employment duties, and an accident occurs while the employee is doing something for the purposes of, and in connection with, the employer's business [*SSCBA 1992, s 98*], he will be covered. For instance, a kitchen porter hung up his apron to dry in a recess near to the ovens where he was forbidden to go. He was injured when he fell into a shallow pit. The hanging up of the apron was for the purposes of his employment, so the accident was deemed to have arisen out of, and in the course of, his employment duties (R(I) 6/55).

Moreover, where a dock labourer was employed on loading a ship by the method of two slings, but he instead used a truck which he had not been authorised to use for this purpose, he was held to be acting in the course of his employment. It was held that he could recover benefit (R(I) 1/70B). This contrasts with the earlier case of *R v D'Albuquerque, ex parte Bresnahan [1966] 1 Lloyd's Rep 69*, where a dock labourer was killed in an accident whilst driving a forklift truck, which he had no authority or permission to use to remove an obstruction. His widow was unable to recover industrial injuries benefit as her husband was held not to have been acting in the course of his employment.

(*c*)   Travelling in an employer's transport – travel to and from work is not covered except where the employee is travelling in transport provided by the employer with his express or implied permission, whether or not the employee was bound to travel in this transport. [*SSCBA 1992, s 99*]. Outside this express provision, the employee will, in most cases, both be required to be on the employer's premises doing what he was authorised to do, unless his work takes him off the premises. A postman was able to recover benefit when he was bitten by a dog on the street, as his job required him to walk along streets (R(I) 10/57). If the journey is preparatory to the start of timed itinerant duties, for example, as a home help, there will be no entitlement to benefit in respect of injury sustained on the way to the first home, though if the employee has more discretion about his movements, he may be entitled to benefit on the way to his first call.

(*d*)   An injury incurred while an employee is trying to prevent a danger to other people, or serious damage to property during an emergency. [*SSCBA 1992, s 100*].

(*e*)   Accidents caused by another's misconduct, boisterousness or negligence (provided that the claimant did not directly induce or contribute to the accident by his own conduct), the behaviour of animals (including birds, fish and insects), if these cause an accident, or if a person is struck by lightning or by any object, respectively confer entitlement to industrial injuries benefit. [*SSCBA 1992, s 101*].

Relevant employment

C6008   'Employed earner's employment' includes all persons who are gainfully employed in Great Britain under a contract of service, or as an office holder, and who are subject to income tax under Schedule E. Self-employed people and private contractors are thus not entitled to industrial injuries benefits.

Certain classes of person are expressly included for the purposes of industrial injuries benefits. They include unpaid apprentices, members of fire brigades (or other rescue brigades), first-aid, salvage or air raid precautions parties, inspectors of mines, special constables, certain off-shore oil and gas workers and certain mariners and air crew. Most trainees on Government training schemes are excluded from the scheme. [*SSCBA 1992, ss 2, 95*].

If an industrial accident occurs outside Great Britain, industrial injuries benefit has since 1 October 1986 been payable when the employee returns to Great Britain, provided the employer is paying UK national insurance contributions, or if the claimant is a voluntary worker overseas and is himself paying UK contributions. Accidents which occur, or prescribed diseases which develop in other EU countries are covered by common rules. An employee who is entitled to make a claim for industrial benefit in another EU member state should make his claim for benefit in that state, regardless of the country which will actually pay the benefit.

Certain types of employment are excluded from cover. [*SSCBA 1992, s 95; Employed Earners' Employments for Industrial Injuries Purposes Regulations 1975 (SI 1975 No 467), Regs 2–7 and Schedules 1, 2*].

Persons treated as employers

C6009   The above regulations also provide (in *Schedule 3*) for cases where certain people who may not have a contract with the employee, or who may be an agency employer, to be the relevant employer for the person who has suffered the industrial injury, or who has developed a prescribed disease. An agency that supplies an office cleaner, or a typist, will be the relevant employer. For casual employees of clubs, the club will be the relevant employer. The Head of Chambers in barristers' chambers is deemed to be the barristers' clerk's employer.

Benefits for prescribed industrial diseases

C6010   The rules for certain prescribed diseases (namely deafness, asthma and asbestos related diseases), differ in some respects from the provisions affecting prescribed diseases outlined below. (See C6045, C6046, below for details of these differing provisions.) The different rules applicable to diseases resulting from exposure to asbestos at work are dealt with for industrial injuries purposes by a special medical board and there is a separate state scheme for statutory compensation where one of these diseases develops and there is no remedy against an employer, or entitlement to state benefits (see C6048 below). (See leaflet NI 272 for help with making a claim.)

To obtain the right to industrial injuries benefits for all other prescribed diseases, the claimant must show:

—   that he is suffering from the prescribed disease;

—   that the disease is prescribed for his particular occupation (where a disease is prescribed for a general activity, for example, contact with certain substances, he must clearly show that this was more than to a minimal extent); and

—   that he contracted the disease through engaging in the particular occupation (there is a presumption that if the disease is prescribed for a particular occupation, the disease was caused by it, in the absence of evidence to the contrary).

(See also OCCUPATIONAL HEALTH AND DISEASES.)

Claims are made on Form BI 100B and there is a right to, and it is advisable to, claim immediately after the disease starts. The 90-day waiting period for receipt of benefit applies as for accidents, as do the percentage disabilities and aggregated assessment rules, except in the case of loss of faculty resulting from diffuse mesothelioma when entitlement begins on the first day of the claim. Assessments are made by two doctors who will decide on the percentage disability and how long the disability will last. Benefit will then be payable for the period stated in the assessment, but if the doctors are not sure of the period, benefit will be paid for a while with a further review. If the disease recurs during that period, there will be no need to make a further claim, but if the condition has worsened, the assessment may be reviewed. If there is a further attack after the period of the assessment, a fresh claim will have to be made, which will be subject to a further 90-day waiting period.

Industrial injuries disablement benefit

Entitlement and assessment

C6011   A person is entitled to an industrial injuries disablement pension if he suffers as a result of the relevant accident, a loss of physical or mental faculty such that the assessed extent of the resulting disablement amounts to not less than 14%. [*SSCBA 1992, s 103, Sch 6*]. He will be similarly entitled if he suffers from a prescribed industrial disease (see C6010 above). An assessment of the percentage disablement up to 100% will be made by an adjudicating medical practitioner who, in the case of accidents, looks at the claimant's physical and mental condition, comparing him in those respects with those of a normal person of the same age and sex. No other factors are relevant. The assessment may cover a fixed period/or the life of the claimant. The degrees of disablement are laid down in a scale so that, for example, loss of one hand is normally 60% and loss of both hands 100%. Disfigurement is included even if this causes no bodily handicap.

Where the claimant suffered from a pre-existing disability before the happening of the industrial accident at the onset of the industrial disease, benefit will only be payable in respect of the industrial accident or disease itself, and the medical adjudicators will compare the original disability with the industrial disability for this purpose. Where one or more disabilities result from industrial accidents or diseases, the level of resulting disability may be aggregated, but not so as to exceed the 100 per cent disability and its corresponding rate of benefit. [*Social Security (General Benefit) Regulations 1982, Reg 11*].

A list of initial application forms is supplied in NI 6 Industrial Injuries Benefit. Once a claim for industrial injuries benefit has been made, the Secretary of State will send Form B1/76 to the claimant. This form asks for full details of the accident or disease. The claimant must then submit to examination by at least two adjudicating medical practitioners and must agree to follow any appropriate medical treatment. If he fails to comply with these requirements, he will be disqualified from receiving this benefit for six months. A decision in writing will be sent to the claimant. It is possible to appeal a refusal of industrial benefit; details of how to appeal will be sent with the decision if it is negative.

This benefit can only be paid 90 days after the date of the accident excluding Sundays. [*SSCBA 1992, s 103*].

Claims in accident cases

C6012   Claims should be made on Form BI 100A obtainable from the post office, job centre, or from the Benefits Agency, by claimants disabled by the accident for nine weeks. Claims should be made within six months of the accident to avoid loss of benefit, as the usual period for which benefit will be backdated is three months. [*Social Security (Claims and Payments) Regulations 1987 (SI 1987 No 1968), Reg 19, Sch 4 para 3*]. It is possible to apply to the DSS for a declaration from an adjudicating officer that an accident is covered by the scheme if a claimant suspects that an accident at work may have lasting effects which may not become apparent until some time later. If a positive finding is made, this will bind the DSS on any later claim for benefit. [*SSCBA 1992, s 44*]. Form BI 95 should be used for making this application. (Claims in respect of prescribed diseases are mentioned at C6010 above; appeals at C6018 below.)

Rate of industrial injuries disablement benefit

C6013   Benefit is paid at one of two rates with the higher being paid to claimants aged over 18. (See C6017 below for current rates and injury percentages.)

Constant attendance allowance and exceptionally severe disablement allowance

C6014   Constant attendance allowance is available if the claimant is receiving industrial injuries disablement benefit based on 100% disablement, or aggregated disablements that total 100% or more. It requires, in addition, that the claimant needs constant care and attention as a result of the effects of an industrial accident or disease. Claims for industrial injuries benefit are made on Form BI 104. It is granted for a fixed period and may be renewed from time to time. There are four rates of payment: part-time (where full-time care is unnecessary); normal rate (if the above conditions are fulfilled and full-time care is required); intermediate (if the claimant is exceptionally disabled and the degree of attendance required is greater, and the care necessary is greater than under the 'normal' classification, the benefit is limited to one and a half times the normal rate); and an exceptional rate (if the claimant is so exceptionally disabled as to be entirely dependent on full-time attendance for the necessities of life). If the intermediate or exceptional rates are payable, an additional allowance (known as exceptionally severe disablement allowance) will be due if the condition is likely to be permanent. Constant attendance allowance may continue to be paid for up to four weeks if the claimant goes into hospital for free medical treatment.

Other sickness/disability benefits

C6015   However, most applicants for industrial injuries benefit will, as their incapacity results from accidents or diseases contracted during their employment, be able to claim statutory sick pay or incapacity benefit up to the date of commencement of industrial injuries benefit as 90 days is less than 28 weeks. The rate of statutory sick pay is higher than that for incapacity benefit for 28 weeks when they are then paid at the same rate. Incapacity benefit rates in the first 28 weeks apply to the self-employed and to the unemployed, or those with too few contributions. For the purposes of claiming incapacity benefit before being entitled to claim a disablement benefit, it should be noted that the presumption that a claimant for benefit for industrial or prescribed diseases has satisfied the contribution requirements for incapacity benefit (as was the case with sickness benefit), has been removed. An age addition is added to incapacity benefit where the claimant is under certain age limits. Claims for incapacity benefit for the first time claimant should be made on Form BI 202. Where entitlement to industrial injuries benefit is below the incapacity benefit rates, then that benefit may be claimed to top up industrial injuries benefit to the current rate of incapacity benefit.

If the carer of the claimant spends at least 35 hours a week looking after him and is of working age and is not earning more than £50 per week (before tax but after deduction of national insurance and other reasonable expenses), invalid care allowance of £39.95 per week (1999/2000) with allowances for the carer's own dependants (if any) may be granted to that carer. If the adult dependant does not live with the claimant, there will be no increase if he is earning more than £38.70 per week. Also, dependant's earnings of over £140 per week in the case of one child, and an extra £18 earnings for each extra child affect dependency benefits.

Income support and other state benefits such as housing benefit and council tax benefit may be available if the claimant with or without dependants does not have sufficient to live on.

Disability working allowance

C6016   This benefit is for people aged 16 years or over who wish to work, but have a physical or mental disability which puts them at a disadvantage in securing a job under criteria set out in the regulations. The applicant must work for at least 16 hours a week to qualify and he receives a credit if he works for 30 hours or more a week. Self-employed people may qualify. This benefit is intended to help those on low incomes, so there are income and capital limits to entitlement. To receive the maximum allowance, the claimant's capital must not exceed £3,000. Capital above £16,000 disqualifies an applicant. An amount between these two figures attracts the maximum allowance less 70 per cent of the difference between the income and applicable amounts where an income of £1 for every £250 is assumed.

In addition to these criteria, he must be in receipt of certain benefits for at least eight weeks before his claim is made. With respect to industrial injuries, the relevant benefits to which he must have been entitled are constant attendance allowance, an increase in disablement pension, higher rate incapacity benefit, housing benefit, or council tax with a higher pensioner premium or he has an invalid carriage or other vehicle provided under the DSS Vehicle Scheme.

Payment

C6017   Industrial injuries benefits are paid weekly in advance on Wednesdays, either by order book cashable at a local post office, or by direct credit transfer if the claimant opts for this.

Table 1

Benefit rates

For financial year 1999/2000 the following weekly benefit rates are payable.

Benefit	Per Week
Statutory sick pay	
Single weekly rate	£59.55
Incapacity benefit	
Up to 28 weeks	£50.35
After 28 weeks to 52 weeks	£59.55
Long-term incapacity benefit	
After 52 weeks	£66.75
Age addition	
Under 35	£14.05
35–44	£ 8.90

Increase for dependants	*Increase for dependent child*	*Increase for adult dependant*
Short-term dependency:		
(a) where beneficiary is under pension age	£9.90/11.35*	£31.15
(b) where the beneficiary is over pension age	£9.90/11.35*	£38.40
Long-term dependency	£9.90/11.35*	£39.95

Industrial injuries disablement benefit		
Disablement	*Over 18*	*Under 18 with no dependants*
100%	£108.10	£66.20
90%	£97.29	£59.58
80%	£86.48	£52.96

70%	£75.67	£46.34
60%	£64.86	£39.72
50%	£54.05	£33.10
40%	£43.24	£26.48
30%	£32.43	£19.86
20%**	£21.62	£13.24

Constant attendance increase

Normal maximum rate   £43.30

Constant attendance allowance

Part-time rate   £21.65

Intermediate rate   £64.95

Exceptional rate   £86.60

In any case, maximum benefit   £86.60

Exceptionally severe disablement increase

Rate   £43.30

Disability working allowance

Single weekly rate   £51.80

Couples or lone parent   £81.05

Credit for working 30 hours or more   £11.05
per week

* The rate of payment of child dependency increase is £9.90 for the first child and £11.35 for each other child.

** Disability must be assessed as at least 14% to be able to claim this 20% payment for a disablement pension.

Appeals

C6018   Appeals relating to all industrial injuries are made to a medical appeal tribunal and should be made within three months of the decision of the adjudicating medical officer(s).

Change of circumstances and financial effects of receipt of benefit

C6019   *Hospital* – if a claimant enters hospital, industrial injuries disablement pension continues to be payable, as does exceptionally severe disablement allowance. Constant attendance allowance will stop after four weeks. Statutory sick pay will be reduced after six weeks.

Taxation – industrial injuries disablement benefit, constant attendance allowance, exceptionally severe disablement allowance and disability working allowance are not taxable. Incapacity benefit is taxable for all claimants who have claimed after 13 April

1995. Those who were in receipt of invalidity benefit before that date are not liable to tax on it. Statutory sick pay is taxable under the PAYE system.

Benefit overlaps

C6020   Industrial injuries benefits may be taken at the same time as incapacity for work benefit with no reduction. Disability living allowance and attendance allowance may not be received at the same time as constant attendance allowance, but if the claimant should receive a higher rate of either of those benefits, constant attendance allowance will be topped-up to bring it up to the higher benefit rate. (For recoupment of benefit after awards of damages see C6041 below.)

Damages for occupational injuries and diseases

C6021   When a person is injured or killed at work in circumstances indicating negligence on the part of an employer, he may be entitled to an award of damages. Damages are normally of two kinds, i.e. liquidated and unliquidated damages. *Liquidated damages* are damages where the amount and circumstances of payment have been agreed in advance by the contracting parties; awards are generally confined to cases of breach of contract.

Where negligent injury and/or death occur, compensation by way of prior agreement is not possible. In other words, employers and employees cannot agree beforehand a set amount of damages for injury, disease or death at work. Such damages, i.e. *unliquidated damages*, are assessed by judges in accordance with precedent; very exceptionally they may be assessed by a jury. Damages are also categorised as general and special damages, according to whether they reflect pre-trial or post-trial losses.

Damages normally take the form of a lump sum; however, 'structured settlements', whereby accident victims are paid a variable sum for the rest of their lives, are now a viable alternative [*Damages Act 1996, s 2*] (see C6025 below). This may well involve greater reliance on actuarial evidence and a rate of return of interest provided by index-linked government securities. Moreover, the rule in *British Transport Commission v Gourley* (see C6021 below), to the effect that damages are paid *net* of tax, may have to be modified, as offering a fiscal subsidy to defendants. In addition, introduction of a conditional fee system (no win no fee) in personal injuries cases, similar to the American contingency fee system (although not entitling lawyers to a share of the litigant's damages), may well result in increased damages.

It should be noted that Green Form legal advice is now only available to those who are on income support or whose income is equivalent to or less than the income support levels. Legal aid is available to help with litigation and there are special financial eligibility income and capital upper limits applicable to those making personal injury claims which are more generous than those for other claims. The Government plans to withdraw legal aid from non-medical personal injury claims in autumn 1998. There will be exceptions for more difficult cases. Conditional fees are expected to enable applicants to bring personal injury claims. The lower income limit for non-contributory legal aid is £2,680 (1999/2000) in respect of all proceedings, and the upper income limit for contributory legal aid is £7,940 (1999/2000) for proceedings that do not include a claim for personal injuries. Where the subject matter of the dispute includes a claim for personal injuries, legal aid is available to a person whose disposable income does not exceed £8,751 per year, but it may be refused if his disposable capital exceeds £8,560 and it appears that he could afford to proceed without legal aid. Capital limits are now subject to an upper limit of £100,000 in relation to the equitable value of the applicant's dwelling-house, that is, after deduction of any mortgage or charge on the property. Stricter rules also apply to financial support from friends and relatives which may be taken into account.

Accident Line, which is part of a scheme run by solicitors who are members of a specialist panel of personal injuries lawyers, provides a free half-hour consultation for claimants who have suffered personal injuries, including industrial accidents. The telephone number is 0500-192-939.

Basis of claim for damages for personal injuries at work

C6022   The basis of an award of unliquidated damages is that an injured employee should be entitled to recoup the loss which he has suffered in consequence of the injury/disease at work. 'The broad general principle which should govern the assessment in cases such as this is that the Tribunal should award the injured party such a sum of money as will put him in the same position as he would have been in if he had not sustained the injuries' (per Earl Jowitt in *British Transport Commission v Gourley [1955] 3 AER 796*). Normally, a lump sum must be awarded. Courts could not order periodical payments instead of a lump sum, unless both parties consented (*Burke v Tower Hamlets Health Authority, The Times, 10 August 1989*). However, following the *Damages Act 1996*, periodical payments may be made in some cases.

It is not necessary that a particular injury be foreseeable, although it normally would be (see further *Smith v Leech Brain & Co Ltd [1962] 2 QB 405*). Moreover, if the original injury has made the plaintiff susceptible to further injury (which would not otherwise have happened), damages will be awarded in respect of such further injuries, unless the injuries were due to the negligence of the plaintiff himself (*Wieland v Cyril Lord Carpets Ltd [1969] 3 AER 1006*). In this case, a woman, who had earlier injured her neck, was fitted with a surgical collar. She later fell on some stairs, injuring herself, because her bifocal glasses had been dislodged slightly by the surgical collar. It was held that damages were payable in respect of this later injury by the perpetrator of the original act of negligence. Conversely, where, in spite of having suffered an injury owing to an employer's negligence, an employee contracts a disease which has no causal connection with the earlier injury, and the subsequent illness prevents the worker from working, any damages awarded in respect of the injury will stop at that point, since the supervening illness would have prevented (and, indeed, has prevented) the worker from going on working.

A dustman who had injured his wrist in the course of his employment made a complaint of breach of statutory duty against D2. His contract of employment with D2 was transferred to D1 by virtue of the *Transfer of Undertakings (Protection of Employment) Regulations 1981*. On a preliminary question of the effect of these regulations, it was held that potential liability for the plaintiff's claim had been transferred to D1. This case highlights the need to consider outstanding litigation on the transfer of a business. [*Taylor v Serviceteam and London Borough of Waltham Forest [1998] PIQR Q1*].

C6023   Listed below are the various losses for which the employee can expect to be compensated. Losses are classified as non-pecuniary and pecuniary.

(a) Non-pecuniary losses

The principal non-pecuniary losses are:

   (i)   pain and suffering prior to the trial;

   (ii)   disability and loss of amenity (i.e. faculty) before the trial;

   (iii)   pain and suffering in the future, whether permanent or temporary;

   (iv)   disability and loss of amenity in the future, whether permanent or temporary;

   (v)   bereavement.

(Damages for loss of expectation of life were abolished by the *Administration of Justice Act 1982, s 1(1)* (see further 'Loss of amenity' at C6031 below).)

There are four main compensatable types of injury, namely (*a*) maximum severity injuries (or hopeless cases), e.g. irreversible brain damage, quadraplegia; (*b*) very serious injuries but not hopeless cases, e.g. severe head injuries/loss of sight in both eyes/injury to respiratory and/or excretory systems; (*c*) serious injuries, e.g. loss of arm, hand, leg; (*d*) less serious injuries, e.g. loss of a finger, thumb, toe etc. There is a scale of rates applicable to the range of disabilities accompanying injury to workers but it is nowhere as precise as the scale for social security disablement benefit. The general (perhaps obvious) principle is that the more serious the disability the greater the damages. Damages for maximum severity cases can vary between £750,000 and £1 million, whereas damages for loss of non-index finger or toe would probably be not much more than £1,000.

(*b*) Pecuniary losses

These consist chiefly of:

   (i)   loss of earnings prior to trial (i.e. special damages);

   (ii)   expenses prior to the trial, e.g. medical expenses;

   (iii) loss of future earnings (see below);

   (iv)   loss of earning capacity, i.e. the handicap on the open labour market following disability.

In actions for pecuniary losses, employees can be required to disclose the general medical records of the whole of their medical history to the employer's medical advisers (*Dunn v British Coal Corporation [1993] ICR 591*).

General and special damages

(*a*) General damages

C6024

General damages are awarded for loss of future earnings, earning capacity and loss of amenity. They are, therefore, awarded in respect of both pecuniary and non-pecuniary losses. An award of general damages normally consists of:

   (i)   damages for loss of future earnings;

   (ii)   pain and suffering (before and after the trial); and

   (iii) loss of amenity (including disfigurement).

(*b*) Special damages

Special damages are awarded for itemised expenses and loss of earnings incurred prior to the trial. Unlike general damages, this amount is normally agreed between the parties' solicitors. When making an award, judges normally specify separately awards for general and special damages. A statement of special damage must be served with the statement of claim which should suffice to give the defendant a fair idea of the case he has to answer. More detailed information must be supplied after the exchange of medical and expert reports.

Structured settlements

C6025

A structured settlement is an agreement for settling a claim or action for damages on terms that the award is made wholly or partly in the form of periodic payments. Such settlements are expected to become more usual in the case of larger awards of damages. Under the *Damages Act 1996*, these periodic payments must be payable in the form of an annuity for life, or for a specified period, and may be held on trust for the plaintiff if that should be necessary. Provision may be added to the settlements for increases, percentages or adjustments where the court or plaintiff's advisers secure these variations in his interest. Structured settlements in favour of plaintiffs may be made for the duration of their life. Knowledge of the plaintiff's special needs is thus vital for the structure to be successful – it should be recognised that structured settlements will not be suitable for all cases. If the plaintiff dies while in receipt of periodic payments, they pass under his estate. Structured settlements may also be made in awards of damages in respect of fatal accidents. Tax-free annuities are payable directly to the plaintiff by the Life Office.

Structured settlements have received special protection in the case of the bankruptcy of the insurer. Under the administration of the Policy Holders Protection Board, the fund collected from other insurers is set at 100%, rather than the usual 90%, of other policy holders' losses (*Damages Act 1996, s 4*).

Structured settlement awards made by the Criminal Injuries Compensation Authority are also tax free.

When agreeing a settlement (whether structured or not), it is better to agree whether payments are net of repayable benefits. If a settlement offer is silent as to repayable benefits, then a deduction will have to be made in respect of them, possibly with unplanned results for the plaintiff.

Structured settlements are advisable where brain damage makes the injured person at risk and suggestible to pressure from relatives. They are also useful where the injured person has little experience or interest in investment, or dislikes the possibility of becoming dependent on the State or relatives should funds run out. Disadvantages are that annuities only last for the lifetime of the injured person. There is also a loss of flexibility to deal with changed circumstances and of the better return gained with the skilful investment of a lump sum.

The Law Commission in Report 224 did not recommend giving the court the power to impose damages in the form of a structured settlement.

Assessment of pecuniary losses (i.e. loss of future earnings)

C6026

Assessing loss of future earnings can be a chancy affair, subject, as it is, to the vagaries and vicissitudes of human life. As was authoritatively said, 'If (the plaintiff) had not been injured, he would have had the prospect of earning a continuing income, it may be, for many years, but there can be no certainty as to what would have happened. In many cases the amount of that income may be doubtful, even if he had remained in good health, and there is always the possibility that he might have died or suffered from some incapacity at any time. The loss which he has suffered between the date of the accident and the date of the trial (i.e. special damages (see above)) may be certain, but his prospective loss is not. Yet damages must be assessed as a lump sum once and for all (see, however, 'Provisional awards' at C6037 below), not only in respect of loss accrued before the trial but also in respect of a prospective loss' (per Lord Reid in *British Transport Commission v Gourley [1955] 3 AER 796*). Moreover, if, at the time of injury, a worker earns at a particular rate, it is presumed that this will remain the same. If, therefore, he wishes to claim more, he must show that his earnings were going to rise, for example, in line with a likely increase in productivity – a probable rise in *national* productivity is not enough.

When the court assesses loss of earnings, the plaintiff has to mitigate his loss by taking work if he can. In *Larby v Thurgood [1993] PIQR 219*, the defendant applied to the court to dismiss an action brought by a fireman who was severely injured in a road traffic accident and who had taken employment as a driver earning £6,000 per annum, unless he agreed to be interviewed by an employment consultant who would then give expert evidence on whether the plaintiff could have obtained better paid employment. This application was refused. Evidence of whether the plaintiff could have obtained better paid employment depended partly on medical evidence of his capabilities and the present and future state of the job market where he lived, which could be established by an employment consultant. His general suitability for employment, his willingness and motivation, were matters of fact for the judge; thus expert opinion was not required for that purpose.

A plaintiff may be earning practically as much as he was before his accident, but may be more at risk of losing his present job, of not achieving expected promotion, or of disadvantages in the labour market. Damages may be claimed for such prospective losses and are known as *Smith v Manchester* damages (after *Smith v Manchester City Council (1974) 118 SJ 597*). In *Thorn v Powergen plc [1997] PIQR Q73*, it was advised that it is good practice to plead for *Smith v Manchester* damages in the statement of claim, but it is not essential if the facts already include such a claim.

Where the injured claimant was a company director or a member of a partnership and will not work again or as well as before, damages for diminution of the value of shares or profits are limited to the injured party's proportionate share (*Anderson v Davis [1995] PIQR Q87*).

Where a marriage has broken down as a result of the personal injury, damages may be recovered if the facts support this conclusion (*Oakley v Walker (1977) 121 SJ 619*).

Capitalisation of future losses

C6027 Loss of future earnings, often spanning many years ahead, particularly in the case of a relatively young employee, is awarded normally as a once-and-for-all capital sum for the maintenance, sometimes for life, of the injured victim. Here it is important to understand that the award of damages is calculated on the basis of the *present* value of future losses – a sum less than the aggregate of prospective earnings because the final amount has to be discounted (or reduced) to give the *present* value (of future losses). Inflation is ignored when assessing future losses in the majority of cases (e.g. pension rights), since this was best left to prudent investment (*Lim Poh Choo v Camden and Islington Area Health Authority [1980] AC 174*). And where injury shortens the life of a worker, he can recover losses for the whole period for which he would have been working (net of income tax and social security contributions, which he would have had to pay), if his life had not been shortened by the accident. The present value of future losses can be gauged from actuarial or annuity tables. Indeed, it is necessary to identify a capital sum which, as income is progressively and periodically deducted for maintenance of the injury victim (with the necessary statutory deductions for income tax and social security contributions), will equate with the net loss of earnings over the working life of the injured victim.

More particularly, the net annual loss (based on rate of earnings at the time of trial and not allowing for inflation) (the multiplicand) has to be multiplied by a suitable number of years' purchase (i.e. multiplier), and often ranging between 8 and 15, and set out in actuarial tables. The multiplier will represent the number of years' purchase necessary to buy an annuity at between 4% and 5% (e.g. 4½%) – a low rate of interest because, in times of inflation, this gives a greater number of years' purchase (or multiplier). However, there is no increase in multiplier for higher rates of tax or as provision for subsequent changes in tax rates.

Example

In the case of a male worker, aged 30 at the date of trial, and earning £10,000 per year net, on a 4½% interest yield, the multiplier will be 17.1. Hence, general damages will be about £170,000, assuming incapacity to work up to age 65.

In the case of a male worker, aged 50 at date of trial, earning £20,000 net, on a 4½% interest yield, the multiplier will be 10.1. Hence, general damages will be about £200,000 assuming incapacity to work until age 65. (The corresponding multipliers for similar female workers are 19.3 (£190,000) and 15.4 (£300,000), assuming same earnings.)

Deductions from awards under this head are made for the actual earnings of the injured plaintiff. Where the plaintiff takes a lighter, less well paid job, and thus suffers a loss of earnings, the courts have held that the fact that he gains more leisure through working shorter hours is not to be taken into account to reduce the amount of damages awarded for loss of earnings (*Arafat v Potter [1994] PIQR Q73*).

Inflation-proof compensation – actuarial tables and index-linked government stock

C6028   It is for an injured plaintiff to invest a lump sum award as best he can in a basket of shares and gilts, so as to replace the lost income for which he is being compensated. Current multipliers assume a discount rate of between 4% and 5% (see C6027 above) – comparable with a rate of 4%–5% currently obtainable on a spread of ordinary shares, if no allowance is made for the effects of future inflation or the relative prosperity (or otherwise) of share-issuing companies (see *Lim*'s case above). Thus, a plaintiff purchasing a spread of gilts and equities will receive interest and prices reflecting variable market forces, and so varying returns.

In this connection, issue (since 1981) of index-linked government stock has made it possible to match receipts from lump sum investment almost precisely with loss of income for which a plaintiff is being compensated. Dividends on these stocks rise pro rata with hikes in the Retail Price Index, as does payment on maturity – so reflecting price inflation almost exactly. Such stock has a discount rate of between 2½–3½% per annum, thereby eliminating speculation. Moreover, investment in index-linked government stock means that the size of multipliers will increase. Actuarial tables (for use in Personal Injury and Fatal Accident cases), first published in 1984 by the Government Actuary's Department, list multipliers calculated on the basis of non-speculative investment in index-linked government stock, showing rates of interest between 1½% and 5%. Though hitherto not binding on the judiciary, these Tables have been widely used by judges at first instance. Use of actuarial tables was cautiously approved by the House of Lords in *Hunt v Severs [1994] 2 AER 385*; while in Scotland the Inner House concluded that such tables can be used to check a multiplier arrived at conventionally (*O'Brien's Curator Bonis v British Steel plc 1991 SLT 477*). These actuarial tables for use in personal injury and fatal accident cases, are admissible in evidence for the purposes of assessing sums to be awarded as general damages for future pecuniary loss [*Civil Evidence Act*

1995, s 10(1)]. Under *s 2* of the *Damages Act 1996*, the Lord Chancellor has the power to prescribe rates of return to ensure the adequate compensation of the plaintiff.

The 1st edition of the Actuarial Tables (HMSO 1984) took account only of mortality risks but not other common risks, such as redundancy, early retirement, child birth or ill-health. These latter are left to the 2nd edition of Actuarial Tables (HMSO 1994) – illustrating by how much multipliers are to be reduced, taking into account those risks. Here multiplier reductions are less for clerical than for manual workers and for those in secure jobs less affected by the threat of redundancy or industrial action, e.g. civil service, professions. Because hitherto the Tables made no allowance for contingencies such as sickness or unemployment, courts tended to deduct around 10% from the final figure. This fact, combined with acceptance that multipliers, based on government stock dividend, have been too low, has resulted in damages being insufficient, and the new Tables may well, therefore, foreshadow awards of considerably greater damages, particularly for younger workers injured at work – perhaps 50% more.

Institutional care and home care

C6029   Expenses of medical treatment may be claimed, except where the victim is maintained at public expense in a hospital or a local authority financed nursing home, in which case any saving of income during his stay will be set off against the claim for pecuniary loss. Alterations to a home, purchase of a bungalow accessible to a wheelchair, adaptations to a car and equipment (such as lifting equipment), which are necessary for care, may be claimed. Nursing and care requiring constant or less attendance may be claimed whether or not the carer is a professional or voluntary carer. It was confirmed by the House of Lords in *Hunt v Severs [1994] 2 AER 385*, that where an injured plaintiff is cared for by a voluntary carer, such as a member of his family, that damages could be recovered for this care, but the plaintiff should hold them in trust for the voluntary carer. In the final ruling on this case, where the person who had caused the injury was the carer, it was held that in these unusual circumstances, damages for the cost of this voluntary care could not be recovered by the plaintiff.

Where voluntary care is undertaken by relatives, compensation for the cost of this care is assessed as a percentage of the Crossroads rate agreed from time to time for community care by most local authorities; the actual percentage awarded being about two-thirds of that rate. A higher percentage of that rate will be awarded where the care being given is beyond the level of care normally provided by home helps (*Fairhurst v St Helens and Knowsley Health Authority [1995] PIQR 41*).

Where a relative gave up work to look after her injured daughter, she could not claim compensation both for the care she had given and has to give and also for her own loss of earnings as this would constitute double recovery which the law does not allow (*Fish v Wilcox, The Times, 18 February 1993*).

Damages for lost years

C6030   Damages may be payable up to retirement age for lost earnings resulting from the shortening of the plaintiff's life expectancy by reason of the industrial accident or disease. Estimated costs of living expenses are deductible from these damages. Damages under this head may also be awarded to dependants if the victim has died.

Normally no damages are awarded for loss of the abilityu to do DIY and gardening. An exception was made in *Gabriel v Nuclear Electric [1996] PIQR Q1*. The plaintiff had been remarkably adept at DIY including home alterations, car maintenance, electrical and plumbing work and had been exceptionally fit for his age until mesothelioma led to his grave illness and very much shortened life expectancy.

Non-pecuniary losses (i.e. loss of amenity)

C6031

It is generally accepted by the courts that quantification of non-pecuniary losses is considerably more difficult than computing pecuniary losses. Clearly, it is more difficult to attach a figure to the loss of a foot or eye than to two years' wages or salary. This becomes even more difficult where loss of sense of taste and smell are involved, or loss of reproductive or excretory organs. Unlike pecuniary losses, loss of amenity generally consists of two awards, i.e. an award for (i) actual loss of amenity and (ii) the impairment of the quality of life suffered in consequence (i.e the psychic loss). That judges recognise the inadequacy of damages here is much in evidence. (In the case of a plaintiff who had suffered grave injuries, 'He is deprived of much that makes his life worthwhile. No money can compensate for the loss. Yet compensation has to be given in money. The problem is insoluble' (per Lord Denning MR in *Ward v James [1965] 1 AER 563*).) Given that damages for non-pecuniary loss have tended to lag behind inflation in recent years, the Law Commission has suggested in its Consultation Paper No 140 (1996), the establishment of a Compensation Advisory Board, consisting of representatives from the medical profession, insurers and employers, to assess such damages.

Victims are generally conscious of their predicament, but in very serious cases they may not be, a distinction underlined in the leading case of *H West & Son Ltd v Shephard [1963] 2 AER 625*. Thus, damages are payable for loss of amenity, whether or not a plaintiff is aware of his predicament. In other words, it is not just subjective or psychic losses which are compensatable. If, however, a victim's injuries are of the maximum severity kind (e.g. tetraplegia) and he is conscious of his predicament, his damages will be greater, since a person who is mentally anguished about his condition, suffers more than one who is not. However, where, as is often, the injuries shorten the life of an accident victim, his damages for non-pecuniary losses will be reduced to take into account the fact of shortened life.

Types of non-pecuniary losses recoverable

C6032

The following are the non-pecuniary losses which are recoverable by way of damages:

(*a*)   pain and suffering;

(*b*)   loss of amenity;

(*c*)   bereavement.

(a) Pain and suffering

This refers principally to actual pain and suffering at the time of the injury and later. Since, however, modern drugs can easily remove acute distress, actual pain and suffering is not likely to be great and so damages awarded will be relatively small.

Additionally, 'pain and suffering' includes 'mental distress' and related psychic conditions; more specifically (i) nervous shock, (ii) concomitant pain or illness following post-accident surgery and embarrassment or humiliation following disfigurement. Claustrophobia and fear are within the normal human emotional experience, but even if causing sweating and vomiting, are not compensatable, unless amounting to a recognised psychiatric condition, such as post-traumatic stress syndrome (*Reilly v Merseyside Regional Health Authority, The Independent, 29 April 1994*).

(i)   *Nervous shock*

Nervous shock refers to actual and quantifiable damage to the nervous system, affecting nerves, glands and blood; and, although normally consequent upon earlier negligent physical injury, an action is nevertheless maintainable, even if shock is caused by property damage (*Attia v British Gas plc [1987] 3 AER 456* where a house caught fire following a gas explosion. The plaintiff, who suffered nervous shock, was held entitled to damages).

Claimants fall into two categories, namely, (*a*) primary and (*b*) secondary victims, the former being directly involved in an accident and normally (though not necessarily) having suffered earlier negligent physical injury; the latter are essentially spectators, bystanders or rescuers (who have not been victims of earlier negligent physical injury). *Primary* victims can sue for damages for nervous shock/psychiatric injury, even if they have not suffered earlier physical injury (*Page v Smith, Current Law, May 1996* in which the appellant, who was physically uninjured in a collision between his car and that of the respondent, had developed myalgic encephalomyelitis and chronic fatigue syndrome, which became permanent. It was held by the House of Lords that the respondent was liable for this condition in consequence of his negligent driving). Foreseeability of physical injury is sufficient to enable a plaintiff directly involved in an accident to recover damages for nervous shock. Thus, in the historic case of *Bourhill v Young [1942] 2 AER 396* a pregnant woman, whilst getting off a tram, heard an accident some fifteen yards away between a motor cyclist and a car, in which the motor cyclist, driving negligently, was killed. In consequence, the plaintiff gave birth to a stillborn child. It was held on the facts of the case that the unknown motor cyclist could not have foreseen injury to the plaintiff who was unknown to him. As for secondary victims, defendants are taken to foresee the likelihood of nervous shock to rescuers attending to an injured person and to their close relatives, though the precise extent of nervous shock need not have been foreseen (*Brice v Brown [1984] 1 AER 997*). Persons who witness distressing personal injuries, who are not related in either of these ways to the victim, are not only considered not to have been foreseen by the defendant, but are expected to be possessed of sufficient fortitude to be able to withstand the calamities of modern life. Only persons with a close tie with the victim or their rescuers who are within sight or sound of the accident or its immediate aftermath will be awarded damages for nervous shock as the law stands at the present. Husbands and wives will be presumed to have a sufficiently proximate tie whilst other relationships are considered on the evidence of the proximity of the relationship.

In *Chadwick v British Railways Board [1967] 1 WLR 912*, following a serious railway accident, for which the defendant was held to be liable, a volunteer rescue worker suffered nervous shock and became psychoneurotic. As administratrix of the rescuer's estate, the plaintiff sued for nervous shock. It was held that (i) damages were recoverable for nervous shock, even though shock was not caused by fear for one's own safety or for that of one's children, (ii) the shock was foreseeable, and (iii) the defendant should have foreseen that volunteers might well offer to rescue and so owed them a duty of care.

The class of persons who can sue for damages for nervous shock is limited, depending on proximity of the plaintiff's relationship with the deceased or injured person (*McLoughlin v O'Brian [1982] 2 AER 298* where the plaintiff's husband and three children were involved in a serious road accident, owing to the defendant's negligence. One child was killed and the husband and other two children were badly injured. At the time of the accident, the plaintiff was two miles away at home, being told of the accident by a neighbour and taken to the hospital, where she saw the injured members of her family and heard that her daughter had been killed. In consequence of hearing and seeing the results of the road accident, the plaintiff suffered severe and recurrent shock. It was held that she was entitled to damages for nervous shock as she was present in the immediate aftermath). This approach was confirmed by the House of Lords in *Alcock v Chief Constable of South Yorkshire Police [1991] 3 WLR 1057*, where it was stated that the class of persons to whom this duty of care was owed as being sufficiently proximate, was not limited to particular relationships such as husband and wife or parent and child, but was based on ties of love and affection, the closeness of which would need to be proved in each case, except that of spouse or parent, when such closeness would be assumed. Similarly, in *Hinz v Berry [1970] 1 AER 1074* the appellant left her husband and children in a lay-by while she crossed over the road to pick bluebells. The respondent negligently drove his car into the rear of the car of the appellant. The appellant heard the crash and later saw her husband and children lying severely injured, the former fatally. She became ill from nervous shock and successfully sued the respondent for damages. On this basis, an employee who suffers nervous shock as a result of witnessing the death of a co-employee at work, will be unlikely to be able to claim damages against his employer for nervous shock, as being a 'bystander who happens to be an employee', as distinct from an active participant in rescue (*Robertson v Forth Bridge Joint Board [1995] IRLR 251* where an employee was blown off the Forth Bridge in a high gale and fell to his death; a co-employee who watched this was unable to sue for damages for nervous shock).

Moreover, in *Vernon v Bosley, The Times, 4 April 1994*, the defendant to a claim for nervous shock argued unsuccessfully that the plaintiff who had been present at the death of his children would have suffered the same psychiatric illness from grief and bereavement if he had not been at the scene. The children's nanny was with the children in a car which she negligently drove into a river. She escaped, but the children were trapped and died despite a rescue attempt at which both parents were present. Although grief and bereavement are not actionable at common law, there was no doubt that the plaintiff had suffered nervous shock in accordance with common law principles. The majority of the Court of Appeal rejected the defendant's appeal, but reduced the damages awarded. (*[1997] PIQR 255*).

In *Young v Charles Church (Southern) Ltd, The Times, 2 May 1997* an employee suffered a psychiatric illness after seeing a workmate electrocuted; the claimant was working close to the victim, and the circumstances were such that he himself was in similar danger. The claimant recovered damages from his employer for breach of statutory duty under electricity regulations – employees are protected by these regulations against foreseeable injury when electrical cable or equipment could become a source of danger to them. It was held in this case that a mental illness was included as a foreseeable injury when the claimant was so close to the electrical shock that killed his workmate.

By contrast, the following cases are concerned with nervous shock to relatives who were not within sight of the tragic event or its aftermath. In *Taylor v*

Somerset Health Authority [1993] 4 Med LR 34 the plaintiff's husband suffered a heart attack at work and died. The plaintiff went to the hospital where, on learning of his death, she suffered nervous shock. Refusing to believe he was dead, she visited his corpse in the mortuary. Her action for damages, on the ground that the defendant had failed to diagnose and treat his heart condition, failed because the main purpose of viewing the corpse was to settle disbelief as to death, and so was not part of the 'immediate aftermath'. Moreover, the viewing related to the death itself rather than the circumstances leading up to it. Similarly, where the mother of an employee crushed to death by a forklift truck sought damages for psychiatric illness resulting from nervous shock, her claim failed, as she had not been present at the accident, at her son's death in hospital, nor saw the body immediately afterwards (*Ravenscroft v Rederiaktiebolaget Transatlantic [1991] 3 AER 73*). Nor will viewing a disaster on television, involving friends/relatives, qualify for entitlement (*Alcock v Chief Constable of South Yorkshire Police* (above)). In any event, reasonable fortitude, on the part of the plaintiff, will be assumed, thereby *ipso facto* disqualifying claims on the part of hypersensitive persons (*McFarlane v EE Caledonia [1994] 1 Lloyds Rep 16* where the owner of a rig did not owe a duty of reasonable care to avoid causing psychiatric injury to a crew member of a rescue vessel who witnessed horrific scenes at the Piper Alpha disaster). (Had he suffered physical injury as well, a claim for additional psychiatric injury might have succeeded.) In rescue situations a distinction is drawn between nervous/post-traumatic stress suffered by voluntary unpaid rescuers, on the one hand, and uniformed or paid rescuers, on the other, the former, in principle, being entitled to damages, ever since *Chadwick*'s case, the latter not being so, in that they are 'fortitudinous bystanders'. (However, in an out-of-court settlement, 14 police officers who suffered mental trauma after rescuing football fans at Hillsborough stadium, were awarded £1.2 million in damages – reported in *The Times, 4 June 1996*.)

(ii)   Illness following post-accident surgery

The plaintiff was employed by the defendant as a train driver. Whilst operating a passenger train, he saw two employees less than thirty yards away on the line he was passing along. He blew the horn but the employees only moved when the train was a few yards away. As a result, the plaintiff suffered shock and was admitted to hospital where he was diagnosed as having suffered a heart attack. He was off work for nine months. When he returned to work he was not able to drive main-line trains because of his heart condition, and was engaged on shunting operations. This in turn revived a serious back injury from which he had suffered for a long time. Eighteen months later he stopped work and several months afterwards he was readmitted to hospital for a laminectomy. Following this back surgery, the plaintiff suffered a further heart attack. It was held that nervous shock was a reasonably foreseeable consequence of the employer's breach of duty; in addition, the employer had to take his victim as he found him, i.e. with a pre-existing symptomless back condition, pre-disposing him to heart attacks, and the employer had to pay damages in respect of both these conditions as well (*Galt v British Railways Board (1983) 133 NLJ 870*).

(b) Loss of amenity

This is a loss, permanent or temporary, of a bodily or mental function, coupled with gradual deterioration in health, e.g. loss of finger, eye, hand etc. Traditionally, there are three kinds of loss of amenity, ranging from maximum severity injury (quadraplegias and irreversible brain damage), multiple injuries (very severe injuries but not hopeless cases) to less severe injuries (i.e. loss of sight, hearing etc.). Obviously, the more grave the injury the greater the award of damages. Moreover, it is clear that, on balance, damages reflect the actual amenity loss rather than the concomitant psychic loss, at least in hopeless cases. Though, if a plaintiff is aware that his life has been shortened, he will be compensated for this loss. Thus, the *Administration of Justice Act 1982, s 1(1)* states:

' (i)   damages are not recoverable in respect of loss of expectation of life caused to the injured person by the injuries; but

(ii)   if the injured person's expectation of life has been reduced by injuries, there shall be taken into account any pain and suffering caused or likely to be caused by awareness that his expectation of life has been reduced.'

(c) Bereavement

A statutory sum of £7,500 is awardable for bereavement by the *Fatal Accidents Act 1976, s 1A* (as amended by the *Administration of Justice Act 1982, s 3(1)* and the *Damages for Bereavement (Variation of Sum) Order 1990 (SI 1990 No 2575)*). This sum is awardable at the suit of husband or wife, or of parents provided the deceased was under eighteen at the date of death if the deceased was legitimate; or of the deceased's mother, if the deceased was illegitimate. (In *Doleman v Deakin, The Times, 30 January 1990* it was held that where an injury was sustained before the deceased's eighteenth birthday, but the deceased actually died after his eighteenth birthday, bereavement damages were not recoverable by his parents.)

Fatal injuries

C6033   Death at work can give rise to two types of action for damages, i.e.

(*a*)   damages in respect of death itself, payable under the *Fatal Accidents Act 1976* (as later amended); and

(*b*)   damages in respect of liability which an employer would have incurred had the employee lived; here the action is said to 'survive' for the benefit of the deceased worker's estate, payable under the *Law Reform (Miscellaneous Provisions) Act 1934*.

Actions of both kinds are, in practice, brought by the deceased workman's dependants, though actions of the second kind technically survive for the benefit of the deceased's *estate*. Moreover, previously paid state benefits are *not* deductible from damages for fatal injuries. [*Social Security Act 1989, s 22(4)(c)*]. Nor are insurance moneys payable on death deductible e.g. life assurance moneys. [*Fatal Accidents (Damages) Act 1908 as re-enacted by the Administration of Justice Act 1982, s 4*]. This also includes any amounts passing to dependants as a result of intestacy (*Wood v Bentall Simplex Ltd, The Times, 3 March 1992* in which an annual income of £5,000, receivable on intestacy, was not to be deducted from damages for fatal accident).

Damages under the Fatal Accidents Act 1976

C6034   'If death is caused by any wrongful act, neglect or default which is such as would (if death had not ensued) have entitled the person injured to maintain an action and recover damages, the person who would have been liable if death had not ensued, shall be liable . . . for damages. . .'. [*Administration of Justice Act 1982, s 3(1)*, amending the Fatal Accidents Act 1976].

Only dependants, which normally means the deceased's widow (or widower) and children and grandchildren can claim – the claim generally being brought by the bereaved spouse on behalf of him/herself and children. [*AJA 1982, s 1(2)*]. The basis of a successful claim is *dependency*, i.e. the claimant must show that he was, prior to the fatality, being maintained out of the income of the deceased. If, therefore, a widow had lived on her own private moneys prior to her husband's death, the claim will fail, as there is no dependency. Nominal damages for loss of life expectancy are abolished. [*AJA 1982, s 1(1)*].

In *Jameson and Another v Central Electricity Generating Board and Another, The Times, 25 February 1997*, the Court of Appeal held that 'full and final settlement' of a claim for compensation following exposure to asbestos does not prevent dependants bringing an action against a concurrent tortfeasor. This case concerned a dependency claim brought by the executors of a deceased employee (J) of a company (B) against another company (C), whom B had sent J to work for. B had already paid J £80,000 before his death in 'full and final settlement' of his claim for breach of statutory duty by exposing J to asbestos at various workplaces (including at C), resulting in his suffering from malignant mesothelioma. C argued that this settlement prevented J's executors subsequently bringing the present claim and that, failing this, C was entitled to recover a contribution towards the damages from B. J's executors contended that J's settlement did not represent full satisfaction of J's claim against B and consequently J was not barred from an action against a concurrent tortfeasor. The judge agreed with this argument and allowed the claim. C appealed.

The Court of Appeal dismissed the appeal. The judge was entitled to find that the settlement did not account for the full value of J's claim. Further, as the current claim concerned compensation for dependants under the *Fatal Accidents Act 1976* this was distinct from J's claim against B in relation to his illness before he died, and so C was not entitled to claim any contribution from B in respect of it.

Originally at common law if a widow remarried, or if her marriage prospects were good, this was taken into account in assessing damages for fatal injuries, since remarriage or its prospects lessened the financial hardship caused by death of a breadwinner. This rule has, however, been abolished. The *Fatal Accidents Act 1976, s 3* provides that remarriage or remarriage prospects are not to be taken into account in assessing fatal damages though likelihood of divorce may be taken into account in some circumstances (see *Martin v Owen* at C6036 below).

However, contributory negligence on the part of the deceased will result in damages on the part of the dependants being reduced. [*Fatal Accidents Act 1976, s 5*].

Survival of actions

C6035 Actions for injury at work which the deceased worker might have had, had he lived, survive for the benefit of his estate, normally for the benefit of his widow, but not necessarily, as he might have willed his estate to someone else, e.g. a mistress. This is provided for in the *Law Reform (Miscellaneous Provisions) Act 1934*. Any damages paid or payable under one Act are 'set off' when damages are awarded under the other Act, as in practice actions in respect of deceased workers are brought simultaneously under both Acts.

Assessment of damages in fatal injuries cases

C6036 Damages in respect of a fatal injury are calculated by multiplying the net annual loss (i.e. earnings minus tax, social security contributions and deductions necessary for personal living (i.e. dependency)) by a suitable number of years' purchase. There is no deduction for things used jointly, such as a house or car. However, where a widow also works, this will reduce the dependency and she cannot claim a greater dependency in future on the ground that she and her deceased husband intended to have children (*Malone v Rowan [1984] 3 AER 402*). In *Crabtree (Administratrix of the Estate of Crabtree) v Wilson [1993] PIQR 24*, it was confirmed that a wife's net dependency percentage of expenditure in an assessment of the damages due to the Crabtree estate must be reduced from the conventional net dependency by the amount of any earnings she makes. The conventional net dependencies, which are based on the assumed expenditure of a male deceased person which is no longer required, leave a dependency of 75% for his dependants if there are children, and 66⅔% where the family was husband and wife. Moreover, if, at the time of death, a widow is separated from her husband, her claim for dependency depends on the likelihood of either being reconciled, or, alternatively, receiving maintenance (*Davies v Taylor [1972] 3 AER 836*). Under *s 3* (see C6034 above) what has to be valued is the expectation of continuing dependency on the deceased, had he lived. Anything that might affect that expectation was relevant including the likelihood of divorce in this particular case (*Martin v Owen, The Times, 21 May 1992*). However, damages for loss of moonlighting (i.e. dependency in respect of undeclared earnings) or for loss of housing or supplementary benefit cannot be recovered (*Hunter v Butler, The Times, 28 December 1995*).

It is possible to agree that fatal injury damages should be paid in the form of a structured settlement (see C6025 above).

Where both parents are dead as a result of negligence or a mother dies, dependency is assessed on the cost of supplying a nanny (*Watson v Willmot [1991] 1 AER 473; Cresswell v Eaton [1991] 1 AER 484*).

Moreover, benefits accruing to a person, such as a widow's pension, are not taken into account in assessing damages. [*Fatal Accidents Act 1976, s 4*].

Provisional awards

C6037

Because medical prognosis can only *estimate* the chance of a victim's recovery, whether partial or total, or alternatively, deterioration or death, it is accepted that there is too much chance and uncertainty in the system of lump sum damages paid on a once-and-for-all basis. 'Chance' refers to 'measurable probabilities' rather than 'fanciful probabilities'. Serious deterioration denotes clear risk of deterioration beyond the norm that could be expected, ruling out pure speculation (*Wilson v Ministry of Defence [1991] 1 AER 638*). Similarly in the case of dependency awards under the *Fatal Accidents Act 1976* it can never be known what the deceased's future would have been, yet courts are expected and called upon to make forecasts as to future income. Therefore, if the doctors get it wrong and a seriously ill victim makes a miraculous recovery, or a victim who was expected to do well suddenly and unforeseeably deteriorates, injustice results from the previous over and under compensation. To meet this problem it is provided that provisional awards may be made. Thus, 'This section applies to an action for damages for personal injuries in which there is proved or admitted to be a chance that at some definite or indefinite time in the future the injured person will, as a result of the act or omission, which gave rise to the cause of action, develop some serious disease or suffer some serious deterioration in his physical or mental condition'. [*Administration of Justice Act 1982, s 6(1)*]. Moreover, 'Provision may be made by rules of the court for enabling the court to award the injured person:

(*a*) damages assessed on the assumption that the injured person will not develop the disease or suffer the deterioration in his condition; and

(*b*) further damages at a future date if he develops the disease or suffers the deterioration'.

[*Administration of Justice Act 1982, s 6(2)*].

A claim in respect of provisional damages must be included in the statement of claim to entitle the claimant to such damages. The disease or type of deterioration in respect of which any future applications may be made must be stated (Rules of the Supreme Court, Order 37 Rule 8). The defendant may make a written offer if the statement of claim includes a claim for provisional damages, offering a specified sum on the basis that the plaintiff's condition will not deteriorate and agreeing to make an award of provisional damages in that sum.

The mere fact that there is a disagreement over future medical prognosis, does not necessarily prevent a sufficient basis of agreement for provisional damages (*Hurditch v Sheffield Health Authority [1989] 2 AER 869* where the plaintiff, suffering from asbestosis, claimed provisional damages against his employer. Part of the medical statement was disputed. It was held that the offer and acceptance of a 'provisional figure' was sufficient for the purposes of *s 6* of the *Administration of Justice Act 1982*).

Interim awards

C6038

In certain limited circumstances a successful plaintiff can apply to the court for an interim payment. This enables a plaintiff to recover *part* of the compensation to which he is entitled before the trial rather than waiting till the result of the trial is known – which may be some time away. This procedure is provided for in Order 29, Part II of the Rules of the Supreme Court, but it only applies where the defendant is either (*a*) insured, (*b*) a public authority, or (*c*) a person whose resources are such as to enable him to make the interim payment. Interim orders cannot be made in 'chance' and 'forecast' cases (see C6034 above).

In *Stringman v McArdle [1994] 1 WLR 1653*, it was held, provided that the usual procedural requirements were fulfilled, that it was not the concern of the judge as to what is to be done with the interim damages awarded to a victim. However, in this case the judge expressed the view that plans for conversion of a dwelling were too elaborate and he doubted that there would be enough left for the maintenance of the victim.

Compensation recovery applies to interim payments as well as to payments into court. Care needs to be taken when applying for interim payments to avoid putting the plaintiff at a disadvantage. Capital of over £8,000, which could include an interim award, removes entitlement to means tested benefits, particularly income support, and there are also reductions on a sliding scale in such benefits for any capital above £3,000.

Payments into court

C6039

A payment into court may be made in satisfaction of a claim even where liability is disputed. From the defendant's point of view, costs from the date of the payment in may be saved if the court does not order a higher payment of damages than that paid into court. The plaintiff may accept the payment in within twenty one days of notification of the payment in. Where the plaintiff is legally aided, he should be advised that the legal aid statutory charge will apply to the defendant's costs if the plaintiff recovers less than the sum paid into court.

Payments into court in settlement of personal injury claims are now statutory subject to recovery of relevant benefits paid to the plaintiff. The liability of the defendant to pay and benefit recovery does not commence until the injured party takes the payment out of court. Practitioners should avoid paying small settlements into court in view of the wide provisions of *s 6* of the *Administration of Justice Act 1982* as the compensator might become liable for all of the relevant benefits payments which have been made.

The defendant may, instead of making a payment in, write a Calderbank letter in which he sets out his terms for settling the action (or makes certain offers). From a defendant's point of view, the letter is helpful in that he may reserve the right to produce it to the attention of the trial judge after judgment on the question of costs. From the plaintiff's point of view, these letters should be studied with care because of applicability of the legal aid statutory charge to the defendant's costs where the defendant recovers less than the amount offered in the letter.

Interest on damages

C6040 Damages constitute a judgment debt; such debt carries interest at 8% (currently) up to date of payment. Courts have a discretion to award interest on any damages, total or partial, prior to date of payment (and this irrespective of whether part payment has already been made [*Administration of Justice Act 1982, s 15*]), though this does not apply in the case of damages for loss of earnings, since they are not yet due. Moreover, a plaintiff is entitled to interest at 2% on damages relating to non-pecuniary losses (except bereavement), even though the actual damages themselves take into account inflation (*Wright v British Railways Board [1983] 2 AC 773*). Under *s 17* of the *Judgments Act 1838* (and *s 35A* of the *Supreme Court Act 1981* and *Schedule 1* to the *Administration of Justice Act 1982*), interest runs from the date of the damages judgment. Thus, where, as sometimes happens, there is a split trial, interest is payable from the date that the damages are quantified or recorded, rather than from the date (earlier) that liability is determined (*Thomas v Bunn, Wilson v Graham, Lea v British Aerospace plc [1991] 2 WLR 27*). Moreover, interest at the recommended rate (of 8%) is recoverable only after damages have been assessed, and not (earlier) when liability has been established (*Lindop v Goodwin Steel Castings Ltd, The Times, 21 May 1990*). The current rate of interest was reduced in 1993 from 15% to 8% [*Judgment Debts (Rate of Interest) Order 1993 (SI 1993 No 564)*] – this interest being tax-free [*Administration of Justice Act 1982, s 74*].

Awards of damages and the new scheme for recovery of state benefits

C6041 The new *Social Security (Recovery of Benefits) Act 1997* and accompanying regulations have made some important changes to the rules for recoupment of benefit from compensation payments. Total costs to business for compliance with the new Scheme have been estimated at between £54 and £70 million.

One key change is that recoupment will not be taken from general damages for pain and suffering and for loss of amenity which it has been accepted should be paid in full. With respect to the other heads of compensation, namely loss of earnings, cost of care and compensation for loss of mobility, they are only to be subject to recoupment from specified benefits relevant to each of these heads of compensation. [*Social Security (Recovery of Benefits) Act 1997, s 8*].

These heads of compensation and relevant benefits are set out overleaf.

Table 2

Calculation of compensation payment

(1) Head of compensation	(2) Benefit
1. Compensation for earnings lost during the relevant period	Disability working allowance
	Industrial injuries disablement pension payable under s 103 of the 1992 Act
	Incapacity benefit
	Income support
	Invalidity pension and allowance
	Jobseeker's allowance
	Reduced earnings allowance
	Severe disablement allowance
	Sickness benefit
	Statutory sick pay
	Unemployability supplement
	Unemployment benefit
2. Compensation for cost of care incurred during the relevant period	Attendance allowance
	Care component of disability living allowance
	Industrial injuries disablement pension increase payable under s 104 or 105 of the 1992 Act
3. Compensation for loss of mobility during the relevant period	Mobility allowance
	Mobility component of disability living allowance

The former sum of £2,500, which was exempt from compensation recovery, is no longer so exempt. The Secretary of State does have the power to exempt small payments under *s 24* of the *Social Security (Recovery of Benefits) Act 1997*.

The retrospective effect of the new provisions should be noted. The new scheme applies to compensation for accidents, injuries or diseases from the date of commencement of the Act unless compensation was made in pursuance of a court order or agreement before the commencement date. Under the *Social Security Administration Act 1992*, the following payments remain exempt from the recoupment of benefits:

(*a*)   any payment made out of property held for the purpose of the charitable trust called the Macfarlane Trust and established partly out of funds provided by the Secretary of State to the Haemophilia Society for the relief of poverty or distress among those suffering from haemophilia;

(*b*)   any compensation payment made by British Coal in accordance with the NCB Pneumoconiosis Compensation Scheme set out in the Schedule to an agreement made on 13 September 1974 between the National Coal Board, the National Union of Mine Workers, the National Association of Colliery Overmen Deputies and Shot-firers and the British Association of Colliery Management;

(*c*)   any payment made to the victim in respect of sensorineural hearing loss where the loss is less than 50 db in one or both ears;

(*d*)   any contractual amount paid to an employee by an employer of his in respect of a day of incapacity for work;

(*e*)   any payment made from the Macfarlane (Special Payments) Trust established on 29 January 1990 partly out of funds provided by the Secretary of State for the benefit of certain persons suffering from haemophilia;

(*f*)   any payment made from the Macfarlane (Special Payments) (No 2) Trust established on 3 May 1991 partly out of funds provided by the Secretary of State, for the benefit of certain persons suffering from haemophilia and other beneficiaries;

(*g*)   any payment made under the *National Health Service (Injury Benefits) Regulations 1974* or the *National Health Service (Scotland) (Injury Benefits) Regulations 1974;*

(*h*)   any payment made by or on behalf of the Secretary of State for the benefit of persons eligible for payment in accordance with the provisions of a scheme established by him on 24 April 1992 or, in Scotland, on 10 April 1992;

(*j*)   Any payment made from the Eileen Trust established on 29 March 1993 out of funds provided by the Secretary of State for the benefit of persons eligible for payment in accordance with its provisions.

Statutory sick pay will not normally be deductible, as most employers are liable to pay in full. Where this is not so in the case of small employers, it will be deductible like other state benefits. [*Statutory Sick Pay Act 1994 (Consequential) Regulations 1994 (SI 1994 No 730)*].

Duties of the compensator

C6042   Before the compensator makes a compensation payment, he must apply to the Secretary of State for a certificate of recoverable benefits (*Social Security (Recovery of Benefits) Act 1997, s 4*). The Secretary of State must send a written acknowledgement of receipt of the application and must supply the certificate within four weeks of receipt of the application (*Social Security (Recovery of Benefits) Act 1997, s 5*).

He must supply the following information with his application:

●   full name and address of the injured person;

●   his date of birth or national insurance number, if known;

●   date of accident or injury when liability arose (or is alleged to have arisen);

●   nature of the accident or disease;

●   his payroll number (where known), if the injured person is employed under a contract of service and the period of five years during which benefits can be recouped includes a period prior to 1994 [*Social Security (Recovery of Benefits) Act 1997, s 21; Recovery of Benefits Regulations 1997, Reg 7*]; and

- the amount of statutory sick pay paid to the injured person for five years since the date when liability first arose, as well as any statutory sick pay before 1994, if the compensator is also the injured person's employer. The causes of his incapacity for work must also be stated.

The certificate of recoverable benefits will show the benefits which have been paid.

The compensator must pay the sum certified within 14 days of the date following the date of issue of the certificate of recoverable benefits (*Social Security (Recovery of Benefits) Act 1997, s 6*). If the compensator makes a compensation payment without having applied for a certificate, or fails to pay within the prescribed fourteen days, the Secretary of State may issue a demand for payment immediately. A county court execution may be issued against the compensator to recover the sum as though under a court order. It is wise for the compensator to check the benefits required to be set off against the heads of compensation payment so that he is sure that the correct reduced compensation is paid to the injured person. Adjustments of recoupable benefits and the issue of fresh certificates are possible.

Where the compensator makes a reduced compensation payment to the injured person, he must inform him that the payment has been reduced. Statements that compensation has been reduced to nil must be made in a specific form. Once the compensator has paid the Secretary of State the correct compensation recovery amount and has made the statement as required, he is treated as having discharged his liability (*Social Security (Recovery of Benefits) Act 1997, s 9*).

Complications

Contributory negligence

C6043   Where damages have been reduced as the result of the plaintiff's contributory negligence, the reduction of compensation is ignored and recovery of benefits is set-off against the full compensation sum.

Structured settlements

The original sum agreed or awarded is subject to compensation recovery and for this purpose, the terms of the structured settlement are ignored and this original sum is treated as a single compensation payment. [*Social Security (Recovery of Benefits) (General) Regulations 1997, Reg 10*].

Complex cases

Where a lump sum payment has been made followed by a later lump sum, both payments are subject to recoupment of benefits where those benefits were recoupable. If the compensator has overpaid the Benefits Agency, he can seek a partial refund. [*Social Security (Recovery of Benefits) (General) Regulations 1997, Reg 9*].

Information provisions

Under *s 23* of the *Social Security (Recovery of Benefits) Act 1997*, anyone who is liable in respect of any accident, injury or disease must supply the Secretary of State with the following information within 14 days of the receipt of the claim against him:

- full name and address of the injured person;

- his date of birth or national insurance number, if known;

- date of accident or injury when liability arose (or is alleged to have arisen); and

- nature of the accident, or disease.

Where the injured person is employed under a contract of service, his employer should also supply the injured person's payroll number (if known) if the period of five years during which benefits may be recouped includes a period prior to 1994 and this is requested by the Secretary of State. [*Social Security (Recovery of Benefits) (General) Regulations 1997, Regs 3, 5 and 6*].

If the Secretary of State requests prescribed information from the injured person, it must be supplied within 14 days of the date of the request. This information includes details of the name and address of the person accused of the default which led to the accident, injury or disease, the name and address of the maker of any compensation claim and a list of the benefits received from the date of the claim. If statutory sick pay was received by the injured person, the name and address of the employer who has paid statutory sick pay during the five-year period from the date of the claim or before 6 April 1994.

Appeals against certificates of recoverable benefits

C6044

Appeals against the certificate of recoverable benefits must be in writing and made not less than three months after the compensation payment was made. The appeal should be made to the Compensation Recovery Unit for a hearing before a tribunal. Leave to appeal to a Commissioner against the decision of the tribunal should be made not later than three months after notice of the tribunal's decision.

In *Hassall and Pether v Secretary of State for Social Security [1995] PIQR 292*, Hassall and Pether were unemployed and in receipt of non-recoupable benefits before they were both injured in an accident. They received exactly the same amount of weekly benefits after the accident but, by contrast, from recoupable benefits. This amount was recouped. The unfairness of this recoupment could have been avoided if the statement of claim had included a claim for special damages for loss of non-recoupable pre-accident benefits.

Treatment of deductible and non-deductible payments from awards of damages

There are three well established exceptions to deductibility of financial gains:

- recovery under an insurance policy to which the plaintiff has contributed all or part of the premiums paid on the policy;

- retirement pensions;

- charitable or ex-gratia payments prompted by sympathy for the claimant's misfortune.

(a) Deductible financial gains

The courts, applying the principles outlined above, have ruled that the following financial gains are deductible:

(i) tax rebates where the employee has been absent from work as a result of his injuries (*Hartley v Sandholme Iron Co [1975] QB 600*);

   (ii)   domestic cost of living expenses (estimated) must be set off against the cost of care (*Lim Poh Choo v Camden and Islington Area Health Authority [1980] AC 174*);

  (iii)   estimated living expenses must be set off against loss of earnings (*Lim Poh Choo*, above);

  (iv)   payment from a job release scheme must be set off against loss of earnings (*Crawley v Mercer, The Times, 9 March 1984*);

   (v)   statutory sick pay must be set off against loss of earnings (*Palfrey v GLC [1985] IRLR 437*);

  (vi)   sick pay provided under an insurance policy must be set off against loss of earnings not paid as a lump sum (*Hussain v New Taplow Paper Mills [1988] AC 514*);

 (vii)   health insurance payment under an occupational pension plan paid before retirement must be set off against loss of earnings where no separate premium had been paid by the employee who had paid contributions to the pension scheme (*Page v Sheerness Steel plc [1996] PIQR 26*);

(viii)   reduced earnings allowance (not a disability benefit) must be set off against loss of earnings (*Flanagan v Watts Blake Bearne & Co plc [1992] PIQR Q144*);

  (ix)   payments under *s* 5 of the *Administration of Justice Act 1982* of any saving to the person who has sustained personal injuries through maintenance at the public expense must be set off against loss of earnings.

(b) Non-deductible financial gains against loss of wages

   (i)   accident insurance payments under a personal insurance policy taken out by the employee (*Bradburn v Great Western Railway Co (1874) LR 10 Exch 1*) (contributory);

  (ii)   lump-sum wage-related accident insurance payment under a personal accident group policy payable regardless of the fault of the employee (*McCamley v Cammell Laird Shipbuilders [1990] 1 AER 854*) (benevolent);

 (iii)   incapacity pension (from contributory insurance scheme) both before and after retirement age (*Longden v British Coal Corporation [1995] PIQR Q48*). It should be noted that even though the incapacity pension was triggered by the accident, benefit flows from the prior contributions paid by the injured party (contributory);

 (iv)   private retirement pensions (*Parry v Cleaver [1970] AC 1; Hewson v Downs [1970] 1 QB 73; Wood v British Coal Corporation [1991] 2 AC 502*) (contributory or benevolent);

  (v)   redundancy payment unconnected with the accident or disease (*Mills v Hassal [1983] ICR 330*). Where the plaintiff was made redundant because he was unfit to take up employment in the same trade, however, the redundancy payment was deductible from damages for lost earnings (*Wilson v National Coal Board [1981] SLT 67*);

 (vi)   ex-gratia payment by an employer (*Cunningham v Harrison [1973] QB 942; Bews v Scottish Hydro-Electric plc, The Times, 25 March 1995*) (benevolent);

(vii)   ill health award and higher pension benefits provided by the employer (*Smoker v London Fire and Civil Defence Authority [1991] 2 AC 502*) (benevolent);

(viii) moneys from a benevolent fund, paid through trustees (not directly to the injured person or dependant) in respect of injuries;

(ix)   charitable donations (but not where the tortfeasor is the donor);

(*c*) *Non-deductible financial gains against cost of care*

(i)   Loss of board and lodging expenses awarded despite their being provided voluntarily by parents where the plaintiff had formerly paid such expenses herself (*Liffen v Watson [1940] 1 KB 556*).

Social security and damages for prescribed diseases

C6045   The claims for social security benefits are similar to those for personal injuries. Claims for damages are also similar, with more latitude for late court applications because of recurrence of, or worsening of, industrial diseases. Lists of prescribed diseases are contained in social security leaflet NI 2. It is advisable always to refer to the latest edition of the leaflet, as the list of diseases is subject to amendment from time to time. There are special provisions applicable to asthma and deafness resulting from industrial processes, and also for pneumoconiosis and similar diseases.

(*a*) *Occupational deafness (see DSS leaflet 207)*

If the claimant's deafness was caused by an accident at work, then to qualify for disablement benefit his average hearing loss must have been at least 50 decibels in both ears due to damage of the inner ear. The claimant's disablement must be at least 20 per cent or more for him to qualify for disablement benefit (total deafness being 100 per cent). The claimant must have worked for at least the five years immediately before making his claim, or for at least ten years, in one of the listed jobs set out in the current edition of the leaflet. A claimant who has been refused benefit because the rules were not complied with will have to wait for three more years when he may qualify if he has worked in one of the listed occupations for five years. Leaflet NI 196 '*Social Security Benefits Rates*' shows the rates payable, relevant to each percentage of loss, for a weekly disablement pension.

The claim will be decided by a Medical Board, whose members will also decide on reviews if the claimant believes that his deafness has worsened. They will inform the claimant in detail of their decision. Awards will be made for a period of five years, and there will be a review at the end of that period with another hearing test to determine whether benefit should continue, or be reduced.

Claims must be made on Form BI 100 (OD) which may be obtained free from the Department of the Environment HS ORI Level 4, Caxton House, London SW1H 9NA (tel: 0171 273 5248), or from a post office and some borough libraries.

(*b*) *Asthma because of a job (see DSS leaflet NI 237)*

As is well known, there has been an increase in the number of sufferers from asthma. To be able to claim disablement benefit because of asthma, a claimant must have worked for an employer for at least ten years and have been in contact with prescribed substances, and his disability must amount to at least 14 per cent. In the list of substances, item 23 includes 'any other sensitising agent encountered at work', so claims may be possible even if the offending sensitising substance is not yet on the list.

Claims must be made on Form BI 100 (OA) which may be obtained from the Department of the Environment (see address and telephone number above), or from a post office and some borough libraries.

Once a claim has been made, the claimant will be seen by a Medical Board whose members will decide whether he has asthma because of his job and, if so, how disabled he is by the asthma. They will also determine how long his disability is likely to last and the extent of his disability, and will then communicate all of this information to the claimant. If they consider that no change is likely, they may award benefit for life. If they expect that there will be changes, there will be a review at the end of the period for which benefit was awarded.

(c) Repetitive strain injuries

Repetitive strain injuries are included as item A4 of *Schedule 1* to the *Social Security (Industrial Injuries) (Prescribed Diseases) Regulations.* [See OCCUPATIONAL HEALTH AND DISEASES]. The case of *Pickford v Imperial Chemical Industries, The Times, 31 August 1996,* shows the importance of providing adequate rest periods to users of word processors to avoid the risk of being made liable for damages. In that case, damages were awarded to a secretary who suffered repetitive strain injury as the result of being obliged to type for long periods without a break.

Pneumoconiosis

C6046   Pneumoconiosis is compensatable under different heads; first, as a ground for disablement benefit, under the *Social Security Contributions and Benefits Act 1992* and, secondly, by way of claim made under the *Pneumoconiosis etc. (Workers' Compensation) Act 1979* – the latter being in addition to any disablement benefit previously paid.

Pneumoconiosis/tuberculosis-pneumoconiosis/emphysema – disablement benefit

C6047   Where a person is suffering from pneumoconiosis accompanied by tuberculosis, then, for benefit purposes, tuberculosis is to be treated as pneumoconiosis. [*Social Security Contributions and Benefits Act 1992, s 110*]. This applies also to pneumoconiosis accompanied by emphysema or chronic bronchitis, provided that disablement from pneumoconiosis, or pneumoconiosis and tuberculosis, is assessed at, at least, 50%. [*Social Security Contributions and Benefits Act 1992, s 110*]. However, a person suffering from byssinosis is not entitled to disablement, unless he is suffering from loss of faculty which is likely to be permanent. [*Social Security Contributions and Benefits Act 1992, s 110*].

Benefit may be payable if the claimant's disablement is assessed at 1 per cent or more, instead of the usual minimum of 14 per cent. If the assessment of disablement is 10 per cent or less (but at least 1 per cent), then the industrial injuries disablement pension will be payable at one-tenth of the 100 per cent rate.

See Table 3(C) at the end of this chapter for details of sums payable to the dependants of sufferers who have died from one of these diseases.

If the disease dies down and recrudescence questions arise later, the decision on the recrudescence must be determined by qualified adjudicating medical practitioners.

Pneumoconiosis – payment of compensation under the Pneumoconiosis etc. (Workers' Compensation) Act 1979

C6048   Claims made under the *Pneumoconiosis etc. (Workers' Compensation) Act 1979* are in addition to any disablement benefit paid or payable under the *Social Security (Industrial Injuries) (Prescribed Diseases) Regulations 1985 (SI 1985 No 967)*. Indeed, whereas the latter consists of periodical payments, the former resemble damages awarded against an employer at common law and/or for breach of statutory duty, except that under the above Act fault (or negligence) need not be proved. This statutory compensation is available only if the employee is unable to claim compensation from any of his former employers (for example, if the employer has become insolvent). There are no requirements that the employee must have worked in a particular industry to be able to claim compensation under the scheme. Claimants are entitled to benefits from the date of claim. There is no ninety day waiting period under the scheme it is sufficient if the claimant suffers from the prescribed disease. Coal miners are excluded from the scheme because they have their own statutory scheme. Claims made under the *Pneumoconiosis etc. (Workers' Compensation) Act 1979* must be made in the manner set out in the *Pneumoconiosis etc. (Workers' Compensation) (Determination of Claims) Regulations 1985 (SI 1985 No 1645)*. The claim must be made (except in the case of a 'specified disease' – see C6049 below) within 12 months from the date on which disablement benefit (under the *Social Security Regulations*) first become payable; or if the claim is by a dependant, within 12 months from the date of the deceased's death. [*Pneumoconiosis etc. (Workers' Compensation) (Determination of Claims) Regulations 1985, Reg 4(1), (2)*]. Awards for pneumoconiosis/byssinosis have declined slowly recently.

Claims for specified diseases

C6049   Claims for a 'specified disease', i.e.:

(*a*)   pneumoconiosis, including (i) silicosis, (ii) asbestosis and kaolinosis;

(*b*)   byssinosis (caused by cotton or flax dust);

(*c*)   diffuse mesothelioma;

(*d*)   primary carcinoma of the lung coupled with evidence of (i) asbestosis and/or (ii) bilateral diffuse pleural thickening

[*Pneumoconiosis etc. (Workers' Compensation) (Specified Diseases) Order 1985 (SI 1985 No 2034)*], must be made within 12 months from the date when disablement benefit first became payable, or, in the case of a dependant, within 12 months from the date of the deceased's death [*Pneumoconiosis etc. (Workers' Compensation) (Determination of Claims) Regulations 1985, Reg 4(3)(4)*]. These time periods can be extended at the discretion of the Secretary of State. Moreover, where a person has already made a claim and has been refused payment, he can apply for a reconsideration of determination, on the ground that there has been a material change of circumstances since determination was made, or that determination was made in ignorance of, or based on, a mistake as to material fact.

The Pneumoconiosis etc. (Workers' Compensation) (Payment of Claims) Amendment Regulations 1997 (SI 1997 No 1691)

C6050   The *Pneumoconiosis etc. (Workers' Compensation) (Payment of Claims) Amendment Regulations 1997 (SI 1997 No 1691)* which came into force in August 1997 specify the following payments for sufferers of 'specified diseases'.

Table 3

(A) Payments in respect of a prescribed disease to sufferers from pneumoconiosis or byssinosis.

Age of disabled person	Percentage assessment for the relevant period									
	10% or less	11–20%	21–30%	31–40%	41–50%	51–60%	61–70%	71–80%	81–90%	91–100%
	£	£	£	£	£	£	£	£	£	£
37 and under	22,503	40,187	47,151	48,491	49,830	50,901	51,975	53,045	54,117	55,188
38	21,860	38,578	45,731	47,368	48,757	49,830	50,901	51,975	53,045	54,117
39	21,217	36,970	44,311	46,240	47,688	48,757	49,830	50,901	51,975	53,045
40	20,576	35,362	42,892	45,114	46,614	47,688	48,757	49,830	50,901	51,975
41	19,932	33,756	41,472	43,988	45,544	46,614	47,688	48,757	49,830	50,901
42	19,286	32,149	40,052	42,866	44,472	45,544	46,614	47,688	48,757	49,830
43	18,325	30,273	38,631	42,008	43,724	45,009	46,079	47,151	48,223	49,296
44	17,360	28,397	37,211	41,150	42,972	44,472	45,544	46,614	47,688	48,757
45	16,397	26,522	35,792	40,293	42,223	43,936	45,009	46,079	47,151	48,223
46	15,431	24,648	34,373	39,436	41,472	43,401	44,472	45,544	46,614	47,688
47	14,468	22,772	32,952	38,578	40,722	42,866	43,936	45,009	46,079	47,151
48	13,636	22,020	31,828	36,863	39,436	41,362	42,437	43,507	44,578	45,652
49	12,806	21,272	30,702	35,149	38,152	39,863	40,936	42,008	43,081	44,152
50	11,976	20,522	29,598	33,435	36,863	38,363	39,436	40,507	41,578	42,650
51	11,146	19,722	28,450	31,720	35,578	36,863	37,946	39,005	40,079	41,150
52	10,314	19,021	27,327	30,005	34,291	35,362	36,437	37,506	38,578	39,649
53	9,537	17,683	25,611	28,505	33,005	34,291	35,362	36,437	37,506	38,578
54	8,760	16,343	23,896	27,007	31,720	33,221	34,291	35,362	36,437	37,506
55	7,983	15,003	22,184	25,504	30,433	32,149	33,221	34,291	35,362	36,437
56	7,206	13,662	20,468	24,005	29,149	31,077	32,149	33,221	34,291	35,362
57	6,430	12,323	18,754	22,503	27,866	30,006	31,077	32,149	33,221	34,291
58	5,921	11,200	16,746	20,198	25,074	27,059	28,210	29,337	30,433	31,506
59	5,411	10,072	14,734	17,897	22,288	24,111	25,343	26,522	27,648	28,717
60	4,904	8,947	12,725	15,591	19,505	21,165	22,476	23,710	24,863	25,935
61	4,393	7,822	10,717	13,287	16,718	18,218	19,609	20,897	22,076	23,146
62	3,885	6,698	8,707	10,983	13,933	15,271	16,746	18,084	19,286	20,360
63	3,616	6,054	7,822	9,820	12,392	13,715	15,110	16,397	17,574	18,646
64	3,353	5,411	6,938	8,653	10,850	12,163	13,477	14,708	15,859	16,930
65	3,082	4,768	6,054	7,491	9,310	10,609	11,841	13,021	14,146	15,218
66	2,814	4,128	5,171	6,321	7,771	9,005	10,208	11,332	12,432	13,502
67	2,546	3,482	4,285	5,157	6,229	7,503	8,573	9,645	10,717	11,788
68	2,477	3,374	4,139	4,942	6,017	7,206	8,238	9,350	10,380	11,439
69	2,411	3,268	3,993	4,730	5,802	6,913	7,905	9,055	10,049	11,090
70	2,344	3,162	3,843	4,514	5,586	6,616	7,569	8,760	9,711	10,744
71	2,278	3,053	3,698	4,299	5,371	6,321	7,234	8,467	9,378	10,397
72	2,211	2,948	3,550	4,087	5,157	6,029	6,898	8,172	9,040	10,049
73	2,156	2,896	3,497	4,006	5,076	5,894	6,765	7,958	8,774	9,752
74	2,103	2,839	3,443	3,925	4,998	5,759	6,632	7,743	8,507	9,451
75	2,051	2,787	3,390	3,843	4,915	5,626	6,497	7,528	8,238	9,161
76	1,996	2,731	3,334	3,765	4,835	5,494	6,364	7,315	7,969	8,869
77 and over	1,943	2,678	3,282	3,683	4,755	5,358	6,229	7,102	7,702	8,573

(B) Payments to sufferers from pneumoconiosis or byssinosis under the statutory scheme (see C6048).

Age of disabled person	Extent of incapacity for the relevant period	
	Partial	Total
	£	£
37 and under	40,187	55,188
38	38,578	54,117
39	36,970	53,045
40	35,362	51,975
41	33,756	50,901
42	32,149	49,830
43	30,273	49,296
44	28,397	48,757
45	26,522	48,223
46	24,648	47,688
47	22,772	47,151
48	22,020	45,652
49	21,272	44,152
50	20,522	42,650
51	19,772	41,150
52	19,021	39,649
53	17,683	38,578
54	16,343	37,506
55	15,003	36,437
56	13,662	35,362
57	12,323	34,291
58	11,200	31,506
59	10,072	28,717
60	8,947	25,935
61	7,822	23,146
62	6,698	20,360
63	6,054	18,646
64	5,411	16,930
65	4,768	15,218
66	4,128	13,502
67	3,482	11,788
68	3,374	11,439
69	3,268	11,090
70	3,162	10,744
71	3,053	10,397
72	2,948	10,049
73	2,896	9,752
74	2,839	9,451
75	2,787	9,161
76	2,731	8,869
77 and over	2,678	8,573

(C) Payments to dependants of a deceased former sufferer from the prescribed diseases of pneumoconiosis or byssinosis (see C6047).

Age of disabled person at his last birthday preceding death	Percentage assessment for the relevant period				
	10% or less	11%–20%	21%–30%	31%–49%	50% and over
	£	£	£	£	£
37 and under	10,582	20,631	23,575	24,380	25,050
38	10,261	19,719	22,772	23,575	24,432
39	9,941	18,807	21,969	22,772	23,817
40	9,616	17,897	21,165	21,969	23,200
41	9,296	16,986	20,360	21,165	22,584
42	8,977	16,078	19,556	20,360	21,969
43	8,397	14,897	18,833	19,637	21,380
44	7,822	13,715	18,108	18,914	20,783
45	7,248	12,538	17,387	18,191	20,198
46	6,670	11,357	16,601	17,466	19,609
47	6,095	10,179	15,942	16,746	19,021
48	5,654	9,858	15,407	16,182	18,298
49	5,210	9,537	14,868	15,620	17,574
50	4,768	9,215	14,335	15,056	16,851
51	4,327	8,894	13,798	14,494	16,129
52	3,885	8,573	13,262	13,933	15,407
53	3,683	7,822	12,245	13,154	14,814
54	3,482	7,072	11,225	12,378	14,226
55	3,282	6,321	10,208	11,601	13,636
56	3,082	5,572	9,189	10,825	13,045
57	2,879	4,823	8,172	10,049	12,457
58	2,692	4,285	7,007	8,682	10,825
59	2,502	3,750	5,841	7,315	9,189
60	2,318	3,216	4,674	5,947	7,556
61	2,132	2,678	3,510	4,582	5,921
62	1,943	2,144	2,344	3,216	4,285
63	1,943	2,103	2,265	2,959	3,819
64	1,943	2,062	2,182	2,706	3,353
65	1,943	2,024	2,103	2,451	2,879
66	1,943	1,984	2,024	2,197	2,411
67 and over	1,943	1,943	1,943	1,943	1,943

(D) Payments to dependants of a deceased former sufferer from pneumoconiosis or byssinosis under the statutory scheme (see C6048).

Age of disabled person at his last birthday preceding death	Payment
	£
37 and under	25,050
38	24,432
39	23,817
40	23,200
41	22,584
42	21,969
43	21,380
44	20,783
45	20,198
46	19,609
47	19,021
48	18,298
49	17,574
50	16,851
51	16,129
52	15,407
53	14,814
54	14,226
55	13,636
56	13,045
57	12,457
58	10,825
59	9,189
60	7,556
61	5,921
62	4,285
63	3,819
64	3,353
65	2,879
66	2,411
67 and over	1,943

(E) Payments to dependants of persons who died as a result of diffuse mesothelioma.

Age of disabled person at his last birthday preceding death	Extent of incapacity for the relevant period	
	Partial	Total
	£	£
37 and under	20,631	25,050
38	19,719	24,432
39	18,807	23,817
40	17,897	23,200
41	16,986	22,584
42	16,078	21,969
43	14,897	21,380
44	13,715	20,783
45	12,538	20,198
46	11,357	19,609
47	10,179	19,021
48	9,858	18,298
49	9,537	17,574
50	9,215	16,851
51	8,894	16,129
52	8,573	15,407
53	7,822	14,814
54	7,072	14,226
55	6,321	13,636
56	5,572	13,045
57	4,823	12,457
58	4,285	10,825
59	3,750	9,189
60	3,216	7,556
61	2,678	5,921
62	2,144	4,285
63	2,103	3,819
64	2,062	3,353
65	2,024	2,879
66	1,984	2,411
67 and over	1,943	1,943

Construction and Building Operations

Introduction to construction work

C8001   The series of construction Regulations made under the *Factories Act 1961* referred to 'building operations' and 'works of engineering construction'. A major revision of these Regulations gives a more comprehensive definition of 'construction work', which is based on a much broader concept and also includes the installation and removal of services which are part of a structure and the installation and removal of fixed plant where there is a risk of falling two metres or more (see also WORK AT HEIGHTS).

All construction activities are now contained in three sets of Regulations bearing the prefix 'Construction'.

—   the *Construction (Head Protection) Regulations 1989 (SI 1989 No 2209 as amended)* (see C8096 below);

—   the *Construction (Design and Management) Regulations 1994 (CDM) (SI 1994 No 3140)* (see C8014 below);

—   the *Construction (Health, Safety and Welfare) Regulations 1996 (CHSW) (SI 1996 No 1592)* (see C8030 below).

Generally, the definition of construction work covers the activities on all kinds of construction sites, from the smallest internal jobs to large-scale complex projects including:

—   general building and construction work;

—   refurbishment work;

—   maintenance and repair work;

—   engineering construction work;

—   civil engineering work.

The exploration and extraction of mineral resources and the preparatory activities are excluded from the definition of construction work, which is extensively defined in the principal regulations. Reference to the full definitions should be made in any case of doubt or for litigation purposes. [*CDM Reg 2(1); CHSW Reg 2(1)*].

The two principal sets of Regulations have different applications:

—   *CDM* applies to construction sites only when the 'construction work' is notifiable to the HSE and where more than five people are likely to be employed at any one time;

—   *CHSW* applies to all construction sites (that is, any place where the principal activity carried on is 'construction work') and when a person is at work on a construction site.

Associated statutory requirements

C8002   The protection of the workforce who carry out construction work stems from the *Health and Safety at Work etc. Act 1974 (HSWA)* and the *Management of Health and Safety at Work Regulations 1992 (MHSWR) (SI 1992 No 2051 as amended)*.

In particular, under the Act itself:

(*a*)   contractors (as employers) owe health and safety duties to their employees [*s 2*];

(*b*)   employees owe such duties to their employers (i.e. contractors/subcontractors) [*s 7*];

(*c*)   building owners (i.e contractors' employers) owe health and safety duties to subcontractors and their employees [*s 3(1)*] (also see *R v Associated Octel Co Ltd* at *C8134);*

(*d*)   self-employed contractors/workmen owe health and safety duties to other self-employed persons (e.g. building owners to main contractors), and to employees (but who are not their own) [*s 3(2)*].

Self-styled 'labour-only' subcontractors have been held to be employees of a large main contractor and so were entitled to the protection of some of the *Construction Regulations (Ferguson v John Dawson & Partners (Contractors) Ltd [1976] IRLR 346* where a nominated subcontractor was liable to a 'self-employed labour-only subcontractor' for breach of *Reg 28(1)* of the *Construction (Working Places) Regulations 1966* (now repealed), requiring provision of guard-rails and toe-boards at working platforms and places);

(*e*)   building owners and occupiers have duties to employees of contractors and subcontractors. [*s 4(1), (2)*]. Thus, *HSWA s 4* states that anyone 'having control to any extent' of premises, must take reasonable care in respect of persons working there, who are *not* employees. This duty can be subject to indemnity clauses in a lease and/or contract (see further OCCUPIERS' LIABILITY), it is strict and must be carried out so far as is reasonably practicable, that is, subject to cost-effective constraints;

(*f*)   although ostensibly applicable to all workplaces, the *Workplace (Health, Safety and Welfare) Regulations 1992 (SI 1992 No 3004)* do *not* extend to building operations and works of engineering construction, unless some other activity is being carried on there (see further WORKPLACES – HEALTH, SAFETY AND WELFARE).

Main Regulations relating to the construction industry

C8003   The following list gives the main Regulations which apply to the construction industry:

—   *Highly Flammable Liquids and Liquefied Petroleum Gases Regulations 1972 (SI 1972 No 917 as amended);*

—   *Health and Safety (First-Aid) Regulations 1981 (SI 1981 No 917 as amended);*

—   *Asbestos (Licensing) Regulations 1983 (SI 1983 No 1649 as amended)* (see C8004*);*

—   *Control of Major Accident Hazards Regulations 1999 (COMAH) (SI 1999 No 743) (*see C8108*);*

—   *Ionising Radiation Regulations 1985 (SI 1985 No 1333 as amended);*

—   *Control of Pesticides Regulations 1986 (SI 1986 No 1510 as amended);*

—   *Control of Noise (Codes of Practice for Construction and Open Sites) Orders 1984 (SI 1984 No 1992) and 1987 (SI 1987 No 1730)* (see C8124);

—   *Control of Asbestos at Work Regulations 1987 (SI 1987 No 2115 as amended)* (see C8004);

—   *Construction Plant and Equipment (Harmonisation of Noise Emission Standards) Regulations 1988 (SI 1988 No 361 as amended)* (see C8124);

—   *Electricity at Work Regulations 1989 (SI 1989 No 635 as amended);*

—   *Noise at Work Regulations 1989 (SI 1989 No 1790 as amended)* (see C8124);

—   *Construction Products Regulations 1991 (SI 1991 No 1620 as amended)* (see C8105);

—   *Notification of Cooling Towers and Evaporative Condensers Regulations 1992 (SI 1992 No 2225)* (see C8119);

—   *Manual Handling Operations Regulations 1992 (SI 1992 No 2793);*

—   *Provision and Use of Work Equipment Regulations 1998 (PUWER) (SI 1998 No 2306);*

—   *Personal Protective Equipment at Work Regulations 1992 (PPE) (SI 1992 No 2966 as amended)* (see C8100);

—   *Waste Management Licensing Regulations 1994 (SI 1994 No 1056 as amended)* (see C8106);

—   *Control of Substances Hazardous to Health Regulations 1999 (COSHH) (SI 1999 No 437);*

—   *Reporting of Injuries, Diseases and Dangerous Occurrences Regulations 1995 (RIDDOR) (SI 1995 No 2023 as amended);*

—   *Health and Safety (Safety Signs and Signals) Regulations 1996 (SI 1996 No 341);*

—   *Pipelines Safety Regulations 1996 (SI 1996 No 825);*

—   *Special Waste Regulations 1996 (SI 1996 No 972 as amended)* (see C8106);

—   *Health and Safety (Consultation with Employees) Regulations 1996 (SI 1996 No 1513);*

—   *Work in Compressed Air Regulations 1996 (SI 1996 No 1656)* (see C8080);

—   *Health and Safety (Young Persons) Regulations 1997 (SI 1997 No 135);*

—   *Lifts Regulations 1997 (SI 1997 No 831);*

—   *Confined Spaces Regulations 1997 (SI 1997 No 1713)* (see C8057);

—   *Health and Safety (Enforcing Authority) Regulations 1998 (SI 1998 No 494);*

—   *Control of Lead at Work Regulations 1998 (SI 1998 No 543).*

Environmental safety aspects during asbestos removal

C8004   Under *Regulation 3* of the *Control of Asbestos at Work Regulations 1987*, employers have duties not only to their own employees but also to, for example:

(*a*)   visitors to the place where work with asbestos is being carried out;

(b)   the occupier's employees if the work is done in someone else's premises;

(c)   people in the neighbourhood who might be accidentally exposed to asbestos dust arising from the work.

Whenever two or more employers work with asbestos at the same time at one workplace they should co-operate in order to meet their separate responsibilities (for further detail see ASBESTOS).

Contractors undertaking work on materials containing asbestos were warned of the serious health hazards associated with such work when the *Control of Asbestos at Work Regulations 1987 (SI 1987 No 2115)* came into force in 1988. The warning was reiterated in 1995 when a court case involving contractors cleaning an asbestos roof ruled that such contractors had a duty to take reasonable care and skill in the work including the taking of necessary precautions (*Barclays Bank plc v Fairclough Building Ltd (No 2) [1995] IRLR 605 CA*).

There have been numerous cases involving incidents during demolition and the removal of asbestos in the three years following the above case and its warning. In a very significant case where the lives of children had been put at risk, the Health and Safety Executive (HSE) and the Environment Agency co-operated and raised a joint prosecution.

The case (*R v Rollco Screw and Rivet Co and Others [1998] HSE E198:98*) resulted in a defendant being jailed for nine months (the second custodial sentence for an asbestos offence) and five others and a company were ordered to pay fines and costs totalling £98,000. Birmingham Crown Court heard disturbing evidence of the casual attitude of the people carrying out the stripping of an asbestos roof and the subsequent disposal of blue, white and brown asbestos. The contractors were not licensed in accordance with the requirements of the *Asbestos (Licensing) Regulations 1983 (SI 1983 No 1649)*. The HSE inspector who conducted the investigation emphasised the importance of property owners and managers checking the qualifications of any person employed to carry out asbestos removal work. The inspector was especially critical of the clear attempt to gain financially from decisions taken which put the public at risk.

The QC for the Environment Agency gave evidence of nine contraventions of the *Environmental Protection Act 1990* (the keeping or disposal of controlled waste in such a way that pollution of the environment or harm to human health was likely . . .) where approximately 300 bags of asbestos were dumped at different locations around the city. Some of the bags had been left open and others had burst, releasing asbestos fibres into the air. The court heard that children had been playing with loose asbestos material since it had been dumped recklessly and indiscriminately in a playground and in a supermarket car park as well as other locations.

Judge Charles Harris QC, in imposing the sentences, singled out one man for the custodial sentence and said that, unlike the others in the case, he knew the risks, he lied steadily and showed manifest dishonesty. He told him 'This was an act of the most astonishing criminal irresponsibility. You understood the nature of asbestos and yet you distributed it around Birmingham in places where people, including children, had easy access to it'. He described the co-defendants as being ignorant of the dangers of asbestos but their neglect had put others in serious danger.

See, however, the sentences imposed on brothers Andrew and Neil Medley (10. INTRODUCTION).

Practical safety criteria

C8005 Falling from a height is the most frequent cause of fatal accidents in the construction industry, hence the considerable attention paid to aspects such as the erection, inspection and maintenance of scaffolds, and the more general aspects of roof work in the *Construction (Health, Safety and Welfare) Regulations 1996*. Accidents associated with ladders are also a common feature of this industry.

Good safety practice dictates the following.

Ladders

C8006 (*a*) Only ladders in a sound condition should be used.

(*b*) The 'one out four up' rule should be strictly adhered to in all situations (i.e. that the vertical height from the ground to the ladder's point of rest should be four times the distance between the base of the vertical dimension and the foot of the ladder).

(*c*) Ladders should be securely fixed near to their upper resting place or, where this is impracticable, 'footed' by an individual or securely fixed at the base to prevent slipping.

(*d*) Ladders should be inspected on a regular basis and a record of such inspections maintained.

(See W9017 WORK AT HEIGHTS for statutory requirements.)

Working platforms

C8007 (*a*) Working platforms should be adequately fenced by means of guard-rails and toe-boards.

(*b*) Platforms should be adequately covered with sound boards.

(*c*) Where mobile platforms are used, they should be stationed on a firm level base and, where possible, tied to the structure to prevent sideways movement. Wheel-locking devices should be provided and used.

(*d*) The following height to base ratios should be applied for all mobile working platforms:

outdoor work – 3:1; indoor work – 3.5:1.

(See W9012 WORK AT HEIGHTS for statutory requirements.)

Materials

C8008 (*a*) Meticulous standards of housekeeping must be maintained on working platforms and other elevated working positions to prevent materials, tools and other items falling on to people working directly below. The correct positioning of toe-boards is most important here.

(*b*) Lifting operations should ensure correct hooking and slinging prior to raising, correct assembly of gin-wheels and a high degree of supervision.

(*c*) Catchment platforms or 'fans' should be installed to catch small items which may fall during construction, particularly where work is undertaken above a public thoroughfare.

Excavations

C8009   (a)   Trenches should be adequately timbered with regard to the depth and width of the trench, the nature of the surrounding ground and the load imposed by subsoil.

(b)   Excavated ground and building materials should be stored well away from the verge of any excavation.

Powered hand tools and machinery

C8010   (a)   Electrically operated hand tools, such as drills, should comply with British Standard 2769: Series and, unless 'all insulated' or 'double insulated', must be effectively earthed.

(b)   Portable tools and temporary lighting arrangements should operate through reduced voltages, using 110 volt mains isolation transformers with the secondary winding centre tapped to earth.

(c)   Power take-offs, cooling fans, belt drives and other items of moving machinery should be securely fenced to prevent workers coming into contact with them. All machinery should comply with the *Provision and Use of Work Equipment Regulations 1998 (SI 1998 No 2306)* (see further MACHINERY SAFETY).

Site transport

C8011   (a)   Employees should not travel on site transport, such as dumper trucks, and notices should be affixed to such vehicles to that effect.

(b)   All vehicle movement and tipping operations on site should be supervised by a person outside the driver's cab.

(c)   Site vehicles should be subject to regular maintenance, particular attention being paid to braking and reversing systems.

(d)   Only competent and trained drivers should be allowed to drive site vehicles.

(e)   Site roadways should be maintained in a sound condition, free from mud, debris, obstructions and large puddles. The verges of the roadway should be clearly defined and adequate lighting provided, particularly at tipping points, reversing and turning areas.

(f)   Site speed limits should be established and clearly marked with signs corresponding to speed limit signs on public roads.

Demolition

C8012   (a)   A pre-demolition survey should always be undertaken, making use of the original plans if available.

(b)   Catching platforms should be installed not more than 6 m below the working level wherever there is a risk to the public.

(c)   Employees should be provided with safety helmets incorporating chin straps, goggles, heavy duty gloves and safety boots with steel insoles. In certain cases, respiratory protection, safety belts or harnesses may also be necessary.

(d)   Demolition should be undertaken, wherever possible, in the reverse order of erection.

(*e*)   When using working platforms, all debris should be removed on a regular basis.

(*f*)   Independently supported working platforms over reinforced concrete slabs should be demolished.

(*g*)   Members of framed structures should be adequately supported and temporary props, bracing or guys installed to restrain remaining parts of the building.

(*h*)   Employees should not work from the floor of a building which is currently being demolished.

(*j*)   Where pulling arrangements, demolition ball, explosives or pusher arms are to be used, employees should be kept well away until these stages have been completed.

(*k*)   Frequent inspections must be made of the demolition site to detect dangers which may have arisen following commencement of demolition.

Fire

C8013   (*a*)   All sources of ignition should be carefully controlled, e.g. welding activities, the use of blow lamps, gas or liquid fuel fired appliances.

(*b*)   All flammable materials, including waste materials, should be carefully stored away from the main construction activity.

(*c*)   All employees should be aware of the fire warning system, training sessions being undertaken according to need.

(*d*)   There should be sufficient access for fire brigade appliances in the event of fire.

(*e*)   There should be adequate space between buildings, e.g. site huts, canteen, etc.

(*f*)   High-risk buildings should be separated from low-risk buildings.

(*g*)   Controlled areas, where smoking and the use of naked lights are forbidden, should be established and suitably marked with warning signs.

(*h*)   An adequate supply of water should be available for fire brigade appliances and on-site fire-fighting.

(*j*)   Fire wardens should be appointed to undertake routine site inspections, together with the operation of a fire patrol, particularly at night and weekends.

(See also FIRE AND FIRE PRECAUTIONS.)

Construction (Design and Management) Regulations 1994 (SI 1994 No 3140)

C8014   The *Construction (Design and Management) Regulations 1994 (CDM)* implement (with minor exceptions) EU Directive 92/57/EEC on the minimum safety and health requirements at temporary or mobile construction sites. The regulations are supported by an Approved Code of Practice, L54: *Managing construction for health and safety* (ISBN 0 7176 0792 5).

Generally, the *CDM Regulations* apply to construction work (as defined) carried out on a construction site which is notifiable to the HSE, that is, a construction project which:

—   is scheduled to last for more than 30 days; or

—   will involve more than 500 man-days of work; or

—   includes any demolition work regardless of the size or duration of the work; or

—   involves five or more workers being on site at any one time.

The Regulations always apply when construction design work is involved.

Notification of project

C8015   Notification of a construction project (where notifiable) (see 'Exclusions' at C8016 below) should be given to HSE in writing (ideally) as soon as practicable after appointment of the planning supervisor, or (failing that), after the appointment of the principal contractor, but before construction work starts, specifying:

(*a*)   date of forwarding;

(*b*)   exact address of construction site;

(*c*)   name and address of client(s);

(*d*)   type of project;

(*e*)   name and address of the planning supervisor;

(*f*)   declaration of appointment by the planning supervisor;

(*g*)   name and address of principal contractor;

(*h*)   declaration of appointment of the principal contractor;

(*j*)   date planned for start of the construction phase;

(*k*)   planned duration of the construction phase;

(*l*)   estimated maximum number of people at work on the construction site;

(*m*)   planned number of contractors on construction site;

(*n*)   name and address of any contractor(s) already chosen.

[*Reg 3, Sch 1*].

Exclusions

C8016   These regulations are inapplicable (mainly) to construction work:

(*a*)   where a client reasonably believes that

     (i)   a project is not notifiable, and

     (ii)   no more than four people are working at any one time (except for demolition and dismantling)

     [*Reg 3(2), (3)*];

(*b*)   of a minor nature where the local authority is the enforcing authority [*Reg 3(4)*];

(c)   carried out for a domestic client, unless (as a result of agreement/arrangement with the developer):

    (i)   land is transferred to the client,

    (ii)   the developer undertakes to build on the land, or

    (iii)   after construction, the land will incorporate premises to be occupied by the client

[*Reg 3(8)*].

Objectives of the CDM Regulations

C8017   The *CDM Regulations* introduce a control framework which requires the effective management of all stages of a construction project from conception, design, commissioning of work, its planning and execution, and in particular construction activities which are likely to pose significant risks to workers.

The overall aim of *CDM Regulations* is to raise construction safety standards by improving co-ordination between various parties involved at both preparation and execution stage. More particularly, clients are required to appoint co-ordinators for preparation (planning supervisors) and execution stages (principal contractors), the co-ordinators being required to prepare and update the health and safety plan, which is the key to the operation of *CDM Regulations*, planning supervisors dealing mainly with designers and principal contractors dealing mainly with other contractors. The health and safety plan (see C8024 below) is initiated by the planning supervisor and forms part of tendering documentation. Before actual construction work begins, the plan should be scrutinised by the principal contractor in order to ensure that it is properly adjusted to contractors and site activities. By *Reg 6*, clients must ensure that adequate financial provision is made and adequate time allowed for completion of the project, with the main health and safety costs being assessed and included in tenders, the basis of this assessment being the health and safety plan. By *Reg 14*, planning supervisors must be competent to assess the project and advise the client, who must then set the budget and timescale and finance the project. As companies, individuals or partnerships, they will often be the lead member of the design team (e.g. architect or engineer); sometimes a main contractor may be a planning supervisor, sometimes even a client. But both planning supervisors and principal contractors should be appointed as early as possible during the planning stage of the project.

It is incumbent on clients to specify that contractors comply with the health and safety plan; in turn, contractors should price compliance, with clients requiring that contractors include in tender identifiable sums for the management of health and safety and to deal with specific hazards. For that reason, tenderers should advise clients of any hazards not identified in the plan which appear in their assessments. It is then for the planning supervisor to advise the client on adequacy of tender (and provision for health and safety), who should take this into account when awarding contracts. In this way, contracts should only be awarded to contractors/tenderers prepared to comply with health and safety requirements and standards.

Duties and responsibilities

C8018   Because the United Kingdom construction industry has characteristics which were not recognised by the EU Temporary or Mobile Construction Sites Directive, it was necessary to specify that the 'client' (a term which includes clients' agents and developers) must appoint other principals for the planning and the carrying out of the construction work within the scope of the Directive. These are the 'planning supervisor' and the 'principal contractor'.

The *CDM Regulations* give detailed 'job descriptions' for the various parties involved in the construction contract. It should be noted that the following duties imposed by the Regulations are additional to those imposed by the *Management of Health and Safety at Work Regulations 1992 (MHSWR)* and other similar health and safety legislation.

Clients

C8019   Clients (including clients' agents) [*Reg 4(1)*] must, prior to construction work, and in respect of each project:

(*a*)   appoint

    (i)   a competent planning supervisor [*Reg 6(1)(3)*], and

    (ii)   a competent principal contractor (who must be a contractor) [*Reg 6(1)-(3)*].

Such appointments can be terminated, changed or renewed (where necessary) to ensure that these roles are filled until construction is completed [*Reg 6(5)*]. So long as competent to perform both roles, planning supervisors can also be principal contractors; and clients can be planning supervisors or principal contractors (or both) [*Reg 6(6)*]. However, clients must not appoint planning supervisors, designers and contractors, unless satisfied as to their competence [*Reg 8(1)-(3)*], and that all three have allocated, or will allocate, appropriate resources for the performance of their respective roles [*Reg 9*];

(*b*)   so far as is reasonably practicable, ensure that the construction phase of any project does not begin without preparation of a satisfactory health and safety plan [*Reg 10*];

(*c*)   as soon as is reasonably practicable but before commencement of work, ensure that the planning supervisor is provided with information relevant to the state of the premises on which construction work is to take place [*Reg 11*];

(*d*)   ensure that information in the health and safety file is kept available for inspection by any person, for the purposes of compliance with statutory requirements and prohibitions [*Reg 12(1)*].

Designers

C8020   Designers must:

(1)   advise clients as to their duties; and

(2)   ensure that any design has regard to the need:

    (*a*)   to avoid foreseeable risks to the health and safety of any person involved in construction or cleaning work in or on the structure at any time, or anyone who may be affected by the work of such person (e.g. a member of the public);

    (*b*)   to combat at source risks to the health and safety of any person at work involved in construction, cleaning work or any person who may be affected by such work;

    (*c*)   to give priority to measures for protecting those involved in construction, cleaning and those who may be affected;

(*d*)   to ensure that the design includes adequate information about any aspect of the project or structure of materials which might affect construction or cleaning workers or those who may be affected by their work; and

(*e*)   to co-operate with the planning supervisor (and any other designer preparing a design in connection with the project) for the purposes of compliance with statutory requirements and prohibitions.

[*Reg   13(2)*].

Planning supervisors

C8021   Planning supervisors must:

(*a*)   ensure that the project is notified to the HSE (unless it is reasonably believed that the project is not notifiable (see 'Exclusions' at C8016 above));

(*b*)   ensure that the design of a project includes

(i)   reference to health and safety management, and

(ii)   adequate information regarding structure and materials;

(*c*)   ensure co-operation between designers, for the purposes of compliance with their duties as designers (under *Reg 13*);

(*d*)   be able to give adequate advice to

(i)   any client/contractor regarding competence of personnel/allocation of resources, and

(ii)   any client regarding competence of a contractor and a contractor's allocation of resources as well as the health and safety plan;

(*e*)   ensure preparation of a health and safety file, containing

(i)   information concerning aspects of the project, structure or materials that may affect health and safety, and

(ii)   any other information which, foreseeably, will be necessary to ensure health and safety of persons involved in construction, cleaning and maintenance or demolition work;

(*f*)   ensure that, on completion of the project, the health and safety file is delivered to the client

[*Reg   14*]; and

(*g*)   ensure that the health and safety plan is made available to every contractor before arrangements are made for them to manage or carry out construction work.

[*Reg   15(1), (2)*].

Principal contractors

C8022   Principal contractors must:

(*a*)   take reasonable steps to ensure co-operation between all contractors, for the purposes of compliance with statutory requirements and/or prohibitions;

(*b*)   so far as is reasonably practicable, ensure that every contractor and every employee complies with the health and safety plan;

(c)   take reasonable steps to ensure that only authorised persons are allowed where construction work is carried on;

(d)   ensure that notification particulars (see C8015 above) are displayed prominently so that they can be read by construction personnel; and

(e)   provide the planning supervisor promptly with any of the following information,

    (i)   which is in possession of the principal contractor, or which the latter could ascertain by making reasonable enquiries of a contractor,

    (ii)   which, reasonably, the planning supervisor would include in the health and safety file (in order to comply with his duties (under *Reg 14* above)), and

    (iii)   which is not in possession of the planning supervisor.

[*Reg 16(1)*].

For the purposes of compliance with *Reg 16(1)*, principal contractors can

    (i)   give any necessary directions to any contractor, and

    (ii)   include in the health and safety plan rules for the management of construction work reasonably required for health and safety management; such rules being in writing and brought to the attention of those affected

[*Reg 16(2), (3)*];

(f)   so far as is reasonably practicable, ensure that every contractor is provided with comprehensible information on health and safety risks to that contractor or to employees or other persons under that contractor's control;

(g)   so far as is reasonably practicable, ensure that every contractor who is an employer provides his employees engaged in construction work with:

    (i)   information relating to

      —   health and safety risks,

      —   protective measures,

      —   procedures to be followed in imminent danger and in danger areas, and

      —   persons appointed to implement those procedures, and

    (ii)   health and safety training, both on recruitment and/or exposure to new/increased risks; such training to be repeated periodically

[*Reg 17*];

(h)   ensure that:

    (i)   employees/self-employed personnel are able to discuss, and offer advice on, matters foreseeably affecting their health and safety, and

    (ii)   there are arrangements for the co-ordination of employees' views (or their representatives')

[*Reg 18*].

Contractors

C8023   Contractors must:

(*a*)   co-operate with the principal contractor, so that both can comply with their statutory duties;

(*b*)   so far as is reasonably practicable, provide the principal contractor promptly with any information (including risk assessments for the purposes of the *Management of Health and Safety at Work Regulations 1992*), which might affect the health and safety of construction workers, or those who might be affected by construction work, or which might justify a review of the health and safety plan;

(*c*)   comply with directions given by the principal contractor, for the purposes of compliance by contractors;

(*d*)   comply with rules applicable to them in the health and safety plan;

(*e*)   provide the principal contractor promptly with information relating to deaths, injuries, conditions and dangerous occurrences notifiable under the *Reporting of Injuries, Diseases and Dangerous Occurrences Regulations 1995* (see further ACCIDENT REPORTING);

(*f*)   provide the principal contractor promptly with any information which:

(i)   is in the possession of the contractor, or which he could ascertain by reasonable enquiries, and

(ii)   it is reasonable to suppose the principal contractor would provide to the planning supervisor, for the purposes of inclusion in the health and safety file, which is not in the possession of the planning supervisor or the principal contractor

[*Reg   19(1)*];

(*g*)   not allow any employee to work on construction work, unless provided with:

(i)   the name of the planning supervisor,

(ii)   the name of the principal contractor, and

(iii)   the contents of the health and safety plan relating to work being carried out by the employee.

Self-employed personnel must also be provided with this information [*Reg 19(2)-(4)*].

Health and safety plan

C8024   Before construction work starts, a duty is placed on the 'client' (as defined) to ensure that the appointed planning supervisor prepares a document known as the 'health and safety plan' which is to serve two purposes:

(*a*)   during the pre-construction phase, to bring together the health and safety information obtained from the client and designers;

(*b*)   during the construction phase, to include the principal contractor's health and safety policy and risk assessments.

The health and safety plan will continue to evolve and provide a focus for the co-ordination of health and safety matters as the construction work progresses.

The health and safety plan forms the basis of the health and safety management structure, being part of the tender documents. It should:

(*a*)   indicate (in general terms) the approach to health and safety to be adopted by everyone (as per the *Management of Health and Safety at Work Regulations 1992*);

(*b*)   identify the main health and safety hazards likely to occur to employees, self-employed operatives and the general public – these having been specified earlier by the client and/or designers (e.g. work in compressed air);

(*c*)   specify precautions to be taken; and

(*d*)   require work to be done to recognised technical standards and in accordance with published guidance (which should be specified in the plan).

Before the commencement of work, the planning supervisor should acquaint both principal contractor and contractors with the health and safety plan, so that they can agree to it or to modifications in it, and then draw up tenders.

The planning supervisor

C8025   Planning supervisors should:

—   prepare the health and safety plan;

—   ensure that the plan forms part of the tender documentation;

—   investigate significant differences in tender documents relating to the plan;

—   assess the adequacy of sums specified in tenders vis-à-vis the plan;

—   advise the client on the adequacy of tenders; and

—   review the plan if the basis of the original advice changes.

The principal contractor

C8026   Principal contractors should ensure that the health and safety plan:

—   translates into an intelligible working document for all those involved in the construction phase;

—   incorporates arrangements submitted by individual contractors for the overall management of health and safety; and

—   includes arrangements for compliance with the duties of the principal contractor (see C8022 above);

—   specifies detailed arrangements for monitoring compliance with health and safety law;

—   includes arrangements for assessing competence of subcontractors; and

—   can be modified/updated in the light of the experience and information of contractors.

Health and safety file

C8027   The health and safety file is a permanent record containing information about the particulars and arrangements relating to the design, methods and materials, maintenance and other information relating to the construction. In practice, the 'file' amounts to a manual to alert those who will be responsible for the structure after construction on safety matters which must be managed after handover. The manual should contain appropriate information regarding maintenance, repair, renovation and demolition.

Prosecution – defence and civil liability

Defence

C8028 A defence is provided against prosecution where it can be shown that an employer or a self-employed person made all reasonable enquiries and reasonably believed either that the Regulations did not apply to the work in question or that he had been given the names of the planning supervisor and the principal contractor together with the relevant contents of the health and safety plan [*Reg 19(5)*].

Civil liability

C8029 Generally, breach of the *CDM Regulations* is not actionable, except as regards:

(*a*)   the preparation of the health and safety plan, prior to construction work, under *Reg 10*; or

(*b*)   allowing only authorised personnel onto premises where construction work is going on, under *Reg 16(1)(c)*.

[*Reg 21*].

Construction (Health, Safety and Welfare) Regulations 1996 (SI 1996 No 1592)

C8030 The *Construction (Health, Safety and Welfare) Regulations 1996 (CHSW)* promote the health and safety of everyone carrying out 'construction work' (as defined, and see also C8001 above) but the Regulations do not apply to workplaces on construction sites which are set aside for non-construction purposes. However, the *CHSW Regulations* give protection to other people who may be affected by the construction work.

A 'construction site' is defined in the Regulations as 'any place where the principal work activity being carried out is construction work' [*Reg 2(1)*].

For details of the requirements and standards of protection regarding falls from access equipment [*Reg 6*], see:

Schedule 1: Requirements for guardrails etc;

Schedule 2: Requirements for working platforms;

Schedule 3: Requirements for personal suspension equipment;

Schedule 4: Requirements for means of arresting falls;

Schedule 5: Requirements for ladders.

For details of the requirements for welfare facilities [*Reg 22*] see:

Schedule 6: Welfare facilities.

Training and site inspection by competent persons followed by preparation of a report to be kept on site and available for inspection by HSE inspectors are especially important requirements. In particular, anyone involved in construction work, which requires training, technical knowledge or experience for reduction of risk of injury, must possess such training, knowledge etc. or be under the supervision of a person with such knowledge. In addition, places of work on construction sites must only be used following inspection by competent persons and preparation of a report to the effect that such place is safe (see C8054 below).

These regulations implement Annex IV of the Temporary or Mobile Construction Sites Directive, thereby extending to construction sites the health, safety and welfare requirements imposed on all other workplaces by the *Workplace (Health, Safety and Welfare) Regulations 1992*. The regulations revoke the *Construction Regulations 1961–1966* (with the exception of the *Construction (Lifting Operations) Regulations 1961* – which have been replaced by the *Lifting Operations and Lifting Equipment Regulations 1998 (SI 1998 No 2307)*.

These regulations lay duties principally on employers, self-employed contractors and employees, and, to a lesser extent, on persons in control of construction sites. [*Regs 4, 22, 29(2)*]. All contractors, big or small, are covered. Breach of duty, followed by conviction, will be visited with criminal sanction (normally payment of a fine). There is also strict civil liability where breach of the regulations results in injury or damage (see ENFORCEMENT). Characteristically, 'I find it necessary to make some general observations about the interpretation of regulations of this kind. They are addressed to practical people skilled in the particular trade or industry, and their primary purpose is to prevent accidents by prescribing appropriate precautions. Any failure to take prescribed precautions is a criminal offence. The right to compensation, which arises when an accident is caused by a breach is a secondary matter. The regulations supplement, but in no way supersede the ordinary common law obligations of an employer to care for the safety of his men, and they ought not to be expected to cover every possible kind of danger' (*Gill v Donald Humberstone & Co Ltd [1963] 3 AER 180*, per Lord Reid).

Duties under the regulations

C8031   The following duties are laid on employers (and self-employed persons) in respect of employees involved in construction work and any persons under their control.

Safe place of work

C8032   Except in the case of a person making such place safe [*Reg 5(4)*]:

(*a*)   every place of work must be made and kept safe and free from health risks for any person at work there, so far as is reasonably practicable [*Reg 5(2)*];

(*b*)   so far as is reasonably practicable, suitable and sufficient safe access/egress, to/from, every place of work and any other place provided for use of a person at work, must be provided and properly maintained [*Reg 5(1)*];

(*c*)   so far as is reasonably practicable, suitable and sufficient steps must be taken to deny access to any place not complying with (*a*) and (*b*) above [*Reg 5(3)*]; and

(*d*)   so far as is reasonably practicable, every place of work must have sufficient working space and be so arranged as to be suitable for any person working or likely to work there [*Reg 5(5)*].

(For requirements relating to falls, fall-preventative equipment, scaffolds, personal suspension equipment, working platforms and ladders, see WORK AT HEIGHTS.)

Stability of structures

C8033   The regulations require that:

(*a*)   in order to prevent danger to any person, all practicable steps must be taken to ensure that any new or existing structure which may become unstable through construction work (including excavations) does not accidentally collapse [*Reg 9(1)*];

(*b*)   no part of a structure must be so loaded as to make it unsafe [*Reg 9(2)*]; and

(*c*)   any buttress, temporary support or structure (used to support a permanent structure) must be erected or dismantled under the surveillance of a competent person [*Reg 9(3)*].

Demolition or dismantling

C8034   Suitable and sufficient steps must be taken to ensure that demolition or dismantling of structures is planned and executed so as to prevent, so far as practicable, danger to any person. Planning and execution of demolition must be carried out under the supervision of a competent person [*Reg 10*].

Explosives

C8035   Explosive charges can only be used or fired if suitable and sufficient steps have been taken to ensure that no one is exposed to any risk of injury from the explosion or flying material [*Reg 11*].

Excavations

C8036   The regulations require that:

(*a*)   to prevent danger to any person, all practicable steps must be taken to ensure that new or existing excavations which are temporarily unstable due to the carrying out of construction work (including other excavation work) do not collapse accidentally [*Reg 12(1)*];

(*b*)   so far as is reasonably practicable, suitable and sufficient steps must be taken to prevent any person being buried or trapped by a fall or dislodgement of material. [*Reg 12(2)*]. In particular, as early as practicable in the course of the work, the excavation must be sufficiently supported so as to prevent, so far as reasonably practicable, that fall or dislodgement of material [*Reg 12(3)*]; suitable and sufficient supporting equipment must be provided [*Reg 12(4)*]; and installation, alteration or dismantling must be carried out only under the supervision of a competent person [*Reg 12(5)*];

(*c*)   suitable and sufficient steps must be taken to prevent any person, vehicle, plant and equipment, accumulation of earth or other material, from falling into an excavation [*Reg 12(6)*];

(*d*)   where collapse of an excavation would endanger a person, no material, vehicle or plant and equipment must be placed or moved near any excavation [*Reg 12(7)*]; and

(*e*)   no excavation work must be carried out unless suitable and sufficient steps have been taken to identify and, so far as reasonably practicable, to prevent any risk of injury arising from any underground cable or service [*Reg 12(8)*].

Cofferdams and caissons

C8037   The regulations require that:

(*a*)   every cofferdam or caisson must be:

    (i)   of suitable design and construction,

    (ii)   of suitable and sound material,

    (iii)   of sufficient strength and capacity for the purpose used, and

    (iv)   properly maintained

    [*Reg 13(1)*]; and

(*b*)   construction, installation, alteration or dismantling must be under the supervision of a competent person [*Reg 13(2)*].

Prevention of drowning

C8038   The regulations require that where:

(*a*)   after falling, any person is liable to fall into water (or other liquid) with a risk of drowning, suitable and sufficient steps must be taken to:

    (i)   prevent, so far as is reasonably practicable, such person from falling,

    (ii)   minimise the risk of drowning, and

    (iii)   ensure the provision and maintenance of suitable rescue equipment

    [*Reg 14(1)*]; and

(*b*)   where there are conveyances by water, there must be provision of safe transport to or from a place of work by water [*Reg 14(2)*]. Vessels used for conveyance purposes must be:

    (i)   of suitable construction,

    (ii)   properly maintained,

    (iii)   under the control of a competent person, and

    (iv)   not overcrowded or overloaded

    [*Reg 14(3)*].

Traffic routes

C8039   Pedestrians and vehicles should be able to move safely and without health risks. To that end, traffic routes should be:

(*a*)   suitable for persons and vehicles using them;

(*b*)   sufficient in number;

(*c*)   in suitable positions;

(*d*)   of sufficient size; and

(*e*)   indicated by suitable signs (see WORKPLACES – HEALTH, SAFETY AND WELFARE).

[*Reg 15(1), (2), (6)*].

These requirements are not satisfied unless:

(i)   pedestrians or vehicles can use a traffic route without causing danger to the health or safety of persons near it;

(ii)   any door or gate (intended for use by pedestrians) leading on to a traffic route for vehicles is so separated from that traffic route as to enable pedestrians to see any approaching vehicle or plant from a place of safety;

(iii)   there is sufficient separation between vehicles and pedestrians to ensure safety, or if that is not reasonably practicable that:

(1)   other means are provided for the protection of pedestrians, and

(2)   effective arrangements are made for warning a person liable to be crushed or trapped by a vehicle of the vehicle's approach;

(iv)   a loading bay has at least one exit point for exclusive use of pedestrians; and

(v)   where it is unsafe for pedestrians to use any gate intended primarily for vehicles, one or more doors for pedestrians is provided in the immediate vicinity of such gate (such door(s) being clearly marked and obstruction free).

[*Reg 15(3)*].

Vehicles must not be driven on traffic routes unless, so far as is reasonably practicable, the route is free from obstruction and permits sufficient clearance [*Reg 15(4)*]. Where this is not reasonably practicable, drivers and persons riding on vehicles must be warned of any approaching obstruction or lack of clearance, e.g. by a sign. (For requirements relating to traffic routes generally, see ACCESS, TRAFFIC ROUTES AND VEHICLES.)

Vehicles

C8040   The regulations require:

(*a*)   unintended movement of vehicles (including mobile plant, locomotives and towed vehicles) must be either prevented or controlled [*Reg 17(1)*];

(*b*)   where persons may be endangered by vehicle movement, the person in effective control of the vehicle must warn any person at work of the risk of injury [*Reg 17(2)*];

(*c*)   construction work vehicles, when being driven, operated or towed, must be:

(i)   driven, operated or towed safely, and

(ii)   be so loaded as to be able to be driven, operated or towed safely

[*Reg 17(3)*];

(*d*)   no person must ride or be required or permitted to ride on any construction work vehicle other than in a safe place provided for that purpose [*Reg 17(4)*]. (For civil liability consequences of failure to do so, see ACCESS, TRAFFIC ROUTES AND VEHICLES.);

(*e*)   no person must remain or be required or permitted to remain on a vehicle during the loading or unloading of loose material unless a safe place is provided and maintained [*Reg 17(5)*];

(*f*)   excavating, handling and tipping vehicles must be prevented from:

(i)   falling into an excavation, pit or water, or

       (ii)   overturning the edge of an embankment or earthwork

[*Reg 17(6)*]; and

    (*g*)   in the case of rail vehicles, plant and equipment must be provided for replacing them on their track, or moving them, if derailed [*Reg 17(7)*].

Doors and gates (not forming part of mobile plant and equipment)

C8041   The regulations require that:

    (*a*)   where necessary to prevent risk of injury, any door, gate, hatch (including temporary ones) – must incorporate (or be fitted with) suitable safety devices [*Reg 16(1)*]; and

    (*b*)   compliance with the regulations presupposes that:

       (i)   any sliding door, gate or hatch has a device to prevent it coming off its track during use,

       (ii)   any upward opening door, gate or hatch has a device to prevent it falling back,

       (iii)   any powered door, gate or hatch has suitable and effective features to prevent it trapping persons, and

       (iv)   any powered door, gate or hatch can be operated manually unless it opens automatically if the power fails

[*Reg 16(2)*].

Prevention of fire risks

C8042   The regulations require that:

    (*a*)   so far as reasonably practicable, suitable and sufficient steps must be taken to prevent risk of injury from:

       (i)   fire or explosion,

       (ii)   flooding, or

       (iii)   substances liable to cause asphyxiation

[*Reg 18*];

    (*b*)   if a work activity gives rise to risk of fire, such activity must not be carried out unless the worker is suitably instructed to prevent risk [*Reg 21(6)*];

    (*c*)   there must also be provision of:

       (i)   suitable and sufficient fire-fighting equipment, suitably located (e.g. in emergency routes),

       (ii)   suitable and sufficient fire detectors and alarm systems, suitably located (e.g. in emergency routes);

       (iii)   training of all persons on site in the correct use of appliances

[*Reg 21(5)*];

    (*d*)   fire-fighting equipment, detectors and alarm systems must be:

       (i)   properly maintained, examined and tested [*Reg 21(3)*],

       (ii)   indicated by suitable signs [*Reg 21(7)*], and

(iii)   easily accessible, if not designed to come into use automatically [*Reg 21(4)*].

Emergency routes and exits

C8043   The regulations require:

(*a*)   a sufficient number of suitable emergency routes and exits, indicated by suitable signs (see WORKPLACES – HEALTH, SAFETY AND WELFARE), must be provided to enable any person to reach a place of safety quickly in the event of danger. [*Reg 19(1)*]. This should lead, as directly as possible, to an identified safe area [*Reg 19(2)*]; and

(*b*)   emergency routes (and traffic routes or doors thereto) must be kept clear and obstruction free and, if necessary, be provided with emergency lighting [*Reg 19(3)*].

Emergency procedures

C8044   There must be prepared and implemented suitable and sufficient arrangements (to be tested by being put into effect at regular intervals) for dealing with any foreseeable emergency, including procedures for site evacuation. Moreover, persons likely to be affected must be acquainted with such arrangements. [*Reg 20(1), (3)*].

Welfare facilities

C8045   Duties in connection with the provision of welfare facilities on construction sites are laid principally on those in control of sites (i.e. occupiers, see generally C8129 below, and OCCUPIERS' LIABILITY). The fact that occupation (or control) of construction sites can be, and frequently is, shared between the building owner and contractor(s) means that both have obligations to see that welfare facilities are provided. In practice, actual provision would be made by the contractor(s). Hence, although overall duties are imposed on occupiers, employers (and self-employed persons) must ensure that workers under their control are provided with welfare facilities.

Facilities to be provided are:

(*a*)   suitable and sufficient sanitary conveniences at readily accessible places [*Reg 22(3)*]. So far as is reasonably practicable, such conveniences must be:

(i)   adequately ventilated and lit,

(ii)   kept in a clean and orderly condition, with

(iii)   separate rooms containing sanitary conveniences provided for men and women (except where each convenience is in a separate room, the door of which can be secured from the inside)

[*Sch 6*];

(*b*)   suitable and sufficient washing facilities (including, where necessary, showers) at readily accessible places. So far as is reasonably practicable, washing facilities must:

(i)   be provided in the immediate vicinity of sanitary conveniences (except showers), and in the vicinity of changing rooms (whether or not provided elsewhere),

(ii)   include a supply of clean hot and cold (or warm) water (ideally running water), and soap, towels etc.

Rooms containing washing facilities must be:

(iii)   sufficiently ventilated and lit,

(iv)   kept in a clean and orderly condition, and

(v)   must have separate washing facilities provided for men and women (except for washing hands, forearms and face only) unless provided in a room the door of which can be secured from the inside and the facilities in each such room are intended for use by only one person at a time

[*Sch 6*];

(c)   an adequate supply of wholesome drinking water at readily accessible places [*Reg 22(5)*]. So far as is reasonably practicable, every supply of drinking water must:

(i)   be conspicuously marked, and

(ii)   be provided with a sufficient number of suitable cups or other drinking vessels, unless the supply is from a jet

[*Sch 6*];

(d)   suitable and sufficient accommodation for:

(i)   accommodating the clothing of any person at work which is not worn during working hours, and

(ii)   special clothing worn by a person at work but which is not taken home

[*Reg 22(6)*].

So far as is reasonably practicable, clothing accommodation should include facilities for drying clothing [*Sch 6*];

(e)   suitable and sufficient accommodation for changing clothing where:

(i)   a person has to wear special clothing at work, and

(ii)   that person cannot be expected to change elsewhere

[*Reg 22(7)*].

Where necessary, facilities for changing clothing must be separate facilities for men and women [*Sch 6*];

(f)   suitable and sufficient rest facilities at readily accessible places [*Reg 22(8)*]. So far as reasonably practicable, rest facilities must include:

(i)   suitable arrangements to protect non-smokers from discomfort caused by tobacco smoke, and where necessary

(ii)   facilities for pregnant women or nursing mothers

[*Sch 6*].

(For welfare facilities generally, see WORKPLACES – HEALTH, SAFETY AND WELFARE.)

Fresh air

C8046   Every workplace on a construction site must, so far as reasonably practicable, have a supply of fresh or purified air so as to ensure safety and absence of health risks; and plant used for supply purposes must, where necessary, contain effective devices for giving visible or audible warning of failure. [*Reg 23*].

(For ventilation requirements generally, see VENTILATION.)

Temperature

C8047   During working hours, so far as reasonably practicable, temperature at any indoor place of work must be reasonable, having regard to the purpose of the workplace. [*Reg 24(1)*].

(For temperature requirements generally, see WORKPLACES – HEALTH, SAFETY AND WELFARE.)

Weather protection

C8048   Every place of work outdoors must, where necessary, be so arranged, so far as is reasonably practicable, as to provide protection from adverse weather. [*Reg 24(2)*].

Lighting

C8049   Every place of work and traffic route must have suitable and sufficient lighting. In the case of artificial lighting where there would be a risk to a person's health or safety from failure of primary artificial lighting, suitable and sufficient secondary lighting must be provided. [*Reg 25(1), (3)*].

(For lighting requirements generally see LIGHTING.)

Plant and equipment

C8050   The regulations require that, so far as is reasonably practicable, all plant and equipment used for construction work must be safe and without health risks, and be:

(*a*)   of good construction,

(*b*)   of suitable and sound materials,

(*c*)   of sufficient strength and suitability for its intended purpose, and

(*d*)   so used and maintained that it remains safe and without health risks

[*Reg 27*].

Good order

C8051   So far as reasonably practicable, every part of a construction site must be kept in good order and every place of work in a reasonable state of cleanliness. Perimeters should be identified by suitable signs (see WORKPLACES – HEALTH, SAFETY AND WELFARE), and sites arranged so that their extent is readily identifiable. Moreover, no timber material with projecting nails must be used in work where nails might be dangerous or allowed to remain in a place where nails could be a source of danger. [*Reg 26*].

Training

C8052   Any person who carries out construction work where training, technical knowledge or experience is necessary to reduce risk of injury, must either:

(*a*)   possess such training, knowledge or experience, or (*b*)   be under the supervision of a person who so does.

[*Reg 28*].

Inspection

C8053   The regulations require that in the case of the following places of work:

(*a*)   working platforms or personal suspension equipment,

(*b*)   excavations, and

(*c*)   cofferdams or caissons

work can only be carried out if such place has been inspected by a competent person as follows.

(1)   Working platforms and personal suspension equipment must be inspected by a competent person:

    (i)   before being taken into use for the first time,

    (ii)   after substantial addition, dismantling or other alteration,

    (iii)   after any event likely to have affected their strength or stability, and

    (iv)   at regular intervals not exceeding 7 days following the last inspection.

(2)   Excavations must be inspected by a competent person:

    (i)   before a person carries out work at the start of every shift,

    (ii)   after any event likely to have affected the strength or stability of the excavation, and

    (iii)   after an accidental fall of rock/earth.

(3)   Cofferdams and caissons should be inspected by a competent person:

    (i)   before the start of every shift, and

    (ii)   after any event likely to have affected their strength or stability.

[*Reg 29(1), Sch 7*].

Where, following inspection, a place of work or plant and materials is not safe, this must be communicated to those in control and such place of work must not be used until defects have been remedied. [*Reg 29(3), (4)*].

In addition to the general duty to inspect places of work (above), in the case of scaffolds, excavations, cofferdams and caissons forming part of a place of work, employers must ensure that they are stable and of sound construction and that the requisite safeguards are in place before workers use such place of work for the first time. [*Reg 29(2)*].

Reports

C8054   Following inspection, a report must be prepared before the end of the working period in which the inspection was completed, and presented within 24 hours to the person on whose behalf it was carried out. [*Reg 30(1), (2)*]. The report (or a copy) must be kept at the site of such place of work and, after work there is completed, retained at the office of the person on whose behalf the inspection was made, for a minimum of three months. Such a report is available for inspection by an HSE inspector and, should he so require, extracts or copies must be sent to the inspector. [*Reg 30(3), (4)*].

Reports are not necessary in the following cases:

(i)   working platforms where persons are not liable to fall more than 2 metres; and

(ii) mobile towers (unless remaining erect for 7 days or more).

[*Reg 30(5), (6)*].

Enforcement

C8055   Penalties and defences in connection with the *Construction (Health, Safety and Welfare) Regulations 1996* are as for *HSWA 1974* (see ENFORCEMENT).

Civil liability for breach of the regulations

C8056   Breach of these regulations (and the *Work in Compressed Air Regulations 1996* and the *Construction (Head Protection) Regulations 1989* – see C8080 and C8096 below), resulting in injury to an employee, will give rise to civil liability, since safety regulations, even if silent regarding civil liability, are actionable (see further INTRODUCTION).

Confined spaces and harmful atmospheres

C8057   The *Confined Spaces Regulations 1997 (SI 1997 No 1713)* apply in all premises and work situations in Great Britain subject to the *Health and Safety at Work etc Act 1974*, with the exception of diving operations and below ground in a mine.

The Regulations are supported by an Approved Code of Practice and guidance – *Safe work in confined spaces (L101)* – providing practical guidance with respect to the requirements of:

—   the *Confined Spaces Regulations 1997 (SI 1997 No 1713)* and *sections 2-4, 6 and 7 of the Health and Safety at Work etc Act 1974*;

—   the *Management of Health and Safety at Work Regulations 1992 (SI 1992 No 2051)*;

—   the *Control of Substances Hazardous to Health Regulations 1999 (SI 1999 No 437)*.

   Note: the *COSHH Regulations* apply to all substances hazardous to health (other than lead or asbestos), such as toxic fume and injurious dust. The *Ionising Radiations Regulations 1985* may apply where radon gas can accumulate in confined spaces, such as sewers, and where industrial radiography is used to look at, for example, the integrity of welds in vessels.

—   the *Personal Protective Equipment at Work Regulations 1992 (SI 1992 No 2966)*;

—   the *Provision and Use of Work Equipment Regulations 1998 (SI 1998 No 2306)*.

Entry into confined spaces

C8058   A 'confined space' has two defining features. Firstly, it is a place which is substantially (though not always entirely) enclosed and, secondly, there will be a reasonably foreseeable risk of serious injury from hazardous substances or conditions within the space or nearby. [*Reg 1(2)*].

Examples:

— ducts, vessels, culverts, tunnels, boreholes, bored piles, manholes, shafts, excavations, sumps, inspection pits, cofferdams, freight containers, building voids, some enclosed rooms (particularly plant rooms) and compartments within them, including some cellars, enclosures for the purpose of asbestos removal, and interiors of machines, plant or vehicles.

Some confined spaces are fairly easy to identify, for example closed tanks, vessels and sewers. Others are less obvious but may be equally dangerous, for example open-topped tanks and vats, closed and unventilated or inadequately ventilated rooms and silos, or constructions that become confined spaces during their manufacture. A confined space may not necessarily be enclosed on all sides.

Respiratory protective equipment

C8059   Where respiratory protective equipment (RPE) is provided or used in connection with confined space entry or for emergency or rescue, it should be suitable for the purpose for which it is intended, that is, correctly selected and matched both to the job and the wearer.

Where the intention is to provide emergency breathing apparatus to ensure safe egress or escape, or for self-rescue in case of emergency, the type commonly called an 'escape breathing apparatus' or 'self-rescuer' (escape set) may be suitable. These types are intended to allow time for the user to exit the hazard area. They are generally carried by the user or stationed inside the confined space, but are not used until needed. This equipment usually has a breathable supply of only short duration and provides limited protection to allow the user to move to a place of safety or refuge. This type of equipment is not suitable for normal work.

In some circumstances entry without the continuous wearing of breathing apparatus may be possible. Several conditions must be satisfied to allow such work including:

— a risk assessment must be done and a safe system of work in place including all required controls, and continuous ventilation;

— any airborne contamination must be of a generally non-toxic nature, or present in very low concentrations well below the relevant occupational exposure limits.

Duties and responsibilities

C8060   There have been several court cases involving accidents and fatalities in sewers and other confined spaces (see for instance *Baker v Hopkins & Son [1959] AER 225*). More recently, in 1998 at Cardiff Crown Court, a record fine was imposed on Neath Port Talbot Council following the deaths of two employees (*R v Neath Port Talbot Council*). The judge, John Prosser, said that the accident should never have happened; the dangers of toxic gases associated with sewer work were well known. The case demonstrated the need for employers to carry out, with strict care, the undertaking of such work and that the difficulty and danger must not be underestimated.

Duties to comply with the *Confined Spaces Regulations* are placed on:

— employers in respect of work carried out by their own employees and work carried out by any other person (for example, contractors) in so far as that work is to any extent under the employers' control [*Reg 3(1)*]; and

— the self-employed in respect of their own work and work carried out by any other person in so far as that work is to any extent under the control of the self-employed [*Reg 3(2)*].

Duty to prevent entry

C8061   The principal duty imposed on employers is to prevent entering or working inside a confined space where it is reasonably practicable to undertake the work by other means [*Reg 4*].

The duty extends to others who are to any extent within the employers' control (such as contractors) and in many cases it will be necessary to modify working practices following a risk assessment of each requirement to enter a confined space.

Examples:

— modifying the confined space itself to avoid the need for entry, or to enable the work to be undertaken from outside;

— testing the atmosphere or sampling the contents of confined spaces from outside using appropriate long tools and probes.

Another case where it may be necessary to modify working practices is where employers or the self-employed have duties in relation to people at work who are not their employees – then the duty is to do what is 'reasonably practicable' in the circumstances. In many cases, the employer or self-employed will need to liaise and co-operate with other employers to agree the respective responsibilities in terms of the regulations and duties. It is also necessary to take all reasonably practicable steps to engage competent contractors.

Associated duties and responsibilities

C8062   In addition to the requirements of the *Health and Safety at Work etc. Act 1974*, other legislation imposes duties with regard to the design, construction and operation within confined spaces.

Some duties extend to erectors and installers of equipment and would include situations where plant and equipment unavoidably involved confined spaces. Where it is not possible to eliminate a confined space completely, procedures must be drawn up to minimise the need to enter such spaces both during normal use or working, and for cleaning and maintenance.

Regarding the type of PPE to be provided, this will depend on the identified hazards and the type of confined space. It may be necessary, for example, to include safety lines and harnesses, and suitable breathing apparatus.

Examples:

— the wearing of some respiratory protective equipment and personal protective equipment can contribute to heat stress;

— footwear and clothing may require insulating properties, e.g. to prevent softening of plastics that could lead to distortion of components such as visors, air hoses and crimped connections.

Risk assessment – the development of a safe system of work

C8063   The priority when carrying out a confined space risk assessment is to identify the measures needed so that entry into the confined space can be avoided. If it is not reasonably practicable to prevent work in a confined space the employer (or the self-employed) must assess the risks connected with persons entering or working in the space and also to others who could be affected by the work. The assessor(s) must understand the risks involved, be experienced and familiar with the relevant processes, plant and equipment and be competent to devise a safe system of working.

If, in the light of the risks identified, it cannot be considered reasonably practicable to carry out the work without entering the confined space, then it will be necessary to secure a safe system for working. The precautions required to create a safe system of work will depend on the nature of the confined space and the hazards identified during the risk assessment.

Use of a permit-to-work procedure

C8064   Not all work involving confined spaces requires the use of a permit-to-work system. For example, it is unlikely that a system would be needed where:

— the assessed risks are low and can be controlled easily; and

— the system of work is very simple; and

— it is known that other work activities being carried out cannot affect safe working in the confined space.

Although there is no set format for a permit system, it is often appropriate to include certain information relevant to all confined space working. In all cases, it is essential that a system is developed which ensures that:

(*a*)   the people working in the confined space are aware of the hazards involved and the identity, nature and extent of the work to be carried out;

(*b*)   there is a formal and methodological system of checks undertaken by competent people before the confined space is entered and which confirms that a safe system of work is in place;

(*c*)   other people and their activities are not affected by the work or conditions in the confined space.

Isolation requirements, that is, the need to isolate the confined space to prevent dangers arising from outside, should also be included in the permit system. Permits are particularly appropriate if essential supplies and emergency services such as sprinkler systems, communications etc., are to be disconnected. The most effective isolation technique is to disconnect the confined space completely by removing a section of pipe or duct and fitting blanks. Other methods include the use of spectacle blinds and lockable valves.

Workforce involvement

C8065   Employees and their representatives should be consulted when assessing the risks connected with entering or working in a confined space. Particular attention is required where the work circumstances change frequently such as at construction sites or steel fabrications.

Model or generic risk assessments

C8066   Where a number of confined spaces (for example, sewers or manholes) are broadly the same in terms of the conditions and the activities being carried out, model risk assessments are permitted provided that the risks and measures to deal with them are the same. Any differences in particular cases which would alter the conclusions of the model risk assessment must be identified.

Planning an entry into a confined space

C8067   To satisfy the safe system requirement of *Reg 4*, it is necessary to plan the work thoroughly and to organise various facilities and arrangements. For a large confined space and multiple entries, a logging or tally system may be necessary in order to check everyone in and out and to control duration of entry.

Competence for confined space working

C8068   The competent person carrying out the risk assessment for work in confined spaces will need to consider the suitability of individuals in view of the particular work to be done.

Examples:

—   suitable build of individuals for exceptional constraints in the physical layout of the space (this may be necessary to protect both the individual and others who could be affected by the work to be done);

—   medical fitness concerning claustrophobia or the wearing of breathing apparatus.

Procedures and written instructions

C8069   To be effective a safe system of work needs to be in writing – in the form of written instructions setting out the work to be done and the precautions to be taken. Each procedure should contain all appropriate precautions to be taken and in the correct sequence.

In particular, procedures for confined space working should include instructions and guidance for:

(*a*)   *First aid* — the availability of appropriate first aid equipment for emergencies until professional medical help arrives.

(*b*)   *First aiders* — the strategic positioning of trained personnel to deal with foreseeable injuries.

(*c*)   *Limiting working time* — for example, when respiratory protective equipment is used, or when the work is to be carried out under extreme conditions of temperature and humidity.

(*d*)   *Communications* — that is, the system of adequate arrangements to enable efficient communication between those working inside the confined space and others to summon help in case of emergency.

(*e*)   *Engine driven equipment* — that is, the rules regarding the siting of such equipment which should be well away from the working area and downwind of any ventilator intakes.

(*f*)   *Water surges* — especially the anticipation that sewers can be affected over long distances by water surges, for example following sudden heavy rainfall upstream of where the work is being carried out.

(*g*)   *Toxic gas, fume or vapour* — procedures to ensure that work can be undertaken safely to include the availability of additional facilities and arrangements where residues may be trapped in sludge, scale or other deposits, brickwork, or behind loose linings, in liquid traps, joints in vessels, in pipe bends, or in other places where removal is difficult.

(h)   *Testing/monitoring the atmosphere* — procedures for the regular testing for hazardous gas, fume or vapour or to check the concentration of oxygen before entry or re-entry into the confined space.

(j)   *Gas purging* — the availability of suitable equipment to purge the gas or vapour from the confined space.

(k)   *Ventilation requirements* — the provision of suitable ventilation equipment to replace oxygen levels in the space, and to dilute and remove gas, fume or vapour produced by the work.

(l)   *Lighting* — procedures to ensure that the confined space is well lit by lighting equipment, including emergency lighting, which must be suitable for use in flammable or potentially explosive atmospheres.

(Generally all lighting to be used in confined spaces should be protected against knocks – for example, by a wire cage – and be waterproof. Where water is present in the space, suitable plug/socket connectors capable of withstanding wet or damp conditions should be used and protected by residual current devices (RCDs) suitable for protection against electric shock. The position of lighting may also be important, for example to give ample clearance for work or rescue to be carried out unobstructed.)

Fire prevention and protection procedures

C8070   The presence of flammable substances and oxygen enrichment in a confined space creates a serious hazard to workers inside the space. There is also a risk of explosion from the ignition of airborne flammable contaminants. In addition, a fire or explosion can be caused by leaks from adjoining plant or processes and the use of unsuitable equipment.

Note: in the case of *R v Associated Octel Co Ltd [1996] 4 AER 846* (see C8134 below) a contractor was badly burned when an explosion occurred in the confined space (a chemical storage tank) he was working in. The principal cause of the accident was unsuitable lighting which broke and ignited some acetone solvent contained in an old emulsion bucket.

There are many fire precautions necessary for safe working in confined spaces; some of the more important of these are outlined below:

(a)   *Fire prevention measures* — procedures to ensure that no flammable or combustible materials are stored in confined spaces that have not been specifically created or allocated for that purpose. In any event, the quantity of the material should be kept to a minimum and stored in suitable fire-resistant containers.

(b)   *Fire protection and fire-fighting equipment* — procedures to ensure the availability of appropriate fire-fighting equipment where the risk of fire has been identified. In some situations, a sprinkler system may be appropriate.

(c)   *Smoking* — procedures to ensure the prohibition of all smoking within and around all confined spaces.

(d)   *Static electricity* — procedures to ensure that the build-up of static in a confined space is minimised. It may be necessary to obtain specialist advice regarding insulating characteristics (for example, most plastics), steam or water jetting equipment, clothing containing cotton or wool, flowing liquids or solids such as sand.

Supervision and training

C8071   It is likely that the risk assessment will identify a level of risk requiring the appointment of a competent person to supervise the work and ensure that the precautions are adhered to. Competence for safe working in confined spaces requires adequate training – in addition, experience in the particular work involved is essential. Training standards must be appropriate to the task, and to the individuals' roles and responsibilities as indicated during the risk assessment.

Emergency arrangements and procedures

C8072   The arrangements for the rescue of persons in the event of an emergency must be suitable and sufficient and, where appropriate, include rescue and resuscitation equipment. The arrangements should be in place before any person enters or works in a confined space [*Reg 5*].

The arrangements must cover any situation requiring the recovery of a person from a confined space, for example incapacitation following a fall.

Size of openings to enable rescue from confined spaces

C8073   Experience has shown that the minimum size of an opening to allow access with full rescue facilities including self-contained breathing apparatus is 575 mm diameter. This size should normally be used for new plant, although the openings for some confined spaces may need to be larger depending on the circumstances, for example to take account of a fully equipped employee, or the nature of the opening.

Public emergency services

C8074   In some circumstances, for example where there are prolonged operations in confined spaces and the risks justify it, there may be advantage in prior notification to the local emergency services before the work is undertaken. In all cases, however, arrangements must be in place for the rapid notification of the emergency services should an accident occur. On arrival, the emergency services should be given all known information about the conditions and risks of entering and/or leaving the confined space before a rescue is attempted.

Training for emergencies and rescue

C8075   To be suitable and sufficient the arrangements for training site personnel for rescue and resuscitation should include consideration of:

—   rescue and resuscitation equipment;

—   raising the alarm and rescue;

—   safeguarding the rescuers;

—   fire safety;

—   control of plant;

—   first aid.

Regular refresher training in the emergency procedures is essential and practice drills including emergency rescues will help to check that the size of openings and entry procedures are satisfactory. The risk assessment may indicate that at least one person, dedicated to the rescue role, should be stationed outside the confined space to keep those inside in constant direct visual sight.

All members of rescue parties should be trained in the operation of appropriate fire extinguishers which should be strategically located at the confined space. In some situations, a sprinkler system may be appropriate. In all cases, in the event of a fire the local fire service should be called in case the fire cannot be contained or extinguished by first-aid measures.

The training syllabus should include the following, where appropriate:

— the likely causes of an emergency;

— rescue techniques and the use of rescue equipment, for example breathing apparatus, lifelines, and where necessary a knowledge of its construction and how it works;

— the checking procedures to be followed when donning and using breathing apparatus;

— the checking of correct functioning and/or testing of emergency equipment (for immediate use and to enable specific periodic maintenance checks);

— identifying defects and dealing with malfunctions and failures of equipment during use;

— works, site or other local emergency procedures including the initiation of an emergency response;

— instruction on how to shut down relevant plant as appropriate (this knowledge would be required by anyone likely to perform a rescue);

— resuscitation procedures and, where appropriate, the correct use of relevant ancillary equipment and any resuscitation equipment provided (if intended to be operated by those receiving emergency rescue training);

— emergency first aid and the use of the first aid equipment provided;

— liaison with local emergency services in the event of an incident, providing relevant information about conditions and risks, and providing appropriate space and facilities to enable the emergency services to carry out their tasks.

Rescue equipment

C8076   When safety harness and lines are provided, it is essential that proper facilities to secure the free end of the line are available. In most cases the line should be secured outside the entry to the confined space. Lifting equipment may be necessary and the harness should be of suitable construction, and made of suitable material to recognised standards capable of withstanding both the strain likely to be imposed, and attack from chemicals.

Maintenance of safety and rescue equipment

C8077   All equipment provided or intended to be used for the purposes of securing the health and safety of people in connection with confined space entry or for emergency or rescue, should be maintained in an efficient state, in efficient working order and in good repair. This should include periodic examination and testing as necessary. Some types of equipment, for example breathing apparatus, should be inspected each time before use.

Atmospheric monitoring equipment – and special ventilating or other equipment provided or used in connection with confined space entry – needs to be properly maintained by competent persons. It should be examined thoroughly, and where necessary calibrated and checked at intervals in accordance with recommendations accompanying the equipment or, if these are not specified, at such intervals determined from the risk assessment.

Records of the examination and tests of equipment should normally be kept for at least five years. The records may be in any suitable format and may consist of a suitable summary of the reports. Records need to be kept readily available for inspection by the employees, their representatives, or by inspectors appointed by the relevant enforcing authority or by employment medical advisers.

Equipment for use in explosive atmospheres

C8078   When selecting equipment for use in confined spaces where an explosive atmosphere may be present, the requirements of the EU-originated Regulations – *Equipment and Protective Systems Intended for Use in Potentially Explosive Atmospheres Regulations (SI 1996 No 192)* – must be complied with. These Regulations apply to 'equipment' and 'protective systems' intended for use in potentially explosive atmospheres. Some of the terms used in the Regulations are defined below:

—   *equipment* means machines, apparatus, fixed or mobile devices, control components and instrumentation thereof and detection or prevention systems which, separately or jointly, are intended for the generation, transfer, storage, measurement, control and conversion of energy or the processing of material and which are capable of causing an explosion through their own potential sources of ignition;

—   *protective systems* means design units which are intended to halt incipient explosions immediately and/or to limit the effective range of explosion flames and explosion pressures; protective systems may be integrated into equipment or separately placed on the market for use as autonomous systems;

—   *devices* means safety devices, controlling devices and regulating devices intended for use outside potentially explosive atmospheres but required for or contributing to the safe functioning of equipment and protective systems with respect to the risks of explosion;

—   *explosive atmosphere* means the mixture with air, under atmospheric conditions, of flammable substances in the form of gases, vapours, mists or dusts in which, after ignition has occurred, combustion spreads to the entire unburned mixture.

Selection and use of equipment

C8079   All equipment must bear the approved CE mark properly fixed in accordance with the requirements of the 1996 Regulations.

Any equipment provided for use in a confined space needs to be suitable for the purpose. Where there is a risk of a flammable gas seeping into a confined space, which could be ignited by electrical sources (for example a portable hand lamp), specially protected electrical equipment must be used.

To be suitable the equipment should be selected on the basis of its intended use – proper earthing is essential to prevent static charge build-up; mechanical equipment may need to be secured against free rotation, as people may tread or lean on it.

Work in compressed air on construction sites – Work in Compressed Air Regulations 1996 (SI 1996 No 1656)

C8080   Replacing the *Work in Compressed Air Special Regulations 1958*, the *Work in Compressed Air Regulations 1996*, which came into effect on 16 September 1996, reflect more modern decompression criteria, being more concerned with the long-term effects of rapid return to atmospheric pressure than the short-term effects which were addressed by earlier regulations. The new regulations require principal contractors to appoint competent compressed air contractors, and the compressed air contractors to appoint contract medical advisers. In addition, greater provision is required in connection with fire prevention and protection measures (including, in particular, emergency means of escape and rescue). Duties are laid on principal contractors, employers (including the self-employed – tunnellers to whom these regulations are substantially addressed are generally self-employed), and employees.

Principal contractor's duties

C8081   The principal contractor must appoint a compressed air contractor in respect of work in compressed air, who must be competent. A compressed air contractor may be the principal contractor himself, if competent. [*Reg 5(1), (2)*].

Compressed air contractor's duties – notification

C8082   The regulations require that:

(*a*)   the compressed air contractor must not allow work in compressed air to be carried out unless written notice has been forwarded to the HSE at least 14 days before commencement of work. Where this is not practicable, owing to an emergency, notice must be given as soon as practicable after the necessity for such work becomes known to the compressed air contractor, and, anyway, before work commences. [*Reg 6(1), (2)*];

(*b*)   no person must work in compressed air unless written notice is forwarded to:

(i)   the nearest suitably equipped hospital,

(ii)   the local ambulance service,

(iii)   the local fire service, and

(iv)   other establishments in the vicinity with an operable medical lock.

[*Reg 6(3), (4)*];

(*c*)   notification should be in writing and contain the following information:

(i)   the fact that work in compressed air is being undertaken,

(ii)   the location of the site,

(iii)   date of commencement and anticipated completion of work,

(iv)   name of compressed air contractor and a 24 hour contact telephone number,

(v)   name, address and telephone number of the contract medical adviser,

(vi)   intended pressure at which the work is to be undertaken,

(vii)   anticipated pattern of work (e.g. shifts), and

(viii)   number of workers likely to be in each shift

[*Reg 6(4), Sch 1*].

Competent persons

C8083   The compressed air contractor must ensure that no person works in (or leaves) compressed air, except in accordance with a system of work which, so far as is reasonably practicable, is safe and without health risks. [*Reg 7(1)*]. To this end, he must ensure that a sufficient number of 'competent persons' are immediately available on site to supervise execution of work in compressed air at all times and for up to 24 hours when work is being undertaken at or above a pressure of 0.7 bar. [*Reg 7(2)*].

Plant and equipment

C8084   The compressed air contractor must ensure that all plant and equipment is:

(*a*)   of a proper design and construction and of sufficient capacity;

(*b*)   safe and without health risks and safely maintained; and

(*c*)   where such plant and equipment is used for the purpose of containing air at a pressure greater than 0.15 bar, it is

(i)   examined and tested by a competent person and any faults rectified prior to use, and

(ii)   re-examined and re-tested after modification or alteration.

[*Reg 8*].

Compression and decompression procedures

C8085   The compressed air contractor must ensure that:

(*a*)   compression or decompression is only carried out as per procedures approved by the HSE;

(*b*)   no worker is subjected to a pressure greater than 3.5 bar (except in emergencies);

(*c*)   no worker is subjected to 'decanting' (i.e. rapid decompression in an airlock to atmospheric pressure followed promptly by rapid compression in an alternative airlock and subsequent decompression to atmospheric pressure – except in an emergency); and

(*d*)   an adequate record is made of exposure in respect of times and pressures at which work in compressed air is carried out, and kept for a minimum of 40 years (including individual exposure records). Such records must be made available to the worker himself and his employer, the latter being required to keep the record for at least 40 years.

[*Reg 11*].

Provision and maintenance of adequate medical facilities

C8086   The compressed air contractor must ensure provision and maintenance of adequate medical facilities (e.g. medical lock, recompression therapy) for the treatment of people working in compressed air and those who have worked in compressed air in the previous 24 hours. Where work is carried out at a pressure greater than 0.7 bar, facilities should include a medical lock; and where work is carried out at a pressure greater than 1.0 bar, a medical lock attendant should be present. [*Reg 12*].

Emergencies

C8087   The compressed air contractor must ensure that no work in compressed air takes place in the absence of suitable and sufficient arrangements in the event of emergencies as follows:

(*a*)   provision and maintenance of a sufficient number of suitable means of access;

(*b*)   preparation of a suitable rescue plan which can be put into effect immediately (including the provision and maintenance of plant and equipment necessary to put the rescue plan into operation);

(*c*)   provision and maintenance of suitable lighting;

(*d*)   provision and maintenance of suitable means of raising the alarm; and

(*e*)   in cases where an airlock is required, maintenance of the airlock, so that it is fit to receive persons in the event of emergency (with particular regard to air supply and temperature of the airlock).

[*Reg 13*].

Fire precautions

C8088   The compressed air contractor must ensure provision of suitable and sufficient means for fighting fire and that any airlock or working chamber is maintained and operated so as to minimise the risk of fire, and must ensure the enforcement of the prohibition against smoking. [*Reg 14*].

Information, instruction and training

C8089   The compressed air contractor must ensure provision of adequate information, instruction and training to employees, including, particularly, information relating to the risks arising from the work and the precautions to be observed. [*Reg 15*].

Fitness for work

C8090   The compressed air contractor must ensure that no one works in compressed air where he has reason to believe that the worker is subject to a medical or physical condition likely to make him unfit or unsuitable for such work. [*Reg 16*].

Prohibition against alcohol and drugs

C8091   The compressed air contractor must prohibit anyone from working in compressed air where he believes such worker to be under the influence of drink and/or drugs. [*Reg 17*].

Employees' duties

C8092   Employees, including the self-employed, must:

(*a*)   when required to do so, and at the cost of the employer, submit to medical surveillance procedures during working hours [*Reg 10(6)*];

(*b*)   avoid smoking or carrying smoking materials [*Reg 14(2)*];

(*c*)   avoid consumption of alcohol or drugs [*Reg 17(2)*]; and

(*d*)   wear a badge or label for 24 hours after leaving work in compressed air [*Reg 19(2)*].

Contract medical adviser

C8093   Owing to the potentially serious dangers arising from pressure itself, or the construction work being done, appointment of a contract medical adviser is essential. Ideally, such person would be a doctor appointed by the HSE, who can carry out statutory medical examinations on compressed air workers on site. His principal role is to actively monitor incidence of decompression illness during work. In the event of decompression illness arising, the contract medical adviser should advise the medical lock attendant regarding appropriate treatment. Both the contract medical adviser and medical lock attendant are responsible for collation and maintenance of exposure records and completion of the worker's health and exposure record, and, on completion of the contract, assist the compressed air contractor in the preservation of formal health and exposure records for the statutory 40-year period.

Competent persons

C8094   The phrase 'competent persons' can refer to:

(*a*)   the engineer in charge;

(*b*)   the compressor attendants;

(*c*)   the lock attendants;

(*d*)   the medical lock attendants (for work in compressed air over 1.0 bar); and

(*e*)   the contract medical adviser.

Enforcement

C8095   In any proceedings for an offence consisting of a contravention of *Reg 14(3)* or *17(3)* (compressed air contractor's duty to ensure compliance with prohibitions against smoking, alcohol or drugs), it is a defence for any person to prove that he took all reasonable precautions and exercised all due diligence to avoid the commission of the offence. [*Reg 20*].

Construction (Head Protection) Regulations 1989 (SI 1989 No 2209)

C8096   Head injuries account for nearly one-third of all construction fatalities, but fell significantly after the introduction of the *Construction (Head Protection) Regulations 1989 (SI 1989 No 2209)*. These regulations specify requirements for head protection during construction work, including offshore operations, but not diving operations at work. They place duties on employers, persons in control of construction sites, self-employed persons and employees regarding the wearing of head protection. The purpose of head protection is to prevent/mitigate head injury caused by: falling/swinging objects, e.g. materials and/or crane hooks; and striking the head against something, as where there is insufficient headroom. Circumstances where head injury is not reasonably foreseeable on construction sites are limited, but it probably would not be required on/in:

(*a*)   sites where buildings are completed and there is no risk of falling materials/objects;

(*b*)   site offices, cabins, toilets, canteens or mess rooms;

(*c*)   cabs of vehicles, cranes etc.;

(*d*)   work at ground level, e.g. road works.

Duties of employers

C8097   The following duties are laid on employers:

(a) Provision/maintenance of head protection

Every employer (that is, main contractor, subcontractor etc.) must provide each employee, while at work on building/construction operations, with suitable head protection, and keep it maintained/replaced (as recommended by the manufacturer). [*Reg 3(1), (2)*].

Moreover, head protection equipment must be kept in good condition and stored, when not in use, in a safe place, though not in direct sunlight or hot or humid conditions. It should be inspected regularly and have defective harness components replaced, and sweatbands regularly cleaned or replaced.

(b) Ensuring head protection is worn

So far as reasonably practicable (for meaning, see E15015 ENFORCEMENT), every employer must ensure that each of his employees, whilst on construction work, wears suitable head protection, unless there is no foreseeable risk of injury to his head (other than by falling). [*Reg 4(1)*].

Moreover, every employer (or employee) who has control (for meaning, see below) over any other person engaged in construction work, must ensure, so far as is reasonably practicable, that such persons wear suitable head protection, unless there is no foreseeable risk of injury to the head, other than by falling. [*Reg 4(2)*].

Persons in control of construction sites

C8098   For the purposes of these regulations, the following persons may be deemed to be 'in control' of construction sites:

(*a*)   main contractor;

(*b*)   managing contractor;

(*c*)   contractor bringing in subcontractors;

(*d*)   contract manager;

(*e*)   site manager;

(*f*)   subcontractor;

(*g*)   managers, including foremen, supervisors;

(*h*)   engineers and surveyors;

(*j*)   (sometimes) clients and architects with control over persons at work.

Procedures and rule making

C8099   Employers and others in control must:

(*a*)   identify when/where head protection should be worn;

(*b*)   inform site personnel procedurally when/where to wear head protection and post suitable safety signs to that effect;

(*c*)   provide adequate supervision;

(*d*)   check that head protection is, in fact, worn.

Supervision by those responsible for ensuring head protection is worn, is an on-going requirement, including monitoring helmet use at all times, starting early in the day and taking in arrivals on site.

Persons in control of construction works can (and should) make rules regulating the wearing of suitable head protection. Such rules must be in writing and be brought clearly to the attention of those involved. Such procedure is particularly useful to main/managing contractors on multi-contractor sites, and rules/regulations on head protection should form part of overall site safety procedures, such as construction phase safety plans in accordance with the *CDM Regulations* (see C8024 above).

Wearing suitable head protection – duty of employees

C8100   Employees must also make full and proper use of head protection and return it to the accommodation provided for it after use. [*Reg 6 as amended by the Personal Protective Equipment at Work Regulations 1992, Sch 2 para 24*]. They must also comply with the rules and regulations made for the wearing of head protection mentioned in C8097 above (see also PERSONAL PROTECTIVE EQUIPMENT). All employees, provided with suitable head protection, must take reasonable care of it and report any loss of it or obvious defect in it, to the employer etc. [*Reg 7*].

Suitable head protection

C8101   Suitable head protection refers to an industrial safety helmet conforming to British Standard BS EN 397: 1995 'Industrial Safety Helmets' – Specification for construction and performance (or an equivalent standard). For work in confined spaces, 'bump caps' conforming to BS EN 812: 1998 are more suitable.

Suitability of head gear involves the following factors: (*a*) fit, (*b*) comfort, (*c*) compatibility with work to be done, and (*d*) user choice.

(a) Fit

Head protection should be of an appropriate shell size for the person who is to wear it, and have an easily adjustable headband, nape and chin strap. The range of size adjustment should be sufficient to accommodate thermal liners in cold weather.

(b) Comfort

Head gear should be as comfortable as possible, including:

(*a*)   a flexible headband of adequate width and contoured vertically and horizontally to fit the forehead;

(*b*)   an absorbent, easily cleanable or replaceable sweatband;

(*c*)   textile cradle straps;

(*d*)   chin straps (when fitted) which

(i)   fit round the ears,

(ii)   are compatible with any other personal protective equipment needed,

(iii)   are fitted with smooth, quick release buckles which do not dig into the skin,

(iv)   are made from non-irritant materials,

(v)   are capable of being stowed on the helmet when not in use.

(c) Compatibility with work to be done

Head gear should not impede work to be done. For instance, an industrial safety helmet with little or no peak is functional for a surveyor taking measurements, using a theodolite or to allow unrestricted upward vision for a scaffold erector. If a job involves work in windy conditions, at heights, or repeated bending or constantly looking upwards, a secure retention system is necessary. Flexible headbands and Y-shaped chin straps can help to secure the helmet on the head. If other personal protective equipment, such as ear defenders or eye protectors, are required, the design must allow them to be worn safely and in comfort.

(d) User choice

In order to avoid possibly unpleasant industrial relations consequences or a possible action for unfair dismissal (see further EMPLOYMENT PROTECTION), it is sensible and advisable to allow the user to participate in selection of head gear.

Duties of self-employed personnel

C8102   Every self-employed person involved in construction/building operations, must:

(i)   provide himself with suitable head protection and maintain/replace it, whenever necessary [*Reg 3(2)*];

(ii)   ensure that any person over whom he has control, wears suitable head gear, unless there is no foreseeable risk of injury [*Reg 4(2)*];

(iii)   give directions to any other self-employed person regarding wearing of suitable head gear [*Reg 5(4)*];

(iv)   wear properly suitable head protection, unless there is no foreseeable risk of injury to the head, and make full and proper use of it and return it to the accommodation provided for it after use [*Reg 6(2)-(4)*];

(v)   where the presence of more than one risk to health or safety makes it necessary for him to wear or use simultaneously more than one item of personal protective equipment, see that such equipment is compatible and continues to be effective against the risk or risks in question [*Personal Protective Equipment at Work Regulations 1992 (SI 1992 No 2966), Reg 5(2)*].

Exceptions

C8103   The following categories of workers on construction sites are exempt from the regulations:

(*a*)   divers actually diving or preparing to dive;

(*b*)   Sikhs wearing turbans on construction sites [*Employment Act 1989, ss 11, 12*], though the regulations do apply to Sikhs not normally wearing turbans at work. (The probability is that this exemption, under *s 11* of the *Employment Act 1989*, is now subordinate to the requirements of the *Construction (Head Protection) Regulations 1989* and *HSWA*, with the result that Sikhs working on construction sites will have to wear hard hats (*SS Dhanjal v British Steel plc (Case No 50740/91)*).)

Visitors on site

C8104   It is not necessary that visitors are provided with or, even less, wear head protection, under these regulations. Nevertheless, in order to satisfy their general duty under *s 2* of the *Health and Safety at Work etc. Act 1974*, and additionally avoid any civil liability for injury at common law in an action for negligence (see further EMPLOYERS' DUTIES TO THEIR EMPLOYEES) and/or under the *Occupiers' Liability Act 1957* (see OCCUPIERS' LIABILITY), employers should provide visitors to the site with suitable head protection where there is a reasonably foreseeable likelihood of injury. This contention is further reinforced by the requirement for every employer to consider the risks inherent in his business which have the potential to harm his employees or any other persons who might be affected, and to take measures to remove or reduce such risks [*Management of Health and Safety at Work Regulations 1992, Reg 3*].

Composition of construction products

C8105   Products must be suitable for construction works and works of civil engineering and can then carry the 'CE' mark. To that end, when incorporated into design and building, construction products should satisfy the following criteria, namely,

(*a*)   mechanical resistance and stability;

(*b*)   safety in case of fire;

(*c*)   hygiene, health and the environment;

(*d*)   safety in use;

(*e*)   protection against noise; and

(*f*)   energy economy and heat retention.

[*Construction Products Regulations 1991 (SI 1991 No 1620), Reg 3, Sch 2 as amended by SI 1994 No 3051*].

Manufacturers must show that their products conform to these specifications, if necessary, by submitting to third party testing (see also PERSONAL PROTECTIVE EQUIPMENT for products generally).

Protecting visitors and the public

C8106   The HSE have issued revised guidance, HS(G)151 *Protecting the public – your next move* (June 1997), which provides practical advice on the measures to be taken to minimise risks to the public and others not directly involved in construction activities. The advice is aimed at preventing accidents and ill health and, to a limited extent, at reducing incidents of nuisance. The guidance does not cover deliberate illegal trespass or forced entry on to sites by protest groups or those intent on criminal activity.

In addition, reference should be made to the following related statutory provisions which have aspects relating to public safety during construction or building operations:

(a) Roads and streets

Highways Act 1980:

> — *s 168* (building operations affecting public safety);

> — *s 169* (the control of scaffolding on highways);

> — *s 174* (the erection of barriers, signs and lighting etc.).

New Roads and Street Works Act 1991:

> — *s 50* (lays down particular safety requirements for work in the street and, specifically, the measures to be taken to minimise inconvenience to the disabled).

Environmental Protection Act 1990:

> — *s 79 as amended by the Noise and Statutory Nuisance Act 1993* (noise or vibration emitted from buildings and from or caused by a vehicle, machinery or equipment in a street).

(b) Waste from building and demolition sites

Waste produced on construction sites is classed as controlled waste and as such must be controlled to comply with EU-based Directives:

Environmental Protection Act 1990:

> — *ss 33–46* (deal with waste management and licensing control).

Controlled Waste (Registration of Carriers and Seizure of Vehicles) Regulations 1991 (SI 1991 No 1624 as amended) (carriage of controlled waste by registered carriers only).

Waste Management Licensing Regulations 1994 (SI 1994 No 1056 as amended) (registers, applications and waste regulation authorities for the recovery and disposal of waste).

Special Waste Regulations 1996 (SI 1996 No 972 as amended) (hazardous properties of waste).

Identifying hazards and evaluating risks

C8107   Construction work is by its nature carried out by workers away from the home base and may not be open to direct management and supervision. The employer's general duty of care to ensure that employees are not put at risk by their work activities (*HSWA, s 2*) still applies. In addition, if the work activities impinge on others, such as another organisation or members of the public, a further duty of care (*HSWA, s 3*) applies.

Section 4 of HSWA relates to the control of premises, rather than the control of undertakings. Persons who control premises used by people who are at work, but who are not their employees, need to ensure, so far as is reasonably practicable, that the premises, access to them and plant and substances used on them are safe and free from risks to health and safety. Site occupiers therefore share a duty of care with contractors (as both are employers) to ensure that all reasonably practicable precautions are taken to safeguard their own employees, other persons on site and the public.

Under the *Occupiers' Liability Act 1957* and the *Occupiers' Liability Act 1984* a duty of care is imposed on occupiers of existing premises regarding visitors. The duty of care extends to children – it should be noted that a child is regarded as being at greater risk than an adult (see O3010 OCCUPIERS' LIABILITY). The 1984 Act further extends the duty of an occupier to people other than lawful visitors, such as trespassers, to ensure that they are not injured whilst on the premises. This may involve making unauthorised access more difficult or putting up suitable warning signs regarding hazards on site.

Safety policies and written arrangements

C8108

Section 2(3) of HSWA requires written safety arrangements only with regard to employee safety. However, by virtue of the *Management of Health and Safety at Work Regulations 1992 (MHSWR), Reg 4* (health and safety arrangements) written arrangements are also required with regard to the protection of the public and other non-employees.

MHSWR refer expressly to occupiers' responsibility to co-ordinate arrangements *(Reg 9)* and to provide information on risks and precautions *(Regs 10 and 13)*. These duties apply whether or not payment is involved, for example free surveys, estimates, measurements, maintenance and servicing under warranty, etc.

Measures to ensure the safety of visitors and members of the public must be one result of the risk assessment task as required by *MHSWR, Reg 3* (see R3004 RISK ASSESSMENT). Chemical installations or other high risk manufacturing or chemical storage premises are also subject to specific duties towards the general public under the *Control of Major Accident Hazards Regulations 1999* (see CONTROL OF MAJOR ACCIDENT HAZARDS).

Companies with cooling towers on site are also subject to specific controls ultimately designed to protect the public. In *R v Board of Trustees of the Science Museum [1993] The Times, March 15, CA* the prosecution had alleged that members of the public outside the Science Museum had been exposed to risks to their health from *legionella pneumophila*, because of inadequate maintenance of the museum's air conditioning system. The basis of their case had been that it is sufficient for the prosecution to show that there has been a risk to health.

The Court of Appeal decided that the word 'risks' in *HSWA, s 3(1)* implied the idea of potential danger. There was nothing in the subsection which narrowed this meaning. *HSWA* should be interpreted so as to make it effective in its role of protecting public health and safety. *Section 3(1)* was intended to be an absolute prohibition, subject to the defence of reasonable practicability.

Insurance cover

C8109

The *Employers' Liability (Compulsory Insurance) Act 1969* states that an employer's legal liability for death, disease or bodily injury suffered by employees as a consequence of employment must be insured by the employer for their mutual protection under the duty of care owed by *HSWA, s 2*. A copy of the current certificate of insurance (issued annually) must be displayed within all working premises. Other insurances, for example reflecting the risk of liability to non-employees under the duty of care imposed by *HSWA, s 3*, are likely to be essential even if not compulsory.

Site planning and layout

C8110   Risk assessment should decide how the site perimeters will be defined, what type of barriers and fencing will be most effective and where they should be placed.

For most sites the perimeter will be the geographical area within which the construction work will be carried out. Determining the perimeter is an important aspect of managing public risk. It must always be recognised that site perimeters need to be changed as the work progresses.

Under the *Construction, Design and Management Regulations 1994 (CDM)* the duties of the principal contractor are wide and varied. Importantly, *CDM* is excluded from use in civil proceedings, except for *Reg 10* which requires the client to ensure that an adequate health and safety plan has been prepared before the construction phase of the project commences, and *Reg 16(1)(c)* which requires the principal contractor to take appropriate steps to ensure that only authorised access is permitted to premises where construction work is continuing.

Similarly, where construction work is taking place on an occupied site, the client will impose existing security rules on everyone entering and leaving the site.

Under the *CDM Regulations*, other contractors involved in the construction work are required to co-operate with the principal contractor and comply with any directions or site rules. In addition, all contractors must provide appropriate information, including information relating to any injuries, diseases and dangerous occurrences.

Employers' liability for the actions and safety of the public and non-employees

C8111   Under *HSWA*, both employers and the self-employed have duties not only to their own workpeople but also to outside contractors, workers employed by them and to members of the public – whether within or outside the workplace – who may be affected by work activities. Undertakings must be conducted in such a way as to ensure, so far as is reasonably practicable, that they do not expose people who are not their employees to risks to their health and safety. The duty extends to, for example, risks to the public outside the workplace from fire or explosion, from falls of unsafely erected scaffolding or from the release of harmful substances into the atmosphere.

In general, the standard of protection required for visitors and others within a construction site will be similar to that given to employees. There may, however, be a need to apply different criteria to achieve these standards when assessing the risks to members of the public. For example, it will be necessary to consider that certain people, such as the very young or disabled, may be more vulnerable than others and that people visiting or passing a workplace may have less knowledge of the potential hazards and of how to avoid them.

The responsibilities of employers and the self-employed to non-employees will in certain circumstances extend to people entering workplaces without permission. This is apart from any liability under common law towards trespassers. The duty under *HSWA* to conduct the business in such a way as not to expose people to risks to health and safety implies taking certain precautions to deter people from unlawfully entering the workplace, for example by the provision of fences, barriers and notices warning of the danger. The duty towards 'unauthorised' people is qualified 'so far as is reasonably practicable', and on construction sites and other open-air workplaces, which have particular dangers as far as children are concerned, simply locking or guarding main doors and gates may not be adequate.

Duties of all people

C8112   *HSWA* imposes one duty on all people, both people at work and members of the public, including children: this is not intentionally to interfere with or misuse anything that has been provided in the interests of health, safety or welfare, whether it has been provided for the protection of employees or other people. The purpose of the provision is clearly to protect things intended to ensure people's safety, including fire escapes and fire extinguishers, perimeter fencing, warning notices for particular hazards, protective clothing, guards on machinery and special containers for dangerous substances.

Control measures

C8113   The general duties of protection owed to visitors apply equally to the emergency services who should be given a plan or map of the premises together with information on specific high risk areas where high voltage or dangerous chemicals may be present. In addition, to comply with occupier's liability legislation the duty of care towards visitors includes contractors.

(a) Visitors

C8114   In general, visitors to a construction site should not be left unaccompanied and they should not, if possible, be taken into any hazardous areas. All visitors should be made to sign in on arrival and sign out on departure and, ideally, be given basic instructions on what to do in the event of an emergency. The main element of looking after visitors is to ensure that they are accompanied at all times, so that the host can lead them to safety in the event of fire or other emergency. Constant accompaniment of visitors will, of course, also improve security arrangements.

(b) Contractors

C8115   Under *MHSWR* the occupier of the premises must ensure that contractors on site are provided with comprehensible information on:

—   the risks to health and safety arising out of the activities on site; and

—   the measures taken by the occupier to ensure compliance with statutory requirements.

[*Reg 10*].

The ideal situation is where contractors can be provided with a completely separated area which can be designated as being under their control. Such an arrangement will normally only apply when the contractors are on site to undertake a major engineering or construction project; and it will only be successful if a contractor is actually given full control of the area – and the main site occupier and his or her employees only enter the area when authorised by the contractor. However, the main site occupier will retain the key responsibility for safety matters – as illustrated in the case of a south coast town council which employed contractors to remove part of a damaged pier. The council had accepted by far the lowest quote and did not discuss the system of work. During the demolition, there was a huge explosion which removed the derelict part of the pier but also caused considerable damage to cars and buildings on the seafront. The contractor and town council were held jointly responsible but the council suffered the larger fine because it failed to employ reputable contractors and did not request a method statement from them.

(c) General public

C8116   Measures to ensure the safety of the general public are usually more difficult and must be one result of the risk assessment task as required by *MHSWR, Reg 3*. Members of the public are owed a duty of care under *HSWA, ss 3 and 4*, to ensure that they are not put at risk by the employer's undertaking. For example, an employer engaged in construction work near a public place must ensure that risks are assessed and adequately controlled. The Act also imposes a duty on employees to co-operate with their employer on health and safety matters and not to do anything which puts others at risk.

As far as protecting the public is concerned, adequate control measures must be determined which should not rely on the use of protective equipment.

Risk assessments

C8117   Risk assessments are an integral part of the *Construction (Design and Management) Regulations 1994 (CDM)* and the *Confined Spaces Regulations 1997*. Additionally, with respect to visitors and the general public, employers may be liable to pay compensation to people injured on their premises under the terms of the *Occupiers' Liability Act 1957*.

When carrying out a risk assessment to safeguard members of the public it is necessary to adopt a very wide approach and consider all the possible hazards and subsequent risks. This would include, but not be limited to, compiling data and control measures for:

(*a*)   *chemical hazards* — e.g., mist, vapour, gas, smoke, dust, aerosol, fumes;

(*b*)   *physical hazards* — e.g., noise, temperature, lighting, vibration, radiation (ionising and non-ionising), pressure;

(*c*)   *biological hazards* — e.g., bacteria, parasites.

Public vulnerability

C8118   Experience has shown that members of the public are particularly vulnerable to those hazards and risks which are not readily identifiable by the normal senses of sight, smell or hearing. The problem may be exacerbated by disabilities and sensory impairments as well as by physical and mental conditions. These conditions would have been assessed for everyone inside the confines of the site but the employer must address the specific needs of all people who may be affected by the work when the hazards may extend outside the site boundaries. The needs of children and the elderly must always be given top priority.

Cooling towers

C8119   The public is particularly vulnerable to cooling towers, and employers must therefore ensure, so far as is reasonably practicable, that no one is put at risk from legionellosis as a result of work activities. Plant of this type includes hot and cold water services, air conditioning and industrial cooling systems, spas and whirlpool baths, humidifiers and air washers.

Designers, manufacturers, importers, suppliers and installers of such plant or water systems – and water treatment contractors – have a duty to ensure, so far as is reasonably practicable, that the plant or system is so designed and constructed that it will be without risks to health. Appropriate information must be provided to users, and tests carried out if required [*HSWA s 6*].

The use of this type of plant must be notified to the local authority under the *Notification of Cooling Towers and Evaporative Condensers Regulations 1992* and the requirements of the *COSHH Regulations* must be complied with, particularly the provisions relating to:

— *risk assessment* – to include breakdowns, abnormal operation and the possibility of exposure of susceptible people (for example in hospitals) [*Reg 6*]. The assessment must be reviewed at least once every five years or if there is a change in plant or operation;

— *prevention or control of exposure* [*Regs 7, 8 and 9*]. Where potential exposure to infection cannot be prevented there must be a written control scheme to minimise exposure;

— *health surveillance* where appropriate [*Reg 11*];

— *information, instruction and training* [*Reg 12*].

(See further L8: *The prevention or control of legionellosis (including legionnaires' disease)*. Approved Code of Practice. (ISBN 0 7176 0732 1).)

Dusts and fibres

C8120   Dust in the form of particulates suspended in air is generated from a number of construction work activities, including, but not limited to:

— cutting bricks, blocks, tiles, slabs etc.;

— sawing wood;

— mixing cement, plasters etc.;

— grinding operations;

— blasting;

— demolition operations.

Fibres from asbestos demolitions are particularly harmful and strict precautions must be taken in case of an uncontrolled release of asbestos fibres from the workplace.

Fumes, mists and vapours

C8121   Most dangers associated with fumes, mists and vapours from operations such as spreading adhesives, mixing and thinning paints and coatings and spraying are well known. In addition, care should be taken and appropriate precautions put in place for operations such as:

— cleaning operations;

— heat treatment processes;

— disturbance of sludge and scale from vessels;

— the release of gases from sewers and similar operations;

— emissions from extraction equipment, LEV systems and the venting of relief valves etc.;

— the use of aerosols;

— the use of pesticides.

Fumes from cutting, welding, soldering and brazing operations are particularly dangerous and require a thorough assessment.

Radiations and hazardous waves

C8122   The dangers associated from the use of equipment emitting radiations, radio-frequency waves and micro-waves are well documented and the precautions to be observed during the use of such equipment must be strictly adhered to at all times. Some operations where the public may be at risk from uncontrolled releases or discharges from the equipment or, in some cases, from natural causes are:

—   infra-red and ultraviolet radiations during cutting and welding;

—   ionising radiation from radiography;

—   laser rays (for example the use of lasers during accurate alignment operations of machinery or structures);

—   X-rays from high voltage sources (for example non-destructive testing operations);

—   the presence of radon on some soils and rocks.

Fire and smoke inhalation

C8123   In addition to the dangers of fire spreading to areas and premises occupied by members of the public, it is necessary to consider the effects of smoke from burning refuse and discarded materials. Advice should be sought from appropriate specialists and approval granted before commencing any burning operations.

Noise control on construction sites

C8124   In addition to the *Noise at Work Regulations 1989 (SI 1989 No 1790)* and HSE's supporting guidance to the Regulations (L108 – ISBN 0 7176 1511 1), there are other legislative requirements and codes designed to protect the public from noise on construction sites. Some of the most important are:

—   *Control of Pollution Act 1974, s 71* – approval of codes and standards regarding noise control;

—   the *Control of Noise (Codes of Practice for Construction and Open Sites) Orders 1984 (SI 1984 No 1992) and 1987 (SI 1987 No 1730)*; and

—   the *Construction Plant and Equipment (Harmonisation of Noise Emission Standards) Regulations 1988 (SI 1988 No 361 as amended)* – noise from plant used in or about building or civil engineering operations.

General construction operations

C8125   The public are also at risk, but perhaps to a lesser degree, from normal construction work activities. Policies and procedures should be in place to cover contingencies and incidents arising from:

—   electricity;

—   excavations;

—   explosives;

—   flooding;

—   lifting operations;

—   materials handling;

—   mechanical plant and general construction equipment;

—   overhead working;

—   piling;

—   scaffolding;

—   underground services;

—   vehicles;

—   vibration.

References

C8126   There are numerous publications available as reference documents which provide advice on the measures to be taken to protect visitors and members of the public during construction activities. In particular, the following HSE publications and Approved Codes of Practice (ACoPs) may be useful when formulating safety policies and procedures.

Construction management

HSR21 Guide to the Control of Industrial Major Accident Hazards Regulations 1984 (ISBN 0 11 885579 4);

HSR25 Memorandum of Guidance on the Electricity at Work Regulations 1989 (ISBN 0 7176 1602 9);

L1 A guide to the Health and Safety at Work etc Act 1974 (ISBN 0 7176 0441 1);

L21 Management of health and safety at work: ACoP to the 1992 Regulations (ISBN 0 7176 0412 8);

L24 Workplace health, safety and welfare: ACoP to the 1992 Regulations (ISBN 0 7176 0413 6);

L54 Managing construction for health and safety: ACoP to the CDM Regulations 1994 (ISBN 0 7176 0792 5);

L55 Preventing asthma at work: How to control respiratory sensitisers (ISBN 0 7176 0661 9);

L64 Safety signs and signals: guidance to the Health and Safety (Safety Signs and Signals) Regulations 1996 (ISBN 0 7176 0870 0);

L73 A guide to the Reporting of Injuries, Diseases and Dangerous Occurrences Regulations 1995 (ISBN 0 7176 1012 8).

Dangerous substances

COP2 Control of lead at work: ACoP (ISBN 0 7176 1506 5);

L5 Control of substances hazardous to health (general ACoP), Control of carcinogenic substances (carcinogens ACoP) and Control of biological agents (biological agents ACoP) – all ACoPs published as one document (ISBN 0 7176 1308 9);

L27 The control of asbestos at work: ACoP (ISBN 0 7176 1673 8);

L28 Work with asbestos insulation, asbestos coating and asbestos insulating board: ACoP (ISBN 0 7176 1674 6);

L62 Safety datasheets for substances and preparations dangerous for supply: guidance on regulation 6 of the Chemicals (Hazard Information and Packaging for Supply) Regulations 1994: ACoP (ISBN 0 7176 0859 X);

L86 Control of substances hazardous to health in fumigation operations: ACoP (ISBN 0 7176 1195 7).

Explosives

L10 A guide to the Control of Explosives Regulations 1991 (ISBN 0 11 885670 7).

Gas

COP20 Standards of training in safe gas installation: ACoP (ISBN 0 7176 0603 1);

L56 Safety in the installation and use of gas systems and appliances: ACoP to the 1994 Regulations (ISBN 0 7176 1635 5);

L80 A guide to the Gas Safety (Management) Regulations 1996 (ISBN 0 7176 1159 0);

L81 The design, construction and installation of gas service pipes: ACoP to the Pipelines Safety Regulations 1996 (ISBN 0 7176 1172 8).

LPG and petroleum spirit

COP6 Plastic containers with nominal capacities up to 5 litres for petroleum spirit: Requirements for testing and marking or labelling (ISBN 0 11 883643 9).

Pesticides

L9 Safe use of pesticides for non-agricultural purposes. Control of Substances Hazardous to Health Regulations 1994: ACoP (ISBN 0 7176 0542 6).

Pressure systems

COP37 Safety of pressure systems. Pressure Systems and Transportable Gas Containers Regulations 1989: ACoP (ISBN 0 7176 0477 2);

L96 A guide to the Work in Compressed Air Regulations 1996 (ISBN 0 7176 1120 5).

Radiations

COP23 Exposure to radon. The Ionising Radiations Regulations 1985: ACoP (ISBN 0 11 883978 0);

L7 Dose limitation – restriction of exposure: additional guidance on regulation 6 of the Ionising Radiations Regulations 1985: ACoP (ISBN 0 11 885605 7);

L58 The protection of persons against ionising radiation arising from any work activity (ISBN 0 7176 0508 6).

Site vehicles

COP26 Rider-operated lift trucks – operator training: ACoP (ISBN 0 7176 0474 8).

Responsibility for contractors and subcontractors

C8127   Most industrial/commercial organisations delegate corporate functions and duties, placed on them by statute, regulation and common law, to contractors and subcontractors. This practice is particularly common in the construction industry, where a main contractor, in order the more competently and expeditiously to discharge his contractual obligations towards his employer (or builder owner), sublets performance of parts of the contract, e.g. steel erection, to specialists.

Significantly, this practice of subletting performance of parts of the entire contract is regarded as sufficiently important in the building industry to justify the existence of a Standard Form of Building Contract (the JCT Standard Form). This means that the rights/obligations of all interested parties, namely, the employer, main contractors and subcontractors, both nominated and domestic, are specified in a formal jointly witnessed contract, known as the Joint Contracts Tribunal (JCT). When a dispute arises between any of the interested parties, for example, who is liable for an injury to an employee of a subcontractor, reference is made to the Conditions of Contract (or Subcontract).

If necessary, such a dispute will be decided by arbitration, since the contract provides for independent arbitration machinery in the form of the RIBA (Royal Institute of British Architects). RIBA arbitration does not exclude jurisdiction of the courts but, in practice, that is often the result, since arbitration is quicker and cheaper. In other words, the building industry has its own quasi-judicial internal disputes machinery and procedures. This is preferable to no machinery at all, since all interested parties know where they stand – at least, that is the theory.

Multiple occupation of construction sites – standard form work

C8128   Where, as is normal on large construction sites, standard form (JCT) building work is being carried out, multiplicity of occupation (or control) is not uncommon. Here control will be shared among building owner(s), main contractor(s) and subcontractor(s). It has been decided that the legal nature of the relationship between a building owner and main contractor is that of licensor and licensee (*Hounslow London Borough Council v Twickenham Garden Developments Ltd [1970] 3 AER 326*).

This vests in the building owner some degree of control over the works e.g. if the contractor does not carry out and complete the works (in accordance with the requirements of Clause 2(1) of the JCT Standard Form Contract) the licence can, subject to certain exceptions, be terminated. Moreover, (given that some statutory duties can be modified) Clause 20(1) of the Conditions of Contract states that 'the contractor shall be liable for, and shall indemnify the employer against any expense, liability, loss or claim or proceedings whatsoever arising under any statute or at common law in respect of personal injury to or the death of any person whomsoever arising out of, or in the course of, or caused by the carrying out of the works, unless due to any act or neglect of the employer or of any person for whom the employer is responsible' (e.g. employee). The proviso to the clause 'unless due to any act or neglect of the employer' is limited solely to common law negligence and does not extend to statutory negligence.

In consequence, the building owner can insist that the main contractor(s) must take out insurance to meet that indemnity, and likewise the main contractor(s) can insist that the subcontractor(s) does the same (Clause 21.1 JCT Standard Form Contract). Thus, for the purposes of common law liability, based on occupation, persons injured on building sites can sue the building owner, main contractor and any subcontractor who may be responsible, the question of indemnity as between the liable parties being governed and determined by the terms of the JCT Contract.

Liability of employer/occupier in connection with contract work

C8129   In practice, two sorts of situation give rise to liability:

(*a*)   injuries/diseases, or the risk of them, to employees of the contractor as a result of working on the occupier's premises; or, alternatively, injuries or the risk of them to the employer's own workforce as a result of the employer failing to acquaint the contractor's workforce with dangers, thereby endangering his own employees (see *R v Swan Hunter Shipbuilders Ltd* below);

(*b*)   injuries/damage to members of the public, or pollution or nuisance to neighbouring landowners.

Such liability can be both criminal and civil (often strict).

Criminal liability

C8130   Criminal liability can arise under several statutes and at common law (e.g. where, owing to gross negligence, employers commit manslaughter – in practice, this is rare). Particularly relevant is the *Health and Safety at Work etc. Act 1974, ss 3(1), 4(2)*.

Health and Safety at Work etc. Act 1974, s 3(1)

C8131   In particular, *HSWA, s 3(1)* states: 'It shall be the duty of every employer to conduct his undertaking in such a way as to ensure, so far as is reasonably practicable, that persons not in his employment who may be affected thereby are not thereby exposed to risks to their health or safety'.

The Swan Hunter case

C8132   An instructive case involving this section was *R v Swan Hunter Shipbuilders Ltd [1982] 1 AER 264.* During construction of a ship at a shipbuilder's yard, subcontractors, who had no contract with the shipbuilders, were working on the ship while it was being fitted out. The shipbuilders were aware that, because of use of oxygen hoses with fuel gases in welding, there was a risk of fire due to the atmosphere in confined and poorly ventilated spaces in the ship becoming oxygen enriched. In regard to that danger they had provided information and instruction for their own employees by way of a book of rules which stipulated that at the end of the day's work, all oxygen hoses should be returned from the lower decks to an open deck, or, where impracticable, the hoses should be disconnected at the cylinder or manifold. This rule book was *not* distributed to the subcontractor's employees working on the ship, and an employee of the subcontractor failed to disconnect the oxygen hose and oxygen was discharged during the night. In consequence, on the next morning, when a welder working in the lower deck lit his welding torch, a fierce fire escaped.

The shipbuilders were charged with failing to provide/maintain a safe system of work, contrary to *s 2(2)(a)*, and failing to provide such information/instruction as was necessary to ensure the health/safety of their employees, contrary to *s 2(2)(c)*.

The shipbuilders were also charged with failing to conduct their undertaking in such a way as to ensure that persons not in their employment, who might be affected thereby, were not exposed to risks to health and safety, contrary to *s 3(1)*.

On appeal against conviction on all three counts, it was held by the Court of Appeal that:

(i) duties imposed on an employer by *ss 2 and 3* followed the common law duty of care of the main contractors to co-ordinate operations at a place of work so as to ensure not only the safety of his own employees but also that of the subcontractor's employees. The main contractor had to prove, on a balance of probabilities, that it was not reasonably practicable for him to carry out the duties under *ss 2 and 3*;

(ii) the shipbuilders were under a duty, under *s 2(2)(a)*, to provide/maintain a safe system of work for the subcontractor's employees, so far as was reasonably practicable, and provide them with information/instruction so as to ensure their safety.

Accordingly, the main contractor, Swan Hunter Shipbuilders Ltd, was fined £3,000 and the subcontractor, Telemeters Ltd, £15,000 after eight men were trapped and killed on board HMS Glasgow.

Furthermore, if the main contractor fails, as in *Swan Hunter*, to comply with *s 3(1)*, in his duties towards subcontracted labour, it is likely that he would be in breach of his duty towards his own employees, under *s 2*. Thus, anyone who is responsible for co-ordinating work has to ensure that reasonable safety precautions are taken for the workmen of a contractor or subcontractor.

The Rhone-Poulenc Rorer case

C8133   Responsibility for contractors' work has been considered in several cases since the *Swan Hunter Shipbuilders* case resulting in further interpretation of *s 3* and the prosecution of employers. Decisions made in the courts have continued to emphasise the role of the main employer in organising and sharing responsibility for the safety of work carried out by contractors. One of these cases concerned a breach of the *Construction (Working Places) Regulations 1966, Reg 36(2)* (now revoked) in addition to *HSWA, s 3* – the case of *R v Rhone-Poulenc Rorer Ltd [1996] ICR 1054* concerned the provision of suitable means for preventing a fall through fragile materials.

Counsel for the prosecution alleged that some sort of physical safety device is required to fulfil an employer's duty to prevent employees from falling through fragile material: neither a system of work based on instruction nor a Code of Practice will suffice.

The court heard that an employee of a subcontractor was instructed to repair a roof light at the company's factory in Dagenham. The company provided one of its own employees to supervise the work. The subcontractor was told not to climb on to the roof. He did so, and fell through the roof light on to a concrete floor 28 feet below and was killed. Rhone-Poulenc was charged under the 1974 Act and the 1966 Regulations. The company was fined £7,500 in respect of the former and £2,500 in respect of the latter, with £55,000 costs.

The company appealed and argued that the trial judge had misdirected the jury in telling them that it was necessary to prove that it had been impracticable to comply with the Regulations, not merely that it was not reasonable to do so.

The Court of Appeal rejected this argument. Wright J stated that the requirement under *Reg 36(2)* was absolute and that employers had a duty to provide such suitable means as might be necessary for preventing, so far as was reasonably practicable, persons from falling through fragile material. This meant that some sort of physical device, for example a safety harness, was required, where in the circumstances guard rails or covering could not be supplied. Falls through fragile material could not be prevented by the provision of a supervisor, a body of instructions, or a code of practice.

In relation to *HSWA, s 3* it was held that because the occupier (Rhone-Poulenc Rorer Ltd) had been in breach of Regulations which applied to its own employees, it was also in breach of *s 3* so far as the contractor's employees were concerned.

The Associated Octel case

C8134   It was 1996 before the House of Lords had to deal with the interpretation of *s 3*. In *R v Associated Octel Co Ltd [1996] 4 AER 846* it was decided that the duty placed on the employer of contractors extended to persons not in his employment.

In 1990, during the course of an annual shutdown for planned maintenance a specialist contractor, RGP, was called in for the purposes of cleaning and repairing a tank at Octel's chlorine plant at Ellesmere Port. Octel had effectively approved the system of work by virtue of having issued a permit-to-work that required the contractor's employee to enter the tank, taking lighting with him, and grind the internal surfaces of the tank and clean residues with an acetone solvent. In the event the light broke causing an explosion in which the contractor's employee was badly injured.

The HSE inspector who investigated the incident was critical of the system of work and identified aspects of the operations which were unsafe. The points raised included:

— the acetone was carried in an old emulsion bucket;

— Octel provided an unsuitable lamp from its own stores;

— there was inadequate ventilation;

— the precautions listed on the permit-to-work referred only to the grinding work and did not specify adequate precautions relating to work in a confined space.

The inspector referred to the fact that the site was a major hazard site and under the control of the *Control of Industrial Major Accident Hazard Regulations 1984 (CIMAH) (SI 1984 No 1902 as amended)* which required a safety case to be submitted and complied with. RGP had employees at Octel's site on a regular basis and had worked for Octel over a number of years. Previously, Octel had exercised a degree of control over RGP's work performance and had a high level of understanding of the dangers involved in tank cleaning operations.

The case argued in the Crown Court and the Court of Appeal was a complex one where the central issue concerned 'control' of the work of the contractor. Octel's counsel referred to the Robens Report of 1972, and cited, *inter alia*, as precedents *R v Board of Trustees of the Science Museum [1993] 3 AER 853*, *R v Swan Hunter Shipbuilders Ltd [1982] 1 AER 264*, *Mailer v Austin Rover Group Ltd [1989] 2 AER 1087* and *RMC Roadstone Products Ltd v Jester [1994] 4 AER 1037*. Octel argued consistently that there was no case to answer because it could not be shown that it was the conduct of Octel's undertaking that endangered the RGP employee. RGP is a specialist contractor and Octel claimed that it had no right to control the manner in which its independent contractor did its work.

Octel lost its argument before the trial judge, as well as before the Court of Appeal for different and complicated legal reasons. However, it was decided that the chemical business was Octel's undertaking, and the undertaking included having the tank cleaned, whether by its own employees or by contractors.

Lord Hoffmann delivered the judgment of the House of Lords, upholding the decisions of the Crown Court and the Court of Appeal. *The Times* (15 November 1996) reported the following points made by Lord Hoffmann:

— it was a question of fact in each case whether an activity which caused a risk to the health and safety of persons other than employees amounted to 'conduct of an undertaking';

— *section 3* of the 1974 Act was not concerned with vicarious liability, but imposed a duty upon the employer himself;

— if the employer engaged an independent contractor to do work forming part of the 'undertaking', then the employer had to stipulate whatever conditions were needed to avoid risks to health and safety;

— the question was simply whether the activity in question could be described as part of the employer's undertaking. Octel's undertaking was running a chemical plant and it was part of the conduct of that undertaking to have the factory cleaned by contractors;

— the tank was part of Octel's plant. The work formed part of a maintenance programme planned by the firm. The workers, although employed by an independent contractor, were almost permanently integrated into the firm's larger operations. In these circumstances, a properly instructed jury would undoubtedly have convicted.

The Port Ramsgate ferry walkway case

C8135

In this case a harbour operator, two foreign marine engineering companies (designers and builders) and Lloyd's Register of Shipping were all prosecuted and found guilty of failing to ensure the safety of passengers after the collapse of a walkway to a cross-channel ferry led to the deaths of six people and injured many more.

The case centred around the 'reasonably practicable' element of *HSWA s 3(1)* and concerned the design, construction, installation and the supervision and approval inspection of the walkway, contracted by the Port of Ramsgate Ltd. The accident occurred only four months after the walkway was commissioned because of the failure of a weld joining one of the feet to an axle. The walkway collapsed and fell some 30 feet on to a floating pontoon.

The QC who was prosecuting on behalf of the HSE gave evidence that the failure was the result of inaccurate stress calculations and also of inferior welding.

During the trial, many legal arguments took place as to who exactly was responsible. Port of Ramsgate Ltd was adamant that it had acted properly in placing contracts with appropriate, experienced contractors and that, by arranging for Lloyd's to manage the design, construction and installation, there was nothing else it could have done regarding the safety of its passengers. It argued strongly that there was no way of foreseeing the profound errors of judgment made by the various parties concerned.

The prosecution continued with its argument that there were measures that could have been taken to satisfy the 'reasonably practicable' element and that one of these might have been the inclusion of a simple fail-safe device such as safety chains.

The judge directed the jury to treat the question of the Port of Ramsgate's undertaking as a question of fact and left it for the jury to decide whether sufficient had been done to satisfy the grounds of 'reasonably practicability'. In the event, the jury found that all three companies were guilty of failing to satisfy the requirement. The judge imposed very high fines:

—   Port of Ramsgate Ltd: £200,000;

—   Lloyd's Register of Shipping: £500,000;

—   Fartygsentreprenader AB and Others (Sweden): £1 million.

It should be noted that this was a highly complex case and its implications for further cases will be considerable.

Although the case was brought before the implementation of the *Construction (Design and Management) Regulations 1994*, it should be noted that these Regulations do not expressly require quality assurance checks to be carried out.

If the same type of case occurred offshore, the *Offshore Installations and Wells (Design and Construction) Regulations 1996* would probably apply and in particular the requirement for 'verification' and the effect on the installation's safety case.

Civil liability

C8136   Normally employers are only liable for the negligent acts/omissions of their own employees or agents but there are certain important exceptions, such as where an employee of an occupier is injured by the contractor's negligence but overall control rests with the occupier.

The McDermid Nash case

C8137   An important case was heard in 1987 concerning a safe system of work, the delegation of the performance of that work and the competency of the person in charge of a situation where an individual, not being in the employ of that person, was injured.

During the case (*McDermid v Nash Dredging & Reclamation Co Ltd [1987] 2 AER 878*) several points were made regarding the legal responsibilities of the various people concerned when contracting an employee of another employer:

—   the employer's safety duties towards his employees are owed personally to those employees – they cannot be got rid of by delegation;

—   an employer who arranges for work to be done by another person, whether under contract or any other relationship, where that other will use employees of the employer, is vicariously liable for acts of negligence of the contractor or other person;

—   liability arises not because the contractor or other person is, for the time being, the employer of the employee in the legal sense but merely from the fact that the usual employer has entrusted the safety of his employee to that other person;

—   the employer still remains liable for the proper performance and the legal duties of his employee;

—   this continued liability does not rely on any contract between the employer and the other party. It arises whenever an employer entrusts the performance of safety duties to another by asking that other party to perform work on his behalf using his employees.

The UK subsidiary of a Dutch company secured a contract to dredge a fjord in Sweden. It was to be an enterprise where some 100 of the UK company's employees were to work on board Dutch vessels under the joint captaincy of a UK and a Dutch captain, each working alternate shifts. Mr McDermid's job was to keep the deck tidy and to tie up and untie the tug from its moorings when it went alongside the dredger.

While the Dutch captain was in charge, Mr McDermid's leg got caught in one of the ship's hawsers and was so badly injured it had to be amputated. The evidence showed that the Dutch captain had not set up a safe system to be sure that Mr McDermid was free of the ropes before applying power to move the tug away from its mooring.

Because of the difficulties of suing a Dutch company while operating in Swedish territorial waters, Mr McDermid sought damages from his UK employer, even though at the time he was working under the control of a foreign captain who was clearly not an employee of the UK company.

The court decided that there was no need to prove even a temporary relationship of employer and employee between the Dutch company and Mr McDermid. Under the common law of vicarious liability, the employer's safety duties are owed to the employee personally. They cannot be got rid of by delegation. Further, when an employer puts his employee into the hands of another he is entrusting the performance of his own safety duties to that other but the employer remains responsible.

Taking all the factors into account, the court ruled that Mr McDermid's employer was vicariously liable for the negligence of the Dutch tug captain and stated:

'It is clear therefore that if an employer delegates to another person, whether an employee or not, his personal duty to take reasonable care for the safety of his employees, the employer is liable for injury caused through the negligence of that person because it is in the eyes of the law his own negligence.'

The employer's appeal to the House of Lords was dismissed, and it was held that an employer's duty to his employee to exercise reasonable care to ensure that the system of work provided for him is safe, is 'personal' and 'non-delegable'. It is no defence for the employer to show that he delegated its performance to a person whom he reasonably believed to be competent to perform it.

It was also stated in court that the negligence of the Dutch captain was not casual but central. It involved abandoning a safe system and operating in its place a manifestly unsafe system.

Hazards left on highways

C8138   An occupier is not under a duty of care to check that a contractor removes hazards from a highway, and so is not liable for consequential injuries. In *Rowe v Herman and others, The Times, 9 June 1997*, the plaintiff (R) sought damages for injuries sustained by tripping over some metal plates left lying on the pavement by an independent contractor (L), which had been carrying out (and had finished) some building work for the occupier (H). H contended that he was not liable for L's negligence under the general principle that an employer is not liable for an independent contractor's negligence. There are two main exceptions to this basic principle – an employer is liable:

(i)   where the work commissioned involved extra hazardous acts; and

(ii)   where danger was created by work on a highway.

The county court held that although H was not liable for the hazard whilst work was being carried out, he became liable under the principle in (ii) once L had finished the work. H appealed.

The Court of Appeal allowed H's appeal. Previous cases, where the employer was held liable, concerned obstructions to the highway being caused as a result of work being carried out under statutory powers, such obstructions arising directly from the work which the employer was required to do (being integral to it). In this case H was not obliged to carry out the building work, and it was not an integral part of the work to obstruct the footway (the plates had merely been laid to prevent lorries from damaging the pavement). It was clear that if the accident had occurred whilst L was carrying out the work, H would not have been liable; it made no sense to suddenly place H under such a duty once L had left the site. Following the general principle that H had no control over the manner in which L carried out its work, so too H had no control over the way that L cleared up.

Control of Major Accident Hazards

Introduction

C10001
The *Control of Major Accident Hazards Regulations 1999 (SI 1999 No 743)* implement the requirements of the 'Seveso II' Directive (96/82/EC) on the control of major accident hazards involving dangerous substances. Seveso II replaced the original Seveso Directive (82/501/EEC) which was implemented in Great Britain by the *Control of Industrial Major Accident Hazards Regulations 1984 (CIMAH)* which in turn have been replaced by the *Control of Major Accident Hazards Regulations 1999 (COMAH)*. *COMAH* came into force on 1 April 1999. The provisions of Article 12 of Seveso II concerning land-use planning have been implemented in the *Planning (Control of Major Accident Hazards) Regulations 1999 (SI 1999 No 981)*.

Control of Major Accident Hazards Regulations 1999 (SI 1999 No 743)

C10002
COMAH gives effect to a safety regime for the prevention and mitigation of major accidents resulting from ultra-hazardous industrial activities. The emphasis is on controlling risks to both people and the environment through demonstrable safety management systems, which are integrated into the routine of business rather than dealt with as an add-on.

An occurrence is regarded as a major accident if:

— it results from uncontrolled developments (i.e. they are sudden, unexpected or unplanned) in the course of the operation of an establishment to which the Regulations apply; and

— it leads to serious danger to people or to the environment, on or off-site; and

— it involves one or more dangerous substances defined in the Regulations.

Major emissions, fires and explosions are the most typical major accidents.

The duties placed on operators by *COMAH* fall into two categories: 'lower tier' and 'top tier'. Lower tier duties fall upon all operators. Some operators are subject to additional, top-tier, duties.

An 'operator' is a person (including a company or partnership) who is in control of the operation of an establishment or installation. Where the establishment or installation is to be constructed or operated, the 'operator' is the person who proposes to control its operation – where that person is not known, then the operator is the person who has commissioned its design and construction.

The HSE and the Environment Agency (in England and Wales) or the Scottish Environment Protection Agency are jointly responsible as the competent authority (CA) for *COMAH*. A co-ordinated approach will be adopted with the HSE likely to act as the primary contact for operators. A charging regime has been introduced and fees are payable by the operator to the HSE for work carried out by the HSE and the

Environment Agency. Under *Reg 19*, the CA must organise an adequate system of inspections of all establishments, and then must prepare a report on the inspection.

Application

C10003   The Regulations apply to an *establishment* where:

(*a*)   dangerous substances are present; or

(*b*)   their presence is anticipated; or

(*c*)   it is reasonable to believe that they may be generated during the loss of control of an industrial chemical process.

'Loss of control' excludes expected, planned or permitted discharges.

'Industrial chemical process' means that premises with no such chemical process do not fall within the scope of the Regulations solely because of dangerous substances generated during an accident.

An 'establishment' means the whole area under the control of the same person where dangerous substances are present in one or more installations. Two or more areas under the control of the same person and separated only by a road, railway or inland waterway are to be treated as one whole area.

'Dangerous substances' are those which:

(*a*)   are named at the appropriate threshold (see Table 1); or

(*b*)   fall within a generic category at the appropriate threshold (see Table 2).

There are two threshold levels: lower tier (Column 2 of the Tables) and top tier (Column 3).

Table 1

Column 1	Column 2	Column 3
Dangerous substances	*Quantity in tonnes*	
Ammonium nitrate (see note below)	350	2,500
Ammonium nitrate (see note below)	1,250	5,000
Arsenic pentoxide, arsenic (V) acid and/or salts	1	2
Arsenic trioxide, arsenious (III) acid and/or salts	0.1	0.1
Bromine	20	100
Chlorine	10	25
Nickel compounds in inhalable powder form (nickel monoxide, nickel dioxide, nickel sulphide, trinickel disulphide, dinickel trioxide)	1	1
Ethyleneimine	10	20
Fluorine	10	20
Formaldehyde (concentration=90%)	5	50

Hydrogen	5	50
Hydrogen chloride (liquefied gas)	25	250
Lead alkyls	5	50
Liquefied extremely flammable gases (including LPG) and natural gas (whether liquefied or not)	50	200
Acetylene	5	50
Ethylene oxide	5	50
Propylene oxide	5	50
Methanol	500	5,000
4, 4-Methylenebis (2-chloraniline) and/or salts, in powder form	0.01	0.01
Methylisocyanate	0.15	0.15
Oxygen	200	2,000
Toluene diisocyanate	10	100
Carbonyl dichloride (phosgene)	0.3	0.75
Arsenic trihydride (arsine)	0.2	1
Phosphorus trihydride (phosphine)	0.2	1
Sulphur dichloride	1	1
Sulphur trioxide	15	75
Polychlorodibenzofurans and polychlorodibenzodioxins (including TCDD), calculated in TCDD equivalent	0.001	0.001
The following CARCINOGENS:	0.001	0.001
4-Aminobiphenyl and/or its salts, Benzidine and/or salts, Bis(chloromethyl) ether, Chloromethyl methyl ether, Dimethylcarbamoyl chloride, Dimethylnitrosomine, Hexamethylphosphoric triamide, 2-Naphthylamine and/or salts, 1, 3 Propanesultone and 4-nitrodiphenyl		
Automotive petrol and other petroleum spirit	5,000	50,000

[*Schedule 1, Part 2*].

Ammonium nitrate:

(*a*)   The 350 / 2500 quantities apply to ammonium nitrate and ammonium nitrate compounds in which the nitrogen content as a result of the ammonium nitrate is more than 28 per cent by weight (except for those compounds referred to in (*b*) below) and to aqueous ammonium nitrate solutions in which the concentration of ammonium nitrate is more than 90 per cent by weight.

(*b*)   The 1250 / 5000 quantities apply to simple ammonium-nitrate based fertilisers which conform with the requirements of the *Fertilisers Regulations 1991* and to composite fertilisers in which the nitrogen content as a result of the ammonium nitrate is more than 28 per cent in weight (a composite fertiliser contains ammonium nitrate with phosphate or potash, or phosphate and potash).

[Notes 1 and 2 of *Part 2 of Schedule 1*].

Substances are classified according to *Regulation 5* of the *Chemicals (Hazard Information and Packaging for Supply) Regulations 1994*.

Table 2

Column 1	Column 2	Column 3
Categories of dangerous substances	*Quantity*	*in tonnes*
1. VERY TOXIC	5	20
2. TOXIC	50	200
3. OXIDISING	50	200
4. EXPLOSIVE (see C10004 below)	50	200
5. EXPLOSIVE (see C10004 below)	10	50
6. FLAMMABLE (as defined in Sch 1 Part 3)	5,000	50,000
7a. HIGHLY FLAMMABLE (as defined in Sch 1 Part 3)	50	200
7b. HIGHLY FLAMMABLE liquids (as defined in Sch 1 Part 3)	5,000	50,000
8. EXTREMELY FLAMMABLE (as defined in Sch 1 Part 3)	10	50
9. DANGEROUS FOR THE ENVIRONMENT in combination with risk phrases:		
R50: 'Very toxic to aquatic organisms'	200	500
R51: 'Toxic to aquatic organisms'; and R53: 'May cause long-term adverse effects in the aquatic environment'	500	2,000
10. ANY CLASSIFICATION not covered by those given above in combination with risk phrases:		
R14: 'Reacts violently with water' (including R14/15)	100	500
R29: 'in contact with water, liberates toxic gas'	50	200

[*Schedule 1, Part 3*].

Where a substance or group of substances named in Table 1 also falls within a category in Table 2, the qualifying quantities set out in Table 1 must be used.

Dangerous substances present at an establishment only in quantities not exceeding 2 per cent of the relevant qualifying quantity are ignored for the purposes of calculating the total quantity present, provided that their location is such that they cannot initiate a major accident elsewhere on site.

Explosives

C10004   Note 2 to *Part 3 of Schedule 1* defines an '*explosive*' as:

(*a*)   (i)   a substance or preparation which creates the risk of an explosion by shock, friction, fire or other sources of ignition;

(ii)   a pyrotechnic substance is a substance (or mixture of substances) designed to produce heat, light, sound, gas or smoke or a combination of such effects through non-detonating self-sustained exothermic chemical reactions; or

(iii)   an explosive or pyrotechnic substance or preparation contained in objects;

(*b*)   a substance or preparation which creates extreme risks of explosion by shock, friction, fire or other sources of ignition.

Aggregation

C10005   There is a rule for aggregation of dangerous substances set out in Note 4 to *Part 3 of Schedule 1*. The rule will apply in the following circumstances:

(i)   for substances and preparations appearing in Table 1 at quantities less than their individual qualifying quantity present with substances having the same classification from Table 2, and the addition of substances and preparations with the same classification from Table 2;

(ii)   for the addition of categories 1, 2 and 9 present at an establishment together;

(iii)   for the addition of categories 3, 4, 5, 6, 7a, 7b and 8, present at an establishment together.

The sub-threshold quantities of named dangerous substances or categories of dangerous substances are expressed as partial fractions of the threshold quantities in column 3 of Table 1 or of Table 2, and added together. When the total exceeds 1, top-tier duties apply.

If the total is less than or equal to 1, the sub-threshold quantities of named dangerous substances or categories of dangerous substances are expressed as partial fractions of the threshold quantities in column 2 of Table 1 or of Table 2, and added together. If the total exceeds 1, lower tier duties apply.

Definitive guidance on aggregation can be found in HSE's '*Guide to the Control of Major Accident Hazards Regulations 1999*'.

Exclusions

C10006   *COMAH* does not apply to:

—   Ministry of Defence establishments;

—   extractive industries exploring for, or exploiting, materials in mines and quarries;

—   waste land-fill sites;

—   transport related activities;

—   substances at nuclear licensed sites which create a hazard from ionising radiation.

COMAH does apply to explosives and chemicals at nuclear installations.

Lower tier duties

General duty

C10007   Under *Reg 4*, every operator is under a general duty to take *all measures necessary* to prevent major accidents and limit their consequences to persons and the environment.

Although the best practice is to completely eliminate a risk, the Regulations recognise that this is not always possible. Prevention should be considered in a hierarchy based on the principle of reducing risk to a level as low as is reasonably practicable, taking account of what is technically feasible and the balance between the costs and benefits of the measures taken. Operators must be able to demonstrate that they have adopted control measures which are adequate for the risks identified. Where hazards are high, high standards will be expected by the enforcement agencies to ensure that risks are acceptably low.

Major accident prevention policy (MAPP)

C10008   Under *Reg 5(1)*, every operator must prepare and keep a document (MAPP) setting out his policy with respect to the prevention of major accidents.

The requirement for a MAPP is new. The document must be in writing and must include sufficient particulars to demonstrate that the operator has established an appropriate safety management system. *Schedule 2* sets out the principles to be taken into account when preparing a MAPP document and at *para 4* lists the following specific issues to be addressed by the safety management system:

(*a*)   *organisation and personnel* – the roles and responsibilities of personnel involved in the management of major hazards at all levels in the organisation. The identification of training needs of such personnel and the provision of the training so identified. The involvement of employees and, where appropriate, sub-contractors;

(*b*)   *identification and evaluation of major hazards* – adoption and implementation of procedures for systematically identifying major hazards arising from normal and abnormal operation and the assessment of their likelihood and severity;

(*c*)   *operational control* – adoption and implementation of procedures and instructions for safe operation, including maintenance of plant, processes, equipment and temporary stoppages;

(*d*)   *management of change* – adoption and implementation of procedures for planning modifications to, or the design of, new installations, processes or storage facilities;

(*e*)   *planning for emergencies* – adoption and implementation of procedures to identify foreseeable emergencies by systematic analysis and to prepare, test and review emergency plans to respond to such emergencies;

(*f*)   *monitoring performance* – adoption and implementation of procedures for the on-going assessment of compliance with the objectives set by the operator's major accident prevention policy and safety management system, and the mechanisms for investigation and taking corrective action in the case of non-compliance. The procedures should cover the operator's system for reporting major accidents or near misses, particularly those involving failure of protective measures, and their investigation and follow-up on the basis of lessons learnt;

(g)   *audit and review* – adoption and implementation of procedures for periodic systematic assessment of the major accident prevention policy and the effectiveness and suitability of the safety management system; the documented review of performance of the policy and safety management system and its updating by senior management.

The MAPP is a concise but key document for operators which sets out the framework within which adequate identification, prevention/control and mitigation of major accident hazards is achieved. Its purpose is to compel operators to provide a statement of commitment to achieving high standards of major hazard control, together with an indication that there is a management system covering all the issues set out in (*a*)–(*g*) above. The guidance to the Regulations suggests that the essential questions which operators must ask themselves are:

—   does the MAPP meet the requirements of the Regulations?

—   will it deliver a high level of protection for people and the environment?

—   are there management systems in place which achieve the objectives set out in the policy?

—   are the policy, management systems, risk control systems and workplace precautions kept under review to ensure that they are implemented and that they are relevant?

Not only must the MAPP be kept up to date (*Reg 5(4)*), but also the safety management system described in it must be put into operation (*Reg 5(5)*).

Notifications

C10009   Notification requirements are set out in *Reg 6*. 'Notify' means notify in writing.

Within a reasonable period of time before the start of construction of an establishment and before the start of the operation of an establishment, the operator must send to the CA a notification containing the information which is specified in *Schedule 3*. There is no need for the notification sent before start-up to contain any information which has already been included in the notification sent before the start of construction, if that information is still valid.

The operator of an existing establishment must send a notification containing the specified information by 3 February 2000, unless a report has been sent to the HSE in accordance with *Reg 7 of the Control of Industrial Major Accident Hazards Regulations 1984*.

The following information is specified in *Schedule 3* for inclusion in a notification:

(*a*)   the name and address of the operator;

(*b*)   the address of the establishment concerned;

(*c*)   the name or position of the person in charge of the establishment;

(*d*)   information sufficient to identify the dangerous substances or category of dangerous substances present;

(*e*)   the quantity and physical form of the dangerous substances present;

(*f*)   a description of the activity or proposed activity of the installation concerned;

(g)   details of the elements of the immediate environment liable to cause a major accident or to aggravate the consequences thereof.

Notification is a continuing duty. *Regulation 6(4)* provides that an operator must notify the CA forthwith in the event of:

— any significant increase in the quantity of dangerous substances previously notified;

— any significant change in the nature or physical form of the dangerous substances previously notified, the processes employing them or any other information notified to the CA in respect of the establishment;

— *Regulation 7* ceasing to apply to the establishment as a result of a change in the quantity of dangerous substances present there; or

— permanent closure of an installation in the establishment.

Information that has been included in a safety report does not need to be notified.

Duty to report a major accident

C10010   Where a major accident has occurred at an establishment, the operator must immediately inform the CA of the accident [*Reg 15(3)*].

This duty will be satisfied when the operator notifies a major accident to the HSE in accordance with the requirements of the *Reporting of Injuries, Diseases and Dangerous Occurrences Regulations 1995.*

The CA must then conduct a thorough investigation into the accident [*Reg 19*].

Top-tier duties

Safety report

C10011   Operators of top-tier sites are required to produce a safety report – its key requirement is that operators must show that they have taken all necessary measures for the prevention of major accidents and for limiting the consequences to people and the environment of any that do occur.

Safety reports are now required before construction as well as before start-up. *Regulation 7(1)* requires that within a reasonable period of time before the start of construction of an establishment the operator must send to the CA a report:

— containing information which is sufficient for the purpose specified in *paragraph 3(a) of Part 1 of Schedule 4* (see below); and

— comprising at least such of the information specified in *Part 2 of Schedule 4* (see below) as is relevant for that purpose.

Within a reasonable period of time before the start of the operation of an establishment the operator must send to the CA a report containing information which is sufficient for the purposes specified in *Part 1 of Schedule 4*, and comprising at least the information specified in *Part 2 of Schedule 4* [*Reg 7(5)*].

The report sent before start-up is not required to contain information already contained in the report sent before the start of construction.

An operator must ensure that neither construction of the establishment, nor its operation, is started until he has received the CA's conclusions on the report. The CA must communicate its conclusions within a reasonable period of time of receiving a safety report [*Reg 17(1)(a)*].

The operator of an existing establishment must send to the CA a report meeting the requirements of *Parts 1 and 2 of Schedule 4*. Current *CIMAH* top-tier sites that have submitted *CIMAH* safety reports in parts can continue to submit *COMAH* reports in parts. If a *CIMAH* report, or any part of it, is up for its three-yearly review before 3 February 2000, a *COMAH* report must be sent before that date or such later date (no later than 3 February 2001) as may be agreed by the CA. If the review would have fallen after that date a *COMAH* report must be sent by 3 February 2001. In any other case the safety report must be sent by 3 February 2002.

PURPOSE OF SAFETY REPORTS

1. Demonstrating that a major accident prevention policy and a safety management system for implementing it have been put into effect in accordance with the information set out in *Schedule 2;*

2. Demonstrating that major accident hazards have been identified and that the necessary measures have been taken to prevent such accidents and to limit their consequences to persons and the environment;

3. Demonstrating that adequate safety and reliability have been incorporated into the

    (a)   design and construction, and

    (b)   operation and maintenance,

    of any installation and equipment and infrastructure connected with its operation, and that they are linked to major accident hazards within the establishment;

4. Demonstrating that on-site emergency plans have been drawn up and supplying information to enable the off-site plan to be drawn up in order to take the necessary measures in the event of a major accident;

5. Providing sufficient information to the competent authority to enable decisions to be made in terms of the siting of new activities or developments around establishments.

    [Schedule 4, Part 1]

MINIMUM INFORMATION TO BE INCLUDED IN SAFETY REPORT

1. Information on the management system and on the organisation of the establishment with a view to major accident prevention.

    This information must contain the elements set out in *Schedule 2*.

2. Presentation of the environment of the establishment:

    (a)   a description of the site and its environment including the geographical location, meteorological, geographical, hydrographic conditions and, if necessary, its history;

    (b)   identification of installations and other activities of the establishment which could present a major accident hazard;

    (c)   a description of areas where a major accident may occur.

3.   Description of installation:

(a)   a description of the main activities and products of the parts of the establishment which are important from the point of view of safety, sources of major accident risks and conditions under which such a major accident could happen, together with a description of proposed preventive measures;

(b)   description of processes, in particular the operating methods;

(c)   description of dangerous substances:

(i)   inventory of dangerous substances including –

—   the identification of dangerous substances: chemical name, the number allocated to the substance by the Chemicals Abstract Service, name according to International Union of Pure and Applied Chemistry nomenclature;

—   the maximum quantity of dangerous substances present;

(ii)   physical, chemical, toxicological characteristics and indication of the hazards, both immediate and delayed, for people and the environment;

(iii)   physical and chemical behaviour under normal conditions of use or under foreseeable accidental conditions.

4.   Identification and accidental risks analysis and prevention methods:

(a)   detailed description of the possible major accident scenarios and their probability or the conditions under which they occur including a summary of the events which may play a role in triggering each of these scenarios, the causes being internal or external to the installation;

(b)   assessment of the extent and severity of the consequences of identified major accidents;

(c)   description of technical parameters and equipment used for the safety of the installations.

5.   Measures of protection and intervention to limit the consequences of an accident:

(a)   description of the equipment installed in the plant to limit the consequences of major accidents;

(b)   organisation of alert and intervention;

(c)   description of mobilisable resources, internal or external;

(d)   summary of elements described in sub-paragraphs (a), (b) and (c) necessary for drawing up the on-site emergency plan.

[*Schedule 4, Part 2*]

All or part of the information required to be included in a safety report can be so included by reference to information contained in another report or notification furnished by virtue of other statutory requirements. This should be done only where the information in the other document is up to date, and adequate in terms of scope and level of detail.

If an operator can demonstrate that particular dangerous substances are in a state incapable of creating a major accident hazard, the CA can limit the information required to be included in the safety report [*Reg 7(12)*].

An operator must provide the CA with such further information as it may reasonably request in writing following its examination of the safety report [*Reg 7(13)*].

Review and revision of safety report

C10012   Where a safety report has been sent to the CA, the operator must review it:

—   at least every five years;

—   whenever a review is necessary because of new facts or to take account of new technical knowledge about safety matters; and

—   whenever the operator makes a change to the safety management system, which could have significant repercussions.

Where it is necessary to revise the report as a result of the review, the operator must carry out the revision immediately and inform the CA of the details [*Reg 8(1)*].

An operator must inform the CA when he has reviewed the safety report but not revised it [*Reg 8(2)*].

Current *CIMAH* top-tier sites that have submitted *CIMAH* safety reports in parts must review each part within five years from the time when that part was sent to the CA.

When modifications which could have significant repercussions are proposed (to the establishment or an installation in it, to the process carried on there or the nature or quantity of dangerous substances present there), the operator must review the safety report and where necessary revise it, in advance of any such modification. Details of any revision must be notified to the CA.

On-site emergency plan

C10013   *Regulation 9(1)* requires operators of top-tier establishments to prepare an on-site emergency plan. The plan must be adequate to secure the objectives specified in *Part 1 of Schedule 5*, namely:

—   containing and controlling incidents so as to minimise the effects, and to limit damage to persons, the environment and property;

—   implementing the measures necessary to protect persons and the environment from the effects of major accidents;

—   communicating the necessary information to the public and to the emergency services and authorities concerned in the area;

—   providing for the restoration and clean-up of the environment following a major accident.

The plan must contain the following information:

—   names or positions of persons authorised to set emergency procedures in motion and the person in charge of and co-ordinating the on-site mitigatory action;

—   name or position of the person with responsibility for liaison with the local authority responsible for preparing the off-site emergency plan (see below);

— for foreseeable conditions or events which could be significant in bringing about a major accident, a description of the action which should be taken to control the conditions or events and to limit their consequences, including a description of the safety equipment and the resources available;

— arrangements for limiting the risks to persons on site including how warnings are to be given and the actions persons are expected to take on receipt of a warning;

— arrangements for providing early warning of the incident to the local authority responsible for setting the off-site emergency plan in motion, the type of information which should be contained in an initial warning and the arrangements for the provision of more detailed information as it becomes available;

— arrangements for training staff in the duties they will be expected to perform, and where necessary co-ordinating this with the emergency services;

— arrangements for providing assistance with off-site mitigatory action.

[*Schedule 5, Part 2*].

Current *CIMAH* top-tier sites that were subject to *CIMAH* requirements for the preparation of an on-site emergency plan must prepare a *COMAH* emergency plan by 3 February 2001. Any other existing establishment must prepare an on-site emergency plan by 3 February 2002. New establishments must prepare such a plan before start-up.

When preparing an on-site emergency plan, the operator must consult:

— employees at the establishment;

— the Environment Agency (or the Scottish Environment Protection Agency);

— the emergency services;

— the health authority for the area where the establishment is situated; and

— the local authority, unless it has been exempted from the requirement to prepare an off-site emergency plan.

Off-site emergency plan

C10014   The local authority for the area where a top-tier establishment is located must prepare an adequate emergency plan for dealing with off-site consequences of possible major accidents. As with the on-site plan, it should be in writing.

The objectives set out in *Part 1 of Schedule 5* (see above) also apply to off-site emergency plans.

The plan must contain the following information:

— names or positions of persons authorised to set emergency procedures in motion and of persons authorised to take charge of and co-ordinate off-site action;

— arrangements for receiving early warning of incidents, and alert and call-out procedures;

— arrangements for co-ordinating resources necessary to implement the off-site emergency plan;

— arrangements for providing assistance with on-site mitigatory action;

— arrangements for off-site mitigatory action;

— arrangements for providing the public with specific information relating to the accident and the behaviour which it should adopt;

— arrangements for the provision of information to the emergency services of other Member States in the event of a major accident with possible trans-boundary consequences.

An operator must supply the local authority with the information necessary for the authority's purposes, plus any additional information reasonably requested in writing by the local authority.

In preparing the off-site emergency plan, the local authority must consult:

— the operator;

— the emergency services;

— the CA;

— each health authority for the area in the vicinity of the establishment; and

— such members of the public as it deems appropriate.

[*Reg 10(6)*].

In the light of the safety report, the CA may exempt a local authority from the requirement to prepare an off-site emergency plan in respect of an establishment [*Reg 10(7)*].

Reviewing, testing and implementing emergency plans

C10015   *Regulation 11* requires that emergency plans are reviewed and, where necessary, revised, at least every three years. Reviewing is a key process for addressing the adequacy and effectiveness of the components of the emergency plan – it should take into account:

— changes occurring in the establishment to which the plan relates;

— any changes in the emergency services relevant to the operation of the plan;

— advances in technical knowledge;

— knowledge gained as a result of major accidents either on-site or elsewhere; and

— lessons learned during the testing of emergency plans.

There is a new requirement to test emergency plans at least every three years. Such tests will assist in the assessment of the accuracy, completeness and practicability of the plan: if the test reveals any deficiencies, the relevant plan must be revised. Agreement should be reached beforehand between the operator, the emergency services and the local authority on the scale and nature of the emergency plan testing to be carried out.

Where there have been any modifications or significant changes to the establishment, operators should not wait for the three-year review before reviewing the adequacy and accuracy of the emergency planning arrangements.

When a major accident occurs, the operator and local authority are under a duty to implement the on-site and off-site emergency plans [*Reg 12*].

Local authority charges

C10016   A local authority may charge the operator a fee for performing its functions under *Regs 10 and 11*, i.e. for preparing, reviewing and testing off-site emergency plans.

The charges can only cover costs that have been reasonably incurred. If a local authority has contracted out some of the work to another organisation, the authority may recover the costs of the contract from the operator, provided that they are reasonable.

In presenting a fee to an operator, the local authority should provide an itemised, detailed statement of work done and costs incurred.

Provision of information to the public

C10017   The operator must supply information on safety measures to people within an area without their having to request it. The area is notified to the operator by the CA as being one in which people are liable to be affected by a major accident occurring at the establishment. The minimum information to be supplied to the public is specified in *Schedule 6*:

INFORMATION TO BE SUPPLIED TO THE PUBLIC

—   name of operator and address of the establishment;

—   identification, by position held, of the person giving the information;

—   confirmation that the establishment is subject to these regulations and that the notification referred to in *Reg* 6 or the safety report has been submitted to the competent authority;

—   an explanation in simple terms of the activity or activities undertaken at the establishment;

—   the common names or, in the case of dangerous substances covered by *Part 3 of Schedule 1*, the generic names or the general danger classification of the substances and preparations involved at the establishment which could give rise to a major accident, with an indication of their principal dangerous characteristics;

—   general information relating to the nature of the major accident hazards, including their potential effects on the population and the environment;

—   adequate information on how the population concerned will be warned and kept informed in the event of a major accident;

—   adequate information on the actions the population concerned should take, and on the behaviour they should adopt, in the event of a major accident;

—   confirmation that the operator is required to make adequate arrangements on site, in particular liaison with the emergency services, to deal with major accidents and to minimise their effects;

—   a reference to the off-site emergency plan for the establishment. This should include advice to co-operate with any instructions or requests from the emergency services at the time of an accident;

> — details of where further relevant information can be obtained, unless making that information available would be contrary to the interests of national security or personal confidentiality or would prejudice to an unreasonable degree the commercial interests of any person.

Under *Sch 8*, the CA must maintain a public register which will include:

— the information included in the notifications submitted by the operators under *Reg 6*;

— top-tier operators' safety reports;

— the CA's conclusions of its examination of safety reports.

Powers to prohibit use

C10018   The CA is required to prohibit the operation or bringing into operation of any establishment or installation or any part of it where the measures taken by the operator for the prevention and mitigation of major accidents are seriously deficient [*Reg 18(1)*].

The CA may prohibit the operation or bringing into operation of any establishment or installation or any part of it if the operator has failed to submit any notification, safety report or other information required under the Regulations within the required time. Where the CA proposes to exercise its prohibitory powers, it must serve on the operator a notice giving reasons for the prohibition and specifying the date when it is to take effect. A notice may specify measures to be taken. The CA may, in writing, withdraw any notice.

Enforcement

C10019   The Regulations are treated as if they are health and safety regulations for the purpose of *HSWA 1974*. The provisions as to offences of the 1974 Act, *sections 33–42*, apply. A failure by the CA to discharge a duty under the Regulations is not an offence [*Reg 20(2)*], although the remedy of judicial review is available.

Public Information for Radiation Emergencies Regulations 1992 (SI 1992 No 2997)

C10020   In the wake of Chernobyl, the *Public Information for Radiation Emergencies Regulations 1992* require employers in control of nuclear installations, from which radiation emergencies are reasonably foreseeable, to apprise the general public of the danger in tandem with local authorities. Ministry of Defence installations are exempt from these requirements if the interests of national security so dictate.

Potential radiation emergency

C10021   An employer (or self-employed person) who conducts an undertaking, where a radiation emergency is reasonably foreseeable, must:

(*a*)   supply members of the public likely to be in an area in which they are liable to be affected by a radiation emergency arising from the undertaking with information, without their having to request it, concerning:

(i)   basic facts about radioactivity and its effects on persons/environment;

     (ii)   the various types of radiation emergency covered and their consequences for people/environment;

     (iii) emergency measures to alert, protect and assist people in the event of a radiation emergency;

     (iv) action to be taken by people in the event of an emergency;

     (v)   authority/authorities responsible for implementing emergency measures;

(*b*)   make the information publicly available; and

(*c*)   update the information at least every three years.

[*Reg 3 and Schedule 2*].

Actual radiation emergency

C10022   It is incumbent on county councils to prepare and update information, including advice on appropriate health protection measures, relating to a radiation emergency. The information must be supplied at regular intervals to members of the public actually affected by the radiation emergency. The following information should be supplied:

(*a*)   the type of emergency that has occurred and, where possible, its characteristics, for example, its origin, extent and probable development;

(*b*)   advice on health protection measures which, depending on the type of emergency, might include:

     (i)   restrictions on consumption of certain foodstuffs and water supply likely to be contaminated;

     (ii) hygiene and decontamination;

     (iii) recommendation to stay indoors;

     (iv) distribution/use of protective substances;

     (v)   evacuation arrangements;

     (vi) special warnings for certain population groups;

(*c*)   announcements concerning co-operation with instructions or compliance with competent authorities;

(*d*)   if there has been no release of radioactivity/ionising radiations, but this is likely:

     (i)   advice to listen to radio/television;

     (ii) preparatory advice to establishments with particular collective responsibilities;

     (iii) recommendations to occupational groups particularly affected;

(*e*)   if time permits, information on the basic facts of radioactivity and its effects on persons/environment.

[*Reg 4 and Schedule 3*].

Dangerous Substances I – at the Workplace

Background and classification

D1001 Over the last hundred years the number of dangerous substances used at the workplace has multiplied enormously, as has the variety of processes, machinery and gadgetry generating dusts, fumes, gases and vapours. With technological development came a series of ad hoc regulations aimed at controlling the effects of dangerous substances in particular industries. Following the *Health and Safety at Work etc. Act 1974*, earlier legislation and regulations were replaced by regulations containing codes of practice, requiring employers to *assess* the health risks to employees and implement health-oriented and risk-preventive strategies – an example being the *Control of Substances Hazardous to Health Regulations 1994* (*COSHH*), now replaced by the *Control of Substances Hazardous to Health Regulations 1999* (see D1024 below).

The great majority of hazardous substances used in industry and commerce, as well as in research establishments, are chemical compounds, including several naturally occurring substances, such as asbestos (see ASBESTOS), heavy metals (such as zinc, chromium and lead), silica, mineral oils and compressed air. In addition, workers may be exposed to hazards from biological agents, such as bacteria, moulds and fungi, some of which are respiratory sensitisers (see D1043 below).

Exposure to a whole range of hazardous substances at work can lead to the onset of identifiable diseases and adverse health effects, including some diseases which are prescribed and for which disablement benefit is payable (see O1046 OCCUPATIONAL HEALTH). This section examines:

  (i) notification of new substances (D1003);

  (ii) notification of sites handling hazardous substances (D1008);

  (iii) marking of hazardous sites (D1009);

  (iv) classification, packaging and labelling of dangerous substances for supply (D1013);

  (v) control of substances hazardous to health (including biological agents, carcinogens and respiratory sensitisers) (D1024, D1039, D1043);

  (vi) controls over lead (D1044);

  (vii) controls over radioactive substances (D1045);

  (viii) controls over explosives (D1064).

New and existing substances

D1002 The European Inventory of Existing Commercial Chemical Substances (EINECS) lists all 100,000 substances marketed for commercial purposes between 1 January

1971 and 18 September 1981. These 'existing substances' are controlled by Council Regulation 793/93/EEC, the *Existing Substances Regulations*, whilst *HSWA* enforcement powers regarding such substances are conferred by the *Notification of Existing Substances (Enforcement) Regulations 1994 (SI 1994 No 1806)*. By contrast, a new substance is one not listed in EINECS and controlled by the *Notification of New Substances Regulations 1993 (SI 1993 No 3050)*.

Notification of new substances – Notification of New Substances Regulations 1993 (SI 1993 No 3050)

D1003   These regulations govern notification of new chemical substances scheduled for commercial circulation, and new substances, notified to the Secretary of State and HSE under these regulations, may appear in the European List of Notified Chemical Substances (ELINCS), subject to certain agreed information being kept confidential [*Reg 19*]. The regulations require:

(a)   *Full notification* – a person must not place a new substance on the market, in a total quantity of one tonne or more per year, unless he has sent to the 'competent authority' (i.e. the Secretary of State for the Environment and the HSE acting together):

   (i)   a technical dossier evaluating foreseeable risks;

   (ii)   a written certificate to the effect that tests, in accordance with good laboratory practice, have been carried out on the new substance;

   (iii)   a declaration relating to the unfavourable effects of the substance; and

   (iv)   in the case of 'dangerous substances' (see D1013 below), methods of proposed compliance with the *Chemicals (Hazard Information and Packaging for Supply) Regulations 1994 (CHIP 2)*.

[*Reg 4*].

(b)   *Follow-up information* – the competent authority must be notified of:

   (i)   changes in the annual or total quantity;

   (ii)   new knowledge of the effects on health or environment;

   (iii)   new uses for substances;

   (iv)   change in the composition of the substance;

   (v)   change in status of manufacturer/importer.

[*Reg 10*].

(c)   *Further testing* – in respect of substances already notified, the competent authority must be notified of:

   (i)   when the quantity of the substance placed on the market reaches 10 tonnes per year from a single manufacturer, or when the total quantity reaches 50 tonnes per manufacturer, the competent authority *may* require some/all of the tests in *Schedule 3, level 1*, i.e. physico-chemical studies, toxicological and ecotoxicity studies;

   (ii)   when the quantity of the substance placed on the market reaches 100 tonnes per year from a single manufacturer, or when the total quantity reaches 500 tonnes per manufacturer, the competent authority *shall* require the tests in *Schedule 3, level 1* (as in (c)(i) above), to be carried out;

    (iii)   when the quantity of the substance placed on the market reaches 1,000 tonnes per year from a single manufacturer or when the total quantity of the substance reaches 5,000 tonnes per manufacturer, the competent authority *shall* draw up a programme of tests at *Schedule 3, level 2*, i.e. toxicological and ecotoxicological studies.

[*Reg 5*].

Reduced notification requirements – substances in small quantities

D1004   There are reduced notification requirements for substances placed on the market in a total quantity of less than one tonne per year by a single manufacturer, and, indeed, some substances are deemed to have been notified, namely:

(*a*)   polymers (generally);

(*b*)   substances in quantities of less than 10 kg per manufacturer, accompanied by a technical dossier containing information necessary for the competent authority to assess risks to humans and the environment [*Sch 2, Part C*];

(*c*)   substances in quantities of less than 100 kg, intended for scientific research and development;

(*d*)   substances for process-oriented research and development with a limited number of registered customers in similarly limited quantities.

[*Reg 6*].

Placing notified substances on the market

(*a*) Full notification of substances

D1005   In the absence of objection by the competent authority, notified substances can be placed on the market after expiry of 60 days following receipt of notification.

(*b*) Reduced notification of substances

In the absence of objection by the competent authority, reduced notification substances can be placed on the market after expiry of 30 days following receipt of notification.

[*Reg 8*].

In the case of both types of substances, the competent authority (i.e. HSE and the Department of the Environment) must carry out an on-going risk assessment to human health and the environment. [*Reg 16*].

Enforcement

D1006   Enforcement of these regulations is by the HSE, and where breach of duty causes injury/damage, there is consequent civil liability. [*Reg 21*].

Excluded substances

D1007   Some substances, when new, do not have to be notified, namely:

(*a*)   medicines;

(*b*)   food substances;

(*c*)   animal feeding stuffs;

(*d*)   plant protection products;

(*e*)   radioactive substances;

(*f*)   waste;

(*g*)   cosmetics;

(*h*)   substances in transit;

(*j*)   substances for export outside the EU; and

(*k*)   a new substance no longer a polymer (i.e. placed on the market before 31 October 1993 and not notified under the *New Substances Regulations 1982 (SI 1982 No 1496)*).

[*Reg 3*].

Notification of sites handling hazardous substances – Notification of Installations Handling Hazardous Substances Regulations 1982 (SI 1982 No 1357)

D1008   Activities involving a notifiable quantity (or more) of a 'hazardous substance' must not be carried on at any site or in (most) pipelines, unless the HSE has been notified in writing at least three months before such activity commences, or within such shorter time as the HSE specifies. [*Reg 3(1)*]. The notification should include all of the following matters:

(*a*)   *In the case of sites:*

(i)   the name and address of the person making the notification;

(ii)   the address of the site where the notifiable activity will take place (including ordnance survey grid reference);

(iii)   the area of the site in question;

(iv)   the date when it is anticipated that the notifiable activity will commence, or, if already commenced, a statement to that effect;

(v)   a general description of the activities carried on or intended to be carried on;

(vi)   the name and address of the planning authority; and

(vii)   the name and maximum quantity of each hazardous substance liable to be on site.

[*Notification of Installations Handling Hazardous Substances Regulations, Reg 3(1), Sch 2 Pt I*].

(*b*)   *In the case of pipelines:*

(i)   the name and address of the person making the notification;

(ii)   the address of the place from which the pipeline activity is controlled and the addresses of the places where the pipeline starts and finishes, an ordnance survey grid reference of where the pipeline starts and finishes, and a map showing the pipeline route;

(iii)   the date when it is anticipated that the notifiable activity will commence, or, if already commenced, a statement to that effect;

(iv) the name and address of the planning authorities in the area(s) where the pipeline lies; and

(v) the total length of the pipeline, its diameter and normal operating pressure, coupled with the name and maximum quantity of each hazardous substance liable to be in the pipeline.

[*Reg 3(1), Sch 2 Pt II*].

Reg 3(1) applies in the case of hazardous substances:

(i) within 500 metres of the site of a pipeline and connected to it;

(ii) any other site controlled by the same person within 500 metres of the site; and

(iii) in any vehicle, vessel, aircraft or hovercraft under the control of the same person, used for storage purposes at the site, or within 500 metres of it, but *not* if used for transporting hazardous substances (for regulations and requirements relating to transportation of hazardous substances, see DANGEROUS SUBSTANCES II).

[*Reg 3(2)*].

Activities involving the following quantities of hazardous substances on sites or in pipelines must be notified to the HSE:

Table 1

Notifiable quantities of named hazardous substances in relation to sites

1 Substance	2 Notifiable quantity tonnes
Liquefied petroleum gas, such as commercial propane and commercial butane, and any mixture thereof held at a pressure greater than 1.4 bar absolute	25
Liquefied petroleum gas, such as commercial propane and commercial butane, and any mixture thereof held under refrigeration at a pressure of 1.4 bar absolute or less	50
Phosgene	2
Chlorine	10
Hydrogen fluoride	10
Sulphur trioxide	15
Acrylonitrile	20
Hydrogen cyanide	20
Carbon disulphide	20
Sulphur dioxide	20
Bromine	40
Ammonia (anhydrous or as solution containing more than 50% by weight of ammonia)	100

Hydrogen	2
Ethylene oxide	5
Propylene oxide	5
tert-Butyl peroxyacetate	5
tert-Butyl peroxyisobutyrate	5
tert-Butyl peroxymaleate	5
tert-Butyl peroxy isopropyl carbonate	5
Dibenzyl peroxydicarbonate	5
2,2-Bis(*tert*-butylperoxy)butane	5
1,1-Bis(*tert*-butylperoxy)cyclohexane	5
Di-sec-butyl peroxydicarbonate	5
2,2-Dihydroperoxypropane	5
Di-*n*-propyl peroxydicarbonate	5
Methyl ethyl ketone peroxide	5
Sodium chlorate	25
Some cellulose nitrate	50
Some ammonium nitrate	500
Aqueous solutions containing more than 90 parts by weight of ammonium nitrate per 100 parts by weight of solution	500
Liquid oxygen	500
[*Sch 1 Pt I*].	

Table 2

Classes of substances not specifically named in Part I above

	1 Class of Substance		2 Notifiable quantity tonnes
1.	Gas or any mixture of gases which is flammable in air and is held in the installation as a gas.	15	
2.	A substance or any mixture of substances which is flammable in air and is normally held in the installation above its boiling-point (measured at 1 bar absolute) as a liquid or as a mixture of liquid and gas at a pressure of more than 1.4 bar absolute.	25	being the total quantity of substances above the boiling points whether held singly or in mixtures.

3.	A liquefied gas or any mixture of liquefied gases, which is flammable in air, has a boiling point of less than 0°C (measured at 1 bar absolute) and is normally held in the installation under refrigeration or cooling at a pressure of 1.4 bar absolute or less.	50	being the total quantity of substances having boiling points below 0°C whether held singly or in mixtures.
4.	A liquid or any mixture of liquids not included in items 1 to 3 above, which have a flash point of less than 21°C.	10,000	

[*Sch 1 Pt II*].

Marking of sites by signs – Dangerous Substances (Notification and Marking of Sites) Regulations 1990 (SI 1990 No 304)

D1009

These regulations are principally for the benefit of fire and emergency services attending the site. Where there is a total quantity of 25 tonnes (or more) of dangerous substances present on site, the *Dangerous Substances (Notification and Marking of Sites) Regulations 1990 (SI 1990 No 304)* require the *notification* and *marking* of such sites with appropriate safety signs. These regulations require that those in control of sites ensure that there are not more than 25 tonnes of 'dangerous substances' on site, unless there has first been notification to:

(*a*)   the local fire authority, and

(*b*)   HSE,

of

(i)   name and address of person notifying;

(ii)   full postal address of site;

(iii)   general description of nature of business;

(iv)   list of classifications of dangerous substances;

(v)   date when it is anticipated that total quantity of 25 tonnes (or more) of dangerous substances will be present.

[*Reg 4, Sch 2 Part I*].

A further notification is required when there is a cessation or reduction of dangerous substances already notified or if there is a change in the list of any classifications of dangerous substances. [*Reg 4, Sch 2 Part II*].

The following substances are excluded from these requirements:

(1)   radioactive substances (see D1045 below);

(2)   Class 1 explosives (see D1064–D1066 below);

(3)   substances in aerosol dispensers;

(4)   substances buried/deposited in the ground as waste.

[*Sch 2 para 1*].

Signs are to be kept clean and free from obstruction so far as reasonably practicable. [*Reg 7*].

Exceptions to duty to notify

D1010   The following sites have their own notification procedure, namely,

(*a*)   sites notifiable to HSE, in accordance with the *Notification of Installations Handling Hazardous Substances Regulations 1982 (SI 1982 No 1357)* (see D1008 above);

(*b*)   sites controlled by *Reg 7* of the *Control of Major Accident Hazards Regulations 1999 (SI 1999 No 743)* (see CONTROL OF MAJOR ACCIDENT HAZARDS);

(*c*)   sites controlled by the *Petroleum Spirit (Consolidation) Act 1928*;

(*d*)   sites controlled by *Reg 27* of the *Dangerous Substances in Harbour Areas Regulations 1987 (SI 1987 No 37)*;

(*e*)   sites for which there exists a waste management licence under *s 35* of the *Environmental Protection Act 1990*; and

(*f*)   nuclear sites.

Marking requirements

D1011   Where there are 25 tonnes (or more) of dangerous substances present on site, safety signs to BS 5378: 1980/1982 must be displayed, as specified in *Schedule 3*, so as to give adequate warning to firemen before entering a site in an emergency. Moreover, safety signs are required to be displayed at such locations on site as an inspector may direct, carrying the appropriate hazard warning symbol and text, e.g. skull and crossed bones – Toxic. In the case of substances with mixed classifications, the sign must carry the exclamation mark symbol (!) (see Table 3 below) plus the words 'DANGEROUS SUBSTANCE' (in capital letters). [*Reg 5*].

Table 3

Classifications and Hazard Warnings – Site markings (as per Marking of Sites Regulations 1990)

1 *Classification*	2 *Hazard warning symbol and text*
Non-flammable compressed gas	 COMPRESSED GAS

Toxic gas	
	TOXIC GAS
Flammable gas	FLAMMABLE GAS
Flammable liquid	FLAMMABLE LIQUID
Flammable solid	FLAMMABLE SOLID
Spontaneously combustible substance	SPONTANEOUSLY COMBUSTIBLE
Substance which in contact with water emits flammable gas	DANGEROUS WHEN WET

Oxidizing substance	**OXIDIZING AGENT**
Organic peroxide	**ORGANIC PEROXIDE**
Toxic substance	**TOXIC**
Corrosive substance	**CORROSIVE**
Harmful substance Other dangerous substance Mixed hazards	**DANGEROUS SUBSTANCE**

[*Sch 3*].

Enforcement and penalties

D1012   (*a*)   Enforcement of notification requirements is by the HSE;

(*b*)   enforcement of marking requirements is by the fire authority, except as follows:

(i)   cessation of presence of dangerous substances on site,

(ii)   reduction of quantity of dangerous substances below 25 tonnes, and

(iii)   change in list of classifications notified

when notification must be to (*a*) the HSE and (*b*) the fire authority.

[*Reg 8, Sch 2 Part II*].

Penalties for breach are as in the case of a breach of *HSWA* (see E15028 ENFORCE-MENT).

Classification, packaging and labelling of dangerous substances for supply – the Chemicals (Hazard Information and Packaging for Supply) Regulations 1994 (SI 1994 No 3247) (CHIP 2)

Definitions

D1013   Classification, packaging and labelling controls over substances dangerous for commercial/industrial supply are contained in the *Chemicals (Hazard Information and Packaging for Supply) Regulations 1994 (SI 1994 No 3247)*, as amended by *SI 1996 No 1092*. Similar controls over chemicals conveyed by road are contained in the *Carriage of Dangerous Goods (Classification, Packaging and Labelling) and Use of Transportable Pressure Receptacles Regulations 1996 (SI 1996 No 2092)* (see D3005 DANGEROUS SUBSTANCES II).

These regulations apply to any substance/preparation except (mainly):

(*a*)   radioactive substances (see D1045 below);

(*b*)   animal feed stuffs;

(*c*)   cosmetics;

(*d*)   medicines;

(*e*)   drugs;

(*f*)   micro-organisms;

(*g*)   samples for enforcement purposes;

(*h*)   munitions;

(*j*)   foods;

(*k*)   products under Customs' control;

(*l*)   substances/preparations for export to non-EU states;

(*m*)   pesticides;

(*n*)   substances/preparations transferred from one workplace to another under common ownership and in the immediate vicinity; and

(*o*)   wastes.

[*Reg 3(1)*].

They impose classification, packaging and labelling duties on suppliers/importers into the EU of chemical substances/preparations classified as dangerous for supply.

Classification of substances/preparations dangerous for supply

D1014 Suppliers are expected to know the classification of substances and provide up-to-date safety data sheets. In particular, suppliers must not supply substances/preparations dangerous for supply, unless:

(*a*)   they have first been classified;

(*b*)
    (i)   a record of classification is kept for a minimum of three years, and

    (ii)   made available for inspection (where necessary) to the enforcement authorities.

[*Regs 5(1)(4), 13 and 16(2)*].

CHIP 97, the *Chemicals (Hazard Information and Packaging for Supply) (Amendment) Regulations 1997*, ensures that users of dangerous chemicals are provided with adequate information about the hazards of those chemicals in order to protect people and the environment. The regulations also contribute to a single market in the supply of dangerous chemicals within the European Union.

The *Chemicals (Hazard Information and Packaging for Supply) (Amendment) Regulations 1998* ('*CHIP 98*') (*SI 1998 No 3106*) came into force on 6 January 1999. *CHIP 98* amends the *Chemicals (Hazard Information and Packaging for Supply) Regulations 1994* ('*CHIP 2*') and introduces a fourth edition of the 'Approved Supply List' (which prescribes agreed classification and labelling for many common chemical substances) so as to include mineral wools, refractory ceramic fibres and special purpose fibres in that list.

The *Chemicals (Hazard Information and Packaging for Supply) (Amendment) Regulations 1999 (SI 1999 No 197)* – '*CHIP 99*' – came into force on 1 March 1999, although suppliers of dangerous chemicals are allowed a transitional period of eight months in which to make the necessary changes to labels and safety data sheets. They introduce a supplement to the 4th edition of the Approved Supply List by amending about 60 substance entries and adding a similar number of new entries.

Classification of substances and preparations dangerous for supply

D1015

Table 4			
Classification of Substances and Preparations for Supply			
CATEGORIES OF DANGER			
	Category of danger	*Symbol letter*	*Indication of danger*	*Symbol (orange background)*
Physico-chemical	Explosive	E	Explosive	

	Oxidising	O	Oxidising
	Extremely flammable	F+	Extremely flammable
	Highly flammable	F	Highly flammable
	Flammable		Flammable
Health	Very toxic	T+	Very toxic
	Toxic	T	Toxic
	Harmful	Xn	Harmful
	Corrosive	C	Corrosive
	Irritant	Xi	Irritant
	Sensitising	Xn	Harmful
		Xi	Irritant

Carcinogenic				
	Categories 1 and 2	T	Toxic	
	Category 3	Xn	Harmful	
Mutagenic				
	Categories 1 and 2	T	Toxic	
	Category 3	Xn	Harmful	
Toxic for reproduction				
	Categories 1 and 2	T	Toxic	
	Category 3	Xn	Harmful	
Environmental	Dangerous to the environment	N	Dangerous to the environment	

Source: HSE IND(G) 181 (L)

Provision of safety data sheets

D1016   Suppliers of dangerous substances/preparations must provide recipients with dated safety data sheets, updated as and when necessary, containing the following information:

   (i)   identification of substance/preparation and company;

  (ii)   composition/information on ingredients;

 (iii)   hazards identification;

  (iv)   first-aid measures;

   (v)   fire-fighting measures;

  (vi)   accidental release measures;

(vii)   handling and storage;

(viii) exposure controls/personal protection;

(ix)   physical/chemical properties;

(x)   stability and reactivity;

(xi)   toxicological data;

(xii)   ecological data;

(xiii) disposal considerations;

(xiv) transport information;

(xv)   regulatory information;

(xvi) other matters.

[*Reg 6, Sch 6*].

This is not necessary in cases where substances/preparations are sold to the general public from a shop (e.g. medicines), if sufficient information is given with the product to enable users to take the necessary health and safety measures but this exception does not apply if the product is to be used at work. [*Reg 6(5)*]. Safety sheets have to be supplied free of charge and with data in English except where the recipient is in another Member State, when it should be in that language. [*Reg 6(4)(6)*].

Packaging requirements for substances dangerous for supply

D1017   Such substances must not be supplied/consigned, unless packaged suitably for the purpose. In particular,

(*a*)   the receptacle containing the substance/preparation must be designed/constructed/maintained and closed, so as to prevent escape/spillage of contents – a requirement which can be satisfied by fitting a suitable safety device;

(*b*)   the receptacle, if likely to come into contact with the substance/preparation, must be made of materials which are not liable to be adversely affected nor, in combination, constitute a health and safety risk;

(*c*)   where the receptacle is fitted with a replaceable closure, the closure must be designed so that the receptacle can be repeatedly re-closed, without allowing escape of contents.

[*Reg 8*].

Labelling requirements for substances/preparations dangerous for supply

(a) Substances

D1018   With the exception of:

(i)   substances transferred from one workplace to another [*Reg 9(6)*];

(ii)   substances supplied in small quantities – except those which are (*a*) explosive, (*b*) very toxic and (*c*) toxic [*Reg 9(7)*], suppliers must not supply substances, unless the following particulars are clearly shown:

(i)   name/full address/telephone number of supplier (whether manufacturer, importer, distributor);

(ii)   name of substance;

(iii)   (*a*)   indication(s) of danger and danger symbol(s),

        (*b*)   risk phrases (as per Part III approved supply list – e.g. highly flammable, risk of serious damage to eyes, may cause cancer) [*Reg 9(8)*],

        (*c*)   safety phrases (not necessary on packages containing fewer than 125 millilitres, unless (i) highly flammable, (ii) flammable, (iii) oxidising, (iv) irritant, and (v) (in the case of substances not intended for public sale) harmful) [*Reg 9(8)*],

        (*d*)   the EEC number (if any) and if the substance is dangerous for supply in the 'Approved Supply List', the words 'EEC label'.

(*b*) Preparations

Suppliers must not supply preparations unless the following particulars are clearly shown:

(i)   name/address/telephone number of supplier (whether manufacturer, importer, distributor);

(ii)   trade name or designation;

(iii)   (*a*)   identification of constituents,

        (*b*)   indication(s) of danger and danger symbol(s),

        (*c*)   risk phrases,

        (*d*)   safety phrases,

        (*e*)   if a pesticide,

            (i)   trade name,

            (ii)   name and concentration of active ingredients – to be expressed as percentage by weight (pesticides supplied as solids, in aerosol dispensers or as volatile/viscous liquids);

        (*f*)   in the case of a preparation intended for sale to the general public, in a nominal quantity, risk phrases and safety phrases may be omitted so long as the substance is not classified as harmful and they may also be omitted in certain other cases involving less dangerous substances.

[*Reg 9(3)*].

Misleading phrases such as 'non-harmful', 'non-toxic' should be avoided in order to avoid possible expensive civil liability for injury/damage (*Vacwell Engineering Co Ltd v BDH Chemicals Ltd [1969] 3 AER 1681*) (see P9033 PRODUCT SAFETY).

Particular labelling requirements for certain preparations

Labelling requirements for certain preparations dangerous for supply

D1019   Certain preparations carry particular labelling requirements as follows.

(*a*)   Preparations to be supplied to the general public:

'Keep locked up.
Keep out of reach of children.
In case of accident, seek medical advice.'.

If such preparations are very toxic, toxic or corrosive, and it is impossible to give information on the package itself, there must be precise and easily intelligible instructions relating to (*inter alia*) destruction of empty package.

(*b*)   Preparations intended for use by spraying:

'Do not breathe gas/fumes/vapour/spray.
In case of insufficient ventilation, wear suitable respiratory equipment.
Use only in well-ventilated areas.'.

(c)   Preparations containing risk of cumulative effects:

'Risk of cumulative effects.'.

(d)   Preparations that may cause harm to breastfed babies:

'May cause harm to breastfed babies.'.

[*Reg 10, Sch 6, Part IIA*].

Labelling requirements for certain preparations whether or not dangerous for supply

D1020   Certain preparations carry particular labelling requirements as follows.

(*a*)   Paints and varnishes containing lead:

(i)   labels of packages of paints and varnishes containing lead in quantities exceeding 0.15% expressed as weight of metal of the total weight of the preparation, as determined in accordance with ISO Standard 6503/1984, shall show the following particulars –

'Contains lead. Should not be used on surfaces that are liable to be chewed or sucked by children.';

(ii)   in the case of packages containing less than 125 millilitres of such preparations the particulars may be –

'Warning. Contains lead.'.

(*b*)   Cyanoacrylate based adhesives:

(i)   the immediate packages of glues based on cyanoacrylates shall bear the following inscription –

'Cyanoacrylate.
Danger.
Bonds skin and eyes in seconds.
Keep out of the reach of children.';

(ii)   appropriate safety advice shall accompany the package.

(*c*)   Preparations containing isocyanates:

the package labels of preparations containing isocyanates (whether as mono-mers, oligomers, prepolymers etc. or as mixtures thereof) shall bear the following inscriptions –

'Contains isocyanates.
See information supplied by the manufacturer.'.

(*d*)   Certain preparations containing epoxy constituents:

the package labels of preparations containing epoxy constituents with an average molecular weight LZ700 shall bear the following inscriptions –

'Contains epoxy constituents.
See information supplied by the manufacturer.'.

(*e*)   Preparations intended to be sold to the general public that contain active chlorine:

the package labels of preparations containing more than 1% of active chlorine which are intended to be sold to the general public shall bear the following inscription –

'Warning! Do not use with other products. May release dangerous gases (chlorine).'.

(*f*)   Preparations containing cadmium (alloys) intended to be used for brazing or soldering:

the package labels of preparations containing cadmium (alloys) intended to be used for brazing or soldering shall bear the following inscription –

'Warning. Contains cadmium.
Dangerous fumes are formed during use.
See information supplied by the manufacturer.
Comply with the safety instructions.'.

[*Reg 10, Sch 6, Part IIB*].

Substances to be labelled 'Restricted to professional user'

D1021   Certain Category 1 and 2 carcinogenic, mutagenic and toxic for reproduction substances require to be labelled 'Restricted to professional user', as follows:

Substance	CAS Number
Carcinogenic substances of Category 1	
2-naphthylamine; ß-naphthylamine	91–59–8
biphenyl-4-ylamine; xenylamine; 4-aminobiphenyl	92–67–1
benzidine; 4,4'-diaminobiphenyl; biphenyl-4,4'-ylenediamine	92–87–5
chromium trioxide	1333–82–0
arsenic acid and its salts	—
arsenic pentoxide; arsenic oxide	1303–28–2
diarsenic trioxide; arsenic trioxide	1327–52–3
asbestos	132207–33–1
	132207–32–0
	12172–73–5
	77536–66–4
	77536–68–6
	77536–67–5

Substance	CAS Number
benzene	71–43–2
bis (chloromethyl) ether	542–88–1
chloromethyl methyl ether, chlorodimethyl ether	107–30–2
dinickel trioxide	1314–06–3
erionite	12510–42–8
nickel dioxide	12035–36–8
nickel monoxide	1313–99–1
nickel subsulphide	12035–72–2
nickel sulphide	16812–54–7
salts of 2–naphthylamine	—
salts of biphenyl–4–ylamine; salts of xenylamine; salts of 4–aminobiphenyl	—
salts of benzidine	—
vinyl chloride; chloroethylene	75–01–4
zinc chromates including zinc potassium chromate	—
Carcinogenic substances of Category 2	
1–methyl–3–nitro–1–nitrosoguanidine	70–25–7
1, 2–dibrimo–3–chloropropane	96–12–8
1,2–dimethylhydrazin	540–73–8
1,3–butadiene, buta–1,3–diene	106–99–0
1,3–dichloro–2–propanol	96–23–1
1,3–propanesultone	1120–71–4
3–propanolide; 1,3–propiolactone	57–57–8
1,4–dichlorobut–2–ene	764–41–0
2–nitronaphthalene	581–89–5
2–nitropropane	79–46–9
2,2'–dichloro–4,4'–methylenedianiline; 4,4'–methylene bis (2–chloroaniline)	101–14–4
2–2'–(nitrosoimino) bisethanol	1116–54–7
3,3'–dichlorobenzidine; 3,3'–dichlorobiphenyl–4,4'– ylenediamine	91–94–1
3,3'–dimethoxybenzidine; o–dianisidine	119–90–4
3,3'–dimethylbenzindine; o–toluidine	119–93–7
4–aminoazobenzene	60–09–3
4–amino–3–fluorophenol	399–95–1
4–methyl–m–phenylenediamine	95–80–7

Substance	CAS Number
4-nitrobiphenyl	92-93-3
4,4'-methylenedi-o-toluidine	838-88-0
4,4'-diaminodiphenylmethane; 4,4'-methylenedianiline	101-77-9
5-nitroacenaphthene	602-87-9
4-o-tolylazo-o-toluidine; 4-amino-2',3-dimethylazobenzene; fast garnet GBC base, AAT; o-aminoazotoluene	97-56-3
disodium-5[4'-((2,6-hydroxy-3-((2-hydroxy-5-sulphophenyl)azo)-phenyl)azo)(1,1'-biphenyl)-4-yl)azo]salicylato(4-)cuprate(2-); Cl Direct Brown 95	16071-86-6
cadmium oxide	1306-19-0
Extracts (petroleum), heavy naphthenic distillate solvent	64742-11-6
Extracts (petroleum), heavy paraffinic distillate solvent	64742-04-7
Extracts (petroleum), light naphthenic distillate solvent	64742-03-6
Extracts (petroleum), light paraffinic distillate solvent	64742-05-8
Extracts (petroleum), light vacuum gas oil solvent	91995-78-7
Hydrocarbons, C26-55, arom. rich	97722-04-8
N,N-dimethylhydrazine	57-14-7
acrylamide	79-06-1
acrylonitrile	107-13-1
ga, ga, ga–trichlorotoluene; benzotrichloride	98-07-7
benzo[a]anthracene	56-55-3
benzo[a]pyrene; benzo[d,e,f]chrysene	50-32-8
benzo[b]fluoranthene;benzo[e]acephenanthrylene	205-99-2
benzo[j]fluoranthene	205-82-3
benzo[k]fluoranthene	207-08-9
beryllium	7440-41-7
beryllium compounds with the exception of aluminium	
beryllium silicates	—
cadmium chloride	10108-64-2
cadmium sulphate	10124-36-4
calcium chromate	13765-19-0
captafol (ISO); 1,2,3,6-tetrahydro-N-(1,1,2,2- tetrachloroethylthio)phthalimide	2425-06-1
carbadox (INN); methyl-3-(quinoxalin-2-ylmethylene)carbazate 1,4-dioxide; 2-(methoxycarbonylhydrazonomethyl)quinoxaline 1,4-dioxide	6804-07-5

Substance	CAS Number
chromium III chromate; chromic chromate	24613-89-6
diazomethane	334-88-3
dibenz[a,h]anthracene	53-70-3
diethyl sulphate	64-67-5
dimethyl sulphate	77-78-1
dimethyl carbamoyl chloride	79-44-7
N-nitrosodimethylamine; dimethylnitrosamine	62-75-9
dimethylsulfamochloride	13360-57-1
1-chloro-2,3-epoxypropane; epichlorohydrin	106-89-8
1,2-dichloroethane; ethylene dichloride	107-06-2
ethylene oxide; oxirane	75-21-8
ethyleneimine; aziridine	151-56-4
hexachlorobenzene	118-74-1
hexamethylphosphoric triamide; hexamethylphosphoramide	680-31-9
hydrazine	302-01-2
hydrazobenzene; 1,2-diphenylhydrazine	122-66-7
methyl acrylamidomethoxyacetate (containing ⩾ 0.1% acrylamide)	77402-03-0
methyl-ONN-azoxymethyl acetate; methyl azoxy methyl acetate	592-62-1
nitrofen (ISO); 2,4-dichlorophenyl 4-nitrophenyl ether	1836-75-5
nitrosodipropylamine	621-64-7
2-methoxyaniline; o-anisidine	90-04-0
potassium bromate	7758-01-2
propylene oxide; 1,2-epoxypropane; methyloxirane	75-56-9
o-toluidine	95-53-4
2-methylaziridine; propyleneimine	75-55-8
salts of 2,2'-dichloro-4,4'-methylenedianiline; salts of 4,4'- methylenebis (2-chloroaniline)	—
salts of 3,3'-dichlorobenzidine; salts of 3,3'-dichlorobiphenyl- 4,4'-ylenediamine	—
salts of 3,3'-dimethoxybenzidine; salts of o–dianisidine	—
salts of 3,3'-dimethylbenzidine; salts of o-toluidine	—
strontium chromate	7789-06-2
styrene oxide; (epoxyethyl)benzene; phenyloxirane	96-09-3
sulfallate (ISO); 2-chlorallyl diethyldithiocarbamate	95-06-7

Substance	CAS Number
thioacetamide	62-55-5
urethane (INN); ethyl carbamate	51-79-6

Mutagenic substances of Category 1

There are no substances classified in this category

Mutagenic substances of Category 2

1,2–dibromo–3–chloropropane	96-12-8
acrylamide	79-06-1
benzo[a]pyrene; benzo[d,e,f]chrysene	50-32-8
diethyl sulphate	64-67-5
ethylene oxide; oxirane	75-21-8
ethyleneimine, aziridine	151-56-4
hexamethylphosphoric triamide; hexamethylphosphoramide	680-31-9
methyl acrylamidomethoxyacetate (containing [00b3] 0.1% acrylamide)	77402-03-0

Toxic for reproduction substances of Category 1

lead hexafluorosilicate	25808-74-6
lead acetate	1335-32-6
lead alkyls	—
lead azide	13424-46-9
lead chromate	7758-97-6
lead compounds, with the exception of those specified elsewhere in this Part of this Schedule	—
lead di(acetate)	301-04-2
lead 2,4,6-trinitroresorcinoxide; lead styphnate	15245-44-0
lead (II) methanesulfonate	17570-76-2
trilead bis(orthophosphate)	7446-27-7
warfarin; 4-hydroxy-3-(3-oxo-1-phenylbutyl)coumarin	81-81-2

Toxic for reproduction substances of Category 2

2-ethoxyethanol; ethylene glycol monoethyl ether	110-80-5
2-ethylhexyl 3,5-bis(1,1-dimethylethyl)-4-hydroxyphenyl methyl thio acetate	80387-97-9
2-methoxyethanol, ethylene glycol monoethyl ether	109-86-4
benzo[a]pyrene; benzo[d,e,f]chrysene	50-32-8

Substance	CAS Number
binapacryl (ISO); 2-sec butyl-4,6-dinitrophenyl-3- methylcrotonate	485-31-4
N,N-dimethylformamide; dimethyl formamide	68-12-2
dinoseb; 6-sec butyl-2,4-dinitrophenol	88-85-7
dinoterb; 2-tert-butyl-4,6-dinitrophenol	1420-07-1
ethylene thiourea; imidazolidine- 2-thione; 2-imidazoline-2-thiol	96-45-7
2-ethoxyethyl acetate; ethylglycol acetate	111-15-9
methyl-ONN-azoxymethyl acetate; methyl azoxy methyl acetate	592-62-1
2-methoxyethyl acetate; methylglycol acetate	110-49-6
nickel tetracarbonyl	13463-39-3
nitrofen (ISO); 2,4-dichlorophenyl 4-nitrophenyl ether	1836-75-5
salts and esters of dinoseb, with the exception of those specified elsewhere in this Part of this Schedule	—
salts and esters of dinoterb	—
chloroform	67-66-3
carbon tetrachloride	56-23-5
1,1,2-trichloroethane	79-00-5
1,1,2,2-tetrachloroethane	79-34-5
1,1,1,2-tetrachloroethane	630-20-6
pentachloroethane	76-01-7
1,1-dichloroethylene	75-35-4
1,1,1-trichlororethane	71-55-6

[*Reg 9(3A), (3B), Sch 6 Part III A, B, as inserted by SI 1996 No 1092*].

Further labelling requirements

D1022   All labels for supply purposes must be indelibly marked and securely fixed to the package and the hazard warning sign must stand out from its background so that it is clearly noticeable. It must be possible to read the label horizontally when the package is set down normally and it must have a side length of 100 square millimetres. If it is not possible to comply with any of the requirements because of the shape of the package, it should be attached in some other appropriate manner.

The dimensions of the label for substances and preparations dangerous for supply are reproduced below.

Capacity of package	Dimensions of label
(a) not exceeding 3 litres	if possible at least 52 × 74 millimetres
(b) exceeding 3 litres but not exceeding 50 litres	at least 74 × 105 millimetres
(c) exceeding 50 litres but not exceeding 500 litres	at least 105 × 148 millimetres
(d) exceeding 500 litres	at least 148 × 210 millimetres

[*Reg 11*].

Enforcement/penalties and civil liability

(*a*) *Enforcement*

D1023   The HSE is the enforcing authority for *CHIP Regulations*, except where the dangerous substance is supplied from a registered chemist, where the Pharmaceutical Society of Great Britain is the enforcing authority. If the supply is from a shop, mobile vehicle or market stall, or to members of the public, the local Weights and Measures Authority is the enforcing authority. [*Reg 16(2)*].

(*b*) *Penalties*

Breach of the provisions of the *Chemicals (Hazard Information and Packaging for Supply) Regulations 1994* carries the same penalties as breach of the *HSWA* itself (see E15028 ENFORCEMENT).

(*c*) *Defence*

It is a defence to a charge under these regulations that a person took all reasonable care and exercised all due diligence to avoid commission of that offence [*Reg 16(4)*] – a difficult test to satisfy (see *J H Dewhurst Ltd v Coventry Corporation [1969] 3 AER 1225*).

(*d*) *Civil liability*

Where breach of duty causes damage/injury, this can give rise to civil liability. [*Reg 16(1)(b)*].

Control of substances hazardous to health – Control of Substances Hazardous to Health Regulations 1999 (SI 1999 No 437) (COSHH)

D1024   *The Control of Substances Hazardous to Health Regulations 1999 (SI 1999 No 437) came into force on 25 March 1999 and revoke and replace the following Regulations: the Control of Substances Hazardous to Health Regulations 1994 (SI 1994 No 3246), the Control of Substances Hazardous to Health (Amendment) Regulations 1996, the Control of Substances Hazardous to Health (Amendment) Regulations 1997, and the Control of Substances Hazardous to Health (Amendment) Regulations 1998.* The new Regulations re-enact, with minor modifications, the 1994 Regulations as amended.

COSHH provides a comprehensive and systematic approach to the control of hazardous substances at work, where risk to health and the costs of failure are often substantial in both human and economic terms. The Regulations require employers to:

— assess risks to health arising from exposure to hazardous substances;

— prevent or adequately control exposure;

— ensure control measures are used, maintained, examined and tested;

— in some instances, monitor exposure and carry out appropriate health surveillance; and

— inform, instruct and train employees.

In addition to minor and drafting amendments, the 1999 Regulations make the following changes of substance:

(*a*) provide for the approval by the Health and Safety Commission of maximum exposure limits for substances in place of the provisions previously contained in *Schedule 1* to the *1994 Regulations*;

(*b*) include certain further definitions, including:

• expanding the definition of 'a substance hazardous to health' to include trigger limits for 'total inhalable dust' or 'respirable dust';

• minor changes to the definitions of 'carcinogen' and 'Member State';

(*c*) require personal protective equipment provided by an employer in pursuance of these Regulations to comply with the *Personal Protective Equipment (EC Directive) Regulations 1992 (SI 1992 No 3139)*;

(*d*) give members of the armed forces an appeal against suspension from work on medical grounds; and

(*e*) revise the Schedule of *Other substances and processes to which the definition of 'carcinogen' relates.*

The 1999 Regulations thus see the removal of the schedule listing the substances assigned maximum exposure limits.

For maximum exposure limits (MELs) and occupational exposure standards (OESs), see Appendix A at D1077 below.

More particularly, a 'substance hazardous to health' is a substance (or preparation):

(*a*) listed in Part I of the 'Approved Supply List' as dangerous (see D1014 above);

(*b*) for which the HSE has approved –

(i) a maximum exposure limit (MEL), or

(ii) an occupational exposure standard (OES)

(see Appendix A at D1077 below);

(*c*) a biological agent (including micro-organisms, endoparasites, cell cultures);

(*d*) a substantial concentration of airborne dust (see VENTILATION); or

(*e*) any other substance creating a comparable health hazard.

[*Control of Substances Hazardous to Health Regulations 1999, Reg 2(1)*].

Although not specified above, these regulations also extend to (*a*) carcinogens (see D1039 below) and (*b*) respiratory sensitisers (see D1043 below).

However, the regulations do not cover:

(i)   asbestos but may do so eventually (see ASBESTOS);

(ii)   lead (see D1044 below);

(iii) ionising radiations (see D1046 below); and

(iv)   highly flammable liquids and liquefied petroleum gases.

Duties under COSHH

(*a*) *Employers*

D1025   Employers owe duties to employees, indirect workers and self-employed personnel, except as regards:

(*a*)   health surveillance (duty owed to employees only) [*Reg 11*]; and

(*b*)   monitoring information and training [*Regs 10, 12*] (duties owed to employees but also to others on premises where work is being carried on).

[*Reg 3(1)*].

The main duties are as follows:

(1)   to carry out (and review) a formal independent assessment of health risks to employees [*Reg 6*] (see D1026 below);

(2)   to prevent/control exposure of employees to health risks [*Reg 7*] (see D1027 below);

(3)   to institute proper use of controls and personal protective equipment [*Reg 8*] (see also PERSONAL PROTECTIVE EQUIPMENT');

(4)   to maintain, examine and test controls and keep records [*Reg 9*] (see D1029 below);

(5)   to monitor workplace exposure of employees [*Reg 10*] (see D1030 below);

(6)   provide health surveillance for employees, where necessary [*Reg 11*] (see D1031 below);

(7)   provide information, instruction and training regarding hazardous substances [*Reg 12*].

(*b*) *Employees*

(1)   to make full and proper use of control measures and personal protective equipment [*Reg 8(2)*];

(2)   at the cost of the employer, to present themselves for health surveillance [*Reg 11(9)*] (see D1032 below).

Risk assessments (Regulation 6)

D1026   The object of a risk assessment is to enable decisions to be made regarding measures necessary to impose the requisite controls on 'substances hazardous to health'; in addition, a formal assessment system is proof that a particular organisation has taken cognisance of health hazards and has implemented, or is about to do so, steps to eliminate/minimise their incidence. More particularly, assessments should identify:

(i)   risks posed to the health of the workforce;

(ii)   steps necessary to control exposure to those hazards;

(iii)   other action necessary to achieve compliance with regulations relating to maintenance requirements and personal protective equipment; and

(iv)   the extent of exposure.

Merely following suppliers' product data is not necessarily sufficient for compliance purposes; HSE Guidance Notes and manufacturers' standards should also be consulted. Not to do so is to be left open to the charge that one has not done all that was 'reasonably practicable' – this statutory requirement implying that employers should keep up to date with the latest HSE, industrial and technical publications (*Stokes v Guest, Keen & Nettlefold (Bolts and Nuts) Ltd [1968] 1 WLR 1776*) (see E11006 EMPLOYERS' DUTIES TO THEIR EMPLOYEES).

Controlling exposure (Regulation 7)

D1027   Employers must ensure that employees are not exposed to substances hazardous to health, where this can be prevented; if not possible, however, exposure must be adequately controlled. [*Reg 7(1)*]. So far as reasonably practicable, measures not requiring use of personal protective equipment should be used (except in the case of (*a*) carcinogens (see D1039 below) and (*b*) biological agents [*Reg 7(2)*]). Whilst maximum exposure must be below maximum exposure limits, control is only adequate if exposure is reduced to the lowest reasonably practicable. (Approved methods for averaging over specified reference periods appear year-on-year in updated form in Guidance Note EH 40 – 'Occupational exposure limits'.) There is no liability if exposure does not exceed the approved occupational standard, or if the employer acts quickly to remedy any excess, as soon as reasonably practicable.

Where measures do not prevent or adequately control exposure, employers must, in addition, supply employees with suitable personal protective equipment. [*Reg 7(4)*]. Such personal protective equipment/clothing must conform with statutory requirement and/or EU specification/standard; similarly, respiratory equipment (see PERSONAL PROTECTIVE EQUIPMENT). [*Reg 7(5)(8)*]. Moreover, employers must ensure that control measures and personal protective equipment/respiratory equipment are properly used and applied as well as regularly maintained in conjunction with systematic defects reporting. Records of tests/examinations, and any repairs consequent thereupon, should be kept for up to five years. [*Reg 9(4)*].

Measures for preventing or controlling exposure

D1028   These consist either exclusively or in combination of the following:

(*a*)   for preventing exposure;

(i)   elimination of the use of the substance;

(ii)   substitution by a less hazardous substance or by the same substance in a less hazardous form;

(*b*)   for controlling exposure:

(i)   totally enclosed process and handling systems;

(ii)   plant or processes or systems of work which minimise generation of, or suppress or contain, the hazardous dust, fume, micro-organisms etc. and which limit the area of contamination in the event of spills and leaks;

(iii)   partial enclosure, with local exhaust ventilation;

(iv)   local exhaust ventilation;

(v)   sufficient general ventilation;

(vi)   reduction of numbers of employees exposed and exclusion of non-essential access;

(vii) reduction in the period of exposure for employees;

(viii) regular cleaning of contamination from, or disinfection of, walls, surfaces etc;

(ix)   provision of means for safe storage and disposal of substances hazardous to health;

(x)   suitable personal protective equipment;

(xi)   prohibition of eating, drinking, smoking etc. in contaminated areas;

(xii) provision of adequate facilities for washing, changing and storage of clothing, including arrangements for laundering contaminated clothing.

In existing work situations, the present control measures should be carefully reviewed, and improved, extended or replaced as necessary to be capable of achieving, and sustaining, adequate control.

If, in spite of the above control measures, leaks, spills or uncontrolled releases of a hazardous substance could still occur, means should be available for limiting the extent of risks to health and for regaining adequate control as soon as possible. The means should include, where appropriate, established emergency procedures, safe disposal of the substance and sufficient suitable personal protective equipment to enable the source of the release to be safely identified and repairs to be made. All persons not concerned with the emergency action should be excluded from the area of contamination.

The Health & Safety Executive has published a free leaflet, '*Solvents and You*' – it advises people who work with solvents about the precautions they should be aware of. It specifically draws attention to the danger of working in confined spaces with solvents where particularly high exposures can occur.

The key aspects of emergency procedures in respect of chemical spillages or releases of corrosive, toxic or flammable materials, dust explosions and fires are detailed in another free HSE leaflet, '*Prepared for Emergency*' (ref: IND(G) 246L).

Engineering controls – records of examination and test

D1029   Engineering controls should be subject to regular examination and test and records kept as follows:

(*a*)	local exhaust ventilation plant – every 14 months;	
(*b*)	local exhaust ventilation plant in the following specific industries:	
	— blasting for the cleaning of metal castings	– every month
	— 12 hours in any week (not gold, platinum or iridium):	– every 6 months
	— non-ferrous metal castings	– every 6 months
	— jute cloth manufacture	– every month
(*c*)	any other case	– at suitable intervals

[*Control of Substances Hazardous to Health Regulations 1999, Reg 9, Sch 4*].

Monitoring exposure at the workplace

D1030   Where employees are exposed to substances hazardous to health, employers must ensure that there is adequate monitoring of exposure and records kept for 40 years. In particular, in the case of exposure to

(*a*)   vinyl chloride monomer – monitoring must be continuous;

(*b*)   vapour/spray emitted by electrolytic chromium processes (except trivalent chromium) – every 14 days.

[*Control of Substances Hazardous to Health Regulations 1999, Reg 10, Sch 5*].

Provision of health surveillance

D1031   Health surveillance must be arranged by employers for employees following certain classifications as follows:

(A)   Schedule 6 employees;

(B)   where exposure is associated with either an identifiable disease (see OCCUPATIONAL HEALTH AND DISEASES) or adverse health effects (see, for instance, legionella at D1034 below).

(A) Schedule 6 employees

Schedule 6 requires that health surveillance of employees under an employment medical adviser or appointed doctor must be arranged by employers at intervals of not more than 12 months, i.e. employees exposed to:

(*a*)   vinyl chloride monomer (VCM) whilst engaged in

(i)   manufacture,

(ii)   production,

(iii)   reclamation,

(iv)   storage,

(v)   discharge,

(vi)   transport,

    (vii)   use,

    (viii) polymerisation,

(unless exposure is insignificant);

(*b*)   nitro/amino derivatives of phenol/benzene (or its homologues) whilst engaged in

    (i)   manufacture of nitro/amino derivatives of phenol/benzene, and

    (ii)   making of explosives with such substances;

(*c*)   potassium or sodium chromate or dichromate, whilst engaged in manufacture;

(*d*)   1-naphthylamine, orthotolidine, dianisidine, dichlorbenzidine, whilst engaged in manufacture;

(*e*)   auramine, magenta, whilst engaged in manufacture;

(*f*)   carbon disulphide, disulphur dichloride, benzene (and benzol), carbon tetrachloride, trichlorethylene, whilst engaged in processes in which these substances are

    (i)   used,

    (ii)   given off as vapour,

in the manufacture of indiarubber or its articles or goods;

(*g*)   pitch, whilst engaged in manufacture of blocks of fuel consisting of

    (i)   coal,

    (ii)   coal dust,

    (iii) coke/slurry,

with pitch as a binding ambience.

(B) Exposure-related identifiable diseases

Exposure to a whole range of substances at work can lead over a period of time to the onset of identifiable diseases and/or adverse health effects. Indeed, exposure to certain substances can lead to diseases which are prescribed, that is, for which disablement benefit is payable, without the employee having to establish negligence against his employer(s) (see OCCUPATIONAL HEALTH AND DISEASES); or to non-notifiable diseases (e.g. legionnaire's disease). Legionnaire's disease is neither notifiable (except in Scotland) (see Appendix B at A3028 ACCIDENT REPORTING) nor is it a prescribed occupational disease (see OCCUPATIONAL HEALTH AND DISEASES) though it is serious enough to have resulted in fatalities.

Medical examinations

D1032   Medical examination must be carried out by employment medical advisers or appointed doctors in the case of *Schedule 6* employees, e.g. exposure to VCM, and, preferably, in other (non-*Schedule 6*) cases as well. In the case of *Schedule 6* employees, medical examinations must take place annually. They must be paid for by employers and employees are entitled to see employment health records, on giving reasonable notice. Correspondingly, employees must submit to medical examination, when required to do so by the employer, during working hours. [*Reg 11(9)*]. If the employment medical adviser concludes that an employee should no longer be engaged in such work or only under specified conditions, the employer must not permit the employee to do such work or, alternatively, only under specified conditions. [*Reg 11(6)*]. In such circumstances, employees may be entitled to paid leave following suspension on medical grounds. Employers (or employees) who are dissatisfied with such suspension order, can apply to the HSE within 28 days for a review of the decision. [*Reg 11(11)*]. Medical records must be kept by the employer for at least 40 years [*Reg 11(3)*] and, on being given reasonable notice, employers must allow employees access to health records [*Reg 11(8)*].

Disclosure of information to employees regarding hazardous substances

D1033   Given that prevention is better than cure, the regulations oblige employers to acquaint their employees with the dangers arising from working with substances hazardous to health, and, in consequence, the precautions that they should take.

Specifically, information must

(*a*)   include the results of monitoring exposure;

(*b*)   be given to the employees (or safety representative) where the maximum exposure (MEL) is exceeded in the case of *Schedule 1* substances, e.g. cadmium, carbon disulphide, isocyanates; and

(*c*)   be given about the collective results of health surveillance.

[*Reg 12*].

Legionella

D1034   Between 100 and 200 cases of legionella are reported each year in England and Wales. *COSHH Regulations* extend to the prevention and control of risks from hazardous micro-organisms, including legionella. Occupiers of non-domestic premises must inform the local authority in writing where a 'notifiable device' exists on their premises. [*Notification of Cooling Towers and Evaporative Condensers Regulations 1992 (SI 1992 No 2225), Reg 3(1)*]. A 'notifiable device' is a cooling tower or an evaporative condenser, but not one

(*a*)   containing no water exposed to air; or

(*b*)   whose water/electricity supply is not connected.

[*Notification of Cooling Towers and Evaporative Condensers Regulations 1992, Reg 2*].

So far as reasonably practicable, employers (and occupiers), as regards factories, hospitals, laboratories, schools and construction sites with

(i)   water systems incorporating a cooling tower,

(ii)   water systems incorporating an evaporative condenser,

(iii)   hot water services (except where the volume of water does not exceed 300 litres),

(iv)   hot/cold water services (irrespective of size) in particularly susceptible premises (e.g. health care premises),

(v)   humidifiers/air washers, creating water droplets, where water temperature is likely to exceed 20°C,

(vi)   spa baths/pools where warm water is recirculated,

must

(1)   identify/assess sources of risk;

(2)   prepare schemes for preventing/controlling risk;

(3)   implement precautions;

(4)   keep records of precautions.

All systems (particularly those in nursing homes/hospitals) susceptible to colonisation by legionella should be assessed, with particular regard to

(A)   droplet formation potential;

(B)   water temperature;

(C)   risk to anyone inhaling water droplets;

(D)   means of preventing/controlling risk.

Vulnerable areas of the workplace

D1035   The two most vulnerable areas of the workplace are (*a*) hot (and sometimes cold) water services and (*b*) air conditioning and industrial cooling systems.

(a) Hot (and cold) water systems

Colonising typically storage tanks, calorifiers, pipework, dead legs, water softeners and filters, as well as taps and showers, legionella can proliferate in warm water temperatures. Cold water services normally are not so vulnerable, except in the case of large cold water systems where use is intermittent or where water temperatures can exceed 20°C.

(b) Air conditioning/industrial cooling systems

Typically heated to 30°C, water from the cooling tower can become heavily contaminated by dust, slime and sludge, thereby providing ideal conditions for legionella to breed. Emanating from cooling towers, legionnaire's disease has resulted to date in a number of fatalities at work, and passers-by, as well as employees, are also at risk. Indeed, most industrial cooling systems operate at temperatures ideal for germination of legionella. Also, evaporative condensers have an industrial cooling function and are used for air conditioning purposes. Since the volume of water in such condensers is less than in a cooling tower, control of water quality is more difficult.

Suitable precautions

D1036   *(a) Hot water systems*

Water services should be checked regularly and well maintained, particularly

(i)   water temperatures at calorifiers;

(ii)   water temperatures at taps after one minute's running (in any case, all taps should be inspected at least once a year);

(iii)   tanks, for organic/bacteriological material (should be inspected at least annually);

(iv)   calorifiers, for organic/bacteriological material;

(v)   accessible pipework and insulation.

Where there is risk of legionnaire's disease, water systems should be disinfected, to BS 6700 'Specification for the design, installation, testing and maintenance of services supplying water for domestic use within buildings'. This can be achieved chemically, by chlorination, or thermally, by simply raising the temperature of the water to such level that legionella cannot survive.

In addition,

(vi)   avoid water temperatures between 20°C and 45°C;

(vii) avoid water stagnation;

(viii) avoid use of materials that harbour bacteria;

(ix)   keep system clear so as to avoid accumulation of sediment harbouring bacteria;

(x)   make use of water treatment systems and chemicals;

(xi)   ensure the whole system operates safely.

(*b*) *Cooling towers / air conditioning systems*

Precautions here include

(i)   designing cooling towers to ensure that aerosol release is minimised;

(ii)   locating towers away from ventilation inlets, opening windows and populated areas (in practice, cooling towers and air inlets are often situated together at roof level);

(iii) maintaining the system in a clean and sound condition;

(iv)   controlling water quality.

Prosecutions for legionella

D1037   Where an employer is prosecuted (under *Sec 3(1)* of the *Health and Safety at Work etc. Act 1974*) with exposing members of the public to health risks from legionella, it is not necessary to show that members of the public had actually inhaled bacterium, or that it had been there to be inhaled; it was enough that there had been a risk of its being there (*R v Board of Trustees of the Science Museum [1994] IRLR 25*).

Prohibition on use at work of certain hazardous substances

D1038   Certain substances are prohibited from importation which are also not to be used at work, namely:

(*a*)   2-napthylamine, benzidine, 4-aminodiphenyl, 4-nitrodiphenyl, their salts and any substance containing any of those compounds in a total concentration [equal to or greater than 0.1 per cent by mass];

(*b*)   matches filled with white phosphorus.

Benzene must not be supplied for use at work if its use is prohibited by Item 11 in the table below. [*Reg 4*].

In addition to specifying preventive measures, *COSHH* imposes prohibitions on the use at work of the following substances:

PROHIBITION OF CERTAIN SUBSTANCES HAZARDOUS TO HEALTH FOR CERTAIN PURPOSES		
Item No.	*Column 1*	*Column 2*
	Description of substance	*Purpose for which the substance is prohibited*
1.	2-naphthylamine; benzidine; 4-aminodiphenyl; 4-nitrodiphenyl; their salts and any substance containing any of those compounds, in a total concentration equal to or greater than 0.1 per cent by mass.	Manufacture and use for all purposes including any manufacturing process in which a substance described in column 1 of this item is formed.
2.	Sand or other substance containing free silica.	Use as an abrasive for blasting articles in any blasting apparatus.
3.	A substance–	Use as a parting material in connection with the making of metal castings.
	(a) containing compounds of silicon calculated as silica to the extent of more than 3% by weight of dry material other than natural sand, zirconium silicate (zircon), calcinated china clay, calcinated aluminous fireclay, sillimanite, calcinated or fused alumina olivine; or	
	(b) composed of or containing dust or other matter deposited from a fettling or blasting process.	
4.	Carbon disulphide.	Use in the cold-cure process of vulcanising in the proofing of cloth with rubber.
5.	Oils other than white oil, or oil of entirely animal or vegetable origin or entirely of mixed animal and vegetable origin.	Use for oiling the spindles of self-acting mules.
6.	Ground or powdered flint or quartz other than natural sand.	Use in relation to the manufacture or decoration of pottery for the following purposes–
		(a) the placing of ware for the biscuit fire;
		(b) the polishing of ware;
		(c) as the ingredient of a wash for saggars, trucks, bats, cranks, or other articles used in supporting ware during firing; and
		(d) as dusting or supporting powder in potters' shops.

7.	Ground or powdered flint or quartz other than–		Use in relation to the manufacture or decoration of pottery for any purpose except–
	(a)	natural sand; or	(a) use in a separate room or building for–
	(b)	ground or powdered flint or quartz which forms part of a slop or paste.	(i) the manufacture of powdered flint or quartz; or
			(ii) the making of frits or glazes or the making of colours or coloured slips for the decoration of pottery;
			(b) use for the incorporation of the substance into the body of ware in an enclosure in which no person is employed and which is constructed and ventilated to prevent the escape of dust.

8.   Dust or powder of a refractory material containing not less than 80 per cent. of silica other than natural sand.

Use for sprinkling the moulds of silica bricks, namely bricks or other articles composed of refractory material and containing not less than 80 per cent. of silica.

9.   White phosphorus.

Use in the manufacture of matches.

10.   Hydrogen cyanide.

Use in fumigation except when–

(a)   released from an inert material in which hydrogen cyanide is absorbed;

(b)   generated from a gassing powder; or

(c)   applied from a cylinder through suitable piping and applicators other than for fumigations in the open air to control or kill mammal pests.

11.   Benzene and any substance containing benzene in a concentration equal to or greater than 0.1 per cent by mass, other than–(a) motor fuels covered by Council Directive 85/210/EEC (OJ No L96, 3.4.85, p 25);(b) waste covered by Council Directives 75/442/EEC (OJ No L194, 25.7.75, p 39), as amended by Council Directive 91/156/EEC (OJ No L78, 26.3.91, p 32), and 91/689/EEC (OJ No L377, 31.12.91, p 20)..

Use for all purposes except–(a) use in industrial processes; and (b) for the purposes of research and development or for the purpose of analysis.

12. The following substances–Chloroform CAS No 67-66-3;Carbon Tetrachloride CAS No 56-23-5;1,1,2 Trichloroethane CAS No 79-00-5;1,1,2,2 Tetrachloroethane CAS No 79-34-5;1,1,2 Tetrachloroethane CAS No 630-20-6;Pentachloroethane CAS No 76-01-7;Vinylidene chloride (1,1 Dichloroethane) CAS No 75-35-4;1,1,1 Trichloroethane CAS No 71-55-6;and any substance containing one or more of those substances in a concentration equal to or greater than 0.1 per cent by mass, other than– (a) medicinal products; (b) cosmetic products.	Supply for use at work in diffusive applications such as in surface cleaning and the cleaning of fabrics except for the purposes of research and development or for the purpose of analysis.

Carcinogens

D1039   Every employer must ensure that exposure of his employees to substances hazardous to their health is prevented, or if this is not reasonably practicable, is adequately controlled. If it is not reasonably practicable to prevent exposure of any employees to a *carcinogen* by using an alternative substance or process, then these measures must be taken:

(*a*)   the total enclosure of the process and handling systems unless this is not reasonably practicable;

(*b*)   plant, process and systems of work which minimise the generation of, or suppress and contain, spills, leaks, dust, fumes and vapours of carcinogens;

(*c*)   limitation of the quantities of a carcinogen at the place of work;

(*d*)   keeping the number of persons who might be exposed to a carcinogen to a minimum;

(*e*)   prohibiting eating, drinking and smoking in areas that may be contaminated by carcinogens;

(*f*)   the provision of hygiene measures including adequate washing facilities and regular cleaning of walls and surfaces;

(*g*)   the designation of those areas and installations which may be contaminated by carcinogens, and the use of suitable and sufficient warning signs; and

(*h*)   the safe storage, handling and disposal of carcinogens and use of closed and clearly labelled containers.

[*COSHH Regulations 1999, Reg 7(3)*].

If control measures fail and this results in the escape of carcinogens into the workplace, only persons charged with repairs must be allowed into the affected area and they must be provided with appropriate respiratory equipment. Employees must be informed immediately of the risk. [*COSHH Regulations 1999, Reg 7*].

Definition of a carcinogen

D1040   A carcinogen is any substance/preparation classified as per the *Chemicals (Hazard Information and Packaging for Supply) Regulations 1994, Sch 3 para 15*, and requiring to be labelled with risk phrase R 45 'may cause cancer' or R 49 'may cause cancer by inhalation', whether or not the substance/preparation requires to be classified anyway under *COSHH 1999, Reg 2*, namely:

(*a*)   any of the carcinogenic substances which must be labelled R 45 or R 49, and

(*b*)   any of the following substances/processes, namely,

   (i)   aflatoxins;

   (ii)   arsenic;

   (iii)   auramine manufacture;

   (iv)   calcining, sintering or smelting of nickel copper matte or acid leaching or electro-refining of roasted matte;

   (v)   coal soots, coal tar, pitch and coal tar fumes;

   (vi)   hardwood dusts;

   (vii)   isopropyl alcohol manufacture;

   (viii)   leather dust in boot and shoe manufacture, arising during preparation and finishing;

   (ix)   magenta manufacture;

   (x)   mustard gas;

   (xi)   rubber manufacturing and processing giving rise to rubber process dust and rubber fume;

   (xii)   used engine oils.

[*COSHH 1999, Sch 1*].

Apart from specific requirements relating to the labelling of carcinogens, where it is not reasonably practicable to prevent exposure to a carcinogen employers should institute certain controls (see 'Measures for preventing or controlling exposure' at D1028 above).

Prohibition on importation of carcinogens

D1041   Importation of the following substances/articles into the United Kingdom is forbidden as being carcinogenic, nor must any such substance/article be supplied for use at work:

(*a*)   2-naphthylamine,
benzidine,
4-aminodiphenyl,
4-nitrodiphenyl,
(and their salts and substances containing any of those compounds in a total concentration exceeding 0.1 per cent);

(*b*)   matches made with white phosphorus;

(*c*)   benzene (except in industrial processes or research).

[*Reg 4*].

Penalties and defences under COSHH

D1042   Penalties for breach of *COSHH 1999* are as for those of *HSWA* (see E15028 ENFORCEMENT). It is a defence that an accused took all reasonable precautions and exercised all due diligence to avoid commission of the offence. [*Reg 16*].

Respiratory sensitisers

D1043   A respiratory sensitiser is a substance which can cause the respiratory system to develop a condition liable to make it over-react – sensitisation – if the substance is inhaled again; as well as causing serious chronic diseases, such as asthma and farmer's lung (see OCCUPATIONAL HEALTH AND DISEASES). Symptoms can include rhinitis and mild asthma attacks. Significantly, since sensitisation affects only a minority of workers (or categories of workers), control can be difficult if not elusive, principally because employers may often not recognise the health hazard when present. Particular culprits are allergens and isocyanates, but not untypical are certain anhydrides, reactive dyes and platinum salts. Industries potentially at risk are polyurethane manufacture, food packaging, adhesives, plastics, resins, textile processes and platinum refining. Sensitisation can also occur from nickel in the plating industry, henna in hairdressing, hardwood dust in woodworking and furniture making, as well as in pharmaceutical manufacture, enzyme preparations and foodstuffs – such as egg proteins in food processing and crustaceans in sea-food processing. Flour being baked, grain milled and hay gathered can also have similar effects.

Once sensitised, an employee continually exposed to the sensitising agent will, in all probability, suffer severe symptoms and eventually, possibly, permanent lung damage. For instance, attacks of asthma can be brought on by inhalation of tobacco smoke and cold air, and can persist years after sensitisation. Employers should, therefore, establish a health surveillance programme, using skills of an occupational health doctor and nurse. Once done, such work can be continued by a trained responsible person who should, however, refer symptoms of sensitisation to a doctor.

In order to comply with *COSHH Regulations*, employers should prevent exposure of sensitive employees to respiratory sensitisers but, if this is not 'reasonably practicable', control it. This involves both formal assessment of risks and inventory of necessary control measures as well as provision of adequate information and training. Sensitised employees should be medically advised about the sort of work they can do without further risk to health.

Control of lead at work – the Control of Lead at Work Regulations 1998 (SI 1998 No 543)

D1044   Many processes can lead to lead poisoning, most commonly lead smelting, melting and burning, vitreous enamelling on glass and metal, pottery glazing, manufacture of lead compounds and accumulators, painting, plumbing, soldering, and rubber production. The *Control of Lead at Work Regulations 1980 (SI 1980 No 1248)* have been revoked and re-enacted with modifications by the *Control of Lead at Work Regulations 1998 (SI 1998 No 543)* which came into force on 1 April 1998.

Employers must:

(i)   assess the health risks to employees created by work involving exposure to lead [*Reg 5*];

(ii) provide employees with suitable and sufficient information, instruction and training so that the employees know not only the risks to health created by exposure to lead but also the precautions which should be taken [*Reg 11(1)*];

(iii) ensure, where any employees are liable to receive significant exposure to lead, that a suitable procedure is in place to measure the concentration of lead in air to which the employees are exposed [*Reg 9(1)*], and that records of such air monitoring exercises are kept for at least five years [*Reg 9(5)*];

(iv) ensure that the exposure of employees to lead is prevented by use of controls other than the mere provision of personal protective equipment – but where this is not reasonably practicable, such exposure to lead must be adequately controlled by way of appropriate control measures (other than the mere provision of personal protective equipment, so far as is reasonably practicable) [*Reg 6(1), (2)*];

(v) provide personal protective equipment to employees, where necessary, and such equipment must comply with EU requirements or otherwise be approved by the Health and Safety Executive [*Reg 6(4), (6)*];

(vi) take all reasonable steps to ensure that any control measure or personal protective equipment is properly used or applied, as the case may be [*Reg 6(7)*];

(vii) ensure that at suitable intervals non-disposable respiratory protective equipment is thoroughly examined and tested [*Reg 8(3)*], and for at least five years employers must keep a record of such examinations and tests [*Reg 8(4)*];

(viii) take adequate steps to ensure, so far as is reasonably practicable, that employees do not eat, drink or smoke in any place which is contaminated by lead (or liable to be contaminated by lead) [*Reg 7(1)*].

In respect of employees who are, or are liable to be, exposed significantly to lead, employers must ensure that they are under surveillance by an appointed doctor or an employment medical adviser [*Reg 10(1)*]. Where medical surveillance is carried out on the premises of the employer, the employer must make sure that suitable facilities are made available [*Reg 10(6)*]. The medical surveillance should be begun, so far as is reasonably practicable, before an employee for the first time commences any work giving rise to exposure to lead, and in any event within fourteen working days of such commencement – and should subsequently be conducted at intervals of not more than twelve months or such shorter intervals as the doctor or employment medical adviser may require [*Sch 2*]. An adequate health record of the medical surveillance of employees should be kept for at least forty years from the date of the last entry made in it [*Reg 10(3)*].

Furthermore, the Regulations introduce various blood-lead action levels and blood-lead suspension levels and urinary lead suspension levels for (i) women of reproductive capacity and (ii) young persons and (iii) other employees, and specify the maximum intervals at which the biological monitoring of such categories of employees must be carried out. In addition, *Sched 1* provides that young persons or women of reproductive capacity may not be employed in any of the following activities:

(*a*) in lead smelting and refining processes:

— work involving the handling, treatment, sintering, smelting or refining of ores or materials containing not less than 5 per cent lead; and

— the cleaning of any place where any of the above processes are carried out;

(*b*)   in lead-acid battery manufacturing processes:

— the manipulation of lead oxides;

— mixing or pasting in connection with the manufacture or repair of lead-acid batteries;

— the melting or casting of lead;

— the trimming, abrading or cutting of pasted plates in connection with the manufacture or repair of lead-acid batteries; and

— the cleaning of any place where any of the above processes are carried out.

Radioactive substances

D1045   Radiation is energy released variously as gamma rays, X-rays, visible light, infra-red and ultraviolet light and microwaves, in the form of waves or particles. The length and frequency of waves (the electromagnetic spectrum) is determined by the quantity of energy released by an atom. It is inherently harmful to people but has also been indispensable in the treatment of certain illnesses and has important industrial uses, such as lasers and welding. Radiation can be natural or of artificial origin; an example of the former is a gamma ray, of the latter an X-ray, such as is used in hospitals, clinics and dental practices. The main danger associated with exposure to radiation is cancer, with exposure to natural radiation being less controllable. To date, however, radiation workers are on par with textile and food workers in a relatively safe industry – 1 in 57,000 deaths per year (HSE statistics 1982).

There are two main kinds of radiation, namely, (*a*) ionising radiations, which are potentially more dangerous (ion – Greek – charged atom) as producing a chemical effect, and (*b*) non-ionising radiations, that is, sources lacking the energy to shatter or ionise atoms. Occupationally, the main example of ionising radiation is an X-ray; whilst examples of non-ionising radiations, in the form of visible, ultraviolet and infra-red light, microwave heat and radio frequency, characterise industries as various as textiles, furniture, paper, automotive, rubber, plastics, construction, communications and power. Legislation has grafted itself onto the distinction between ionising and non-ionising radiations, the former being controlled currently by the *Ionising Radiations Regulations 1985*, whilst the latter are the subject of a draft EU directive on Physical Agents. In addition, new requirements can be expected shortly, in connection with the production, processing, handling and transport and disposal of ionising radiations.

Effect of radiation exposure

(a) Ionising radiations

D1046   Ionising radiations cause tissue damage and the extent of tissue reaction depends on the density of ionisation in the path of radiation – a linear energy transfer (LET). Direct action of radiation on cells can cause cell death or induce mutation. Health effects of radiation can be genetic or somatic, the former affecting offspring, the latter the irradiated individual. Somatic effects take the form of early or late responses, the latter sometimes resulting in induction of malignant disease. Here there may be a latency of several decades between irradiation and tumour appearance.

Workers in hospitals, medical establishments, dental departments, laboratory staff and university researchers are vulnerable to hazards from ionising radiations. Radiation hazards can be emitted from two kinds of sources (*a*) a sealed source, and (*b*) an unsealed source. With the former, a sealed source, the source is contained so that the radioactive material cannot be released, e.g. an X-ray machine. Such radioactive material is usually solid, whereas unsealed sources take the form of gases, liquids or particulates and, because they are unsealed, entry into the body is fairly easy.

(b) Non-ionising radiations

Non-ionising radiations – such as lasers used in welding and cutting, ultraviolet radiation associated with arc welding and infra-red radiation emitted by radiant fires – particularly threaten the eye. Laser beams can cause blindness and exposure to ultraviolet radiation 'arc eye', if goggles or protective glasses are not worn.

Ionising radiations – the Ionising Radiations Regulations 1985 (SI 1985 No 1333)
Duties of employers

D1047

(1)   Not to undertake for the first time work with ionising radiation (except in the case of exposure to the short-lived daughters of radon 222 – where notification after commencement of work is sufficient), unless at least 28 days prior to commencement of work, he

   (*a*)   has notified HSE of the intention to carry out such work;

   (*b*)   has supplied the following particulars:

      (i)   name/address of employer;

     (ii)   address of premises where work is to be carried out;

    (iii)   nature of business;

   (iv)   on type of radiation, e.g. sealed source, unsealed radioactive substance, radiation generator, atmosphere containing the short-lived daughters of radon 222;

     (v)   whether any source is to be used at other premises;

   (vi)   dates of notification and commencement of work.

[*Reg 5(2), Sch 4*].

There are certain exceptions to the general duty to notify, e.g. nuclear installations, radioactive substances having an activity concentration of more than 100 Bqg^{-1}. Material changes in work activity have to be notified, though not cessation, except where (*a*) the site has been or is to be vacated, and (*b*) the work involves a radioactive substance other than a radioactive substance solely in the form of a sealed source.

Defence to notification requirement

It is a defence for a person to prove that

   (*a*)   he neither knew nor had reasonable cause to believe that he had undertaken (or might be required to undertake) work with ionising radiation, and (*b*)   where he had discovered that he had undertaken (or was undertaking) work with ionising radiation, he had forthwith notified HSE of the necessary details.

[*Reg 5(8)*].

(2)   To restrict, so far as is reasonably practicable (for the meaning of this expression, see E15024 ENFORCEMENT), the exposure of employees, and other persons foreseeably affected, to ionising radiations. [*Reg 6(1)*]; this is to be done preferably by engineering controls and shielding and ventilation containment of radioactive substances; warning devices and safety features are only ancillary protection. [*Reg 6(2)*].

(3)   To provide employees and others (e.g. outside maintenance workers) with adequate and suitable personal protective equipment. [*Reg 6(3)*].

(4)   To prevent any radioactive substance, in the form of a sealed source (see D1046 above) from being held in the hand or manipulated directly by hand, unless the instantaneous dose rate to the skin of the hand is less than 75 mSvh^{-1}. [*Reg 6(5)*].

(5)   So far as is reasonably practicable, to prevent any unsealed radioactive substance (or article containing a radioactive substance) from being held in the hand or directly manipulated by hand. [*Reg 6(5)*].

(6)   To ensure that employees (and others foreseeably affected) are not exposed to dose limitations of ionising radiations for the whole body greater than the following:

(*a*)   for employees of 18 or over 50 mSv

(*b*)   for trainees under 18 15 mSv

(*c*)   for any other person (e.g. member of the public) 5 mSv

[*Reg 7, Sch 1*].

(7)   To designate as *controlled areas* any area where doses are likely to exceed 30% of any dose limit for employees aged 18 or more [*Reg 8(1)*] (controlled area).

(8)   To designate as a *supervised area* any area (not being a controlled area) where any person is likely to be exposed to more than 30% of ionising radiations than he would be exposed to in a controlled area. [*Reg 8(2)*] (supervised area).

(9)   Not to permit employees (or others) to enter or remain in a controlled area, unless the employee (or other person)

(*a*)   is a classified person (see (10) below);

(*b*)   enters or remains in the area under a written system of work preventing:

(i)   an employee of 18 or more from receiving a dose of ionising radiations more than 30% of any relevant dose limit (see (6) above),

(ii)   any other person from receiving a dose of ionising radiations greater than the statutory dose limit (see (6) above).

[*Reg 8(6)*] (permit to work system).

(10)   In the case of employees of 18 or over, who are likely to receive a dose of ionising radiations greater than 30% of any relevant dose limit, to designate them as '*classified persons*'. [*Reg 9(1)*] (classified persons).

No such designation may be made, however, unless the medical adviser or appointed doctor has certified in the health record that in his professional opinion a person is fit to be classified. [*Reg 9(3)*]. He must also inform the employees of relevant health hazards, precautions to be taken and the importance of complying with medical and technical requirements. He must also provide the employees with appropriate training in radiation protection. [*Reg 12(c)*].

(11)   To appoint qualified persons as radiation protection advisers where

(*a*)   any employees are exposed to an instantaneous dose rate of more than 7.5 mSvh^{-1} and provide them with adequate information and facilities [*Reg 10(5)*]; or

(*b*)   a controlled area has been designated (see (7) above)

[*Reg 10(1)*] (radiation protection advisers).

(12)   In the case of classified persons, to ensure that all significant doses of ionising radiations received are assessed (preferably by use of personal dosemeters), and that health records of (*a*) classified persons and (*b*) employees who have been overexposed, are kept for at least 50 years. [*Reg 13(2)(3)*] and to send to the Executive within three months of the end of each calendar year or other agreed period summaries of all dose records for the year.

(13)   To control radioactive substances (see D1050 below).

(14)   To assess radiation hazards to employees and the general public and to prepare a contingency plan in order to minimise exposure (see below).

(15)   In the case (mainly) of

(*a*)   classified persons;

(*b*)   employees who have received overexposure (but are not classified persons);

(*c*)   employees engaged in work with ionising radiation on conditions imposed by an employment medical adviser (see above) or appointed doctor;

(i)   to provide adequate medical surveillance, and

(ii)   to have and maintain a health record (or copy) for at least fifty years from the date of the last entry and make it available to the Employment Medical Adviser or appointed doctor.

[*Reg 16(1)-(3) and (9)*].

The European Council adopted in 1997 a Directive on limits for exposures to ionising radiations as a result of work activities. The revised Directive introduced a new maximum exposure limit for workers of 100 milliSieverts (mSv) in a consecutive five-year period, thus giving an 'average limit' of 20 mSv per year, subject to a maximum of 50 mSv a year. Member States are allowed to set a simple annual limit of 20 mSv if they wish. For a member of the public, the revised Directive introduced a new limit of 1 mSv a year. This compared with the previous limit of 5 mSv.

Duties of employees

D1048   Employees are required to

(1)   (in the case of women), inform the employer as soon as they discover that they are pregnant [*Reg 12(d)*];

(2)   present themselves for medical examination and tests during working hours (for medical surveillance purposes) (see above) [*Reg 16(7)*];

(3)   not to expose themselves (or any other persons) to ionising radiation more than is reasonably necessary for carrying out the work [*Reg 6(4)(a)*];

(4)   exercise reasonable care while working [*Reg 6(4)(a)*];

(5)   make full and proper use of personal protective equipment [*Reg 6(4)(b)*];

(6)   report to the employer any defects in personal protective equipment [*Reg 6(4)(c)*];

(7)   not to eat, drink or smoke, take snuff or apply cosmetics in a controlled area, but may drink from a drinking fountain, if the water is not contaminated [*Reg 6(6)*].

Designation of controlled areas

(a) External radiation

D1049   Employers must designate as a *controlled area*, any area in which the instantaneous dose rate exceeds (or is likely to do so) 7.5 μSvh^{-1} but, where the dose rate does not exceed that amount, this designation need not be made because a radioactive substance is in the area (and certain other conditions are satisfied which are beyond the scope of this publication). [*Sch 6 Part I*].

(b) Internal radiation

Employers must designate as a *controlled area* any area where either:

(i)   the air concentration of radionuclide, averaged over any 8-hour working period, exceeds (or is likely to do so) the concentration specified for that radionuclide in Column 3 of *Schedule 2*; or

(ii)   the level of contamination of any surface by a radionuclide, as determined by a suitable method, exceeds (or is likely to do so) the contamination level for that radionuclide specified in Column 4 of *Schedule 2*.

An area is not required to be designated as a *controlled area* if the only potential or actual source of contamination is a radioactive substance present in the area and the total activity of the radionuclide in the area does not exceed the quantity for that radionuclide specified in Column 5 of *Schedule 2*. [*Sch 6 Part II*].

(c) Short-lived daughters of radon 222

Employers must designate as a *controlled area* any area in which the concentration in the air of short-lived daughters of radon 222, averaged over an 8-hour working period, exceeds 2×10^{-6} Jm^{-3} (~0.1 working levels). [*Sch 6 Part IV*].

Control of radioactive substances

D1050   Control over radioactive substances must be exercised as follows:

(a)　so far as reasonably practicable, the substance should be in the form of a sealed source (see D1046 above); the design, construction and maintenance of articles containing and embodying radioactive substances, must prevent leakage [*Reg 18(1)(2)*];

(b)　records relating to quantity and location of radioactive substances, should be kept for at least two years [*Reg 19*];

(c)　radioactive substances must be kept in suitable receptacles in a suitable store [*Reg 20*]; during transportation, radioactive substances must be kept in a suitably labelled receptacle [*Reg 21*].

Assessments and notifications

D1051　(1)　Work must not be carried out with ionising radiations, unless employers have first made an assessment identifying the nature and magnitude of radiation hazards to (a) employees and (b) the general public. [*Reg 25*].

(2)　Where the assessment reveals that employees or the general public are likely to receive a dose of ionising radiations above the statutory dose limit (see (6) at D1047 above) the employer must prepare a contingency plan in order to minimise exposure. [*Reg 27*].

(3)　Where overexposure to radiation has already taken place, the employer must carry out an investigation to determine whether there are circumstances which show beyond reasonable doubt that no overexposure could have occurred. Failing this, he must notify

(a)　the HSE;

(b)　the employee's employer;

(c)　in the case of his own employee, an employment medical adviser.

[*Reg 29*].

Penalties

D1052　Penalties under the *Ionising Radiations Regulations 1985* are as in *HSWA* (see further E15028 ENFORCEMENT).

Persons undergoing medical examinations

D1053　In the interest of persons (or patients) undergoing medical examination, employers must ensure that their employees, carrying out such examinations with ionising radiation, are qualified and can produce a certificate to that effect. Employers must also retain a record of their training. [*Ionising Radiation (Protection of Persons Undergoing Medical Examination or Treatment) Regulations 1988 (SI 1988 No 778)*].

Ionising Radiations (Outside Workers) Regulations 1993 (SI 1993 No 2379)

D1054　The *Ionising Radiations (Outside Workers) Regulations 1993 (SI 1993 No 2379)* cover the health and safety of outside workers, i.e. those who work in an EU country other than their own and who work in a controlled area. The outside employer has to provide those of his employees who may be exposed to radiation in a controlled area with a uniquely identified radiation passbook containing prescribed particulars. The person in charge of the works on site (the operator) has to ensure that the employee is able to undertake the work safely, that he is suitably monitored and that the estimated radiation doses are entered in the radiation passbook.

The management of the outside undertaking also has to obtain information about the risks and estimated doses from the operator and will have to arrange instruction and training for the employees.

Duties of outside contractors

D1055   Outside contractors must ascertain what radiation hazards outside workers will be exposed to and accordingly send only workers who are suitable. Outside workers must have received the necessary information and training regarding risks and an estimate must be made of the dose receivable by the worker. [*Reg 4*]. Following this, the worker must be issued with an individual radiation passbook and a record kept of its issue. This should contain

(*a*)   individual serial number;

(*b*)   date of issue;

(*c*)   name/address of outside contractor, signed by authorised person;

(*d*)   name, date, birth, gender of outside worker;

(*e*)   date of last medical review of outside worker and his classification;

(*f*)   name of organisation where work is undertaken, period of assignment, latest dose assessment prior to assignment and estimated dose information.

[*Reg 5, Sch*].

Duties of operators

D1056   Operators of organisations receiving outside workers must disclose to outside contractors details relating to radiological and other risks involved; and ensure, by reference to the passbook, that workers have received the necessary training, are medically fit and know how to use personal protective equipment. Upon completion of work, operators must enter details of the dose received by the outside worker in the passbook. (This may not be necessary in the case of short duration visits.) [*Reg 6*]. Where an employer is informed by an employee (or other person) that overexposure has occurred, or it is suspected that it has occurred, the operator must carry out an investigation to show beyond reasonable doubt that there are no circumstances in which overexposure could have occurred; failing this, the operator must notify

(i)   the HSE;

(ii)   the outside worker's employer.

[*Ionising Radiations Regulations 1985, Reg 29*].

Duties of outside workers

D1057   Outside workers must take reasonable care of passbooks, must not falsify information in it, must return the passbook on leaving their employment and make it available to the operator. [*Reg 7*].

Defence

D1058

It is a defence for outside contractors to show that breach of duty arose because the *operator* did not fulfil a term of a written contract entered into by him; and for an operator to show that an *outside* contractor failed to fulfil such term. [*Reg 8*].

Non-ionising radiations – EU Directive on Physical Agents

D1059

Regulation for both optical and non-optical radiation is proposed as follows:

(a) *Optical radiation* (i.e. infra-red, visible and ultraviolet light) – threshold level to be *half* the ceiling value (the ceiling value equating with exposure limits recommended by the American Congress of Governmental Industrial Hygienists (ACGIH)). At threshold value, workers

(i) must be given adequate information and training;

(ii) must be supplied with personal protective equipment, on request;

(iii) are entitled to health surveillance.

At ceiling level

(i) employers would have to establish a regime of control strategies – copies being sent to safety representatives;

(ii) personal protective equipment would have to be used;

(iii) hazard areas would have to be designated; and

(iv) systematic health surveillance would have to be carried out.

(b) *Non-optical radiation* (electric and magnetic fields with frequencies up to 300 GHz) – threshold level to be *one-fifth* of the ceiling level, ceiling values of electric currents and specific absorption rate of energy in the human body as well as contact current being tabulated. In addition, there are three action levels. At first action level, employers must

(i) carry out a risk assessment;

(ii) provide workers with information and training;

(iii) provide workers with personal protective equipment, on request (in the case of electric fields).

At second action level (1.6 times the value of fields serving as first action levels), employers will have to

(i) establish a regime of control strategies;

(ii) designate hazard areas, restricting access;

(iii) train operators and check their competence.

At third action level (three times the value of first action level) offending work activities must be notified to HSE. Equipment producing this level will have to be marked.

Radioactive substances and the environment – Radioactive Substances Act 1993

D1060

Radioactive material – defined mainly as actinium, lead, polonium, protoactinium, radium, radon, thorium and uranium – must not be kept on premises, or permitted or caused to be kept, for trade purposes, unless the premises are registered, following application to the appropriate agency (EA or SEPA) [*Sec 6*], who must copy the same to all interested local authorities [*Sec 7*]. The appropriate agency can grant or refuse such application, the former conditionally or unconditionally. [*Sec 7*]. Following registration (and/or authorisation for disposal purposes (see D1061 below)), copies of registration/authorisation documents must be posted at the premises in a prominent position so as to be accessible to employees and members of the public. [*Sec 19*]. On registration, copies of registration documents must be circulated to all interested local authorities, though there is an exemption from registration during currency of a nuclear site licence. [*Secs 7, 8*]. Copies of registration and authorisation documents must be made available for inspection by the general public at all reasonable times on payment of a reasonable fee; and they are entitled to take copies. [*Sec 39*]. Moreover, documentation concerning site and disposal authorisation must be retained, if necessary, for production to an inspector on demand. [*Sec 20*]. The registration requirement extends to use of mobile radioactive apparatus, such as might be used in testing or measuring radioactive substances or emitting them into the environment. [*Sec 9*]. In the case of registration or authorisation (for disposal) being refused, cancelled or revoked, an aggrieved operator can appeal directly to the Secretary of State [*Sec 26*]; this also applies where he wishes to appeal against enforcement and/or prohibition notices (see D1062 'Enforcement' below).

Disposal of radioactive waste

D1061   The *Radioactive Substances Act 1993* prohibits disposal of radioactive waste from trade premises – save in the case of waste from clocks and watches [*Sec 15*] – except in accordance with authorisation granted by the appropriate agency [*Secs 13, 14*]. Such authorisation can be revoked or varied at any time, with or without conditions. In some cases, prior to grant of authorisation, consultation with public and local authorities may be necessary. [*Sec 18*].

Enforcement

D1062   Failure to comply with a registration or authorisation, or with one or more of its conditions can lead to service of an enforcement notice against an offender – a copy being sent to interested local authorities. [*Sec 21*]. However, where retention, use, accumulation or disposal of radioactive material or apparatus – even in furtherance of registration or more particularly disposal – involves *imminent* risk of environmental pollution or harm to human health, the offending operator can be served with a prohibition notice. [*Sec 22*]. The purpose of an enforcement notice is remedial; that of a prohibition notice to stop the offending activity (see further E15006 ENFORCEMENT). Inspectors (who are indemnified against any subsequent criminal and civil liability) are empowered to enter premises on which there are, or are suspected to be, radioactive substances, at all reasonable times, to carry out tests, require co-operation and assistance on the part of occupiers and to compel occupiers to leave premises undisturbed.

Offences and penalties

D1063   Offences are mainly concerned with (*a*) registration and disposal authorisation, (*b*) display of documentation concerning registration and disposal authorisation and (*c*) retention of documentation concerning site suitability and disposal. More particularly:

(*a*)　　Violation of registration and/or authorisation requirements (or attaching conditions) carries

　　(i)　　on summary conviction, a maximum fine of £20,000 or up to six months' imprisonment (or both);

　　(ii)　　on conviction on indictment, an indefinite fine, or up to five years' imprisonment (or both).

　　[*Sec 32*].

(*b*)　　Failure to display the necessary documents (relating to registration and authorisation) carries

　　(i)　　on summary conviction, a maximum fine of £5,000;

　　(ii)　　on conviction on indictment, an indefinite fine.

　　[*Sec 33(1)*].

(*c*)　　Failure to retain site and disposal documents carries

　　(i)　　on summary conviction, a maximum fine of £5,000;

　　(ii)　　on conviction on indictment, an indefinite fine.

　　[*Sec 33(2)*].

Companies and other bodies corporate, whether nationalised or not, are subject to the same penalties as individual functional directors, managers and secretaries found guilty of consent, connivance or neglect. So, too, 'other persons', who are not the 'alter ego' of the organisation and generally lower down the corporate tree [*Secs 36, 37*] (see further E15034 ENFORCEMENT). The *Radioactive Substances Act 1993* binds the Crown, although the latter cannot be liable in any criminal proceedings, with the exception of Crown employees. [*Sec 42*].

Classification and labelling of explosives – Classification and Labelling of Explosives Regulations 1983 (SI 1983 No 1140) as amended by the Carriage of Explosives by Road Regulations 1996 (SI 1996 No 2093)

D1064　　Explosive articles and substances fall into one of the following categories, namely those with

		Division
(*a*)	mass explosion hazard	1.1
(*b*)	projection hazard (but not mass explosion hazard)	1.2
(*c*)	fire hazard and either:	
	(i)　minor blast hazard, or	
	(ii)　minor projection hazard, or	1.3
	(iii)　both	
	(but not mass explosion hazard)	
(*d*)	no significant hazard	1.4

		Division
(e)	very insensitive substances with mass explosion hazard	1.5
(f)	extremely insensitive articles which do not have a mass explosion hazard	1.6

[*Classification and Labelling of Explosives Regulations 1983, Sch 1, as amended by SI 1996 No 2093*].

Explosive articles/substances must not be conveyed, kept or supplied, unless

(i)   they have been classified according to composition, and in the form and packaging necessary, and

(ii)   they and their packaging are correctly labelled.

[*Reg 3*].

Exceptions

(1)   explosives being manufactured/tested [*Reg 4(2)*];

(2)   explosives removed from their packaging for immediate use;

(3)   fireworks, small arms ammunition kept by a retailer, or so obtained [*Reg 4(3)*].

Moreover, both the explosives themselves and their inner and outer packagings must be correctly labelled.

Labelling requirements of explosives

Packaged explosives

D1065   (a)   Packaged explosives in Class 1 Divisions 1.1, 1.2 and 1.3 must be labelled as in the following figure. (The number relates to the explosives Division Number i.e. 1.2, 1.4, and the letter to its Compatibility Group.)

(*b*)   Packaged explosives of Divisions 1.4 and 1.5 as follows:

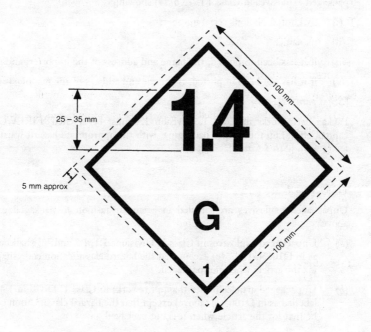

(c)   packaged explosives not within Class 1 as follows:

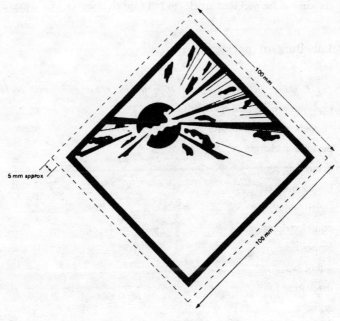

All the above labels are orange with black pictographs, numbers and letters. [*Sch 3 paras 10, 11*]. In addition to the above labels, a second label must be attached to packaged explosives in Class 1 [*Reg 6(1)*] showing:

(i)   its United Nations serial number;

(ii)   its name;

(iii) if it has been imported, the name and address of the importer; and

(iv)   if it has not been imported, the name and address of the manufacturer.

[*Sch 3 para 12*].

Packaged fireworks in Class 1, Division 1.4 must be labelled 'FIREWORK' (in capital letters) on their outer packaging, with the appropriate hazard warning code i.e. (1.4 S). [*Sch 3 para 8*].

Unpackaged explosives

D1066   Unpackaged explosives are labelled in a similar fashion to packaged explosives above.

(*a*)   Unpackaged explosives in Class 1, Divisions 1.1, 1.2 and 1.3 shall be labelled as in D1065(*a*) (above) except that the hazard classification code shall be that for the article when not packaged.

(*b*)   Unpackaged articles (other than a firework) in Class 1, Division 1.4 shall be labelled as in D1065(*b*) (above) except that the hazard classification code shall be that for the article when it is not packaged, or

the word 'EXPLOSIVE' (in capital letters), followed by the hazard classification code (when not packaged) shall be displayed. If the article falls within Division 1.4, Compatibility Group 'S', then 1.4 S shall be displayed.

Unpackaged articles also require a second label to be used. [*Reg 6(2)(4)*]. This is the same as for packaged articles in D1065(i)-(iv) (above). [*Sch 3 para 13*].

Labelling of packaging

(a) Explosive articles in respect of which outer packaging must be labelled:

D1067   explosive articles (not specified)

boosters without detonator

demolition charges

detonating cord

igniter cord

electric detonator

non–electric detonator

igniter fuse

safety fuse

detonating fuse

igniters

sounding devices

[Reg 8(1), Sch 4].

(*b*) *Explosive substances in respect of which both inner and outer packaging must be labelled:*

barium azide

gunpowder

diazodinititrophenol (wetted)

blasting explosives

lead azide (wetted)

mercury fulminate

nitrocellulose

nitroglycerin

nitrostarch

pentolite

powdercake

explosive samples

explosive substances (not specified)

trinitrotoluene (TNT)

tritonal

[Reg 8(1)(2), Sch 5].

In all cases, labelling should be durable and fixed on the packaging and article/substance or on a piece of paper securely fixed to the packaging and article/substance. *[Reg 10]*.

Defence

D1068   It is a defence that a person charged took all reasonable precautions *and* exercised all due diligence to comply. *[Reg 12]*. Generally speaking, this 'due diligence' defence has not been invoked with much success.

Control of explosives at work – Control of Explosives Regulations 1991 (SI 1991 No 1531)

Duties of employers

D1069   With the exception of *Schedule 1* explosives, before an employer can acquire and keep explosives, he must

(*a*)   possess a valid explosives certificate to the effect that he is a fit person (i.e. free from criminal conviction);

(*b*)   acquire and keep

   (i)   no more than the specified quantity, and

  (ii)   only specified explosives

(*a*)   in a specified place, and

(*b*)   for specified purposes

[*Reg 7*].

(*c*)   keep up-to-date records of the explosives and their source for at least three years, which must be made available for inspection by a police officer [*Reg 12, Sch 3*];

(*d*)   report the loss of any explosive [*Reg 13*];

and he must not

(*e*)   transfer explosives, unless the transferee is in possession of a valid explosives licence and is a fit person [*Reg 8*].

Enforcement

D1070   The enforcement agency for these regulations is the police. [*Reg 15*].

Certificate for the purposes of acquiring/keeping explosives

D1071

FORM OF EXPLOSIVES CERTIFICATE
HEALTH AND SAFETY AT WORK ETC. ACT 1974
CONTROL OF EXPLOSIVES REGULATIONS 1991

CERTIFICATE TO *ACQUIRE/ACQUIRE AND KEEP EXPLOSIVES

1. I the undersigned *being/being duly authorised by the chief officer of police for ....police force, do hereby certify that (name) ....of (address) ....is a fit person to *acquire/acquire and keep explosives in accordance with this certificate.

Alternative A—acquisition only

2. The maximum amount of explosives acquired on any one occasion shall not exceed ....

3. The only explosives which may be acquired are those of the following descriptions, namely
....

4. Explosives may only be acquired for the purpose(s) of ....

5. This certificate shall be valid until....................................(maximum one year), unless notice of revocation by or on behalf of the chief officer of police has been served on the certificate holder at an earlier date.

(*Notes:*
(a) If this certificate relates to acquisition only, this section must be completed in accordance with these Notes and "alternative B" deleted.
(b) Each of paragraphs 2, 3 and 4 may be completed or deleted.
(c) Paragraph 5 must be completed.)

Alternative B—acquisition and keeping

2. The explosives may only be kept at the

　　*licensed factory
　　*licensed magazine
　　*registered premises　　　　⎫
　　*store　　　　　　　　　　　⎬ at ....
　　*premises occupied by the Secretary of State
　　*premises used for keeping for private use　⎭

3. The only explosives which may be acquired or kept are those of the following descriptions, namely
....

4. The amount of explosives kept may not exceed the amount which may lawfully be kept at the said premises.

5. This certificate shall be valid until....................................(maximum three years), unless notice of revocation by or on behalf of the chief officer of police has been served on the certificate holder at an earlier date.

(*Notes:*
(a) If this certificate relates to acquisition and keeping, this section must be completed in accordance with these Notes and "alternative A" deleted.
(b) In paragraph 2 all but one of the alternatives marked with a * must be deleted. No address should be inserted if the explosives are to be kept at premises used for keeping for private use. An address must be inserted in all other cases.
(c) If paragraph 2 allows explosives to be kept at a store, registered premises or premises used for keeping for private use paragraph 3 must be completed. If paragraph 2 refers to keeping explosives at premises used for keeping for private use, the description of explosives in paragraph 3 must not include any explosives other than one or more of those mentioned in regulation 10(1) of the Regulations.
(d) Paragraph 4 needs no change.
(e) Paragraph 5 must be completed.)

Signed..

Date..
* Delete as applicable　　　　　　　　　*fig.2*

fig.2

Marketing and transfer of explosives – Placing on the Market and Supervision of Transfers of Explosives Regulations 1993 (SI 1993 No 2714)

Design/manufacture and marketing

D1072　With the exception of firearms, explosives for use by the police/armed forces, pyrotechnical articles, explosives used immediately at the place of manufacture, and for life saving purposes in a motor vehicle [*Reg 3(2)*], explosives must not be put into circulation unless:

(*a*)　they satisfy certain essential safety requirements [*Reg 4*], though there is sufficient compliance until 31 December 2002 if the explosives comply with statutory requirements existing on 31 December 1994 (see D1064 'Classification and labelling of explosives' above, and DANGEROUS SUBSTANCES II);

(*b*)　their conformity with *SI 1993 No 2714* is attested [*Reg 5*]; and

(*c*)　CE marking has been affixed to the explosives [*Reg 7*].

Safety criteria

D1073　Design and manufacture of explosives must be such as to render minimal any risk to the safety of human life and health, property damage and to the environment. Explosives must be tested as to:

(i)　construction, including chemical composition;

(ii)　physical/chemical stability;

(iii)　sensitiveness to impact and friction;

(iv)　compatibility of all components;

(v)　chemical purity;

(vi)　resistance against influence of water;

(vii)　resistance to high/low temperatures;

(viii)　suitability for use in hazardous conditions;

(ix)　prevention of untimely or inadvertent ignition;

(x)　correct loading and functioning;

(xi)　suitable instructions/markings regarding safe handling, storage, use and disposal (in language of the recipient state);

(xii)　ability to withstand deterioration during storage; and

(xiii)　specification of all devices and accessories necessary for reliable and safe functioning.

[*Sch 1*].

Conformity attestation

D1074　Attestation of conformity with these regulations consists of:

(i)　EU type examination, and

(ii)　unit verification.

CE marking

D1075 CE marking must be visible, easily legible, indelible and, if durable, must remain so during transport/storage. It must be affixed either to the explosives themselves, or an identification plate which cannot be re-used, or to the packaging. [*Sch 3*].

Transfer of explosives

D1076 Before any explosives are moved within Great Britain (except movement on the same site), the transferee must obtain transfer approval from the HSE, the document to be retained for three years. [*Reg 8*]. This is not applicable to the Crown, as regards explosives for defence purposes, or explosives transferred to or by the HSE. [*Reg 3(3)*].

In addition, as regards plastic explosives, it is proposed by the draft *Marketing of Plastic Explosives for Detection Regulations* that plastic explosives must contain a chemical detection agent before they can be manufactured, imported or possessed.

Appendix A

Maximum exposure limits and occupational exposure standards – COSHH Regulations

(a) Maximum exposure limits

D1077   A maximum exposure limit (MEL) is the maximum concentration of a substance, averaged over a reference period, to which employees may be exposed, e.g. by inhalation, as specified in the *Control of Substances Hazardous to Health Regulations 1999* (*COSHH 1999*). The combined effect of *Regs 7* and *16* of the *COSHH Regulations 1994* is to require all employers to take reasonable precautions not to exceed MELs. Thus, in the case of substances with an 8-hour long-term reference period (unless statutory assessment shows that the level of exposure is unlikely to exceed MEL), in order to comply, an employer should carry out a monitoring programme (in accordance with *Reg 10*) as proof that MEL is not *normally* exceeded. Alternatively, where a substance has a short-term MEL (e.g. 15 minutes), brief exposure is likely to have acute effects. Here short–term exposure limits should *never* be exceeded.

LIST OF SUBSTANCES ASSIGNED TO MAXIMUM EXPOSURE LIMITS

The maximum exposure limits of the dusts included in the list below refer to total inhalable dust fraction, unless otherwise stated.

		Reference periods			
		Long-term maximum exposure limit (8-hour TWA reference period)		Short-term maximum exposure limit (15-minute reference period)	
Substance	Formula	ppm	mg m^{-3}	ppm	mg m^{-3}
Acrylamide	CH_2=$CHCONH_2$	—	0.3	—	—
Acrylonitrile	CH_2=CHCN	2	4.4	—	—
Antimony & antimony compounds except stibine (as Sb)	Sb	—	0.5	—	—
Arsenic & compounds except arsine (as As)	As	—	0.1	—	—
Azodicarbonamide	$C_2H_4N_4O_2$	—	1.0	—	3.0
Benzene	C_6H_6	5	16	—	—
Beryllium and beryllium compounds (as Be)	Be	—	0.002	—	—
Bis (chloromethyl) ether	$ClCH_2OCH_2Cl$	0.001	0.005	—	—
Buta-1, 3-diene	CH_2=CHCH=CH_2	10	22	—	—
Cadmium & cadmium compounds, except cadmium oxide fume, cadmium sulphide and cadmium sulphide pigments (as Cd)	Cd	—	0.025	—	—
Cadmium oxide fume (as Cd)	CdO	—	0.025	—	0.05

Substance	Formula	Reference periods			
		Long-term maximum exposure limit (8-hour TWA reference period)		Short-term maximum exposure limit (15-minute reference period)	
		ppm	mg m^{-3}	ppm	mg m^{-3}
Cadmium sulphide and cadmium sulphide pigments (respirable dust as Cd)	CdS	—	0.03	—	—
Carbon disulphide	CS$_2$	10	32	—	—
1-Chloro-2,3-epoxypropane (Epichlorohydrin)	OCH$_2$CHCH$_2$Cl	0.5	1.9	1.5	5.8
Chromium (VI) compounds (as Cr)	Cr	—	0.05	—	—
Cobalt and cobalt compounds (as Co)	Co	—	0.1	—	—
Cotton dust		—	2.5	—	—
1,2-Dibromoethane (Ethylene dibromide)	BrCH$_2$CH$_2$Br	0.5	3.9	—	—
1,2-Dichloroethane (Ethylene dichloride)	ClCH$_2$CH$_2$Cl	5	21	—	—
Dichloromethane	CH$_2$Cl$_2$	100	350	300	1060
2,2'-Dichloro–4,4'-methylene dianiline (MbOCA)	CH$_2$(C$_6$H$_3$ClNH$_2$)$_2$	—	0.005	—	—
Diethyl sulphate	C$_4$H$_{10}$O$_4$S	0.05	0.32	—	—
Dimethyl sulphate	C$_2$H$_6$O$_4$S	0.05	0.26	—	—
2-Ethoxyethanol	C$_2$H$_5$OCH$_2$CH$_2$OH	10	37	—	—
2-Ethoxyethyl acetate	C$_2$H$_5$OCH$_2$CH$_2$OOCCH$_3$	10	55	—	—
Ethylene oxide	CH$_2$CH$_2$O	5	9.2	—	—
Ferrous foundry particulate					
total inhalable dust		—	10	—	—
respirable dust		—	4	—	—
Formaldehyde	HCHO	2	2.5	2	2.5
Grain dust		—	10	—	—
Halogeno-platinum compounds		—	0.002	—	—
Hardwood dust		—	5	—	—
Hydrazine	N$_2$H$_4$	0.02	0.03	0.1	0.13
Hydrogen cyanide	HCN	—	—	10	11
Iodomethane	CH$_3$I	2	12	—	—
Isocyanates, all (as-NCO)		—	0.02	—	0.07
Maleic anhydride	C$_4$H$_2$O$_3$	—	1	—	3
Man–made mineral fibre		—	5	—	—
2-Methoxyethanol	CH$_3$OCH$_2$CH$_2$OH	5	16	—	—
2-Methoxyethyl acetate	CH$_3$COOCH$_2$CH$_2$OCH$_3$	5	25	—	—

Substance	Formula	Reference periods			
		Long-term maximum exposure limit (8-hour TWA reference period)		Short-term maximum exposure limit (15-minute reference period)	
		ppm	mg m^{-3}	ppm	mg m^{-3}
4,4'-Methylenedianiline	$CH_2(C_6H_4NH_2)_2$	0.01	0.08	—	—
Nickel and its inorganic compounds (except nickel carbonyl):	Ni				
water-soluble nickel compounds (as Ni)		—	0.1	—	—
nickel and water-insoluble nickel compounds (as Ni)		—	0.5	—	—
2-Nitropropane	$CH_3CH(NO_2)CH_3$	5	19	—	—
Phthalic anhydride	$C_8H_4O_3$	—	4	—	12
Polychlorinated biphenyls (PCB)	$C_{12}H_{(10-X)}Cl_X$	—	0.1	—	—
Propylene oxide	C_3H_6O	5	12	—	—
Rubber fume		—	0.6	—	—
Rubber process dust		—	6	—	—
Silica, respirable crystalline	SiO_2	—	0.3	—	—
Softwood dust		—	5	—	—
Styrene	$C_6H_5CH=CH_2$	100	430	250	1080
o-Toluidine	$CH_3C_6H_4NH_2$	0.2	0.89	—	—
Trichloroethylene	$CCl_2=CHCl$	100	550	150	820
Triglycidyl isocyanurate (TGIC)	$C_{12}H_{15}N_3O_6$	—	0.1	—	—
Trimellitic anhydride	$C_9H_4O_5$	—	0.04	—	0.12
Vinyl chloride	$CH_2=CHCl$	7	—	—	—
Vinylidene chloride	$CH_2=CCl_2$	10	40	—	—
Wool process dust		—	10	—	—

[*HSE (EH 40/98)*].

(b) Occupational exposure standards

An occupational exposure standard (OES), as approved by the HSC, is the concentration of a substance, daily exposure to which over a given period, is not, according to present knowledge, likely to have injurious effects on employees. Where a substance has been assigned an OES, employers should do what is reasonably practicable (see E15024 ENFORCEMENT) to reduce exposure to that standard. Nevertheless, if exposure exceeds the OES, control is still adequate if the employer has indicated why the OES has been exceeded *and* is doing all that is reasonably practicable to comply with the OES.

The Health & Safety Executive publishes *EH64: Summary criteria for occupational exposure limits.* EH64 is a looseleaf publication containing summarised data and reasoning behind occupational exposure limits (OELs) for many toxic substances.

EH64 is also used for consultation on new or revised occupational exposure standards (OESs) or the withdrawal of old standards, and on new biological monitoring guidance values (BMGVs) which are limits set for blood and urine samples.

The summaries give information on established and proposed OELs, and are intended to help employers, employees, occupational hygienists and occupational health practitioners to approach the control of exposure to toxic substances as required under the *Control of Substances Hazardous to Health Regulations 1994* in a more informed way. The summaries contain information on why particular exposure limits have been set, and also on the reasoning behind the values chosen.

Substances included for the first time in the 1998 supplement to *EH64* include:

- Acetaldehyde;

- Barium sulphate;

- Butan-2-one;

- Metallic silver;

- 4-Methylpentan-2-one;

- Methyltertbutyl ether.

In October 1997 the Health and Safety Executive issued Chemical Hazard Alert Notices (CHANs) for eight substances where the current scientific information indicates that no safe level of exposure can be identified.

The Health and Safety Commission's expert scientific panel, Working Group on the Assessment of Toxic Chemicals, judged that the criteria for an Occupational Exposure standard (OES) can no longer be met for aniline, bromoethane, 3-chloropropene, a-chlorotoluene, 1,2-diaminoethane, glutaraldehyde, 2-furaldehyde and phenylhydrazine. An OES is set at a level where there will be no ill-health to workers, if exposed on a daily basis.

The CHANs offer interim advice and urge employers, safety representatives, users and suppliers to put in place appropriate measurement and risk management strategies in advance of any Maximum Exposure Limit being set.

Appendix B

Approved List of Classified Biological Agents

D1078
Classified biological agents, comprising bacteria, viruses, parasites and fungi, are listed below.

Notes.

A: Possible allergic effects.

D: List of workers exposed to this biological agent to be kept for 40 years after the end of the last known exposure.

T: Toxin production.

V: Effective vaccine available.

BACTERIA

Biological Agent	Classification	Notes
Acinetobacter calcoaceticus	2	
Acinetobacter lwoffi	2	
Actinobacillus actinomycetemcomitans	2	
Actinomadura madurae	2	
Actinomadura pelletieri	2	
Actinomyces gerencseriae	2	
Actinomyces israelii	2	
Actinomyces pyogenes	2	
Actinomyces spp	2	
Aeromonas hydrophila	2	
Alcaligenes spp	2	
Arcanobacterium haemolyticum (Corynebacterium haemolyticum)	2	
Arizona spp	2	
Bacillus anthracis	3	V
Bacillus cereus	2	
Bacteroides fragilis	2	
Bacteroides spp	2	
Bartonella bacilliformis	2	
Bordetella bronchiseptica	2	
Bordetella parapertussis	2	
Bordetella pertussis	2	V
Borrelia burgdorferi	2	
Borrelia duttonii	2	
Borrelia recurrentis	2	
Borrelia spp	2	
Brucella abortus	3	

Biological Agent	Classification	Notes
Brucella canis	3	
Brucella melitensis	3	
Brucella suis	3	
Burkholderia cepacia	2	
Burkholderia mallei (Pseudomonas mallei)	3	
Burkolderia pseudomallei (Pseudomonas pseudomallei)	3	
Burkholderia spp	2	
Campylobacter fetus	2	
Campylobacter jejuni	2	
Campylobacter spp	2	
Cardiobacterium hominis	2	
Chlamydia pneumoniae	2	
Chlamydia psittaci (non avian strains)	2	
Chlamydia psittaci (avian strains)	3	
Chlamydia trachomatis	2	
Clostridium botulinum	2	T, V
Clostridium perfringens	2	
Clostridium tetani	2	T, V
Clostridium spp	2	
Corynebacterium diphtheriae	2	T, V
Corynebacterium minutissimum	2	
Corynebacterium pseudotuberculosis	2	
Corynebacterium spp	2	
Coxiella burnetti	3	
Edwardsiella tarda	2	
Ehrlichia sennetsu (Rickettsia sennetsu)	3	
Ehrlichia spp	3	
Eikenella corrodens	2	
Enterobacter aerogenes/cloacae	2	
Enterobacter spp	2	
Enterococcus spp	2	
Erysipelothrix rhusiopathiae	2	
Escherichia coli (with the exception of non-pathogenic strains)	2	
Flavobacterium meningosepticum	2	
Fluoribacter bozemanae (formerly Legionella)	2	
Francisella tularensis (Type A)	3	
Francisella tularensis (Type B)	2	V
Fusobacterium necrophorum	2	
Fusobacterium spp	2	
Gardnerella vaginalis	2	

Biological Agent	Classification	Notes
Haemophilus ducreyi	2	
Haemophilus influenzae	2	
Haemophilus spp	2	
Helicobacter pylori	2	
Klebsiella oxytoca	2	
Klebsiella pneumoniae	2	
Klebsiella spp	2	
Legionella pneumophila	2	
Legionella spp	2	
Leptospira interrogans (all serovars)	2	
Listeria ivanovii	2	
Listeria monocytogenes	2	
Moraxella catarrhalis	2	
Moraxella lacunata	2	
Morganella morganii	2	
Mycobacterium africanum	3	V
Mycobacterium avium / intracellulare	3	
Mycobacterium bovis (BCG strain)	2	
Mycobacterium bovis	3	V
Mycobacterium chelonae	2	
Mycobacterium fortuitum	2	
Mycobacterium kansasii	3	
Mycobacterium leprae	3	V
Mycobacterium malmoense	3	
Mycobacterium marinum	2	
Mycobacterium microti	3	
Mycobacterium paratuberculosis	2	
Mycobacterium scrofulaceum	3	
Mycobacterium simiae	3	
Mycobacterium szulgai	3	
Mycobacterium tuberculosis	3	V
Mycobacterium ulcerans	3	
Mycobacterium xenopi	3	
Mycoplasma hominis	2	
Mycoplasma pneumoniae	2	
Neisseria elongata	2	
Neisseria gonorrhoeae	2	
Neisseria meningitidis	2	V
Nocardia asteroides	2	
Nocardia brasiliensis	2	

Biological Agent	Classification	Notes
Nocardia farcinica	2	
Nocardia nova	2	
Nocardia otitidiscaviarum	2	
Nocardia spp	2	
Pasteurella multocida	2	
Pasteurella spp	2	
Peptostreptococcus anaerobius	2	
Peptostreptococcus spp	2	
Plesiomonas shigelloides	2	
Porphyromonas spp	2	
Prevotella spp	2	
Proteus mirabilis	2	
Proteus penneri	2	
Proteus vulgaris	2	
Providencia alcalifaciens	2	
Providencia rettgeri	2	
Providencia spp	2	
Pseudomonas aeruginosa	2	
Pseudomonas mallei – see Burkholderia mallei		
Pseudomonas pseudomallei – see Burkolderia pseudomallei		
Rhodococcus equi	2	
Rickettsia akari	3	
Rickettsia canada	3	
Rickettsia conorii	3	
Rickettsia montana	3	
Rickettsia prowazekii	3	
Rickettsia rickettsii	3	
Rickettsia tsutsugamushi	3	
Rickettsia typhi		
(Rickettsia mooseri)	3	
Rickettsia spp	3	
Rochalimaea spp *(formerly Bartonella)*	2	
Rochalimaea quintana	2	
Salmonella arizonae	2	
Salmonella enteritidis	2	
Salmonella (other serovars)	2	
Salmonella paratyphi A,B,C	**3**	
Salmonella typhi	3	V
Salmonella typhimurium	2	
Serpulina spp	2	

Biological Agent	Classification	Notes
Serratia liquefaciens	2	
Serratia marcescens	2	
Shigella boydii	2	
Shigella dysenteriae (Type 1)	3	T
Shigella dysenteriae (other than Type 1)	2	
Shigella flexneri	2	
Shigella sonnei	2	
Staphylococcus aureus	2	T
Stenotrophomonas maltophilia	2	
Streptobacillus moniliformis	2	
Streptococcus pneumoniae	2	
Streptococcus pyogenes	2	
Streptococcus spp	2	
Treponema carateum	2	
Treponema pallidum	2	
Treponema pertenue	2	
Treponema spp	2	
Ureaplasma urealyticum	2	
Vibrio cholerae (including El Tor)	2	T, V
Vibrio parahaemolyticus	2	
Vibrio spp	2	
Yersinia enterocolitica	2	
Yersinia pestis	3	V
Yersinia pseudotuberculosis	2	
Yersinia spp	2	

VIRUSES

Biological Agent	Classification	Notes
Adenoviridae	2	
Arenaviridae		
Amapari	2	
Flexal	3	
Guanarito	4	
Ippy	2	
Junin	4	
Lassa Fever	4	
Latino	2	
Lymphocytic choriomeningitis	3	
Machupo	4	

Biological Agent	Classification	Notes
Mobola	2	
Mopeia	3	
Parana	2	
Pichinde	2	
Sabia	4	
Tamiami	2	
Astroviridae	2	
Bunyaviridae		
Akabane	3	
Bunyamwera	2	
California encephalitis	2	
Germiston	3	
Oropouche	3	
Hantaviruses:		
Hantaan (Korean haemorrhagic fever)	3	
'Muerto Canyon'	3	
Prospect Hill	2	
Puumala	2	
Seoul	3	
Other Hantaviruses	2	
Nairoviruses:		
Bhanja	3	
Crimean/Congo haemorrhagic fever	4	
Hazara	2	
Phleboviruses:		
Rift valley fever	3	V
Sandfly fever	2	
Toscana	2	
Uukuviruses	2	
Other Bunyaviridae known to be pathogenic	2	
Caliciviridae:		
Hepatitis E	3	
Norwalk	2	
Other Caliciviridae	2	
Coronaviridae	2	
Filoviridae		
Ebola	4	
Marburg	4	
Reston	4	
Flaviviridae:		

Biological Agent	Classification	Notes
Flaviviruses		
Dengue viruses Types 1-4	3	
Israel turkey meningitis	3	
Japanese B encephalitis	3	V
Murray Valley encephalitis	3	
Rocio	3	
Sal Vieja	3	
San Perlita	3	
Spondweni	3	
St. Louis encephalitis	3	
Wesselsbron	3	
West Nile fever	3	
Yellow fever	3	V
Tick-borne virus group:		
Absettarov	3	V
Hanzalova	3	V
Hypr	3	V
Kumlinge	3	
Kyasanur forest disease	4	V
Louping ill	3	V
Negishi	3	
Omsk haemorrhagic fever	4	V
Powassan	3	
Russian spring summer encephaltis	4	V
Hepatitis C group viruses:		
Hepatitis C	3 D	
Other Flaviviruses known to be pathogenic	2	
Hepadnaviridae		
Hepatitis B	3	V, D
Hepatitis D (delta)	3	V, D
Herpesviridae:		
Cytomegalovirus	2	
Epstein-Barr virus	2	
Herpesvirus simiae (B virus)	3	
Herpes simplex types 1 and 2	2	
Herpesvirus varicella-zoster	2	
Human B-cell lymphotropic virus 6 (HHV6)	2	
Human B-cell lymphyotropic virus 7 (HHV7)	2	
Orthomyxoviridae:		
Influenza virus types A, B and C	2	V

Biological Agent	Classification	Notes
Tick-borne orthomyxoviridae: Dhori and Thogoto	2	
Papovaviridae:		
BK and JC viruses	2	D
Human papillomaviruses	2	D
Paramyxoviridae		
Measles	2	V
Mumps	2	V
Newcastle disease	2	
Parainfluenza (Types 1 to 4)	2	
Respiratory syncytial virus	2	
Parvoviridae		
Human parvovirus (B19)	2	
Picornaviridae		
Acute haemorrhagic conjunctivitis virus (AHC)	2	
Coxsackieviruses	2	
Echoviruses	2	
Polioviruses	2	V
Rhinoviruses	2	
Hepatoviruses: Hepatitis A (human enterovirus type 72)	2	V
Poxviridae		
Buffalopox	2	
Cowpox[1]	2	
Milker's nodes virus	2	
Molluscum contagiosum virus	2	
Monkeypox	3	V
Orf	2	
Vaccinia[2]	2	
Variola (major and minor)[3]	4	V
Yatapox (Tana & Yaba)	2	
Reoviridae		
Coltivirus	2	
Human rotaviruses	2	
Orbiviruses	2	
Reoviruses	2	
Retroviridae		
Human immunodeficiency viruses	3	D
Human T-cell lymphotropic viruses (HTLV) types 1 and 2	3	D
Rhabdoviridae		
Duvenhage	2	V
Piry	3	

Biological Agent	Classification	Notes
Rabies	3	V
Vesicular stomatitis	2	
Togaviridae		
Alphaviuses:		
Bebaru	2	
Chikungunya	3	
Eastern equine encephalomyelitis	3	V
Everglades	3	
Getah	3	
Mayaro	3	
Middleburg	3	
Mucambo	3	
Ndumu	3	
O'nyong-nyong	3	
Ross river	2	
Sagiyama	3	
Semliki forest	2	
Sindbis	2	
Tonate	3	
Venezuelan equine encephalomyelitis	3	V
Western equine encephalomyelitis	3	V
Other known alpha viruses	2	
Rubiviruses: Rubella	2	V
Unclassified viruses		
Blood-borne hepatitis viruses not yet identified	3	D
Unconventional agents associated with:		
Creutzfeldt-Jakob disease	3	D[4]
Gerstmann-Sträussler-Scheinker syndrome	3	D[4]
Kuru	3	D[4]

[1] including strains isolated from cats and exotic species e.g. elephants, cheetahs. [2] including strains originally classified as rabbitpox virus. [3] all strains including 'whitepox virus'. [4] long term record keeping is not required where the results of the assessment made under *Regulation 6* of the *COSHH Regulations 1994* indicate that the activity does not involve a deliberate intention to work with or use that biological agent; and there is no significant risk to the health of employees associated with that agent.

PARASITES

Biological Agent	Classification	Notes
Acanthamoeba castellanii	2	
Acanthamoeba spp	2	
Ancylostoma duodenale	2	

Biological Agent	Classification	Notes
Angiostrongylus cantonensis	2	
Angiostrongylus costaricensis	2	
Ascaris lumbricoides	2	A
Ascaris suum	2	A
Babesia divergens	2	
Babesia microti	2	
Balantidium coli	2	
Blastocystis hominis	2	
Brugia malayi	2	
Brugia pahangi	2	
Brugia timori	2	
Capillaria philippinensis	2	
Capillaria spp	2	
Clonorchis – see *Opisthorchis*		
Cryptosporidium parvum	2	
Cryptosporidium spp	2	
Cyclospora cayetanensis	2	
Cyclospora app	2	
Dientamoeba fragilis	2	
Dipetalonema – see *Mansonella*		
Diphyllobothrium latum	2	
Dracunculus medinensis	2	
Echinococcus granulosus	3	
Echinococcus multilocularis	3	
chinococcus vogeli	3	
Entamoeba histolytica	2	
Enterobius vermicularis	2	
Fasciola gigantica	2	
Fasciola hepatica	2	
Fasciolopsis buski	2	
Giardia lamblia (Giardia intestinalis)	2	
Hymenolepis diminuta	2	
Hymenolepis nana	2	
Isopora belli	2	
Leishmania aethiopica	2	
Leishmania braziliensis	3	
Leishmania donovani	3	
Leishmania mexicana	2	
Leishmania peruviana	2	
Leishmania major	2	

Biological Agent	Classification	Notes
Leishmania tropica	2	
Leishmania spp	2	
Loa loa	2	
Mansonella ozzardi	2	
Mansonella perstans	2	
Mansonella streptocerca	2	
Naegleria fowleri	3	
Necator americanus	2	
Onchocerca volvulus	2	
Opisthorchis sinensis (Clonorchis sinensis)	2	
Opisthorchis viverrini (Clonorchis viverrini)	2	
Opisthorchis felineus	2	
Opisthorchis spp	2	
Paragonimus westermani	2	
Paragonimus spp	2	
Plasmodium falciparum	3	
Plasmodium spp (human & simian)	2	
Sarcocystis suihominis	2	
Schistosoma haematobium	2	
Schistosoma intercalatum	2	
Schistosoma japonicum	2	
Schistosoma mansoni	2	
Schistosoma mekongi	2	
Schistosoma spp	2	
Strongyloides stercoralis	2	
Strongyloides spp	2	
Taenia saginata	2	
Taenia solium	3	
Toxocara canis	2	
Toxocara cati	2	
Toxoplasma gondii	2	
Trichinella nativa	2	
Trichinella nelsoni	2	
Trichinella pseudospiralis	2	
Trichinella spiralis	2	
Trichomonas vaginalis	2	
Trichostrongylus orientalis	2	
Trichostrongylus spp	2	
Trichuris trichiura	2	
Trypanosoma brucei brucei	2	

Biological Agent	Classification	Notes
Trypanosoma brucei gambiense	2	
Trypanosoma brucei rhodesiense	3	
Trypanosoma cruzi	3	
Trypanosoma rangeli	2	
Wuchereria bancrofti	2	

FUNGI

Biological Agent	Classification	Notes
Aspergillus fumigatus	2	A
Blastomyces dermatitidis (Ajellomyces dermatitidis)	3	
Candida albicans	2	A
Candida spp	2	
Coccidioides immitis	3	A
Cryptococcus neoformans var neoformans (Filobasidiella neoformans var neoformans)	2	A
Cryptococcus neoformans var gattii (Filobasidiella bacillispora)	2	A
Emmonsia parva var *parva*	2	
Emmonsia parva var *crescens*	2	
Epidermophyton floccosum	2	A
Fonsecaea compacta	2	
Fonsecaea pedrosoi	2	
Histoplasma capsulatum var *capsulatum (Ajellomyces capsulatus)*	3	
Histoplasma capsulatum var *duboisii*	3	
Histoplama capsulatum var *farcinimosum*	3	
Madurella grisea	2	
Madurella mycetomatis	2	
Microsporum spp	2	A
Neotestudina rosatii	2	
Paracoccidioides brasiliensis	3	
Penicillium marneffei	3	A
Sporothrix schenckii	2	
Trichophyton rubrum	2	
Trichophyton spp	2	
Xylohypha bantiana	2	

Dangerous Substances II – Transportation

Introduction – transportation of dangerous substances by road and rail

D3001   In view of the risk of accidents and spillages in connection with transportation of dangerous goods and substances, and to harmonise EU law in relation to the transportation of dangerous goods by road and rail, considerable statutory duties are placed on consignors and operators of companies involved in the transportation of dangerous goods (including radioactive material) by both road and rail. Recent regulatory changes in this area are the result of the UK incorporating the international 'ADR' and 'RID' agreements into its domestic law.

The duties placed on consignors and operators essentially relate to:

(*a*)   classification, packaging and labelling;

(*b*)   physical transportation (or carriage) requirements relating to the dimensions and suitability of vehicles; and

(*c*)   the competence of drivers and attendants (where necessary).

The transportation of dangerous goods is covered in the following regulations:

(1)   the *Carriage of Dangerous Goods (Classification, Packaging and Labelling) and Use of Transportable Pressure Receptacles Regulations 1996 (SI 1996 No 2092)*;

(2)   the *Carriage of Dangerous Goods by Road Regulations 1996 (SI 1996 No 2095)*;

(3)   the *Carriage of Dangerous Goods by Rail Regulations 1996 (SI 1996 No 2089)*;

(4)   the *Carriage of Explosives by Road Regulations 1996 (SI 1996 No 2093)*;

(5)   the *Carriage of Dangerous Goods by Road (Driver Training) Regulations 1996 (SI 1996 No 2094)*;

(6)   the *Transport of Dangerous Goods (Safety Advisers) Regulations 1999 (SI 1999 No 257)*;

(7)   the *Radioactive Material (Road Transport) (Great Britain) Regulations 1996 (SI 1996 No 1350)*; and

(8)   the *Packaging, Labelling and Carriage of Radioactive Material by Rail Regulations 1996 (SI 1996 No 2090)*.

The Health and Safety Executive has finalised the production of the series of six guidance documents which support the new regulations on the carriage of dangerous goods by road and rail.

The six guidance documents comprise a free introductory booklet and five priced publications which take the reader step by step through the new regulations. They are:

- Are you involved in the Carriage of Dangerous Goods by Road or Rail (Free Booklet);

- Carriage of Dangerous Goods Explained, Part 1 – Guidance for Consignors of Dangerous Goods by Road and Rail (Classification, Packaging, Labelling and Provision of Information) (Ref. HS(G)160), price £9.95 – provides guidance for consignors on classification, packaging and labelling requirements, as well as the use of transportable pressure receptacles;

- Carriage of Dangerous Goods Explained, Part 2 – Guidance for Road Vehicle Operators and others Involved in the Carriage of Dangerous Goods by Road, (Ref. HS(G)161), price £12.20 – provides guidance, principally for road vehicle operators and drivers,on requirements relating to the vehicle and its operation, such as design and construction, vehicle marking,transport documentation and the training of drivers. It also provides guidance on the design and construction of tankers, brought forward from the Approved Codes of Practice made under the 1992 tanker regulations;

- Carriage of Dangerous Goods Explained, Part 3 – Guidance for Rail Operators and Others Involved in the Carriage of Dangerous Goods by Rail, (Ref. HS(G)163), price £7.50 – covers areas similar to Part 2 but in relation to carriage by rail;

- Carriage of Dangerous Goods Explained, Part 4 – Guidance for Operators, Drivers and Others Involved in the Carriage of Explosives by Road, (Ref. HS(G)162), price £10.95 – provides guidance on the quantities of dangerous goods that may be carried (and mixing of loads), vehicle construction, driver training, loading and unloading, journey planning, provision of information, vehicle marking, ensuring safe carriage and handling emergencies; and

- Carriage of Dangerous Goods Explained, Part 5 – Guidance for Consignors, Rail Operators and Others Involved in the Carriage of Radioactive Material by Rail, (Ref. HS(G)164), price £8.95 – sets out guidance for consignors, rail operators and others involved in thepackaging, labelling and carriage of radioactive material by rail, including suitability of containers and wagons, loading, emergency arrangements, information and training.

All of the above publications are available from HSE Books.

This section concerns the regulations in (1)–(6) above.

Dangerous goods

D3002   'Dangerous goods' means any:

(*a*)   explosives;

(*b*)   radioactive material;

(*c*)   goods named individually in the Approved Carriage List (ACL);

(*d*)   any other goods having one or more hazardous properties; and

(*e*)   certain environmentally hazardous substances as stated in the *Health and Safety at Work etc. Act 1974 (Application to Environmentally Hazardous Substances) Regulations 1996 (SI 1996 No 2075)*.

[*The Carriage of Dangerous Goods (Classification, Packaging and Labelling) and Use of Transportable Pressure Receptacles Regulations 1996 (SI 1996 No 2092), Reg 2(1)*].

Transit and carriage

D3003   Dangerous goods are deemed to be carried from the time when they are placed on a vehicle for the purposes of carriage by road or on a railway, until either:

(*a*)   they are removed from the vehicle etc.; or

(*b*)   any receptacle containing the goods has been cleaned, so that any goods or their vapour which remain in the receptacle, are not sufficient to create or increase a significant risk to health and safety, whether or not the vehicle is actually on the road or railway.

'Carriage' or 'consignment' of dangerous goods includes where packages still contain sufficient dangerous goods (or their vapours) to create or increase risks to health and safety.

[*Carriage of Dangerous Goods (Classification, Packaging and Labelling) and Use of Transportable Pressure Receptacles Regulations 1996, Reg 3(2)(a)–(b)*].

Defence under the regulations

D3004   The regulations detailed in (1)–(5) at D3001 above, all have a common defence, namely, that the person charged with an offence under those regulations can prove that:

(*a*)   the commission of the offence was due to the act or default of another person, not being an employee (see further ENFORCEMENT); and

(*b*)   he took all reasonable precautions and exercised all due diligence to avoid the commission of the offence (e.g. the *Carriage of Dangerous Goods (Classification, Packaging and Labelling) and Use of Transportable Pressure Receptacles Regulations 1996, Reg 19*). The penalties applied for breaches of these regulations are the same as for breaches of *HSWA* itself (see ENFORCEMENT).

Classification, packaging and labelling of dangerous goods for carriage by road and rail – the Carriage of Dangerous Goods (Classification, Packaging and Labelling) and Use of Transportable Pressure Receptacles Regulations 1996 (SI 1996 No 2092)

D3005   These regulations, which came into force on 1 September 1996, specify requirements for the classification, packaging and labelling of dangerous goods (and substances) transported by road and rail. In any proceedings for an offence consisting of a contravention of the regulations prior to 1 January 1999, compliance with the *Chemicals (Hazard Information and Packaging) Regulations 1993 (SI 1993 No 1746)* is a defence in the case of goods classified, packaged or labelled prior to 1 July 1995 in accordance with the *1993 Regulations*. [*Reg 20(1)*].

Classification requirements

D3006   Dangerous goods must not be conveyed by road or rail unless classified according to:

(*a*)   the Approved Carriage List (ACL);

(b)   the Approved Requirements and Test Methods for Classification and Packaging of Dangerous Goods for Carriage; and

(c)   the Approved Requirements for Transportable Pressure Receptacles (where applicable).

Regulation 5 requires that, classification must refer to –

(i)   in the case of goods named individually in the Approved Carriage List:

—   classification code,

—   packaging group,

—   subsidiary hazard code,

—   proper shipping names,

—   UN number,

—   appropriate danger sign (see Table 1 below),

—   subsidiary hazard sign (if any); and

(ii)   in the case of all other goods:

—   classification code,

—   packing group,

—   subsidiary hazards,

—   proper shipping names,

—   UN number,

—   appropriate danger sign (see Table 1 below),

—   subsidiary hazard sign (if any).

[*Reg 5, Sch 1 Parts I, II, Sch 2 Parts I, II*].

Optional lettering may be used as well, e.g. 'COMPRESSED GAS', 'TOXIC GAS', 'FLAMMABLE LIQUID', 'OXIDISING AGENT'. [*Sch 1 Part I, column 7*]. In the case of 'TOXIC' substances, the word 'POISON' may be used, and, in the case of 'FLAMMABLE' substances, the word 'INFLAMMABLE'. [*Sch 1 Part II, para 2(c)-(d)*].

Exemptions from classification

D3007   Certain viscous substances are exempt from classification as flammable liquids. These are:

(a)   substances not having properties of a toxic or corrosive substance;

(b)   solutions which do not contain more than 20% nitro-cellulose, containing not more than 12.6% nitrogen by mass;

(c)   substances where the flash point is equal to or greater than 23°C;

(d)   solvents, where in solvent separation tests, the solvent which separates is not more than 3% of the volume of the substance;

(*e*)   substances where the viscosity of the substance when determined at 23°C in a flow cup conforming to ISO 2431-1984 or ES EN 535-1991, and having a jet diameter of 6mm is

(i)   in a case where the substance contains not more than 60% of a flammable liquid with a flashpoint of 61°C or less, not less than 40 seconds, and

(ii)   in any other case, not less than 60 seconds.

[*Sch 1, Part III*].

Table 1

Labelling requirements for dangerous substances carried by road and rail

SCHEDULE 1	CLASSIFICATION AND ASCERTAINMENT OF OTHER PARTICULARS OF DANGEROUS GOODS					Regulation 5
	PART I TABLE OF CLASSIFICATIONS AND OTHER PARTICULARS					
(1) Classification	*(2)* Hazardous properties	*(3)* Relevant properties	*(4)* Packing group	*(5)* Class number	*(6)* Danger sign	*(7)* Optional lettering
Non-flammable, non-toxic gas	A substance which— (a) at 50°C has a vapour pressure greater than 300 kilopascals absolute or is completely gaseous at 20°C at a standard pressure of 101.3 kilopascals; and (b) is carried at an absolute pressure of not less than 280 kilopascals or in liquefied form. other than a toxic gas or a flammable gas.	—	—	2.2		COMPRESSED GAS
Toxic gas	A substance which at 50°C has a vapour pressure greater than 300 kilopascals absolute or is completely gaseous at 20°C at a standard pressure of 101.3 kilopascals and which is toxic.	—	—	2.3		TOXIC GAS

SCHEDULE 1 *(continued)*

(1) Classification	(2) Hazardous properties	(3) Relevant properties	(4) Packing group	(5) Class number	(6) Danger sign	(7) Optional lettering
Flammable gas	A substance which— (a) at 50°C has a vapour pressure greater than 300 kilopascals absolute or is completely gaseous at 20°C at a standard pressure of 101,3 kilopascals and is flammable; or (b) is packed in an aerosol dispenser where that dispenser contains either— (i) more than 45 per cent by mass of a flammable substance, or (ii) more than 250 grammes of a flammable substance, and in this sub-paragraph flammable substance means a flammable gas or flammable liquid having a flash point less than or equal to 100°C	—	—	2.1		FLAMMABLE GAS
Flammable liquid	A liquid with a flash point— (a) above 61°C and which is carried at a temperature above its flashpoint; or (b) of 61°C or below except— (i) a liquid which has a flash-point equal to or more than 35°C, and when tested in accordance with the appropriate approved method does not support combustion.	(a) (in the case of any liquid having a flash point of less than 23°C and containing either not more than 5% of toxic or corrosive substances with a packing group of I or II or not more than 5% of flammable liquids with a packing group of I and a subsidiary hazard of toxic or corrosive)—	III	3		FLAMMABLE LIQUID

SCHEDULE 1 *(continued)*

(1)	(2)	(3)	(4)	(5)	(6)	(7)
Classification	Hazardous properties	Relevant properties	Packing group	Class number	Danger sign	Optional lettering
	(ii) a viscous substance which complies with the provisions of Part III of this Schedule and is contained in a receptacle with a capacity of less than 450 litres, or	(i) less than 3% of it separates out into a clear solvent layer following a suitable solvent separation test,				
		(ii) the flash point of it is specified in column 1 of the table set out in Part IV of this Schedule,				
	(iii) a substance which is classified as a flammable gas because it has the hazardous properties specified in sub-paragraph (b) of this column corresponding to the entry for a 'flammable gas' in column 1 of this Part.	(iii) the kinematic viscosity of it is within the range specified in column 2 of the table set out in Part IV of the Schedule which is opposite to the flash point of that liquid referred to in head (ii) of this sub-paragraph, and				
		(iv) is contained in a receptacle with a capacity of less than 450 litres, or				
		(b) (in the case of any other liquid) it has–				
		(i) an initial boiling point not greater than 35°C,				
		(ii) an initial boiling point above 35°C and a flash point of less than 23°C, or	II			
		(iii) an initial boiling point above 35°C and a flash point of 23°C or above.	III			

SCHEDULE 1 *(continued)*

(1)	(2)		(3)			(4)	(5)	(6)	(7)
Classification	*Hazardous properties*		*Relevant properties*			*Packing group*	*Class number*	*Danger sign*	*Optional lettering*
Flammable solid	(a)	a solid which, under conditions encountered in transport, is readily combustible or may cause or contribute to fire through friction;	A substance which is—				4.1		FLAMMABLE SOLID
	(b)	a self-reactive or related substance which is liable to undergo a strongly exothermic reaction; or	(a)		water-wetted and (when in a dry state) required to be classified (as defined by regulation 2(1) of the Classification and Labelling of Explosives Regulations 1983) in pursuance of regulation 3(2)(a) of those Regulations;	I			
	(c)	a desensitised explosive where the explosive properties have been suppressed.	(b)	(i)	a self-reactive substance, or	II			
				(ii)	a readily combustible solid which, when ignited, burns very vigorously or intensely and is difficult to extinguish; or				
			(c)		a readily combustible solid which, when ignited, burns vigorously or intensely.	III			
Spontaneously combustible substance	A substance which is liable to spontaneous heating under conditions encountered in carriage or to heating in contact with air being then liable to catch fire.		A substance which is—				4.2		SPONTANE-OUSLY COMBUSTIBLE
			(a)		a pyrophoric substance which ignites instantly on contact with air;	I			
			(b)		liable to ignite on contact with air within a short space of time, particularly under conditions of spillage; or	II			
			(c)		any other substance which is liable to ignite on contact with air.	III			

SCHEDULE 1 (*continued*)

(1) Classification	(2) Hazardous properties	(3) Relevant properties	(4) Packing group	(5) Class number	(6) Danger sign	(7) Optional lettering
Substance which in contact with water emits flammable gas	A substance which in contact with water is liable to become spontaneously combustible or to give off a flammable gas.	A substance which— (a) either reacts vigorously with water at ambient temperatures and demonstrates generally a tendency for the gas produced to ignite spontaneously or reacts readily with water at ambient temperatures so that the rate of evolution of flammable gas is equal to or greater than 10 litres per kilogram of substance over any period of one minute;	I	4.3		DANGEROUS WHEN WET
		(b) reacts readily with water at ambient temperatures so that the maximum rate of evolution of flammable gas is equal to or greater than 20 litres per kilo gram of substance per hour; or	II			
		(c) reacts slowly with water at ambient temperatures so that the maximum rate of evolution of flammable gas is greater than 1 litre per kilogram of substance per hour.	III			
Oxidizing substance	A substance other than an organic peroxide which, although not necessarily combustible, may by yielding oxygen or by a similar process cause or contribute to the combustion of other material.	A solid substance which, when mixed with cellulose in a ratio of either 1:4 or 1:1 by mass, exhibits a burning rate at least as fast as that for a– (a) 3:2 mixture by mass of potassium bromate and cellulose;	I	5.1		OXIDIZING AGENT
		(b) 2:3 mixture by mass of potassium bromate and cellulose; or	II			
		(c) 3:7 mixture by mass of potassium bromate and cellulose.	III			
		A liquid substance which, when mixed with cellulose in a ratio of 1:1 by mass, exhibits a pressure rise at least as fast as that of a 1:1 mixture by mass of–				

SCHEDULE 1 *(continued)*

(1) Classification	(2) Hazardous properties	(3) Relevant properties	(4) Packing group	(5) Class number	(6) Danger sign	(7) Optional lettering
	A substance which is—	(a) 50% perchloric acid and cellulose;	I			
		(b) 40% aqueous sodium chlorate solution and cellulose; or	II			
		(c) 65% aqueous nitric acid and cellulose.	III			
Organic peroxide		Any substance classified as an organic peroxide	II	5.2		ORGANIC PEROXIDE
	(a) an organic peroxide; and					
	(b) an unstable substance which may undergo exothermic self-accelerating decomposition.					
Toxic substance	A substance which is liable either to cause death or serious injury or to harm human health if swallowed or inhaled or by skin contact.	A substance which has been allocated to—		6.1		TOXIC
		(a) packing group I in accordance with the criteria set out in Part V of this Schedule;	I			
		(b) packing group II in accordance with the criteria set out in Part V of this Schedule; or	II			
		(c) packing group III in accordance with the criteria set out in Part V of this Schedule.	III			

SCHEDULE 1 (continued)

(1) Classification	(2) Hazardous properties	(3) Relevant properties	(4) Packing group	(5) Class number	(6) Danger sign	(7) Optional lettering
Infectious substance	A substance which either contains viable micro-organisms that are known or reasonably believed to cause disease in animals or humans or genetically-modified micro-organisms and organisms which are infectious.	—	—	6.2		INFECTIOUS SUBSTANCE
Corrosive substance	A substance which by chemical action will— (a) cause severe damage when in contact with living tissue; or (b) materially damage freight or equipment if leakage occurs.	A substance which— (a) causes full thickness destruction of skin tissue at the site of contact with an observation period of 60 minutes starting on the intact skin of an animal for a period of 3 minutes or less,	I	8		CORROSIVE
		(b) causes full thickness destruction of skin tissue at the site of contact with an observation period of 14 days starting after testing on the intact skin of an animal for a period of more than 3 minutes but not more than 60 minutes, or	II			
		(c) (i) causes full thickness destruction of skin tissue at the site of contact with an observation period of 14 days starting after testing on the intact skin of an animal for a period of more than 60 minutes but not more than 4 hours; or	III			
		(d) causes corrosion in steel or aluminium surfaces at a rate exceeding 6.25 mm a year at a test temperature of 55°C.	III			

SCHEDULE 1 *(continued)*

(1) Classification	*(2)* Hazardous properties	*(3)* Relevant properties	*(4)* Packing group	*(5)* Class number	*(6)* Danger sign	*(7)* Optional lettering
Miscellaneous dangerous goods	A substance which–					
	(a) is listed in the approved carriage list and which may create a risk to the health or safety of persons in the conditions encountered in carriage whether or not it has any of the hazardous properties of any other classification; or	—	—	9		—
	(b) contains a genetically-modified micro-organism which is capable of altering animals, plants or microbiological substances in a way which is not normally the result of natural reproduction but excluding any infectious substance;					
	(c) is hazardous to the environment but excluding any substance which–					
	(i) is an explosive or radioactive material,					
	(ii) possesses any of the hazardous properties of any other classification, or					
	(iii) constitutes dangerous goods for any other reason.					

[*Reg 5, Sch 1 Pt I*].

Table 2
Subsidiary hazard signs for such substances and optional lettering

(1) Subsidiary hazard	(2) Subsidiary hazard sign	(3) Optional lettering
Liable to explosion		—
Danger of fire (flammable gas)		FLAMMABLE GAS
Danger of fire (flammable liquid)		FLAMMABLE LIQUID
Danger of fire (flammable solid)		FLAMMABLE SOLID
Liable to spontaneous ignition		SPONTANEOUSLY COMBUSTIBLE
Danger of emission of flammable gas on contact with water		DANGEROUS WHEN WET

(1)	(2)	(3)
Subsidiary hazard	*Subsidiary hazard sign*	*Optional lettering*
Fire intensifying hazard		OXIDISING AGENT
Toxic		TOXIC
Corrosive		CORROSIVE

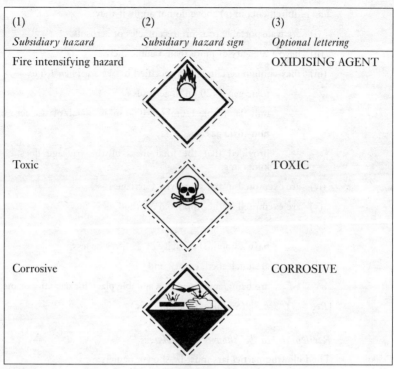

[*Reg 5, Sch 2 Pt I*].

Packaging requirements

Composition and design

D3008 Consignors shall not consign any dangerous goods for carriage in packages unless those packages are suitable, and in particular unless:

(*a*) the packages, and any packaging or overpack associated with the packages are designed, constructed, maintained, filled and closed so as to prevent any of the contents of those packages from escaping when subjected to the stresses and strains of normal handling and conditions encountered in carriage;

(*b*) the packages, and any packagings or overpack associated with the packages, are made of materials which, if they come into contact with the contents of those packages, are not made of materials which are likely to be damaged by the contents so as to create a health and safety risk;

(*c*) (where fitted) receptacle closures must be able to be repeatedly re-closed without letting the contents escape;

(*d*) any conditions relating to packaging specified in the special provision code of the ACL are complied with; and

(*e*) packages have been tested and approved, a competent authority has approved the test, and the packagings allocated an ADR mark, RID mark, UN mark, or joint ADR/RID mark.

[*Reg 6(1)*].

The requirements in (*e*) above do not apply if they:

  (i) are transportable pressure receptacles or aerosols;

  (ii) have a capacity of more than 3 cubic metres;

  (iii) they contain certain goods specified in *Sch 3 column 1*, i.e.

     — toxic gas   120 ml in aerosols

     — non-flammable 120ml (or 1000 ml in metal/plastic aerosols)

     — non-toxic gas

     — provided that the total mass of the package does not exceed 30 kilograms;

  (iv) are exempted in the Approved Carriage List;

  (v) are exempted in the Approved Method; or

  (vi)

     — have a nominal capacity of 25 litres or less,

     — are uncleaned, empty, and

     — are being consigned to a suitable place for cleaning or disposal.

[*Reg 6(3), Sch 3*]. (See also Table 3 below.)

Particulars to be shown on packages

D3009   The following particulars must be shown, namely:

(*a*)   designation of the goods;

(*b*)   UN number;

(*c*)   danger sign; and

(*d*)   subsidiary hazard signs (if any);

and must,

  (i) be so displayed as to be easily read;

  (ii) stand out from their background so as to be readily noticeable;

  (iii) either be

     — clearly and indelibly marked on the package, or

     — clearly and indelibly printed on a label securely fixed to the package, or attached in some appropriate manner; and

  (iv) be in English or the language of the recipient state.

[*Regs 8, 11*].

Table 3

Packages/receptacles exempt from showing particulars under Regulation 8

(1) Goods/Classification	(2) Packing group	(3) Maximum quantity per receptacle
Non-flammable, non-toxic, gas, except one with a fire intensifying subsidiary hazard	—	120 ml (or 1.000 ml in metal or plastic aerosols).
Flammable gas or a non-flammable, non-toxic gas with a fire intensifying subsidiary hazard	—	120 ml in glass aerosols. 1.000 ml in metal or plastic aerosols.
Toxic gas	—	120 ml in aerosols.
Flammable liquid	II	1 litre in metal packagings. 500 ml in glass or plastic packagings.
	III	5 litres
Flammable solid	II	500 g
	III	3 kg
Substance (liquid or solid) which in contact with water emits flammable gas	II	500 g
	III	1 kg
Oxidizing substance (liquid or solid)	II	500 g
	III	1 kg
Organic peroxide (solid, of Type B or C as defined in the appropriate approved method, and not requiring temperature control)	II	100 g
Organic peroxide (liquid, of Type B or C as defined in the appropriate approved method, and not requiring temperature control)	II	25 ml
Organic peroxide (solid, of Type D, E or F as defined in the appropriate approved method, and not requiring temperature control)	II	500 g
Organic peroxide (liquid, of Type D, E or F as defined in the appropriate approved method, and not requiring temperature control)	II	125 ml
Toxic substance (solid)	II	500 g
Toxic substance (liquid)	II	100 ml
Toxic substance (solid)	III	3 kg
Toxic substance (liquid)	III	1 litre
Corrosive substance (solid)	II	1 kg
Corrosive substance (liquid)	II	500 ml. If glass, porcelain or stoneware receptacles are used they must be enclosed in compatible and rigid intermediate packagings.
Corrosive substance (solid)	III	2 kg
Corrosive substance (liquid)	III	1 litre

(1) Goods/Classification	(2) Packing group	(3) Maximum quantity per receptacle
Diagnostic specimens in Group (b) (within the meaning of the approved methods)	—	100 ml packed in accordance with the appropriate approved method.
Dibromodifluoromethane	—	5 litres
Benzaldehyde	III	5 litres
Environmentally hazardous substance (solid), NOS	III	5 kg
Environmentally hazardous substance (liquid), NOS	III	5 litres

[*Regs 6(3)(c), 8(4), Sch 3*].

Exempted goods and substances

D3010   The following goods are exempted from the regulations:

(*a*)   infectious substances affecting animals only (UN 2900);

(*b*)   environmentally hazardous substance (solid) (UN 3077);

(*c*)   environmentally hazardous substance (liquid) (UN 3082);

(*d*)   genetically modified micro-organisms (UN 3245);

carried in

(i)   an agricultural or forestry tractor;

(ii)   mobile machinery;

(iii)   a vehicle with less than 4 wheels;

(iv)   a vehicle with a maximum design speed of 25 km/h or less; or

(v)   armed forces vehicles.

[*Reg 3(7)*].

Main exempted operations

D3011   These include:

(*a*)   international transport operations within the meaning of COTIF (the Convention concerning international carriage by rail), where goods are classified, packaged and labelled in accordance with RID;

(*b*)   international transport operations within the meaning of ADR;

(*c*)   goods carried by sea and classified etc. in accordance with the International Maritime Dangerous Goods Code issued by the International Maritime Organisation;

(*d*)   goods carried by air and classified etc. in accordance with the Technical Instructions for the Safe Transport of Dangerous Goods by Air issued by the International Civil Aviation Organisation;

(*e*)   goods carried in a vehicle which is not being used for, or in connection with, work;

(*f*)   goods carried

    (i)   between private premises and another vehicle in the vicinity of those premises, or

    (ii)   between one part of the premises and another;

(*g*)   goods carried in connection with the provision of emergency services, solely for the purpose of re-packaging or disposal at the destination (so long as they are clearly marked as dangerous and sealed to prevent them escaping);

(*h*)   goods carried as a sample by an enforcement authority;

(*j*)   goods carried on a railway from one part of a factory, mine, quarry or harbour area to another part;

(*k*)   explosives;

(*l*)   live animals;

(*m*)   fuel, batteries or fire safety equipment used for the operation of the vehicle;

(*n*)   petroleum spirit; and

(*o*)   radioactive material (governed by the *Radioactive Material (Road Transport) (Great Britain) Regulations 1996*).

[*Reg 3(1)*].

Importance of the approved information

D3012   Information relating to the classification, packaging and labelling criteria, for the purposes of transportation of dangerous goods by road and rail is contained in:

(*a*)   the Approved Carriage List (ACL);

(*b*)   the Approved Requirements and Test Methods for Classification and Packaging of Dangerous Goods for Carriage; and

(*c*)   the Approved Requirements of Transportable Pressure Receptacles (formerly 'transportable gas containers').

The Health and Safety Commission has published a revision of the Approved Carriage List; Approved Requirements and Test Methods for the Classification and Packaging of Dangerous Goods for Carriage; and Approved Requirements for Transportable Pressure Receptacles. In addition to the classification of dangerous goods (as per *Schedule 1*), vehicles carrying dangerous goods or substances by road and rail must, where necessary, be labelled with subsidiary hazard signs (as per *Schedule 2*). [*Regs 4, 5*]. (See Table 2 above.)

Transitional defence

D3013   Apart from the general defence under these regulations (see D3001 above), it is also a defence that goods were classified, packaged and labelled for carriage prior to 1 July 1995, in accordance with the previous regulations (the *Carriage of Dangerous Goods by Road and Rail (Classification, Packaging and Labelling) Regulations 1994 (SI 1994 No 669)*). [*Reg 20*].

Training of drivers of vehicles carrying dangerous goods – the Carriage of Dangerous Goods by Road (Driver Training) Regulations 1996 (SI 1996 No 2094)

D3014   These regulations, which came into force on 1 September 1996, require that operators of vehicles engaged in the carriage of dangerous goods ensure that drivers are instructed and trained in the dangers associated with the carriage of dangerous goods and hold vocational training certificates. For the first time this instruction and training covers:

(*a*)   certain environmentally hazardous substances;

(*b*)   radioactive material; and

(*c*)   flammable liquids.

Under the regulations, vehicles are considered to be engaged in the 'carriage' of dangerous substances from the commencement of loading until the vehicle has been unloaded and cleaned or purged of the goods to the extent that it no longer creates a significant health and safety risk to any person regardless of whether the vehicle is on the road at any time. [*Reg 2(4)*].

In particular, drivers of the following vehicles carrying dangerous goods must receive adequate training and instruction:

(i)   road tankers with a capacity of 1,000 litres (or less);

(ii)   tank containers with a capacity greater than 3,000 litres (excluding the carriage of

—   explosives,

—   goods in transport category 4, and

—   radioactive material (generally))

[*Reg 2(1)(a), (2)*];

(iii)   vehicles having a permissible maximum weight exceeding 3.5 tonnes

—   in bulk,

—   in a road tanker with a capacity of 1,000 litres (or less),

—   in a tank container with a capacity of 3,000 litres (or less),

—   where any of the goods are in transport category 0,

—   where goods carried are in packages, none of the goods is in transport category 0,

—   where goods carried are in packages, none of the goods is in transport category 0 and the total mass or volume is greater than 20,

—   where goods carried are in packages, none of the goods is in transport category 0 or 1, and the total mass or volume is greater than 200, or

—   where goods carried are in packages, none of the goods is in transport category 0, 1 or 2, and the total mass or volume is greater than 500.

[*Reg 2(1)(a)*].

Instruction and training requirements – (main) duties of operators

D3015   Operators of vehicles (other than those registered outside the United Kingdom), engaged in the carriage of dangerous goods, must ensure that drivers of such vehicles have received adequate instruction and training to enable them to understand:

(a)   the nature of dangers and risks involved, and action to be taken in emergencies;

(b)   their duties under the *HSWA 1974*; and

(c)   any regulations relevant to the operation, e.g. the *Carriage of Dangerous Goods by Road Regulations 1996*.

[*Reg 3(1)*].

The operator must keep a record of such training and, where necessary, make a copy available to the driver. [*Reg 3(2)*]. More particularly, operators must ensure that drivers hold a valid 'vocational training certificate' issued by the Secretary of State. [*Reg 4(1)*]. It is sufficient compliance if a driver holds a training certificate issued under the previous regulations (the *Road Traffic (Training of Drivers of Vehicles Carrying Dangerous Goods) Regulations 1992 (SI 1992 No 744)*). [*Reg 5*]. Exceptions occur in the case of certain radioactive material. [*Reg 4(9)*]. Drivers must keep such certificates for the whole of the period of carriage [*Reg 6*], and may be required to produce them to a police constable or goods vehicle examiner [*Reg 7*].

Transitional defence

D3016   Where there is a breach of training or vocational certificate requirements prior to 1 January 1997, it is a defence for an accused person to prove that he complied with *Regulation 4* or *5(1)* of the *1992 Regulations*. [*Reg 11(1)*].

Appointment of safety advisers for the transport of dangerous goods – the Transport of Dangerous Goods (Safety Advisers) Regulations 1999 (SI 1999 No 257)

D3017   The *Transport of Dangerous Goods (Safety Advisers) Regulations 1999 (SI 1999 No 257)* came into force on 1 March 1999 (except as regards its key requirement, *reg 4*, for which the date is 31 December 1999). The Regulations implement Council Directive 96/35/EC on the appointment and vocational qualification of safety advisers for the transport of dangerous goods by road, rail and inland waterway. *Reg 3* provides that the Regulations are applicable to self-employed people in the same way as they are applicable to employers.

Reg 4(1) provides that, before any employer transports dangerous goods by road, rail or inland waterway, he must have appointed an individual as a safety adviser for the purpose of advising him on health, safety and environmental matters relating to the transportation of those dangerous goods. 'Dangerous goods' have the meaning given them by the *Carriage of Dangerous Goods (Classification, Packaging and Labelling) and Use of Transportable Pressure Receptacles Regulations 1996 (SI 1996 No 2092)* (see D3002). Under the Regulations, employers are required to provide adequate information, time and other resources to allow the safety advisers to fulfil their functions. Employers must ensure that a sufficient number of safety advisers have been appointed under *reg 4(1)* to enable them to carry out their duties effectively. The exact number of advisers to appoint is a matter for each employer to determine – it depends upon what is appropriate, bearing in mind the scale of the operation, the number of sites involved, and how far duties are allocated to advisers themselves or to other staff. Crucially, where a number of employers frequently use the same site, such as a port or marshalling yard, they may co-operate and appoint the same person as their safety adviser.

Schedule 2 to the Regulations lists the functions of safety advisers as including:

— monitoring compliance with the rules relating to the transportation of dangerous goods;

— advising the employer on the transportation of dangerous goods;

— ensuring that an annual report to the employer is prepared on the activities of the employer concerning the transport of dangerous goods;

— monitoring the procedures for compliance with the rules governing the identification of dangerous goods being transported;

— monitoring the practice of the employer in taking into account, when buying means of transport, any special requirements in connection with the dangerous goods to be transported;

— monitoring the procedures for checking the equipment used in connection with the transport of dangerous goods;

— monitoring the training of the employer's employees and the maintenance of records of such training;

— implementing proper emergency procedures on the occurrence of any accident or incident which may affect safety during the transport of dangerous goods;

— investigating and preparing reports on serious accidents, incidents or infringements recorded during the transportation of dangerous goods;

— implementing measures to avoid the recurrence of serious accidents, incidents or infringements;

— verifying that employees involved in transporting dangerous goods have detailed operational procedures and instructions;

— implementing verification procedures to ensure that the documents and safety equipment which must accompany the transportation of the goods are indeed on board the vehicle and that they comply with health and safety regulations; and

— implementing verification procedures to ensure compliance with legislation governing the loading and unloading of dangerous goods.

If dangerous goods are being transported by the employer, and an accident occurs which affects the health or safety of any person or causes damage to the environment or to property, the safety adviser must ensure that a report on the accident is prepared and provided to the employer, who must keep the report for at least five years.

Reg 7 provides that safety advisers must hold vocational training certificates, obtainable only after training has been completed and an examination passed. The safety adviser's certificate must be appropriate to the modes of transport used by the employer and to all dangerous goods specified and transported by the employer. Each certificate will be valid for five years: advisers will then need to pass a 'refresher' examination.

Carriage of dangerous goods by road – the Carriage of Dangerous Goods by Road Regulations 1996 (SI 1996 No 2095)

D3018　These regulations, which came into force on 1 September 1996, impose requirements on (mainly) operators in connection with the transportation of dangerous goods by road in containers, tanks and vehicles (other than radioactive material and explosives) as well as storage of petrol and its distribution from terminals to service stations. [*Sch 12*]. Additionally, designers, manufacturers, importers, suppliers and repairers of such vehicles as well as examiners and testers of tanks have duties. (For exempted operations see D3010, D3011 above.)

Compliance with certification requirements

D3019　It is incumbent on:

(*a*)　operators of tanks and vehicles to comply with the Approved Carriage List (ACL);

(*b*)　designers, manufacturers, importers, suppliers and repairers of vehicles to comply with the Approved Vehicle Requirements (see D3003 above); and

(*c*)　designers, manufacturers, importers, suppliers, repairers, examiners and testers to comply with the Approved Tank Requirements.

[*Reg 6*].

Definitions

D3020　The relevant definitions relating to these regulations are as follows.

(A) *Operator*

The operator of a 'container' or 'vehicle' is:

(*a*)　the person who, having a place of business in Great Britain, has the management of the container or vehicle for the time being, or, if there is no person falling within this definition;

(*b*)　the driver of the vehicle or, in the case of a container, the driver of the vehicle on which the container is carried.

The operator of a 'tank' (other than the carrying tank of a road tanker), shall be:

(i)　the person who, having a place of business in Great Britain owns the tank, or, if there is no person falling within this definition;

(ii)　the person who, having a place of business in Great Britain, has the management of that tank; or

(iii)　the person who, having a place of business in Great Britain, has the management of that tank for the time being; or

(iv)　if there is no person who satisfies the requirements of (i)-(iii) above, the driver of the vehicle on which the tank is carried.

[*Reg 4*].

(B) *Consignor*

'Consignor' is defined by *Reg 2(1)* as:

(*a*)   a person who, having a place of business in Great Britain, consigns, whether as a principal or agent for another, dangerous goods for carriage; or

(*b*)   the consignee of the goods insofar as that person has control over the carriage of those goods in Great Britain.

(C) *Containers*

The definition of 'container' in the regulations has the same meaning as in the *Carriage of Dangerous Goods (Classification, Packaging and Labelling) and Use of Transportable Pressure Receptacles Regulations 1996 (SI 1996 No 2092), Reg 2(1).* This is an article of carriage equipment with an internal volume of not less than 1 cubic metre which is:

(*a*)   of a permanent character and strong enough for repeated use;

(*b*)   designed to facilitate the carriage of goods, by one or more modes of carriage, without intermediate reloading;

(*c*)   designed to be readily handled; and

(*d*)   designed to be easy to fill and empty,

but does not include

(i)   an intermediate bulk container;

(ii)   any packagings;

(iii)   a tank;

(iv)   a transportable pressure receptacle or vehicle.

(D) *Road tanker, tank, tank container, tank wagon*

The definitions of 'road tanker', 'tank', 'tank container', 'tank wagon' have the same meanings as in the *Carriage of Dangerous Goods (Classification, Packaging and Labelling) and Use of Transportable Pressure Receptacles Regulations 1996 (SI 1996 No 2092), Reg 2(1).* These are as follows.

(*a*)   *Road tanker* – means a vehicle or trailer constructed or adapted for the carriage of goods which has a tank ('carrying tank') which is

(i)   attached to the frame of the vehicle (whether structurally or otherwise) and (except when empty) is not intended to be removed from the vehicle;

(ii)   an integral part of the vehicle; or

(iii)   a demountable tank.

(*b*)   *Tank* – means a tank which is

(i)   used for the carriage of a liquid, gaseous, powdery or granular material or a sludge; and

(ii)   so constructed that it can be securely closed (except for the purpose of relieving excess pressure) during the course of carriage,

and includes an assembly of transportable pressure receptacles interconnected by a manifold and mounted on a frame where

(iii)   the frame is permanently fixed to a vehicle; or

(iv)   the receptacles have a total volume of 1,000 litres or more,

but   does not include

(v)   an intermediate bulk container;

(vi)   a hopper with a loose-fitting lid;

(vii)   a transportable pressure receptacle;

(viii)   an aerosol; or

(ix)   packagings which satisfy *Regulation 6* (see D3007 above) or are excluded from the regulations.

(*c*)   *Tank container* – means a tank (other than the carrying tank of a road tanker or tank wagon), whether or not divided into separate compartments, having a total capacity of more than 450 litres (or 1,000 litres in the case of tanks used for the carriage of a gas).

(*d*)   *Tank wagon* – comprises of a superstructure of one or more tanks (including their openings and closures), their items of equipment, and an underframe fitted with its own items of equipment (including running gear, suspension, buffing, traction, braking gear and inscriptions).

Main duties of consignors

D3021   Consignors who engage operators to carry dangerous substances have duties to ensure that any operator engaged by him to carry those goods is provided with certain information. [*Reg 13(1)*]. The duty is imposed to enable operators to comply with their duties (see below). Operators break the law if they undertake the carriage of dangerous goods without the receipt of such information. This does not apply to consignors who also act as the operator, provided that they carry the goods on their own behalf. [*Reg 13(3)*].

Information to be provided by consignors

D3022   Any consignor of dangerous goods must ensure that any operator engaged by him is provided with information in documentary form prior to the carriage of the goods. This includes:

(*a*)   the designation of the dangerous goods;

(*b*)   the classification code;

(*c*)   the UN number;

(*d*)   any extra information that may be required to determine the transport category of the dangerous goods;

(*e*)   the control and emergency temperatures (where appropriate);

(*f*)   where the dangerous goods are carried in packages, either:

(i)   the mass or volume of each individual package and the number of packages consigned,

(ii) for each transport category, the sum of the mass or volume of the individual packages consigned;

(g) where the dangerous goods are carried other than in packages, either:

(i) the mass or volume of the dangerous goods consigned in each container, tank or vehicle and the number of containers or tanks, or

(ii) for each transport category, the sum of the mass or volume of all the dangerous goods consigned in containers, tanks or vehicles;

(h) the name and address of the consignor;

(j) the name and address of the consignee (if known);

(k) any other relevant information; and

(l) a statement signed or authenticated by or on behalf of the consignor (a 'consignor's declaration') confirming that in accordance with the *Carriage of Dangerous Goods by Road Regulations 1996* and the *Carriage of Dangerous Goods (Classification, Packaging and Labelling) and Use of Transportable Pressure Receptacles Regulations 1996*:

(i) the dangerous goods as presented may be carried,

(ii) the dangerous goods and any packaging, intermediate bulk container or tank in which they are contained are in a fit condition for carriage and properly labelled (see D3027 below), and

(iii) where several packages are packed together in an overpack or in a single container, this mixed packing is not prohibited.

Main duties of operators

D3023   Operators carrying dangerous goods are subject to the following duties, namely to ensure the following. (For the definition of 'operator' see D3020 above.)

(a) The letter 'Y' appears in column 8 of the Approved Carriage List, where goods are carried in bulk in a container or vehicle. [*Reg 8*]. Operators of 'vehicles' carrying such dangerous goods in bulk also have to comply with the requirements of *Schedule 5*, and operators of 'containers' carrying dangerous goods in bulk with *Schedule 6*.

(b) The letter 'Y' appears in column 7 of the Approved Carriage List, where goods are carried in a tank. [*Reg 9*].

(c) A container, tank and vehicle being used for the carriage of dangerous goods is:

(i) suitable for such carriage, having regard to the journey itself and the hazardous properties of the cargo, and

(ii) has been adequately maintained.

[*Reg 10(1)*].

(d) Any vehicle which is being used for the carriage of dangerous goods:

(i) has only one trailer or semi-trailer;

(ii) if used for carriage of packages, with packaging sensitive to moisture, is either

— sheeted, or

—   closed; and

(iii)   has complied with the requirements of *Schedule 7* 'Types of vehicle to be used for the carriage of certain dangerous goods'.

[*Reg 10(2)*].

(*e*)   A certificate has been signed, dated and issued by a competent authority, in relation to a tank (before carrying dangerous goods), stating that the tank:

(i)   has been examined and tested in accordance with requirements which have been approved and published in the Approved Tank Requirements,

(ii)   conforms to the approved design, and

(iii)   is suitable for its intended purpose,

and is kept at the operators' principal place of business.

[*Reg 11(3)(7)*].

Where the operator is not the tank owner, it is sufficient compliance if:

(i)   an authenticated copy of the certificate is kept:

—   at the operator's principal place of business in Great Britain, or

—   if there is no place of business in Great Britain, on the vehicle; or

(ii)   the certificate is readily available from the owner of the tank.

[*Reg 11(8)*].

(*f*)   That he has:

(i)   obtained the consignor's declaration (if applicable), or an authenticated copy in relation to the dangerous goods carried; and

(ii)   he has taken reasonable steps to ensure that the goods are in a condition fit for carriage.

[*Reg 12(1)*].

(*g*)   In the case of vehicles:

(i)   used for the carriage of infectious substances or toxic goods; or

(ii)   which are empty but uncleaned after the carriage of such goods,

that the operator has ensured that no food is carried in the vehicle unless effectively separated from the infectious substance or toxic goods to avoid the risk of contamination by those goods.

[*Reg 12(7)*].

(*h*)   That any other operators engaged by them who are engaging in the carriage of dangerous goods are provided with the requisite transport documentation prior to the journey commencing. This includes:

(i)   name and address of the consignor;

(ii)   name and address of the consignee;

(iii)   designation of dangerous goods;

(iv)   classification code;

(v)   UN number;

(vi)   any other information required to determine the transport category of the goods;

(vii)   control and emergency temperatures;

(viii)   details of total mass of volume of dangerous goods;

(ix)   emergency action code (where appropriate);

(x)   prescribed temperature (where appropriate); and

(xi)   emergency information.

[*Regs 13(1)(2), 14(1)-(3)*].

(*j*)   That all steps as it is reasonable for them to take to ensure that nothing in the way that goods are loaded, stowed or unloaded from any container, tank or vehicle is liable to create a significant risk or significantly increase any existing risk to the health or safety of any person arising out of the presence of those dangerous goods. [*Reg 19(1), (2)(b), Sch 11*]. The same duties as are imposed on drivers (see (*g*)-(*q*) at D3027 below) apply to operators.

(*k*)   That any vehicle which is being used to convey dangerous goods is:

(i)   equipped so that the driver can take those measures detailed in the emergency information; and

(ii)   where toxic gases are being carried, that the vehicle crew are supplied with suitable respiratory protective equipment to enable them to escape safely in the event of any emergency.

[*Reg 21(1)*].

(*l*)   Ensure that the vehicle is equipped with:

(i)   at least one portable fire extinguisher with a minimum capacity of 2kg of dry powder (or other suitable extinguishant) suitable for fighting a fire in the engine or cab of the vehicle; and, if it is to be used to fight a fire involving the load, it does not aggravate the fire, and if possible, controls it; and

(ii)   at least one portable fire extinguisher with a minimum capacity of 6kg of dry powder (or other suitable extinguishant) suitable for fighting a tyre or brake fire or a fire involving the load, which does not aggravate the fire, and if possible, controls it,

and that the extinguishants contained therein, will not release toxic gases into the drivers cab when under the influence of the heat of a fire. [*Reg 23(2), (7)*].

The extinguisher must:

(1)   bear a mark of compliance with a standard issued by a recognised competent authority;

(2)   be fitted with a seal verifying that it has not been used; and

(3)   where it was manufactured after 31 December 1996, bear an inscription as to the date when it should next be inspected.

[*Reg 23(4)*].

If the load only comprises of infectious substances, the extinguisher in (ii) above need not be provided. [*Reg 23(3)(b)*].

(*m*) Ensure that when the vehicle is parked it is parked to comply with certain requirements. The same duties that are imposed on drivers in this regard (see (*u*) at D3026 below) apply to operators.

(*n*) No container, vehicle or tank shall carry any dangerous goods which are required by the *Carriage of Dangerous Goods (Classification, Packaging and Labelling) and Use of Transportable Pressure Receptacles Regulations 1996 (SI 1996 No 2092)* to be labelled with a subsidiary hazard sign 'liable to explosion' with any other dangerous goods unless effective measures are taken to ensure that carriage of the mixed load is no more dangerous than the total quantity of the unmixed load. [*Reg 18(1)*].

Emergency information to be provided by operators

D3024 The operator shall provide to other operators engaged by him details of measures to be taken by the driver in the event of an accident or emergency, and any other safety information concerning the goods. This includes:

(*a*) the nature of the danger inherent in the dangerous goods being carried and the safety measures to be taken to avert such danger;

(*b*) the measures to be taken and treatment to be given in the event of any person coming into contact with the dangerous goods being carried or with any substances which might evolve;

(*c*) the measures to be taken in the case of fire, and, in particular, the fire-fighting appliances or equipment which must not be used;

(*d*) the measures to be taken in the case of breakage or deterioration of packagings, especially where such breakage or deterioration can lead to the spillage of goods onto the road; and

(*e*) any additional information required to be given in *Schedule 9* 'Additional emergency information relating to the carriage of certain dangerous goods'.

Information to be kept by operators

D3025 Operators of any vehicle which is used for the carriage of dangerous substances must also ensure that a record of information contained in the transport documentation (other than emergency information) is kept for at least three months after the completion of the journey. [*Reg 16*].

Main duties of drivers

D3026 The following are the main duties of drivers:

(*a*) Not to permit a person to be carried in the vehicle or tanker, other than a member of the vehicle crew, for the sole purpose of transporting that person. [*Reg 12(2)*].

(*b*) Not to open a package containing dangerous goods, unless authorised by the operator of the vehicle. [*Reg 12(3)*].

(*c*) Not to bring portable lighting apparatus onto a vehicle if such apparatus can produce a flame or has a metallic surface liable to produce sparks (except where only infectious substances are carried). [*Reg 12(4)-(5)*].

(*d*)   Not to enter a closed vehicle, which is being used for the carriage of liquids having a flash point of 61°C or below or flammable gases, carrying a lighting apparatus other than a portable lamp designed that it cannot ignite any flammable vapours or gases which may have penetrated into the interior of the vehicle. [*Reg 12(6)*].

(*e*)   In cases of a vehicle:

   (i)   used for carriage of infectious substances/toxic goods, or

   (ii)   which is empty and uncleaned after the carriage of such goods,

   not to carry food therein, unless effectively separated from infectious substances and toxic goods. [*Reg 12(7)*].

(*f*)   To ensure transport documentation (see above) is:

   (i)   readily available during carriage, and

   (ii)   produced, on request, to a police constable or goods vehicle examiner.

   [*Reg 15(1)*].

(*g*)   To ensure documentation relating to dangerous goods not being carried, is removed from the vehicle or placed in a securely closed container and clearly marked, indicating that it does not relate to any dangerous goods which are being carried. [*Reg 15(3)*].

(*h*)   To take such steps as is reasonably practicable to ensure that no dangerous goods are loaded, stowed or unloaded so as to create or increase significantly health and safety hazards associated with their presence. [*Reg 19(1), (2)(b), Sch 11*].

(*j*)   To load, stow, unload goods so as to prevent significant displacement in relation to each other and the sides of the vehicle. [*Reg 19(3)*].

(*k*)   Where dangerous goods have escaped from any package into a container or vehicle in which they are being carried, to ensure that the container or vehicle is cleaned as soon as possible, and definitely before re-loading. [*Reg 19(4)*].

(*l*)   To ensure that containers and vehicles which have been used for the carriage of dangerous goods in bulk, shall be properly cleaned before re-loading unless the new load consists of dangerous goods with the same designation as the preceding load. [*Reg 19(5)*].

(*m*)   Not to smoke in the vicinity of or inside the vehicle, during loading or unloading operations. [*Reg 19(6)*].

(*n*)   To ensure that where goods with a flash-point of 61°C or below are being carried in a tank that the chassis is earthed before the tank is filled or emptied, and the rate of filling is limited to avoid an electrostatic discharge which could cause ignition of any vapour present. [*Reg 19(7)*].

(*o*)   To shut off vehicle engines during loading and unloading operations. [*Reg 19(8)*].

(*p*)   Not to overfill tank or compartments with dangerous goods. [*Reg 19(9)*].

(*q*)   To ensure, so far as is practicable, that:

   (i)   all openings in a tank, and

   (ii)   valves and cap

are securely closed prior to the start of and throughout a journey. [*Reg 19(10)*].

(*r*)   In the event of accident or emergency, to take all reasonable steps to comply with instructions in the emergency information. [*Reg 22(1)*].

(*s*)   In the event of emergency, to notify emergency services by the quickest practical means. [*Reg 22(2)*].

(*t*)   Not to do anything liable to create or increase significantly the risk of fire or explosion. [*Reg 23(1)*].

(*u*)   When parked, that the vehicle (after being properly secured) is:

(i)   supervised by a competent person, either over 18 or a member of the armed forces; and

(ii)   is parked in an isolated position, either

—   unsupervised in an open space in a secure depot or factory, or (failing that)

—   in a vehicle park supervised by an appropriate person who has been notified of the nature of the load and the whereabouts of the driver, or (failing that)

—   in a public/private vehicle park, where the vehicle is not likely to suffer damage, or (failing that)

—   in a suitable open space separated from the public highway and dwellings, where the public does not normally pass or assemble

(except where the vehicle has been either damaged or has broken down and the driver has gone for assistance, and has taken all reasonable steps to secure the vehicle and its contents before leaving it). [*Reg 24(1)(2)*].

Information to be displayed on containers, tanks and vehicles

D3027   In general, the following information must be displayed on the vehicle:

(*a*)   an orange-coloured panel, containing the UN number and emergency action code of the dangerous goods carried;

(*b*)   a telephone number where additional specialist information can be obtained concerning the load;

(*c*)   danger signs and subsidiary hazard signs; and

(*d*)   a hazard warning panel.

The requirements of the regulations relating to information which must be displayed is contained in *Regulation 17* and *Schedule 10*.

The operator of any container, tank or vehicle which is being used for the carriage of dangerous goods has a duty to ensure that the information displayed on the container, tank or vehicle concerned is in accordance with *Schedule 10*. [*Reg 17(1)*]. No information, referred to in *Schedule 10* must remain on any container, tank or vehicle when it is not being used for the carriage of dangerous goods [*Reg 17(2)*], and no additional information which may cause confusion to the emergency services when read in conjunction with information required by *Schedule 10* should be attached [*Reg 17(3)*]. The operator and the driver must ensure that any danger sign, hazard warning panel, orange-coloured panel or subsidiary hazard sign which is displayed is kept clean and free from obstruction [*Reg 17(4)*], and that when dangerous goods are no longer contained in the vehicle (e.g. after discharge or unloading) that the signs are covered, and that the material being used to cover them would withstand 15 minutes' engulfment in fire [*Reg 17(5)*].

Schedule 10 contains detailed requirements as to the marking of vehicles.

Orange-coloured panels, UN numbers and emergency action codes

D3028   Orange-coloured panels shall be displayed at the front and back of any vehicle carrying dangerous goods. [*Reg 17(1), Sch 10, Pt I*]. An example of an orange-coloured panel is illustrated as *Figure 1* below.

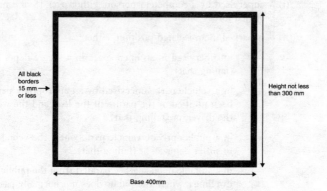

Where a vehicle is carrying only one of the dangerous goods listed in the Approved Carriage List in a 'tank' the following information shall be displayed:

(*a*)   an orange-coloured panel at the rear of the vehicle bearing the appropriate UN number and the appropriate emergency action code (see *Figure 2* below); and

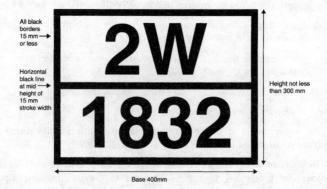

(*b*)   an orange-coloured panel as in (*a*) above on both sides of

  (i)   the tank,

  (ii)   the frame of the tank, or

  (iii) the vehicle, provided that the panel is positioned immediately below the tank.

Where a vehicle is carrying a multi-load in tanks, the following information shall be displayed:

(*a*)   an orange-coloured panel at the rear of the vehicle bearing the appropriate emergency action code (see *Figure 3* below);

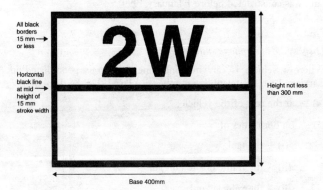

All black borders 15 mm → or less

Horizontal black line at mid → height of 15 mm stroke width

Height not less than 300 mm

Base 400mm

(*b*)   an orange-coloured panel on the sides of each tank, or where the tank has more than one compartment, on each compartment, which are

    (i)   at least one on each side which conforms to that illustrated as *Figure 3* above, and

    (ii)   the remainder which bear the appropriate UN number (see *Figure 4* below); or

All black borders 15 mm → or less

Height not less than 150 mm

Base 400mm

(*c*)   on both sides of the frame of each tank or on both sides of the vehicle provided they are positioned immediately below the tank or tank compartment concerned.

Where the vehicle is carrying only one of the dangerous goods listed in the Approved Carriage List in bulk, in the vehicle or container on the vehicle, it shall be labelled with:

(*a*)   an orange-coloured panel as in *Figure 2* above at the rear of the vehicle; and

(*b*)   an orange-coloured panel as in *Figure 2* above on each side of the vehicle.

Where a vehicle is carrying a multi-load in bulk, in separate compartments of the vehicle or in separate containers on the vehicle, it shall be labelled with:

(*a*)   an orange-coloured panel as in *Figure 3* above at the rear of the vehicle bearing the appropriate emergency action code; and

(*b*)   an orange-coloured panel displayed on each side of each compartment or on each container, of which

    (i)   at least one conforms to *Figure 2* above, and

(ii) the remainder conform to *Figure 4* above.

Any UN numbers or emergency action codes displayed need to be in black digits, measuring not less than 100mm in height and not less than 15mm stroke width. They also need to be able to be legible after 15 minutes engulfment in fire (unless the tank was constructed before 1 January 1999).

Display of telephone number

D3029 Where a vehicle is carrying only one dangerous good listed in the Approved Carriage List, the telephone number displayed shall be displayed:

(*a*) at the rear of the vehicle;

(*b*) on both sides of

(i) the tank,

(ii) the frame of the tank, or

(iii) the vehicle; and

(*c*) in the immediate vicinity of the orange-coloured panels.

Where a vehicle is carrying a multi-load in tanks, the telephone number shall be displayed:

(*a*) at the rear of the vehicle;

(*b*) on both sides of

(i) the tank,

(ii) the frame of the tank, or

(iii) the vehicle; and

(*c*) is in the immediate vicinity of the orange-coloured panels which conform to *Figures 2* or *3* (see D3028 above).

The telephone number shall consist of black digits of not less than 30mm in height and be displayed on an orange-coloured background. (See *Figure 5* below.) The telephone number may be substituted by the words 'consult local depot' or 'contact local depot'.

Danger signs and subsidiary hazard signs

D3030 The regulations require that where a vehicle is carrying dangerous goods in packages in a container, any danger sign or subsidiary hazard sign which is required by the *Carriage of Dangerous Goods (Classification, Packaging and Labelling) and Use of Transportable Pressure Receptacles Regulations 1996 (SI 1996 No 2092)* shall be displayed on at least one side of the container.

Where the vehicle is carrying dangerous goods in a tank container or in bulk in a container, required danger signs or subsidiary hazard signs should be shown on each side of the container, and if not visible from the outside of the vehicle, the same signs should also be displayed on the rear of the vehicle.

These signs are required to be not less than 250mm in height, and have a line of the same colour as the symbol 12.5 mm inside the edge and running parallel to it.

Hazard warning panels

D3031   The labelling requirements in D3028-D3030 above may be displayed on a hazard warning panel as in *Figure 5* below.

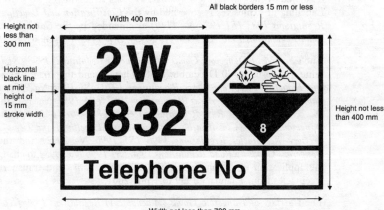

Petroleum deliveries at filling stations

D3032   The regulations lay down requirements for the unloading of petrol at petroleum filling stations and other premises licensed for the unloading of petrol from the tank of a road tanker. [*Reg 20(1)*]. *Schedule 12* lays down detailed requirements. *Sch 12, Part II* lays down detailed requirements for licensee-controlled deliveries, and *Sch 12, Part III* for driver-controlled deliveries. A Part III Licence is required for driver-controlled deliveries.

Sch 12, para 20 lays down requirements to be met by licensees who intend to use driver-controlled deliveries under the Part III procedure.

Defence

D3033   It is a defence to a charge under these regulations for the person charged to prove:

(*a*)   that the commission of the offence was due to the act or default of another person not being one of his employees; and

(*b*)   that he took all reasonable precautions and excercised all due diligence to avoid the commission of the offence.

[*Reg 26(1)*].

Transitional defence

D3034   In any proceedings for an offence under these regulations prior to 1 January 1997, it is a defence for the accused to prove that the goods were carried:

(*a*)   in a road tanker in accordance with the *Road Traffic (Carriage of Dangerous Substances in Road Tankers and Tank Containers) Regulations 1992 (SI 1992 No 743)*; or

(*b*)   in bulk or in packages in accordance with the *Road Traffic (Carriage of Dangerous Substances in Packages etc.) Regulations 1992 (SI 1992 No 742)*.

[*Reg 28*].

Transportation of explosives by road

D3035   Packaging of explosives is governed by the *Packaging of Explosives for Carriage Regulations 1991 (SI 1991 No 2097)*. Requirements concerning transportation are regulated by the *Carriage of Explosives by Road Regulations 1996 (SI 1996 No 2093)*. Labelling of explosives is governed by the *Classification and Labelling of Explosives Regulations 1983 (SI 1983 No 1140)* as amended by the *Carriage of Explosives by Road Regulations 1996 (SI 1996 No 2093), Sch 9* (see DANGEROUS SUBSTANCES I).

The *Carriage of Dangerous Goods (Amendment) Regulations 1998 (SI 1998 No 2885)* came into force on 30 December 1998. They amend the *Highly Flammable Liquids and Liquefied Petroleum Gases Regulations 1972 (SI 1972 No 917)*, the *Dangerous Substances in Harbour Areas Regulations 1987 (SI 1987 No 37)*, the *Carriage of Dangerous Goods by Rail Regulations 1996 (SI 1996 No 2089)*, the *Carriage of Dangerous Goods (Classification, Packaging and Labelling) and Use of Transportable Pressure Receptacles Regulations 1996 (SI 1996 No 2092)* and the *Carriage of Dangerous Goods by Road Regulations 1996 (SI 1996 No 2095)* to change the date for the application of certain provisions relating to tanks and transportable pressure receptacles from 1 January 1999 to 1 July 2001.

The *Carriage of Dangerous Goods (Amendment) Regulations 1999 (SI 1999 No 303)* came into force on 5 March 1999. They amend the following Regulations:

- the *Classification and Labelling of Explosives Regulations 1983*;

- the *Pressure Systems and Transportable Gas Containers Regulations 1989*;

- the *Packaging of Explosives for Carriage Regulations 1991*;

- the *Carriage of Dangerous Goods by Rail Regulations 1996*;

- the *Packaging, Labelling and Carriage of Radioactive Material by Rail Regulations 1996*;

- the *Carriage of Dangerous Goods (Classification, Packaging and Labelling) and Use of Transportable Pressure Receptacles Regulations 1996*;

- the *Carriage of Explosives by Road Regulations 1996*;

- the *Carriage of Dangerous Goods by Road (Driver Training) Regulations 1996*;

- the *Carriage of Dangerous Goods by Road Regulations 1996*; and

- the *Health and Safety Fees Regulations*.

The effect of the amendments is to align the above-mentioned Regulations with the latest versions of the ADR and RID agreements, as defined in the *Carriage of Dangerous Goods (Classification, Packaging and Labelling) and Use of Transportable Pressure Receptacles Regulations 1996, Reg 2(1)*.

The main changes are as follows:

(*a*)   a general disapplication:

— where goods are carried in an emergency for the purposes of saving life or protecting the environment;

— with regard to goods, except explosives, which are part of machinery or equipment;

— for certain pharmaceutical products packaged for retail sale and intended for personal or household use; and

— with regard to certain radioactive materials carried by rail;

(*b*) a new requirement for large containers to meet international standards;

(*c*) the carriage in bulk of used batteries to be allowed under certain conditions;

(*d*) revisions to the content and format of emergency information for the carriage of dangerous goods by road;

(*e*) a new training requirement for employees with responsibilities related to the carriage of dangerous goods by road;

(*f*) training for the drivers of road vehicles which carry dangerous goods to be in the form of a theoretical course in specified subjects accompanied by practical exercises;

(*g*) the introduction of additional arrangements for the carriage of certain oxidizing, toxic and corrosive substances in composite intermediate bulk containers;

(*h*) the carriage in bulk of certain high temperature goods to be permitted in special vehicles, wagons and large containers;

(*i*) greater flexibility in the carriage of mixed loads of explosives and other dangerous goods;

(*j*) the requirement for an ADR (B3) certificate for Types II and III explosives vehicles constructed after 1 January 1997;

(*k*) the introduction of transitional provisions in relation to the publication of a new edition of an Approved Document; and

(*l*) the substitution of fixed fees for applications for approvals of training or refresher courses under the *Carriage of Dangerous Goods by Road (Driver Training) Regulations 1996*.

Carriage of explosives – The Carriage of Explosives by Road Regulations 1996 (SI 1996 No 2093)

D3036   These regulations, which came into effect on 1 September 1996, specify requirements in relation to the carriage of explosives by road, placing duties mainly (but not exclusively) on the operators of vehicles carrying explosives. The regulations do not apply to any explosive nuclear device or certain dangerous goods. [*Reg 3(5)-(6)*].

Definitions

D3037   The relevant definitions contained in these regulations are as follows.

(A) *Explosives*

These are explosive articles or substances which:

(i)   have been assigned on a classification to Class 1; or

(ii) are unclassified.

(B) *Explosive substances*

These are:

(i)   a solid or liquid substance; or

(ii)   a mixture of solid or liquid substances or both,

which are capable by chemical reaction in itself of producing a gas at such a temperature and pressure and at such a speed as could cause damage to surroundings or which is designed to produce an effect by heat, light, sound, gas or smoke or a combination of these as a result of non-detonative self-sustaining exothermic chemical reactions.

(C) *Carriage*

Under the regulations a vehicle or container shall be deemed to be engaged in the 'carriage' of explosives:

(i)   in the case of a vehicle, from the commencement of loading it with the explosives concerned for the purpose of carrying those explosives by road until that vehicle (or any compartment within it) has been unloaded, and, if necessary cleaned, so that any explosives which remain do not create a significant health or safety risk to any person;

(ii)   in the case of a container which is to be placed on a vehicle, from the commencement of loading, until the container is either

— removed from the vehicle, or

— unloaded, and where necessary cleaned, so that any explosives which remain are not significant to create a risk to the health and safety of any person.

It is immaterial in (i) and (ii) above, whether or not the vehicle or container is on a road at any material time.

(D) *Operator*

Under the regulations an 'operator' is defined as:

(i)   a person who, having a place of business in Great Britain, has the management of a vehicle or container for the time being; or

(ii)   the driver of the vehicle or, in the case of a container, the driver of the vehicle on which the container is carried.

However, a person is not to be regarded as being the operator of a vehicle or container solely because he has management of it during loading or unloading, or the vehicle or container is on premises which are under his control.

(E) *Consignor*

This means:

(i)   the person who, having a place of business in Great Britain, consigns, whether as a principal or agent for another, explosives for carriage; or

(ii)   the person who has control over the carriage of explosives within Great Britain.

(F) *Packaging, container, dangerous goods, trailer*

Packaging – has the same definition as in the *Carriage of Dangerous Goods (Classification, Packaging and Labelling) and Use of Transportable Pressure Receptacles Regulations 1996 (SI 1996 No 2092), Reg 2(1)*. (See D3020 above.)

Container – has the same definition as in the *Carriage of Dangerous Goods (Classification, Packaging and Labelling) and Use of Transportable Pressure Receptacles Regulations 1996 (SI 1996 No 2092), Reg 2(1)*. (See D3020 above.)

Dangerous goods – has the same definition as in the *Carriage of Dangerous Goods (Classification, Packaging and Labelling) and Use of Transportable Pressure Receptacles Regulations 1996 (SI 1996 No 2092), Reg 2(1)*. (See D3020 above.)

Trailer – is defined in the *Road Vehicles (Construction and Use) Regulations 1986 (SI 1986 No 1078), Reg 3(2)*.

Main duties of consignors

D3038   Any consignor of explosives shall ensure that prior to carriage of any explosives by an operator engaged by him, that the operator is provided with information in documentary form as specified below. [*Reg 16(1), Sch 6*].

In relation to each type of explosive being carried this will be:

(*a*)   the designation;

(*b*)   the classification;

(*c*)   the UN Number;

(*d*)   the total net mass in tonnes or kilograms of explosives carried; and

(*e*)   whether, in the case of explosives in Compatibility Group C, D, or G, the explosives carried are explosive substances or explosive articles.

In relation to the consignment as a whole this will be:

(i)   the number of packages consigned;

(ii)   the name and address of the consignor;

(iii)   the name and address of the consignee;

(iv)   any other relevant information; and

(v)   a statement signed or authenticated by or on behalf of the consignor confirming that the explosives as presented to the operator are carried in conformity with the regulations, and that the labelling and packaging conform with the *Packaging of Explosives for Carriage Regulations 1991 (SI 1991 No 2097)*, and the *Classification and Labelling of Explosives Regulations 1983 (SI 1983 No 1140)*.

[*Reg 16(1), Sch 6, Part I*].

Duties of operators

D3039   These are as follows.

(*a*)   Not to carry explosives of Compatibility Group K in a vehicle. [*Reg 7(1)*].

(*b*)   Not to carry unclassified explosives in a vehicle (with certain exceptions). [*Reg 7(2)*].

(*c*)   Not to carry explosives in a vehicle being used to carry passengers for hire (with certain exceptions). [*Reg 8(1)*].

(*d*)   Not to carry in bulk explosives which are explosive substances. [*Reg 9*].

(*e*)   To ensure that the vehicle and any container used for carriage is suitable for the safety and security of explosives. [*Reg 10*].

(*f*)　To ensure that any vehicles used comply with any requirements entitled 'Approved Requirements for the Construction of Vehicles Intended for the Carriage of Explosives by Road' published by the Health and Safety Commission have been complied with. [*Reg 11*].

(*g*)　Not to carry explosives which are in different compatibility groups together unless it is permitted by *Schedule 4* of the regulations or effective measures have been taken to ensure that the carriage of such a mixed load is no more dangerous than the carriage of the same quantity of explosives in any of the compatibility groups carried (with certain restrictions). [*Reg 14(1)(2)*].

(*h*)　To display requisite information on the vehicle concerning explosives. [*Reg 15, Sch 5*].

(*j*)　Not to display any information, orange-coloured panel, danger sign or subsidiary hazard sign when the vehicle or container is not being used for the carriage of explosives. [*Reg 15(5)*].

(*k*)　Not to allow any information to be displayed on a vehicle or container which is likely to confuse the emergency services when read in conjunction with any information displayed in accordance with *Schedule 5* 'Information to be displayed on vehicles and containers'. [*Reg 15(6)*].

(*l*)　To provide information to another operator engaged by him, with information provided by the consignors. [*Reg 17(1)*].

(*m*)　To provide information to any driver engaged by him, with information provided by the consignors, called the 'transport documentation'. [*Reg 17(2)*]. This transport documentation consists of the information provided by the consignors (see D3038 (*a*)-(*e*) and (i)-(v) above) together with:

　(i)　the total number of packages;

　(ii)　the name and address of the operator of the vehicle;

　(iii)　emergency information, consisting of details of measures to be taken by the driver in the event of an accident or emergency and other safety information concerning the explosives being carried. This includes

　　—　the nature of the danger inherent in the explosives being carried and the safety measures to be taken to avert any such danger,

　　—　the action to be taken and treatment to be given in the event of any person coming into contact with the explosives being carried or with any substances which might be evolved,

　　—　the measures to be taken in the case of fire and, in particular, the fire-fighting appliances or equipment which must not be used,

　　—　the measures to be taken in the case of breakage or deterioration of the packagings or of the explosives being carried, especially where such deterioration results in a spillage of the explosives onto the road, and

　　—　the measures to be taken to avoid or minimise damage in the event of spillage of explosives which are pollutant to the aquatic environment.

(*n*)　To ensure that explosives are loaded, stowed, and unloaded so as not to create a significant health and safety risk. [*Reg 19(1)*].

(*o*)　To ensure that food is not carried with explosives, unless effectively separated and protected from the risk of contamination. [*Reg 19(3)*].

(*p*)　To ensure that when the vehicle:

(i)　is not parked, an attendant accompanies the driver, and

(ii)　is parked, and the driver is not present, a person competent to ensure security of explosives is constantly with the vehicle.

[*Reg 20(1)*].

(*q*)　To ensure that where more than 5 tonnes of explosives in Division 1 (see below) are being carried, to follow the route agreed with the police. [*Reg 21(1)*].

(*r*)　To take steps to

(i)　prevent accidents and minimise the harmful effects of any which may occur; and

(ii)　prevent unauthorised access to, or removal from, part of the load.

[*Reg 22*].

(*s*)　To ensure that people do not smoke whilst carrying explosives or during their unloading, or bring portable lighting equipment onto a vehicle if such equipment has any flame or is liable to produce sparks. [*Reg 23*].

(*t*)　To ensure that the vehicle is so equipped that the driver can take steps detailed in the emergency information. [*Reg 24*].

(*u*)　To ensure that there is not a significant risk of fire or explosion during the carriage of explosives. [*Reg 25*].

(*v*)　To ensure that in the event of accidents or emergencies, proper precautions are taken:

(i)　for the safety of persons from ignition, and

(ii)　for the security of explosives.

[*Reg 26(3)*].

(*w*)　Where an operator is informed of any emergency where the situation cannot be brought under immediate control, the operator shall inform the Health and Safety Executive by the quickest practicable means. [*Reg 26(2)*].

(*x*)　To ensure that not more than the specified quantity of explosives is carried. This is as follows:

Division	Compatibility Group	Maximum quantity (kilograms)
1.1	A	50
1.1	B, F, G or L	5,000
1.1	C, D, E or J	16,000
1.2	Any	16,000
1.3	Any	16,000
1.4	Any	16,000

Division	Compatibility Group	Maximum quantity (kilograms)
1.5	Any	16,000
1.6	Any	16,000

[*Reg 13, Sch 3, Part III*].

(*y*)   Where explosives have escaped from any package into a container or vehicle in which they are being carried, to ensure that the vehicle concerned is cleaned as soon as possible. [*Reg 19(2), Sch 7 para 2*].

(*z*)   To clean any surfaces onto which explosives will be loaded. [*Reg 19(2), Sch 7 para 3*].

(*aa*)   Except where the engine has to be used to drive pumps or other appliances for loading or unloading, to ensure that the vehicle's engine shall be shut off during loading and unloading operations. [*Reg 19(2), Sch 7 para 4*].

Duties of drivers

D3040   These are as follows.

(*a*)   To ensure that the orange-coloured panel, danger sign or subsidiary hazard sign is affixed and displayed on the vehicle/container. [*Reg 15(5)*].

(*b*)   To ensure that Transport Documentation (e.g. designation, classification code, UN number etc.) is

   (i)   kept on the vehicle during carriage, and

   (ii)   produced, on request, to a police constable or goods vehicle examiner.

[*Reg 18(1)*].

(*c*)   To ensure that where a trailer which is being used for the carriage of explosives becomes detached from the motor vehicle, that:

   (i)   he gives the Transport Documentation to the occupier of any premises on which his trailer is parked, or

   (ii)   he attaches the Transport Documentation to the trailer in a readily visible position.

(*d*)   To ensure that any documentation relating to explosives not being carried in the vehicle is placed in a securely closed container, and clearly marked to show that it does not relate to any explosives being carried.

(*e*)   Not to load, stow, unload explosives, so as to create a significant health and safety risk. [*Reg 19(1)*].

(*f*)   Where explosives have escaped from any package into a container or vehicle in which they are being carried, to ensure that the vehicle concerned is cleaned as soon as possible. [*Reg 19(2), Sch 7 para 2*].

(*g*)   To clean any surfaces onto which explosives will be loaded. [*Reg 19(2), Sch 7 para 3*].

(*h*)   Except where the engine has to be used to drive pumps or other appliances for loading or unloading, to ensure that the vehicle's engine shall be shut off during loading and unloading operations. [*Reg 19(2), Sch 7 para 4*].

(*j*)   Not to carry food with explosives, unless the food is effectively separated. [*Reg 19(3)*].

(*k*)   Not to open a package containing explosives unless so authorised. [*Reg 19(4)*].

(*l*)   To ensure that when a vehicle:

    (i)   is not parked, an attendant accompanies the driver; and

    (ii)   when it is parked, and the driver is not present, a competent person constantly remains with the vehicle.

    [*Reg 20(1)*].

(*m*)   Not to carry another person in a vehicle which is being used to carry explosives for the sole reason of transporting them. [*Reg 20(6)*].

(*n*)   If carriage is more than 5 tonnes of explosives in Division 1.1, to follow the route agreed with the police. [*Reg 21(1)*].

(*o*)   Where the driver's vehicle is part of a convoy carrying explosives, to keep a distance of at least 50 metres between each vehicle. [*Reg 21(2)*].

(*p*)   To apply the parking brake, when parking. [*Reg 21(3)*].

(*q*)   Where the driver is in control of the explosives during carriage, he shall take such steps as are reasonable to:

    (i)   prevent accidents and minimise the harmful effects of any accident which may occur; and

    (ii)   shall prevent unauthorised access to, or removal of, all or part of the load.

    [*Reg 22*].

(*r*)   Not to smoke or produce an open flame where explosives are being carried or unloaded, or bring portable lighting apparatus which could produce a flame or spark near explosives. [*Reg 23(1), (2)*].

(*s*)   Not to cause or permit anything to be done which is liable to create a significant risk of explosion, or to increase any existing risk. [*Reg 25(1)*].

(*t*)   To ensure that at least one fire extinguisher is located in a trailer, located in such a way as to be easily accessible. [*Reg 25(2), Sch 8 paras 3, 7*].

(*u*)   In the event of an emergency or accident, to notify:

    (i)   the emergency services; and

    (ii)   the operator

    by the quickest practical means.

[*Reg 26(1)*].

(*v*)   In the event of an emergency or accident, to ensure that precautions are taken for:

    (i)   the safety of persons likely to be affected by ignition; and

    (ii)   the security of explosives.

    [*Reg 26(3)*].

Drivers and attendants, or persons responsible for the security of explosives must (generally) be over 18 years. [*Reg 28*].

Marking of vehicles

D3041   Both operators and drivers of vehicles used for the carriage of explosives must ensure that such *vehicles* are marked with:

(a)   two black rectangular reflectorised orange-coloured panels at the front and back, having a black border not more than 15 millimetres wide. This panel should be clearly visible, and so far as is reasonably practicable be kept clean and free from obstruction at all times when explosives are being carried. Where explosives have been unloaded, the panel should be covered or removed, the covering being able to withstand engulfment in fire for 15 minutes.

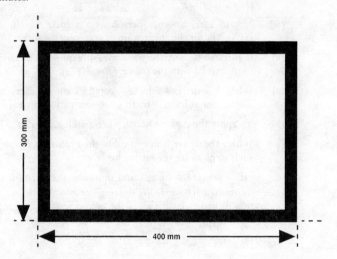

and in the case of explosives of divisions 1.1, 1.2 or 1.3 (i.e. more dangerous varieties);

(b)   two danger signs on each side of the *vehicle* or *container*, with orange-coloured background, having a black border (the Division Number 1.2 and the compatibility group letter 'E' are only examples)

or, in the case of explosives of divisions 1.4, 1.5 or 1.6 (less powerful)

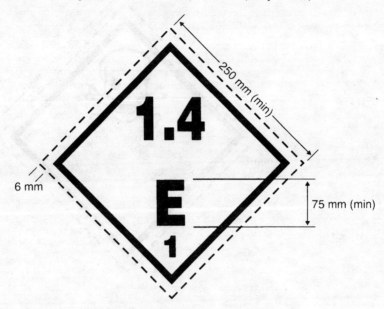

Where explosives are carried in a *vehicle* or *container* solely in connection with an application for their classification, the following danger sign shall be displayed:

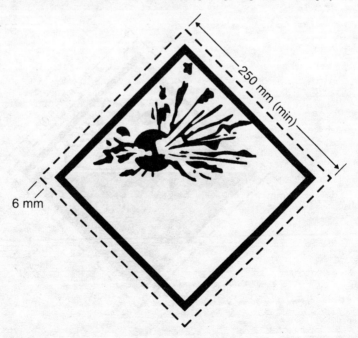

where explosives are allocated on classification UN Number 0018, 0019, 0020, 0021, 0076, 0077, 0143, 0224 or 03001 the *vehicle* or *container* shall be labelled with the subsidiary hazard sign:

where explosives are allocated on classification the UN number 0015, 0016, 0018, 0019, 0301 or 0303 the following subsidiary hazard sign shall be displayed:

In the case of a *vehicle* or *container* carrying explosives of different compatibility groups, no compatibility letter shall be written on any danger or subsidiary hazard sign required to be displayed. [*Sch 5 para 14*].

Training for drivers carrying explosives

D3042   The *Carriage of Dangerous Goods by Road (Driver Training) Regulations 1996 (SI 1996 No 2094)* (see D3014 above) apply to drivers transporting explosives in or on a vehicle not being used to carry passengers for hire or reward [*Reg 2(1)(b)*] (with some exceptions [*Sch 1, Sch 2, Part II*]).

Provision of information

D3043   Consignors must furnish operators with accurate and up-to-date information about explosives to be carried, so that operators can comply with their duties. [*Reg 16, Sch 6, Part I*]. (See D3038 above.)

In turn, operators must ensure that drivers (or their attendants) possess written information at the start of the journey. [*Reg 17(2), Sch 6, Part II*]. (See D3039(*m*) above.)

The requirement for written information does not apply to those explosives listed in *Schedule 1, Parts I-III* (see below). For explosives listed in *Sch 1, Part II* the maximum amount of the explosives must not exceed 50 kilograms.

PART I

1	2
Explosives	*UN Number*
ARTICLES, PYROTECHNIC for technical purposes	0432
CARTRIDGES, POWER DEVICE	0323
CARTRIDGES, SIGNAL	0405
CARTRIDGES, SMALL ARMS	0012
CARTRIDGES SMALL ARMS, BLANK	0014
CASES CARTRIDGE, EMPTY, WITH PRIMER	0055
CUTTERS, CABLE EXPLOSIVE	0070
FIREWORKS	0337
FLARES, AERIAL	0404
FUSE, SAFETY	0105
IGNITERS	0454
LIGHTERS, FUSE	0131
PRIMERS, CAP TYPE	0044
SIGNAL DEVICES, HAND	0373
SIGNALS, RAILWAY TRACK, EXPLOSIVE	0193

PART II

1	2
Explosives	*UN Number*
CARTRIDGES, SMALL ARMS*	0328
CARTRIDGES, SMALL ARMS	0339
CARTRIDGES, SMALL ARMS, BLANK*	0327
CARTRIDGES, SMALL ARMS, BLANK	0338
CASES, CARTRIDGE, EMPTY WITH PRIMER	0379
FIREWORKS*	0333
FIREWORKS*	0334
FIREWORKS*	0335
FIREWORKS	0336
SIGNAL DEVICES, HAND	0191
SIGNAL, DISTRESS, SHIP*	0195

PART III

1	2
Explosives	*UN Number*
ARTICLES, PYROTECHNIC for technical purposes	0428
ARTICLES, PYROTECHNIC for technical purposes	0429
ARTICLES, PYROTECHNIC for technical purposes	0430
ARTICLES, PYROTECHNIC for technical purposes	0431
CARTRIDGES, OIL WELL	0277
CARTRIDGES, OIL WELL	0278
CARTRIDGES, POWER DEVICE	0275
CARTRIDGES, POWER DEVICE	0276
CARTRIDGES, POWER DEVICE	0381
CARTRIDGES, SIGNAL	0054
CARTRIDGES, SIGNAL	0312
CASES, COMBUSTIBLE EMPTY, WITHOUT PRIMER	0446
CASES, COMBUSTIBLE EMPTY, WITHOUT PRIMER	0447
CORD, IGNITER	0066
DINITROSOBENZENE	0406
FLARES, AERIAL	0093

1	2
Explosives	*UN Number*
FLARES, AERIAL	0403
FLARES, SURFACE	0092
FLASH POWDER	0094
FLASH POWDER	0305
FUSE, INSTANTANEOUS NON-DETONATING: (QUICKMATCH)	0101
IGNITERS	0121
IGNITERS	0314
IGNITERS	0315
IGNITERS	0325
5-MERCAPTO-TETRAZOLE-l-ACETIC ACID	0448
POTASSIUM SALTS OF AROMATIC NITRO-DERIVATIVES, explosive	0158
PRIMERS, CAP TYPE	0377
PRIMERS, CAP TYPE	0378
ROCKETS, LINE THROWING	0238
ROCKETS, LINE THROWING	0240
ROCKETS, LINE THROWING	0453
SIGNALS, DISTRESS, ship	0194
SIGNALS, RAILWAY TRACK, EXPLOSIVE	0192
SIGNALS, SMOKE with explosive sound unit	0196
SIGNALS, SMOKE without explosive sound unit	0197
SODIUM DINITRO-o-CRESOLATE, dry or wetted with less than 15% water by mass	0234
SODIUM PICRAMATE, dry or wetted with less than 20% water by mass	0235
TETRAZOLE-1-ACETIC ACID	0407
ZIRCONIUM PICRAMATE, dry or wtted with less than 20% water by mass	0236

Enforcing authority

D3044   The enforcing authority for these regulations is the Health and Safety Executive.

Defence

D3045   It is a defence to a charge under these regulations for the person charged to prove that:

(*a*)   the commission of the offence was due to the act or default of another person not being one of his employees; and (*b*)   that he took all reasonable precautions and exercised all due diligence to avoid the commission of the offence.

[*Reg 31*].

Transitional provisions

D3046   Until 1 January 1997 it was sufficient compliance with the requirements of the regulations to have complied with the requirements of the *Road Traffic (Carriage of Explosives) Regulations 1989 (SI 1989 No 615)*.

Packaging of Explosives for Carriage Regulations 1991 (SI 1991 No 2097)

D3047   These regulations cover the packaging of explosives, whereas the *Carriage of Explosives by Road Regulations 1996 (SI 1996 No 2093)* cover the labelling requirements of tankers and vehicles carrying those packaged explosives. The main requirements of these regulations are:

(1)   explosives must not be transported unless they are in packaging which complies with the regulations [*Reg 4*];

(2)   the packaging must be designed/constructed so that it will

(*a*)   protect the explosives,

(*b*)   prevent the escape of explosives,

(*c*)   avoid increased risk of ignition,

(*d*)   be able to be safely handled,

(*e*)   be able to withstand loading in the course of foreseeable stacking,

and so that

(*f*)   the inner packaging and interior of the outer packaging is free from grit or rust,

(*g*)   the explosives are not likely to come into contact with another substance or article that could cause an explosion.

[*Reg 5*].

The export of dangerous chemicals outside the EU

D3048   The *Export of Dangerous Chemicals Regulations 1992 (SI 1992 No 2415)* relate to the EU common notification system for dangerous chemicals being imported from non-EU member states. These regulations ban an exporter from providing false or misleading information relating to any requirement or prohibition relating to this form of export. The Health and Safety Executive is the enforcing authority and enforcement follows the *HSWA* rules (see further ENFORCEMENT). It is proposed to add the following chemicals to the current list: pentachlorophenol, ugilec 121, ugilec 141, DBBT, ethylene oxide, dinoseb, binapacryl, captafol, dicofol, maleic hydrazide, choline/potassium and sodium salts of maleic hydrazide, quintozene, 2-Naphthylamine, benzedine, 4-Nitrobiphenyl, and 4-Aminobiphenyl.

Carriage of dangerous goods by rail – The Carriage of Dangerous Goods by Rail Regulations 1996 (SI 1996 No 2089)

D3049   These regulations which came into force on 1 September 1996, specify precautions in relation to the carriage of dangerous goods by train. As with the regulations concerning the carriage of dangerous goods by road, the classification and packaging requirements overlap with the *Carriage of Dangerous Goods (Classification, Packaging and Labelling) and Use of Transportable Pressure Receptacles Regulations 1996 (SI 1996 No 2092)*.

The regulations apply to the carriage of any dangerous goods in a container, package, tank container, tank wagon or wagon, except where the carriage falls into one of the exceptions listed in *Regulation 2*. The exceptions include where:

(*a*)   the dangerous goods carried are carried for use solely in connection with the operation of the locomotive, container, tank container, tank wagon or wagon;

(*b*)   the carriage commences and terminates within the same factory, harbour area, military establishment, mine or quarry;

(*c*)   the goods are being carried solely for use in connection with the provision of train catering facilities; and

(*d*)   the carriage forms part of an international transport operation which is subject to any bi-lateral or multilateral agreement and where the carriage is made under the Convention concerning International Carriage by Rail.

Definitions

D3050   The relevant definitions relating to these regulations are as follows.

(A) *Operator*

The operator of a container, tank container, tank wagon or wagon is:

(*a*)   the person who, having a place of business in Great Britain, owns the container, tank container, tank wagon or wagon concerned; or

(*b*)   the person who, having a place of business in Great Britain, acts as agent for the owner of the container, tank container, tank wagon or wagon concerned; or

(*c*)   the operator of the train on which the container or tank container is carried or of which the tank wagon or wagon forms part.

The members of the crew includes the driver, guard and any other person on board who has responsibilities in relation to the carriage of dangerous substances on the train. [*Reg 1(3)*].

A person to whom a container, tank container, tank wagon or wagon is leased or hired shall be deemed to be the owner, unless the lessor or hirer has made a written agreement with the person to whom he has leased or hired the container, to the effect that the lessor or hirer shall assume the responsibilities of the owner imposed by the regulations. [*Reg 1(4)*].

(B) *Consignor*

The consignor has the same definition as in the *Carriage of Dangerous Goods (Classification, Packaging and Labelling) and Use of Transportable Pressure Receptacles Regulations 1996 (SI 1996 No 2092), Reg 2(1)*.

Meaning of carriage

D3051   A container, package, tank container, tank wagon or wagon is deemed to be engaged in the carriage of dangerous goods throughout the period where such an item is:

(*a*)   loaded and brought on to the railway; or

(*b*)   where the item is brought on to the railway before loading, from the commencement of loading;

until

(*c*)   the item is removed from the railway; or

(*d*)   where any compartment of the item has been unloaded (and where necessary cleaned and decontaminated) that any of the vapours which remain are not sufficient to create a significant risk to the health and safety of any person.

[*Reg 2(8)*].

Duties/obligations imposed on all persons concerned with carriage

D3052   These include the following.

(*a*)   That no tank container or tank wagon, or any compartment is filled beyond its safe level with dangerous goods. [*Reg 16*].

(*b*)   Not to carry any mixed loads specified in *Schedule 6* unless they are adequately segregated to prevent the creation of a mixture which is a greater risk than when the goods are carried separately. [*Reg 17*].

(*c*)   Not to allow food to be carried in any container etc. unless the food is effectively separated from those goods or is otherwise adequately protected from the risk of contamination. [*Reg 18(4)*].

(*d*)   To take all reasonable care to ensure that:

(i)   nothing is done during carriage to create a significant risk or significantly increase any risk to health and safety; and

(ii)   unauthorised access to dangerous goods is prevented.

[*Reg 21*].

(*e*)   To ensure that no person shall cause or permit anything to be done which increases any existing risk of fire or explosion. [*Reg 22*].

Duties of consignors

D3053   Consignors of dangerous goods must ensure that any operator of a container, tank container, tank wagon or wagon engaged by him to carry the goods is provided with the following information in documentary form before carriage. The information as a whole is called the 'Carriage Information' and consists of:

(*a*)   in relation to each of the dangerous goods being carried –

    (i)   the designation,

    (ii)   the classification code,

    (iii)   the UN number,

    (iv)   the packaging group (where appropriate),

    (v)   in the case of explosives, the Compatibility Group and Division of each type of explosive being carried,

    (vi)   in the case of explosives within a Compatibility Group whose Compatibility Group letter is C, D or G, whether the explosives are explosive articles or explosive substances,

    (vii)   the mass or volume of the goods, and

    (viii)   the words 'salvage packaging' (if used); and

(*b*)   in relation to the consignment as a whole –

    (i)   the total mass or volume of the dangerous goods consigned,

    (ii)   the name and address of the consignor,

    (iii)   the name and address of the consignee (if known),

    (iv)   the name and telephone number where specialist advice can be obtained in English at any time,

    (v)   any other information relevant, and

    (vi)   a statement dated and signed or authenticated by or on behalf of the consignor confirming that any of the following regulations have been complied with:

        —   the *Classification and Labelling of Explosives Regulations 1983 (SI 1983 No 1140)*;

        —   the *Packaging of Explosives for Carriage Regulations 1991 (SI 1991 No 2097)*; and

        —   the *Carriage of Dangerous Goods (Classification, Packaging and Labelling) and Use of Transportable Pressure Receptacles Regulations 1996 (SI 1996 No 2092)*;

and that therefore

        —   the dangerous goods as presented may be carried,

        —   the dangerous goods and any packaging, intermediate bulk container, tank container or tank wagon in which they are contained are in a fit condition for carriage and properly labelled, and

        —   where several packages are packed together in an overpack or single container, that this is not prohibited.

    [*Reg 11(2)*].

Consignors shall also ensure that any train operator engaged by him is supplied with the Carriage Information. [*Reg 12(2)*].

Duties of operators

D3054   Operators of containers, tank containers, tank wagons or wagons carrying dangerous goods must ensure the following.

(*a*)   That all reasonable steps are taken to ensure that the requirements specified in any of the approved documents relevant to the container, tank container, tank wagon or wagon are complied with. [*Reg 4(a)*].

(*b*)   That a wagon or large container will not be permitted to carry dangerous substances in bulk unless:

(i)   the letter 'Y' appears in column 8 of the Approved Carriage List;

(ii)   any requirements specified in *Schedule 2* to the regulations 'Requirements for the carriage in bulk of certain dangerous goods in wagons and large containers' is complied with;

(iii)   in the case of a wagon, it is:

—   closed,

—   open and sheeted, or

—   has a movable roof; and

(iv)   in the case of a large container, it is:

—   closed, or

—   open and sheeted.

[*Reg 5*].

(*c*)   That small containers shall not carry dangerous goods unless the requirements in *Schedule 3* 'Requirements for the carriage in small containers of certain dangerous goods' are complied with. [*Reg 6*].

(*d*)   That no tank container or tank wagon shall carry dangerous goods unless the letter 'Y' appears in column 7 of the Approved Carriage List. [*Reg 7(1)*].

(*e*)   That no tank container or tank wagon shall carry dangerous goods unless the information relating to certification of tanks specified in the Approved Tank Requirements is indelibly marked on one or more corrosion-resistant plates which are securely fastened to the item concerned. [*Reg 7(3)*].

(*f*)   That any container, tank container, tank wagon or wagon shall not be used to carry dangerous goods unless:

(i)   it is suitable for the purpose of such carriage; and

(ii)   it has been adequately maintained.

[*Reg 8(1)*].

'Suitable for such carriage' means that it is suitable with regard to:

(1)   the nature and circumstances of the journey being undertaken; and

(2)   the hazardous properties and quantities of dangerous goods and of all other goods to be carried with them.

(*g*)   That no explosives are carried unless:

(i)   he has taken all reasonable steps to ensure that those goods have been classified and labelled in accordance with the *Classification and Labelling of Explosives Regulations 1983 (SI 1983 No 1140)* as amended by the *Carriage of Explosives by Road Regulations 1996 (SI 1996 No 2093)* (see DANGEROUS SUBSTANCES I and D3037 above);

(ii) where the *Packaging of Explosives for Carriage Regulations 1991 (SI 1991 No 2097)* apply, he has taken all reasonable steps to comply with the regulations; and

(iii) any requirements under the *Carriage of Dangerous Goods (Classification, Packaging and Labelling) and Use of Transportable Pressure Receptacles Regulations 1996 (SI 1996 No 2092)* have been complied with.

[*Reg 10*].

Part VII of the regulations 'Special requirements concerning the carriage of explosives' contains detailed requirements, including restrictions on the carriage of certain explosives, the carriage of explosives on passenger trains and the security measures to be taken.

(*h*) That any train operator engaged by him is provided with the Carriage Information. [*Reg 12(3)*].

(*j*) To keep a record of information contained within the Carriage Information for at least three months following the completion of each journey. [*Reg 13*].

(*k*) To display information concerning the dangerous goods in the container, tank container, tank wagon or wagon. [*Reg 14(1), Sch 5*]. These requirements as to the display of information are similar to those concerning the transport of dangerous substances by road (see D3027 above). Such information should not be displayed when the container etc. no longer contains the dangerous goods [*Reg 14(2)*]; no information should be displayed which might confuse the emergency services if read in conjunction with the information displayed pursuant to *Schedule 5* [*Reg 14(3)*]; the information displayed (i.e. danger sign, hazard warning panel, subsidiary hazard sign etc.) is free from obstruction when the container etc. is handed over to the train operator [*Reg 14(5)*]; and he has taken all reasonable steps to ensure that the information displayed is in accordance with *Schedule 5* [*Reg 14(6)*].

(*l*) To ensure that dangerous goods are so loaded, stowed or unloaded as not to create a significant health and safety risk or increase one significantly. [*Reg 18(1)*].

(*m*) To ensure that any product remaining in a container etc. will not cause a significant risk to health, or increase an already existing risk if other dangerous goods are loaded. [*Reg 18(3)*].

(*n*) Ensure that all openings and discharge or filling openings are fitted with more than one valve or cap, and that all are closed prior to carriage. [*Reg 19(1)*].

Duties of train operators

D3055 Operators are under a duty to ensure the following.

(*a*) That all reasonable steps are taken to ensure that the requirements specified in any of the approved documents relevant to the container, tank container, tank wagon or wagon are complied with. [*Reg 4(b)*].

(*b*) That any container, tank container, tank wagon or wagon shall not be used to carry dangerous goods unless:

(i) it is suitable for the purpose of such carriage; and

(ii)   it has been adequately maintained.

[*Reg 8(2)*].

(c)   That any other train operator engaged by him to carry dangerous goods is supplied with the Carriage Information. [*Reg 12(4)*].

(d)   Where the train operator is considered to be the operator to keep a record of information contained within the Carriage Information for at least three months following the completion of each journey. [*Reg 13*]. (See D3050(A) above for meaning of 'operator'.)

(e)   Shall take measures to ensure that any train being used for the carriage of dangerous goods during marshalling or formation does not create a significant increase in risk. [*Reg 20*].

(f)   Shall, with facility operators and infrastructure controllers:

(i)   draw up, and where necessary give effect to, such safety systems and procedures that will adequately deal with any emergency involving dangerous goods; and

(ii)   co-operate with each other so as to ensure effective co-ordination of their respective safety systems and procedures.

[*Reg 23*].

Duties in relation to tanks

D3056   *Regulation 9* contains detailed requirements as to the examination, testing and certification of tanks. The provisions in *Regulation 9* only apply to tanks constructed after 31 December 1998.

No person shall manufacture, import or supply a tank intended for the use of the carriage of dangerous goods unless it is of an 'approved design' which has been certified by a competent authority. It must:

(a)   conform with requirements published in the Approved Tank Requirements; and

(b)   be suitable for the purpose for which it was intended.

Similarly, operators must comply with the above requirements and additionally:

(c)   ensure that it has been examined and tested in accordance with the Approved Tank Requirements.

[*Reg 9(2)(3)*].

Information to be displayed on containers, tank containers, tank wagons and wagons

D3057   In general, *Regulation 14* as supplemented by *Schedule 5* requires that the following information is displayed.

(a)   The UN number for the goods specified in the Approved Carriage List.

(b)   The emergency action code.

(c)   The danger sign for the goods ascertained in accordance with the *Carriage of Dangerous Goods (Classification, Packaging and Labelling) and Use of Transportable Pressure Receptacles Regulations 1996 (SI 1996 No 2092)*.

(d)   The subsidiary hazard sign.

(*e*)   A telephone number where specialist advice can be obtained in English at any time during the carriage of the goods.

The information is required to be displayed as follows.

(1)   The UN number and emergency action code in black letters of 100mm height and 15mm stroke thickness.

(2)   Where the emergency action code in column 5 of the Approved Carriage List indicates a white letter on a black background, that letter shall be displayed as an orange letter on a black rectangle, which has a height and a width at least 10mm greater than the height and width of the letter.

(3)   The danger and subsidiary hazard sign shall have sides which measure not less than 250mm.

(4)   The telephone number shall consist of black digits of 30mm height and shall be displayed on an orange-coloured background.

The orange-coloured panels and hazard warning panels shall be:

 (i)   in the form of a plate;

 (ii)   securely attached; and

 (iii)   visible.

[*Sch 5 para 2*].

(For examples of these panels see *Figures 1* and *5* at D3028 above.)

Tank containers and tank wagons carrying dangerous goods shall display:

(A)   an orange-coloured panel on each side of the tank or tank container, bearing the UN Number and emergency action code;

(B)   the danger sign and subsidiary hazard sign, adjacent to the orange-coloured panel; and

(C)   the telephone number.

[*Sch 5 para 5*].

For containers and wagons carrying dangerous goods in bulk,

(I)   an orange-coloured panel bearing the emergency action code and UN number shall be displayed on each side of the container or wagon; and

(II)   the danger sign or subsidiary hazard sign shall be displayed adjacent to the orange-coloured panel.

[*Sch 5 para 4*].

Defence

D3058

In any proceedings for an offence under the regulations, it is a defence for the person charged to prove:

(*a*)   that the commission of the offence was due to the act or default of another person not being one of his employees; and

(*b*)   that he took all reasonable precautions and exercised all due diligence to avoid the commission of the offence.

[*Reg 31*].

Transitional defence

D3059   In any proceedings for an offence under the regulations prior to 1 January 1997, it shall be a defence to prove that the goods were carried in accordance with the *Carriage of Dangerous Goods by Rail Regulations 1994 (SI 1994 No 670)*.

[*Reg 33*].

Electricity

Introduction

E3001 Electricity, properly used, is a safe, convenient and efficient source of energy for heat, light and power. Between 1990 and 1995, however, 533 people were killed in electrical incidents in Great Britain. In 1995 alone there were 121 serious electrical fires costing more than £45 million in insurance claims. These are just two facts that can be gleaned from '*Electrical Incidents in Great Britain Statistical Summary*', published by the Health and Safety Executive (HSE). It gives information on a wide range of electrical incidents, including examples of some of the most commonly recurring in a variety of locations, such as offices, farms, construction sites and the home. The HSE aims to promote a greater awareness and understanding of the causes of electrical accidents so that those responsible for electrical safety are more fully aware of the risks involved. '*Electrical Incidents in Great Britain Statistical Summary*' is available from HSE Books, PO Box 1999, Sudbury CO10 6FS.

Inadvertent contact with overhead electric power lines usually results in a serious injury: indeed, one-third of such contacts are fatal. The HSE has published a revised guidance aimed at those working near overhead lines – this includes separate sections dealing with agriculture and horticulture, arboriculture and forestry, construction, railways and other transport systems with overhead conductors. '*Guidance Note GS6*', revised in 1997, is available from HSE Books.

As the electrical accidents that do happen at work often result in severe injuries or damage, high standards of electrical installation, and of electrical plant and apparatus, are essential. Adequate systems of control and maintenance are also essential, and those who work on or use such installations, plant and apparatus must be sufficiently competent. Accordingly, they must be suitably trained, instructed and supervised.

Electrical hazards

E3002 Electrical hazards may arise from bad design, construction or installation, or as a result of inadequate standards of protection or maintenance, or from inappropriate usage of the equipment or, indeed, its misuse.

Such hazards can lead to electric shock or electric burns to the individual concerned, or can result in damaged equipment, an explosion or even a general fire.

Good design and construction of electrical equipment can be assumed if they comply with the recognised standards. Good installation, protection and maintenance require the employment of competent staff or contractors. Correct operation and use will also depend on competence, achieved through adequate training, instruction and supervision.

An electric shock is the result of an electric current flowing through a part of the body. It can affect the nervous system and bodily organs and functions. The value of the current and the time it flows through the body are the two critical factors that determine the effect on the body. The heart is particularly susceptible to a condition known as ventricular fibrillation from currents as low as 50 milliamps flowing for a few seconds. No accidental current should be allowed to pass through the body but the risk of any effects – should it occur – should be kept to a minimum by ensuring that the current passing will be as small as possible and that it will pass for as short a time as possible.

One effect of a shock may be a rapid movement away from the source, which might lead to a fall. When an individual is working above ground level, such a fall could be fatal. Extensive and deep burns, at both the point of entry and at the point of exit, can result from a current passing through the body.

Preventative action

E3003   Preventive action against shock and burns includes the following:

(*a*)   inspection of all electrical equipment, particularly portable hand-held tools;

(*b*)   checking suitable equipment is installed for circuit protection;

(*c*)   testing of equipment installed for circuit protection;

(*d*)   regular inspection of equipment to minimise the risks of shocks to personnel;

(*e*)   avoidance of work near live conductors;

(*f*)   the use of proper systems and methods of working;

(*g*)   ensuring that those using the equipment or involved with it are competent so to do.

Precautions against electrical dangers must be taken in the light of legal requirements, relevant standards and codes of practice.

Legal requirements

E3004   Although not in every case specifically mentioned, the safety of electrical installations and the use of electricity are covered in the following:

(*a*)   the *Health and Safety at Work Act 1974*;

(*b*)   the *Management of Health and Safety at Work Regulations 1992*;

(*c*)   the *Construction (Design and Management) Regulations 1994*;

(*d*)   the *Electricity at Work Regulations 1989*;

(*e*)   the *Provision and Use of Work Equipment Regulations 1998*;

(*f*)   the *Electrical Equipment for Explosive Atmospheres (Certification) Regulations 1990*.

General duties under the Health and Safety at Work Act 1974

E3005   The 1974 Act provides a comprehensive legal framework for occupational health and safety. Although the Act does not expressly refer to electricity, many of its general requirements – for example, safe methods of working, training and supervision – are relevant to electricity and its use.

The Management of Health and Safety at Work Regulations 1992

E3006   As with the *Health and Safety at Work Act 1974*, these regulations do not specifically refer to electricity. The assessment of risks required by these regulations, however, certainly includes the use of electricity.

The Construction (Design and Management) Regulations 1994

E3007   Although not expressly mentioned, the use of electricity and the installation of electrical equipment certainly come within the responsibilities of such persons as the designer, the client and the main contractor. The HSE specifies electricity in its guidance, '*Health and safety for small construction sites*', HS(G)130, and '*Health and Safety in Construction*', HS(G)150.

The Electricity at Work Regulations 1989 (SI 1989 No 635)

E3008   These regulations are aimed at the users rather than the suppliers or manufacturers of electrical equipment. They apply to all places of work, including factories, shops, offices, laboratories and educational establishments. In accordance with the *Health and Safety at Work Act 1974* they lay down the principles of electrical safety in general terms. Details of the design, selection, erection, inspection and testing of electrical installations have been published by the Institution of Electrical Engineers in its '*IEE Wiring Regulations*' (currently 16th edition).

The HSE's leaflet, '*Electrical Safety and You*', ref: IND(G)23(L), is especially aimed at small firms. It describes the main hazards, gives simple guidance on risk assessment and outlines the basic measures, common to all industries, to help control the risks of using electricity at work. It also directs readers to more specific guidance produced by the HSE and other organisations.

The regulations refer to the duties to prevent danger or injury – the prevention of danger amounts to the avoidance of risk of injury.

The regulations provide for different levels of duty, ranging from reasonably practicable to an absolute duty. In the case of an alleged breach of an absolute duty, it is a defence that reasonable measures have been taken and all due diligence observed.

Safe system of work – general requirements

E3009   There is an overriding need to provide and maintain a proper safe system of work in connection with work on electrical systems, irrespective of whether they are alive or have been made dead (*regs 4, 13, 14*).

Employers should use safety signs where there is a significant risk to health and safety that has not been avoided or controlled – this frequently involves the use of the 'Danger electricity' warning sign.

Design, construction and maintenance of electrical systems – general requirement

E3010   All systems must be constructed and maintained so as to prevent danger, so far as is reasonably practicable. Construction includes design of the system, selection of equipment used in it and installation.

Although the regulations are user-orientated and do not impose duties on manufacturers and designers of electrical equipment, the *Provision and Use of Work*

Equipment Regulations 1998 provide that every employer must ensure that work equipment is so constructed or adapted as to be suitable for the purpose for which it is used or provided. This means that the equipment supplied must be suitable for the work to be undertaken and that therefore any electrical use associated with the equipment must also be suitable for the purpose for which the equipment is supplied. Generally any system complying with the current *IEE Wiring Regulations* will go a long way to satisfying the *Electricity at Work Regulations*.

Portable electrical equipment

E3011   Since many accidents occur when portable tools are being used, the HSE has emphasised three stages of inspection and testing.

The first stage is a frequent visual inspection by the user which includes checking that the cable sheath is not damaged; the plug is not damaged; that there are no inadequate joints in the cable; that the sheath of the cable is securely attached to the plug and equipment on entry to both; that the equipment has not been used for work for which it is not suited, causing it, for example, to become wet or contaminated; that there is no damage to the external casing of the equipment and that there is no evidence of overheating or burns.

The second stage involves a more formal regular visual inspection by a competent person and might include the checking of connections within the plug and equipment; that the correct fuse is being used in the plug, and that there is no indication of any overheating or burning.

The third stage comprises a regular inspection and testing of the equipment by a competent person.

There are two levels of competency: (i) where the person is not skilled in electrical work and uses a simple pass/fail type of portable appliance tester (PAT); and (ii) where more sophisticated electrical skills are used and the readings on the instruments used need interpretation. [HSE: '*Maintaining portable and transportable electrical equipment*', HS(G) 107 (1994)].

Strength and capability of electrical equipment

E3012   No electrical equipment must be put into use where its strength and capability may be exceeded in such a way as may give rise to danger (*reg 5*). This is an absolute requirement and therefore must be complied with, irrespective of whether risk or injury is foreseeable. *Reg 29* provides a defence if it can be shown that reasonable steps have been taken and all due diligence observed to avoid a breach. Before electrical equipment is put into use, it must therefore be properly selected and adequately rated for the work to be carried out.

Siting of equipment in adverse or hazardous environments

E3013   *Reg 6* provides that where it is reasonably foreseeable that electrical equipment is going to be exposed to:

(*a*)   mechanical damage;

(*b*)   the effects of weather, natural hazards, temperature or pressure;

(*c*)   the effects of wet, dirty, dusty or corrosive conditions; or

(*d*)   any flammable or explosive substances, including dusts, vapours and gases, it must be so constructed or protected so as to prevent, so far as reasonably practicable, danger from such exposure.

This is aimed at conditions both indoors and outdoors, and includes the weather-proofing of switchboards housing electrical equipment.

Insulation, protection and placement of conductors

E3014   *Reg 7* provides that all conductors in a system giving rise to danger must either:

(*a*)   be suitably covered with insulating material and protected, so far as is reasonably practicable to prevent danger; or

(*b*)   have such precautions taken as will prevent danger, including being suitably placed.

The purpose of this requirement is to prevent danger from conductors in a system that can give rise to danger, such as an electric shock, by resorting to permanently safeguarding the live conductors. Where it is not possible to insulate fully, such as an electric overhead travelling crane, this requirement can be satisfied by live conductors being out of reach and therefore in a safe position. If they intermittently come within reach, perhaps when a ladder is used, then a safe system of work should be used to limit or control such access.

Earthing or other suitable precautions

E3015   Precautions must be taken, either by earthing or other suitable means, to prevent danger arising when any conductor (other than a circuit conductor) which, it is reasonably foreseeable, may become charged, does become charged. This might occur when a system is misused or there is a fault in the system.

Reg 29 provides a defence if it can be shown that reasonable steps have been taken and all due diligence observed to avoid a breach.

The usual precaution is to earth such conductive parts that can be touched, i.e. the connection of such parts to the earth. This will include metal-cased equipment that can be touched. A way of earthing such equipment, along with pipes for water, gas or oil, is to connect them all together. Such cross-bonding or equipotential bonding avoids the risk of dangerous voltages running through different exposed metal items.

The bonding conductors must be capable of carrying any fault current for the time it flows. The time will be dependent on the fuse or other protective system used.

Another way of reducing the risks of danger when using electrical equipment is to use a residual current device (RCD) designed to operate rapidly if a small leakage current flows.

Reducing voltage will reduce the risk from a shock. 110-volt centre-tapped transformers are frequently used to do this on construction sites. Reduced voltage is particularly appropriate when working inside metal containers, such as boilers, with portable tools.

A way of removing the path to earth is to work in an earth-free area. This means that even if the electricity source is earth-referenced there can be no current path back to earth from the earth-free area and therefore no shock through an individual by a current to earth. This type of system is often used for testing electrical equipment.

Integrity of referenced connectors

E3016   If a circuit conductor is connected to earth or to any other reference point, nothing which might reasonably be expected to give rise to danger, by breaking the electrical continuity or introducing high impedance, must be placed in that conductor unless suitable precautions are taken to prevent that danger (*regs 9 and 10*).

This requirement is especially important in the case of three-phase supplies, where the neutral conductor is connected to earth at source in the distribution system, so that phase voltages are not adversely affected by unbalanced loading. This does not mean that certain electrical devices, like joints or bolted links, cannot be connected in referential circuit conductors as long as suitable precautions have been taken to ensure that no danger is caused from their use or from their installation or removal. Fuses, thyristors, transistors and the like must not be installed in this way as they could give rise to danger if they become open circuit.

Every joint or connection in a system must be both mechanically and electrically suitable for use (*reg 10*). This requirement includes the connections to plugs, sockets and other means of joining or connecting conductors, whether these connections are permanent or temporary. *Regulation 29* provides a defence if it can be shown that reasonable steps have been taken and all due diligence observed to avoid a breach.

Excess current protection

E3017   Efficient means, suitably located, must be provided for protecting from excess of current every part of a system as may be necessary to prevent danger (*reg 11*). This duty is absolute, but the defence of *reg 29* is available.

The provision recognises that faults may occur in electrical systems and requires that protective devices, such as fuses or circuit breakers, are installed to ensure that all parts of an electrical system are safeguarded from the consequences of fault conditions.

The main fault conditions are (i) overloads, (ii) short circuits, and (iii) earth faults. In all cases the protective device aims to detect the abnormal current flowing and then to interrupt the fault current before the danger causes damage or injury. The '*IEE Wiring Regulations*' give detailed guidance on selection and rating of protective devices.

Cutting off supply and isolation of electrical equipment

E3018   Suitable means must exist for cutting off the electrical supply to any electrical equipment and for the isolation of any electrical equipment (*reg 12*). This will include means of identifying circuits.

Isolation means the disconnection and separation of the electrical equipment from every source of electrical energy in such a way that this disconnection is secure.

Precautions for work on equipment made dead

E3019   Adequate precautions must be taken in respect of electrical equipment which has been made dead in order to ensure that, while work is being carried out on or near that equipment, there is no danger of the equipment becoming electrically charged during the work.

Several accidents occur each year because of work on a de-energised system which inadvertently is still live or becomes live whilst the work is being carried out. A safe system of work must therefore be used. This can include the following:

(*a*)   isolation from all points of supply;

(*b*)   securing each point of isolation, for example by locking off;

(*c*)   earthing the equipment that is being worked upon;

(*d*)   testing and thereby verifying that the equipment is dead before working on it;

(*e*)   creating a safe working zone only accessible to authorised persons;

(*f*)   safeguarding from other live conductors in proximity, for example by screening; and

(*g*)   issuing a permit to work.

Work on or near live conductors

E3020   *Regulation 14* provides that no person must carry out work on or so near to any live conductor (other than one suitably covered with insulating material to prevent danger) that danger may arise, unless:

(*a*)   it is unreasonable for it to be dead; and

(*b*)   it is reasonable for him to be at work on or near it, while it is live; and

(*c*)   suitable precautions, including provision of suitable protective equipment, are taken to prevent injury.

There are limited circumstances where live working is permitted, such as where it is not practicable to carry out work with the equipment dead, for example during testing; or where making the equipment dead might endanger other users of the equipment. This requirement imposes an absolute duty not to work on live electrical equipment unless the circumstances justify it. If such work does proceed, suitable precautions must be taken to prevent injury, including a written company policy specifying the criteria for live working and the precautions to be taken.

Precautions

E3021   Live work should only be done by competent employees (see E3023 below) who are in possession of adequate information about the nature of the work and the system. Appropriate insulated tools, equipment and protective clothing, e.g. rubber gloves or rubber mats, should be used as well as screens. Such work should be done with another competent person present if this would minimise the risk of injury. In addition, access to the work area should be restricted and earth-free work areas established.

Working space, access and lighting

E3022   To prevent injury, adequate working space, adequate means of access and adequate lighting must be provided at all electrical equipment on which or near which work is being done in circumstances that might give rise to danger (*reg 15*). (For access and lighting provisions, see ACCESS, TRAFFIC ROUTES AND VEHICLES and LIGHTING respectively.)

Competent person

E3023   No person shall be engaged in any work activity where technical knowledge or experience is necessary to prevent danger or injury, unless he possesses such knowledge or experience, or is under such degree of supervision, as may be appropriate having regard to the nature of the work.

Any supervision on electrical work, particularly live electrical work, must be by a suitably competent person.

The Provision and Use of Work Equipment Regulations 1998

E3024   Electricity is not specifically mentioned in these Regulations, but *reg 4* provides that 'work equipment shall be so constructed or adapted as to be suitable for the purpose for which it is used or provided'.

Use of electrical equipment in explosive atmospheres

E3025   The *Equipment and Protective Systems Intended for Use in Potentially Explosive Atmospheres Regulations 1996 (SI 1996 No 192)* now govern electrical equipment for use in potentially explosive atmospheres, e.g. mines, with the exception of equipment placed on the market before 30 June 2003 which complies with existing electrical safety requirements as indicated below in the *Electrical Equipment for Explosive Atmospheres (Certification) Regulations 1990*, which will be revoked as from 1 July 2003.

Certain equipment and systems are exempt, e.g. medical devices, equipment for domestic use and personal protective equipment (*Sch 5*). Manufacturers of such electrical equipment and components are under a duty to ensure that it complies with the necessary health and safety requirements (e.g. relating to potential ignition sources/hazards arising from external effects) (*Sch 3*), and appropriate conformity assessment procedures (*regs 6 and 8*). Suppliers of such equipment must also see that it is safe to put into circulation, though not in the case of products put into circulation before 1 March 1996 or previously supplied within the EU (*reg 7*).

Conformity assessment procedures (for which fees are payable) are to be determined by notified bodies, with personnel appointed, if necessary, by the Secretary of State (*regs 11 and 13*). Breach of these regulations is an offence, leading to a maximum period of imprisonment or a fine (*regs 16 and 17*), but it is a defence that due diligence was taken to avoid the commission of the offence (*reg 18*).

Electrical Equipment for Explosive Atmospheres (Certification) Regulations 1990 (SI 1990 No 13)

E3026   Manufacturers of such equipment may apply to a certification body for a certificate which states that the electrical equipment conforms to the standards specified in the directive. The certification bodies are empowered to carry out checks. Manufacturers may also apply to the appropriate certification body for a certificate stating that the equipment offers a degree of safety equivalent to EC standards.

When issued with a certificate, the manufacturer can fix to the equipment the appropriate distinctive community mark, namely:

(*a*)   that specified in Annex II to the First Specific Directive – in the case of the Framework Directive;

(*b*)   that specified in Annex C – in the case of the Gassy Mines Directive.

[*Reg 11(1)*].

Affixation of community marks, otherwise than in accordance with *reg11(1)*, is punishable as a breach of health and safety regulations.

Where a certification body refuses to issue a certificate of conformity or inspection, or withdraws one already issued, the certification body must forthwith send a written notice of the decision to the manufacturer (*reg 6*). In such a case, a manufacturer can apply to the Secretary of State for a review of the decision of the certification body within 60 days of receipt of the written notice (*reg 7*). The application must be made in writing, stating the grounds on which it is made and copies of documents supplied by the manufacturer to the certification body and a copy of the notice of decision should be included with the application. The Secretary of State then has a discretion to direct the holding of an inquiry (*reg 8*).

Product liability

E3027   Electricity is a product for the purposes of the *Consumer Protection Act 1987*. Consequently, where a defect in an electrical installation or system results in an injury, damage and/or death, liability is strict (see PRODUCT SAFETY).

Non-statutory standards and codes

E3028   The Institution of Electrical Engineers (IEE) has been producing the IEE Wiring Regulations since 1882 – they are now in their sixteenth edition. This edition includes requirements for design, installation, inspection, testing and maintenance of electrical installations in or about buildings generally. Although they have no statutory force, they provide a good indication of good industrial practice for the purposes of the *Electricity Regulations 1989*.

The National Inspection Council for Electrical Installations Contracting (NICEIC) enrols contractors whose work is of an approved standard. NICEIC surveys work to check that it complies with IEE Wiring Regulations.

The British Standards Institution, BSI, has issued many British Standards and codes of practice for electrical equipment and practice. Such standards and codes are subject to revision and supplementation. The standards range from insulation, earthing terminals and electrical connections of small equipment, to a complex set of precautions and specialised electrical equipment, based on the IEC concepts of flameproofing, intrinsic safety and other types of protection for electrical equipment in flammable atmospheres.

A few of the BSI codes are for earthing, street lighting, electrical equipment for industrial use and for office machines and the distribution of electricity on construction and building sites.

The British Approvals Service for Electrical Equipment in Flammable Atmospheres, BASEEFA, linked with the HSE, is the official UK body for testing and certificating electrical apparatus for use in hazardous atmospheres, to IEC standards as accepted by CENELEC and BSI.

The British Electrical and Allied Manufacturers' Association, BEAMA, issues a specialised range of standards and codes drawn up in consultation with users and others.

The British Electrical Approvals Board for Household Equipment, BEAB, gives its seal of approval to such domestic type equipment as satisfies design and safety standards.

The HSE has published a guidance note, PM 82, '*The selection, installation and maintenance of electrical equipment for use in and around buildings containing explo-*

sives', to assist those responsible for design selection, installation, operation and maintenance of electrical equipment (including mobile mechanical handling equipment) used at premises where explosives are manufactured, handled or stored. It aims to prevent fires and explosions due to electrical causes. The main topics covered by the guidance note include:

(*a*)   site supplies;

(*b*)   area and building zoning and categorisation;

(*c*)   selection and siting of equipment;

(*d*)   lighting protection;

(*e*)   radio frequency ignition hazards;

(*f*)   portable equipment;

(*g*)   fork-lift trucks;

(*h*)   maintenance and testing of equipment and systems.

Electricity (Standards of Performance) Regulations 1993 (SI 1993 No 1193)

E3029   The *Electricity (Standards of Performance) Regulations 1993* provide for compensation to be payable by electricity suppliers for interruptions to supply and breach of any other performance standards. These regulations have been made under the *Competition and Service (Utilities) Act 1992* which itself introduced requirements for information on each public electricity supplier's performance standards and for each of them to establish a complaints procedure.

Emissions into the Atmosphere

Introduction

E5001   Statutory controls over industrial pollution have existed since the *Alkali Act 1863*, intended to deal with the worst effects of Victorian smokestack industries and their foul emissions. Laying emphasis, as it did, on control of (mainly) smoke emission, legislation has traditionally identified industrial pollution with air pollution. Indeed, until the *Environmental Protection Act 1990 (EPA 1990)*, the main regulatory machinery for controlling *industrial* pollution, based on the *Alkali etc. Works Regulation Act 1906* and *s 5* of the *Health and Safety at Work etc. Act 1974*, sought to ensure the use of best practicable means to prevent, or render harmless, the emission into the atmosphere of noxious or offensive substances. After completion of the phasing in of the new regime under *EPA 1990*, the *1906 Act* and *s 5 HSWA 1974* were repealed on 16 December 1996. The *Health and Safety (Emissions into the Atmosphere) Regulations 1983 (SI 1983 No 943)* and *1989 (SI 1989 No 319)*, and the *Control of Industrial Air Pollution (Registration of Works) Regulations 1989 (SI 1989 No 318)*, ceased to have effect.

Environmental Protection Act 1990: pollution control

E5002   The *Environmental Protection Act 1990 Part I* has established two separate but related systems of pollution control: integrated pollution control (IPC) and air pollution control (APC). The IPC system applies to the most potentially polluting or technologically complex industrial processes. IPC is administered by the Environment Agency, a body corporate established by the *Environment Act 1995, s 1*, which took over the functions of Her Majesty's Inspectorate of Pollution on 1 April 1996.

The purpose of IPC is to prevent or minimise pollution of the environment due to the release of substances into any environmental medium (i.e. the air, water or land) [*EPA 1990, s 4(2)*].

APC, which applies to less polluting types of processes, is administered by local authorities for the purpose of preventing or minimising pollution of the environment due to emissions (only) into the air [*EPA 1990, s 4(3)*].

The IPC system is currently being reviewed because the requirements of EU Council Directive 96/61/EC of 24 September 1996, concerning integrated pollution prevention and control (IPPC), must be transposed into national legislation by 30 October 1999. The IPPC Directive applies to 'installations' rather than 'processes', so IPPC will apply to a much wider range of installations than is currently covered by IPC or APC.

Industrial atmospheric pollution – EPA 1990, Part I

E5003   Under *EPA 1990* no person shall carry on a 'prescribed process' except under an authorisation granted by the 'enforcing authority' and in accordance with the conditions to which the authorisation is subject [*EPA 1990, s 6(1)*].

The 'enforcing authority' for processes designated for central control (IPC) is the Environment Agency [*s 4(2)*]; for processes designated for local control (APC) this is the local authority [*s 4(3)*].

Prescribed processes

E5004 The *Environmental Protection (Prescribed Processes and Substances) Regulations 1991 (SI 1991 No 472)* as amended, prescribe the processes for which an authorisation is required under *s 6* and prescribe the substances the release of which into the air, water or land is subject to control under *ss 6* and *7*.

The regulations also classify them either as 'Part A' processes subject to integrated pollution control (IPC) by the Environment Agency or 'Part B' processes under local authority air pollution control (APC). The processes are described in the regulations under the following chapter headings.

Chapter 1	**Fuel Production, Combustion Processes, Power Generation**
1.1	Gasification
1.2	Carbonisation
1.3	Combustion
1.4	Petroleum
Chapter 2	**Metal Production and Processing**
2.1	Iron and steel
2.2	Non-ferrous
Chapter 3	**Mineral Industries**
3.1	Cement and lime
3.2	Asbestos
3.3	Fibre
3.4	Other
3.5	Glass
3.6	Ceramic
Chapter 4	**Chemical Industry**
4.1	Petrochemical
4.2	Organic
4.3	Acid
4.4	Halogen
4.5	Inorganic
4.6	Fertiliser
4.7	Pesticide
4.8	Pharmaceutical
4.9	Bulk storage
Chapter 5	**Waste Disposal and Recycling**
5.1	Incineration
5.2	Recovery
5.3	Waste derived fuel
Chapter 6	**Other Industries**
6.1	Paper and pulp
6.2	Di-isocyanate
6.3	Tar and bitumen
6.5	Coating and printing
6.6	Dye and ink
6.7	Timber

6.8   Rubber
6.9   Animal or vegetable matter

[*Environmental Protection (Prescribed Processes and Substances) Regulations 1991 (SI 1991 No 472), Sch 1* as amended by *SI 1992 No 614, SI 1993 No 1749, SI 1993 No 2405, SI 1994 No 1271, SI 1994 No 1329, SI 1995 No 2678*].

Prescribed substances

E5005   The following substances are prescribed for the purposes of local authority air pollution control:

—   oxides of sulphur and other sulphur compounds

—   oxides of nitrogen and other nitrogen compounds

—   oxides of carbon

—   organic compounds and partial oxidation products

—   metals, metalloids and their compounds

—   asbestos, glass fibres and mineral fibres

—   halogens and their compounds

—   phosphorus and its compounds

—   particulate matter

[*Sch 4*].

Applications for authorisation

E5006   An application to an enforcing authority for an authorisation under *s 6* must be in writing, containing:

(*a*)   the name, address and telephone number of the applicant;

(*b*)   where prescribed processes will not be carried on by means of mobile plant:

    (i)   the name of the local authority where the prescribed process will be carried on,

    (ii)   the address of the premises where the process will be carried on,

    (iii)   a map/plan showing the location of the premises,

    (iv)   if part of the premises only is to be used for carrying on the process, a plan identifying it;

(*c*)   in the case of mobile plant:

    (i)   the name of the local authority where the applicant has his main place of business,

    (ii)   the address of that place of business;

(*d*)   a description of the prescribed process;

(*e*)   a list of prescribed substances (and any other substances which might cause harm if released into any environmental medium) which will be used in or result from that process;

(*f*)   a description of techniques for preventing release of substance(s), for reducing release to a minimum, and rendering harmless any released;

(*g*)   details of any proposed release of such substances, and assessment of environmental consequences;

(*h*)   proposals for monitoring release, environmental consequences and use of techniques;

(*j*)   matters on which the applicant relies to secure compliance with *Sec 7(2), (4)* and *(7)* of *EPA 1990*;

(*k*)   any additional information which the applicant wants taken into account.

[*Environmental Protection (Application, Appeals and Registers) Regulations 1991 (SI 1991 No 507), Reg 2 (as amended by SI 1996 No 667)*].

The application must be accompanied by the prescribed fee.

The enforcing authority must either grant the authorisation subject to conditions (see E5007 below) or refuse the application [*s 6(3)*]. The authorisation must not be granted unless the authority considers that the applicant will be able to carry on the process so as to comply with the conditions which would be included in the authorisation [*s 6(4)*]. It is clear from the decision in *R v Secretary of State for the Environment and Compton ex parte West Wiltshire DC [1997] JPL 210* that the authority must refuse to grant the authorisation if it believes the applicant does not have the ability to comply with necessary conditions, even if the applicant is willing to do so. The authority must review the conditions of an authorisation at least every four years [*s 6(6)*].

Conditions of authorisation

E5007   Every authorisation for the carrying on of a prescribed process must contain conditions to ensure:

(*a*)   that, in carrying on the prescribed process, the 'best available techniques not entailing excessive cost' (BATNEEC) will be used for preventing the release of substances prescribed for any environmental medium into that medium or, where that is not practicable, for reducing the release to a minimum and for rendering harmless any such substances which are so released *and* for rendering harmless any other (i.e. non-prescribed) substances which might cause harm if released into any environmental medium (see E5008 below);

(*b*)   compliance with any directions given by the Secretary of State for the implementation of any obligations of the UK under European Community or international law. (The *Municipal Waste Incineration Directions 1991* relating to Council Directives 89/369/EEC and 89/429/EEC and the *Large Combustion Plant (New Plant) Directions 1995* relating to Council Directive 88/609/EEC as amended have been made);

(*c*)   compliance with any limits or requirements and achievement of any environmental quality standards or objectives prescribed by the Secretary of State under relevant enactments (such as those of the *Air Quality Regulations 1997 (SI 1997 No 3043)* made under the *Environment Act 1995, s 87*); and

(*d*)   compliance with any relevant requirements specified in a plan made by the Secretary of State under *s 3(5)* establishing limits or quotas for the release of substances [*s 7(2)*];

but no conditions can be imposed for the purpose only of securing the health of persons at work [*s 7(1)*].

Best available techniques not entailing excessive cost (BATNEEC)

E5008 There is implied in every IPC authorisation a general condition that the person carrying on the process must use the best available techniques not entailing excessive cost:

(*a*)   for preventing the release of substances prescribed for any environmental medium into that medium or, where that is not practicable by such means, for reducing the release of such substances to a minimum and for rendering harmless any such substances which are so released; and

(*b*)   for rendering harmless any other (i.e. non-prescribed) substances which might cause harm if released into any environmental medium.

[*s 7(4)*].

In the case of APC authorisations granted by the local authority, references to the release of substances into *any* environmental medium are to be read as references to the release of substances into the air [*s 7(5)*].

Guidance issued by the Department of the Environment in March 1996 entitled *Integrated Pollution Control: A Practical Guide* states:

' "Best" means most effective in preventing, minimising or rendering harmless polluting releases . . . there may be more than one set of "best" techniques.

"Available" should be taken to mean procurable by the operator of the process. It does not imply that the technique has to be in general use, but it does require general accessibility.

"Techniques" is defined in Section 7(1). The term embraces both the plant in which the process is carried on and how the process is operated. It should be taken to mean the components of which it is made up and the manner in which they are connected together to make the whole. It also includes matters such as numbers and qualifications of staff, working methods, training and supervision and also the design, construction, lay-out and maintenance of buildings, and will affect the concept and design of the process.

"Not entailing excessive cost" (NEEC) needs to be taken in two contexts, depending on whether it is applied to a new process or existing processes. Nevertheless, in all cases BAT can properly be modified by economic considerations where the costs of applying best available techniques would be excessive in relation to the nature of the industry and to the environmental protection to be achieved.

New Processes

In many cases, for new processes it is expected that BAT and BATNEEC will be synonymous. However, the following principles should apply:

–   the cost of the best available techniques must be weighed against the environmental damage from the process; the greater the environmental damage, the greater the costs of BAT that can be required before costs are considered excessive;

–   the objective is to prevent damaging releases or to reduce such releases so far as this can be done without imposing excessive costs. If after applying BATNEEC serious harm would still result, the application can be refused; and

– an objective approach to the consideration of what is BATNEEC is required. The concern is with what costs in general are excessive; the lack of profitability of a particular business should not affect determination.

Existing Processes

In relation to existing processes, the Environment Agency is concerned additionally with establishing timescales over which old processes will be upgraded to new standards, or as near to new standards as possible, or ultimately closed down.

Even though it relates to a single medium, the Secretary of State considers that the approach adopted in the EC Air Framework Directive is helpful in relation to the operation of IPC across all three media. Article 12 of the Directive, for example, which applies to all plants requiring an authorisation under the Directive, requires, where necessary, the imposition of appropriate conditions in authorisations, on the basis of developments as regards BAT and the environmental situation and also on the basis of the desirability of avoiding excessive costs for the plants in question, having regard to the economic circumstances of the industrial sector concerned.

Article 13, which applies only to processes existing prior to July 1987, requires certain factors to be taken into account:

In the light of an examination of developments as regards best available technology and the environmental situation, the Member States shall implement policies and strategies, including appropriate measures, for the gradual adaption of (specified) existing plants to the best available technology, taking into account in particular:

– the plant's technical characteristics;

– its rate of utilisation and length of its remaining life;

– the nature and volume of polluting emissions from it; and

– the desirability of not entailing excessive costs for the plant concerned, having regard in particular to the economic situation of undertakings belonging to the category in question.'

It is apparent therefore that the concept of 'excessive cost' allows commercial considerations relevant to an individual existing plant to be taken into account in determining what technology should be regarded as the 'best available' for control of polluting emissions from it.

Best practicable environmental option (BPEO)

E5009   If a process subject to IPC (not APC) is likely to involve the release of substances into more than one environmental medium, then there is an obligation to use BATNEEC for minimising the pollution which may be caused to the environment taken as a whole by the releases, having regard to the best practicable environmental option available as respects the substances which may be released [*s 7(7)*].

The *Practical Guide* states:

'BPEO can be defined as the option which minimises pollution to the environment as a whole, at acceptable cost, in the long term as well as the short term. A BPEO assessment for IPC should normally include an assessment of the environmental effects of releases and the economic implications of a number of options for carrying on the IPC process in question, along with a justified choice of which is the BPEO.'

Guidance Notes

E5010
The Department of the Environment (now the Department of the Environment, Transport and the Regions) has published a wide range of *General Guidance Notes* and APC *Process Guidance Notes*. IPC *Process Guidance Notes* are issued by the Environment Agency. All are available from HMSO. APC *Process Guidance Notes* have statutory force as guidance issued by the Secretary of State to local authorities to which they must have regard under *s 7(11)*. IPC *Process Guidance Notes*, whilst lacking statutory force, 'represent the view of the Environment Agency on best available techniques for particular processes and are therefore a material considera-tion to be taken into account in every case'. [*Practical Guide* para 7.19].

Transfer of authorisations

E5011
An authorisation for the carrying on of any prescribed process may be transferred by the holder to another person [*s 9(1)*]. The transferee must notify the enforcing authority in writing of the transfer within 21 days [*s 9(2)*].

Variation of authorisations by enforcing authority

E5012
The enforcing authority (EA or LA) may at any time (subject to the requirements of *s 7* – see above) vary an authorisation by adding, changing or removing conditions. The authority must do so if it appears that *s 7* requires conditions to be imposed which are different from the subsisting conditions [*s 10(1)*].

The procedure is for the authority to serve a *variation notice* on the holder:

– specifying the proposed variations and the date(s) when they are to take effect [*s 10(3)*]; and

– requiring the holder to notify the authority of what action (if any) he proposes to take to comply with the notice and to pay the prescribed charge or fee [*s 10(4)*].

If the variation will involve a 'substantial change' to the way that the process is being carried on (i.e. one that would make a substantial change to the release of substances from the process), the proposal must be advertised by the holder in accordance with the requirements of *Sch 1, Pt II*.

Variation of conditions: applications by holders

E5013
The holder of an authorisation who wishes to make a 'relevant change' in the process being carried on (i.e. one that could alter the release of substances from the process) may request the enforcing authority to determine:

(*a*) whether the proposed change would involve a breach of any condition of the authorisation;

(*b*) if not, whether the authority would be likely to vary the conditions as a result of the change;

(*c*) if breach of a condition would be involved, whether the authority would consider varying the conditions to enable the change to be made;

(d)   whether a 'substantial change' in the way the process is being carried on would be involved.

[*s 11(1),(2)*].

If the authority determines that the change would require the variation of conditions under (*b*) or (*c*) or would involve a substantial change, then it must notify the holder who can, if he wishes to proceed with the change, make the necessary application for variation [*s 10(3),(4)*]. Again, any such application must be accompanied by the prescribed fee.

Revocation of authorisation

E5014   The enforcing authority may at any time revoke an authorisation by giving not less than 28 days' notice in writing to the holder [*s 12*].

Enforcement of EPA 1990

E5015   *EPA 1990* gives enforcing authorities considerable enforcement powers analogous with those of HSE inspectors, for the purposes of *HSWA 1974* (see ENFORCEMENT) as follows.

(a)   An enforcement notice can be served if the enforcing authority (i.e. the Environment Agency or a local authority) is of the opinion that the conditions of authorisation have been or are likely to be contravened, specifying the matters constituting the contravention and the necessary remedial action which must be taken within a specified period. [*s 13*].

(b)   A prohibition notice can be served where the enforcing authority is of the opinion that there is an 'imminent risk of serious pollution of the environment', relating to any aspects of the process, whether regulated by conditions of authorisation or not. A prohibition notice can suspend an authorisation and specify remedial action necessary before the suspension is lifted. [*s 14*].

Appeals against notices

E5016   A person who has been refused an authorisation or who is dissatisfied with conditions attaching to an authorisation, or an operator who has been refused a variation of his authorisation or whose authorisation has been revoked, can appeal to the Secretary of State [*s 15*]. The latter can

(a)   affirm the decision;

(b)   grant/vary the authorisation;

(c)   quash the conditions of the authorisation;

(d)   quash the decision revoking the authorisation.

[*s 15(6)*].

Public registers of information

E5017   Enforcing authorities must establish and maintain a public register of information, in which records relating to applications for authorisation, authorisations, enforcement and prohibition notices, revocations and convictions are to be kept. [*s 20*].

(This equates with the position under the *Environment and Safety Information Act 1988* regarding notices served under *HSWA 1974* – see E15022 ENFORCEMENT.) Enforcing authorities must

(*a*)   ensure that registers are available, at all reasonable times, for inspection by the public free of charge; and

(*b*)   afford members of the public facilities for obtaining copies of entries, on payment of a reasonable charge.

[*s 20(7)*].

Information is not included in the register if that would affect national security [*s 21*] or if the local authority (or, on appeal, the Secretary of State) agree that it is commercially confidential [*s 22*].

Offences/penalties/burden of proof

Offences

E5018   The following are the main offences:

(*a*)   carrying on a prescribed process without an authorisation or without complying with the conditions to which it is subject;

(*b*)   failing to give due notice to an enforcing authority, of transfer of an authorisation;

(*c*)   failing to comply with or contravening a requirement/prohibition of an enforcement or prohibition notice;

(*d*)   making a false, misleading or reckless statement connected with authorisations;

(*e*)   making a false entry in any record connected with authorisations;

(*f*)   failing to comply with a court order to remedy the cause of an offence.

[*s 23(1)*].

Penalties

E5019   (1)   For breach of (*a*), (*c*) or (*f*) in E5018 above:

(i)   on summary conviction, a maximum fine of £20,000 or a maximum of three months' imprisonment, or both;

(ii)   on conviction on indictment, an unlimited fine or a maximum of two years' imprisonment, or both.

[*s 23(2)*].

(2)   For breach of (*b*), (*d*) or (*e*) in E5018 above:

(i)   on summary conviction, a fine not exceeding the statutory maximum;

(ii)   on conviction on indictment, an unlimited fine or a maximum of two years' imprisonment, or both.

[*s 23(3)*].

Burden of proof

E5020   In any proceedings for an offence relating to failure to comply with the implied general condition requiring use of BATNEEC [*s 7(4)* – see E5008 above], it is for the accused to prove that there was no better available technique not entailing excessive cost than was, in fact, used to satisfy the condition [*s 25(1)*].

Where an entry is required in a record concerning observance of any condition of authorisation, and the entry has *not* been made, that fact is admissible as evidence that the condition has *not* been observed. [*s 25(2)*].

Offences of bodies corporate and 'other persons'

Offences by bodies corporate

E5021   Where an offence under *EPA 1990*, committed by a body corporate, is proved to have been committed with the consent or connivance, or attributable to neglect on the part of any

(*a*)   director,

(*b*)   manager,

(*c*)   secretary,

(*d*)   other similar officer, or

(*e*)   a person who was purporting to act in any such capacity,

he, as well as the body corporate, is guilty of an offence [*s 157(1)*]. (This is analogous with *HSWA 1974, s 37(1)* (see E15032 ENFORCEMENT and E11013 EMPLOYERS' DUTIES TO THEIR EMPLOYEES).) A conviction may lead to disqualification from being a company director, under the *Company Directors' Disqualification Act 1986, s 2*.

Offences by 'other persons'

E5022   Where the commission by any person of an offence is due to the act or default of some other person, that other person may be charged with and convicted of the offence, whether or not proceedings are taken against the first person committing the offence [*s 158*]. Analogous with *HSWA 1974, s 36(1)*, this provision could be used to prosecute employees whose activities cause their employer to commit an offence (see E15032, E15034 ENFORCEMENT).

Application to Crown

E5023   *EPA 1990* applies to the Crown but breach of the Act itself, or any regulations made under it, will *not* give rise to *criminal* liability [*s 159(1) and (2)*]. (This compares with the position of the Crown under *HSWA 1974* (see E15035 ENFORCEMENT).)

Statutory nuisances – criminal liability under EPA 1990

E5024   Dust, steam, smells or other effluvia arising on industrial, trade or business premises, and being prejudicial to health or a nuisance, are statutory nuisances [*s 79(1)(d)*]. A local authority cannot without the consent of the Secretary of State institute proceedings for statutory nuisance in certain cases where proceedings could be brought for an offence in relation to IPC or APC (see E5018 above).

Where a local authority is satisfied that a statutory nuisance exists, or is likely to occur or recur, it must serve an *abatement notice* on the person responsible for the nuisance or, where the nuisance arises from a structural defect, on the owner of the premises; or, if the person responsible for the nuisance cannot be found, on the owner or occupier of the premises [*s 80(1), (2)*]. An abatement notice may:

– require abatement of the nuisance or prohibit or restrict its occurrence or reoccurrence;

– require execution of such works and taking of such other steps as may be necessary for any of those purposes;

and must specify the time(s) within which compliance is required.

In *Network Housing Association Ltd v Westminster City Council, The Times 8 November 1994* a noise abatement notice served under *s 80* was held to be invalid because it required only a particular result to be achieved without indicating what work was to be carried out.

An appeal against an abatement notice may be made to a magistrates' court within 21 days of the date of service [*s 80(3)*].

A person on whom an abatement notice is served who, without reasonable excuse, contravenes or fails to comply with any requirement or prohibition imposed by the notice, is guilty of an offence [*s 80(4)*] and liable on summary conviction to a fine not exceeding level 5 on the standard scale and a daily fine of up to 10 per cent of that level if the offence continues after conviction [*s 80(5)*]. But an offence committed on industrial, trade or business premises carries a maximum fine on summary conviction of £20,000 [*s 80(6)*].

In the case of most statutory nuisances arising on industrial, trade or business premises and in some other cases, it is a defence to show that the 'best practicable means' were used to prevent, or to counteract the effects of, the nuisance [*s 80(7)*]. 'Best practicable means' is to be interpreted as follows:

(*a*)   'practicable' means reasonably practicable having regard, for example, to local conditions and circumstances, to the current state of technical knowledge and to the financial implications;

(*b*)   'means' include the design, installation, maintenance and operation of plant and machinery, and the design, construction and maintenance of buildings and structures;

(*c*)   the test is to apply only so far as compatible with any duty imposed by law, with safety and safe working conditions.

[*s 79(9)*].

If a local authority forms the opinion that criminal proceedings under *s 80(4)* would provide an inadequate remedy for any statutory nuisance, it may institute proceedings in the High Court for an injunction [*s 81(5)*]. Such proceedings cannot be brought unless the local authority has actually considered whether criminal proceedings would be inadequate (*Vale of White Horse DC v Allen & Partners [1997] Env LR 212*).

A person who is aggrieved by the existence of a statutory nuisance may make a complaint to a magistrates' court [*s 82(1)*]. If the court is satisfied that the alleged nuisance exists, or that although abated it is likely to recur, it must make an order:

(*a*)   requiring the defendant to abate the nuisance within a specified time and execute any necessary works; and/or (*b*)   prohibiting a recurrence of the nuisance and requiring the defendant to execute any necessary works within a specified time;

and may impose a fine not exceeding level 5 on the standard scale [*s 82(2)*].

As proceedings for statutory nuisance under *s 82* are criminal in nature, the court has jurisdiction to make orders for compensation under the *Powers of Criminal Courts Act 1973, s 35* to those aggrieved by the nuisance (*Botross v Hammersmith and Fulham LBC, The Times 7 November 1994*).

If the court finds that the alleged nuisance existed at the date of the complaint, it must order the defendant to pay 'expenses properly incurred' by the complainant, including legal costs, even if the defendant had abated the nuisance by the time of the hearing (*s 82(12)* and see *R v Dudley Magistrates' Court ex parte Hollis [1998] 1 AER 759*).

A person against whom proceedings are brought under *s 82* can avoid liability by showing that he is not the person by whose act, default or sufferance the nuisance arose or continued (*Carr v Hackney LBC, The Times 9 March 1995*).

Civil liability for environmental damage

E5025

Civil liability for environmental damage may arise under the common law relating to trespass, negligence, nuisance and what is known as the 'rule' in *Rylands v Fletcher*.

Trespass

E5026

An action for trespass can be brought against a person who causes direct physical interference with land. For example, if soot from a chimney is deposited on land in sufficient quantities to cause physical interference, then the person in possession of the land would have the right to sue the person responsible for trespass. There is no need to prove physical damage to the land in order to bring an action for trespass.

Negligence

E5027

Liability in negligence may arise where the defendant breaches a duty of care that he owes to the plaintiff, which causes the plaintiff to suffer damage which is foreseeable. A case in which liability in negligence was found to exist as the result of emissions into the atmosphere was *Margereson and Hancock v JW Roberts Ltd, The Times 17 April 1996*. A former factory owner was held to be liable to two people who contracted mesothelioma as a result of playing, when children, in a factory loading bay, where there were high concentrations of asbestos dust. 'The test in every case ought to be whether the defendant can reasonably foresee that his conduct will expose the plaintiff to the risk of personal injury.' [See A5032 ASBESTOS].

Nuisance

E5028

An unlawful interference with the use or enjoyment of land, or of some right over it, is a nuisance. Since the right of one person to do what he likes with his land must always be balanced against the rights of others to the enjoyment of their land, a use of land must be unreasonable in order to give rise to an action for nuisance. Therefore a use of land for industrial purposes which causes pollution of the atmosphere and affects activities on adjoining premises will be a nuisance if that use is unreasonable. If the use is reasonable, the fact that it may give rise to an adverse effect on adjoining premises because the activities carried out on those other premises are abnormally sensitive to atmospheric pollution will not give rise to an action for nuisance.

The 'rule' in Rylands v Fletcher

E5029

Rylands v Fletcher (1866) LR 1 Exch 265 held that a person who brings on to his land something which causes damage if it escapes has strict liability to any person who suffers loss or damage as the natural consequence of that escape.

The principles established by *Rylands v Fletcher* were considered by the House of Lords in *Cambridge Water v Eastern Counties Leather plc [1994] 2 AC 264*. In that case, the defendants operated a tannery from which, over a period of years and unbeknown to them, a solvent had leaked. The solvent was later found in water extracted from a borehole operated by the plaintiffs. The borehole became unusable for supplying water for public consumption after the *Water Supply (Water Quality) Regulations 1989 (SI 1989 No 1147)* came into force. The plaintiffs suffered damage as the result of having to sink a new borehole at a cost of £1 million. The House of Lords held that the defendants were not liable to the plaintiffs under 'the rule' because the damage had not been foreseeable.

Clean Air Act 1993

E5030

The *Clean Air Act 1993* consolidates the *Clean Air Acts 1956 and 1958*, and *Part IV of the Control of Pollution Act 1974*.

The *Clean Air Act 1993* prohibits the emission of dark smoke from a chimney of any building or one which serves the furnace of any fixed boiler or industrial plant [*s 1(1), (2)*], except in cases prescribed in regulations made by the Secretary of State [*s 1(3)*]. The *Dark Smoke (Permitted Periods) Regulations 1958 (SI 1958 No 498)* and the *Dark Smoke (Permitted Periods) (Vessels) Regulations 1958 (SI 1958 No 878)* have been made.

'Dark smoke' means smoke as defined by reference to the Ringelmann Chart [*s 3*] although in any proceedings the court may be satisfied that smoke is or is not dark smoke notwithstanding that there has been no actual comparison of the smoke with the Ringelmann Chart [*s 3(2)*].

A person guilty of an offence shall be liable on summary conviction, in the case of a contravention as respects a chimney of a private dwelling, to a fine not exceeding level 3 on the standard scale and, in any other case, level 5 [*s 1(5)*].

The emission of dark smoke from any industrial or trade premises is prohibited and the occupier of the premises and any person who causes or permits the emission shall be guilty of an offence [*s 2(1)*]. *Section 2* does not apply to the emission of dark smoke caused by the burning of any matter prescribed by regulations made by the Secretary of State [*s 2(2)(b)*]. The *Clean Air (Emission of Dark Smoke) (Exemption) Regulations 1969 (SI 1969 No 1263)* prescribe six categories of exempted matter, subject to compliance with conditions. A person guilty of an offence under *s 2* shall be liable on summary conviction to a fine not exceeding £20,000 [*s 2(5)*].

New furnaces must, so far as practicable, be smokeless [*s 4*].

Limits on the rates of emission of grit and dust from chimneys of furnaces may be prescribed by regulations made by the Secretary of State [*s 5(2)*]. The *Clean Air (Emission of Grit and Dust from Furnaces) Regulations 1971 (SI 1971 No 162)* prescribe limits on the emission of grit and dust from certain furnaces.

In certain cases, application must be made to the local authority for approval of the height of chimneys of furnaces [*ss 14 and 15*].

Part III Clean Air Act 1993 empowers a local authority to establish by order a smoke control area [*s 18*]. Breach of a prohibition on emission of smoke in a smoke control area is an offence [*s 20*] unless exemptions under *s 21* or *s 22* apply.

Parts I to III Clean Air Act 1993 (i.e. *ss 1–29*) do not apply in relation to prescribed processes under *Part I EPA 1990* (see E5003 above).

Air pollution

E5031   *Part IV Clean Air Act 1993* replaces *Part IV Control of Pollution Act 1974* and provides powers for the Secretary of State to make regulations for the purpose of limiting or reducing air pollution by:

(*a*)   imposing requirements as to the composition of motor fuel [*s 30*]; and

(*b*)   imposing limits on the sulphur content of furnace or engine fuel oil [*s 31*].

Cable burning is made an offence, punishable on summary conviction by a fine not exceeding level 5 on the standard scale, unless the burning is part of a process subject to *Part I EPA 1990* [*s 33*] (see E5003 above).

A local authority may obtain information about the emission of pollutants and other substances into the air by:

(*a*)   issuing notices under *s 36* (information about emissions from premises);

(*b*)   measuring and recording the emissions, and for that purpose entering on any premises, whether by agreement or in exercise of the power conferred by *s 56* (rights of entry and inspection); and

(*c*)   entering into arrangements with occupiers of premises under which they measure and record emissions on behalf of the local authority (other than private dwellings or caravans) [*s 35(1)*].

The power of entry cannot be exercised unless the authority has given to the occupier of the premises 21 days' notice in writing and the occupier has not given notice to the authority requesting it to serve on him a notice under *s 36* [*s 35(2)*].

The local authority has the power to serve written notice requiring the occupier of any premises to furnish specified information concerning the emission of pollutants and other substances into the air from the premises [*s 36(1)*].

If the notice relates to a process subject to *Part I EPA* (see E5003 above), the person served with the notice is not obliged to supply any information which, as certified by an inspector appointed under *Part I*, is not of a kind which is being supplied to the inspector for the purposes of that Part [*s 36(3)*].

Air quality

E5032   Under *Part IV Environment Act 1995*, local authorities must review and assess the air quality in their area. The *Air Quality Regulations 1997 (SI 1997 No 3043)* require local authorities to assess whether the air quality standards and objectives set out in the regulations are likely to be achieved by 2005. Where objectives will not be met by that deadline, the authority must set up an air quality management area (AQMA) and state the steps that it expects to take in order to secure compliance with the regulations. The objectives to be achieved aim to reduce the level of certain substances such as carbon monoxide and lead in the air to specified levels and are contained in full in *Reg 4* and the *Schedule*.

To help local authorities interpret the Act and regulations, the DETR has issued circular 15/97, '*The United Kingdom National Air Quality Strategy and Local Air Quality Management: Guidance for Local Authorities*'. This explains the National Air Quality Strategy which the Government was required by the Act to adopt. The

Strategy contains the Government's policies for the assessment and management of air quality. The DETR has also published the following Guidance Notes:

- *Framework for review and assessment of air quality.* LAQM.G1(97)

- *Developing local air quality strategies and action plans: the principal considerations.* LAQM.G2(97)

- *Air quality and traffic management.* LAQM.G3(97)

- *Air quality and land use planning.* LAQM.G4(97)

- *Monitoring for air quality reviews and assessments.* LAQM.TG1(98)

- *Preparation and use of atmospheric emission inventories.* LAQM.TG2(98)

- *Selection and use of dispersion models.* LAQM.TG3(98)

Provisions of *Part IV Environment Act 1995* also give local authorities powers to contribute to the management of air quality. *Section 4(4A) EPA 1990* requires local authorities to consider the National Air Quality Strategy (under *s 80 Environment Act 1995*) when exercising their responsibilities to prevent or reduce air pollution caused by operations in their area.

Control of Asbestos in the Air Regulations 1990 (SI 1990 No 556)

E5033   Emissions of asbestos dust into the atmosphere are governed specifically by the *Control of Asbestos in the Air Regulations 1990 (SI 1990 No 556)*.

Any person undertaking activities involving the working of products containing asbestos must ensure that those activities do not cause significant environmental pollution by asbestos fibres or dust emitted into the air. Any person undertaking the demolition of buildings, structures and installations containing asbestos and the removal from them of asbestos or materials containing asbestos, involving the release of asbestos fibres or dust into the air, must ensure that significant environmental pollution is not caused. [*Control of Asbestos in the Air Regulations 1990, Reg 4*].

Contravention of these provisions is an offence, punishable on conviction on indictment by a fine or on summary conviction by a fine not exceeding level 4 on the standard scale [*Reg 5*]. *HSWA 1974, s 37* (offences by bodies corporate) applies to offences under *Reg 5*.

Employers' Duties to their Employees

Introduction

E11001   The purpose of this chapter is to provide a brief introduction to the common law duties and statutory duties of employers towards their employees, and the consequences of any breach of those duties.

Common law duties

Negligence

E11002   For there to be liability for negligence, the plaintiff must prove:

—   that the defendant owed him a duty of care;

—   that the defendant acted in breach of that duty; and

—   that the breach caused loss or injury of a kind which is recoverable at law.

The duty of care

E11003   The question of whether a duty of care exists can be approached in two slightly different ways, one general and the other incremental. The general approach was summarised by Lord Wilberforce in *Anns v Merton London Borough Council [1978] AC 728* when he said:

> '. . . the position has now been reached that in order to establish that a duty of care arises in a particular situation, it is not necessary to bring the facts of that situation within those of previous situations in which a duty of care has been held to exist. Rather the question has to be approached in two stages. First one has to ask whether, as between the alleged wrongdoer and the person who has suffered damage there is a sufficient relationship of proximity or neighbourhood such that, in the reasonable contemplation of the former, carelessness on his part may be likely to cause damage to the latter, in which case a *prima facie* duty of care arises. Secondly, if the first question is answered affirmatively, it is necessary to consider whether there are any considerations which ought to negative, or to reduce or limit the scope of the duty or the class of person to whom it is owed or the damages to which a breach of it may give rise.'

The incremental approach was set out by Lord Roskill in *Caparo Industries v Dickman [1990] 2 AC 605* when he said:

> 'Phrases such as "foreseeability", "proximity", "neighbourhood", "just and reasonable", "fairness", "voluntary acceptance of risk" or "voluntary assumption of responsibility" will be found used from time to time in the different cases. But . . . such phrases are not precise definitions. At best they are but labels or phrases descriptive of the very different factual situations which can exist in particular cases and which must be carefully examined in

each case before it can be pragmatically determined whether a duty of care exists and, if so, what is the scope and extent of that duty. If this conclusion involves a return to the traditional categorisation of cases as pointing to the existence and scope of any duty of care . . . I think this is infinitely preferable to recourse to somewhat wide generalisations which leave their practical application matters of difficulty and uncertainty.'

Either approach allows the duty of care placed upon an employer to develop over time so that as new risks to an employee's health and safety are recognised the scope of the duty of care expands to include them and impose liability.

Vicarious liability

E11004   Employers are of course sometimes personally negligent. However, in a large number of cases an employee will be injured by the negligence of his fellow employees. The concept of vicarious liability renders the employer liable for the acts of his employees carried out in the course of their employment and when not 'off on a frolic' of their own. There will be responsibility even where an employee is carrying out an authorised act in an unauthorised way or in a manner prohibited by his employer – see *Rose v Plenty [1976] 1 AER 97* where a boy was injured on a milk float in circumstances where the driver, an employee, had been forbidden to 'employ' children to deliver milk and collect empties. Similarly, in *Kay v ITW Ltd [1967] 3 AER 22* a forklift truck driver, finding a lorry in his way, got in and moved it – although he was not authorised to drive lorries, this act was regarded to be in the course of his employment.

Liability arises even where an employee has been grossly negligent. In *Century Insurance Co Ltd v Northern Ireland Road Transport Board [1942] 1 AER 491*, an employee of the respondent was employed to deliver petrol in tankers to garages. Whilst delivering petrol at a garage forecourt, and whilst petrol was actually being transferred from the tanker to an underground tank at the garage, the employee decided to have a smoke. Having lit a match, he then threw it away while still alight, and it landed by the underground tank. There was an explosion which caused considerable damage. It was held that the employer was liable, since the employee was doing what he was employed to do, namely delivering petrol, even though he was acting in a grossly negligent way.

In addition, where an employee gives orders to a co-employee by way of a practical joke, he is still acting in the course of employment, and the employer is liable. In *Chapman v Oakleigh Animal Products (1970) 8 KIR 1063* the plaintiff employee was told to put his hand in the nozzle of a machine to clear an obstruction. Fellow employees wanted to spray him with crushed ice out of the machine. Another employee slipped and accidentally turned on the machine. The plaintiff's hand was injured in the machine. The employer was found to be liable.

An act or omission causing injury arises during the course of employment even if committed before work starts or after it finishes, so long as it is reasonably incidental to work. As regards travelling to and from work, the rule is that an employee is acting in the course of his employment only if he is going about his employer's business at the time. In *Vandyke v Fender [1970] 2 QB 292*, men travelling to work in a car provided by their employers and paid a travelling allowance (but no wages for travelling time) were not on duty and not in the course of their employment. By contrast, an employee required by his employer to travel from his home to a place away from his usual workplace to carry out work there, and who was paid wages for the travelling time, was acting in the course of his employment while travelling (*Smith v Stages and Another [1989] ICR 272 (HL)*).

There is a considerable body of case law on vicarious liability, establishing the following:

(*a*)   an employee is acting within the course of employment even if he performs his work or a task in contravention of a statute or regulation (*National Coal Board v England [1954] 1 AER 546*);

(*b*)   an employee who takes a lunch break during the course of a journey whilst at work, is acting within the course of employment (*Harvey v RG O'Dell Ltd [1958] 1 AER 657*);

(*c*)   an employee is acting within the course of employment if injured doing something incidental to work, e.g. having a cup of tea (*Davidson v Handley Page Ltd [1945] 1 AER 255*);

(*d*)   an employee may act within the course of employment if he stays in a dangerous workplace, contrary to instructions (*Stapley v Gypsum Mines Ltd [1953] 2 AER 478* – roof of gypsum mine);

(*e*)   an employee is acting within the course of employment if he uses an uninsured private car for company business (*Canadian Pacific Railway Co v Lockhart [1942] AC 591*);

(*f*)   an employee who uses a private car rather than a company lorry on a job, is acting within the course of employment (*McKean v Raynor Bros (Nottingham) Ltd [1942] 2 AER 650*);

(*g*)   by contrast, an employee who does an unauthorised act which is not so connected with an authorised act as to be a mode of doing it, but an independent act, is not acting within the course of his employment (*Aldred v Naconco [1987] IRLR 292* where an employee pushed an unsteady washbasin against another employee who suffered back injury from turning quickly and was unsuccessful in his action for damages);

(*h*)   an employer is vicariously liable for the negligence of an independent contractor, if the latter becomes part of his workforce and causes the death of an employee (*Marshall v Sharp & Sons 1991 SLT 114*).

There is recent Scottish authority that an employer is not vicariously liable for sexual harassment of an employee by another (*Ward v Scotrail Railways Ltd [1999] May CL*). In this case the male employee had sent the plaintiff a letter of a sexual nature, blocked her daily route to work and swapped shifts so as to work alongside her. It was held that the male employee had not been acting within the course of his employment and was motivated purely by personal emotions. It must be doubted whether the same result would have occurred in England.

Specific duties

E11005   The classic expression of the employer's duty of care towards his employee is that the employer must provide competent and safe fellow employees, safe equipment and place of work, and a safe system of work (*Wilson v Clyde Coal Co Ltd & English [1937] 3 AER 628*). All three are ultimately only manifestations of the duty of the employer to take reasonable care to carry out his operations so as not to subject those employed by him to unnecessary risk. However, the tripartite division is a convenient way of approaching the subject. The important points to note are:

(*a*)   *Competent and safe fellow employees.* This is generally important only where the employer has been negligent in selecting staff for particular work. Thus an untrained or inexperienced employee should not be put in charge of others in the carrying out of a task beyond his capacity. The duty also extends to cover the effects of persistent practical jokers who injure their fellow employees, where such behaviour was foreseeable. Obviously a failure to train employees will also result in their not being competent.

(b)   *Safe plant and machinery and a safe place of work.* The employer is responsible for defective equipment which he has purchased and which injures his employee. The *Employers' Liability (Defective Equipment) Act 1969, s 1(1)* provides:

'Where after the commencement of this Act–

(a)   an employee suffers personal injury in the course of his employment in consequence of a defect in equipment provided by his employer for the purposes of the employer's business; and

(b)   the defect is attributable wholly or in part to the fault of a third party (whether identified or not),

the injury shall be deemed to be also attributable to negligence on the part of the employer (whether or not he is liable in respect of the injury apart from this subsection), but without prejudice to the law relating to contributory negligence and to any remedy by way of contribution or in contract or otherwise which is available to the employer in respect of the injury.'

The employer's failure to comply with the duty can take the form of a failure to provide proper equipment for the job or failure to maintain it. It can also consist of a failure to supply proper personal protection equipment.

The duty to provide *a safe place of work* extends to entrance and egress and the general condition of premises.

(c)   *Safe system of work.* This is by far the most important aspect of the employer's duty. It is also the most difficult to describe in that there are as many systems of work as there are varieties of it. Illustrations of defective systems have sometimes been set out under the following headings:

—   faulty co-ordination of departments or branches of work;

—   faulty planning for a particular task or layout of plant;

—   unsafe method of using machinery or using machinery for the wrong process;

—   not enough men for the task;

—   insufficient supervision and instruction;

—   poor communication.

To these might be added the obligation to insist that safety aids and protective clothing etc. are used, the duty to warn where the employee is exposed to a risk against which it is not practicable to protect him (see below) and the obligation to assess the risks to employees of carrying out particular tasks and operations.

A system of work is not automatically unsafe because it is potentially hazardous. In *Nilsson v Redditch BC [1995] PIQR P199* a dustman was injured by a shard of glass poking from a refuse sack. The court held that although the 'black bag' system was potentially hazardous, it was not unsafe and so the local authority did not have to replace it with the wheelie bin system.

The duties apply even though an employee:

(i)   is working away on third party premises. Here the employer remains liable for any injuries arising in connection with the system of work on the third party premises, whilst in addition the occupier will (and the employer may) be responsible for defects in the structure of the premises or in respect of any defect in plant or substances provided by the occupier for use by persons not in his employment; or

(ii)   has been hired out to another employer, but control over the job he is performing remains with his permanent employer (*Mersey Docks and Harbour Board v Coggins and Griffiths (Liverpool) Ltd [1947] AC 1* where the Board hired out the services of a skilled crane driver to a firm of stevedores, and the former was held liable for injury negligently caused by the crane driver whilst working for the stevedores).

There is doubt as to how far an employer is obliged to go in protecting his employees from the criminal acts of third parties. Any employee dealing with large numbers of members of the public, especially where money is involved, could be at foreseeable risk; it is probable, therefore, that an employer will be liable if he fails to take at least the standard sensible precautions where there is foreseeable risk to the employee.

The standard of the duty of care and the duty to warn

E11006   The standard of care which the employer must adopt is not absolute. In *Stokes v GKN (Bolts and Nuts) Ltd [1968] 1 WLR 1776*, Swanwick J stated the law as follows:

'. . . the overall test is still the conduct of the reasonable and prudent employer, taking positive thought for the safety of his workers in the light of what he knows or ought to know; where there is a recognised and general practice which has been followed for a substantial period in similar circumstances without mishap, he is entitled to follow it, unless in the light of common sense or newer knowledge, it is clearly bad; but, where there is developing knowledge, he must keep reasonably abreast of it and not be too slow to apply it; and where he has in fact greater than average knowledge of the risks, he may be thereby obliged to take more than the average or standard precautions. He must weigh up the risk in terms of the likelihood of injury occurring and the potential consequences if it does; and he must balance against this the probable effectiveness of the precautions that can be taken to meet it and the expense and inconvenience they involve. If he is found to have fallen below the standard to be properly expected of a reasonable and prudent employer in these respects, he is negligent.'

Where an employer knows that employees will be injured as a consequence of, for instance, using a particular tool, then that does not mean that he is liable even though the injury is foreseeable. Thus Mustill J in *Thompson v Smiths Shiprepairers [1984] QB 405* (a deafness case) placed the following gloss on Swanwick J's words:

'In the passage just cited, Swanwick J drew a distinction between a recognised practice followed without mishap, and one which in the light of common sense or increased knowledge is clearly bad. The distinction is indeed valid and sufficient for many cases. The two categories are not, however, exhaustive as the present actions demonstrate. The practice of leaving employees unprotected against excessive noise had never been followed "without mishap". Yet even the plaintiffs have not suggested that it was "clearly bad", in the sense of creating a potential liability in negligence, at any time before the mid-1930s. Between the two extremes is a type of risk which is regarded at any given time (although not necessarily later) as an inescapable feature of the industry. The employer is not liable for the consequences of such risks, although subsequent changes in social awareness, or improvements in knowledge and technology, may transfer the risk into the category of those against which the employer can and should take care. It is unnecessary, and perhaps impossible, to give a comprehensive formula for identifying the line between the acceptable and the unacceptable.'

When a practice shifts from acceptable to unacceptable, the first obligation on an employer to do something about a particular problem will frequently be to warn an employee of risks to which his work might expose him. Thus, in a case involving Vibration White Finger (VWF), Lawton LJ stated:

'Generally speaking, if a job has risks to health and safety which are not common knowledge, but of which an employer knows or ought to know and against which he cannot guard by taking precautions, then he should tell everyone to whom he is offering the job what those risks are if, on the material then available to him, knowledge of those risks would be likely to affect the decision of a sensible, level headed prospective employee about accepting the offer.' (*White v Holbrook Precision Castings Ltd [1985] IRLR 215 (CA)*).

There are difficulties for a plaintiff in relying on such an argument because he would have to convince the court that having received the warning he would not have taken the employment, or, if the warning was given during the employment, that he would have left it.

In *Pickford v Imperial Chemical Industries plc [1998] 3 AER 462* the defendants avoided liability for a secretary's writer's cramp after appealing to the House of Lords. It was noted that the prescribed disease A4 (cramp of the hand or forearm due to repetitive movements) is not easily identifiable or understood and, in cases such as this, great caution should be exercised in imposing on the employer a duty to warn of the risks and of the need to take rest breaks. The trend has been for the courts to insist on the need for warnings where there is a risk of harm; the conclusion of the House of Lords in this case that no warning of the risks was necessary reverses this trend where symptoms of disease are diffuse and of uncertain origin.

Liability for industrial diseases

E11007   The consequence of the court's approach that the standard of care is not absolute has meant that liability sometimes tends to lag some way behind scientific and medical knowledge.

Whilst it has been known for hundreds of years that exposure to loud noise caused deafness, it was only in the early 1970s that liability was recognised. Likewise the first common law liability for asbestosis and mesothelioma dates back to the same time. In *Smith v P&O Bulk Shipping Ltd [1998] 2 Lloyd's Rep 81*, an employee of the defendants died from mesothelioma as a result of asbestos exposure between 1954 and 1971. It was not until 1977 when the Department of Trade issued a circular to ship-owners warning of the dangers of asbestos that a reasonable ship-owner would have been aware of the risks. The employee had retired from work before then so the claim against P&O for negligence failed.

Unlike industrial accidents, diseases arise out of the working environment and system of work and are not referable to single identifiable incidents. In many conditions the damage or injury is cumulative, extending over decades, with long latent periods. Liability may commence only after significant injury has already been caused. In deafness cases it is not uncommon for proceedings to be issued in relation to working conditions which existed as long ago as the 1950s even though liability is unlikely to commence before 1963.

The most recent cases concerning the recognition of industrial diseases involve Repetitive Strain Injury and Vibration White Finger.

Repetitive Strain Injury (RSI) is an area bedevilled by disagreement between medical experts and by confusion of terminology. The phrase Repetitive Strain Injury has been called into question as failing to describe adequately the totality of the various illnesses, and has been replaced by Work Related Upper Limb Disorders (WRULDs).

In *Mughal v Reuters [1993] IRLR 571* Judge Prosser rejected a claim for damages for generalised RSI. On the medical evidence in front of him he found that the diagnosis was meaningless. It is possible to argue that even though there are no physical signs of the illness, there is a mental element which causes the plaintiff to believe that he is suffering pain, which is indistinguishable from the real thing (Dr Paul Riley, RSI, *PC Today*, April 1994). However, if that is the case, then presumably unless there is a recognisable mental illness, there can be no recovery.

Others reject that suggestion and, for instance, state:

> 'On the basis of this accumulating body of experimental evidence alone, the notion that "RSI is all in the mind" may now be ruled out as scientifically insupportable.' (S Pheasant, RSI, [*1994*] *JPIL 228*).

Since the *Reuters* case there have been cases where medical evidence in this field has been questioned or praised by judges in a far more definite way than would be expected in less contentious cases (e.g. *Moran v South Wales Argus (1994) (unreported); Ball v Post Office [1995] PIQR P5*).

The reported cases since *Reuters* show the tide generally running against claimants. For example:

Land v Volex (January 1994) (unreported) – RSI claim. No pathology and therefore no award of damages.

Astbury v Post Office (July 1994) (unreported) – occupational cramp. The medical evidence was divided, but there was no pathology. None the less, the judge found that the plaintiff was suffering from occupational cramp, but that there was no liability on the part of the employer because the employer could not have foreseen the onset of this injury.

Ball v Post Office (June 1994) (unreported) – the plaintiff was diagnosed as having tenosynovitis. Although the judge accepted that this condition had been aggravated by the plaintiff's work as a sorter, the employer was found not liable as there had been no evidence of any significant history of upper limb disorders amongst sorters.

Moran v South Wales Argus (1994) (unreported) – RSI claim. The judge accepted the defendant's view that the plaintiff had suffered no physical injury. The workstation had been poorly designed, however, and in this regard the employer was in breach of its duty of care. Yet the employer was held not to be liable, because the plaintiff had suffered no physical injury.

In *Amosu and Others v Financial Times (August 1998, unreported)*, the Financial Times avoided liability for specific musculo-skeletal disorders which were familiar in everyday practice. The judge remained unpersuaded that the plaintiffs had established that they suffered from physical problems on the balance of probabilities. 'There was a long history of outbreaks of socially determined conditions which lacked any organic cause and went back to complaints about the replacement of the quill by steel nibbed pens' from clerks in the Civil Service in the last century.

This line of authority culminates in the House of Lords case of *Pickford v Imperial Chemical Industries plc* (above). In order to establish liability for the Industrial

Disease A4 ('cramp of the hand or forearm due to repetitive movements', e.g. writer's cramp), the plaintiff had to prove that there was an organic cause for her symptoms, even though writer's cramp is a recognised prescribed disease. The plaintiff's tactical amendment to the pleadings, replacing 'RSI' with 'writer's cramp', failed and the defendants avoided liability.

There has been a recent reversal of the tide in favour of claimants. In *McPherson v London Borough of Camden (1999, unreported)*, the High Court judge found that the claimant was suffering from De Quervain's stenosing tenosynovitis caused by excessive movement of the thumb during keyboard use in poor ergonomic and working time conditions between June 1993 and January 1994. Damages for pain, suffering and loss of amenity were assessed at £3,500. The total award was £98,194, including a substantial loss of earnings award.

The message therefore seems to be that, to have a reasonable chance of succeeding, the plaintiff must suffer from a foreseeable non-generalised organic injury caused by the defendant's negligence. Although it was noted in *Pickford* that the Court of Appeal had been wrong to consider that advances in medical knowledge and technology meant that the psychogenic approach had been largely discredited, it remains more difficult to establish a recognised psychiatric injury in the absence of any organic cause.

With VWF there is less medical uncertainty. Unlike RSI, it is distinct from other upper limb disorders. Like RSI, it is not susceptible to objective clinical tests. In the case of *Armstrong & Others v British Coal Corporation (1996) (unreported)* the preliminary issues to be decided were:

'From what date, if at all, ought the defendants to have recognised:

(i)   that the work with the tools complained of . . . gave rise to a foreseeable risk of VWF, and

(ii)   that effective precautions to guard against that risk could and ought to have been taken in respect of that work.'

The plaintiffs contended for dates in the late 1960s and early 1970s, whilst the defendants argued for a date not earlier than the commencement of proceedings.

VWF has been known since the 1900s to have been produced by the use of vibrating hand tools. As already explained, where an employer knows that employees will be injured as a consequence of, for instance, using a particular tool, then that does not necessarily mean that he is liable even though the injury is foreseeable. He will only become liable when the risk becomes something which he should and indeed could guard against.

There had never been any obvious problem with VWF amongst miners. Virtually no cases were reported to the National Coal Board's very large in-house medical service. However, in 1967 the medical service carried out a small investigation into VWF at four collieries. The survey dealt with only a tiny sample of 22 miners, but identified VWF in some 18% of those surveyed. It was held that this should have tilted the balance in favour of carrying out a full survey. It was held that such a survey would have disclosed a large incidence of VWF. The judge considered that a full survey would have taken several years and decided that it would have been completed by 1 January 1973. From that date the defendants should have recognised that there was a foreseeable risk of VWF.

This did not, however, mean that they were liable at that stage. It was the answer to the second question which determined when, in Mustill J's words, the defendants should have taken steps to prevent the injuries. The judge in fact decided that there was more than one date, and that a system of warnings and routine medical examinations should have been introduced by 1 January 1975, and a job rotation by 1 January 1976. On the adaptation of tools and eradication of the jobs, the judge could make no finding other than that the date would be after 1 January 1976. The date seems to have been based:

> '. . . on general grounds of human experience and on the basis of the defendants' strength in the market and the agreed qualities of their own research department, not on any specific scientific engineering evidence.'

The Court of Appeal has since broadly agreed with the approach adopted by the court.

Many of the plaintiffs had received substantial vibration doses before 1975 and damages were not reduced to reflect this non-negligent exposure where the plaintiffs' symptoms first began after 1975. Only nominal deductions of about £750 each were made to reflect latent damage already sustained at the beginning of 1975.

In *Allen and Others v BREL and RFS (1998, unreported)*, Smith J held that the defendants' engineering evidence provided an adequate basis on which to apportion the injury between the pre-negligent period (up to 1976 in most cases) and the negligent period (post-1976). She did not apportion the damage on a strictly straight-line basis but took into account varying vibration exposure labels and discounted somewhat those periods of exposure where damage was symptomless. This resulted in a significant reduction in damages.

In addition, she made a finding that it would have been impossible to eradicate vibration exposure completely. A further discount in damages was made to reflect non-negligent exposure post-1976.

This 'discovery' of more and more occupational diseases, giving rise to liability at common law, is likely to be a continuing process.

Industrial diseases and third parties

E11008   An employer can in certain circumstances, and especially with regard to industrial diseases, owe a duty of care to the family of an employee.

In the case of *Hewett v Alf Brown's Transport Ltd [1992] ICR 530* the plaintiff's husband worked as a lorry driver engaged in carrying lead-contaminated waste arising from the demolition of a gas works. In a nine-month period, six individuals suffered from lead poisoning although none were drivers. The plaintiff's husband wore overalls and a mask when involved in loading the lorry, and thus avoided poisoning. The plaintiff's wife suffered lead poisoning. The judge concluded, on the balance of probabilities, that her being poisoned was a consequence of her having washed her husband's overalls.

However, the plaintiff did not succeed. The court concluded that while the defendant would otherwise have owed a duty of care, the standard of care to be adopted by a reasonable employer was in effect codified by the *Control of Lead at Work Regulations 1980 (SI 1980 No 1248)*. These required certain precautions to be adopted, including the provision of washing and changing facilities where the exposure to lead of an employee was significant. Under the definition contained in the Regulations the exposure to lead of the plaintiff's husband was not significant, and accordingly he could have brought no claim himself. As he had no right of action, the court held that the plaintiff could not 'as a matter of law' succeed.

A very similar case, which involved asbestos, was *Gunn v Wallsend Slipway & Engineering Company, The Times, 23 January 1989*. Here the plaintiff's wife was exposed to asbestos dust from washing her husband's overalls before 1965. On occasions the plaintiff's husband would return from his employer's shipyard 'white with dust'. Waterhouse J concluded that until the publication of a paper in the *Journal of Industrial Medicine* in 1965 ('the Newhouse paper') no one engaged in shipbuilding or industry generally, or having responsibilities in that field, foresaw that there was a risk of injury to a person in the plaintiff's position. The judge rejected the plaintiff's argument that it was known that those living in the vicinity of asbestos mines could develop asbestos-related diseases, or that under *Smith v Leech Brain [1962] 2 QB 405* the defendants owed a duty of care because it could be foreseen that the plaintiff would suffer some lung injury, even if it was not mesothelioma.

He said:

'The reality of the matter is that, on the evidence before me, no one in the industrial world before October 1965 directed his or her mind to the risk of physical injury from domestic exposure to asbestos dust, except in what I will call "the asbestos neighbourhood cases". In particular, no one directed his or her mind to the risk to another from an asbestos worker's person or working clothes. There was no medical literature on the subject, no warnings or guidance in industrial or official publications even hinting at the problem, and no approved practice in relation to the storage and washing of working clothes. Even if the defendants had employed appropriate medical and safety personnel, it is most unlikely that they would have become aware of the risk from domestic exposure to asbestos dust before about the end of 1965.'

The plaintiff's claim accordingly failed.

It might therefore be expected that a date of guilty knowledge for mesothelioma caused to those who suffered heavy exposure to dust through living near an asbestos factory could be no earlier than 1960.

That is not, however, what Holland J decided in the case of *Hancock and Margereson v Turner & Newall (1995) (unreported)*.

Mrs Margereson claimed as widow and administratrix of her deceased husband. Mr Margereson had lived in the immediate vicinity of Turner & Newall's factory from his birth in 1925 until 1943, and thereafter between 1948 and 1957. He died of mesothelioma. Mrs Hancock had spent her childhood living adjacent to the factory between 1938 and 1951.

Within the factory the whole process of producing asbestos materials was carried out and inevitably produced a great deal of dust. The staple asbestos produced for much of the period was blue.

Witnesses described how children played on bales of blue asbestos at the factory loading bay, and how the dust got everywhere in the immediately adjacent houses and streets. One witness stated:

'I also remember that on occasions my bedroom would change colour overnight with the dust. The walls of my bedroom were supposed to be pink, but overnight it would change to blue or white depending on the dust . . . I remember dry dust and fibre all round on the streets near the factory. A lot of the time it would look like candy floss or cotton wool . . . I have seen it blow around like a snow storm.'

The judge found that this and similar evidence was unexaggerated.

The judge also concluded that from around 1930 the defendants very well knew that exposure to asbestos within the factory was such as to injure their employees. The factory had an inadequate dust control system.

On the basis of the medical evidence the judge found that:

'1.   Neither at any material time nor now would any of the medical witnesses have foreseen asbestosis as likely to be caused by environmental exposure, that is, by exposure to asbestos dust other than within the confines of a factory workroom.

2.   At no material time was there established a level of exposure to dust that was safe, nor one that was not dangerous.

3.   There was then a perceived relationship between tuberculosis and asbestosis so that it was thought that anyone suffering or likely to suffer from the former condition was more at risk of contracting the latter.

4.   As the material period progresses, the notion of a potential association between asbestosis and lung cancer developed.

5.   At no material time was mesothelioma a concept known to medicine, neither was the potential for such being caused by lesser levels of exposure to asbestos such as could be available in the vicinity of the defendant's factory.

6.   There is no evidence that anyone has ever contracted asbestosis by reason of environmental exposure in this country.'

The judge then went on to consider the *Asbestos Industry Regulations 1931 (SI 1931 No 1140)*. These were absolute in their terms and effectively prohibited the exposure of workers to visible asbestos dust. They also prohibited the employment of young persons within the factory because of the perceived connection between exposure and tuberculosis and to minimise the length of exposure of employees.

The test adopted by Holland J to decide liability was:

'Ought the defendants at any material time to have reasonably foreseen that their conduct would expose the plaintiffs to the risk of personal injury so as to come under a duty of care to them?'

He concluded that there was no doubt that the defendants owed a duty of care to their employees. He went on:

'If the evidence shows with respect to a person outside the factory that he or she was exposed to the knowledge of the defendants, actual or constructive, to conditions in terms of dust emissions not materially different to those giving rise within the factory to duty of care then I see no reason not to extend to that extramural "neighbour" a comparable duty of care.'

There were no material differences between exposure in the offices of the factory, and in the adjacent houses, between the factory yard and the outside street and this gave rise to the same foresight of potential injury to those exposed for prolonged periods.

In the light of the facts concerning the exposure of children, the judge considered that:

'. . . no responsible contemporaneous medical opinion could have discounted the risk of injury to such children through inhalation as "a mere possibility which would not occur to the mind of a reasonable man".'

The injury to the plaintiffs was therefore foreseeable. Holland J was thus following the approach of Lord Ackner in *Page v Smith [1995] 2 WLR 644* where it was said in an entirely different context (a very minor road traffic accident giving rise to myalgic encephalomyelitis) that:

> 'Assuming in favour of the respondent that the circumstances of the accident were such that (1) the risk of injury by nervous shock was remote and (2) such a risk, although a possibility, would become an actuality only in very exceptional circumstances, nevertheless the risk could not be said to be so far-fetched or fantastic as to be "a mere possibility which would never occur to the mind of a reasonable man" (per Lord Dunedin in *Fardon v Harcourt-Rivington (1932) 146 LT 391 at 392*). The risk was a real risk in the sense that it was justifiable not to take steps to eliminate it only if the circumstances were such that a reasonable man, careful of the safety of his neighbours, would think it right to neglect it.'

Accordingly in the *Hancock and Margereson* case the defendants were liable because they had exposed the plaintiffs as children to asbestos dust.

The judge did not find liability on the basis that the defendants owed a duty of care to the whole area because neither of the plaintiffs fell within that category and because he envisaged:

> '. . . real difficulty in holding that the defendants as factory occupiers should have anticipated such a level of inhalation at such a remove from their premises as then (that is, before knowledge of mesothelioma and the level of exposure capable of inducing such) would raise foresight of personal injury. Introduce the fact of distance and the balance of probabilities favours the defendants. The inhalation that was condemned in the 1930 Report and that founded the 1931 Regulations is a concept that was then to be readily associated with the immediate environs of this factory, but not elsewhere.'

The Court of Appeal upheld the judge's decision in robust terms and it would appear to be only a matter of time, depending on the particular circumstances, before a spouse case succeeds.

Liability for psychological injury

E11009   The law concerning psychological injury can be distilled into seven propositions (*per* Law Commission Consultation Paper 137, *Liability for Psychiatric Illness*). These are:

(*a*)   The plaintiff must have suffered from a recognised psychiatric illness that, at least where the plaintiff is a secondary victim, must be shock induced. The primary victim is the person who is injured as a direct result of the defendant's negligence. The secondary victim is the person who witnesses the primary victim's injury and suffers from psychiatric injury himself as a consequence.

(*b*)   It must have been reasonably foreseeable that the plaintiff might suffer a physical or psychiatric illness as a result of the defendant's negligence.

It was initially thought that the psychiatric injury itself must be foreseeable.

In *Page v Smith [1995] 2 WLR 644* the plaintiff was driving a car involved in a minor collision. No one suffered any physical injury in the accident. The plaintiff had suffered from chronic fatigue syndrome ('CFS') on an intermittent basis for some 20 years. It was alleged that his condition had become chronic and permanent as a result of the collision. Understandably, perhaps, the defendants seem to have been most reluctant to pay the plaintiff any compensation.

Otton J at first instance found that it was foreseeable that such an accident could cause CFS. The Court of Appeal, however, held that it was not foreseeable that a person of ordinary fortitude would have suffered any psychiatric illness as a result of the accident.

In the House of Lords, Lord Lloyd stated the majority view that, where the plaintiff was the primary victim, foreseeability of physical injury was enough to enable the plaintiff to recover damages for psychiatric injury. He said:

'It could not be right that a negligent defendant should escape liability for psychiatric injury just because, although serious physical injury was foreseeable, it did not in fact transpire.'

'Since liability depends on foreseeability of physical injury, there could be no question of the defendant finding himself liable to all the world.'

'Nor in the case of a primary victim is it appropriate to ask whether he is a person of "ordinary phlegm". In the case of physical injury there is no such requirement. The negligent defendant, or more usually his insurer, takes his victim as he finds him.'

'In claims by secondary victims the law insists on certain control mechanisms, in order as a matter of policy to limit the number of potential claimants. Thus, the defendant will not be liable unless psychiatric injury is foreseeable in a person of normal fortitude.'

'In an age when medical knowledge is expanding fast, and psychiatric knowledge with it, it would not be sensible to commit the law to a distinction between physical and psychiatric injury, which may already seem somewhat artificial, and may soon be altogether outmoded.'

Page v Smith has since been followed in *Giblett v P & NE Murray Ltd [1999] The Times 21 May*. There the trial judge had erred in holding that cessation of sexual activity as a consequence of a car accident which caused whiplash was not foreseeable. The Court of Appeal held that the correct test was to determine whether, on balance of probabilities, the accident caused or materially contributed to the development, or increased the duration, of a pre-existing psychiatric illness. The plaintiff had only to show that her physical or psychiatric injury was reasonably foreseeable and that negligence had caused her injury. On the facts she failed because there was no proved causal link between the accident and the cessation of sexual activity.

Thus with the primary victim there is need only to foresee the risk of personal injury in order to be able to claim damages for psychiatric injury. Only in the case of the secondary victim is there any requirement that it must be reasonably foreseeable that mental injury will result.

(*c*)   The plaintiff can recover damages if the foreseeable psychiatric illness arose from a reasonable fear of immediate physical injury to himself. An employee who is put in fear for his own physical safety but escapes with only mental injury will be able to recover damages. Psychiatric harm suffered by an employee as a result of witnessing the electrocution of a fellow employee who was working close by so that he was lucky not to have been electrocuted himself may fall within the ambit of this proposition (see *Young v Charles Church (Southern) Ltd (unreported, May 1997, Court of Appeal*).

(*d*)   Where the defendant has negligently injured or imperilled someone other than the plaintiff, and the plaintiff, as a result, has foreseeably suffered a shock-induced psychiatric illness, the plaintiff can recover if he can establish the requisite degree of proximity in terms of:

(i)   the class of persons whose claims should be recognised, and

(ii)   the closeness of the plaintiff to the accident in time and space, and

(iii)   the means by which the shock is caused.

In respect of the class of persons, those with a tie of love and affection to the primary victim are included. This will normally include parents and their children, but not, it seems, siblings. Rescuers and those who are involuntary participants are included, but mere bystanders are not.

The requirement for closeness as to time and space includes coming on the immediate aftermath. The perception must be through one's own unaided senses. This was broadly confirmed in *Alcock v Chief Constable of South Yorkshire Police [1992] 1 AC 310*. There it was held by the House of Lords that the Chief Constable was entitled to rely on the television companies complying with their own codes of practice and not broadcasting pictures which contemporaneously showed the suffering of recognisable individuals. Leading counsel for some of the plaintiffs indeed accepted that had such pictures been shown there would have been a *novus actus interveniens*.

Lord Nolan and Lord Ackner, however, both foresaw circumstances in which it would be possible to claim on the basis of television pictures transmitted live. It can only be a matter of time before such claims are successfully made.

(*e*)   Where the defendant has negligently damaged or imperilled property belonging to the plaintiff, and the plaintiff as a result has suffered a psychiatric illness, it would appear that in certain circumstances the plaintiff can recover.

(*f*)   It is unclear whether there can be liability for the negligent communication of news to the plaintiff which has foreseeably caused him to suffer psychiatric illness.

(*g*)   There are miscellaneous cases where the primary victim can recover, particularly involving employees who have suffered stress at work as in *Walker v Northumberland County Council [1995] 1 AER 737*.

The first English case indicating an expansion of the previously perceived boundaries of the employer's duty of care to his employee came in *Johnstone v Bloomsbury Health Authority [1992] QB 333*.

In that case a junior hospital doctor alleged that he had suffered from depression because he had been required to work excessive hours. His contract of employment enabled his employers to require him to work 48 hours per week on average. In fact he worked for up to 100 hours per week, and on at least one occasion worked for 36 hours with only 30 minutes' sleep.

Although the doctor's contract of employment would have ostensibly enabled his employer to require him to work such hours, so long as on some kind of average calculation he did not work more than 48 hours per week, the Court of Appeal held that the employer's ability to require him to work overtime must be exercised reasonably and hence with proper regard to the employee's health. The claim was settled, before its merits could be decided one way or another, for a sum in the region of £5,000.

The case of *Walker* re-emphasised the existence of an employer's duty of care to his employees not to cause them psychiatric injury through stress. Mr Walker was employed by the defendants as an area social services officer which was a middle manager position. In that role he had to deal with an increasing number of child care problems which were by their very nature extremely stressful. There was plainly too much work and in November 1986 Mr Walker suffered a nervous breakdown.

He was away from work until March 1987. When he returned he was promised additional support which did not materialise. Indeed the amount of work had increased while he had been away and perhaps inevitably he suffered a second nervous breakdown in September 1987. He was unable to return to work again.

Colman J commented:

'There has been little judicial authority on the extent to which an employer owes to his employees a duty not to cause them psychiatric damage by the volume or character of the work which the employees are required to perform. It is clear law that an employer has a duty to provide his employee with a reasonably safe system of work and to take reasonable steps to protect him from risks which are reasonably foreseeable. Whereas the law on the extent of this duty has developed almost exclusively in cases involving physical injury to the employer as distinct from injury to his mental health, there is no logical reason why risk of psychiatric damage should be excluded from the scope of an employer's duty of care or from the co-extensive implied term in the contract of employment. That said, there can be no doubt that the circumstances in which claims based on such damage are likely to arise will often give rise to extremely difficult evidential problems of foreseeability and causation. This is particularly so in the environment of the professions, where the plaintiff may be ambitious and dedicated, determined to succeed in his career in which he knows the work to be demanding, and may have a measure of discretion as to how and when and for how long he works, but where the character or volume of the work given to him eventually drives him to breaking point. Given that the professional work is intrinsically demanding and stressful, at what point is the employer's duty to take protective steps engaged? What assumption is he entitled to make about the employee's resilience, mental toughness and stability of character, given that people of clinically normal personality may have a widely differing ability to absorb stress attributable to their work?'

The judge held that in assessing an employer's conduct the law calls for no more than a reasonable response to the danger which is being guarded against. He stated that what is reasonable depends on the nature of the relationship, the magnitude of the risk of injury which was reasonably foreseeable, the seriousness of the consequences for the person owed the duty, and the cost and practicability of preventing the risk.

Colman J decided that the case turned on the question of:

'. . . whether it ought to have been foreseen that Mr Walker was exposed to a risk of mental illness materially higher than that which would ordinarily affect a social services middle manager in his position with a really heavy workload. For if the foreseeable risk were not materially greater than that, there would not, as a matter of reasonable conduct, be any basis upon which the council's duty to act arose.'

He decided that as there was no prior indication that the stress Mr Walker underwent before his first illness would cause such an illness there was no liability for it. However, the first illness made the second entirely foreseeable and hence the council was found to be liable.

Since then, there has been an out-of-court settlement of £100,000 to a deputy teacher in a primary school who alleged he had suffered two nervous breakdowns after being bullied by the headmistress (*Ratcliff v Pembrokeshire County Council (1998, unreported)*).

In many ways *Walker* raises more questions than it answers. The employer could presumably have dismissed Mr Walker after the first illness and avoided any possibility of paying damages beyond wages for the period of notice.

Contributory negligence and causation

E11010   The employee is under a duty of care not to injure himself. The defence of *volenti non fit injuria* is generally unavailable, that is the employer cannot say he is not liable because the employee has voluntarily accepted a risk of injury in carrying out a particular task.

An employee's damages will be reduced to the extent that he can be shown to have been contributorily negligent. However, what would otherwise be the effect of such negligence is mitigated by the attitude of the law which excuses an employee's inadvertence. Thus Lord Wright said in *Caswell v Powell Duffryn Associated Collieries [1940] AC 152*:

> 'The jury have to draw the line where mere thoughtlessness or inadvertence ceases, and where negligence begins. What is all important is to adapt the standard of negligence to the facts and to give due regard to the actual conditions under which men work in a factory or mine, to the long hours and the fatigue, to the slackening of attention which naturally comes from constant repetition of the same operation, to the noise and confusion in which the man works, to his preoccupation in what he is actually doing at the cost of some inattention to his own safety.'

This approach developed as a means of preventing contributory negligence vitiating the strict civil liability placed on employers in respect of their statutory duties under the *Factories Acts*. It has, however, been of fairly general application. Mere inadvertence is therefore unlikely to be penalised.

When considering contributory negligence, it is important not to confuse it with questions of causation. In *Chapman v Tangmere Airfield Nurseries Ltd (1998)* the plaintiff fell while reaching for a tomato after attempting to steady himself on a trolley which he thought was there but which had in fact run ahead on its rails. At first instance the judge held that while the defendant had been negligent in failing to ensure that the trolley did not move, there was no liability because 'but for' the plaintiff's failure to look first for the trolley there would have been no accident. The Court of Appeal held that this was an incorrect approach, and that a defendant should be held liable if the consequence of his negligence was 'a' cause of an accident, even if it was not 'the' cause of it. The only question was as to the degree of the plaintiff's contributory negligence.

Breach of statutory duties

E11011   Various statutes impose duties on employers to look after the health and welfare of their employees. Duties are also imposed on employees to look after their work-mates' and their own health and safety.

The principal legislation is contained in the *Health and Safety at Work etc. Act 1974*, the *Management of Health and Safety at Work Regulations 1992 (SI 1992 No 2051)* and the *Workplace (Health, Safety and Welfare) Regulations 1992 (SI 1992 No*

3004). These statutes and regulations set out both general duties and duties specific to particular circumstances and processes.

The *Workplace Regulations* are not examined here as they are dealt with in WORKPLACES – HEALTH, SAFETY AND WELFARE.

Statutory duty and negligence compared

E11012

Statutory duties are distinct from common law duties but they tend to be broadly similar. Statutes and regulations generally describe the nature and scope of an employer's duty in more detail than is provided by the law of negligence. They constitute a clearer framework of what the law requires in specific circumstances.

Nevertheless, an action for breach of statutory duty involves different principles from those applicable in a negligence action. Foreseeability of injury, for example, will often be irrelevant to an action for breach of statutory duty. A person may establish liability in negligence but fail to prove a breach of statutory duty, because statutory duties tend to be strictly defined. The statutory duty may or may not require the same actions by an employer as the common law of negligence.

Criminal sanctions

E11013

The general duties set out in *HSWA* and in the *Management of Health and Safety at Work Regulations 1992* do not confer a civil right of action for damages on an injured individual except where the person is a new or expectant mother. It is likely that an injured baby would also have a right of action.

Instead, breach of the provisions is a criminal offence rendering an employer or employee liable to prosecution. The case may be heard in the magistrates' court or the Crown Court. The penalty is a fine. The maximum fine that the magistrates can impose is £20,000. The Crown Court has unlimited powers to fine.

A statutory duty may not be delegated. An employer remains responsible for the safety of employees (and of independent contractors where they are engaged in work which forms part of the employer's undertaking – see *R v Associated Octel Co Ltd [1996] 1 WLR 1543 (HL)*) even where, for instance, outside consultants have been employed to devise and implement safety standards. If they perform their brief so that there is a breach of statutory duty, and injury results, a prosecution against the employer remains a possibility. The employer may attempt to argue, in mitigation, that he himself was not at fault and that any fine should be reduced accordingly.

This approach might prove counter-productive. In *R v Mersey Docks and Harbour Company (1995) 16 Cr App R (S) 806* the Court of Appeal held that it was no mitigation to say that matters of safety were left to other people. The court should impose fines which left people in no doubt that it was their duty and they had to discharge it. In this case the employers had wholly disregarded the risk, and the steps taken to carry out its duty were superficial and inadequate. There may be situations, however, in which this case might be distinguished and similar mitigation might be successful.

The employer is generally a legal entity and not an individual. It has been settled since the middle of the last century that a corporate employer may be convicted for a breach of statutory duty.

Corporate criminal liability arises in respect of breaches of statutory duty because the duty imposed on the employer is non-delegable and the statute provides that breach is a criminal offence.

Under *HSWA s 37* a director, manager or other similar member of a corporation may be prosecuted personally in addition to the corporation. He will be convicted if it is proved that he consented to the commission of the offence by the corporation or if the offence is attributable to his neglect.

Corporate manslaughter

E11014   The commission of a criminal offence generally involves two elements: a particular state of mind accompanied by a particular act.

It was formerly thought that a corporation could not commit a criminal offence because, although it was a legal entity, it had no mind or body. It is now settled that a corporation can commit a criminal offence.

In every corporation there is a mind and body in the form of its controlling or directing officers. Their acts and decisions are the company's acts and decisions.

It is a question for both the judge and the jury to decide whether an employee in a given case exercises a sufficient degree of control as to become part of the corporation. If not, he is merely the company's servant or agent as opposed to the company, and the company is unlikely to be vicariously liable for his criminal acts.

A corporation can only be convicted of offences punishable by a fine. These include most offences but exclude murder.

Until *P&O European Ferries (Dover) Ltd (1991) 93 Cr App R 72* it was thought that a corporation could not be convicted of an offence involving personal violence. It was argued that since 1601 authoritative books had described manslaughter as 'the killing of a human being by a human being'. The argument was rejected and it was held that an indictment for manslaughter would lie against the company allegedly responsible for the Zeebrugge disaster.

Similarly, a manslaughter prosecution against an employer might arise out of a fatal accident at work.

There are two types of manslaughter, voluntary and involuntary. Voluntary manslaughter involves an intent to kill or do serious injury with mitigating circumstances which include provocation or diminished responsibility.

Involuntary manslaughter comprises all other unlawful killings. These are divided into two categories: (i) manslaughter by an unlawful and dangerous act, and (ii) manslaughter by reckless or possibly gross negligence.

The *P&O* case fell into category (ii). At the time the test was largely one of subjective recklessness involving appreciation of an obvious and serious risk by the directing mind of the company (i.e. its directors and senior managers). One of the reasons why the prosecution failed was that there was insufficient evidence to prove that any of the individuals making up the directing mind had sufficient knowledge of the risk that a ferry might sail with its bow doors open to make them reckless. None of them knew that there had been five earlier instances of P&O ferries putting to sea with the bow doors open.

The situation was altered to an extent by the introduction of a new test in *R v Adomako [1995] AC 171*:

> 'The jury will have to decide whether the extent to which the defendant's conduct departed from the proper standard of care incumbent upon him . . .was such that it should be judged criminal.'

This injected an element of objectivity. On this test it might have been open to the jury to conclude that one of the causes of the disaster was the failure of the company to provide a safe system for the operation of ferries; and that failure fell far below what could reasonably have been expected.

However, that would not necessarily have overcome the difficulty of proving that an individual forming part of the directing mind had sufficient knowledge to mean the company was guilty. The trial judge specifically declined to adopt the aggregation principle which would have allowed the faults of a number of individuals, none whose faults were sufficient to make them guilty of manslaughter, to be aggregated so that in their totality there was such a high degree of fault that the company was guilty.

This has meant that smaller companies with basic management structures are more likely to be convicted of an offence. Thus in *R v Kite and OLL Ltd (1994)*, both OLL Ltd and its managing director were convicted of manslaughter following the death of four youths in a canoeing accident at Lyme Regis. Given the simplicity of OLL's management structure, it was relatively straightforward to establish liability because the managing director had personal knowledge of the inadequacies of the safety systems and the consequent risks which were said by the prosecution to be 'obvious and serious'.

Since *OLL* there has been only one other successful prosecution for corporate manslaughter. This was in 1996 when Jackson Transport (Ossett) Ltd was convicted with its managing director. Whilst Jackson Transport was a larger company than OLL with approximately 40 employees, the prosecution succeeded against the company because it had a basic management structure and it was possible to identify a guilty directing mind.

In 1996, the Law Commission's Report on Involuntary Manslaughter considered the specific problems associated with corporate manslaughter. The report commented, 'the problems that confront a prosecution for corporate manslaughter explain why there has only been one successful prosecution [the report was published before the *Jackson Transport* case], . . . we have welcomed the opportunity to consider the principles of corporate liability in the light of great obstacles now confronting those wishing to bring a prosecution'.

The report's central recommendation was that there should be a new offence of corporate killing, committed where a company's conduct in causing death falls far below what could reasonably be expected. Unlike common law manslaughter it would not require the risk of death to be obvious or that the company be capable of appreciating the risk. The requirement would be for a death to have been caused by a company's failure in the way in which its activities are managed and organised.

No legislation has resulted. However, there are signs that the common law is moving beyond the identification principle into new ways of attributing liability to a company.

In the Privy Council case of *Meridian Global Funds Management Asia Ltd v Securities Commission [1995] 2 AC 500*, two senior investment managers in Meridian, a large Hong Kong investment company, improperly used their authority to buy into a New Zealand company with a view to gaining control of it. Whether the knowledge of the managers could be attributed to the company was debated and Lord Hoffmann held that in attributing knowledge to a company the identification principle was not always appropriate or necessary.

Civil liability for breach of statutory duty

E11015   A person injured in the course of employment is likely to assert that the employer was both negligent and in breach of its statutory duty. Breach of the subsidiary regulations under *HSWA* and a wide variety of other regulations give rise to civil liability.

In a successful action for breach of statutory duty, the following issues will be proved.

(*a*)   The statute imposes a duty on the defendant. Occupational health and safety legislation is generally directed at the employer with a view to reducing injuries at work.

(*b*)   The defendant has failed to perform the duty. Statutory duties incorporating the word 'shall' are absolute duties unless qualified. Anything which an Act specifies shall be done must be done irrespective of any constraints imposed by particular circumstances.

If, for instance, a flywheel is insecurely fenced and injury ensues, the employer is liable even if he did everything in his power to ensure that the fencing was safe under *s 12* of the *Factories Act 1961*. It is irrelevant that fencing might make the machine unusable. A finding of negligence would be unlikely in similar circumstances.

Occupational health and safety legislation generally qualifies the absolute nature of the duty with the words 'practicable' or 'as far as is reasonably practicable.' New and recent legislation tends to use the word 'practicable'.

To do what is 'practicable' means to do what is feasible or what is capable of being done, given current knowledge, irrespective of inconvenience or difficulty. Financial considerations do not enter the equation. It may be practicable or feasible to remove an obstruction from a gangway while the duty of reasonable care in negligence requires no more than that a warning be given.

To do what is 'reasonably practicable' often involves something more than the negligence test of reasonable care. Inconvenience and expense may be taken into account and a view may be formed on whether or not the necessary time and money are proportionate to the result to be achieved. Any such computation should be made before any accident occurs and with the benefit of all available current knowledge on the level of risk and the steps possible to reduce it.

The onus of establishing that something was not practicable or reasonably practicable lies on the defence in both civil and criminal actions.

There is a substantial body of case law on the application of the practicability and reasonable practicability tests in particular circumstances.

Employers are expected to be aware of official HSE publications, including Codes of Practice. They should also keep abreast of relevant recent legislation and statutory instruments published by the Stationery Office. They should also keep abreast of current technical publications and developments potentially affecting their product and/or business.

(*c*)   The breach of duty has caused the plaintiff injury. The same principle applies as in the law of negligence: an injured person will not recover damages from the employer unless he shows that it was the employer's wrongdoing which caused or contributed to his injuries. Where an employer has been at fault but that fault has not caused any injuries, no compensation is payable.

(*d*)   The injury was of the kind envisaged by the statute. There may be difficulties in proving that the nature of the injury was of the kind envisaged by the statute if the injury occurs in an unusual way which the provision was not designed to prevent. There are a variety of cases on this point dealing with particular circumstances. The tendency of the courts is to lean in favour of compensation for injured employees.

Defences

E11016   Contributory negligence may reduce the extent of the employer's liability in a civil action but it is rarely a complete defence. Where there is a breach of a duty imposed on the injured party personally, it is equivalent to contributory negligence.

The defence of *volenti non fit injuria* is not available in an action for breach of statutory duty.

In exceptional circumstances where the breach has occurred solely as a result of the plaintiff's conduct without any fault on the part of the defendant or anyone for whom he is responsible, the defendant will not be liable.

Duties under the Health and Safety at Work etc. Act 1974

E11017   *Duty owed by employer to his employees.* An employer owes a general duty to his employees to ensure their health, safety and welfare at work [*s 2*].

An employer or self-employed person, save where it is an educational establishment, owes a duty to his trainees even where there is no contract of employment with the trainee (see the *Health and Safety (Training for Employment) Regulations 1990 (SI 1990 No 1380)*).

The following aspects of the duty are highlighted [*s 2(2)(a)-(e)*]:

(*a*)   the provision and maintenance of safe plant and systems of work;

(*b*)   adequate arrangements for the safe use, handling, storage and transport of articles and substances;

(*c*)   the provision of information, instruction, training and supervision necessary to ensure health and safety;

(*d*)   the maintenance in a safe condition of the place of work and access to it and egress from it; and

(*e*)   the provision and maintenance of a working environment that is safe and without health risks, including adequate arrangements for the welfare of employees while at work.

There is a duty on every employer who employs five employees or more to prepare and revise as appropriate a written statement of his general policy on the health and safety at work of his employees and the arrangements in force for carrying out that policy. The statement and any revisions should be brought to the notice of the employees. Reference may be made to any no smoking policy. [*s 2(3)*].

There is a duty to consult any safety representatives appointed by a recognised trade union on safety matters. [*s 2(4)*]. This duty has recently been extended to any employees who are not members of a group covered by trade union safety representatives (see the *Health and Safety (Consultation with Employees) Regulations 1996 (SI 1996 No 1513)*).

Duty owed by employer and self-employed to those who are not employees. An employer owes a duty not only to his employees but also to those others who may be affected by the way he conducts his undertaking. The duty extends to members of the general public. He must ensure that their health and safety is not at risk. A self employed person owes the same duty. [*s 3(1) and (2)*].

Proof of harm is not necessary to prove a breach of this section. A risk or possibility of danger is sufficient.

Duty owed by those with control of premises to non-employees using the premises as a place of work. Where a person has a degree of control over premises, he owes a duty to those who use the premises as a place of work or for the use of machinery or substances to ensure that the premises and any machinery or substances in the premises are safe and without risks to health.

The duties set out above are not absolute but are qualified by the words 'so far as is reasonably practicable'.

Duty owed by employee. An employee owes a duty while at work to take reasonable care for the health and safety of himself and those who may be affected by his acts or omissions. He must co-operate with his employer so far as is necessary to enable him to comply with his duties. [*s 7*].

Management of Health and Safety at Work Regulations 1992 (SI 1992 No 2051)

E11018
The regulations are a new departure in the law relating to both statutory duty and negligence. They impose a positive duty on employers to investigate the existence of possible risks to health, irrespective of whether an employer has been put on notice of any risks. The assumption is that there may be risks even if there is no evidence of any.

A failure to implement the regulations is likely to be persuasive evidence of negligence.

Readers should note that, at the time of going to press, the Health and Safety Commission had published a Consultative Document containing proposals to amend the *Management of Health and Safety at Work Regulations 1992* (the Management Regulations) and revise their accompanying Approved Code of Practice (ACoP).

The proposed *Health and Safety (Miscellaneous Modifications) Regulations 1999* would introduce minor changes to the Management Regulations (and others), to clarify the UK's implementation of the European Framework Directive (89/391/EEC) following enquiries from the European Commission.

The proposed regulations would:

- clarify that employers should, where possible, use competent employees *in preference to* external sources for competent advice and assistance on health and safety;

- implement principles of prevention in the Regulations, rather than through the ACoP;

- include a specific requirement to arrange necessary contacts with emergency services regarding first-aid, emergency medical care and rescue; and

- make it explicit that employers cannot be afforded a defence for contravention of their obligations by reason of any act or default by employees or competent persons.

The ACoP has been revised to take account of the new regulations and previous amendments to the Management Regulations relating to: new or expectant mothers (the *Management of Health and Safety at Work (Amendment) Regulations 1994 (SI 1994 No 2865)* which implemented the European Pregnant Workers Directive), young people (the *Health and Safety (Young Persons) Regulations 1997 (SI 1997 No 135)* which implemented the Young Workers Directive), and fire safety (the *Fire Precautions (Workplace) Regulations 1997 (SI 1997 No 1840)* which implemented the fire precautions provisions of the Framework Directive). The ACoP also introduces general guidance material into the document in line with HSC's state-ment on the role and status of ACoPs and takes account of comments arising from HSC's earlier consultation exercise on changing patterns of employment.

On completion of the consultation exercise, it is HSC's intention to consolidate the Regulations, taking account of past amendments, and publish them alongside the revised ACoP.

'*Proposals for the Health and Safety (Miscellaneous Modifications) Regulations 1999 and the amendment of the Management of Health and Safety at Work Approved Code of Practice*' is available free of charge from HSE Books.

Risk assessments

E11019   The purpose of the employer's assessment is to identify any measures necessary to keep his employees safe. [*Reg 3*]. The duty is likely to extend to temporary workers.

Assessments must not be confined to employees but must extend to the health and safety of any person likely to be affected by the employer's undertaking.

Self-employed persons have identical duties which encompass the assessment of any risk to which they themselves might be exposed as well as the assessment of any risk to those affected by their undertakings or businesses.

Employers who share the same workplace should co-operate with each other in assessing risks and implementing preventative measures.

An employer of five or more employees must record in writing the significant findings of any assessment. The record should identify the risk, specify the group affected and set out preventative measures taken.

The Approved Code of Practice accompanying the regulations sets out the assess-ment required. This is a systematic examination of the workplace, examining the hazards present and the likelihood of their arising.

A Health and Safety Executive guide sets out a simple and practical approach which every employer should take.

The assessment should address the risk of stress.

The regulations have been amended to impose a specific duty towards new and expectant mothers. Where risks to the mother or her baby cannot be avoided, the employer should alter the working conditions or hours worked 'if it is reasonable to do so'. If such an alteration is not possible, the pregnant employee should be suspended.

Information

E11020   The employer should supply his employees with information on the risks identified. The same information should be provided to any other employer who shares the workplace. Information on risks should be provided to anyone working in the undertaking; that this duty extends to temporary workers. Employers of employees working in a host employer's undertaking must be informed of any risks and preventative measures adopted by the host employer.

An employer owes a duty to temporary workers, who are working under a fixed term contract or are employed by an agency, to provide them with comprehensible information on the qualifications or skills required to carry out the work safely and any health surveillance required to be provided [*Management of Health and Safety at Work Regulations 1992 (SI 1992 No 2051), Reg 13*]. Where temporary workers are provided by an agency, the necessary health and safety information must be provided to the agency for passing to the temporary staff. The employment agency must take all necessary steps to acquaint itself with the risks its employees will face, wherever they work, and to ensure their protection accordingly.

Control, monitoring and review

E11021   Where preventative measures are implemented, arrangements must be made for their control, monitoring and review. The arrangements must be recorded in writing where more than five persons are employed.

Competent assistance

E11022   Every employer, with certain limited exceptions, must appoint one or more competent persons to assist in undertaking the health and safety measures required. A competent person will have sufficient training and experience or knowledge to enable him properly to assist [*Reg 6*].

Health surveillance

E11023   Appropriate health surveillance must be provided where risks to health and safety have been identified by the assessment [*Reg 5*].

Duty to train employees in safe working practices

E11024   *Regulation 11* imposes a duty on an employer to ensure that his employees are provided with adequate health and safety training. This applies both to when they are recruited and on their being exposed to any new or increased risks. Training should also be provided when new working practices are introduced.

Employers using subcontracted labour are under a duty to train and instruct subcontract personnel where there is a risk to their safety. This is part of the general duty imposed by *s 3* of the *1974 Act*.

In entrusting an employee with a task the employer must take into account the person's capabilities as regards health and safety.

Employees are under a corresponding duty to act in accordance with the training given. Failure to do so can lead to prosecution and/or, more often, dismissal.

Arrangements for the provision of safety training should be included in a company's health and safety policy.

Procedures for serious and imminent danger

E11025   The employer must keep under review procedures to deal with serious and imminent danger, to appoint staff to take charge of evacuating buildings in emergencies (such as fire marshals), to take measures to prevent untrained staff from having access to places where particular hazards exist, and to permit employees to take action to save themselves (if necessary, without managerial approval) [*Reg 7*]. These procedures must be communicated to all employees [*Reg 8*].

Damages and limitation of actions

Egg-shell skull

E11026 Generally a defendant is only liable for the foreseeable loss and damage which will be caused by his negligence. However, an employer may well be liable for 'most' direct consequences, whether foreseeable or not, on the principle that a 'wrongdoer takes his victim as he finds him' (and that if he happens to have an egg-shell skull, so much the worse).

In *Smith v Leech Brain & Co Ltd [1961] 3 AER 1159* the plaintiff's husband had been a galvaniser at the defendant's factory. He suffered a burn on the lip from a splash of molten metal. The injury would not have happened if the employer had taken adequate statutory precautions. The burn led to terminal cancer, to which the deceased had a predisposition, as he had earlier worked in a gasworks. It was held that the employer was liable for the cancer. 'It has always been the law of this country that a tortfeasor takes his victim as he finds him . . . The test is not whether these defendants could reasonably have foreseen that a burn would cause cancer and that Mr Smith would die. The question is whether these defendants could reasonably foresee the type of injury which he suffered, namely, the burn' (*per* Lord Parker).

Moreover, when the act of a third person intervenes between the original act or omission (i.e. original act of negligence) and the damage, the original act or omission is still the direct cause of damage, if the intervention of the third person might reasonably have been expected: *Robinson v Post Office [1974] 2 AER 737* in which the appellant suffered a minor wound at work when he slipped on a ladder with an oily rung. He was given anti-tetanus serum and later developed encephalitis. The doctor had not followed the correct procedure for giving a test dose before administering a full dose. However, even if the test dose had been correctly given, the appellant would have shown no reaction. It was held that although the doctor had been negligent, his negligence had not caused encephalitis. The Post Office were liable for the encephalitis suffered by the plaintiff – they were bound to take the plaintiff as they found him, i.e. with an allergy to the serum.

Pure economic loss

E11027 Where a person suffers purely economic loss as a result of another's negligence, this loss has traditionally been considered to be too remote to be recoverable: *Weller & Co v Foot and Mouth Disease Research Institute [1965] 3 AER 560* where financial loss suffered by auctioneers as a result of the negligent escape of a virus which had infected cattle was found too remote to be claimed; and *Spartan Steel & Alloys Ltd v Martin (Contractors) & Co Ltd [1972] 3 AER 557* where the loss of profit from being unable to melt metal in the foundry as a result of an electric cable being negligently damaged was only recoverable loss if physical damage had been done as well. No remedy was available in respect of economic loss unconnected with physical damage. Economic loss following from physical damage can be recovered so long as it is foreseeable.

General and special damages

E11028   It would not be appropriate to discuss in any detail how damages for personal injury are assessed, save to say that damages are paid for pain and suffering as well as for economic losses. In the case of death the dependants are able to claim for the value of their lost dependency.

Limitation

E11029   The standard limitation period for personal injuries is three years from when the cause of action arose. There are a variety of complicated exceptions the effect of which, *inter alia*, that claims for industrial diseases can frequently be made many years after the exposure to the substance or thing which caused the injury.

Employers' Liability Insurance

Introduction

E13001
Most employers carrying on business in Great Britain are under a statutory duty to take out insurance against claims for injuries/diseases brought against them by employees. When such a compulsory insurance policy is taken out the insurance company issues the employer with a certificate of insurance, and the employer must keep a copy of this displayed in a prominent position at his workplace, so that employees can see it. It is a criminal offence to fail to take out such insurance and/or to fail to display a certificate (see E13013–E13015 below); however, such a failure does not give rise to any civil liability on the part of a company director (*Richardson v Pitt-Stanley [1995] 1 AER 460*. Here the plaintiff suffered a serious injury to his hand in an accident at work, and obtained judgment against his employer, a limited liability company, for breach of the *Factories Act 1961, s 14(1)* (failure to fence dangerous parts of machinery). Before damages were assessed, the company went into liquidation and there were no assets remaining to satisfy the plaintiff's judgment. The company had also failed to insure against liability for injury sustained by employees in the course of their employment, as required by the *Employers' Liability (Compulsory Insurance) Act 1969, s 1. Sec 5* of that Act makes failure to insure a criminal offence. The plaintiff then sued the directors and secretary of the company who, he alleged, had committed an offence under *Sec 5*, claiming as damages a sum equal to the sum which he would have recovered against the company, had it been properly insured. His action failed. It was held that the *Employers' Liability (Compulsory Insurance) Act 1969* did not create a civil as well as criminal liability). These duties are contained in the *Employers' Liability (Compulsory Insurance) Act 1969* (referred to hereafter as the '*1969 Act*') and in the *Employers' Liability (Compulsory Insurance) Regulations 1998 (SI 1998 No 2573)* (referred to hereafter as the '*1998 Regulations*'). In addition, the requirements of the *1969 Act* extend to offshore installations but do not extend to injuries suffered by employees when carried on or in a vehicle, or entering or getting onto or alighting from a vehicle, where such injury is caused by, or arises out of use, by the employer, of a vehicle on the road. [*1998 Regulations, Reg 9 and Schedule 2 para 14*]. Such employees would normally be covered under the *Road Traffic Act 1988, s 145* as amended by the *Motor Vehicles (Compulsory Insurance) Regulations 1992 (SI 1992 No 3036)*. As from 1 July 1994, liability for injury to an employee whilst in a motor vehicle has been that of the employer's motor insurers.

Purpose of compulsory employers' liability insurance

E13002
The purpose of compulsory employers' liability insurance is to ensure that employers are covered for any legal liability to pay damages to employees who suffer bodily injury and/or disease during the course of employment and as a result of employment. It is the liability of the employer towards his employees which has to be covered; there is no question of compulsory insurance extending to employees, since employers are under no statutory or common law duty to insure employees against

risk of injury, or even to advise on the desirability of insurance; it is their potential legal liability to employees which must be insured against (see E13008 below). Such liability is normally based on negligence, though not necessarily personal negligence on the part of the employer. Moreover, case law suggests that employers' liability is becoming stricter. The rule that employers must 'take their victims as they find them' underlines the need for long-tail cover because the employer may find himself liable for injuries/diseases which 'trigger off' or exacerbate existing conditions. (See further E11025 EMPLOYERS' DUTIES TO THEIR EMPLOYEES.)

An employers' liability policy is a legal liability policy. Hence, if there is no legal liability on the part of an employer, no insurance moneys will be paid out. Moreover, if the employee's action against the employer cannot succeed, the action for damages cannot be brought against an employer's insurer (*Bradley v Eagle Star Insurance Co Ltd [1989] 1 AER 961* where the employer company had been wound up and dissolved before the employer's liability to the injured employee had been established) (see below for the transfer of an employer's indemnity policy to an employee). The effect of this decision has been reversed by the *Companies Act 1989, s 141*, amending the *Companies Act 1985, s 651* which allows the revival of a dissolved company within two years of its dissolution for the purpose of legal claims and, in personal injuries cases, the revival can take place at any time subject to the existing limitation of action rules contained in the *Limitation Act 1980*. For example, in the case of *Re Workvale Ltd (No 2) [1992] 2 AER 627*, the court exercised its discretion under *Sec 33* of the *Limitation Act 1980* to allow a personal injuries claim to proceed after the three-year limitation period had expired. This meant that the company could also be revived under the provisions of *CA 1985, s 651(5)* and *(6)* (as amended). Thus, proceedings under the *Third Parties (Rights against Insurers) Act 1930, s 1, 1(b)* may be brought in this manner.

If the employer becomes bankrupt or if a company becomes insolvent, the employer's right to an indemnity from his insurers is transferred to the employee who may then keep the sums recovered with priority to his employer's creditors. This is only so if the employer has made his claim to this indemnity by trial, arbitration or agreement before he is made bankrupt or insolvent (*Bradley v Eagle Star Insurance Co Ltd [1989] 1 AER 961*). The employee must also claim within the statutory limitation period from the date of his injury (see E13007 below for subrogation rights generally).

The policy protects an employer from third party claims; an employee as such is not covered since he normally incurs no liability. Although offering wide cover an employers' liability policy does not give cover to third party non-employees (e.g. independent contractors and members of the public). Such liability is covered by a public liability policy which, though advisable, is not compulsory.

This section examines:

— the general law relating to contracts of insurance (see E13003–E13006 below);

— the insurer's right of recovery (i.e. subrogation) (see E13007 below);

— the duty to take out employers' liability insurance (see E13008–E13012 below);

— issue and display of certificates of insurance (see E13013 below);

— penalties (see E13014, E13015 below);

— scope and cover of policy (see E13016–E13019 below);

— 'prohibition' of certain terms (see E13020 below);

— trade endorsement for certain types of work (see E13021, E13022 below).

General law relating to insurance contracts

E13003   Insurance is a contract. When a person wishes to insure, for example, himself, his house, his liability towards his employees, valuable personal property or even loss of profits, he (the proposer) fills in a proposal form for insurance, at the same time making certain facts known to the insurer about what is to be insured. On the basis of the information disclosed in the proposal form, the insurer will decide whether to accept the risk or at what rate to fix the premium. If the insurer elects to accept the risk, a contract of insurance is then drawn up in the form of an insurance policy. (Incidentally, it seems to matter little whether the negotiations leading up to contract took place between the insured (proposer) and the insurance company or between the insured and a broker, since the broker is often regarded as the agent of one or the other, generally of the proposer (*Newsholme Brothers v Road Transport & General Insurance Co Ltd [1929] 2 KB 356)*.) However, a lot depends on the facts. If he is authorised to complete blank proposal forms, he may well be the agent of the insurer.

Extent of duty of disclosure

E13004   A proposer must disclose to the insurer all material facts within his actual knowledge. This does not extend to disclosure of facts which he could not reasonably be expected to know. 'The duty is a duty to disclose, and you cannot disclose what you do not know. The obligation to disclose, therefore, necessarily depends on the knowledge you possess. This, however, must not be misunderstood. The proposer's opinion of the materiality of that knowledge is of no moment. If a reasonable man would have recognised that the knowledge in question was material to disclose, it is no excuse that you did not recognise it. But the question always is – Was the knowledge you possessed such that you ought to have disclosed it?' (*Joel v Law Union and Crown Insurance Co [1908] 2 KB 863* per Fletcher Moulton LJ).

The knowledge of those who represent the directing mind and will of a company and who control what it does, e.g. directors and officers, is likely to be identified as the company's knowledge whether or not those individuals are responsible for arranging the insurance cover in question (*PCW Syndicates v TCW Reinsurers [1996] 1 Lloyd's Rep 241*).

An element of consumer protection, in favour of insureds, was introduced into insurance contracts by the Statement of General Insurance Practice 1986, a form of self-regulation applicable to many but not to all insurers. This has consequences for the duty of disclosure, proposal forms (E13005 below), renewals and claims. In particular, with regard to the last element (claims), an insurer should not refuse to indemnify on the grounds of:

(*a*)   non-disclosure of a material fact which a policyholder could not reasonably be expected to have disclosed; or

(*b*)   misrepresentation (unless it is a deliberate non-disclosure of, or negligence regarding a material fact). Innocent misrepresentation is not a ground for avoidance of payment.

The trend towards greater consumer protection in (*inter alia*) insurance contracts is reflected in the *Unfair Terms in Consumer Contracts Regulations 1994 (SI 1994 No 3159)*. These regulations which came into force on 1 July 1995 apply in the case of 'standard form' (or non-individually negotiated) contracts. [*Reg 3*]. They:

(i)   invalidate any 'unfair terms' therein, in favour of the insured [*Reg 5*] – an 'unfair term' being one which, contrary to the requirement of 'good faith'

[*Reg 4(3), 2 Sch*], 'causes a significant imbalance in the parties' rights and obligations, to the insured's detriment' [*Reg 3, 3 Sch*];

(ii)   require a written contract term to be expressed in plain, intelligible language, if there is doubt about the meaning of terminology, a construction in favour of the insured will prevail [*Reg 6*]; and

(iii)   where the seller/supplier claims that a term was individually negotiated, he must prove it [*Reg 3(5)*].

Complaints (other than frivolous or vexatious ones) relating to 'unfair terms' in standard form contracts, are addressable by the Director General of Fair Trading, who may prevent their continued use. [*Reg 8*]. See also P9056 PRODUCT SAFETY.

Filling in proposal form

E13005   Generally only failure to make disclosure of relevant facts will allow an insurer subsequently to invalidate the policy and refuse to compensate for the loss. The test of whether a fact was or was not relevant is whether its omission would have influenced a prudent insurer in deciding whether to accept the risk, or at what rate to fix the premium.

The arm of *uberrima fides* (i.e. the utmost good faith) is a long one. If, when filling in a proposal form, a statement made by the proposer is at that time true, but is false in relation to other facts which are not stated, or becomes false before issue of the insurance policy, this entitles the insurer to refuse to indemnify. In *Condogianis v Guardian Assurance Co Ltd [1921] 2 AC 125* a proposal form for fire cover contained the following question: 'Has proponent ever been a claimant on a fire insurance company in respect of the property now proposed, or any other property? If so, state when and name of company'. The proposer answered 'Yes', '1917', 'Ocean'. This answer was literally true, since he had claimed against the Ocean Insurance Co in respect of a burning car. However, he had failed to say that in 1912 he had made another claim against another insurance company in respect of another burning car. It was held that the answer was not a true one and the policy was, therefore, invalidated.

Loss mitigation

E13006   There is an implied term in most insurance contracts that the insured will take all reasonable steps to mitigate loss caused by one or more of the insured perils. Thus, in the case of burglary cover of commercial premises, this could extend to provision of security patrols, the fitting of burglar alarm devices and guard dogs. In the case of employers' liability, it will extend to appointment or use of services of an accredited safety officer and/or occupational hygienist, either permanently or temporarily, particularly in light of the *Management of Health and Safety at Work Regulations 1992 (SI 1992 No 2051)*, to oversee, for example, application of the *COSHH Regulations 1994*. Again, in the case of fire cover, steps to mitigate the extent of the loss on the part of the insured, might well extend to regular visits by the local fire authority and/or advice on storage of products and materials by reputable risk management consultants. Indeed, it is compliance with this implied duty in insurance contracts that accounts for the growth of the practice of risk management, and good housekeeping on the part of more and more companies.

Subrogation

E13007   Subrogation enables an insurer to make certain that the insured recovers no more than exact replacement of loss (i.e. indemnity). 'It (the doctrine of subrogation) was introduced in favour of the underwriters, in order to prevent their having to pay more than a full indemnity, not on the ground that the underwriters were sureties, for they are not so always, although their rights are sometimes similar to those of sureties, but in order to prevent the assured recovering more than a full indemnity' (*Castellain v Preston (1883) 11 QBD 380* per Brett LJ). *Subrogation does not extend to accident insurance moneys, whereby the insured (normally self-employed) is promised a fixed sum in the event of injury or illness (Bradburn v Great Western Railway Co (1874) LR 10 Exch 1* where the appellant was injured whilst travelling on a train, owing to the negligence of the respondent. He had earlier bought personal accident insurance to cover him for the possibility of injury on the train. It was held that he was entitled to both damages for negligence *and* insurance moneys payable under the policy (see further COMPENSATION FOR WORK INJURIES/DISEASES)). The right of subrogation does not arise until the insurer has paid the insured in respect of his loss, and has been invoked infrequently in employers' liability cases. In *Morris v Ford Motor Co Ltd [1973] 2 AER 1084* the Ford Motor Co had subcontracted cleaning at one of their plants to the X company, for which the appellant worked. Whilst engaged on this work at the plant, the appellant was injured owing to the negligence of an employee whilst driving a forklift truck. The appellant claimed damages from the respondent company for the negligence of their employee, on the grounds of vicarious liability. X company had, however, entered into a contract of indemnity with the respondent company, agreeing to indemnify the company for all losses or claims for injury arising out of the cleaning operations. Although accepting that they were bound by the terms of this contract of indemnity, the X company argued that they should be subrogated against the negligent Ford employee, on the ground that the employee had carried out his work negligently. It was held that the agreement by the British Insurance Association that they would not sue an employee of an insured employer in respect of injury caused to a co-employee, unless there was either (*a*) collusion and/or (*b*) wilful misconduct on the part of the employee, was binding and that the X company could not recoup its loss from the negligent employee.

Duty of employer to take out and maintain insurance

E13008   'Every employer carrying on business in Great Britain shall insure, and maintain insurance against liability for bodily injury or disease sustained by his employees, and arising out of and in the course of their employment in Great Britain in that business.' [*Employers' Liability (Compulsory Insurance) Act 1969, s 1(1)*].

Such insurance must be provided under one or more 'approved policies'. An 'approved policy' is a policy of insurance not subject to any conditions or exceptions prohibited by regulations (see E13020 below). [*Sec 1(3)*]. This now includes insurance with an approved EU insurer. [*Insurance Companies (Amendment) Regulations 1992 (SI 1992 No 2890)*].

There is no duty under the *1969 Act* to warn or insure the employee against risks of employment outside Great Britain (*Reid v Rush Tompkins Group plc [1989] 3 AER 228*) although the *1998 Regulations* require the employer to insure employees employed on or from offshore installations or associated structures – see E13009 below.

Employees covered by the Act

E13009   Cover is required in respect of liability to employees who:

(*a*)   are ordinarily resident in Great Britain; or

(b)   though not ordinarily resident in Great Britain, are present in Great Britain in the course of employment here for a continuous period of not less than 14 days; or

(c)   though not ordinarily resident in the United Kingdom, have been employed on or from an offshore installation or associated structure for a continuous period of not less than seven days.

[*Employers' Liability (Compulsory Insurance) Regulations 1998, Reg 1(2)*].

Employees not covered by the Act

E13010   An employer is not required to insure against liability to an employee who is (*a*) a spouse, (*b*) father, (*c*) mother, (*d*) son, (*e*) daughter, (*f*) other close relative. [*Sec 2(2)(a)*]. Those who are not ordinarily resident in the UK are not covered by the Act except as above. Nor are employees working abroad covered. Such employees can sue under English law in limited circumstances (*Johnson v Coventry Churchill International Ltd [1992] 3 AER 14* where an employee, working in Germany for an English manpower leasing company, was injured when he fell through a rotten plank. He was unable to sue his employer under German law; although he was working in Germany, it was held that England was the country with the most significant relationship with the claim because he had made the contract in England, his employers had covered him with personal liability insurance and he therefore expected them to compensate him through these insurers for any personal injury sustained in Germany).

Degree of cover necessary

E13011   The amount for which an employer is required to insure and maintain insurance is £5 million in respect of claims relating to any one or more of his employees, arising out of any one occurrence. [*Employers' Liability (Compulsory Insurance) Regulations 1998, Reg 3(1)*].

Between 1 January 1972 (when the *Employer's Liability (Compulsory Insurance) Act 1969* came into force) and 1994, insurers, in practice, provided unlimited cover under employers' liability policies. As from 1 January 1995, as a result of payments made in respect of claims exceeding the amount of premiums received during the period 1989–1993, unlimited liability was withdrawn, but most insurers continued to offer a minimum of £10 million indemnity for onshore work. A consultative document issued by the Department of the Environment, Transport and the Regions entitled *The Draft Employers' Liability (Compulsory Insurance) General Regulations [C4857 September 1997]* (hereafter referred to as 'the 1997 consultative document') which preceded the *1998 Regulations* assumed that this practice would continue.

Where a company has subsidiaries, there will be sufficient compliance if a company insures/maintains insurance for itself *and* on behalf of its subsidiaries for £5 million in respect of claims affecting any one or more of its own employees and any one or more employees of its subsidiaries arising out of any one occurrence. [*Employers' Liability (Compulsory Insurance) Regulations 1998, Reg 3*].

Insurers and the courts have interpreted the legislation to mean that all injuries resulting from one incident (e.g. an explosion) are treated as one occurrence, and each individual case of gradually occurring injury or disease is treated as an individual occurrence – the only exception being a situation where a sudden and immediate outbreak of a disease amongst the workforce is clearly attributable to an identifiable incident (e.g. the escape of a biological agent). The introduction to the

1997 consultative document suggested that this interpretation might be challenged and set out a possible alternative regulation to be used instead of what is now *Reg 3* of the *1998 Regulations* if clarification was felt necessary. This was not adopted so presumably the Government are now satisfied that the position is clear.

Exempted employers

E13012   The following employers are exempt from the duty to take out and maintain insurance:

(*a*)   nationalised industries;

(*b*)   any body holding a Government department certificate that any claim which it cannot pay itself will be paid out of moneys provided by Parliament;

(*c*)   any Passenger Transport Executive and its subsidiaries, London Regional Transport and its subsidiaries;

(*d*)   statutory water undertakers and certain water boards;

(*e*)   the Commission for the New Towns;

(*f*)   health service bodies, National Health Service Trusts;

(*g*)   probation and after-care committees, magistrates' court committees, and any voluntary management committee of an approved bail or approved probation hostel;

(*h*)   governments of foreign states or commonwealth countries and some other specialised employers;

(*j*)   Railtrack Group plc and its subsidiaries (the exemption ceasing when it is no longer owned by the Crown);

(*k*)   the Qualifications & Curriculum Authority.

There are other types of employer specified in the regulations, but these are the main exceptions. [*Employers' Liability Compulsory Insurance Act 1969, s 3; Employers' Liability (Compulsory Insurance) Regulations 1998, Schedule 2*].

Issue, display and retention of certificates of insurance

E13013   The insurer must issue the employer with a certificate of insurance, which must be issued not later than 30 days after the date on which insurance was commenced or renewed. [*Employers' Liability (Compulsory Insurance) Act 1969, s 4(1); Employers' Liability (Compulsory Insurance) Regulations 1998, Reg 4*]. Where there are one or more contracts of insurance which jointly provide insurance cover of not less than £5 million, the certificate issued by any individual insurer must specify both the amount in excess of which insurance cover is provided by the individual policy, and the maximum amount of that cover. [*Employers' Liability (Compulsory Insurance) Regulations 1998, Reg 4(3)*].

A copy or copies of the certificate must be displayed at each place of business where there are any employees entitled to be covered by the insurance policy and the copy certificate(s) must be placed where employees can easily see and read it and be reasonably protected from being defaced or damaged. [*Employers' Liability (Compulsory Insurance) Regulations 1998, Reg 5*]. The exception is where an employee is employed on or from an offshore installation or associated structure, when the employer must produce, at the request of that employee and within ten days from such request, a copy of the certificate. [*Employers' Liability (Compulsory Insurance) Regulations 1998, Reg 5(4)*].

An employee must, if a notice has been served on him by the Health and Safety Executive, produce a copy of the policy to the officers specified in the notice and he must permit inspection of the policy by an inspector authorised by the Secretary of State to inspect the policy. [*Employers' Liability (Compulsory Insurance) Regulations 1998, Regs 7, 8*].

A change introduced by the *1998 Regulations* is that employers are now required by law to retain any certificate of employers' liability insurance (or a copy) for a period of 40 years beginning on the date on which the insurance to which it relates commences or is renewed [*Employers' Liability (Compulsory Insurance) Regulations 1998, Reg 4(4)*]. Companies may retain the copy in any eye-readable form in any one of the ways authorised by the *Companies Act 1985, ss 722 and 723* [*Employers' Liability (Compulsory Insurance) Regulations 1998, Reg 4(5)*].

Penalties

Failure to insure or maintain insurance

E13014   Failure by an employer to effect and maintain insurance for any day on which it is required is a criminal offence, carrying a maximum penalty on conviction of £2,500. [*Criminal Justice Act 1991, s 17(1)*].

Failure to display a certificate of insurance

E13015   Failure on the part of an employer to display a certificate of insurance in a prominent position in the workplace is a criminal offence, carrying a maximum penalty on conviction of £2,500. [*Criminal Justice Act 1991, s 17(1)*].

In the 1997 consultative document, the Government suggests that penalties should be increased to become the same as those under the *Health and Safety at Work etc Act 1974*, i.e. fines of £20,000 in a magistrates' court and unlimited in the Crown Court. To implement this change will require primary legislation, and the Government says that it will be 'looking for opportunities in a Criminal Justice Bill'.

Cover provided by a typical policy

Persons

E13016   Cover is limited to protection of employees. Independent contractors are not covered; liability to them should be covered by a public liability policy. Directors who are employed under a contract of employment are covered, but directors paid by fees who do not work full-time in the business are generally not regarded as 'employees'. Liability to them would normally be covered by a public liability policy. Similarly, since the judicial tendency is to construe 'labour-only' subcontractors in the construction industry as 'employees' (see CONSTRUCTION AND BUILDING OPERATIONS), employers' liability policies often contain the following endorsement: 'An employee shall also mean any labour master, and persons supplied by him, any person employed by labour-only subcontractors, any self-employed person, or any person hired from any public authority, company, firm or individual, while working for the insured in connection with the business'. The public liability policy should then be amended to exclude the insured's liability to 'employees' so designated.

In the 1997 consultative document, the Government points out that the issue as to what constitutes 'an employee' cannot be completely resolved without primary legislation, but proposes to issue guidance on interpretation.

Scope of cover

E13017   The policy provides for payment of:

(*a*)   costs and expenses of litigation, incurred with the insurer's consent, in defence of a claim against the insured (i.e. civil liability);

(*b*)   solicitor's fees, incurred with the insurer's consent, for representation of the insured at proceedings in any court of summary jurisdiction (e.g. magistrates' court or Crown Court), coroner's inquest, or a fatal accident inquiry (i.e. criminal proceedings), arising out of an accident resulting in injury to an employee. It does *not* cover payment of a fine imposed by a criminal court.

The policy will often contain an excess negotiated between the insurer and employer, i.e. a provision that the employer pay the first £x of any claim. For the purposes of the *1969 Act*, any condition in a contract of insurance which requires a relevant employee to pay, or an insured employer to pay the relevant employee, the first amount of any claim or any aggregation of claims, is prohibited. Agreements will still be permitted which provide that the insurer will pay the claim in full and may then seek some reimbursement from the employer. [*Employers' Liability (Compulsory Insurance) Regulations 1998, Reg 2*].

Geographical limits

E13018   Cover is normally limited to Great Britain, Northern Ireland, the Channel Islands and the Isle of Man, in respect of employees normally resident in any of the above, who sustain injury whilst working in those areas. Cover is also provided for such employees who are injured whilst temporarily working abroad, so long as the action for damages is brought in a court of law of Great Britain, Northern Ireland, the Channel Islands or the Isle of Man – though even this proviso is omitted from some policies.

Employers must also have employers' liability insurance in respect of employees who, though not ordinarily resident in the United Kingdom, have been employed on or from an offshore installation or associated structure for a continuous period of not less than seven days; or who, though not ordinarily resident in Great Britain, are present in Great Britain in the course of employment for not less than fourteen days. [*Employers' Liability (Compulsory Insurance) Regulations 1998, Reg 1(2)*].

Conditions which must be satisfied

E13019   (*a*)   Cover only relates to bodily injury or disease; it does not extend to employee's property. This latter cover is provided by an employers' public liability policy.

(*b*)   Injury must arise out of and during the course of employment (see E11004 EMPLOYERS' DUTIES TO THEIR EMPLOYEES). If injury does not so arise, cover is normally provided by a public liability policy.

(*c*)   Bodily injury must be caused during the period of insurance. Normally with injury-causing accidents there is no problem, since injury follows on from the accident almost immediately. Certain occupational diseases, however, may not manifest themselves until much later, e.g. asbestosis, mesothelioma, pneumoconiosis, deafness. Here legal liability takes place when the disease manifests itself, or is 'discovered'. Moreover, at least as far as occupational deafness is concerned, liability between employers can be apportioned, giving rise to contribution between insurers (see further NOISE AND VIBRATION).

(*d*)   Claims must be notified by the insured to the insurer as soon as possible, or as stipulated by the policy.

Regulation 2 does not fetter the freedom of underwriters to apply certain conditions in connection with intrinsically hazardous work; for instance, exclusion of liability for accidents arising out of demolition work, or in connection with use of explosives.

'Prohibition' of certain conditions

E13020

All liability policies contain conditions with which the insured must comply if the insurer is to 'progress' his claim, e.g. notification of claims. Failure to comply with such condition(s) could jeopardise cover under the policy: the insured would be legally liable but without insurance protection. In the case of an employers' liability policy, an insurer might seek to avoid liability under the policy if the condition requiring the insured to take reasonable care to prevent injuries to employees, and/or comply with the provisions of any relevant statutes/statutory instruments (e.g. *HSWA; Ionising Radiations Regulations 1985*), or to keep records, was not complied with.

The object of the *1969 Act* was to ensure that an employer who had a claim brought against him would be able to pay the employee any damages awarded. Regulations made under the Act, therefore, seek to prevent insurers from avoiding their liability by relying on breach of a policy condition, by way of 'prohibiting' certain conditions in policies taken out under the Act. More particularly, insurers cannot avoid liability in the following circumstances:

(*a*)   some specified thing being done or being omitted to be done after the happening of the event giving rise to a claim (e.g. omission to notify the insurer of a claim within a stipulated time) [*Employers' Liability (Compulsory Insurance) Regulations 1998, Reg 2(1)(a)*];

(*b*)   failure on the part of the policy-holder to take reasonable care to protect his employees against the risk of bodily injury or disease in the course of employment [*Employers' Liability (Compulsory Insurance) Regulations 1998, Reg 2(1)(b)*]. As to the meaning of 'reasonable care' or 'reasonable precaution' here, 'It is eminently reasonable for employers to entrust . . . tasks to a skilled and trusted foreman on whose competence they have every reason to rely'. (*Woolfall and Rimmer Ltd v Moyle and Another [1941] 3 AER 304*). The prohibition is therefore, not broken by a negligent act on the part of a competent foreman selected by the employer. Where, however, an employer acted wilfully (in causing injury) and not merely negligently (though this would be rare), the insurer could presumably refuse to pay (*Hartley v Provincial Insurance Co Ltd [1957] Lloyd's Rep 121* where the insured employer had not taken steps to ensure that a stockbar was securely fenced for the purposes of the *Factories Act 1937, s 14(3)* in spite of repeated warnings from the factory inspector, with the result that an employee was scalped whilst working at a lathe. It was held that the insurer was justified in refusing to indemnify the employer who was in breach of statutory duty and so liable for damages). This was confirmed in *Aluminium Wire and Cable Co Ltd v Allstate Insurance Co Ltd [1985] 2 Lloyd's Rep 280*;

(*c*)   failure on the part of the policy-holder to comply with statutory requirements for the protection of employees against the risk of injury [*Employers' Liability (Compulsory Insurance) Regulations 1998, Reg 2(1)(c)*] – the reasoning in *Hartley v Provincial Insurance Co Ltd* (see (*b*) above), that wilful breach may not be covered, probably applies here too;

(*d*) failure on the part of the policy-holder to keep specified records and make such information available to the insurer [*Employers' Liability (Compulsory Insurance) Regulations 1998, Reg 2(1)(d)*] (e.g. accident book or accounts relating to employees' wages and salaries (see ACCIDENT REPORTING));

(*e*) by means of the use of an excess in policies [*Employers' Liability (Compulsory Insurance) Regulations 1998, Reg 2(2)*] – see E13017 above

Trade endorsements for certain types of work

E13021 There are no policy exceptions to the standard employers' liability cover. Trade endorsements, however, are used frequently in underwriting employers' liability risks, and there is nothing in the *1969 Act* to prevent insurers from applying their normal underwriting principles and applying trade endorsements where they consider it necessary, i.e. they will amend their standard policy form to exclude certain risks. Thus, there may be specific exclusions of liability arising out of types of work, such as demolition, or the use of mechanically driven woodworking machinery, or work above certain heights, unless the appropriate rate of premium is paid. This does mean that there are still circumstances where an employee will not obtain compensation from his employer based on the employer's insurance cover.

Measure of risk and assessment of premium

E13022 Certain trades or businesses are known to be more dangerous than others. For most trades or businesses insurers have their own rate for the risk, expressed as a rate per cent on wages (other than for clerical, managerial or non-manual employees for whom a very low rate applies). This rate is used as a guide and is altered upwards or downwards depending upon:

(*a*) previous history of claims and cost of settlement;

(*b*) size of wage roll;

(*c*) whether certain risks are not to be covered, e.g. the premium will be lower if the insured elects to exclude from the policy certain risks, such as the use of power driven woodworking machinery;

(*d*) the insured's attitude towards safety.

Many insurers survey premises with the object of improving the risk and minimising the incidence of accidents and diseases. This is an essential part of their service, and they often work in conjunction with the insured's own safety staff.

Extension of cover

E13023 In addition to employers' liability insurance, it is becoming increasingly common for companies to buy insurance in respect of directors' personal liability. Indeed, in the United States, some directors refuse to take up appointments in the absence of such insurance being forthcoming.

Employment Protection

Introduction

Legislative changes introduced by the Labour government have had a significant impact on the characterisation of the employment relationship. Government policy has been to promote a flexible labour market based on effective partnership at work. This policy reduces the importance of correctly categorising whether a person is a worker or an employee. Some employment protection is not dependent on there being a relationship of employer-employee as defined by established law. For example, the *Public Interest Disclosure Act 1998* applies to 'workers' and defines this term broadly, and the *Working Time Regulations 1998* apply to 'workers' which is a wider category than persons categorised as employees under traditional English employment law analysis.

As a result, this is a period of some change in terms of the approach taken by Parliament to employment protection and to employment law in general. The *Employment Relations Act 1999* is, at the time of writing, waiting to receive royal assent and is expected to enter into force soon. It introduces some important changes to the treatment of the employment relationship – including the relative roles of trade unions and individuals. Such topics as recognition of unions and consultation with employee representatives in various fields may take on a more significant role than has been the case in the last ten or fifteen years.

None the less, despite changes to the emphases of employment law, the employer-employee relationship retains its importance as a central concept in understanding how to interpret the employment relationship.

The relationship between an employer and an employee is a contractual one and as such must have all the elements of a legally binding contract to render it enforceable. In strict contractual terms an offer is made by the employer which is then accepted by the employee. This acceptance may be oral, in writing, or by conduct, for example by the employee turning up for work. The consideration on the employer's part is the promise to pay wages and on the employee's part to provide his services for the employer. Once the employer's offer has been accepted, the contract comes into existence and both parties are bound by any terms contained within it (*Taylor v Furness, Withy & Co Ltd (1969) 6 KIR 488*).

The contractual analysis of the employment relationship is not entirely satisfactory in explaining the relationship between worker and employer. To fit the contract model, various elements comprising the reality of the employment relationship become part of the contract by implication.

An employment contract is unlike many other contracts, because many of the terms will not have been individually negotiated by the parties. The contract will contain the express terms that the parties have agreed – most commonly hours, pay, job description – and there will be a variety of other terms which will be implied into the contract from other sources and which the parties have not agreed. Many of these are relevant to health and safety. If any of the express or implied terms in the contract are broken, the innocent party will have certain remedies. The fact that various employee rights, particularly in relation to health and safety, are implied into the contractual terms and conditions is important for this reason.

In addition to terms implied into the contract by the common law, statute (now the *Employment Rights Act 1996*) has created additional employment protection rights for employees, including some specific rights in relation to health and safety. These are in addition to detailed rights and duties arising from health and safety legislation and regulations which are discussed elsewhere. An employer will often lay down health and safety rules and procedures. While the law allows an employer the ultimate sanction of dismissal as a method of ensuring that safety rules are observed, such dismissals should be lawful, that is generally with notice, and should be fair. Furthermore, statute has created specific protection from victimisation for employees who are protecting themselves or others against perceived health and safety risks. All of these provisions are the subject of this section.

As a specific health and safety protection measure, the *Health and Safety at Work etc. Act 1974* ('*HSWA*') *s 2* lays a general duty on all employers to ensure, so far as is reasonably practicable (for the meaning of this expression, see E15017 ENFORCEMENT), the health, safety and welfare of all their employees

Sources of contractual terms

Express terms

E14002   These are the terms agreed by the parties themselves and may be oral or in writing. Normally the courts will uphold the express terms in the contract because these are what the parties have agreed, although if the term is ambiguous the court may be called upon to interpret the ambiguity, for example what the parties meant by 'reasonable overtime'.

Generally the express terms cause no legal problems and the parties can insert such terms into the contract as they wish, subject to the following:

(*a*)   An employer cannot restrict his liability for the death or personal injury of his employees caused by his negligence. Further, he can only restrict liability for damage to his employee's property if such a restriction is reasonable (*Unfair Contract Terms Act 1977, s 2*).

(*b*)   The terms in the contract cannot infringe the *Equal Pay Act 1970*, and the *Sex Discrimination Acts 1975* and *1986*.

(*c*)   The terms in the contract cannot infringe the *Race Relations Act 1976*.

(*d*)   The terms cannot infringe the *Disability Discrimination Act 1995*.

(*e*)   The employer cannot have a notice provision which gives the employee less than the statutory minimum notice guaranteed by *s 86* of the *Employment Rights Act 1996*.

(*f*)   Until the coming into force of the *Employment Relations Act 1999*, there was provision for an employee under a fixed term contract of one year or more to agree to waive the right to unfair dismissal. From the coming into force of the Act, this kind of waiver will no longer be possible. Any term which prevents the employee from suing for unfair dismissal is void. A term preventing the employee from pursuing a claim for a redundancy payment is void unless it is contained in a fixed term contract of two years or more (*Employment Rights Act 1996, s 203*).

(g)   Some judges have suggested that any express terms regarding hours are subject to the employer's duty to ensure his employee's safety and must be read subject to this, so that a term requiring an employee to work 100 hours a week will not be enforceable (see for example Stuart-Smith LJ in *Johnstone v Bloomsbury Health Authority [1991] IRLR 118*). More specifically, the provisions of the *Working Time Regulations 1998* affect the contractual term in relation to working hours. The Regulations implement the European Working Time Directive and set a maximum working week of 48 hours calculated over a 17-week reference period. In addition, the Regulations provide for an obligatory daily rest period, a maximum of night work and minimum annual leave and otherwise regulate working time. In *Barber v KTB Mining UK Ltd [1999] IRLR 308*, the court decided that the maximum imposed on weekly working time by the Regulations was part of the employees' contract. This decision gives some protection to employees who refuse to work beyond the statutorily stated maximum.

As well as preventing unlawful discrimination, the effect of the *Sex Discrimination Acts 1975* and *1986* has been to remove some of the restrictions on women and their employment generally and health and safety specifically. In particular, the *Sex Discrimination Act 1975* allowed machine attendants, for the purposes of the *Operations at Unfenced Machinery Regulations 1938 (SR & O 1938 No 641)* (which remained in force until 1 January 1997), to be women. Moreover, restrictions on the employment of women by night imposed in the *Hours of Employment (Conventions) Act 1936* were removed by the *Sex Discrimination Act 1986, s 7(1)*. The further restrictions on employment of women as regards hours of employment, holidays etc. specified in the *Factories Act 1961, ss 86-94* (and the corresponding restrictions of the *Mines and Quarries Act 1954*) have also been repealed by *s 7*.

However, some restrictions/prohibitions on certain types of employment by women, in the interests of health and safety at work, still remain.

Under the *Control of Lead at Work Regulations 1998 (SI 1998 No 543)*, which came into force on 1 April 1998, an employer is prohibited from employing women of reproductive capacity or young people in particular activities relating to lead processes as follows:

(*a*)   In the lead smelting and refining process:

(i)   handling, treating, sintering, smelting or refining any material containing 5 per cent or more of lead; or

(ii)   cleaning where any of the above activities have taken place.

(*b*)   In the lead acid manufacturing process:

(i)   manipulating lead oxides;

(ii)   mixing or pasting;

(iii)   melting or casting;

(iv)   trimming, abrading or cutting of pasted plates; or

(v)   cleaning where any of the above activities have taken place.

Common law implied terms

E14003   The court will imply terms into the contract when a situation arises which was not anticipated by the parties at the time they negotiated the express terms. As such, the court is 'filling in the gaps' left by the parties' own negotiations. The courts use two tests to see if a term should be implied, (i) the 'business efficacy' test (*The Moorcock*

(*1889*) *14 PD 64*) or (ii) the 'officious bystander' or 'oh of course' test (*Shirlaw v Southern Foundries Ltd [1939] 2 KB 206*). Once the court has decided, by virtue of one of these tests, that a term should be implied, it will use the concept of reasonableness to decide the content of the term. Often this will involve looking at how the parties have worked the contract in the past. For example, if the contract does not contain a mobility clause, but the employee has always worked on different sites, the court will normally imply a mobility clause into the contract (*Courtaulds Northern Spinning Ltd v Sibson [1988] IRLR 305*). Terms can also be implied by custom and practice. The test for this is relatively difficult to fulfil – the term must be notorious and certain and, in effect, everyone in the industry/enterprise must know that it is part of the contract. Arguments based on custom and practice come into play in relation to issues such as statutory holidays and redundancy policies.

Collective agreements

E14004   Collective agreements are negotiated between an employer or employer's association and a trade union or unions. This means that they are not contracts between an employer and his individual employees because the employee was not one of the negotiating parties. Some terms of the collective agreement will be procedural and will govern the relationship between the employer and the union; some, on the other hand, will impact on the relationship between the employer and each individual employee, for example a collectively bargained pay increase. As the employee is not a party to the collective agreement, the only way he can enforce a term which is relevant to him is if the particular term from the collective agreement has become a term of his individual employment contract. Procedural provisions, policy and more general aspirations are not suitable for incorporation into an individual contract of employment. Incorporation is important because the collective agreement is not a legally binding contract between the employer and the union (*Trade Union and Labour Relations (Consolidation) Act 1992, s 179(1)*) and thus needs to be a term of an employment contract to make it legally enforceable.

The two main ways that a term from a collective agreement becomes a term of an employment contract is by express or implied incorporation. Until recently, implied incorporation was the most common and was complex. It generally required the employee to be a member of the union which negotiated the agreement, to have knowledge of the agreement and of the existence of the term, and to have conducted himself in such a way as to indicate that he accepted the term from the collective agreement as a term of his contract. A recent EAT case, *Healy & Others v Corporation of London (24 June 1999)*, illustrates that habitual acceptance of the benefits of a collective agreement does not, in itself, lead to the conclusion that the terms of that collective agreement have become contractually binding on an individual employee. There can be many reasons for an individual to accept the benefits of collective bargaining which do not amount to an acceptance that the underlying agreement forms part of his or her contract.

Express incorporation meant that the employee had expressly agreed (normally in his contract) that any term collectively agreed would become part of his contract. This used to be unusual, but with the change made to the statutory statement which must be given to all employees (see below) employees must be told of collective agreements which apply to them, and this has been held as expressly incorporating those agreements into the contract.

Statutory statement of terms and conditions

E14005   By the *Employment Rights Act 1996, s 1* every employee no later than two months after starting employment, must receive a statement of his basic terms and conditions. The statement must contain:

(*a*)   the names of the employer and employee;

(*b*)   the date the employment began;

(*c*)   the date the employee's continuous employment began;

(*d*)   the scale or rate of remuneration and how it is calculated;

(*e*)   the intervals when remuneration is paid;

(*f*)   terms and conditions relating to hours;

(*g*)   terms and conditions relating to holidays;

(*h*)   terms relating to sick pay (if any);

(*i*)   terms and conditions relating to pensions;

(*j*)   notice requirements;

(*k*)   job description;

(*l*)   title of the job;

(*m*)   if the job is not permanent, the period of employment;

(*n*)   place of work, or if various the address of the employer;

(*o*)   any collective agreements which affect terms and conditions and, if the employer is not a party to the agreements, the persons with whom they were made;

(*p*)   if the employee is required to work outside the UK for more than one month, the period he will be required to work, the currency in which he will be paid, any additional benefits paid to him and any terms and conditions relating to his return to the UK.

The terms in (*a*), (*b*), (*c*), (*d*), (*e*), (*f*), (*g*), (*l*) and (*n*) must all be contained in a single document. In relation to pensions and sick pay the employer may refer the employee to a reasonably accessible document, and in respect of notice the employer can refer the employee to a reasonably accessible collective agreement or to the *Employment Rights Act 1996, s 86* which contains provisions relating to minimum notice periods.

In addition, if the employer employs more than twenty employees, he must give them details of any disciplinary and grievance procedures which apply to them. If the employer employs fewer than twenty employees, he must let them know to which person they can take a grievance – there is no requirement for him to give details of the disciplinary procedures. There is also no duty on any employer to give details of any disciplinary or grievance procedures relating to health and safety. Given the employer's duties under the *Health and Safety at Work etc. Act 1974, s 2*, however, and given the law relating to unfair dismissal, it is good industrial relations practice to ensure that all employees know of all the disciplinary procedures which could be invoked against them.

Works rules

E14006   Works rules may or may not be part of the contract. If they are part of the contract and thus contractual terms, they can be altered only by mutual agreement, that is the employee must agree to any change. It is unusual, however, for such rules to be contractual – to be so, there would have to be some reference to them within the contract and an intention that they are terms of the contract. The more usual position with regard to the employer's rules was stated in *Secretary of State for Employment v ASLEF (No 2) [1972] 2 QB 455* where Lord Denning said that they were merely instructions from an employer to an employee. This means that they are non-contractual and the employer can alter the rules without the consent of the employees. The fact that they are not contractual does not mean that they cannot be enforced against an employee. All employees have a duty to obey lawful, reasonable orders (see E14008 below) and thus failing to comply with the rules will be a breach of this duty and therefore a breach of contract. The only requirement that the law stipulates is that the order must be lawful and reasonable and it is unlikely that an order to comply with any health and safety rules would infringe these requirements.

Disciplinary and grievance procedures

E14007   It has already been noted that the employer must give details of grievance procedures to all employees. Failing to do so could lead to the employee resigning and claiming constructive dismissal (*W A Goold (Pearmak) Ltd v McConnell [1995] IRLR 516 and below*). In addition, if the employer employs more than twenty employees he must give details of the disciplinary procedures to those employees. Many employers adopt the ACAS Code of Practice on Disciplinary Powers and Procedures (1977) (as amended). This gives guidelines as to the sanctions which can be employed for breaches of the employer's rules. It seems that most employers have chosen to follow these guidelines to the extent of allowing employees to be accompanied to disciplinary hearings. However, the *Employment Relations Act 1999* will create a statutory right to be accompanied by a fellow employee or by a trade union representative during grievance procedures about serious issues and for disciplinary proceedings. This right will be enforceable in the Employment Tribunal and compensation payable for any failure. It is worth noting that fellow employees are under no duty to perform the role of accompanying individual.

Subject to the above, employers may establish their own disciplinary procedures. Such procedures may become part of the contract. If, for example, the employer gives the employee a copy of the procedures with the contract, and the contract refers to the procedures and the employee signs for receipt of the contract and the procedures, it is likely that they will be contractual. Employers may prefer their disciplinary procedures not to be contractual. If the procedures are contractual, any employee will be able to claim that his or her contract has been breached if they are not followed. This possibility also applies to those employees who have been employed for less than the one year qualifying period required to bring a claim for unfair dismissal. In response to a claim of breach of contract, a court may award damages against the employer. These damages are based on an assessment of the time for which, if the procedure had been followed, the employee's employment would have continued.

Common law implied duties

E14008   Both the employer and employee owe duties towards each other. These are duties implied into every contract of employment and should be distinguished from the implied terms discussed above which are implied into a particular individual contract. Although there are a number of different duties, three are of major importance for the purposes of this work: the duty on the part of the employee to obey lawful reasonable orders and to perform his work with reasonable care and skill, and the duty on the part of the employer to ensure his employee's safety. The duty to obey lawful reasonable orders ensures that the employer's safety rules can be enforced and, as it is a contractual duty, breach will allow the employer to invoke certain sanctions against the employee, the ultimate of which may be dismissal. The same is true of the duty to perform his work with reasonable care and skill. Should the employee be in breach of this duty and place his or others' safety at risk, the employer may impose sanctions against him including dismissal. The imposition of the employer's duty is to complement the statutory provisions. Statutes such as the *Health and Safety at Work etc. Act 1974* provide sanctions against the employer should he fail to comply with the legislation or any regulations made thereunder. The common law duty provides the employee with a remedy should the duty be broken, either in the form of compensation if he is injured, or, potentially, with a claim of unfair dismissal. The employer's duty to ensure his employees' safety is one of the most important aspects of the employment relationship. At least one judge has argued that it is so important that any express term must be read subject to it (see *Johnstone* at E14002 above). Breach of this duty can lead to the employee resigning and claiming constructive dismissal (see below). In *Walton & Morse v Dorrington [1997] IRLR 488*, an employee claimed that she had been constructively dismissed (unfairly) because her employer had breached the implied term of her contract of employment that it would provide, so far as reasonably practicable, a suitable working environment. The employee had been forced to work in a smoke-filled environment for a prolonged period of time and her employer did not take appropriate steps to redress the problem when she raised the issue. The EAT agreed that she had been constructively dismissed because the employer had breached its duty to her.

Employee employment protection rights

Right not to suffer a detriment in health and safety cases

E14009   By the *Employment Rights Act 1996, s 44* every employee has the right not to be subjected to a detriment, by any act or any failure to act, by his employer on the grounds that:

(*a*)   having been designated by the employer to carry out activities in connection with preventing or reducing risks to health and safety at work, the employee carried out (or proposed to carry out) any such activities;

(*b*)   being a representative of workers on matters of health and safety at work or a member of a safety committee –

   (i)   in accordance with arrangements established under or by virtue of any enactment; or

   (ii)   by reason of being acknowledged as such by the employer;

   the employee performed (or proposed to perform) any functions as such a representative or a member of such committee;

(*ba*)   the employee took part (or proposed to take part) in consultation with the employer pursuant to the *Health and Safety (Consultation with Employees) Regulations 1996* or in an election of representatives of employee safety within the meaning of those Regulations (whether as a candidate or otherwise);

(*c*)   being an employee at a place where –

   (i)   there was no such representative or safety committee; or

   (ii)   there was such a representative or safety committee but it was not reasonably practicable for the employee to raise the matter by those means;

he brought to his employer's attention, by reasonable means, circumstances connected with his work which he reasonably believed were harmful or potentially harmful to health or safety;

(*d*)　in circumstances of danger which the employee reasonably believed to be serious and imminent and which he could not reasonably have been expected to avert, he left (or proposed to leave) or (while the danger persisted) refused to return to his place of work or any dangerous part of his place of work; or

(*e*)　in circumstances of danger which the employee reasonably believed to be serious and imminent, he took (or proposed to take) appropriate steps to protect himself or other persons from the danger.

In regarding whether the steps the employee took or proposed to take under (*e*) were reasonable, the court must have regard to all the circumstances including the employee's knowledge and the facilities and advice available to him (*s 44(2)*). In *Kerr v Nathan's Wastesavers Ltd (1995) IDS Brief 548*, however, the Employment Appeal Tribunal stressed that tribunals should not place too onerous a duty on the employee to make enquiries to determine if his belief is reasonable. Various actions by the employer can constitute a detriment to the employee (such as disciplining the employee). Likewise, a failure to act on the part of the employer can also constitute a detriment (for example not sending the employee on a training course). Furthermore, the section is not restricted to the health and safety of the employee or his colleagues. In *Barton v Wandsworth Council (1995) IDS Brief 549* a tribunal ruled that an employee had been unlawfully disciplined when he voiced concerns over the safety of patients due to what he considered to be the lack of ability of newly introduced escorts. This shows that the legal protection is triggered in relation to any health and safety issue and includes cases where the employee voices concerns, and is not limited to only those circumstances where the employee commits more positive action. *Section 44(3)*, however, provides that an employee is not to be regarded as subjected to a detriment if the employer can show that the steps the employee took or proposed to take were so negligent that any reasonable employer would have treated him in the same manner. Furthermore, if the detriment suffered by the employee is dismissal, there is special protection under *s 100* (see below).

If the employee should suffer a detriment within the terms of *s 44* he may present a complaint to an employment tribunal (*s 48*). The complaint must be presented within three months of the act (or failure to act) complained of, or, if there is a series of acts, within three months of the date of the last act. The tribunal has a discretion to waive this time limit if it was not reasonably practicable for the employee to present his complaint in time. If the tribunal finds the complaint well founded, it must make a declaration to that effect and may make an award of compensation to the employee, the amount of compensation being what the tribunal regards as just and reasonable in all the circumstances (*s 49(2)*). The amount of compensation shall take into account any expenses incurred by the employee in consequence of the employer's action and any loss of benefit caused by the employer's action. Compensation can be reduced because of the employee's contributory conduct.

The protection from being dismissed or subjected to a detriment on the health and safety grounds specified in *s 44* and *s 100* of the *Employment Rights Act 1996* has been reinforced by a new, more general protection for whistleblowers.

The Public Interest Disclosure Act 1998 came into force on 2 July 1999. It is applicable not only to health and safety matters, but also offers protection to workers who whistleblow in relation to criminal acts, failure to comply with legal obligations, miscarriages of justice, danger to the environment and deliberate concealment of these matters. Under the Act, which inserts new sections into the *Employment Rights*

Act 1996, a worker who makes a 'qualifying disclosure' which he reasonably believes shows one of these matters, may be protected.

Disclosures are only protected if they are made to appropriate persons – which, generally, will mean that the employer ought to be approached in the first instance. There are other possibilities available under the Act: disclosure to a legal adviser, disclosure to a prescribed person (e.g. the FSA or the Inland Revenue), and a more general category for disclosures made provided that all the conditions specified are met. The *Public Interest Disclosure (Prescribed Persons) Order 1999 (SI 1999 No 1549)* deals with 'prescribed persons', i.e. organisations to whom a worker may 'blow the whistle';

In terms of health and safety risks, protection under the 1998 Act for proper disclosures is not limited to cases of imminent or serious danger – it can apply where the health and safety of any individual has been, is being or is likely to be, endangered. In all cases the worker must be acting in good faith.

If a disclosure is protected, any detriment to which the worker is subjected or dismissal made as a result will be unlawful. A dismissal in these circumstances will be deemed to be unfair, and there is no minimum qualifying period for entitlement to make an unfair dismissal claim for this reason. The *Public Interest Disclosure (Compensation) Order 1999 (SI 1999 No 1548)* provides that there are no limits on the compensation available to whistleblowers who are unfairly dismissed because they have made a protected disclosure.

Dismissal on health and safety grounds

E14010 In addition to the normal protection against dismissal (see below), where an employee is dismissed and the reason or principal reason for the dismissal is one of the grounds listed in *s 44*, the dismissal will be unfair. The only defence available to the employer applies when the dismissal was due to the actions taken by the employee to protect himself or others from danger that the employee reasonably believed was serious and imminent (*s 44(1)(e)* and *s 100(1)(e)*). The employer can escape a finding of unfair dismissal if he can show that the actions taken or proposed by the employee were so negligent that any reasonable employer would have dismissed. In respect of a dismissal falling within *s 100*, the normal qualifying period of employment does not apply nor does the upper age limit (*s 108(3)(c)* and *s 109(2)(c)*). Thus an employee who has only been employed for a few weeks or who is over the normal retirement age for the job can claim unfair dismissal for a breach of *s 100*.

The *Employment Relations Act 1999* removes any limit on compensation for any unfair dismissal on health and safety grounds.

Dismissal for assertion of a statutory right

E14011 By *s 104*, an employee will be deemed to be unfairly dismissed where the reason or principal reason for that dismissal was that the employee –

(*a*)   brought proceedings against an employer to enforce a right of his which is a relevant statutory right, or

(*b*)   alleged that the employer had infringed a right of his which is a relevant statutory right.

It is immaterial whether or not the employee has the right or whether or not the right has been infringed as long as the employee made it clear to the employer what the right claimed to have been infringed was and the employee's claim is made in good faith. A statutory right for the purposes of the section is any right under the *Employment Rights Act* in respect of which remedy for infringement is by way of complaint to an employment tribunal, a right under *s 86* (minimum notice requirements), or rights in relation to trade union activities under the *Trade Union and Labour Relations (Consolidation) Act 1992*.

This is an important right for employees. If, for example, after the employee has successfully claimed compensation from his employer for a breach of s *44* he is dismissed, the dismissal will be unfair by *s 104*. Again, if the employer unlawfully demotes or suspends without pay as a disciplinary sanction for breach of health and safety rules, and after proceedings against him for an unlawful deduction the employer dismisses the employee, this will be unfair by *s 104*. As with dismissal in health and safety cases under *s 100*, the normal qualifying period of employment does not apply – neither does the upper age limit.

Enforcement of safety rules by the employer

The rules

E14012   Given the statutory duty on the employer, under the *Health and Safety at Work etc. Act 1974, s 2*, to have a written statement of health and safety policy, and the common law duty on the employer to ensure his employees' safety, the employer should lay down health and safety rules, breach of which will lead to disciplinary action against the employee. These rules must be communicated to the employee and be clear and unambiguous so that the employee knows exactly what he can and cannot do.

The employer's disciplinary rules will often classify misconduct, e.g. as minor misconduct, serious misconduct and gross misconduct. It is unlikely that a tribunal would uphold as fair a dismissal for minor misconduct. It will underline the importance of health and safety rules if their breach is deemed to be serious or gross misconduct. The tribunal will, however, look at all the circumstances of the case – it does not automatically follow, therefore, if an employer has stated that a breach of a particular rule will be gross misconduct, that a tribunal will find a resultant dismissal fair.

The procedures

E14013   Once an employer has laid down his rules, he must ensure that he has adequate procedures to deal with a breach. The procedures used by an employer are scrutinised by a tribunal in any unfair dismissal claim and many an employer has lost such a claim because his procedures were inadequate. As discussed below, an employer in an unfair dismissal claim must show the tribunal that he acted reasonably. This concentrates on the fairness of the employer's actions and not on the fairness to the individual employee (*Polkey v A E Dayton Services Ltd [1987] IRLR 503*). This means that an employer cannot argue that a breach of procedures has made no difference to the final outcome and that he would have dismissed the employee even if he had adhered to his procedure. Breach of procedures themselves is likely to render a dismissal unfair regardless of which rule was broken. Following the introduction of a statutory rule in relation to the conduct of disciplinary proceedings (the right under the *Employment Relations Act 1999* to be accompanied – see E14007 above), the employer must be particularly careful that proper procedures are followed.

Many employers adopt the ACAS procedures. Essentially any disciplinary procedure should contain three elements: an investigation, a hearing and an appeal.

(*a*) *Investigation*

The law requires that the employer has a genuine belief in the employee's 'guilt', and that the belief is based on reasonable grounds after a reasonable investigation (*British Home Stores v Burchell [1978] IRLR 379*). If the employer suspends the employee during the investigation, this suspension should be with pay unless there is a contractual right to suspend without pay. An investigation is important because it may reveal defects in the training of the employee, or reveal that the employee was not told of the rules, or that another employee was responsible for the breach. In all of these cases, disciplinary action against the suspended employee will be unfair. Any investigation should be as thorough as possible and should take place as soon as possible. If other employees are to be questioned as witnesses, memories fade quickly. Likewise, taking too long a time to start an investigation may lead the employee to think no action will be taken and to then discipline him may itself be unfair.

(*b*) *Hearing*

Once the employer has investigated, he must conduct a hearing to make a decision as to the sanction he will impose. To act fairly, the employer must comply with the rules of a fair hearing. These are:

 (i)   The employee must know the case against him to enable him to answer the complaint. This also means that the employee should be given sufficient time before the hearing to enable him to prepare his case.

 (ii)   The employee should have an opportunity to put his side of the case, i.e. the employer should listen to the employee's side of the story and allow the employee to put forward any mitigating circumstances.

 (iii) The employee must be allowed to be accompanied at the hearing by a fellow employee or a trade union representative (*Employment Relations Act 1999*).

 (iv)   The hearing should be unbiased, i.e. the person chairing the hearing should come to it with an open mind and not have prejudged the issue.

 (v)   The employee should be informed of his right to appeal to a higher level of management which has not been involved in the first hearing. If the employee fails to exercise his right of appeal, however, he will not have failed to mitigate his loss, if ultimately a tribunal finds that he has been unfairly dismissed and thus his compensation will not be reduced (*William Muir (Bond 9) Ltd v Lamb [1985] IRLR 95*). Failing to allow an employee to exercise a right of appeal will almost certainly render any dismissal unfair (*West Midlands Co-operative Society Ltd v Tipton [1986] IRLR 112*).

(*c*) *Appeal*

In an unfair dismissal case a tribunal is required to consider the reasonableness of the employer's action taking into account the resources of the employer and the size of the employer's undertaking. This means that in the case of all but very small undertakings, the tribunal will expect the employer to have provided an appeal for the employee. All the rules of a fair hearing equally apply to an appeal. An appeal which is a complete rehearing of the case (rather than merely a review of the written notes of the disciplinary hearing) can rectify procedural flaws committed earlier on in the procedure. An appeal, however, cannot endorse the sanction imposed by the earlier hearing for a different reason, unless the employee has had notice of the new reason and has been given an opportunity to put his side of the case in respect of it.

Sanctions other than dismissal

E14014   There are a variety of sanctions, apart from dismissal, that an employer may impose. It is important, however, that the 'punishment fits the crime'. The imposition of too harsh a sanction may entitle the employee to resign and claim constructive dismissal (see below).

(a) Warnings

The ACAS Code recommends three warnings in cases of normal misconduct before dismissing: the first oral, the second written and a final written warning stating that a repetition will result in dismissal. These are only guidelines, however, and it clearly depends on the circumstances of the case. A minor breach of a health and safety rule, for example, may justify a final written warning given the potential seriousness of breaches of such rules. The ACAS Code urges that, apart from gross misconduct, no employee should be dismissed for a first breach of discipline, although, again, breaches of health and safety rules have been held to be gross misconduct. The Code also recommends that warnings should remain on the employee's record for a definite period of time (six to twelve months). Once this time has expired, the warnings will be ignored when looking to see if the procedure has been followed in later cases of misconduct, but can be considered when the employer is looking at the employee's work record to decide what sanction to impose.

(b) Fines or deductions

The employer must have contractual authority or the written permission of the employee before he can make a deduction from the employee's wages as a disciplinary sanction. Deducting without such authority is a breach of the *Employment Rights Act 1996, s 13* and gives the employee the right to sue for recovery in the industrial tribunal. It will also lead to a potential constructive dismissal claim.

(c) Suspension without pay

Any suspension without pay will have the same consequences as a fine or deduction if there is no contractual authority or written authorisation from the employee to impose such a sanction.

(d) Demotion

Most demotions will involve a reduction in pay, and thus without written or contractual authority the employer will be in breach of the *Employment Rights Act 1996, s 13* and liable to a constructive dismissal claim.

Suitable alternative work

E14015   Where an employee is suspended from work for health and safety reasons, the employer must offer suitable alternative work. Alternative work will only be suitable if:

(a)   the work is of a kind which is both suitable in relation to the employee and appropriate for the employee to do in the circumstances; and

(b)   the terms and conditions applicable for performing the work are not substantially less favourable than corresponding terms and conditions applicable for performing the employee's usual work.

If an employer fails to provide suitable alternative work, the employee may bring a claim before an employment tribunal which can award 'just and equitable' compensation. Such complaint must normally be lodged within three months of the first day of the suspension (*Employment Rights Act 1996, s 70*).

Remuneration on suspension from work

E14016 An employee who is suspended if no suitable alternative work is available is entitled to normal remuneration for the duration of the suspension. However, if the employee unreasonably refuses an offer of suitable alternative work, no remuneration is payable for the period during which the offer applies. An employee may bring a complaint to an employment tribunal if an employer fails to pay the whole or any part of the remuneration to which the employee is entitled (*Employment Rights Act 1996, ss 68, 70(1)*).

Dismissal

E14017 Dismissal is the ultimate sanction that an employer can impose for breach of health and safety rules. All employees are protected against wrongful dismissal at common law, but, in addition, some employees have protection against unfair dismissal. The protection against unfair dismissal comes from statute (the *Employment Rights Act 1996*) and therefore the employee must satisfy any qualifying criteria laid down by the statute before he can claim. Given that the protection against wrongful and unfair dismissal rest alongside each other, an employee may claim for both, although he will not be compensated twice. Wrongful dismissal is based on a breach of contract by the employer and compensation will be in the form of damages for that breach – that is, the damage the employee has suffered because the employer did not comply with the contract. Unfair dismissal, on the other hand, is statute created and is not based on a breach of contract by the employer. Compensation for such dismissal is based on a formula within the statute and not calculated on the loss suffered by the employee.

Wrongful dismissal

E14018 A dismissal at common law is where the employer unilaterally terminates the employment relationship with or without notice. A wrongful dismissal is where the employer either gives no notice or shorter notice than is required by the employee's contract and the employee's conduct does not warrant this. An employer is entitled to dismiss without notice only if the employee has committed gross misconduct – in all other circumstances the employer must give contractual notice to end the relationship, or pay wages in lieu of notice. This needs qualification, however. First, the law decides what is gross misconduct and not the employer. Just because the employer has stated that certain actions are gross misconduct does not mean that the law will regard it as such. Only very serious misconduct is regarded by the law as gross, such as refusing to obey orders, gross neglect, theft. Second, although the contract will lay down notice periods, the *Employment Rights Act 1996, s 86* lays down minimum notice periods, and any attempt by the contract to give less than the statutory minimum is void. These periods apply to all employees who have been employed for one month or more and are:

(*a*)   not less than one week if the employee has been employed for less than two years;

(*b*)   after the employee has been employed for two years, one week for each year of service, subject to a statutory maximum of twelve weeks.

The employee can waive his right to notice or accept wages in lieu of notice. If the contract gives notice periods which are greater than the statutory minimum, the contractual notice prevails. Therefore, if the employer has an employee who has been employed for six years, and the employer sacks him with four weeks' notice, the employee can sue for a further two weeks' wages in the employment tribunal. Finally, if the employer fundamentally alters the terms of the employee's contract, without his consent, in reality the employer is terminating (repudiating) the original contract and substituting a new one. The employee should therefore be given the correct notice before the change comes into effect.

Unfair dismissal

Dismissal

E14019   While all employees are protected against wrongful dismissal, generally employees must be employed for one year or more before they gain protection from unfair dismissal. In respect of certain reasons, however, an employee is protected immediately and does not need a year of employment. One of these is dismissal on certain health and safety grounds discussed above. The qualifying period was reduced from two years by way of statutory instrument with effect from June 1999.

The two-year qualifying period rule has been challenged as being discriminatory to women and the House of Lords has referred the issue to the European Court of Justice (*R v Secretary of State for Employment ex parte Seymour-Smith and Perez [1997] The Times 13 March*). The ECJ did not decide whether the two-year qualifying period was discriminatory but remitted this particular question to the House of Lords for determination on the facts in the United Kingdom – i.e. whether a significantly smaller proportion of women than of men could comply with the two-year qualifying period. The judgment was given early in 1999 and at the time of writing the House of Lords has not yet given a ruling. Pending the result of this case, a significant number of cases in the employment tribunal have been stayed. If the House of Lords finds that the two-year qualification period was indeed indirectly discriminatory towards women, individuals with a shorter period of employment who have lodged their claims in the tribunals may be able to take their claims forward.

The reduction of the qualifying period to one year only may have resolved any concerns about discrimination but, depending on the result in the *Seymour-Smith* case, this may be the subject of some debate.

Once an employee is protected against unfair dismissal the *Employment Rights Act, s 95* recognises three situations which the law regards as dismissal. These are:

(a)   the employer terminating the contract;

(b)   a fixed term contract which expires and is not renewed;

(c)   the employee resigning in circumstances in which he is entitled to do so because of the employer's conduct – a constructive dismissal.

The first situation is the same as the common law, that is the employer is unilaterally ending the relationship. Even if the employer gives the correct amount of notice so that the dismissal is lawful, it does not necessarily follow that the dismissal will be fair.

The second situation needs no explanation. If a fixed term contract has come to an end and is not renewed, this is, in effect, the employer deciding to end the relationship. Until the entry into force of the *Employment Relations Act 1999*, an employee who is on a fixed term contract of one year or more can, by a term of that contract, waive his right to sue for an unfair dismissal when the contract ends. Once the 1999 Act becomes effective, such a waiver will no longer be possible.

The third situation, the constructive dismissal, is much more complex. On the face of it the employee has resigned, but if the reason for his resignation is the employer's conduct, and the employee is protected against unfair dismissal (the general rule being, as seen above, that he has been employed for one year), then the law treats the resignation as an employer termination. The action on the part of the employer which entitles the employee to resign and claim constructive dismissal is a repudiatory breach of contract. In other words, the employer has committed a breach which goes to the root of the contract and has, therefore, repudiated it. This means that not all breaches by the employer are constructive dismissals but that serious breaches may be. It is also important to recognise that, as discussed above, the terms of the contract may include those which have not been expressly agreed by the parties and therefore rules, disciplinary procedures, terms collectively bargained, and all the implied duties discussed in E14008 above, may all be contractual terms. Breach of the health and safety duties owed to all employees will set up a constructive dismissal claim. In addition, the law requires that both the employer and employee treat each other with mutual respect and do nothing to destroy the trust and confidence each has in the other. Breach of this duty will establish a constructive dismissal claim. In one case, a demotion imposed as a disciplinary sanction was held to be excessive by the Employment Appeal Tribunal. Its very excessiveness was a breach of the duty of mutual respect which entitled the employee to resign and claim constructive dismissal.

Obviously, however, the employee must resign before he can make a claim for unfair dismissal. In the majority of cases the repudiatory breach by the employer is a fundamental alteration of the contractual terms (for example hours). In this situation, the employer still wishes to continue the relationship, albeit on different terms. The employee has two choices: he can resign or he can continue to work under the new terms. If the employee continues to work and accepts the changed terms, the contract is mutually varied and no action will lie, provided that the employee was given the correct notice before the change was implemented. If the employee resigns, however, he will have been dismissed. In *Walton & Morse v Dorrington [1997] IRLR 488*, the employee waited to find alternative employment before she resigned. The EAT decided that, in her circumstances, this was a reasonable thing to have done and agreed that she had not accepted her employer's breach of its duty to her and had been constructively dismissed (see E14008 above).

Reasons for dismissal

E14020   *Section 98* of the *Employment Rights Act 1996* gives five potentially fair reasons for dismissal. These are:

(*a*)   capability or qualifications;

(*b*)   conduct;

(*c*)   redundancy;

(*d*)   contravention of statute;

(*e*)   some other substantial reason.

Dismissal on health and safety grounds could potentially fall within most of these reasons. It should, however, be remembered that, where an employee is dismissed in circumstances where continued employment involves a risk to the employee's health and safety, the employer may be open to claims of unfair dismissal if an employee is dismissed under such circumstances. Before terminating employment, an employer should consider all the circumstances of the case and assess the risk involved and take measures which are reasonably necessary to eliminate the risk.

Illness may now make it unsafe to employ the employee; breach of health and safety rules will normally fall under misconduct; to continue to employ the employee may contravene health and safety legislation or it may be that the employer has had to reorganise his business on health and safety grounds and the employee is refusing to accept the change. This latter situation could be potentially fair under 'some other substantial reason'.

Reasonableness

E14021

Merely having a fair reason to dismiss does not mean that the dismissal is fair. *Section 98(4)* of the *Employment Rights Act* requires the tribunal in any unfair dismissal case to consider whether the employer acted reasonably in all the circumstances. This means that the tribunal will look at two things – (i) was the treatment of the employee procedurally fair, and (ii) was dismissal a fair sanction in relation to the employee's actions and all the circumstances of the case.

Procedures have already been discussed at E14013 above. If the employer has complied with his procedures, he will not be found to have acted unfairly unless the procedures themselves are unfair. This is unlikely if the employer is following the ACAS Code.

In respect of the fairness of the decision, the tribunal will look at three things – (i) has the employer acted consistently, (ii) has he taken the employee's past work record into account, and (iii) has the employer looked for alternative employment. The latter aspect is of major importance in relation to redundancy, incapability due to illness or dismissal because of a contravention of legislation, but will not be relevant in dismissals for misconduct.

When looking at consistency, the tribunal will look for evidence that the employer has treated the same misconduct the same way in the past. If the employer has treated past breaches of health and safety rules leniently it will be unfair to suddenly dismiss for the same breach, unless he has made it clear to the employees that his attitude has changed and breaches will be dealt with more severely in the future. Employees have to know the potential disciplinary consequences for breaches of the rules, and if the employer has never dismissed in the past he is misleading employees unless he tells them that things have changed. The law, however, only requires an employer to be consistent between cases which are the same. This is where a consideration of the employee's past work record is important. It is not inconsistent to give a long-standing employee with a clean record a final warning for a breach of health and safety rules and to dismiss another shorter-serving employee with a series of warnings behind him, as long as both employees know that the penalty for breach of the rules could be dismissal. The cases are not the same. It would, however, be unfair if both the employees had the same type of work record and length of service and only one was dismissed, and dismissal had never been imposed as a sanction for that type of breach in the past.

Remedies for unfair dismissal

(a) Reinstatement

E14022

The first remedy that the tribunal is required to consider is reinstatement of the employee. When doing so the tribunal must take into account whether the employee wishes to be reinstated, whether it is practicable for the employer to reinstate him and, if the employee's conduct contributed to or caused his dismissal, whether it is just to reinstate him. Reinstatement means that the employee must return to his old job with no loss of benefits. If reinstatement is ordered and the employer refuses to comply with the order, or only partially complies, compensation will be increased. Reinstatement, however, is rarely ordered by tribunals.

(b) Re-engagement

If the tribunal does not consider that reinstatement is practicable, it must consider whether to order the employer to re-engage the employee. In making its decision the tribunal looks at the same factors as when it considers reinstatement. Re-engagement is an order requiring the employer to re-employ the employee on terms which are as favourable as those he enjoyed before his dismissal, but it does not require the employer to give the employee the same job back. Failure on the part of the employer to comply with an order of re-engagement will lead to increased compensation, although tribunals rarely make re-engagement orders.

(c) Compensation

Compensation falls under a variety of different heads. In an unfair dismissal case the employee will receive:

Basic award: This is based on his age, years of service and salary –

(i)　　one and a half weeks' pay for each year of service over the age of 41;

(ii)　　one week's pay for each year of service between 41 and 22;

(iii)　　half a week's pay for each year of service below the age of 22.

This is subject to a statutory maximum of £220 a week (at present) and a maximum of twenty years' service. Compensation is reduced by one-twelfth for each month the employee works during his 64th year. Where the employee is unfairly dismissed for health and safety reasons under *s 100*, the minimum basic award is £2,900 (at present).

Compensatory award: This is payable in addition to the basic award to compensate the employee for loss of future earnings, benefits etc, which are in excess of the basic award. As with the basic award the compensatory award can be reduced for contributory conduct. The present maximum compensatory award is £12,000.

Additional award: If the employer fails to comply with a reinstatement or re-engagement order, the tribunal may make an additional award. This will be between 13 and 26 weeks' pay (at a maximum of £220 per week) if the dismissal is non-discriminatory, and between 26 and 52 weeks' pay if the reason for the dismissal was sex or race discrimination. These limits do not apply, however, when the combination of the basic and compensatory award would not fully reflect the actual loss sustained by the employee.

Special award: Where the reason for the dismissal was health and safety grounds under *s 100*, the tribunal must make a special award. (There are other reasons which attract a special award which will not be dealt with here.) This is one week's actual pay multiplied by 104 or £14,500, whichever is the greater, subject to a statutory maximum of £29,000. Where the tribunal orders reinstatement or re-engagement and the employer fails to comply, then the award is increased to one week's actual pay multiplied by 156 or £21,800, whichever is the greater. There is no statutory maximum in this circumstance. A special award can be reduced for contributory conduct or where the employee has prevented an order being complied with or has unreasonably refused an offer by the employer which would have had the effect of reinstating him. The amount of the reduction is what the tribunal considers to be just and equitable.

Note: The *Employment Relations Act 1999* will remove the limit on compensation for employees who are dismissed for health and safety reasons (see E14010). In addition, the maximum compensatory award will be increased to £50,000 and then subject to index-linked increases in the future. The Act will replace special awards with additional awards as a simplifying measure. In cases previously covered by special awards, the ex-employee will be entitled to an additional award.

The *Sex Discrimination and Equal Pay (Remedies) Regulations 1993 (SI 1993 No 2798)* abolished the limit on awards of compensation in sex discrimination and equal pay cases and made provision for interest to be included in such awards. Employers could therefore be faced with claims leading to the award of large amounts of compensation in cases of unlawful sex discrimination.

Health and safety duties in relation to women at work

Sex discrimination

E14023

Since health and safety issues may give rise to sex discrimination claims under the *Sex Discrimination Act 1976* (*SDA 1976*), it is appropriate to examine what particular considerations an employer needs to bear in mind in its relations with female employees.

The steps necessary to be taken by an employer, in order to comply with his duties under *HSWA s 2*, may differ for women.

New or expectant mothers are particularly vulnerable to adverse or indifferent working conditions. Indeed, most employers have probably taken measures to guard against risks to new and expectant mothers, in accordance with their general duties under *HSWA, s 2*, and the *Management of Health and Safety at Work Regulations 1992 (SI 1992 No 2051)* (see EMPLOYERS' DUTIES TO THEIR EMPLOYEES). In addition, the *Management of Health and Safety at Work (Amendment) Regulations 1994 (SI 1994 No 2865)* require employers to protect new and expectant mothers in their employment from certain specified risks if it is reasonable to do so, and to carry out a risk assessment of such hazards. If the employer cannot avoid the risk(s), he must alter the working conditions of the employee concerned or the hours of work, offer suitable alternative work and, if no suitable alternative work is available, suspend the employee on full pay (see E14024 below).

Although *SDA 1976* prohibits discrimination on grounds of sex, *s 51(1)* provides that any action taken to comply with certain existing health and safety legislation (e.g. *HSWA*) will *not* amount to unlawful discrimination. In *Page v Freight Hire (Tank Haulage) Ltd [1981] IRLR 13*, the complainant was an HGV driver. The employer, acting on the instructions of the manufacturer of the chemical dimethyl-formamide (DMF), refused to allow her to transport the chemical which was potentially harmful to women of child bearing age. She brought a complaint of unfair discrimination. It was held that the fact that the discriminatory action was taken in the interests of safety did not of itself provide a defence to a complaint of unlawful discrimination. However, the employer was protected by *s 51(1)* of *SDA* because the action taken was necessary to comply with the employer's duty under *HSWA*.

Pregnant workers, new and breastfeeding mothers

E14024   The *Management of Health and Safety at Work (Amendment) Regulations 1994 (SI 1994 No 2865)* which implemented the European Directive on Pregnant Workers introduced new *Regs 13A to 13C* to the *Management of Health and Safety at Work Regulations 1992*. The principal duty of an employer under these regulations is to protect new or expectant mothers from any process or working conditions or certain physical, chemical and biological risks at work (see E14025 below). The phrase 'new or expectant mother' is defined as a worker who is pregnant, who has given birth within the previous six months, or who is breastfeeding. 'Given birth' is defined as having delivered a living child or, after 24 weeks of pregnancy, a stillborn child.

Risk assessment

E14025   The 1994 regulations require employers to carry out an assessment of the specific risks posed to the health and safety of pregnant women and new mothers in the workplace and then to take steps to ensure that those risks are avoided. Risks include those to the unborn child or child of a woman who is still breastfeeding – not just risks to the mother.

An interesting development in relation to this requirement is the case of *Day v T Pickles Farms Ltd [1999] IRLR 217*, where the employee suffered nausea when pregnant as a result of the smell of food at her workplace. As a result of the nausea, she was unable to work and was eventually dismissed after a prolonged absence.

The EAT found that she had not been constructively dismissed, but decided that her employers should have carried out a risk assessment when employing her, a woman of childbearing age. The question of whether the applicant had been subjected to a detriment was remitted to the employment tribunal.

The EAT's interpretation of the *Management of Health and Safety at Work Regulations 1992* was that the obligation to carry out a risk assessment which considers possible risks to the health and safety of a pregnant female employee is relevant from the moment an employer employs a woman of childbearing age.

The Health and Safety Executive has published a booklet entitled '*New and expectant mothers at work – A guide for employers*'. The booklet provides guidance on what employers need to do to comply with the legislation. The booklet includes a list of the known risks to new and expectant mothers and suggests methods of avoidance.

The main risks to be avoided are as follows:

(*a*)   Physical agents:

—   shocks/vibrations/movement (including travelling and other physical burdens),

—   handling of loads entailing risks,

—   noise,

—   non-ionising radiation,

—   extremes of heat and cold.

(*b*)   Biological agents:

— such as listeria, rubella and chicken pox virus, toxoplasma, cytomega-lovirus, hepatitis B and HIV.

(*c*)   Chemical agents:

— such as mercury, antimiotic drugs, carbon monoxide, chemical agents of known and percutaneous absorption and chemicals listed under various Directives.

(*d*)   Working conditions:

— such as mining work and work with display screen equipment (VDUs).

Where a risk has been identified following the assessment, affected employees or their representatives should be informed of the risk and the preventive measures to be adopted. The assessment should be kept under review.

In particular, employers must consider removing the hazard or seek to prevent exposure to it. If a risk remains after preventive action has been taken, the employer must take the following course of action:

(i)   temporarily adjust her working conditions or hours of work (*Management of Health and Safety at Work Regulations 1992, Reg 13A(2)*).

If it is not reasonable to do so or would not avoid the risk:

(ii)   offer suitable alternative work (*Employment Rights Act 1996, s 67*).

If neither of the above options is viable:

(iii)   suspend her on full pay for as long as necessary to protect her health and safety or that of her child (*Management of Health and Safety at Work Regulations 1992, Regs 13A(3) and 13B; Employment Rights Act 1996, s 67*).

Appendix 1 of the booklet lists aspects of pregnancy such as morning sickness, varicose veins, increasing size etc. that may affect work and which employers may take into account in considering working arrangements for pregnant and breastfeeding workers. These are merely suggestions and not requirements of the law.

Night work by new or expectant mother

E14026   Where a new or expectant mother works at night and has been issued with a certificate from a registered doctor or midwife stating that night work would affect her health and safety, the employer must first offer her suitable alternative daytime work, and suspend her as detailed at E14015 above if no suitable alternative employment can be found (*Management of Health and Safety at Work (Amendment) Regulations 1994, Reg 13B*).

Notification

E14027   An employer is not required to alter a woman's working conditions or hours of work or suspend her from work until she notifies him in writing that she is pregnant, has given birth within the previous six months or is breastfeeding. Additionally, the amended working conditions do not have to be maintained if the employee fails to produce a medical certificate confirming her pregnancy in writing within a reasonable time if the employer requests her to do so. The exemption also applies once the employer knows that the employee is no longer a new or expectant mother or if the employer cannot establish whether she remains so. However, an employer has a general duty under *HSWA* and the *Management of Health and Safety at Work*

Regulations 1992 to take steps to protect the health and safety of a new or expectant mother, even if she has not given written notification of her condition.

Maternity leave

E14028   All pregnant workers have a right to 14 weeks' maternity leave, regardless of length of service and number of hours worked. The maternity leave period starts from:

(*a*)   the notified date of commencement; or

(*b*)   the first day of absence because of pregnancy or childbirth after the beginning of the sixth week before the expected week of confinement; or

(*c*)   the date of childbirth;

and continues for 14 weeks or until the birth of the child, whichever is later (*Employment Rights Act 1996, ss 71-73*).

If an employee is prohibited from working for a specified period after childbirth by virtue of a legislative requirement (e.g. under the *Public Health Act 1936, s 205*), her maternity leave period must continue until the expiry of that later period. The *Maternity Leave (Compulsory Leave) Regulations 1994 (SI 1994 No 2479)* provide that an employee entitled to maternity leave should not work or be permitted to work by her employer during the period of two weeks beginning with the date of childbirth.

Enforcement

Introduction

E15001 In the last decade there has been a movement away from a purely legalistic approach towards health and safety at work to one concerned with loss prevention, asset protection, accountability and consultation with the workforce, a situation without parallel under previous protective legislation. An effective system of enforcement is still, however, essential if workplaces are to be kept safe and accidents prevented. Prior to the *Health and Safety at Work etc. Act 1974 (HSWA)*, the principal sanction against breach of a statutory requirement was prosecution. This preoccupation with criminal proceedings was criticised by the Robens Committee (para 142) as being largely ineffective in securing the most important end result, namely that the breach should be remedied as soon as possible. *HSWA*, therefore, has given HSE inspectors a range of enforcement powers which do not necessarily depend on prosecution for their efficacy. Most important of these are the powers to serve improvement and prohibition notices. Contravention of an improvement/prohibition notice carries with it, on summary conviction, a maximum fine of £20,000 or, alternatively, six months' imprisonment and on conviction on indictment an unlimited fine or two years' imprisonment (see E15028 below). In particular, a prohibition notice may be served by an inspector where he believes there to be a risk of serious personal injury, regardless of whether any offence has actually been committed. Equally important, though less obvious perhaps, HSE inspectors and environmental health officers, the two principal enforcement authorities, can use powers given to them by *HSWA*, i.e. serve improvement and prohibition notices, in order to enforce remaining pre-*HSWA* statutory requirements, e.g. duties under the *Factories Act 1961* and *Offices, Shops and Railway Premises Act 1963 (OSRPA)*, since these qualify as 'relevant statutory provisions' (see E15002 below). Recently, however, greater enforcement powers have been conferred on local authorities by the *Health and Safety (Enforcing Authority) Regulations 1989 (SI 1989 No 1903)* (see E15004 below).

More recently, the *Environmental Protection Act 1990* and the *Environment Act 1995* have conferred similar notice-serving powers on the Environment Agency. The *Radioactive Material (Road Transport) Act 1991* has given transport inspectors powers to detain, search and generally 'quarantine' vehicles carrying radioactive packages in breach of that Act and the *Radioactive Substances Act 1993* similarly empowers inspectors in respect of premises containing radioactive substances and mobile radioactive apparatus.

Such enforcement powers apart, breach of a statutory requirement is still a criminal offence. Prosecution, albeit a 'reserve weapon', is an important one; in 1994/95 there were nearly 2,300 prosecutions for health and safety offences. Persons committing a breach, or permitting one to occur, should be in no doubt that they stand to be prosecuted. It is not just the employer who is liable to prosecution: employees and junior and middle management and even visitors to the workplace can also be prosecuted, either in tandem with the employer or alone. If the employer is a company or local authority, the company, its directors and/or officers, as well as councillors may be charged with an offence (see E15032 below).

Prosecutions and other enforcement procedures are the responsibility of the appropriate 'enforcing authority' (see E15003–E15005 below). In addition, where an employee is injured or killed as a result of negligence or breach of a statutory requirement, a civil action may be brought against the employer for damages. (Although possibly an additional form of enforcement, civil liability is mainly discussed in EMPLOYERS' DUTIES TO THEIR EMPLOYEES.)

This section deals with the following aspects of enforcement:

— The 'relevant statutory provisions' which can be enforced under *HSWA* (see E15002 below).

— The 'enforcing authorities' (see E15003–E15005 below).

Part A: Enforcement Powers of Inspectors

— Improvement and prohibition notices (see E15006–E15011 below).

— Appeals against improvement and prohibition notices (see E15012, E15013 below).

— Grounds for appeal against a notice (see E15014–E15018 below).

— Inspectors' investigation powers (see E15019 below).

— Inspectors' powers of search and seizure (see E15020 below).

— Indemnification by enforcing authority (see E15021 below).

— Public register of notices (see E15022 below).

Part B: Offences and Penalties

— Prosecution for contravention of the relevant statutory provisions (see E15023, E15024 below).

— Main offences and penalties (see E15025–E15030 below).

— Offences committed by particular types of persons, including the Crown (see E15031–E15035 below).

(For offences under the *Environmental Protection Act 1990* see EMISSIONS INTO THE ATMOSPHERE.)

'Relevant statutory provisions' covered by the Health and Safety at Work etc. Act 1974

E15002   The enforcement powers conferred by *HSWA* extend to any of the 'relevant statutory provisions'. These comprise:

(*a*)   the provisions of *HSWA Part I* (i.e. *ss 1–53*); and

(*b*)   any health and safety regulations passed under *HSWA*, e.g. the *Ionising Radiations Regulations 1985 (SI 1985 No 1333)*, the *Management of Health and Safety at Work Regulations 1992 (SI 1992 No 2051)* and the *Workplace (Health, Safety and Welfare) Regulations 1992 (SI 1992 No 3004)*; and

(*c*)   the 'existing statutory provisions', i.e. all enactments specified in *HSWA Sch 1*, including any regulations etc. made under them, so long as they continue to have effect; that is, the *Explosives Acts 1875–1923*, the *Mines and Quarries Act 1954*, the *Factories Act 1961*, the *Public Health Act 1961*, the *Offices, Shops and Railway Premises Act 1963* and (by dint of the *Offshore Safety Act 1992*) the *Mineral Workings (Offshore Installations) Act 1971* [*HSWA s 53(1)*].

Enforcing authorities

The Health and Safety Executive (HSE)

E15003   The HSE is the central body entrusted with the enforcement of health and safety legislation (see HEALTH AND SAFETY COMMISSION AND EXECUTIVE). In any given case, however, enforcement powers rest with the body which is expressed by statute to be the 'enforcing authority'. Here the general rule is that the 'enforcing authority', in the case of industrial premises, is the HSE and, in the case of commercial premises within its area, the local authority (the enforcing authority in over a million premises), except that the HSE cannot enforce provisions in respect of its own premises, and similarly, local authorities' premises are inspected by the HSE. Each 'enforcing authority' is empowered to appoint suitably qualified persons as inspectors for the purpose of carrying into effect the 'relevant statutory provisions' within the authority's field of responsibility. [*HSWA s 19(1)*]. Inspectors so appointed can exercise any of the enforcement powers conferred by *HSWA* (see E15006–E15011 below) and bring prosecutions (see E15023, E15024 below).

The appropriate 'enforcing authority'

E15004   The general rule is that the HSE is the enforcing authority, except to the extent that:

(*a*)   regulations specify that the local authority is the enforcing authority instead; the regulations that so specify are the *Health and Safety (Enforcing Authority) Regulations 1989 (SI 1989 No 1903)*; or

(*b*)   one of the 'relevant statutory provisions' specifies that some other body is responsible for the enforcement of a particular requirement.

[*HSWA s 18(1), (7)(a)*].

Table 1

Activities for which the HSE is the enforcing authority

The HSE is specifically the enforcing authority in respect of the following activities (even though the main activity on the premises is listed in *Sch 1*, see below). Note that water and telecommunications systems are now excluded under the *1989 Regs*.

1.   Any activity in a mine or quarry;

2.   fairground activity;

3.   any activity in premises occupied by a radio, television or film undertaking, where broadcasting, recording, filming, or video-recording is carried on;

4.   (*a*)   construction work (with modifications);

    (*b*)   installation, maintenance or repair of gas systems or work in connection with a gas fitting;

    (*c*)   installation, maintenance or repair of electricity systems;

    (*d*)   work with ionising radiations;

---

5. use of ionising radiations for medical exposure;

6. any activity in radiography premises where work with ionising radiations is carried on;

7. agricultural activities, including agricultural shows;

8. any activity on board a sea-going ship;

9. ski slope, ski lift, ski tow or cable car activities;

10. fish, maggot and game breeding (but not in a zoo).

[*Health and Safety (Enforcing Authority) Regulations 1989 (SI 1989 No 1903), Reg 4(5)(b) and Sch 2*].

The HSE is the enforcing authority against the following, and for any premises they occupy, including parts of the premises occupied by others providing services for them. (This is so even though the main activity is listed in 1 Sch, see below.)

11. Local authorities;

12. parish councils and community councils;

13. police authorities;

14. fire authorities;

15. international HQs and defence organisations and visiting forces;

16. United Kingdom Atomic Energy Authority (UKAEA);

17. the Crown (except where premises are occupied by HSE itself).

The HSE is also the enforcing authority for:

18. indoor sports activity (with conditions);

19. enforcement of HSWA s 6 (duties of manufacturers/suppliers of industrial products).

[*Health and Safety (Enforcing Authority) Regulations 1989, Reg 4(3)(4) and Sch 1*].

20. Offshore installations. [*Offshore Safety (Repeals and Modifications) Regulations 1993*].

Table 2

Activities for which local authorities are the enforcing authorities

Where the main activity carried on in non-domestic premises is one of the following, the local authority is the enforcing authority (i.e. the relevant county, district or borough council).

1. Sale or storage of goods for retail/wholesale distribution (including sale and fitting of motor car tyres, exhausts, windscreens or sunroofs), except:

   (*a*) where it is part of a transport undertaking;

(*b*)   at container depots where the main activity is the storage of goods in course of transit to or from dock premises, an airport or railway;

(*c*)   where the main activity is the sale or storage for wholesale distribution of any dangerous substances;

(*d*)   where the main activity is the sale or storage of water or sewage or their by-products or natural or town gas;

2.   display or demonstration of goods at an exhibition, being offered or advertised for sale;

3.   office activities;

4.   catering services;

5.   provision of permanent or temporary residential accommodation, including sites for caravans or campers;

6.   consumer services provided in a shop, except:

(i)   dry cleaning;

(ii)   radio/television repairs;

7.   cleaning (wet or dry) in coin-operated units in launderettes etc.;

8.   baths, saunas, solariums, massage parlours, premises for hair transplant, skin piercing, manicuring or other cosmetic services and therapeutic treatments, except where supervised by a doctor, dentist, physiotherapist, osteopath or chiropractor;

9.   practice or presentation of arts, sports, games, entertainment or other cultural/recreational activities, unless carried on:

(*a*)   in a museum;

(*b*)   in an art gallery;

(*c*)   in a theatre;

(*d*)   where the main activity is the exhibition of a cave to the public;

10.   hiring out of pleasure craft for use on inland waters;

11.   care, treatment, accommodation or exhibition of animals, birds or other creatures, except where the main activity is:

(i)   horse breeding/horse training at stables;

(ii)   agricultural activity;

(iii)   veterinary surgery;

12.   undertaking, but not embalming or coffin making;

13.   church worship/religious meetings;

[*Health and Safety (Enforcing Authority) Regulations 1989, Reg 3(1) and Sch 1*].

14.   temporary grandstands.

> Where non-domestic premises are occupied by more than one occupier, each part separately occupied is 'separate premises', for the purposes of enforcement. [*Reg 3(2)*]. This, however, does not apply in the case of:
>
> (*a*)   airport land;
>
> (*b*)   the Channel Tunnel system;
>
> (*c*)   offshore installations;
>
> (*d*)   building/construction sites;
>
> (*e*)   university, polytechnic, college, school etc. campuses;
>
> (*f*)   hospitals;
>
> where HSE is the enforcing authority for the whole of the premises. [*Reg 3(4) and Sch 1*].

The division of enforcement responsibility between the HSE and local authorities in the 1989 Regulations, as set out in the tables above, was amended in 1998. The *Health and Safety (Enforcing Authority) Regulations 1998 (SI 1998 No 494)* came into force on 1 April 1998. They revoke and re-enact with amendments the *Health and Safety (Enforcing Authority) Regulations 1989*, which determined whether responsibility for enforcement of the *Health and Safety at Work etc. Act 1974* and the other relevant statutory provisions within the meaning of that Act should rest with local authorities or with the Health and Safety Executive (HSE). The revised regulations, which follow a similar structure to the 1989 regulations, are designed to minimise the need for dual inspection of premises by the HSE and local authorities.

Thus *reg 3(1)* provides that local authorities are the enforcing authority for such activities as are listed in *Sch 1*. These include most situations involving the storage of goods for wholesale or retail distribution – or the sale of goods – and such activities as:

- office activities;

- catering services;

- the provision of residential accommodation;

- consumer services provided in a shop (except dry-cleaning services or radio and television repairs);

- the practice or presentation of the arts, sports, games, entertainment or other cultural or recreational activities;

- the provision of child care, or playgroup or nursery facilities.

Schedule 2 lists activities in respect of which the Health and Safety Executive is the enforcing authority. These include:

- any activity in a fairground;

- any activity in a mine or quarry;

- agricultural activities (activities at a garden centre are excluded from the definition of 'agricultural activities');

- the installation or repair of a gas or electricity system.

David Eves, Deputy Director General of the HSE, and co-Chair of the HSE/Local Authority Enforcement Liaison Committee (HELA) said, 'There have been considerable changes in the workplace since the Regulations were last updated in 1989.

Although some of these changes have resulted in increased safety for workers and a reduction in those risks that are harmful to health, it is important that employers, workers and others clearly understand which authority has responsibility for enforcing health and safety legislation to make the work activities better still.

'The HSE has consulted local authorities, industry and independent health and safety specialists to make sure that there is agreement that these revisions ensure an appropriate and clear allocation of enforcement responsibility between HSE inspectors and local authority inspectors.'

The main changes are the transfer to local authorities of enforcement responsibility for:

● pre-school childcare except where they are in domestic premises;

● storage of goods in retail or wholesale premises which are part of a transport undertaking;

● mobile vendors;

● horticultural activities in garden centres; and

● theatres, art galleries and museums.

Other changes include:

● local authority owned indoor sports halls are now treated the same as other local authority owned premises;

● a clarification of HSE's enforcement responsibility for common parts of domestic premises;

● land within the perimeter of an airport is treated as other premises in multiple occupation;

● an amendment to the definition of 'fairground' to make it clearer;

● go-karts and bouncy castles are excluded from being relevant in determining whether premises are fairgrounds.

The new Regulations will result in an overall increase in the premises enforced by local authorities and a reduction in those enforced by the HSE. This increase can be accommodated within local authorities' planned priority inspection system and confers no cost to business and industry. The Regulations will reduce dual enforcement in many small businesses.

Transfer of responsibility between the HSE and local authorities

E15005   Enforcement can be transferred (though not in the case of Crown premises), by prior agreement, from the HSE to the local authority and vice versa. The Health and Safety Commission is also empowered to effect such a transfer, without the necessity of such agreement. In either case, parties who are affected by such transfer must be notified. [*Health and Safety (Enforcing Authority) Regulations 1989, Reg 5*]. Transfer is effective even though the above procedure is not followed (i.e. the authority changes when the main activity changes) (*Hadley v Hancox (1987) 85 LGR 402*, decided under the previous regulations).

Where there is uncertainty, a new provision allows responsibility to be assigned by the HSE and the local authority jointly to either body. [*Reg 6(1)*].

Part A: Enforcement Powers of Inspectors

Improvement and prohibition notices

E15006   It was recommended by the Robens Committee that 'Inspectors should have the power, without reference to the courts, to issue a formal improvement notice to an employer requiring him to remedy particular faults or to institute a specified programme of work within a stated time limit.' (Cmnd 5034, para 269). 'The improvement notice would be the inspector's main sanction. In addition, an alternative and stronger power should be available to the inspector for use where he considers the case for remedial action to be particularly serious. In such cases he should be able to issue a prohibition notice.' (Cmnd 5034, para 276). *HSWA* put these recommendations into effect.

Improvement notices

E15007   An inspector may serve an improvement notice if he is of the opinion that a person:

(*a*)   is contravening one or more of the 'relevant statutory provisions' (see E15002 above); or

(*b*)   has contravened one or more of those provisions in circumstances that make it likely that the contravention will continue or be repeated.

[*HSWA s 21*].

In the improvement notice the inspector must:

(i)   state that he is of the opinion in (*a*) and (*b*) above; and

(ii)   specify the provision(s) in his opinion contravened; and

(iii)   give particulars of the reasons for his opinion; and

(iv)   specify a period of time within which the person is required to remedy the contravention (or the matters occasioning such contravention).

[*HSWA s 21*].

The period specified in the notice within which the requirement must be carried out (see (iv) above) must be at least 21 days – this being the period within which an appeal may be lodged with an employment tribunal (see E15012 below) [*HSWA s 21*]. In order to be validly served on a company, an improvement notice relating to the company's actions as an employer must be served at the registered office of the company, not elsewhere. Service at premises occupied by the company will only be valid if the notice relates to a contravention by the company in the capacity of occupier (*HSE v George Tancocks Garage (Exeter) [1993] COD 284*).

The 'notice of intent' procedures which were used to enforce health and safety law were withdrawn with effect from 1 April 1998, in an attempt to help improve the effectiveness of health and safety inspection at the workplace and to simplify administrative procedures.

Previously, the Health and Safety Executive and local authority inspectors had to issue a notice of intent (NOI) to businesses when they proposed to serve an improvement notice. Such notice of intent would explain what was wrong, what needed to be done to rectify the matter, and the date by which such action must be taken.

When inspectors propose to issue an improvement notice, they must first discuss with the duty holder the breaches of law concerned, and the action that will be needed to comply. The duty holder is given an opportunity to discuss issues with the inspector before formal action is taken and, if possible, to resolve points of difference. When an inspector decides that an improvement notice should be issued, the inspector should tell the duty holder what needs to be done, why and by when. An improvement notice includes such explanation.

Failure to comply with an improvement notice can have serious penal consequences (see E15028 below).

Prohibition notices

E15008 If an inspector is of the opinion that, with regard to any activities to which s *22(1)* applies (see below), the activities involve or will involve a risk of serious personal injury, he may serve on that person a notice (a prohibition notice). [*HSWA s 22(2)*].

It is incumbent on an inspector to show, on a balance of probabilities, that there is a risk to health and safety (*Readmans Ltd v Leeds CC [1992] COD 419* where an environmental health officer served a prohibition notice on the appellant regarding shopping trolleys with child seats on them, following an accident involving an eleven-month-old child. The appellant alleged that the industrial tribunal had wrongly placed the burden of proof on them, to show that the trolleys were not dangerous. It was held by the High Court (allowing the appeal), that it was for the inspector to prove that there was a health and/or safety risk).

Prohibition notices differ from improvement notices in two important ways, as follows:

(*a*)   with prohibition notices, it is not necessary that an inspector believes that a provision of *HSWA* or any other statutory provision is being or has been contravened;

(*b*)   prohibition notices are served in *anticipation* of danger.

Section 22 applies where, in the inspector's opinion, there is a hazardous activity or state of affairs generally. It is irrelevant that the hazard or danger is not mentioned in *HSWA*; it can exist by virtue of other legislation, or even in the absence of any relevant statutory duty. In this way notices are used to enforce the later statutory requirements of *HSWA* and the earlier requirements of the *Factories Act 1961* and other protective occupational legislation.

A prohibition notice must:

(*a*)   state that the inspector is of the opinion stated immediately above;

(*b*)   specify the matters which create the risk in question;

(*c*)   where there is actual or anticipatory breach of provisions and regulations, state that the inspector is of the opinion that this is so and give reasons;

(*d*)   direct that the activities referred to in the notice must not be carried out on, by or under the control of the person on whom the notice is served, unless the matters referred to in (*b*) above have been remedied.

[*HSWA s 22(3)*].

Failure to comply with a prohibition notice can have serious penal consequences (see E15028 below).

Differences between improvement and prohibition notices

E15009 Unlike an improvement notice, where time is allowed in which to correct a defect or offending state of affairs, a prohibition notice can take effect immediately.

A direction contained in a prohibition notice shall take effect:

(a)   at the end of the period specified in the notice; or

(b)   if the notice so declares, immediately.

[*HSWA s 22(4) as substituted by Consumer Protection Act 1987, 3 Sch*].

Risk of injury need not be imminent, even if the notice is to take immediate effect (*Tesco Stores Ltd v Kippax COIT No 7605-6/90*).

An improvement notice gives a person upon whom it is served time to correct the defect or offending situation. A prohibition notice, which is a direction to stop the work activity in question rather than put it right, can take effect immediately on issue; alternatively, it may allow time for certain modifications to take place (i.e. deferred prohibition notice). Both types of notice will generally contain a schedule of work which the inspector will require to be carried out. If the nature of the work to be carried out is vague, the validity of the notice is not affected. If there is an appeal, an employment tribunal may, within its powers to modify a notice, rephrase the schedule in more specific terms (*Chrysler (UK) Ltd v McCarthy [1978] ICR 939*).

Effect of non-compliance with notice

E15010   If, after expiry of the period specified in the notice, or in the event of an appeal, expiry of any additional time allowed for compliance by the tribunal, an applicant does not comply with the notice or modified notice, he can be prosecuted. If convicted of contravening a prohibition notice, he may be imprisoned. [*HSWA s 33(1)(g), (3)(b)(i)*]. In *R v Kerr; R v Barker (1996) unreported* the directors of a company were each jailed for four months after allowing a machine which was subject to a prohibition notice – following an accident in which an employee lost an arm – to continue to be operated.

Service of notice coupled with prosecution

E15011   Where an inspector serves a notice, he may at the same time decide to prosecute for the substantive offence specified in the notice. The fact that a notice has been served would not be relevant to the prosecution. Nevertheless, an inspector would not normally commence proceedings until after the expiry of 21 days, i.e. until he was satisfied that there was to be no appeal against the notice or until the tribunal had heard the appeal and affirmed the notice, since it would be inconsistent if conviction by the magistrates were followed by cancellation of the notice by the tribunal. The fact that an employment tribunal has upheld a notice would not be binding on a magistrates' court hearing a prosecution under the statutory provision of which the notice alleged a contravention; it would be necessary for the prosecution to prove all the elements in the offence (see E15024 below).

Employment tribunals are mainly concerned with hearing unfair dismissal claims by employees; only a tiny proportion of cases heard by them relate specifically to health and safety. Moreover, they are not empowered to determine breaches of criminal legislation.

Appeals against improvement and prohibition notices

E15012   A person on whom either type of notice is served may appeal to an employment tribunal within 21 days from the date of service of the notice. The tribunal may extend this time where it is satisfied, on application made in writing (either before or after expiry of the 21-day period), that it was not reasonably practicable for the appeal to be brought within the 21-day period. On appeal the tribunal may either affirm or cancel the notice and, if it affirms it, may do so with modifications in the form of additions, omissions or amendments. [*HSWA ss 24(2), 82(1)(c); Industrial Tribunals (Constitution and Rules of Procedure) Regulations 1993 (SI 1993 No 2687), Reg 8(4) and 4 Sch*].

Effect of appeal

E15013   Where an appeal is brought against a notice, the lodging of an appeal automatically suspends operation of an improvement notice, but a prohibition notice will continue to apply unless there is a direction to the contrary from the tribunal. Thus:

(*a*)   in the case of an improvement notice, the appeal has the effect of suspending the operation of the notice;

(*b*)   in the case of a prohibition notice, the appeal only suspends the operation of the notice in the following circumstances:

(i)   if the tribunal so directs, on the application of the appellant; and

(ii)   the suspension is then effective from the time when the tribunal so directs.

[*HSWA s 24(3)*].

Grounds for appeal

E15014   The main grounds for appeal are:

(*a*)   the inspector wrongly interpreted the law (see E15015 below);

(*b*)   the inspector exceeded his powers, though not necessarily intentionally, under an Act or regulation (see E15016 below);

(*c*)   breach of law is admitted but the proposed solution is not 'practicable' or not 'reasonably practicable', or that there was no 'best practicable means' other than that used where 'best practicable means' is also a defence to a charge of statutory nuisance (depending on the terminology of the particular statute) (see E15017 below);

(*d*)   breach of law is admitted but the breach is so insignificant that the notice should be cancelled (see E15018 below).

The merits of appealing the issue or terms of an enforcement notice should always be considered carefully as, in practice, this may be the employer's only opportunity to dispute the reasonableness of the requirements imposed. Failure to comply with a notice is a strict liability offence and if a prosecution is brought it is not open to the employer to argue that he did everything 'reasonably practicable' to comply with the notice (*Deary v Mansion Hide Upholstery Ltd [1983] ICR 610*, see E15024 below).

The delay involved in lodging an appeal can have important practical consequences. It is not uncommon for up to four months to elapse before an appeal against an improvement notice can be heard by the tribunal (in the case of prohibition notices it is about one month). For this reason particularly, and in view of the fact that notice of appeal suspends operation of an improvement notice, many companies opt for appealing, since at the time of service of notice they may not be in a position to meet the requirements of the notice; whereas, three or four months later, the position may have changed. If, however, the sole reason for appealing is to gain time and nothing else, the tribunal is not likely to be sympathetic and costs could be awarded against the unsuccessful appellant, though this is rare. [*Industrial Tribunals*

(Constitution and Rules of Procedure) Regulations 1993, Reg 8(4), Sch 4]. This provision states that: 'a tribunal may make an Order that a party shall pay to another party either a specified sum in respect of the costs of or in connection with an appeal incurred by that other party or, in default of agreement, the taxed amount of those costs'.

Inspector's wrong interpretation of the law

E15015 It is doubtful whether many cases have succeeded, or indeed would succeed on this ground. Two situations are possible. First, a statute or regulation imposes on an employer a strict duty. This occurs in the case of certain sections of the *Factories Act 1961*, e.g. *ss 12, 13* (applicable to existing factories until 1 January 1997), dealing with prime movers and transmission machinery. Here there is virtually no scope for argument for the employer.

The second situation is where a statute permits latitude and requires a duty to be carried out 'so far as reasonably practicable'. The definition of 'reasonably practicable' was authoritatively laid down in *Edwards v National Coal Board [1949] 1 AER 743* where it was said that ' "reasonably practicable" is a narrower term than "physically possible", and seems . . . to imply that a computation must be made by the owner in which the quantum of risk is placed on one scale and the sacrifice involved in the measures necessary for averting the risk (whether in money, time or trouble) is placed in the other, and that, if it be shown that there is a gross disproportion between them – the risk being insignificant in relation to the sacrifice – the defendants discharge the onus on them'. Here an employer has more scope for argument. For example, in *Canterbury City Council v Howletts and Port Lympne Estates Limited (The Times, 13 December 1996)*, a prohibition notice was served on Howletts Zoo following the death of a keeper while he was cleaning the tigers' enclosure. It was Howletts' policy to allow their animals to roam freely; the local authority argued that the zoo's keepers could have carried out their tasks in the tigers' enclosure with the animals secured. The High Court affirmed the industrial tribunal's decision to set aside the notice, holding that *HSWA s 2* was not intended to render illegal certain working practices simply because they were dangerous.

Employers should note that contesting a prohibition notice on the ground that there has been no legal contravention is pointless, since valid service of a prohibition notice does not depend on legal contravention (*Roberts v Day, COIT No 1/133, Case No 3053/77*). In addition, inspectors can use their powers under *HSWA ss 21, 22* and *25* ('search and destroy dangerous articles and substances') in respect of one or more of the 'relevant statutory provisions' (see E15002 above).

Inspector exceeded powers under statute

E15016 It can happen that an inspector exceeds his powers under statute by reason of misinterpretation of the statute or regulation (*Deeley v Effer, COIT No 1/72, Case No 25354/77*). This case involved the requirement that 'all floors, steps, stairs, passages and gangways must, so far as is reasonably practicable, be kept free from obstruction and from any substance likely to cause persons to slip'. [*OSRPA s 16(1)*] (now replaced by equivalent duties under the *Workplace (Health, Safety and Welfare) Regulations 1992*). The inspector considered that employees were endangered by baskets of wares in the shop entrance. The tribunal ruled that the notice had to be cancelled, since the only persons endangered were members of the public, and *OSRPA* is concerned with dangers to employees.

Proposed solution not practicable

The position in a case where, although breach of the law is admitted, the proposed solution is not considered practicable, depends upon the nature of the obligation. The duty may be strict, or have to be carried out so far as practicable or, alternatively, so far as reasonably practicable. In the first two situations cost of compliance is irrelevant; in the latter case, where a requirement has to be carried out 'so far as reasonably practicable', cost effectiveness is an important factor but has to be weighed against the risks to health and safety involved in failing to implement the remedial measures identified in the enforcement notice. Where there is a real danger of serious injury the cost of complying with the notice is unlikely to be decisive. Thus in a leading case, the appellant was served with an improvement notice requiring secure fencing on transmission machinery. An appeal was lodged on the ground that the proposed modifications were too costly (£1,900). It was argued that because of the intelligence and integrity of the operators a safety screen costing £200 would be adequate. The tribunal dismissed the appeal: the risk justified the cost (*Belhaven Brewery Co Ltd v McLean [1975] IRLR 370*).

The cost of complying with a notice is likely to carry less weight in the case of a prohibition notice than an improvement notice, as there must be 'a risk of serious personal injury' for a prohibition notice to be served (*Nico Manufacturing Co Ltd v Hendry [1975] IRLR 225*, where the company argued that a prohibition notice in respect of the worn state of their power presses should be cancelled on the ground that it would result in a 'serious loss of production' and endanger the jobs of several employees. The tribunal dismissed this argument, having decided that using the machinery in its worn condition could cause serious danger to operators). Similarly, an undertaking by a company to take additional safety precautions against the risk of injury from unsafe plant until new equipment was installed was not sufficient (*Grovehurst Energy Ltd v Strawson (HM Inspector) COIT No 5035/90*).

Where cost is a factor this is not to be confused with the current financial position of the company. A company's financial position is irrelevant to the question whether a tribunal should affirm an enforcement notice. Thus in *Harrison (Newcastle-under-Lyme) Ltd v Ramsay (HM Inspector) [1976] IRLR 135*, a notice requiring cleaning, preparation and painting of walls had to be complied with even though the company was on an economy drive.

Tribunals have power under *HSWA s 24* to alter or extend time limits attaching to improvement and prohibition notices (*D J M and A J Campion v Hughes (HM Inspector of Factories) [1975] IRLR 291*, where even though there was an imminent risk of serious personal injury, a further four months were allowed for the erection of fire escapes as it was not practicable to carry out the remedial works within the time limits set). Extensions of time in which to comply with notices are most commonly granted where the costs of the improvements and modifications required by the notice are significant.

In *R v British Steel plc [1994] IRLR 540* the Court of Appeal held that *HSWA s 2(1)* (and hence each of the other analogous duties) . . .[0091]creates an absolute prohibition. And the defence [of reasonable practicability] is a narrow one comparable to the defence under *section 29(1) of the Factories Act 1961*, which simply comprehends the idea of measures necessary to avert the risks to health and safety'. That view was subsequently, and conclusively, endorsed by the House of Lords in *R v Associated Octel Co Ltd [1996] 1 WLR 1543* (another *HSWA s 3(1)* decision). Of course, that raised a further, fundamental question: what was the scope of the defence of 'reasonable practicability'? That issue was central to the significant Court of Appeal decision, *R v Nelson Group Services (Maintenance) Ltd* (judgment 30 July 1998).

The company, Nelson Group Services, had been involved in the installation, servicing and maintenance of gas appliances. One of their employees, a fitter, had, while removing a gas fire from a house, left the gas fittings in a condition exposing the occupier to health and safety risks. The fitter had been properly trained by the company, so enabling him to carry out his work safely and competently.

The company was prosecuted under *HSWA s 3(1)*, which provides that 'It shall be the duty of every employer to conduct his undertaking in such a way as to ensure, so far as is reasonably practicable, that persons not in his employment who may be affected thereby are not thereby exposed to risks in their health and safety'.

The Crown Court convicted the company of failing to discharge its duty under the above provision. The company appealed. In the Crown Court the judge had directed the jury that if they found that the fitter had left the fittings in a condition exposing the occupier to health or safety risks, the defence of 'reasonable practicability' was unavailable to the defendants.

That was wrong. In the leading Court of Appeal judgment Roch LJ said that the fact that the employee carrying out the work had done so negligently did not of itself preclude the employer from establishing that everything 'reasonably practicable' had been done in accordance with *HSWA s 3(1)*.

It had been, he continued, '. . . sufficient for the adequate protection of the public that the employer was required to show that everything "reasonably practicable" had been done to see that a person doing the work had safe systems of work laid down for him, had the appropriate skill and instruction, had been subject to adequate supervision and had been provided with safe plant and equipment for the proper performance of the work, and it had not been necessary that the employer be held criminally liable even for an isolated negligent act by the employee performing the work, such persons themselves being liable to criminal sanctions under the Act and relevant regulations.'

Breach of law is insignificant

E15018   Tribunals will rarely cancel a notice which concerns breach of an absolute duty where the breach is admitted but the appellant argues that the breach is trivial: *South Surbiton Co-operative Society Ltd v Wilcox [1975] IRLR 292*, where a notice had been issued in respect of a cracked wash-hand basin, being a breach of an absolute duty under the *Offices, Shops and Railway Premises Act 1963*. It was argued by the appellant that, in view of their excellent record of cleanliness, there was no need for officials to visit the premises. The appeal was dismissed.

Inspectors' investigation powers

E15019   Inspectors have wide ranging powers under *HSWA* to investigate suspected health and safety offences. These include powers to:

(*a*)   enter and search premises;

(*b*)   direct that the premises or anything on them be left undisturbed for so long as is reasonably necessary for the purpose of the investigation;

(*c*)   take measurements, photographs and recordings;

(*d*)   take samples of articles or substances found in the premises and of the atmosphere in or in the vicinity of the premises;

(*e*)   dismantle or test any article which appears to have caused or be likely to cause danger;

(*f*)   detain items for testing or for use as evidence;

(*g*)   interview any person;

(*h*)   require the production and inspection of any documents. Copies may also be taken; and

(*j*)   require the provision of facilities and assistance for the purpose of carrying out the investigation.

[*HSWA s 20*].

Under these powers inspectors may require interviewees to answer such questions as they think fit and sign a declaration that those answers are true. [*HSWA s 20(1)(j)*]. However, evidence given in this way is inadmissible in any proceedings subsequently taken against the person giving the statement or his or her spouse. [*HSWA s 20(7)*]. Where prosecution of an individual is contemplated the inspector will, therefore, usually exercise his evidence-gathering powers under the *Police and Criminal Evidence Act 1984 (PACE)*. Evidence given in this way is admissible against that person in later proceedings. Interviews conducted under PACE are subject to strict legal controls, for example, interviewees must be cautioned before the interview takes place, they have certain 'rights to silence' (although these were qualified by the *Criminal Justice and Public Order Act 1994*), and there are rules relating to the recording of the interview.

Inspectors' powers of search and seizure in case of imminent danger

E15020   Where an inspector has reasonable cause to believe that there are on premises 'articles or substances ("substance" includes solids, liquids and gases – *HSWA s 53(1)*) which give rise to imminent risk of serious personal injury', he can:

(*a*)   seize them; and

(*b*)   cause them to be rendered harmless (by destruction or otherwise).

[*HSWA s 25(1)*].

Enforcing authorities are given similar powers regarding environmental pollution, under the *Environment Act 1995, ss 108, 109*.

Before an article forming 'part of a batch of similar articles', or a substance is rendered harmless, an inspector must, if practicable, take a sample and give to a responsible person, at the premises where the article or substance was found, a portion which has been marked in such a way as to be identifiable. [*HSWA s 25(2)*]. After the article or substance has been rendered harmless, the inspector must sign a prepared report and give a copy of the report to:

(i)   a responsible person (e.g. safety officer); and

(ii)   the owner of the premises, unless he happens to be the 'responsible person'. (See A3004 ACCIDENT REPORTING for the meaning of this term.)

[*HSWA s 25(3)*].

Analogous powers are given to transport inspectors under the *Radioactive Material (Road Transport) Act 1991, s 5* in respect of vehicles carrying radioactive packages.

A customs officer may assist the enforcing authority or the inspector in his enforcement duties under the *Health and Safety at Work etc. Act 1974* by seizing any imported article or substance and he may then detain it for not more than two working days and he may disclose information about it to the enforcing authorities or inspectors. [*HSWA ss 25A, 27A, inserted by Consumer Protection Act 1987, 3 Sch*].

Indemnification by enforcing authority

E15021   Where an inspector has an action brought against him in respect of an act done in the execution or purported execution of any of the 'relevant statutory provisions' (see E15002 above) and is ordered to pay damages and costs (or expenses) in circumstances where he is not legally entitled to require the enforcing authority which appointed him to indemnify him, he may be able to take advantage of *HSWA s 26*. By virtue of that provision, the authority nevertheless has the power to indemnify the inspector against all or part of such damages where the authority is satisfied that the inspector honestly believed:

(*a*)   that the act complained of was within his powers; and

(*b*)   that his duty as inspector required or entitled him to do it.

Public register of improvement and prohibition notices

E15022   Improvement (though not in the case of the *Fire Precautions Act 1971*) and prohibition notices relating to public safety matters have to be entered in a public register as follows:

(*a*)   within 14 days following the date on which notice is served in cases where there is no right of appeal;

(*b*)   within 14 days following the day on which the time limit expired, in cases where there is a right of appeal but no appeal has been lodged within the statutory 21 days;

(*c*)   within 14 days following the day when the appeal is disposed of, in cases where an appeal is brought.

[*Environment and Safety Information Act 1988, s 3*].

Notices which impose requirements or prohibitions solely for the protection of persons at work are not included in the register. [*Environment and Safety Information Act 1988, s 3(3)*].

In addition, registers must be kept of notices served by:

(i)   fire authorities, under the *Schedule* to the *Environment and Safety Information Act 1988* for the purpose of *s 10* of the *Fire Precautions Act 1971* (not improvement notices);

(ii)   local authorities, under the *Schedule* to the *Environment and Safety Information Act 1988* for the purpose of *s 10* of the *Safety of Sports Grounds Act 1975*;

(iii)   responsible authorities (as defined by the *Environment and Safety Information Act 1988, s 2(2)*) and the Minister of Agriculture, Fisheries and Food under *s 2* of the *Environment and Safety Information Act 1988* for the purpose of *s 19* of the *Food and Environment Protection Act 1985*;

(iv)   enforcing authorities, under *s 20* of the *Environmental Protection Act 1990*; and

(v)   enforcing authorities, under the *Radioactive Substances Act 1993*.

These registers are open to inspection by the public free of charge at reasonable hours and, on request and payment of a reasonable fee, copies can be obtained from the relevant authority. [*Environment and Safety Information Act 1988, s 1*]. Such records can also be kept on computer.

Part B: Offences and Penalties

Prosecution for breach of the 'relevant statutory provisions'

E15023 Prosecutions can follow non-compliance with an improvement or prohibition notice, but equally inspectors will sometimes prosecute without serving notice. Service of notices remains the most usual method of enforcement. In 1994/95 approximately 22,600 enforcement notices were issued by all enforcement authorities compared with nearly 2,300 prosecutions for health and safety offences. Prosecutions are most commonly brought after a workplace accident or dangerous incident (such as a fire or explosion). Investigations by the enforcing authorities may take many months to complete and, in complex cases, it is not unusual for prosecutions to be commenced up to a year after the original incident. Prosecutions normally take place before the magistrates but there is provision in *HSWA* for prosecution on indictment before the Crown Court. [*HSWA, s 33(3)(b)*]. The determining factor behind prosecution on indictment is the gravity of the particular offence.

Burden of proof

E15024 Throughout criminal law the burden of proof of guilt is on the prosecution to show that the accused committed the particular offence (*Woolmington v DPP [1935] AC 462*). The burden is a great deal heavier than in civil law, requiring proof of guilt beyond a reasonable doubt as distinct from on a balance of probabilities. While not eliminating the need for the prosecution to establish general proof of guilt, *HSWA s 40* makes the task of the prosecution easier by transferring the onus of proof to the accused for one element of certain offences. *Section 40* states that in any proceedings for an offence consisting of a failure to comply with a duty or requirement to do something so far as is practicable or so far as is reasonably practicable, or to use the best practicable means to do something, the onus is on the accused to prove (as the case may be) that it was not practicable or not reasonably practicable to do more than was in fact done to satisfy the duty or requirement, or that there was no better practicable means than was in fact used to satisfy the duty or requirement. However, *s 40* does not apply to an offence created by *s 33(1)(g)* – failing to comply with an improvement notice.

In *Deary v Mansion Hide Upholstery Ltd [1983] ICR 610*, an improvement notice was served on the defendant company requiring it to provide fire resistant storage for polyurethane form. The company did not comply, nor did it appeal. It was irrelevant that the company had complied with the notice so far as 'reasonably practicable' as that was not a requirement of the offence charged. A similar burden of proof exists under the *Environmental Protection Act 1990* (see E5020 EMISSIONS INTO THE ATMOSPHERE).

Main offences and penalties

E15025 Health and safety offences are either (*a*) triable summarily (i.e. without jury before the magistrates), or (*b*) triable summarily and on indictment (i.e. triable either way), or (*c*) triable only on indictment. Most health and safety offences, however, fall into categories (*a*) and (*b*).

Summary offences and offences triable either way

E15026 The main health and safety offences triable (*a*) summarily, or (*b*) either way (i.e. summarily or on indictment) are the following:

Summary only offences

(*a*) contravening a requirement imposed under *HSWA s 14* (power of the HSC to order an investigation);

(*b*) contravening a requirement imposed by an inspector under *HSWA s 20*;

(*c*) preventing or attempting to prevent a person from appearing before an inspector, or from answering his questions;

(*d*) intentionally obstructing an inspector or customs officer in the exercise of his powers;

(*e*) falsely pretending to be an inspector.

'Either way' offences

(*a*) failure to carry out one or more of the general duties of *HSWA ss 2-7*;

(*b*) contravening either:

(i) *HSWA s 8* – intentionally or recklessly interfering with anything provided for safety;

(ii) *HSWA s 9* – levying payment for anything that an employer must by law provide in the interests of health and safety (e.g. personal protective clothing);

(*c*) contravening any health and safety regulations;

(*d*) contravening a requirement imposed by an inspector under *HSWA s 25* (power to seize and destroy articles and substances);

(*e*) contravening a requirement of a prohibition or improvement notice;

(*f*) intentionally or recklessly making false statements, where the statement is made:

(i) to comply with a requirement to furnish information; or

(ii) to obtain the issue of a document;

(*g*) intentionally making a false entry in a register, book, notice etc. which is required to be kept;

(*h*) failing to comply with a remedial court order, made under *HSWA s 42*.

[*HSWA s 33(1)*].

In England and Wales there is no time limit for bringing prosecutions for offences, except for offences tried summarily in the magistrates' courts – where the time limit is six months from the date the complaint was laid. [*Magistrates' Courts Act 1980, s 127(1)*]. In Scotland the six months' time limit extends to 'either way' offences tried summarily. The period may be extended in the case of special reports, coroners' court hearings or in cases of death generally. [*HSWA s 34(1)*]. There is no time limit for commencing hearings in the Crown Court.

Summary trial or trial on indictment

E15027 Generally, offences triable either way are tried summarily. They could, however, be tried on indictment e.g. if the magistrates felt that the matter was too serious for them and required a penalty greater than they could impose under their powers under *HSWA s 33(3)(a)* (see E15028 below).

Trial on indictment could well take place where an offence created serious risk to life or disclosed flagrant disregard of health and safety duties, or alternatively, the offender was a persistent one. Here the Crown Court can impose an unlimited fine. [*HSWA s 33(3)(b)(ii)*]. In addition, the prosecution may ask for trial on indictment, or the defendant may refuse consent to summary trial.

Penalties for health and safety offences

E15028 Penalties tend to relate to the three main categories of offences characterising breach of health and safety legislation, namely:

(*a*) breaches of *ss 2-6* of the *Health and Safety at Work etc. Act 1974* – serious offences:

(i) summary conviction – a maximum £20,000 fine,

(ii) conviction on indictment – an unlimited fine (but no imprisonment);

(*b*) breaches of improvement or prohibition orders, or orders under *s 42* of the *Health and Safety at Work etc. Act* to remedy the cause of offence – serious offences:

(i) summary conviction – a maximum £20,000 fine, or imprisonment for up to six months or both,

(ii) conviction on indictment – an unlimited fine or imprisonment for up to two years or both;

(*c*) most other offences including breaches of health and safety regulations:

(i) summary conviction – a maximum fine of £5,000,

(ii) conviction on indictment – an unlimited fine or up to two years' imprisonment (or both) for licence breaches and explosives offences (see, for example, *R v Hill (1996) unreported*, where a demolition contractor was jailed for three months for breach of asbestos licensing regulations).

[*HSWA s 33(1A), (2) and (2A)* as inserted by the *Offshore Safety Act 1992*, and *HSWA s 33(3)*].

In *R v F Howe & Son (Engineers) Ltd [1999] 2 All ER 249* the Court of Appeal considered an appeal against fines totalling £48,000 and an order for costs of £7,500 imposed in respect of four offences under the *Health and Safety at Work etc. Act 1974* and related regulations. The prosecution had been brought as a result of a fatal accident when an employee of the appellant had been electrocuted while operating an electric vacuum machine. The appellant contended that the total fine was excessive.

The Court of Appeal held that this was a bad case and that the Crown Court judge had been right to describe the state of the electrical equipment as appalling – there appeared to have been a flagrant disregard for the safety of the company's employees. Corners were cut and no real attention had been paid to electrical safety. In determining an appropriate fine for an offence under the *Health and Safety at Work etc. Act 1974* and related regulations, aggravating features include: death resulting in consequence of a breach; a failure to heed warnings; and a risk run specifically to save money. Mitigating features include: prompt admission of responsibility and a timely plea of guilty; steps to remedy deficiencies after they are drawn to the defendant's attention; and a good safety record. Other relevant factors are: the degree of risk and extent of the danger created by the offence; the extent of the breach; and the defendant's resources and the effect of the fine on its business.

Although it is not possible to set out a tariff or to stipulate that a fine should bear a specific relationship to the turnover or net profit of the defendant, a fine must be large enough to bring home the message, both to managers and to shareholders, that the purpose of prosecutions for health and safety offences in the workplace is to achieve a safe environment for those who work there and for other members of the public who may be affected. Although the penalty should reflect public disquiet at the unnecessary loss of life, the Court of Appeal held that the fine in this case should not be so large as to imperil the earnings of employees or create a risk of bankruptcy.

This was not a case where the offences were so serious that the company ought not to be in business, but it was one which required a substantial penalty. The Court of Appeal held that the order for costs should be left undisturbed, but that, because of the limited resources of the appellant company, the fine imposed upon it should be reduced to £15,000, thereby reducing the total financial burden upon it from £55,500 to £22,500.

In *R v Rollco Screw and Rivet Co Ltd and Others, The Times 29 April 1999*, the Lord Chief Justice gave unqualified support to the observations of Scott Baker J in *R v F Howe & Son (Engineers) Ltd* which amounted to a clear and correct statement of the principles which should guide the court. In *Rollco*, it was held that where a company and its directors are convicted of offences under the *Health and Safety at Work etc Act 1974*, the court must ensure that the financial penalties imposed are appropriate to mark the gravity of the case. Although in a small company the directors might also be the shareholders, the penalties fixed should make clear that directors have a personal responsibility which cannot be shuffled off to the company. In considering the period over which a financial penalty might be ordered to be payable, the court could properly fix a longer period in the case of a corporate defendant than in the case of an individual defendant. The proper approach is to pose two questions:

What financial penalty did the offence merit?

What financial penalty could a defendant, whether corporate or personal, reasonably be ordered to meet?

On the first question, the court held that the total penalty imposed on the company and directors of £50,000, split as to £40,000 payable by the company and £10,000 by the directors, was, in the circumstances, appropriate recognition of the gravity of the offences committed under the *Health and Safety at Work etc Act 1974, ss 2(1) and 3(1)* in respect of a serious incident of asbestos contamination.

On the second question, the company had submitted that its means were such that together with the costs order, the total sum of £70,000 payable was grossly excessive and not an amount it could meet. The Court of Appeal held that the total period for payment – six years and five months – was excessive and reduced it to five years and seven months, not by reducing the fine but by reducing the sum payable by way of costs from £30,000 to £20,000.

Compare, however, the penalties meted out to Andrew and Neil Medley at Leeds Crown Court in April 1999 (see 10 INTRODUCTION).

Defences

E15029   Although no general defences are specified in the *Health and Safety at Work etc. Act 1974*, some regulations passed under the Act carry the defence of 'due diligence' (for example, the *Control of Substances Hazardous to Health Regulations 1999 (SI 1999 No 437))*.

Manslaughter

E15030   In cases of workplace death, manslaughter charges may also be brought if there is sufficient evidence. The decision to prosecute rests with the Crown Prosecution Service, not the enforcing authorities under health and safety legislation. Manslaughter convictions linked to breaches of safety legislation are rare but are becoming more common. There have been a series of individual prosecutions for manslaughter of directors or managers responsible for workplace deaths and in 1994 the first successful prosecution for corporate manslaughter involved OLL Ltd, the activity centre responsible for organising the Lyme Bay canoeing trip in which four teenagers died. (See EMPLOYERS' DUTIES TO THEIR EMPLOYEES at E11014).

Offences committed by particular types of persons

Corporate offences – delegation of duties to junior staff

E15031   Companies cannot avoid liability for breach of the general duties of the *HSWA* by arguing that the senior management and 'directing mind' of the company had taken all reasonable precautions, and that responsibility for the offence lay with a more junior employee or agent who was at fault. The *HSWA* generally imposes strict criminal liabilities on employers and others (subject to the employer being able to establish that all reasonably practicable precautions had been taken) and it is not open to corporate employers to seek to avoid liability by arguing that their general duties have properly been delegated to someone lower down the corporate tree. In *R v British Steel plc [1994] IRLR 540*, British Steel were prosecuted under *HSWA s 3* after a fatal accident to a subcontractor who was carrying out construction work under the supervision of a British Steel engineer. British Steel argued that it was not responsible under *s 3* for the actions of the supervising engineer as the engineer was not part of the 'directing mind' of the company and all reasonable precautions to ensure the safety of the work had been taken by senior management. The Court of Appeal dismissed this argument. A similar decision was reached in *R v Gateway Foodmarkets Ltd, The Times, 2 January 1997*, which concerned a breach of *HSWA s 2* arising out of a fatal accident to an employee who fell through a trap door in the floor of a lift control room. The accident occurred while the store manager was manually attempting to rectify an electrical fault in the lift in accordance with a local practice which was not authorised by Gateway's head office. The Court of Appeal held that the failure at store manager level was attributable to the employer.

However, where there is a defence of due diligence to the legislation allegedly breached, the company may be able to avoid liability if the members of senior management responsible for actual control of the company's operations have exercised due diligence and the failure occurs because of the actions of a junior member of staff: *Tesco Supermarkets Ltd v Nattrass [1972] AC 153*, a House of Lords decision on the wording of the *Trade Descriptions Act 1968*. The case was considered by the Court of Appeal in *R v British Steel plc [1994] IRLR 540* who distinguished it from the factual circumstances before them on the basis that the *Tesco* decision involved application of a due diligence defence which was not part of *HSWA s 3*.

Offences of directors or other officers of a company

E15032   Where an offence is committed by a body corporate, senior persons in the hierarchy of the company may also be individually liable. Thus, where the offence was committed with the consent or connivance of, or was attributable to any neglect on the part of any of the following, that person is himself guilty of an offence and liable to be punished accordingly. Those who may be so liable are:

(*a*)   any functional director;

(*b*)   manager (which does not include an *employee* in charge of a shop while the manager is away on a week's holiday (*R v Boal [1992] 1 QB 591*), concerning *s 23* of the *Fire Precautions Act 1971* – identical terminology to *HSWA s 37*));

(*c*)   company secretary;

(*d*)   other similar officer of the company;

(*e*)   anyone purporting to act as any of the above.

[*HSWA s 37(1)*].

It is not sufficient that the company through its 'directing mind' (its board of directors) has committed an offence – there must be some degree of personal culpability in the form of proof of consent, connivance or neglect by the individual concerned. Evidence of this sort can be difficult to obtain and prosecutions under *s 37(1)* have, in the past, been few compared with prosecutions of companies (although they are increasing in number).

Directors, managers and company secretaries can be personally liable for ensuring that corporate safety duties are performed throughout the company (for example, failure to maintain a safe system of work can give rise to personal liability). Not just duties imposed by law but also obligations placed on individuals by their employment contracts and job descriptions, for example under a safety policy, must be met. In the case of *Armour v Skeen (Procurator Fiscal, Glasgow) [1977] IRLR 310*, an employee fell to his death whilst repairing a road bridge over the River Clyde. The appellant, who was the Director of Roads, was held to be under a duty to supervise the safety of council workmen. He had not prepared a written safety policy for road work, despite a written request that he do so, and was found to have breached *HSWA s 37(1)*.

Similar duties exist under the *Environmental Protection Act 1990* and the *Environment Act 1995, s 95(2)-(4)*, see E5021 EMISSIONS INTO THE ATMOSPHERE. Directors convicted for breach of *HSWA s 37* may also be disqualified, for up to two years, from being a director of a company, under the provisions of the *Company Directors Disqualification Act 1986, s 2(1)* as having committed an indictable offence connected with (*inter alia*) the *management* of a company. In *R v Chapman (1992), unreported*, a director of a quarrying company was disqualified and fined £5,000 for contravening a prohibition notice on an unsafe quarry where there had been several fatalities and major injuries.

Directors' insurance

E15033   Companies can now buy insurance in order to protect directors. [*Companies Act 1985, s 310(3)*]. Moreover, directors need not contribute towards premiums, as they had to previously. Such insurance, which must be mentioned in the Annual Report and Accounts, may (subject to the terms of the policy), protect directors against:

(*a*)   civil liability for claims made against them in breach of directorial duties, e.g. by shareholders when directors have acted in breach of their duty of care to the company, as well as legal costs and expenses incurred in defence or settlement of such claim;

(*b*)   legal costs and expenses involved in defending criminal actions (e.g. breach of *HSWA s 37*), but not the fine or other penalty incurred, it being illegal to insure against payment of penalties (see further E13017 EMPLOYERS' LIABILITY INSURANCE).

Companies can also indemnify directors against such costs and damages, but only where judgment is ultimately given in the individual's favour or he is acquitted.

Offences due to the act of another person

E15034   *Section 36(1)* of *HSWA* makes clear that although provision is separately made for the prosecution of less senior corporate staff, e.g. safety officers, works managers, this does not prevent a further prosecution against the company itself. *Section 36(1)* states that where an offence under *HSWA* is due to the act or default of some other person, then:

(*a*)   that other person is guilty of the offence; and

(*b*)   a second person can be charged and convicted, whether or not proceedings are taken against the first-mentioned person.

Where the enforcing authorities rely on *HSWA s 36*, this must be made clear to the defendant. In *West Cumberland By Products Ltd v DPP, The Times, 12 November 1987*, the conviction of a company operating a road haulage business for breach of regulations relating to the transport of dangerous substances was set aside as the offence charged related to the obligations of the driver of the vehicle and, in prosecuting the operating company, reliance was not placed on *HSWA s 36*.

Position of the Crown

E15035   The general duties of *HSWA* bind the Crown. [*HSWA s 48(1)*]. (For the position under the *Factories Act 1961*, see W11048 WORKPLACES – HEALTH, SAFETY AND WELFARE.) However, improvement and prohibition notices cannot be served on the Crown, nor can the Crown be prosecuted. [*HSWA s 48(1)*]. Crown employees, however, can be prosecuted for breaches of *HSWA*. [*HSWA s 48(2)*]. Crown immunity is no longer enjoyed by health authorities, nor premises used by health authorities (defined as Crown premises) including hospitals (whether NHS hospitals or NHS trusts or private hospitals) [*National Health Service and Community Care Act 1990, s 60*]. Health authorities are also subject to the *Food Safety Act 1990*. Most Crown premises can be inspected by authorised officers in the same way as privately run concerns, though prosecution against the Crown is not possible. [*Food Safety Act 1990, s 54(2)*].

Environmental Management

Introduction

E16001 The management of environmental performance is now well-accepted as a critical issue for organisations in both the public and private sectors.

Broadly speaking, environmental management refers to the controls implemented by an organisation to minimise the adverse environmental impacts of its operations; in many cases this leads to opportunities to improve business performance in general.

Historically, environmental management tends to have been driven by a complex and interacting array of external pressures, to which business somewhat reluctantly responded.

However, business is becoming more proactive in its approach to environmental management, as the business benefits of it become more apparent. External pressures are still important influences, but increasingly they tend to shape the nature and scope of business' environmental management practices, rather than triggering them in the first place. The emergence of co-operative and constructive stakeholder dialogue as an element of corporate environmental management is an encouraging indication that business recognises the value of effective and proactive environmental management. Furthermore, the ongoing development of new and increasingly innovative approaches to environmental management reflects the fact that there is commercial value to be gained from continuous improvement, and that environmental management is more than a passing fad.

Examples of sources of pressure on business to adopt more sustainable management practices include:

- changing corporate governance expectations;
- management information needs;
- employees;
- legislation;
- market mechanisms;
- the financial community;
- the supply chain;
- community and environmental groups;
- environmental crises;
- the business community;
- customers; and
- competitor initiatives.

Internal drivers

Corporate governance

E16002   The concept of corporate governance has changed substantially during the last decade, reflecting the changed conditions in which business operates. The removal of trade barriers, the subsequent growth and political influence of trans-national companies, the opening of previously restricted markets and a general reduction in corporate taxation rates have contributed to radical changes in the way business operates, including increasing the extent to which it controls its own performance. Consequently, the notion of corporate responsibility has also changed. Society is looking less to government to control the social and environmental impacts of business activity, and instead is seeing business as being accountable for those impacts. Good corporate governance is no longer merely a reflection of responsible fiscal performance. As a result, the mandate of corporate directors and managers is expanding and they are recognising the need to operate in a more transparent and inclusive manner. Proactive environmental management is a key aspect of that.

Management information needs

E16003   Effective business management relies on timely and reliable information on the multitude of factors that influence it. As managers' understanding of the relationship between environmental performance and business performance increases, so too does their requirement for information pertaining to environmental performance. Such information assists to increase their control over those factors.

This reflects the growing acceptance of the sustainability concept, which recognises that long term business success requires environmental, social and economic factors to be balanced. While there is no clear guidance or agreement on how such a balance should be achieved, it is clear that it must be based on appropriate information on all three primary elements. Thus the recognition of the relevance of environmental performance to business performance, the value of controlling it and the need for expanded management information is an increasingly important driver of environmental management practices. Structured environmental management systems not only provide a means of controlling environmental performance *per se*, but also allow more informed strategic and operational decisions to be made by management.

Employees

E16004   Employees have a potentially strong influence over the environmental management practices of an organisation. The desire to minimise staff turnover means that companies are becoming more responsive to employee enquiries and suggestions regarding corporate environmental performance. Conversely, companies wishing to attract high calibre recruits are increasingly realising the importance of maintaining a strong and positive corporate image, which is often dependent on environmental performance, amongst a number of other things.

External drivers

Legislation

E16005   UK companies are influenced by a range of international treaties, conventions and protocols; European regulations and directives; and domestic legislation. The latter may be a tool for implementing European directives, or they may have been enacted independently of any requirement of the European Union.

Enforcement of the various legal instruments within England and Wales is primarily the responsibility of the Environment Agency, although local authorities also play a role. In Scotland, responsibility lies with the Scottish Environment Protection Agency.

Good corporate environmental management requires a thorough understanding of the legal requirements imposed on a company, in addition to evidence that the company has made reasonable attempts to ensure ongoing compliance with them, either through technological, procedural and/or administrative mechanisms.

It is interesting that a large number of published corporate environmental policies now commit to going 'beyond compliance'. That is, legislative compliance is increasingly being seen as a minimum standard.

Market mechanisms

E16006   While the command and control approach embodied in environmental legislation and regulations represents a significant pressure on business, policy makers have begun to examine new tools to encourage better management of environmental performance.

A range of measures is beginning to emerge designed to influence the economics of polluting activities. These so-called market-based instruments impose costs on pollution-causing activities and provide incentives for companies to look for ways of minimising environmental damage. Such instruments being discussed or implemented within the European Union include:

(*a*)   a carbon tax aimed at raising the cost of all fossil fuels, and those with a high carbon content becoming more expensive than others. This is designed to encourage energy conservation and a switch to cleaner fuels. Thus businesses will need to manage carefully their use of energy;

(*b*)   tradable emissions permits which set pollution quotas. Companies that reduce their emissions below the quota can sell the unused part of their quota to other firms. Businesses thus have the incentive to improve their emissions performance;

(*c*)   taxes and credits. A number of initiatives within the UK suggest that taxes and credits will increasingly be used as a mechanism for controlling environmental performance. For example, the UK introduced a Landfill Tax in October 1996 to encourage companies to reduce their waste streams. The tax is payable by landfill operators at a standard rate, which increased in April 1999 from £7 per tonne to £10 per tonne. A lower charge of £2 per tonne applies to inactive waste.

Additionally, in the March 1999 budget the Chancellor announced 'the biggest ever package of environmental tax reforms'. It included a levy on the business use of energy to be introduced from April 2001, changes to company car taxation which will favour those with lower CO_2 emission rates, the introduction of higher rates of duty on some categories of lorries and overall increases in road fuel duty. Plans to introduce a quarrying tax have been put on hold while the government and industry attempt to negotiate a voluntary agreement.

The financial community

E16007   The emerging realisation of the link between environmental performance and business performance has encouraged investors, shareholders and insurers to develop a direct interest in the environmental performance of companies. The financial community is therefore increasingly seeking information on how environmental issues will potentially impact on the long term viability of the companies in which they have a commercial interest. In particular, they are concerned about the extent to which environmental risks are being controlled. They want reassurance that companies are not in breach of legal requirements with the consequent threats of fines, reputational damage and the need for unanticipated expenditure. They need to be sure that assets, in the form of plant, equipment, property and brand value, against which they have lent money, are correctly valued. Raw materials, by-products and end products may need to be replaced, modified and/or discontinued, which may require provisions or contingent liabilities to be included in the corporate accounts. Such a situation may arise as a result of substances being phased out (for example, legal controls on CFC production), or it may reflect changing market attitudes such that the demand for less environmentally damaging products begins to decline. Additional research and development costs are likely to be associated with such changes.

Consideration of environmental risks is now an established component of acquisitions, mergers, flotations, buyouts or divestments. Management of companies involved in any of these deals must be able to demonstrate that environmental liabilities do not constitute an unacceptable risk for investors or insurers.

Supply chain

E16008   Most businesses are both purchasers and suppliers of a range of goods and services. This means that one company can directly influence the environmental performance of another. As a result, many companies are taking active steps to control their environmental performance throughout the supply chain. For example, it is quite common for purchasing companies to require their suppliers to demonstrate ongoing compliance with formal environmental management standards such as ISO 14001 or EMAS, and to provide information on the environmental performance of the supplier and the products and services it provides.

Community and environment group pressure

E16009   The majority of public pressure on companies to improve their environmental performance is initiated by local communities which experience the direct effects of pollution. Most companies recognise the importance and value of working co-operatively with local communities. In fact many have established community liaison panels, which comprise representatives of the local community. Such panels interact with the company on a regular basis and provide input on environmental and other community issues.

Environmental pressure groups, often supported by a high level of legal and technical expertise, are also influential. Previously the relationship between environmental pressure groups and business was characterised by mutual mistrust and reactive criticism. The emergence of the concept of 'stakeholder engagement', whereby companies take a more inclusive approach to business management, means that environmental pressure groups can be expected to have more direct access to companies and management in the future. In fact their opinions are already actively sought by many organisations, who recognise the importance of constructive dialogue. While companies will not necessarily implement all suggestions made by external pressure groups, the trend towards more timely and constructive dialogue is likely to continue.

The evolution of the Internet and other sophisticated communication media has significantly increased public awareness of and access to information about corporate environmental performance, as well as increasing the speed with which such information can be transferred and responded to. The result of this is that sources of pressure on companies to improve environmental performance have broadened into the international arena. Companies are finding it necessary to develop and adopt consistent environmental and social performance standards in all markets in which they operate, since their performance is increasingly subject to international scrutiny.

Environmental crises

E16010   High profile environmental crises are, unfortunately, often a trigger for improved environmental management. There are two main types:

(*a*)   crises that are generated as a result of the actions of an individual company, the effects of which are generally experienced at a local scale;

(*b*)   crises that are generated by collective action or by natural forces, the effects of which are often experienced at the national or international scale.

Individual companies that have been associated with environmentally damaging events such as oil spills generally find themselves exposed to intense pressure to improve their environmental management practices in the immediate future. The need to correct the reputational damage caused by environmental crises is a further incentive to respond quickly. Obviously the costs of responding to pressures arising from catastrophic environmental incidents can be extremely high, and most companies seek to avoid those by incorporating environmental issues into their corporate risk management programmes.

Global or national environmental crises tend to emerge more gradually, and with considerably more debate about accountability and appropriate responses. Nevertheless, there are a number of examples of global environmental issues that have facilitated more systematic and intensive environmental management practices than may otherwise have occurred in the same time period. The most obvious examples are the depletion of the ozone layer and the greenhouse effect. At a national level, issues such as water shortages, topsoil losses and regional air pollution have triggered the adoption of improved environmental management practices on an extensive scale.

Business community

E16011   Trade associations and business groups such as the Confederation of British Industry (CBI) and the International Chamber of Commerce (ICC) have played a leading and effective role in encouraging businesses to adopt environmental management practices. Increasingly the importance of doing this within a sustainable development framework is being accepted.

For example, the ICC *Business Charter for Sustainable Development* is a set of 16 principles to guide company strategies and operations towards sustainable development. The principles have been adopted widely by companies throughout the world. The principles require adherents to make environmental management a high priority, with detailed programmes and practices for its implementation integrated with existing management systems and procedures. The charter highlights such areas as employee and customer education, research facilities and operations, contractors and suppliers and emergency preparedness. It requires organisations to support the transfer of technology, be open to concerns expressed by the public and employees and carry out regular environmental reviews and report progress.

In 1995 the World Industry Council on the Environment (WICE) and the Business Council for Sustainable Development (BCSD) merged to become the World Business Council for Sustainable Development (WBCSD), a coalition of 120 international companies which are committed to the principles of sustainable development. WBCSD seeks to promote the effective implementation of these principles through a combination of advocacy, research, education, knowledge-sharing and policy development.

The Responsible Care programme is an example of an international initiative from a specific industry sector. The programme has been adopted by 41 national chemical industry associations, including the Chemical Industries Association (CIA) in the UK. All of those associations have made acceptance of Responsible Care requirements compulsory for individual member companies. Responsible Care is designed to promote continuous improvement, not only in environmental management, but also health and safety. In June 1998 the CIA published guidelines on implementing Responsible Care Management Systems. From December 2000 self-assessment against those guidelines will be compulsory for all CIA members, unless external verification has been achieved.

In the UK, the Prince of Wales Business Leaders Forum (PWBLF), which incorporates Business in the Environment (BiE), has played a major role in raising awareness of the relevance of environmental management and sustainable development to business, and promoting practical tools for improving performance.

The Confederation of British Industry (CBI) has urged companies to commit to evaluating the environmental impacts of their operations, setting targets and publicly reporting performance. To assist in this, the CBI has developed a computerised environmental management benchmarking programme, designed to enable companies to evaluate their environmental management practices relative to current best-practice.

Individual companies have also contributed to the development of improved environmental performance standards. As the relevance of good environmental management to overall business performance has become more apparent, progressive companies have voluntarily adopted a number of innovative and unique approaches to corporate environmental management. This has had the effect of constantly moving the frontiers of 'acceptable' environmental management practices and created substantial peer pressure which in turn has encouraged other companies to adopt similar or even more effective practices.

Environmental management guidelines

Standards for environmental management

E16012 Various guidelines exist for responding to those many pressures to minimise damage to the environment and health. Effective environmental management, like quality management or financial management, requires *inter alia*:

(a) the setting of objectives and performance measures;

(b) the definition and allocation of responsibilities for implementing the various components of environmental management;

(c) the measurement, monitoring and reporting of information on performance;

(d) a process for ensuring feedback on systems and procedures so that the necessary changes can be actioned.

There are two main instruments which influence current approaches to environmental management. The first is the EU Eco-Management and Audit Scheme

(EMAS) Regulation. The second is the International Standards Organisation Series of Environmental Management Standards.

The Eco-Management and Audit Scheme (EMAS) Regulation

E16013   This voluntary scheme applies in all member States and has two main aims:

(*a*)   to encourage better environmental management at individual production sites within particular industries; and

(*b*)   to improve the disclosure of information on the impacts of those sites on the environment.

The Regulation sets out a number of elements of systematic environmental management. Sites that can demonstrate ongoing compliance with those requirements to an independent assessor have the right to be registered under EMAS.

Following the adoption of a company policy, an initial environmental review is made to identify the potential impacts of a site's operations, and an internal environmental protection system must be established. The system must include specific objectives for environmental performance and procedures for implementing them. The system, and the results of the initial environmental review, must be described in an initial environmental statement. The statement must be validated by an accredited external organisation before being submitted to nominated national authorities in individual States for registration of the site under the scheme.

There are a number of key points here:

(*a*)   the first stage in developing environmental management is to carry out a thorough review of impacts on the environment;

(*b*)   setting up an environmental management system is a prerequisite of registration under the scheme;

(*c*)   external validation of the environmental statement is intended to ensure consistency in environmental management systems;

(*d*)   the description of the environmental management system within the statement will be on the public record.

Once a site has been registered under the scheme, it will require regular audits to review the effectiveness of the environmental management system as well as giving information on environmental impacts of the site. Here it is sufficient to note that development of procedures for internal auditing is a crucial part of an environmental management system. In addition to the audit, the preparation and external validation of an environmental statement, submitted to the competent authority for continued registration and made public, are elements of an on-going procedure.

EMAS has been operating in the UK since April 1995. At the beginning of 1999, 64 UK sites were registered. A total of more than 2,300 sites are registered throughout Europe, the majority of which are in Germany.

International standards on environmental management (the ISO 14000 series)

E16014   The International Standards Organisation is continuing to develop a series of standards for various aspects of environmental management. All are designed to assist organisations with implementing more effective environmental management systems. Table 1 outlines the various standards and guidelines within the series.

The most high profile of these standards is ISO 14001, published in June 1996, which sets out the characteristics for a certifiable environmental management system (EMS). ISO 14001 was based on the British Standard on Environmental Management Systems (BS 7750), although the latter has been superseded by the international standard.

The format of ISO 14001 reflects the procedures and manuals approach of the ISO 9000 quality management systems series. In practice this means that organisations which operate to the requirements of ISO 9000 can extend their management systems to incorporate the environmental management standard, although the existence of a certified quality management system is not a prerequisite for ISO 14001.

ISO 14001 requires an organisation to develop an environmental policy which provides the foundation for the rest of the system. The standard includes guidance on the development and implementation of other elements of an EMS, which is ultimately designed to allow an organisation to manage those environmental aspects over which it has control, and over which it can be expected to have an influence. ISO 14001 does not itself stipulate environmental performance criteria.

Almost 8,000 companies had been certified to ISO 14001 at the beginning of 1999. The UK has the third largest number of certified companies, after Germany and Japan.

Table 1: The ISO 14000 series

ISO 14001: 1996	Environmental management systems – Specifications with guidance for use
ISO 14004: 1996	Environmental management systems – General guidelines on principles, systems and supporting techniques
ISO 14010: 1996	Guidelines for environmental auditing – General principles
ISO 14011: 1996	Guidelines for environmental auditing – Audit procedures – Auditing of environmental management systems
ISO 14012: 1996	Guidelines for environmental auditing – Qualification criteria for environmental auditors
ISO 14040: 1997	Environmental management – Life cycle assessment – Principles and framework
ISO 14041: 1998	Environmental management – Life cycle assessment – Goal and scope definition and inventory analysis
ISO 14050: 1998	Environmental management – Vocabulary
ISO/FDIS 14020	Environmental labels and declarations – General principles
ISO/DIS 14021	Environmental labels and declarations – Environmental labelling – Self-declared environmental claims – Terms and definitions
ISO/DIS 14024	Environmental labels and declarations – Environmental labelling TYPE 1 – Guiding principles and procedures
ISO/FDIS 14031	Environmental performance evaluation – Guidelines
ISO/DIS 14042	Environmental management – Life cycle assessment – Impact assessment

Differences between ISO 14001 and EMAS

E16015   The key differences between ISO 14001 and EMAS are:

(*a*)   ISO 14001 can be applied on a company-wide basis, whereas EMAS registration is only granted at individual site level;

(*b*)   there is no restriction on the type of organisations to which ISO 14001 can apply, whereas EMAS is generally limited to defined industrial activities; and

(*c*)   ISO 14001 does not currently include a requirement for public reporting of environmental performance information, whereas sites registered under EMAS must produce an independently validated, publicly available environmental statement.

Implementing environmental management

Practical requirements

E16016   Both EMAS and ISO 14001 set a pattern for companies wishing to develop environmental management systems. The key steps in implementing such systems involve:

(*a*)   conducting an initial review, designed to establish the current situation with respect to legislative requirements, potential environmental impacts and existing environmental management controls;

(*b*)   developing an environmental policy which will provide the basis of environmental management practices as well as informing day to day operational decisions;

(*c*)   establishing specific objectives and performance improvement targets;

(*d*)   developing a programme to implement the objectives and establish operational control over environmental performance;

(*e*)   ensuring information systems are adequate to provide management with complete, reliable and timely information; and

(*f*)   auditing the system to compare intended performance with actual performance.

Review

E16017   In order to be able to actively manage its interactions with the environment, an organisation needs to understand the relationship between its business processes and its environmental performance. An environmental review should therefore be conducted, which clarifies how various business activities could potentially affect (or be affected by) the quality of different components of the environment (air, land, water, natural resources). This will allow an organisation to understand which of its activities have the greatest potential impact on the environment (usually, but not always, these will relate to procurement and/or manufacturing processes), and also which elements of environmental management and performance have the greatest potential impact on business performance (for example, high profile environmental prosecutions can have a significant impact on corporate reputation and brand value).

The initial (and subsequent) review should also consider the current and likely future legislative requirements that the company must comply with. It should also consider the overall organisational strategy, any other relevant corporate policies, customer specifications and community expectations which could influence environmental management practices. The review also offers the opportunity to establish a baseline of actual management organisation, systems and procedures, its compliance record and the range of initiatives already in place to improve performance.

Ideally, an environmental review should involve input from a range of stakeholders, both internal and external to the organisation. This promotes a wider perspective on potential environmental impacts, and ensures that the resulting policies and programmes to be developed by the organisation will reflect a comprehensive range of issues and risks. Consequently, the chances of unidentified and therefore uncontrolled risks emerging will be minimised.

Policy

E16018   The results of the initial review should inform the development of a written environmental policy. The policy directs and underpins the remainder of the EMS, and represents a statement of intent with regard to environmental performance standards and priorities.

The policy should be endorsed by the highest level of management in the company, and should be communicated to all stakeholders.

Objectives

E16019   It is important that the policy be supported by objectives that are both measurable and achievable. They should be cascaded throughout an organisation, so that at each level there are defined targets for each function to assist in the achievement of the objectives. A key part of ensuring continuous improvement in environmental performance is to review and update objectives in the light of progress and changing regulations and standards.

Objectives should be developed in conjunction with the groups and individuals who will have responsibility for achieving them. They should also be clearly linked to the overall business strategy and as far as possible with operational objectives. This ensures that environmental management is viewed as relevant and integral to business performance, rather than being seen as an isolated initiative.

The process of objective setting also needs to consider the most appropriate performance measures for tracking progress towards the ultimate objective. For example, if an objective is to reduce waste by 20 per cent over five years, a number of parameters could be used to reflect different aspects of the organisation's waste reduction efforts towards that, including volumes of waste recycled, efficiency with which raw materials are converted to product, and proportion of production staff that have received waste management training.

The current draft of ISO 14031 provides useful guidance on the principles to be applied in the selection of appropriate environmental performance indicators. Performance in whichever parameters are selected should be measured regularly to enable corrective actions to be taken in a timely manner. As far as possible, performance measures and the achievement of quantified targets should be linked to existing appraisal systems for business units or individuals.

Responsibilities

E16020   Allocation of responsibilities is vital for successful environmental management. Its implementation will typically involve changes in management systems and operations, training and awareness of personnel at all levels and in marketing and public relations.

A wide range of business functions will therefore need to be involved in developing and implementing environmental management systems. The commitment of senior personnel to introduce sound environmental management throughout the organisation, and to communicate it to all staff is vital.

Companies have adopted a range of organisational approaches as part of their environmental management systems. In some cases there is a single specialist function with responsibility for monitoring and auditing the system. An alternative is to have a central environmental function with only an advisory role which can also undertake verification of the internal audits carried out by other divisions or departments. The approach needs to be adapted to the culture and structure of the organisation, but whatever system is adopted, there are a number of crucial elements:

(*a*)   access to expertise in assessing environmental impacts and developing solutions;

(*b*)   a degree of independence in the auditing function;

(*c*)   a clear accountability for meeting environmental management objectives;

(*d*)   adequate information systems to help those responsible for evaluating performance against objectives, to identify problem areas and to ensure that action is taken to solve them.

Training and communications

E16021   Both ISO 14001 and EMAS include training and communications as a key requirement of the EMS. In particular, they focus on ensuring that employees at all levels, in addition to contractors and other business partners, are aware of company policy and objectives; of how their own work activities impact on the environment and the benefits of improved performance; what they need to do in their jobs to help meet the company's environmental objectives; and the risks to the organisation of failing to carry out standard operating procedures.

This can involve a significant investment for companies, but if integrated with existing training modules and reinforced regularly, many hours of essential training can be achieved. An important benefit of training is that it can be a fertile ground for new ideas to minimise adverse environmental impacts.

Communication with, for example, regulators, investors, public bodies and local communities is an important part of good environment management and requires a preparedness to be open, honest and informative. It also requires clear procedures for liaising with external groups.

Operational controls

E16022   The operational control elements of an EMS define its scope and essentially set out a basis for effective day-to-day management of environmental performance. Typically, such controls would include:

(*a*)   a register of relevant legislation and corporate policies that must be complied with;

(*b*)   a plan of action for ensuring that the policy is met, objectives are achieved and environmental management is continuously improved. This sets out the various initiatives to be proactively implemented and milestones to be achieved, and could be considered a 'road map' for guiding environmental performance;

(c)   a compilation of operating procedures which define the limits of acceptable and unacceptable practices within a company and which incorporate consideration of the environmental interactions identified in the review and the objectives and targets that were defined subsequently;

(d)   an emergency response plan to be implemented in the event of a sudden, unexpected and potentially catastrophic event which could potentially influence a company's environmental performance in an adverse manner;

(e)   a programme for monitoring, measuring, recording and reviewing environmental performance. This should incorporate a mechanism for regularly reporting back to senior management, since they are the key enablers of the EMS and because they retain ultimate responsibility of business performance.

These operational controls, and indeed all elements of an EMS, should be documented.

Information management and public reporting

E16023   The critical factor in an EMS is the quality and timeliness of information to internal and external users. The importance of providing performance information to external users is increasing as expectations of greater transparency and corporate accountability continue to grow. Such expectations have been supported in the UK by strong encouragement from Government for companies to voluntarily and publicly report on their environmental performance. Public environmental reporting is encouraged, but not mandated, by ISO 14001, although EMAS has always included a requirement for the preparation of an environmental statement as a condition of registration under the scheme.

Regardless of whether they have adopted EMAS, ISO 14001, or neither, many companies have a statutory duty to report on some aspects of their environmental performance to demonstrate legislative compliance. Some of that information is publicly available. An increasing number of companies are choosing to provide information on their environmental performance, either in their annual report and accounts, or in a stand-alone document. In most cases, the information provided extends well beyond a demonstration of legislative compliance, and tends towards a general overview of all significant aspects of environmental management and performance. Furthermore, many companies, recognising the importance of sustainability, are beginning to measure and report on their performance in terms of social impact.

As stakeholders and communication media become more sophisticated, and our understanding of environmental interactions increases, so information requirements become more complex. This means that management information systems must incorporate database management, modelling, measuring, monitoring and flexible reporting. The trend also means that environmental reports that have been produced solely as a means of improving public relations and to defuse external pressures are becoming less acceptable to many stakeholders. The main reasons for this appear to be that they are seldom generated in response to internal management information needs, which in turn means that they tend to focus on statements of management intent, qualitative claims and descriptive anecdotes rather than actual performance. They are therefore less likely to include detailed and verifiable information.

Instead, companies are recognising the value of maintaining a constructive and open dialogue with stakeholders, and published reports are being used as part of those efforts. KPMG has tracked environmental reporting practices within the FTSE 100 for several years, and identified a steady increase in the proportion of those companies that are publishing environmental reports. In 1998, 32 per cent of companies in the FTSE 100 produced environmental performance reports.

While no standards on environmental reporting currently exist, a number of sources of guidance are available. Current 'best practice' environmental reporting in the UK is dictated by the United Nations Environment Program (UNEP)/ SustainAbility benchmark study into corporate environmental reporting, the results of which have been published annually since 1996. The Global Reporting Initiative (GRI), launched in draft form in March 1999, represents an attempt to provide an expanded model for non-financial reporting, and reflects the move towards broader sustainability reporting. It has been developed with global, multi-stakeholder input from business, non-government organisations and accounting organisations from North America, Europe, Asia and Latin America. A number of companies are currently piloting the GRI model, which will be re-released in an updated form in early 2000.

In an attempt to increase the credibility of published reports and identify opportunities for improving management information systems, a number of companies are seeking independent assurance on the reliability, completeness and likely accuracy of information contained in their reports. Although there are no standards for providing an independent opinion on corporate environmental reports, the long-established financial audit model provides a useful framework. Contemporary financial audit practice does not require reconciling and cross-checking every individual figure included in a report. Instead it relies on a review of the effectiveness of the systems, procedures and controls that have been used to generate the information included in the report. That review is supplemented by testing, on a sample basis, of the application of a number of the procedures, and correlation of resulting information with that included in the report. In 1998, 50 per cent of FTSE 100 companies that produced an environmental report included an independent assurance opinion in the report, according to data collected by KPMG.

Auditing and review

E16024   Auditing of environmental management systems, whether conducted by internal or external parties, is a means of identifying potential risk areas and can assist in identifying actions and system improvements required to facilitate ongoing system and performance improvement.

Benefits of environmental management

Effective environmental management

E16025   Effective environmental management will involve changes across all business functions. It requires commitment from senior management and is likely to need additional human and financial resources initially. However, it can also offer significant benefits to businesses. These include:

(*a*)   avoidance of liability and risk. Good environmental management allows businesses to choose when and how to invest in better environmental performance, rather than reacting at the last minute to new legislation or consumer pressures. Unforeseen problems will be minimised, prosecution and litigation avoided;

(*b*)   gaining competitive advantage. A business with sound environmental management is more likely to make a good impact on its customers. The business will be better placed to identify and respond rapidly to opportunities for new products and services, to take advantage of 'green' markets and also respond to the increasing demand for information on supplier environmental performance;

(c)   achievement of a better profile with investors, employees and the public. Increasingly investors and their advisers are avoiding companies with a poor environmental record. The environmental performance of businesses is an increasing concern for existing staff and potential recruits. Some businesses are finding that a good environmental record helps to boost their public image;

(d)   cost savings from better management of resources and reduction of wastes through attention to recovering, reusing and recycling; and reduced bills from more careful use of energy;

(e)   an improved basis for corporate decision-making. Effective environmental management can provide valuable information to corporate decision-makers by expanding the basis of such decisions beyond financial considerations. Companies that understand the interactions between their business activities and environmental performance are in a strong position for integrating environmental management into their business, thereby incorporating key elements of the principles of sustainable development.

Effective environmental management can turn environmental issues from an area of threat and cost to one of profit and opportunity. As standards for environmental management systems are adopted and are widely applied, the question will increasingly become, as with quality management, can a company afford not to adopt environmental management? The external pressures on organisations to improve environmental performance are unlikely to abate. Environmental management systems can help companies respond to the pressures in a timely and cost-effective way.

The future

E16026   Environmental management is now well-established as an essential component of effective business management. Environmental management systems have been widely adopted and in most cases these have facilitated demonstrable and ongoing improvements in environmental performance. The involvement of a range of stakeholders in corporate environmental management is no longer the exception; the constructive contribution that they make is actively sought. The publication of environmental reports has also come to be relatively common among leading companies; most include a mechanism for obtaining feedback from external stakeholders, and an increasing number are independently assured in a similar way to annual financial reports and accounts.

However, there is already a noticeable trend towards sustainability management, whereby companies are attempting to systematically balance economic, environmental and social considerations in business strategies and operations. The strong inter-relationships and inter-dependence between these three elements of sustainable development make it imperative for companies to move towards a more integrated approach to managing them.

In late 1998, the UK Government announced a number of national 'sustainability indicators' to be used to assess the effectiveness of Government policies and initiatives. Pressures on business to do likewise will increase, and the efforts of a number of organisations including WBCSD, UNEP, the GRI consortium and organisations seeking to implement their guidelines will help to respond to those pressures.

The UK Government has recently launched an updated national strategy for sustainable development, entitled *A Better Quality of Life*, which clearly acknowledges the role that business must play in facilitating sustainable development. Already, companies are developing systems for achieving that, as demonstrated by recent efforts by several companies to produce public sustainability reports.

Model reports such as *Sooner, Sharper, Simpler* by the Centre for Tomorrow's Company and *Prototype plc* by the Institute of Chartered Accountants of England and Wales (ICAEW) provide useful guidance on the direction in which corporate performance reporting is likely to go. Initiatives such as the GRI are expected to further facilitate a change in approach and foster a more sustainable approach to business management.

Therefore, while environmental management will remain a critical issue for business to address, it will increasingly become integrated with other aspects of business management, reflecting a growing acceptance of the importance of sustainability.

Kate Murphy is an Executive Consultant at KPMG. The views expressed in this chapter are her own and do not necessarily reflect the views of KPMG.

Fire and Fire Precautions

Introduction – the parameters of fire safety legislation

F5001   Fire safety legislation is dually but separately concerned with (*a*) the imposition of controls on the design and construction of buildings (building control law, applying to all *new* buildings, including private individual dwellings), and (*b*) the safe management of *existing* buildings (i.e. premises) by way of imposition of specified precautionary measures, e.g. regular inspection to ensure in particular that occupants are able to leave safely in the event of fire.

'Existing buildings' are:

(*a*)   some workplaces (mainly factories, offices and shops), and

(*b*)   places to which the public has access (shops, libraries, swimming pools, theatres, hotels, boarding houses), but not private dwellings.

The precautionary measures are of two types:

(i)   general fire precautions (e.g. alarms, drills), and

(ii)   process fire precautions (e.g. control of hazardous work activities and substances).

This section deals, almost exclusively, with the safe management of the workplace.

In this connection, the current *Fire Precautions Act 1971* introduced a series of controls, by way of regulations passed thereunder, for the protection of workers in factories, offices and shops as well as various sections of the general public. The basis of this protection is 'certification', this being dependent on 'designation'. Moreover, the *Fire Precautions (Workplace) Regulations 1997 (SI 1997 No 1840)* extend protection to nearly all other workplaces. Fire safety signs must be provided and maintained where indicated by risk assessment to ensure that occupants leave safely in event of fire (*Health and Safety (Safety Signs and Signals) Regulations 1996, Reg 4*).

The current position – overview

F5002   Statute law relating to fire and fire precautions is extensive and located mainly in the *Fire Precautions Act 1971 (FPA)* (and regulations and orders made thereunder), the *Fire Safety and Safety of Places of Sport Act 1987*, the *Fire Precautions (Workplace) Regulations 1997* as amended by the *Fire Precautions (Workplace) (Amendment) Regulations 1999*, the *Health and Safety at Work etc. Act 1974 (HSWA)* (in the form of the *Fire Certificates (Special Premises) Regulations 1976 (SI 1976 No 2003)* (see F5033 below)), the *Petroleum Acts* (and regulations made thereunder), the *Public Health Acts 1936-1961*, the *Building Act 1984* (and the *Building Regulations 1991* made thereunder), the *Fire Services Act 1947* and the *Fires Prevention (Metropolis) Act 1774* as well as certain regulations, made under the *Factories Act 1961*, such as the *Highly Flammable Liquids and Liquefied Petroleum Gases Regulations 1972*.

The *Fire Precautions Act 1971* imposes requirements relating to fire precautions upon occupiers of premises (whether or not employers) where there is a fire risk; whilst the *Fire Safety and Safety of Places of Sport Act 1987* is a deregulating measure modifying some of the duties of the *Fire Precautions Act 1971* (see F5012-F5023 below). Meanwhile, *HSWA* is concerned specifically with premises containing dangerous materials and/or where hazardous processes are carried on. The *Petroleum Spirit (Consolidation) Act 1928* imposes requirements on storage and transportation of petroleum spirit, whilst the *Public Health Acts* and, more particularly, the *Building Act 1984* (and *Building Regulations 1991*) apply health, safety and welfare requirements to *new* buildings (industrial, commercial and private) and buildings under construction and altered buildings, in the interests of occupants, both present and future. The *Fire Services Act 1947* specifies the duties of local fire authorities and the *Fires Prevention (Metropolis) Act 1774*, *inter alia*, regulates liability of occupiers of premises to adjoining occupiers for damage caused by fire spread. The *Fire Precautions (Workplace) Regulations 1997* and the 1999 amendment Regulations impose a requirement on the employer to conduct a fire risk assessment.

The first four Acts, the *Fire Precautions Act 1971*, the *Fire Safety and Safety of Places of Sport Act 1987*, *HSWA 1974* and the *Public Health Acts 1936* and *1961* are predominantly penal measures, whilst the *Fires Prevention (Metropolis) Act 1774* concerns civil liability. More particularly, the *Fire Precautions Act 1971* (as amended by the *Fire Safety and Safety of Places of Sport Act 1987*) and *HSWA* specify fire precautions in relation to commercial and industrial (and a limited number of other) buildings already in existence (see F5006 below), whilst the *Public Health Acts* and the *Building Regulations* apply mainly to *new* buildings – industrial, commercial and private, and *buildings under construction as well as altered buildings*.

The Government is currently conducting a review of fire safety legislation. The results of this review will appear in the form of a *Fire Safety Bill* which is expected to pass through Parliament some time in 2000. It is intended that this Bill will consolidate current fire safety legislation.

The Health and Safety Executive is reviewing the *Petroleum Spirit (Consolidation) Act 1928* and it is expected that many of the provisions in this Act will be incorporated into current regulations dealing with dangerous substances.

Specific fire precautions regulations

F5003   The main legislation relating to fire safety in workplaces is the *Fire Precautions Act 1971* (as amended by the *Fire Safety and Safety of Places of Sport Act 1987*), the effect of which latter Act was to deregulate, to a limited extent, fire precautions law. The key to operation of the *Fire Precautions Act 1971* was (and still is) *certification* – that is, if premises were to be put to certain uses, they would require a valid fire certificate. The *Fire Precautions (Workplace) Regulations 1997* ('the Workplace Regulations') and the recent *Fire Precautions (Workplace) (Amendment) Regulations 1999 (SI 1999 No 1877)* require all employers to conduct a fire risk assessment of the workplaces for which they are responsible. However, application must still be made for a fire certificate for premises designated under the *Fire Precautions Act 1971*, i.e. hotels and boarding houses, offices, factories and railway premises. Fire certificates are also required for 'special premises' (see below.)

The 1997 Workplace Regulations originally allowed designated premises, i.e. those with fire certificates or with certificate applications pending, to be excepted from the requirement to carry out a risk assessment, but the exception was removed by the *Fire Precautions (Workplace) (Amendment) Regulations 1999* (see F5024 and F5025). Thus virtually all places of employment are now caught by the Workplace Regulations.

The Workplace Regulations do not allow the contents of a fire certificate to be such that people complying with the certificate will contravene these regulations. The Workplace Regulations allow fire authorities to modify certificates accordingly.

Similarly, safety certificates issued under the *Safety of Sports Grounds Act 1975* or the *Fire Safety and Safety of Places of Sport Act 1987* are not allowed to require anyone to do anything that would cause them to contravene the Workplace Regulations.

The principal regulations made under the *Fire Precautions Act 1971, s 12* (the regulation-enabling section) are:

(*a*)   the *Fire Precautions (Factories, Offices, Shops and Railway Premises) Order 1989 (SI 1989 No 76)*;

(*b*)   the *Fire Precautions (Hotels and Boarding Houses) Order 1972 (SIs 1972 Nos 238, 382)*;

(*c*)   the *Fire Certificates (Special Premises) Regulations 1976 (SI 1976 No 2003)* (the *'Special Premises' Regulations*); and

(*d*)   the *Fire Precautions (Workplace) Regulations 1997 (SI 1997 No 1840)*.

((*a*) to (*d*) above are collectively known as the 'fire regulations'). (For offences and penalties in connection with the 'fire regulations', see F5012 below.)

Fire certification – anchor of the Fire Precautions Act 1971

F5004   The anchor of the *Fire Precautions Act 1971* was the requirement for 'designated' premises to be 'fire-certificated' – normally by the local fire authority, though in the case of exceptionally hazardous industrial premises (i.e. special premises) by the HSE. To date, two designation orders have been made affecting factories, offices and shops *and* hotels and boarding houses (see further F5005 below). A fire certificate must be produced on demand to a fire officer, for inspection purposes, or a copy of it (*Fire Precautions Act 1971, s 19(1)(c)*). (For offences/penalties, see F5012 below.)

Fire certificates specify:

(*a*)   use/uses of premises;

(*b*)   means of escape in case of fire;

(*c*)   how means of escape can be safely and effectively used;

(*d*)   alarms and fire warning systems; and

(*e*)   fire-fighting apparatus to be provided in the building.

Moreover, at its discretion, the fire authority can, additionally, impose requirements relating to:

(i)   maintenance of means of escape and fire-fighting equipment;

(ii)   staff training; and

(iii) restrictions on the number of people within the building.

Prior to the issue of a fire certificate, premises must be inspected by the fire authority, though failure to do so or inadequate inspection or advice cannot involve the fire authority in liability for negligence (see F5007 below).

Fire-certificated (or designated premises)

F5005   The *Fire Precautions Act 1971* allowed the Secretary of State responsible to issue designation orders from time to time whereby premises put to certain designated uses would be required to have fire certificates. Although a range of uses was provided for in the Act, to date only two such orders have been issued. These have designated hotels and boarding houses (see F5003(*b*)) and factories, offices, shops and railway premises (see F5003(*a*)).

Work premises requiring a fire certificate

F5006   Under the *Fire Precautions (Factories, Offices, Shops and Railway Premises) Order 1989 (SI 1989 No 76)* a certificate must be applied for in the following situations:

(*a*)   (i)   where more than 20 people are at work, or

       (ii)   more than 10 are at work elsewhere than on the ground floor

       (in shops, factories, offices and railway premises);

(*b*)   in buildings in multiple occupation containing two or more individual factory, office, shop or railway premises, when the aggregate of people at work exceeds the same totals;

(*c*)   in factories where explosive or highly flammable materials are stored, or used in or under the premises, unless, in the opinion of the fire authority, there is no serious risk to employees.

[*Fire Precautions (Factories, Offices, Shops and Railway Premises) Order 1989 (SI 1989 No 76), Reg 5*].

In light of the amendment of the *Fire Precautions Act 1971* by the *Fire Safety and Safety of Places of Sport Act 1987*, some relaxation of earlier requirements is now possible (see F5013 below).

Applications for local authority fire certificate

F5007   Where a fire certificate is required in respect of premises, that is premises which have not been granted exemption, as low risk (see F5013 below), from certification under the *Fire Safety and Safety of Places of Sport Act 1987*, applications for a fire certificate relating to appropriate premises (see F5006 above) must be made to the local fire authority on the correct form (see F5008 below), obtainable from each fire authority. Plans may be required and the premises will be inspected before issue of a certificate. If the fire authority is not satisfied as to existing arrangements, it will specify the steps to be taken before a certificate is issued, and notify the occupier or owner that they will not issue a certificate until such steps are taken within the specified time (*Fire Precautions Act 1971, s 5*). (Hospitals, NHS trusts and private hospitals must conform to the requirements of FIRECODE. For the position of hospitals, see generally E15035 ENFORCEMENT and F5021 below.)

Despite the fact that the *Fire Precautions Act 1971, s 5(3)* lays a duty on a fire authority to carry out an inspection of premises in respect of which an occupier has applied for a fire certificate, it seems that if the fire authority fails to do so it cannot be sued for negligence, as this would amount to provision of 'gratuitous insurance' for damage (see further F5055 below). Nor is the fire authority under a duty to advise hoteliers not to reopen (see F5010 and F5058 below, *Hallett v Nicholson*).

Form for application for fire certificate

F5008   Applications for a fire certificate must be made on the form prescribed by the *Fire Precautions (Application for Certificate) Regulations 1989 (SI 1989 No 77)*.

FIRE PRECAUTIONS ACT 1971, s.5

APPLICATION FOR A FIRE CERTIFICATE

For Official Use Only

* In the case of
Crown
premises,
substitute H.M.
Inspector of
Fire Services.

To the Chief Executive of the Fire Authority*

I hereby apply for a fire certificate in respect of the premises of which details are given below. I make the application as, or on behalf of, the occupier/owner of the premises.

Signature ....

Name: Mr/Mrs/Miss ....
(in block capitals)

If signing on behalf of a company or some other person, state the capacity in which

signing ....

Address...

Telephone number... Date.............

To be completed by the Applicant:–
1. Postal address of the premises ....
....
....
....

2. Name and address of the owner of the premises

Name ....

Address ....
....
....

(In the case of premises in plural ownership the names and addresses of all owners should be given.)

3. Details of the premises
(If the fire certificate is to cover the use of two or more sets of premises in the same building, details of each set of premises should be given on a separate sheet.)

(a) Name of occupier ....

(and any trading name, if different) ....

....

(b) Use(s) to which premises put ....

(c) Floor(s) in building on which premises situated (e.g. basement(s), ground floor, first floor etc.) ....

....

(d) Number of persons employed to work in the premises ....

(e) Maximum number of persons at work or it is proposed will work in the premises at any one time (including employees, self-employed persons and trainees)–

    (i) below the ground floor of the building ....

    (ii) on the ground floor of the building ....

    (iii) on the first floor of the building ....

    (iv) in the whole of the premises ....

(f) Maximum number of persons other than persons at work likely to be in the premises at any one time ....

(g) Number of persons (including staff, guests and other residents) for whom sleeping accommodation is provided in the premises–

    (i) below the ground floor of the building ....

    (ii) above the first floor of the building ....

    (iii) in the whole of the premises ....

4. If the premises consist of part only of a building, the uses to which the other parts of the building are put (on a floor by floor basis):

....

....

....

5. (a) Total number of floors (excluding basements) in the building in which the premises are situated ....

    (b) Total number of basements in that building ....

6. Approximate date of construction of the premises ....

7. Nature and quantity of any explosive or highly flammable materials stored or used in or under the premises

Materials	Maximum quantity stored	Method of storage	Maximum quantity liable to be exposed at any one time

(Continue on a separate sheet if necessary)

8. Details of fire-fighting equipment available for use in the premises

Nature of equipment	Number Provided	Where installed	Is the equipment regularly maintained?
(a) Hosereels			Yes/No
(b) Portable fire extinguishers			Yes/No
(c) Others			Yes/No
(specify types e.g. sand/water buckets. fire blanket)			

(Continue on a separate sheet if necessary)

Who should apply?

F5009 Application should normally be made by the occupier in the case of factories, offices and shops. In the following cases it must be made by the owner or owners:

(*a*) premises consisting of part of a building, all parts of which are owned by the same person (i.e. multi-occupancy/single ownership situations);

(*b*) premises consisting of part of a building, the different parts being owned by different persons (i.e. multi-occupancy/plural ownership situations).

[*Fire Precautions Act 1971, s 5, Sch 2 Part II*].

Categories of fire risk premises

F5010 Where there is in the opinion of the fire authority a serious risk to persons from fire on premises, unless steps are taken to minimise that risk, and the fire authority thinks that a particular use of premises should be either prohibited or restricted, it may apply to the court for an order prohibiting or restricting that use of premises until remedial steps are taken (*Fire Precautions Act 1971, s 10(2)*). This requirement does not impose a duty on a fire authority to advise an occupier not to reopen; hence, if he reopens and suffers loss from fire, the fire authority will not be liable (*Hallett v Nicholson*, see F5058 below).

Contents of a fire certificate

F5011 A fire certificate specifies:

(*a*) the particular use or uses of premises which it covers;

(*b*) the means of escape in the case of fire (as per plan);

(*c*) the means for securing that the means of escape can be safely and effectively used at all relevant times (e.g. direction signs/emergency lighting/fire or smoke stop doors);

(*d*) the means for fighting fire for use by persons in the building;

(*e*) the means for giving warnings in the case of fire;

(*f*)   in the case of any factory, particulars as to any explosives or highly flammable materials stored or used on the premises.

[*Fire Precautions Act 1971, s 6(1)*].

In addition, a fire certificate may require:

(i)   maintenance of the means of escape and their freedom from obstruction;

(ii)   maintenance of other fire precautions set out in the certificate;

(iii)   training of employees on the premises as to what to do in the event of fire and keeping of suitable records of such training;

(iv)   limitation of number of persons who at any one time may be on the premises;

(v)   any other relevant fire precautions.

[*Fire Precautions Act 1971, s 6(2)*].

Offences/penalties for breach of the Fire Precautions Act 1971

F5012   Failure to have/exhibit a valid fire certificate, or breach of any condition(s) in such certificate is an offence, committed by the holder, carrying:

(*a*)   on summary conviction, a maximum fine of £5,000; and

(*b*)   on conviction on indictment, an indefinite fine or up to two years' imprisonment (or both).

[*Fire Precautions Act 1971, s 7(1)(5) as amended by the Criminal Justice Act 1991, s 17(1)*].

An occupier also commits an offence if the fire authority or inspectorate is not informed of a proposed structural or material alteration (*Fire Precautions Act 1971, s 8*). Breach carries the same penalties as for breach of *s 7* (above). Other offences include obstructing a fire inspector (*s 19(6)*) and forging/falsifying a fire certificate (*s 22(1)*).

Waiver of certification for designated premises

F5013   Under the insertions in the *Fire Safety and Safety of Places of Sport Act 1987*, a fire authority can grant exemption from certification requirements in the case of 'designated use' premises (*Fire Precautions Act 1971, s 1(3A)*). The powers to grant exemption are given to the local fire authority by the amended *Fire Precautions Act 1971, s 5A*. Exemption from certification requirements can be granted, either on application for a fire certificate, or at any time during the currency of a fire certificate. Fire certificates are not necessary, in the case of factory, office, shop and railway premises, where either

(*a*)   a fire authority has granted exemption (under *Sec 5A* of the *Fire Precautions Act 1971* (as amended)) in the case of 'low-risk' premises, or

(*b*)   there are fewer than

(i)   20 employees in buildings containing two or more factory and/or office premises at any one time, or

(ii)   10 employees in buildings containing two or more factory and/or office premises at any one time, elsewhere than on the ground floor.

(1989 Code of Practice for fire precautions in factories, offices, shops and railway premises not required to have a fire certificate, operational as from 1 April 1989.)

It is not necessary formally to apply for exemption (*Fire Precautions Act 1971 (as amended), s 5A(2)*). Normally, however, exemption would not be granted unless the fire authority had first carried out an inspection within the previous twelve months. Hence, if exemption is granted on application for a fire certificate, the grant disposes of the application; alternatively, if the grant is made during the currency of a fire certificate, the certificate ceases to have effect. Any exemption certificate must specify the greatest number of persons who can safely be in the premises at any one time. Such exemptions can be withdrawn by the fire authority without an inspection/inquiry as to the degree of seriousness of risk from fire to persons on the premises etc., in which case notice of withdrawal must be given.

Change of conditions affecting premises for which exemption is granted

F5014   If, while an exemption is in force an occupier proposes to carry out material changes in the premises, the occupier must inform the fire authority of the proposed changes. Not to do so is to commit an offence (*Fire Precautions Act 1971, s 8A(1)*). This applies where it is proposed:

(*a*)   to make an extension of, or structural alteration to the premises which would affect the means of escape from the premises; or

(*b*)   to make an alteration in the internal arrangement of the premises, or in the furniture or equipment, which would affect the means of escape from the premises; or

(*c*)   to keep explosive or highly flammable materials under, in or on the premises, in a quantity or aggregate quantity greater than the prescribed maximum; or

(*d*)   (where an exemption grant depends on a specified number of persons being on the premises) to make use of the premises which involves there being a greater number of persons on the premises.

[*Fire Precautions Act 1971, s 8A(2)*].

Offences/penalties – exempted premises

F5015   Any person found guilty of any of these offences is liable:

(*a*)   on summary conviction to a maximum fine of £5,000,

(*b*)   on conviction on indictment, to an indefinite fine or imprisonment for up to two years (or both).

[*Fire Precautions Act 1971, s 8A(3)*].

Duty to provide/maintain means of escape – exempted premises

F5016   Premises which are exempt from fire certification must be provided with:

(*a*)   means of escape in the case of fire; and

(*b*)   means of fighting fire;

as may reasonably be required by the fire authority (*Fire Precautions Act 1971, s 9A(1)*, but this section does not apply where *Part II* of the *Fire Precautions*

(Workplace) Regulations 1997 applies. *Part II* of the *1997 Regulations* is entitled 'Fire Precautions in the Workplace' and comprises *Regs 3–6*).

Breach of this duty carries with it a maximum fine of £5,000 (*Fire Precautions Act 1971, s 9A(3)*). However, it is important to note that there is no breach of duty to provide means of escape/fire-fighting equipment where the fire authority has served an *improvement notice* in respect of the premises (see F5018 below). Moreover, it is anticipated that codes of practice relating to means of escape and fire-fighting methods and equipment, which are not themselves legally enforceable, will be issued. This means that an occupier who failed to follow a provision of a code of practice would have non-compliance taken into account under proceedings for breach of the Act. Compliance with such codes of practice will be admissible as a defence.

Definition of 'escape'

F5017   In relation to premises 'escape' means 'escape from them to some place of safety beyond the building, which constitutes or comprises the premises, and any area enclosed by it or within it; accordingly, conditions or requirements can be imposed as respects any place or thing by means of which a person escapes from premises to a place of safety' (*Fire Precautions Act 1971, s 5(5) as amended by FSSPSA 1987, s 4(2)*).

Improvement notices

F5018   Use of improvement notices, which have proved effective in general health and safety law for upgrading standards of health and safety at the workplace, has been duplicated in fire precautions law. Thus, where a fire authority is of the opinion that the duty to provide:

(*a*)   means of escape; and

(*b*)   means of fire-fighting;

has been breached, they can serve on the occupier an improvement notice, specifying, particularly by reference to a code of practice (see F5016 above), what measures are necessary to remedy the breach and requiring the occupier to carry out this remedial work within three weeks, or alternatively appeal (*Fire Precautions Act 1971, s 9D*). Service of such notice need not be recorded in a public register (see further E15022 ENFORCEMENT).

Relevance of Building Regulations

F5019   Where premises are those to which, during erection, the *Building Regulations 1991* impose requirements as to means of escape in case of fire, and in consequence plans were deposited with the local authority, the fire authority cannot serve an improvement notice requiring structural or other alterations, unless the fire authority is satisfied that the means of escape in case of fire are inadequate, by reason of matters/circumstances of which particulars were not required by the *Building Regulations*. (*Fire Precautions Act 1971, s 9D(3)*).

More particularly, the following requirements are specified in respect of new premises:

(1)   The building must be designed/constructed so that there are *means of escape* in case of fire, to a place of safety outside.

Internal fire spread

(2)   To inhibit internal fire spread, internal linings must:

    (*a*)   resist flame spread over surfaces;

    (*b*)   if ignited, have a reasonable rate of heat release.

(3)   The building must be designed and constructed so that, in the event of fire, its stability will be maintained for a reasonable period; and a common wall should be able to resist fire spread between the buildings.

(4)   The building must be designed and constructed so that unseen fire/smoke spread within concealed spaces in its fabric and structure, is inhibited.

External fire spread

(5)   External walls must be able to resist fire spread over walls and from one building to another.

(6)   A roof should be able to resist fire spread over the roof and from one building to another.

Finally:

(7)   The building must be designed and constructed to provide facilities to firefighters and enable fire appliances to gain access.

[*Building Regulations 1991, Sch 1*].

Practical guidance is given in '*Approved Document B*' in the *Building Regulations 1991*, published by the Stationery Office.

Appeals against improvement notices

F5020   An appeal must be lodged against an improvement notice within 21 days from the date of service. Moreover, unlike prohibition notices, the effect of an appeal is to suspend operation of the improvement notice. Presumably, a ground of appeal would be that occupiers of 'low risk' premises have achieved satisfactory fire safety standards by means other than those specified in a code of practice.

If the appeal fails, the occupier must carry out the remedial work specified in the notice. Failure to do so carries with it:

(*a*)   on summary conviction a maximum fine of £5,000;

(*b*)   on conviction on indictment, an indefinite fine or imprisonment for up to two years (or both).

[*Fire Precautions Act 1971, ss 9E, 9F*].

Premises involving serious risk of injury to persons – prohibition notices

F5021   In places of work generally, health and safety inspectors can serve prohibition notices requiring a hazardous activity to cease in cases where there is thought to be a serious risk of personal injury. Now, in the case of fire hazards where there is thought to be a serious risk of injury to persons from fire, the fire authority is in a similar way empowered to serve on the occupier a prohibition notice. The effect of such notice (which need not affect all the premises) will be to prohibit use of the premises or activity until the risk is removed. The original *s 10* of the *Fire Precautions Act 1971* was replaced by a new *s 10*, empowering fire authorities to issue prohibition notices. This replacement section applies to the following premises, in respect of which prohibition notices can be served, i.e. premises:

(*a*)   providing sleeping accommodation;

(*b*)   providing treatment/care;

(*c*)   for the purposes of entertainment, recreation or instruction, or for a club, society or association;

(*d*)   for teaching, training or research;

(*e*)   providing access to members of the public, whether for payment or otherwise;

(*f*)   places of work.

(This includes hospitals, factories and places of public worship, but not private dwellings (*Fire Safety and Safety of Places of Sport Act 1987, s 13*). Thus, a fire authority could restrict/prohibit the use of any part of a hospital, factory or place of religious worship, presenting a serious fire risk to persons – premises which are also subject to the *Building Act 1984* and *Building Regulations 1991* (see W11042 WORKPLACES – HEALTH, SAFETY AND WELFARE). In particular, after consultation with the fire authority, if a local authority is not satisfied with the means of escape in case of fire, it can serve a notice requiring the owner to carry out remedial work in residential premises of all kinds, including inns, hotels and nursing homes and certain commercial premises with sleeping accommodation above them, whether a fire certificate is in force or not (*Building Act 1984, s 72*).)

The fire authority is most likely to serve prohibition notices in cases where it considers that means of escape are inadequate or could be improved. As with prohibition notices served generally in respect of workplaces, it can be immediate or deferred. Occupiers must lodge an appeal within 21 days; moreover, the appeal does not, as with improvement notices (above), suspend operation of the notice which remains in force.

Entry of such notices must appear in a public register (*Environment and Safety Information Act 1988, ss 1, 3 and Sch*).

Offences/penalties

F5022   A person found guilty of contravening a prohibition notice is liable to:

(*a*)   a maximum fine of £5,000 on summary conviction; and

(*b*)   on conviction on indictment, an indefinite fine or up to two years' imprisonment (or both).

[*Fire Precautions Act 1971, s 10B(3) as inserted by Fire Safety and Safety of Places of Sport Act 1987, s 9*].

It is, however, a defence that the person did not know *and* had no reason to believe that the prohibition notice had been served (*Fire Precautions Act 1971, s 10B(2) as inserted by Fire Safety and Safety of Places of Sport Act 1987, s 9*).

Civil liability/actionability

F5023   Any person suffering injury/damage as a result of breach of or failure to comply with the provisions of the *Fire Precautions Act 1971*, must in most cases prove negligence at common law if he wishes to secure compensation. There is an action for breach of statutory duty in the case of *s 9A* (duty as to means of escape and for fighting fire) but otherwise the Act excludes civil proceedings. The regulations made under the Act also exclude civil proceedings unless they provide otherwise. [*Fire Precautions Act 1971, s 27A (as amended)*]. This means that the effect of the decision in *Hallett v Nicholson* (F5058 below), which was concerned with fire certificate requirements, exempts fire authorities from civil liability (but see further F5055 below).

The Fire Precautions (Workplace) Regulations 1997 as amended by the Fire Precautions (Workplace) (Amendment) Regulations 1999

Extension of statutory requirements to 'non-designated' workplaces

F5024 By way of implementation of the Framework and Workplace Directives in relation to fire safety, the *Fire Precautions (Workplace) Regulations 1997* pursuant to the *Fire Precautions Act 1971, s 12*, extend fire precautions requirements to most places of work. This includes some workplaces currently designated and certificated under the *Factories Act 1961* and the *Offices, Shops and Railway Premises Act 1963*.

Regulation 8 amends various regulations of the *Management of Health and Safety at Work Regulations 1992*, in particular *Reg 3* (risk assessment). Now employers, occupiers and persons in control of premises must carry out a risk assessment of fire. Where five or more employees are at work, the assessment must be in writing and must identify those at risk.

The *Fire Precautions (Workplace) (Amendment) Regulations 1999* make amendments to the 1997 Workplace Regulations. The main changes are to extend the scope of the Regulations by removing some of the excepted categories of workplace that appeared in the 1997 Workplace Regulations. These amendments have been brought in to address concerns expressed by the European Union that the 1997 Regulations did not fully implement the Framework and Workplace Directives (see above) and to resolve the resulting legislative overlaps.

Workplaces to which the Regulations do not apply

F5025 These include the following:

- Workplaces used only by the self-employed.

- Private dwellings.

- Mine shafts and mine galleries, other than surface buildings.

- Construction sites (any workplace to which the *Construction (Health, Safety and Welfare) Regulations 1996* apply).

- Ships within the meaning of the *Docks Regulations 1988* (including those under construction or repair by persons other than the crew).

- Means of transport used outside the workplace and workplaces which are in or on a means of transport.

- Agricultural or forestry land situated away from the undertaking's main buildings.

- Offshore installations (workplaces to which the *Offshore Installations and Pipelines Works (Management and Administration) Regulations 1995* apply).

[*Fire Precautions (Workplace) Regulations 1997, Reg 3(5)* as amended by *Fire Precautions (Workplace) (Amendment) Regulations 1999, Reg 5(c)*].

Fire risk assessment

F5026   The fire risk assessment may involve six stages:

Stage 1 – identifying the fire hazards;

Stage 2 – identifying the people at risk;

Stage 3 – removing or reducing the hazards;

Stage 4 – assigning a risk category;

Stage 5 – deciding if existing arrangements are satisfactory or need improvement;

Stage 6 – recording the findings. This is a statutory requirement if more than five people are employed.

Further, detailed guidance is available in *The Loss Prevention Council Library of Fire Safety, Volume 5 – Fire Risk Management in the Workplace.*

Fire-fighting and fire detection

F5027   Where necessary (whether due to the features of a workplace, the activity carried on there, any hazard present there or any other relevant circumstances) in order to safeguard the safety of employees in case of fire:

(*a*)   a workplace must, to the extent that is appropriate, be equipped with appropriate fire-fighting equipment and with fire detectors and alarms; and

(*b*)   any non-automatic fire-fighting equipment so provided must be easily accessible, simple to use and indicated by signs,

and for the purposes of sub-paragraph (*a*) what is appropriate is to be determined by the dimensions and use of the building housing the workplace, the equipment it contains, the physical and chemical properties of the substances likely to be present and the maximum number of people that may be present at any one time (*Reg 4(1)*).

Where necessary in order to safeguard the safety of his employees in case of fire, an employer must:

(*a*)   take measures for fire-fighting in the workplace, adapted to the nature of the activities carried on there and the size of his undertaking and of the workplace concerned and taking into account persons other than his employees who may be present;

(*b*)   nominate employees to implement those measures and ensure that the number of such employees, their training and the equipment available to them are adequate, taking into account the size of, and the specific hazards involved in, the workplace concerned; and

(*c*)   arrange any necessary contacts with external emergency services, particularly as regards rescue work and fire-fighting (*Reg 4(2)*).

Emergency routes and exits

F5028   Routes to emergency exits from a workplace and the exits themselves must be kept clear at all times, where this is necessary for safeguarding the safety of employees in case of fire (*Reg 5(1)*).

The following requirements must be complied with in respect of a workplace where necessary (whether due to the features of the workplace, the activity carried on there, any hazard present there or any other relevant circumstances) in order to safeguard the safety of employees in case of fire:

(*a*)   emergency routes and exits must lead as directly as possible to a place of safety;

(*b*)   in the event of danger, it must be possible for employees to evacuate the workplace quickly and as safely as possible;

(*c*)   the number, distribution and dimensions of emergency routes and exits must be adequate having regard to the use, equipment and dimensions of the workplace and the maximum number of persons that may be present there at any one time;

(*d*)   emergency doors must open in the direction of escape;

(*e*)   sliding or revolving doors must not be used for exits specifically intended as emergency exits;

(*f*)   emergency doors must not be so locked or fastened that they cannot be easily and immediately opened by any person who may require to use them in an emergency;

(*g*)   emergency routes and exits must be indicated by signs; and

(*h*)   emergency routes and exits requiring illumination must be provided with emergency lighting of adequate intensity in the case of failure of their normal lighting (*Reg 5(2)*).

Maintenance

F5029   The workplace and any equipment and devices provided in respect of the workplace under *Regs 4 and 5* must be subject to a suitable system of maintenance and be maintained in an efficient state, in efficient working order and in good repair, where this is necessary for safeguarding the safety of employees in case of fire (*Reg 6*).

Enforcement

F5030   The duty of enforcing the workplace fire precautions legislation falls on fire authorities, who may appoint inspectors for this purpose (*Reg 10*).

A fire authority can issue an enforcement notice in respect of a serious breach. The enforcement notice must notify the person who is served with it that the fire authority is of the opinion that he is in breach of the workplace fire precautions legislation and that such breach is putting one or more employees at serious risk. The notice must also:

—   specify the steps required to remedy the breach;

—   require those steps to be taken within a given time; and

—   provide details of the appeals procedure relating to enforcement notices.

[*Reg 13*].

Offences and penalties

F5031   A person is guilty of an offence if:

(*a*)   being under a requirement to do so, he fails to comply with any provision of the workplace fire precautions legislation;

(*b*)   that failure places one or more employees at serious risk (i.e. subject to a risk of death or serious injury which is likely to materialise) in case of fire; and

(*c*)   that failure is intentional or is due to his being reckless as to whether he complies or not.

[*Reg 11(1)*].

Any person guilty of an offence under *Reg 11(1)* is liable:

(*a*)   on summary conviction, to a fine; or

(*b*)   on conviction on indictment, to a fine, or to imprisonment for a term not exceeding two years, or both.

[*Reg 11(2)*].

A person is not guilty of an offence under *Reg 11(1)* in respect of any failure to comply with the workplace fire precautions legislation which is subject to an enforcement notice (*Reg 11(3)*).

Application to the Crown

F5032   These regulations do not extend to premises used solely by the armed forces, but otherwise apply to premises which are Crown occupied and Crown owned. *Section 10* of the *Fire Precautions Act 1971* only binds the Crown in so far as it applies to premises and workplaces owned by the Crown but not occupied by the Crown (*Reg 18*).

Ultra-hazardous premises – (special premises) – the Fire Certificates (Special Premises) Regulations 1976 (SI 1976 No 2003)

F5033   In the case of premises containing hazardous materials or processes (i.e. special premises), a fire certificate must be obtained from HSE. This applies even if only a small number of persons is employed there. Exemption from this requirement may be granted where the regulations are inappropriate or not reasonably practicable of implementation.

When a certificate has been issued by the HSE the occupier of those premises must post a notice in those premises, stating:

(*a*)   that the certificate has been issued; and

(*b*)   the places where it (or a copy) can be inspected easily by any person who might be affected by its provisions; and

(*c*)   the date of the posting of the notice.

[*Fire Certificates (Special Premises) Regulations 1976, Reg 5(5)(6)*].

These conditions do not override those applicable to a licence for the storage of petroleum spirit under the *Petroleum Spirit (Consolidation) Act 1928*.

'Special premises' for which a fire certificate is required from the HSE

F5034   The 'special premises' for which a fire certificate is required from the HSE are set out for reference in Table 1 below.

Table 1

'Special premises' for which a fire certificate is required by HSE

1   Any premises at which are carried on any manufacturing processes in which the total quantity of any highly flammable liquid under pressure greater than atmospheric pressure and above its boiling point at atmospheric pressure may exceed 50 tonnes.

2   Any premises at which is carried on the manufacturing of expanded cellular plastics and at which the quantities manufactured are normally of, or in excess of, 50 tonnes per week.

3   Any premises at which there is stored, or there are facilities provided for the storage of, liquefied petroleum gas in quantities of, or in excess of, 100 tonnes except where the liquefied petroleum gas is kept for use at the premises either as a fuel, or for the production of an atmosphere for the heat-treatment of metals.

4   Any premises at which there is stored, or there are facilities provided for the storage of, liquefied natural gas in quantities of, or in excess of, 100 tonnes except where the liquefied natural gas is kept solely for use at the premises as a fuel.

5   Any premises at which there is stored, or there are facilities provided for the storage of, any liquefied flammable gas consisting predominantly of methyl acetylene in quantities of, or in excess of, 100 tonnes except where the liquefied flammable gas is kept solely for use at the premises as a fuel.

6   Any premises at which oxygen is manufactured and at which there are stored, or there are facilities provided for the storage of, quantities of liquid oxygen of, or in excess of, 135 tonnes.

7   Any premises at which there are stored, or there are facilities provided for the storage of, quantities of chlorine of, or in excess of, 50 tonnes except when the chlorine is kept solely for the purpose of water purification.

8   Any premises at which artificial fertilizers are manufactured and at which there are stored, or there are facilities provided for the storage of, quantities of ammonia of, or in excess of, 250 tonnes.

9   Any premises at which there are in process, manufacture, use or storage at any one time, or there are facilities provided for such processing, manufacture, use or storage of, quantities of any of the materials listed below in, or in excess of, the quantities specified —

Phosgene	5 tonnes
Ethylene oxide	20 tonnes
Carbon disulphide	50 tonnes

Acrylonitrile	50 tonnes
Hydrogen cyanide	50 tonnes
Ethylene	100 tonnes
Propylene	100 tonnes
Any highly flammable liquid not otherwise specified	4,000 tonnes

10   Explosives, factories or magazines which are required to be licensed under the Explosives Act 1875.

11   Any building on the surface at any mine within the meaning of the Mines and Quarries Act 1954.

12   Any premises in which there is comprised —

(*a*)   any undertaking on a site for which a licence is required in accordance with section 1 of the Nuclear Installations Act 1965 or for which a permit is required in accordance with section 2 of that Act; or

(*b*)   any undertaking which would, except for the fact that it is carried on by the United Kingdom Atomic Energy Authority, or by, or on behalf of, the Crown, be required to have a licence or permit in accordance with the provisions mentioned in sub-paragraph (a) above.

13   Any premises containing any machine or apparatus in which charged particles can be accelerated by the equivalent of a voltage of not less than 50 megavolts except where the premises are used as a hospital.

14   Premises to which Regulation 26 of the Ionising Radiations Regulations 1985 (SI 1985 No 1333) applies.

15   Any building, or part of a building, which either —

(*a*)   is constructed for temporary occupation for the purposes of building operations or works of engineering construction; or

(*b*)   is in existence at the first commencement there of any further such operations or works

and which is used for any process of work ancillary to any such operations or works (but see F5035 below).

[*Fire Certificates (Special Premises) Regulations 1976, Sch 1 Part I*].

Temporary buildings used for building operations or construction work – exempted

F5035   By virtue of the *Special Premises Regulations 1976, Sch 1 para 15* a fire certificate is required in the case of buildings constructed for temporary occupation for the purposes of building operations or works of engineering construction (see CON-STRUCTION AND BUILDING OPERATIONS), and buildings already in existence for such purposes when such operations or works begin. An exemption is available, however, if:

(*a*)   fewer than 20 persons are employed at any one time, or fewer than 10 elsewhere than on the ground floor; and

(*b*)   the nine conditions set out in *Sch 1 Pt II* are satisfied.

[*Special Premises Regulations, Reg 3(1), Sch 1 para 15*].

There must, however, be provided suitable means of escape in case of fire, adequate fire-fighting equipment, exit doorways that can be easily and immediately opened from inside, unobstructed passageways as well as distinctive and conspicuous marking of fire exits.

Other dangerous processes

F5036   Certain particularly dangerous processes are controlled, as far as fire prevention measures are concerned, by specific regulations. These are:

(*a*)   the *Celluloid (Manufacture, etc.) Regulations 1921 (SR & O 1921 No 1825)* – applying to the manufacture, manipulation and storage of celluloid and the disposal of celluloid waste;

(*b*)   the *Manufacture of Cinematograph Film Regulations 1928 (SR & O 1928 No 82)* – applicable to the manufacture, repair, manipulation or use of cinematograph film;

(*c*)   the *Cinematograph Film Stripping Regulations 1939 (SR & O 1939 No 571)* – applicable to the stripping, drying or storing of cinematograph film;

(*d*)   the *Highly Flammable Liquids and Liquefied Petroleum Gases Regulations 1972 (SI 1972 No 917)* – applicable to premises containing highly flammable liquids and liquefied petroleum gases;

(*e*)   the *Magnesium (Grinding of Castings and Other Articles) Special Regulations 1946 (SR & O 1946 No 2017)* – prohibition on smoking, open lights and fires;

(*f*)   the *Factories (Testing of Aircraft Engines & Accessories) Special Regulations 1952 (SI 1952 No 1689)* – applicable to the leakage or escape of petroleum spirit;

(*g*)   the *Electricity at Work Regulations 1989 (SI 1989 No 635), Reg 6(d)* – electrical equipment which may reasonably foreseeably be exposed to any flammable or explosive substance, must be constructed or protected so as to prevent danger from exposure;

(*h*)   the *Dangerous Substances in Harbour Areas Regulations 1987 (SI 1987 No 37)* – applicable to risks of fire and explosion in harbour areas. A fire certificate is not required for these premises [*Special Premises Regulations, Reg 3A, as amended*];

(*j*)   the *Gas Safety (Installation and Use) Regulations 1994 (SI 1994 No 1886)* (as amended by *SI 1996 No 550*) – to avoid explosion/fire as a result of gas fitting of appliances/pipes/tanks;

(*k*)   the *Offshore Installations (Prevention of Fire and Explosion, and Emergency Response) Regulations 1995 (SI 1995 No 743)* – to prevent and minimise the effects of fire and explosion on offshore installation;

(*l*)   the *Construction (Health, Safety and Welfare) Regulations 1996 (SI 1996 No 1592), Reg 21*; and

(*m*)   the *Work in Compressed Air Regulations 1996 (SI 1996 No 1656), Reg 14.*

Application for fire certificate for 'special premises'

F5037   In order to obtain a fire certificate for 'special premises' (see F5034 above for definition), the occupier or owner (see F5009 above) must apply to the relevant HSE inspectorate, e.g. the factory inspectorate in respect of factory premises. No form is prescribed but certain particulars must be provided, including:

(*a*)   the address and description of the premises;

(*b*)   the nature of the processes carried on or to be carried on there;

(*c*)   nature and approximate quantities of any explosive or highly flammable substance kept or to be kept on the premises;

(*d*)   the maximum number of persons likely to be present on the premises;

(*e*)   the name and address of the occupier.

Plans may be required to be deposited and premises will be inspected, and the occupier may well have to make improvements to the fire precautions before a certificate is issued (*Special Premises Regulations, Reg 4*).

Appeals relating to the issue of a fire certificate

F5038   An appeal may be made to the magistrates' court by an applicant for a fire certificate in relation to:

(*a*)   a requirement specified by a fire authority or the HSE; or

(*b*)   the fire authority or the HSE refusing to issue a certificate; or

(*c*)   the contents of a certificate.

An appeal must be lodged within 21 days of the date of notice from the fire authority (*Special Premises Regulations, Reg 12*).

Duty to keep fire certificate on the premises

F5039   Every fire certificate must be kept on the premises to which it relates (and preferably displayed), as long as it is in force (*Fire Precautions Act 1971, s 6(8)*). Failure to comply with this subsection is an offence (*Fire Precautions Act 1971, s 7(6)*).

Notification of alteration to premises

F5040   Any proposed structural alterations or material internal alteration to premises for which a fire certificate has been issued, must first be notified to the local fire authority or inspectorate (as appropriate). Similarly, any proposed material alteration to equipment in the premises, or furniture, must be so notified. Not to do so is to commit an offence (see F5012 above). The premises may be inspected by staff from the relevant enforcement agency at any reasonable time while the certificate is in force (*Fire Precautions Act 1971, s 8(1)(2)*).

Penalties

F5041   A person found guilty of an offence under the *Fire Precautions Act 1971, s 7(1)* is liable to:

(*a*)   a fine not exceeding £5,000 (on summary conviction); or

(*b*)   an unlimited fine or imprisonment for not more than two years, *or both* (on indictment).

[*Fire Precautions Act 1971, s 7(1) as amended by the Criminal Justice Act 1991, s 17(1)*].

Licensed premises and fire safety

F5042   Some premises, other than work premises, which must have a current licence in order to operate, will have a licence refused or not renewed by the local magistrates if the local fire authority is not satisfied as to the fire precautions necessary in the premises. (As far as these premises are places of work, the *Fire Precautions (Workplace) Regulations 1997* will apply.) The premises are as follows:

Cinemas

F5043   Safety in cinemas is controlled by the *Cinematograph (Safety) Regulations 1955 (SI 1955 No 1129)* (as subsequently amended). Cinemas must be provided with:

(*a*)   adequate, clearly marked exits, so placed as to afford safe means of exit;

(*b*)   doors which are easily and fully openable outwards;

(*c*)   passages and stairways kept free from obstruction

[*Reg   2*];

(d)   suitable and properly maintained fire appliances;

(*e*)   proper instruction of licensee and staff on fire precautions;

(*f*)   treatment of curtains so that they will not readily catch fire;

(*g*)   use of non-flammable substances for cleaning film or projectors

[*Reg   5*];

(h)   prohibition on smoking in certain parts of the premises (*Reg 6*);

(*j*)   appropriate siting of heating appliances (*Reg 24*).

Theatres

F5044   Under *s 12(1)* of the *Theatres Act 1968* premises used for the public performance of a play must be licensed. The conditions for obtaining or having renewed a licence include compliance with rules relating to safety of persons in the theatre, and particularly, staff fire drills, provision of fire-fighting equipment, maintenance of a safety curtain and communication with the fire service; gangways and seating correctly arranged and free from obstruction, doors and exits, marking and method of opening, lighting arrangements; also scenery and draperies must be non-flammable and there are controls over smoking and overcrowding.

Gaming houses (casinos, bingo halls etc.)

F5045   Issue or retention of a licence to operate depends *inter alia* on compliance with fire requirements (*Gaming Act 1968*).

Premises for music, dancing etc.

F5046   Issue or retention of a licence to operate premises for public music or entertainment depends on compliance with the fire requirements (*Local Government (Miscellaneous Provisions) Act 1982, Sch 1*).

Similarly, in the case of premises used for private music/dancing, e.g. dancing schools, there must be compliance with the fire requirements (*Private Places of Entertainment (Licensing) Act 1967*).

Schools

F5047   In the case of local authority controlled schools, including special schools, the 'health and safety of their occupants, and in particular, their safe escape in the event of fire, must be reasonably assured', with particular reference to the design, construction, limitation of surface flame spread and fire resistance of structure and materials therein (*Standards for School Premises Regulations 1972 (SI 1972 No 2051)*).

As far as a school is a place of work, the *Fire Precautions (Workplace) Regulations 1997* also apply.

Children's and community homes

F5048   Both these local authority controlled establishments must carry out fire drills and practices and, in addition, consult with the fire authorities (*Children's Homes Regulations 1991 (SI 1991 No 1506)*; *Community Homes Regulations 1972 (SI 1972 No 319)*).

As far as a children's or community home is a place of work, the *Fire Precautions (Workplace) Regulations 1997* also apply.

Residential and nursing homes

F5049   Similar requirements apply in the case of:

(a)   residential homes (*National Assistance (Conduct of Homes) Regulations 1962 (SI 1962 No 2000)*); and

(b)   nursing homes (*Nursing Homes and Mental Nursing Homes Regulations 1981 (SI 1981 No 932) as amended*).

In particular, satisfactory arrangements must be made for the evacuation of patients and staff in the event of fire.

As far as a residential or nursing home is a place of work, the *Fire Precautions (Workplace) Regulations 1997* also apply.

Crown premises

F5050   As with other health and safety duties and regulations, generally speaking, statutory fire duties and fire regulations apply to the Crown (*Fire Precautions Act 1971, s 40*; *Fire Precautions (Workplace) Regulations 1997, Reg 18*) but, owing to Crown immunity in law – itself referable to the fiction that the king can do no wrong – proceedings cannot be enforced against the Crown (see further E15035 ENFORCE-MENT). This has the effect that Crown premises, that is, government buildings such as the Treasury and the Foreign Office as well as royal palaces, are required to be fire-certificated but, if they fail to apply for certification, they cannot, like other occupiers, be prosecuted. Secondly, failure to acquire fire-certificate status could prejudice the safety of fire-fighters called upon to combat fires in Crown premises (see further F5056 below). Moreover, fire certificates are not required in (a) prisons, (b) special hospitals for the mentally incapacitated and (c) premises occupied exclusively by the armed forces (*Fire Precautions Act 1971, s 40(2)*).

Civil liability at common law and under the Fires Prevention (Metropolis) Act 1774 for fire damage

F5051   Civil liability, in respect of fire damage, can arise in one of several ways: an occupier of premises from which fire escapes and does damage can be liable to adjoining occupiers and/or fire-fighters, or even members of the public injured or killed whilst fighting the fire on the premises; conversely, the occupier of premises may be injured as a consequence of damage negligently caused to his property by the fire authority whilst fighting a fire on his premises. Again, a fireman may be injured whilst fighting a fire owing to the negligence of his superior officers in failing to ascertain the dangerous state of the premises where the fire is to be fought, or a member of the public, assisting the fire authority to fight a fire on his premises, because he has not been given suitable equipment or proper fire-fighting instructions or protective clothing, may be injured. In addition, a fire-fighter or third party, whether pedestrian or motorist, may be injured as a result of a fire appliance being driven dangerously on the way to a fire or as a result of crossing adverse traffic lights. All these situations are potential 'candidates' for the imposition of civil liability. Moreover, liability for damage done by fire spread is not necessarily confined to negligence; such liability can be strict if fire spread is within the rule in *Rylands v Fletcher* (see F5054 below). In order to ensure therefore that occupiers and others involved may minimise their liability, insurance cover, though not compulsory, is highly desirable. The basic principles relating to fire cover are considered below (see F5060 below).

Liability of occupier

F5052   An occupier of premises where fire breaks out can be liable to (*a*) lawful visitors to the premises injured by the fire or falling debris (and is also liable to unlawful visitors, i.e. trespassers, as the principle of 'common humanity', enunciated in *Herrington v British Railways Board* applies as does the *Occupiers' Liability Act 1984*, see OCCUPIERS' LIABILITY); (*b*) firemen injured during fire-fighting operations; and (*c*) adjoining occupiers.

Fire-fighters

F5053   The main principles established by case law are as follows:

(*a*)   The occupier owes a duty to a fire-fighter not to expose him to unexpected hazards (i.e. hazards over and above that of fire – *Hartley v British Railways Board, The Times, 2 February 1981* where a fireman was injured whilst searching the roof space of the respondent's premises which had caught fire. He had been told that the station building was occupied when in fact it was not. The respondents were held liable for the confusion as to whether the station was occupied or not, the confusion having led to the hazardous situation causing injury).

(*b*)   The occupier is liable to a fire-fighter for any hazard for which he is responsible, if the hazard is over and above the normal fire-fighting hazard (*Hartley v Mayoh [1953] 2 AER 525* where a fireman was killed whilst fighting a fire at a pickle manufacturing factory. The attempt to cut off electricity supply failed, owing to the novel construction of the switches, with the result that unknown to him power continued to flow. It was held that the occupier was liable because he should have known how the switches worked; the fact that he did not constituted an additional hazard for the fireman). In

Salmon v Seafarer Restaurants [1983] 1 WLR 1264, the proprietor of a fish and chip shop failed to extinguish a light under a chip fryer and was held liable for a fireman's injury.

(c)   Decisions and conduct resulting from them which, in other circumstances, could well be regarded as negligent, may well not be negligent in an emergency (*Bull v London County Council, The Times, 29 January 1953* where an experienced fireman fell from the extension ladder at the height of a fire and was seriously injured. It was held that climbing the extension ladder in a fire emergency was not negligence on the part of the fireman).

(d)   More recently, occupiers, in the form of householders, were held liable to a fireman who was injured, on normal grounds of foreseeability and causation. The respondent, when burning off paint on his house, negligently set fire to roof timbers. The appellant, a fireman, sprayed water on the fire and the resulting steam caused him injuries. It was held that the appellant was so closely and directly affected by the respondent's act that the respondent ought reasonably to have had him in contemplation when directing his mind to the acts or omissions in question, namely, using the blowlamp without taking care to avoid setting the rafters alight (*Ogwo v Taylor [1987] 3 AER 961*). This includes the reasonably foreseeable *consequences* of an occupier's negligence, e.g. post-traumatic stress (*Hale v London Underground Ltd, The Times, 5 November 1992* concerning £147,000 damages awarded to a fireman injured going to the rescue of another fireman at the King's Cross fire in 1987).

Adjoining occupier

F5054   Originally liability for fire spread causing damage to adjoining property was strict (and in certain limited circumstances, still is (see below *Rylands v Fletcher*)). Current law, however, is traceable back to the *Fires Prevention (Metropolis) Act 1774, s 86* which provides that unless an occupier has been negligent he will not be liable for damage to adjoining property caused by fire spread. This extends to failure on the part of an occupier to take effective measures to prevent fire spread once a fire has started (*Goldman v Hargrave [1967] 1 AC 645*).

If, however, fire spreads and does damage in circumstances within the rule in *Rylands v Fletcher [1861-73] AER Rep 1*, liability is strict. The point here is that fire in itself is not regarded as ultra-hazardous and hence not governed by strict liability criteria; if however fire is caused by some activity/operation on land, or container capable of self-propulsion or explosion (e.g. petrol in storage), and it escapes and causes injury and/or damage to adjoining property, there will be liability irrespective of negligence. The main purpose of the rule in *Rylands v Fletcher* is to ensure that those putting land to ultra-hazardous use, e.g. electrical supply, water storage in bulk, petrol storage, keep the danger in 'at their peril'. Thus, 'Where a person for his own purposes brings and keeps on land in his occupation anything likely to do mischief if it escapes, (he) must keep it in at his peril, and if he fails to do so, he is liable for all damage naturally accruing from the escape' (Blackburn J). This applies to fire (*Emanuel v Greater London Council (1970) 114 SJ 653* where a contractor, who was an employee of the Ministry of Public Building and Works, removed prefabricated bungalows from the council's land. He then lit a fire and the sparks spread to the plaintiff's land, where buildings and products belonging to the plaintiff were damaged. It was held that, although the council had not been negligent, they were still liable). In fairness, however, it should be emphasised that the rule in *Rylands v Fletcher* has been interpreted restrictively. Thus, 'I should hesitate to hold that in these days and in an industrial community it was a non-natural use of land to build a factory on it and conduct there the manufacture of explosives' (per Lord Macmillan in *Read v J Lyons & Co Ltd [1947] AC 156*). Indeed, given the dominance of planning decisions in land development over the past forty years, presumptively, if planning permission has been obtained by an operator for a particular use(s) of land (as will be normal), it is impossible to say that use of said land is 'non-natural'; hence in most cases potentially dangerous activities are outside the scope of the rule of strict liability.

Liability of fire authority

General

F5055   Civil liability of fire brigades and fire authorities for injury or damage to members of the public and their property must be regarded as an unsettled area of law. Such uncertainty arises because

(a)   neither the *Fire Services Act 1947* nor the *Fire Precautions Act 1971* make express provision for civil liability in connection with their operational activities;

(b)   the leading case on civil liability of statutory authorities/undertakers generally (*East Suffolk Rivers Catchment Board v Kent [1941] AC 74*) was concerned with damage caused in exercise of a statutory *discretion* (or power), whereas fire brigades/fire authorities are under a statutory *duty* to attend fires. Thus, the *Fire Services Act 1947, s 1* imposes a general duty on every fire authority to make provision for firefighting purposes. In particular, the services of a fire brigade and equipment necessary to meet all normal requirements should be secured, as well as arrangements for dealing with calls for fire brigade assistance in cases of fire; and

(c)   *Atkinson v Newcastle & Gateshead Waterworks Co (1877) LR 2 Ex D 441* had established that statutory utility authorities (e.g. water, fire) were not indiscriminate providers of gratuitous insurance to beleaguered property owners/occupiers, with the consequence that there was no liability upon such authorities at common law for negligence. Property owners/occupiers had to provide their own insurance against risks such as fire/water damage. In *Atkinson's* case the plaintiff's timber yard was gutted by fire, there being insufficient water in the mains to extinguish it. The defendants were required by statute to maintain a certain pressure of water in their pipes, with a daily penalty for failure to do so. The plaintiff sued the defendants for loss caused by fire on the ground that they were in breach of a statutory duty to maintain a specified water pressure in the pipes. It was held that the statute did not disclose a cause of action, since it was not the intention of Parliament to make water authorities indiscriminate providers of gratuitous insurance. A rash of recent cases illustrates the uncertainty.

In *Duff v Highland and Islands Fire Board 1995 SLT 1362* Lord Macfadyen stated that, should injury befall a fire-fighter or member of the public whilst attending or going to a fire, or damage occur to attended property or adjoining ones, as a general principle, in such operational matters, the fire brigade/fire authority did not enjoy immunity from civil action analogous with that enjoyed by the police in the investigation of crime. This view was recently confirmed in *Capital and Counties plc v Hampshire CC, The Times, 26 April 1996*, where a fire brigade was held liable in negligence when a fireman ordered a sprinkler system to be turned off in a burning building; the brigade was not immune from liability to the owner of the building on the ground of public policy. Similarly, in *Crown River Cruises Ltd v Kimbolton Fireworks Ltd and the London Fire and Civil Defence Authority (Queen's Bench),*

27 February 1996, during the course of a fireworks display a small fire started on a dumb barge, caused by hot and burning debris falling during the display, and was attended by the London Fire and Civil Defence Authority. Subsequently, a passenger vessel moored alongside the barge as usual. Later that night fire broke out on that vessel with substantial damage being caused to the barge as well. The fire on board the passenger vessel was the result of the fire authority's negligent failure to extinguish the original fire properly. It was held that both the firework display organiser and the London Fire Authority were liable 25% and 75% to the plaintiff.

A different view prevailed, however, in *Church of Jesus Christ of Latter-Day Saints (Great Britain) v Yorkshire Fire and Civil Defence Authority, The Times, 9 May 1996.* Here an entire chapel as well as a classroom were gutted by fire because hydrants did not work and water had to be obtained from a dam half a mile away. An action for negligence brought against the fire brigade because (*a*) hydrants had not been regularly inspected, and (*b*) defects had not been observed and repaired, failed because the *Fire Services Act 1947* did not confer a private right of action, and this was the outcome in the slightly later case of *John Munroe (Acrylics) Ltd v London Fire and Civil Defence Authority, The Times, 22 May 1996.* Here four fire engines arrived in response to emergency calls, by which time most of the burning debris and fires on wasteland had (apparently) been put out. Firemen, however, did not inspect one unit, which abutted the wasteland, where there was combustible material visible. It was held that neither the fire brigade directly nor the fire authority vicariously was liable for damage ensuing. In particular, there was not sufficient proximity between a fire brigade and an owner/occupier of premises which might be on fire so as to impose upon the fire brigade directly, and upon the fire authority vicariously, a duty at common law to respond to a call for assistance. On the contrary, imposition of a duty at common law might well lead to defensive fire-fighting. If the efficiency of the emergency services were to be tested, this should be done, not by way of private litigation, but by national and/or local inquiries instituted by local authorities.

Injury to fire-fighters

F5056   Just as any other employer, a fire authority can be vicariously liable when a fire-fighter is injured whilst being driven negligently to a fire; or when he suffers injuries fighting a fire, though in practice such cases are likely to be rare. Moreover, as an employer a fire authority has duties to its employees under *HSWA*, and particularly under *s 2*, to provide a safe system of work and adequate information/ training in connection with fire-fighting. Thus, if a fire authority sent an insufficient number of men to fight a large fire this could be regarded as a defective system of work for the purposes of *HSWA s 2(2)(a)*; similarly, where a fireman was injured or killed whilst fire-fighting and it was shown that he had received inadequate training, there might well be breach of *HSWA s 2(2)(c)*.

Of course, a fire-fighter can only be instructed and trained in fire-fighting and its hazards within the 'state of the art'. If the hazards of a particular type of fire are not known or not documented, the fire authority would not be liable for the fire-fighter's injury (*Biggerstaff v Glasgow Corporation (1962) (unreported)* where a huge fire broke out in a bonded warehouse containing millions of gallons of whisky. Whilst the fire was being fought an explosion ripped out the walls, killing some firemen and injuring the plaintiff, the driver of a turntable ladder. He sued his employer, the fire authority, on two grounds: (*a*) that they had not removed non-essential personnel from the immediate area of the explosion, and (*b*) that training given to fire officers to fight hazards associated with whisky vapour fires was inadequate. The action failed, principally because this type of accident was (then) unique and the true hazards of whisky vapour were not appreciated).

Injury to members of the public fighting a fire

F5057 　A fire authority could be liable to other persons legitimately and foreseeably (i.e. invited and/or allowed to participate by fire-fighters at the incident) fighting a fire who are injured or killed, e.g. ambulance staff, staff on the premises where a fire breaks out or spreads to, the in-house fire brigade (if any), or the owner or occupier of premises which have caught fire and who assists in fire-fighting. In such cases the fire authority can be liable if it fails to take similar precautions as it would take in respect of its own members (*Burrough v Berkshire & Reading Joint Fire Authority (1972) (unreported)* where the plaintiff suffered head injuries whilst helping to fight a fire at his barn. He had not been provided with a protective helmet. The fire authority was held to be liable).

Injury to visitors of the occupier's premises

F5058 　Where a fire causes injury or death to visitors of an occupier, e.g. a hotelier, it is doubtful whether the fire authority can be sued for negligence for breach of the *Fire Precautions Act 1971, s 5(3)* (granting of a fire certificate to premises for particular use, following inspection) (*Hallett v Nicholson 1979 SC 1* where hoteliers were sued by children whose parents had died in a fire at the hotel. The hoteliers had applied for a certificate under *FPA 1971, s 1* and they argued that the fire authority was under a duty under *s 5(3)* to inspect the hotel; and, in addition, that the fire authority had failed to advise the hotelier not to reopen, under *s 10(2)*. It was held that the fire authority was not liable because (*a*) acts/omissions on the part of a statutory authority in the proper exercise of its statutory duties were not actionable; (*b*) the failure of the fire authority to advise the hoteliers not to reopen under *s 10(2)* was not obligatory but discretionary; (*c*) the *Fire Precautions Act 1971* did not empower, even less impose, a duty on a fire authority to recommend interim measures; and (*d*) in the absence of a request on the part of the hoteliers for advice on interim measures, the fire authority was under no duty to give such advice). Moreover, a fire authority was not liable when a fireman deliberately drove very slowly during an industrial dispute and the plaintiff's premises were destroyed by a fire. Their manner of driving was not merely a wrongful and unauthorised mode of doing an act authorised by their employers, but was so unconnected with what they were authorised to do that it was not a mode of performing an authorised act at all (*General Engineering Services Ltd v Kingston and Saint Andrew Corp [1988] 3 AER 867*).

Injury to third party road user, whilst speeding to scene of fire

F5059 　An innocent third party road user is entitled to assume that a fire engine will stop at adverse traffic signals, and so, if he suffered injury or death as a result of its not stopping, the fire authority would be liable (*Ward v London County Council [1938] 2 AER 341*). The contrary is the position where, however, a fire engine stops and proceeds with caution at adverse traffic signals (*Buckoke v Greater London Council [1971] Ch 655* where the chief London Fire Brigade officer issued an order that adverse traffic lights could and should be passed through with caution; this order laid the onus of avoiding accidents on the driver of the fire engine. Some firemen went to court to test the order's legality. It was held by the Court of Appeal that the order was lawful).

Fire insurance

F5060 　There is no statutory definition of fire, as there is of certain other insurable risks, e.g. theft, burglary. What is insured is loss or damage caused by fire. Hence, fire must be the proximate cause of loss/damage. This is not always easy to determine where there are several vying causes. For example, a shopkeeper insured his plateglass against loss/damage arising from any cause except fire. Fire broke out in a neighbour's property, in consequence of which a mob gathered. The mob rioted and broke the plateglass. It was held that the riot not the fire was the cause of the loss and so the insured was entitled to recover (*Marsden v City and County Insurance (1865) LR 1 CP 232*).

Where the fire insured against is imminent, loss caused to property by action taken to avert the risk, is covered. A cargo of cork insured against loss by fire and stored on a pier, was thrown into the sea in order to prevent an existing fire spreading. It was held that the damage by water loss was covered, since the dominant (or proximate) cause of the cork loss was the fire, itself an insured peril (*Symington v Union Insurance of Canton (1928) 97 LJKB 646*).

In order for there to be a fire, actual ignition is necessary. In *Austin v Drewe (1816) 6 Taunt 436*, stock in a sugar refinery was insured against loss by fire. A flue went up through all the floors of the refinery from a stove situated on the ground floor. There was a register, which was closed at night to retain heat, but opened when a fresh fire was lit in the morning. One morning an employee of the insured forgot to open the register. Intense heat in the flue damaged sugar on the top floor. There were smoke and sparks but the sugar did not ignite. It was held that there was no loss by fire.

In order to qualify for compensation for loss/damage caused by fire:

(*a*)   there must be actual ignition;

(*b*)   the outbreak of fire (from the insured's point of view) was accidental; and

(*c*)   something must be on fire which should not be on fire. Thus, a fire lit for a particular purpose would not qualify, e.g. fire to burn rubbish. But if such fire escaped, doing damage, the insurer would be liable (*Upjohn v Hitchens [1918] 2 KB 18*).

Fire prevention and control

Elements of fire

F5061   There are three prerequisites for fire:

(*a*)   oxygen;

(*b*)   fuel (or combustible substance);

(*c*)   source of energy;

the so-called 'fire triangle'.

Fire is a mixture in gaseous form of a combustible substance and oxygen, given sufficient energy to start a fire. Once a fire is under way, energy output guarantees a continuous source of sustainable energy, with excess taking the form of sensible heat. Fire takes place in a gaseous state, though it may be convenient to label fires as solids (e.g. wood), liquid (e.g. petrol) and gas (e.g. gas flame). In the former two cases, close inspection reveals that the flame burns a little way away from the wood or liquid.

This part of the chapter considers generally the practical aspects of fire prevention and control. It should be borne in mind that *special risks* involving flammable or toxic liquids, metal fires or other hazards should be separately evaluated for loss prevention and as regards control techniques. (For precautions against fire hazards from flammable liquids, see the *Highly Flammable Liquids and Liquefied Petroleum Gases Regulations 1972 (SI 1972 No 917)*, and HSE Guidance documents HS(G) 51 and HS(G) 176).

It is the responsibility of management to consider how safe is safe: that is, to balance the costs of improvement against the financial consequences of fire. Considerable improvement can often be made immediately at little or no cost. Other recommendations which may require a financial appraisal must be related to loss effect values. In certain cases, however, due to high loss effect, special protection may be needed almost regardless of cost.

Modern developments in fire prevention and protection can now provide a solution to most risk management problems within economic acceptability. It must be pointed out, however, that it is a waste of time and money installing protective equipment unless it is designed to be functional and the purpose of such equipment is understood and accepted by all personnel. The reasons for providing such equipment should, therefore, be fully covered in any fire training course. Fire routines should also be amended as necessary to ensure that full advantage is taken of any new measures implemented.

Common causes of fires

F5062   The following, in no particular order of significance, are the commonest causes of fires in industrial and non-industrial premises:

(*a*)   wilful fire raising and arson;

(*b*)   careless disposal of cigarettes, matches;

(*c*)   combustible material left near to sources of heat;

(*d*)   accumulation of easily ignitable rubbish or paper;

(*e*)   inadvertence on the part of contractors, maintenance workers;

(*f*)   electrical equipment left on inadvertently when not in use;

(*g*)   misuse of portable heaters;

(*h*)   obstructing ventilation of heaters, machinery or office equipment;

(*j*)   inadequate cleaning of work areas;

(*k*)   inadequate supervision of cooking activities.

Fire classification

F5063   There are four common categories of fire which are related to the fuel involved and the method of extinction, as follows.

(*a*)   *Class A*. Fires generally involving solid organic materials, such as coal, wood, paper and natural fibres, in which the combustion takes place with the formation of glowing embers. Extinction is achieved through the application of water in jet or spray form.

(*b*)   *Class B*. Fires involving:

(i)   liquids, which can be separated into those liquids which mix with water e.g. acetone, acetic acid and methanol; and those which do not mix with water e.g. waxes, fats, petrol and solvents; and

(ii)   liquefiable solids e.g. animal fats, solid waxes, certain plastics.

Foam, carbon dioxide and dry powder can be used on all these types of fire. However, some types of foam break down on contact with water-miscible liquids – special alcohol-resistant foam is needed for large volumes of such liquids. Water spray can be used on liquids that mix with water. Water must not be used on fats, petrol, etc. For foam, carbon dioxide and dry powder, extinction is principally achieved by smothering, with a certain degree of cooling in some cases. Water acts primarily by cooling.

(*c*)   *Class C.* Fires involving gases should only be controlled by stopping the gas supply if safe to do so. Burning gas should not be extinguished as a build-up of unburnt gas may explode.

(*d*)   *Class D.* Fires involving certain flammable metals, such as aluminium or magnesium. These fires burn with very high temperatures, and their extinction is achieved by the use of special powders.

(*e*)   A new classification – *Class F* – is being developed for deep-fat fryer fires to enable special extinguishers to be tested for this type of fire.

Electrical fires

F5064

Fires involving electrical apparatus must always be tackled by first isolating the electricity supply and then by the use of carbon dioxide, vaporising liquid or dry powder.

Table 2 below classifies fires which can be controlled by portable fire appliances (see also BS EN 3 and BS 6643).

Table 2

Class of fire	Description	Appropriate extinguisher
A	Solid materials, usually organic, with glowing embers	Water (foam, dry powder or CO2 will work but may be less effective than water)
B	Liquids and liquefiable solids:	Foam, CO2, dry powder
	miscible with water e.g. acetone, methanol	Alcohol-resistant foam, CO2, dry powder, skilled use of water spray
	immiscible with water e.g. petrol, benzene, fats, waxes	Foam, dry powder, CO2

Fire extinction – active fire protection measures

F5065

Extinction of a fire is achieved by one or more of the following:

(*a*)   *starvation* – this is achieved through a reduction in the concentration of the fuel. It can be effected by:

(i)   removing the fuel from the fire;

(ii)   isolating the fire from the fuel source; and

(iii)   reducing the bulk or quantity of fuel present;

(*b*)   *smothering* – this brings about a reduction in the concentration of oxygen available to support combustion. It is achieved by preventing the inward flow of more oxygen to the fire, or by adding an inert gas to the burning mixture;

(*c*)   *cooling* – this is the most common means of fire-fighting, using water. The addition of water to a fire results in vaporisation of some of the water to steam, which means that a substantial proportion of the heat is not being returned to the fuel to maintain combustion. Eventually, insufficient heat is added to the fuel and continuous ignition ceases. Water in spray form is more efficient for this purpose as the spray droplets absorb heat more rapidly than water in the form of a jet.

Property risk

F5066

Fire safety precautions needed for the protection of life are dealt with by legislation, as detailed in F5001–F5050 above.

In order to ensure the survival of a business in the event of fire, property protection must be considered and a business risk assessment carried out. The involvement of a company's insurer is essential as insurers have considerable experience in this field. The business risk assessment follows similar stages to the life risk assessment (see F5024 above) but assesses the importance of each area to the function of the business and how vulnerable they are to fire.

For example, an area where essential records or documents are stored is likely to have a serious effect should a fire occur; essential equipment, plant or stock which, if destroyed or severely damaged by fire, might be difficult to replace or have a serious effect on production would require special consideration, and often high fire protection requirements to minimise such an effect.

These risks should be determined by management; they need to be identified, considered and evaluated. A report should be produced by each departmental head, outlining areas which may require special consideration. Such a report should also include protection of essential drawings, records and other essential documents.

A typical area of high loss effect would be the telephone equipment room. The loss of this equipment could have a serious and immediate effect upon communications generally. Fire separation (to keep a fire out) is therefore considered essential, and automatic fire suppression by self-contained extinguishing units should be strongly recommended.

Essential data, usually on computer magnetic media, should be duplicated and the copy stored in a safe area which preferably is off-site. Paper records can be copied and reduced photographically and similarly stored.

Passive and active fire protection

F5067

Passive fire protection is where part of the structure of a building is inherently fire resistant. Most buildings are divided into fire-resisting compartments. These serve two functions. One is to limit the spread of fire and can be a property protection measure as well as life safety. The other is to protect escape routes by making the escape route a fire-resisting compartment. All fire escape stairways are fire-resisting compartments. In day-to-day work these compartments are most obvious where doorways pass through the compartment walls. The doors in these openings are nearly always self-closing fire resisting door sets. It is essential that these doors are not obstructed and are allowed to self-close freely at all times. Any glazing in such doors must also be fire resisting and if damaged must be repaired to the appropriate standard. (Guidance on the most common types of fire door is given in BS 8214: 1990. *Code of practice for fire door assemblies with non-metallic leaves.*)

Active fire protection involves systems that are activated when a fire occurs, for example automatic fire detection or automatic sprinkler systems. As such systems are only required in an emergency it is essential that they are routinely tested and maintained.

Fire procedures and portable equipment

Fire procedures

F5068
The need for effective and easily understood fire procedures cannot be over-emphasised. It may be necessary to provide a fire procedure manual, so arranged that it can be used for overall fire defence arrangements, and sectioned for use in individual departments or for special risks.

It is essential that three separate procedures are considered:

(a)   procedure during normal working hours;

(b)   procedure during restricted manning on shifts;

(c)   procedure when only security staff are on the premises.

All procedures should take into consideration absence of personnel due to sickness, leave, etc. The fire brigade should be called immediately any fire occurs, irrespective of the size of the fire. Any delay in calling the fire brigade must be added to the delay before the fire brigade's actual arrival, which will be related to the traffic conditions or the local appliances already attending another fire.

A person should be given the responsibility for ensuring that pre-planned action is carried out when a fire occurs. Large fires often result from a delayed call, which may be due not to delayed discovery but to wrong action being taken in the early stages following discovery of a fire. A pre-planned fire routine is essential for fire safety. The fire brigade, when called, should be met on arrival by a designated person available to guide them directly to the area of the fire. It is essential that all fire routines, when finalised, be made known to the fire brigade.

Fire equipment

F5069
There has been a number of cases where a person using an extinguisher has been seriously injured. Investigations have shown that either the wrong type of extinguisher was supplied or the operator had no training in the correct use of the extinguisher. The latter should not need to be over-emphasised, especially in areas of special risk, oil dipping tanks, furnace areas, highly flammable liquids, gas or cylinder fires etc.

The following recommendations are given in order to allow an evaluation of an existing problem and may need to be related to process risks:

(a)   it is essential that persons be trained in the use of extinguishers, especially in areas where special risks require a specific type of extinguisher to be provided;

(b)   any person employed to work, who is requested to deal with a fire, should be clearly instructed that at no time should that person jeopardise his own safety or the safety of others;

(*c*)   persons who may be wearing overalls contaminated with oil, grease, paint or solvents should not be instructed to attack a fire. Such contaminated materials may vaporise due to heat from the fire, and ignite.

Types of fire extinguisher

F5070   The type of extinguisher provided should be suitable for the risk involved, adequately maintained and appropriate records kept of all inspections, tests etc. All fire extinguishers should be fitted on wall brackets. It has been found that if this is not done, extinguishers are removed or knocked over and damaged. Extinguishers should be sited near exits or on the line of exit.

Water extinguishers

F5071   This type of extinguisher is suitable for ordinary combustible fires, for example wood and paper, but are not suitable for flammable liquid fires. Such extinguishers should also be labelled 'not to be used on fires involving live electricity'. Water spray extinguishers are recommended.

Foam extinguishers

F5072   These are suitable for small liquid spill fires or small oil tank fires where it is possible for the foam to form a blanket over the surface of the flammable liquids involved. Foam extinguishers may not extinguish a flammable liquid fire on a vertical plane. Where foam is required for hydro-carbon fires, light water is recommended, preferably by spray applicator. Alcohols miscible with water, when on fire, will break down ordinary foam and should be considered a special risk.

Dry powder extinguishers

F5073   This type will deal effectively with flammable liquid fires and is recommended, as it is capable of quick knock-down of a fire. The size of the extinguisher is important and it must be capable of dealing effectively with the possible size of the spill fire which may occur, with some extinguishant in reserve. The recommended minimum size is a 20 lb trigger-controlled extinguisher with CO_2 discharge. (Dry powder extinguishers will also deal with fires involving electrical equipment.)

Bcf extinguishers

F5074   The extinguishing medium in these is a halon. Manufacture of this class of chemicals is no longer permitted due to their adverse effect on the environment. New extinguishers of this type are no longer available although some old ones may still be in service. Recharging of existing extinguishers is no longer practised and replacement by dry powder or carbon dioxide extinguishers is recommended. This type of extinguisher is suitable for fires where electrical or electronic equipment may be involved. This type of extinguisher can also be used on flammable liquid fires; such use may, however, produce large quantities of toxic irritant gases. The hotter the fire, the more toxic the vapours produced. Therefore, a quick knock-down is essential. Bcf extinguishers should not be used on high temperature, metal or deep fat fires, especially in confined areas.

Carbon dioxide extinguishers

F5075   For fires involving electrical equipment, carbon dioxide extinguishers are recommended. Carbon dioxide (CO_2) extinguishers are quite heavy and may be at high pressure. A minimum size of 2 kg is recommended. CO_2 is not recommended for flammable liquid fires, except for small fires. Training in the use of CO_2 extinguishers is essential.

Dry powder or CO_2 extinguishers which are too small can be hazardous due to the danger of re-ignition or flash-back.

Colour coding of portable fire extinguishers

F5076   All new certified fire extinguishers for use throughout the EU are to be coloured red, as from 1 January 1997, following the introduction of BS EN 3 and the removal of the current British Standard BS 5423. Manufacturers will be allowed, under BS 7863 (new), to affix different coloured panels on or above the operation instructions label. Existing extinguishers need not be replaced until they have served their useful life.

Fire alarms in 'certificated' premises

F5077   A manually operated fire alarm system is required in any 'certificated' premises (see F5005 above), and will be indicated on the fire certificate. The system should comply with the British Standard Code of Practice for the installation of fire alarms, and any equipment used should comply with the appropriate British Standard specification. The system should be tested weekly.

Good 'housekeeping'

F5078   The need for good 'housekeeping' cannot be over-emphasised. Poor housekeeping is the greatest single cause of fire. A carelessly discarded cigarette end, especially into a container of combustible waste or amongst combustible storage, often results in fire. The risk is higher in an area which is infrequently used. The following are essential guidelines:

(*a*)   where smoking is permitted, suitable deep metal ashtrays should be provided. Ashtrays should not be emptied into combustible waste unless the waste is to be removed from the building immediately. It is recommended that smoking ceases before close of work so that if smouldering occurs this will be detected before staff leave the premises;

(*b*)   combustible waste and contaminated rags should be kept in separate metal bins with close fitting metal lids;

(*c*)   cleaners should, preferably, be employed in the evenings when work ceases. This will ensure that combustible rubbish is removed from the building to a place of safety before the premises are left unoccupied;

(*d*)   rubbish should not be kept in the building overnight, or stored in close proximity to the building;

(*e*)   'no smoking' areas should be strictly enforced, especially in places which are infrequently used, e.g. stationery stores, oil stores, or telecommunications intake room. Suitable 'smoking prohibited' notices should be displayed throughout such areas – notices should comply with BS 5499 and the *Health and Safety (Safety Signs and Signals) Regulations 1996 (SI 1996 No 341)*;

(*f*)   where 'no smoking' is enforced due to legal requirements (for example, areas where flammable liquids are used or stored) or in areas of high risk or high loss effect, it is recommended that the notice read 'Smoking prohibited – dismissal offence';

(*g*)   materials should not be stored on cupboard tops, and all filing cabinets should be properly closed, and locked if possible, at the end of the day.

Pre-planning of fire prevention

F5079   A pre-planned approach to fire prevention and control is essential. Fire spreads extremely fast, the temperature can rise to 1,000°C in only one minute. Smoke can be flammable and toxic. The essential factor is to re-evaluate the risk, identify areas of high loss effect or high risk, and plan accordingly to meet requirements and legal responsibilities.

Means of escape

F5080   Means of escape should be designed and constructed around fire travel. This consists of three stages as follows:

(*a*)   travel within rooms;

(*b*)   travel from rooms to a stairway or exit;

(*c*)   travel within stairways to a final exit.

In particular, for offices:

(i)   total travel distance between any point in a building and the nearest final exit should not exceed

— 25m, if there is only one exit, or

— 45m, if more than one exit;

(ii)   two or more exits are necessary

— from a room in which more than 60 people work, or

— if any point in the room is more than 12m from the nearest exit;

(iii)   minimum width of exit should be 750mm;

(iv)   — corridors should be at least 1m wide;

— office corridors should be divided by fire-resisting doors if they are longer than 45m;

(v)   stairways should be at least 800mm wide and fire-resistant; so, too, should doors connecting them;

(vi)   one stairway is adequate in a building of up to four storeys only; fire doors must open outwards only;

(vii)   escape doors should never be locked. If, for security reasons, they have to be secured against external entry, panic bolts or similar fastenings (complying with BS 5499) should be fitted;

(viii)   fire exit notices should be affixed to or above fire escape doors;

(ix)   corridors and stairways, which are a means of escape, should have half-hour fire resistance and preferably be constructed from brick or concrete with a non-combustible surface;

(x)   fire alarms should be audible all through the building. In multi-storey buildings such alarms will normally be electrically operated, whereas in smaller buildings a bell or gong is sufficient;

(xi) it should not normally be necessary for a person to travel more than 30m to the nearest alarm point.

In any certificated premises the means of escape certificate or fire certificate must be available on demand. The following are essential:

(*a*) all doors affording means of escape in case of fire should be maintained easily and readily available for use at all times that persons are on the premises;

(*b*) all doors not in continuous use, affording a means of escape in case of fire, should be clearly indicated;

(*c*) sliding doors should also clearly indicate the direction of opening and, where possible, not be used on escape routes;

(*d*) doors should be adequately maintained and should not be locked or fastened in such a way that they cannot be easily and immediately opened by persons leaving the premises. Moreover, all gangways and escape routes should be kept clear at all times.

Unsatisfactory means of escape

F5081   The following are unsatisfactory means of escape in case of fire:

(*a*) lifts;

(*b*) portable ladders;

(*c*) spiral staircases;

(*d*) escalators;

(*e*) lowering lines.

Fire drill

F5082   As well as being a statutory requirement in procedures relating to 'events of serious and imminent danger' (*Management of Health and Safety at Work Regulations 1992, Reg 7(1)*), as a matter of good housekeeping (in addition to being probably required as well by the fire certificate (see F5011 above, 'Contents of a fire certificate')), employers should acquaint the workforce with the arrangements for fire drill. This consists of putting up a notice in a prominent place stating the action employees should take on

(*a*) hearing the alarm, or

(*b*) discovering the fire.

Ideally, employees should receive regular fire drill, even though normal working is interrupted. Indeed, fire alarms should be sounded weekly so that employees may familiarise themselves with the sound, and evacuation drills should be carried out at least annually. Trained employees should be designated as fire wardens and carry out head counts on evacuation, as well as acting as last man out and generally advising and shepherding the public. In addition, selected employees should be trained in the proper use of fire extinguishers. Moreover, periodical visits by the local fire authority should be encouraged by employers, since this provides a valuable source of practical information on fire fighting, fire protection and training.

Typical fire drill notice

F5083   When the fire alarm sounds:

1.   Switch off electrical equipment and leave room, closing doors behind you.

2.   Walk quickly along escape route to open air.

3.   Do not use lifts.

4.   Report to fire warden at assembly point.

5.   Do not re-enter building.

When you discover a fire:

1.   Raise alarm (normally by operating a break glass call point).

2.   Leave the room, closing doors behind you.

3.   Leave the building by escape route.

4.   Report to fire warden at assembly point.

5.   Do not re-enter building.

Fires on construction sites

F5084   Each year there are numerous fires, of a major kind, on construction sites and in buildings undergoing refurbishment. For that reason the *Joint Code of Practice on the Protection from Fire of Construction Sites and Buildings Undergoing Renovation* (published by the Loss Prevention Council, Melrose Avenue, Borehamwood WD6 2BJ) proposes that the main contractor should appoint a *site fire safety co-ordinator*, responsible for assessing the degree of fire risk and for formulating and regularly updating the *site fire safety plan*; he should liaise with the co-ordinator for the design phase (see F5087 below). The site fire safety plan should detail:

(*a*)   organisation of and responsibilities for fire safety;

(*b*)   general site precautions, fire detection and warning alarms;

(*c*)   requirements for a Hot Work Permit system;

(*d*)   site accommodation;

(*e*)   fire escape and communications system (including evacuation plan and procedures for raising the fire brigade);

(*f*)   fire brigade access, facilities and co-ordination;

(*g*)   fire drill and training;

(*h*)   effective security measures to minimise the risk of arson;

(*j*)   materials storage and waste control system.

Role of site fire safety co-ordinator

F5085   The site fire safety co-ordinator must:

(*a*)   ensure that all procedures, precautionary measures and safety standards (as specified in the site fire safety plan) are clearly understood and complied with by all those on the project site;

(*b*)   ensure establishment of Hot Work Permit systems;

(*c*)   carry out weekly checks of firefighting equipment and test all alarm and detection devices;

(*d*)   conduct weekly inspections of escape routes, fire brigade access, firefighting facilities and work areas;

(*e*)   liaise with local fire brigade for site inspections;

(*f*)   liaise with security personnel;

(*g*)   keep a written record of all checks, inspections, tests and fire drill procedures;

(*h*)   monitor arrangements/procedures for calling the fire brigade;

(*j*)   during the alarm, oversee safe evacuation of site, ensuring that all staff/visitors report to assembly points;

(*k*)   promote a safe working environment.

Emergency procedures

F5086   The following emergency procedures should be implemented, where necessary,

(*a*)   establish a means of warning of fire, e.g. handbells, whistles etc.;

(*b*)   display written emergency procedures in prominent locations and give copies to all employees;

(*c*)   maintain clear access to site and buildings;

(*d*)   alert security personnel to unlock gates/doors in the event of an alarm;

(*e*)   install clear signs in prominent positions, indicating locations of fire access routes, escape routes and positions of dry riser inlets and fire extinguishers.

Designing out fire

F5087   Construction works should be designed and sequenced to accommodate

(*a*)   permanent fire escape stairs, including compartment walls;

(*b*)   fire compartments in buildings under construction, including installation of fire doors;

(*c*)   fire protective materials to structural steelwork;

(*d*)   planned firefighting shafts duly commissioned and maintained;

(*e*)   lightning conductors;

(*f*)   automatic fire detection systems;

(*g*)   automatic sprinkler and other fixed fire fighting installations.

Moreover, adequate water supplies should be available and hydrants suitably marked and kept clear of obstruction.

Other fire precautions on site

F5088   Portable fire extinguishers can represent the difference between a conflagration and a fire kept under control. Therefore, personnel must be trained in the use of portable firefighting equipment and adequate numbers of suitable types of portable extinguishers should be available. They should be located in conspicuous positions near exits on each floor. In the open, they should be 500 mm above ground bearing the sign 'Fire Point' and be protected from both work activities and adverse weather conditions. In addition, all mechanically-propelled site plant should carry an appropriate fire extinguisher, and extinguishers, hydrants and fire protection equipment should be maintained and regularly inspected by the site fire safety co-ordinator.

Plant on construction sites also constitutes a potential danger. All internal combustion engines of powered equipment, therefore, should be positioned in the open air or in a well-ventilated non-combustible enclosure. They should be separated from working areas and sited so that exhaust pipes/gases are kept clear of combustible materials. Moreover, fuel tanks should not be filled whilst engines are running and compressors should be housed singly away from other plant in separate enclosures.

Consequences of failure to comply with code

F5089

Non-compliance with the provisions of this code could well result in insurance ceasing to be available or being withdrawn, thereby constituting a breach of a Standard Form contract (see C8127 CONSTRUCTION AND BUILDING OPERATIONS). Where fire damage is caused to property by the negligence of employees of a subcontractor, then, in accordance with Clause 6.2 of the JCT Contract, to the effect that the contractor is liable for 'injury or damage to property', the contractor is liable and not the employer (or building owner); even though, under Clause 6.3B, the employer is required to insure against loss or damage to existing structures, to the work in progress, and to all unfixed materials and goods intended for, delivered to or placed on the works (*National Trust v Haden Young Ltd, The Times, 11 August 1994*). The practical implementation of fire precautions on construction sites forms part of the overall construction health and safety plan (see C8024 CONSTRUCTION AND BUILDING OPERATIONS).

First-Aid

Introduction

F7001
The *Health and Safety (First-Aid) Regulations 1981 (SI 1981 No 917)*, which came into operation on 1 July 1982, require employers to have facilities for the provision of first-aid in their place of work.

Medical treatment should be provided at the scene promptly, efficiently and effectively before the arrival of any medical teams that may have been called. First-aid can save lives and can prevent minor incidents from becoming major incidents. Employers are responsible for making arrangements for the immediate management of any illness or injury suffered by a person at work. First-aid at work covers the management of first-aid in the workplace – it does not include treating ill or injured people at work with medicines.

However, the Regulations do not prevent specially trained staff taking action above the initial management of the injured or ill at work.

The employer's duty to make provision for first-aid

F7002
Employers must provide such equipment and facilities as are adequate and appropriate for rendering first-aid if any of their employees are injured or become ill at work. Employers must make sure that there are an adequate and appropriate number of suitable persons who:

(*a*)   are trained and have such qualifications as the Health and Safety Executive may approve for the time being; and

(*b*)   have additional training, if any, as may be appropriate in the circumstances.

Where such a suitable person is absent in temporary and exceptional circumstances, an employer can appoint a person, or ensure that a person is appointed:

(*a*)   to take responsibility for first-aid in situations relating to an injured or ill employee who needs help from a medical practitioner or nurse;

(*b*)   to ensure that equipment and facilities are adequate and appropriate in the circumstances.

With regard to any period of absence of the first-aider, consideration must be given to:

(*a*)   the nature of the undertaking;

(*b*)   the number of employees at work; and

(*c*)   the location of the establishment.

The assessment of first-aid needs

F7003   The employer should assess his first-aid needs and requirements as appropriate to the circumstances of his workplace. The employer's principal aim must be the reduction of the effects of injury and illness at the place of work. Adequate and appropriate first-aid personnel and facilities should be available for rendering assistance to persons with common injuries or illnesses and those likely to arise from specific hazards at work. Similarly, there must be adequate facilities for summoning an ambulance or other professional medical help.

The extent of first-aid provision in a particular workplace that an employer must make depends upon the circumstances of that workplace. There are no fixed levels, of first-aid – the employer must assess what personnel and facilities are appropriate and adequate. Employers with access to advice from occupational health services may wish to use these resources for the purposes of conducting such assessment, and then take the advice given as to what first-aid provision would be deemed appropriate.

In workplaces that employ:

● qualified medical doctors registered with the General Medical Council; or

● nurses whose names are registered in Part 1, 2, 10 or 11 of the Single Professional Register maintained by the United Kingdom Central Council for Nursing, Midwifery and Health Visiting,

the employer may consider that there is no need to appoint first-aiders.

There is no requirement for the results of the first-aid risk assessment to be recorded in writing, although it may nevertheless be a useful exercise for the employer – for he may subsequently be asked to demonstrate that the first-aid provision is adequate and appropriate for the workplace.

When assessing first-aid needs, employers must consider the following:

— the hazards and risks in the workplace;

— the size of the organisation;

— the history of accidents in the organisation;

— the nature and distribution of the workforce;

— the distance from the workplace to emergency medical services;

— travelling, distant and lone workers' needs and requirements;

— employees working on shared or multi-occupied sites;

— annual leave and other absences of first-aiders and appointed persons.

The hazards and risks in the workplace

F7004   *The Management of Health and Safety at Work Regulations 1992* require employers to make a suitable and sufficient assessment of the risks to health and safety at work of their employees. The assessment must be designed to identify the measures required for controlling or preventing any risks to the workforce: highlighting what types of accidents or injuries are most likely to occur will help employers address such key questions as the appropriate nature, quantity and location of first-aid personnel and facilities.

Where the risk assessment conducted by a company identifies a low risk to health and safety, employers need only provide (i) a first-aid container clearly identified and suitably stocked, and (ii) an appointed person to look after first-aid arrangements and resources and to take control in emergencies.

Where risks to health and safety are high, employers may need to ensure the following:

- the provision of an adequate number of first-aiders so that first-aid can be given immediately;

- the training of first-aiders to deal with specific risks or hazards;

- informing the local emergency services in writing of the risks and hazards on the site and the processes being undertaken; and

- the provision of a first-aid room(s).

Employers will need to consider the different risks in each part of their company or organisation. Where an organisation occupies a large building with different processes being performed in different parts of the premises, each area's risks must be assessed separately. It would not be appropriate to conduct a generic assessment of needs to cover a variety of activities – the parts of the building with higher risks will need greater first-aid provision than those with lower risk.

The size of the company

F7005   In general, the amount of first-aid provision that is required will increase according to the number of employees involved. Employers should be aware, however, that in some organisations there may be few employees but the risks to their health and safety might be high – and, as a result, their first-aid needs will also be high.

The history of incidents and accidents

F7006   When assessing first-aid needs, employers might find it useful to collate data on accidents that have occurred in the past, and then analyse, for example, the numbers and types of accidents, their frequency and consequences. Organisations with large premises should refer to such information when determining the first-aid equipment, facilities and personnel that are required to cover specific areas.

The character and dispersion of the workforce

F7007   The employer should bear in mind that the size of the premises can affect the time it might take a first-aider to reach an incident. If there are a number of buildings on the site, or the building in question comprises several storeys, the most suitable arrangement might be for each building or floor to be provided with its own first-aiders. Where employees work in shifts or in self-contained areas, first-aid arrangements may need to be tailored to reflect that fact.

Employees who are potentially at higher risk, such as trainees, young workers or people with disabilities, will need to be given special consideration.

The distance from the workplace to emergency medical services

F7008   Where a workplace is far from emergency medical services, it may be necessary to make special arrangements for ensuring that appropriate transport can be provided for taking an injured person to the emergency medical services.

In every case where the place of work is remote, the very least that an employer should do is to give written details to the local emergency services of the layout of the workplace, plus any other relevant information, such as information on specific hazards.

Travelling, distant and lone workers' needs and requirements

F7009   Employers are responsible for meeting the needs of their employees whilst they are working away from the main company premises.

When assessing the needs of staff who travel long distances or who are constantly mobile, consideration should be given to the question of whether they ought to be provided with a personal first-aid kit.

Organisations with staff working in remote areas must make special arrangements for those employees in respect of communications, special training and emergency transport.

Personnel on sites that are shared or multi-occupied

F7010   Employers with personnel working on shared or multi-occupied sites can agree to have one employer on the site who is solely responsible for providing first-aid cover for all the workers. It is strongly recommended that this agreement is written to avoid confusion and misunderstandings between the employers. It will highlight the risks and hazards of each company on the site, and will make sure that the shared provision is suitable and sufficient. After the employers have agreed the arrangement, the personnel must be informed accordingly.

Workers who are contracted out to other companies must have access to first-aid facilities and equipment. The user employer bears the responsibility for providing such facilities and equipment.

First-aiders on annual leave or absent from the workplace

F7011   Adequate provision of first-aid must be available at all times. Employers should therefore ensure that the arrangements they make for the provision of first-aid at the workplace are adequate to cover for any annual leave of their first-aiders or appointed persons. Such arrangements must also be able to cover for any unplanned or unusual absences from the workplace of first-aiders or appointed persons.

Other important points

F7012   Employers are not obliged by these regulations to provide first-aid facilities for members of the public. Although the regulations are aimed at employees, including trainees, many organisations like health authorities, schools and colleges, places of entertainment, fairgrounds and shops do make first-aid provision for persons other than their employees. Other legislation deals with public safety and first-aid facilities for the public – for example, the *Road Traffic Act 1960* regulates first-aid provision on buses and coaches.

Where employers extend their first-aid provision to cover more than merely their employees, the provision for the employees must not be diminished and should not fall below the standard required by these regulations.

The compulsory element of employers' liability insurance does not cover litigation resulting from first-aid given to non-employees. It is advised that employers check their public liability insurance policy on this issue.

Reassessing first-aid needs

F7013   In order to ensure that first-aid provision continues to be adequate and appropriate, employers should from time to time review the first-aid needs in the workplace, particularly when changes have been made to working practices.

Duty of the employer to inform employees of first-aid arrangements

F7014   Employers are under a duty to inform employees of the arrangements that have been made for first-aid in their workplace. One method of doing this is to distribute guidance to all employees which highlights the key issues in the first-aid arrangements, such as listing the names of all first-aiders and describing where first-aid resources are located.

Employers should consider nominating an employee to ensure that the guidance is kept up to date and is distributed to all staff, and to act also as information officer for first-aid in the workplace.

Internal memos can be used as a method of keeping the personnel informed of any changes in the first-aid arrangements. Announcements posted up on notice-boards are another good way of informing employees of the first-aid arrangements and of any changes to those arrangements. Any person with a reading or language problem must be given the information in a way that they can understand.

First-aid and the self-employed

F7015   Self-employed people may find that, having assessed their first-aid needs, they should make provision for first-aid. The self-employed who work in low-risk areas, for example at home, are required merely to make first-aid provision appropriate to a domestic environment.

When self-employed people work together on the same site, they are each responsible for their own first-aid arrangements. If they wish to collaborate on first-aid provision, they may agree a joint arrangement to cover all personnel on that particular site.

First-aiders

F7016   Sufficient numbers of first-aiders should be located on the premises to administer first-aid quickly when the occasion arises. The assessment of first-aid needs may have helped to highlight the extent to which there is a need for first-aiders. The table below gives suggested numbers of first-aiders or appointed persons who should be available at the workplace. The suggested numbers are not a legal requirement – they are merely for guidance.

There are no hard and fast rules on numbers – employers will have to make a judgement, taking into account all the circumstances of their organisation. If the company is a long way from a medical facility or there are shift workers on site or premises spanning a large area, the numbers of first-aid personnel set out below may not be sufficient – the employer may have to make provision for a larger number of first-aiders to be on site.

Selection of first-aiders

F7017   First-aiders must be reliable and of good disposition. Not only should they have good communication skills, but they must also possess the ability and aptitude for acquiring new knowledge and skills and must be able to handle physical and stressful emergency incidents and procedures. Their position in the company should be such that they are able to leave their place of work immediately to respond to an emergency.

Table 1
First-aid personnel

Category of risk	Numbers employed at any location	Suggested number of first-aid personnel
Lower risk – e.g. shops, offices, libraries	Fewer than 50	At least one appointed person
	50–100	At least one first-aider
	More than 100	One additional first-aider for every 100 employed
Medium risk – e.g. light engineering and assembly work, food processing, warehousing	Fewer than 20	At least one appointed person
	20–100	At least one first-aider for every 50 employed (or part thereof)
	More than 100	One additional first-aider for every 100 employed
Higher risk – e.g. most construction, slaughterhouse, chemical manufacturer, extensive work with dangerous machinery or sharp instruments	Fewer than 5	At least one appointed person
	5–50	At least one first-aider
	More than 50	One additional first-aider for every 50 employed
	Where there are hazards for which additional first-aid skills are necessary	In addition, at least one first-aider trained in the specific emergency action

The training and qualifications of first-aid personnel

F7018   Individuals nominated to be first-aiders must complete a programme of competence-based training in first-aid at work run by an organisation approved by the HSE. See F7027 below for a range of first-aid competencies which make up a basic curriculum. Organisations that are contracted to train first-aid personnel may be notified of any particular risks or hazards in a workplace so that the first-aid course that is provided may be tailored to include the risks specific to that workplace.

Additional special training may be undertaken to deal with unusual risks and hazards. This will enable the first-aider to be competent in dealing with such risks. Such special training may be separate from the basic course or an extension to it but does not need approval by the HSE. The first-aid certificate awarded may include the special hazard training undertaken and be indicated on the certificate.

It is important for employers to understand that first-aid at work certificates are valid for three years. Employers wishing to arrange refresher training must do so before the original first-aid certificate expires. If the certificate of any first-aider expires, he or she will have to attend a full course of training to regain their first-aid at work certificate. Employers can arrange refresher training up to three months before the expiry date of the certificate – the new first-aid at work certificate will then run from the date of the expiry of the old certificate. It is advisable for employers to keep a record of first-aiders in the company, together with their certification dates, in order to assist them in organising refresher training. Employers should develop a programme of knowledge and skills training for their first-aiders to enable them to be updated on new skills and to make them aware of suitable sources of first-aid information, such as occupational health services and training organisations qualified by the HSE to conduct first-aid at work training.

Appointed persons

F7019

An appointed person is an individual who looks after first-aid resources for the company and will call emergency services if required. The appointed person is allocated these duties when it is found through the first-aid needs assessment that a first-aider is not necessary. The appointed person is the minimum requirement an employer can have in the workplace. Clearly, even if the company is considered a low health and safety risk and, in the opinion of the employer, a first-aider is unnecessary, an accident or illness still may occur – therefore somebody should be nominated to call the emergency services, if required.

Appointed persons are not first-aiders – and therefore they should not be called upon to administer first-aid if they have not received the relevant training. However, employers may consider it prudent to send appointed persons on first-aid training courses. Such a course normally last for four hours and includes the following topics:

- action in an emergency;

- cardio-pulmonary resuscitation;

- first-aid treatment for the unconscious casualty;

- first-aid treatment for the bleeding or the wounded.

HSE approval is not required for this training.

The only time an appointed person can replace a first-aider is when the first-aider is absent, due to circumstances which are temporary, unforeseen and exceptional. Appointed persons cannot replace first-aiders who are on annual leave. If the first-aid assessment has identified a requirement for first-aiders, they should be available whenever there is a need for them in the place of work.

Records and record keeping

F7020

It is considered good practice to keep records of incidents which required the attendance of a first-aider and treatment of an injured person. It is advisable for smaller companies to have one record book but for larger organisations this may not be practicable.

The data entered in the record book should include the following:

- the date, time and place of the incident;

- the injured person's name and job title;

- a description of the injury or illness and of the first-aid treatment administered;

- details of where the injured person went after the incident, i.e. hospital, home or back to work;

- the name and signature of the first-aider or person who dealt with the incident.

This information may be collated, which might help the employer improve the environment with regard to health and safety in the workplace. It can be used in future first-aid needs assessment and will be helpful for insurance and investigative purposes. The statutory accident book is not the same as the record book, but they may be combined.

First-aid resources

F7021   Having completed the first-aid needs assessment, the employer must provide the resources, i.e. the equipment, facilities and materials, that will be needed to ensure that an appropriate level of cover is available to the employees at all relevant times. First-aid equipment, suitably marked and obtainable, must be made available at specific sites in the workplace.

First-aid containers

F7022   First-aid equipment must be suitably stocked and contained in a properly identifiable container. One first-aid container with sufficient quantity of first-aid materials must be made available for each worksite – this is the minimum level of first-aid equipment. Larger premises, for example, will require the provision of more than one container.

First-aid containers should be easily accessible and, where possible, near hand-washing facilities. The containers should be used only for first-aid equipment. Tablets and medications should not be kept in them. The first-aid materials within the containers should be protected from damp and dust.

Having completed the first-aid needs assessment, the employer will have a good idea as to what first-aid materials should be stocked in the first-aid containers. If there is no specific risk in the workplace, a minimum stock of first-aid materials would normally comprise the following (there is no mandatory list):

- a leaflet giving guidance on first-aid (for example, HSE leaflet *Basic advice on first aid at work*);

- 20 individually wrapped sterile adhesive dressings (assorted sizes), appropriate to the type of work;

- two sterile eye pads;

- four individually wrapped triangular bandages (preferably sterile);

- six safety pins;

- six medium-sized individually wrapped sterile unmedicated wound dressings – approximately 12cm x 12cm;

- two large sterile individually wrapped unmedicated wound dressings – approximately 18cm x 18cm;

- one pair of disposable gloves.

This list is a suggestion only – other equivalent materials will be deemed acceptable.

An examination of the first-aid kits should be conducted frequently. Stocks should be replenished as soon as possible after use, and ample back-up supplies should be kept on the company premises. Any first-aid materials found to be out of date should be carefully discarded.

All first-aid containers should have a white cross on a green background as identification.

Additional first-aid resources

F7023   If the results of the assessment suggest a need for additional resources such as scissors, adhesive tape, disposable aprons, or individually wrapped moist wipes, they can be kept in the first-aid container if space allows. Otherwise they may be kept in a different container as long as they are ready for use if required.

If the assessment highlights the need for such items as protective equipment, they must be securely stored next to first-aid containers or in first-aid rooms or in the hazard area itself. Only persons who have been trained to use these items may be allowed to use them.

If there is a need for eye irrigation, and mains tap water is unavailable, at least a litre of sterile water or sterile normal saline solution (0.9%) in sealed, disposable containers should be provided. If the seal is broken, the containers should be disposed of and not reused. Such containers should also be disposed of when their expiry date has been passed.

First-aid kits for travelling

F7024   First-aid kits for travelling may contain the following items:

- a leaflet giving general guidance on first-aid (for example, HSE leaflet *Basic advice on first aid at work*);

- six individually wrapped sterile adhesive dressings;

- one large sterile unmedicated dressing – approximately 18cm x 18cm;

- two triangular bandages;

- two safety pins;

- individually wrapped moist cleansing wipes;

- one pair of disposable gloves.

This list is a suggestion only – it is not mandatory.

Rooms designated as first-aid areas

F7025   A suitable room should be made available for first-aid purposes where the first-aid needs assessment found such a room to be necessary. Such room(s) should have sufficient first-aid resources, be easily accessible to stretchers and be easily identifiable, and where possible should be used only for administering first-aid.

First-aid rooms are normally necessary in organisations operating within high-risk industries. Therefore they would be deemed to be necessary on, for example, petrochemical sites and large construction industry sites. A person should be made responsible for the first-aid room.

On the door of the first-aid room a list of the names and telephone extensions of all the first-aiders should be displayed, together with details as to how and where they may be contacted on site.

First-aid rooms should:

- have enough space to hold a couch with space in the room for people to work, a desk, a chair and any other resources found necessary (see below);

- where possible, be near an access point in the event that a person needs to be taken to hospital;

- have heating, lighting, and ventilation;

- have surfaces that can be easily washed;

- be kept clean and tidy; and

- be available and ready for use whenever employees are in the workplace.

The following is a list of resources that may be found in a first-aid room:

- a record book for logging incidents where first-aid has been administered;

- a telephone;

- a storage area for storing first-aid materials;

- a bed/couch with clean pillows and blankets;

- a chair;

- a refuse bin with disposable yellow clinical waste bags or some receptacle suitable for the safe disposal of clinical waste;

- a sink that has hot and cold running water – also drinking water and disposable cups;

- soap and some form of disposable paper towel.

If the designated first-aid room has to be shared with the working processes of the company, the employer must consider the implications of the room being needed in an emergency and whether the working processes in that room could be stopped immediately. Can the equipment in the room be removed in an emergency so as not to interfere with any administration of first-aid? Can the first-aid resources and equipment be stored in such a place as to be available quickly when necessary? Lastly, the room must be appropriately identified and, where necessary, be sign-posted by white lettering or symbols on a green background.

Appendix A

Assessment of first-aid needs – checklist

F7026   The minimum first-aid provision for each worksite is:

- a suitably stocked first-aid container;
- an appointed person to take charge of first-aid arrangements;
- information for employees on first-aid arrangements.

This checklist will help you assess whether you need to make any additional provisions.

	Aspects to consider	Impact on first-aid provision
1.	What are the risks of injury and ill health arising from the work as identified in your risk assessment?	If the risks are significant you may need to employ first-aiders.
2.	Are there any specific risks, such as: • hazardous substances; • dangerous tools; • dangerous machinery; • dangerous loads or animals?	You will need to consider: • specific training for first-aiders; • extra first-aid equipment; • precise siting of first-aid equipment; • informing emergency services; • a first-aid room.
3.	Are there parts of your establishment where different levels of risk can be identified (e.g. a university with research labs)?	You will probably need to make different levels of provision in different parts of the establishment.
4.	Are large numbers of people employed on site?	You may need to employ first-aiders to deal with the higher probability of an accident.
5.	What is your record of accidents and cases of ill-health? What type are they and where did they happen?	You may need to: • locate your provision in certain areas; • review the contents of the first-aid box.
6.	Are there inexperienced workers on site, or employees with disabilities or special health problems?	You will need to consider: • special equipment; • local siting of equipment.
7.	Are the premises spread out, e.g. are there several buildings on the site or multi-floor buildings?	You will need to consider provision in each building or on several floors.
8.	Is there shiftwork or out-of-hours working?	Remember that there needs to be first-aid provision at all times people are at work.

9.	Is your workplace remote from emergency medical services?	You will need to: • inform local medical services of your location; • consider special arrangements with the emergency services.
10.	Do you have employees who travel a lot or work alone?	You will need to: • consider issuing personal first-aid kits and training staff in their use; • consider issuing personal communicators to employees.
11.	Do any of your employees work at sites occupied by other employers?	You will need to make arrangements with the other site occupiers.
12.	Do you have any work experience trainees?	Remember that your first-aid provision must cover them.
13.	Do members of the public visit your premises?	You have no legal responsibilities for non-employees, but HSE strongly recommends that you include them in your first-aid provision.
14.	Do you have employees with reading or language difficulties?	You will need to make special arrangements to give them first-aid information.

Do not forget to allow for leave or absences of first-aiders and appointed persons. First-aid personnel must be available at all times when people are at work.

Appendix B

First-aid competencies

F7027   Employees who have successfully completed first-aid training must be able to apply the following competencies:

(*a*)   to act safely, promptly and effectively when an incident occurs at work;

(*b*)   to administer cardio–pulmonary resuscitation (CPR) promptly and effectively;

(*c*)   to administer first-aid safely, promptly and effectively to a casualty who is unconscious;

(*d*)   to administer first-aid safely, promptly and effectively to a casualty who is wounded or bleeding;

(*e*)   to administer first-aid safely, promptly and effectively to a casualty who:

— is burnt or scalded;

— has an injury to bones, muscles or joints;

— is in shock;

— has an eye injury;

— is suffering from poisoning;

— has been rendered unconscious by gas or fumes;

(*f*)   the transportation of the casualty safely in the workplace;

(*g*)   the recognition and management of common major illnesses;

(*h*)   the recognition and management of minor illnesses;

(*i*)   the management of records and the provision of written information to medical staff if required.

First-aiders must also know and understand the following elements of first-aid at work:

(*a*)   the legal requirements relating to the provision of first-aid at work;

(*b*)   first-aider responsibilities and procedures in an emergency;

(*c*)   safety and hygiene in first-aid procedures;

(*d*)   how to use first-aid equipment provided in the workplace.

Health and Safety Commission and Executive

Introduction

H3001   One of the fundamental changes brought about by the *Health and Safety at Work etc. Act 1974 (HSWA)* was the establishment of a new, unified system for the administration and enforcement of health and safety. The two bodies it created for this purpose were the Health and Safety Commission (HSC) and the Health and Safety Executive (HSE). The HSC is the body given overall responsibility for administering and overseeing health and safety matters, including the effective operation of health and safety law. It is a quasi-independent body, directly responsible to the relevant Secretary of State (the Secretary of State for the Environment). In addition to keeping all aspects of health and safety under review, the HSC's specific functions include submitting proposals for regulations to the Secretary of State, and approval of codes of practice. The HSE is, in effect, the 'executive arm' of the HSC and is responsible to the HSC and the Secretary of State. The purpose of this section is to examine briefly the composition and functions of these two bodies.

Establishment and composition of the Commission and Executive

H3002   The Health and Safety Commission and the Health and Safety Executive were established by *HSWA s 10*. Both are bodies corporate. The HSC came into being on 1 October 1974, and the HSE on 1 January 1975.

The HSC consists of a Chairman and not fewer than six, nor more than nine, other members. Of the other members, three represent employers, three represent employees, and the remainder are from bodies such as local authorities and professional organisations. [*HSWA s 10(2)(3)*].

The HSE consists of three people. One is appointed by the HSC to be the Director of the HSE, and the other two are appointed by the HSC after consultation with the Director. All three appointments require the approval of the Secretary of State. [*HSWA s 10(5)*].

The Commission has its own Secretariat, but in general the civil service staff which undertake the administration and enforcement of health and safety come under the wing of the Executive.

Functions of the Commission

H3003   The function of the HSC is to carry out the general purpose of *Part I* of *HSWA*. [*HSWA s 11(1); Employment Protection Act 1975, s 116, Sch 15 para 4*]. In particular, the Commission has the following duties:

(*a*)   to assist and encourage people concerned with matters within *Part I* of *HSWA* to further those purposes;

(b)   to make appropriate arrangements for research, publication of the results of research and provision of training and information in connection with these purposes, including encouraging research and training by others;

(c)   to advise and keep informed as it considers appropriate, government departments, employers, employees, and organisations representing employers and employees, on matters relevant to these purposes;

(d)   to submit proposals for regulations to the relevant authority (see further H3005 below);

(e)   to replace/update existing law and regulations and prepare approved codes of practice [*HSWA s 1(2)*].

[*HSWA s 11(2); Employment Protection Act 1975, s 116, Sch 15 para 4*].

The HSC is given consequential powers to make agreements with other government departments, establish advisory committees, etc. for the purpose of discharging its functions. [*HSWA s 13*]. It may also delegate the exercise of certain of its functions to the HSE (see H3011 below).

Relationship between HSC/HSE and the Secretary of State

H3004   The HSC and HSE are both independent of any government department. However, the HSC is under a continuing duty to submit particulars of its functions to the Secretary of State. [*HSWA s 11(3)(a)*]. The Secretary of State also has the power to give specific directions with which the HSC (and, if appropriate, HSE) must comply. [*HSWA s 11(3)(c),(4)*].

Power of HSC to propose regulations

H3005   The Secretary of State can approve, with or without modification, any proposals submitted to him by the HSC, but he has a duty to consult the HSC before making any regulations himself. [*HSWA s 50(2)*]. This is by far the most important function of the HSC; it means, in effect, that the HSC is responsible for all new statutory instruments, often emanating from EU Directives, relating to health and safety at work. Since its establishment several sets of regulations with an important effect on health and safety at work have appeared, some of the more recent being the *Control of Lead at Work Regulations 1998*, the *Control of Asbestos at Work (Amendment) Regulations 1998* and the *Control of Substances Hazardous to Health Regulations 1999*. Such regulations are normally finalised following consultation with both sides of industry, particular trades and industries, and any other interested bodies e.g. local authorities and educational establishments. Publication of a consultative document and draft regulations precedes the final statutory instrument.

Nature of health and safety regulations

H3006   Health and safety regulations, proposed by the HSC, can do one of the following:

(a)   repeal or modify any of the 'relevant statutory provisions' (for definition of this expression, see E15002 ENFORCEMENT);

(b)   exclude or modify any of the 'existing statutory provisions'. An example of this is the *Employers' Health and Safety Policy Statements (Exception) Regulations 1975 (SI 1975 No 1584)*, which exempts employers employing fewer than *five* employees from issuing a written company safety policy, as required by *HSWA s 2(3)* (see further STATEMENTS OF HEALTH AND SAFETY POLICY);

(*c*)   make a specified authority responsible for the enforcement of any of the relevant statutory provisions.

[*HSWA s 15(3)(c)*].

Areas likely to be the subject of future regulation are set out in *HSWA Sch 3 para 3*.

Issue and approval of codes of practice

H3007   While it does not have the power to *make* regulations, the HSC is given the power to approve and issue codes of practice for the purpose of providing practical guidance on the requirements of health and safety legislation or regulations. [*HSWA s 1(2)*]. The HSC may arrange for such a code of practice to be prepared by some other body on its behalf, and it may also grant approval for any code of practice drawn up and issued by some other body. In all cases, the HSC is required to consult any appropriate government department, or other body, beforehand and it must also obtain the consent of the Secretary of State to its approval of the code. There are additional provisions relating to publicising approval of a code, revising codes, withdrawing approval in appropriate cases, etc. [*HSWA s 16*].

A code of practice approved in this way is an 'approved code of practice' [*HSWA s 16(7)*] a recent example being the Approved Code of Practice relating to the *Control of Major Accident Hazards Regulations 1999*.

Investigations and inquiries

H3008   The HSC is given the following powers:

(*a*)   to request the HSE (or any other person) to investigate any accident, occurrence, situation or matter which the HSC considers ought to be investigated and present a special report to the HSC on the findings of the investigation;

(*b*)   if the Secretary of State consents, to direct that an inquiry be held into any accident, occurrence, situation or matter.

[*HSWA s 14*].

Functions of the Executive

Arrangements for enforcement of duties

H3009   The principal function of the HSE is to make adequate arrangements for the *enforcement* of the general duties of *HSWA* and any other relevant statutory provisions, contained in other protective Acts (or regulations passed thereunder), e.g. the *Offices, Shops and Railway Premises Act 1963* and the *Fire Precautions Act 1971*, unless the responsibility for enforcement lies with some other enforcing body such as a local authority (see ENFORCEMENT). [*HSWA s 18(1)*].

The *Health and Safety (Fees) Regulations 1999 (SI 1999 No 645)* came into force on 1 April 1999. They update and replace the *Health and Safety (Fees) Regulations 1997 (SI 1997 No 2505)*. They fix or determine the fees payable by an applicant to the Health and Safety Executive in respect of an application made, *inter alia*, for:

(*a*)   an approval under mines and quarries legislation;

(*b*)   an approval of certain respiratory protective equipment;

(*c*)   an approval of a scheme or programme under the *Freight Containers (Safety Convention) Regulations 1984*;

(*d*)   a licence under the *Asbestos (Licensing) Regulations 1983* (see A5030 ASBESTOS);

(*e*)   an approval of dosimetry services and type approval of radiation generators or apparatus containing radioactive substances under the *Ionising Radiations Regulations 1985*;

(*f*)   an approval under the *Carriage of Dangerous Goods by Road (Driver Training) Regulations 1996*;

(*g*)   a vocational training certificate under the *Carriage of Dangerous Goods by Road (Driver Training) Regulations 1996*; and

(*h*)   a vocational training certificate under the *Transport of Dangerous Goods (Safety Advisers) Regulations 1999*.

Transfer of responsibilities

H3010   The Secretary of State may by regulation transfer responsibility for enforcing regulations from the HSE to local authorities and vice versa. [*HSWA s 18(2)(b)(i)*].

Duties delegated by the HSC

H3011   The HSC may direct the HSE to exercise certain functions, or perform certain duties on its behalf. [*HSWA s 11(4)(a)*]. These relate in practice to the carrying out of research into health and safety matters; provision for the education of persons concerned with health and safety, and publicity regarding health and safety at work.

Appointment of inspectors

H3012   In order to carry out its duty of enforcing the general duties under *HSWA* and other relevant legislation (see H3005 above), the HSE is empowered to appoint inspectors (known as HSE inspectors), subject to their having the necessary suitable qualifications, and to terminate such appointments, if and when necessary. [*HSWA s 19(1)*]. Moreover, as an enforcing authority, the HSE may indemnify inspectors mistakenly acting outside their statutory powers against any damages, costs or expenses incurred if the HSE is satisfied that the inspector honestly believed that he was empowered to do what he did. [*HSWA s 26*]. (For the enforcement powers of inspectors, see ENFORCEMENT.)

HSE publications

H3013   The HSE (through HSE Books) publishes a series of guidance notes/advisory literature for employers, local authorities, trade unions, insurance companies etc. on most aspects of health and safety of concern to industry. These are divided into five main areas, i.e. Chemical Safety (CS); Environmental Hygiene (EH); General Series (GS); Medical Series (MS); and Plant and Machinery (PM).

In addition, there are the Health and Safety (Guidance) Series (HS(G)); the Health and Safety (Regulations) Series (HS(R)); Legal Series (L); Best Practicable Means Leaflets (BPM); Emission Test Methods (ETM); Health and Safety Commission Leaflets (HSC); Health and Safety Executive Leaflets (HSE); Industry General Leaflets (IND(G)); Industry Safety Leaflets (IND(S)); similarly, Methods for the Determination of Hazardous Substances (MDHS); Toxicity Reviews (TR); Occasional Papers; Agricultural Safety Leaflets (AS). (See further, APPENDIX 2.)

It is in the interests of employers to be familiar with these publications and their recommendations, or at least the more important ones. Since employers can be liable for negligence for injury/disease to employees (see EMPLOYERS' DUTIES TO THEIR EMPLOYEES), they will be liable for failure to take account, not only of developments which they were actually aware of, but also of developments which, as good prudent employers, they ought to have known about.

H3014   **HSE STRUCTURE**

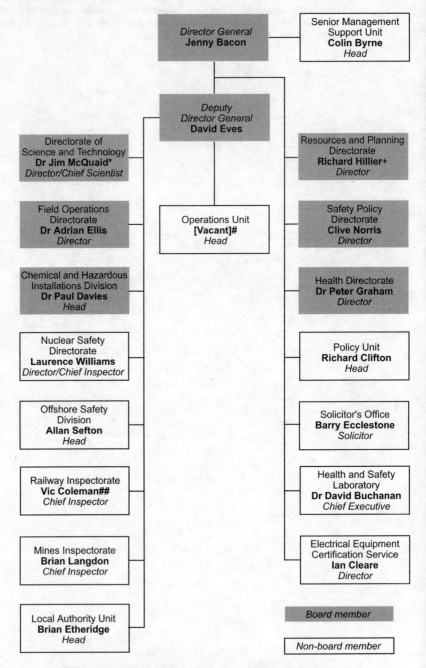

Director General **Jenny Bacon**	Senior Management Support Unit **Colin Byrne** Head

Deputy Director General **David Eves**

| Directorate of Science and Technology **Dr Jim McQuaid*** Director/Chief Scientist | Resources and Planning Directorate **Richard Hillier+** Director |

| Field Operations Directorate **Dr Adrian Ellis** Director | Operations Unit **[Vacant]#** Head | Safety Policy Directorate **Clive Norris** Director |

| Chemical and Hazardous Installations Division **Dr Paul Davies** Head | Health Directorate **Dr Peter Graham** Director |

| Nuclear Safety Directorate **Laurence Williams** Director/Chief Inspector | Policy Unit **Richard Clifton** Head |

| Offshore Safety Division **Allan Sefton** Head | Solicitor's Office **Barry Ecclestone** Solicitor |

| Railway Inspectorate **Vic Coleman##** Chief Inspector | Health and Safety Laboratory **Dr David Buchanan** Chief Executive |

| Mines Inspectorate **Brian Langdon** Chief Inspector | Electrical Equipment Certification Service **Ian Cleare** Director |

| Local Authority Unit **Brian Etheridge** Head | |

Board member

Non-board member

*	Director, Directorate of Science and Technology reports to Director General as Chief Scientist
+	Richard Hillier is the third member of the Executive
#	David Ashton was the head of Operations Unit until 14 September 1998
##	Vic Coleman took up post on 14 July 1998 following the retirement of Stan Robertson on 13 July 1998

Joint Consultation – Safety Representatives and Safety Committees

Introduction

J3001

The provision of 'information, consultation and participation' and of 'health protection and safety at the workplace' are outlined as two of the 'fundamental social rights of workers' in accordance with the Community Charter of Fundamental Rights of 1989. Combined with the signing of the Social Chapter in 1998, these have been great stimuli for the introduction of extensive obligations to consult on health and safety issues. This can be seen as recently as October 1998 with the introduction of the *Working Time Regulations 1998*. With a European Council proposal for European Works Councils to be introduced into all workplaces with 50 or more workers, consultation with the workforce is likely to become a central issue for industrial relations and health and safety over the next few years.

This chapter looks at the existing domestic legislation that places an employer under an obligation to consult with its workforce.

Regulatory framework

J3002

The legal requirements for consultation are more convoluted than might be expected, principally because there are two groups of workers who are treated as distinct for consultation purposes. Until 1996 only those employers who recognised a trade union for any collective bargaining purpose were obliged to consult the workforce through safety representatives. The *Safety Representatives and Safety Committees Regulations 1977 (SI 1977 No 500)* ('the Safety Representatives Regulations'), which were made under the provisions of the *Health and Safety at Work etc. Act 1974 (HSWA 1974), s 2(6)*, came into effect in 1978 and introduced the right for recognised trade unions to appoint safety representatives. The *Safety Representatives Regulations* were amended in 1993 – by the *Management of Health and Safety at Work Regulations 1992 (SI 1992 No 2051)* – to extend employers' duties to consult and provide facilities for safety representatives.

The duty to consult was extended on 1 October 1996 by virtue of the *Health and Safety (Consultation with Employees) Regulations 1996 (SI 1996 No 1513)*. These regulations were introduced as a 'top up' to the *Safety Representatives Regulations*, extending the obligation upon employers to consult all of their employees about health and safety measures. The 1996 Regulations have therefore expanded the obligation beyond just trade union appointed representatives which, in turn, has addressed the general reduction of union recognition over the last five years.

The obligation of consultation, its enforcement and the details of the role and functions of safety representatives and representatives of employee safety, whether under the *Safety Representatives Regulations* or the *Health and Safety (Consultation with Employees) Regulations 1996*, are almost identical but, for the sake of clarity, are dealt with separately below. The primary distinction is that different obligations apply depending upon whether the affected workers are unionised or not. The respective regulations also cover persons working in host employers' undertakings.

There are specific supplemental provisions which apply for offshore installations, which are governed by the *Offshore Installations (Safety Representatives and Safety Committees) Regulations 1989 (SI 1989 No 971)*. The *Coal Industry Nationalisation Act 1946* contains an express statutory obligation for the National Coal Board to enter into consultation with trade unions representing coal miners on questions relating to the safety, health or welfare of coal miners.

Although the *Health and Safety (Consultation with Employees) Regulations 1996* and the *Safety Representatives Regulations* are based upon good industrial relations practice, there is still the possibility of a prosecution by the Health and Safety Executive (HSE) inspectors of employers who fail to consult their workforce on health and safety issues. There is substantial overlap, however, with employment protection legislation and the obligations in respect of consultation – as can be seen from the protective rights which are conferred upon safety representatives, such as the right not to be victimised or subjected to detriment for health and safety activities, together with the consequential right to present a complaint to an employment tribunal if they are dismissed or suffer a detriment as a result of carrying out their duties.

The *Health and Safety (Consultation with Employees) Regulations 1996* also extend these rights to the armed forces. However, armed forces representatives are to be appointed rather than elected, and no paid time off is available. The *Health and Safety (Consultation with Employees) Regulations 1996* do not apply to sea-going ships.

Unionised workforce – consultation obligations

J3003

Under the *Safety Representatives Regulations*, a trade union has the right to appoint an individual to represent the workforce in consultations with the employer on all matters concerning health and safety at work, and to carry out periodic inspections of the workplace for hazards. Every employer has a duty to consult such union-appointed safety representatives on health and safety arrangements (and, if they so request him, to establish a safety committee to review the arrangements – see J3017 below). [*HSWA 1974, s 21*].

General duty

J3004

The general duty of the employer under the *Safety Representatives Regulations* is to 'consult with safety representatives with regard to both the making and maintaining of arrangements that will enable the employer and its workforce to co-operate in promoting and developing health and safety at work, and monitoring its effectiveness'. See the Health and Safety Commission publications, '*Safety Representatives and Safety Committees Regulations and Guidance Notes 1977*' and the Approved Code of Practice (HSC 9) '*Time Off for the Training of Safety Representatives*'.

Appointment of safety representatives

J3005

The right of appointment of safety representatives was, until 1 October 1996, restricted to independent trade unions who are recognised by employers for collective bargaining purposes. The *HSCER 1996* extended this to duly elected representatives of employee safety, as detailed above.

The terms 'independent' and 'recognised' are defined in the *Safety Representatives Regulations* and follow the definitions laid down in the *Trade Union and Labour*

Relations (Consolidation) Act 1992, ss 5 and *178(3)* respectively. The regulations make no provision for dealing with disputes which may arise over questions of independence or recognition (this is dealt with in the *Trade Union and Labour Relations (Consolidation) Act 1992, ss 6* and *8*). Safety representatives must be representatives of recognised independent trade unions, and it is up to each union to decide on its arrangements for the appointment or election of its safety representatives [*Reg 3*]. Employers are not involved in this matter, except that they must be informed in writing of the names of the safety representatives appointed and of the group(s) of employees they represent [*Reg 3(2)*].

The *Safety Representatives Regulations, Reg 8*, state that safety representatives must be employees except in the cases of members of the Musicians' Union and actors' Equity. In addition, where reasonably practicable, safety representatives should have at least two years' employment with their present employer or two years' experience in similar employment. The HSC guidance notes advise that it is not reasonably practicable for safety representatives to have two years' experience, or employment elsewhere, where:

(*a*)   the employer is newly established,

(*b*)   the workplace is newly established,

(*c*)   the work is of short duration, or

(*d*)   there is high labour turnover.

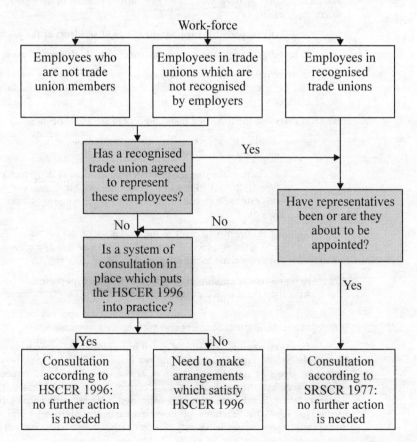

The same general guidance is followed for employee safety representatives under the *HSCER 1996*.

Number of representatives for workforce

J3006 The *Safety Representatives Regulations* do not lay down the number of safety representatives that unions are permitted to appoint for each workplace. This is a matter for unions themselves to decide, having regard to the number of workers involved and the hazards to which they are exposed. The HSE's view is that each safety representative should be regarded as responsible for the interests of a defined group of workers. This approach has not been found to conflict with existing workplace trade union organisation based on defined groups of workers. The size of these groups does vary from union to union and from workplace to workplace. While normally each workplace area or constituency would need only one safety representative, additional safety representatives are sometimes required where workers are exposed to numerous or particularly severe hazards; where workers are distributed over a wide geographical area or over a variety of workplace locations; and where workers are employed on shiftwork.

Role of safety representatives

J3007 The *Safety Representatives Regulations, Reg 4(1)* (as amended by the *Management of Health and Safety at Work Regulations 1992*) lists a number of detailed functions for safety representatives:

(a) to investigate potential hazards and causes of accidents at the workplace;

(b) to investigate employee complaints concerning health etc. at work;

(c) to make representations to the employer on matters arising out of (a) and (b) and on general matters affecting the health etc. of the employees at the workplace;

(d) to carry out the following inspections (and see J3008 below):

— of the workplace (after giving reasonable written notice to the employer – see *Reg 5*);

— of the relevant area after a reportable accident or dangerous occurrence (see ACCIDENT REPORTING) or if a reportable disease is contracted, if it is safe to do so and in the interests of the employees represented (see *Reg 6*);

— of documents relevant to the workplace or the employees represented which the employer is required to keep (see *Reg 7*) – reasonable notice must be given to the employer;

(e) to represent the employees they were appointed to represent in consultations with the HSE inspectors, and to receive information from them (see J3016 below);

(f) to attend meetings of safety committees.

These functions are interrelated and are to be implemented proactively rather than reactively. Safety representatives should not just represent their members' interests when accidents or near-misses occur or at the time of periodic inspections, but should carry out their obligations on a continuing day-to-day basis. The *Safety Representatives Regulations* make this obligation clear by stating that safety representatives have the functions of investigating potential hazards and members' complaints *before* accidents, as well as investigating dangerous occurrences and the causes of accidents *after* they have occurred. These functions are only assumed when the employer has been notified in writing by the trade union or workforce of the identity of the representative.

Thus safety representatives may possibly be closely involved not only in the technical aspects of health, safety and welfare matters at work, but also in those areas which could be described as quasi-legal. In other words, they may become involved in the interpretation and clarification of terminology in the *Safety Representatives Regulations*, as well as in discussion and negotiation with employers as to how and when the regulations may be applied. This would often happen in committee meetings.

As a result of the amendment of the *Safety Representatives Regulations* introduced by the *Management of Health and Safety at Work Regulations 1992 (SI 1992 No 2051)*, as of 1 January 1993 the subjects on which consultation 'in good time' between employers and safety representatives should take place are:

(*a*)   the introduction of any new measure at a workplace which may substantially affect health and safety;

(*b*)   arrangements for appointing competent persons to assist the employer with health and safety and implementing procedures for serious and imminent risk;

(*c*)   any health and safety information the employer is required to provide; and

(*d*)   the planning and organisation of health and safety training and health and safety implications of the introduction (or planning) of new technology.

[*Reg 4A(1)* as inserted by the *Management of Health and Safety at Work Regulations 1992, Sch*].

The safety representative's terms of reference are, therefore, broad, and exceed the traditional 'accident prevention' area. For example, *Reg 4(1)* empowers safety representatives to investigate 'potential hazards' and to take up issues which affect standards of health, safety and welfare at work. In practice it is becoming clear that four broad areas are now engaging the attention of safety representatives and safety committees:

—   health;

—   safety;

—   environment;

—   welfare.

These four broad areas effectively mean that safety representatives can, and indeed often do, examine standards relating, for example, to noise, dust, heating, lighting, cleanliness, lifting and carrying, machine guarding, toxic substances, radiation, cloakrooms, toilets and canteens. The protective standards that are operating in the workplace, or the lack of them, are now coming under much closer scrutiny than hitherto.

Workplace inspections

J3008   Arrangements for three-monthly and other more frequent inspections and reinspections should be by joint arrangement. The TUC advises that the issues to be discussed with the employer can include:

—   more frequent inspections of high risk or rapidly changing areas of work activity;

—   the precise timing and notice to be given for formal inspections by safety representatives;

—   the number of representatives taking part in any one formal inspection;

—   the breaking-up of plant-wide formal inspections into smaller, more manageable inspections;

—   provision for different groups of safety representatives to carry out inspections of different parts of the workplace;

—   the kind of inspections to be carried out, e.g. safety tours, safety sampling or safety surveys;

—   the calling in of independent technical advisers by the safety representatives.

Although formal inspections are not intended to be a substitute for day-to-day observation, they have on a number of occasions provided an opportunity to carry out a full-scale examination of all or part of the workplace and for discussion with employers' representatives about remedial action. They can also provide an opportunity to inspect documents required under health and safety legislation, e.g. certificates concerning the testing of equipment. It should be emphasised that, during inspections following reportable accidents or dangerous occurrences, employers are not required to be present when the safety representative talks with his members. In workplaces where more than one union is recognised, agreements with employers about inspections should involve all the unions concerned. It is generally agreed that safety representatives are also allowed under the regulations to investigate the following:

—   potential hazards;

—   dangerous occurrences;

—   the causes of accidents;

—   complaints from their members.

This means that imminent risks, or hazards which may affect their members, can be investigated right away by safety representatives without waiting for formal joint inspections. Following an investigation of a serious mishap, safety representatives are advised to complete a hazard report form, one copy being sent to the employer and one copy retained by the safety representative.

Rights and duties of safety representatives

Legal immunity

J3009   Ever since the *Trade Disputes Act 1906*, trade unions (and employers' associations) have enjoyed immunity from liability in tort for industrial action, taken or threatened, in contemplation or furtherance of a trade dispute (although such freedom of action was subsequently curtailed by the *Trade Union and Labour Relations (Consolidation) Act 1992, s 20* consolidating the *Employment Act 1982, s 15*). Not surprisingly, perhaps, this immunity extends to their representatives acting in a lawful capacity. Thus, the *Safety Representatives Regulations* state that none of the functions of a safety representative confers legal duties or responsibilities [*Reg 4(1)*]. As safety representatives are not legally responsible for health, safety or welfare at work, they cannot be liable under either the criminal or civil law for anything they may do, or fail to do, as a safety representative under these Regulations. This protection against criminal or civil liability does not, however, remove a safety representative's legal responsibility as an employee. Safety representatives must carry out their responsibilities under *HSWA 1974, s 7* if they are not to be liable for criminal prosecution by an HSE inspector. These duties as an employee are to take reasonable care for the health and safety of one's self and others, and to co-operate with one's employer as far as is necessary to enable him to carry out his statutory duties on health and safety.

Time off with pay

General right

J3010   Under the *Safety Representatives Regulations* safety representatives are entitled to take such paid time off during working hours as is necessary to perform their statutory functions, and reasonable time to undergo training in accordance with a code of practice approved by the Health and Safety Commission.

Definition of 'time off'

J3011   The *Safety Representatives Regulations, Reg 4(2)* provides that the employer must provide the safety representative with such time off with pay during the employee's working hours as shall be necessary for the purposes of:

(a)   performing his statutory functions; and

(b)   undergoing such training in aspects of those functions as may be reasonable in all the circumstances.

Further details of these requirements are outlined in the code of practice attached to the *Safety Representatives Regulations* and the HSC approved code of practice on time off for training. The Code of Practice is for guidance purposes only – its contents are recommendations rather than requirements.

The combined effect of the ACAS Code No 3: '*Time Off for Trade Union Duties and Activities*' (1991) issued under the *Employment Protection Act 1975* and the HSC approved code on time off is that shop stewards who have also been appointed as safety representatives are to be given time off by their employers to carry out both their industrial relations duties and their safety functions, and also paid leave to attend separate training courses on industrial relations and on health and safety at work – this includes a TUC course on *COSHH* (*Gallagher v The Drum Engineering Co Ltd, COIT 1330/89*).

An employee is not entitled to be paid for time taken off in lieu of the time he had spent on a course. This was held in *Hairsine v Hull City Council [1992] IRLR 211* when a shift worker, whose shift ran from 3 pm to 11 pm, attended a trade union course from 9 am to 4 pm and then carried out his duties until 7 pm. He was paid from 3 pm to 7 pm and he could claim no more. However, where more safety representatives have been appointed than there are sections of the workforce for which safety representatives could be responsible, it is not unreasonable for an employer to deny some safety representatives time off for fulfilling safety functions (*Howard and Peet v Volex plc (HSIB 181)*).

A decision of the EAT seems to favour jointly sponsored in-house courses, except as regards the representational aspects of the functions of safety representatives, where the training is to be provided exclusively by the union (*White v Pressed Steel Fisher [1980] IRLR 176*). Moreover, one course per union per year is too rigid an approach (*Waugh v London Borough of Sutton (1983) HSIB 86*).

Definition of 'pay'

J3012   The amount of pay to which the safety representative is entitled is contained in the Schedule to the Regulations.

Recourse for the safety representative

J3013   Where the employer's refusal to allow paid time off is unreasonable, he must reimburse the employee for the time taken to attend [*Reg 4(2), Schedule*]. *Scarth v East Herts DC (HSIB 181)*: the test of reasonableness is to be judged at the time of the decision to refuse training.

Safety representatives who are refused time off to perform their functions or who are not paid for such time off are able to make a complaint to an employment tribunal [*Reg 11*].

Facilities to be provided by employer

J3014   The type and number of facilities that employers are obliged to provide for safety representatives are not spelled out in the regulations, code of practice or guidance notes, other than a general requirement in the *Safety Representatives Regulations, Reg 5(3)* which states, *inter alia*, that 'the employer shall provide such facilities and assistance as the safety representatives shall require for the purposes of carrying out their functions'. Formerly, the requirement to provide facilities and assistance related only to inspections.

Trade unions consider that the phrase 'facilities and assistance' includes the right to request the presence of an independent technical adviser or trade union official during an inspection, and for safety representatives to take samples of substances used at work for analysis outside the workplace. The TUC has recommended that the following facilities be made available to safety representatives:

(*a*)   a room and desk at the workplace;

(*b*)   facilities for storing correspondence;

(*c*)   inspection reports and other papers;

(*d*)   ready access to internal and external telephones;

(*e*)   access to typing and duplicating facilities;

(*f*)   provision of notice-boards;

(*g*)   use of a suitable room for reporting back to and consulting with members;

(*h*)   other facilities should include copies of all relevant statutes, regulations, approved codes of practice and HSC guidance notes; and copies of all legal or international standards which are relevant to the workplace.

Disclosure of information

J3015   Employers are required by the *Safety Representatives Regulations* to disclose information to safety representatives which is necessary for them to carry out their functions [*Reg 7(2)*] – for a parallel provision see the *Management of Health and Safety at Work Regulations 1992, Reg 8* (see CHILDREN AND YOUNG PERSONS C3013).

Regulation 7 details the health and safety information 'within the employer's knowledge' that should be made available to safety representatives. The code of practice to the regulations outlines that this should include:

(*a*)   plans and performance and any changes proposed which may affect health and safety;

(*b*)   technical information about hazards and precautions necessary, including information provided by manufacturers, suppliers and so on;

(c)   information and statistical records on accidents, dangerous occurrences and notifiable industrial diseases; and

(d)   other information such as measures to check the effectiveness of health and safety arrangements and information on articles and substances issued to homeworkers.

The exceptions to this requirement are where disclosure of such information would be 'against the interests of national security'; where it would contravene a prohibition imposed by law; any information relating to an individual (unless consent has been given); information that would damage the employer's undertaking; and information obtained for the sole purpose of bringing, prosecuting or defending legal proceedings.

However, the decision in *Waugh v British Railways Board [1979] 2 AER 1169* established that where an employer seeks to withhold a report made following an accident on grounds of privilege, he can only do so if its dominant purpose is related to actual or potential hostile legal proceedings. In this particular case, a report was commissioned for two purposes following the death of an employee: (a) to recommend improvements in safety measures, and (b) to gather material for the employer's defence. It was held that the report was not privileged.

This was followed in *Lask v Gloucester Health Authority [1986] HSIB 123* where a circular '*Reporting Accidents in Hospitals*' had to be discovered by order after an injury to an employee whilst he was was walking along a path. The relevant information to be disclosed by employers is contained in paragraph 6 of the approved code of practice on Safety Representatives and Safety Committees. Where differences of opinion arise as to the evaluation or interpretation of technical aspects of safety information or health data, unions are advised to contact the local offices of the HSE, because of the HSE expertise and access to research.

Technical information

J3016   HSE inspectors are also obliged under *HSWA 1974, s 28(8)*, to supply safety representatives with technical information – factual information obtained during their visits (i.e. any measurements, testing the results of sampling and monitoring), notices of prosecution, copies of correspondence and copies of any improvement or prohibition notices issued to their employer. The latter places an absolute duty on an inspector to disclose specific kinds of information to workers or their representatives concerning health, safety and welfare at work. This can also involve personal discussions between the HSE inspector and the safety representative. The inspector must also tell the representative what action he proposes to take as a result of his visit. Where local authority health inspectors are acting under powers granted by *HSWA 1974* (see ENFORCEMENT), they are also required to provide appropriate information to safety representatives.

Safety committees

J3017   There is a duty on every employer, in cases where it is prescribed (see below), to establish a safety committee if requested to do so by safety representatives. The committee's purpose is to monitor health and safety measures at work [*HSWA 1974, s 2(7)*]. Such cases are prescribed by the *Safety Representatives Regulations* and limit the duty to appoint a committee to requests made by trade union safety representatives.

Establishment of a safety committee

J3018   If requested by at least two safety representatives in writing, the employer must establish a safety committee [*Safety Representatives Regulations, Reg 9(1)*].

When setting up a safety committee, the employer must:

(*a*)   consult with both:

—   the safety representatives who make the request; and

—   the representatives of recognised trade unions whose members work in any workplace where it is proposed that the committee will function;

(*b*)   post a notice, stating the composition of the committee and the workplace(s) to be covered by it, in a place where it can easily be read by employees;

(*c*)   establish the committee within three months after the request for it was made.

[*Reg 9(2)*].

Function of safety committees

J3019   In practical terms, trade union appointed safety representatives are now using the medium of safety committees to examine the implications of hazard report forms arising from inspections, and the results of investigations into accidents and dangerous occurrences, together with the remedial action required. A similar procedure exists with respect to representatives for tests and measurements of noise, toxic substances or other harmful effects on the working environment.

Trade unions regard the function of safety committees as a forum for the discussion and resolution of problems that have failed to be solved initially through the intervention of the safety representative in discussion with line management. There is, therefore, from the trade unions' viewpoint, a large measure of negotiation with its consequent effect on collective bargaining agreements.

If safety representatives are unable to resolve a problem with management through the safety committee, or with the HSE, they can approach their own union for assistance – a number of unions have their own health and safety officers who can, and do, provide an extensive range of information on occupational health and safety matters. The unions, in turn, can refer to the TUC for further advice.

The 'Brown Book', which contains the *Safety Representatives Regulations*, code of practice and guidance, was revised in 1996 to include the amendments made in 1993 by the *Management of Health and Safety at Work Regulations 1992* (see above) and the *Health and Safety (Consultation with Employees) Regulations 1996* (see below).

Non-unionised workforce – consultation obligations

J3020   A representative of employee safety is an elected representative of a non-unionised workforce who is assigned with broadly the same rights and obligations as a safety representative in a unionised workforce.

General duty

J3021   The *Health and Safety (Consultation with Employees) Regulations 1996* introduced a new duty to consult any employees who are not members of a group covered by safety representatives (appointed under the *Safety Representatives Regulations*). Employers therefore have the choice of consulting their employees either directly or by way of an appointed representative of employee safety. The obligation is to consult those employees in good time on matters relating to their health and safety at work.

Number of representatives for workforce

J3022   Guidance notes on the *Health and Safety (Consultation with Employees) Regulations 1996* state that the number of safety representatives who can be appointed depends on the size of the workforce and workplace, whether there are different sites, the variety of different occupations, the operation of shift systems and the type and risks of work activity. The most recent DTI Workplace Survey states that in a non-unionised workplace which has appointed worker representatives, it is usual for there to be several representatives, with the median being three. The survey estimated that there are approximately 218,000 representatives across all British workplaces with 25 or more employees.

Role of safety representatives

J3023   The functions of representatives of employee safety are:

(*a*)   to make representations to the employer of potential hazards and dangerous occurrences at the workplace which affect or could affect the group of employees he represents;

(*b*)   to make representations to the employer on general matters affecting the health and safety at work of the group of employees he represents, and in particular on such matters as he has been consulted about by the employer under the 1996 Regulations; and

(*c*)   to represent that group of employees in consultations at the workplace with inspectors appointed under *HSWA 1974*.

Rights and duties of representatives of employee safety

Time off with pay

J3024   Under the *Health and Safety (Consultation with Employees) Regulations 1996, Reg 7(1)(b)*, the right that a representative of employee safety has to take time off with pay is generally the same as that for safety representatives.

Definition of 'time off'

J3025   An employer is under an obligation to permit a representative of employee safety to take such time off with pay during working hours as shall be necessary for:

(*a*)   performing his functions; and

(*b*)   undergoing such training as is reasonable in all the circumstances.

A candidate standing for election as a representative of employee safety is also allowed reasonable time off with pay during working hours in order to perform his functions as a candidate [*Reg 7(2)*].

Definition of 'pay'

J3026   *Schedule 1* to the 1996 Regulations deals with the definition of pay, and generally the definition is the same as that for union safety representatives.

Provision of information

J3027   The employer must provide such information as is necessary to enable the employees or representatives of employee safety to participate fully and effectively in the consultation. In the case of representatives of employee safety, the information must also be sufficient to enable them to carry out their functions under the Regulations.

Information provided to representatives must also include information which is contained in any record which the employer is required to keep under *RIDDOR* and which relates to the workplace or the group of employees represented by the representatives. Note that there are exceptions to the requirement to disclose information similar to those under the *Safety Representatives Regulations, Reg 7* (see J3015 above).

Relevant training

J3028   Representatives of employee safety must be provided with reasonable training in respect of their functions under the *Health and Safety (Consultation with Employees) Regulations 1996*, for which the employer must pay.

Recourse for a representative of employee safety

J3029   A representative of employee safety, or candidate standing for election as such, who is denied time off or who fails to receive payment for time off may make an application to an employment tribunal for a declaration and/or compensation. As in the case of safety representatives, the remedies obtainable (set out in *Schedule 2* to the 1996 Regulations) are similar to those granted to complainants under the *Trade Union and Labour Relations (Consolidation) Act 1992, s 168* (time off for union duties).

A representative of employee safety, or candidate standing for election as such, also has the right not to be subjected to any detriment on the grounds that he took part (or proposed to take part) in consultation with the employer or (as the case may be) in an election of representatives of employee safety (*Employment Rights Act 1996, s 44(1)(ba)*, inserted by the *Health and Safety (Consultation with Employees) Regulations 1996, Reg 8*). A complaint may be made to an employment tribunal which can make a declaration and also award compensation (*Employment Rights Act 1996, ss 48, 49*). There is no minimum qualifying period of service nor upper age limit for bringing such a claim.

If a representative of employee safety, or candidate standing for election as such, is dismissed and the reason, or principal reason, for the dismissal is that he took part (or proposed to take part) in consultation with the employer pursuant to the 1996 Regulations or (as the case may be) in an election of representatives of employee safety, that dismissal shall be deemed automatically unfair (*Employment Rights Act 1996, s 100(1)(ba)*, inserted by the *Health and Safety (Consultation with Employees) Regulations 1996, Reg 8*). It will also be automatically unfair dismissal to select a representative or candidate for redundancy for such a reason (*Employment Rights Act 1996, s 105*). The normal minimum qualifying period of service and the normal upper age limit for bringing unfair dismissal claims do not apply (*Employment Rights Act 1996, ss 108, 109*).

European development in health and safety

J3030   Health and safety law will continue to be subject to change in the future with the implementation of further European directives and the HSC programme of modifying and simplifying health and safety law.

The election of the Labour Government in May 1997 has led to a change of approach to health and safety issues. Legislation has already been introduced on working time (see WORKING TIME). The most important type of European health and safety legislation is the directives made under Article 118A of the Treaty of Rome. The Framework Directive, from which the *Health and Safety (Consultation with Employees) Regulations 1996* were derived, will continue to drive forward developments in UK health and safety law.

Lifting Machinery and Equipment

Introduction

L3001
There are several distinct categories or groups of machinery which relate to lifting. Each group is dealt with within the regulatory framework in a slightly different way.

The legislation separates lifting machinery from lifts which are permanently installed in buildings. The latter are covered by the EU's Lifts Directive which is implemented into UK law by the *Lifts Regulations 1997 (SI 1997 No 831)*. The *Lifts Regulations 1997* make reference to the Machinery Directive and the Construction Products Directive.

The lifting machinery which is not covered by the Lifts Directive is covered by the Machinery Directive which is implemented into UK law by the *Supply of Machinery (Safety) Regulations 1992 (SI 1992 No 3073 as amended by SI 1994 No 2063)*. The Machinery Directive deals directly with safety for suppliers of lifting machines and lifting accessories.

There are specific requirements for lifting machinery in addition to the common requirements for all machinery. These extra requirements deal with matters such as lifting coefficients for tests, whether machines lift goods and/or people, and what control systems are appropriate (see the *Supply of Machinery (Safety) Regulations 1992, Schedule 3 section 4* 'Essential health and safety requirements to offset the particular hazards due to a lifting operation').

In addition, specific types of lifting equipment including lifting devices which raise people to a height of more than three metres, and vehicle servicing lifts, are within the *Supply of Machinery (Safety) Regulations 1992, Schedule 4*, and require the conformity to be subject to scrutiny by a notified body within the Machinery Directive. 'State-of-the-art' for safety is established in some cases in the relevant transposed harmonised standards, e.g. EN 1493: 1998 – Vehicle lifts.

Lifts controlled by electrical equipment are also subject to the relevant parts of the *Electrical Equipment (Safety) Regulations 1994 (SI 1994 No 3260)* implementing the Low Voltage Directive, and the *Electromagnetic Compatibility Regulations 1992 (SI 1992 No 2372 as amended by SI 1994 No 3080)*. Lifts installed in buildings are also subject to the IEE Wiring Regulations (BS 7671: 1992 – Requirements for electrical installations).

These above rules and regulations apply to the supply of lift equipment. In addition the *Lifting Operations and Lifting Equipment Regulations 1998 (SI 1998 No 2307)* apply to their use and upkeep.

This chapter examines:

   (i)   hoists and lifts;

   (ii)   forklift trucks;

   (iii)   lifting machinery other than hoists and lifts – particularly cranes and the safe use of mobile cranes;

(iv)   lifting tackle (ropes, rings, hooks and slings);

(v)   lifting operations on construction sites; and

(vi)   statutory requirements relating to lifting equipment, namely:

(i)   the *Lifts Regulations 1997 (SI 1997 No 831)*;

(ii)   the *Lifting Operations and Lifting Equipment Regulations 1998 (SI 1998 No 2307)*.

Hoists and lifts

L3002   A hoist or lift is a 'platform or cage, the direction or movement of which is restricted by a guide or guides'. [*Factories Act 1961, s 25(1)*].

Examples include goods lifts, man hoists (for example those found in flour mills), paternoster lifts (for transporting passengers vertically – usually up to six). Although not within the statutory definition, powered working platforms are commonly used for fast and safe access to overhead machinery/plant, stored products, lighting equipment and electrical installations as well as for enabling maintenance operations to be carried out on high-rise buildings. Their height, reach and mobility give them distinct advantages over scaffolding, boatswain's chairs and platforms attached to fork lift trucks. Typical operations are characterised by self-propelled hydraulic booms, semi-mechanised articulated booms and self-propelled scissors lifts. Platforms should always be sited on firm level working surfaces and their presence indicated by traffic cones and barriers. Location should be away from overhead power lines – but, if this is not practicable, a permit to work system should be instituted. A key danger arises from overturning as a consequence of overloading the platform. Maximum lifting capacity should, therefore, be clearly indicated on the platform as well as in the manufacturer's instructions, and it is inadvisable to use working platforms in high winds (i.e. above Force 4 or 16 mph). Powered working platforms should be regularly maintained and only operated by trained personnel.

Fork lift trucks

L3003   Fork lift trucks are the most widely used item of mobile mechanical handling equipment. There are several varieties which are as follows:

(1)   *Pedestrian-operated stackers – manually-operated and power-operated*

Manually-operated stackers are usually limited in operation, for example, for moving post pallets, and cannot pick up directly from the floor. Whereas power-operated stackers are pedestrian-operated or rider-controlled, operate vertically and horizontally and can lift pallets directly from the floor.

(2)   *Reach trucks*

Reach trucks enable loads to be retracted within their wheel base. There are two kinds, namely, (*a*) moving mast reach trucks, and (*b*) pantograph reach trucks. Moving mast reach trucks are rider-operated, with forward-mounted load wheels enabling carriage to move within wheel base – mast, forks and load moving together. Pantograph reach trucks are also rider-operated, reach movement being by pantograph mechanism, with forks and load moving away from static mast.

(3)　*Counterbalance trucks*

Counterbalance trucks carry loads in front counterbalanced to the weight of the vehicle over the rear wheels. Such trucks are lightweight pedestrian-controlled, lightweight rider-controlled or heavyweight rider-controlled.

(4)　*Narrow aisle trucks*

With narrow aisle trucks the base of the truck does not turn within the aisle in order to deposit/retrieve load. There are two types, namely, side loaders for use on long runs down narrow aisles, and counterbalance rotating load turret trucks, having a rigid mast with telescopic sections, which can move sideways in order to collect/deposit loads.

(5)　*Order pickers*

Order pickers have a protected working platform attached to the lift forks, enabling the driver to deposit/retrieve objects in or from a racking system. Conventional or purpose-designed, they are commonly used in racked storage areas and operate well in narrow aisles.

Lifting machinery (other than hoists/lifts)

L3004　Lifting machinery (other than hoists/lifts) refers to a 'crane, crab, winch, teagle, pulley block, gin wheel, transporter or runway'. [*Factories Act 1961, s 27(9)*]. In practice, cranes are the most important.

Cranes

L3005　Cranes are widely used in lifting/lowering operations in construction, dock and shipbuilding works. The main hazard, generally associated with overloading or incorrect slewing, is collapse or overturning, the latter in consequence of the crane driver exceeding the 'maximum permitted moment' (mpm). Contact with overhead power lines is also a danger. In such cases, the operator should normally remain inside the cab and not allow anyone to touch the crane or load; the superintending engineer should immediately be informed. (For reportable dangerous occurrences in connection with cranes etc., see ACCIDENT REPORTING at A3027.)

There are several varieties of crane in frequent use, namely, fixed cranes used at docks and railway sidings; tower cranes on construction sites; mobile cranes used for lifting/lowering loads onto particular locations; overhead travelling cranes – these last operating along a fixed railtrack; in addition, on construction sites there are rough-terrain cranes as well as crawler and wheeled cranes all carrying suspended loads. Persons in the foreseeable impact area of an overhead travelling crane are especially at risk. In order to avoid accidents, electrical supply to the crane should be isolated and a permit to work system instituted. Trained signallers (or banksmen) should be on hand to direct movement of the crane and in a position to see the load clearly and be clearly seen by the driver.

Safe lifting operations by mobile cranes

L3006　A mobile crane is a crane which is capable of travelling under its own power, but not on a line or rails. [*Construction (Lifting Operations) Regulations 1961, Reg 4(1)*].

Safe lifting operations – as per BS 7121 'Safe use of cranes' – depend on co-operation between supervisor (or appointed person), slinger (and/or signaller) and crane driver.

(*a*)   *Appointed person*

Overall control of lifting operations rests with an 'appointed person', who can, where necessary, stop the operation. Failing this, control of operations will be in the hands of the supervisor (who, in some cases, may be the slinger). The appointed (and competent) person must ensure that:

   (i)   lifting operations are carefully planned and executed;

   (ii)   weights and heights are accurate;

   (iii)   suitable cranes are provided;

   (iv)   the ground is suitable;

   (v)   suitable precautions are taken, if necessary, regarding gas, water and electricity either above or below ground;

   (vi)   personnel involved in lifting/lowering are trained and competent.

(*b*)   *Supervisor*

Supervisors must:

   (i)   direct the crane driver where to position the crane;

   (ii)   provide sufficient personnel to carry out the operation;

   (iii)   check the site conditions;

   (iv)   report back to the appointed person in the event of problems;

   (v)   supervise and direct the slinger, signaller and crane driver;

   (vi)   stop the operation if there is a safety risk.

(*c*)   *Crane driver*

Crane drivers must:

   (i)   erect/dismantle and operate the crane as per manufacturer's instructions;

   (ii)   set the crane level before lifting and ensure that it remains level;

   (iii)   decide which signalling system is to apply;

   (iv)   inform the superviser in the event of problems;

   (v)   carry out inspections/weekly maintenance relating to

   —   defects in crane structure, fittings, jibs, ropes, hooks, shackles,

   —   correct functioning of automatic safe load indicator, over hoist and derrick limit switches.

Drivers should always carry out operations as per speeds, weights, heights and wind speeds specified by the manufacturer, mindful that the weight of slings/lifting gear is part of the load. Such information should be clearly displayed in the cab and not obscured or removed. Windows and windscreens should be kept clear and free from stickers containing operational data. Any handrails, stops, machinery guards fitted to the crane for safe access should always be replaced following removal for maintenance; and tools, jib sections and lifting tackle properly secured when not in use.

After a load has been attached to the crane hook by the lifting hook, tension should be taken up slowly, as per the slinger's instructions, the latter being in continuous communication with the driver. In the case of unbalanced loads, drivers/slingers should be familiar with a load's centre of gravity – particularly if the load is irregularly shaped. Once in operation, crane hooks should be positioned directly over the load, the latter not remaining suspended for longer than necessary. Moreover, suspended loads should not be directed over people or occupied buildings.

(*d*) *Slingers*

Slingers must:

  (i) attach/detach a load to/from the crane;

  (ii) use correct lifting appliances;

  (iii) direct movement of a load by correct signals. Any part of a load likely to shift during lifting/lowering must be adequately secured by the slinger beforehand. Spillage or discharge of loose loads (e.g. scaffolding) can be a problem, and such loads must be properly secured/fastened. Nets are useful for covering palletised loads (e.g. bricks).

(*e*) *Signallers*

Not infrequently, signallers are responsible for signalling in lieu of slingers. Failing this, their remit is to transmit instructions from slinger to crane driver, when the former cannot see the load.

Lifting tackle

L3007   Lifting tackle refers to:

(*a*) chain slings;

(*b*) rope slings;

(*c*) rings;

(*d*) hooks;

(*e*) shackles;

(*f*) swivels.

[*Factories Act 1961, s 26(3)*].

Chains

L3008   A chain is a classic example of lifting tackle, in spite of an increase in use of wire ropes. There are several varieties, including mild high-tensile, and alloy steel. The principal risk is breakage, usually occurring in consequence of a production defect in a link, or through application of excessive loads.

Ropes

L3009   Ropes are used quite widely throughout industry in lifting/lowering operations, the main hazard being breakage through overloading and/or natural wear and tear. Ropes are either of natural (e.g. cotton, hemp) or man-made fibre (e.g. nylon, terylene). Natural fibre ropes, if they become wet or damp, should be allowed to dry naturally and kept in a well-ventilated room. They do not require certification prior to service but six months' examination thereafter is compulsory. If the specified safe working load (SWL) cannot be maintained by a rope, it should forthwith be withdrawn from service. Of the two, man-made fibre ropes have greater tensile strength, are not subject so much to risk from wear and tear, are more acid/corrosion-resistant and can absorb shock loading better.

Wire ropes are much in use in cranes, lifts, hoists, elevators etc. and are normally lubricant-impregnated to minimise corrosion and reduce wear and tear.

Slings, hooks, eyebolts, pulley blocks etc.

L3010   Slings are chains or ropes (either fibre or wire) and should be of adequate strength. Wire rope slings should always be well lubricated and, where multiple slings are in use, the load should be evenly distributed. Hooks are of forged steel and should be fitted with a safety catch to ensure that the load does not slip off. Eyebolts are mainly for lifting heavy concentrated loads; there being several types, namely, dynamo, collar and eyebolt incorporating link. Pulley blocks, ideally made from shock-resistant metal, are also widely used in lifting and lowering operations. In particular, however, blocks designed for use with fibre rope should not be operated with wire rope.

Lifting operations on construction sites

L3011   Lifting/lowering activities are typical on construction sites. Hazards peculiar to this environment, which crane drivers should beware of, are:

(a)   adverse weather, e.g. heavy rain, causing ground sinkage, thereby necessitating levelling checks or mat packing;

(b)   underground services, e.g. drains, sewers, mains;

(c)   uncompacted landfill;

(d)   excavations. Crane operators should always check with supervisors before travelling close to excavations, and, in any case, regularly check the excavation face, especially after heavy rainfall. Moreover, crane travel, whether with or without loads on site, should proceed only when accompanied by a slinger to keep an eye open for obstructions and hazards and warn other people in the vicinity. When travelling minus load, chains/slings should be detached from the hook and the hookblock secured. Similarly, cranes should not be left unattended unless:

   (i)   loads have been detached,

   (ii)   the lifting device has been secured,

   (iii) the engine has been turned off,

   (iv)   brakes and locks have been applied,

   (v)   the ignition key has been removed.

Cranes travelling on public highways are governed by the same rules and regulations as apply to other road users; drivers must be in possession of a valid current driving licence and over 21. They should be aware of the crane's overall clearance height and see that slings, shackles etc. are either removed or secured.

Statutory requirements relating to lifting equipment

L3012   The *Lifts Regulations 1997 (SI 1997 No 831)* came into force on 1 July 1997 and the *Lifting Operations and Lifting Equipment Regulations 1998 (SI 1998 No 2307)* came into force on 5 December 1998. These two regulations replaced the previous provisions contained in the *Factories Act 1961*, the *Offices, Shops and Railway Premises (Hoists and Lifts) Regulations 1968*, the *Construction (Lifting Operations) Regulations 1961* and the *Lifting Plant and Equipment (Records of Test and Examination etc.) Regulations 1992*.

This section examines:

(*a*)   the *Lifts Regulations 1997 (SI 1997 No 831)*; and

(*b*)   the *Lifting Operations and Lifting Equipment Regulations (SI 1998 No 2307)*.

In this context certain words need explanation:

'Lift' – this means an appliance serving specific levels, having a car moving along guides which are rigid – or along a fixed course even where it does not move along guides which are rigid (for example, a scissor lift) – and inclined at an angle of more than 15 degrees to the horizontal and intended for the transport of:

—   persons,

—   persons and goods, or

—   goods alone if the car is accessible, that is to say, a person may enter it without difficulty, and fitted with controls situated inside the car or within reach of a person inside;

'Accessory for lifting' – this means 'work equipment for attaching loads to machinery for lifting';

'Lifting equipment' – this means 'work equipment for lifting or lowering loads and includes its attachments used for anchoring, fixing or supporting it'.

The Lifts Regulations 1997

L3013   These Regulations apply to lifts permanently serving buildings or constructions; and safety components for use in such lifts. [*Reg 3*].

These Regulations do not apply to:

(*a*)   the following lifts – and safety components for such lifts:

—   cableways, including funicular railways, for the public or private transportation of persons,

—   lifts specially designed and constructed for military or police purposes,

—   mine winding gear,

—   theatre elevators,

—   lifts fitted in means of transport,

—   lifts connected to machinery and intended exclusively for access to the workplace,

—   rack and pinion trains,

—   construction-site hoists intended for lifting persons or persons and goods.

[*Reg 4, Schedule 14*].

(*b*) any lift or safety component which is placed on the market (i.e. when the installer first makes the lift available to the user, but see L3019 below) and put into service before 1 July 1997 [*Reg 5*].

(*c*) any lift or safety component placed on the market and put into service on or before 30 June 1999 which complies with any health and safety provisions with which it would have been required to comply if it was to have been placed on the market and put into service in the United Kingdom on 29 June 1995.

This exclusion does not apply in the case of a lift or a safety component which;

— unless required to bear the CE marking pursuant to any other Community obligation, bears the CE marking or an inscription liable to be confused with it; or

— bears or is accompanied by any other indication, howsoever expressed, that it complies with the Lifts Directive.

[*Reg 6*].

(*d*) any lift insofar as and to the extent that the relevant essential health and safety requirements relate to risks wholly or partly covered by other Community directives applicable to that lift [*Reg 7*].

General requirements

General duty relating to the placing on the market and putting into service of lifts

L3014 (i) Subject to *Reg 12* (see L3019 below), no person who is a responsible person shall place on the market and put into service any lift unless the requirements of paragraph (ii) below have been complied with in relation to it [*Reg 8(1)*].

(ii) *Regulation 8(2)* provides that the requirements in respect of any lift are that:

— it satisfies the relevant essential health and safety requirements and, for the purpose of satisfying those requirements:

— where a transposed harmonised standard covers one or more of the relevant essential health and safety requirements, any lift constructed in accordance with that transposed harmonised standard shall be presumed to comply with that (or those) essential health and safety requirement(s); and

— by calculation, or on the basis of design plans, it is permitted to demonstrate the similarity of a range of equipment to satisfy the essential safety requirements;

— the appropriate conformity assessment procedure in respect of the lift has been carried out in accordance with *Reg 13(1)* (see L3020 below);

— the CE marking has been affixed to it by the installer of the lift in accordance with *Schedule 3*;

— a declaration of conformity has been drawn up in respect of it by the installer of the lift; and

— it is in fact safe.

Note: Reg 18(1) provides that a lift which bears the CE marking, and is accompanied by an EC declaration of conformity in accordance with *Reg 8(2)*, is taken to conform with all the requirements of the *Lifts Regulations 1997*, including *Reg 13* (see L3020 below), unless reasonable grounds exist for suspecting that it does not so conform.

(iii)   Any technical documentation or other information in relation to a lift required to be retained under the conformity assessment procedure used must be retained by the person specified in that respect in that conformity assessment procedure for any period specified in that procedure [*Reg 8(3)*].

In these Regulations, 'responsible person' means:

—   in the case of a lift, the installer of the lift;

—   in the case of a safety component, the manufacturer of the component or his authorised representative established in the Community; or

—   where neither the installer of the lift nor the manufacturer of the safety component nor the latter's authorised representative established in the Community, as the case may be, have fulfilled the requirements of *Reg 8(2)* (see above) or *9(2)* (see L3015 below), the person who places the lift or safety component on the market.

General duty relating to the placing on the market and putting into service of safety components

L3015   Safety components include devices for locking landing doors; devices to prevent falls; overspeed limitation devices; and electric safety switches.

(i)   Subject to *Reg 12* (see L3019 below), no person who is a responsible person shall place on the market and put into service any safety component unless the requirements of paragraph (ii) below have been complied with in relation to it [*Reg 9(1)*].

(ii)   *Regulation 9(2)* provides that the requirements in respect of any safety component are that:

—   it satisfies the relevant essential health and safety requirements and for the purpose of satisfying those requirements where a transposed harmonised standard covers one or more of the relevant essential health and safety requirements, any safety component constructed in accordance with that transposed harmonised standard shall be presumed to be suitable to enable a lift on which it is correctly installed to comply with that (or those) essential health and safety requirement(s);

—   the appropriate conformity assessment procedure in respect of the safety component has been carried out in accordance with *Reg 13(1)* (see L3020 below);

—   the CE marking has been affixed to it, or on a label inseparably attached to the safety component, by the manufacturer of that safety component, or his authorised representative established in the Community, in accordance with *Schedule 3* (which specifies the requirements for CE marking);

—   a declaration of conformity has been drawn up in respect of it by the manufacturer of the safety component or his authorised representative established in the Community; and

—   it is in fact safe.

Note: Reg 18(1) provides that a safety component – or its label – which bears the CE marking, and is accompanied by an EC declaration of conformity in accordance with *Reg 9(2)*, is taken to conform with all the requirements of the *Lifts Regulations 1997*, including *Reg 13* (see L3020 below), unless reasonable grounds exist for suspecting that it does not so conform.

(iii) Any technical documentation or other information in relation to a safety component required to be retained under the conformity assessment procedure used must be retained by the person specified in that respect in that conformity assessment procedure for any period specified in that procedure [*Reg 9(3)*].

General duty relating to the supply of a lift or safety component

L3016 Subject to *Reg 12* (see L3019 below) any person who supplies any lift or safety component but who is not a person to whom *Reg 8* or *9* applies (see L3014 and L3015 above) must ensure that that lift or safety component is safe [*Reg 10*].

Penalties for breach of Regs 8, 9 or 10

L3017 A person who is convicted of an offence under *Reg 8, 9* or *10* above is liable to imprisonment (not exceeding three months) or to a fine not exceeding level 5 on the standard scale, or both. *Reg 22*, however, provides a defence of due diligence: i.e. the defendant must show that he took all reasonable steps and exercised all due diligence to avoid committing the offence.

Specific duties relating to the supply of information, freedom from obstruction of lift shafts and retention of documents

L3018

(i) The person responsible for work on the building or construction where a lift is to be installed and the installer of the lift must keep each other informed of the facts necessary for, and take the appropriate steps to ensure, the proper operation and safe use of the lift. Shafts intended for lifts must not contain any piping or wiring or fittings other than that which is necessary for the operation and safety of that lift.

(ii) Where, in the case of a lift, for the purposes of *Reg 8(2)* (see L3014 above) the appropriate conformity assessment procedure is one of the procedures set out in *Reg 13(2)(a), (b) or (c)* (see L3020 below), the person responsible for the design of the lift must supply to the person responsible for the construction, installation and testing all necessary documents and information for the latter person to be able to operate in absolute security.

A person who is convicted of an offence under (i) or (ii) above is liable to imprisonment (not exceeding three months) or to a fine not exceeding level 5 on the standard scale, or both. *Reg 22*, however, provides a defence of due diligence: i.e. the defendant must show that he took all reasonable steps and exercised all due diligence to avoid committing the offence.

(iii) A copy of the declaration of conformity mentioned in *Reg 8(2)* or *9(2)* must:

— in the case of a lift, be supplied to the EC Commission, the member states and any other notified bodies, on request, by the installer of the lift together with a copy of the reports of the tests involved in the final inspection to be carried out as part of the appropriate conformity assessment procedure referred to in *Reg 8(2)*; and

— be retained, by the person who draws up that declaration, for a period of ten years – in the case of a lift, from the date on which the lift was placed on the market; and in the case of a safety component, from the date on which safety components of that type were last manufactured by that person.

A person who fails to supply or keep a copy of the declaration of conformity, as required above, is liable on summary conviction to a fine not exceeding level 5 on the standard scale. *Reg 22*, however, provides a defence of due diligence: i.e. the defendant must show that he took all reasonable steps and exercised all due diligence to avoid committing the offence.

[*Reg 11*].

Exceptions to placing on the market or supply in respect of certain lifts and safety components

L3019   For the purposes of *Reg 8, 9* or *10*, a lift or a safety component is not regarded as being placed on the market or supplied:

(i) where that lift or safety component will be put into service in a country outside the Community; or is imported into the Community for re-export to a country outside the Community – but this paragraph does not apply if the CE marking, or any inscription liable to be confused with such a marking, is affixed to the lift or safety component or, in the case of a safety component, to its label; or

(ii) by the exhibition at trade fairs and exhibitions of that lift or safety compo-nent, in respect of which the provisions of these Regulations are not satisfied, if:

— a notice is displayed in relation to the lift or safety component in question to the effect that it does not satisfy those provisions; and that it may not be placed on the market or supplied until those provisions are satisfied; and

— adequate safety measures are taken to ensure the safety of persons.

[*Reg 12*].

Conformity assessment procedures

L3020   For the purposes of *Reg 8(2)* or *9(2)* (see L3014 and L3015 above), the appropriate conformity assessment procedure is as follows:

For lifts – one of the following procedures:

— if the lift was designed in accordance with a lift having undergone an EC type-examination as referred to in *Schedule 5*, it must be constructed, installed and tested by implementing:

— the final inspection referred to in *Schedule 6*; or

— the quality assurance system referred to in *Schedule 11* or *Schedule 13*; and

the procedures for the design and construction stages, on the one hand, and the installation and testing stages, on the other, may be carried out on the same lift;

— if the lift was designed in accordance with a model lift having undergone an EC type-examination as referred to in *Schedule 5*, it must be constructed, installed and tested by implementing:

— the final inspection referred to in *Schedule 6*; or

— one of the quality assurance systems referred to in *Schedule 11* or *Schedule 13*; and

all permitted variations between a model lift and the lifts forming part of the lifts derived from that model lift must be clearly specified (with maximum and minimum values) in the technical dossier required as part of the appropriate conformity assessment procedure;

— if the lift was designed in accordance with a lift for which a quality assurance system pursuant to *Schedule 12* was implemented, supplemented by an examination of the design if the latter is not wholly in accordance with the harmonised standards, it must be installed and constructed and tested by implementing, in addition, the final inspection referred to in *Schedule 6* or one of the quality assurance systems referred to in *Schedule 11* or *Schedule 13*;

— the unit verification procedure, referred to in *Schedule 9*, by a notified body (see L3022 below); or

— the quality assurance system in accordance with *Schedule 12*, supplemented by an examination of the design if the latter is not wholly in accordance with the transposed harmonised standards.

For safety components – one of the following procedures:

— submit the model of the safety component for EC type-examination in accordance with *Schedule 5* and for production checks by a notified body (see L3022 below) in accordance with *Schedule 10*;

— submit the model of the safety component for EC type-examination in accordance with *Schedule 5* and operate a quality assurance system in accordance with *Schedule 7* for checking production; or

— operate a full quality assurance system in accordance with *Schedule 8*.

[*Reg 13*].

Requirements fulfilled by the person who places a lift or safety component on the market

L3021   Where in the case of a lift or a safety component, any of the requirements of *Regs 8, 9, 11* and *13* to be fulfilled by the installer of the lift or the manufacturer of the safety component or, in the case of the latter, his authorised representative established in the Community, have not been so fulfilled such requirements may be fulfilled by the person who places that lift or safety component on the market [*Reg 14*].

This provision, however, does not affect the power of an enforcement authority to take action in respect of the installer of the lift, the manufacturer of the safety component or, in the case of the latter, his authorised representative established in the Community in respect of a contravention of or a failure to comply with any of those requirements.

Notified bodies

L3022   For the purposes of these Regulations, a notified body is a body which has been appointed to carry out one or more of the conformity assessment procedures referred to in *Reg 13* which has been appointed as a notified body by the Secretary of State in the United Kingdom or by a member State.

[*Reg 15*].

The Lifting Operations and Lifting Equipment Regulations 1998

L3023   The requirements imposed by these Regulations on an employer in relation to lifting equipment apply in respect of lifting equipment provided for use or used by an employee of his at work. They also apply to a self-employed person, with regard to lifting equipment he uses at work, and to anyone with control, to any extent, of:

— lifting equipment;

— a person at work who uses or supervises or manages the use of lifting equipment; or

— the way in which lifting equipment is used,

and to the extent of his control.

General requirements

Strength and stability

L3024   Every employer must ensure that lifting equipment is of adequate strength and stability for each load, having regard in particular to the stress induced at its mounting or fixing point – and that every part of a load and anything attached to it and used in lifting it is of adequate strength [*Reg 4*].

Lifting equipment for lifting persons

L3025   Every employer must ensure that lifting equipment for lifting persons:

(i)   subject to (ii) below, is such as to prevent a person using it being crushed, trapped or struck or falling from the carrier;

(ii)   is such as to prevent so far as is reasonably practicable a person using it, while carrying out activities from the carrier, being crushed, trapped or struck or falling from the carrier;

(iii)   has suitable devices to prevent the risk of a carrier falling, and, if the risk cannot be prevented for reasons inherent in the site and height differences, the employer must ensure that the carrier has an enhanced safety coefficient suspension rope or chain which is inspected by a competent person every working day;

(iv)   is such that a person trapped in any carrier is not thereby exposed to danger and can be freed.

[*Reg 5*].

Positioning and installation

L3026   Employers must ensure that lifting equipment is positioned or installed in such a way as to reduce to as low as is reasonably practicable the risk of the lifting equipment or a load striking a person, or the risk from a load:

—   drifting;

—   falling freely; or

—   being released unintentionally,

and that otherwise it is safe.

Employers must also ensure that there are suitable devices for preventing anyone from falling down a shaft or hoistway [*Reg 6*].

Marking of lifting equipment

L3027   Employers must ensure that:

(i)   subject to (ii) below, machinery and accessories for lifting loads are clearly marked to indicate their safe working loads;

(ii)   where the safe working load of machinery for lifting loads depends on its configuration, either the machinery is clearly marked to indicate its safe working load for each configuration, or information which clearly indicates its safe working load for each configuration is kept with the machinery;

(iii)   accessories for lifting are also marked in such a way that it is possible to identify the characteristics necessary for their safe use;

(iv)   lifting equipment which is designed for lifting persons is appropriately and clearly marked to this effect; and

(v)   lifting equipment which is not designed for lifting persons but which might be mistakenly so used is appropriately and clearly marked to the effect that it is not designed for lifting persons.

[*Reg 7*].

Organisation of lifting operations

L3028   Every employer must ensure that any lifting or lowering of a load which involves lifting equipment is properly planned by a competent person, appropriately supervised and carried out in a safe manner [*Reg 8*].

Thorough examination and inspection

L3029   An employer is under a duty to ensure:

(i)   before lifting equipment is put into service for the first time by him, that it is thoroughly examined for any defect unless:

—   the lifting equipment has not been used before; and

—   in the case of lifting equipment for which an EC declaration of conformity could or (in the case of a declaration under the *Lifts Regulations 1997*) should have been drawn up, the employer has received such declaration made not more than twelve months before the lifting equipment is put into service; or

—   if obtained from the undertaking of another person, it is accompanied by physical evidence referred to in (iv) below;

[*Reg 9(1)*].

(ii)   where the safety of lifting equipment depends on the installation conditions, that it is thoroughly examined – after installation and before being put into service for the first time and after assembly and before being put into service at a new site or in a new location, to ensure that it has been correctly installed and is safe to operate [*Reg 9(2)*];

(iii)   that lifting equipment which is exposed to conditions causing deterioration which is liable to result in dangerous situations is:

thoroughly examined;

—   at least every six months, in the case of lifting equipment for lifting persons or an accessory for lifting;

—   at least every twelve months, in the case of other lifting equipment; or

—   in either case, in accordance with an examination scheme; and

—   whenever exceptional circumstances which are liable to jeopardise the safety of the lifting equipment have occurred, and

if appropriate for the purpose, is inspected by a competent person at suitable intervals between thorough examinations,

to ensure that health and safety conditions are maintained and that any deterioration can be detected and remedied in good time;

[*Reg 9(3)*].

(iv)   that no lifting equipment leaves his undertaking; or, if obtained from the undertaking of another person, is used in his undertaking, unless it is accompanied by physical evidence that the last thorough examination required to be carried out under this regulation has been carried out.

[*Reg 9(4)*].

Reports and defects

L3030   (i)   A person making a thorough examination for an employer under *reg 9* must:

—   immediately notify the employer of any defect in the lifting equipment which in his opinion is or could become a danger to anyone;

—   write a report of the thorough examination (see L3031 below) to the employer and any person from whom the lifting equipment has been hired or leased;

—   where there is in his opinion a defect in the lifting equipment involving an existing or imminent risk of serious personal injury send a copy of the report to the relevant enforcing authority ('relevant enforcing authority' means, where the defective lifting equipment has been hired or leased by the employer, the Health and Safety Executive – and otherwise, the enforcing authority for the premises in which the defective lifting equipment was thoroughly examined).

(ii)   A person making an inspection for an employer under *Reg 9* must immediately notify the employer of any defect in the lifting equipment which in his opinion is or could become a danger to anyone, and make a written record of the inspection.

(iii)   Every employer who has been notified under (i) above must ensure that the lifting equipment is not used before the defect is rectified; or, in the case of a defect which is not yet but could become a danger to persons, after it could become such a danger.

[*Reg 10*].

Prescribed information

L3031   *Schedule 1* specifies the information that must be contained in a report of a thorough examination, made under *Reg 10* (see L3030 above). The information must include the following:

(i)   The name and address of the employer for whom the thorough examination was made.

(ii)   The address of the premises at which the thorough examination was made.

(iii)   Particulars sufficient to identify the lifting equipment including its date of manufacture, if known.

(iv)   The date of the last thorough examination.

(v)   The safe working load of the lifting equipment or, where its safe working load depends on the configuration of the lifting equipment, its safe working load for the last configuration in which it was thoroughly examined.

(vi)   In respect of the first thorough examination of lifting equipment after installation or after assembly at a new site or in a new location:

—   that it is such thorough examination; and

—   if in fact this is so, that it has been installed correctly and would be safe to operate.

(vii)   In respect of all thorough examinations of lifting equipment which do not fall within (vi) above:

(a)   whether it is a thorough examination under *Reg 9(3)*:

—   within an interval of six months;

—   within an interval of twelve months;

—   in accordance with an examination scheme; or

—   after the occurrence of exceptional circumstances;

(b)   if in fact this is so, that the lifting equipment would be safe to operate.

(viii)   In respect of every thorough examination of lifting equipment:

(a)   identification of any part found to have a defect which is or could become a danger to anyone, and a description of the defect;

(b)   particulars of any repair, renewal or alteration required to remedy a defect found to be a danger to anyone;

    (c)   in the case of a defect which is not yet but could become a danger to anyone:

— the time by which it could become such a danger;

— particulars of any repair, renewal or alteration required to remedy the defect;

    (d)   the latest date by which the next thorough examination must be carried out;

    (e)   particulars of any test, if applicable;

    (f)   the date of the thorough examination.

(ix)   The name, address and qualifications of the person making the report; that he is self-employed or, if employed, the name and address of his employer.

(x)   The name and address of a person signing or authenticating the report on behalf of its author.

(xi)   The date of the report.

Keeping of information

L3032   An employer who obtains lifting equipment to which the 1998 Regulations apply, and who receives an EC declaration of conformity relating to it, must keep the declaration for so long as he operates the lifting equipment [*Reg 11(1)*].

Regulation 11(2)(a) provides that the employer must ensure that the information contained in every report made to him under *Reg 10(1)* (see L3030 above) is kept available for inspection:

— in the case of a thorough examination under *Reg 9(1)* (see L3029 above) of lifting equipment other than an accessory for lifting, until he stops using the lifting equipment;

— in the case of a thorough examination under *Reg 9(1)* (see L3029 above) of an accessory for lifting, for two years after the report is made;

— in the case of a thorough examination under *Reg 9(2)* (see L3029 above), until he stops using the lifting equipment at the place it was installed or assembled;

— in the case of a thorough examination under *Reg 9(3)* (see L3029 above), until the next report is made under that paragraph or the expiration of two years, whichever is later.

The employer must ensure that every record made under *Reg 10(2)* (see L3030 above) is kept available until the next such record is made [*Reg 11(2)(b)*].

Cranes, hoists and lifting equipment – common causes of failure

General

L3033   The principal cause of failure in all forms of lifting equipment is that of overloading, i.e. exceeding the specified safe working load (SWL) of the crane, forklift truck, hoist, chain, etc. in use for a specific lifting job. Every year there are numerous accidents and scheduled dangerous occurrences reported which are caused as a result of overloading. A second common cause of failure, and one which is inexcusable, is associated with neglect of the equipment while not in use. Neglect may be associated with poor or inadequate maintenance of the fabric of a crane or its safety devices, or simply a failure to store rope slings properly while not in use. One of the results of neglect is corrosion of metal surfaces resulting in weakened crane structures, wire ropes and slings.

Specific causes of failure are outlined below.

Cranes

L3034   (a)   Failure to lift vertically, e.g. dragging a load sideways along the ground before lifting.

   (b)   'Snatching' loads, i.e. not lifting slowly and smoothly.

   (c)   Exceeding the maximum permitted moment, i.e. the product of the load and the radius of operation.

   (d)   Excessive wind loading, resulting in crane instability.

   (e)   Defects in the fabrication of the crane, e.g. badly welded joints.

   (f)   Incorrect crane assembly in the case of tower cranes.

   (g)   Brake failure (rail-mounted cranes).

   (h)   In the case of mobile cranes:

      (i)   failure to use outriggers;

      (ii)   lifting on soft or uneven ground; and

      (iii) incorrect tyre pressures.

Hoists and lifts

L3035   (a)   Excessive wear in wire ropes.

   (b)   Excessive broken wires in ropes.

   (c)   Failure of the overload protection device.

   (d)   Failure of the overrun device.

Ropes

Fibre ropes

L3036   (a)   Bad storage in wet or damp conditions resulting in rot and mildew.

   (b)   Inadequate protection of the rope when lifting loads with sharp edges.

   (c)   Exposure to direct heat to dry, as opposed to gradual drying in air.

   (d)   Chemical action.

Wire ropes

L3037   (a)   Excessive broken wires.

   (b)   Failure to lubricate regularly.

   (c)   Frequent knotting or kinking of the rope.

   (d)   Bad storage in wet or damp conditions which promotes rust.

Chains

L3038   (*a*)   Mechanical defects in individual links.

(*b*)   Application of a static in excess of the breaking load.

(*c*)   Snatch loading.

Slings

L3039   Slings are manufactured in natural or man-made fibre or chain. The safe working load of any sling varies according to the angle formed between the legs of the sling.

The relationship between sling angle and the distance between the legs of the sling is also important. (See Table 1 below.)

Table 1
Safe working load for slings

Sling Angle	Distance between legs
30°	½ leg length
60°	1 leg length
90°	1⅓ leg length
120°	1⅔ leg length

For a one tonne load, the tension in the leg increases as shown in Table 2 below.

Table 2
Safe working load for slings – increased tension

Sling leg angle	Tension in leg (tonnes)
90°	0.7
120°	1.0
151°	2.0
171°	6.0

Other causes of failure in slings are:

(*a*)   Cuts, excessive wear, kinking and general distortion of the sling legs.

(*b*)   Failure to lubricate wire slings.

(*c*)   Failure to pack sharp corners of a load, resulting in sharp bends in the sling and the possibility of cuts or damage to it.

(*d*)   Unequal distribution of the load between the legs of a multi-leg sling.

Hooks

L3040   (*a*)   Distortion of the hook due to overloading.

(*b*)   Use of a hook without a safety catch.

(*c*)   Stripping of the thread connecting the hook to the chain fixture.

Forklift trucks

L3041 (*a*) Uneven floors, steeply inclined ramps or gradients, i.e. in excess of 1:10 gradient.

(*b*) Inadequate room to manoeuvre.

(*c*) Inadequate or poor maintenance of lifting gear.

(*d*) The practice of driving forwards down a gradient with the load preceding the truck.

(*e*) Load movement in transit.

(*f*) Sudden or fast braking.

(*g*) Hidden obstructions in the path of the truck.

(*h*) Use of the forward tilt mechanism with a raised load.

(*j*) Generally bad driving, including driving too fast, taking corners too fast, striking overhead obstructions, particularly when reversing and excessive use of the brakes.

Safe stacking of materials

L3042 Once materials, containers etc. have been lifted, they must remain stable until it is necessary to bring them down again. Whether 'block stacked', i.e. self-supporting, or stored in shelving or racks, there is a hazard and attention to basic principles is important.

Methods of storage depend on the shape and fragility of the material or package. Cylinders stored 'on the roll' are one of the more hazardous materials. The bottom layer must be properly secured to prevent movement; subsequent layers can rest on the one below, or be laid on battens and wedged. Progressively, as forklift trucks – and particularly reach trucks and narrow aisle stackers – lift to greater heights, so storage racking has been constructed higher. The Storage Equipment Manufacturers' Association has published a code of practice, which covers pallet racks, drive-in and drive-through racks and cantilever racks, setting out guidance to users. ('*Code of practice for the use of static racking*', Storage Equipment Manufacturers' Association, McLaren Building, 35 Dale End, Birmingham B4 7LN. Tel: 0121-200 2100).

Racking

L3043 A manufacturer will install racking to customer's requirements in terms of loading, pallet height and aisle width depending on the type of handling equipment used. Heavier loads must not be used; if there is to be a change of load stored, the manufacturer must be consulted. Racking has collapsed through either overloading or impact damage to an upright member.

Where trucks are used the following are to be recommended:

(*a*) bolting to the floor; and

(*b*) a column guard or guide rail to protect corners at the ends of aisles.

Pallets

L3044 Many types of load are carried on pallets and, whilst there are many metal pallets in use, the vast majority are of timber for economy of cost and weight. When damaged they are hazardous – and they are easily damaged by the dangerous forks of a truck.

The pallet should, therefore, be designed according to the load it is to carry and, if it is to be stored in racking, the type of rack.

There is a useful HSE Guidance Note which indicates some of the considerations of design, and makes recommendations for inspection of new and used pallets. ('*Safety in the use of timber pallets*', HSE Guidance Note PM 15, HMSO). See also British Standard BS ISO 6780: '*General purpose flat pallets for through transit of goods. Principal dimensions and tolerances*' (1988).

Forklift trucks

L3045   Forklift trucks (for legal requirements, see L3003 above) are potentially hazardous for a variety of reasons:

(*a*)   they usually work in fairly congested areas;

(*b*)   when elevating a heavy load, stability is bound to be reduced;

(*c*)   there is always the possibility of a load falling down;

(*d*)   when travelling with a load in the lowered position, the driver's visibility is often impaired;

(*e*)   even when travelling unladen, the forks projecting at the front are dangerous.

Truck population in the UK is now reckoned to be more than a quarter of a million; there are, therefore, a great many older machines in use which can exhibit many faults. In recent years many manufacturers have been fitting load guards, overhead guards, and warning horns as standard. Some now include a transparent window in the overhead guard (a wise extra where there is a possibility of small items falling down and being able to pass through the guard members) and masts with improved forward visibility. There are British and International Standards Organisation (ISO) standards for stability testing and practically all manufacturers test accordingly. (British Standards BS 3726, BS 5777). Another safety move has been the introduction of standard control symbols, particularly useful now that more trucks are being imported. (BS 5829 '*Specification for control symbols for powered industrial trucks*').

Requirements for safe forklift truck operation

L3046   An analysis of safe truck operation identifies three principal aspects as the potential cause of truck accidents: the driver, the truck and the system of work.

The driver

L3047   Drivers should be in good health, with sound vision and hearing. They should be over 18 years of age and trained within an approved training scheme. Drivers should observe the following precautions:

(*a*)   regulate speed with visibility;

(*b*)   use the horn whenever turning a blind corner;

(*c*)   be constantly aware of pedestrians and vehicles on roadways, loading bays, storage areas and transfer points (the use of convex mirrors located at strategic points greatly reduces the risk of collision);

(*d*)   drive in reverse when the load obscures vision;

(*e*)   travel with the forks down, and not operate the forks when in motion;

(*f*)   use prescribed lanes/routes; *no short cuts*;

(g)   stick to factory speed limits, e.g. 10 mph;

(h)   slow down on wet or uneven surfaces;

(j)   use the handbrake and tilt mechanism correctly;

(k)   take care on ramps (max 1 : 10);

(l)   when leaving the truck at any time, put the controls in neutral position, switch the power off, apply the brakes, and ensure the key or connector plug is removed.

Drivers should not:

(i)   carry passengers;

(ii)   park in front of fire appliances or fire exits;

(iii)   turn around on ramps;

(iv)   permit unauthorised use, e.g. by contractors.

The truck

L3048   On no account should trucks in a defective or dangerous condition be used.

A daily check system should be operated, prior to starting or on handover to another driver, which covers brakes, lights, steering, horn, battery, hydraulics and speed controls.

The system of work

L3049   On no account should the maximum rated load capacity be exceeded. Loads should always be placed dead centre on the forks.

The truck should be driven with the forks well under the load, with the load located firmly against the fork carriage and the mast tilted to suit the stability of the load being carried.

The following general points should be observed:

(a)   slinging should be undertaken only at designated slinging points;

(b)   a load which looks unsafe should never be moved;

(c)   broken, defective or inadequate strength pallets should never be used;

(d)   care must be taken at overhead openings, pipework, ducting, conduits, etc.;

(e)   the stability of a stack should always be checked before moving the forks.

Training of truck operators

L3050   Although training in safe handling, storage and transportation is necessary under the general legal duties imposed by *HSWA* (see above), special hazards exist with respect to forklift trucks (see further L3003 ABOVE). DEMONSTRABLY, PROPER TRAINING OF OPERATORS IS THE ONLY WAY TO SAFER USE OF LIFT TRUCKS. RTITB LTD PUBLISH '*LIFT TRUCK OPERATOR AND INSTRUCTOR TRAINING RECOMMENDATIONS*'.

Although there are no specific regulations on this area, the HSE ACoP requires, following general principles under *HSWA s 2*, that employers ensure their employees are sufficiently trained for the job. Competence, of course, can be demonstrated by the employees having completed a training course provided by a training provider accredited by one of the four accrediting bodies. The HSE recognises four accrediting bodies. These are:

(*a*)   RTITB Ltd,
Ercall House,
8 Pearson Road,
Central Park,
Telford
TF2 9TX
Telephone: (01952) 777777

(*b*)   Lantra National Training,
National Agricultural Centre,
Stoneleigh,
Near Kenilworth,
Warwickshire
CV8 2LG
Telephone: (01203) 696996

(*c*)   Association of Industrial Truck Trainers,
Independent Training Standards Scheme and Register,
Scammell House,
High Street,
Ascot,
Berkshire
SL5 7JF
Telephone: (01530) 417234

(*d*)   Construction Industry Training Board (CITB),
Bircham Newton Training Centre,
King's Lynn,
Norfolk
PE31 6RH
Telephone: (01485) 577577

After completing a course and receiving a certificate of competence, an operator needs proper supervision by a qualified person. Lamentably, many trainees (and so-called operators, in many cases) fail to understand the theory of counterbalancing. Most appreciate the effect of load weight, but not many grasp the effect of *load centre* which is equally essential to safe truck operation (e.g. the overturning moment: load weight × distance from pivot point, which is the front wheels).

Pedestrian-controlled lift trucks

L3051   Useful information for operators of pedestrian-controlled lift trucks is published by the British Industrial Truck Association in pocket book format. (*'Operator's safety code for powered industrial trucks'*, British Industrial Truck Association, Scammell House, High Street, Ascot SL5 7JF. Tel: 01344 623 800). Features which are increasingly being built in by manufacturers are:

(*a*)   toe guards around the wheels; and

(*b*)   a safety button in the head of the control handle to reverse the machine in the event of the operator being trapped between the machine and some other object.

Lighting

Introduction

L5001   Increasingly employers have become aware that indifferent lighting at work is bad economics, bad ergonomics, can lead to bad industrial relations and can make accidents at work more likely, whereas good lighting uses energy more efficiently, helps to improve productivity and quality of work, improves workforce morale, and helps to reduce accidents at work.

The factors that need to be considered for good lighting conditions include the following:

(a)   horizontal illuminance;

(b)   vertical illuminance and illuminance in other planes;

(c)   uniformity of illuminance over the working area;

(d)   colour appearance;

(e)   colour rendering;

(f)   glare and any associated discomfort;

(g)   the reflectance from the environment, ceilings, walls and floors;

(h)   the reflectance from the equipment and materials being used in the job;

(j)   the ratios of variation of illuminances associated with the job.

Statutory lighting requirements

General

L5002   The *Health and Safety at Work etc. Act 1974, s 2(2)(e)* requires employers to provide and maintain a working environment that is, so far as is reasonably practicable, safe and without risks to health, including adequate arrangements for the welfare of employees at work. Adequate lighting in all workplaces thus falls within this section, and is therefore enforceable.

People should be able to work and move around their workplace without suffering eye strain and without being subject to any risks associated with shadows. Hence local lighting may be necessary at individual workstations. All areas should be risk assessed and appropriate action taken to minimise any risks thereby identified.

The assessment should include the actual people who might be in that area and should include those with special needs (*Lighting at Work, HS(G)38*).

There are inherent risks in all areas with traffic and pedestrians, particularly after dark. Headlights can cause dazzle and fixed lights can cause glare. The position of lights and their associated switches should be carefully considered, bearing in mind other hazards such as fire, radiation and electricity. Access to switches and fittings should also be considered as bulbs need changing and fittings need cleaning.

Warehouses with materials stacked high can create shadows and as a result cause unnecessary risks. Frequently the lighting in a warehouse has been designed for the warehouse without racking, and the racking has been placed directly under the light fittings causing shadows in the access ways rather than having the lighting over the access ways.

Where individuals are particularly exposed to high risks when lighting fails, suitable emergency lighting should be available (*Workplace (Health, Safety and Welfare) Regulations 1992, Reg 8(3)*).

Sources of light

Natural light

L5003   People generally prefer to work in natural rather than artificial light. Workstations should be positioned to take advantage of available natural light.

This is frequently not possible and therefore other lighting must be available to supplement the natural light. Any plant operating outside daylight hours will need further lighting. Most large floor areas need further lighting even though the roof may have been designed to use natural light. Certain situations demand a light level which is high – on overcast days such a level may not be achievable by natural light, and there will be a need for supplementary electric lighting.

When considering windows for lighting purposes, other factors such as heat retention in winter and reduction in summer, noise, air-conditioning and security may also have to be considered.

Electric lighting

L5004   The costs of buying, installing and running any light fitting, and what it costs to replace, all affect the purchasing decision, together with such considerations as size, heat produced, expected life and colour effects.

The efficacy of lamps is measured as the light output per unit of electricity supplied, i.e. lumens per watt.

Type of lamp	Lumens per watt
Incandescent lamps	10 to 18
Tungsten halogen	18 to 24
High pressure mercury	25 to 55
Tubular fluorescent	30 to 80 (depending on colour)
Mercury halide	66 to 84
High pressure sodium	65 to 120

Generally the common incandescent lamps are relatively cheap to install but more expensive to run, whereas the fluorescent tubes are more expensive to install but less costly to run. The mercury discharge lamps and the low pressure sodium lamps have restricted colour performance – high pressure sodium lamps and colour corrected mercury lamps do not have this disadvantage.

Standards of lighting or illuminance

The technical measurement of illuminance

L5005   The standard of illuminance, i.e. the amount of light, required in a given situation depends on several factors, including general comfort considerations and the visual efficiency required. The unit of illuminance is the 'lux': one lux is one lumen per square metre. The lumen is the unit of luminous flux used to describe the quantity of light emitted by a source or received by a surface.

Light meters can be used to measure the degree of illuminance.

Average illuminance and measured illuminance on the task

L5006   The HSE Guidance note HS(G)38, *Lighting at Work*, which was revised in 1997, relates illuminance levels to the degree of detail which is needed to be seen in a particular task or situation. The table below (from HS(G)38) indicates the average illuminance recommended for the work area as a whole as well as the minimum measured illuminance at any position within it. As the illuminance produced by any lighting installation is seldom uniform, the use of the average figure alone could result in the presence of a few positions with a much lower illuminance which may well pose a threat to health and safety. The minimum measured illuminance is therefore the lowest illuminance permitted within that work area for purposes of health and safety.

The planes on which the illuminances should be provided depend on the layout of the task. If the task is predominantly on one plane, e.g. horizontal, as with an office desk, or vertical as in a warehouse, the recommended illuminances are those recommended for that plane. Where there is no well defined plane or more than one, the recommended illuminance should be provided on the horizontal plane and care taken to ensure that the reflectances in the working areas are high.

Table 1
Average illuminances and minimum measured illuminances for different types of work

General activity	Typical locations/types of work	Average illuminance (Lx)	Minimum measured illuminance (Lx)
Movement of people, machines and vehicles[1]	Lorry parks, corridors, circulation routes	20	5
Movement of people, machines and vehicles in hazardous areas; rough work not requiring any perception of detail	Construction site clearance, excavation and soil work, docks, loading bays, bottling and canning plants	50	20

Work requiring limited perception of detail	Kitchens, factories, assembling large components, potteries	100	50
Work requiring perception of detail	Offices, sheet metal work, bookbinding	200	100
Work requiring perception of fine detail	Drawing offices, factories assembling electronic components, textile production	500	200

Notes

1. Only safety has been considered, because no perception of detail is needed and visual fatigue is unlikely. However, where it is necessary to see detail to recognise a hazard or where error in performing the task could put someone else at risk, for safety purposes as well as to avoid visual fatigue the figure should be increased to that for work requiring the perception of detail. The *CIBSE Code for Interior Lighting 1994* gives more information and recommendations.

2. The purpose is to avoid visual fatigue: the illuminances will be adequate for safety purposes.

Illuminance ratios

L5007   The relationship between the lighting of the work area and adjacent areas is significant. Large differences in illuminance between these areas may cause visual discomfort or even affect safety levels where there is frequent movement, e.g. fork-lift trucks. This problem arises most often where local or localised lighting in an interior exposes a person to a range of illuminance for a long period, or where there is movement between interior and exterior working areas exposing a person to a sudden change of illuminance. To guard against danger and discomfort the recommendations in Table 2 should be followed.

Table 2
Maximum ratios of illuminance for adjacent areas

Situations to which recommendation applies	Typical location	Maximum ratio of illuminances		
		Working area		*Adjacent area*
Where each task is individually lit and the area around the task is lit to a lower illuminance	Local lighting in an office	5	:	1
Where two working areas are adjacent, but one is lit to a lower illuminance than the other	Localised lighting in a works store	5	:	1

Where two working areas are lit to different illuminances and are separated by a barrier but there is frequent movement between them	A storage area inside a factory and a loading bay outside	10	:	1

Maintenance of light fitments

L5008

The lighting output from a given lamp will reduce gradually in the course of its life. The total light output from a light fitting and its lamp can greatly be improved by regular cleaning and maintenance, which should include the reflector, the diffuser and any other part of the luminaire. Often it is sensible and economic to change a batch of lamps on a planned basis rather than wait until each one fails and then replace it.

Qualitative aspects of lighting

L5009

Although the quantity of light afforded to a task in terms of standard service illuminance is an important feature of any lighting design, there are several qualitative aspects of lighting which can affect the way people perceive their work activities and any dangers that may be present.

Glare

L5010

Glare occurs whenever one part of the visual field is much brighter than the average brightness to which the eye or visual system is adapted. There are three different forms of glare:

(*a*)   disability glare – the direct interference with vision. Driving at night towards a car with headlights on full beam is an example of this;

(*b*)   discomfort glare – when there is discomfort, irritability, annoyance or distraction. This can lead to visual fatigue and headaches;

(*c*)   reflected glare – is the reflection of bright lights on shiny or wet surfaces which can almost entirely conceal the detail in or behind the object which is glinting.

The Illuminating Engineering Society (IES) publishes a Limiting Glare Index for each of the effects in (*a*) and (*b*) above. This is an index representing the degree of discomfort glare which will be just tolerable in any particular location.

Distribution

L5011

The distribution of light is concerned with the way that it is spread. The British Zonal Method, BZM, classifies luminaires (light-fittings) according to the way they distribute the light, from BZ1, where all the light is in a narrow column – as with a torch – to BZ10 where the light is distributed in all directions – as with a spherical lamp source which has no reflectors.

The position of any light source, the shape of the area being lit and the degree of reflection from any surfaces will all affect the light distribution.

The actual spacing of the light sources is also important for good, even distribution. In normal circumstances, the evenness of illuminance in an office will be satisfactory if the ratio of the height of the luminaire above the working position to the spacing between luminaires is between 1*1/2*:1 and 1:1, depending on the type of luminaires used.

Brightness

L5012   Brightness or 'luminosity' is a subjective sensation and therefore cannot be measured. It is possible, however, to consider a brightness ratio, which is the ratio of the apparent luminosity between a task object and its surroundings. To ensure the correct brightness ratio, the ability of all surfaces to reflect light should be maintained. As a general guide, if the task illuminance value (i.e. the recommended illuminance level for a particular task) is 1, the effective reflectance values should be about 0.6 for ceilings, between 0.3 and 0.8 for walls, and between 0.2 and 0.3 for floors.

Diffusion

L5013   Diffusion is the projection of light in all directions, with no predominant direction. The direction of light can often determine the density of shadows which may prejudice safety standards or reduce the evenness of lighting. A diffuser as part of a light fitting will reduce the glare from that fitting.

Colour rendition

L5014   Colour rendition refers to the appearance of an object under a specific light source, compared to its colour under a reference illuminant, usually natural light. Good standards of colour rendition allow the colour of an object to be properly perceived. Generally the colour rendering properties of luminaires should not clash with those of natural light and should be just as effective at night.

Stroboscopic effect

L5015   Under certain circumstances the frequency of the electric signals to a light source when it is used on a rotating object can cause the eye to perceive that the rotating object has stopped or is moving very slowly either forwards or backwards. If the object is rotating fast and an individual approaches it under the impression that it is stationary, the situation is extremely dangerous.

Angle selection

L5016   The direction and elevation of the light flux can minimise the reflectance from light sources on visual display screens. To help to achieve this, light fittings which restrict the light level above a specified angle to the vertical from the fitting have been developed and are categorised as follows:

—   category 1 is above 55 degrees;

—   category 2 is above 65 degrees; and

—   category 3 is above 75 degrees.

The categories are not a measure of the efficacy of the luminaires.

Machinery Safety

Introduction

M1001

Every six hours, throughout all sectors of industry, someone is seriously injured whilst using work equipment – whether a power press, lawn mower or photocopier – resulting possibly in limb amputation, disfigurement or even death. It is not surprising, therefore, that traditionally machinery safety has always been in the vanguard of safety at work, being a fertile source of case law – case law under the (now defunct) *s 14* of the *Factories Act 1961*, for instance, achieving almost biblical significance. More particularly, a substantial part of *Part II* of the *Factories Act 1961* was devoted to specifying requirements relating to safe operation of machinery in factories, and a succession of regulations passed thereunder (ranging from the *Horizontal Milling Machines Regulations 1928*, through the *Operations at Unfenced Machinery Regulations 1938* and the *Power Presses Regulations 1965* to the *Abrasive Wheels Regulations 1970* and the *Woodworking Machines Regulations 1974*) were equally concerned with imposition of maximum safety standards and training of operators. Such regulations sometimes set standards more draconian than those of the *Factories Act 1961* itself, e.g. the *Woodworking Machines Regulations 1974*. Some machinery was regarded as dangerous *per se* (e.g. prime movers and transmission machinery), where breach of fencing requirement causing injury entitled an operator to damages automatically, without having to establish negligence; other machinery had to be demonstrably dangerous, that is, the cause of reasonably foreseeable injury – often by reference to past track accident record (e.g. parts of machinery other than prime movers and transmission machinery).

'A part of machinery is dangerous if it is a possible cause of injury to anybody acting in a way in which a human being may be reasonably expected to act in circumstances which may be reasonably expected to occur' (*Walker v Bletchley-Flettons [1937] 1 AER 170 per* du Parcq J).

Because design of accident-free machinery was regarded as idealistic, statutory requirement tended to underline the importance of fencing and guarding, with the corollary that duties were laid on employers, as distinct from designers and manufacturers of industrial machinery. In more recent times, however, legislation increasingly reflects a sea change of emphasis, with equal (if not more) responsibility being allocated to designers and manufacturers, a trend initially sign-posted by *s 6* of *HSWA* (see P9011 PRODUCT SAFETY) and later compounded by the *Supply of Machinery (Safety) Regulations 1992* and *1994*. Moreover, earlier law (i.e. the *Factories Act 1961*) was anachronistic and reflected the absence of a general statutory requirement or criterion throughout industry to machinery safety. Thus, the fencing requirements of the *Factories Act 1961* applied only to factories, safety requirements relating to agricultural machinery were out of date and the *Operations at Unfenced Machinery Regulations* did not extend to robots.

Currently, statutory duties are dually (but separately) laid on both manufacturers of machinery for use at work and employers and users of such machinery and equipment, prior compliance, on the part of manufacturers leading to compliance on the part of employers/users. General and specific duties are imposed on manufacturers by the *Supply of Machinery (Safety) Regulations 1992 (SI 1992 No 3073)* as amended by the *Supply of Machinery (Safety) (Amendment) Regulations 1994 (SI 1994 No 2063)*. Correspondingly, general and specific duties (of a parallel nature) are laid on employers and users of work machinery by the *Provision and Use of Work Equipment Regulations 1998 (SI 1998 No 2306) (PUWER 1998)*. These two sets of regulations interface as follows: designers and manufacturers are required to design and manufacture machinery and equipment suitable for specified work purposes (that is, equipment accommodating reasonably foreseeable injury precautions) in alignment with BS 5304 (1988 'Code of Practice for Safety of Machinery', as updated by BS EN 292 'Basic Concepts, General Principles for Design' (1991)). Employers and users, on the other hand, are required, by inspection, to identify foreseeable hazards (if any) during risk assessment.

The importance of design as regards machine safety

M1002 A machine is defined as an assembly of linked parts or components, at least one of which moves, with the appropriate machine actuators, control and power circuits, joined together for a specific application, in particular for the processing, treatment, moving or packaging of a material. More particularly, machines embrace:

(*a*) operational parts, performing the principal output function of the machine (i.e. manufacture) (e.g. chuck, drill bit of a vertical drill); and

(*b*) non-operational parts, conveying power/motion to the operational parts (e.g. motor drives).

An operator is liable to injury from machinery in a variety of ways, such as:

(i) coming into contact with it;

(ii) being trapped between machinery and material in it;

(iii) being struck by machinery or becoming entangled in its motion;

(iv) being struck by parts of machinery ejected from it; or

(v) being struck by material ejected from machinery.

These dangers sought to be addressed previously by the fencing/guarding requirements of the *Factories Act 1961* and are currently the remit of *PUWER 1998* and the *Supply of Machinery (Safety) Regulations 1992* (see M1019 below). Because the legal requirements are generally stringent, Great Britain has a good accident record by international standards. Engineering design of safeguards, however, is often poor, indicating that the law is honoured in the breach rather than in the observance. The HSE states that about three-quarters of all moving machinery accidents are preventable with reasonably practicable precautions. Half the number of preventable accidents arise as a consequence of a failure on the part of employers to provide proper safeguards. The other half are largely caused by workmen removing safety devices.

Design of machine guards to date has not been particularly successful, though design standards, in recent years, were set by BS 5304: 1975 'Code of Practice for safe guarding of machinery'. Progress was made on certain machines, partly as a result of innovative guard design and partly as a result of operative training, thus minimising the level of serious injuries. Design of machine guards is covered by EN 953; this is complemented by several other BS EN standards for machinery safety (see APPENDIX 3), replacing the old BS 5304: 1975 and its later version BS 5304:

1988. These standards, together with the General Product Safety Directive (see P9001 PRODUCT SAFETY) and the regulations on the safety of machinery (see M1014 and M1019 below) are expected to succeed in further reducing operator injuries.

Responsibility for poor guard design rests predominantly with the fact that the law has laid emphasis on the user's obligations in respect of factory machinery, rather than considering the measure of involvement which designers and manufacturers of factory machinery should carry. It seems true to say that in some cases injured workmen have been blamed, or lost all or part of their compensation, for what amounts to lack of commitment on the part of design engineers. To some extent this regressive state of affairs has been ameliorated by the introduction of *HSWA s 6* placing for the first time, general duties regarding product safety upon designers, manufacturers, importers and suppliers, and by the *Consumer Protection Act 1987* (see PRODUCT SAFETY). The stricter safeguards in the new legislation should make further improvements.

Practical control methods to prevent accidents

M1003   There are two main reasons why accidents happen: either because of a failure to identify danger or acknowledge the possibility of harm, or because control measures are inadequate. Historically three control methods have prevailed:

(*a*)   motivation of personnel at risk in an effort to make them cope better with danger;

(*b*)   provision of protective clothing (which complies with legal requirements but does not embrace machine operation and unpredictable behaviour);

(*c*)   provision and maintenance of physical safeguards to meet the needs of those at risk and to cope with unpredictable behaviour.

The success of (*a*) and (*b*) depends on changing people's attitudes and skills regarding safety, or on employing people with the requisite attitudes and skills. Evidence shows overwhelmingly that the benefits here are likely to be short term. Conversely, adoption of the approach in (*c*) has proved highly successful, especially where it is written into legal requirement.

Machinery hazards

M1004   Hazards associated with machinery can be classified as follows.

(*a*) Traps

Traps created by machinery are of three basic types:

(i)   *In-running nips*: a common feature of conveyorised systems, traps are created where a moving chain meets a toothed wheel, where a moving belt meets a roller, or at the point where two revolving drums, rollers or toothed wheels meet. See *fig. 1* below:

(ii)   *Reciprocating traps*: these are a feature particularly of presses operating under vertical or horizontal motion. See *fig. 2* below:

(iii)   *Shearing traps*: where a moving part of machinery traverses a fixed part, or where two moving parts traverse each other, as with a pair of garden shears, and a guillotine effect is produced. See *fig. 3* below:

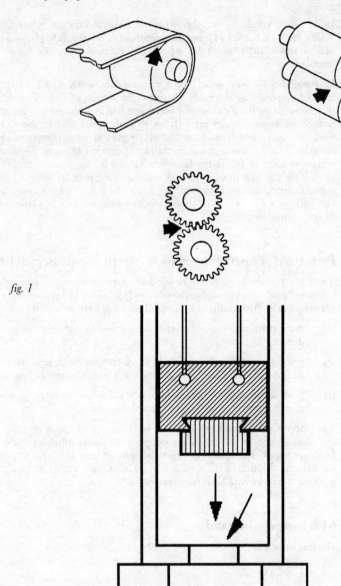

fig. 1

fig. 2 Vertical reciprocating operation of a power press

(*b*) *Entanglement*

The risk of entanglement of clothing, hair and limbs is associated with unfenced revolving shafts, pulleys, drills or chucks to drills. See *fig. 4* below:

(*c*) *Contact*

Contact with machinery may cause injury, for instance abrasions due to contact with a grinding wheel, burns from hot surfaces, or amputations through contact with a circular saw.

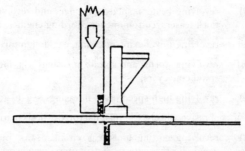

fig. 3 Shearing trap

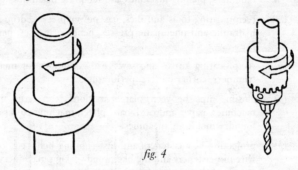

fig. 4

(*d*) *Ejection*

Machines may frequently eject particles of wood or metal during a processing operation, or parts of the machine may be thrown out of it.

(*e*) *Impact*

Certain fast-moving machines could cause injury if an individual gets in the way during the cycle of the machine, e.g. certain types of meat slicing machine.

Classified dangerous parts of machinery

M1005   The HSE has classified the following parts of machinery as inherently dangerous and, as such, they must be securely fenced:

(*a*)   revolving shafts, spindles, mandrels and bars, e.g. line and counter shafts, machine shafts, drill spindles, chucks and drills, etc., boring bars, stock bars, traverse shafts;

(*b*)   in-running nips between pairs of rotating parts, e.g. gear wheels, friction wheels, calendar bowls, mangle rolls, metal manufacturing rolls, rubber washing, breaking and mixing rolls, dough brakes, printing machines, paper-making machines;

(*c*)   in-running nips of the belt and pulley type, e.g. belts and pulleys, plain, flanged or grooved, chain and sprocket gears, conveyor belts and pulleys, metal coiling and the like;

(*d*)   projections on revolving parts, e.g. key heads, set screws, cotter pins, coupling bolts;

(*e*)   discontinuous rotating parts, e.g. open arm pulleys, fan blades, spoked gear wheels and spoked flywheels;

(*f*)   revolving beaters, spiked cylinders and revolving drums, e.g. scutchers, rag flock teasers, cotton openers, carding engines, laundry washing machines;

(*g*)   revolving mixer arms in casing, e.g. dough mixers, rubber solution mixers;

(*h*)   revolving worms and spirals in casings, e.g. meat mincers, rubber extruders, spiral conveyors;

(*j*)   revolving high speed cages in casings, e.g. hydro-extractors, centrifuges;

(*k*)   abrasive wheels, e.g. manufactured wheels, natural sandstone wheels;

(*l*)   revolving cutting tools, e.g. circular saws, milling cutters, circular shears, wood slicers, routers, chaff cutters, woodworking machines such as spindle moulders, planing machines and tenoning machines;

(*m*)   reciprocating tools and dies, e.g. power presses, drop stamps, relief stamps, hydraulic and pneumatic presses, bending presses, hand presses, revolution presses;

(*n*)   reciprocating knives and saws, e.g. guillotines for metal, rubber and paper, trimmers, corner cutters, perforators;

(*o*)   closing nips between platen motions, e.g. letter press platen printing machines, paper and cardboard platen machine cutters, some power presses, foundry moulding machines;

(*p*)   projecting belt fasteners and fast-running belts, e.g. bolt and nut fasteners, wire pin fasteners and the like, woodworking machinery belts, textile machinery side belting, centrifuge belts;

(*q*)   nips between connecting rods or links, and rotating wheels, cranks or discs, e.g. side motion of certain flat-bed printing machines, jacquard motions or looms;

(*r*)   traps arising from the traversing carriages of self-acting machines, e.g. metal planing machines.

Machinery guards

M1006   A guard is part of a machine used to provide protection by means of a physical barrier. Depending on its construction, a guard may be called casing, cover, screen, door or enclosing guard. A guard may act alone: it is then effective only when it is closed. Alternatively a guard may be used in conjunction with an interlocking device (with or without guard locking – see below): in this case, protection is certain whatever the position of the guard. A wide range of guards or guarding systems is available.

(*a*) *Fixed guard*

EN 953: 1997 '*Safety of machinery – Guards – General requirements for the design and construction of fixed and movable guards*' defines a fixed guard as 'a guard kept in place (i.e. closed)', either permanently or by means of fasteners (screws, nuts) making removal/opening impossible without using tools.

There are two kinds of fixed guards:

—   an enclosing guard which prevents access to the danger zone from all sides;

—   a distance guard which does not completely enclose a danger zone, but which prevents or reduces access because of its dimensions and its distance from the danger zone, e.g. a perimeter fence or tunnel guard. A tunnel guard is commonly used with metal cutting machinery: the strip metal can only be fed through the tunnel to the cutters, thereby ensuring that users have no access to the cutting mechanism.

(*b*) *Movable guard*

According to EN 953: 1997, this is a guard which is connected by mechanical means (e.g. hinges or slides) to the machine frame or an attached element and which can be opened without the use of tools.

There are three basic kinds of movable guards:

— a power operated guard: this is operated with the assistance of power from a source other than manual effort or gravity;

— a self-closing guard: this works by means of gravity, a spring or other external power;

— a control guard: this is a guard associated with an interlocking device so that the hazardous machine functions 'covered' by the guard cannot operate until the guard is closed, and the closing of the guard initiates the operation of these functions.

(*c*) *Adjustable guard*

This is defined by EN 953: 1997 as a fixed or movable guard which is adjustable as a whole or which incorporates an adjustable part or parts. The adjustment remains fixed during a particular operation. Such guards are appropriate for many band saws, drilling machines and circular saws.

(*d*) *Interlocking guard*

EN 953: 1997 defines this form of guard as one associated with an interlocking device so that:

— the hazardous machine functions 'covered' by the guard cannot operate until the guard is closed;

— if the guard is opened while hazardous machine functions are operating, a stop instruction is given;

— when the guard is closed, the hazardous machine functions 'covered' by the guard can operate, but the closure of the guard does not itself initiate their operation.

(*e*) *Interlocking guard with guard locking*

This is a guard associated with an interlocking device and a guard locking device so that:

— the hazardous machine functions 'covered' by the guard cannot operate until the guard is closed and locked;

— the guard remains closed and locked until the risk of injury from the hazardous machine functions has passed;

— when the guard is closed and locked, the hazardous machine functions 'covered' by the guard can operate, but the closure and locking of the guard do not by themselves initiate their operation.

Safety devices

M1007   A safety device is a protective appliance, other than a guard, which eliminates or reduces risk, alone or associated with a guard. There are many forms of safety device available.

(a) Trip device

A trip device is one which causes a machine or machine elements to stop (or ensures an otherwise safe condition) when a person or a part of his body goes beyond a safe limit (EN 292-1: 1991). Trip devices take a number of forms – for example, mechanical, electro-sensitive safety systems and pressure-sensitive mat systems.

Trip devices may be:

— mechanically actuated – e.g. trip wires, telescopic probes, pressure-sensitive devices; or

— non-mechanically actuated – e.g. photo-electric devices, or devices using capacitive or ultrasonic means to achieve detection.

(b) Mechanical restraint device

Such a device introduces into a mechanism a mechanical obstacle (for example, a wedge, spindle, strut or scotch) which, by virtue of its own strength, can prevent any hazardous movement, such as the fall of a ram, due to the failure of the normal retaining system.

(c) Interlocking device (interlock)

The purpose of this sort of device, which may be mechanical, electrical or some other type, is to prevent the operation of machine elements under specified conditions (generally as long as a guard is not closed).

(d) Enabling (control) device

This is an additional manually operated control device used in conjunction with a start control and which, when continuously actuated, allows a machine to function.

(e) Hold-to-run control device

This device initiates and maintains the operation of machine elements for only as long as the manual control (actuator) is actuated. The manual control returns automatically to the stop position when released.

(f) Two-hand control device

A hold-to-run control device which requires at least simultaneous actuation by the use of both hands in order to initiate and to maintain, whilst hazardous condition exists, any operation of a machine thus affording a measure of protection only for the person who actuates it. EN 574:1996 lays down specific recommendations relating to the design of such devices.

(g) Limiting device

Such a device prevents a machine or machine elements from exceeding a designed limit (e.g. space limit, pressure limit).

(*h*) *Limited movement control device*

The actuation of this sort of device permits only a limited amount of travel of a machine element, thus minimising risk as much as possible; further movement is precluded until there is a subsequent and separate actuation of the control.

(*j*) *Deterring/impeding device*

This comprises any physical obstacle which, without totally preventing access to a danger zone, reduces the probability of access to this zone by preventing free access.

Other aspects of machinery safety

(*a*) *Position of controls*

M1008

Control should be so positioned and spaced as to provide safe and easy operation with ample clearance between each control. Two-hand control devices should not be used as an alternative to guarding, but as an extra safeguard. Actuators which are used to initiate a start function or the movement of machine elements ought to be constructed and mounted so as to minimise inadvertent operation. Push button start controls should be shrouded and pedal-operated controls should be protected to prevent accidental operation. Controls should be clearly identifiable and readily distinguishable from each other. (BS 3641: 1983 and EN 60204-1: 1997).

(*b*) *Emergency stops*

Each machine must be fitted with one or more emergency stop devices to enable actual or impending danger to be averted. The following exceptions apply:

— machines in which an emergency stop device would not lessen the risk, either because it would not reduce the stopping time or because it would not enable the special measures required to deal with the risk to be taken;

— hand-held portable machines and hand-guided machines.

An emergency stop device must stop the dangerous process as quickly as possible, without creating additional hazards. The emergency stop control must remain engaged; it must be possible to disengage it only by an appropriate operation on the control device itself. Disengaging the control must not restart the machinery, but only permit restarting. The stop control function must not trigger the stopping function before being in the latched position. (Essential Health and Safety Requirements, and EN 418: 1992).

(*c*) *Colour*

It may be necessary to paint certain parts of machines a distinguishing colour which will only be visible when a danger exists, e.g. the insides of hinged or sliding covers which, when open, expose dangerous machine parts or a part of the machine which remains with the source of danger.

(*d*) *Spindles*

Spindles should be able to be brought to rest quickly and consistently. Spindle brakes which are activated by mechanical, hydraulic, pneumatic or electrical means should bring the spindle to rest, or retain their capability of bringing the spindle to rest, in the event of a power failure. The braking system should be such that the spindle will not automatically rotate when power is resumed after a power failure.

Rotating parts and equipment fastened to rotating parts should be so secured as to prevent dislodgement in consequence of the brake action.

(e) Handles and handwheels

Cranked handles or handwheels used to operate a mechanism, which can also be operated under power at a peripheral speed of the handwheel of more than 20 metres per minute, should be designed to prevent rotation under power, be solid and be provided with a device that stalls rotation if obstructed. (Machine Tool Traders Association Standards Instruction Sheet No 11.)

(f) Power-operated workholding devices

These devices should be designed so that a dangerous situation is prevented in the event of failure of the power supply. On automatic machines the control system should be interlocked to prevent the machine from being operated until power is supplied to the workholding device and the workpiece is clamped. The control system should be such that the power-operating system for the workholding device cannot be operated to unclamp the workpiece whilst the machine is in operation.

(g) Equipment

— Electrical equipment should comply with EN 60204-1: 1997;

— Hydraulic equipment should comply with EN 982: 1996;

— Pneumatic equipment should comply with EN 983: 1996.

(h) Coolants

Where a coolant is used, machines should be designed to contain the coolant at least during the more usual operations. It may also be necessary to add a bactericide to the coolant to prevent bacterial growth. Coolant reservoirs should be covered where possible. The coolant system should be designed so that coolant troughs, reservoirs, etc. can be easily cleaned. Nozzles should be designed so that they will stay firmly in position when set and not require adjustment by the operator during the machining process. On-off volume controls should not be adjacent to the nozzle and should be positioned so as to ensure operator safety when adjustments are made. Additional splash guards should be used where necessary. Means should be provided for the safe removal of swarf from the work area.

(j) Lubrication

Lubrication points should be easily accessible. Care should be taken to avoid any accidental mixing of coolant, cutting fluids and lubricants. Excess lubricants should be prevented from reaching the surrounding floor area. On machines in which the failure of an automatic lubrication system could cause a hazard to the operator, such a lubrication system should incorporate a suitable indication of its correct functioning.

(k) Counterweights and enclosures

Counterweights, related machine elements and their movements which constitute a hazard, should be safeguarded.

Enclosures used within the machine to house mechanical, electrical, hydraulic equipment, etc. which constitute a hazard should be provided with fixed covers and guards.

(*l*) *Lifting gear*

All fixtures used on the machine and other externally-mounted devices should be provided with means for their safe loading and unloading. When a machine is provided with lifting gear and appliances, the supplier should provide details of the safe working load and notify the user of the need to obtain a certificate of test and examination. [*Factories Act 1961, s 27*] (disapplied with regard to supply of new machinery by the *Supply of Machinery (Safety) Regulations 1992*). Eyebolts and eyebolt holes should be identified to prevent mismatching. (HSE Guidance Note PM 16; BS 4278: 1984). (See LIFTING MACHINERY AND EQUIPMENT.)

Non-mechanical machinery hazards

M1009   Other hazards associated with machinery operation, which can be a contributory factor in accidents and/or occupational ill-health, include:

(*a*)   inadequate temperature, lighting and ventilation control of the machine area, frequently resulting in steep temperature gradients, shadows, glare and general discomfort;

(*b*)   noise from machinery, which reduces the chance of operators hearing warning signals, such as the fire alarm or a forklift truck horn, and can result in operators going deaf over a period of time;

(*c*)   chemical substances used in machinery-operated processes, which can cause dermatitis or even result in a gassing accident;

(*d*)   ergonomic design faults, leading to postural fatigue, visual fatigue, back and other body strains, and an increased risk of operator error;

(*e*)   ionising radiation, due to inadequate containment of sealed and unsealed sources of radiation; and resulting in various occupational cancers; and

(*f*)   dust and fume emission, resulting in certain conditions of the respiratory tract, such as silicosis, and the potential for dust explosions.

All these factors should be considered in the assessment of machinery hazards.

Legal requirements in connection with machinery
Background

M1010   Since 1 January 1997, when *PUWER 1992* came fully into effect for all workplaces using workplace machinery (including vehicles), the fencing/guarding requirements of the *Factories Act 1961* (as well as *OSRPA 1963*) were repealed, in tandem with the revocation (either total or partial) of a gamut of regulations variously concerned with machine safety (e.g. the *Operations at Unfenced Machinery Regulations 1938* (as amended), the *Agriculture (Power Take-off) Regulations 1957*, the *Abrasive Wheels Regulations 1970* and the *Woodworking Machines Regulations 1974*).

Repeals

M1011   The following sections of primary legislation were repealed from 1 January 1993, except in respect of equipment provided for use before 1 January 1993, where the repeal came into effect from 1 January 1997:

(*a*)   *Factories Act 1961, ss 12-17* and *19*; and

(*b*)   *Offices, Shops and Railway Premises Act 1963, s 17*.

Revocations

M1012   The following regulations were revoked from 1 January 1993, except in respect of equipment provided for use before 1 January 1993, where the revocation came into effect from 1 January 1997:

(*a*)   *Horizontal Milling Machines Regulations 1928*;

(*b*)   *Operations at Unfenced Machinery Regulations 1938*;

(*c*)   *Agriculture (Power Take-off) Regulations 1957*;

(*d*)   *Agriculture (Stationary Machinery) Regulations 1959*;

(*e*)   *Abrasive Wheels Regulations 1970* (partial); and

(*f*)   *Woodworking Machines Regulations 1974* (partial).

Notwithstanding these repeals and revocations, residual civil liability, in connection with these requirements and regulations, is set to continue.

Definition of machinery for use at work

M1013   'Machinery for use at work' (for manufacturing purposes) means machinery

(*a*)   designed for use/operation, whether exclusively or not, by persons at work, or

(*b*)   designed for use/operation, otherwise than at work, in non-domestic premises made available to persons at a place where they may use the machinery provided for their use there.

[*Supply of Machinery (Safety) Regulations 1992, 6 Sch 9*].

'Work equipment' (for employer/user purposes) means

'any machinery, appliance, apparatus, tool or installation for use at work (whether exclusively or not)'.

[*PUWER 1998, Reg 2(1)*].

Duties of employers – Provision and Use of Work Equipment Regulations 1998 (SI 1998 No 2306) (PUWER)

M1014   Statutory duties of employers regarding machinery used, almost exclusively, to be concerned with fencing and guarding – witness *Secs 12-16* of the *Factories Act 1961*. Now, in the light of *PUWER 1998*, employers are required to select suitably safe new or second-hand equipment for use at work, maintain it properly and inform operators of foreseeable dangers, in the interests of the general safety of legitimate users of such machinery.

'Use' of machinery refers to any activity involving work equipment, including 'starting, stopping, programming, setting, transporting, repairing, modifying, maintaining, servicing and cleaning'. [*PUWER 1998, Reg 2(1)*].

The main aim of *PUWER 1998* is to protect workers against dangerous machinery and parts (that is, machinery and parts that could foreseeably cause operators injury when properly used). In this connection, there is an overriding strict duty (*a*) to prevent access to dangerous parts and (*b*) to stop movement of dangerous parts before a person (or any part of him/her) enters a danger zone. Guarding and the establishment of safe work systems should be the objective of all employers, whenever reasonably practicable. (Alternatively, if dangerous parts cannot be completely guarded, instructions and training courses coupled with safe work systems represent a fall-back position.) The regulations, applicable to all workplaces, including factories, offices, service industries, construction sites and offshore installations, and covering employees, self-employed personnel and members of the public using work equipment in public places, specify both general and specific requirements in relation to machinery, its installation and use.

General requirements

M1015   Every employer must ensure:

(*a*)   *Selection of equipment* – that he has regard to the working conditions and to the risks, existing on the premises, to the health and safety of persons and to any additional risk posed by use of that work equipment. [*Reg 4*].

(*b*)   *Suitability of work equipment* – that work equipment is

   (i)   constructed or adapted so as to be suitable for the purpose for which it is provided;

   (ii) used only for operations for which, and under conditions for which, it is suitable (i.e. will not affect the health or safety of any person).

[*Reg 4*].

(*c*)   *Maintenance* – that work equipment is maintained in an efficient state and working order, and in good repair, and, where there is a maintenance log for machinery, that the log is kept up to date. [*Reg 5*].

(*d*)   *Inspection* – that work equipment is inspected and that the result of an inspection is recorded and kept until the next inspection is recorded. Inspection should be carried out:

   (i)   where the safety of work equipment depends on the installation conditions – after installation and before being put into service for the first time, or after assembly at a new site/location;

   (ii) where work equipment exposed to conditions causing deterioration is liable to result in dangerous situations – at suitable intervals, and each time that exceptional circumstances which are liable to jeopardise the safety of the work equipment have occurred.

[*Reg 6*].

It must be clear who is responsible for the inspection of the equipment – it is not acceptable to disown the equipment.

(e)   *Specific risks* – that where any use of work equipment is likely to involve a specific risk to the health or safety of any person

(i)   use of that work equipment must be restricted to those persons given the task of using it, and

(ii)   repairs, modifications, maintenance or servicing be restricted to persons specifically designated to carry out such operations (whether or not also authorised to carry out other operations) who must have received adequate training.

[*Reg 7*].

(f)   *Information/instructions* – that all persons who use equipment or who supervise or manage the use of work equipment must have available to them adequate health and safety information and, where appropriate, written instructions readily comprehensible to the workers concerned, including instructions relating to:

(i)   the conditions in which, and the methods by which, the work equipment is to be used;

(ii)   foreseeable abnormal situations and the action to be taken in such circumstances;

(iii)   any conclusions to be drawn from experience in using the equipment.

[*Reg 8*].

(g)   *Training* – that all persons using work equipment or who supervise or manage same must have adequate training. [*Reg 9*].

(h)   *Conformity with EU requirements* – that work equipment has been designed and constructed in compliance with any statutory instruments, listed in *Sch 1*, which give effect to EU directives concerning product safety [*Reg 10*].

Specific requirements

M1016   The following requirements came into effect from 1 January 1993 in respect of new equipment and from 1 January 1997 as regards existing equipment.

1.   *Dangerous parts of machinery* – in order

(a)   to prevent access to dangerous parts of machinery or any rotating stock-bar, or

(b)   to stop movement of any dangerous parts of machinery or rotating stock-bar before any part of a person enters a danger zone (i.e. a zone where a person is exposed to risk from dangerous parts of machinery),

guards/protection devices must be provided, so far as practicable.

A hierarchy of such measures consists of:

(i)   fixed guards enclosing every dangerous part; if not practicable then –

(ii)   other guards or protection devices where fixed guards are not possible; if not practicable then –

(iii)   provision of jigs, holders, push-sticks or similar protection if practicable; if not practicable then –

(iv)   information, instruction, training and supervision must be provided.

Guards must:

(1)   be suitable for their purpose;

(2)   be of good construction, sound material and adequate strength;

(3)   be properly maintained;

(4)   not create additional risks to health or safety;

(5)   not be easily bypassed or rendered inoperative;

(6)   be situated at sufficient distance from a danger zone;

(7)   not restrict more than necessary any view of the operation of work equipment; and

(8)   allow for fitting, replacing of parts, and maintenance work, without having to remove the guard or protective device.

[*Reg 11*].

2.   *Protection against failure* – so far as is reasonably practicable (see E15017 ENFORCEMENT), that work equipment is protected or, if it is not reasonably practicable, adequately controlled without the use of PPE against risks to health or safety from:

—   ejected/falling objects;

—   rupture/disintegration;

—   overheating/catching fire;

—   unintended/premature discharge or ejection of any article, gas, dust, liquid or vapour;

—   unintended/premature explosion of work equipment or material produced, used or stored in it.

[*Reg 12*].

3.   *High/low temperature* – that parts of work equipment and material produced or used in it, which might burn, scald or sear, be protected to prevent persons being so injured. [*Reg 13*].

4.   *Controls for starting equipment* – that work equipment is provided with one or more controls to:

(*a*)   start equipment (as well as re-start); and

(*b*)   change speed, pressure or operating conditions,

and it must not be possible to perform any of the above operations except by deliberate action (other than in the case of an automatic device). [*Reg 14*].

5.   *Stop controls* – that work equipment is provided with readily accessible stop controls (including emergency stop controls [*Reg 16*]), which

(*a*)   must bring equipment to a complete stop safely, and

(*b*)   if necessary, disconnect all energy sources, and

(*c*)   must operate in priority to controls which start or change the work equipment's operating conditions.

[Reg 15].

6.   *Position of controls* – that controls of work equipment are clearly visible and identifiable, have appropriate marking where necessary and are not in a danger zone (except where necessary). In particular, no one should be in a danger zone *vis-à-vis* the position of any control affecting a danger zone hazard; but, if not reasonably practicable, no one should be in a danger zone when work equipment is about to start; but, if the latter is not reasonably practicable, audible/visible warning should be given when work equipment is about to start. [*Reg 17*].

7.   *Control systems* – must be safe so far as practicable and chosen – making due allowance for the failures, faults and constraints to be expected in the planned circumstances of use – so that

   (*a*)   their operation does not create increased risk to health or safety;

   (*b*)   no fault in them can result in increased risk to health or safety; and

   (*c*)   they do not hinder the operation of stop or emergency stop controls.

   [*Reg 18*].

8.   *Isolation from energy sources* – that equipment must be provided with appropriate means to isolate it from its sources of energy; such means must be clearly identifiable and accessible. Reconnection of energy sources to work equipment must not expose operatives to risk. [*Reg 19*].

9.   *Stability* – that work equipment is stabilised by clamping, etc. [*Reg 20*].

10.   *Lighting* – that any place where work equipment is used, be adequately lit. [*Reg 21*].

11.   *Maintenance operations* – that, so far as is reasonably practicable, maintenance operations which involve a risk to health or safety can be carried out while the equipment is shut down, or otherwise without exposing anyone carrying them out to such risk, or, alternatively, appropriate protective measures can be taken. [*Reg 22*].

12.   *Markings* – that equipment be appropriately marked (i.e. CE markings). [*Reg 23*].

13.   *Warnings* – that equipment incorporate clear and unambiguous warnings or warning devices. [*Reg 24*].

(These requirements are applicable also to offshore operations.)

Mobile work equipment

M1017   Every employer must ensure:

   (*a*)   *Employees carried on mobile work equipment* – that no employee is carried by mobile work equipment unless:

      (i)   it is suitable for carrying persons; and

      (ii)   it incorporates features – for reducing risks to their safety – to as low as is reasonably practicable.

[*Reg 25*].

(*b*)   *Rolling over of mobile work equipment* – that where there is a risk to an employee riding on mobile work equipment from its rolling over, it is minimised by:

    (i)   stabilising the work equipment;

    (ii)   a structure which ensures that the work equipment does no more than fall on its side;

    (iii) a structure giving sufficient clearance to anyone being carried if it overturns further than that; or

    (iv) a device giving comparable protection.

This regulation does not apply to a fork-lift truck having a structure as described in (*b*)(ii) and (*b*)(iii) above.

The employer must ensure that the mobile work equipment has a suitable restraining system where there is a risk of anyone on it being crushed if it rolls over.

Compliance with this regulation is not required where:

—   it would increase the overall risk to safety;

—   it would not be reasonably practicable to operate the mobile work equipment in consequence; or

—   in relation to an item of work equipment provided for use in the undertaking or establishment before 5 December 1998 it would not be reasonably practicable.

[*Reg 26*].

(*c*)   *Overturning of fork-lift trucks* – that a fork-lift truck having a structure as described in (*b*)(ii) and (*b*)(iii) above and which carries an employee is adapted or equipped to reduce the risk to safety from its overturning to as low as is reasonably practicable. [*Reg 27*].

(*d*)   *Self-propelled work equipment* – that where it may, while in motion, involve risk to the safety of persons:

    (i)   it has facilities for preventing its being started by an unauthorised person;

    (ii)   it has appropriate facilities for minimising the consequences of a collision where there is more than one item of rail-mounted work equipment in motion at the same time;

    (iii) it has a device for braking and stopping;

    (iv) where safety constraints so require, emergency facilities operated by readily accessible controls or automatic systems are available for braking and stopping the work equipment in the event of failure of the main facility;

    (v)   where the driver's direct field of vision is inadequate to ensure safety, there are adequate devices for improving his vision so far as is reasonably practicable;

    (vi) if provided for use at night or in dark places – it is equipped with lighting appropriate to the work to be carried out, and is otherwise sufficiently safe for such use;

(vii) if it, or anything carried or towed by it, constitutes a fire hazard, appropriate fire-fighting equipment should be carried or kept close to it.

[*Reg 28*].

(*e*)   *Remote-controlled self-propelled work equipment* – that where it involves a risk to safety while in motion, it stops automatically once it leaves its control range; and, where the risk is of crushing or impact, it has features to guard against such risk unless other appropriate devices are able to do so.

[*Reg 29*].

(*f*)   *Drive shafts* – that where the seizure of the drive shaft between mobile work equipment and its accessories or anything towed is likely to involve a risk:

(i)   the work equipment has a means of preventing such seizure; or

(ii)   where such seizure cannot be avoided, take every possible measure to avoid an adverse effect on the safety of an employee.

The employer must also ensure that the work equipment has a system for safeguarding the shaft, where:

(i)   the mobile work equipment has a shaft for the transmission of energy between it and other mobile work equipment; and

(ii)   the shaft could become soiled or damaged by contact with the ground while uncoupled.

[*Reg 30*].

Power presses

M1018   'Power press means a press or press brake for the working of metal by means of tools, or for die proving, which is power driven and which embodies a flywheel and clutch'. [*PUWER 1998, Reg 2(1)*].

(*a*)   *Power presses to which regulations 32–35 do not apply:*

(i)   a power press for the working of hot metal;

(ii)   a power press not capable of a stroke greater than 6 mm;

(iii)   a guillotine;

(iv)   a combination punching and shearing machine, turret punch press or similar machine for punching, shearing or cropping;

(v)   a machine, other than press brake, for bending steel sections;

(vi)   a power press for the compacting of metal powders;

(vii)   machines for straightening, upsetting, heading, riveting, eyeletting, press-stud attaching, zip fastener bottom stop attaching, stapling or wire stitching.

[*Reg 31*].

(*b*)   *Thorough examination of power presses, guards and protection devices* – every employer shall ensure that:

(i)   a power press is not put into service for the first time after installation, or after assembly at a new site or in a new location, unless it has been thoroughly examined to ensure that:

—   it has been installed correctly;

—   it is safe to operate; and

—   any defect has been remedied;

(ii)   a guard, other than one to which paragraph (iii) relates – or protection device – is not put into service for the first time on a power press unless it has been thoroughly examined when in position on that power press to ensure that it is effective for its purpose, and any defect has been remedied;

(iii)   part of a closed tool which acts as a fixed guard is not used on a power press unless it has been thoroughly examined when in position on any power press in the premises to ensure that it is effective for its purpose, and any defect has been remedied;

(iv)   for the purposes of ensuring that health and safety conditions are maintained, and that any deterioration can be detected and remedied in good time: every power press must be thoroughly examined – if it only has fixed guards at least every twelve months; otherwise at least every six months – and whenever exceptional circumstances have occurred which are liable to jeopardise the safety of the power press or its guards or protection devices. Any defects must be remedied before reusing the power press.

[*Reg 32*].

(c)   *Inspection of guards and protection devices*

(i)   every employer must ensure that a power press is not used after the setting, re-setting or adjustment of its tools, except in trying out its tools or die proving, unless its every guard and protection device has been inspected and tested while in position on the power press by a person appointed in writing by the employer who is:

—   competent; or

—   undergoing training for that purpose and acting under the immediate supervision of a competent person,

and who has signed a certificate which complies with paragraph (iii) below; or

—   the guards and protection devices have not been altered or disturbed in the course of the adjustment of its tools;

(ii)   every employer must ensure that a power press is not used after the expiration of the fourth hour of a working period unless its every guard and protection device has been inspected and tested while in position on the power press by a person appointed in writing by the employer who is:

—   competent; or

—   undergoing training for that purpose and acting under the immediate supervision of a competent person,

and who has signed a certificate which complies with paragraph (iii) below;

(iii)   a certificate referred to in (i) and (ii) above:

—   must contain sufficient particulars to identify every guard and protection device inspected and tested and the power press on which it was positioned at the time of the inspection and test;

— must state the date and time of the inspection and test;

— must state that every guard and protection device on the power press is in position and effective for its purpose.

[*Reg 33*].

(*d*)   *Reports*

(i)   a person making a thorough examination for an employer under *reg 32* must:

— immediately notify the employer of any defect in a power press (or its guard or protection device) which in his opinion is or could become a danger to persons;

— write a report of the thorough examination to the employer;

— where there is in his opinion a defect in a power press (or its guard or protection device) which is or could become a danger to persons, send a copy of the report to the enforcing authority for the premises in which the power press is situated;

[*Reg 34(1)*]

(ii)   a person making an inspection and test for an employer under *reg 33* must immediately notify the employer of any defect in a guard or protection device which in his opinion is or could become a danger to persons and the reason for his opinion.

[*Reg 34(2)*].

(*e*)   *Keeping of information* – every employer must ensure that reports that comply with *reg 34(1)* are kept available for inspection for two years, and that certificates belonging to supervising persons under *reg 33* are kept available for inspection – at or near the power press to which they relate until superseded by a later certificate – and, after that, until six months have elapsed since it was signed. [*Reg 35*].

Duties on designers and manufacturers – Supply of Machinery (Safety) Regulations 1992 (SI 1992 No 3073), as amended

M1019   General and specific duties relating to machinery safety are laid on designers and manufacturers of machinery for use at work by the *Supply of Machinery (Safety) Regulations 1992*, as amended by the *Supply of Machinery (Safety) (Amendment) Regulations 1994 (SI 1994 No 2063)*.

Supply of safe machinery (including safety components, roll-over protective structures and industrial trucks) is governed by these regulations. The *Supply of Machinery (Safety) (Amendment) Regulations 1994* extends to machinery for lifting people [*Reg 4, Sch 2 para 10*] (e.g. elevating work platforms). The combined effect of the two sets of regulations requires that, when machinery or components are properly installed, maintained and used for their intended purposes, there is no risk (except a minimal one) of their being a cause or occasion of death or injury to persons, or damage to property [*Reg 2(2), as amended by SI 1994 No 2063, Reg 4, Sch 2 para 5*].

Relevant machinery

M1020 The *Supply of Machinery (Safety) Regulations 1992* do not apply to:

(*a*) specific machinery or safety components supplied before 1 January 1995 [*Reg 7A, as inserted by SI 1994 No 2063, Reg 4, Sch 2 para 7*];

(*b*) machinery complying with health and safety requirements as at 31 December 1992, which has been put into service before 31 December 1994;

(*c*) machinery covered by other directives (see P9001 PRODUCT SAFETY); and

(*d*) electrical equipment.

The regulations cover:

(i) safety components [*SI 1992 No 3073, Reg 3 as amended by SI 1994 No 2063, Reg 4, Sch 2 para 5*];

(ii) machinery/components for lifting or moving persons [*SI 1992 No 3073, Reg 5, Sch 5 as amended by SI 1994 No 2063, Reg 4, Sch 2 para 10*];

(iii) roll-over protective structures; and

(iv) industrial trucks.

Excluded machinery

M1021 Certain machinery is outside the ambit of these regulations namely:

(*a*) machinery whose only power source is directly applied manual effort unless it is a machine used for lifting or lowering loads;

(*b*) machinery for medical use used in direct contact with patients;

(*c*) special equipment for use in fairgrounds and/or amusement parks;

(*d*) steam boilers, tanks and pressure vessels;

(*e*) machinery specially designed or put into service for nuclear purposes which, in the event of failure, may result in an emission of radioactivity;

(*f*) radioactive sources forming part of a machine;

(*g*) firearms;

(*h*) storage tanks and pipelines for petrol, diesel fuel, flammable liquids and dangerous substances;

(*j*) means of transport, that is vehicles and their trailers intended solely for transporting passengers by air or on road, rail or water networks, as well as means of transport in so far as such means are designed for transporting goods by air, on public road or rail networks or on water. Vehicles used in the mineral extraction industry shall not be excluded;

(*k*) seagoing vessels and mobile offshore units together with equipment on board such vessels or units;

(*l*) cableways, including funicular railways, for the public or private transportation of persons;

(*m*) agricultural and forestry tractors;

(*n*) machines specifically designed and constructed for military or police purposes;

(*o*)   lifts which permanently serve specific levels of buildings and constructions, having a car moving between guides which are rigid and inclined at an angle of more than 15 degrees to the horizontal and designed for the transport of:

—   persons,

—   persons and goods,

—   goods alone if the car is accessible, that is to say, a person may enter it without difficulty, and fitted with controls situated inside the car or within reach of a person inside;

(*p*)   means of transport of persons using rack and pinion rail mounted vehicles;

(*q*)   mine winding gear;

(*r*)   theatre elevators; and

(*s*)   construction site hoists for lifting persons or persons and goods.

[*Supply of Machinery (Safety) Regulations 1992 (SI 1992 No 3073), Sch 5 as amended by the Supply of Machinery (Safety) (Amendment) Regulations 1994 (SI 1994 No 2063), Reg 4, Sch 2 para 23*].

General machinery and machinery posing special hazards

M1022   The regulations draw a distinction between general machinery and machinery posing special hazards, in that the latter's – machinery posing special hazards – technical file, which must be prepared in either case for relevant machinery, must be sent to

(i)   an approved body for retention/verification – in the case of machinery manufactured according to transposed harmonised standards [*Reg 14*], and

(ii)   an approved body, coupled with an example of machinery for EU-type-examination – in the case of machinery not manufactured according to transposed harmonised standards.

[*Regs 13, 15*].

Machinery posing special hazards – Schedule 4 machinery

M1023   Such machinery includes:

(A) Machinery:

(1)   circular saws (single or multi-blade) for working with wood and analogous materials or for working with meat and analogous materials;

(2)   sawing machines with fixed tool during operation, having a fixed bed with manual feed of the workpiece or with a demountable power feed;

(3)   sawing machines with fixed tool during operation, having a manually operated reciprocating saw-bench or carriage;

(4)   sawing machines with fixed tool during operation, having a built-in mechanical feed device for the workpieces, with manual loading and/or unloading;

(5)   sawing machines with movable tool during operation, with a mechanical feed device and manual loading and/or unloading;

(6)   hand-fed surface planing machines for woodworking;

(7)   thicknessers for one-side dressing with manual loading and/or unloading for woodworking;

(8)   band-saws with a fixed or mobile bed and band-saws with a mobile carriage, with manual loading and/or unloading, for working with wood and analogous materials or for working with meat and analogous materials;

(9)   combined machines of the types referred to in (1) to (8) and (11) for working with wood and analogous materials;

(10)   hand-fed tenoning machines with several tool holders for woodworking;

(11)   hand-fed vertical spindle moulding machines for working with wood and analogous materials;

(12)   portable chain saws for woodworking;

(13)   presses, including press-brakes, for the cold working of metals, with manual loading and/or unloading, whose movable working parts may have a travel exceeding 6 mm and a speed exceeding 30 mm/s;

(14)   injection or compression plastics-moulding machines with manual loading or unloading;

(15)   injection or compression rubber-moulding machines with manual loading or unloading;

(16)   machinery for underground working of the following types:

    —   machinery on rails, locomotives and brake-vans,

    —   hydraulic-powered roof supports,

    —   internal combustion engines to be fitted to machinery for under-ground working;

(17)   manually-loaded trucks for the collection of household refuse incorporating a compression mechanism;

(18)   guards and detachable transmission shafts with universal joints;

(19)   vehicles servicing lifts;

[*Supply of Machinery (Safety) Regulations 1992 (SI 1992 No 3073), Sch 4 as amended by the Supply of Machinery (Safety) (Amendment) Regulations 1994 (SI 1994 No 2063), Reg 3, Sch 1 para 4*]

and

(20)   devices for the lifting of persons involving a risk of falling from a vertical height of more than three metres;

(21)   machines for the manufacture of pyrotechnics.

[*Supply of Machinery (Safety) Regulations 1992 (SI 1992 No 3073), Sch 4 as amended by the Supply of Machinery (Safety) (Amendment) Regulations 1994 (SI 1994 No 2063), Reg 4, Sch 2 para 22*].

(B) Safety components:

(1)   electro-sensitive devices designed specifically to detect persons in order to ensure their safety (non-material barriers, sensor mats, electromagnetic detectors, etc.);

(2)   logic units which ensure the safety functions of bi-manual controls;

(3)   automatic movable screens to protect presses;

(4)   roll-over protective structures (ROPS); and

(5)   falling object protective structures (FOPS).

[*Supply of Machinery (Safety) Regulations 1992 (SI 1992 No 3073), Sch 4 as amended by the Supply of Machinery (Safety) (Amendment) Regulations 1994 (SI 1994 No 2063), Reg 4, Sch 2 para 22*].

Technical file

Machinery posing special hazards

M1024   In respect of relevant machinery which is Schedule 4 machinery manufactured in accordance with transposed harmonised standards, the responsible person must select one of the following paths:

—   draw up a technical file and forward it to an approved body for retention by that body;

—   submit the technical file to an approved body requesting (i) verification by that body that the transposed harmonised standards have been correctly applied, and (ii) that the body draw up a certificate of adequacy for the file; or

—   submit the technical file to an approved body together with an example of the relevant machinery for EC type-examination or, where appropriate, a statement as to where such an example might be EC type-examined.

In the case of relevant machinery which is Schedule 4 machinery and which is not or only partly manufactured in accordance with transposed harmonised standards, or in respect of which there are no transposed harmonised standards, the responsible person must submit a technical file to an approved body together with an example of the machinery for EC type-examination or, where appropriate, a statement as to where such an example might be EC type-examined.

The technical file must include:

(*a*)   an overall drawing of the machinery together with drawings of the control circuits;

(*b*)   full, detailed drawings, accompanied by any calculation notes, test results and such other data as may be required to check the conformity of the machinery with the essential health and safety requirements;

(*c*)   a description of methods adopted to eliminate hazards presented by the machinery, a list of transposed harmonised standards used or, alternatively, a list of standards used;

(*d*)   a copy of the instructions for the machinery drawn up; and

(*e*)   for series manufacture, the internal measures that will be implemented to ensure that all the items of machinery so produced are in conformity with the provisions of the Machinery Directive.

The technical file must be drawn up in an official language of the member state in which the approved body is established or in such other language as is acceptable to the approved body, always provided that the instructions for the machinery are in one of the EU languages. On being put into service, the machinery must be accompanied not only by the instructions in the original language, but also by a translation of the instructions in the language(s) of the country in which the machinery is used.

General machinery

M1025 In the case of relevant machinery which is not Schedule 4 machinery, the responsible person must draw up a technical file which consists of:

(*a*) an overall drawing of the machinery together with drawings of the control circuits;

(*b*) full, detailed drawings, accompanied by any calculation notes, test results and such other data as may be required to check the conformity of the machinery with the essential health and safety requirements;

(*c*) a list of the essential health and safety requirements, transposed harmonised standards, relevant standards and other technical specifications which were used when the machinery was designed;

(*d*) a description of the methods adopted to eliminate the hazards presented by the machinery;

(*e*) if he so desires, any technical report or certificate obtained from a competent body or laboratory;

(*f*) if he declares conformity with a transposed harmonised standard which provides therefor, any technical report giving the results of tests carried out at his choice either by himself or by a competent body or laboratory; and

(*g*) a copy of the instructions for the machinery.

For series manufacture, the responsible person must also have available documentation in respect of the internal measures that will be implemented to ensure that all the items of machinery so produced are in conformity with the provisions of the Machinery Directive.

Where the technical file is drawn up in the United Kingdom, it must be in English – always provided that the instructions for the machinery referred to above at (*g*) are in one of the EU languages. On being put into service, the machinery must be accompanied not only by the instructions in the original language, but also by a translation of the instructions in the language(s) of the country in which the machinery is used.

Essential health and safety requirements for general machinery and machinery posing special hazards

M1026 Essential health and safety features relate to:

(1) general design features;

(2) controls;

(3) mechanical hazards;

(4) non-mechanical hazards;

(5) maintenance;

(6) indicators.

The key objective of the regulations is to integrate safety into workplace machinery throughout the process which begins with the design and development stage of the machinery and ends with its distribution.

(1) General design features

M1027 To that end the following general design features should be incorporated:

(*a*) machinery must be constructed so as to be fit for function, and adjustable/ maintainable without endangering operators;

(*b*) in order to do this, manufacturers should

(i) eliminate and/or reduce inherent risks as far as possible,

(ii) take necessary protection measures in relation to risks that cannot be eliminated,

(iii) inform users of residual risks owing to shortcomings in protection measures,

(iv) specify training needs,

(v) specify personal protection needs;

(*c*) design of machinery should envisage not just normal use but also reasonably foreseeable use, and machinery should be designed to prevent reasonably foreseeable abnormal use;

(*d*) discomfort, fatigue and psychological stress faced by an operator must be reduced to a minimum;

(*e*) constraints upon operators must be accommodated, including requisite and foreseeable use of personal protective equipment;

(*f*) supply of machinery must be accompanied by special equipment and accessories for use, adjustment and maintenance purposes;

(*g*) machinery should not endanger the operator when being filled or used with or drained of fluids;

(*h*) integral lighting should be supplied where there is a risk from lack of it, in spite of normal ambient lighting;

(*j*) machinery must be capable of being handled and stored safely.

[*Sch 3*].

(2) Controls – starting and stopping

M1028 Control systems must be safe and reliable, in a way that they can withstand the rigours of normal use and external factors and that errors in logic do not lead to dangerous situations. Control devices must be:

(*a*) clearly visible and appropriately marked;

(*b*) positioned for safe operation;

(*c*) located outside a danger zone, except for emergency stops or consoles;

(*d*) positioned so that their operation cannot cause additional risk;

(*e*) designed so that risk cannot occur without intentional operation;

(*f*) made to withstand foreseeable strain, especially as regards emergency stop devices;

(*g*) in the case of a multi-action control, the action to be performed, must be clearly displayed;

(*h*) fitted with indicators which the operator can read;

(*j*)   prevented from exposing persons in danger zones – and the operator must be able to ensure this from the main control position; failing this, an acoustic and/or visual warning signal must be given whenever machinery is about to start.

Starting and stopping

(*a*) Starting

M1029   It must be possible to

(i)   start machinery, only by deliberate intended action;

(ii)   re-start machinery after stoppage;

(iii)   effect change in speed pressure only by voluntary action of control (though not from the normal sequence of the automatic cycle).

(*b*) Stopping

M1030   Stopping devices must accommodate both normal and emergency stopping.

(i)   *Normal stop.* Machinery must be fitted with a control to bring it safely to a complete stop and each workstation, too, to stop some or all of the moving parts, so that it is made safe. Stop controls must have priority over start controls, and, once machinery is stopped, energy supply must be cut off.

(ii)   *Emergency stop.* Emergency stops/devices must be easily identifiable, clearly visible and quickly accessible, and able to stop a dangerous process as quickly as possible. The emergency stop must remain engaged, and disengagement must not reactivate machinery. Further, stop controls must not trigger the stopping function before being in the engaged position. Once active operation of the emergency stop control has ceased following stop command, that command must be sustained by engagement of the emergency stop device until that engagement is specifically overridden. It must not be possible to engage the device without triggering a stop command. Disengaging the stop device must not reactivate machinery but only permit restarting.

(iii)   *Mode selection.* Control mode selected must override all other control systems, except the emergency stop. If, for certain operations, machinery has to operate with protection devices neutralised, the mode selector must simultaneously

(*a*)   disable automatic control mode;

(*b*)   permit movements only by controls requiring sustained action;

(*c*)   permit operation of dangerous moving parts only in enhanced safety conditions (e.g. reduced speed);

(*d*)   prevent any movement liable to pose a danger by acting voluntarily or involuntarily on a machine's internal sensors.

(iv)   *Failure of power supply/failure of control circuit.* Neither failure of power supply or of control circuit must lead to:

(*a*)   machinery starting unexpectedly;

(*b*)   machinery being prevented from stopping if the command has been given;

(*c*)   any moving part/piece falling out or being ejected;

(*d*)   impeding of automatic or manual stopping of moving parts;

(*e*)   protection devices becoming ineffective.

[*Sch 3*].

(3) Protection against mechanical hazards

M1031   Machinery must:

(*a*)   be stable enough for use without risk of overturning, falling or unexpected movement. If necessary, anchorage must be incorporated (and indicated);

(*b*)   be able to withstand workplace stresses and not be likely to break up, including fatigue, ageing, corrosion and abrasion. In particular, manufacturers must indicate the type and frequency of inspection and maintenance and specify the parts likely to need replacement. Where a workpiece comes into contact with a tool, the tool must be operating normally; when the tool starts or stops, intentionally or accidentally, feed and tool movement must be co-ordinated;

(*c*)   prevent objects, such as tools/workpieces, being ejected;

(*d*)   not have sharp edges/angles/rough surfaces;

(*e*)   where intended to carry out various operations, be able to be used separately, and it must be possible to start and stop separately;

(*f*)   where designed to perform under different conditions or speeds, selection and adjustment must be able to be completed safely;

(*g*)   prevent hazards arising from moving parts of machinery, or if hazards are not avoidable, moving parts must be fixed with guards. In particular, manufacturers should indicate how, if necessary, equipment can be safely unblocked.

[*Sch 3*].

Guards

M1032   In order to ensure maximum safety with machinery, guards (or safety devices) should be used (see M1006, M1007 above for varieties) to protect the operator against the risk from

(*a*)   moving transmission parts; and/or

(*b*)   moving parts directly involved in the work process.

In principle, machinery with moving transmission parts (e.g. belts/pulleys) can have fixed or movable guards – the latter being preferable where frequent access is foreseeable; but, whichever is used, it should always:

(i)   be of robust construction;

(ii)   not give rise to any additional risk;

(iii)   not be easily by-passable or rendered non-operational;

(iv)   be located at an adequate distance from a danger zone;

(v)   cause minimum obstruction to the view of those involved in the production process; and

(vi) enable installation, replacement or maintenance work to be carried out, if possible, without the guard having to be dismantled.

However, where moving parts cannot be made wholly or even partially inaccessible during operation, requiring operator intervention, either (*a*) fixed or (*b*) adjustable guards (i.e. incorporating an adjustable element which, once adjusted, remains *in situ* during operation) should be used.

Fixed guards – special requirements

M1033   Fixed guards should be:

(*a*)   securely held in place;

(*b*)   fixed by systems that can be opened with tools; and

(*c*)   where possible, unable to remain in place without their fixings.

Movable guards – special requirements

M1034

(*a*) *Movable guards offering protection against moving transmission parts*

These should

(i)   remain fixed to machinery when open, as far as possible;

(ii)   be interlocking

—   to prevent activation of moving parts, and

—   give stop command when they are no longer closed.

(*b*) *Movable guards offering protection against moving parts directly involved in work process*

These should ensure that:

(i)   moving parts cannot start up while within the operator's reach;

(ii)   the exposed person cannot reach the moving parts once activated;

(iii) they can be adjusted only by means of an intentional action, such as the use of a tool or key;

(iv)   the absence or failure of one of the component parts prevents starting, or stops moving parts;

(v)   the protection against any risk of ejection is proved by means of an appropriate barrier.

Adjustable guards (resisting access to parts involved)

M1035   These should:

(*a*)   be adjustable manually or automatically;

(*b*)   be readily adjustable without use of tools;

(*c*)   reduce as far as possible the likelihood of ejection.

Interlocking systems may be mechanical, electrical (e.g. control interlocking, power interlocking), hydraulic, pneumatic (or any permutation) and should be 'fail-safe'.

Guards can also be automatic, in which case, they are activated by the mechanism of the machinery (see further M1006 above). These are frequently used on power presses.

[*Sch 3*].

(4) Protection against non-mechanical hazards

M1036   Additionally, machinery must protect against:

(*a*)   electrical hazards – voltage limits must be observed;

(*b*)   a build-up of electrostatic charges and/or be fitted with a discharging system;

(*c*)   all potential hazards from energy supplies other than electricity (e.g. hydraulic, pneumatic or thermal energy);

(*d*)   fitting errors – in particular, incorrect fluid connections, electrical conductors, via information on pipes, cables etc.;

(*e*)   hazards of extreme temperatures, either high or low;

(*f*)   fire, either through overheating of machinery or caused by gases, liquids, dusts, vapours;

(*g*)   explosion;

(*h*)   noise – airborne noise must be reduced to the lowest practicable level;

(*j*)   vibration – must be reduced to the lowest practicable level;

(*k*)   radiation – the effects on exposed persons must be eliminated or reduced to safe levels, and external radiation must not interfere with its operation;

(*l*)   accidental radiation, in the case of laser equipment; as for optical equipment, this must not create health risks from laser rays; and laser equipment on machinery must not create health risks through reflection or diffusion;

(*m*)   emissions of dust, gases, liquids and vapours. If such hazard exists, machinery must be able to contain or evacuate it; and if not enclosed during normal operation, containment/evacuation devices must be as close as possible to emission source;

(*n*)   the risk of being trapped – a person should be able to summon help;

(*o*)   the risk of slipping or tripping or falling.

[*Sch 3*].

(5) Maintenance

M1037   (*a*)   Adjustment, maintenance, repair, cleaning and servicing must be able to be carried out while machinery is at a standstill; but if for technical reasons these operations cannot be undertaken while the machinery is at a standstill, at least it must be possible to carry them out without risk. In case of automated machinery and, where necessary, other machinery, the manufacturer must make provision for a connecting device for mounting diagnostic fault-finding equipment. Automated machine components, which have to be changed frequently, must be easily and safely removable and replaceable.

(*b*)   Safe means of access to areas of production, adjustment and maintenance should be provided and designed to prevent falls.

(*c*)   The machinery must be fitted with means of isolating it from all energy sources, clearly identifiable and capable of being locked where an operator cannot check whether energy is still cut off.

(*d*)   If operator intervention cannot be avoided, it must be possible to carry out maintenance easily and in safety.

(*e*)   Cleaning of internal parts with dangerous substances or preparations must be possible without entry; and unblocking should take place from outside. If cleaning by entry is necessary, this should be able to be done with a minimum of danger.

[*Sch 3*].

(6) Indicators

M1038   Machinery must be fitted with indicators and the necessary unambiguous and intelligible information to control it easily. Indicators can consist of:

(*a*)   *Information devices.* Information given must not be excessive to the extent of overloading the operator. Where the health and safety of exposed persons may be endangered by a fault in the operation of unsupervised machinery, the machinery must be equipped to give an appropriate acoustic or light signal as a warning.

(*b*)   *Warning devices.* The operator must have facilities which enable him to check the operation of warning devices at all times. Any warning of residual risks should preferably be given in readily understandable pictograms and/or be given in one of the languages of the country in which the machinery is to be used.

(*c*)   *Markings.* All machinery (including interchangeable equipment and safety components) must be marked legibly and indelibly as follows:

    (i)   name/address of manufacturer;

    (ii)   CE mark, including year of construction;

    (iii)   designation of series or type;

    (iv)   use in an explosive atmosphere;

    (v)   safe use specifications (e.g. maximum speed of rotating parts);

    (vi)   its mass, if machinery is to be handled.

(*d*)   *Instructions.* Machinery must be accompanied by the following instructions:

    (i)   marking information;

    (ii)   maintenance information (e.g. address of importer);

    (iii)   foreseeable use;

    (iv)   likely workstation of operator;

    (v)   instructions for

        —   safe putting into service,

        —   safe use,

        —   safe handling,

        —   safe assembly and dismantling,

- safe maintenance, servicing, repair,

- safe adjustment,

- training instructions, if necessary,

- properties of tools to be fitted,

- incorrect use of machinery.

Instructions

M1039   (a)   The instructions for the machinery must be in one of the EU languages. On being put into service, the machinery must be accompanied by a translation of the instructions in the language or languages of the country in which the machinery is used and by the instructions in the original language.

(b)   They must contain drawings and diagrams for putting into service, maintenance, inspection and repair as well as for safety purposes.

(c)   Installation and assembly requirements for reducing noise and vibration.

(d)   (With reference to airborne noise emissions):

- equivalent continuous A-weighted sound pressure (see N3005 NOISE AND VIBRATION) at workstations where this exceeds 70 dB(A); if not in excess of 70 dB(A), this must be shown;

- peak C-weighted instantaneous sound pressure value at workstations, where this exceeds 63Pa (130 dB in relation to 20 μ Pa);

- sound power level emitted by machinery where equivalent continuous A-weighted sound pressure level at workstations exceeds 85 dB(A).

(e)   If necessary, precautions relating to use in explosive atmospheres.

(f)   In case of machinery which may also be intended for use by non-professional operators, the wording and layout of the instructions for use must take into account the general level of education and ability that can reasonably be expected from such operators.

[*Sch 3*].

Health and safety requirements applicable to machinery for lifting/moving persons

M1040   The devices must be located so that:

(a)   the floor of the lifting/moving device must be designed and constructed so as to offer space and strength according to the maximum number of persons and the maximum working load specified by the manufacturer;

(b)   persons inside the device must be able to control movements upwards and downwards or move it horizontally;

(c)   excess speeds must not cause hazards;

(d)   if necessary, devices must be fitted with a sufficient number of anchorage points for persons possibly using it, which are strong enough for attachment of personal protective equipment against the danger of falling;

(e)   trapdoors in floors/ceilings/side doors must open in a direction that prevents the risk of falling, if they open unexpectedly;

(*f*)   when the device is moving, floors must not tilt to an extent that occupants are in danger of falling, and must be slip-resistant;

(*g*)   the device must be designed/constructed so as to prevent its falling or overturning;

(*h*)   acceleration/braking of the device must not endanger persons; and

(*j*)   essential safety information must be provided to occupants.

[*Supply of Machinery (Safety) (Amendment) Regulations 1994 (SI 1994 No 2063), Reg 4, Sch 2 para 21*].

Enforcement

M1041   Enforcement is by HSE, since these regulations qualify as 'relevant statutory provisions' (see ENFORCEMENT). [*Sch 6*].

(*a*) Offences/Defences

Breach of these regulations, as well as failing to comply with the necessary marking requirements, is an offence under the *Health and Safety at Work etc. Act 1974*. [*Reg 29, Sch 6*].

(*b*) Defences

It is a defence that a person charged took all reasonable steps *and* exercised all due diligence to avoid committing the offence. [*Reg 31(1)*]. Where the substance of the defence is that commission of the offence was due either to

(*a*)   act or default of another, or

(*b*)   reliance on information given by another,

the accused cannot rely on this defence, unless

(i)   he served notice of this on the prosecutor at least seven days before the hearing,

(ii)   the notice sufficiently identifies the other person,

(iii)   it was reasonable for him to have relied on the information.

[*Reg 31(2), (3), (4)*].

In such circumstances the 'other person' may be proceeded against, though this is no bar to prosecution against the original accused [*Reg 31(1)*] (see further E15034 ENFORCEMENT). Similarly, offences may be committed by bodies corporate, companies and directors under these regulations (see E15032 ENFORCEMENT).

(*c*) Penalties

Breach of an offence under *Regulation 11* – duty to supply safe machinery – carries a maximum penalty

(*a*)   on summary conviction, of a fine of £5,000; or

(*b*)   on conviction on indictment, an indefinite fine, except for

(i)   breach of an improvement/prohibition notice, or

(ii)   failure to disclose information to the HSC or an enforcement officer

which can invoke imprisonment for up to two years, or a fine (or both).
[*Sch 6 para 3*].

Civil liability

M1042   Breach of these regulations causing injury/damage will give rise to civil liability, even though the regulations, as here, are silent on the point, since they do not state otherwise [*HSWA s 47(2)*].

Checklist for machinery safeguards

M1043   The following is a list of safeguards for machine accident prevention:

(*a*)   Does the safeguard totally prevent dangerous access (or otherwise eliminate danger) when in its correct position and when working properly?

(*b*)   Is the guard reasonably convenient to use (i.e. does it interfere with either the speed or quality of the work); are there foreseeable reasons why it should be defeated?

(*c*)   How easy is it to defeat or misuse the safeguard? (The 'cost' of defeating a safeguard should always outweigh the benefits. It is wise never to underestimate the ingenuity of the man who spends all day, every day, working with what he believes is a perverse and unnecessary safety device.)

(*d*)   Are the components of the safeguard:

(i)   reliable;

(ii)   fail-safe?

(*e*)   Does the safeguard cope with foreseeable machine failures?

(*f*)   Is the safeguard straightforward to inspect and maintain?

(*g*)   Are all controls to the machine safely located, correctly designed and clearly identified?

(*h*)   Is there an efficient emergency stopping device? Is it clearly identified? (NB: There is a sign specified for this purpose in the *Health and Safety (Safety Signs and Signals) Regulations 1996.*)

(*j*)   Does all electrical equipment comply with EN 60204–1? Is there an effective system for checking and maintaining such equipment?

(*k*)   Are coolant systems effective and easy to maintain?

(*l*)   Is access for lubrication readily and safely available? Are all lubrication points clearly identified?

(*m*)   Is the machine safely located so that other workers are not exposed to danger? Does the current layout of the machining area permit easy movement between machines, workbenches and other items?

(*n*)   What is the sound pressure level emitted by the machine? Is it in excess of 90 dBA? If so, what modifications must be made to control noise at source, or should the machine be installed in a soundproof enclosure? If hearing protection is provided for operators and other workers in the immediate vicinity, are they appropriate to the noise risks and are they being worn all the time during machine operation?

(*o*)   What is the procedure to ensure effective preventive maintenance? Is the procedure documented, including allocation of responsibilities? What are the mechanical and other hazards which may arise during routine maintenance of the machine?

(*p*)   What chemical substances are used in the machine process? Have they been checked for toxicity, flammability and other dangerous properties? Have operators been trained to recognise these hazards and to take suitable precautions?

(*q*)   Does the machine emit:

  (i)   dust;

  (ii)   fumes;

  (iii) gases; or

  (iv)   other airborne contaminants?

What is the system for removing these contaminants at the point of emission? How frequently is the efficiency of the system checked to ensure it is operating effectively?

(*r*)   Is the general lighting in the machine area adequate? Is lighting at specific danger points adequate?

(*s*)   Does the machine emit heat? Are there hot surfaces which could cause burns on contact?

(*t*)   Is the level of ventilation in the machine area satisfactory?

Manual Handling

Introduction

M3001　More than one-third (36.5%) of accidents reported to the Health and Safety Executive (HSE) and local authority environmental health departments result from manual handling. It is the single most common cause of workplace injury and research suggests that over 600,000 people in Britain consider that they have a health problem caused by manual handling at work.

Many of these accidents relate to back injuries, but injuries to the feet, hands, arms and legs, including fractures and lacerations, also occur. The three main risks are accidental injury, over-exertion and cumulative damage. Many manual handling injuries build up over a long period of time rather than being caused by a single incident.

Such injuries are not restricted to areas seen as traditionally heavy industries, but occur across the range of industry and service sectors, in offices, shops and warehouses, hospitals, banks, laboratories, factories, farms and building sites, and while making deliveries.

On average, each injury results in 20 days being taken off work, and in some cases, workers are unable to return to work as a result of becoming permanently disabled. For example, many nurses are invalided out of the health service as a result of back injuries caused by manual handling. And back injuries represent the biggest single group of claims for incapacity benefit.

It is estimated that back injuries, many caused by manual handling, cost British employers in the region of £6 billion every year in lost production. In addition, there have been a number of large compensation awards for damages paid out to workers who have been injured through manual handling as a result of their employer's negligence.

For example, in 1998, nursery nurse Jenny Bentley received £78,000 in compensation from Stockport City Council after a lifting injury damaged her back so severely that she was unable to work in the four years it took for her case to be settled. She had been asked to move a locker weighing up to 75 pounds across a busy main road, a distance of up to 600 yards.

Public services union, Unison, which backed her claim for compensation, said that employers should be more aware of the risks of back injury before they ask staff to lift heavy or awkward loads. Most accidents resulting in injury are prevented by taking very simple steps.

Employers' legal duties to prevent injury

Health and Safety at Work etc. Act 1974

M3002　Under the *Health and Safety at Work etc. Act 1974* (*HSWA*), employers have a general duty to ensure the health, safety and welfare at work of their employees. In particular, they have a duty to ensure the safe use, handling, storage and transport of articles and substances so far as is reasonably practicable [*HSWA, s 2(2)a*].

The term 'reasonably practicable' is used throughout health and safety legislation and means that the costs of carrying out a measure must be weighed up against the risks if it is not carried out.

Management of Health and Safety at Work Regulations 1992 (SI 1992 No 2051)

M3003

Regulation 3(1) of the *Management of Health and Safety at Work Regulations 1992* requires employers to assess the risks to health and safety arising from their work activities. This general risk assessment should identify whether there is a risk of injury from manual handling operations in the workplace. If this is the case, the employer should comply with the more specific requirements of the *Manual Handling Operations Regulations 1992*.

Manual Handling Operations Regulations 1992 (SI 1992 No 2793)

M3004

These regulations are based on an ergonomic approach to preventing manual handling injuries. This involves fitting the job to the worker, taking into account anatomy, physiology and psychology. Whereas previous legislation set limits on the weight of loads that could be lifted, these regulations require a number of relevant factors to be taken into consideration, including the nature of the task, the load, the working environment and the individual capability of workers.

The Regulations define manual handling operations as: 'any transporting or supporting of a load (including lifting, putting down, pushing, pulling, carrying or moving thereof) by hand or by bodily force'.

A load is a discrete movable object, and includes people and animals. However, the definition of an injury excludes those caused by corrosive or toxic spillages, which are covered instead by the *Control of Substances Hazardous to Health Regulations 1999 (COSHH) (SI 1999 No 437)*.

The Regulations set out a hierarchy of measures employers should work through in order to prevent or reduce the risk of injury to their employees from the manual handling of loads:

(i)   Avoid hazardous manual handling operations so far as is reasonably practicable (*Reg 4(1)(a)*). This maybe done by redesigning the task to avoid moving the load or by automating or mechanising the process;

(ii) Make a suitable and sufficient assessment of any hazardous manual handling tasks that cannot be avoided (*Reg 4(1)(b)(i)*);

(iii) Reduce the risk of injury from those operations to the lowest level reasonably practicable (*Reg 4(1)(b)(ii)*).

People working under the control and direction of others, even if they are treated as being self-employed for tax and National Insurance purposes, are classed as employees for health and safety purposes and are therefore covered by these regulations.

The HSE published revised guidance to support the Regulations in 1998. The new guidance includes a revised Appendix 1, which sets out a detailed assessment guidelines filter. It also has an example of an assessment checklist with notes on its completion and a worked example of a pallet process operation in Appendix 2. The guidance also contains expanded advice on:

(*a*)   duties of the self-employed working under the direction of other people;

(*b*)   the increased risk to pregnant workers and the advantages of having a well-defined plan to respond to a worker becoming pregnant;

(*c*)   the *Disability Discrimination Act 1995* and advice on the needs of disabled people;

(*d*)   the risk associated with lifting loads from floor level;

(*e*)   the duties of manufacturers and suppliers;

(*f*)   how the risk may be affected if reducing the weight of the load means increasing the frequency of handling; and

(*g*)   the use of abdominal and back support belts.

Avoiding manual handling operations

M3005   Employers should firstly look at how manual handling operations can be avoided or minimised, either by redesigning the workplace or work organisation, or automating or mechanising tasks. Automation includes palletisation, vacuum handling, lift trucks and conveyors.

If the operations are automated or mechanised, an assessment of the new risks involved will be necessary since, for example, conveyors can present trapping hazards, while forklift trucks have caused crush injuries and may lead to the build up of diesel fumes in the workplace. There also needs to be consideration as to whether additional manual handling problems are caused, particularly at loading or off-loading points.

Some handling aids need to be maintained and the *Lifting Operations and Lifting Equipment Regulations 1998 (SI 1998 No 2307)* may apply. These require certain pieces of equipment to be regularly examined and tested. If vehicles are used, such as forklift trucks, the *Workplace (Health, Safety and Welfare) Regulations 1992 (SI 1992 No 3004)* require that traffic routes are organised so that vehicles and people can circulate safely in the workplace, and are kept apart where practicable.

HSE guidance

M3006   In the HSE publication, *Manual handling – solutions you can handle*, the HSE advises that avoiding manual handling operations can be very simple, and gives the example of fitting a hosepipe to a tap to avoid having to lift a bucket into a sink to fill it. It gives an intermediate solution – palletising operations so that loads can be lifted with a forklift truck rather than manually – and says that a more complicated solution could involve redesigning the workplace to minimise the amount of handling.

The guidance gives the following examples of steps to avoid or reduce manual handling:

(*a*)   Where powders, granules or liquids have to be transferred, these can be fed into a machine from a bulk container by suction or using a pump, rather than workers carrying loads up steps.

(*b*)   Where loads are transferred between conveyor belts and weighing machines, ensuring that these are in line can reduce manual handling.

(c)   Where patients are liable to fall out of bed, fitting side guards prevents this, reducing the amount of manual handling because staff do not have to lift them back into bed, and reducing injuries to patients.

Another HSE publication, *A pain in your workplace? Ergonomic problems and solutions*, gives some examples of how manual handling operations have been reduced or eliminated in particular types of workplaces.

In one example, longer retractable handles and a vertical handle were fitted into a hospital toilet used by geriatric and infirm patients. They had needed manual assistance from hospital staff in order to be able to use the toilet, but with the new handles, most were able to support themselves with little or no assistance. This gave the patients increased independence as well as reducing the amount of handling, and therefore the risk of injury to staff.

In another example at a wine merchants, changing the way customers collected cases of beer reduced the amount of manual handling required. The cases had been delivered to a garage at the back of the shop, brought into the shop by the shop assistant, and then the customer would carry the cases out to the car park after purchasing them. The system was changed so that the cases were left in the garage; customers paid in the shop and received a voucher. The cases were then collected from the garage by customers in their cars, meaning less manual handling for the customer as well as the shop assistant.

Carrying out the risk assessment

M3007   In some situations it may not be reasonably practicable to avoid the need for employees to carry out manual handling tasks. The Regulations require that where this is the case, a 'suitable and sufficient' assessment of manual handling operations should be carried out.

HSE guideline figures

M3008   Where the general assessment under the *Management of Health and Safety at Work Regulations 1992 (SI 1992 No 2051)* has indicated the possibility of injury, but manual handling operations cannot be avoided, an appendix to the HSE's Guidance on the *Manual Handling Operations Regulations 1992 (SI 1992 No 2793)* provides guideline figures.

Lifting and lowering: The basic guideline figures for identifying when manual lifting and lowering operations may not need a detailed assessment are set out in Figure 1. If the handler's hands enter more than one of the box zones during the operation, the smallest weight figures apply. It is important to remember, however, that the transition from one box zone to another is not abrupt; an intermediate figure may be chosen where the handler's hands are close to a boundary. Where lifting or lowering with the hands beyond the box zones is unavoidable, a more detailed assessment should always be made.

These basic guideline figures for lifting and lowering are for relatively infrequent operations – up to approximately 30 operations per hour. The guideline figures will have to be reduced if the operation is repeated more often. As a rough guide, the figures should be reduced by 30% where the operation is repeated once or twice per minute, by 50% where the operation is repeated around five to eight times per minute and by 80% where the operation is repeated more than about 12 times per minute.

Even if the operations are within the guidelines, a more detailed assessment should still be made where the pace of work is not under the control of the worker, there is

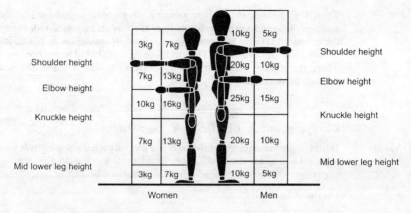

Fig. 1: Lifting and lowering

no change of activity providing the opportunity for other muscles to be used, there are inadequate rest periods, or where the handler must support the load for any length of time.

Carrying: The guideline figures can be used where loads are held against the body and carried up to about ten metres before resting. If loads are carried greater distances without a rest, or the hands are below knuckle height, a more detailed assessment will be needed.

Pushing and pulling: The guideline figures can also be used where pushing and pulling operations are being carried out and the hands are between knuckle and shoulder height. The guideline figure for starting or stopping a load is a force of about 25kg for men and 16kg for women, and for keeping it in motion, 10kg and 7kg respectively. There is no specific limit to the distance over which the load may be pushed or pulled, provided that there are adequate opportunities for rest or recovery.

Handling while seated: The basic guideline figure for handling operations carried out while seated, shown in Figure 2, is 5kg for men and 3kg for women. These guidelines only apply when the hands are within the box zone indicated. If handling beyond the box zone is unavoidable, a more detailed assessment should be made.

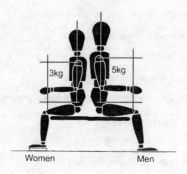

Fig. 2: Handling while seated

The HSE advises that where twisting or turning is involved, a detailed risk assessment should normally be made as there is an increased risk of injury, unless the operation is fairly infrequent (up to about 30 operations an hour), and there are no other posture problems. The guideline figures should be reduced by about 10% where the worker twists through 45 degrees, and 20% where the worker twists through 90 degrees.

Carrying out a detaile risk assessment

M3009   Where an initial assessment shows that a more detailed assessment is necessary, this must take into account the factors listed in *Schedule 1* to the *Manual Handling Operations Regulations 1992* which are summarised below.

Do the tasks involve:

(*a*)   holding or manipulating loads at a distance from the trunk;

(*b*)   unsatisfactory bodily movement or posture, particularly twisting the trunk, stooping, reaching upwards;

(*c*)   excessive movement of loads, especially lifting, lowering or carrying distances;

(*d*)   excessive pushing or pulling of loads;

(*e*)   risk of sudden movement of loads;

(*f*)   frequent or prolonged physical effort;

(*g*)   insufficient rest or recovery periods; or

(*h*)   a rate of work imposed by a process?

Are the loads:

(*a*)   heavy;

(*b*)   bulky or unwieldy;

(*c*)   difficult to grasp;

(*d*)   unstable or with contents likely to shift; or

(*e*)   sharp, hot or otherwise potentially damaging?

In the working environment, are there:

(*a*)   space constraints preventing good posture;

(*b*)   uneven, slippery or unstable floors;

(*c*)   variations in the level of floors or work surfaces;

(*d*)   extremes of temperature or humidity;

(*e*)   conditions causing ventilation problems or gusts of wind; or

(*f*)   poor lighting conditions?

Does the job:

(*a*)   require unusual strength, height etc;

(*b*)   create a hazard to those who may reasonably be considered to be pregnant or have a health problem; or (*c*)   require special information or training for its safe performance?

Is movement or posture hindered by personal protective equipment or clothing?

Pregnant workers

M3010   Although the HSE advises that variations in individual capability are generally less important than the nature of the manual handling operations in causing injury, there are nevertheless, particular issues around manual handling and pregnancy which employers need to consider. The health of pregnant women and the foetus can be affected by manual handling, particularly if it involves prolonged standing or walking, and as size increases, it can be difficult to achieve and maintain correct postures. In addition, hormonal changes during pregnancy can affect the ligaments and joints, increasing the risk of injury, and women returning to work after maternity leave may still be vulnerable to injury.

In addition to the duties set out under the *Manual Handling Operations Regulations 1992*, the *Management of Health and Safety at Work (Amendment) Regulations 1994 (SI 1994 No 2865)* require that when a woman has informed her employer that she is pregnant, the employer must assess the risks to her health and safety to which she is exposed.

The HSE advises that it is good practice for the following measures to be considered when assessing the risks to the health and safety of pregnant workers from manual handling tasks:

(*a*)   a reassessment of manual handling tasks to look at what improvements can be made;

(*b*)   provision of training in how work may be altered to accommodate changes in posture and physical capability, including taking breaks;

(*c*)   job rotation, relocation or suspension on full pay;

(*d*)   liaison with the GP to ensure capability; and

(*e*)   monitoring following a return to work after maternity leave to assess the need for any changes.

Disabled workers

M3011   Under the *Disability Discrimination Act 1995* employers must make reasonable adjustments to the workplace or employment arrangements so that a disabled person is not at a substantial disadvantage compared to other workers or job applicants. With regard to manual handling operations, this could include limiting the size, weight or number of loads, or providing suitable manual handling aids.

HSE guidance

M3012   The HSE guidance to the *Manual Handling Operations Regulations 1992* says that assessments should be based on a thorough practical understanding of manual handling tasks, the loads and the working environment, and points out that employers or managers should be better placed to know about manual handling operations in their own organisations than someone from outside. However, it says that there may be a place for outside organisations to provide training for in-house assessors.

It advises that setting up teams of people with different specialisms, for example in legal requirements, the operations being carried out, human capabilities, high-risk activities and the measures necessary to reduce the risks, can be effective.

The guidance also says that safety representatives and employees should play a positive part in the assessment, since they will have practical experience of carrying out the tasks and will know about any problems in the working environment. Analysing accident and ill-health records can also be useful in identifying problem areas.

Reducing the risk of injury

M3013 *Regulation 4(1)(b)(iii)* of the *Manual Handling Operations Regulations 1992* requires that where manual handling operations that involve a risk of injury cannot be avoided, appropriate steps must be taken to reduce the risk of injury to as low a level as reasonably practicable. This will involve an examination of the task, load, working environment and individual capability.

HSE guidance

M3014 Again, the HSE publication, *A pain in your workplace? Ergonomic problems and solutions*, gives some examples of how the risk of manual handling injury can be reduced in different types of workplaces.

For example, a woman working in radio equipment assembly carried out a job involving lifting and moving heavy pieces of radio equipment from one workbench to another several times an hour. She developed pain in her shoulder and was diagnosed as having a frozen shoulder. The safety manager moved the two workbenches together so that she did not have to lift the equipment, only push it on to the other bench. This very simple modification improved the work routine and the pain stopped.

In another example, there were high levels of sickness absence due to back pain among airport baggage handlers. A number of improvements were implemented, including labelling baggage over 25kg with its weight, to enable workers to prepare for a lift, standardising the height of conveyors to 650 millimetres in order to reduce stooping, and improving the spread of work between teams of staff more evenly.

The HSE guidance to the *Manual Handling Operations Regulations*, and the HSE publication *Manual handling – solutions you can handle* give a number of examples of how manual handling injuries can be reduced, by making improvements to various aspects of the work.

Making alterations to the load

M3015 Loads can be made lighter, smaller or provided with handles to make them easier to hold. However, where loads are made smaller or lighter, if this means that handling is more frequent, this must be taken into account as it could make the situation worse.

Containers with liquids or loose powder should be filled almost full so that the contents are not liable to shift suddenly. Sharp corners and rough surfaces should be avoided, as should corrosive or oily deposits.

Metal containers can be drilled with holes to make them lighter, smaller containers can be used for filling, with these being continually refilled from a supply tank, or the load can be put on wheels. For example, a bucket used for cleaning purposes can be fitted with castors so it can be pushed along with the mop rather than being carried.

Improvement to the task

M3016   This means reducing the amount of bending, stooping, stretching, pushing and pulling required. For example, storage heights can be changed to waist level, obstacles that have to be reached over or into can be removed, and lifting can be replaced with controlled pulling or pushing. Job rotation can allow one group of muscles to rest while another group is being used, or heavy work can be interspersed with lighter work.

Height and angle adjustable worktables can be adjusted to suit particular jobs and reduce bending, platforms can be provided to avoid lifts above shoulder height for shorter workers, and containers with removable sides which allow access to the bottom can reduce stooping.

In addition, changes can be made to allow the body to be used more efficiently. In general, any change that allows loads to be held closer to the body will be an improvement. When lifting of loads at or near floor level is unavoidable, handling techniques which allow the use of the legs rather than the back are preferable, as long as the load is small enough to be held close to the trunk.

Mechanical assistance

M3017   Handling aids can be provided so that although there is still some manual handling, there is less risk of injury. These include levers, hoists, roller conveyors, trucks, trolleys, chutes and handling devices, such as hand-held hooks and suction pads.

For example, lifting hooks can help lift large awkward loads, and paving slab handlers are available. Platform trucks that can be raised and lowered further reduce handling by avoiding the need for bending. Tracks and chutes allow heavy and bulky loads to be moved manually or by gravity under their own weight. If portable conveyors are used to reduce manual handling, they should be at a height of around 0.9m where loads are light enough to be lifted with one hand; around 0.75m height where heavier loads such as cases and cartons are loaded, and at around floor level for heavy loads like drums.

Workers who will be using handling aids should be able to express their preference. The moving and handling co-ordinator at Wigan and Leigh Health Service NHS Trust told the 1998 NHS workforce conference that allowing nurses to choose new lifting equipment resulted in a six-fold reduction in sickness absence due to manual handling injuries. She estimated the trust had saved £2 million over a four-year period.

The working environment

M3018   Having a workplace with adequate space to manoeuvre, clear floor spaces and adequate headroom can reduce the risk of injury. The ground should be stable and level, spillages should be dealt with promptly, and there should be a comfortable working environment with adequate lighting.

Where there are space constraints, it may be necessary to increase the width of openings to ease manoeuvring of loads. If there are uneven, slippery or unstable floors which mean there is a risk that workers could lose their balance, improvements may include good housekeeping, special floor surfaces and coatings, and as a temporary measure, large boards over an uneven area may help. Where there are variations in floor levels, ramps instead of stairs can allow wheeled handling aids to be used.

Individual capability

M3019   Particular consideration should be given to those who are pregnant (see above) or who have a history of back, knee or hip trouble or hernia problems, but in general medical screening is not recommended as a way of reducing the risk of injury.

Safety representatives and employees should be involved in redesigning work in order to minimise injuries.

Abdominal and back support belts

M3020   The merits of abdominal and back support belts is controversial, since although manufacturers and suppliers claim that they can reduce manual handling injuries, some research has shown they have no effect, and there are concerns that they may put some people at additional risk of injury. In addition, there is some concern that muscles could be weakened in the long term and this has yet to be studied.

The HSE advice is that although the decision as to whether to use them or not rests with employers, it is normally possible to reduce risks more effectively with safe systems of work, providing protection to all workers not just particular individuals. It also says that relying solely on support belts will not meet the employer's duties under the regulations.

In general, health and safety legislation always prioritises the control or prevention of hazards at source, with the provision of personal protective clothing and equipment as a last resort to control risks where they cannot be controlled by other means.

Providing additional information about the load

M3021   *Regulation 4(1)(b)(iii)* requires that where it is not reasonably practicable to avoid the need for employees to undertake manual handling operations which involve a risk of injury, employees should be provided with general indications, and where reasonably practicable to do so, precise information on the weight of each load and the heaviest side where the centre of gravity is not positioned centrally.

General indications should generally be given during basic training on manual handling. Where employers originate loads, the best way of giving precise information is to mark it on the loads. Suppliers should also be asked to do this.

Training

M3022   Training should be seen as complementing safe systems of work, and not as an alternative to such systems. Safety representatives and employees should be involved in the development of manual handling training. This should cover:

(*a*)   avoiding hazards;

(*b*)   dealing with unavoidable or unfamiliar manual handling operations;

(*c*)   proper use of handling aids and personal protective equipment;

(*d*)   features of the working environment contributing to safety;

(*e*)   the importance of good housekeeping;

(*f*)   factors affecting capability; and

(*g*)   good handling technique.

It should include recognition of loads whose weight or shape could cause injury, and assessing weight before attempting to lift a load. It is important that the practices taught on training courses can actually be used in the workplace.

Good handling techniques

M3023   Again, training in good handling techniques is not a substitute for other measures to reduce injury, but it can be valuable alongside other risk reduction measures, as long as it can actually be put into practice at the workplace. It should also be tailored to the particular handling operations being undertaken.

The HSE guidance to the *Manual Handling Operations Regulations* provides an example of a lifting task to illustrate the following advice:

(*a*)   plan the lift, asking whether help or handling aids are required;

(*b*)   place the feet apart to give a balanced and stable base for lifting;

(*c*)   adopt a good posture with the knees bent and the hands level with the waist when grasping the load, the back straight, maintaining its natural curve and the chin tucked in;

(*d*)   get a firm grip with the arms within the boundary formed by the legs;

(*e*)   carry out the lifting movement smoothly, raising the chin as the lift begins and keeping control of the load;

(*f*)   move the feet rather than twisting the trunk when turning to the side;

(*g*)   keep close to the load for as long as possible, keeping the heaviest side of the load next to the trunk; and

(*h*)   put down the load, then adjust the positioning afterwards.

Reviewing the assessment

M3024   *Regulation 4(2)* of the *Manual Handling Operations Regulations 1992* requires that assessments are kept up to date and reviewed where there has been a significant change in manual handling operations, there is reason to suspect that the assessment is no longer valid, or where a reportable injury occurs. (See *Reporting of Injuries, Diseases and Dangerous Occurrences Regulations 1995* (*RIDDOR*) in ACCIDENT REPORTING).

Employees' duties

M3025   *Regulation 5* of the *Manual Handling Operations Regulations 1992* requires employees to make full and proper use of any system of work for handling of loads laid down by the employer.

The Millennium Bug

Introduction

M7001   For almost as long as computers have existed programmers, anxious to save memory space, have used a chronological shorthand. Instead of writing the year in a four digit form, such as 1969, they abbreviated this to two digits and invariably wrote 69.

The use of this practice became almost universal in the computer and information technology market. As a result, it also became the norm in integrated microchips which formed an integral part of most items of sophisticated electronic equipment. These microchips are often described as embedded systems, and so numerous and integrated are they that it has proved difficult to identify them all, let alone try to repair or replace them.

Long past is the time when the two digit software could easily be remedied with a few overriding programming instructions. Long gone is the opportunity to rewrite all the offending microchips.

Against what criteria does one measure these lost opportunities for the computer industry? It is against one of the few events which cannot be delayed, deferred or deflected. It is the arrival of the year 2000.

The advent of the year 2000 means that two digit year codes can no longer be relied on to be accurate. What does '59' mean as a year? The computer, being by nature an extremely rapid moron, could interpret it as 1959 or 2059 or some totally different date.

Similarly, embedded microchips are likely to struggle when asked to 'interpret' data in the light of the forthcoming Millennium. To some extent this has already occurred with bar-coding microchip based scanners rejecting consignments of supermarket food with sell-by dates of 2001 on the basis that they interpreted 01 as being 1901 which meant they 'decided' the products were 98 years past their sell-by date!

The third ingredient in the Y2K cocktail is that 2000 is a leap year and therefore computers need to be able to recognise and deal with the date 29.02.2000.

The extent of the problem

M7002   There have been three distinct evolutionary phases when assessing the Y2K problem, or Millennium Bug as it is now known.

The first phase was to regard it as an isolated, rather esoteric technical problem, only of concern to computer technicians and programmers.

The second phase was an awareness that it was actually a business or commercial issue, perhaps posing more of a threat to the continuity and smooth running of business than anything else this century. The problem is now being recognised for the major threat it truly represents. Consequently it has been discussed in detail by the G8 countries at their latest summit meeting, and in the nuclear sector OECD and NEA are in the process of obtaining, from member states, detailed action plans which set out the remedial measures they are currently taking.

The third and most important phase was the realisation that the Y2K problem is no respecter of business sectors. Far from being confined to the information technology, high-tech, and defence sectors, the Millennium Bug can strike at any manufacturing or service industry that uses an operating system that may contain software code or microchips.

So, in addition to the obvious risk areas such as computer networks and data processing plants, the Phase 3 realisation is that lifts, fax machines, motor cars, machine control panels, burglar and fire alarms are all in jeopardy. Businesses are now realising that equipment which shows no outward sign of a displayed date may be critically affected by the Millennium Bug because it nevertheless receives and/or processes date-critical data as part of its daily function.

Interdependency and common cause failure

M7003

Hot on the heels of the Phase 3 awareness has come the realisation that commercially 'no business is an island'. There is a real vulnerability to many links in the chain, be they customers, suppliers, utility providers or trading partners. In an ideal world, each organisation would be able to scrutinise the Y2K preparation of all other participants in the food chain to ensure that they were equally ready for the year 2000. After all, there is only a limited value to a business being totally prepared for the Millennium on a stand-alone basis if its telephone or electricity providers are knocked out of action by the Millennium Bug. In this sense each business is as strong as the weakest link in its commercial chain.

Additionally, a Y2K problem in one system or area is likely to affect other systems also and create a domino effect. Such a defect could involve a number of items in one system malfunctioning or, worse, it could result in a number of different and apparently independent systems all failing together. Such an occurrence is known as a 'common cause' defect.

Best endeavours

M7004

No matter how dependent a business is on its chain of suppliers and customers, the starting point for ensuring Y2K readiness is a detailed examination of one's own state of readiness. Although, when viewed in its widest context, the task is daunting, businesses should remember that the largest journey starts with a single step.

So what are the steps that businesses should be taking in their quest to use their best endeavours to avoid being bitten by the Millennium Bug?

Health and safety priorities

M7005

The first step is to identify by way of list, and then to investigate, safety critical systems. Having been investigated, the systems should be marked in terms of safety criticality. In this way the opening initiative will identify safety critical systems which may be defective due to a Y2K related problem.

As part of this first step it is of course necessary to understand what is meant by Y2K defective or Y2K compliant. It is for this reason that at least two codes of compliance have been published. The first and probably most widely used in the UK is the BSI Code of Compliance (BSI-Document PD2000-13). However, the code produced by the Electronics and Information Industries Forum (EIIF) is also a perfectly good yardstick against which to measure the Y2K readiness of a system.

Suppliers' duties and disclosure

M7006　Any system that is new or has recently been purchased should have included a supplier's statement of the Y2K readiness of that system. Even if such a statement was absent, the law relating to the sale and supply of goods may mean that hardware sold in the last twelve months would not be of a reasonable quality if not Y2K compliant. Furthermore, if older systems have been supplied with the benefit of a maintenance agreement, the supplier's duty under the maintenance agreement may be to supply upgrades and enhancements which will make the system Y2K compliant.

It should also be stressed that a supplier faces an ongoing legal duty to provide customers with information if its system could jeopardise health and safety. This duty survives sale and includes data relating to health and safety issues about which the supplier learns subsequently.

Testing

M7007　Having identified equipment which is both health and safety critical and date-sensitive, it is important to test those systems both in isolation – through simulated Y2K handling procedures – and in conjunction with interconnecting systems or dependent procedures. Great care needs to be taken in carrying out such tests because random or ill-conceived testing may actually create Y2K problems where none previously existed. It is also important to consider whether, in anticipating, for example, the events of Friday 31 December 1999, the system will work with today's passwords or whether password protection will need to be removed.

Part of the testing process should ensure that all personnel involved in the testing adequately represent the business interests they are seeking to protect. So in addition to the IT manager and production manager, the financial controller should be involved in terms of likely cash flow and order book disruption. Perhaps the HR function should also be represented, particularly if the contingency planning is likely to involve committing further personnel to dealing with the Y2K problem whenever it arises. The resultant contingency plan should be a physical document to which all involved personnel subscribe and which identifies the practical and business-critical problems and the contingencies in place to resolve those problems. It should also include cold-starting or restarting procedures for systems that have ceased to operate because of internal Y2K problems or those of others in the supply chain.

Such testing and contingency planning should not be a one-off event. Particularly in the case of safety critical systems it needs to be a continual regular process. Indeed, it is unlikely that a business will obtain (or retain) insurance cover for Y2K issues such as business interruption unless it demonstrates to its insurers that the testing and planning is a rolling, continuing process.

It is also true to say that if the Y2K problems of a business are not investigated at all, or if they are investigated but no attempt is then made to remedy them, the directors of that business face personal liability. In the case of health and safety systems that liability could include personal liability for corporate manslaughter.

Safety critical systems

M7008　The threats to safety critical systems have been examined but how are these systems to be identified and defined? The test applied in this chapter is that the systems must be both safety critical and dependent upon date processing or manipulation.

In terms of assessing how vital a health and safety role is played by a system it is necessary to consider the role that system plays in terms of risk management and risk mitigation. It is also necessary to consider what the safety implications would be if the system proved to be Y2K defective. Again prioritisation of perceived risk is vital here. Perhaps the most useful approach is a scale of 1–5 where Priority 1 is the most serious. The following gradations may be used.

Priority 5 – no health and safety consequences;

Priority 4 – risk of curable injury;

Priority 3 – risk of permanent injury;

Priority 2 – risk to individual life;

Priority 1 – risk to many lives.

Such prioritisation of the health and safety systems can then be factored into the Y2K contingency planning and the testing and replicating programme so that most date-based systems are identified first and correlated to the Priority 1 health and safety systems.

In this way not only will planning enable the highest health and safety, date-dependent systems to be concentrated upon first, but also systems with the longest lead times will also be prioritised.

Legislation

The US position

M7009

A word of caution to anyone doing business with organisations in the USA. UK organisations which sell goods or services into the USA should be aware of the *Year 2000 Information and Readiness Disclosure Act*, generally known as the Good Samaritan Act, which became law on 19 October 1998.

This Act was passed because, in America's litigious culture, many businesses were very reluctant to describe their level of Y2K readiness. What the Act provides, therefore, is a genuine attempt to persuade suppliers to make a full and candid statement about their Y2K readiness. If they do this, even if they admit that their products are not Y2K ready, they will not be liable in a private civil action in an American court. Businesses will be liable if their Y2K statement was material and they made it knowing that it was false, inaccurate or misleading, but not otherwise.

A Year 2000 readiness disclosure can be written or stored electronically. So the posting of a statement on a business website for a commercially reasonable duration could well be adequate. However, the Act makes it clear that this will only be permitted where it does not run counter to earlier agreements about service of notices and entire agreement provisions.

Domestic legislation

M7010

The UK Government has not passed any overarching Y2K legislation. Two pieces of legislation were going through the Parliamentary process in the autumn of 1998 but both were lost due to lack of time and, some would say, lack of Government commitment.

In terms of UK health and safety legislation there is a substantial volume of law that will apply to Y2K. For example, *sections 2, 3 and 6 of the Health and Safety at Work etc. Act 1974* are all being interpreted to include employers, consultants, designers, manufacturers and installers. Health and safety inspectors are specifically sanctioned to raise Y2K issues in so far as they relate to health and safety in the workplace and, if they find that inadequate attention has been given to this issue, then an improvement notice may well be issued. There are of course penalties such as fines and even imprisonment for failure to comply with an improvement notice.

In addition such legislation as the *Supply of Machinery (Safety) Regulations 1992*, the *Electrical Equipment (Safety) Regulations 1994*, the *Management of Health and Safety at Work Regulations 1992*, the *Offshore Installations and Wells (Design and Construction) Regulations 1996*, the *Construction (Design and Management) Regulations 1994* and the *Provision and Use of Work Equipment Regulations 1998* will all lend themselves to a Y2K enforcement regime in so far as health and safety is concerned.

Conclusion

M7011   Statistics tell us that 90 per cent of all businesses in the UK will suffer Y2K problems in critical systems that could affect health and safety. Despite this risk only 30 per cent have in place contingency plans as to how they will deal with these problems. It is estimated that the world-wide cost for software and systems correction could be as high as £333 billion, and the total cost of the problem, including damages and litigation costs, could well exceed £1,000 billion.

No business can guarantee the Y2K compliance of any other member of its supply chain. Well-informed and well-managed businesses, however, can and should resolve their internal Y2K problems, particularly in respect of health and safety, by taking the steps outlined above.

To recap and conclude, those steps are:

1.   create a definitive list of all hardware, software and date-dependent components and systems;

2.   list, study and if necessary take advice upon the contracts under which all such systems have been or are about to be supplied;

3.   prepare the health and safety priority analysis;

4.   create a detailed plan as to how high priority systems' problems are to be resolved;

5.   carry out detailed testing of high priority systems, new systems and the interface between the two;

6.   repeat Y2K tests in genuine Y2K circumstances involving appropriate personnel;

7.   ensure that during the most critical Y2K dates (namely 9.9.99, 31.12.99, 1.1.2000, 29.2.2000, 1.3.2000, 31.12.2000 and 1.1.2001) sufficiently expert staff and adequate systems are in place to overcome any Y2K problems.

Each of these measures is even more vital if the effect of a Y2K bug is to cause health and safety problems. In the case of Y2K and health and safety, precaution and preparation are most certainly better than cure.

Note: The author of this chapter has taken all due care and consideration, taking into account the nature and subject matter of the chapter. However, in view of the uncertain, unprecedented and unforeseeable nature of the Millennium Bug and Y2K, no liability whatsoever can be accepted by the author in respect of any reliance placed upon, or acts or omissions occurring in relation to, the contents of this chapter.

Noise and Vibration

PART A: Noise at Work

Introduction

N3001

Around 80 per cent of claims for occupational disease against employers' liability insurance relate to deafness, compared with a total of about 6 per cent for lung diseases and 4 per cent for upper limb disorders. This corresponds to about 34,000 claims for noise-induced deafness in 1995, according to statistics from the Association of British Insurers.

The Department of Social Security pays disablement benefit to people who suffer at least 50 decibels (dB) of noise-induced hearing loss in both ears. This level of hearing loss is roughly equivalent to listening to the television or a conversation through a substantial brick wall. Moreover, claimants must have been employed for at least ten years in a specified noisy occupation. Despite these restrictions, there were 763 new awards in 1995. There are currently 14,200 people, 99 per cent of them men, receiving the benefit from the DSS. Yet this seems to be only the tip of the iceberg, since the 1990 Labour Force Survey estimate was of 121,400 people in England and Wales reporting work-related deafness or other ear problems, which would have included many sufferers who did not meet the DSS criteria. Statistics from audiological examinations show approximately 1,200 claimants annually with between 35 and 49 decibels of hearing loss, still a severe disability, equivalent to listening through a substantial partition wall in a house.

Over the five-year period since 1990, when the *Noise at Work Regulations 1989* (see N3012 below) were introduced to provide statutory enforcement of hearing protection, the Health and Safety Executive undertook 31 prosecutions. Over the same period, it issued 2,089 improvement notices and 139 prohibition notices relating to breaches of the regulations.

Hearing damage

N3002

We all lose hearing acuity with age, and this loss is accelerated and worsened by exposure to excessive noise. Fortunately, in early life, we have much greater hearing acuity than modern life demands, and a small loss is readily compensated by turning up the volume of the radio or TV.

Loud noises cause permanent damage to the nerve cells of the inner ear in such a way that a hearing aid is ineffective. At first, the damage occurs at frequencies above normal speech range, so that the sufferer may have no inkling of the problem, although it could be identified easily by an audiogram, which measures the sensitivity of the ear at a number of frequencies across its normal range. As exposure continues, the region of damage progresses to higher and lower frequencies. Damage starts to extend into the speech range, making it difficult to distinguish consonants, so that words start to sound the same. Eventually, speech becomes a muffled jumble of sounds.

Some people are much more susceptible to hearing damage than others. A temporary dullness of hearing, or tinnitus (a ringing or whistling sound in the ears) when emerging from a noisy place are both indicative of damage to the nerve cells of the inner ear. Because these symptoms tend to disappear with continued exposure, they are often misinterpreted as the ear becoming 'hardened', whereas in fact it is losing its ability to respond to the noise. Even when hearing has apparently returned to normal, a little of the sensitivity is likely to have been lost. Therefore, anyone who experiences dullness of hearing or tinnitus after noise exposure must take special care to avoid further exposure. They may also be advised to seek medical advice and an audiogram.

Apart from catastrophic exposures (usually to explosive sounds), the risk of hearing loss is closely dependent on the 'noise dose' received, and especially on the cumulative effect over a period of time. British Standard BS 5330 gives a procedure for estimating the risk of 'hearing handicap' due to noise exposure. Handicap is there defined as a hearing loss of 30 dB, which is sufficiently severe to impair the understanding of conversational speech or the appreciation of music. This may be compared with the loss of 50 dB required for DSS disability benefit.

The perception of sound

N3003   Sound is caused by a rapid fluctuation in air pressure. The human ear can hear a sensation of sound when the fluctuations occur between 20 times a second and 20,000 times a second. The rate at which the air pressure fluctuates is called the frequency of the sound and is measured in Hertz (Hz). The loudness of the sound depends on the amount of fluctuation in the air pressure. Typically, the quietest sound that can be heard (the threshold of hearing) is zero decibels (0 dB) and the sound becomes painful at 120 dB. Surprisingly perhaps, zero decibels is not zero sound. The sensitivity and frequency range of the ear vary somewhat from person to person and deteriorate with age and exposure to loud sounds.

The human ear is not equally sensitive to sounds of different frequencies (i.e. pitch): it tends to be more sensitive in the frequency range of the human voice than at higher or lower frequencies (peaking at about 4 kHz). When measuring sound, compensation for these effects can be made by applying a frequency weighting, usually the so-called 'A' weighting, although other weightings are sometimes used for special purposes.

The ear has an approximately logarithmic response to sound: for example, every doubling or halving in sound pressure gives an apparently equal step increase or decrease in loudness. In measuring environmental noise, sound pressure levels are therefore usually quoted in terms of a logarithmic unit known as a decibel (dB). To signify that the 'A' weighting has been applied, the symbol of dB(A) is often used. However, current practice tends to prefer the weighting letter to be included in the name of the measurement index, see below. For example, dB(A) Leq and dB LAeq both refer to the 'A' weighted equivalent sound level in decibels.

Depending upon the method of presentation of two sounds, the human ear may detect differences as small as 0.5 dB(A). However, for general environmental noise the detectable difference is usually taken to be between 1 and 3 dB(A), depending on how quickly the change occurs. A 10 dB(A) change in sound pressure level corresponds, subjectively, to an approximate doubling or halving in loudness. Similarly, a subjective quadrupling of loudness corresponds to a 20 dB(A) increase in sound pressure level (SPL). When two sounds of the same SPL are added together, the resultant SPL is approximately 3 dB(A) higher than each of the individual sounds. It would require approximately *nine* equal sources to be added to an original source before the subjective loudness is doubled.

Noise indices

N3004 The sound pressure level of industrial and environmental sound fluctuates continuously. A number of measurement indices have been proposed to describe the human response to these varying sounds. It is possible to measure the physical characteristics of sound with considerable accuracy and to predict the physical human response to characteristics such as loudness, pitch and audibility. However, it is not possible to predict *subjective* characteristics such as annoyance with certainty. This should not be surprising: one would not expect the light meter on a camera to be able to indicate whether one was taking a good or a bad photograph, although one would expect it to get the physical exposure correct. Strictly speaking, therefore, a meter can only measure sound and not noise (which is often defined as sound unwanted by the recipient): nevertheless, in practice, the terms are usually interchangeable.

Equivalent continuous 'A' weighted sound pressure level, LAeq

N3005 This unit takes into account fluctuations in sound pressure levels. It can be applied to all types of noise, whether continuous, intermittent or impulsive. LAeq is defined as the steady, continuous sound pressure level which contains the same energy as the actual, fluctuating sound pressure level. In effect, it is the energy-average of the sound pressure level over a period which must be stated, e.g. LAeq, (18-hour).

This unit is now being put forward as a universal noise index, because it can be used to measure all types of noise, although it has yet to supplant older units in certain cases, particularly for the assessment of road traffic noise where calculation techniques and regulatory criteria have not been updated.

Levels measured in LAeq can be added using the rules mentioned earlier. There is also a time trade-off: if a sound is made for half the measurement period, followed by silence, the LAeq over the whole measurement period will be 3 dB less than during the noisy half of the period. If the sound is present for one-tenth of the measurement period, the LAeq over the whole measurement period will be 10 dB less than during the noisy one-tenth of the measurement period. This is a cause of some criticism of LAeq: for discontinuous noise, such as may arise in industry, it does not limit the maximum noise level, so it may be necessary to specify this as well.

Daily personal noise exposure, LEP,d

N3006 This is used in the *Noise at Work Regulations 1989* as a measure of the total sound exposure a person receives during the day. It is formally defined in a Schedule to the regulations.

LEP,d is the energy-average sound level (LAeq) to which a person is exposed over a working day, disregarding the effect of any ear protection which may be worn, adjusted to an 8-hour period. Thus, if a person is exposed to 90 dB LAeq for a 4-hour working day, their LEP,d is 87 dB, but if they work a 12-hour shift, the same sound level would give them an LEP,d of 91.8 dB.

Maximum 'A' weighted sound pressure level, LAmax,T

N3007 The maximum 'A'-weighted root-mean-square (rms) sound pressure level during the measurement period is designated LAmax. Sound level meters indicate the rms sound pressure level averaged over a finite period of time. Two averaging periods *(T)* are defined, S (slow) and F (fast), having averaging times of 1 second and 1/8th second. It is necessary to state the averaging period. Maximum SPL should not be confused with Peak SPL which is a measure of the instantaneous peak pressure.

Peak sound pressure

N3008   Instantaneous peak sound pressure can only be measured with specialist instruments. It is used in the assessment of explosive sounds, such as from gunshots and blasting, and in hearing damage assessments of this type of sound. Where the maximum sound level exceeds 125 dB LAmax,F, then an accurate measurement of peak pressure is advisable to check for compliance with the peak action level of the *Noise at Work Regulations*.

Background noise level, LA90

N3009   LA90 is the level of sound exceeded for 90 per cent of the measurement period. It is therefore a measure of the background noise level – in other words, the sound drops below this level only infrequently. (The term 'background' should not be confused with 'ambient', which refers to *all* the sound present in a given situation at a given time.)

Sound power level, LWA

N3010   The sound output of an item of plant or equipment is frequently specified in terms of its sound power level. This is measured in decibels relative to a reference power of 1 pico-Watt (dB re 10-12 W), but it must not be confused with sound pressure level. The sound pressure level at a particular position can be calculated from a knowledge of the sound power level of the source, provided the acoustical characteristics of the surrounding and intervening space are known. As a crude analogy, the power of a lamp bulb gives an indication of its light output, but the illumination of a surface depends on its distance and orientation from the source, and the presence of reflecting and obstructing objects in the surroundings.

To give a rough idea of the relationship between sound power level and sound pressure level, for a noise source which is emitting sound uniformly in all directions close above a hard surface in an open space, the sound pressure level 10 metres from the source would be 28 dB below its sound power level.

General legal requirements

N3011   Statutory requirements relating to noise at work *generally* are contained in the *Noise at Work Regulations 1989 (SI 1989 No 1790)*. Replacing the previous Department of Employment (voluntary) Code of Practice on Noise (1972), these regulations require employers to take reasonably practicable measures, on a long-term on-going basis, to reduce employees' exposure to noise at work to the lowest possible level, and to lower noise exposure where employees are exposed to levels of 90 dB(A) or above, or to peak action level or above (200 Pascals). In addition, ear protectors must be provided and worn and ear protection zones designated. Estimates throughout industry overall suggest that about 1.7 million workers may be exposed above 85 dB(A), the first action level, and 630,000 above 90 dB(A), the second action level.

At present, there are no specific provisions relating to *vibration* other than those contained in the *Social Security (Industrial Injuries) (Prescribed Diseases) Regulations 1985 (SI 1985 No 967)* and the *Reporting of Injuries, Diseases and Dangerous Occurrences Regulations 1985 (SI 1985 No 2023)*. Occupational deafness and certain forms of vibration-induced conditions, i.e. vibration-induced white finger, are prescribed industrial diseases for which disablement benefit is payable (though the 14 per cent disablement rule will obviously limit the number of successful claimants. Damages may also be awarded against the employer (see further N3021 below).

Noise At Work Regulations 1989 (SI 1989 No 1790)

N3012   The following duties are laid on employers.

1.   To make (and update where necessary) a formal noise assessment, where employees are likely to be exposed to:

   (*a*)   first action level or above (85 dB(A)),

   (*b*)   peak action level or above (200 Pascals).

   [*Regs 2(1), 4(1)*].

   Such assessment should be made by a competent person and adequately:

   (i)   identify which employees are exposed, and

   (ii)   provide the employer with such information as will enable him to carry out his statutory duties, and

   (iii)   when there is reason to suppose that the assessment is no longer valid, or when there has been a significant change in the work to which the assessment relates, review noise levels and make any changes recommended by the review.

   [*Reg 4(2)*].

2.   To keep an adequate record of such assessment until a further assessment is made. [*Reg 5*].

3.   (As a long-term strategy, and on an on-going basis), to reduce the risk of damage to the hearing of their employees from exposure to noise to the lowest level reasonably practicable. [*Reg 6*].

4.   To reduce, so far as is reasonably practicable, the exposure to noise of employees (other than by provision of personal ear protectors), where employees are likely to be exposed to (*a*) 90 dB(A) or above or (*b*) peak action level (200 Pascals) or above. [*Reg 7*].

5.   To provide, at the request of an employee, suitable and efficient personal ear protectors where employees are likely to be exposed to 85 dB(A) or above but less than 90 dB(A). [*Reg 8(1)*].

6.   To designate ear protection zones, indicating:

   (*a*)   that it is an ear protection zone, and

   (*b*)   the need for employees to wear personal ear protectors whilst in such zone where any employee is likely to be exposed to 90 dB(A) or above, or to peak action level or above. Moreover, no employee should enter such zone unless he is wearing personal ear protectors.

   [*Reg 9*].

   Ear protection so provided must be maintained in an efficient state and employees must report any defects in it to the employer and see that it is fully and properly used. [*Reg 10*].

7.   To provide employees, likely to be exposed to 85 dB(A) or above, or to peak action level or above, with adequate information, instruction and training with regard to:

   (*a*)   risk of damage to that employee's hearing,

   (*b*)   steps the employee can take to minimise the risk, (*c*)   the requirement on employees to obtain personal ear protectors from the employer, and

(*d*)   the employee's duties under the regulations.

[*Reg 11*].

In addition, there are specific legal requirements applying to tractor cabs and offshore installations and construction sites (see below).

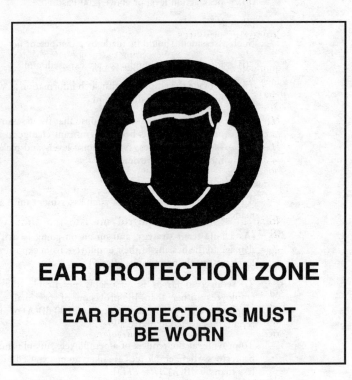

EAR PROTECTION ZONE

EAR PROTECTORS MUST BE WORN

Fig. 1 Sign for informing that ear protectors must be worn (white on a circular blue background)

From the Health and Safety (Safety Signs and Signals) Regulations 1996 (SI 1996 No 341)

Legal obligations of designers, manufacturers, importers and suppliers of plant and machinery

N3013   The *Supply of Machinery (Safety) Regulations 1992 (SI 1992 No 3073)* require manufacturers and suppliers of noisy machinery to design and construct such machinery so that the risks from noise emissions are reduced to the lowest level taking account of technical progress. Information on noise emissions must be provided when specified levels are reached.

If a machine is likely to cause people at work to receive a daily personal noise exposure exceeding the first or peak action levels, adequate information on noise must be provided. If the second or peak action levels are likely to be exceeded, this should include a permanent sign or label, or if the machine may be noisy in certain types of use, an instruction label which could be removed following noise testing.

Specific legal requirements

Agriculture

N3014   The *Agriculture (Tractor Cabs) Regulations 1974 (SI 1974 No 2034)* (as amended by *SI 1990 No 1075*) provide that noise levels in tractor cabs must not exceed 90 dB(A) or 86 dB depending on which annex is relevant in the certificate under Directive 77/311/EEC. [*Reg 3(3)*].

Construction sites

N3015   There are 23 EC directives relating to the noise emission of construction plant and equipment. These govern the maximum permissible levels of noise from a wide range of construction plant, and the way in which the emitted level is to be determined and marked. The directives are implemented in the UK via a series of statutory instruments, with titles of the form *Construction Plant and Equipment (Harmonisation of Noise Emission Standards) Regulations (SI 1985 No 1968; SI 1988 No 361; SI 1989 No 1127; SI 1992 No 488; SI 1995 No 2357)*; *Lawnmowers (Harmonisation of Noise Emission Standards) Regulations (SI 1986 No 1795; SI 1987 No 876; SI 1992 No 168)*; and *Supply of Machinery (Safety) Regulations 1992 (SI 1992 No 3073)*.

Noise and vibration control on construction and open sites, BS 5228: Parts 1 to 5

N3016   This code of practice gives detailed guidance on the assessment of noise and vibration from construction sites, open–cast coal extraction, piling operations, and surface mineral extraction. Part 1, revised in 1997, gives detailed noise calculation and assessment procedures. Its predecessor (published in 1984) was an approved code of practice under the *Control of Pollution Act 1974*. Part 1 of the code of practice is principally concerned with environmental noise and vibration, but also briefly recites the *Noise at Work Regulations 1989*.

Compensation for occupational deafness

Social security

N3017   Prescription rules for occupational deafness have been extended three times, in 1980, 1983 and 1994. On the first two occasions the number of awards increased substantially but then fell back. Since the most recent extension, occupational deafness has been the largest single category of *compensated* occupational disease (1,128 cases in 1990 though new awards declined to 972 in 1991/92 and 763 in 1995).

The most common condition associated with exposure to noise is occupational deafness. Deafness is prescribed occupational disease A 10 (see OCCUPATIONAL HEALTH AND DISEASES) and is defined as: 'sensorineural hearing loss amounting to at least 50 dB in each ear being the average of hearing losses at 1, 2 and 3 kHz frequencies, and being due, in the case of at least one ear, to occupational noise'. [*Social Security (Industrial Injuries) (Prescribed Diseases) Amendment Regulations 1989 (SI 1989 No 1207), Sch 1 Pt I*]. Thus, the former requirement for hearing loss to be measured by pure tone audiometry no longer applies. Extensions of benefit criteria relating to occupational deafness are contained in the *Social Security (Industrial Injuries) (Prescribed Diseases) Regulations 1985 (SI 1985 No 967)*, which are amended, as regards assessment of disablement for benefit purposes, by the *Social Security (Industrial Injuries) (Prescribed Diseases) Amendment Regulations 1994 (SI 1994 No 2343)*.

Conditions for which deafness is prescribed

N3018   Any occupation involving:

(*a*)   the use of powered (but not hand-powered) grinding tools on metal (other than sheet metal or plate metal), or work wholly or mainly in the immediate vicinity of those tools whilst they are being so used; or

(*b*)   the use of pneumatic percussive tools on metal, or work wholly or mainly in the immediate vicinity of those tools whilst they are being so used; or

(*c*)   the use of pneumatic percussive tools for drilling rock in quarries or underground or in mining coal, or in sinking shafts or for tunnelling in civil engineering works, or work wholly or mainly in the immediate vicinity of those tools whilst they are being so used; or

(*d*)   the use of pneumatic percussive tools on stone in quarry works, or work wholly or mainly in the immediate vicinity of those tools whilst they are being so used; or

(*e*)   work wholly or mainly in the immediate vicinity of plant (excluding power press plant) engaged in the forging (including drop stamping) of metal by means of closed or open dies or drop hammers; or

(*f*)   work in textile manufacturing where the work is undertaken wholly or mainly in rooms or sheds in which there are machines engaged in weaving man-made or natural (including mineral) fibres or in the high speed false twisting of fibres; or

(*g*)   the use of, or work wholly or mainly in the immediate vicinity of, machines engaged in cutting, shaping or cleaning metal nails; or

(*h*)   the use of, or work wholly or mainly in the immediate vicinity of, plasma spray guns engaged in the deposition of metal; or

(*j*)   the use of, or work wholly or mainly in the immediate vicinity of, any of the following machines engaged in the working of wood or material composed partly of wood, that is to say: multi-cutter moulding machines. This does not extend to multi-cross cutting machines used for cutting newsprint (R(I)2/ 92), planing machines, automatic or semi-automatic lathes, multiple cross-cut machines, automatic shaping machines, double-end tenoning machines, vertical spindle moulding machines (including high speed routing machines), edge banding machines, bandsawing machines with a blade width of not less than 75 millimetres and circular sawing machines in the operation of which the blade is moved towards the material being cut; or

(*k*)   the use of chain saws in forestry; or

(*l*)   air arc gouging or work wholly or mainly in the immediate vicinity of air arc gouging; or

(*m*)   the use of band saws, circular saws or cutting discs for cutting metal in the metal founding or forging industries, or work wholly or mainly in the immediate vicinity of those tools whilst they are being so used; or (*n*)   the use of circular saws for cutting products in the manufacture of steel, or work wholly or mainly in the immediate vicinity of those tools whilst they are being so used; or

(*o*)   the use of burners or torches for cutting or dressing steel based products, or work wholly or mainly in the immediate vicinity of those tools whilst they are being so used; or

(*p*)   work wholly or mainly in the immediate vicinity of skid transfer banks; or

(*q*)   work wholly or mainly in the immediate vicinity of knock out and shake out grids in foundries; or

(*r*)   mechanical bobbin cleaning or work wholly or mainly in the immediate vicinity of mechanical bobbin cleaning; or

(*s*)   the use of, or work wholly or mainly in the immediate vicinity of, vibrating metal moulding boxes in the concrete products industry; or

(*t*)   the use of, or work wholly or mainly in the immediate vicinity of, high pressure jets of water or a mixture of water and abrasive material in the water jetting industry (including work under water); or

(*u*)   work in ships' engine rooms; or

(*v*)   the use of circular saws for cutting concrete masonry blocks during manufacture, or work wholly or mainly in the immediate vicinity of those tools whilst they are being so used; or

(*w*)   burning stone in quarries by jet channelling processes, or work wholly or mainly in the immediate vicinity of such processes; or

(*x*)   work on gas turbines in connection with:

   (i)   performance testing on test bed,

   (ii)   installation testing of replacement engines in aircraft, and

   (iii)   acceptance testing of Armed Service fixed wing combat planes; or

(*y*)   the use of, or work wholly or mainly in the immediate vicinity of:

   (i)   machines for automatic moulding, automatic blow moulding or automatic glass pressing and forming machines used in the manufacture of glass containers or hollow ware,

   (ii)   spinning machines using compressed air to produce glass wool or mineral wool,

   (iii)   continuous glass toughening furnaces.

[*Social Security (Industrial Injuries) (Prescribed Diseases) Regulations 1985 (SI 1985 No 967); Social Security (Industrial Injuries) (Prescribed Diseases) Amendment No 2 Regulations 1987 (SI 1987 No 2112); Social Security (Industrial Injuries) (Prescribed Diseases) Amendment Regulations 1994 (SI 1994 No 2343); Social Security (Industrial Injuries and Diseases) (Miscellaneous Amendments) Regulations 1996 (SI 1996 No 425)*].

'Any occupation' covers activities in which an employee is engaged under his contract of employment. The fact that the workforce is designated, classified or graded by reference to function, training or skills (e.g. labourer, hot examiner, salvage and forge examiner) does not of itself justify a conclusion that each separate designation, classification or grading involves a separate occupation (*Decision of the Commissioner No R(I) 3/78*).

'Assistance in the use' of tools qualifies the actual *use* of tools, not the process in the course of which tools are employed. Thus, a crane driver who positions bogies to enable riveters to do work on them and then goes away, assists in the process of getting bogies repaired, which requires use of pneumatic tools, but this is not assistance in the actual use of tools, for the purposes of disablement benefit. The position is otherwise when a crane holds a bogie in suspension to enable riveters to work *safely* on them. Here the crane driver assists in the actual *use* of pneumatic percussive tools (*Decision of the Commissioner No R(I) 4/82*).

Conditions under which benefit is payable — 1985 Regulations

N3019   For a claimant to be entitled to disablement benefit for occupational deafness, the following conditions currently apply:

(*a*)   he must have been employed:

    (i)   at any time on or after 5 July 1948, and

    (ii)   for a period or periods amounting (in the aggregate) to at least ten years.

(*b*)   there must be permanent sensorineural hearing loss, and loss in each ear must be at least 50 dB; and

(*c*)   at least loss of 50 dB in one ear must be attributable to noise at work. [*Sch 1, Pt I*].

(There is a presumption that occupational deafness is due to the nature of employment [*1985 Regulations, Reg 4(5)*]);

(*d*)   the claim must be made within five years of the last date when the claimant worked in an occupation prescribed for deafness [*1985 Regulations, Reg 25(2)*];

(*e*)   any assessment of disablement at less than 20% is final [*1985 Regulations, Reg 33*].

A person, whose claim for benefit is turned down because he/she had not worked during the five years before the claim in one of the listed occupations, may claim if he/she continued to work and later met the time conditions. If a claim is turned down as the disability is less than 20 per cent, the claimant must wait three years before re-applying. If, by waiting three years, it would be more than five years since the applicant worked in one of the listed occupations, the three-year limit is waived.

Assessment of disablement benefit for social security purposes

N3020   The extent of disablement is the percentage calculated by:

(*a*)   determining the average total hearing loss due to all causes for each ear at 1, 2 and 3 kHz frequencies; and

(*b*)   determining the percentage degree of disablement for each ear; and then

(*c*)   determining the average percentage degree of binaural disablement.

[*Social Security (Industrial Injuries) (Prescribed Diseases) Amendment Regulations 1989, Reg 4(2)*].

The following chart (Table 1 below) shows the scale for all claims made on/after 3 September 1979.

Table 1

Percentage degree of disablement in relation to hearing loss

Hearing loss	*Percentage degree of disablement*
50–53 dB	20
54–60 dB	30
61–66 dB	40
67–72 dB	50
73–79 dB	60
80–86 dB	70
87–95 dB	80
96–105 dB	90
106 dB or more	100

[*Social Security (Industrial Injuries) (Prescribed Diseases) Regulations 1985, Reg 34, Sch 3 Pt II, as amended*].

Any degree of disablement, due to deafness at work, assessed at less than 20 per cent, must be disregarded for benefit purposes. [*Social Security (Industrial Injuries) (Prescribed Diseases) Amendment Regulations 1990 (SI 1990 No 2269)*].

Action against employer at common law

N3021   There is no separate action for noise at common law; liability comes under the general heading of negligence (see EMPLOYERS' DUTIES TO THEIR EMPLOYEES). Indeed, it was not until as late as 1972 that employers were made liable for deafness negligently caused to employees (*Berry v Stone Manganese Marine Ltd [1972] 1 Lloyd's Rep 182*). Absence of a previous general statutory requirement on employers regarding exposure of employees to noise sometimes led to the law being strained to meet the facts *(Carragher v Singer Manufacturing Co Ltd 1974 SLT (Notes) 28 relating to the Factories Act 1961, s 29*: 'every place of work must, so far as is reasonably practicable, be made and kept safe for any person working there', to the effect that this is wide enough to provide protection against noise). Admittedly, it is proper to regard noise as an aspect of the working environment (*McCafferty v Metropolitan Police District Receiver [1977] 2 AER 756* where an employee, the plaintiff, who was a ballistics expert, suffered ringing in the ears as a result of the sounds of ammunition being fired from different guns in the course of his work. When he complained about ringing in the ears – the ballistics room had no sound-absorbent material on the walls and he had not been supplied with ear protectors – he was advised to use cotton wool, which was useless. It was held that his employer was liable since it was highly foreseeable that the employee would suffer hearing injury if no steps were taken to protect his ears, cotton wool being useless). Moreover, although there are specific statutory requirements to minimise exposure to noise (in agriculture and offshore operations and construction operations, see N3014, N3015 above), these have generated little or no case law.

The main points established at common law are as follows.

(*a*)   As from 1963, the publication date by the (then) Factory Inspectorate of 'Noise and the Worker', employers have been 'on notice' of the dangers to hearing of their employees arising from over-exposure to noise (*McGuinness v Kirkstall Forge Engineering Ltd 1979, unreported*). Hence, consistent with their common law duty to take reasonable care for the health and safety of their employees, employers should 'provide and maintain' a sufficient stock of ear muffs.

This was confirmed in *Thompson v Smiths, etc.* (see (*d*) below). However, more recently, an employer was held liable for an employee's noise-induced deafness, even though the latter's exposure to noise, working in shipbuilding, had occurred *entirely before* 1963. The grounds were that the employer had done virtually nothing to combat the *known* noise hazard from 1954–1963 (apart from making earplugs available) (*Baxter v Harland & Wolff plc, Northern Ireland Court of Appeal 1990 (unreported)*).

This means that, as far as Northern Ireland is concerned, employers are liable at common law for noise-induced deafness as from 1 January 1954 – the earliest actionable date. Limitation statutes preclude employees suing prior to that date (*Arnold v Central Electricity Generating Board [1988] AC 228*).

(*b*)   Because the true nature of deafness as a disability has not always been appreciated, damages have traditionally not been high (*Berry v Stone Manganese Marine Ltd [1972]* – £2,500 (halved because of time limitation obstacles); *Heslop v Metalock (Great Britain) Ltd (1981)* –£7,750; *O'Shea v Kimberley-Clark Ltd (1982)* – £7,490 (tinnitus); *Tripp v Ministry of Defence [1982] CLY 1017* – £7,500).

(*c*)   Damages will be awarded for exposure to noise, even though the resultant deafness is not great, as in tinnitus (*O'Shea v Kimberley-Clark Ltd, The Guardian, 8 October 1982*).

(*d*)   Originally the last employer of a succession of employers (for whom an employee had worked in noisy occupations) was exclusively liable for damages for deafness, even though damage (i.e. actual hearing loss) occurs in the early years of exposure (for which earlier employers would have been responsible) (*Heslop v Metalock (Great Britain) Ltd, The Observer, 29 November 1981*). More recently, however, the tendency is to *apportion* liability between offending employers (*Thompson, Gray, Nicholson v Smiths Ship Repairers (North Shields) Ltd; Blacklock, Waggott v Swan Hunter Shipbuilders Ltd; Mitchell v Vickers Armstrong Ltd [1984] IRLR 93*). This is patently fairer because some blame is then shared by the original employer(s), whose negligence would have been responsible for the actual hearing loss.

(*e*)   Because of the current tendency to apportion liability, even in the case of pre-1963 employers (see *McGuinness v Kirkstall Forge Engineering Ltd* above), contribution will take place between earlier and later insurers.

(*f*)   Although judges are generally reluctant to be swayed by scientific/statistical evidence, the trio of shipbuilding cases (see (*d*) above) demonstrates, at least in the case of occupational deafness, that this trend is being reversed (see Table 2 below, the 'Coles-Worgan classification'); in particular, it is relevant to consider the 'dose response' relationship published by the National Physical Laboratory (NPL), which relates long-term continuous noise exposure to expected resultant hearing loss. This graph always shows a rapid increase in the early years of noise exposure, followed by a trailing off (see N3022 below, 'Relevance of Coles-Worgan scale').

(*g*)   Current judicial wisdom identifies three separate evolutionary aspects of deafness, i.e. (i) hearing loss (measured in decibels at various frequencies); (ii) disability (i.e. difficulty/inability to receive everyday sounds); (iii) social handicap (attending musical concerts/meetings etc.). That social handicap is a genuine basis on which damages can be (*inter alia*) awarded, was reaffirmed in the case of *Bixby, Case, Fry and Elliott v Ford Motor Group (1990, unreported)*.

Relevance of Coles-Worgan scale

N3022   The Coles-Worgan scale (see Table 2 below) was used to assess disability in the trio of shipbuilding cases; this gives a better assessment of disability than reference to hearing loss alone. This scale takes account of hearing loss at 0.5, 1.0, 2.0 and 4.0 kHz and also clinical symptoms, the subject being assigned to one of ten classes or 'groups' of increasing severity, e.g. 'slight', 'moderate' etc. (0.5, 1.0, 2.0 and 4.0 kHz are the denoted 'frequencies of interest' from a hearing loss point of view. These cover the range of frequencies of principal importance to speech intelligibility and are, therefore, significant in any assessment by audiometry of hearing loss).

Table 2

The Coles-Worgan classification for occupational deafness

Group O	—	No significant auditory handicap.
Group I	—	The hearing is not sufficiently impaired to affect the perception of speech, except for a slight (additional to normal) difficulty in noisy backgrounds.
Groups II & III	—	Slight (II) and moderate (III) difficulty whenever listening to faint speech, but would usually understand normal speech. The subject would also have distinctly greater difficulty when trying to understand speech against a background of noise.
Groups IV & V	—	Frequent difficulty with normal speech and would sometimes (IV) or often (V) have to ask people to 'speak up' in order to hear them, even in face-to-face conversation. Great (IV) or very great (V) difficulty in a background of noise.
Group VI	—	Marked difficulties in communication since he would sometimes be unable to clearly understand even loud speech. In noise the subject would find it impossible to distinguish speech.
Groups VII & VIII	—	Would only understand shouted or amplified speech, and then only moderately well (VII) or poorly (VIII).
Group IX	—	Minimal speech intelligibility even with well-amplified speech.
Group X	—	Virtually totally deaf with respect to the understanding of speech.

General guidance on noise at work

Guidance on the Noise at Work Regulations 1989

N3023   The Health and Safety Executive publishes a series of Noise Guides on the *Noise at Work Regulations*. Volume 1 (Guides 1 and 2) deals with legal duties, whilst Volume 2 (Guides 3 to 8) covers noise assessment, information and control.

Guidance on specific working environments

N3024   Certain working environments carry particular difficulties in the assessment and control of noise exposure, mainly because of the variability of the noise levels and the length of exposure.

The following specific guidance may be of assistance:

— *A Guide to Reducing the Exposure of Construction Workers to Noise*. R A Waller, Construction Industry Research and Information Association. CIRIA Report 120, 1990.

— *Offshore Installations: Guidance on design and construction, Part II, Section 5*. Department of Energy, 1977.

— *Guide to Health, Safety and Welfare at Pop Concerts and Similar Events*. Health and Safety Commission, Home Office and the Scottish Office. HMSO, 1993.

Ear protection

N3025   There are many types of ear protection, falling into two main categories: (i) ear muffs which fit over and surround the ears, and which seal to the head by cushions filled with soft plastic foam or a viscous liquid; and (ii) ear plugs, which fit into the ear canal. Ear protectors will only be effective if they are in good condition, suit the individual and are worn properly. All ear protectors can be uncomfortable, especially if they press too firmly on the head or ear canal, or cause too much sweating. Individuals differ greatly in their preference, and wherever possible the employer should select more than one type of suitable protector and offer the user a personal choice. British Standard BS EN 458: 1994 gives guidance and recommendations for the selection, use, care and maintenance of hearing protectors.

Sound systems for emergency purposes

N3026   Voice messages can be superior to bells or sirens to convey warnings and instructions in emergencies. However, these must be properly audible in noisy places. British Standard BS 7443: 1991 gives specifications for sound systems for emergency purposes.

PART B: Effects of Vibration on People

Introduction

N3027   The effects of vibration on people can be divided into three broad classes:

— people in buildings;

— people in vehicles, etc., and industrial situations;

— hand-arm vibration on people operating certain tools or machines.

The four principal effects of whole-body vibration are considered to be:

(*a*)   degraded health;

(*b*)   impaired ability to perform activities;

(*c*)   impaired comfort;

(*d*)   motion sickness;

Exposure to whole-body vibration causes a complex distribution of oscillatory motions and forces within the body. These may cause unpleasant sensations giving rise to discomfort or annoyance, result in impaired performance (e.g. loss of balance, degraded vision) or present a health risk (e.g. tissue damage or deleterious physiological change). However, there is little evidence that vibration directly affects thought processes. Many factors influence human response to vibration, including the type and direction of vibration and the type of person involved. The present state of knowledge does not permit a definitive dose-effect relationship between whole-body vibration and injury or health.

People can overcome moderate effects of vibration on task performance by making greater effort, and this may initially improve performance, although at the cost of greater fatigue, with ultimate degradation of performance.

Effects on comfort depend greatly on the circumstances, for example whether the person expects to be able to read or write in the prevailing conditions.

Low frequency oscillation of the body can cause the motion sickness syndrome (kinetosis) characterised principally by pallor, sweating, nausea and vomiting.

Buildings and structures

N3028   Vibration can affect buildings and structures, but a detailed treatment of this is beyond the scope of the present chapter. People are more sensitive to vibration than buildings or structures, so vibration within a building is likely to become unacceptable to the occupants at values well below those which pose a threat to a structurally sound building. For detailed technical guidance on the measurement and evaluation of the effects of vibration on buildings, British Standard BS 7385: Part 1: 1990 [ISO 4866: 1990] and BS 7385: Part 2: 1993 may be consulted.

Vibration measurement

Measurement units

N3029   Vibration is the oscillatory motion of an object about a given position. The rate at which the object vibrates (i.e. the number of complete oscillations per second) is called the frequency of the vibration and is measured in Hertz (Hz). The frequency range of principal interest in vibration is from about 0.5 Hz to 100 Hz, i.e. below the range of principal interest in noise control.

The magnitude of the vibration is now generally measured in terms of the acceleration of the object, in metres per second squared (i.e. metres per second, per second) denoted m.s-2 or m/s2. However, vibration magnitude can also be measured in terms of peak particle velocity, in metres per second (denoted m.s-1 or m/s), or in terms of maximum displacement (in metres or millimetres).

For simple vibratory motion, it is possible to convert a measurement made in any one of these terms to either of the other terms, provided the frequency of the vibration is known, so the choice of measurement term is to some extent arbitrary. However, *acceleration* is now the preferred measurement term because modern electronic instruments generally employ an *accelerometer* to detect the vibration. As the name suggests, this responds to the acceleration of the vibrating object and hence this characteristic can be measured directly.

Direction and frequency

N3030   The human body has different sensitivity to vibration in the head to foot direction, the side to side direction, and in the front to back direction, and this sensitivity varies according to whether the person is standing, sitting or lying down. In order to assess the effect of vibration, it is necessary to measure its characteristics in each of the three directions and to take account of the recipient's posture. The sensitivity to vibration is also highly frequency-dependent. BS 6841: 1987 'Measurement and evaluation of human exposure to whole-body mechanical vibration and repeated shock' provides a set of six frequency-weighting curves for use in a variety of situations. The curves may be considered analogous to the 'A'-weighting used for noise measurement. However, few instruments have these weightings built into them.

Vibration dose value

N3031   In most situations, vibration magnitudes do not remain constant, and the concept of vibration dose value (VDV) has been developed to deal with such cases. This is analogous to the concept of noise dose used in the *Noise at Work Regulations*. Again, few instruments are capable of measuring VDV. Taken with the frequency-weighting system, it is possible to introduce a single-number vibration rating, but the present state of research falls short of providing limit values in definitive terms. However, vibration dose values in the region of 15 m.s-1.75 will usually cause severe discomfort, and increased exposure to vibration can be expected to increase the risk of injury.

Structural vibration of buildings can be felt by the occupants at low vibration magnitudes. It can affect their comfort, quality of life and working efficiency. Low levels of vibration may provoke adverse comments, but certain types of highly sensitive equipment (e.g. electron microscopes) or delicate tasks may require even more stringent criteria.

Adverse comment regarding vibration is likely when the vibration magnitude is only slightly in excess of the threshold of perception and, in general, criteria for the acceptability of vibration in buildings are dependent on the degree of adverse comment rather than other considerations such as short-term health hazard or working efficiency.

Vibration levels greater than the usual threshold may be tolerable for temporary or infrequent events of short duration, especially when the risk of a startle effect is reduced by a warning signal and a proper programme of public information.

Detailed guidance on this subject may be found in British Standard BS 6472: 1992 'Evaluation of human exposure to vibration in buildings (1 Hz to 80 Hz)'.

Hand-arm vibration

N3032   Intensive vibration can be transmitted to the hands and arms of operators from vibrating tools, machinery or workpieces. Examples include the use of pneumatic, electric, hydraulic or engine-driven chain-saws, percussive tools or grinders. The vibration may affect one or both arms, and may be transmitted through the hand and arm to the shoulder.

The vibration may be a source of discomfort, and possibly reduced proficiency. Habitual exposure to hand-arm vibration has been found to be linked with various diseases affecting the blood vessels, nerves, bones, joints, muscles and connective tissues of the hand and forearm.

Vibration-induced white finger (VWF)

N3033 Extensive and prolonged exposure to hand-arm vibration can give rise to the condition known as 'vibration white finger' (VWF), which arises from progressive loss of blood circulation in the hand and fingers, sometimes resulting in necrosis (death of tissue) and gangrene for which the only solution may be amputation of the affected areas or complete hand. Initial signs are mild tingling and numbness of the fingers. Further exposure results in blanching of the fingers, particularly in cold weather and early in the morning. The condition is progressive to the base of the fingers, sensitivity to attacks is reduced and the fingers take on a blue-black appearance. The development of the condition may take up to five years according to the degree of exposure to vibration and the duration of such exposure.

Since its recent addition as a prescribed occupational disease, VWF has grown rapidly to become the largest single category of disease to date for benefit purposes. Many of these claims will probably be a first step in suing employers at common law.

VWF is prescribed occupational disease A11. It is described as: 'episodic blanching, occurring throughout the year, affecting the middle or proximate phalanges or in the case of a thumb the proximal phalanx, of:

(*a*) in the case of a person with five fingers (including thumb) on one hand, any three of those fingers;

(*b*) in the case of a person with only four such fingers, any two of those fingers; or

(*c*) in the case of a person with less than four such fingers, any one of those fingers or . . . the remaining one finger.'

[*Social Security (Industrial Injuries) (Prescribed Diseases) Regulations 1985*].

VWF is also actionable at common law against the employer (*Heal v Garringtons Ltd (1984) unreported*; *McFaul v Garringtons Ltd (1985) HSIB 113*). Damages are awarded according to the stage of the disease at the time of the action from the date the employer should have known of the risk.

With regard to the issue of the time when an award for damages should begin for vibration white finger (VWF) the recent case of *Armstrong v British Coal (unreported)*, has established that damages are awarded according to the stage of the disease at the time of the action, from the date that the employer should have known of the risk to his employees, to the current day. The case established that for the mining industry, the relevant time was 1 January 1973.

Foreseeably, prescription may extend to hand arm vibration syndrome (HAVS) instead of vibration white finger (VWF). The former would cover recognised neurological effects as well as the currently recognised vascular effects of vibration. Neurological effects will include numbness, tingling in the fingers and reduced sensibility. Moreover, the current list of occupations, for which VWF is prescribed, may be replaced by a comprehensive list of tools/rigid materials against which such tools are held, including:

(*a*) percussive metal-working tools (e.g. fettling tools, riveting tools, drilling tools, pneumatic hammers, impact screwdrivers);

(*b*)   grinders/rotary tools;

(*c*)   stone working, mining, road construction and road repair tools;

(*d*)   forest, garden and wood-working machinery (e.g. chain saws, electrical screwdrivers, mowers/shears, hedge trimmers, circular saws); and

(*e*)   miscellaneous process tools (e.g. drain suction machines, jigsaws, pounding-up machines, vibratory rollers, concrete levelling vibratibles).

(Cm 2844).

Vibratory hand tools

N3034   The energy level of the hand tool is significant. Percussive action tools, such as compressed air pneumatic hammers, operate within a frequency range of 33–50 Hz. These cause considerable damage whereas rotary hand tools, which operate within the frequency range 40–125 Hz, are less dangerous.

Use, either frequent or intermittent, of hand-held vibratory tools, can result in injury to the wrist. Carpal tunnel syndrome arising in this way is now prescribed occupational disease A12. [*Social Security (Industrial Injuries) (Prescribed Diseases) Amendment Regulations 1993 (SI 1993 No 862), Reg 6(2)*].

Personal protection against hand-arm vibration

N3035   There is no adequate personal protective equipment presently available against hand-arm vibration. Wearing gloves may help, but mainly by keeping hands warm and protecting against injury. 'Anti-vibration' gloves are not generally effective in reducing vibration exposure, and can even increase it. Their bulk may also reduce the ability of workers to control the equipment.

Workers can reduce the risk by keeping the blood flowing while working, for example by keeping warm whilst working, not smoking especially whilst working, and exercising hands and fingers. Tools should be designed for the job, both to lessen vibration and to reduce the strength of grip and amount of force needed. The equipment should be used in short bursts rather than long sessions. Symptoms should not be ignored. Vibration white finger is reportable under the *Reporting of Injuries, Diseases and Dangerous Occurrences Regulations 1995 (RIDDOR)*. The Health and Safety Executive publishes a full guide on *Hand-arm vibration*, HS(G)88, (1994), together with leaflets for employers and employees.

Proposed EC directive physical agents at work

N3036   In early 1993, the European Commission published its proposal for a Directive (ref 93/077/02) on the protection of workers from exposure to physical agents, covering noise, vibration and non-ionising radiation, which would replace the current EC directive on worker noise exposure. Following comments from member states and the European parliament, revised proposals were published in April 1994 (ref 94/C230/03).

For *noise*, this would set 75 dB(A) daily personal exposure as the threshold at which workers should be informed of risks, 80 dB(A) as the level at which personal ear defenders would need to be provided, and 85 dB(A) as the level at which a programme of noise control would need to be established. 90 dB(A) would be the level at which ear defenders must be used, and 105 dB(A) the level at which noisy activities must be declared to the responsible authority.

For *hand-arm vibration*, the threshold would be a daily personal exposure of 1 m/s2, at which workers are to be told of the risks; at 2.5 m/s2, assessments become mandatory; at 5 m/s2 systematic health surveillance would be required; 10 m/s2 is permissible 'for a few minutes', but efforts must be made to reduce the level of vibration, and sufficient work breaks introduced to bring down the average level. Where the daily personal dose would exceed 20 m/s2, the offending equipment must be marked and the activities declared to the responsible authority.

For *whole-body vibration*, the threshold would be a daily personal exposure of 0.25 m/s2, at which workers are to be told of the risks; at 0.5 m/s2 (or at 1.25 m/s2 for a one-hour average), a regime of vibration control strategies would be required; at 0.7 m/s2, health surveillance would be required, and at 1.25 m/s2 daily personal exposure, offending work activities must be notified.

The proposals are accompanied by a number of new administrative requirements. The revised proposals have been resisted as unnecessarily bureaucratic and have not yet progressed further.

Occupational Health and Diseases

Introduction

O1001   'Occupational disease' is a label commonly used, but one which tends to hide the more complex causes of disease. There are nearly 70 prescribed occupational diseases or conditions recognised under the *Social Security (Industrial Injuries) (Prescribed Diseases) Regulations 1985* (as amended) for which benefit may be claimed, subject to certain qualifications. There are also many other conditions which may have an occupational cause and which are not on the prescribed list. However, many of these conditions may have non-occupational causes: for example, lung cancer may be caused from underground work in a coal mine but is more commonly caused by cigarette smoking. Some conditions may have more than one cause: for example, hearing loss in the inner ear may be due to prolonged exposure to excessive noise, but may additionally be due to the effects of ageing (presbyacusis). Some conditions may have a non-occupational origin which is then exacerbated by work. Establishing occupational causation is therefore a complicated exercise that involves the careful elimination of other possible causes.

The compensation factor cannot be overlooked as the confirmation of an occupational cause often opens the door to a possible claim for benefit from the Department of Social Security or for civil liability for an employer or other negligent party (usually through an insurer). Those who suffer from a non-occupational condition will usually visit their GP or hospital in the first instance, but those who believe there is an occupational cause will usually first consult their trade union or a solicitor before seeking medical advice. This different emphasis is important as those who examine the compensation seeker should always have regard to the motive behind the consultation.

Diagnosis of some occupational diseases is difficult: in some cases there are no universally recognised clinical tests and the examiner must rely on the subjective history provided by the patient. For example, in the earlier stages of vibration white finger, the symptoms may be transient and not present at the time of the examination.

The extent of occupational disease in the United Kingdom is unknown. It certainly runs into millions of sufferers but numbers depend on the extent of reporting, the gathering of this information and in some cases, the accuracy of the diagnosis. Department of Social Security statistics suggest that there are at present about 60,000 new claims each year, but this is only the tip of the iceberg as many do not qualify for benefit. Insurance statistics of civil claims made may be a more reliable indicator but reporting is spasmodic and there may be overlap where one person is claiming damages from several parties.

Occupational diseases are widespread amongst those who have worked in hazardous industries such as mining, construction and certain heavy industries. But there is now an increasing amount of 'white collar' disease: the widespread use of visual display units has brought potential risks of musculo-skeletal disorders and eyesight problems. Increasing work pressures may lead to stress although the causes of this condition may include other factors. There is also a shift in emphasis of the legislation. Most of the previous legislation based on the *Factories Act 1961* and the *Offices, Shops and Railway Premises Act 1963*, together with detailed regulations applying to specific trades and processes, has now been repealed and replaced by new legislation which is more widely based and which applies generally to people 'at work'. The first radical change was the *Health and Safety at Work etc. Act 1974 (HSWA)*, but subsequent legislation has been due mainly to the implementation of various EU health and safety at work Directives.

It seems likely that occupational disease will be more common in areas of former heavy industry although it is difficult to generalise. Some national companies carrying out similar operations at different locations may find that one location has a much higher incidence of occupational disease reporting than the others. This may be due partly to the culture within the local community or in the workplace itself but the desire for compensation, and the extent to which it is encouraged should not be overlooked. Employers often find a greater incidence of disease reporting by workers who are being made redundant or where a factory is to close completely.

Some conditions, like dermatitis, are known as short-tail diseases because the symptoms often become manifest within a short period of time from the relevant exposure. Others, like asbestos-related diseases, are long-tail as the symptoms may not arise for many years after the relevant exposure; one particular asbestos disease, mesothelioma, may not become manifest until 40 or 50 years later. This means that there could be generations of workers whose exposure ceased in the 1960s and 1970s but whose symptoms may not appear until the first part of the 21st century. When such conditions do arise, investigation of exposure will be exceedingly difficult with the passage of time. One should also remember that some diseases are suffered by those who do not have direct contact. This so-called 'neighbourhood exposure' could affect others working nearby, those washing a worker's dusty overalls or, as in one case, even children playing in a dusty factory yard. Noise exposure may also cause neighbourhood problems as it may affect not only the user of the noisy equipment but others in the vicinity, or perhaps those who are unfortunate enough to live close to a noisy workplace.

Many diseases are incurable although there may be treatment that alleviates the symptoms. The progression of some diseases may be halted by prompt intervention, but the removal of the worker from the harmful exposure is often necessary and this may mean the loss of a job or the transfer to lower-paid work. Regrettably, some diseases, especially lung conditions, are often fatal. Mesothelioma is invariably so. Most long-tail diseases are caused by past neglect of proper preventative action, even when viewed in the light of knowledge at the time. But strict observance of current legislation and codes of practice should go a long way to ensure that the present epidemic of occupational disease does not continue.

Long-tail diseases

O1002   Most of these diseases originate from the former manufacturing industries and, because of the latent period between the first exposure and the onset of the condition, we are now faced with the legacy of those workers who are suffering because of past neglect. Many of these workers are no longer in the jobs where their exposure occurred and many of their former workplaces have either closed or have been drastically changed. This makes investigation into the cause of the disease somewhat difficult.

Health and safety legislation in the 1990s should help to eradicate many of the old problems that were the root cause of these conditions but it would be naïve to think that no-one remains at risk from some form of hazard. There are also those working today who are already suffering from one or more of these diseases due to past exposures, so it is essential that any present employer is made aware of their pre-existing problems and takes adequate steps to prevent further harm.

Three typical long-tail diseases have been selected for detailed comment:

— asbestos-related diseases;

— noise-induced hearing loss (NIHL); and

— vibration white finger (VWF).

Asbestos-related diseases

O1003   Asbestos is a name given to a group of minerals whose common feature is their fibrous nature. It is found in rock fissures in certain parts of the world, including Canada and southern Africa. It is a very versatile mineral which, when broken down into fibres, may be spun, woven and incorporated into many compounds. There are three main kinds of asbestos:

(*a*)   *Chrysotile (white)*. This, the most commonly used, has strong, silky, flexible fibres which are easily used in the making of asbestos textiles.

(*b*)   *Crocidolite (blue)*. This has brittle fibres with high tensile strength which are highly resistant to chemicals and sea water.

(*c*)   *Amosite (brown)*. This has long, fairly strong fibres with good insulation properties.

It was commonly believed that blue asbestos was the most dangerous of the three types because of its fibre length and diameter, but all three types should be regarded as being dangerous to health because of their indestructible nature. The fibres have the propensity to penetrate all the body's natural defence mechanisms and to lodge permanently in the lungs.

The use of asbestos grew considerably through the first part of the 20th century and probably reached a peak in the 1960s and early 1970s. Its uses are many and varied and include:

(*a*)   manufacture of asbestos textiles;

(*b*)   thermal insulation (lagging), especially in shipyards and power stations;

(*c*)   electrical insulation;

(*d*)   clutch and brake linings;

(*e*)   asbestos cement products (like roofing sheets and pipework).

Dockers who unloaded sacks of raw asbestos may also have been exposed, and there is an ongoing problem with situations where asbestos lagging has to be removed.

From the early part of the 20th century, some of the health problems associated with asbestos were beginning to become apparent. The first statutory controls were contained in the *Asbestos Industry Regulations 1931* but this legislation was limited to the asbestos manufacturing processes. After World War II it was suspected that certain groups of shipyard workers may have been at risk and some asbestos controls were incorporated in the *Shipbuilding and Ship-repairing Regulations 1960*. There were also more general requirements in the *Factories Acts of 1937 and 1961* relating to ventilation and the removal of dust. It is probably fair to say that most of these statutory requirements went unheeded by the majority of employers until the mid-to late 1960s, when the extent of the asbestos problem began to be fully realised.

Firstly, an investigation into conditions in a mining area of South Africa, published in 1960 found a high incidence of a rare cancer, mesothelioma, amongst those who lived and worked there. Secondly, an investigation in 1965 discovered a high incidence of this disease in the London area. Public concern grew and the *Asbestos Regulations 1970* (of much wider application than the 1931 Regulations), were introduced. Further stringent measures have since been taken, culminating in the *Control of Asbestos at Work Regulations 1987* and the *Asbestos (Licensing) Regulations 1983* (amendments to both regulations have been made which came into force in 1999) and the *Asbestos (Prohibitions) Regulations 1992*.

The conditions which may arise from asbestos exposure are:

—   mesothelioma;

—   asbestosis;

—   bronchial carcinoma (lung cancer);

—   diffuse pleural thickening; and

—   pleural plaques.

Mesothelioma

O1004   This is a cancer of the of the pleura, a thin lining which surrounds the lungs. Sometimes it may also affect the peritoneum, the lining of the abdominal cavity. It is believed that only a relatively small degree of exposure is necessary for the disease to be initiated. Blue asbestos is thought to be the culprit but other types cannot be excluded.

As mentioned earlier, there is usually an extremely long latent period between exposure and onset during which time the cells are slowly multiplying but remain undetected. Patients may first suffer chest pains and breathlessness and begin to lose weight, but by the time the condition is diagnosed, it is too late. Progression is rapid, the cancer invades the lungs and the condition becomes extremely painful and distressing. This type of cancer does not respond to treatment or surgical intervention and most patients die within 12 to 18 months of the initial diagnosis. Mesothelioma is quite rare in the normal population, so where there is a history of asbestos exposure, causation is seldom in dispute. The condition may be detected on X-ray or CT scan.

Because the uses of asbestos peaked in the 1960s and 1970s and because the latency period is typically 40 to 50 years, the incidence of mesothelioma is likely to peak in the first quarter of the 21st century.

Asbestosis

O1005   This is a type of scarring or fibrosis of the lungs which is caused by asbestos bodies penetrating through to the alveoli, the tiny vessels at the end of the airways where oxygen is taken into the bloodstream and carbon dioxide removed. The lung's defences cause the fibrosis to occur and this gradually spreads so as to block the actions of the alveoli. Unlike mesothelioma, asbestosis is a dose-related condition: it is believed that causation depends upon a significant degree of exposure over several year for it to take hold, and the severity of the disease may be related to the extent of the exposure and the period of time over which the exposure takes place. The latency period is thought to be at least ten years from first exposure.

Symptoms may include breathlessness on exertion, crackling sounds in the base of the lungs and finger clubbing. The fibrosis may sometimes be seen on X-ray or CT scan and a lung function test may reveal reduced gas transfer. Asbestosis is not invariably fatal but may cause severe respiratory disability. Complications, particularly lung cancer, may arise which will have a significant effect on life expectancy.

Lung cancer

O1006 This disease is of course widely associated with cigarette smoking but it is believed that it can arise directly as a result of asbestos exposure in non-smokers. However, where there is a combination of cigarette smoking and asbestos exposure, the likelihood of lung cancer developing is extremely high.

Diffuse pleural thickening

O1007 This is a fairly uncommon condition where asbestos bodies cause a thickening of the lining of the pleura, resulting in breathlessness. Unlike mesothelioma, it is a benign condition but those suffering from it could develop the malignant condition at a later stage.

Pleural plaques

O1008 These are small areas of fibrous thickening on the walls of the pleura which usually cause no respiratory disability but which may be detected on X-ray examination. They are probably an indication that the individual has had asbestos exposure.

Although there is no disability, the patient who is told about the finding may be understandably anxious about the future. In a small percentage of cases the condition may progress into one of the disabling conditions listed above. For this reason, those who have been advised that they have pleural plaques may seek an award of provisional damages for their anxiety from those responsible for the exposure, with a proviso that they may return to the court for a more substantial award at a later date if they succumb to one of the more serious conditions.

Civil liability

O1009 There are seldom many disputes about the issues of liability to the individual claimant. If there had been exposure and if the *Factories Acts* applied, the stringent requirements of the sections relating to ventilation and the removal of dust would be difficult for most employers to defend. The greater problem arises where there is more than one defendant and in trying to establish how much each is going to pay. Some insurers are parties to sharing arrangements that help to resolve this issue speedily. Because of the latent period it is usually accepted that any exposure that took place within the last ten years before the disease was diagnosed is not relevant.

Damages for asbestos-related diseases vary considerably. Readers should refer to the current edition of the *Judicial Studies Board Guidelines* under the section on lung disease for assistance on general damages for pain, suffering and loss of amenity. However where there is a respiratory disability, those who are of working age are likely to have substantial claims for lost earnings. They may also require considerable care and assistance as the disease progresses. Sadly, those who suffer from mesothelioma may not live to receive their settlement and the claim will then be pursued by the estate and/or the dependants.

Noise-induced hearing loss (NIHL)

O1010 The condition is more commonly called 'occupational deafness' but NIHL is now a more acceptable term because the word 'deafness' implies almost total loss of hearing whereas noise exposure at work causes only a partial hearing loss.

The consensus view is that NIHL is the most common occupational disease. Although no reliable figures are available, it is believed that at least two million workers in the UK may have been exposed to excessive noise for at least a significant period of their employment. The DSS statistics are of little assistance because the benefit is not paid until the claimant has a high level of hearing loss. Although the disease was extremely common in the traditional heavy industries, like shipbuilding, boiler-making, steel manufacture and mining, most factories have some noisy areas and there are many parts of the service industry where workers are at risk.

Noise

O1011   Noise is simply unwanted sound. This is sometimes subjective: a rock band may give one person much pleasure but cause annoyance to another. However, it is generally accepted that excessive noise at work is not only unwanted but potentially harmful.

There are three important factors when considering the effects of noise:

— intensity (or loudness);

— frequency (or pitch); and

— daily dose (or duration of exposure).

Intensity

The louder the sound, the greater the likelihood of hearing damage. The range of intensity levels which may be heard by the human ear varies enormously from the slightest whisper to the sound of a jet engine on take-off. The latter may be 100 million, million (10^{14}) times as loud as the former so a logarithmic scale, known as the decibel (dB) scale, is used to simplify the numbering of the ratios. 0 dB is the threshold of normal hearing, 140 dB would be the sound of a jet engine, whereas factory noise or a heavy goods vehicle would be typically in the 80 to 90 dB range. As the scale is logarithmic, the following examples should be noted:

(a)   90dB is ten times as loud as 80dB.

(b)   ± 1dB represents an increase/decrease of 1.26 (100.1) in the intensity level.

(c)   93 dB is twice as loud as 90dB (3dB = 1.263).

(d)   96 dB is four times as loud as 90dB.

(e)   87dB is half as loud as 90dB.

Noise intensity levels may be measured in the workplace by a noise level meter. Personal dose meters may also be used to assess an individual's noise dose over a period of time.

Frequency

Sounds may occur at various frequencies which range from a low rumble to a high-pitched whine or whistle. The human ear responds differently to sounds of the same intensity but at different frequencies – some high frequency sounds will appear to be louder. Frequencies are banded together in octaves (like the notes on a piano) but when measuring the effects of noise at work, it is usual to average out the bands and to apply a weighting factor which allows for the differing responses of the ear. This is known as the A-weighted scale and a measurement of intensity would be expressed as 90 dB(A), for example.

Frequencies are usually measured at their octave band centres. The unit of measurement is the Hertz (Hz). 1 Hz = 1 cycle per second; 1000Hz = 1 kiloHertz (1 kHz). The range of hearing in a normal healthy young adult is between about 20 Hz and 20 kHz but the range for the understanding of most speech is between about 1 and 3 kHz.

Daily dose

The risk of hearing damage from noise at work is dose related. The unprotected ear may be exposed to a moderately loud noise for a short period of time without harm but if the exposure continues for several hours, there may be a risk of temporary hearing loss. If this daily pattern of exposure continues over a number of years, the temporary hearing loss will inevitably become permanent. The UK control standard is based on daily personal exposure to noise over an 8 hour working day (LEP,d.).

Control measures

O1012   The first official attempt at assessing the risk to hearing from noise at work and advising on preventative steps was a booklet called *'Noise and the worker'*, published by the Ministry of Labour in 1963. The booklet advised employers to measure noise levels and, if they exceeded a level which would now be expressed at approximately 89 dB(A), to take preventative measures. This would include the issue of personal hearing protection, which by that time was reasonably effective in attenuating high noise levels. *'Noise and the worker'* was followed by more detailed and updated guidance in a Code of Practice, published in 1972 by the Department of Employment.

With a few minor exceptions, there was no specific legislation aimed at noise control at work until the *Noise at Work Regulations 1989* (implementing an EU noise at work Directive) were introduced. These regulations had the following main objectives:

(*a*)   general duty to reduce the risk of hearing damage to the lowest level reasonably practicable;

(*b*)   assessments of noise exposure to be made;

(*c*)   reduce noise exposure as far as reasonably practicable;

(*d*)   provision of information to workers;

(*e*)   two main action levels at or above 85 dB(A) and 90 dB(A):

  (i)   at the first level (85), ear protection must be provided to workers on request;

  (ii)   at the second level (90), the protection must be issued to all those exposed and ear protection zones established where all those entering must wear protection.

Damage to hearing by noise

O1013   The human ear is divided into three sections:

(*a*)   the outer ear, which extends along the ear canal to the ear drum;

(*b*)   the middle ear, containing a set of three bones, the ossicles, which link the ear drum to the inner ear; and

(*c*)   the inner ear which contains the cochlea, the organ of hearing.

The cochlea is connected to the brain by the auditory nerve. Inside the cochlea are receptor cells which have hair-like tufts and groups of these cells respond to different frequency ranges. Continuous exposure to loud noise will tend to permanently damage these cells so that the efficiency of the hearing organ is gradually diminished.

The cells which respond to the high frequency ranges are situated close to the oval window in the cochlea, a membrane which connects the cochlea to the ossicles in the middle ear. These cells tend to suffer from the greatest damage by noise and those exposed typically have their greatest hearing loss at or about the 4 kHz frequency. The effect of this is that they have difficulty in distinguishing the high-pitched consonant sounds like sh, th, p etc, especially in crowded places where there others are talking. They may also have problems hearing the doorbell or telephone ringing.

Other typical indicators of NIHL are:

(*a*)   it causes damage only to the inner ear (sensori-neural loss);

(*b*)   it is in both ears (bilateral);

(*c*)   the extent of the loss is about the same in each ear (symmetrical); and

(*d*)   it develops gradually over a period of years of exposure to high noise levels.

There are many other causes of hearing loss, some of which, like presbyacusis (senile deafness) also affect the inner ear. Correct diagnosis will involve the consideration of all the other possible causes. The most common method of measuring hearing loss is by pure tone audiometry, whereby tones are delivered to the subject through an earphone and responses are recorded on a graph. The object is to establish the threshold of hearing for a given frequency, this threshold being measured in dB (i.e. the intensity level at which the subject begins to hear the sound). An audiogram of a typical NIHL subject will show that the hearing threshold is greatest at or around the 4 kHz frequency and this will be shown by a dip or notch in the graph.

Tinnitus

O1014   This is a symptom which consists of a sensation of noises in the ear without external stimulus. Typically, it consists of ringing noises but whistling, buzzing, roaring or clicking sounds are reported by some. Its cause is not well established but it can arise in connection with several conditions of the inner ear, including NIHL but also with presbyacusis and Meniëre's disease, for example.

The effect of tinnitus varies enormously from mild to very severe. Most people have experienced a ringing sensation from time to time, for example after visiting a disco or perhaps during a respiratory infection. These transient symptoms cause few problems, but there are some who suffer from continuous, loud noises in the ear which often disturb sleep, and in rare cases, may even cause them to become suicidal.

Civil liability

O1015   As with asbestos claims, the investigation of noise exposure is often difficult to investigate because of the passage of time. Some employers may have done noise surveys in the past, but these frequently provide only a snapshot of conditions at a particular time, and it is often argued by claimants that these surveys are unrepresentative. Defendants also have the problem of co-ordinating the claim where there are multiple defendants.

Because specific statutory control only started in 1990, many NIHL claims are based on common law. In this context, the actions of a reasonable and prudent employer in the light of current knowledge and invention is relevant (following *Stokes v GKN [1968] 1 WLR 1776*). The so-called guilty knowledge began, for most defendants, only in 1963 when *'Noise and the Worker'* was first published, so, where there was pre-1963 exposure, liability and damages should be apportioned between the 'innocent' and 'guilty' periods (see *Thompson v Smiths Ship-repairers [1984] 1 All ER 881*).

There are a number of NIHL claims held to have been statute barred because of excessive delay in bringing the proceedings. Although *section 33* of the *Limitation Act 1980* provides courts with a discretion to override the three-year time limit for bringing claims, there seems to be an increasing tendency not to exercise this discretion where there has been inexcusable delay which has caused prejudice to the defendant (see for example *Barrand v British Cellophane, The Times, 16 February 1995*).

The latest edition of the *Judicial Studies Board Guidelines* provides suggested brackets of awards for hearing loss due to noise on a full liability basis. The guidelines couple together hearing loss and tinnitus which may be slightly confusing. Not all NIHL sufferers have any tinnitus, and those who do often have mild transient symptoms which attract little or no additional award. The 'bottom end' figure for a mild hearing loss is about £3,500 and most cases are settled at below £7,500. Age is an important factor, the younger claimants receiving higher awards in most cases. The tariff schemes mentioned are no longer operating. It is unlikely that many NIHL sufferers will have to give up work, provided that they wear adequate hearing protection or that the noise levels are otherwise reduced. Therefore most claims are confined to general damages for pain, suffering and loss of amenity.

Vibration white finger (VWF)

O1016 This is an occupationally-induced form of a condition known as Raynaud's phenomenon, which arises from an abnormal response to cold in the fingers. It is caused by exposure to excessive vibration for a prolonged period.

Vibration

O1017 Like NIHL, VWF is dose related and many who suffer from an occupational hearing loss may also have this condition as hand-held tools which are noisy may also vibrate excessively, but VWF is confined to those who actually use the equipment. The measurement factors are:

— magnitude of vibration;

— frequency of the vibration; and

— the daily dose.

Magnitude

Measurement of magnitude is complex and needs to be done by a skilled person. The aim is to measure the acceleration of the tool, the unit of measurement being in meters per second squared (m/s2). An accelerometer is fixed to the handle of the tool and measurements are taken along three axes (x, y and z). Variations in results are likely due to the condition of the tool, the material being worked upon and the way in which the operator grips the tool.

Frequency

As with noise measurement, the frequency range is an important factor, but with vibration exposure the harmful effects are most likely to be in the low frequency range from about 2 Hz to 1250 Hz. A weighted average is normally used.

Daily dose

The current action level is contained in British Standard BS 6842:1987 and applies when the daily dose reaches 2.8 m/s2 over 8 hours. Because of the problems with variable measurement it is suggested that the following guidelines may be appropriate:

(*a*)   Any tool causing tingling and numbness after ten minutes' use should be suspect.

(*b*)   Almost any exposure which exceeds two hours a day is likely to cause harm.

(*c*)   Exposure which exceeds 30 minutes a day with tools like caulking or chipping hammers, rock drills, pneumatic road breakers, or heavy duty portable grinders is likely to cause harm.

Effects of exposure to excessive vibration

O1018   There are two main symptoms of the condition:

(*a*)   vascular: blanching of one or more parts of the fingers; and

(*b*)   neurological: tingling and (sometimes) numbness in the fingers.

In the early stages, the attacks are transient, perhaps lasting up to one hour. As the patient recovers from the attack, there is aching and redness. Initial attacks occur in cold conditions, usually in winter.

It should be emphasised that these symptoms are the same whether the subject suffers from non-occupational Raynaud's phenomenon or from VWF. The former is a naturally occurring condition in the general population and is particularly common in women where it is believed that about 10 per cent suffer from it. Raynaud's phenomenon may arise as a complication of various conditions, including rheumatoid arthritis, frostbite, and vascular disease, and may also arise as a result of cigarette smoking or from trauma or surgery to the hands.

Where the condition is work related, continuous exposure may cause damage to the blood supply to the fingers and to the nerve endings. With time, the attacks become more prolonged and the effects more serious and in a very few cases, gangrene may occur. The condition starts at the tips of the fingers, but as it progresses, more parts of the fingers are affected. It is rare for the thumbs to be involved. As cold conditions may bring on attacks, workers may be advised to wear gloves and perhaps avoid working in exposed locations.

If the disease is diagnosed at an early stage, the worker may be advised to cease work with vibratory tools. If this is done, it is unlikely that the condition will progress and in some cases, a complete recovery may be possible.

Classification of symptoms

O1019   There are two recognised scales for assessing the severity of symptoms. The Taylor-Pelmear scale is the oldest and uses four stages of severity but is perhaps too crude a measure for medico-legal purposes and may rely on some non-clinical factors, such as a change of job. The later Stockholm scale grades symptoms separately for vascular and sensori-neural components and for the number of affected fingers on each hand. This more detailed approach is now favoured by many examiners although they will often refer to both scales in a medico-legal context.

Preventative steps

O1020   These may be summarised as follows:

(*a*)   risk assessment – identifying the processes and individuals at risk;

(*b*)   warnings – advising those at risk of the hazards and action to be taken;

(*c*)   training and adequate supervision;

(*d*)   minimising daily exposure time;

(*e*)   proper tool control and maintenance;

(*f*)   medical surveillance to ensure that symptoms are reported promptly and that harmful exposure does not continue.

It is questionable whether the wearing of gloves will reduce the magnitude of vibration and their use should be confined to the role of keeping the hands warm and/or protection from sharp edges etc.

Civil liability

O1021   There is no specific statutory requirement relating to VWF so most of the claims are based on duty at common law. As with deafness claims there is a date when guilty knowledge commences and, in most cases, this will be 1976 or thereabouts. This date is used following the publication of a book – *Vibration white finger in industry* by Taylor and Pelmear (1975) – and by the introduction of a draft British Standard (DD 43) in the same year. (See *Armstrong v British Coal, 30 September 1997*, Kemp & Kemp at H6A-002 and *White v Holbrook Castings [1985] IRLR 215*.) However, the views of the courts as to apportionment of damages have been varied and no clear guidance can be given.

The latest edition of the *Judicial Studies Board Guidelines* provides a reasonable guide to the brackets of awards for full liability in VWF cases, and it helpfully explains the various stages of the Taylor-Pelmear scale. The awards range from below £2,500 up to £16,000. However, unlike deafness claims, those who suffer from VWF are often advised to cease work and this may result in substantial claims for loss of earnings and/or damages for lost opportunity in the labour market (*Smith v Manchester* claims).

The changing pattern of occupational diseases

O1022   Technological and employment changes have caused an ongoing shift in the pattern and nature of current occupational health conditions. The gradual shift from manufacturing to service-related employment has resulted in the development of many so-called 'new' white collar diseases. Obviously, there is a geographic pattern to the development of these new diseases with particular emphasis on the South of England.

The 1992 'Six Pack Regulations' reflect a partial response to the change in the employment market and a move away from the factory based legislation of yester-year.

Two typical growth areas are:

— stress;

— work-related upper limb disorders (WRULDs).

Stress

O1023   Stress and anxiety are hardly a new problem restricted to modern man. People have suffered from stress-related conditions, one suspects, back to our very earliest stages of evolution. We all suffer stress in one form or another during our lifetime whether it be due to work pressures or difficult life events related to personal tragedy.

What is stress?

O1024   Stress can be defined as the psychological, physiological and behavioural response to external stimuli. Not all stimuli causes excessive stress levels and not all stress is bad. Some professions, especially senior management, are particularly vulnerable, but it is difficult to generalise because personal factors are so important. One person will not necessarily be affected in the same way as another by external 'stressors'.

Common symptoms of stress include depression, anxiety, guilt, apathy and sleeplessness (psychological), and tension, high blood pressure, weight loss and loss of appetite (physical). Behavioural and associated symptoms are also prominent in the workplace.

In recent years there has been a growth in supposedly work related stress claims. Stress by itself is not a prescribed disease under the *Social Security (Industrial Injuries) (Prescribed Diseases) Regulations 1985*. The real difficulty in these claims is the multifactorial nature of stress. Separating occupational from non-occupational causes is extremely difficult and often impossible. Reasonable foreseeability of stress-related illness is essential, although it is often difficult to establish where there is no known history of psychological problems.

Generally courts have not been keen to allow recovery for 'psychiatric illness caused by accumulation over a period of time of more gradual assaults on the nervous system' (see for example *Alcock and Others v Police Constable of South Yorkshire [1992] 1 AC 354*). It has now been confirmed that a duty of care in respect of a psychiatric injury does not arise solely by virtue of a master and servant relationship, there must be other factors (see *White and Others v Chief Constable of South Yorkshire, 3rd December 1998* in the House of Lords).

What causes stress?

O1025   When analysing an individual's employment there are a number of factors or 'stressors' which can contribute towards the levels of stress experienced by that individual:

(*a*)   time pressures;

(*b*)   overload/underload;

(*c*)   interpersonal relationships;

(*d*)   working hours;

(*e*)   working environment; and

(*f*)   personality.

The law

O1026   The Government has sought to address the number of hours worked by any one individual in the *Working Time Regulations 1998 (SI 1998 No 1833)*. These regulations implement Council Directive 93/104 (1992 OJL 307/18) and Council Directive 94/93 (1994 OJL 216/12). Obligations are imposed on employers concerning the maximum average weekly working time of workers, the average normal hours of night workers, the provision of health assessments for night workers, rest breaks to be given to workers engaged in certain kinds of work and keeping records of workers' hours of work.

Under the *Management of Health and Safety At Work Regulations 1992* employers are required to make a suitable and sufficient assessment of the risks to the health and safety of their employees to which they are exposed whilst at work, and this includes excessive stress levels whether it be caused by difficult time pressures or bullying by co-workers.

Over the last few years there have been an increasing number of stress-related cases in the UK courts. *Walker v Northumberland County Council [1995] 1 All ER 737* received significant press attention. Mr Walker managed four teams of social service field workers in a depressed area of Northumberland. He found the strain of the job too much and at the end of November 1986 suffered a nervous breakdown. His symptoms included anxiety, headaches, sleeplessness and an inability to cope with any levels of stress. On medical advice he was absent from work for three months. He returned to work but in September 1987 stress-induced symptoms returned and he was subsequently diagnosed as suffering from stress-related anxiety and was advised to take sick leave. In February 1988 he had a second mental breakdown and was later dismissed on the grounds of permanent ill health. The local authority was held liable. It was found that an employer does owe a duty of care to an employee not to cause him psychiatric injury as a result of the volume or character of work which employees are required to do. Although the first breakdown was found not to be reasonably foreseeable to the defendant, the second was. It was reasonably foreseeable that there was a real risk of repetition of his illness if he was exposed to the same workload and if his duties were not alleviated by effective additional assistance. In continuing to employ him but providing no effective help the council had acted unreasonably and was in breach of its duty of care.

Interpersonal relationships at work are frequently a cause or contributory factor to mental ill health. In *Ratcliffe v Pembrokeshire County Council (1998)* it was claimed that Mr Ratcliffe, a teacher, had suffered a nervous breakdown which he attributed to a systematic system of bullying by his headmistress, Jean Morris. Although the defendants in that case maintained a total denial of liability throughout, the action was subsequently compromised upon terms that resulted in Mr Ratcliffe receiving damages of £101,028. (See also *Firman v British Telecom plc, 13 February 1996 (unreported)*.)

Legislation in this area is under consideration, and a Dignity At Work Bill is expected to be introduced in Parliament.

Work-related upper limb disorders (WRULDs)

Definition

O1027   –   Commonly referred to as repetitive strain injury (RSI). (This terminology as a separate form of injury was rejected by Prosser J in *Mughal v Reuters [1993] IRLR 571*.)

- Claims arise out of a wide variety of jobs. In respect of white collar workers, claims commonly are made by VDU operators, typists and data processors. Claims by blue collar workers usually arise from heavy repetitive manual or routine repetitive line work (for example assembly work).

- Upper limb disorders (ULDs) include a wide range of conditions affecting the fingers, hands, wrists and forearms. Some are prescribed diseases and some are not. Some are known to be work related, some not. Medical opinion remains fairly divided.

See Table 1 below for a list of common upper limb disorders.

Table 1
Common upper limb disorders

Medical condition	Description	Clinical signs and symptoms
Peritendonitis crepitans (PD A8)	Inflammation of tendon of hand or forearm.	Swelling, heat, redness, pain and crepitus (creaking) of wrist. Can be caused by rapid repeated movement and thus caused by work.
Carpal tunnel syndrome	Compression of the medial nerve of the wrist as it passes through the carpal tunnel.	Pain, numbness in palm and fingers on the lateral side of the hand and wrist, difficulty in moving fingers, decreased hand strength. Electro–conductivity diagnostic tests. It is a prescribed disease where associated with vibration.
Tendonitis (PD A8)	Inflammation of tendons.	Pain and swelling. Tendons can become locked in their sheaths so that the fingers become locked in flexion. Repeated extension. Reflexion of fingers thought to be causative.
Tenosynovitis (Trigger digit/trigger thumb) (PD A8)	Inflammation of the tendon sheath.	Swelling, tenderness and pain in the tendon sheath of fingers or thumbs, accompanied by a characteristic 'locking'. Can be caused by repetitive motions of the digits.

De Quervains syndrome (De Quervains stenosing tenovaginitis) (PD A8)	Thickening of the tendon sheath over the radial borders of the wrist at the junction of the thumb/wrist.	Reduction in the grip strength, tenderness and swelling, pain on radial side of wrist. Caused by repeated pinching and gripping with thumb or repeated ulnar deviation of wrist. Can develop spontaneously.
Tennis elbow (Lateral epicondylitis)	Inflammation of the tendons that attach the forearm muscles to the bony knob on the outer elbow.	Tenderness of outer or inner aspect of the elbow, extending into the forearm along a palpable band in line with the extensor muscles. Accompanied by pain and swelling. No clear medical evidence that the conditions are related to work although they are exacerbated by heavy repetitive manual labour.
Golfer's elbow (Medial epicondylitis)	Inflammation of the tendons of the forearm muscles that attach to the inner aspect of the bony knob of the elbow.	
Writer's cramp (PDA4) Ganglions	Cramp of the hand or forearm.	Can be caused by prolonged periods of handwriting, typing or other repetitive movements of the fingers, hand or arms.
Ganglions	Cysts containing viscous, mucinous fluid found in vicinity of joints and tendons in various parts of the body, although the majority are on the wrist.	Not believed to be work related but can be exacerbated by work.

Bringing a claim

O1028   To bring a successful WRULD claim the claimant will need to establish:

(*a*)   that he or she is suffering from a definable medical condition;

(*b*)   that this condition has been caused or exacerbated by his work and as a direct result of any breach of duty owed to him either in common law or pursuant to statute by his employers; and

(c)   that it was foreseeable to a reasonable and prudent employer that the work engaged could give rise to an upper limb disorder.

Problems arise because a claimant has difficulty in satisfying one of the definable medical conditions listed in Table 1 above. In *Mughal* the plaintiff was unable to establish one of the specific upper limb conditions and was suffering from a diffuse range of symptoms. Prosser J could not accept RSI as a separate form of injury and in the absence of a specific organic condition rejected the claim.

It is not enough for a claimant to say that he or she has suffered 'passing minimal discomfort' (see *Griffiths v British Coal Corporation (unreported)*).

Many of the recent cases have turned on the establishment of an organic condition. Following *Mughal* claimants suffering from diffuse symptoms attempted to identify their problem as a specific upper limb condition (see for example *Pickford v Imperial Chemical Industries plc (1998) 1 WLR 1189*). Alternatively a number of alternative labels such as fybro-myalgia or reflex sympathetic dystrophy were adopted on their behalf by the treating or expert medical practitioner.

In *Alexander and Others v Midland Bank (1998)* five female bank employees claimed that they were suffering from regional fybro-myalgia arising from their work as data processor operators. The claimants all worked in the nine district centres set up by Midland Bank to process cheques and vouchers. Their job involved rapid repetitive keying-in work on encoding machines over long periods of time, often one-handed. By 1991 some of the claimants began to report symptoms in the upper limbs. The pain and discomfort became more persistent and intense. It was held that the plaintiffs' symptoms were more than passing minimal discomfort and were sufficient to form an actionable claim for personal injury notwithstanding the obvious lack of precision in the description of pathology of pain. The court found that the pressure of the decoders' work contributed to their injuries, and the bank knew or ought to have reasonably foreseen that these factors invited the risk of injury and were held in breach of their duty.

In *Amosu and Others v The Financial Times, 31 July 1998 (unreported)* the Divisional Court (QBD) considered a claim by five journalists at the *Financial Times* who each claimed to have suffered specific musculo-skeletal disorders following the introduction of a computerised system for the writing, editing and printing of the newspaper. The allegations included the provision of bad and poorly ergonomically designed work stations and the exposure to excessive pressures of work with inadequate rest breaks. On this occasion the court held that each of the claimants had failed to demonstrate or prove on the balance of probabilities that they had suffered from the various physical problems as alleged.

In the majority decision by the House of Lords in *Pickford* the claimant failed to satisfy the court that her symptoms were organic and caused by typing work. Mrs Pickford alleged that she had developed prescribed disease PD A4, commonly known as writer's cramp, because of the large amount of typing work carried out at speed for long periods without breaks. The House of Lords found that it was not reasonably foreseeable that a secretary working in the same work regime as the plaintiff would be likely to suffer from the condition. There were no specific duties on ICI to provide rest breaks as her work was sufficiently varied to allow rotation between typing and other known repetitive work. Further there was no specific duty to warn of the specific risks of developing PD A4 as this was not practice in the industry at the time and such warnings would have been counter-productive precipitating the very condition it was intended to avoid.

Employers' duties and prevention

O1029   The primary source is the *Health and Safety (Display Screen Equipment) Regulations 1992*, but see also the *Management of Health and Safety At Work Regulations 1992* and the *Workplace (Health, Safety and Welfare) Regulations 1992*.

Further guidance can be found in the HSE publication, *Work-related upper limb disorders: A guide to prevention* (1990).

Prudent employers should look to provide:

(*a*)   suitable and adequate health and safety training/information relating to the use of equipment, posture and breaks;

(*b*)   a suitable work station;

(*c*)   suitable rotation and breaks. Employers should carry out risk assessments looking at the necessary application of force, the speed of work, the repetition and the awkwardness of any specific task; and

(*d*)   warnings where appropriate.

Preventative management

Safety policy

O1030   *Section 2(3)* of *HSWA 1974* requires those employing five or more people to have a written statement of general policy on matters of health and safety and to revise it as necessary. The document should detail the organisation and arrangements for carrying out the policy and it should be brought to the notice of all employees.

This is an important document which should be signed by a senior person within the organisation (usually the chief executive). It should clearly set out the obligations of line managers in carrying out the objectives of the organisation. Where there are specific hazards (e.g. asbestos) the policy should deal with the measures to be taken. This may be in the form of an internal code of practice.

Risk assessment

O1031   This is the cornerstone of modern occupational health and safety management and stems from EU Directives on health and safety which have been subsequently implemented by UK legislation.

Regulations which contain the requirement to carry out risk assessments include:

(*a*)   *Control of Asbestos at Work Regulations 1987;*

(*b*)   *Control of Lead at Work Regulations 1998;*

(*c*)   *Control of Substances Hazardous to Health Regulations 1994 (COSHH);*

(*d*)   *Health and Safety (Display Screen Equipment) Regulations 1992;*

(*e*)   *Management of Health and Safety at Work Regulations 1992;*

(*f*)   *Manual Handling Regulations 1992;*

(*g*)   *Noise at Work Regulations 1989;*

(*h*)   *Personal Protective Equipment at Work Regulations 1992;*

(*i*)   *Workplace (Health, Safety and Welfare) Regulations 1992.*

An employer is required to carry out a suitable and sufficient risk assessment where there may be a risk of injury or disease. Having identified the areas of risk, protective measures which either eliminate or minimise the risk must be indicated.

The assessments may be carried out by outside agencies, but are often best done internally where there are staff familiar with the processes and potential hazards. Management should consider seeking the help and advice of employees in this task, particularly where there are employee health and safety representatives. Assessments are not necessarily confined to the risks to employees, but also to others who may be affected by their undertaking: this may include contractors, customers, delivery drivers and others likely to visit the premises. Where employees are working away from the normal workplace, they need to be given special consideration.

Risk assessments are not static: they must be reviewed constantly in the light of changing circumstances. They will normally be in writing and these records should be retained for as long as they are relevant. It is particularly important that where there is a risk of occupational disease, assessments should deal specifically with the problem. For example, where there is a problem with excessive noise, there should be a detailed survey of noisy areas and risks to individuals, but this may also need to be supported by health surveillance in the form of audiometry to test the effectiveness of the control measures. Regular safety audits are also an effective way of checking the effectiveness of the risk assessments.

Ceasing exposure

O1032   In some cases, the risk of harm from a substance or process is so great that consideration should be given to ceasing the exposure entirely. This may mean closing the workplace or discontinuing the hazardous process. Such radical steps may be necessary where the process carries a risk of serious injury and the employer is not satisfied that control measures will eliminate the risk. An example of this might be the total ban on the use or handling of asbestos and the substitution by another insulating material.

Minimising exposure

O1033   A less radical solution may be to reduce the level of exposure to the lowest level that is reasonably practicable. The aim should be to reduce the exposure not only to the occupational exposure standard (which should be regarded as the maximum allowable in any event), but to aim for the lowest level that is reasonably achievable. For example, in a noisy workplace, an employer may aim to reduce exposure to the first action level of 85 dB(A) but cannot be confident that this level may always be achieved. Further engineering measures could bring the level to well below 85 dB(A), ensuring that none of the workforce is at risk and avoiding the necessity to have hearing protection available.

Enclosing the process

O1034   Risks arising from a hazardous process may be substantially reduced if it is enclosed to ensure that there is no escape of the substance. However, there must be provision for access by personnel to carry out essential maintenance and the employer must ensure that such persons are adequately trained and are provided with the necessary personal protection when working in the enclosure.

Enclosing the operator

O1035   This is the reverse of the above system of control. It is especially suitable where the process is on a scale that makes enclosure uneconomic (e.g. a noisy bottling plant). The operator and the plant controls are situated in a sealed control room and access on to the floor of the plant is carefully controlled with the necessary personal protection worn.

Automating or mechanising the process

O1036   The aim of this system is to remove the human element from some or all of the process. Where there is a high incidence of musculo-skeletal problems in the workplace, this may be an appropriate measure to consider. However, the different risks involved with the introduction of new machinery may need to be assessed.

Minimising exposure time

O1037   Many occupational diseases are dose related so every effort should be made to ensure that workers are exposed to hazards for as little time as possible during their working day. In theory, this is a very successful control measure and should be cost effective, but it does need proper supervision and worker co-operation to ensure that it is effective. A simple example is where VDU operators are given adequate rest breaks coupled with other tasks (e.g. filing) which are performed away from the display screen.

Monitoring exposure

O1038   Monitoring is an important part of the process for ensuring that exposure is maintained at or below the maximum safe level. For example, dust levels may be monitored by regular environmental samples and supplemented by personal dose sampling on workers who are at risk. Continuous automatic sampling may be necessary in some cases. Monitoring should be done regularly and proper records maintained.

Personal protective equipment (PPE)

O1039   The use of PPE is now governed by the *Personal Protective Equipment at Work Regulations 1992*. In the guidance notes to the Regulations it is stressed that in the hierarchy of control measures, PPE must be regarded as a last resort: engineering controls and safe systems of work should come first although there may be a need for personal protection whilst such measures are being implemented. The reason for the 'last resort' status is because there are so many problems involved in the reliance upon PPE as a safe method of prevention, and in some workplaces there is reluctance by the workforce to wear the protection provided.

There are, however, circumstances where the employer sees no alternative to the use of PPE. If this is so, there are many points to consider to ensure that the protection is effective, including:

(*a*)   risk assessment to ensure that if PPE is the only means of controlling exposure, the equipment is suitable and effective;

(*b*)   ensuring that the necessary equipment is issued to all workers who may be at risk;

(*c*)   ensuring that the equipment fits correctly and is compatible with other PPE that may be worn;

(*d*)   arrangements for the maintenance and replacement of the equipment;

(*e*)   suitable accommodation for the equipment (e.g. lockers);

(*f*)   information, instruction and training to advise workers about the risks of exposure, the need for the protection, the manner of its use, and how to maintain the equipment;

(*g*)   ensuring that information given is comprehensible to the worker – a point to consider where there may be language difficulties.

If a control system relies on PPE, it is essential that there is adequate supervision to ensure that equipment is being properly worn at all relevant times. Having regard to all the problems, an employer may well be advised to look again at other control measures.

Information, instruction, training and supervision

O1040   These have been discussed in relation to PPE but they are essential ingredients of the total programme of preventative management.

(*a*)   *Information.* Those who are at risk must be told the precise nature of the risks that they face and what they need to do to avoid or minimise these risks. For example, if there is a problem with noise, they should be told how noise can damage hearing, what areas of the workplace are hazardous, and where they must wear hearing protection. Instructional videos are often available for this sort of education.

(*b*)   *Instruction.* In addition to receiving advice on the health risks, a worker should also be given clear instructions as to any steps which need to be taken. This instruction may be oral but is best supplemented by an instruction booklet and perhaps warning notices. Instructions may need to be in foreign languages where appropriate.

(*c*)   *Training.* Following instruction there must be adequate training to ensure that the worker understands what needs to be done. This may include, for example, a demonstration on the correct method of wearing PPE.

(*d*)   *Supervision.* Adequate supervision is the key to effective preventative management. If this does not exist then all the assessments, plans and procedures are so much waste paper. First line supervisors are on the spot and can immediately see what is right or wrong. They can ensure, for example, that protection is being worn or that hazardous dust is not allowed to escape. Employers should ensure that health and safety is an essential part of the supervisor's role and that they are given the time and resources to perform that function.

Medical surveillance

O1041   There are certain statutory requirements for this (e.g. in *COSHH*) but, in addition, employers may choose to implement their own programme. The surveillance may take several forms:

(*a*)   pre-employment questionnaire and/or examination to ensure that new entrants are screened for suitability;

(*b*)   new starters may have initial tests, such as audiometry, which will establish a benchmark against which further progress can be checked;

(*c*)   regular examinations, say every year, to ensure that health is maintained;

(*d*)   providing a service where workers with symptoms may report them immediately (this is particularly beneficial with work-related upper limb disorders, for example); and

(*e*)   a referral procedure where those returning from sickness absence may be examined as to their continuing suitability for certain work.

Future trends

O1042   Increasing technological development will undoubtedly change the risks to which workers are exposed and in consequence the nature of occupational health problems.

Asthma and other environmental conditions are likely to be at the forefront of new claims along with WRULDs and stress.

As individuals become ever more litigious we can expect lawyers to attempt to push open new causes of action founded on new occupational diseases. Repetitive lifting/bending and postural claims are just one example where growth can be expected to be lawyer led.

Although law and practice change to reflect each new risk there is inevitably a time gap and whilst the incidence of many traditional industrial diseases have been halted or reduced we should not expect an eradication of all occupational health diseases. The very technological advancements which have reduced many of the traditional risks in industry bring about a whole new set of occupational health issues and problems.

Current list of prescribed occupational diseases

O1043   The current list of prescribed occupational diseases is contained in the *Social Security (Industrial Injuries) (Prescribed Diseases) Regulations 1985 (SI 1985 No 967)* (the main regulations), the *Social Security (Industrial Injuries) (Prescribed Diseases) Amendment Regulations 1987 (SI 1987 No 335)*, the *Social Security (Industrial Injuries) (Prescribed Diseases) (Amendment No 2) Regulations 1987 (SI 1987 No 2112)*, the *Social Security (Industrial Diseases) (Prescribed Diseases) Amendment Regulations 1989 (SI 1989 No 1207)*, the *Social Security (Industrial Injuries) (Prescribed Diseases) Amendment Regulations 1990 (SI 1990 No 2269)*, the *Social Security (Industrial Injuries) (Prescribed Diseases) Amendment Regulations 1991 (SI 1991 No 1938)*, the *Social Security (Industrial Injuries) (Prescribed Diseases) Amendment Regulations 1993 (SI 1993 No 862)*, the *Social Security (Industrial Injuries) (Prescribed Diseases) Amendment (No 2) Regulations 1993 (SI 1993 No 1985)*, the *Social Security (Industrial Injuries) (Prescribed Diseases) Amendment Regulations 1994 (SI 1994 No 2343)* and the *Social Security (Industrial Injuries and Diseases) (Miscellaneous Amendments) Regulations 1996 (SI 1996 No 425)*. *Schedule 1* to the main regulations and occupations for which they are prescribed are reproduced in Table 2 below. Pneumoconiosis and the occupations for which it is prescribed are set out in *Schedule 2* to the main regulations and is also reproduced below. Compensation for pneumoconiosis etc. is dealt with in COMPENSATION FOR WORK INJURIES AND DISEASES and O1048 below.

The question whether a claimant is suffering from a prescribed disease is a diagnosis one, falling within the remit of the Medical Appeal Tribunal; the question whether a disease is prescribed is for the Adjudicating Officer, the Social Security Appeal Tribunal and the Commissioner. Where a claimant is suffering from a prescribed disease, it is open to the Adjudicating Officer to seek to show that the particular disease was not due to the nature of the claimant's employment (R(I) 4/91 – primary neoplasm C 23, invoking *Reg 4* of the *Social Security (Industrial Injuries)*

(Prescribed Diseases) Regulations 1985). In addition, a Medical Appeal Tribunal can decide disablement issues (R(I) 2/91 – disablement assessed at 7% in respect of vibration white finger, A 11).

Moreover, medical practitioners and specially qualified medical practitioners can now adjudicate upon matters relating to industrial injuries and prescribed diseases (hitherto the exclusive province of medical boards or special medical boards). [*Social Security (Industrial Injuries and Adjudication) Regulations 1993 (SI 1993 No 861); Social Security (Industrial Injuries) (Prescribed Diseases) Amendment (No 2) Regulations 1993 (SI 1993 No 1985)*].

Table 2
Current list of prescribed occupational diseases

Prescribed disease or injury	Occupation
A. *Conditions due to physical agents*	*Any occupation involving:*
1. Inflammation, ulceration or malignant disease of the skin or subcutaneous tissues or of the bones, or blood dyscrasia, or cataract, due to electro-magnetic radiations (other than radiant heat), or to ionising particles.	Exposure to electro-magnetic radiations (other than radiant heat) or to ionising particles.
2. Heat cataract.	Frequent or prolonged exposure to rays from molten or red-hot material.
3. Dysbarism, including decompression sickness, barotrauma and osteonecrosis.	Subjection to compressed or rarified air or other respirable gases or gaseous mixtures.
4. Cramp of the hand or forearm due to repetitive movements.	Prolonged periods of handwriting, typing or other repetitive movements of the fingers, hand or arm.
5. Subcutaneous cellulitis of the hand (Beat hand).	Manual labour causing severe or prolonged friction or pressure on the hand.
6. Bursitis or subcutaneous cellulitis arising at or about the knee due to severe or prolonged external friction or pressure at or about the knee (Beat knee).	Manual labour causing severe or prolonged external friction or pressure at or about the knee.
7. Bursitis or subcutaneous cellulitis arising at or about the elbow due to severe or prolonged external friction or pressure at or about the elbow (Beat elbow).	Manual labour causing severe or prolonged external friction or pressure at or about the elbow.

8.	Traumatic inflammation of the tendons of the hand or forearm, or of the associated tendon sheaths.		Manual labour, or frequent or repeated movements of the hand or wrist.
9.	Miner's nystagmus.		Work in or about a mine.
10.	Substantial sensorineural hearing loss amounting to at least 50dB in each ear, being due in the case of at least one ear to occupational noise, and being the average of pure tone loss measured by audiometry over the 1, 2 and 3 kHz frequencies (occupational deafness).	(*a*)	The use of, or work wholly or mainly in the immediate vicinity of, pneumatic percussive tools or high-speed grinding tools, in the cleaning, dressing or finishing of cast *metal* or of ingots, billets or blooms (but not stone/concrete used in road/railway construction; or
			Any occupation involving:
		(*b*)	the use of, or work wholly or mainly in the immediate vicinity of, pneumatic percussive tools on metal in the shipbuilding or ship repairing industries; or
		(*c*)	the use of, or work in the immediate vicinity of, pneumatic percussive tools on metal, or for drilling rock in quarries or underground, or in mining coal, for at least an average of one hour per working day; or
		(*d*)	work wholly or mainly in the immediate vicinity of drop-forging plant (including plant for drop-stamping or drop-hammering) or forging press plant engaged in the shaping of metal; or
		(*e*)	work wholly or mainly in rooms or sheds where there are machines engaged in weaving man-made or natural (including mineral) fibres or in the bulking up of fibres in textile manufacturing; or
		(*f*)	the use of, or work wholly or mainly in the immediate vicinity of, machines engaged in cutting, shaping or cleaning metal nails; or

(g)   the use of, or work wholly or mainly in the immediate vicinity of, plasma spray guns engaged in the deposition of metal; or

(h)   the use of, or work wholly or mainly in the immediate vicinity of, any of the following machines engaged in the working of wood or material composed partly of wood, that is to say; multi-cutter moulding machines, planing machines, automatic or semi-automatic lathes, multiple cross-cut machines, automatic shaping machines, double-end tenoning machines, vertical spindle moulding machines (including high-speed routing machines), edge banding machines, bandsawing machines with a blade width of not less than 73 millimetres and circular sawing machines in the operation of which the blade is moved towards the material being cut; or

(j)   the use of chain saws in forestry; or

(k)   air arc gouging or work wholly or mainly in the immediate vicinity of air arc gouging; or

(l)   the use of band saws, circular saws or cutting discs for cutting metal in the metal founding or forging industries, or work wholly or mainly in the immediate vicinity of those tools whilst they are being so used; or

(m)   the use of circular saws for cutting products in the manufacture of steel, or work wholly or mainly in the immediate vicinity of those tools whilst they are being so used; or (*n*)   the use of burners or torches for cutting or dressing steel based products, or work wholly or mainly in the immediate vicinity of those tools whilst they are being so used; or

(*o*)   work wholly or mainly in the immediate vicinity of skid transfer banks; or

(*p*)   work wholly or mainly in the immediate vicinity of knock out and shake out grids in foundries; or

(*q*)   mechanical bobbin cleaning or work wholly or mainly in the immediate vicinity of mechanical bobbin cleaning; or

(*r*)   the use of, or work wholly or mainly in the immediate vicinity of, vibrating metal moulding boxes in the concrete products industry; or

(*s*)   the use of, or work wholly or mainly in the immediate vicinity of, high pressure jets of water or a mixture of water and abrasive material in the water jetting industry (including work under water); or

(*t*)   work in ships' engine rooms; or

(*u*)   the use of circular saws for cutting concrete masonry blocks during manufacture, or work wholly or mainly in the immediate vicinity of those tools whilst they are being so used; or

(*v*)   burning stone in quarries by jet channelling processes, or work wholly or mainly in the immediate vicinity of such processes; or

(*w*)   work on gas turbines in connection with:

    (i)   performance testing on test bed,

(ii) installation testing of replacement engines in aircraft,

(iii) acceptance testing of Armed Service fixed wing combat planes; or

(*x*) the use of, or work wholly or mainly in the immediate vicinity of:

(i) machines for automatic moulding, automatic blow moulding or automatic glass pressing and forming machines used in the manufacture of glass containers or hollow ware;

(ii) spinning machines using compressed air to produce glass wool or mineral wool;

(iii) continuous glass toughening furnaces.

Any occupation involving:

11. Episodic blanching, occurring through out the year, affecting the middle or proximal phalanges or in the case of a thumb the proximal phalanx, of –

(*a*) in the case of a person with 5 fingers (including thumb) on one hand, any 3 of those fingers, or

(*b*) in the case of a person with only 4 such fingers, any 2 of those fingers, or

(*a*) The use of hand-held chain saws in forestry; or

(*b*) the use of hand-held rotary tools in grinding or in the sanding or polishing of metal, or the holding of material being ground, or metal being sanded or polished, by rotary tools; or

(*c*) the use of percussive metal-working tools, or the holding of metal being worked upon by percussive tools, in riveting, caulking, chipping, hammering, fettling or swaging; or

(c)	in the case of a person with less than 4 such fingers, any one of those fingers or, as the case may be, the one remaining finger (vibration white finger).	(d)	the use of hand-held powered percussive drills or hand-held powered percussive hammers in mining, quarrying, demolition, or on roads or footpaths, including road construction; or
		(e)	the holding of material being worked upon by pounding machines in shoe manufacture.

12.	Carpal tunnel syndrome..	Use of hand-held vibrating tools whose internal parts vibrate so as to transmit that vibration to the hand, but excluding those which are solely powered by hand

B.	*Conditions due to biological agents*	*Any occupation involving:*
1.	Anthrax.	Contact with animals infected with anthrax or the handling (including the loading or unloading or transport) of animal products or residues.
2.	Glanders.	Contact with equine animals or their carcases.

3.	Infection by leptospira.(See below*)	(a)	Work in places which are, or are liable to be, infested by rats, field mice or voles, or other small mammals; or
		(b)	work at dog kennels or the care or handling of dogs; or
		(c)	contact with bovine animals or their meat products or pigs or their meat products.

Any occupation involving:

4.	Ankylostomiasis.	Work in or about a mine.
5.	Tuberculosis.	Contact with a source of tuberculosis infection.

6.	Extrinsic allergic alveolitis (including farmer's lung).	Exposure to moulds or fungal spores or heterologous proteins by reason of employment in:
		(a)	agriculture, horticulture, forestry, cultivation of edible fungi or malt-working; or
		(b)	loading or unloading or handling in storage mouldy vegetable matter or edible fungi; or

		(*c*) caring for or handling birds; or
		(*d*) handling bagasse.
7.	Infection by organisms of the genus brucella.	Contact with –
		(*a*) animals infected by brucella, or their carcases or parts thereof, or their untreated products; or
		(*b*) laboratory specimens or vaccines of, or containing, brucella.
8.	Viral hepatitis.	Close and frequent contact with –
		(*a*) human blood or human blood products; or
		(*b*) a source of viral hepatitis.
9.	Infection by *Streptococcus suis*.	Contact with pigs infected by *Streptococcus* suis, or with the carcases, products or residues of pigs so infected.
10.	(*a*) Avian chlamydiosis	Contact with birds infected with chlamydia psittaci, or with the remains or untreated products of such birds.
	(*b*) Ovine chlamydiosis	Contact with sheep infected with chlamydia psittaci, or with the remains or untreated products of such sheep.
11.	Q fever.	Contact with animals, their remains or their untreated products.
12.	Orf.	Contact with sheep, goats or with the carcases of sheep or goats.
13.	Hydatidosis.	Contact with dogs.

* (This can also give rise to liability at common law, where an employer fails to set up a system for killing off rats, or, alternatively fails to instruct employees to take proper precautions by washing their hands frequently (*Campbell v Percy Bilton Ltd (1988) (unreported)*). Previously, common law liability for Weil's disease, carried by rats, was unlikely (*Tremain v Pike [1969] 3 AER 1303* where a farmer was held not liable to an employee who contracted Weil's disease on a rat-infested farm, as no warnings had been issued by the local health authority). Today, however, with greater awareness and knowledge of health and hygiene hazards, liability is more likely. Even so, the likelihood of injury, magnitude of risk and cost of an exterminating operation would all be relevant to liability (see further *Paris v Stepney Borough Council* at 30(b) INTRODUCTION).)

C.	*Conditions due to chemical agents*	*Any occupation involving:*
1.	Poisoning by lead or a compound of lead.	The use or handling of, or exposure to the fumes, dust or vapour of, lead or a compound of lead, or a substance containing lead.
2.	Poisoning by manganese or a compound of manganese.	The use or handling of, or exposure to the fumes, dust or vapour of, manganese or a compound of manganese, or a substance containing manganese.
3.	Poisoning by phosphorus or an inorganic compound or phosphorus or poisoning due to the anti-cholinesterase or pseudo anti-cholinesterase action of organic phosphorus compounds.	The use or handling of, or exposure to the fumes, dust or vapour of, phosphorus or a compound of phosphorus, or a substance containing phosphorus.
4.	Poisoning by arsenic or a compound of arsenic.	The use or handling of, or exposure to the fumes, dust or vapour of, arsenic or a compound of arsenic, or a substance containing arsenic.
5.	Poisoning by mercury or a compound of mercury.	The use or handling of, or exposure to the fumes, dust or vapour of, mercury or a compound of mercury, or a substance containing mercury.
6.	Poisoning by carbon bisulphide.	The use or handling of, or exposure to the fumes or vapour of, carbon bisulphide or a compound of carbon bisulphide, or a substance containing carbon bisulphide.
7.	Poisoning by benzene or a homologue of benzene.	The use or handling of, or exposure to the fumes of, or vapour containing benzene or any of its homologues.
8.	Poisoning by nitro-or amino-or chloro-derivative of benzene or of a homologue of benzene, or poisoning by nitrochlorbenzene.	The use or handling of, or exposure to the fumes of, or vapour containing a nitro-or amino-or chloro-derivative of benzene, or of a homologue of benzene, or nitrochlorbenzene.
9.	Poisoning by dinitrophenol or a homologue of dinitrophenol or by substituted dinitrophenols or by the salts of such substances.	The use or handling of, or exposure to the fumes of, or vapour containing, dinitrophenol or a homologue or substituted dinitrophenols or the salts of such substances.
10.	Poisoning by tetrachloroethane.	The use or handling of, or exposure to the fumes of, or vapour containing, tetrachloroethane.

11.	Poisoning by diethylene dioxide (dioxan).	The use or handling of, or exposure to the fumes of, or vapour containing, diethylene dioxide (dioxan).
12.	Poisoning by methyl bromide.	The use or handling of, or exposure to the fumes of, or vapour containing, methyl bromide.

Any occupation involving:

13.	Poisoning by chlorinated naphthalene.	The use or handling of, or exposure to the fumes of, or dust or vapour containing, chlorinated naphthalene.
14.	Poisoning by nickel carbonyl.	Exposure to nickel carbonyl gas.
15.	Poisoning by oxides of nitrogen.	Exposure to oxides of nitrogen.
16.	Poisoning by gonioma kamassi (African boxwood).	The manipulation of gonioma kamassi or any process in or incidental to the manufacture of articles therefrom.
17.	Poisoning by beryllium or a compound of beryllium.	The use or handling of, or exposure to the fumes of, or dust or vapour of, beryllium or a compound of beryllium, or a substance containing beryllium.
18.	Poisoning by cadmium.	Exposure to cadmium dust or fumes.
19.	Poisoning by acrylamide monomer.	The use or handling of, or exposure to, acrylamide monomer.
20.	Dystrophy of the cornea (including ulceration of the corneal surface) of the eye.	(*a*) The use or handling of, or exposure to, arsenic, tar, pitch, bitumen, mineral oil (including paraffin), soot or any compound, product or residue of any of these substances, except quinone or hydroquinone; or (*b*) exposure to quinone or hydroquinone during their manufacture.
21.	(*a*) Localised new growth of the skin, papillomatous or keratotic; (*b*) squamous-celled carcinoma of the skin.	The use or handling of, or exposure to, arsenic, tar, pitch, bitumen, mineral oil (including paraffin), soot or any compound, product or residue of any of these substances, except quinone or hydroquinone.

22.	(*a*) Carcinoma of the mucous membrane of the nose or associated air sinuses;	Work in a factory where nickel is produced by decomposition of a gaseous nickel compound which necessitates working in or about a building or buildings where that process or any other industrial
	(*b*) primary carcinoma of a bronchus or of a lung.	process ancillary or incidental thereto is carried on.

23. Primary neoplasm (including papilloma, carcinoma-in-situ and invasive carcinoma) of the epithelial lining of the urinary tract (renal pelvis, ureter, bladder and urethra).

(*a*) Work in a building in which any of the following substances is produced for commercial purposes:

    (i) alpha-naphthylamine, beta-naphthylamine or methylene-bis-orthochloroaniline;

    (ii) diphenyl substituted by at least one nitro or primary amino group or by at least one nitro and primary amino group (including benzidine);

    (iii) any of the substances mentioned in sub-paragraph (ii) above if further ring substituted by halogeno, methyl or methoxy groups, but not by other groups;

    (iv) the salts of any of the substances mentioned in sub-paragraphs (i) to (iii) above;

    (v) auramine or magenta; or

Any occupation involving:

(*b*) the use or handling of any of the substances mentioned in sub-paragraph (a) (i) to (iv), or work in a process in which any such substance is used, handled or liberated; or

		(*c*)	the maintenance or cleaning of any plant or machinery used in any such process as is mentioned in sub-paragraph (*b*), or the cleaning of clothing used in any such building as is mentioned in sub-paragraph (*a*) if such clothing is cleaned within the works of which the building forms a part or in a laundry maintained and used solely in connection with such works; or
		(*d*)	Soderberg aluminium smelting process. [*SI 1993 No 862*].
24.	(*a*) Angiosarcoma of the liver;	(*a*)	Work in or about machinery or apparatus used for the polymerization of vinyl chloride monomer, a process which, for the purposes of this provision, comprises all operations up to and including the drying of the slurry produced by the polymerization and the packaging of the dried product; or
	(*b*) osteolysis of the terminal phalanges of the fingers;		
	(*c*) non-cirrhotic portal fibrosis.		
		(*b*)	work in a building or structure in which any part of that process takes place.
25.	Occupational vitiligo.		The use or handling of, or exposure to, para-tertiary-butylphenol, para-tertiarybutylcatechol, para-amyl-phenol, hydroquinone or the monobenzyl or monobutyl ether of hydroquinone.
26.	Damage to the liver or kidneys due to exposure to carbon tetrachloride.		Use of or handling of or exposure to the fumes of, or vapour containing carbon tetrachloride.
27.	Damage to the liver or kidneys due to exposure to trichloromethane (chloroform).		Use of or handling of or exposure to fumes of or vapour containing trichloromethane (chloroform).
28.	Central nervous system dysfunction and associated gastro-intestinal disorders due to exposure to chloromethane (methyl chloride).		Use of or handling of or exposure to fumes or vapours containing chloromethane (methyl chloride).

Any occupation involving:

29. Peripheral neuropathy due to exposure to n-hexane or methyl n-butyl ketone.

Use of or handling of or exposure to the fumes of or vapours containing n-hexane or methyl n-butyl ketone.

30. (As from 24 March 1996) chrome dermatitis, or ulceration of the mucous membranes or epidermis, resulting from exposure to chromic acid, chromates or bi-chromates.

Use or handling of, or exposure to, chromic acid, chromates or bi-chromates.

D.   *Miscellaneous Conditions*

1. Pneumoconiosis.

Any occupation involving –

(*a*)   the mining, quarrying or working of silica rock or the working of dried quartzose sand or any dry deposit or dry residue of silica or any dry admixture containing such materials (including any occupation in which any of the aforesaid operations are carried out incidentally to the mining or quarrying of other minerals or to the manufacture of articles containing crushed or ground silica rock);

(*b*)   the handling of any of the materials specified in the foregoing sub-paragraph in or incidental to any of the operations mentioned therein, or substantial exposure to the dust arising from such operations.

Any occupation involving the breaking, crushing or grinding of flint or the working or handling of broken, crushed or ground flint or materials containing such flint, or substantial exposure to the dust arising from any of such operations.

Any occupation involving sand blasting by means of compressed air with the use of quartzose sand or crushed silica rock or flint, or substantial exposure to the dust arising from sand and blasting.

Any occupation involving work in a foundry or the performance of, or substantial exposure to the dust arising from, any of the following operations:

(*a*)   the freeing of steel castings from adherent siliceous substance;

(*b*)   the freeing of metal castings from adherent siliceous substance–

    (i)   by blasting with an abrasive propelled by compressed air, by steam or by a wheel; or

    (ii)   by the use of power-driven tools.

Any occupation in or incidental to the manufacture of china or earthenware (including sanitary earthenware, electrical earthenware and earthenware tiles), and any occupation involving substantial exposure to the dust arising therefrom.

Any occupation involving the grinding of mineral graphite, or substantial exposure to the dust arising from such grinding.

Any occupation involving the dressing of granite or any igneous rock by masons or the crushing of such materials, or substantial exposure to the dust arising from such operations.

Any occupation involving the use, or preparation for use, of a grindstone, or substantial exposure to the dust arising therefrom.

Any occupation involving–

(*a*)   the working or handling of asbestos or any admixture of asbestos;

(*b*)   the manufacture or repair of asbestos textiles or other articles containing or composed of asbestos;

(*c*) the cleaning of any machinery or plant used in any foregoing operations and of any chambers, fixtures and appliances for the collection of asbestos dust;

(*d*) substantial exposure to the dust arising from any of the foregoing operations.

Any occupation involving–

(*a*) work underground in any mine in which one of the objects of the mining operations is the getting of any mineral;

(*b*) the working or handling above ground at any coal or tin mine of any minerals extracted therefrom, or any operation incidental thereto;

(*c*) the trimming of coal in any ship, barge, or lighter, or in any dock or harbour or at any wharf or quay;

(*d*) the sawing, splitting or dressing of slate, or any operation incidental thereto.

Any occupation in or incidental to the manufacture of carbon electrodes by an industrial undertaking for use in the electrolytic extraction of aluminium from aluminium oxide, and any occupation involving substantial exposure to the dust arising therefrom.

Any occupation involving boiler scaling or substantial exposure to the dust arising therefrom.

[*Social Security (Industrial Injuries) (Prescribed Diseases) Regulations 1985 (SI 1985 No 967), 1 Sch, Part II*].

Any occupation involving:

2.   Byssinosis.   Work in any room where any process up to and including the weaving process is performed in a factory in which the spinning or manipulation of raw or waste cotton or of flax, or the weaving of cotton or flax, is carried on.

3.	Diffuse mesothelioma (primary neoplasm of the mesothelium of the pleura or of the pericardium or of the peritoneum).	(a)	The working or handling of asbestos or any admixture of asbestos; or
		(b)	the manufacture or repair of asbestos textiles or other articles containing or composed of asbestos; or
		(c)	the cleaning of any machinery or plant used in any of the foregoing operations and of any chambers, fixtures and appliances for the collection of asbestos dust; or
		(d)	substantial exposure to the dust arising from any of the foregoing operations.
4.	(As from 24 March 1996) allergic rhinitis		Exposure to any of the following agents:
		(a)	isocyanates;
		(b)	platinum salts;
		(c)	fumes or dusts arising from the manufacture, transport or use of hardening agents (including epoxy resin curing agents) based on phthalic anhydride, tetrachlorophthalic anhydride, trimellitic anhydride or triethylene-tetramine;
		(d)	fumes arising from the use of rosin as a soldering flux;
		(e)	proteolytic enzymes;
		(f)	animals including insects and other arthropods used for the purposes of research or education or in laboratories;
		(g)	dusts arising from the sowing, cultivation, harvesting, drying, handling, milling, transport or storage of barley, oats, rye, wheat or maize, or the handling, milling, transport or storage of meal or flour made therefrom;
		(h)	antibiotics;
		(i)	cimetidine;
		(j)	wood dust;

(*k*)   ispaghula;

(*l*)   castor bean dust;

(*m*)   ipecacuanha

(*n*)   azodicarbonamide;

(*o*)   animals including insects and other arthropods or their larval forms, used for the purposes of pest control or fruit cultivation, or the larval forms of animals used for the purposes of research or education or in laboratories;

(*p*)   glutaraldehyde;

(*q*)   persulphate salts or henna;

(*r*)   crustaceans or fish or products arising from these in the food processing industry;

(*s*)   reactive dyes;

(*t*)   soya bean;

(*u*)   tea dust;

(*v*)   green coffee bean dust;

(*w*)   fumes from stainless steel welding.

5.   Non-infective dermatitis of external origin (but excluding dermatitis due to ionising particles or electromagnetic radiations other than radiant heat).

Exposure to dust, liquid or vapour or any other external agent (except chromic acid, chromates or bi-chromates – as from 24 March 1996) capable of irritating the skin (including friction or heat but excluding ionising particles or electro-magnetic radiations other than radiant heat).

6.   Carcinoma of the nasal cavity or associated air sinuses (nasal carcinoma).

(*a*)   Attendance for work in, on or about a building where wooden goods are manufactured or repaired; or

(*b*)   attendance for work in a building used for the manufacture of footwear or components of footwear made wholly or partly of leather or fibre board; or

(c)   attendance for work at a place used wholly or mainly for the repair of footwear made wholly or partly of leather or fibre board.

Any occupation involving:

7.   Asthma which is due to exposure to any of the following agents:

Exposure to any of the agents set out in column 1 of this paragraph.

(a)   isocyanates;

(b)   platinum salts;

(c)   fumes or dusts arising from the manufacture, transport or use of hardening agents (including epoxy resin curing agents) based on phthalic anhydride, tetrachlorophthalic anhydride, trimellitic anhydride or triethylene-tetramine;

(d)   fumes arising from the use of rosin as a soldering flux;

(e)   proteolytic enzymes;

(f)   animals including insects and other anthropods used for the purposes of research or education or in laboratories;

(g)   dusts arising from the sowing, cultivation, harvesting, drying, handling, milling, transport or storage of barley, oats, rye, wheat or maize, or the handling, milling, transport or storage of meal or flour made therefrom;

(h)   antibiotics;

(i)   cimetidine;

(j)   wood dust;

(k)   ispaghula;

(*l*)   castor bean dust;

(*m*)   ipecacuanha;

(*n*)   azodicarbonamide;

(*o*)   animals including insects and other arthropods or their larval forms, used for the purposes of pest control or fruit cultivation, or the larval forms of animals used for the purposes of research, education or in laboratories;

(*p*)   glutaraldehyde;

(*q*)   persulphate salts or henna;

(*r*)   crustaceans or fish or products arising from these in the food processing industry;

(*s*)   reactive dyes;

(*t*)   soya bean;

(*u*)   tea dust;

(*v*)   green coffee bean dust;

(*w*)   fumes from stainless steel welding;

(*x*)   any other sensitising agent; (occupational asthma).

Moreover, the time at which a person shall be treated as having developed prescribed diseases B 12 and B 13, or occupational asthma due to exposure to agents specified in D 7 (o) to (x), is the first day on which that person is incapable of work, or suffering from a loss of faculty as a result of those diseases after 25 September 1991.

Any occupation involving:

8.   Primary carcinoma of the lung where there is accompanying evidence of one or both of the following:

    (*a*)   asbestosis;

(*a*)   The working or handling of asbestos or any admixture of asbestos; or

(*b*)   the manufacture or repair of asbestos textiles or other articles containing or composed of asbestos; or

	(*b*) bilateral diffuse pleural thickening.	(*c*)	the cleaning of any machinery or plant used in any of the foregoing operations and of any chambers, fixtures and appliances for the collection of asbestos dust; or
		(*d*)	substantial exposure to the dust arising from any of the foregoing operations.
9.	Bilateral diffuse pleural thickening.	(*a*)	The working or handling of asbestos or any admixture of asbestos; or
		(*b*)	the manufacture or repair of asbestos textiles or other articles containing or composed of asbestos; or
		(*c*)	the cleaning of any machinery or plant used in any of the foregoing operations and of any chambers, fixtures and appliances for the collection of asbestos dust; or
		(*d*)	substantial exposure to the dust arising from any of the foregoing operations.
10.	Primary carcinoma of the lung.	(*a*)	Work underground in a tin mine; or
		(*b*)	exposure to bis (chloromethyl) ether produced during the manufacture of chloromethyl methyl ether; or
		(*c*)	exposure to pure zinc chromate, calcium chromate or strontium chromate.
11.	Primary carcinoma of the lung with silicosis. (Presumed not to be recrudescent.) [*SI 1993 No 862, Reg 5*].	Any occupation involving exposure to silica dust in the course of	
		(*a*)	manufacture of glass or pottery;
		(*b*)	tunnelling in or quarrying sandstone or granite;
		(*c*)	mining metal ores;
		(*d*)	slate quarrying;
		(*e*)	mining clay;

(*f*)   use of siliceous materials as abrasives;

(*g*)   cutting stone;

(*h*)   stonemasonry;

(*j*)   work in a factory.

Any occupation involving:

12.   Chronic bronchitis or emphysema (or both) (except where claimant is entitled to disablement benefit for pneumoconiosis, under Reg 22(1) – 'where a person is disabled by pneumoconiosis, or pneumoconiosis accompanied by tuberculosis – assessed at, at least, 50%, the effects of any emphysema and chronic bronchitis are to be treated as pneumoconiosis').

Exposure to coal dust by reason of working underground in a coal mine for a period of, or periods amounting in the aggregate to, at least, 20 years (whether before or after 5 July 1948).

(In order to qualify for benefit a claimant must show

(*a*)   by means of a chest radiograph that he has coal dust retention to at least the level of Category 1 in the ILO's publication 'The Classification of Radiographs of Pneumoconioses' (Revised Edition 1980, 8th Impression 1992);

(*b*)   a forced expiratory volume in one second at least one litre below the mean value predicted in accordance with 'Lung function: Assessment and Application in Medicine' (Cotes, 4th Edition 1979) for a person of the claimant's age, height and sex, measured from the position of maximum inspiration with the claimant making maximum effort.)

[*Social Security (Industrial Injuries) (Prescribed Diseases) Regulations 1985 (SI 1985 No 967), 1 Sch; Social Security (Industrial Injuries) (Prescribed Diseases) Amendment Regulations 1987 (SI 1987 No 335); Social Security (Industrial Injuries) (Prescribed Diseases) (Amendment No 2) Regulations 1987 (SI 1987 No 2112), Reg 2, Sch; Social Security (Industrial Injuries) (Prescribed Diseases) Amendment Regulations 1989 (SI 1989 No 1207), Reg 6, Sch; Social Security (Industrial Injuries) (Prescribed Diseases) Amendment Regulations 1990 (SI 1990 No 2269); Social Security (Industrial Injuries) (Prescribed Diseases) Amendment Regulations 1991 (SI 1991 No 1938); Social Security (Industrial Injuries) (Prescribed Diseases) Amendment Regulations 1993 (SI 1993 No 862); Social Security (Industrial Injuries) (Prescribed Diseases) Amendment (No 2) Regulations 1993 (SI 1993 No 1985); Social Security (Industrial Injuries) (Prescribed Diseases) Amendment Regulations 1994 (SI 1994 No 2343); Social Security (Industrial Injuries and Diseases) (Miscellaneous Amendments) Regulations 1996 (SI 1996 No 425)*].

Occupiers' Liability

Introduction

O3001   Inevitably, by far the greater part of this book deals with the duties of employers (and employees) both at common law, and by virtue of the *Health and Safety at Work etc. Act 1974* and other kindred legislation. In addition, however, duties are laid on persons (including companies and local authorities) who merely *occupy* premises which other people either visit or carry out work activities upon, e.g. repair work or servicing.

More particularly, persons in control of premises (see O3004 below for meaning of 'control'), that is, occupiers of premises and employers, where others work (*although not their employees*), have a duty under *HSWA s 4* to take reasonable care towards such people working on the premises. Failure to comply with this duty can lead to prosecution and a fine on conviction (see further ENFORCEMENT). This duty applies to premises not *exclusively* used for private residence, e.g. lifts/electrical installations in the *common parts* of a block of flats, and exists for the benefit of workmen repairing/servicing them (*Westminster City Council v Select Managements Ltd [1985] 1 AER 897*).

Moreover, a person who is injured while working on or visiting premises, may be able to sue the occupier for damages, even though the injured person is not an employee. Statute law relating to this branch of civil liability (i.e. occupiers' liability) is to be found in the *Occupiers' Liability Act 1957* and, as far as trespassers are concerned, in the *Occupiers' Liability Act 1984*. (In Scotland, the law is to be found in the *Occupiers' Liability (Scotland) Act 1960*.)

Duties owed under the Occupiers' Liability Act 1957

O3002   An occupier of premises owes the same duty, the 'common duty of care', to all his lawful visitors. [*OLA 1957, s 2(1)*]. 'The common duty of care is a duty to take such care as in all the circumstances of the case is reasonable to see that the visitor will be reasonably safe in using the premises for the purposes for which he is invited or permitted by the occupier to be there.' [*OLA 1957, s 2(2)*]. Thus, a local authority which failed, in severe winter weather, to see that a path in school grounds was swept free of snow and treated with salt and was not in a slippery condition, was in breach of *Sec 2*, when a schoolteacher fell at 8.30 am and was injured (*Murphy v Bradford Metropolitan Council [1992] 2 AER 908*).

The duty extends only to requiring the occupier to do what is 'reasonable' in all the circumstances to ensure that the visitor will be safe. Some injuries occur where no one is obviously to blame. For example, in *Graney v Liverpool County Council (1995) (unreported)* an employee who slipped on icy paving slabs could not recover damages against his employer. The Court of Appeal held that many people slip on icy surfaces in cold weather – it did not follow that in this particular case the employer was to blame.

Nature of the duty

O3003   *OLA 1957* is concerned only with civil liability. 'The rules so enacted in relation to
an occupier of premises and his visitors shall also apply, in like manner and to like
extent as the principles applicable at common law to an occupier of premises and his
invitees or licensees would apply. . .' [*OLA 1957, s 1(3)*]. This contrasts with *HSWA
1974*, in which the obligations are predominantly penal measures enforced by the
HSE (or some other 'enforcing authority'). *OLA 1957* cannot be enforced by a state
agency – nor does it give rise to criminal liability. Action under *OLA 1957* must be
brought in a private suit between parties.

The liability of an occupier towards lawful visitors at common law was generally
based on negligence; so, too, is the liability under *OLA 1957*. It is never strict. In
Neame v Johnson [1993] PIQR 100, a case concerning an ambulanceman who was
injured in the defendant's house when carrying him unconscious in a chair in poor
lighting conditions, the ambulanceman knocked over a pile of books stacked by a
wall on a landing, and consequently slipped on a book, injuring himself. It was held
that the pile of books did not create a 'reasonably foreseeable risk of injury', and so
there was no liability. Nor does the duty of the occupier extend to replacing glass
panels in an ageing building. In *McGivney v Golderslea Ltd (1997) (unreported)* the
defendant owned a block of flats which had been built in 1955 – the glass in the door
at the foot of the communal stairs had been installed at the same time. When the
plaintiff, who was visiting a friend on the third floor, came down the stairs, he
slipped and his hand went through the glass panel on the front door resulting in
personal injuries. The plaintiff claimed that the defendant was in breach of *OLA
1957, s 2(2)*. However, at the time the flats were built the glass satisfied the building
regulations then in force. Since 1955 building regulations have been updated and, in
such a building being constructed today, stronger glass must be used such that on
the balance of probabilities the plaintiff's accident would not have occurred. The
Court of Appeal found that there was no duty on the defendant to replace the glass
and the plaintiff's claim therefore failed.

The relationship of occupier and visitor is less immediate than that of employer and
employee, and is not, as far as occupiers' liability is concerned, underwritten by
compulsory insurance (but by public liability insurance, which is not obligatory but
advisable).

Who is an 'occupier'?

O3004   'Occupation' is not defined in the Act, which merely states that the 'rules regulate
the nature of the duty imposed by law in consequence of a person's occupation or
control of premises . . . but they (shall) not alter the rules of the common law as to
the persons on whom a duty is so imposed or to whom it is owed . . .'. [*OLA 1957,
s 1(2)*]. The meaning of 'occupation' must, therefore, be gleaned from the rules of
common law. Where premises, including factory premises, are leased or subleased,
control may be shared by lessor and lessee or by sublessor and sublessee. 'Wherever
a person has a sufficient degree of control over premises that he ought to realise that
any failure on his part to use care may result in injury to a person coming lawfully
there, then he is an "occupier" and the person coming lawfully there is his "visitor"
and the "occupier" is under a duty to his "visitor" to use reasonable care. In order to
be an occupier it is not necessary for a person to have entire control over the
premises. He need not have exclusive occupation. Suffice it that he has some degree
of control with others' (per Lord Denning in *Wheat v E Lacon & Co Ltd [1965] 2
AER 700*). In *Jordan v Achara (1988) 20 HLR 607*, the plaintiff, who was a meter
reader, was injured when he fell down stairs in a basement of a house. The defendant
landlord, who was the owner of the house, had divided it into flats. Because of

arrears of payment, the electricity supply had been disconnected. The local authority, having arranged for it to be reconnected for the tenants, recovered payment by way of rents paid directly to the authority. It was held that the landlord was liable for the injury, under the *Occupiers' Liability Act 1957*, since he was the occupier of the staircase and the passageway (where the injury occurred) and his duties continued in spite of the local authority being in receipt of rents.

Liability associated with dangers arising from maintenance and repair of premises will be that of the person responsible, under the lease or sublease, for maintenance and/or repair. 'The duty of the defendants here arose not out of contract, but because they, as the requisitioning authority, were in law in possession of the house and were in practice responsible for repairs . . . and this control imposed upon them a duty to every person lawfully on the premises to take reasonable care to prevent damage through want of repair' (per Denning LJ in *Greene v Chelsea BC [1954] 2 AER 318*, concerning a defective ceiling which collapsed, injuring the appellant, a licensee). Significantly also, managerial control constitutes 'occupation' (*Wheat v Lacon*, see above, concerning an injury to a customer at a public house owned by a brewery and managed by a manager – both were held to be 'in control'). Moreover, if a landlord leases part of a building but retains other parts, e.g. roof, common staircase, lifts, he remains liable for that part of the premises (*Moloney v Lambeth BC (1966) 64 LGR 440*, concerning a guest injured on a defective common staircase in a block of council flats).

However, it is not the occupier's duty to make sure that the visitor is *completely safe*, but only reasonably so. For example, in *Berryman v London Borough of Hounslow, The Times, 18 December 1996*, the plaintiff injured her back when she was forced to carry heavy shopping up several flights of stairs because the lift in the block of flats maintained by the landlord was broken. The landlord's obligation to take care to ensure that the lift he provided was reasonably safe was discharged by employing competent contractors. There was no causal connection between the plaintiff's injury on the stairs and the absence of a lift service. In other words, the injury to the plaintiff was not a 'foreseeable consequence' of the broken lift.

Premises

O3005   *OLA* regulates the nature of the duty imposed by law in consequence of a person's occupation of premises. [*OLA 1957, s 1(2)*]. This means that the duties are not *personal* duties but depend on occupation of *premises*; and extend to a 'person occupying, or having control over, any fixed or movable structure, including any vessel, vehicle or aircraft' [*OLA 1957, s 1(3)(a)*] (e.g. a car, *Houweling v Wesseler [1963] 40 DLR(2d) 956-Canada* or, more recently, a sea wall in *Staples v West Dorset District Council (1995) 93 LGR 536*). In *Bunker v Charles Brand & Son Ltd [1969] 2 AER 59* the defendants were contractors digging a tunnel for the construction of the Victoria Line of London Underground. To this end they used a large digging machine which moved forward on rollers. The plaintiff was injured when he slipped on the rollers. The defendants were held to be occupiers of the tunnel, even though it was owned by London Transport.

To whom is the duty owed?

Visitors

O3006   Visitors to premises entitled to protection under the Act are both (*a*) invitees and (*b*) licensees. This means that protection is afforded to all lawful visitors, whether the visitors enter for the occupier's benefit (clients or customers) or for their own benefit (factory inspectors, policemen), though not to persons exercising a public or private way over premises. [*OLA 1957, s 2(6)*]. The House of Lords in *McGeown v Northern Ireland Housing Executive [1995] 1 AC 233* found that no duty of care was owed by an occupier of land over which a public right of way existed to persons lawfully exercising that right of way. They were not visitors for the purposes of *OLA 1957*, because use of a public right of way was incompatible with the concept of a visitor as defined in *OLA 1957*. This was clear because the defendant housing executive was found to have no power to exclude anyone from using the pathway. The concept of 'visitor' under the Act suggests the person in question has permission to be in a particular place at a particular time. Once a public right of way has been established, the question of permission being granted by the owner to those who choose to use the public right of way is irrelevant. They do so as of right and not by virtue of any licence or invitation.

Nevertheless, occupiers are under a duty to erect a notice warning visitors of the immediacy of a danger (*Rae (Geoffrey) v Mars (UK) [1990] 3 EG 80* where a deep pit was situated very close to the entrance of a dark shed, in which there was no artificial lighting, into which a visiting surveyor fell, sustaining injury. It was held that the occupier should have erected a warning). In some instances it may be necessary not only to provide proper warning notices but also to arrange for the supervision of visitors at the occupier's premises (*Farrant v Thanet District Council (1996) (unreported)*). However, there is no duty on an employer to light premises at night, which are infrequently used by day and not occupied at night. It is sufficient to provide a torch (*Capitano v Leeds Eastern Health Authority, Current Law, October 1989* where a security officer was injured when he fell down a flight of stairs at night, while checking the premises following the sounding of a burglar alarm. The steps were formerly part of a fire escape route but were now infrequently used).

Trespassers

O3007

'. . . a trespasser is not necessarily a bad man. A burglar is a trespasser; but so too is a law-abiding citizen who unhindered strolls across an open field. The statement that a trespasser comes upon land at his own risk has been treated as applying to all who trespass, to those who come for nefarious purposes and those who merely bruise the grass, to those who know their presence is resented and those who have no reason to think so.' (*Commissioner for Railways (NSW) v Cardy [1960] 34 ALJR 134*).

Common law defines a trespasser as a person who:

(*a*)   goes on to premises without invitation or permission; or

(*b*)   although invited or permitted to be on premises, goes to a part of the premises to which the invitation or permission does not extend; or

(*c*)   remains on premises after the invitation or permission to be there has expired; or

(*d*)   deposits goods on premises when not authorised to do so.

Duty owed to trespassers, at common law and under the Occupiers' Liability Act 1984

Common law

O3008

Common law used to be that an occupier was not liable for injury caused to a trespasser, unless the injury was either intentional or done with reckless disregard for the trespasser's presence (*R Addie & Sons (Collieries) Ltd v Dumbreck [1929] AC 358*). In more recent times, however, the common law has adopted an attitude of humane conscientiousness towards simple (as distinct from aggravated) trespassers. '. . . the question whether an occupier is liable in respect of an accident to a trespasser on his land would depend on whether a conscientious, humane man with his knowledge, skill and resources could reasonably have been expected to have done, or refrained from doing, before the accident, something which would have avoided it. If he knew before the accident that there was a substantial probability that trespassers would come I think that most people would regard as culpable failure to give any thought to their safety.' (*Herrington v British Railways Board [1972] 1 AER 749*). The effect of this House of Lords case was that it became possible for a trespasser to bring a successful action in negligence under the common law. However, the precise nature of the occupier's duty to the trespasser remained unclear, leading to Parliamentary intervention culminating in the *Occupiers' Liability Act 1984*.

Occupiers' Liability Act 1984

O3009   The *Occupiers' Liability Act 1984* introduced a duty on an occupier in respect of trespassers, that is persons whether they have 'lawful authority to be in the vicinity or not' who may be at risk of injury on his premises. [*OLA 1984, s 1*]. Thus, an occupier owes a duty of care to a trespasser in respect of any injury suffered on the premises (either because of any danger due to the state of the premises, or things done or omitted to be done) [*OLA 1984, s 1(3)(a)*], in the following circumstances:

(*a*)   if he was aware of the danger or had reasonable grounds to believe that it exists;

(*b*)   if he knows or has reasonable grounds to believe that a trespasser is in the vicinity of the danger concerned, or that he may come into the vicinity of the danger; and

(*c*)   if the risk is one against which, in all the circumstances of the case, he may reasonably be expected to offer some protection.

Where under *OLA 1984*, the occupier is under a duty of care to the trespasser in respect of the risk, the standard of care is 'to take such care as is reasonable in all the circumstances of the case to see that he does not suffer injury on the premises by reason of the danger concerned'. [*OLA 1984, s 1(4)*]. The duty can be discharged by issuing a warning, e.g. posting notices warning of hazards; these, however, must be explicit and not merely vague. Thus, 'Danger' might not be sufficient whereas 'Highly Flammable Liquid Vapours – No Smoking' would be [*OLA 1984, s 1(5)*] (see O3015 below). Moreover, under *OLA 1984* there is no duty to persons who willingly accept risks (see O3016 below). However, the fact that an occupier has taken precautions to prevent persons going on his land, where there is a danger, does not mean that the occupier has reason to believe that someone would be likely to come into the vicinity of the danger, thereby owing a duty to the trespasser, under the *Occupiers' Liability Act 1984, s 1(4)* (*White v St Albans City and District Council, The Times, 12 March 1990*). In *Revil v Newbury, The Times, 3 November 1995*, the court considered the duty of an occupier to an intruder. It found that the intruder could recover damages despite being engaged in unlawful activities at the time the injury occurred. The defendant was held to have injured the intruder by using greater force than was justified (by shooting the intruder through a locked door) in protecting himself and his property. The doctrine of *ex turpi causa non oritur actio* (i.e. no cause of action may be founded on an immoral or illegal act) cannot, without more, be relied upon by the defendant to escape liability. Violence may be returned with necessary violence, but the force used must not exceed the limits of what is reasonable in all the circumstances. For the extent of the intruder's contributory negligence, see O3011 below.

Children

O3010   'An occupier must be prepared for children to be less careful than adults.' [*OLA 1957, s 2(3)(a)*]. Where an adult would be regarded as a trespasser, a child is likely to qualify as an implied licensee, and this in spite of the stricture that 'it is hard to see how infantile temptations can give rights however much they excuse peccadilloes' (per Hamilton LJ in *Latham v Johnson & Nephew Ltd [1913] 1 KB 398*). If there is something or some state of affairs on the premises (e.g. machinery, a boat, a pond, bright berries, a motor car, forklift truck, scaffolding), this may constitute a 'trap' to a child. If the child is then injured by the 'trap', the occupier will often be liable. Though sometimes the presence of a parent may be treated as an implied condition of the permission to enter premises (e.g. when children go on to premises at dusk – *Phipps v Rochester Corporation [1955] 1 AER 129*). Perhaps the current common law position regarding 'child-trespass' was best put as follows: 'The doctrine that a trespasser, however innocent, enters land at his own risk, that in no circumstances is he owed a duty of reasonable or any care by the owners or occupiers of the land, however conscious they may be of the likelihood of his presence and of the grave risk of terrible injury to which he will probably be exposed, may have been all very well when rights of property, particularly in land, were regarded as more sacrosanct than any other human right. . . It is difficult to see why today this doctrine should not be buried' (per Salmon LJ in *Herrington v British Railways Board*, concerning a six-year-old boy electrocuted on the defendant's electrified line) (but see O3017 below, *Titchener v British Railways Board*). Even though the children had been warned of the danger, the defendant company was still held liable in *Southern Portland Cement v Cooper [1974] AC 623*.

A different approach was taken more recently by the Court of Appeal in allowing the council's appeal in *Jolley v London Borough of Sutton, The Times, 23 June 1998*. A 14 year old schoolboy had been awarded damages (reduced by 25 per cent for contributory negligence) for severe injuries sustained when he and a friend were attempting to restore an abandoned cabin cruiser on council land. In order to carry out repairs to the hull, the boys used a car jack to lift the front of the boat off the ground. However, the boat was rotten and no amount of work would have rendered the boat seaworthy. The plaintiff was underneath the boat when it fell on him. Although it was accepted that the council owed the child a duty of care under *OLA 1957, s 2(3)(a)*, and was negligent in failing to remove the boat, the court held that the immediate cause of the accident was the propping up of the boat by the boys: 'Even making full allowance for the unpredictability of children's behaviour, it was not reasonably foreseeable that an accident could occur as a result of the boys deciding to work under a propped up boat. Nor could any reasonably similar accident have been foreseen.' The court criticised the approach traditionally taken in previous cases to accidents involving children: 'There was . . . a tendency to proceed from the proposition that once meddling by children was foreseeable then, whatever form it might take none of its manifestations could be regarded as unexpected. That approach was flawed.' In this case, the council could not reasonably have foreseen that the boys would prop up the boat and that one of them would be injured in this way. Despite owing them a duty of care, it was the boys' actions which actually caused the accident and not the council's negligence in failing to remove the boat.

Contributory negligence

O3011   In a number of cases brought under *OLA 1957*, the question of contributory negligence is often considered and impacts considerably on the amount of damages eventually awarded. This may be because the duty on the occupier is only to take such care as is reasonable to see that the visitor will be reasonably safe in using his premises. Therefore, it is possible to imagine that, even where an occupier is found to have breached his duty of care, the injured party may also, by his own conduct, have contributed to the circumstances giving rise to the injury and may have exacerbated the severity of the injuries sustained. The *Law Reform (Contributory Negligence) Act 1945, s 1(1)* provides that 'where any person suffers damage as the result partly of his own fault and partly of the fault of another person, a claim in respect of that damage shall not be defeated by reason of the fault of the person suffering the damage, but the damage recoverable in respect thereof shall be reduced to such extent as the Court thinks just having regard to the claimant's share in the responsibility of the damage'. There is nothing to suggest that the above provision does not apply to children or trespassers. However, Lord Denning in *Gough v Thorn [1966] 3 All ER 398* held that 'a very young child cannot be guilty of contributory negligence. An older child may be. But it depends on the circumstances'. In *Revil v Newbury* (see O3009 above*), although the defendant's conduct was not reasonable, the plaintiff intruder was found to be two-thirds to blame for the injuries he suffered and his damages were reduced accordingly.

Dangers to guard against

O3012   The duty owed by an occupier to his lawful visitors is a 'common duty of care', so called since the duty is owed to both invitees and licensees, i.e. those having an interest in common with the occupier (e.g. business associates, customers, clients, salesmen) and those permitted by regulation/statute to be on the premises, e.g. factory inspectors/policemen. That duty requires that the dangers against which the occupier must guard are twofold: (*a*) structural defects in the premises; and (*b*) dangers associated with works/operations carried out for the occupier on the premises.

Structural defects

O3013   As regards structural defects in premises, the occupier will only be liable if either he actually knew of a defect or foreseeably had reason to believe that there was a defect in the premises. Simply put, the occupier would not incur liability for the existence of latent defects causing injury or damage, unless he had *special* knowledge in that regard, e.g. a faulty electrical circuit, unless he were an electrician; whereas, he would be liable for patent (i.e. obvious) structural defects, e.g. an unlit hole in the road. This duty now extends to 'uninvited entrants', e.g. trespassers, under *OLA 1984, s 1*.

Workmen on occupier's premises

O3014   'An occupier may expect that a person, in the exercise of his calling, will appreciate and guard against any special risks ordinarily incident to it, so far as the occupier leaves him free to do so.' [*OLA 1957, s 2(3)(b)*]. This has generally been taken to imply that risks associated with system or method of work on customer premises are the exclusive responsibility of the employer (not the customer or occupier) (*General Cleaning Contractors Ltd v Christmas* (see W9034 WORK AT HEIGHTS)), though how far this rule now applies specifically to window cleaners themselves is doubtful (see *King v Smith* at W9034 WORK AT HEIGHTS). This means that risks associated with the system or method of work on third party premises are the responsibility of the employer not the occupier (*General Cleaning Contractors Ltd v Christmas [1952] 2 AER 1110*, concerning a window cleaner who failed to take proper precautions in respect of a defective sash window: it was held that there was no liability on the part of the occupier, but liability on the part of the employer (see EMPLOYERS' DUTIES TO THEIR EMPLOYEES)). The occupier will only incur liability for a structural defect in premises which the oncoming workman would not normally guard against as part of a safe system of doing his job, i.e. against 'unusual' dangers. 'And with respect to such a visitor at least, we consider it settled law that he, using reasonable care on his part for his own safety, is entitled to expect that the occupier shall on his part use reasonable care to prevent damage from unusual danger, which he knows or ought to know' (per Willes J in *Indermaur v Dames [1866] LR 1 CP 274*, concerning a gasfitter testing gas burners in a sugar refinery who fell into an unfenced shaft and was injured).

Case law has highlighted some liability on the part of occupiers to particular classes of employees, namely firemen and, more recently, window cleaners (*King v Smith [1995] ICR 339*).

The law is not entirely settled in the case of firemen (*Sibbald v Sher Bros, The Times, 1 February 1981*): 'It (is) . . . very unlikely that the duty of care owed by the occupier to workers was the same as that owed to firemen,' (per Lord Fraser of Tullybelton), (but) it is arguable that a 'fireman (is) a "neighbour" of the occupier in the sense of Lord Atkin's famous dictum in *Donoghue v Stevenson [1932] AC 562*, so that the occupier owes him some duty of care, as for instance, to warn firemen of an unexpected danger or trap of which he knew or ought to know' (per Waller LJ in *Hartley v British Railways Board (1981) SJ 125*). One's neighbour was defined in law as follows: 'persons who are so closely and directly affected by my act that I ought reasonably to have them in contemplation as being so affected when I am directing my mind to the acts or omissions which are called in question' (per Lord Atkin in *Donoghue v Stevenson [1932] AC 562*).

In sum, an occupier will be liable:

(a)   if he exposes a fireman to the risk of injury/death over and above the normal risks (see further F5052 (*a*) and (*b*) FIRE AND FIRE PRECAUTIONS); and

(b)   in accordance with the general principles of negligence, in non-emergency situations (as per *Ogwo v Taylor [1987] 3 AER 961*, applying the 'neighbour' principle of *Donoghue v Stevenson*).

In both cases, the basis of action is negligence, either at common law or under the *Occupiers' Liability Act 1957* or both.

Dangers associated with works being done on premises

O3015   Where work is being done on premises by a contractor, the occupier is not liable if he:

(a)   took care in selecting a competent contractor; and

(b)   satisfied himself that the work was being properly done by the contractor.

[*OLA 1957, s 2(4)(b)*].

As regards (*b*) it may be highly desirable (indeed necessary) for an occupier to delegate the 'duty of satisfaction', especially where complicated building/ engineering operations are being carried out, to a specialist, e.g. an architect, geotechnical engineer. Not to do so, in the interests of safety of visitors, is probably negligent. 'In the case of the construction of a substantial building, or of a ship, I should have thought that the building owner, if he is to escape subsequent tortious liability for faulty construction, should not only take care to contract with a competent contractor . . . but also cause that work to be supervised by a properly qualified professional . . . such as an architect or surveyor . . . I cannot think that different principles can apply to precautions during the course of construction, if the building owner is going to invite a third party to bring valuable property on to the site during construction' (per Mocatta J in *AMF International Ltd v Magnet Bowling Ltd [1968] 2 AER 789*).

Waiver of duty and the Unfair Contract Terms Act 1977 (UCTA)

O3016   Where damage was caused to a visitor by a danger of which he had been warned by the occupier (e.g. by notice), an explicit notice, e.g. 'Highly Flammable Liquid Vapours – No Smoking' (as distinct from a vague notice such as 'Fire Hazards') used to absolve an occupier from liability. Now, however, such notices are ineffective (except in the case of trespassers, see O3008 above) and do not exonerate occupiers. Thus: 'a person cannot by reference to any contract term or to a notice given to persons generally or to particular persons exclude or restrict his liability for death or personal injury resulting from negligence'. [*UCTA s 2*]. Such explicit notices are, however, a defence to an occupier when sued for negligent injury by a simple trespasser under the *Occupiers' Liability Act 1984*. As regards negligent damage to property, a person can restrict or exclude his liability by a notice or contract term, but such notice or contract term must be 'reasonable', and it is incumbent on the occupier to prove that it is in fact reasonable. [*UCTA ss 2(2), 11*].

The question of whether the defendant did what was reasonable fairly to bring to the notice of the plaintiff the existence of a particular onerous condition, regarding his statutory rights, was considered in *Interfoto Picture Library Ltd v Stiletto Visual Programmes Ltd [1989] QB 433*. It was held that for a condition seeking to restrict statutory rights (e.g. under *OLA 1957*) to be effective it must have been fairly brought to the attention of a party to the contract by way of some clear indication which would lead an ordinary sensible person to realise, at or before the time of making the contract, that such a term relating to personal injury was to be included in the contract.

Risks willingly accepted – 'volenti non fit injuria'

O3017   'The common duty of care does not impose on an occupier any obligation to a visitor in respect of risks willingly accepted as his by the visitor'. [*OLA 1957, s 2(5)*]. However, this 'defence' has generally not succeeded in industrial injuries claims. This is similarly the case with occupiers' liability claims (*Burnett v British Waterways Board [1973] 2 AER 631* where a lighterman was held not to be bound by the terms of a notice erected by the respondent, even though he had seen it many times and understood it). This decision has since been reinforced by the *Unfair Contract Terms Act 1977*. 'Where a contract term or notice purports to exclude or restrict liability for negligence a person's agreement to or awareness of it is not of itself to be taken as indicating his voluntary acceptance of any risk.' [*UCTA s 2(3)*]. *OLA 1957* makes clear that there may be circumstances in which even an explicit warning will not absolve the occupier from liability. Nevertheless, the occupier is entitled to expect a reasonable person to appreciate certain obvious dangers and take appropriate action to ensure his safety. In those circumstances no warning would appear to be required. It was not necessary, for example, to warn an adult of sound mind that it was dangerous to go near the edge of a cliff in *Cotton v Derbyshire Dales District Council, The Times, 20 June 1994*. This is not, however, the position with respect to trespassers. *OLA 1984, s 1(6)* states, 'No duty is owed . . . to any person in respect of risks willingly accepted as his by that person . . .'. This applies even if the trespasser is a child (see O3010 above) (*Titchener v British Railways Board 1984 SLT 192* where a 15-year-old girl and her boyfriend aged 16 had been struck by a train. The boy was killed and the girl suffered serious injuries. They had squeezed through a gap in a fence to cross the line as a short-cut to a disused brickworks which was regularly used. It was held by the House of Lords that the respondent did not owe a duty to the girl to do more than they had done to maintain the fence. It would have been 'quite unreasonable' for the respondent to maintain an impenetrable and unclimbable fence. But the 'duty (to maintain fences) will tend to be higher with a very young or a very old person than with a normally active and intelligent adult or adolescent' (per Lord Fraser). This position might well be otherwise if anti-trespasser devices were not satisfactorily maintained (*Adams v Southern Electricity Board, The Times, 21 October 1993* where the electricity board was held to be liable to a teenage trespasser for injuries sustained when he climbed on to apparatus by means of a defective anti-climbing device).

In the curious case of *Arthur v Anka [1996] 2 WLR 602* a car was parked without permission in a private car park. It was clamped but the driver removed his vehicle with the clamp still attached. The owner of the car park sued the driver for the return of the wheel clamp and payment of the fine for illegal parking. The question of *volenti* was considered in detail. The judge held that the owner parked his car in full knowledge that he was not entitled to do so and that he was therefore consenting to the consequences of his action (payment of the fine); he could not complain after the event. The effect of this consent was to render conduct lawful which would otherwise have been tortious. By voluntarily accepting the risk that his car might be clamped, the driver accepted the risk that the car would remain clamped until he paid the reasonable cost of clamping and de-clamping.

Actions against factory occupiers

O3018 The *Workplace (Health, Safety and Welfare) Regulations 1992 (SI 1992 No 3004)* which came into force, in so far as existing workplaces are concerned, on 1 January 1996 now apply with respect to the health, safety and welfare of persons in a defined workplace. The application of the Regulations is not confined to factories and offices – they also affect public buildings such as hospitals and schools, but they do not apply to, for example, construction sites and quarries. Employers, persons who have control of the workplace and occupiers are all subject to the Regulations, the provisions of which address the environmental management and condition of buildings, such as the day-to-day considerations of ventilation, temperature control and lighting and potentially dangerous activities such as window cleaning. In many ways the Regulations reflect the obligations imposed by the old *Factories Act 1961*. For example, *Regulation 12(3)* requires floors and traffic routes, 'so far as is reasonably practicable', to be kept free from obstacles or substances which may cause a person to 'slip, trip or fall'. These Regulations also closely mirror the general obligation placed on employers by *HSWA s 2* to ensure so far as is reasonably practicable, the health, safety and welfare of their employees whilst at work. Breach of these Regulations gives rise to civil liability by virtue of *HSWA s 47(2)* (for criminal liability, see O3019 below and ENFORCEMENT).

An approved Code of Practice and Guidance to the Regulations is available from the Health and Safety Commission.

Occupier's duties under HSWA 1974

O3019 In addition to civil liabilities under the *Occupiers' Liability Act 1957* and at common law, occupiers of buildings also have duties, the failure of which to carry out can lead to criminal liability under *HSWA*. More particularly, 'each person who has, to any extent, control of premises (i.e. "non-domestic" premises) or the means of access thereto or egress therefrom or of any plant or substance in such premises' must do what is reasonably practicable to see that the premises, means of access and egress and plant/substances on the premises, are safe and without health risks. [*HSWA s 4(2)*]. This section applies in the case of (*a*) non-employees and (*b*) non-domestic premises. [*HSWA s 4(1)*]. In other words, it places health and safety duties on persons and companies letting or sub-letting premises for work purposes, even though the persons working in those premises are not employees of the lessor/ sublessor. The duty also extends to non-working persons, e.g. children at a play centre (*Moualem v Carlisle City Council (1994) 158 JPN 786*). As with most other forms of leasehold tenure, the person who is responsible for maintenance and repairs of the leased premises is the person who has 'control' (see, by way of analogy, O3004 above). [*HSWA s 4(3)*]. Included as 'premises' are common parts of a block of flats. These are 'non-domestic' premises (*Westminster City Council v Select Managements Ltd [1985] 1 AER 897* which held that being a 'place' or 'installation on land', such areas are 'premises'; and they are not 'domestic', since they are in common use by the occupants of more than one private dwelling).

Moreover, the reasonableness of the measures which a person is required to take to ensure the safety of those premises is to be determined in the light of his knowledge of the expected use for which the premises have been made available and of the extent of his control and knowledge, if any, of the use thereafter. More particularly, if premises were not a reasonably foreseeable cause of danger to anyone acting in a way a person might reasonably be expected to act, in circumstances that might reasonably be expected to occur during the carrying out of the work, further measures would not be required against unknown and unexpected events (*Mailer v Austin Rover Group [1989] 2 AER 1087* where an employee of a firm of cleaning contractors, whilst cleaning one of the appellant's paint spray booths and the sump underneath it, was killed by escaping fumes. The contractors had been instructed by the appellants not to use paint thinners from a pipe in the booth (which the appellants had turned off but not capped) and only to enter the sump (where the ventilator would have been turned off) with an approved safety lamp and when no one was working above. Contrary to those instructions, an employee used thinners from the pipe, which had then entered the sump below, where the deceased was working with a non-approved lamp, and an explosion occurred. It was held that the appellant was not liable for breach of *HSWA s 4(2)*).

When considering criminal liability of an occupier under *HSWA* in relation to risks to outside contractors, *s 4* is likely to be of less significance in the future because of the decision of the House of Lords in *R v Associated Octel [1994] ICR 281*, a decision which in effect enables *HSWA, s 3* to be used against occupiers. *Section 3(1)* provides that 'It shall be the duty of every employer to conduct his undertaking in such a way as to ensure, so far as is reasonably practicable, that persons not in his employment who may be affected thereby are not thereby exposed to risks to their health or safety'. The decision establishes that an occupier can still be conducting his undertaking by engaging contractors to do work, even where the activities of the contractor are separate and not under the occupier's control. *Section 3* therefore requires the occupier to take steps to ensure the protection of contractors' employees from risks not merely arising from the physical state of the premises but also from the process of carrying out the work itself.

Offices and Shops

Introduction

O5001   The principal health, safety and welfare requirements in offices and shops are contained in the *Workplace (Health, Safety and Welfare) Regulations 1992* (see W11001 WORKPLACES – HEALTH, SAFETY AND WELFARE). There are only a few remaining provisions of the *Offices, Shops and Railway Premises Act 1963* still in force (although much of the old Act has been preserved in so far as it applies to registrars of births, deaths and marriages and to the police). Although not so intrinsically or potentially hazardous as factories and other workshops, offices and shops can still pose dangers to employees, visitors and members of the public. This chapter considers the main hazards in offices and shops along with recommended remedial action as well as the topical issue of VDUs. Moreover, since shops are workplaces visited daily by members of the public, civil liability relating to injuries suffered by customers has tended to be strict.

Hazards in offices

O5002   The average office would appear to be a relatively safe place compared with, say, a typical factory or workshop. Nevertheless, injuries do occur to office staff by way of slips, trips and falls, often when moving equipment or carrying loads or passing along blocked corridors or passageways. Electricity transmission can also pose dangers as a result of defective plugs or sockets, or of inappropriate loads, and, more topically, VDUs have attracted (and continue to do so) a considerable volume of litigation. In addition, photocopying equipment requires particular precautions. There are certain specified machines which cannot be operated in offices unless the operator has been adequately trained and is under supervision.

Fire is probably the main office hazard. This may be simply associated with human carelessness, such as the inadvertent disposal of cigarette ends. A wide range of flammable materials can be found in offices: spirit-based cleaning fluids, floor polishes, paper and many forms of packaging materials. All these substances are fire hazards if not controlled. Equally important in combating risk of fire is the maintenance of high safety standards in respect of electricity. It is important to bear in mind the following:

(*a*)   the provision of sufficient socket outlets and the minimal use of adaptors;

(*b*)   sockets should not be overloaded;

(*c*)   electrical equipment should be regularly tested;

(*d*)   taped joints for connecting cables should be prohibited;

(*e*)   plugs and leads should be regularly inspected in order to identify damage to cables and signs of overheating;

(*f*)   equipment should be switched off before it is unplugged or cleaned;

(*g*)   faulty switches should be identified;

(h)   malfunctioning electrical equipment should be reported.

The introduction of computerised equipment and word processors can create electrical hazards. The fact is that many of the older offices were not designed for so much electrical equipment, with the result that there is overloading with frequent use of multi-point adaptors, extension leads, wiring of more than one appliance into a 13 amp plug and overfilling of riser shafts. In older offices without central heating, there are freestanding heating appliances which can lead to further overloading of the electricity supply. There is also the risk of such appliances falling or being knocked over, leading to the danger of fire on the premises.

Visual display units and lighting

Health factors

O5003   Introduction of new technology, in the form of VDUs, has ushered in, over the last decade, a rash of complaints from operators, the principal complaint being eye strain or visual fatigue. It is thought that one in three VDU operators suffers from eye strain, back pain or general lethargy, and one in four from headaches attributable to glare discomfort and terminal reflections. Moreover, incidence of ocular discomfort among VDU operators, such as secretaries, journalists, finance dealers and graphic designers, has been reported as being twice that of the rest of the national workforce.

Visual fatigue is common to many tasks requiring a high degree of concentration and visual perception. Common symptoms are eye irritation, aggravated by rubbing; redness and soreness, together with temporary blurring and visual confusion. Spots, shapes in front of the eyes and chromatic effects (i.e. the sensation of coloured shapes before the eyes) surrounding viewed objects, also occur. Some people experience a fear or dislike of light or bright lights (photophobia), resulting in the need to wear dark glasses. Headaches are the most common symptom.

Generally, visual fatigue has a varied and complex pattern of symptoms, a component generally being anxiety. It is a temporary and reversible phenomenon, current optical wisdom arguing that it is impossible to damage eyes through the use of VDUs. Age, visual sharpness and performance are all significant in assessing whether an operator is likely to be affected by visual fatigue (see O5004 below). VDU operators can also suffer from musculo-skeletal strain – stiffness and tenderness of the neck, shoulders and forearms as well as Repetitive Strain Injury (RSI) now referred to as work related upper limb disorder (WRULD) (see further OCCUPATIONAL HEALTH AND DISEASES) caused by repeated finger, hand/arm movements emanating from use of a keyboard, and also stress. More rarely, they may suffer from photogenic epilepsy. Compensation has recently been awarded to employees on the ground of repetitive strain injury (see *McSherry and Lodge v British Telecom Ltd [1992] 3 Med LR 129*.

Methods of combating visual fatigue include investment in the installation of a non-reflective, protective VDU glare filter screen varying employees' visual tasks, with only a specified percentage (say 50%) of a working day devoted to VDU work, and a specified maximum continuous period of work (say 1 hour), followed by a break (say of 15 minutes), location of the display screen to minimise glare, correct specification and use of window coverings, etc.

Operational considerations

O5004   Visual fatigue can be associated with:

(a)   poor legibility, due to factors in the VDU such as 'flicker', 'shimmer' and 'jitter', which are directly related to the 'refresh rate' (i.e. the rate at which the phosphors return to luminosity after they have faded) of the display system;

(*b*)   poor definition of the screen characters against the background field;

(*c*)   glare;

(*d*)   unsuitable background lighting;

(*e*)   poor quality source material; and

(*f*)   visual defects on the part of the operator.

Items (*a*) to (*d*) above can be corrected through good VDU and workplace design. Very few people, however, have perfect vision, the ability to see varying with age, and the presence or absence of visual defects, e.g. myopia (short-sightedness) and hypermetropia (long-sightedness). On this basis, it is recommended that vision screening should be a standard feature of any pre-employment health examination for VDU operators, followed by further vision screening at intervals. Operators may need modifications to their prescription lenses to undertake such work. They should consult their optician whenever discomfort or visual fatigue is experienced, informing the optician of the type of work they perform (see O5005, O5006 below for statutory eyetest rights).

Statutory requirements relating to VDUs – the Health and Safety (Display Screen Equipment) Regulations 1992

O5005   The *Health and Safety (Display Screen Equipment) Regulations 1992 (SI 1992 No 2792)* impose the following duties on employers:

(1)   To assess (and review) health and safety risks to persons exposed at VDU workstations, whether or not provided by the employer, and reduce risks so identified. [*Reg 2*].

Risk assessment

Given the health risks involved (see O5003 above) and the possibility of liability being incurred by an employer for musculo-skeletal disorders, employers will have to assess the extent of such risks in the case of display screen workers who are:

(*a*)   employees, including home-workers;

(*b*)   employees of other employers ('temps'); or

(*c*)   self-employed (e.g. self-employed temps, journalists).

Workstations used at home will also have to be assessed.

The risk assessment should be:

(i)   systematic, with investigation of non-obvious causes, e.g. poor posture may be a response to glare rather than poor furniture;

(ii)   appropriate to the foreseeable degree of risk – itself depending on duration, intensity or difficulty of work; and

(iii)   comprehensive, covering organisational, job, workplace and individual factors.

Probably the best form of assessment is an ergonomic checklist and employees must have received the necessary training (see O5007 below) before completing such checklist. Once done, the assessment must be recorded, if necessary electronically, and kept readily accessible. Assessments should be reviewed in the following cases:

(1)   major change to software;

(2)   major change to hardware;

(3)   major change to workstation furniture;

(4)   relocation of workstation;

(5)   significant modification of lighting; and

(6)   change in the user's VDU related workload, either in terms of quantity or complexity.

(2)   To ensure that display screen equipment (DSE) work is periodically inter-rupted by breaks or changes of activity so as to reduce the workload of employees. [*Reg 4*].

(3)   Provide employees with:

(*a*)   initial eye/eyesight tests on request;

(*b*)   subsequent eye/eyesight tests at regular intervals, with consent of the operator;

(*c*)   additional eye/eyesight tests on request, where users are encountering visual difficulties;

(*d*)   special corrective appliances where tests show that normal corrective appliances cannot be used

[*Reg 5*]

(employees cannot, however, be required to take eyesight tests against their will [*Reg 5(6)*]);

(*e*)   adequate health and safety training in use of the workstation and whenever the workstation is substantially modified [*Reg 6*] (see further O5007 below); and

(*f*)   adequate health and safety information in connection with the work-station and in order to enable them to comply with *Regs 2-6* [*Reg 7*].

Penalties for breach of these regulations coincide with those for breach of *HSWA* (see ENFORCEMENT).

Employee eye care

O5006   Employers can arrange with individual opticians to provide care and examination on site or at an optician's practice; the employee cannot elect which. Sometimes, however, an employer may wish to offer 'vision screening'; if an employee does not want to be screened he can opt for full eye examination; similarly, if he is vision-screened but still has visual symptoms when using the screen. For this reason, many opticians provide a 'vision-work' service, offering on-site facilities for screening and full eyesight testing.

Training and health and safety information

O5007

(*a*)   *Information* should be provided to all operators of VDUs or to employees and/or agency workers and should relate to:

(i)   risks from display screen equipment   – employees

(ii) risk assessments (see O5005 above) and measures to reduce risks and any risks resulting from changes to the workstation	– employees of others (e.g. agency workers or temps)
	– self-employed operators
(iii) breaks/activity changes	– employees
(iv) eye/eyesight tests	– employees
(v) initial training	– employees
(vi) training following modification of workstation – employees	

(*b*)   *Training* (which is only required to be given to employees) should relate to:

(i)   comfort of posture and importance of postural change;

(ii)   use of adjustment mechanisms, especially furniture;

(iii)   use and arrangement of components for good posture and to prevent overreaching and avoid glare and reflections;

(iv)   need for regular cleaning of screens and other equipment;

(v)   need for breaks and activity changes.

Workstation equipment

O5008   (*a*)   *Display screens* must have

(i)   well-defined, clean characters,

(ii)   stable, flicker-free image,

(iii)   adjustable brightness/contrast,

(iv)   easy swivel/tilt, and

(v)   be free of glare/reflections.

(*b*)   *Keyboards* must

(i)   be tiltable and separate from display,

(ii)   have space in front to support arms/hands,

(iii)   have matt, non-reflective surfaces,

(iv)   have adequately contrasted symbols.

(*c*)   *Work desks* must have

(i)   a large, low reflectance surface,

(ii)   a document holder, if necessary,

(iii)   adequate space for comfortable position.

(*d*)   *Work chairs* must

(i)   be stable but allow worker easy freedom of movement,

(ii)   be adjustable in backrest height/tilt and seat height,

(iii)   have a footrest available, if necessary.

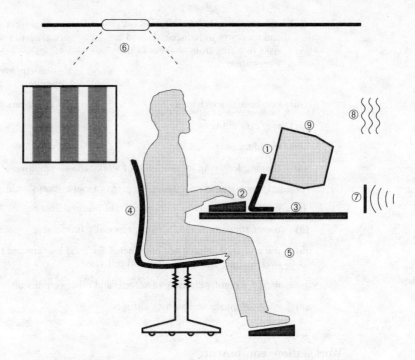

① SCREEN: READABLE AND STABLE IMAGE, ADJUSTABLE, GLARE FREE
② KEYBOARD: USABLE, ADJUSTABLE, KEY TOPS LEGIBLE
③ WORK SURFACE: ALLOW FLEXIBLE ARRANGEMENT, SPACIOUS, GLARE FREE, DOCUMENT HOLDER AS APPROPRIATE
④ WORK CHAIR: APPROPRIATE ADJUSTABILITY PLUS FOOT REST
⑤ LEG ROOM AND CLEARANCES: TO FACILITATE POSTURAL CHANGE

⑥ LIGHTING: PROVISION OF ADEQUATE CONTRAST, NO DIRECT OR INDIRECT GLARE OR REFLECTIONS
⑦ DISTRACTING NOISE MINIMISED
⑧ NO EXCESSIVE HEAT, ADEQUATE HUMIDITY
⑨ SOFTWARE: APPROPRIATE TO THE TASK AND ADAPTED TO USER CAPABILITIES, PROVIDE FEEDBACK ON SYSTEM STATUS, NO CLANDESTINE MONITORING

VDUs – User/Equipment Interface

Workstation environment

O5009   The following environmental conditions should be satisfied.

(*a*)   *Space* – it should be designed to allow for change of posture.

(*b*)   *Lighting* – there should be satisfactory lighting conditions, secondary adjustable lighting, and glare should be avoided by layout and design of light fittings.

(*c*)   *Heat* – equipment heat should not cause discomfort.

(*d*)   *Radiation* – all electromagnetic radiation (except visible light) should be reduced to negligible levels.

(*e*)   *Humidity* – an adequate level of humidity should be maintained.

(*f*)   *Operator/computer interface* – the workstation should:

(i)   be easy to use,

(ii)   be adapted to user's level of knowledge,

(iii)   have a system to provide feedback to user,

(iv)   have information displayed in a format and at a pace adapted to operator,

(v)   accommodate the principles of software ergonomics.

Clandestine monitoring of an operator's performance is not permitted.

Workstation design

O5010   For VDU operation, the head can be inclined 20° forward from the vertical. The centre of the field of view should therefore be at a point where the eyes are cast at an angle of 20° in a downward position. (This assumes that the field of vision is predominantly the screen plus document holder, rather than the keyboard.)

To ensure easy reading of documents and screen, the viewing distance from the eyes should be within the range 450–550 mm and should not exceed 700 mm. The distance from the eyes to the screen and from the eyes to the document should be identical to minimise frequent changes in focus.

Document holders should be used whenever appropriate, to reduce the head and body movements when transferring gaze from documents to screen and back again.

Lighting

O5011   The VDU should, wherever possible, be positioned so that office lights or windows do not reflect directly on the face of the screen.

Office lighting should be adequate but not too bright to interfere with the screen image. For maximum comfort, the background lighting should be in the 300 to 500 lux (see L5006 LIGHTING) range, given that the VDU has a brightness control for use by the operator. The VDU can be operated below 300 lux or above 500 lux if required, depending upon the operator or the task. Local lighting can be introduced to facilitate the reading of documents in low background lighting conditions. Harsh lighting contrasts should be avoided.

Glare can be reduced by:

(*a*)   changing the position of the VDU screen to eliminate reflections from the screen or other surfaces, e.g. by siting the VDU parallel to fluorescent light fittings, or so that the VDU does not pick up reflections from windows;

(*b*)   using a non-reflective VDU screen or filter over the screen;

(*c*)   reducing the brightness of the light source;

(*d*)   fitting lights with suitable diffusers; and

(*e*)   as a last resort, changing the position of troublesome lights.

In certain cases, the provision of window blinds may be necessary where there is reflection from the screen face. Generally, any sort of light used by one operator whether emanating from the screen or otherwise, should be screened from other operators. [*Health and Safety (Display Screen Equipment) Regulations 1992, Sch 1*].

Equipment maintenance

O5012   Regular maintenance and servicing of equipment should be undertaken in accordance with the manufacturer's instructions. Where there is evidence of screen flicker, poor contrast adjustment or other faults, the maintenance contractor or supplier should be contacted.

Display screens and the working environment

O5013   As regards *display screens*:

(a)   characters on screen must be well-defined and clearly formed, of adequate size with adequate spacing between characters and lines;

(b)   the image on the screen must be stable, with no flickering;

(c)   brightness and contrast between characters must be easily adjustable;

(d)   the screen must swivel and tilt easily;

(e)   it must be possible to use a separate base for the screen or an adjustable table;

(f)   the screen must be free of reflective glare and discomfort-causing reflections.

As regards the *keyboard*:

(a)   it must be tiltable and separate from the screen so as to allow the user to find a comfortable working position;

(b)   the space in front of the keyboard must provide support for the hands/arms of the user;

(c)   it must have a matt surface and avoid reflective glare;

(d)   arrangement of keyboard/characteristics of keys must facilitate the use of the keyboard;

(e)   symbols on keys must be adequately contrasted and legible from the design working position.

As regards the *work desk or work surface*:

(a)   it must have a sufficiently large, low-reflectance surface and allow flexible arrangement of screen, keyboard, documents etc.;

(b)   the document holder must be stable and adjustable so as to minimise the need for uncomfortable head/eye movements;

(c)   there must be adequate space for users to find a comfortable position.

As regards the *work chair*:

(a)   it must be stable and allow the user freedom of movement and a comfortable position;

(b)   the seat must be adjustable in height;

(c)   the seat back must be adjustable in height and tilt;

(d)   a footrest must be available, if needed.

As regards the *working environment*:

(a)   the workstation must be dimensioned and designed so as to allow sufficient space for the user to change position/vary movements;

(*b*)   room lighting/spot lighting must ensure satisfactory lighting conditions and appropriate contrast between screen and background environment. Disturbing glare/reflections on the screen must be prevented by co-ordinating the workplace and the workstation layout with positioning of artificial light sources;

(*c*)   workstations must be so designed as to avoid glare from windows, transparent or translucid walls, as well as distracting reflections on screen;

(*d*)   equipment should not be too noisy or produce excess heat, and radiation, with the exception of the visible part of the electro-magnetic spectrum, must be reduced to negligible levels, and an adequate humidity level must be maintained.

As regards the *user/computer interface*:

(*a*)   software must be suitable;

(*b*)   software must be easy to use and adaptable to the user's level of knowledge or experience;

(*c*)   systems must provide feedback on the system's performance;

(*d*)   systems must display information in a format and at a pace adapted to users;

(*e*)   principles of software ergonomics must be applied, in particular to human data processing.

[*Sch 1*].

Repetitive strain injury (RSI)

O5014   The most common affliction of regular keyboard users is repetitive strain injury (RSI) now more commonly described as work related upper limb disorder (WRULD) (see further O1027 OCCUPATIONAL HEALTH AND DISEASES) and, in future, it would seem, it is going to become increasingly more difficult for employers to avoid liability for this condition – at least, if they cannot show that they have provided reasonable safeguards against keyboard-related injuries. More significantly, the developing practices of computer manufacturers of providing explicit warnings about conditions associated with keyboards and other equipment when supplying personal computers will have the following consequences:

(*a*)   employers will no longer be able to rely on the absence of manufacturers' warnings (in order to avoid liability) but will have to show that they have complied with the requirements of the *Health and Safety (Display Screen Equipment) Regulations 1992* (O5005–O5007 above); and

(*b*)   employees/users will have responsibilities themselves to use equipment in a way consistent with the safety and comfort guides provided to them; failure to do so, after being made aware of the health risks in the warning, may well amount to assumption of risk of injury on their part, thereby invalidating a claim for damages (see further EMPLOYERS' DUTIES TO THEIR EMPLOYEES).

Photocopying equipment

O5015   A number of hazards have been identified with photocopiers, including risks of:

(*a*)   inhalation of fumes from aqueous solutions of ammonia (in the case of dyeline copiers only); and

(*b*)   ozone emission created by electrical discharge.

The following precautions should be adopted, particularly where photocopying equipment is located in well-populated office locations:

(i)   the photocopier should be serviced in accordance with the manufacturer's instructions;

(ii)   staff servicing the copier should be adequately trained, especially regarding the cleaning of the drum;

(iii)   the photocopier should be sited in accordance with the manufacturer's guidelines on minimum siting requirements – otherwise additional ventilation may be needed to control heat, humidity and gaseous emissions; and

(iv)   in the case of dyeline copiers only, staff engaged in cleaning and maintenance should be provided with eye protection.

The HSE has issued updated advice on how best to control the possible health risks that could result from exposure at work to ozone*. It is aimed particularly at employers and managers as well as employees and health and safety professionals. The guidance emphasises what needs to be done and what does not.

Significant additions to the guidance include:

(*a*)   practical advice to employers on controlling exposure to ozone in accordance with the requirements of the *Control of Substances Hazardous to Health Regulations 1999 (COSHH)*, and on how best to keep any exposure at or below the new Occupational Exposure Standard (OES). The OES for ozone, which came into force on 1 January 1996, is of 0.2ppm in air averaged over a 15 minute reference period; and

(*b*)   advice to many work situations that involve exposure only to small amounts of ozone with no significant risk to health (for example, in the use of office equipment such as photocopiers, printers and X-ray machines). The document stresses that where this type of equipment is the only source of ozone in a particular workplace, and if the guidance is followed, then an employer need only keep the risk assessment and control measures under review.

The guidance is intended to be read in conjunction with the Health and Safety Commission's ACoP '*General COSHH ACoP (Control of Substances Hazardous to Health)*' (L5) available from HSE Books.

* '*Ozone: Health Hazards and Precautionary Measures*' (EH38 (revised)) is available, price £4, from HSE Books.

Dangerous machines in offices

O5016   It is an offence to allow any person employed to work in an office or shop to work at a dangerous machine, unless:

(*a*)   he has been adequately informed as to dangers (including written instructions, if appropriate, provided in a readily comprehensible form); and

(*b*)   he is adequately trained to use the machine and to take necessary precautions against risks which its use may entail.

[*Provision and Use of Work Equipment Regulations 1998 (SI 1998 No 2306), Regs 8 and 9*].

Specific rules applying to office machinery contained in the *Prescribed Dangerous Machines Order 1964* have been repealed (along with the *Offices, Shops and Railway*

Premises Act 1963, s 19) and replaced by the generally applicable machinery safety requirements of the *Provision and Use of Work Equipment Regulations 1998 (SI 1998 No 2306)* – see MACHINERY SAFETY.

Slips, trips and falls

O5017   Slips, trips and falls tend to happen to office workers when they are moving equipment about or carrying loads. In order to avoid risk of such injuries, trailing leads should not be allowed to create tripping hazards; where necessary, torn floor coverings should be replaced; spillages should always be quickly cleaned up; passageways, doorways and corridors as well as entrances should not become or be left blocked; also handrails should be provided on stairways – stairs and stairwells should be well lit – see the *Workplace (Health, Safety and Welfare) Regulations 1992 (SI 1992 No 3004)* and W11009 WORKPLACES – HEALTH, SAFETY AND WELFARE);

Overall responsibilities of office management

O5018   Office managers should ensure compliance with accident rules and procedures (see ACCIDENT REPORTING). Employers should make sure that there are written safety policies and that these are revised when necessary. All employers should ensure that:

(*a*)   new office premises are duly notified to the local authority pursuant to the *Offices, Shops and Railway Premises Act 1963, s 49*;

(*b*)   workstations are comfortable with seating and footrests (if appropriate) (see W11008 WORKPLACES – HEALTH, SAFETY AND WELFARE);

(*c*)   first-aid boxes are always fully stocked, with someone appointed to take charge in an emergency and call an ambulance (see FIRST-AID);

(*d*)   adequate rest areas are provided for staff (see WELFARE FACILITIES);

(*e*)   air conditioning systems with a water cooling tower are notified to the local authority;

(*f*)   where VDUs are in continuous or intensive use, adequate breaks are arranged and staff taught how to arrange the workstation so as to avoid awkward movements, reflections and general aches and pains;

(*g*)   trolleys and/or castors are provided for moving cabinets, desks and other bulky items so as to minimise risk of back injury (see MANUAL HANDLING);

(*h*)   staff are instructed and provided with necessary protective equipment, to deal with risk of personal violence, particularly when carrying cash or valuables.

Shops

O5019   Although not obviously so hazardous and accident-prone as factories and manufacturing establishments, shops need to maintain high health and safety standards in the interests of both employees and the general public. Special considerations include the need to take into account the risks associated with large numbers of persons visiting shop premises and the potential dangers to children, the elderly and those with disabilities.

Shop management should also consider, for example, the dangers associated with continual use of escalators between floors and lifts, and inform customers accordingly with boldly worded notices. Similarly, entrance and exit points, as well as means of escape in case of fire, should be clearly identified. Shop entrances and exits to and from, in many cases, a main street or busy thoroughfare, should at all times be kept clear from obstructions as well as delivery points, often at the rear of commercial premises, and members of the public should be prohibited from parking in such restricted areas. Special care is needed to ensure that trolleys and other equipment for moving stock (such as ladders) do not block access and are not left accessible to children. Where necessary, staff should see that wandering trolleys are returned to ranks and spillages eliminated as soon as possible (see O5021 below).

Out of bounds areas, such as lift motor rooms and staff offices, should be clearly signposted and marked 'Private. No admittance except for staff'. Latent structural hazards should be clearly identified, e.g. a dark or unlit staircase, and even patent dangers should be drawn to the attention of unattended children (see O3010 OCCUPIERS' LIABILITY). Where repairs are being carried out or remedial or decorative work is going on above, customers and visitors should be alerted to this. Wherever possible, particularly in large multi-storey stores, lighting should be evenly distributed.

Staff should be made aware, as part of induction training, of their health and safety duties to the general public and the possibility of liability, both criminal and civil, if potentially dangerous situations arise or someone is accidentally injured.

More so than with factories and offices, shop staff – in constant contact with the general public – should be au fait with risks to the public (and especially children) and, where necessary, briefed as to first-aid location and provision. Moreover, since fire hazard and risk of fire spread is one of the deadliest dangers in shops, staff should be briefed in fire hazards and routine fire fighting techniques (see also FIRE AND FIRE PRECAUTIONS). A knowledge of the location of fire extinguishers and how to operate them is essential, as well as any dangerous cutting machines at food counters.

Employees operating bacon slicers and similar food processing machines should be instructed in the inherent dangers of such machines and management should make failure to comply with guarding requirements a dismissible offence. Prominent signs should prohibit smoking (by staff on duty as well as customers).

Maintenance of high health and safety and public hygiene standards in shops (as well as restaurants and hotels) is required by a variety of overlapping statutes and regulations. Apart from the *Health and Safety at Work etc. Act 1974*, which applies in a general way to shops, the principal legislation applicable to shops, hotels and restaurants is the *Workplace (Health, Safety and Welfare) Regulations 1992 (SI 1992 No 3004)*, the *Food Safety Act 1990* and subsequent regulations and the *General Product Safety Regulations 1994 (SI 1994 No 2328)* (see further PRODUCT SAFETY).

Law in shops is enforced by environmental health officers, except for the fire regulations which are enforced by the local fire authority, with whom on-going consultation and co-operation by shop management is strongly advised. Since much of the liability associated with shops legislation is criminal and depends on either 'sale' having taken place or with 'offering for sale' products, case law has instructively established that display of products in a supermarket, hypermarket or shop for self-service purposes is not an 'offer for sale' (*Pharmaceutical Society of Great Britain v Boots Cash Chemists Ltd [1953] 1 QB 401*) (see also *Fisher v Bell [1960] 3 AER 731* relating to the display of a flick knife). Actual sale takes place when money is handed over at the check-out in return for goods.

Loading bays and warehousing

O5020   A particular problem with wholesale and commercial premises is the safety of loading bays as everything coming into or leaving a warehouse has to pass the loading dock. With increased efficiency in the distribution industry, loading docks have become very busy areas, in continual use by the likes of heavy forklift trucks and juggernaut road vehicles. Not atypically, where lorries move off unexpectedly or trailers creep away from loading docks, coupled with constant movement from forklift trucks unloading loads, a forklift truck can career off the loading dock or cause an operator to become trapped between handling equipment and a lorry trailer. Together with the often generally low appreciation of the risks involved (given that many trucks are driven by employees of foreign companies with little knowledge of English) this makes for a growing hazard, resulting increasingly in the voluntary installation of vehicle restraints. All parties involved have obligations to ensure adequate safety in such situations under the general duties of the *Health and Safety at Work etc. Act 1974* (*BOC Distribution Services v HSE [1995] JPIL 128*). (See also ACCESS, TRAFFIC ROUTES AND VEHICLES.)

Civil liability for injuries in shops

O5021   A shop, supermarket or hypermarket qualifies as 'premises' for the purposes of the *Occupiers' Liability Act 1957*, and customers visiting shops are 'lawful visitors'. They are therefore entitled to protection under that Act, unless they go or stray to places or parts of the premises (e.g. staff rooms) to which they are not invited/ permitted, or from which they are specifically excluded. In particular, an enormous variety of gadgetry in shops and supermarkets is a fertile source of attraction to children. These range from sweets to medicines, and from coat hangers to lifts and escalators. These can constitute 'traps' which the 'common duty of care' under the Act requires to be dealt with by reasonable measures to protect children.

Res ipsa loquitur – unusual dangers

O5022   Where a customer on shop premises is injured as a result of an accident which, in the ordinary course of things, should not happen if the management is exercising proper care, liability may be established easily without detailed proof of negligence. Thus, 'the duty of the shopkeeper in this class of case is well established. It may be said to be a duty to use reasonable care to see that the shop floor, on which people are invited, is kept reasonably safe, and if an unusual danger is present, of which the injured person is unaware, and the danger is one which would not be expected and ought not to be present, the onus of proof is on the defendants to explain how it was that the accident happened' (per Lord Goddard CJ in *Turner v Arding & Hobbs Ltd [1949] 2 AER 911*).

In *Ward v Tesco Stores Ltd [1976] 1 AER 219* the appellant slipped, while shopping, on some yoghurt which had spilled on to the floor, was injured and sued the respondent for negligence. It was held that it was the duty of the respondents, through their employees, to see that floors were kept clean and free from spillages. Since the appellant's injury was not one which, in the ordinary course of things, would have happened if the floor had been kept clean and spillages dealt with as soon as they occurred, it was for the respondents to demonstrate that the accident had not arisen from lack of reasonable care on their part. In the absence, therefore, of a satisfactory explanation as to how yoghurt got on to the floor, the inference was that the spillage had occurred because the respondents had failed to exercise reasonable care.

The law on the maxim *res ipsa loquitur* was authoritatively laid down by Erle CJ in *Scott v London and St Katharine Docks Co (1865) 3 H & C 596*: 'But where the thing is shewn to be under the management of the defendant or his servants, and the accident is such as in the ordinary course of things does not happen if those who have the management use proper care, it affords reasonable evidence, in the absence of explanation by the defendants, that the accident arose from want of care'. Thus, there are four circumstances in which *res ipsa loquitur* applies:

(*a*)   the 'thing' causing the accident must be under the control of the employer, or under his management;

(*b*)   the injury-causing accident must be one which does not happen in the ordinary course of things;

(*c*)   the accident would not have happened if management had been exercising reasonable care;

(*d*)   absence of explanation, on the part of the defendant, to show that they used reasonable care.

Latterly the courts have declined to adopt overly formulistic approaches to the maxim, stressing that it is to be applied with common sense, as it is no more than a phrase 'to describe the proof of facts which are sufficient to support an inference that a defendant was negligent and therefore to establish a *prima facie* case against him' (per Hobhouse LJ in *Ratcliffe v Plymouth & Torbay Health Authority and Exeter and North Devon Health Authority [1998] PIQR 170*).

Office and shop units and common parts

O5023   The remaining provisions of the *Offices, Shops and Railway Premises Act 1963* impose requirements for the safety, cleanliness and adequate lighting of common parts such as lobbies, stairs and storage areas shared between tenants or other businesses occupying shop or office units. Responsibility lies with the owner of the building (as opposed to the occupiers of the units) or the owner of the common parts in situations of divided ownership (*ss 42 and 43*).

Personal Protective Equipment

Introduction

P3001 Conventional wisdom suggests that 'safe place strategies' are more effective in combating health and safety risks than 'safe person strategies'. Safe systems of work, and control/prevention measures serve to protect everyone at work, whilst the advantages of personal protective equipment are limited to the individual(s) concerned. Given, however, the fallibility of any state of the art technology in endeavouring to achieve total protection, some level of personal protective equipment is inevitable in view of the obvious (and not so obvious) risks to head, face, neck, eyes, ears, lungs, skin, arms, hands and feet. Current statutory requirements for employers to provide and maintain suitable personal protective equipment are contained in the *Personal Protective Equipment at Work Regulations 1992 (SI 1992 No 2966)*, enjoining them to carry out an assessment of their employees' needs.

Adjunct to this, common law insists not only that employers have requisite safety equipment at hand, or available in an accessible place, but also that management ensure that operators use it. In *Bux v Slough Metals Ltd [1974] 1 AER 262* an employer who had complied with his statutory duty to 'provide' goggles for an employee was nevertheless held liable for damages for breach of his general common law duty for failing to supervise the employee adequately to ensure that he wore them. 'In these circumstances it would, in my judgment, be idle for the employers to urge that they had fulfilled their duty of reasonable care for the safety of their workmen by simply providing them with goggles and then stand by while the men did dangerous work with their eyes wholly unprotected' (per Edmund Davies LJ).

That the hallowed duty to 'provide and maintain' has been getting progressively stricter is evidenced by *Crouch v British Rail Engineering Ltd [1988] IRLR 404* to the extent that employers could be in breach of either statutory or common law duty (or both) in the case of injury/disease to a member of the employee's immediate family involved, say, in cleaning protective clothing – but the injury/disease must have been foreseeable (*Hewett v Alf Brown's Transport Ltd [1992] ICR 530*). This chapter deals with the requirements of the *Personal Protective Equipment at Work Regulations 1992*, the *Personal Protective Equipment (EC Directive) Regulations 1992 (SI 1992 No 3139)* as amended by the *Personal Protective Equipment (EC Directive) (Amendment) Regulations 1994 (SI 1994 No 2326)*, the duties imposed on manufacturers and suppliers of personal protective equipment, the common law duty on employers to provide suitable personal protective equipment, and the main types of personal protective equipment and clothing and some relevant British Standards.

The Personal Protective Equipment at Work Regulations 1992 (SI 1992 No 2966)

P3002 With the advent of the *Personal Protective Equipment at Work Regulations 1992*, all employers must make a formal assessment of the personal protective equipment needs of employees and provide ergonomically suitable equipment in relation to foreseeable risks at work (see further P3006 below). Employers cannot be expected to comply with their new statutory duties, however, unless manufacturers of personal protective equipment have complied with theirs under the requirements of the *Personal Protective Equipment (EC Directive) Regulations 1992 (SI 1992 No 3139)* as amended by *SI 1994 No 2326* – that is, had their products independently certified for EU accreditation purposes. Although imposing a considerable remit on manufacturers, EU accreditation is an indispensable condition precedent to sale and commercial circulation (see P3012 below).

It is important that personal protective clothing equipment should be seen as 'last resort' protection – its use should only be prescribed when engineering and management solutions and other safe systems of work do not effectively protect the worker from the danger.

Employees must be made aware of the purpose of personal protective equipment, its limitations and the need for on-going maintenance. Thus, when assessing the need for, say, eye protection, employers should first identify the existence of workplace hazards (e.g. airborne dust, projectiles, liquid splashes, slippery floors, inclement weather in the case of outside work) and then the extent of danger (e.g. frequency/ velocity of projectiles, frequency/severity of splashes). Selection can (and, indeed, should) then be made from the variety of CE-marked equipment available, in respect of which manufacturers must ensure that such equipment provides protection, and suppliers ascertain that it meets such requirements/standards [*HSWA s 6*] (see further PRODUCT SAFETY). Typically, most of the risks will have already been logged, located and quantified in a routine risk/safety audit (see RISK ASSESS-MENT), and classified according to whether they are physical/chemical/biological in relation to the part(s) of the body affected (e.g. eyes, ears, skin).

Selection of personal protective equipment is a first stage in an on-going routine, followed by proper use and maintenance of equipment (on the part of both employers and employees) as well as training and supervision in personal protection techniques. Maintenance presupposes a stock of renewable spare parts coupled with regular inspection, testing, examination, repair, cleaning and disinfection schedules as well as keeping appropriate records. Depending on the particular equipment, some will require regular testing and examination (e.g. respiratory equipment), whilst others merely inspection (e.g. gloves, goggles). Generally, manufacturers' maintenance schedules should be followed and suitable accommodation provided for protective equipment in order to minimise loss or damage and prevent exposure to cold, damp or bright sunlight, e.g. pegs for helmets, pegs and lockers for clothing, spectacle cases for safety glasses.

On-going safety training, often carried out by manufacturers for the benefit of users, identifying the need for personal protective equipment, should combine both theory and practice.

Work activities/processes requiring personal protective equipment

P3003

Examples abound of processes/activities of which personal protective equipment is a prerequisite, from construction work and mining, through work with ionising radiations, to work with lifting plant, cranes, as well as handling chemicals, tree felling and working from heights. Similarly, blasting operations, work in furnaces and drop forging all require a degree of personal protection.

Statutory requirements in connection with personal protective equipment

P3004 General statutory requirements relating to personal protective equipment are contained in *s 2* of the *Health and Safety at Work etc. Act 1974* (see further EMPLOYERS' DUTIES TO THEIR EMPLOYEES), and in the *Personal Protective Equipment at Work Regulations 1992*, 'Every employer shall ensure that suitable personal protective equipment is provided to his employees who may be exposed to a risk to their health or safety at work except where, and to the extent that such risk has been adequately controlled by other means which are equally or more effective'. [*Reg 4(1)*]. More specific statutory requirements concerning personal protective equipment exist in the *Personal Protective Equipment at Work Regulations 1992* (in tandem with the *Personal Protective Equipment (EC Directive) Regulations 1992 (SI 1992 No 3139)* and *SI 1994 No 2326)*), and sundry other recent regulations applicable to particular industries/processes, e.g. asbestos, noise, construction (see P3008 below). It is a characteristic of all statutory requirements that personal protective equipment is provided by employers to employees free of charge [*HSWA s 9*].

General statutory duties – HSWA 1974

P3005 Employers are under a general duty to ensure, so far as reasonably practicable, the health, safety and welfare at work of their employees – a duty which clearly implies provision/maintenance of personal protective equipment. [*HSWA s 2(1)*].

Specific statutory duties – Personal Protective Equipment at Work Regulations 1992 (SI 1992 No 2966)

Duties of employers

P3006 Employers – and self-employed persons in cases (*a*), (*b*), (*c*), (*d*) and (*e*) below, must undertake the following:

(*a*) Formally assess (and review periodically) provision and suitability of personal protective equipment. [*Reg 6(1)(3)*].

The assessment should include:

(i) risks to health and safety not avoided by other means;

(ii) reference to characteristics which personal protective equipment must have in relation to risks identified in (i); and

(iii) a comparison of the characteristics of personal protective equipment having the characteristics identified in (ii).

[*Reg 6(2)*].

The aim of the assessment is to ensure that an employer knows which personal protective equipment to choose; it constitutes the first stage in a continuing programme, concerned also with proper use and maintenance of personal protective equipment and training and supervision of employees.

(*b*) Provide suitable personal protective equipment to his employees, who may be exposed to health and safety risks while at work, except where the risk has either been adequately controlled by other equally or more effective means. [*Reg 4(1)*].

Personal protective equipment is not suitable unless:

(i) it is appropriate for risks involved and conditions at the place of exposure;

(ii) it takes account of ergonomic requirements and the state of health of the person who wears it;

(iii) it is capable of fitting the wearer correctly; and

(iv) so far as reasonably practicable (for meaning, see ENFORCEMENT), it is effective to prevent or adequately control risks involved without increasing the overall risk.

[*Reg 4(3)*].

(c) Provide compatible personal protective equipment – that is, that the use of more than one item of personal protective equipment is compatible with other personal protective equipment. [*Reg 5*].

(d) Maintain (as well as replace and clean) any personal protective equipment in an efficient state, efficient working order and in good repair. [*Reg 7*].

(e) Provide suitable accommodation for personal protective equipment when not being used. [*Reg 8*].

(f) Provide employees with information, instruction and training to enable them to know

(i) the risks which personal protective equipment will avoid or minimise;

(ii) the purpose for which and manner in which personal protective equipment is to be used;

(iii) any action which the employee might take to ensure that personal protective equipment remains efficient.

[*Reg 9*].

(g) Ensure, taking all reasonable steps, that personal protective equipment is properly used. [*Reg 10*].

Summary of employer's duties

(1) duty of assessment

(2) duty to provide suitable PPE

(3) duty to provide compatible PPE

(4) duty to maintain and replace PPE

(5) duty to provide suitable accommodation for PPE

(6) duty to provide information and training

(7) duty to see that PPE is correctly used.

Duties of employees

P3007 Every employee must:

(a) use personal protective equipment in accordance with training and instructions [*Reg 10(2)*];

(b) return all personal protective equipment to the appropriate accommodation provided after use [*Reg 10(4)*]; and

(c) report forthwith any defect or loss in the equipment to the employer [*Reg 11*].

Specific requirements for particular industries and processes

P3008   In addition to the general remit of the *Personal Protective Equipment at Work Regulations 1992*, the following regulations impose specific requirements on employers to provide personal protective equipment up to the EU standard.

(1) *Confined Spaces Regulations 1997 (SI 1997 No 1713)* – supply of suitable breathing apparatus etc. for use in confined spaces;

(2) *Control of Lead at Work Regulations 1998 (SI 1998 No 543)* – supply of suitable respiratory equipment and suitable protective clothing where exposure is not insignificant;

(3) *Control of Asbestos at Work Regulations 1987 (SI 1987 No 2115), Regs 8, 17-28 (as amended by SI 1998 No 3235)* – supply of respiratory protective equipment and suitable protective clothing;

(4) *Control of Substances Hazardous to Health Regulations 1999 (SI 1999 No 437) (COSHH), Reg 7(4), (5)* – supply of suitable protective equipment where exposure of employees to substances hazardous to health cannot otherwise be prevented or adequately controlled;

(5) *Noise at Work Regulations 1989 (SI 1989 No 1790), Reg 8* – personal ear protectors;

(6) *Construction (Head Protection) Regulations 1989 (SI 1989 No 2209), Reg 3* – suitable head protection;

(7) *Ionising Radiations Regulations 1985 (SI 1985 No 1333), Reg 23* – supply of suitable respiratory protective equipment, film badges, dosemeters;

(8) *Shipbuilding and Ship-repairing Regulations 1960 (SI 1960 No 1932), Regs 50, 51* – supply of suitable breathing apparatus, belts, eye protectors, gloves and gauntlets.

[*Miscellaneous Factories (Transitional Provisions) Regulations 1993 (SI 1993 No 2482)*].

Increased importance of uniform European standards

P3009   To date, manufacturers of products, including personal protective equipment (PPE), have sought endorsement or approval for products, prior to commercial circulation, through reference to British Standards (BS), HSE or European standards, an example of the former being Kitemark and an example of the latter being CEN or CENELEC. Both are examples of *voluntary* national and international schemes that can be entered into by manufacturers and customers, under which both sides are 'advantaged' by conformity with such standards. Conformity is normally achieved following a level of testing appropriate to the level of protection offered by the product. With the introduction of the *Personal Protective Equipment (EC Directive) Regulations 1992* as amended by *SI 1994 No 2326* (see P3012 below), this voluntary system of approval was replaced by a statutory certification procedure.

Towards certification

P3010   Certification as a condition of sale is probably some time away. Transition from adherence based on a wide range of voluntary national (and international) standards to a compulsory universal EU standard takes time and specialist expertise. Already, however, British Standards Institution (BSI) has adopted the form BS EN as a British version of a uniform European standard. But, generally speaking, uniformity of approach to design and testing, on the part of manufacturers, represents a considerable remit and so statutory compliance with tougher new European standards is probably not likely to happen immediately. Here, too, however, there is evidence of some progress, e.g. the EN 45000 series of standards on how test houses and certification bodies are to be established and independently accredited. In addition, a range of European standards on PPE is currently being prepared in relation, particularly, to eye protection, hearing protection, respiratory protection and falls from heights.

Interim measures

P3011   Most manufacturers have elected to comply with the current CEN standard when seeking product certification. Alternatively, should a manufacturer so wish, the inspection body can verify by way of another route to certification – this latter might well be the case with an innovative product where standards did not exist. Generally, however, compliance with current CEN (European Standardisation Committee) or, alternatively, BS 5750: Quality Assurance has been the well-trodden route to certification. To date, several UK organisations, including manufacturers and independent bodies, have established PPE test houses, which are independently accredited by the National Measurement Accreditation Service (NAMAS). Such test houses will be open to all comers for verification of performance levels.

Personal Protective Equipment (EC Directive) Regulations 1992 (SI 1992 No 3139) as amended by SI 1994 No 2326

P3012   The *Personal Protective Equipment (EC Directive) Regulations 1992* as amended by *SI 1994 No 2326* require most types of PPE (for exceptions, see P3019 below) to satisfy specified certification procedures [*Art 8*], pass EU type-examination (i.e. official inspection by an approved inspection body) [*Art 10*] and carry a 'CE' mark both on the product itself and its packaging [*Art 13*] before being put into commercial circulation. Indeed, failure on the part of a manufacturer to obtain affixation of a 'CE' mark on his product before putting it into circulation, is a criminal offence under *s 6* of the *Health and Safety at Work etc. Act 1974*, carrying a maximum fine, on summary conviction, of £20,000 (see ENFORCEMENT). Enforcement is through trading standards officers. [*The Personal Protective Equipment (EC Directive) (Amendment) Regulations 1993 (SI 1993 No 3074)*].

CE mark of conformity

P3013   The *Personal Protective Equipment (EC Directive) Regulations 1992* as amended by the *Personal Protective Equipment (EC Directive) (Amendment) Regulations 1994 (SI 1994 No 2326)* specify procedures and criteria with which manufacturers must comply in order to be able to obtain certification. Essentially this involves incorporation into design and production basic health and safety requirements. [*Art 3*]. Hence, by compliance with health and safety criteria, affixation of the 'CE' mark becomes a condition of sale and approval (see *fig. 1* below). Moreover, compliance, on the part of manufacturers, with these regulations, will enable employers to comply with their duties under the *Personal Protective Equipment at Work Regulations 1992. Reg 4(3)(e)* of the *Personal Protective Equipment at Work Regulations 1992* requires the PPE provided by the employer to comply with this and any later EU directive requirements.

CE accreditation is not a synonym for compliance with the CEN standard, since a manufacturer could opt for certification via an alternative route. Still less is it an approvals mark. It is rather a quality mark, since all products covered by the regulations are required to meet formal quality control or quality of production criteria in their certification procedures. [*Arts 8.4, 11, 89/686/EEC*].

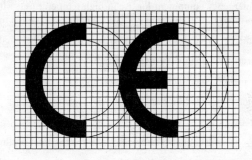

Certification procedures

P3014   In order to obtain certification, manufacturers must submit to an approved body the following documentation (except in the case of PPE of simple design, where risks are minimal, e.g. gardening gloves, thimbles, aprons, headgear, footwear, helmets, sunglasses).

(*a*)   Technical file, i.e.

    (i)   overall and detailed plans, accompanied by calculation notes/results of prototype tests; and

    (ii)   an exhaustive list of basic health and safety requirements and harmonised standards taken into account in the model's design.

(*b*)   Description of control and test facilities used to check compliance with harmonised standards.

(*c*)   Copy of information relating to:

    (i)   storage, use, cleaning, maintenance, servicing and disinfection;

    (ii)   performance recorded during technical tests to monitor levels of protection;

    (iii)   suitable PPE accessories;

    (iv)   classes of protection appropriate to different levels of risk and limits of use;

    (v)   obsolescence deadline;

    (vi)   type of packaging suitable for transport;

    (vii)   significance of markings.

[*Art 1.4, Annex II; Art 8.1, Annex III*].

This must be provided in the official language of the member state of destination.

PPE protection against mortal/serious dangers – requiring compliance with quality control system

P3015   This category of PPE, including:

(*a*)   filtering, respiratory devices for protection against solid and liquid aerosols/irritant, dangerous, toxic or radiotoxic gases;

(*b*)   respiratory protection devices providing full insulation from the atmosphere, and for use in diving;

(*c*)   protection against chemical attack or ionising radiation;

(*d*)   emergency equipment for use in high temperatures, whether with or without infrared radiation, flames or large amounts of molten metal (100°C or more);

(*e*)   emergency equipment for use in low temperatures (–50°C or less);

(*f*)   protection against falls from heights;

(*g*)   protection against electrical risks; and

(*h*)   motor cycle helmets and visors;

must satisfy either

(i)   —   an EU quality control system for the final product, or

—   a system for ensuring EU quality of production by means of monitoring;

and in either case,

(ii)   an EU declaration of conformity.

[*Art 8.4*].

Basic health and safety requirements applicable to all PPE

P3016   All PPE must:

(*a*)   be ergonomically suitable, that is, be able to perform a risk-related activity whilst providing the user with the highest possible level of protection;

(*b*)   preclude risks and inherent nuisance factors, such as roughness, sharp edges and projections and must not cause movements endangering the user;

(*c*)   provide comfort and efficiency by facilitating correct positioning on the user and remaining in place for the foreseeable period of use; and by being as light as possible without undermining design strength and efficiency; and

(*d*)   be accompanied by necessary information – that is, the name and address of the manufacturer and technical file (see P3014 above).

[*Annex II*].

General purpose PPE – specific to several types of PPE

P3017   (*a*)   PPE incorporating adjustment systems must not become incorrectly adjusted without the user's knowledge;

(*b*)   PPE enclosing parts of the body must be sufficiently ventilated to limit perspiration or to absorb perspiration;

(*c*)   PPE for the face, eyes and respiratory tracts must minimise risks to same and, if necessary, contain facilities to prevent moisture formation and be compatible with wearing spectacles or contact lenses;

(*d*)   PPE subject to ageing must contain date of manufacture, the date of obsolescence and be indelibly inscribed if possible. If the useful life of a product is not known, accompanying information must enable the user to establish a reasonable obsolescence date. In addition, the number of times it can be cleaned before being inspected or discarded must (if possible) be affixed to the product; or, failing this, be indicated in accompanying literature;

(*e*)   PPE which may be caught up during use by a moving object must have a suitable resistance threshold above which a constituent part will break and eliminate danger;

(*f*)   PPE for use in explosive atmospheres must not be likely to cause an explosive mixture to ignite;

(*g*)   PPE for emergency use or rapid installation/removal must minimise the time required for attachment and/or removal;

(*h*)   PPE for use in very dangerous situations (see P3015 above) must be accompanied with data for exclusive use of competent trained individuals, and describe procedure to be followed to ensure that it is correctly adjusted and functional when worn;

(*j*)   PPE incorporating components which are adjustable or removable by user, must facilitate adjustment, attachment and removal without tools;

(*k*)   PPE for connection to an external complementary device must be mountable only on appropriate equipment;

(*l*)   PPE incorporating a fluid circulation system must permit adequate fluid renewal in the vicinity of the entire part of the body to be protected;

(*m*)   PPE bearing one or more identification or recognition marks relating to health and safety must preferably carry harmonised pictograms/ideograms which remain perfectly legible throughout the foreseeable useful life of the product;

(*n*)   PPE in the form of clothing capable of signalling the user's presence visually must have one or more means of emitting direct or reflected visible radiation;

(*o*)   multi-risk PPE must satisfy basic requirements specific to each risk.

[*Art 2, Annex II*].

Additional requirements for specific PPE for particular risks

P3018   There are additional requirements for PPE designed for certain particular risks as follows:

PPE protection against

(1)   *Mechanical impact risks*

  (i)   impact caused by falling/projecting objects must be sufficiently shock-absorbent to prevent injury from crushing or penetration of the protected part of the body;

(ii)   falls.

In the case of falls due to slipping, outsoles for footwear must ensure satisfactory adhesion by grip and friction, given the state and nature of the surface. In the case of falls from a height, PPE must incorporate a body harness and attachment system connectable to a reliable anchorage point. The vertical drop of the user must be minimised to prevent collision with obstacles and the braking force injuring, tearing or causing the operator to fall;

(iii)   mechanical vibration. PPE must be capable of ensuring adequate attenuation of harmful vibration components for the part of the body at risk.

(2)   *(Static) compression of part of the body* – must be able to attenuate its effects so as to prevent serious injury of chronic complaints.

(3)   *Physical injury* – must be able to protect all or part of the body against superficial injury by machinery, e.g. abrasion, perforation, cuts or bites.

(4)   *Prevention of drowning* – (lifejackets, armbands etc.) must be capable of returning to the surface a user who is exhausted or unconscious, without danger to his health. Such PPE can be wholly or partially inherently buoyant or inflatable either by gas or orally. It should be able to withstand impact with liquid, and, if inflatable, able to inflate rapidly and fully.

(5)   *Harmful effects of noise* – must protect against exposure levels of the *Noise at Work Regulations 1989* (i.e. 85 and 90 dB(A)) and must indicate noise attenuation level.

(6)   *Heat and/or fire* – must possess sufficient thermal insulation capacity to retain most of the stored heat until after the user has left the danger area and removed PPE. Moreover, constituent materials which could be splashed by large amounts of hot product must possess sufficient mechanical-impact absorbency. In addition, materials which might accidentally come into contact with flame as well as being used in the manufacture of fire-fighting equipment, must possess a degree of non-flammability proportionate to the risk foreseeably arising during use and must not melt when exposed to flame or contribute to flame spread. When ready for use, PPE must be such that the quantity of heat transmitted by PPE to the user must not cause pain or health impairment. Second, ready-to-use PPE must prevent liquid or steam penetration and not cause burns. If PPE incorporates a breathing device, it must adequately protect the user. Accompanying manufacturers' notes must provide all relevant data for determination of maximum permissible user exposure to heat transmitted by equipment.

(7)   *Cold* – must possess sufficient thermal insulating capacity and retain the necessary flexibility for gestures and postures. In particular, PPE must protect tips of fingers and toes from pain or health impairment and prevent penetration by rain water. Manufacturers' accompanying notes must provide all relevant data concerning maximum permissible user exposure to cold transmitted by equipment.

(8)   *Electric shock* – must be sufficiently insulated against voltages to which the user is likely to be exposed under the most foreseeably adverse conditions. In particular, PPE for use during work with electrical installations (together with packaging), which may be under tension, must carry markings indicating either protection class and/or corresponding operating voltage, serial number

and date of manufacture; in addition, date of entry into service must be inscribed as well as of periodic tests or inspections.

(9) *Radiation*

(a)   Non-ionising radiation – must prevent acute or chronic eye damage from non-ionising radiation and be able to absorb/reflect the majority of energy radiated in harmful wavelengths without unduly affecting transmission of the innocuous part of the visible spectrum, perception of contrasts and distinguishment of colours. Thus, protective glasses must possess a spectral transmission factor so as to minimise radiant-energy illumination density capable of reaching the user's eye through the filter and ensure that it does not exceed permissible exposure value. Accompanying notes must indicate transmission curves, making selection of the most suitable PPE possible. The relevant protection-factor number must be marked on all specimens of filtering glasses.

(b)   Ionising radiation – must protect against external radioactive contamination. Thus, PPE should prevent penetration of radioactive dust, gases, liquids or mixtures under foreseeable use conditions. Moreover, PPE designed to provide complete user protection against external irradiation must be able to counter only weak electron or weak photon radiation.

(10) *Dangerous substances and infective agents*

(a)   respiratory protection – must be able to supply the user with breathable air when exposed to polluted atmosphere or an atmosphere with inadequate oxygen concentration. Leak-tightness of the facepiece and pressure drop on inspiration (breath intake), as well as in the case of filtering devices purification capacity, must keep the contaminant penetration from the polluted atmosphere sufficiently low to avoid endangering health of the user. Instructions for use must enable a trained user to use the equipment correctly;

(b)   cutaneous and ocular contact (skin and eyes) – must be able to prevent penetration or diffusion of dangerous substances and infective agents. Therefore, PPE must be completely leak-tight but allow prolonged daily use or, failing that, of limited leak-tightness restricting the period of wear. In the case of certain dangerous substances/infective agents possessing high penetrative power and which limit duration of protection, such PPE must be tested for classification on the basis of efficiency. PPE conforming with test specifications must carry a mark indicating names or codes of substances used in tests and standard period of protection. Manufacturers' notes must contain an explanation of codes, detailed description of standard tests and refer to the maximum permissible period of wear under different foreseeable conditions of use.

(11) *Safety devices for diving equipment* – must be able to supply the user with a breathable gaseous mixture, taking into account the maximum depth of immersion. If necessary, equipment must consist of

(a)   a suit to protect the user against pressure;

(b)   an alarm to give the user prompt warning of approaching failure in supply of breathable gaseous mixture;

(c)   life-saving suit to enable the user to return to the surface.

[*Art 3, Annex II*].

Excluded PPE

P3019

(a)   PPE designed and manufactured for use specifically by the armed forces or in the maintenance of law and order (helmets, shields);

(b)   PPE for self-defence (aerosol canisters, personal deterrent weapons);

(c)   PPE designed and manufactured for private use against

   (i)   adverse weather (headgear, seasonal clothing, footwear, umbrellas),

   (ii)   damp and water (dish-washing gloves),

   (iii)   heat (e.g. gloves);

(d)   PPE intended for the protection or rescue of persons on vessels or aircraft, not worn all the time.

[*Annex I*].

Main types of personal protection

The main types of personal protection covered by the *Personal Protective Equipment at Work Regulations 1992* are (a) head protection, (b) eye protection, (c) hand/arm protection, (d) foot protection and (e) whole body protection.

In particular, these regulations do not cover ear protectors and most respiratory protective equipment – these areas are covered by other existing regulations and guidance, for example the *Noise at Work Regulations 1989* and HSE's guidance booklet HS(G) 53, '*Respiratory protective equipment: a practical guide for users*'.

Head protection

P3020   This takes the form of:

(a)   crash, cycling, riding and climbing helmets;

(b)   industrial safety helmets – to protect against falling objects;

(c)   scalp protectors (bump caps) – to protect against striking fixed obstacles;

(d)   caps/hairnets – to protect against scalping,

and is particularly suitable for the following activities:

   (i)   building work – particularly on scaffolds;

   (ii)   civil engineering projects;

   (iii)   blasting operations;

   (iv)   work in pits and trenches;

   (v)   work near hoists/lifting plant;

   (vi)   work in blast furnaces;

   (vii)   work in industrial furnaces;

   (viii)   ship-repairing;

   (ix)   railway shunting;

   (x)   slaughterhouses;

   (xi)   tree-felling;

(xii)   suspended access work, e.g. window cleaning.

Eye protection

P3021   This takes the following forms:

(*a*)   safety spectacles – these are the same as prescription spectacles but incorporating optional sideshields; lenses are made from tough plastic, such as polycarbonate – provide lateral protection;

(*b*)   eyeshields – these are heavier than safety spectacles and designed with a frameless one-piece moulded lens; can be worn over prescription spectacles;

(*c*)   safety goggles – these are heavier than spectacles or eye shields; they are made with flexible plastic frames and one-piece lens and have an elastic headband – they afford total eye protection; and

(*d*)   faceshields – these are heavier than other eye protectors but comfortable if fitted with an adjustable head harness – faceshields protect the face but not fully the eyes and so are no protection against dusts, mist or gases.

Eye protectors are suitable for working with:

(i)   chemicals;

(ii)   power driven tools;

(iii)   molten metal;

(iv)   welding;

(v)   radiation;

(vi)   gases/vapours under pressure;

(vii)   woodworking.

Hand/arm protection

P3022   Gloves provide protection against:

(*a*)   cuts and abrasions;

(*b*)   extremes of temperature;

(*c*)   skin irritation/dermatitis;

(*d*)   contact with toxic/corrosive liquids,

and are particularly useful in connection with the following activities/processes:

(i)   manual handling;

(ii)   vibration;

(iii)   construction;

(iv)   hot and cold materials;

(v)   electricity;

(vi)   chemicals;

(vii)   radioactivity.

Foot protection

P3023   This takes the form of:

(a)   safety shoes/boots;

(b)   foundry boots;

(c)   clogs;

(d)   wellington boots;

(e)   anti-static footwear;

(f)   conductive footwear,

and is particularly useful for the following activities:

(i)   construction;

(ii)   mechanical/manual handling;

(iii)   electrical processes;

(iv)   working in cold conditions (thermal footwear);

(v)   chemical processes;

(vi)   forestry;

(vii)   molten substances.

Respiratory protective equipment

P3024   This takes the form of:

(a)   half-face respirators,

(b)   full-face respirators,

(c)   air-supply respirators,

(d)   self-contained breathing apparatus,

and is particularly useful for protecting against harmful

(i)   gases;

(ii)   vapours;

(iii)   dusts;

(iv)   fumes;

(v)   smoke;

(vi)   aerosols.

Whole body protection

P3025   This takes the form of:

(a)   coveralls, overalls, aprons;

(b)   outfits to protect against cold and heat;

(c)   protection against machinery and chainsaws;

(d)   high visibility clothing;

(*e*)   life–jackets,

and is particularly useful in connection with the following activities:

  (i)   laboratory work;

  (ii)   construction;

 (iii)   forestry;

 (iv)   work in cold–stores;

  (v)   highway and road works;

 (vi)   food processing;

 (vii)   welding;

(viii)   fire–fighting;

 (ix)   foundry work;

  (x)   spraying pesticides.

Some relevant British Standards for protective clothing and equipment

P3026   Although not, strictly speaking, a condition of sale or approval, for the purposes of the *Personal Protective Equipment at Work (EC Directive) Regulations 1992*, compliance with British Standards (e.g. BS 5750: 'Quality Assurance') may well become one of the well–tried verification routes to obtaining a 'CE' mark. For that reason, if for no other, the following non–exhaustive list of British Standards on protective clothing and equipment should be of practical value to both manufacturers and users.

Table 1
Protective clothing

BS 697 : 1986	Specification for rubber gloves for electrical purposes
BS 3314: 1982	Specification for protective aprons for wet work
BS 5426: 1993	Specification for work wear and career wear
BS 5438: 1976	Methods of test for flammability of vertically oriented textile fabrics and fabric assemblies subject to a small igniting flame
1989 (1995)	Methods of test for flammability of textile fabrics when subjected to a small igniting flame applied to the face or bottom edge of vertically oriented specimens
BS 6408: 1983	Specification for clothing made from coated fabrics for protection against wet weather
BS EN 340: 1993	Protective clothing. General requirements
BS EN 341: 1993	Personal protective equipment against falls from a height. Descender devices
BS EN 348: 1992	Protective clothing. Determination of behaviour of materials on impact of small splashes of molten metal

BS EN 353: 1993	Personal protective equipment against falls from a height. Guided type of fall arresters
BS EN 354: 1993	Personal protective equipment against falls from a height. Lanyards
BS EN 355: 1993	Personal protective equipment against falls from a height. Energy absorbers
BS EN 360: 1993	Personal protective equipment against falls from a height. Retractable type fall arresters
BS EN 361: 1993	Personal protective equipment against falls from a height. Full body harnesses
BS EN 362: 1993	Personal protective equipment against falls from a height. Connectors
BS EN 363: 1993	Personal protective equipment against falls from a height. Fall arrest systems
BS EN 364: 1993	Personal protective equipment against falls from a height. Test methods
BS EN 365: 1993	Personal protective equipment against falls from a height. General requirements
BS EN 366: 1993	Protective clothing. Protection against heat and fire
BS EN 367: 1992	Protective clothing. Protection against heat and flames
BS EN 368: 1993	Protective clothing. Protection against liquid materials
BS EN 369: 1993	Protective clothing. Protection against liquid chemicals
BS EN 373: 1993	Protective clothing: Assessment of resistance of materials to molten metal splash
BS EN 381: 1993	Protective clothing for users of hand-held chain saws
BS EN 463: 1995	Protective clothing. Protection against liquid chemicals. Test method
BS EN 464: 1994	Protective clothing. Protection against liquid and gaseous chemicals including liquid aerosols and solid particles. Test method
BS EN 465: 1995	Protective clothing: Protection against liquid chemicals. Performance requirements for chemical protective clothing type 4 equipment
BS EN 466: 1995	Protective clothing: Protection against liquid chemicals. Performance requirements for chemical protective clothing type 3 equipment
BS EN 467: 1995	Protective clothing: Protection against liquid chemicals.
BS EN 468: 1998	Protective clothing for use against liquid chemicals. Test method
BS EN 469: 1995	Protective clothing for firefighters

BS EN 470: 1995	Protective clothing for use in welding and allied processes. General requirements
BS EN 471: 1994	Specification for high visibility warning clothing
BS EN 510: 1993	Specification for protective clothing where there is a risk of entanglement with moving parts
BS EN 530: 1995	Abrasion resistance of protective clothing material. Test methods
BS EN 531: 1995	Protective clothing for industrial workers exposed to heat
BS EN 532: 1995	Protective clothing. Protection against heat and flame. Test method for limited flame spread
BS EN 533: 1997	Materials and material assemblies used in clothing for protection against heat or flame

Protective footwear

BS 2723: 1956 (1995)	Specification for firemen's leather boots
BS 4676: 1983 (1996)	Specification for gaiters and footwear for protection against burns and impact risks in foundries
BS 5145: 1989	Specification for lined industrial vulcanised rubber boots
BS 6159:	Polyvinyl chloride boots
Part 1: 1987	Specification for general industrial lined or unlined boots
BS EN 344: 1993	Requirements and test methods for safety, protective and occupational footwear for professional use
BS EN 345: 1993	Specification for safety footwear for professional use
BS EN 346: 1993	Specification for protective footwear for professional use
BS EN 347: 1993	Specification for occupational footwear for professional use
BS EN 381: 1993	Protective clothing for users of hand-held chain saws

Head protection

BS 6658: 1995	Specification for protective helmets for vehicle users
BS 4423: 1969	Specification for climbers' helmets
BS EN 443: 1997	Specification for protective helmets for firefighters
BS EN 812: 1997	Specification for industrial scalp protectors (bump caps)
BS EN 1384: 1997	Specification for protective hats for equestrian activities

Face and eye protection

BS 2724: 1987 (1995)	Specification for sunglare eye protectors for general use
BS 4110: 1979	Specification for eye-protectors for vehicle users
BS 7028: 1988	Guide for selection, use and maintenance of eye protection for industrial and other uses
BS EN 166:1996	Specification for eye protectors for industrial and non-industrial users
BS EN 167: 1995	Personal eye protection. Optical test methods
BS EN 168: 1995	Personal eye protection. Non-optical test methods
BS EN 169: 1992	Specification for filters for personal eye protection equipment used in welding and similar operations
BS EN 170: 1992	Specification for filters for ultra violet filters used in personal eye protective equipment
BS EN 171: 1992	Specification for infra-red filters used in personal eye protective equipment
BS EN 172: 1995	Specification for sunglare filters used in personal eye protective equipment for industrial use
BS EN 175: 1997	Specification for eye and face protection during welding and similar operations

Respiratory protection

BS 4001: (1990)	Care and maintenance of underwater breathing apparatus
Part 1 (1998)	Compressed air open circuit type
Part 2 (1967)	Standard diving equipment
BS 4275: 1997	Guide to implementing an effective respiratory protective device programme
BS 4400: 1969 (1995)	Method for sodium chloride particulate test for respirator filters
BS 4667	Specification for breathing apparatus
Part 4: 1989	Specification for open-circuit escape breathing apparatus
BS 7355: 1990	Specification for full masks for respiratory protective devices
BS 7356: 1990 (1995)	Specification for half masks and quarter face masks for respiratory protective devices
BS EN 132: 1991	Respiratory protective devices. Definitions
BS EN 133: 1991	Respiratory protective devices. Classification
BS EN 134: 1991	Respiratory protective devices. Nomenclature of compounds

BS EN 135: 1991	Respiratory protective devices. List of equivalent terms
BS EN 136: 1998	Parts for full face masks for respiratory protective devices. Specification for full face masks for special use
BS EN 137: 1993	Specification for respiratory protective devices, self-contained open-circuit compressed air breathing apparatus
BS EN 138: 1994	Respiratory protective devices. Specification for fresh air hose breathing apparatus for use with full face mask, half mask or mouthpiece assembly
BS EN 139: 1995	Respiratory protective devices. Compressed air line breathing apparatus for use with a full face mask, half mask or a mouthpiece assembly
BS EN 141: 1991	Specification for gas filters and combined filters used in respiratory protective equipment
BS EN 143: 1991	Specification for particle filters used in respiratory protective equipment
BS EN 144: 1992	Respiratory protective devices. Gas cylinder valves
BS EN 145: 1993	Respiratory protective devices. Self contained closed circuit compressed oxygen breathing apparatus
BS EN 146: 1992	Respiratory protective devices. Specification for powered particle filtering devices incorporating helmets or hoods
BS EN 147: 1992	Respiratory protection devices. Specification for power assisted particle filtering devices incorporating full face masks, half masks or quarter masks
BS EN 148: Part 3: 1992	Specification for thread connection M 45 X 3
BS EN 149: 1992	Specification for filtering half masks to protect against particles
BS EN 371: 1992	Specification for AX gas filters and combined filters against low boiling organic compounds used in respiratory protective equipment
BS EN 372: 1992	Specification for SX gas filters and combined filters against specific named compounds used in respiratory protective equipment
Radiation protection	
BS 3664: 1963	Specification for film badges for personnel radiation monitoring
BS EN 175: 1997	Specification for equipment for eye and face protection during welding and similar operations
BS EN 269: 1995	Respiratory protective devices. Specification for powered fresh air hose breathing apparatus incorporating a hood

BS EN 270: 1995	Respiratory protective devices. Compressed air line breathing apparatus incorporating a hood
Hearing protection	
BS EN 352:	Hearing protectors. Safety requirements and testing
Part 1 1993	Ear muffs
Part 2 1993	Ear plugs
Hand protection	
BS EN 374:	Protective gloves against chemicals and micro-organisms
Part 1: 1994	Terminology and performance requirements
Part 2: 1994	Determination of resistance to penetration
Part 3: 1994	Determination of resistance to permeation by chemicals
BS EN 388: 1994	Protective gloves against mechanical risks
BS EN 407: 1994	Protective gloves against thermal risks (heat and/or fire)
BS EN 421: 1994	Protective gloves against ionising radiation and radioactive contaminations
BS EN 511: 1994	Specification for protective gloves against cold

Common law requirements

P3027   In addition to general and/or specific statutory requirements, the residual combined duty, on employers at common law, to provide and maintain a safe system of work, including appropriate supervision of safety duties, still obtains, extending, where necessary, to protection against foreseeable risk of eye injury (*Bux v Slough Metals Ltd* (see P3001 above) and dermatitis/facial eczema (*Pape v Cumbria County Council [1991] IRLR 463*). *Pape* concerned an office cleaner who developed dermatitis and facial eczema after using Vim, Flash and polish. The employer was held liable for damages at common law, since he had not instructed her in the dangers of using chemical materials with unprotected hands and had not made her wear rubber gloves.

Consequences of breach

P3028   Employers who fail to provide suitable personal protective equipment, commit a criminal offence, under the *Health and Safety at Work etc. Act 1974* and the *Personal Protective Equipment at Work Regulations 1992* and sundry other regulations (see P3006-P3008 above). In addition, if, as a result of failure to provide suitable equipment, an employee suffers foreseeable injury and/or disease, the employer will be liable to the employee for damages for negligence. Conversely, if, after instruction and, where necessary, training, an employee fails or refuses to wear and maintain suitable personal protective equipment, he too can be prosecuted and/or dismissed and, if he is injured or suffers a disease in consequence, will probably lose all or, certainly, part of his damages.

Product Safety

Introduction

P9001

With the expansion of EU Directives and other legislation aimed at manufacturers, designers, importers and suppliers, product safety emerges as a fast growth area – a development expedited by the introduction of the *General Product Safety Regulations 1994 (SI 1994 No 2328)*. Indeed, there is an identifiable trend towards placing responsibilities on producers and those involved in commercial circulation as well as on employers and occupiers (see MACHINERY SAFETY and PERSONAL PROTECTIVE EQUIPMENT). Although there is no question of removal of duties from employers and occupiers and users of industrial plant, machinery and products, there is a realisation that the *sine qua non* of compliance on the part of employers and users with their safety duties is compliance with essential health and safety requirements on the part of designers and manufacturers. This trend is likely to continue with more products being brought within the scope of the EU's 'new approach' regime which promotes supply of products throughout the single market provided they meet essential requirements which can be demonstrated by compliance with harmonised European standards. As far as civil liability is concerned, this trend may well result in a long-term shift in the balance of liability for injury away from employers and occupiers towards designers, manufacturers and other suppliers.

It was thalidomide that first focused serious attention on the legal control of product safety, leading to the Medicinal Products Directive (65/65/EEC) and the *Medicines Act 1968*, the first comprehensive regulatory system of product testing, licensing and vigilance. Since then a host of regulations has appeared, covering areas as diverse as pencils, aerosols, cosmetics and electrical products. More recently the General Product Safety Directive (92/59/EEC), implemented by the *General Product Safety Regulations 1994*, requires in a general way that producers of consumer goods place only safe products on the market and undertake appropriate post-marketing surveillance. The significance of these Regulations lies not in their substantive requirements (which are not at all detailed or especially onerous). Their importance lies more in the completion of an all-embracing consumer product safety regime across the European Union. Whilst specific regulatory requirements will take precedence (e.g. duties specified in sectoral directives or directives dealing with particular risks such as the Electromagnetic Compatibility Directive (89/336/EEC)) aspects of the *General Product Safety Regulations 1994* are meant to cover any gaps in the consumer protection network left by existing regulatory requirements.

The regulation of products for use in the workplace has developed along separate lines (although there is increasing overlap by virtue of the 'new approach' Directives, such as those for machinery or electromagnetic compatibility, which apply uniform requirements for consumer and workplace products albeit with separate enforcement regimes). Under *HSWA s 6* all articles and substances for use at work are required to be as safe as is reasonably practicable, and manufacturers and other suppliers are under obligations to provide information and warnings for safety in use. Various product-specific regulations have also been made under *HSWA*, for example the *Chemicals (Hazard Information and Packaging for Supply) Regulations 1994* and the *Asbestos (Prohibitions) Regulations 1992*.

As far as commercial considerations are concerned, quality and fitness for purpose of products has been an implied statutory term in contracts for sale of goods in legislation stemming from the late nineteenth century and which is now found in the *Sale of Goods Act 1979*, as amended by the *Sale and Supply of Goods Act 1994*. These 1994 amendments included a more focused definition of the standard of *satisfactory quality* which a supplier is obliged by contract to provide, the criteria for which now explicitly include safety, durability, and freedom from minor defects. The ability to exclude these statutory terms, or insist that buyers waive the rights they have, is now strictly curtailed by the *Unfair Contract Terms Act 1977* (banning exclusion of the most significant rights in consumer contracts, and subjecting exclusions in standard form commercial contracts to a statutory test of 'reasonableness'). In addition, and based on the Directive on Unfair Terms in Consumer Contracts (93/13/EEC), there are now other restrictions contained in the *Unfair Terms in Consumer Contracts Regulations 1994 (SI 1994 No 3159)* imposing a requirement of fairness on most terms in consumer contracts which are not individually negotiated. These Regulations also lay down a requirement for suppliers to ensure that terms are expressed in plain, intelligible language. The most important restriction of all for present purposes in these two sets of Regulations is the effective ban on notices and contract terms seeking to exclude liability for death or personal injury resulting from negligence, a prohibition which is reinforced in relation to defective products by the *Consumer Protection Act 1987 s 7*.

This section deals with criminal and civil liabilities for unsafe products for consumer and industrial use as well as the duties imposed on sellers and suppliers of consumer products and after-sales personnel as far as contract law is concerned.

Consumer products

General Product Safety Regulations 1994

Duties of producers and distributors

P9002   The *General Product Safety Regulations 1994 (SI 1994 No 2328)* lay down general requirements concerning the safety of products intended for or likely to be used by consumers. Products used solely in the workplace are not covered, but the fact that a product has a wider industrial application will not prevent it being a consumer product for the purposes of these Regulations if it is supplied to consumers. All manner of products are potentially caught, including clothing, primary agricultural products, DIY equipment and motor vehicles.

The Regulations do not apply to:

—   second-hand products which are antiques;

—   products supplied for repair or reconditioning before use, provided that the purchaser is clearly informed accordingly;

—   products exported direct by the UK manufacturer to a country outside the European Union.

Furthermore, the Regulations are disapplied in relation to any product where there are specific provisions in European law governing *all aspects* of the safety of a product. Where there are product-specific provisions in European law which do not cover all aspects, the *General Product Safety Regulations* apply to the extent that specific provision is not made by European law (*Reg 3(c) and Reg 4*).

The main requirements of the Regulations are that:

(*a*)   no producer place a product on the market unless it is safe [*Reg 7*];

(*b*)   producers provide consumers with relevant information, so as to enable them (i.e. consumers) to assess risks inherent in products throughout the normal or foreseeable period of use, where such risks are not immediately obvious without adequate warnings, and to take precautions against those risks [*Reg 8(1)(a)*];

(*c*)   producers update themselves regarding risks presented by their products and take appropriate action (if necessary recall and withdrawal), e.g. by

    (i)   identifying products/batches of products by marking,

    (ii)   sample testing,

    (iii)   investigating and following up *bona fide* complaints,

    (iv)   keeping distributors informed accordingly

[*Reg 8(1)(b), (2)*];

(*d*)   in order to enable producers to comply with their duties distributors must act with due care, and in particular:

    (i)   must not supply products to any person which are known or presumed (on the basis of information in their possession and as professionals) to be dangerous products, and

    (ii)   must participate in monitoring safety of products placed on the market – in particular, by passing on information on product risks and co-operating in action to avoid risks.

[*Reg 9(a)(b)*].

Conformity with safety requirements – presumption of safety

P9003   A 'safe' product is a product which, under normal or reasonably foreseeable conditions of use (as well as duration), does not present any risk (or only minimal risks) compatible with the product's use, considered as acceptable and consistent with a high level of protection for the safety and health of consumers, with reference to:

(*a*)   product characteristics (e.g. composition, packaging, assembly and maintenance instructions);

(*b*)   the effect on other products, where use with other products is reasonably foreseeable;

(*c*)   product presentation (i.e. labelling, instructions for use and disposal); and

(*d*)   categories of consumers at serious risk – in particular, children.

[*Reg 2(1)*].

In this connection, where a product conforms with specific UK safety requirements (e.g. the *Plugs and Sockets etc (Safety) Regulations 1994*) there is a presumption that the product is safe, until the contrary is proved. In the absence of specific regulations governing the health and safety aspects of a product, the assessment of safety is to be made by taking into account:

    (i)   voluntary national standards implementing European standards;

(ii)   EU technical specifications, or, failing these,

—   standards drawn up in the UK, or

—   codes of practice relating to the product, or

—   state of the art and technology

and the safety that consumers may reasonably expect.

[*Reg 10*].

Offences, penalties and defences

P9004   Contravention of *Regs 7–9(a)* (above) is an offence, carrying, on summary conviction, a maximum penalty of:

(*a*)   imprisonment for up to three months, or

(*b*)   a fine of £5,000, or

(*c*)   both.

[*Reg 12*].

Preparatory acts by producers and distributors

P9005   No producer or distributor may:

(*a*)   offer or agree to place on the market any dangerous product, or expose or possess such product for placing on the market, or

(*b*)   offer or agree to supply any dangerous product, or expose or possess same for supply.

Contravention is an offence, carrying the same maximum penalties as breach of *Reg 12* (see P9004 above).

Offence by another person

P9006   As with breaches of *HSWA* and similarly-oriented legislation, where an offence is committed by 'another person' in the course of his commercial activity, that person can be charged, whether or not the principal offender is prosecuted. Similarly, where commission of an offence is consented to or connived at, or attributable to neglect, on the part of a director, manager or secretary, such persons can be charged in addition to or in lieu of the body corporate. [*Reg 15*].

Defence of 'due diligence' – and exceptions

P9007   It is a defence for a person charged under these regulations to show that he took all reasonable steps and exercised all due diligence to avoid committing the offence. [*Reg 14(1)*]. (See further ENFORCEMENT.)

Exceptions

(*a*)   Where, allegedly, commission of the offence was due to:

(i)   the act or default of another, or

(ii)   reliance on information given by another,

a person so charged cannot, without leave of the court, rely on the defence of 'due diligence', unless he has served a notice, within, at least, seven days before the hearing, identifying the person responsible for the commission or default. [*Reg 14(2)(3)*].

(*b*)   A person so charged cannot rely on the defence of 'information supplied by another', unless he shows that it was reasonable in all circumstances for him to have relied on the information. In particular, did he take steps to verify the information or did he have any reason to disbelieve the information? [*Reg 14(4)*].

(*c*)   A distributor charged with an offence cannot rely on the defence where he has contravened *Reg 9(b)* concerning passing on information. [*Reg 14(5)*].

A mere recommendation on the part of an importer that labels should be attached to boxes by retailers does not constitute 'due diligence' for the purposes of *Reg 14(1)*. (In *Coventry County Council v Ackerman Group plc [1995] Crim LR 140*, an egg boiler imported by the defendant failed to contain instructions that eggs should be broken into the container and yolks pricked before being microwaved. The defendant had learned of the problem and had printed instructions which it sent to all retailers, recommending that they be fixed to the boxes.)

Compliance with recognised standards (such as British Standards) will not amount to the defence of due diligence if a product is nevertheless unsafe for the user. In *Whirlpool (UK) Ltd and Magnet Ltd v Gloucestershire County Council (1993, unreported)* cooker hoods which were intrinsically safe and which met applicable standards for the purposes of the *Low Voltage Electrical Equipment (Safety) Regulations 1989* failed to meet the general safety requirement contained in the then applicable consumer protection legislation because they were liable to result in fires when used in conjunction with certain gas hobs.

Industrial products

P9008   The *Health and Safety at Work etc. Act 1974* (*HSWA*) was the first Act to place a *general* duty on designers and manufacturers of industrial products to design and produce articles and substances that are safe and without health risks when used at work. Before this date, legislation had tended to avoid this approach, e.g. the *Factories Act 1961*, on the premise that safety could not be designed into machinery (see M1001 MACHINERY SAFETY). Statutory requirements had tended to concentrate on the duty to guard and fence machinery, and with the placement of a duty upon the user/employer to inspect and test inward products for safety. There is a general residual duty on the employers/users of industrial products to inspect and test them for safety under *s 2* of *HSWA*.

These duties notwithstanding, the trend of legislation in recent years has been towards safer design and manufacture of products for industrial and domestic use. Thus, *HSWA s 6* as updated by the *Consumer Protection Act 1987, Sch 3* imposes general duties on designers, manufacturers, importers and suppliers of products ('articles and substances') for use at work, to their immediate users. Contravention of *s 6* carries with it a maximum fine, on summary conviction, of £20,000 or an unlimited fine in the Crown Court (see ENFORCEMENT). Additionally, a separate duty is laid on installers of industrial plant and machinery. However, because of their involvement in the key areas of design and manufacture, more onerous duties are placed upon designers and manufacturers of articles and substances for use at work than upon importers and suppliers, who are essentially concerned with distribution and retail of industrial products, though under *HSWA s 6(8A)* importers are made liable for the first time for the faults of *foreign* designers/manufacturers.

Criminal liability for breach of statutory duties

P9009   This refers to duties laid down in *HSWA* as revised by *Schedule 3* to the *Consumer Protection Act 1987*. The duties exist in relation to articles and substances for use at work and fairground equipment. There is no civil liability available to employees under these provisions except for breach of safety regulations. (For the specific requirements now applicable to machinery for use at work, see MACHINERY SAFETY.)

Definition of articles and substances

P9010   An article for use at work means:

(*a*)   any plant designed for use or operation (whether exclusively or not) by persons at work; and

(*b*)   any article designed for use as a component in any such plant.

[*HSWA s 53(1)*].

A substance for use at work means 'any natural or artificial substance (including micro-organisms), whether in solid or liquid form or in the form of a gas or vapour'. [*HSWA, s 53(1)*].

An article upon which first trials/demonstrations are carried out is not an article for use at work, but rather an article which *might* be used at work. The purpose of trial/demonstration was to determine whether the article could safely be later used at work (*McKay v Unwin Pyrotechnics Ltd, The Times, 5 March 1991* where a dummy mine exploded, causing the operator injury, when being tested to see if it would explode when hit by a flail attached to a vehicle. It was held that there was no breach of *HSWA s 6(1)(a)*).

Duties in respect of articles and substances for use at work

P9011   *HSWA s 6* (as amended by the *Consumer Protection Act 1987, 3 Sch*) places duties upon manufacturers and designers, as well as importers and suppliers, of (*a*) articles and (*b*) substances for use at work, whether used exclusively at work or not (e.g. lawnmower, hair dryer).

Articles for use at work

P9012   Any person who designs, manufactures, imports or supplies any article for use at work (or any article of fairground equipment) must:

(*a*)   ensure, so far as is reasonably practicable (for the meaning of this expression see E15017 ENFORCEMENT), that the article is so designed and constructed that it will be safe and without risks to health at all times when it is being (i) set, (ii) used, (iii) cleaned or (iv) maintained by a person at work;

(*b*)   carry out or arrange for the carrying out of such testing and examination as may be necessary for the performance of the above duty;

(c)   take such steps as are necessary to secure that persons supplied by that person with the article are provided with adequate information about the use for which the article is designed or has been tested and about any conditions necessary to ensure that it will be safe and without risks to health at all such times of (i) setting, (ii) using, (iii) cleaning, (iv) maintaining *and* when being (v) dismantled, or (vi) disposed of; and

(d)   take such steps as are necessary to secure, so far as is reasonably practicable, that persons so supplied are provided with all such revisions of information as are necessary by reason of it becoming known that anything gives rise to a serious risk to health or safety.

[*HSWA s 6(1)(a)-(d) as amended by the Consumer Protection Act 1987, Sch 3*].

(See P9014 and P9015 below for further duties relevant to articles for use at work.)

In the case of an article for use at work which is likely to cause an employee to be exposed to 85 dB(A) or above, or to peak action level (200 pascals) or above, adequate information must be provided about noise likely to be generated by that article. [*Noise at Work Regulations 1989 (SI 1989 No 1790), Reg 12*] (see further NOISE AND VIBRATION).

Substances for use at work

P9013   Every person who manufactures, imports or supplies any substance must:

(a)   ensure, so far as is reasonably practicable, that the substance will be safe and without risks to health at all times when it is being (i) used, (ii) handled, (iii) processed, (iv) stored, or (v) transported by any person at work or in premises where substances are being installed;

(b)   carry out or arrange for the carrying out of such testing and examination as may be necessary for the performance of the duty in (a);

(c)   take such steps as are necessary to secure that persons supplied by that person with the substance are provided with adequate information about:

(i)   any risks to health or safety to which the inherent properties of the substance may give rise;

(ii)   the results of any relevant tests which have been carried out on or in connection with the substance; and

(iii)   any conditions necessary to ensure that the substance will be safe and without risks to health at all times when it is being (a) used, (b) handled, (c) processed, (d) stored, (e) transported and (f) disposed of; and

(d)   take such steps as are necessary to secure, so far as is reasonably practicable, that persons so supplied are provided with all such revisions of information as are necessary by reason of it becoming known that anything gives rise to a serious risk to health or safety.

[*HSWA s 6(4) as amended by the Consumer Protection Act 1987, Sch 3*].

Additional duty on designers and manufacturers to carry out research

P9014   Any person who undertakes the design or manufacture of any article for use at work must carry out, or arrange for the carrying out, of any necessary research with a view to the discovery and, so far as is reasonably practicable, the elimination or minimisation of any health or safety risks to which the design or article may give rise. [*HSWA s 6(2)*].

Duties on installers of articles for use at work

P9015   Any person who erects or instals any article for use at work in any premises where the article is to be used by persons at work, must ensure, so far as is reasonably practicable, that nothing about the way in which the article is erected or installed makes it unsafe or a risk to health when it is being (*a*) set, (*b*) used, (*c*) cleaned, or (*d*) maintained by someone at work. [*HSWA s 6(3) as amended by the Consumer Protection Act 1987, Sch 3*].

Additional duty on manufacturers of substances to carry out research

P9016   Any person who manufactures any substance must carry out, or arrange for the carrying out, of any necessary research with a view to the discovery and, so far as is reasonably practicable, the elimination or minimisation of any health/safety risks at all times when the substance is being (*a*) used, (*b*) handled, (*c*) processed, (*d*) stored, or (*e*) transported by someone at work. [*HSWA s 6(5) as amended by the Consumer Protection Act 1987, Sch 3*].

No duty on suppliers of industrial articles and substances to research

P9017   It is not necessary to repeat any testing, examination or research which has been carried out by designers and manufacturers of industrial products, on the part of importers and suppliers, in so far as it is reasonable to rely on the results. [*HSWA s 6(6)*].

Custom built articles

P9018   Where a person designs, manufactures, imports or supplies an article for or to another person on the basis of a written undertaking by that other to ensure that the article will be safe and without health risks when being (*a*) set, (*b*) used, (*c*) cleaned, or (*d*) maintained by a person at work, the undertaking will relieve the designer/manufacturer etc. from the duty specified in *HSWA s 6(1)(a)* (see P9012 above), to such extent as is reasonable, having regard to the terms of the undertaking. [*HSWA s 6(8) as amended by the Consumer Protection Act 1987, Sch 3*].

Importers liable for offences of foreign manufacturers/designers

P9019   In order to give added protection to industrial users from unsafe imported products, *Schedule 3* to the *Consumer Protection Act 1987* has introduced a new subsection (*HSWA s 6(8A)*) which, in effect makes importers of unsafe products liable for the acts/omissions of foreign designers and manufacturers. *Section 6(8A)* states that nothing in (*inter alia*) *s 6(8)* is to relieve an importer of an article/substance from any of his duties, as regards anything done (or not done) or within the control of:

(*a*)   a foreign designer; or

(*b*)   a foreign manufacturer of an article/substance.

[*HSWA s 6(8A)*].

Proper use

P9020

The original 1974 wording of *HSWA s 6(1)(a), 6(4)(a) and 6(10)* concerning 'proper use' excluded foreseeable user error as a defence, which had the consequence of favouring the supplier. Thus, if a supplier could demonstrate a degree of operator misuse or error, however reasonably foreseeable, the question of initial product safety was sidestepped. Moreover, 'when properly used' implied, as construed, that there could only be a breach of *s 6* once a product had actually been *used*. This was contrary to the principle that safety should be built into design/production, rather than relying on warnings and disclaimers. The wording in *s 6* is now amended so that only *unforeseeable* user/operator error will relieve the supplier from liability; he will no longer be able to rely on the strict letter of his operating instructions. [*Consumer Protection Act 1987, Sch 3*].

Powers to deal with unsafe imported goods

P9021

HSWA does not empower enforcing authorities to stop the supply of unsafe products at source or prevent the sale of products by foreign producers after they have been found to be unsafe, but enforcement officers have the power to act at the point of entry or anywhere else along the distribution chain to stop unsafe articles/substances being imported by serving prohibition notices (see ENFORCEMENT).

Customs officers can seize any imported article/substance, which is considered to be unsafe, and detain it for up to two (working) days. [*HSWA s 25A (incorporated by Schedule 3 to the Consumer Protection Act 1987)*].

In addition, customs officers can transmit information relating to unsafe imported products to HSE inspectors. [*HSWA s 27A (incorporated by Schedule 3 to the Consumer Protection Act 1987)*].

Civil liability for unsafe products – historical background

P9022

Originally at common law where defective products caused injury, damage and/or death, redress depended on whether the injured user had a contract with the seller or hirer of the product. This was often not the case, and in consequence many persons, including employees repairing and/or servicing products, were remediless. This rule, emanating from the decision of *Winterbottom v Wright (1842) 10 M & W 109*, remained unchanged till 1932, when *Donoghue (or M'Alister) v Stevenson [1932] AC 562* was decided by the House of Lords. This case was important because it established that manufacturers were liable in negligence (i.e. tort) if they failed to take reasonable care in the manufacturing and marketing of their products, and in consequence a user suffered injury when using the product in a reasonably foreseeable way. More particularly, a 'manufacturer of products, which he sells in such a form as to show that he intends them to reach the ultimate consumer in the form in which they left him with no reasonable possibility of intermediate inspection, and with the knowledge that the absence of reasonable care in the preparation or putting up of the products will result in an injury to the consumer's life or property, owes a duty to the consumer to take reasonable care' (per Lord Atkin). In this way, manufacturers of products which were defective were liable in negligence to users and consumers of their products, including those who as intermediaries, repair, maintain and service industrial products, it being irrelevant whether there was a contract between manufacturer and user (which normally there was not).

Donoghue v Stevenson is a case of enormous historical importance in the context of liability of manufacturers, but although the principle has become well established and is still widely applied it did not give a reliable remedy to injured persons, who still had to satisfy the legal burden of proving that the manufacturer had not exercised reasonable care, a serious obstacle to overcome in cases involving technically complex products. In some instances it became possible to avoid this obstacle, by establishing liability on other bases.

Defective equipment supplied to employees

P9023

At common law an employer obtaining equipment from a reputable supplier was unlikely to be found liable to an employee if the equipment turned out to be defective and injured him (*Davie v New Merton Board Mills Ltd [1959] AC 604*). Although it represented no bar to employees suing manufacturers direct for negligence, the effect of this decision was reversed by the *Employers' Liability (Defective Equipment) Act 1969* rendering employers strictly liable (irrespective of negligence) for any defects in equipment causing injury (see EMPLOYERS' DUTIES TO THEIR EMPLOYEES). In such circumstances the employer would be able to claim indemnity for breach of contract by the supplier of the equipment.

Breach of statutory duty

P9024

Whilst legislation and regulations dealing with domestic and industrial safety are principally penal and enforceable by state agencies (trading standards officers and health and safety inspectors) if injury, death or damage occurs in consequence of a breach of such statutory duty, it may be possible to use this breach as the basis of a civil liability claim. Here there may be strict liability if there are absolute requirements, or the duty may be defined in terms of what it is practicable or reasonably practicable to do (see E15017 ENFORCEMENT).

As far as workplace products are concerned, *HSWA s 47* bars a right of action in civil proceedings in respect of any failure to comply with *HSWA s 6* (or the other general duties under the Act) but breach of a duty imposed by health and safety regulations will generally be actionable in this way, unless the particular regulations in question contain a proviso to the contrary.

The position is the same in relation to consumer safety regulations made under the *Consumer Protection Act 1987* (*Consumer Protection Act 1987, s 41(1)*). No provision is made in the *General Product Safety Regulations 1994* for any breach thereof to give rise to civil liability for the benefit of an injured person, and given that the regulations stem from European law it is unlikely that they would be construed in such a way as to give more extensive rights than those contained in the Product Liability Directive (85/374/EEC) (see below).

Consumer Protection Act 1987 – introduction of product liability

P9025

At European level it was deemed necessary to introduce a degree of harmonisation of product liability principles between member states, and at the same time to reduce the importance of fault and negligence concepts in favour of liability being determined by reference to 'defects' in a product. Thus the nature of the product itself would become the key issue, not the conduct of the manufacturer. After protracted debate the Product Liability Directive (85/374/EEC) was adopted.

P9026   The introduction of strict product liability is enshrined in Britain within the *Consumer Protection Act 1987, s 2(1)*. Thus, where any damage is *caused* wholly or partly by a defect (see P9029 below) in a product (e.g. goods, electricity, a component product or raw materials), the following may be liable for damages (irrespective of negligence):

(*a*)   the producer;

(*b*)   any person who, by putting his name on the product or using a trade mark (or other distinguishing mark) has held himself out as the producer;

(*c*)   any person who has imported the product into a member state from outside the EU, in the course of trade/business.

[*Consumer Protection Act 1987, s 2(1), (2)*].

Producers

P9027   Producers are variously defined as:

(*a*)   the person who manufactured a product;

(*b*)   in the case of a substance which has not been manufactured, but rather won or abstracted, the person who won or abstracted it;

(*c*)   in the case of a product not manufactured, won or abstracted, but whose essential characteristics are attributable to an industrial process or agricultural process, the person who carried out the process.

[*Consumer Protection Act 1987, s 1(2)(c)*].

Liability of suppliers

P9028   Although producers are principally liable, intermediate suppliers can also be liable in certain circumstances. Thus, any person who supplied the product is liable for damages if:

(*a*)   the injured person requests the supplier to identify one (or more) of the following:

(i)   the producer,

(ii)   the person who put his trade mark on the product,

(iii)   the importer of the product into the EU; and

(*b*)   the request is made within a reasonable time after damage/injury has occurred *and* it is not reasonably practicable for the requestor to identify the above three persons; and

(*c*)   within a reasonable time after receiving the request, the supplier fails either:

(i)   to comply with the request, or

(ii)   identify his supplier.

[*Consumer Protection Act 1987, s 2(3)*].

No liability attaches here to a supplier of game/agricultural produce, if the supply occurred before the product had undergone an industrial process. [*Consumer Protection Act 1987, s 2(4)*].

Importers of products into the EU and persons applying their name, brand or trade mark will also be directly liable as if they were original manufacturers. [*s 2(2)*].

Defect – key to liability

P9029   Liability presupposes that there is a defect in the product, and indeed, existence of a defect is the key to liability. Defect is defined in terms of the absence of safety in the product. More particularly, there is a 'defect in a product . . . if the safety of the product is not such as persons generally are entitled to expect' (including products comprised in that product). [*Consumer Protection Act 1987, s 3(1)*].

Defect can arise in one of three ways and is related to:

(*a*)   construction, manufacture, submanufacture, assembly;

(*b*)   absence or inadequacy of suitable warnings, or existence of misleading warnings or precautions;

(*c*)   design.

The definition of 'defect' implies an entitlement to an expectation of safety on the part of the consumer, judged by reference to *general* consumer expectations not individual subjective ones. (The American case of *Webster v Blue Ship Tea Room Inc 347 Mass 421, 198 NE 2d 309 (1964)* is particularly instructive here. The plaintiff sued in a product liability action for a bone which had stuck in her throat, as a result of eating a fish chowder in the defendant's restaurant. It was held that there was no liability. Whatever her own expectations may have been, fish chowder would not be fish chowder without some bones and this is a general expectation.)

Consumer expectation of safety – criteria

P9030   The general consumer expectation of safety must be judged in relation to:

(*a*)   the marketing of the product, i.e:

(i)   the manner in which; and

(ii)   the purposes for which the product has been marketed;

(iii)   any instructions/warnings against doing anything with the product; and

(*b*)   by what might reasonably be expected to be done with or in relation to the product (e.g. the expectation that a sharp knife will be handled with care); and

(*c*)   the time when the product was supplied (e.g. a product's short shelf-life).

A defect cannot arise retrospectively by virtue of the fact that, subsequently, a safer product is made and put into circulation. [*Consumer Protection Act 1987, s 3(2)*].

Time of supply

P9031   Liability attaches to the *supply* of a product (see P9040 below). More particularly, the producer will be liable for any defects in the product existing at the time of supply (see P9039(*d*) below); and where two or more persons collaborate in the manufacture of a product, say by submanufacture, either and both may be liable, that is, severally and jointly (see P9037 below).

Contributory negligence

P9032   A person who is careless for his own safety is probably guilty of contributory negligence and, thus, will risk a reduction in damages [*Consumer Protection Act 1987, s 6(4)*] (see also EMPLOYERS' DUTIES TO THEIR EMPLOYEES). However, in the product liability context, carelessness of the user may mean that there is no liability at all on the part of the producer: if, for example, clear instructions and warnings provided with the product had been disregarded, when compliance would have avoided the accident, it is highly unlikely that the product would be found to be defective for the purposes of the Act. No off-setting of damages for contributory fault of the plaintiff would arise.

Absence or inadequacy of suitable/misleading warnings

P9033   The common law required that the vendor of a product point out any latent dangers in a product which he either knew about or ought to have known about. Misleading terminology/labelling on a product or product container could result in liability for negligence (*Vacwell Engineering Ltd v BDH Chemicals Ltd [1969] 3 AER 1681* where ampoules containing boron tribromide, which carried the warning 'Harmful Vapours', exploded on contact with water, killing two scientists. It was held that this consequence was reasonably foreseeable and accordingly the defendants should have researched their product more thoroughly). In a similar product liability action today, the manufacturers would be strictly liable (subject to statutory defences) and, if injury/damage followed the failure to issue a written/pictorial warning, as required by regulation (e.g. the *Chemicals (Hazard Information and Packaging for Supply) Regulations 1994 (SI 1994 No 3247)*), there would be liability.

The duty, on manufacturers, to research the safety of their products, before putting them into circulation (see *Vacwell Engineering Ltd v BDH Chemicals Ltd*) is even more necessary and compulsory now, given the introduction of strict product liability. This includes safety in connection with directions for use on a product. A warning refers to something that can go wrong with the product; directions for use relate to the best results that can be obtained from products, if the directions are followed. In the absence of case law on the point it is reasonable to assume that in order to avoid actions for product liability, manufacturers should provide both warnings, indicating the worst results and dangers, and directions for use, indicating the best results; the warning, in effect, identifying the worst consequences that could follow if directions for use were not complied with.

Defect must exist when the product left the producer's possession

P9034   This situation tends to be spotlighted by alteration of, modification to or interference with a product on the part of an intermediary, for instance, a dealer or agent. If a product leaves an assembly line as per its intended design, but is subsequently altered, modified or generally interfered with by an intermediary, in a manner outside the product's specification, the manufacturer is probably not liable for any injury so caused. In *Sabloff v Yamaha Motor Co 113 NJ Super 279, 273 A 2d 606 (1971)*, the plaintiff was injured when the wheel of his motor-cycle locked, causing it to skid, then crash. The manufacturer's specification stipulated that the dealer attach the wheel of the motor-cycle to the front fork with a nut and bolt, and this had not been done properly. It was held that the dealer was liable for the motor-cyclist's injury (as well as the assembler, since the latter had delegated the function of tightening the nut to the dealer and it had not been properly carried out).

Role of intermediaries

P9035   If a defect in a product is foreseeably detectable by a legitimate intermediary (e.g. a retailer in the case of a domestic product or an employer in the case of an industrial product), liability used to rest with the intermediary rather than the manufacturer, when liability was referable to negligence (*Donoghue (or M'Alister) v Stevenson [1932] AC 562*). This position does not duplicate under the *Consumer Protection Act 1987*, since the main object of the legislation is to fix producers with strict liability for injury-causing product defects to users. Nevertheless, there are common law and statutory duties on employers to inspect/test inward plant and machinery for use at the workplace, and failure to comply with these duties may make an employer liable. In addition, employers, in such circumstances, can incur liability under the *Employers' Liability (Defective Equipment) Act 1969* (see EMPLOYERS' DUTIES TO THEIR EMPLOYEES) and so may seek to exercise contractual indemnity against manufacturers.

Comparison with negligence

P9036   Product liability differs from negligence in that it is no longer necessary for injured users to prove absence of reasonable care on the part of manufacturers. All that is now necessary is proof of (*a*) defect (see P9029 above) and (*b*) that the defect caused the injury. It will, therefore, be no good for manufacturers to point to an unblemished safety record and/or excellent quality assurance programmes, since the user is not trying to establish negligence. How or why a defect arose is immaterial; what is important is the fact that it exists.

The similarity between product liability and negligence lies in causation. Defect must be the material *cause* of injury. The main arguments against this are likely to be along the lines of misuse of a product by a user (e.g. knowingly driving a car with defective brakes), or ignoring warnings (a two-pronged defence, since it also denies there was a 'defect'), or – as is common in chemicals and pesticides cases – a defence based on alternative theories of causation of the claimant's injuries.

Joint and several liability

P9037   If two or more persons/companies are liable for the same damage, the liability is joint and several. This can, for example, refer to the situation where a product (e.g. an aircraft) is made partly in one country (e.g. England) and partly in another (e.g. France). Here both partners are liable (joint liability) but in the event of one party not being able to pay, the other can be made to pay all the compensation (several liability). [*Consumer Protection Act 1987, s 2(5)*].

Parameters of liability

P9038   Liability for certain types of damage including (*a*) death, (*b*) personal injury and (*c*) loss or damage to property, is included relevant to private use, occupation and consumption by consumers [*s 5(1)*]. However, producers and others will not be liable for:

(*a*)   damage/loss to the defective product itself, or any product supplied with the defective product [*Consumer Protection Act 1987, s 5(2)*];

(*b*)   damage to property not 'ordinarily intended for private use, occupation or consumption' e.g. car/van used for business purposes [*Consumer Protection Act 1987, s 5(3)*]; and

(*c*)   damage amounting to less than £275 (to be determined as early as possible after loss) [*Consumer Protection Act 1987, s 5(4)*].

Defences

P9039   The following statutory defences are open to producers, etc:

(*a*)   the defect was attributable to compliance with any requirement imposed by law/regulation or a European Union rule/regulation [*Consumer Protection Act 1987, s 4(1)(a)*];

(*b*)   the defendant did not supply the product to another (i.e. did not sell/hire/lend/exchange for money/give goods as a prize etc. (see below 'supply')) [*Consumer Protection Act 1987, s 4(1)(b)*];

(*c*)   the supply to another person was not in the course of that person's business [*Consumer Protection Act 1987, s 4(1)(c)*];

(*d*)   the defect did not exist in the product at the relevant time (i.e. it came into existence after the product had left the possession of the defendant). This principally refers to the situation where, e.g. a retailer fails to follow the instructions of the manufacturer for storage or assembly [*Consumer Protection Act 1987, s 4(1)(d)*];

(*e*)   that the state of scientific and technical knowledge at the relevant time was not such that a producer 'might be expected to have discovered the defect if it had existed in his products while they were under his control' (i.e. development risk) [*Consumer Protection Act 1987, s 4(1)(e)*] (see P9043 below);

(*f*)   that the defect was:

(i)   a defect in a subsequent product (in which the product in question was comprised); and

(ii)   was wholly attributable to:

(A)   design of the subsequent product; or

(B)   compliance by the producer with the instructions of the producer of the subsequent product.

[*Consumer Protection Act 1987, s 4(1)(f)*]. This is known as the component manufacturer's defence.

The meaning of 'supply'

P9040   Before there can be liability under the *Consumer Protection Act 1987*, that is, strict liability, a product must have been '*supplied*'. This is defined as follows:

(*a*)   selling, hiring out or lending goods;

(*b*)   entering into a hire-purchase agreement to furnish goods;

(*c*)   performance of any contract for work and materials to furnish goods (e.g. making/repairing teeth);

(*d*)   providing goods in exchange for a consideration other than money (e.g. trading stamps);

(*e*)   providing goods in or in connection with the performance of any statutory function/duty (e.g. supply of gas/electricity by public utilities);

(*f*)   giving the goods as a prize or otherwise making a gift of the goods.

[*Consumer Protection Act 1987, s 46(1)*].

Moreover, in the case of hire-purchase agreements/credit sales the effective supplier (i.e. the dealer) and not the ostensible supplier (i.e. the finance company) is the 'supplier' for the purposes of strict liability. [*Consumer Protection Act 1987, s 46(2)*].

Building work is only to be treated as a supply of goods in so far as it involves provision of any goods to any person by means of their incorporation into the building/structure, e.g. glass for windows. [*Consumer Protection Act 1987, s 46(3)*].

No contracting out of strict liability

P9041   The liability of a person who has suffered injury/damage under the *Consumer Protection Act 1987*, cannot be (*a*) limited or (*b*) excluded:

(*a*)   by any contract term; or

(*b*)   by any notice or other provision.

[*Consumer Protection Act 1987, s 7*].

Time limits for bringing product liability actions

P9042   No action can be brought under the *Consumer Protection Act 1987, Part I* (i.e. product liability actions) after the expiry of ten years from the time when the product was first put into circulation (i.e. the particular item in question was supplied in the course of business/trade etc.). [*Limitation Act 1980, s 11A(3); Consumer Protection Act 1987, Sch 1*].

In other words, ten years is the cut-off point of liability. Moreover, actions for personal injury caused by product defects must be initiated within three years of whichever event occurs later, namely:

(*a*)   the date when the cause of action accrued (i.e. injury occurred); or

(*b*)   the date when the injured person had the requisite knowledge of his injury/damage to property.

[*Limitation Act 1980, s 11A(4); Consumer Protection Act 1987, Sch 1*].

But if during that period the injured person died, his personal representative has a further three years from his death to bring the action. (This coincides with actions for personal injuries against employers, except of course in that case there is no overall cut-off period of ten years.) [*Limitation Act 1980, s 11A(5)*].

Development risk

P9043   This will probably emerge as the most important defence to product liability actions. Manufacturers have argued that it would be wrong to hold them responsible for the consequences of defects which they could not reasonably have known about or discovered. The absence of this defence would have the effect of increasing the cost of product liability insurance and stifle the development of new products. On the other hand, consumers maintain that the existence of this defence threatens the whole basis of strict liability and allows manufacturers to escape liability by, in effect, pleading a defence associated with the lack of negligence. For this reason, not all EU states have allowed this defence; the states in favour of its retention are the United Kingdom, Germany, Denmark, Italy and the Netherlands. The burden of proving development risk lies on the producer and it seems likely that he will have to show that no producer of a product of that sort could be expected to have discovered the existence of the defect. 'It will not necessarily be enough to show that he (the producer) has done as many tests as his competitor, nor that he did all the tests required of him by a government regulation setting a minimum standard.' (Explanatory memorandum of EC Directive on Product Liability, Department of Trade and Industry, November 1985).

Additionally, the fact that judgments in product liability cases are 'transportable' could have serious implications for the retention of development risk in the United Kingdom (see P9044 below).

Transportability of judgments

P9044   The Brussels Convention of 17 September 1968 on Jurisdiction and Enforcement of Judgments in Civil and Commercial Matters requires judgments given in one of the original six EC member states to be enforced in another. The United Kingdom is bound by this Convention, which, by virtue of the *Civil Jurisdiction and Judgments Act 1982*, is part of United Kingdom law. Where product liability actions are concerned, litigation can be initiated in the state where the defendant is based or where injury occurred and the judgment of that court 'transported' to another member state. This could pose a threat to retention of development risk in the United Kingdom and other states in favour of it from a state against it, e.g. France, Belgium, Luxembourg.

Contractual liability for substandard products

P9045   Contractual liability is concerned with defective products which are substandard (though not necessarily dangerous) regarding quality, reliability and/or durability. Liability is predominantly determined by contractual terms implied by the *Sale of Goods Act 1979* and the *Sale and Supply of Goods Act 1994*, in the case of goods sold; the *Supply of Goods (Implied Terms) Act 1973*, where goods are the subject of hire purchase and conditional and/or credit sale; and the *Supply of Goods and Services Act 1982*, where goods are supplied but not sold as such, primarily as a supply of goods with services; hire and leasing contracts are subject to the 1982 Act as well.

Exemption or exclusion clauses in such contracts are generally invalid by dint of the *Unfair Contract Terms Act 1977*, which also applies to such transactions. Moreover, 'standard form' contracts with consumers where the terms have not been individually negotiated, which contain 'unfair terms' – that is, terms detrimental to the consumer – will have such terms excised, if necessary, by the Director General of Fair Trading, under the *Unfair Terms in Consumer Contracts Regulations 1994 (SI 1994 No 3159)*. This Act extends to most consumer contracts but not to contracts of employment [*Reg 3(1), Sch 1*] (see P9056 below).

Contractual liability is strict. It is not necessary that negligence be established (*Frost v Aylesbury Dairy Co Ltd [1905] 1 KB 608* where the defendant supplied typhoid-infected milk to the plaintiff, who, after its consumption, became ill and required medical treatment. It was held that the defendant was liable, irrespective of the absence of negligence on his part).

Sale of Goods Acts

P9046   Conditions and warranties as to fitness for purpose, quality and merchantability were originally implied into contracts for the sale of goods at common law. Then those terms were codified in the *Sale of Goods Act 1893*, which, however, was not a blanket consumer protection measure, since sellers were still allowed to exclude liability by suitably worded exemption clauses in the contract. This practice was finally outlawed, at least as far as consumer contracts were concerned, by the *Supply of Goods (Implied Terms) Act 1973* and later still by the *Unfair Contract Terms Act*

1977, the current statute prohibiting contracting out of contractual liability and negligence. Indeed, consumer protection has reached a height with the *Unfair Terms in Consumer Contracts Regulations 1994*, invalidating 'unfair terms' in most consumer contracts of a standard form nature (see P9056 below).

More recently, the law relating to sale and supply of goods has been updated by the *Sale of Goods Act 1979* and the *Sale and Supply of Goods Act 1994*, the latter replacing the condition of 'merchantable quality' with 'satisfactory quality'. The difference between the 'merchantability' requirement, under the *1979 Act*, and its replacement 'satisfactory quality', under the *1994 Act*, is that, under the former Act, products were 'usable' (or, in the case of food, 'edible'), even if they had defects which ruined their appearance; now they must be free from minor defects as well as being safe and durable. Further, under the previous law, a right of refund disappeared after goods had been kept for a reasonable time; under current law, there is a right of examination for a reasonable time after buying.

Sale of Goods Act 1979

P9047

In 1979 a consolidated *Sale of Goods Act* was passed and current law on quality and fitness of products is contained in that Act. Another equally important development has been the extension of implied terms, relating to quality and fitness of products, to contracts other than those for the sale of goods, that is, to hire purchase contracts by the *Supply of Goods (Implied Terms) Act 1973*, and to straight hire contracts by the *Supply of Goods and Services Act 1982*. In addition, where services are performed under a contract, that is, a contract for work and materials, there is a statutory duty on the contractor to perform them with reasonable care and skill. In other words, in the case of services liability is not strict, but it is strict for the supply of products. This is laid down in *s 4* of the *Supply of Goods and Services Act 1982*. This applies whether products are simultaneously but separately supplied under any contract, e.g. after-sales service, say, on a car or a contract to repair a window by a carpenter, in which latter case service is rendered irrespective of product supplied.

Products to be of satisfactory quality – sellers/suppliers

P9048

The *Sale of Goods Act 1979* (as amended) writes two quality conditions into all contracts for the sale of products, the first with regard to satisfactory quality, the second with regard to fitness for purpose.

Where a seller sells goods in the course of business, there is an implied term that the goods supplied under the contract are of satisfactory quality, according to the standards of the reasonable person, by reference to description, price etc. [*Sale of Goods Act 1979, s 14(2) as substituted by the Sale and Supply of Goods Act 1994, s 1(2)*]. The 'satisfactory' (or otherwise) quality of goods can be determined from:

(*a*)   their state and condition;

(*b*)   their fitness for purpose (see P9051 below);

(*c*)   their appearance and finish;

(*d*)   their freedom from minor defects;

(*e*)   their safety; and

(*f*)   their durability.

However, the implied term of 'satisfactory quality' does not apply to situations where:

(i) the unsatisfactory nature of goods is specifically drawn to the buyer's attention prior to contract; or

(ii) the buyer examined the goods prior to contract and the matter in question ought to have been revealed by that examination.

[*Sale of Goods Act 1979, s 14(2) as substituted by the Sale and Supply of Goods Act 1994, s 1(2A), (2B) and (2C)*].

Sale by sample

P9049 In the case of a contract for sale by sample, there is an implied condition that the goods will be free from any defect making their quality unsatisfactory, which would not be apparent on reasonable examination of the sample. [*Sale of Goods Act 1979, s 15(2) as substituted by the Sale and Supply of Goods Act 1994, s 1(2)*].

Conditions implied into sale – sales by a dealer

P9050 The condition of satisfactory quality only arises in the case of sales by a dealer to a consumer, not in the case of private sales. *Sec 14(2)* also applies to second-hand as well as new products. It is not necessary, as it is with the 'fitness for purpose' condition (see P9051 below), for the buyer in any way to rely on the skill and judgment of the seller in selecting his stock, in order to invoke *Sec 14(2)*. However, if the buyer has examined the products, then the seller will not be liable for any defects which the examination should have disclosed. Originally this applied if the buyer had been given opportunity to examine but had not, or only partially, exercised it. In *Thornett & Fehr v Beers & Son [1919] 1 KB 486*, a buyer of glue examined only the outside of some barrels of glue. The glue was defective. It was held that he had examined the glue and so was without redress.

Products to be reasonably fit for purpose

P9051 'Where the seller sells goods in the course of a business and the buyer, expressly or by implication, makes known

(*a*) to the seller, or

(*b*) where the purchase price or part of it is payable by instalments and the goods were previously sold by a credit-broker to the seller, to that credit-broker,

any particular purpose for which the goods are being bought, there is an implied condition that the goods supplied under the contract are reasonably fit for that purpose, whether or not that is a purpose for which such goods are commonly supplied, except where the circumstances show that the buyer does not rely or that it is unreasonable for him to rely, on the skill or judgment of the seller or credit-broker.' [*Sale of Goods Act 1979, s 14(3)*].

Reliance on the skill/judgment of the seller will generally be inferred from the buyer's conduct. The reliance will seldom be express: it will usually arise by implication from the circumstances; thus to take a case of a purchase from a retailer, the reliance will be in general inferred from the fact that a buyer goes to the shop in the confidence that the tradesman has selected his stock with skill and judgment (*Grant v Australian Knitting Mills Ltd [1936] AC 85*). Moreover, it is enough if the buyer relies partially on the seller's skill and judgment. However, there may be no reliance where the seller can only sell goods of a particular brand. The plaintiff bought beer in a public house which he knew was a tied house. He later became ill as a result of drinking it. It was held that there was no reliance on the seller's skill and so no liability on the part of the seller (*Wren v Holt [1903] 1 KB 610*).

Even though products can only be used normally for one purpose, they will have to be reasonably fit for that particular purpose. The plaintiff bought a hot water bottle and was later scalded when using it because of its defective condition. It was held that the seller was liable because the hot water bottle was not suitable for its normal purpose (*Priest v Last [1903] 2 KB 148*). But, on the other hand, the buyer must not be hypersensitive to the effects of the product. The plaintiff bought a Harris Tweed coat from the defendants. She later contracted dermatitis from wearing it. Evidence showed that she had an exceptionally sensitive skin. It was held that the coat was reasonably fit for the purpose when worn by a person with an average skin (*Griffiths v Peter Conway Ltd [1939] 1 AER 685*).

Like *s 14(2)*, *s 14(3)* extends beyond the actual products themselves to their containers and labelling. A plaintiff was injured by a defective bottle containing mineral water, which she had purchased from the defendant, a retailer. The bottle remained the property of the seller because the plaintiff had paid the seller a deposit on the bottle, which would be returned to her, on return of the empty bottle. It was held that, although the bottle was the property of the seller, the seller was liable for the injury caused to the plaintiff by the defective container (*Geddling v Marsh [1920] 1 KB 668*).

Like *s 14(2)* (above), *s 14(3)* does not apply to private sales.

Strict liability under the Sale of Goods Act 1979, s 14

P9052   Liability arising under the *Sale of Goods Act, s 14* is strict and does not depend on proof of negligence by the purchaser against the seller (*Frost v Aylesbury Dairy Co Ltd* (see P9045 above)). This fact was stressed as follows in the important case of *Kendall v Lillico [1969] 2 AC 31*. 'If the law were always logical one would suppose that a buyer who has obtained a right to rely on the seller's skill and judgment, would only obtain thereby an assurance that proper skill and judgment had been exercised, and would only be entitled to a remedy if a defect in the goods was due to failure to exercise such skill and judgment. But the law has always gone further than that. By getting the seller to undertake his skill and judgment the buyer gets . . . an assurance that the goods will be reasonably fit for his purpose and that covers not only defects which the seller ought to have detected but also defects which are latent in the sense that even the utmost skill and judgment on the part of the seller would not have detected them' (per Lord Reid).

Dangerous products

P9053   As distinct from applying to merely substandard products, both these subsections, *s 14(2)* and *(3)* can be invoked where a product is so defective as to be unsafe, but the injury/damage must be a reasonably foreseeable consequence of breach of the implied condition. If, for instance, therefore, the chain of causation is broken by contributory negligence on the part of the user, in using a product knowing it to be defective, there will be no liability. In *Lambert v Lewis [1982] AC 225*, manufacturers had made a defective towing coupling which was sold by retailers to a farmer. The farmer continued to use the coupling knowing that it was unsafe. As a result, an employee was injured and the farmer had to pay damages. He sought to recover these against the retailer for breach of *s 14(3)*. It was held that he could not do so.

Credit sale and supply of products

P9054   Broadly similar terms to those under the *Sale of Goods Act 1979, s 14* exist, in the case of hire purchase, credit sale, conditional sale and hire or lease contracts, by virtue of the Acts described above at P9045 having been modified by the *Sale and Supply of Goods Act 1994*.

Unfair Contract Terms Act 1977 (UCTA)

P9055   In spite of its name, this Act is not directly concerned with 'unfairness' in contracts, nor is it confined to the regulation of contractual relations. The main provisions are as follows:

(*a*)   Liability for death or personal injury resulting from negligence cannot be excluded by warning notices or contractual terms (*s 2*). (This does not necessarily prevent an indemnity of any liability to an injured person being agreed between two other contracting parties: if A hires plant to B on terms that B indemnifies A in respect of any claims by any person for injury, the clause may be enforceable (see *Thompson v T Lohan (Plant Hire) Ltd [1987] 2 All ER 631)*.)

(*b*)   In the case of other loss or damage, liability for negligence cannot be excluded by contract terms or warning notices unless these satisfy the requirement of reasonableness.

(*c*)   Where one contracting party is a consumer, or when one of the contracting parties is using written standard terms of business, exclusions or restrictions of liability for breach of contract will be permissible only in so far as the term satisfies the requirement of reasonableness (*s 3*); as far as contracts with consumers are concerned, it is not possible to exclude or restrict liability for the implied undertakings as to quality and fitness for purpose contained in the *Sale of Goods Act 1979* (as amended) or in the equivalent provisions relating to hire purchase and other forms of supply of goods (*s 6(2)*). Separate provisions make it an offence to include this type of exclusion clause in a consumer contract (*Consumer Transactions (Restrictions on Statements) Order 1976*).

(*d*)   In all cases where the reasonableness test applies, the burden of establishing that a clause or other provision is reasonable will lie with the person who is trying to rely on the term in question. The consequence of contravention of the Act is, however, limited to the offending term being treated as being ineffective; the courts will give effect to the remainder of the contract so far as it is possible to do so.

Unfair Terms in Consumer Contracts Regulations 1994 (SI 1994 No 3159)

P9056   Consumers faced with standard form contracts are given more ammunition to combat terminological obscurity, legalese and inequality of bargaining power, by the *Unfair Terms in Consumer Contracts Regulations 1994*. These regulations have the effect of invalidating any 'unfair terms' in consumer contracts involving products and services, e.g. sale, supply, servicing agreements, insurance and, as a final resort, empowering the Director General of Fair Trading to scrutinise 'standard form' terms, with a view to recommending, where necessary, their discontinued use. Contracts affected by the Act will remain enforceable minus the unfair terms (which will be struck out), in so far as this result is possible. [*Reg 5(2)*].

The contracts affected are only 'standard form' ones, that is, contracts whose terms have not been 'individually negotiated' between seller/supplier and consumer [*Reg 3(1)*]; and a term is taken not to have been 'individually negotiated', where it has been drafted in advance and the consumer has not been able to influence the substance of the term [*Reg 3(3)*]. Significantly, it is incumbent on the seller/supplier, who claims that a term was 'individually negotiated' (i.e. not unfair) to prove that it so was [*Reg 3(5)*]. However, if the terms of the contract are in plain, intelligible language, fairness, relating to subject matter or price/remuneration, cannot be questioned [*Reg 3(2)*].

The key provisions are:

(*a*)   an 'unfair term' is one which causes a significant imbalance in the parties' rights and obligations, detrimentally to the consumer, contrary to the underlying tenet of good faith [*Reg 4(1)*];

(*b*)   'good faith' in bargaining is determined by

   (i)   strength of bargaining positions of the parties,

   (ii)   whether the consumer had an inducement to agree to the term,

   (iii)   whether products/services were sold/supplied to the special order of the consumer, and

   (iv)   the extent to which the seller/supplier has dealt fairly with the consumer

[*Sch 2*];

(*c*)   an 'unfair term' is not binding on the consumer [*Reg 5(1)*];

(*d*)   terms of standard form contracts must be expressed in plain, intelligible language and, if there is doubt as to the meaning of a term, it must be interpreted in favour of the consumer [*Reg 6*];

(*e*)   complaints about 'unfair terms' in standard forms are to be considered by the Director General of Fair Trading, who may bring proceedings for an injunction to prevent use of the terms in future if the proponent of the unfair terms does not agree to desist from using them [*Reg 8*].

Examples of 'unfair terms'

P9057   Terms which have the object or effect of:

(*a*)   excluding or limiting the legal liability of a seller or supplier in the event of the death of a consumer or personal injury to the latter resulting from an act or omission of that seller or supplier;

(*b*)   inappropriately excluding or limiting the legal rights of the consumer vis-à-vis the seller or supplier or another party in the event of total or partial non-performance or inadequate performance by the seller or supplier of any of the contractual obligations, including the option of offsetting a debt owed to the seller or supplier against any claim which the consumer may have against him;

(*c*)   making an agreement binding on the consumer whereas provision of services by the seller or supplier is subject to a condition whose realisation depends on his own will alone;

(*d*)   permitting the seller or supplier to retain sums paid by the consumer where the latter decides not to conclude or perform the contract, without providing for the consumer to receive compensation of an equivalent amount from the seller or supplier where the latter is the party cancelling the contract;

(*e*) requiring any consumer who fails to fulfil his obligation to pay a disproportionately high sum in compensation;

(*f*) authorising the seller or supplier to dissolve the contract on a discretionary basis where the same facility is not granted to the consumer, or permitting the seller or supplier to retain the sums paid for services not yet supplied by him where it is the seller or supplier himself who dissolves the contract;

(*g*) enabling the seller or supplier to terminate a contract of indeterminate duration without reasonable notice except where there are serious grounds for doing so;

(*h*) automatically extending a contract of fixed duration where the consumer does not indicate otherwise, when the deadline fixed for the consumer to express this desire not to extend the contract is unreasonably early;

(*j*) irrevocably binding the consumer to terms with which he had no real opportunity of becoming acquainted before the conclusion of the contract;

(*k*) enabling the seller or supplier to alter the terms of the contract unilaterally without a valid reason which is specified in the contract;

(*l*) enabling the seller or supplier to alter unilaterally without a valid reason any characteristics of the product or service to be provided;

(*m*) providing for the price of goods to be determined at the time of delivery or allowing a seller of goods or supplier of services to increase their price without in both cases giving the consumer the corresponding right to cancel the contract if the final price is too high in relation to the price agreed when the contract was concluded;

(*n*) giving the seller or supplier the right to determine whether the goods or services supplied are in conformity with the contract, or giving him the exclusive right to interpret any term of the contract;

(*o*) limiting the seller's or supplier's obligation to respect commitments undertaken by his agents or making his commitments subject to compliance with a particular formality;

(*p*) obliging the consumer to fulfil all his obligations where the seller or supplier does not perform his;

(*q*) giving the seller or supplier the possibility of transferring his rights and obligations under the contract, where this may serve to reduce the guarantees for the consumer, without the latter's agreement;

(*r*) excluding or hindering the consumer's right to take legal action or exercise any other legal remedy, particularly by requiring the consumer to take disputes exclusively to arbitration not covered by legal provisions, unduly restricting the evidence available to him or imposing on him a burden of proof which, according to the applicable law, should lie with another party to the contract.

[*Sch 3*].

Risk Assessment

Introduction and background

R3001   Although the Industrial Revolution began in Britain 200 years ago, the term 'risk assessment' has only been commonly used since the inception of the 'single European market' in January 1993, when the *Management of Health and Safety at Work Regulations 1992 (SI 1992 No 2051)* came into force, thereby ratifying the European Framework Directive (89-391).

Reg 3 of the *Management of Health and Safety at Work Regulations 1992* requires every employer to develop and publish risk assessments relating to risks which their operations might pose to their own employees, and to any other persons who might be affected by them. *Reg 3* is discussed later in this chapter.

It is remarkable that risk assessments had not been required in earlier legislation, given that risks at work have always existed. These increased dramatically as the United Kingdom moved from an agrarian towards an industrial economy.

The notion of risk assessment had been implied by legislation, however, if not actually stated. For example, *s 2(2)(a)* of the *Health and Safety at Work Act (HSWA) 1974* requires employers to provide and maintain plant and systems of work that are, so far as is reasonably practicable, safe and without risks to health.

Section 2(3) of *HSWA* requires employers to prepare and revise, when appropriate, a written statement of their general policy with respect to health and safety, together with details of the organisation and arrangements for ensuring compliance with the policy.

Clearly compliance with such requirements – and with many other health and safety regulations which are referred to in this chapter – necessitates risk assessment.

It is not possible to develop an effective safe system, or write a meaningful safety policy, if no attempt has been made to identify (i) the risks that exist in the business, and (ii) which of these risks calls for the greatest degree of management focus. In short, risk assessment is fundamental to the whole health and safety equation.

Legislation quite properly focuses upon risks to the health and safety of employees and others, whereas businesses must also be concerned with questions of commercial survival.

Risk and risk management should therefore be seen as a means of protecting people, plant, assets and reputation, but within the confines of profitability. There is not much use having a business in which all the people are totally protected from harm, if that business fails commercially!

In recent years many businesses have appreciated the fact that humanitarian and commercial considerations are interwoven and indivisible where workplace risks are concerned, and this has given rise to the emergence of new terminology to describe the subject.

'Risk manager' and 'risk management' are terms which are rapidly replacing the 'safety manager' and 'health and safety management', and the portents are that the latter terms will be relegated to history within the next few years. Similarly health and safety consultancies are discovering that they are more marketable if described as risk management consultants.

Table 1 illustrates how risks at work have the potential to harm a business in a variety of ways; the 'knock-on' effect of any one of them could, in the final analysis, affect the viability of the business.

Table 1

Comparison of potential consequences of risk exposure

Damage/harm	Consequence
To people – as a result of injury or ill-health	Lost time, training of replacements, compensation, damage to plant/materials, production
To plant, processes or materials	Lost output/production, restitution or replacement costs, business interruption, lost business
To product	As above, plus liability and loss of confidence/market share
To environment	Effect on company reputation/image and clean-up costs

Damage or harm as described in Table 1 above might also lead to criminal prosecution, depending on the circumstances.

'Assessment'

R3002   If the statutory requirement for 'risk assessment' is novel in the UK, so is the notion of 'assessment' itself. Before 1974 – indeed before 1993 – the pattern of most legislation was a precise statement of what was required in order to comply with the law, coupled with the penalties for failing to do so!

The *Control of Substances Hazardous to Health Regulations 1988 (COSHH)* – now replaced by the *COSHH Regulations 1999 (SI 1999 No 437)* – heralded a change of emphasis which was not just different, but which wrong-footed many employers, and which remains a mystery to many to this day!

This was because employers were not told precisely what the law demanded, but were charged with ensuring, so far as reasonably practicable, that they had 'assessed' their own business, and had taken whatever measures were necessary for them to take in order to eliminate or mitigate the risks which the *COSHH Regulations* were intended to address.

This change in the legislative approach, while apparently giving individual employers more flexibility about the way they manage their businesses, and implying less official intervention, is not quite what it seems.

Reg 3 of the *Management of Health and Safety at Work Regulations 1992* calls for risk assessments which are 'suitable and sufficient', a definition capable of wide interpretation, and which leaves open the possibility that statutory inspectors may conclude that an employer's risk assessment, however conscientiously developed, is either unsuitable or insufficient, or both.

Given the vagueness of the qualification 'suitable and sufficient', it is perhaps not surprising that official guidance on the risk assessment process is scarce and often unhelpful. Hitherto no case law exists to indicate how the courts will judge allegedly unsuitable risk assessments, although there have been cases where employers have been charged with not having a risk assessment at all!

Inevitably an accident will occur in circumstances in which those compiling the risk assessment have overlooked or attached insufficient importance to the risk which gave rise to the accident. No doubt cases of this kind will be determined by the court's decision as to whether the accident could have been 'reasonably foreseen'. This emphasises the importance of thoroughly reviewing every aspect of an organisation's operations when developing the risk assessment.

Other law requiring risk management

R3003   Although the requirement for a 'general' risk assessment appears in *Reg 3* of the *Management of Health and Safety at Work Regulations 1992*, there are a number of other regulations calling for risk assessment.

As stated in R3002 above, the first time risk assessment requirements appeared in legislation was in connection with the *COSHH Regulations* in 1988 – even before universal risk assessment was introduced by the *Management of Health and Safety at Work Regulations, 1992*, which took effect from 1 January 1993.

The introduction of the *COSHH Regulations* was the first intimation that the law relating to health and safety would move towards self-regulation, i.e. announcing broad principles in regulation, and requiring employers to apply these principles to the situation in their business or organisation. This fundamental change in approach has resulted in some businesses being uncertain whether the measures they have taken for the purposes of complying with *COSHH* are sufficient.

One certainty is that keeping a collection of data sheets covering every substance in use in a business, and doing nothing else *does not constitute compliance*, although the possession of this information is key to the process.

The objective of the assessment called for in the *COSHH Regulations* is to establish which substances used are hazardous or potentially so, and to take measures to eliminate or at least mitigate the risks posed by these substances.

In many cases, the quantities used, and the length of time during which there is exposure to a substance, together with many other factors, have a bearing on the situation, and it is by taking into consideration these and other relevant factors that an employer develops his *COSHH* assessment.

For example a substance which should not be used in confined spaces may be relatively harmless if used in the open air; substances which are incompatible with others must be stored and used in isolation of each other, and so on.

There are some general hierarchical principles to be followed in the treatment of risks, which are applicable to *COSHH* and all other regulations calling for risk assessment. These are described in R3011 below.

Other regulations demanding risk assessment are the *Health and Safety (Display Screen Equipment) Regulations 1992*, the *Manual Handling Operations Regulations 1992*, the *Construction (Design and Management) Regulations 1994* and the *Fire Precautions (Workplace) Regulations 1997*.

The principal regulations dealing with risk assessment (the *Management of Health and Safety at Work Regulations 1992*) have been amended since 1992 to take account of two categories of employee who might be at greater risk than others. These additional regulations are *Regs 13A–13C* (risks to new or expectant mothers) and *Reg 13D* (protection of young persons).

Regulation 3 of the Management of Health and Safety at Work Regulations 1992, as amended

R3004

Paragraph 1:	requires every employer to make a 'suitable and sufficient' assessment of the risks to all employees while at work, and to persons not in his employment who might be affected by the way he conducts his operations.
	This is so that he can identify the measures needed to ensure compliance with applicable health and safety law, including the *Fire Precautions (Workplace) Regulations 1997.*
Paragraph 2:	a variation of paragraph 1, this covers the responsibilities of the self-employed. It enjoins the self-employed person to assess the risks to himself while at work, and to others who might be affected by his work.
Paragraph 3:	the assessments made to comply with paragraphs 1 and 2 above should be kept under review and amended to reflect any material changes, and the new measures necessary to eliminate or reduce the new or different risks must be identified.
Paragraph 4:	employers must record 'the significant findings' of the assessment carried out, and also identify any group of employees who are especially at risk, if the workforce totals five or more.
	The term 'the significant findings' has no further quantification, and so most employers opt to write the whole of their risk assessment down.
	The word 'record' is also misleading. In fact the duty is actually to publish the assessment, and to bring it to the attention of all employees (see the *Management of Health and Safety at Work Regulations 1992, Reg 8*).

There is no doubt that the duty to develop risk assessments to comply with *Reg 3* is more important and more onerous than all the other requirements in the *Management of Health and Safety at Work Regulations*, which are concerned with a number of aspects of health and safety management, many of them novel, while others redefine earlier statutory requirements.

Confirmation of this, in print terms alone, is conclusive: although the four paragraphs of *Reg 3* occupy only part of a single page of print, the guidance to these four short paragraphs extends to six pages!

Summary of official guidance on Regulation 3

R3005   It is recognised that in a great many cases, risk assessment, whether or not referred to as such, is a continual process. The essential difference now is that there is a requirement for a systematic general examination of *every work activity* in order to ensure that consideration is given to all work activities which pose a risk to health and safety.

Hazard is defined as the potential to cause harm.

Risk is defined as the likelihood that the harm is realised.

For example a sealed container of acid is a hazard, which could become a risk once the container is opened or damaged or disposed of.

The objective in carrying out a risk assessment is to enable employers and the self-employed to confirm that they have considered all the risks present in their operations, or caused by them, and taken all the measures necessary to eliminate or reduce the risks in order to comply with applicable health and safety legislation, so far as is reasonably practicable.

When any risk is identified, therefore, the measures taken to remove or ameliorate that risk must at least comply with the standards of any regulations that are concerned with the risk, for example the *Control of Lead at Work Regulations 1998*, the *Noise at Work Regulations 1989*, the *Electricity at Work Regulations 1989*, and so on.

Suitable and sufficient is a term which features prominently in these regulations; for a risk assessment to be suitable and sufficient it should satisfy the following:

(*a*)   It should identify the significant risks resulting from work, i.e. focusing on risks liable to arise from work activity.

Trivial risks, i.e. risks which would be associated with life in general, can be ignored unless the particular work activity increases the risks, or is of significant relevance to the work activity in question.

It is the responsibility of employers and the self-employed to keep themselves abreast of workplace risks by reading HSE guidance, professional journals, trade, company or supplier manuals and literature, where applicable.

(*b*)   The employer or self-employed person should be able to identify and prioritise the measures that are required to comply with relevant law and regulation.

(*c*)   The assessment should be appropriate given the nature of the work, and likely to remain valid for a reasonable period of time.

This means that risks which are capable of resolution or rectification quickly, for example basic maintenance work, need not be included in the assessment, but should be dealt with routinely as and when they arise.

It can be seen that none of this guidance is quantified, and the onus of deciding what is suitable and sufficient must rest with those who are responsible for developing the risk assessment.

The guidance recognises that where repetitive risk situations occur, a generic risk assessment can be developed. In such cases, however, it is important to consider local conditions or circumstances which could create the need for review and reappraisal of a generic assessment.

It can be seen, therefore, that where a business or organisation has a number of branches that perform the same function, for example retail store chains, regional offices and the like, a 'generic' risk assessment is acceptable and desirable in the interests of uniform management of the risks.

However, it is essential in such cases that each branch of the enterprise critically reviews the generic assessment (i) to ensure that all the risks described in it are applicable to them, and (ii) to add any risks which are peculiar only to that branch. Such risks might be related to the geography of the area or site, or to other businesses with which they share the building or development.

Emphasis is placed upon continuous monitoring of risk assessments to ensure that if the conditions applicable when they were developed do not remain the same, reassessment is undertaken.

Above all, the risk assessment must be responsive to change of every kind, including changes in organisation, local conditions, methods of working, materials in use, legislation and guidance, and technological advances.

If assessment has been carried out to comply with other regulations (see R3003 above), it need not be repeated in this (general) risk assessment. It will be sufficient, for the sake of completeness, simply to refer in this general risk assessment to any other assessments.

If the workforce exceeds four, the assessments must be recorded. This may be in hard copy form, or it may be on computer provided that the computer records can be quickly retrieved for reference or perusal by a statutory inspector.

The assessment might refer to other documents or procedures which describe in greater detail the measures taken to eliminate or reduce the risks identified; these might include, for example, method statements, safe systems of work, and the company health and safety policy.

The risk assessment must include the following:

(*a*)   risks and their relative seriousness compared with the other risks (see R3007 *et seq* below);

(*b*)   the control measures to address the risks, not necessarily in detail but where appropriate quoting the document that contains the detail, for example 'Method Statement No: . . .';

(*c*)   the population which may be affected (numbers, percentages, etc).

Preventative and protective measures

R3006   The preventative and protective measures taken to address the risks identified must at least comply with any relevant legal provision, for example legislation relating to noise levels and machinery safety, where this type of risk is identified.

The following principles should be followed:

(*a*)   Avoid the risk altogether if possible.

Many tasks are carried out in a particular way because 'that is how we have always done it'. Yet manufacturers are constantly improving their products in order to reduce or eliminate risk. For example, in terms of manual handling, many manufacturers of heavy products, such as cement or containerised fresh water, have introduced smaller bags or containers in order to reduce the risk of back injury.

(*b*) Combat the risk at source.

It is better to use safer tools, equipment and materials than to use palliative measures to overcome problems caused by old, obsolete tools, etc. It is better to use non-slip surfaces than to try to overcome the problems associated with slippery surfaces.

(*c*) Adapt work to the individual wherever possible.

The science of ergonomics has improved dramatically in recent years. Efforts have been made to design workstations and work equipment to suit the worker, rather than expecting workers to stretch, squat or even have to lie down to reach controls, cable connections etc. More still needs to be done, however, in respect of the accessibility of equipment and installations for maintenance purposes.

(*d*) Take full advantage of technical and technological progress.

(*e*) Measures to ameliorate risks should form part of a cohesive company strategy, rather than being taken in isolation. Often the improvements will only be effective if linked to improved supervision, changes in routine, better designed and more user friendly systems of work, etc.

(*f*) Opt for measures which protect the greatest number, rather than those measures with limited effect as regards the number of individuals likely to benefit.

(*g*) People at work need to understand what has to be done by them to make their workplace safe. Communication, as ever, is key.

(*h*) Develop and maintain a health and safety culture, i.e. a culture where *everyone* in the organisation shares ownership of and responsibility for health and safety.

The risk assessment process – stage 1

(a) Who will be involved?

R3007 The risk assessment process should involve those individuals who have most knowledge of the area or operation being assessed. This does not mean just the management of the area or operation, but those who have most 'hands-on' experience of the work involved.

It should certainly include operatives, since these are the people who have to do the work, and who must therefore know more about the risks associated with it than anyone else.

The *Safety Representatives and Safety Committees Regulations 1977* require firms having no registered trade unions to arrange elections for workers to elect representatives to speak on their behalf in respect of health and safety at work matters. In unionised firms similar arrangements apply, except that the representatives are nominated by the unions concerned.

Patently these representatives are best placed and best qualified to serve as members of the group who will develop the risk assessment; this group is referred to in the remainder of this chapter as 'the risk assessment group'.

Exclusion of these elected representatives from the risk assessment group would be difficult to justify, bearing in mind that they have been elected to comply with regulations aimed at ensuring that workers have a voice in such matters at risk assessment.

The competent safety adviser to the company, appointed to comply with *Reg 6* of the *Management of Health and Safety at Work Regulations 1992*, should be in attendance to provide advice.

(b) What aids should be available to assist the risk assessment group?

The following should be made available to the risk assessment group:

   (i)   a full and detailed description of the work processes being assessed for risks;

   (ii)   the accident history of the work area being assessed;

   (iii)   any in-company, trade or professional information related to the type of work being assessed, such as details of accidents or information about risks or similar matters connected with the type of work under review;

   (iv)   copies of any regulations which relate to or affect the type of work being assessed. Examples are the *Noise at Work Regulations 1989*, the *Electricity at Work Regulations 1989*, and the *Provision and Use of Work Equipment Regulations 1998 (PUWER)*;

   (v)   blank assessment forms – see Appendix A.

The risk assessment process – stage 2

R3008

   (i)   If the work process being reviewed is complex or lengthy, break it down into phases or stages before commencing the assessment.

   For risk assessments being carried out for the purposes of complying with the *Construction (Design and Management) Regulations 1994*, the phases of the overall project are identified under the following key generic headings:

   — feasibility;

   — design;

   — execution;

   — completion.

   For such projects the design and execution phases usually present the greatest number of potential risks.

   (ii)   When the phases of the work have been agreed, list all the risks associated with each phase, using the method best suited to the business. 'Brainstorming' is a popular method.

   Appendix B contains a non-exhaustive list of potential risks covering most types of businesses.

   (iii)   When all the risks in each phase of the work under review have been listed, commence the risk assessment. The process for this is described in R3009 below.

   (iv)   On completion of the risk assessment, ensure that all the measures to remove or reduce risk as shown on the risk assessment sheets (see R3009 below) have been initiated, and responsibilities assigned and completion dates agreed and confirmed.

(v)   Hold briefings for all staff affected by the risk assessment. Ensure that they understand the purpose of the risk assessment and how it affects them. Invite comments for consideration at the next review of the assessment; if the comments are sufficiently important, incorporate them into the current version of the risk assessment.

(vi) Monitor implementation measures until all are completed; keep the situation under continuous review, taking note of any changes in work processes, new or altered risks, new or amended regulations, etc. Where any change occurs, either convene a special meeting of the risk assessment group, or put it on the agenda for the next scheduled meeting of the risk assessment group.

The risk assessment process – methodology

R3009   Appendix A to this chapter is an example of a risk assessment worksheet (RAW) or record sheet.

There is no official guidance on the most appropriate methodology for ranking or recording risks. The procedure suggested here is used by many businesses and organisations, and found to be a suitable method of developing and recording the results of their risk assessments.

Before describing the process, it is important to stress that all risk assessments are subjective; how could it be otherwise? If two or more people are assembled to discuss any matter, some differences of opinion are found to arise. When carrying out a risk assessment, provided that there is a general consensus, and no member of the risk assessment group has a significantly different opinion from the rest, there is no problem.

In the final analysis, if the risk assessment group applies the same methodology at all times, and the group includes employees who are closer to the operation than anyone else, their opinion about the risks and the measures to combat them is probably the best there is.

Even if the order of final risk ranking is debatable, this is not critical provided that all the important risks are considered, and sensible measures are taken to reduce or eliminate them.

Ranking risks

In a commercial office, where the risks are likely to be few in number and relatively simple in nature, it is acceptable for the risk assessment group to decide by a show of hands whether the risks identified are of low, medium or high importance; nothing more sophisticated than that.

At the opposite end of the spectrum, for example in a steelworks or chemical plant, the above method would clearly not suffice, and a great deal more care must be taken to classify the risks. Courses are available which cover more advanced methods of risk assessment such as failure modes and effects analysis (FMEA), and hazard and operability studies (HAZOP).

However, there is an approach between these two extremes which is used much more widely, and which is appropriate to most businesses and organisations. This is a process called the '5 × 5 method of risk assessment'.

The '5 × 5' method measures each risk identified against the two constituents of risk – hazard severity (seriousness) and probability (likelihood of occurrence), giving a value to each on a scale of 1-5 and multiplying the two answers together – see Table 2.

Table 2
Risk assessment calculation – risks to people

Seriousness	Score
Fatal or multi-fatal outcome	5
Major injury outcome (i.e. RIDDOR reportable)	4
Three-day injury as determined in RIDDOR	3
Minor injury – first-aid only	2
Accident or incident where no injury occurs	1
Probability/likelihood/frequency	*Score*
Daily occurrence	5
Weekly occurrence	4
Monthly occurrence	3
Quarterly occurrence	2
Annual occurrence	1
or	
Very likely to occur	5
Probable	4
Possible	3
Remote	2
Improbable	1

From this table it can be seen that the highest 'score' possible is 25, i.e. 5 for likelihood/frequency and 5 for severity/seriousness.

In terms of prioritising action to reduce risks – a specific requirement of *the Management of Health and Safety at Work Regulations 1992, Reg 3* – the risk assessment group might conclude that a score of 16 and over should be rated as 'high', between 9 and 15 'medium'; and below 9 as 'low'.

The advantage of this system is that each risk has its own discrete score, and even within the three groupings 'high', 'medium' and 'low' each risk has its own numerical value, and therefore ranking within that group. The thresholds for each of the three groupings do not have to be as shown in the preceding paragraph; this is a matter for the risk assessment group to determine.

In the seriousness scale in Table 2, it will be seen that reference is made to reportable major injuries and to reportable three-day injuries. These injury conditions are described in the *Reporting of Injuries, Diseases and Dangerous Occurrences Regulations 1995 (RIDDOR)* in the following terms.

Reportable major injury
—   any fracture, other than to fingers, thumbs or toes;
—   any amputation;

—   dislocation of the shoulder, hip, knee or spine;

—   temporary or permanent loss of sight;

—   a chemical or hot metal burn to the eye or any penetrating injury to the eye;

—   any injury resulting from electric shock or electrical burn (including any electrical burn caused by arcing or arcing products) leading to unconsciousness or requiring resuscitation or admittance to hospital for more than 24 hours;

—   any other injury:

   •   leading to hypothermia, heat-induced illness or to unconsciousness;

   •   requiring resuscitation; or

   •   requiring admittance to hospital for more than 24 hours;

—   loss of consciousness caused by asphyxia or by exposure to a harmful substance or biological agent;

—   either of the following conditions which result from the absorption of any substance by inhalation, ingestion or through the skin:

   •   acute illness requiring medical treatment; or

   •   loss of consciousness;

—   acute illness requiring medical treatment where there is reason to believe that this resulted from exposure to a biological agent or its toxins or infected material.

Three-day injury

—   any injury which is not classified as a reportable major injury as above, but which none the less prevents the injured employee from carrying out his/her normal work for more than three consecutive days, excluding the day of the accident, but including every day thereafter, whether or not these days would normally have been working days.

It should be noted that in the event of a three-day injury, the employee may or may not be at work. The criterion is inability to carry out their normal work.

The values in Table 2 relate to risk of injury to people. In the case of risks to property/plant or other assets, the seriousness and consequences factors would be different, as would the probability/likelihood/frequency values – for example, see Table 3.

Table 3
Risk assessment calculation – risks to property/plant/assets

Seriousness	Consequences	Score
Catastrophic:	complete destruction of facility	5
Major damage:	parts of operation at standstill; significant contractual failure; or total rescheduling	4

Severe damage:	significant loss of production or significant delays; or substantial costs/resources required to restore 'status quo'	3
Minor damage:	short delays in process etc; or possibility of requiring outside assistance to restore situation	2
Negligible:	capable of same-day repair or restitution by own staff and no interference with normal company operations	1

Probability/likelihood/frequency	Score
Regular occurrence	5
Frequent occurrence	4
Occasional occurrence	3
Rare occurrence	2
Remote occurrence	1
or	
At least once each day	5
Three or four times a month	4
Two or three times a year	3
Once every two years	2
Unlikely to happen at all	1

Using the table at Appendix A it is now possible to list the risks identified (column B), show their consequence/severity and frequency/likelihood (columns G and H) and the total score in the risk level column (column I). Appendix A describes the purpose of every column of the risk assessment form.

This completes the risk assessment phase; the next phase is the 'action plan', i.e. taking or implementing measures in order to eliminate or reduce the risks identified.

NB: When determining the numerical status of each risk as described above, the risk assessment group should ignore at this stage any statutory or in-company actions already taken, and evaluate the risk as though no measures of any kind had been taken to reduce the risk. In essence, the risk evaluated is the 'raw risk'.

The 'action plan' phase

R3010   The risk assessment group should now focus on the existing controls imposed by the law, together with any in-company controls or measures in place to reduce the risk (column J). The effect of these might be to reduce the numerical risk value to be inserted in the 'revised risk' column (column K).

Finally, consideration should be given to any further controls that might be possible (column L); the effect of these, if any, will produce a 'final risk' (column M).

It is this final risk rating which is critical, and if the rating at the final stage remains 'high' or 'medium' it will be necessary to review the operation in question in order to bring about a safer working environment.

If a risk is determined as low at the outset, or it becomes low following the action plan measures, it might be decided to take no further action on the risk, instead focusing effort on risks with higher classifications.

The procedure for calculating the numerical risk value in columns K and M is the same as that for column I, although space has not allowed for a 'consequence and frequency' score to be shown separately. It is recommended that, for completeness' sake, columns K and M should show the constituent figures of the score shown, for example 20 (5 × 4).

Risk assessment – hierarchy of measures

R3011   Risk assessment groups should keep in mind the following hierarchy of measures when considering the identification, control, etc. of risks:

Stage 1: Assessing the problem

- Identification – what are the risks and where do they exist?

- Evaluation and quantification – the risk assessment process itself as described in this chapter.

Stage 2: Solving the problem

- Eliminating, reducing and/or controlling the risk. If the risk cannot be eliminated or reduced, how can it be controlled? By reducing the exposure of workers to the risk, by training, improved systems of work, issue and use of personal protective equipment (PPE), etc.

Stage 3: Verification

- Monitoring and review – to ensure that the measures taken are eliminating or reducing the risks as effectively as was intended. If not, review and reassess.

Appendix A

Risk assessment record sheet

Purpose

R3012   This record sheet represents a simple way to record risks as required by the *Management of Health and Safety at Work Regulations 1992, Reg 3*, by showing the process by which the risk assessment team has arrived at its conclusion as to the ranking of the risk, together with the measures used to reduce the level of each risk. Before using this record sheet, paragraphs R3007–R3011 should be read carefully.

The layout of the record sheet can be amended or modified to suit the requirements of individual companies.

Layout and use of the record sheet – an explanation of the columns

Column reference	Title	Meaning/purpose of column
A	No	For reference purposes only; it has nothing to do with risk assessment as such. If the total assessment includes, for example, 30 risks, readers can find a particular risk quickly.
B	Risk identified	A short description might be sufficient. Alternatively, a range of risks might be related to a particular item or process: in such cases, this column might be completed by showing the phases or stages of a work process as a head, with the risks associated with each phase beneath (or a permutation of this approach).
C, D, E & F	Persons at risk – EMP, CON, PUB, VIS	*Regulation 3* specifically calls for the identification of any groups of people especially at risk. These columns facilitate this by providing columns for employees, contractors, the public at large, and visitors respectively. Users of the form may wish to use other groupings or abbreviations.
G, H & I	Consequence & frequency categories and risk level	This is the 'first pass' assessment, considering the risk without taking account of any measures already in place or envisaged, i.e. the 'raw risk'. Using Table 2, assign a numerical value between 1-5 for (i) the seriousness of the consequence, and (ii) for the probability/likelihood of such a risk occurring. Multiply the two answers together and insert the score (between 1 and 25) in column I – the risk level.

J & K	Existing controls and revised risk	The purpose of these two columns is to improve (reduce) the risk level score (column I) by describing measures which are already in place either for the purposes of complying with legal requirements or they are in-company measures determined as being necessary. Taking account of these measures, recalculate the numerical exercise in Table 2 and insert the revised score in column K.
L & M	Any additional controls required and final risk	As part of the risk assessment process, the risk assessment group may decide upon further measures to reduce the risk level. These measures will be listed in column L and their numerical benefit reassessed using the Table 2 formula to provide the final numerical value (column M).

Notes

1. The initial risk assessment process comprises columns A – I, whilst the action plan comprises columns J – M.

2. It might be the case that no additional controls (column L) are possible or necessary because all the ameliorating measures are covered by column J, and these bring the numerical ranking to an acceptable level, i.e. the risk is classified as 'low'.

3. In many cases, the measures to combat the identified risks will include safe systems of work, method statements or permits to work. Clearly the detail of these systems/statements/permits does not need to appear in this record. Instead, such systems etc. Should be numbered for ease of reference, and the information in columns J and/or L will simply state that one of the measures to address a particular risk is, for example, 'method statement No 10'.

   Copies of method statements or other documentation supporting the entries in the risk assessment record sheet should be readily available.

4. The model risk assessment record sheet on page R30/X is for illustrative purposes only. It cannot be assumed that its numerical conclusions are correct in relation to the risks identified in the model, as determination of numerical values in each case must be made by the risk assessment group of the organisation.

5. In this model, risks scoring 16 or over are rated 'high', those scoring 9-15 are 'medium' risks, and risks scoring below 9 are 'low'.

6. In respect of each risk identified, the 'additional control' options will not be necessary or possible in every case. The object of column L is to suggest further ways of eliminating or reducing the risks identified.

7. Although not stated in the model, it is possible that many of the 'existing controls' and 'additional controls' in columns J and L would in fact constitute or be part of a published procedure or system of work. Where this is the case, such systems/procedures should be numbered for ease of reference, and copies should be kept with the 'master' copy of the company risk assessment record sheet.

Risk assessment record sheet

Numerical values: 16–25 High risk; 9–15 Medium risk; Below 9 Low risk

LOCATION: Smith & Sons, Anytown

A	B	C	D	E	F	G	H	I	J	K	L	M
		Persons at Risk				Consequence Category	Frequency Category	Risk Level	Existing Controls	Revised Risk	Any Additional Controls required	Final Risk
No	Risk Identified	EMP	CON	PUB	VIS							
1	Working alone or in isolation from others											
1A	Working alone; ie after 6pm Mon–Fri, at weekends or Bank Holidays	10%	–	–	–	5	2	10	None	10	Banning out-of-hours working	0
											– Requiring minimum of 2 when working alone	see notes
											– Security to check on those working alone	
											– Manager to telephone to check on well-being of those working alone	
											– Staff working alone to ring designated number at intervals	
1B	Working in isolation	4%	–	–	–	5	4	20	Issued with 2-way radio	12 (4 × 3)	Must advise supervisor when commencing work in isolation, and on return	6 (3 × 2)
											Must 'phone-in' every 30 minutes while working in isolation. If not done, Supr to investigate	
2	Fork lift Truck – collision with pedestrians	100%	–	–	yes	4	4	16	FLT drivers trained and certificated	12 (4 × 3)	– Designated pedestrian walking routes and crossing points	6 (3 × 2)
											– Training for all staff in dangers from FLTs	
3	Improper entry to works with felonious intent	100%	–	–	–	4	3	12	Visual check by Security at main gate	12 (4 × 3)	– Must sign-in, wear badge	4 (2 × 2)
											– Be met at Reception and accompanied while on premises. Escorted to Reception to sign-out	

◄——— Risk assessment ———►   ◄——— Action plan ———►

Risk assessment record sheet Numerical values: 16–25 High risk; 9–15 Medium risk; Below 9 Low risk

Appendix B

Non-exhaustive list of potential risks

This list is a combination of generic and specific aspects of work which could pose risks; it is not exhaustive. The purpose is to provide risk assessment groups with an *aide-mémoire* for use when preparing the list of risks applicable to the operations of their business or organisation.

For ease of reference the contents are arranged under the following headings, and within each group the risk areas are arranged alphabetically.

1.   Electrical

2.   Emergency response

3.   Environment – general

4.   Environment – working

5.   Fire and explosion

6.   Health

7.   Mechanical

8.   Permits to work

9.   Personnel

10.   Persons at particular risk

11.   Place of work

12.   Production

13.   Security and violence

14.   Substances materials

1. Electrical

Direct contact

Flash testing

Ignition source

Indirect contact

Overhead power lines

Portable tools

Short circuit/overload

Trailing leads

25 KV overhead

2. Emergency response

Emergency equipment missing/faulty

Emergency plan non-existent/outdated

Emergency vehicle access blocked

First-aid – none or insufficient

3. Environment – general

Discharge to drains

Disposal of waste

Drain overflow

Failure/inadequacy of bunds

Ground contamination

Noise nuisance

Solvent emissions

Spillages

Stack emissions

4. Environment – working

Ambient temperature

Cleanliness

Hot/cold surfaces

Humidity

Hygiene

Lighting (day & night)

Noise

Ventilation

5. Fire and explosion

Combustible waste

Electrical overload

Fire loading

Flammable atmospheres

Flammable dust

Flammable liquids

Gas cylinders

Ignition sources

Smoking/naked flame

6. Health

Dermatitis

Food poisoning

Hearing impairment

Ingestion of substances

Lasers

Legionella

Manual handling (back etc)

Microbiological

Radiation

Repetitive strain injury (RSI/WRULD)

Respiratory

Sensitisers

Sun rays

Vibration White Finger

Welding flash

7. Mechanical

Abrasion

Compressed air

Crushing

Cutting/shearing

Drawing-in/trapping

Entanglement

Flying particles

High pressure injection

High pressure systems

Impact

Lifting equipment

Lifting tackle failure

Machinery failures

Mobile equipment

Moving rail vehicles

Rotating shafts

Sharp surfaces

Stabbing

Vibrating

8. Permits to work

Effluent discharge consent

Environmental Protection Act 1990

Fire certificate

Licence to operate

9. Personnel (see also 10. Persons at particular risk)

Competent

Disabilities/restrictions

Fit

Hazardous behaviour (horseplay)

Informed

10. Persons at particular risk (see also 13. Security and violence)

Cleaners

Contractors

Disabled

Maintenance staff

Novices/new staff

Operatives

Postal staff

Pregnant staff

Receptionists

Security staff

Visitors

Young persons

Any employee working in isolation of other staff, or who works alone after normal working hours or during week-ends or public holidays.

When employees work at these times, their employer is under a greater duty of care than when they work normal hours alongside other employees.

11. Place of work

Access/egress

Confined spaces

Demolition

Fall of persons

Falling objects

High risk areas

Holes/pits

Housekeeping

Lack of oxygen

Movement – fork-lift trucks/vehicles

Obstructed gangways

Overhead cables

Overhead loads

Piped liquid and gas

Restricted height

Scaffolding/false work

Slips/trips

Stability of fixed equipment

Stability of workplace

Trench collapse

Underground cables

Working above liquids

Working at heights

Working near or above water

12. Production

Method of work (is system safe?)

Quality control

Software integrity

Storage of materials

Stored energy

Testing

13. Security and violence

Computer installation

Highly flammable vaults

High value items

Material stores

Money

Sensitive information

Substations (incoming services)

Violence – under this generic heading acts of violence may be generated/motivated for different reasons. It is therefore important for risk assessment groups to consider whether any of the causes/motivations could be present in their operations, for example:

● violence caused by frustration, e.g. passengers on transport systems;

- politically motivated violence (bombs, attacks on individuals);
- violence during robberies;
- violence as the by-product of acts of vandalism;
- violence induced by drugs/alcohol.

See Appendix C for practical advice and guidance in respect of workplace violence.

14. Substances/materials

Asbestos

Chemicals (*COSHH Regulations 1999*)

Dust/gases

Fumes/vapour/mist

Ionising radiations

Lead

Vehicle exhausts

Appendix C

Working in safety: practical advice and guidance

A leaflet, *'Working Alone in Safety'*, has been published by the HSE because there are many people who work by themselves, without close or direct supervision.

Working alone may be an occasional part of a job for some or it might be routine for others. People working alone may be in fixed premises such as one person working in a small workshop, petrol station, or kiosk. They could also be mobile workers in construction, agriculture or in services such as postal delivery or health visiting.

The guidance has been updated to reflect the legal duty for risk assessment. It points out that risk assessment should be used to determine whether it is safe to work alone and what precautions are necessary. It guides the reader on issues to be considered in risk assessment and determining the right level of precautions. Control measures may include instruction, training, supervision, protective equipment etc.

Questions addressed by the leaflet include the following:

—   Who are lone workers and what jobs do they do?

—   Can people legally work alone?

—   Can the risks of the job be adequately controlled by one person?

—   Is the person medically fit and suitable to work alone?

—   What training is required to ensure competency in safety matters?

—   How will the person be supervised?

—   What happens if a person becomes ill, has an accident, or there is an emergency?

'Working Alone in Safety' is available free of charge from HSE Books.

The Suzy Lamplugh Trust, the national charity for personal safety, undertakes research and provides talks and training, advice and guidance, particularly for employers and employees. Practical advice on personal safety is given in its free twenty-page leaflet, *'Working Safely in Other People's Homes'*. Whilst primarily aimed at those whose work takes them into other people's homes, this leaflet includes a number of general principles in respect of risk assessment and risk avoidance which are equally important to anyone to bear in mind when out and about on their own. For further information on this, and on courses, conferences and resources – including employers' guidances, manuals and videos – contact the Training Department, The Suzy Lamplugh Trust, 14 East Sheen Avenue, London SW14 8AS (tel: 0181 876 0305; fax: 0181 876 0891).

Statements of Health and Safety Policy

Requirement for a written policy

S7001   The *Health and Safety at Work Act 1974, s 2(3)* states that 'It shall be the duty of every employer to prepare and as often as may be appropriate revise a written statement of his general policy with respect to the health and safety at work of his employees and the organisation and arrangements for the time being in force for carrying out that policy, and to bring the statement and any revision of it to the notice of all of his employees'.

Section 3(1) HSWA 1974 imposes a duty upon every employer to conduct his undertaking in such a way as to ensure, so far as is reasonably practicable, that persons not in his employment who may be affected thereby are not thereby exposed to risks to their health or safety.

Exception

S7002   Those employers carrying on an undertaking in which fewer than five persons are being employed are excepted from the provisions of *s 2(3)* (*Employers' Health and Safety Policy Statements (Exception) Regulations 1975 (SI 1975 No 1584)*.

Statement of health and safety policy

Format

S7003   Essentially, a policy statement should consist of three parts, as follows:

—   *A general statement of intent.* This should outline the organisation's health and safety philosophy and should indicate that overall responsibility for health and safety rests with senior management. In a company this would be the board of directors and/or the managing director.

—   *Organisation.* This should outline the health and safety responsibilities of all concerned within the organisation. It will indicate who is responsible for what and to whom he reports, and will also indicate how the systems are monitored. If safety officers or safety representatives and safety committees are part of the system, it will indicate how they are involved and what their functions are.

—   *Arrangements.* This part of the policy deals with the practical arrangements by which the policy will be implemented. These include safety training; safe systems of work; environmental control; noise control; sufficient light; dust control; the control of substances hazardous to health; fire safety and prevention; suitable medical and first-aid facilities; accident reporting and investigation procedures; emergency procedures; and details of how to work safely with particular hazards such as radiation or in particular situations such as confined spaces.

Basic objectives

S7004   The health and safety policy statement should include the following:

(*a*)   a statement that senior management are responsible for health and safety throughout the organisation. In the case of a company, the whole policy should be signed by the managing director or at least by a member of the board;

(*b*)   an indication that it is the duty of management to ensure that a safe and healthy place of work is maintained and that everything reasonably practicable is done to prevent injury to any personnel in any situation whilst at work. Health and safety considerations must be addressed in all aspects of design, construction and operation of plant, machinery and equipment, including, for example, the question of how raw materials are to enter the workplace and how the finished products will leave it;

(*c*)   a statement reminding all employees that it is their duty to act responsibly, and to do everything they can to prevent danger or injury.

Organisation (people and their responsibilities)

S7005   Policies will show – both in written and diagrammatic form (where appropriate) – the responsibilities of management and staff for health and safety throughout the organisation, including the following:

(*a*)   the unbroken chain of delegation of duties through line management and supervisors;

(*b*)   the identification of key personnel, both by name and position, who are responsible for ensuring that detailed arrangements for safe working are drawn up, implemented and updated;

(*c*)   the definition of the responsibilities of both line and functional management. Detailed job descriptions should be drawn up accordingly;

(*d*)   the provision of suitable support for both line and functional management to ensure that health and safety is kept to a satisfactory standard. This may involve safety advisers, medical advisers, designers, hygienists, ergonomists, chemists, radiation experts, engineers, etc;

(*e*)   the nomination of personnel with the competence and authority to measure and monitor safety performance;

(*f*)   the provision of means to deal with failures;

(*g*)   the arrangements for accountability for the management of health and safety of all staff throughout the organisation;

(*h*)   the organisation must ensure that each individual is clearly informed what he must do in his role, and what resources both in time and money are available;

(*j*)   the individual must be certain of the extent to which he is realistically supported by the policy and by the organisation needed to fulfil it.

Arrangements (systems and procedures)

S7006   Safe systems of working must be designed to ensure that all risks associated with work are minimised. The following aspects should be used as a guide when preparing arrangements for ensuring health and safety at work:

(*a*)   the involvement of the safety adviser and relevant management at the design and planning stages of any activity;

(*b*)   the provision of criteria for the safe use of all articles, products and substances – this may well require the co-operation of designers, suppliers or manufacturers;

(*c*)   the provision of clear instructions for the installation, maintenance and use of machines, and for controlling any hazardous substances associated with their use or cleaning. Method statements for each part of the work associated with a machine may be used;

(*d*)   ensuring that each individual is competent to carry out his specific work. This will include, where necessary, the following:

—   the training of employees to ensure that they are aware of the risks involved with their specific work and that they are able to minimise such risks in the appropriate manner;

—   the undertaking of medical surveillance and biological monitoring. It may be necessary to carry out such monitoring before the work is started, during its operation and when it is finished;

—   ensuring that the individual concerned is physically and mentally able to carry out the work;

(*e*)   the availability of suitable personal protective equipment, and ensuring that it is used where necessary;

(*f*)   the development and utilisation of safe systems of work. Such systems of work may well be developed from (*c*) above. For certain work a permit to work system should be used and developed to ensure that the situation is as safe as possible;

(*g*)   the consideration of emergency conditions, what each individual should do under such conditions, what services are available such as medical and fire services and how the risks of any emergency ever happening are kept to a minimum.

(*h*)   the provision of procedures for contractors and visitors.

Such arrangements should be put in writing and circulated to all members of staff.

Appendices to statements

S7007   If the arrangements are kept in general terms, it will be helpful to use appendices for details of work at specific machines or in specific situations or with specific substances.

Examples of this are when there are several machines carrying out similar work but one of those machines is using a very hazardous material, or there may be specific tasks that involve manual handling in a particular manner, or there may be one area where humidity becomes very high and certain specific additional procedures must be used.

Policy monitoring

S7008   To detect how the health and safety policy is working within an organisation the following should be monitored:

(*a*)   the policy itself, to ensure that the management of health and safety at work is kept within the legal requirements;

(*b*)   the accident and ill-health records to give an indication of where the policy could be improved, and how the operation of the policy is reducing the accidents that are occurring throughout the organisation;

(*c*)   the extent to which the organisation specifies and achieves certain clearly defined aims and objectives, both short and long term. This will include the time taken between specifying the aims and objectives and achieving them;

(*d*)   the extent of compliance with the policy statement, including the allocation of responsibilities.

Checklist for statements of health and safety policy

S7009

—   Does the statement express a commitment to health and safety?

—   Are the obligations of the organisation to its employees made clear?

—   Are the obligations of the organisation to any others, who are affected by its undertaking, clear?

—   Is it clear who is responsible for seeing that the policy is implemented?

—   How is this being done?

—   Is it clear who is keeping it under review?

—   How is it being reviewed?

—   Is it signed by a partner or a senior director?

—   Have the views of managers, supervisors, competent persons, safety representatives and the safety committee been taken into account?

—   Have the duties and responsibilities of those involved in specific tasks been discussed with them, and did they accept and understand them?

—   Are staff aware of how their performance in relation to health and safety will be assessed and what facilities are available to them?

—   Does the statement make clear that co-operation by all employees is vital to the success of the health and safety policy?

—   Does the statement describe how employees are to be involved in the organisation's health and safety as well as in their own safety?

—   Does the statement include clear responsibilities for each individual at each level throughout the organisation?

—   Does the statement detail who is responsible for:

  •   reporting and recording accidents and investigations;

  •   fire precautions, fire drills, fire evacuation procedures;

  •   first-aid;

  •   safety inspections;

- the training programme;
- ensuring that legal requirements are met and that suitable action has been taken in the light of Approved Codes of Practice and HSE guidance on regulations?

Arrangements

(a) General

S7010   Keeping the workplace, including the staircases, floors, entrances and exits, washrooms, etc. in a safe, clean condition by cleaning, maintenance and repair (*Workplace (Health, Safety and Welfare) Regulations 1992, HSE Guidance L24*).

(b) Plant

Maintenance and proper use of plant, machinery and guards for all work equipment including mobile and lifting equipment (*Provision and Use of Work Equipment Regulations 1998, HSE Guidance L22*).

Maintenance of equipment such as tools, ladders etc. Are they in a safe condition?

Regular testing and maintenance of lifts, hoists, cranes, pressure systems, boilers and other dangerous machinery, emergency repair work, and safe methods of carrying out such work.

Maintenance of electrical installations and equipment.

Introduction of new plant and equipment into the workplace by examination, testing and consultation with the workforce.

(c) Substances

Safe storage, handling and, where applicable, packaging, labelling and transport of dangerous substances (*Control of Substances Hazardous to Health Regulations 1999, HSE Guidance* and *Chemicals (Hazard Information and Packaging for Supply) Regulations 1994, HSE Guidance L63*).

Controls on work involving harmful substances such as lead and asbestos.

(d) Protective safety equipment

Maintenance and proper use of protective safety equipment such as helmets, goggles, respirators etc. (*Personal Protective Equipment at Work Regulations 1992, HSE Guidance L25*).

(e) Other hazards

Noise – control noise at source; wear ear protectors ('*Guidance on the Noise at Work Regulations 1989*', *HSE Guidance L108*).

Preventing unnecessary or unauthorised entry into hazardous areas.

Ensuring safe lifting of heavy or awkward loads (*Manual Handling Regulations 1992, HSE Guidance L23*).

Protecting employees against assault when handling or transporting money or valuables.

Assessing special hazards to employees when working on unfamiliar sites, including discussions with site manager where necessary.

(f) Emergencies

Ensuring that fire exits are marked, unlocked and free from obstruction.

Maintenance and testing of fire-fighting equipment, fire drills and evacuation procedures.

Provision of first-aid, including the name and location of the person responsible for first-aid and the deputy, and the location of the first-aid box.

(g) Communication

Giving employees information about the general duties under *HSWA 1974* and specific legal requirements relating to their work.

Giving employees necessary information about substances, plant, machinery and equipment with which they come into contact.

Ensuring there is a route for employees to communicate with management.

Discussing with contractors, before they start working on site, what risks they may create for employees, and what action needs to be taken to minimise such risks. This may mean a segregated area or a shut-down plant.

(h) Training

Training managers, supervisors and employees to enable them to carry out their health and safety responsibilities and to work safely.

(j) Supervising

Supervising employees as far as is necessary, for their safety and for the safety of others.

Providing special supervision of young workers, new employees and employees carrying out unfamiliar tasks (*Young people at work: a guide for employers, HS(G)165*).

(k) Keeping check

Regular inspections and checks of health and safety in the workplace, of the use of machinery, appliances and working methods should be undertaken.

A specimen outline health and safety policy

S7011
1. The Company recognises its health and safety duties under the *Health and Safety etc. Act 1974* and associated regulations that have followed the original Act.

2. The Company has appointed to constantly review and keep up to date the Company's Health and Safety Policy and the workplace procedures, and to liaise with the Health and Safety Executive when necessary.

3. The Company has instituted a system for the reporting of accidents, diseases and dangerous occurrences to the local enforcing authority, in our case the HSE.

4. The Company has an accident book which is available for inspection by an HSE inspector at any time.

5. The Company will so far as is reasonably practicable —

(a)   provide and maintain a safe place of work, a safe system of work, safe appliances for work and a safe and healthy environment; and

(b)   provide such information and instruction as may be necessary to ensure the health and safety of its employees and to promote awareness and understanding of health and safety throughout its workforce. This will include updating and refresher training where necessary.

6. The Company has taken out insurance against liability for death, injury and/or disease suffered by any employee whilst at work, provided only that it was caused by the negligence and/or breach of statutory duty on the part of the Company. The certificate of insurance is available for inspection at all reasonable times by employees and any health and safety inspector.

7. All employees of the Company agree, as a term of their contract of employment, to comply with their health and safety responsibilities for themselves and others and that they will generally co-operate with their employer to enable their employer to carry out his health and safety duties towards them. Failure to comply with health and safety duties can lead to instant dismissal.

8. Prime responsibility for health and safety lies with the Managing Director and Board of Directors of the Company. The Company regards itself bound by any acts or omissions of the Managing Director, any executive director or senior manager, giving rise to liability, provided only that such acts and/or omissions arise out of or during company business. The prosecution of any director or senior manager shall not prevent a further prosecution against the Company.

9. The Company recognises its duties to the general public and all lawful visitors to the Company's premises. In particular, where visitors must wear personal protective clothing or otherwise take reasonable precautions for their own health and safety, failure to do so will be regarded as a breach of Company policy, which will entitle the Company to take appropriate measures which may include asking the visitor to leave the premises.

10. This Policy has been prepared in accordance with the *Health and Safety at Work etc. Act 1974* and binds all directors, managers and employees, in the interests of employees and customers. We request that our customers and visitors respect this Policy, a copy of which can be obtained on demand.

Signed:

Managing Director.

Date:

Ventilation

Introduction

V3001 Air being invisible and intangible, there is a dangerous tendency to take it for granted. As breathing is predominantly an involuntary activity, it underlines the need to be selective about what we breathe, with whom we do so, and in what conditions. Moreover, given that an average individual needs an intake of over thirty pounds of air per day (or about six pints of air every minute), the dangers to employees (and others) of an inadequate or polluted air supply are obvious. The twin objectives of good ventilation are the elimination or dispersal of particulate matter (see V3010 below) and the replacement of stale, hot or humid air (often associated with production processes or equipment) with fresh air free from impurity, the aim being to induce a sense of individual comfort in employees. The composition of pure dry air is 20.94% oxygen, 0.03% carbon dioxide and 79.03% nitrogen and inert gases.

Satisfactory ventilation is normally achievable by means of windows (or other similar apertures), as well as by recycled air, particularly in warm weather or hot workplaces. Air recirculated via mechanical ventilation or air conditioning systems should be adequately filtered and impurities removed, and be impregnated with fresh air prior to recirculation. To that end, ventilation systems should be designed with fresh air inlets and kept open, regularly and properly cleaned, tested and maintained. In order to avoid uncomfortable draughts the velocity of ventilation systems may have to be controlled. Employers who fail to ventilate effectively and follow relevant official guidance on medical surveillance of workers can be liable at common law if an employee becomes sensitised to a respiratory sensitiser in the workplace, even in the absence of evidence that the relevant occupational exposure limits have been exceeded (*Douglas Reilly v Robert Kellie & Sons Ltd (1989) HSIB 166* where an employee contracted occupational asthma whilst working with low levels of isocyanate fumes. It was held that the employer was liable at common law for breach of the *Factories Act 1961, s 63* (now repealed), since the hazards associated with isocyanate fumes had been known about since the early 1980s).

This chapter deals with current statutory requirements, contained in the *Health and Safety at Work etc. Act 1974* (general) (see V3004 below), the *Workplace (Health, Safety and Welfare) Regulations 1992* (specific) (see V3005 below), and certain specific processes where adherence to ventilation requirements is paramount (see V3006 below). (For requirements relating to ventilation on construction sites see C8046 CONSTRUCTION AND BUILDING OPERATIONS.) Origins of pollution of the working atmosphere, specific pollutants and their insidious effect on health, along with strategies for controlling them, are also covered.

Pollution of the working environment and dangers of exposure to dust and fumes

V3002 Pollution of the working environment can occur through the generation of airborne particulates, such as dusts, fumes, mists and vapours (as defined in V3003 below).

Of these, probably dust and fumes pose the principal hazard to workers, some of the situations being well documented, e.g. tungsten and silicon processes resulting in pneumonia followed by progressive fibrosis, milling cotton resulting in byssinosis, weaving hemp in chronic bronchitis, underground mining in emphysema and copper welding/electroplating with cadmium also causing emphysema (see further OCCUPATIONAL HEALTH AND DISEASES). Dusts can be fibrogenic, that is they can lead to fibrotic changes to lung tissue, or, alternatively be toxic, eventually leading to poisoning of body systems. Examples of fibrogenic dusts are: silica, cement dust and certain metals such as tungsten; toxic dusts include: arsenic, lead, mercury and beryllium. More particularly, dusts are classified according to the response on the worker, as follows:

(*a*)   benign pneumoconiosis, such as siderosis, associated with work with iron particles; here there is no permanent lung disorder;

(*b*)   pneumonitis or acute inflammation of lung tissue, caused by inhalation of metallic fumes, e.g. zinc oxide fumes; this can result in death;

(*c*)   extrinsic allergic alveolitis, e.g. farmer's lung; this can eventuate into a disabling condition;

(*d*)   tumour-forming, e.g. asbestosis, plural mesothelioma (caused by work with crocidolite); characterised by a high mortality rate;

(*e*)   nuisance particulates, e.g. dust from combustion of solid fuels; however causing no permanent lung damage.

Dust at the workplace has a variety of origins ranging from:

(i)   dust arising in connection with cleaning and treatment of raw materials, e.g. sandblasting in foundries;

(ii)   dust emitted in operations such as refining, grinding, milling, cutting, sanding; and

(iii) dusts manufactured for specific treatments or dressings; to

(iv)   general environmental dust, e.g. caused by sweeping factory floors or by fuel combustion.

Fumes are formed through vaporisation or oxidation of metals, e.g. typically lead and welding fumes. Lead processes emitting dust and fume should be enclosed and maintained under negative pressure by an enclosing hood. Moreover, the fume should be treated before any escape into the atmosphere. Welding fume, caused by action of heat and ultraviolet light, produces carbon monoxide and ozone and is potentially harmful, leading to 'welder's lung'. For that reason, welding should only be carried out in ventilated areas. Welding workshops should be equipped with adequate mechanical ventilation, and local exhaust ventilation should be incorporated at the point of fume emission as a supplement to general ventilation. If welding is carried out in a confined space (see the *Confined Spaces Regulations 1997 (SI 1997 No 1713)*), a permit to work system should be in force. Welders should of necessity be familiar with various relevant forms of respiratory protection (see further PERSONAL PROTECTIVE EQUIPMENT).

Polluting agents

V3003   Pollution of the workplace environment may take place through the generation of airborne particulates, such as dusts, fumes, mists and vapours. These are defined below.

Particulate: a collection of solid particles, each of which is an aggregation of many molecules.

Dust: an aerosol composed of solid inanimate particles. (Standard ILO definition).

Fumes: airborne fine solid particulates formed from a gaseous state, usually by vaporisation or oxidation of metals.

Mist: airborne liquid droplets.

Vapour: a substance in the form of a mist, fume or smoke emitted from a liquid.

Statutory requirements
General – HSWA 1974

V3004

The general duty upon employers under the *Health and Safety at Work etc. Act 1974 (HSWA)* to 'ensure, so far as reasonably practicable, the health, safety and welfare at work of all their employees' [*HSWA s 2(1)*], must be regarded as including a duty to provide employees with an adequate and renewable supply of pure and uncontaminated air. Employers must also provide and maintain a safe working environment. [*HSWA s 2(2)(e)*]. In consequence, employers may be in breach if the workplace is not adequately ventilated and specific dust and fume hazards not controlled. In addition, all employers must inform, instruct and train their employees in health and safety procedures. This means that they, or their representatives, must know how to use, test and maintain equipment for ensuring air purity and ventilation as well as dust control (*R v Swan Hunter Shipbuilders Ltd [1981] ICR 831,* where the deaths of the subcontractor employees might have been avoided, had they been properly instructed and trained in the use of respirators). (See further C8132 CONSTRUCTION AND BUILDING OPERATIONS.)

Facilities managers (i.e. those responsible for the well-being of occupants and visitors) are required to maintain a clean and healthy ventilation system in the workplace. This may mean the procurement of ventilation hygiene services from a specialist contractor which often demands a level of technical expertise outside the scope of the majority.

The Heating and Ventilating Contractors' Association (HVCA) have published a Guide to Good Practice, '*Cleanliness of Ventilation Systems – TR/17*'. This Guide and others on ventilation are available from HVCA Publications (tel: 01768 864771).

Responding to industry needs, the Building Services Research and Information Association has developed a Standard Specification for Ventilation Hygiene* to allow competitive tenders to be provided by contractors on an equal basis. The client thereby achieves optimum value for money by securing complete but not excessive action by the contractor. Correspondingly, contractors face less ambiguity in performance expectations.

The Standard Specification is in two parts, the basic specification with accompanying detailed guidance. Supported by the Department of Environment Transport and Regions, this is the first of a range of specifications written for facilities managers. It provides straightforward, easy to use clauses of industry-standard performance requirements. The guidance document explains in detail the scope of work required to fulfil a ventilation hygiene contract.

* '*Guidance and Standard Specification for Ventilation Hygiene*', price £40, is available from BSRIA publications sales, tel: 01344 426511.

Specific – Workplace (Health, Safety and Welfare) Regulations 1992 (SI 1992 No 3004)

V3005   Effective and suitable provision must be made to ensure that every enclosed workplace is ventilated by a sufficient quantity of fresh or purified air. Plant designed and used for such purposes must be accompanied with visible and/or audible means of warning of any failure, which might affect health or safety. [*Workplace (Health, Safety and Welfare) Regulations 1992, Reg 6*].

Specific processes or industries

Highly flammable liquids and liquefied petroleum gases

V3006   Where a dangerous concentration of vapours from a highly flammable liquid may be expected, the process must be carried on within a cabinet or other enclosure, which is:

(*a*)   effective to prevent the escape of such vapours into the general atmosphere;

(*b*)   adequately ventilated; and

(*c*)   fire-resistant.

[*Highly Flammable Liquids and Liquefied Petroleum Gases Regulations 1972 (SI 1972 No 917), Reg 10(2)*].

Where compliance with this requirement is not reasonably practicable the workroom must have exhaust ventilation adequate to remove vapours from the workroom. [*Reg 10(3)*].

Lead processes

V3007   The *Control of Lead at Work Regulations 1998 (SI 1998 No 543)* came into force on 1 April 1998. They were introduced in order that work involving lead might be covered by a single set of regulations.

Regulations revoked include the *Control of Lead at Work Regulations 1980 (SI 1980 No 1248)*. See the *Control of Lead at Work Regulations 1998, Sch 3* for a full list of revocations. *Sections 74, 128, 131 and 132* of the *Factories Act 1961* have been repealed by *Reg 14(1)*.

The aims of the new Regulations and Approved Code of Practice, Regulations and Guidance, (COP2) are to:

(*a*)   protect the health of people at work by preventing or, where this is not practicable, adequately controlling their exposure to lead;

(*b*)   monitor the amount of lead that employees absorb so that individuals whose work involves significant exposure (as defined by *Reg 2*) to lead at work can be taken off such work before their health is affected.

The Regulations apply to all work which exposes employees to lead in any form in which it may be inhaled, ingested or absorbed through the skin, for example as dust, fume or vapour.

The duties imposed by these Regulations extend not only to employers but also to self-employed persons. [*Reg 3(2)*].

Control of Lead at Work Regulations 1998 (SI 1998 No 543)

V3008   An employer who is working with lead, or a substance or material containing it has a duty to ensure that his employees are not exposed to lead, or, where this is not reasonably practicable (see E15017 ENFORCEMENT), to ensure that appropriate control measures are adequately controlling the exposure to lead of his employees and of anyone else who may be affected by their work with lead and/or lead-based products – such persons may include:

—   persons working for other employers, such as maintenance staff or cleaners;

—   visitors to the work area; and

—   families of those exposed to lead at work who may be affected by lead carried home unintentionally on clothing and/or footwear.

Exposure to lead covers all routes of possible exposure, i.e., inhalation, absorption throught the skin and ingestion.

Without prejudice to the *Management of Health and Safety at Work Regulations 1992, Reg 3*, employers must not carry on any work which is liable to expose any employees to lead at work unless they have first made an assessment as to whether the exposure of any employees to lead is liable to be significant. [*Reg 5*].

Measures for controlling exposure to lead may include one or more of the following:

(*a*)   using substitutes, i.e. lead-free or low-solubility lead compounds;

(*b*)   using lead or lead compounds in emulsion or paste form to minimise the formation of dust;

(*c*)   using temperature controls to keep the temperature of molten lead below 500°C, the level above which fume emission becomes significant, though the formation of lead oxide and the emission of dust is still possible below this temperature;

(*d*)   the containment of lead, lead materials, compounds, fumes or dust in totally enclosed plant and in enclosed containers such as drums and bags. The container must be so designed that no lead is allowed to leak out. Where it is necessary to open such containers, this should be carried out under exhaust ventilation conditions, if reasonably practicable;

(*e*)   where total enclosure is not reasonably practicable, an effective ventilation system must be in operation before work is allowed to commence. This may consist of:

(i)   partial enclosure such as booths designed to prevent the lead escaping – these should be fitted with exhaust ventilation;

(ii)   various types of exhaust hoods which should be as close to the lead source as is reasonably practicable so that they may take the lead dust, fume or vapour away from the employee's breathing zone;

(iii)   an extract ductwork system that is adequate to remove the dust, fume or vapour from the source area;

(iv)   a dust and/or fume collection unit with a sound and adequate filtration system that will both remove the lead source from the workplace and prevent it from re-entering;

(v)   fans of a suitable type placed in the system after the collection and filtration units so that the units are kept under negative pressure, thus ensuring that any escape of lead is minimised;

(f)   wet methods which include:

(i)   the wetting of lead and lead materials, e.g. wet grinding and pasting processes. Wet methods should be used during rubbing and/or scraping lead-painted surfaces;

(ii)   the wetting of floors and work benches whilst certain types of work are being carried out, e.g. work with dry lead compounds and pasting processes in the manufacture of batteries.

Wetting should be sufficiently thorough to prevent dust forming, and the wetted materials or surfaces should not be allowed to dry out since this can create dry lead dust which then is liable to be hazardous if it becomes airborne. Water sprays are not a fully effective method of controlling airborne dust.

Wetting methods should not be used when they are liable to be unsafe, such as:

(i)   at furnaces where they could cause an explosion;

(ii)   when lead materials containing arsenides or antimonides could, on contact with water, produce highly toxic arsine or stibine gases;

(g)   providing and maintaining a high standard of cleanliness.

Special care and attention should be given to the design of plant and systems to eliminate possible areas which might increase the risk to the employee of exposure from lead.

Before any plant, equipment or systems are used in lead or lead compound work, there should be an adequate checking procedure in place to ensure that such plant, equipment or systems are as designed and that they meet the standard required under the *Control of Lead at Work Regulations 1998* for the safety of all those who could be affected by lead.

Asbestos

V3009   No process must be carried on in any factory unless exhaust equipment is provided, maintained and used, which prevents the entry into air of asbestos dust. [*Control of Asbestos at Work Regulations 1987 (SI 1987 No 2115), Reg 13(2)*].

In addition, where it is not reasonably practicable to reduce exposure of employees to below the 'control limits', employers must provide employees concerned with suitable respiratory protective equipment. [*Reg 8(2)*].

Moreover, where the concentration of asbestos is likely to exceed any 'control limit', the employer must designate that area a 'respirator zone' and ensure that only permitted employees enter/remain in that zone. [*Reg 14(2)*]. (See further ASBESTOS.)

Control of airborne particulates

V3010   Airborne particulates may be controlled in the following ways.

(*a*) *Substitution replacement*

The use of a less harmful toxic substance or modification to a process may minimise or totally eliminate the hazard. For example, substitution of soap solutions for organic solvents is sometimes possible in cleaning operations.

(*b*) *Suppression*

The use of a wet process for handling powders or other particulates is an effective form of control. In the cleaning process, it may be possible to damp down floors prior to removal of dust sooner than resorting to dry sweeping.

(*c*) *Isolation*

This form of control entails enclosure of all or part of a process or the actual point of dust production and may be incorporated in machinery/plant, in which case it is necessary to ensure seals are maintained. Total enclosure of large processes involving grinding of metals or other materials, linked to an extract ventilation system, is an effective method of isolating dust from the operator's breathing zone.

(*d*) *Extract/exhaust ventilation*

Removal of dust or fume at the point of emission by entraining it in a path of fresh air and taking it to an extract hood or other collection device is the role of extract/exhaust ventilation (see the HSE's guidance booklet HSG54: '*The maintenance, examination and testing of local exhaust ventilation*'). The air velocity required to provide this movement depends upon the type of material, varying from about 0.5 metres per second for gases to 10 metres per second or above for some dusts. In fact for large dense dust particles from grinding or cutting operations, it may be necessary to arrange for the trajectory of the emitted particles to be encompassed by the exhaust hood so that the material is literally thrown into the hood by its own energy.

Extract ventilation systems generally take three distinct forms:

(i)   *Receptor systems*: the contaminant enters the system without inducement, and is transported from the hood through ducting to a collection point by the use of a fan.

(ii)   *Captor systems*: in this system moving air captures the contaminant at some point outside the hood and induces its flow into it. The rate of air flow must be sufficient to capture the contaminant at the furthest point of origin, and the air velocity induced at this point must be high enough to overcome the effects of cross currents created by open doors, windows or moving parts of machinery.

(iii)   *High velocity low volume systems*: dusts from high speed grinding machines in particular require very high capture velocities. With an HVLV system high velocities at the source are created by extracting from small apertures very close to the source of the contaminant. These high velocities can be achieved with quite low air flow rates.

(*e*) *Dilution ventilation*

In certain cases, it may not be possible to extract particulates close to their point of origin. Where the quantity of contaminant is small, uniformly evolved and of low toxicity, it may be possible to dilute it by inducing large volumes of air to flow through the contaminated region. Dilution ventilation is most successfully used to control vapours from low toxicity solvents, but is seldom satisfactory in the control of dust and fumes.

(f) Cleaning procedures

Whilst the above methods may be effective in preventing environmental contamination of the workplace, there will inevitably be a need for efficient cleaning procedures wherever dusty processes are operated. Hand sweeping should be replaced by the use of industrial vacuum cleaning equipment, or in situ (ring main) systems which incorporate hand-held suction devices connected via ducting to a central collection point.

(g) Air cleaning

Air cleaning is often employed, either to prevent emission of noxious substances into the atmosphere or to enable some of the air to be recirculated during winter months, thus reducing heated air costs and lowering fuel bills. For particulates such as dusts and grit, air cleaning may involve some form of inertial separator, such as settling chambers or cyclones, usually followed by bag filters. For very fine dusts and fumes, bag filters are often used as the pre-filter, followed by absolute or electrostatic filters. For gases and vapours, the cleaning is usually achieved by wet scrubbers (device where the air is passed in close contact with a liquid) to take the gas into solution or react chemically with it. Scrubbers can also be used for particulate material. The selection of air cleaning types will depend upon the properties of the materials emitted and the size ranges of the particulates.

To generate air flow in the duct, various types of fans are available. The type of fan must be suitable for the system in which it is installed. This requires a knowledge of the system resistance and the fan characteristics in order to generate the desired air flow with minimum noise and power consumption.

For systems with little ducting and airflow resistance, axial fans may be used to generate high air flows. For ducted systems, centrifugal fans are often used, creating generally lower air flows per size, but at the higher air pressures required to overcome the resistances imposed by ducting and air cleaners. The fan should not be used outside its duty range. It should be sited either outside the building or as near to the discharge as possible, so that air cleaners and all ducting within the building are on the negative static pressure side of the fan, thus preventing leakage of the contaminant through cracks or defects in the duct.

Guidance* on the use of the dust lamp for observing the presence of airborne particles in the workplace has been published by the Health & Safety Executive (HSE) in the series 'Method for the Determination of Hazardous Substances' (MDHS). The guidance has been written for occupational hygienists, ventilation engineers, and health and safety practitioners. It briefly explains the principle of the dust lamp, its use in observing the presence of airborne particles and identifies its advantages and limitations. Despite its name, the dust lamp can be used to reveal the presence of many different types of airborne particulates both solids (dusts, fumes, fibres) and liquids (organic or inorganic mists). The dust lamp can be used to gauge the size and direction of movement of a particle cloud, but it does not give a quantitative measure of either concentration or particle size.

* '*MDHS 82: The dust lamp: A simple tool for observing the presence of airborne particles*', price £15.00, is available from HSE Books.

Respiratory protection

V3011   Respiratory protection implies the provision and use of equipment such as dust masks, general purpose dust respirators, positive pressure powered dust respirators, self-contained breathing apparatus or other forms of such protection. Where dust emission is intermittent or other controls are not available (as above), then resort may be made to respiratory protection. The work and care required in the selection and establishment of a respiratory protection programme, including the training of operators in the correct use of the equipment, is likely to be at least as great as any other control system. The protection must be selected to give adequate cover and minimum discomfort and the need for other personal protective devices should not be ignored. (See also PERSONAL PROTECTIVE EQUIPMENT.)

Work at Heights

Introduction

W9001 Work at heights characterises many occupations – construction and maintenance workers, plant and equipment installers, personnel servicing passenger lifts, heating and air conditioning systems, window cleaners. The risk of a fall, often with fatal results, is a common hazard in such activities. Indeed, two-fifths of all reported major injuries are caused by falls from a height; and half the fatal injuries to construction workers are caused by falls from a height. It is the most common cause of fatality to employees generally. Falls generally come into one of two causal categories, as being associated with either (*a*) means of access to the workstation or (*b*) the system of work. As regards means of access to the working position, this can be a portable ladder, roof ladder or powered working platform. In many cases, this has proved to be singularly inadequate or unsuitable for the task at hand, resulting in falls through fragile roofs, from a roof edge or from an item of plant above floor level. In this connection, all workplaces (temporary as well as permanent) must have suitable and effective safeguards for preventing people from being injured as a result of falling a distance likely to cause personal injury (see W9003 below). [*Workplace (Health, Safety and Welfare) Regulations 1992 (SI 1992 No 3004), Reg 13*]. (Construction works are covered separately by the *Construction (Health, Safety and Welfare) Regulations 1996 (SI 1996 No 1592)*. (See CONSTRUCTION AND BUILDING OPERATIONS.) However, the duty of architects etc. to pay adequate regard to the avoidance or reduction of risk to future maintenance workers when designing both new structures and repairs or alterations to existing ones should be noted, particularly as this duty will also protect many not usually thought to be construction workers. [*Construction (Design and Management) Regulations 1994, Reg 13*]. A further point to be noted is that if the occupier intends to control the way that construction work is done he could well acquire typical contractor duties. [*Construction (Health, Safety and Welfare) Regulations 1996, Reg 4*].

The second most common cause of accident/fatality is the system of work adopted once the working position is reached. If the system has been correctly planned, operators briefed in the system and the appropriate precautions to be taken prior to commencement of work, should be able to work safely at a height. Such system will include compulsory provision, maintenance, replacement and wearing of safety helmets to protect those working at heights and those working or visiting below, by dint of the *Construction (Head Protection) Regulations 1989 (SI 1989 No 2209)*, and bump caps for those working in confined spaces. However, work at heights is frequently undertaken in a situation of emergency or crisis. For instance, a fault may have developed on an item of plant which needs immediate attention for production to continue or the factory roof may be leaking, resulting in damage to stored products below. In both cases, urgent action is required and there is insufficient time to consider any precautions necessary to ensure safe working at height; therefore there should be emergency procedures planned and in force to deal with this sort of contingency.

Another aspect of work at heights is window cleaning. Windows in factories, workplaces and high-rise commercial and office blocks must be regularly and periodically cleaned [*Workplace (Health, Safety and Welfare) Regulations 1992, Reg 16*]. Frequency of cleaning depends on type of establishment, whether office, shop or factory etc. (see W9038 below) – but in any case the method selected should ensure protection for window cleaners (see W9036, W9037 and W9039 below). The inescapable fact is that window cleaning, particularly in high-rise commercial properties with vast oceans of glass has posed serious safety problems for contract window cleaning companies and self-employed window cleaners, requiring, on the one hand, contract cleaning companies to use best available window cleaning equipment and methods, and, on the other, building owners/occupiers to make safety anchorage points, in so far as they are permitted to do so, conveniently accessible on the building (see further BS 8213: Part 1: '*Code of practice for safety in use and during cleaning of windows and doors (including guidance on cleaning materials and methods*' (1991) for excellent guidance). Crucially, in this connection, buildings, windows and skylights on buildings may need to be fitted with suitable devices (see W9040-W9042 below) to allow windows and skylights to be securely cleaned to satisfy the safety requirements. [*Workplace (Health, Safety and Welfare) Regulations 1992, Reg 16(1)*]. More generally, the building designer has a duty to pay adequate regard to the avoidance or reduction of risk to those cleaning windows and any transparent or translucent wall, ceiling or roof where they might fall more than two metres. [*Construction (Design and Management) Regulations 1994, Regs 2(1), 13(2)(a)*]. Falls from heights accounting for by far the greater majority of major injuries, the need to comply with fall-preventive statutory requirements and window cleaning regulations at all times is paramount.

Current statutory requirements

W9002   Current statutory requirements relating to falls from heights are contained in the *Workplace (Health, Safety and Welfare) Regulations 1992*. There are also specific requirements relating to prevention of falls on construction sites, in the form of the *Construction (Health, Safety and Welfare) Regulations 1996, Regs 5–8*. Requirements relating to windows and window cleaning are contained in the *Workplace (Health, Safety and Welfare) Regulations 1992, Regs 14–16*.

Falls from a height – all workplaces (except construction sites)

W9003   So far as reasonably practicable (for meaning, see E15017 ENFORCEMENT), suitable and effective measures must be taken (other than by provision of personal protective equipment, training, information, supervision etc.) to prevent:

(*a*)   any person falling a distance likely to cause personal injury; or

(*b*)   any person being struck by a falling object likely to cause personal injury.

Any area from which this might happen must be clearly indicated – particularly in the case of pits or tanks. [*Workplace (Health, Safety and Welfare) Regulations 1992, Reg 13*].

Suitable and effective measures are:

(i)   fencing;

(ii)   covering; and

(iii)   fixed ladders.

Fencing

W9004

This should primarily prevent people falling from edges and objects falling on to people, and where it has to be removed temporarily (as where goods/materials are admitted), temporary measures should be put in train (e.g. provision of handholds). Except in the case of roof edges or other points to which there is no general legitimate access, secure fencing should be provided where a person might fall:

(*a*)   2 metres or more, or

(*b*)   less than 2 metres, where the risk of injury is otherwise greater (e.g. internal traffic route below).

Fencing should be sufficiently high to prevent falls, both of people and objects, over or through it. Minimally, it should consist of two guard-rails at suitable heights. The top of the fencing should generally be at least 1,100 mm above the surface from which a person might fall, be of adequate strength and stability to restrain any person or object liable to fall against it.

Covers

W9005

Pits, tanks, vats, sumps, kiers etc. can be securely covered (instead of fenced). Covers must be strong and able to support loads imposed on them as well as passing traffic; nor should they be easily detachable and removable. They should be kept securely *in situ* except for purposes of inspection or access. Uncovered tanks, pits or structures must be fenced if there is a traffic route over them.

Fixed ladders

W9006

Assuming a staircase is impracticable, fixed ladders – sloping ones are safer than vertical ones – (which should be provided in pits etc.) should be:

(*a*)   of sound construction,

(*b*)   properly maintained,

(*c*)   securely fixed.

Rungs should be horizontal and provide adequate foothold without reliance on nails or screws. In the absence of an adequate handhold, stiles should extend to at least 1,100 mm above any landing (or the highest rung) to step or stand on. Fixed ladders with a vertical distance of more than 6 m should normally have a landing at every 6 m point. Where possible, each run should be out of line with the previous run to reduce falling distance. And where a ladder passes through a floor, the opening should be as small as possible, fenced (if possible) and a gate provided to prevent falls.

(For ladders on construction sites, see W9017 below and C8006 CONSTRUCTION AND BUILDING OPERATIONS.)

Pits, tanks, vats, kiers etc. – new workplaces

W9007

Serious accidents have occurred as a result of workers, often maintenance workers, falling into or overreaching or overbalancing (and falling) into pits etc. containing dangerous corrosive or scalding substances. Thus, where there is a risk of a person or employee falling into a dangerous or corrosive or scalding substance, (so far as is reasonably practicable) pits, tanks (or similar vessels) must be either:

(*a*)   fenced, or

(*b*)   covered

[*Reg 13(5)*]

and means of access/egress into pits/tanks – in the form (preferably) of fixed ladders (or the equivalent) – should be provided [*Reg 13(6)*].

Construction sites – the Construction (Health, Safety and Welfare) Regulations 1996 (SI 1996 No 1592)

W9008   Construction work is associated with a large number of falls, some of which are fatal. A fair proportion of serious accidents occur as a result of workers falling off (or through) working platforms, scaffolds, toe boards, fragile roofs and personal suspension equipment. This situation is now addressed by *Regulations 6–8* of the *Construction (Health, Safety and Welfare) Regulations 1996*. In the first place, however, there are the duties of employers to assess risks [*Management of Health and Safety at Work Regulations 1992, Reg 3*] (see particularly the advice to *Reg 3* in para 27 of the Approved Code of Practice (L 21)) and of designers to pay adequate regard to the avoidance or reduction of risk. [*Construction (Design and Management) Regulations 1994, Reg 13(2)(a)*]. These duties will entail such matters as reviewing the need firstly to have the work – or so much of it – done at heights, and where such avoidance and reduction cannot be achieved, as will often be the case, giving preference to collective measures such as secure working platforms over individual ones such as safety harnesses.

See the HSE's free publication CIS 49: '*General access scaffolds and ladders*' (1997).

Working platforms, scaffolds, toe-boards, guard-rails, personal suspension equipment – fall preventative requirements

W9009   Suitable and sufficient steps must be taken to prevent any person (direct or indirect employees) from falling, so far as is reasonably practicable. [*Reg 6(1)*]. This will usually involve the provision of:

(*a*)   suitable working platforms;

(*b*)   guard-rails, toe-boards (not required in respect of stairway or rest platforms of a scaffold used as a means of access or egress to or from a place of work) [*Reg 6(9)*]; and

(*c*)   barriers.

These can be removed for movement of materials, but must be replaced as soon as practicable. [*Reg 6(4)*].

Definition

W9010   A working platform refers to any platform used (*a*) as a place of work, or (*b*) a means of access or egress (to or from) a place of work, including:

(*a*)   a scaffold;

(*b*)   a suspended scaffold;

(*c*)   a cradle;

(*d*)   a mobile platform;

(*e*)   a trestle;

(*f*)   a gangway;

(*g*)   a run;

(*h*)   a gantry;

(*j*)   a stairway; and

(*k*)   a crawling ladder.

[*Reg 2(1)*].

Requirements relating to guard-rails and toe boards

W9011   The regulations require that:

(*a*)   guard-rails, toe-boards and barriers and other similar means of protection must be:

    (i)   suitable and of sufficient strength and rigidity for the purpose for which they are being used, and

    (ii)   so placed, secured and used as to ensure, so far as is reasonably practicable, the avoidance of accidental displacement;

(*b*)   structures supporting guard-rails, toe-boards, barriers and other means of protection, or a structure to which these are attached, must be of a suitable and sufficient strength for the purpose for which they are used;

(*c*)   main guard-rails must be at least 910 millimetres above the edge from which a person is liable to fall;

(*d*)   there must not be an unprotected gap of more than 470 millimetres between any guard-rail, toe-board or barrier and the walking surface;

(*e*)   toe-boards must be not less than 150 millimetres high; and

(*f*)   guard-rails, toe-boards, barriers and other similar means of protection must be so placed as to prevent, so far as is reasonably practicable, the fall of a person, material or objects from a place of work.

[*Sch 1*].

Requirements relating to working platforms

W9012   The regulations require work platforms to conform to the following requirements.

(*a*)   *Stability* – they must be:

    (i)   suitable and of sufficient strength and rigidity for the intended use,

    (ii)   erected and used to ensure, so far as is reasonably practicable, the avoidance of accidental displacement,

    (iii)   remain stable and if modified or altered, remain stable after modification or alteration, and

    (iv)   dismantled so as to avoid accidental displacement.

(*b*)   *Safety* – they must be:

    (i)   of sufficient dimensions to permit free passage of persons and safe use of equipment and materials, and, so far as is reasonably practicable, be a safe working area,

    (ii)   at least 600 millimetres wide,

(iii)   so reasonably constructed that the surface has no gap likely to cause injury, or from which there is any risk of any person below the platform being struck by falling objects,

(iv)   so erected, used and maintained to prevent, so far as is reasonably practicable, any slipping or tripping, or any person being caught between a working platform and an adjacent structure, and

(v)   provided with such handholds and footholds as are necessary to prevent, so far as is reasonably practicable, any person from slipping or falling from a working platform.

(c)   *Load* – they must not be so loaded as to give rise to danger of collapse or deformation which could affect its safe use.

(d)   *Supporting structures* – must be:

(i)   of suitable and sufficient strength and rigidity for the intended purpose,

(ii)   so erected and, where necessary, securely attached to another structure as to ensure stability,

(iii)   so altered or modified as to ensure stability when altered or modified, and

(iv)   erected on surfaces which are stable and of a sufficient strength and suitable composition to ensure the safe support of the structure, working platform and any load intended to be placed upon the working platform.

[*Sch 2*].

Personal suspension equipment – fall preventative requirements

W9013   'Personal suspension equipment' refers to suspended access (other than a working platform) for use by an individual, including a boatswain's chair and abseiling equipment, but does not include a suspended scaffold or cradle. [*Reg 2(1)*].

Where compliance with guard-rail, toe-board or working platform duties (see above) is not reasonably practicable, (e.g. owing to short-term work), suitable personal suspension equipment must be provided and used. [*Reg 6(3)(c)*].

Requirements relating to personal suspension equipment

W9014   Personal suspension equipment must be:

(a)   of suitable and sufficient strength, having regard to the work being carried out and the load, including any person it is intended to bear;

(b)   securely attached to a structure or plant, and the structure or plant must be suitable and of sufficient strength and stability to support the equipment and load;

(c)   installed or attached so as to prevent uncontrolled movement of equipment; and

(d)   suitable and sufficient steps must be taken to prevent any person from falling or slipping from personal suspension equipment.

[*Sch 3*].

Means of arresting falls

W9015   Where compliance with guard-rail, toe-board, working platform or personal suspension equipment requirements is not reasonably practicable, suitable and sufficient means for arresting falls must be (i) provided, and (ii) used. [*Reg 6(3)(d)*].

Equipment provided for arresting falls must adhere to the following requirements.

(*a*)   The equipment must be suitable and of sufficient strength to safely arrest the fall of any person liable to fall.

(*b*)   The equipment must be securely attached to a structure or to a plant, and the structure or plant (and the means of attachment) must be suitable and of sufficient strength and stability to safely support the equipment and any person liable to fall.

(*c*)   Suitable and sufficient steps must be taken to ensure, so far as is reasonably practicable, that in the event of a fall, equipment does not cause injury to a person.

[*Sch 4*].

Installation and erection of scaffolds, personal suspension equipment and fall-arresting devices

W9016   Installation and erection of any scaffold, personal suspension equipment or fall-arresting devices, or substantial addition or alteration thereto (not including personal attachment of any equipment or fall-arresting devices to a person for whose safety such equipment or device is provided) must be carried out under the supervision of a competent person. [*Reg 6(8)*].

Ladders

W9017   Owing to a growing number of fatalities and serious injuries to workers involving the use of ladders, ladders can no longer be used as:

(*a*)   a place of work, or

(*b*)   a means of access or egress, to or from a place of work,

unless it is reasonable to do so, having regard to:

(c)   the nature of work and the duration of work, and

(*d*)   the risk to the safety of any person at work arising from the use of a ladder.

[*Reg 6(5)*].

Ladders must be:

(i)   of suitable and sufficient strength for their intended purpose;

(ii)   so erected as to avoid displacement;

(iii)   (where they are of three metres in height or more), secured, so far as is practicable, and where not practicable, a person must be positioned at the foot of the ladder to prevent it slipping during use (see further the case of *Boyle v Kodak Ltd [1969] 2 AER 439*, where an experienced painter failed to secure a ladder, contrary to the *Building (Safety, Health and Welfare) Regulations 1948, Reg 29* and was injured).

(iv)   (where ladders are used as a means of access between places of work), sufficiently secured to prevent slipping and/or falling.

In addition, ladders must:

(v) (where the top of the ladder is used as a means of access to another level), extend to a sufficient height above the level to which it gives access, so as to provide a safe handhold (unless a suitable alternative handhold is provided);

(vi) (where a ladder or run of ladders rises vertically 9 metres or more above its base), be provided, where practicable, with a safe landing area or rest platform at suitable intervals;

(vii) be erected on surfaces which are stable and firm, of sufficient strength, and of suitable composition safely to support the ladder and its load.

[*Sch 5*].

(For practical safety criteria in the use of ladders, see also C8006 CONSTRUCTION AND BUILDING OPERATIONS.)

Maintenance of fall-preventative equipment

W9018   All scaffolds, working platforms, toe-boards, guard-rails, personal suspension equipment, fall-arresting devices and ladders must be properly maintained. [*Reg 6(7)*].

Fragile materials

W9019   Suitable and sufficient steps must be taken to prevent any person falling through any fragile material. [*Reg 7(1)*]. In particular:

(*a*) no person must pass or work on or from fragile material, through which he would be liable to fall 2 metres (or more), unless suitable and sufficient platforms, coverings or other similar means of support are provided and used so that the weight of any person so passing or working is supported by such supports;

(*b*) no person must pass or work near fragile materials through which he would be liable to fall 2 metres (or more), unless suitable and sufficient guard-rails or coverings are provided and used to prevent any person working or passing from falling; and

(*c*) in the above cases, prominent warning notices must be affixed to the place where the material is located.

[*Reg 7(2)*].

(For the possible effect of such notices, see OCCUPIERS' LIABILITY.)

Falling objects

W9020   With relation to this hazard the regulations require:

(*a*) that in order to prevent danger to any person, suitable and sufficient steps must be taken to prevent, so far as is reasonably practicable, the fall of any material or object (e.g. the provision of working platforms or guard-rails etc.) [*Reg 8(1)*];

(*b*) where compliance is not reasonably practicable, suitable and sufficient steps must be taken to prevent any person being struck by any falling material or object likely to cause injury (e.g. the provision of a covered traffic route or roadway) [*Reg 8(3)*];

(c)   that no material or object must be thrown or tipped from a height, where it is likely to cause injury [*Reg 8(4)*]; and

(d)   that materials or equipment must be so stored as to prevent danger to any person from:

   (i)   collapse,

   (ii)   overturning, or

   (iii)   unintentional movement of such materials and equipment

   [*Reg 8(5)*].

Inspection of working platforms etc.

W9021

Working platforms and personal suspension equipment must be inspected by a competent person:

(a)   before being taken into use for the first time;

(b)   after any substantial addition, dismantling or other alteration;

(c)   after any event likely to have affected its strength or stability; and

(d)   at regular intervals not exceeding seven days.

[*Reg 29(1), Sch 7*].

Also, the employer or person who controls the way that construction work is done by anyone using a scaffold must ensure that it is stable and complies with the safeguards required by the Regulations before it is used by such persons for the first time. [*Reg 29(2)*].

Where a person may fall more than two metres, the competent person must make a report within the working period in which the inspection is completed. The report must contain the following:

—   the name and address of the person for whom the inspection was carried out;

—   the location of the place of work inspected;

—   a description of what was inspected;

—   date and time of the inspection;

—   details of anything that could cause risk;

—   details of any consequent action;

—   details of further action considered necessary;

—   name and position of the person making the report.

   [*Reg 30(1), (5), Sch 8*].

The report must be provided within 24 hours to the person for whom it was prepared. It must be kept on site until completion and for a further three months at the office of the person for whom it was prepared; in addition, it must be available to an inspector at all reasonable times and copies or extracts must be sent to an inspector if required. [*Reg 30(2)–(4)*].

No report is required on a mobile tower scaffold unless it has remained in the same place for seven days or more [*Reg 30(6)(a)*] and only report of an addition, dismantling or alteration (see (b) above) is required in any period of 24 hours. [*Reg 30(6)(b)*].

Practical guidelines

W9022   Construction or extensive maintenance work will probably entail risks both to those carrying it out and to the ordinary workers. These risks must be assessed, any existing precautions reviewed and the appropriate control measures taken. [*Management of Health and Safety at Work Regulations 1992, Reg 3*]. Where work must be done at heights, suitable access equipment or other safeguards must be provided and attention paid to the following:

(*a*)   Who is in control and what is the amount of co-ordination necessary, i.e. have the responsibilities of the occupier, employer and contractor been clearly defined?

(*b*)   What level of supervision and training is required with regard to the type of hazard and level of risk? (including selection of the appropriate method, and the use of approved equipment).

(*c*)   What other considerations are necessary, e.g. is there any danger to works employees from the contractors' operations, or vice-versa?

Many of these matters may seem obvious, but lives have been lost because the contractor or maintenance worker did not appreciate the fragile nature of a roof or the fact that it had been weakened owing to the nature of the process. These considerations point to the need for careful preparation and planning of such work to ensure that there is proper co-ordination and co-operation [*Management of Health and Safety at Work Regulations 1992, Reg 9*]. The contractor must be aware of any risks from the operations on the premises that might affect his workforce and of the precautions that the occupier is taking to control them. Furthermore, the occupier must ensure that comprehensible information about this has been passed on to the construction workers. [*Reg 10(1), (3)*]. The contractor must be provided with the names of the relevant persons who have been appointed to ensure evacuation in an emergency, while the occupier must take all reasonable steps to ensure that the contractor's employees themselves know who is to implement their own evacuation. [*Reg 10(4)*].

Where the *Construction (Design and Management) Regulations 1994* apply, the occupier (as client) must give the planning supervisor information about the premises. This information should be taken into account by the designers in the avoidance or reduction of risk and in the subsequent preparation of the health and safety plan. It is important to note that this information must include anything that the client could find out by making reasonable enquiries. For instance, the obvious risks to construction workers of falling should not obscure the possible danger that work at heights may disturb any asbestos that might be there – it should not be forgotten that asbestos is a greater cause of death in the construction trades than falling.

Since the inception of the *Management of Health and Safety at Work Regulations 1992* and *Construction (Design and Management) Regulations 1994*, larger firms should have well-established systems to deal with these matters, including the appointment of competent principal and other contractors. Smaller firms, or those that do not regularly commission construction work, while they are entitled to the advice of the planning supervisor where the *Construction (Design and Management) Regulations 1994* apply, may care to consider the following as appropriate when selecting contractors or in subsequent dealings with them:

(*a*)   the time for the tendering contractor to respond to the initial (pre-tender) stage of the health and safety plan;

(*b*)   the time for the contractor's own investigation of health and safety matters (e.g. a survey) where the Regulations do not apply;

(*c*)   the response to the significant risks – knowledge of precautions; possession of advisory booklets etc; any safety training of managers and supervisors; signs that the impact of risks arising from the operations has been appreciated;

(*d*)   how the contractor checks his health and safety performance;

(*e*)   how staff (including casuals) engaged for this job are or will be trained;

(*f*)   the protective clothing and equipment that will be provided (see PERSONAL PROTECTIVE EQUIPMENT);

(*g*)   the resources to be devoted to health and safety management (ask to see the person who will actually do the managing);

(*h*)   the arrangements for necessary liaison throughout the job (not forgetting the contractor's arrangements for delivering file information to the planning supervisor);

(*j*)   potential risks associated with adverse weather conditions, such as a sudden downpour, dense fog, snow lying on a roof or high winds; in particular, the responsibility for calling operators off a roof or high-level position given adverse weather conditions;

(*k*)   the provision of safety harnesses and belts, including the necessary anchorage points for them, or safety nets in certain situations (see W9031 below).

In addition the occupier/employer should ensure that his maintenance supervisor or clerk of works, etc. has access to the information contained in the health and safety at work guidance/advisory booklets, such as HSG 33 '*Health and safety in roofwork*' (1998), HSG 150 '*Health and safety in construction*' (1996) and L 54 '*Managing construction for health and safety*' (1995, Approved Code of Practice on the *Construction (Design and Management) Regulations 1994*), all available from HSE Books. He may also provide simple checklists to cover his own operations.

Windows and window cleaning – all workplaces

W9023   Window cleaning hazards occur principally in high-rise properties such as office blocks and residential tower blocks. These contain vast areas of glass which should be maintained in a clean state on both inner and outer surfaces. Cleaning the interior surfaces generally presents no difficulties, though accidents have arisen from the unsafe practice of window cleaners reaching up to clean windows from step ladders which have not been securely placed on highly-polished office floors and, in consequence, falling through the glass windows and injuring themselves. Moreover, if windows can be cleaned from inside, company safety rules and procedures should prevent employees going out onto sills in cases where a window/windows, if in proper working order, can be cleaned from inside. Failure to operate this rule can involve the employer in both criminal and civil liability. Equally important, if not more so, the customer or client must ensure that his windows are in proper working order and regularly inspected and maintained, if they are capable of being cleaned from inside (*King v Smith [1995] ICR 339* (see W9034 below)).

It is the cleaning of outer surfaces that can present serious hazards if proper precautions are not taken, and this part of the section is concerned with the duties of workplace occupiers in relation to windows and window-cleaning on their premises (see W9031 below); in addition, liability of employers at common law in relation to window cleaning personnel is also covered (see W9034 below), and methods of protection for window cleaners as well as methods of cleaning (see W9036–W9042 below).

See BS 8213: Part 1: '*Code of practice for safety in use and during cleaning of windows and doors (including guidance on cleaning materials and methods*' (1991).

Statutory requirements relevant to windows in all workplaces (except construction sites) – the Workplace (Health, Safety and Welfare) Regulations 1992 (SI 1992 No 3004)

Composition of windows

W9024   Every window (and every transparent or translucent surface in a door or gate) where necessary for reasons of health or safety must be:

   (*a*)   (i)   of safety material (e.g. polycarbonates, glass blocks, glass which breaks safely (laminated glass) or ordinary annealed glass meeting certain minimal criteria),

           (ii)   protected against breakage of transparent or translucent material (e.g. by a screen or barrier); and

   (*b*)   appropriately (and conspicuously) marked so as to make it apparent (e.g. with coloured lines or patterns).

[*Workplace (Health, Safety and Welfare) Regulations 1992, Reg 14*].

The HSC in October 1996 approved a change to its publication '*Workplace health, safety and welfare*', the Approved Code of Practice (ACoP) which supports the *Workplace (Health, Safety and Welfare) Regulations 1992 (SI 1992 No 3004)*. The change became necessary as the HSC acknowledged that there was confusion in the business world on what the law says about glazing in existing workplaces that became subject to the *Workplace Regulations* on 1 January 1996. The change relates to workplace glazing and now reads:

'In assessing whether it is necessary, for reasons of health and safety, for transparent or translucent surfaces in doors, gates, walls and partitions to be of a safety material or be adequately protected against breakage, particular attention should be paid to the following cases:

   (*a*)   in doors and gates, and door and gate side panels, where any part of the transparent or translucent surface is at shoulder height or below;

   (*b*)   in windows, walls and partitions, where any part of the transparent or translucent surface is at waist level or below, except in glasshouses where people there will be likely to be aware of the presence of glazing and avoid contact.

This paragraph does not apply to narrow panes up to 250mm wide measured between glazing beads.'

Position and use of windows

W9025   No window, skylight or ventilator, capable of being opened, must be likely to be:

   (*a*)   opened,

   (*b*)   closed,

   (*c*)   adjusted, or

(*d*)   in a position when open,

so as to expose the operator to risk of injury. [*Workplace (Health, Safety and Welfare) Regulations 1992, Reg 15*].

In other words, it must be possible to reach openable windows safely; and window poles or a stable platform should be kept ready nearby. Window controls should be so positioned that people are not likely to fall out of or through the window. And where there is a danger of falling from a height, devices should prevent the window opening too far. In order to prevent people colliding with them, the bottom edge of opening windows should generally be 800 mm above floor level (unless there is a barrier to stop or cushion falls). Staircase windows should have controls accessible from a safe foothold, and window controls beyond normal reach should be gear-operated or accessible by pole. Manually operated window controls should not be higher than 2 metres above floor level.

Cleaning windows

W9026   All windows and skylights in workplaces must be designed and constructed to allow safe cleaning. [*Workplace (Health, Safety and Welfare) Regulations 1992, Reg 16(1)*]. If they cannot be cleaned from the ground (or similar surface), the building should be fitted with suitable safety devices to be able to comply with the general safety requirement (see above). [*Workplace (Health, Safety and Welfare) Regulations 1992, Reg 16(2)*].

Civil liability in connection with fall-preventive regulations

W9027   Because regulations give rise to civil liability when breached, even if silent (which these are), if breach leads to injury or damage, an action for breach of statutory duty would lie.

Window cleaners as employees or self-employed contractors

W9028   Where window cleaners are employees of a contract window cleaning company, the company as employer owes a duty to its employees, under *HSWA s 2(1)* and *(2)*, to provide a safe method of work, and instruction and training in job safety, e.g. provision of information as to how to tackle the job and the use of safety harnesses etc. All workplaces, buildings, windows and skylights should be fitted with suitable devices to allow the window or skylight to be cleaned safely, to comply with *Reg 16* of the *Workplace (Health, Safety and Welfare) Regulations 1992* (see W9026 above).

Alternatively, window cleaners may be self-employed. In such cases they themselves commit an offence if they fail to provide themselves with adequate protection, e.g. safety harnesses, because of the requirement of *HSWA s 3(2)*.

Who provides protection to window cleaners on high-rise properties?

W9029   Where multi-storey properties are concerned, the duty of protection may fall upon one of three parties (or, at least, there may be division of responsibility between them):

(*a*)   the contract window cleaning firm or the self-employed window cleaner;

(*b*)   the building owner;

(*c*)   the building occupier or business operator (i.e. the building occupier who is not the owner of the building).

Contract window cleaning firms and self-employed window cleaners

W9030   Both the contract window cleaning firm and the self-employed window cleaner have a statutory duty to provide protection (under *HSWA ss 2(1), (2), 3(2)*) and the employer/occupier, under *Regs 15* and *16* of the *Workplace (Health, Safety and Welfare) Regulations 1992* (see W9025, W9026 above). This applies to contract cleaning companies (not just of windows) in respect of equipment left on the occupier's premises and used by the occupier's employees, even though the contract cleaning company is not actually working (*R v Mara [1987] 1 WLR 87* where one of the occupier's employees was electrocuted when using polisher/scrubber, which had a defective cable, to clean loading bay on a Saturday afternoon, when cleaning company did not operate its undertaking. It was held that the director of the cleaning company was in breach of *HSWA s 3(1)*). In addition, if an accident arose from the work, the window cleaning company could, as employer, be liable at common law, if it failed to take reasonable care and exercise control. There is no action for damages for breach of statutory duty under *HSWA* (see EMPLOYERS' DUTIES TO THEIR EMPLOYEES). In this connection, any employer, when prosecuted under *HSWA* or sued at common law would have to show that he had clearly instructed employees not to clean windows where no proper safety precautions had been taken, in order to avoid liability. Also, window cleaning companies would have to satisfy themselves, before instructing employees to clean windows, as to what safety precautions (if any) were provided, and that, if necessary, employees were told to test for defective sashes (see further *King v Smith* at W9034 below).

Division of responsibility between window cleaning firm or self-employed window cleaner and building owner or occupier (i.e. employer)

W9031   Although a window cleaner, whether an employee or self-employed, would be expected to have his own safety harness, it would be up to the contractor to provide fixing points for harness attachment. The responsibility for provision of harness anchorage points (e.g. safe rings, i.e. eyebolts) will be with either the building owner or building occupier (business operator) whose windows are being cleaned. Two situations are possible here:

(*a*)   the building occupier is the owner of the building; or

(*b*)   the building occupier (as is usual) is not the owner of the building.

Where the building occupier is the building owner

W9032   Here, the window cleaning contract is placed by the building occupier/owner and the latter, having control of the building, is therefore responsible under *HSWA s 3(1)*, *Regs 15* and *16* of the *Workplace (Health, Safety and Welfare) Regulations 1992*, and at common law (and under the contract) to protect window cleaning personnel on his premises. Courts may also be prepared to imply terms into such contracts that such premises be reasonably safe to work on.

This position (that is, where the building owner and the building occupier are the same person) is not, however, the norm. On the contrary, the normal position is that the building owner and business operator are separate persons or companies.

Where the building occupier (that is, the employer) is not the building owner

W9033   Given that the employee or self-employed window cleaner must provide his own safety harness (see W9031 above), the responsibility of providing a safe ring for harness attachment lies with the building owner or occupier. More precisely, where the building owner employs a contract window cleaning firm, then it is up to the building owner (*inter alia*, as an implied contractual term) to make safety anchorage provision. He cannot escape from this contractual obligation owing to the strictures of the *Unfair Contract Terms Act 1977* (see OCCUPIERS' LIABILITY). He would also be required to do so by virtue of *HSWA s 3(1)* – the duty towards persons working on premises who are not one's employees (see EMPLOYERS' DUTIES TO THEIR EMPLOYEES).

This is the exception, not the norm. Generally, window cleaning contracts are placed by building occupiers (business operators), and so in the great majority of cases it is the *building occupier* who is responsible under *HSWA s 3(1)* and under the *Workplace (Health, Safety and Welfare) Regulations 1992*, under the express or implied terms of a contract, and/or at common law (should an accident occur) for ensuring the safety of window cleaning personnel. Thus, the building occupier would have to provide a safety ring for harness attachment. A problem could arise here if the building owner refused permission for such attachment – resort to legal action would be, it is thought, the only ultimate solution. And occupiers should be under no illusion that failure to provide safety anchorage points can (and will, in all probability) result in the imposition of heavy fines! (By way of consolation, however, the cost of making available certain types of protection to window cleaners may often be less than the penalty incurred for failing to provide it.)

Common law liability to window cleaners

W9034   At common law (and under *HSWA s 2(2)*), an employer must provide and maintain a safe system of work. This extends to provision of safe appliances, tools etc. and giving information/training on how to carry out tasks safely (see EMPLOYERS' DUTIES TO THEIR EMPLOYEES). Nevertheless, there is a division of responsibility between employer and occupier of premises where a window cleaner is working. The former, the employer, must see that the employee is provided with a safe method of work; but this did not extend to defects in the premises (e.g. window sills) of the occupier causing injury to employees (*General Cleaning Contractors Ltd v Christmas [1952] 2 AER 1110* where an experienced employee window cleaner was injured whilst cleaning windows at a club. There were no fittings on the building to which safety belts could have been attached. A defective sash dropped onto the employee's hand, causing him to lose his handhold and fall. It was held that the employer was liable; he should have provided wedges to prevent sashes from falling and also instructed employees to test for dangerous sashes). Modern conventional wisdom suggests, however, that an employer does not provide a safe system of work if a window cleaner has to clean windows from an outside window sill, which are capable of being cleaned from inside if they are in proper working order. It is incumbent on the customer-occupier to ensure that such windows are in a good state of maintenance and proper working order. (In the case of *King v Smith [1995] ICR 339*, a window cleaner was injured when he fell from a sill on a local authority building. The court held both employer and customer liable, the former 70%, the latter 30%.)

Much of the earlier common law liability will, in all probability, be replaced in due course by case law arising in connection with breach of duty under the *Workplace (Health, Safety and Welfare) Regulations 1992*, where such duties are strict.

In practice it is important that owners and occupiers of buildings assure themselves that the proposed method of cleaning the windows by the cleaning contractor is safe and in compliance with *Reg 16*, and the owners/occupiers should verify that the agreed system of work is being followed by the contractor's employees, or by a self-employed contractor, as the case may be.

Accidents to window cleaners – typical causes

W9035
(a) The most common fatal accident is that of a cleaner falling from an external window sill, ledge, or similar part of a building, due to loss of balance as the result of a slip, or the breakage of part of a sill, or the failure of a pull handle or part of a building being used as a handhold.

(b) Other fatalities have been due to falls through fragile roofing where cleaners have relied upon the roof for support when cleaning or glazing windows, or gaining access for such work, and falls from suspended scaffolds or boatswain's chairs due to failure of the equipment.

(c) Falls from ladders, which account for a substantial proportion of injuries, are occasionally fatal; they include falls due to the unexpected movement of a ladder such as the top sliding sideways or the foot slipping outwards, failure of part of the ladder, and falls when stepping on or off it.

Methods of protection for window cleaners

W9036
(a) If the building was designed with totally self-pivoting windows, this is probably the ideal situation in terms of safeguarding the window cleaner. Note the qualified duty in this regard on the building designer in the *Construction (Design and Management) Regulations 1994, Reg 13(2)(a)*. However, a wide variety of window designs are used in buildings – sliding sashes, louvred sashes, hinged casements and fixed lights. All require a slightly different technique for cleaning.

(b) Ordinary ladders are not suitable (and should not be used) for multi-storey properties of more than two storeys.

(c) Hydraulic platforms are effective but work can only safely proceed at a relatively slow rate; moreover, their maximum reach is sometimes limited, and they cause nuisance to passers-by.

(d) Gondola cages are used on high-rise buildings with good results, but are of little use for low and medium-rise blocks. They can also be dangerous to window cleaning personnel, as they are inclined to sway about in high winds. Moreover, this method of window cleaning is expensive.

Probably the most practical and economical method of complying with legal requirements for the safety of window cleaning personnel is provision of safe ring/harness combinations, but note the presumption in favour of collective over individual precautions that is contained in para 27 of the Approved Code of Practice to the *Management of Health and Safety at Work Regulations 1992, Reg 3*, and the similar duty imposed upon building designers by the *Construction (Design and Management) Regulations 1994, Reg 13(2)(a)(iii)*. These bolts can be installed rapidly, without damaging the building structurally, and without impairing its aesthetic appearance.

Safety rings should be installed by a specialist company operating in the field. In this way a window cleaner can clip his harness on to the ring and step on to the window ledge and clean the window safely. After proper installation, anchorage points should be professionally examined from time to time to ensure that they remain firm and safe.

Another (relatively inexpensive) device for use in cleaning outer surfaces on high-rise office blocks and industrial multi-storey properties is the new mobile safety anchor. The cost is often shared between the contract window cleaning company (or self-employed window cleaner) and the building owner or occupier.

Suspended scaffolds are commonly used for window cleaning in high-rise buildings. Guidance on the design, construction and use of suspended scaffolds is given in:

(i)   BS 6037: 1990 *'Code of practice for permanently installed suspended access equipment'*; and

(ii)   BS 5974: 1990 *'Code of practice for temporarily installed suspended scaffolds and access equipment'*.

Whether a suspended scaffold is used, either permanently or temporarily installed, it is essential to ensure that:

—   safe means of access to and egress from the cradle are provided;

—   properly planned inspection and maintenance procedures for each installation are carried out;

—   there are instructions that work shall be carried out only from the cradle; and

—   operatives are properly trained in the use of the cradle.

Where power-driven equipment is used, operatives should be familiar with:

—   relevant instructions from the manufacturer or supplier;

—   any limitations on use, for example, due to wind conditions or length of suspension rope;

—   the correct operation of the controls, particularly those affecting the raising or lowering of the cradle;

—   the safety devices fitted to the equipment; and

—   the procedure if the equipment does not work properly.

Precautions against the failure of a cradle having a single suspension rope at each end are described in BS 6037, for example, the provision at each suspension point of a second rope (safety rope) and an automatic device to support the platform. In some cases, protection against suspension rope failure at the cradle end can be obtained by fitting a manually operated clamping device.

Travelling ladders are permanently installed in some buildings. In other cases a ladder can be suspended from a specially designed frame on the roof. In such cases, the cleaner should wear a safety harness or belt, attached to an automatic fall arresting device on the side of the ladder, and have a safe place at which he can step on or off the ladder.

Cleaning methods

W9037   Window glass can normally be cleaned satisfactorily using plain water, liberally applied, followed by leather off and polishing with a scrim. The use of squeegees is on the increase and, although they cannot safely be used by a person standing on a window sill, they can be safely operated from the ground. Very dirty glazing in factories, foundries or railway premises may need treatment with ammonia or strong soda solution; and hydrofluoric acid in diluted solution may be necessary when cleaning skylights or roof glazing which has remained uncleaned for a long time. Here the working area should be adequately sheeted to protect passers-by, and, in the case of roof glazing, the interior of the building should be protected against penetrating drops. Stringent personal precautions are necessary when handling acids (e.g. eye shields, rubber gloves, boots (see further PERSONAL PROTECTIVE EQUIPMENT), which should only be used as a last resort) and such work should only be carried out by specialist firms. Hydrofluoric acid should never be used on vertical glazing.

Frequency of cleaning

W9038 The recommended frequencies of external and internal cleaning, as dictated by current good practice, are as follows:

Shops	weekly
Banks	twice a month
Offices/hotels	monthly
Hospitals	monthly
Factories – light industry	monthly
Heavy industry	every two months
Schools	every two months

Access for cleaning

W9039 There are three ways in which windows can be cleaned, affecting access:

(*a*) external cleaning (with access exclusively from the outside);

(*b*) internal cleaning;

(*c*) a mixed system, whereby windows accessible from the inside are cleaned internally, and the rest are cleaned externally, access being through the opening lights of the facade.

Moreover, in factories and other industrial concerns windows are, not infrequently, obstructed by machines, reflecting in-plant lay-out at initial design – a matter for safety officers and safety representatives when carrying out safety audits (see JOINT CONSULTATION – SAFETY REPRESENTATIVES AND SAFETY COMMITTEES).

Cleaning from the outside

W9040 Assuming windows cannot be cleaned from inside the workplace or building, as a matter of design, there should be safe external access in the form of permanent walkways, with guard-rails or other protective devices to prevent cleaners (and other users) from falling down. Such walkways should be at least 400 mm wide and guard-rails at least 900 mm above the walkway, with a knee rail. Safety of window cleaners is best guaranteed by installation of totally self-pivoting windows (see W9036 above). However, a wide variety of window designs is currently in use in buildings – sliding sashes, louvred sashes, fixed lights and hinged casements, all requiring different cleaning techniques.

(a) Cleaning from ladders

Portable ladders, aluminium or timber, should rest on a secure base and reasonably practicable precautions, to avoid sliding outwards at the base and sideways at the top, should be taken to:

(i)   secure fixing at the top to preclude lateral or outward movement, e.g. by fastening to an eyebolt/ringbolt;

(ii)   fasten rung to eyebolt/ringbolt or other anchorage point (see further W9036 above) at a height of 2 metres;

(iii) failing this, a person should be stationed at the base in order to steady the ladder or an approved base anchoring device should be used.

The '1 out 4 up' rule (for ladders) suggests that ladders are safest when placed at an angle of 75° to the horizontal; lesser angles indicate that the ladder is more likely to slide outwards at the base. Moreover, window cleaners (and other users) should avoid:

—   overreaching (as this can unbalance the ladder);

—   proximity with moving objects either above or below (e.g. overhead travelling crane or vehicles operating in the workplace or delivering to the workplace);

—   positioning near to vats or tanks containing dangerous fluids/substances or near to unguarded machinery or exposed electrical equipment. (As for *in situ* travelling ladders, see W9036 above.)

BS EN 131-1: 1993 covers, in respect of ladders, the general design characteristics which are of importance for safety, handling and manufacture. See also the HSE's free publication CIS 49: '*General access scaffolds and ladders*' (1997).

(b) Safety harnesses

In the absence of other, more satisfactory means of cleaning windows, e.g. suspended scaffolds, hydraulic platforms etc., the other reasonably practicable alternative is a safety harness. However, this has the shortcoming that, if a window cleaner falls, he is still likely to be injured. For this reason, harnesses and safety belts must be up to 'free fall' distance (that is, the distance preceding arrest of fall) of, at least,

(i)   2 metres – safety harness, or

(ii)   0.6 metres – safety belt.

Because some walls may not be strong enough or otherwise suitable, inspection by a competent person should always precede selection of permanent fixed anchorage points. Permanent fixed anchorages should comply with BS EN 795: 1997 '*Protection against falls from a height. Anchor devices. Requirements and testing*' (to be read in conjunction with BS 7883: 1997 '*Code of practice for application and use of anchor devices conforming to BS EN 795*') and be periodically inspected and tested for exposure to elements. Failing this, temporary anchorage or even mobile anchorage, given the same built-in safeguards, may suffice (see W9036 above).

Specific requirements, test methods, instructions for use etc. relating to personal protective equipment against falls from a height can be found in the following standards, all published in 1993: BS EN 354 (lanyards), BS EN 358 (work positioning systems), BS EN 361 (full body harnesses), and BS EN 363 (fall arrest systems). See also BS EN 813: 1997 (sit harnesses).

Cleaning from the inside

W9041   Outer surfaces by design should be able to be cleaned from inside the workplace without use of steps or stepladders. Also, size of aperture and weight of window is relevant. Different types of windows present different dangers; for example, in the case of reversible pivoted/projecting windows, a safety catch is necessary to maintain the window in a fully reversed position; in the case of louvres, there should be sufficient space for a cleaner's hand to pass between the blades, which should incorporate a positive hold-open position to avoid the danger of blowing shut (see BS 8213, Part 1 1991: *'Safety in use and during cleaning of windows'*).

Maximum safe reach to clean glass immediately beneath an open window is 610 mm downwards (that is, 2' 0″), 510 mm upwards (1' 8″) and 560 mm sideways (1'10″). Horizontally or vertically pivoted windows, reversible for cleaning purposes, are probably the best safety option (see W9036 above). Given that windows should be accessible without resort to a ladder, short-of-stature window cleaners should invariably make use of cleaning aids to reach further up glazing panels. Built-in furniture should never be placed near windows to obstruct access; nor should blinds or pelmets inhibit the operation of windows and window controls.

Mixed system of cleaning

W9042   Where window cleaners clean windows externally without facilities for ladders or cradles, the building designer should appreciate that the cleaner's safety depends on good foothold and good handhold. The practice of cleaners having to balance, like trapeze artists, on narrow sills or transoms, is patently dangerous. Owing to the frequency of failure of apparently safe and adequate footholds and handholds, it is imperative that suitable and convenient safety bolts or fixings, to which the cleaner may fix his safety belt, should be provided. Where possible, the safety eyebolt should be fitted on the inside of the wall. Moreover, internal bolts are not weakened by the weather. Where safety eyebolts are fitted to the window frame, architects should pay particular regard at design stage to the fixing of the frame to the building structure, so as to ensure that fixings can withstand the extra load, imposed on the frame, in the event of the cleaner falling.

Where glazing areas are incorporated in roofs, provision should be made for cleaning both sides of the glass, and, where possible, walkways should be provided, both externally and internally. Internal walkways can also be designed to serve for maintenance of electric lighting installations. Where walkways are not feasible, access by permanent travelling ladders should be considered.

The *Construction (Design and Management) Regulations 1994* place specific responsibility upon designers to ensure that their designs enable maintenance to be carried out (including window cleaning) safely and without risks to health (see C8020 CONSTRUCTION AND BUILDING OPERATIONS). Practical advice for designers on this subject, and on cleaning buildings in general, will be found in CIRIA report 166, *CDM Regulations – work sector guidance for designers*, at section D6.

Working Time

Introduction

W10001   *The Working Time Regulations 1998* (the Regulations) came into force on 1 October 1998. This is the first time under English law that there are specific rules governing working hours, rest breaks and holiday entitlement for the majority of workers (as opposed to those in specialised industries). The Regulations will implement into national legislation the provisions of the Working Time Directive (93/104/EC) and the Young Workers Directive (94/33/EC). This chapter deals only with the Regulations as they govern adult workers, i.e. those aged 18 or over.

The Working Time Directive has led a fairly controversial life. It was adopted on 23 November 1993 as a health and safety measure under Article 118a of the Treaty of Rome, requiring only a qualified majority, rather than a unanimous vote. As such, the UK Government, which was opposed to the Directive, was unable to avoid its impact. The UK Government challenged the Directive on the basis that it was not truly a health and safety measure and should, in fact, have been introduced under Article 100 as a social measure which would have required a unanimous vote. This argument was lost when on 12 November 1996, the European Court of Justice upheld the status of the Directive as a health and safety measure. As a result, the UK Government was obliged to implement the Directive into national legislation by 23 November 1996. The former Conservative Government issued a consultation document with this in mind; however, there was then a delay due to the change of Government in May 1997. The current Labour Government published its consultative document and a set of draft Regulations in April 1998 and on 30 July the Regulations (*SI 1998 No 1833*) were laid before Parliament in their current form.

The stated purpose of the Working Time Directive, acknowledged by the European Court of Justice, is to lay down a minimum requirement for health and safety as regards the organisation of working time. This will, of course, be significant to the extent that the English courts and tribunals will interpret the Regulations in accordance with the Directive by adopting the 'purposive' approach, which is now accepted under English law.

The structure of the Regulations is to prescribe various limits and entitlements for workers and then to set out a sequence of exceptions and derogations from these provisions. The structure of this chapter will roughly follow that format.

Definitions

W10002   *Regulation 2* sets out a number of basic concepts (some more familiar than others), which recur consistently and which underpin the legislation. These are as follows.

Working time

W10003   Working time is defined, in relation to a worker, as:

    (a)   any period during which he is working, *at his employer's disposal* and carrying out his activity or duties;

(*b*)   any period which he is receiving relevant training; and

(*c*)   any *additional* period which is to be treated as working time for the purposes of the Regulations under a relevant agreement (see W10006 below).

As was highlighted by the Labour Government's consultative document, this definition raises numerous uncertainties; for example, in relation to workers who are 'on call' or who operate under flexible working arrangements. This is something which will have to be clarified by employment tribunals in due course. However, the DTI, in their Guidance to the Working Time Regulations, state that time when a worker is 'on call' but otherwise free to pursue their own activities would not be working time. Similarly if a worker was required to be at the place of work 'on call', but was sleeping though available to work if necessary, a worker would not be working and so the time spent asleep would not count as working time.

It should be noted that although the consultative document suggested that the definition of working time could be clarified in a relevant agreement between the parties, it is only any *additional* period which can be treated as working time by means of a relevant agreement. The relevant agreement cannot alter, in particular it cannot narrow, the absolute definition of working time.

Worker

W10004   A worker is any individual who has entered into or works under (or where the employment has ceased), worked under:

(*a*)   a contract of employment; or

(*b*)   any other contract, whether express or implied and (if express) whether oral or in writing, whereby the individual undertakes to do or perform personally any work or services for another party to the contract whose status is not by virtue of the contract that of a client or customer of any profession or business undertaking carried on by the individual.

This definition is wider than just employees and covers any individuals who are carrying out work for an employer, unless they are genuinely self employed, in that the work amounts to a business activity carried out on their own account (see also the reference to agency workers below).

Agency workers

W10005   *Regulation 36* makes specific provision in relation to agency workers who do not otherwise fall into the general definition of workers. This provides that where (i) any individual is employed to work for a principal under an arrangement made between an agent and that principal, and (ii) the individual is not a worker because of the absence of a contract between the individual and the agent or principal, then the Regulations will apply as if that individual were a worker employed by whichever of the agent or principal is responsible for paying or actually pays the worker in respect of the work. Again, individuals who are genuinely self-employed are excluded from this definition.

Collective, workforce and relevant agreements

W10006   These play a significant role in the Regulations as employers and employees can, by entering into such agreements (where the Regulations so allow), effectively supplement or derogate from the strict application of the Regulations. Employers and employees who need a certain amount of flexibility in their working arrangements may well find one or other of these agreements will facilitate compliance with the Regulations.

Collective agreement

W10007   This is an agreement with an independent trade union within the meaning of the *Trade Union and Labour Relations (Consolidation) Act 1992, s 178.*

Workforce agreement

W10008   This is a concept new to English law. It is an agreement between an employer and the duly elected representatives of its employees or, in the case of small employers (i.e. those with 20 or fewer employees), potentially the employees themselves. In order for a workforce agreement to be valid, it must comply with the conditions set out in *Schedule 1* to the Regulations, which provides that a workforce agreement must:

(*a*)   be in writing;

(*b*)   have effect for a specified period not exceeding five years;

(*c*)   apply either to

   (i)   all of the relevant members of the workforce, or

   (ii)   all of the relevant members of the workforce who belong to a particular group;

(*d*)   be signed by

   (i)   the representatives of the workforce or of the particular group of workers, or

   (ii)   where an employer employs 20 or fewer workers on the date on which the agreement is first made available for signature, either appropriate representatives or by a majority of the workers employed by him;

(*e*)   before the agreement was made available for signature, the employer must have provided all the workers to whom it was intended to apply with copies of the text of the agreement and such guidance as they might reasonably require in order to understand it fully.

'Relevant members of the workforce' are defined as all of the workers employed by a particular employer (excluding any worker whose terms and conditions of employment are provided for wholly or in part in a collective agreement). Therefore, as soon as a collective agreement is in force in respect of any worker, the provisions of any workforce agreement in respect of that worker would cease to apply.

Paragraph 3 of Schedule 1 to the Regulations sets out the requirements relating to the election of workforce representatives. These are as follows:

(*a*)   the number of representatives to be elected shall be determined by the employer;

(*b*)   candidates for election as representatives for the workforce must be relevant members of the workforce, and the candidates for election as representatives of a particular group must be members of that group;

(*c*)   no worker who is eligible to be a candidate can be unreasonably excluded from standing for election;

(*d*)   all the relevant members of the workforce must be entitled to vote for representatives of the workforce and all the members of a particular group must be entitled to vote for representatives of that group;

(*e*)   the workers must be entitled to vote for as many candidates as there are representatives to be elected;

(*f*)   the election must be conducted so as to secure that (i) so far as is reasonably practicable those voting do so in secret, and (ii) the votes given at the election are fairly and accurately counted.

Relevant agreement

W10009   This is an 'umbrella provision' and means a workforce agreement which applies to a worker, any provision of a collective agreement which forms part of a contract between a worker and his employer, or any other agreement in writing which is legally enforceable as between the worker and his employer. A relevant agreement could, of course, include the written terms of a contract of employment. It would only include the provisions of staff handbooks, policies etc. where it could be shown that these were 'legally enforceable' as between the parties.

Maximum weekly working time

48-hour working week

W10010   It is, of course, the 48-hour working week which has caused so much controversy. *Regulation 4* provides that an employer shall take all reasonable steps, in keeping with the need to protect the health and safety of workers, to ensure that a worker's *average* working time (including overtime) shall not exceed 48 hours for each 7-day period.

Regulation 4(6) provides a specific formula for calculating a worker's average working time over a reference period, which the Regulations have determined as 17 weeks (for exceptions, see below). This is as follows:

$$\frac{a + b}{c}$$

where

a   is the total number of hours worked during the reference period;

b   is the total number of hours worked during the period which

   (i)   begins immediately after the reference period, and

   (ii)   consists of the number of working days equivalent to the number of 'excluded days' during the reference period; and

c   is the number of weeks in the reference period.

'Excluded days' are days comprised of annual leave, sick leave or maternity leave and any period in respect of which an individual has opted out of the 48-hour limit (see below).

In *Barber v RJB Mining (UK) Ltd [1999] IRLR 308*, the plaintiffs were pit deputies who had a contractual working week of 42 hours, but usually had to work more than 48 hours per week. They sought a declaration of their rights under *Reg 4(1) of the Working Time Regulations 1998, claiming that it imposes a mandatory, contractual obligation on an employer not to require an employee to work more than an average of 48 hours per week. The argument put forward by their employer was that breach of Reg 4(1) conferred no justiciable right, and that Reg 4(1) must be read with, and subject to, Reg 4(2), which provides that an employer must take all reasonable steps to comply with the 48-hour limit. The High Court allowed the plaintiffs' application and granted them a declaration that they need not work until such time as their average hours fell to 48 hours.*

Reference period

W10011   The crucial issue in calculating the average number of hours worked is the question of when the reference period starts. The reference period is any period of 17 weeks in the course of a worker's employment, unless a relevant agreement provides for the application of successive 17-week periods (*Reg 4(3)*). This means that unless the parties specify that the reference period is a defined period of 17 weeks, followed by a successive period of 17 weeks, then the reference period will become a 'rolling' 17-week period. This could be significant where there is a marked variation in the hours that an individual works in a particular period, from week to week. In such a situation an employer would be recommended to include provision in a relevant agreement for successive 17-week reference periods to ensure that it can comply with the maximum weekly working requirements. Such a provision may be desirable in any event, for ease of administration.

For the first 17 weeks of employment, the average is calculated by reference to the number of weeks actually worked (*Reg 4(4)*).

Exceptions and derogations to Regulation 4

W10012   There are various exceptions to the maximum working week.

(*a*)   *Regulation 5* provides that an individual can agree with his employer to opt out of the 48-hour week (see W10013 below).

(*b*)   The 48 hour limit does not apply at all in the case of certain workers whose working time is unmeasured (*Reg 20* – see W10028 below).

(c)   In special cases (as described in *Reg 21* – see W10029 below), the 17-week reference period over which the 48 hours are averaged will be automatically extended to 26 weeks (*Reg 4(5)*).

(*d*)   A collective or workforce agreement can extend the 17-week reference period to a period not exceeding 52 weeks, if there are objective or technical reasons concerning the organisation of work (*Reg 23*).

Agreement to exclude 48-hour working week

W10013   The 48-hour limit on weekly working time will not apply where a worker agrees with his employer in writing that the maximum 48-hour working week should not apply in the individual's case, provided that certain requirements are satisfied. These are:

(*a*)   the agreement must be in writing;

(*b*)   the agreement may specify its duration or be of an indefinite length – however, it is always open to the worker to terminate the agreement by giving notice, which will be the length specified in the agreement (subject to a maximum of three months), or, if not specified, seven days;

(c)   the employer must maintain up-to-date records which—

    (i)   identify each of the workers who has agreed to waive the 48-hour limit,

    (ii)   set out any terms on which the worker has agreed that the limit does not apply,

    (iii) specify the number of hours worked by the worker during each reference period since the agreement came into effect, extending back at least two years;

(d)   permit any inspector appointed by the Health and Safety Executive (or any other authority responsible for enforcement of the Regulations) to inspect the records on request; and

(e)   provide any such inspector with any further information he may request regarding any case in which a worker has agreed that the 48-hour limit will not apply to him.

This Regulation was one of the more controversial adopted by the Government. Although it is specifically permitted by the Directive, arguably it runs a 'coach and horses' through the spirit of the Regulations. However, a worker cannot be forced to sign such an agreement. Moreover, the Regulations provide protection where an employee has suffered any detriment on the grounds that he has refused to waive any benefit conferred on him/her by the Regulations (*Employment Rights Act 1996, s 45A(1)(b)*, inserted by *Reg 31(1)(b)* – see W10036 below). Furthermore, a worker will always have the right to terminate the agreement and work no more than 48 hours on giving, at most, three months' notice.

On a practical note, the agreement by a worker to exclude the 48-hour working week must be a written agreement between the employer and the individual worker. It cannot take the form of or be incorporated in a collective or workforce agreement. However, it could, of course, be part of the contract of employment, although it would be advisable for an employer to clearly delineate the agreement to work more than 48 hours from the rest of the contract of employment.

Rest periods and breaks

Daily rest period

W10014   Adult workers are entitled to an uninterrupted rest period of not less than 11 consecutive hours in each 24-hour period (*Reg 10*).

Exceptions and derogations

W10015   The provisions regarding daily rest periods do not apply where a worker's working time is unmeasured (*Reg 20*).

Derogations from the rule may be made with regard to shift work (*Reg 22*), or by means of collective or workforce agreements (*Reg 23*) or where there are special categories of workers (*Re, 21*). However, in all cases (except for workers with unmeasured working time under *Reg 20* – see W10028 *et seq.* below) compensatory rest must be provided (*Reg 24*).

Weekly rest period

W10016   Adult workers are entitled to an uninterrupted rest period of not less than 24 hours in each seven-day period (*Reg 11*). However, if his employer so determines, an adult worker will be entitled to either two uninterrupted rest periods (each of not less than 24 hours) in each 14-day period or one uninterrupted rest period of not less than 48 hours in each 14-day period.

The entitlement to weekly rest is in addition to the 11-hour daily rest entitlement which must be provided by virtue of *Regulation 10*, except where objective or technical reasons concerning the organisation of work would justify incorporating all or part of that daily rest into the weekly rest period.

For the purposes of calculating the entitlement, the 7 or 14-day period will start immediately after midnight between Sunday and Monday, unless a relevant agreement provides otherwise. The Regulations do not require Sunday to be included in the minimum weekly rest period.

Derogations from the entitlement to weekly rest periods are the same as those for daily rest.

Rest breaks

W10017   By virtue of *Regulation 12*, adult workers are entitled to a rest break where their daily working time is more than six hours. Details of this rest break, including duration and the terms on which it is granted, can be regulated by a collective or workforce agreement. If no such agreement is in place, the rest break will be for an uninterrupted period of not less than 20 minutes and the worker will be entitled to spend that break away from his work station, if he has one.

Derogations from the entitlement to rest breaks include cases specified in *Regulation 21* (see above), where working time is unmeasured and cannot be predetermined (*Reg 20*), and also by means of a collective or workforce agreement (*Reg 23*). As before, compensatory rest must be provided other than where *Regulation 20* applies (*Reg 24*).

Monotonous work

W10018   *Regulation 8* provides that where the pattern according to which an employer organises work is such as to put the health and safety of a worker employed by him at risk in particular, because the work is monotonous or the work rate is predetermined, the employer shall ensure that the employee is given adequate rest breaks. This Regulation is phrased in virtually identical terms to Article 13 of the Working Time Directive and unfortunately, its incorporation into the Regulations has not clarified its meaning in any way!

It is not clear how rest breaks in *Regulation 8* would differ from those under *Regulation 12*. It may be that in the case of monotonous work, an employer might have to consider giving employees shorter breaks more frequently as opposed to one longer continuous break. This was the suggestion in the Government's consultative document.

No derogations from these provisions apply except in the case of domestic workers.

Night work

Definitions

W10019   Before considering the detailed provisions in relation to night work contained in *Regulation 6*, an understanding of the definitions of 'night time' and 'night worker' contained in *Regulation 2*, is necessary. These are as follows.

Night time in relation to a worker means a period:

(*a*)   the duration of which is not less than seven hours; and

(*b*)   which includes the period between midnight and 5 a.m.,

which is determined for the purposes of the Regulations by a relevant agreement or, in the absence of such an agreement, the period between 11 p.m. and 6 a.m.

Night worker means a worker –

(i)   who *as a normal course* works at least three hours of his daily working time during night time (for the purpose of this definition, a person works hours 'as a normal course' if he works such hours on a majority of days on which he works – a person who performs night work as part of a rotating shift pattern may also be covered); or

(ii)   who is likely during night time to work at least such proportion of his annual working time as may be specified for the purposes of the Regulations in a collective or workforce agreement.

A case heard by the Northern Ireland High Court, *R v Attorney-General for Northern Ireland, ex parte Burns [1999] IRLR 315* considered, *inter alia*, the definition of 'night worker' in the EC Working Time Directive: 'any worker who, during night time, works at least three hours of his daily working time as a normal course' – 'night time' is defined as 'any period of not less than seven hours . . . which must include . . . the period between midnight and 5 am'. From January 1993 until September 1995, Miss Burns, a production operative, had worked a night shift between 9.00 pm and 7.00 am one week in every three. From September 1995 she worked on cycles of 15 shifts which were eight hours long. During five of these shifts, at least three hours of her working time fell between 11.00 pm and 6.00 am. Kerr J held that Miss Burns fell within the definition of a 'night worker' – it was inconceivable that the definition should be confined, as the Government had argued, to those who work night shifts exclusively or even predominantly.

Length of night work

W10020   If a worker falls within these definitions, then he or she is a night worker for the purposes of the Regulations. *Regulation 6* then goes on to provide that an employer shall take all reasonable steps to ensure that the normal working hours of a night worker do not exceed an average of 8 hours in any 24-hour period. This is averaged over a 17-week reference period which is calculated in the same way as in *Regulation 4* (see W10011 above).

As with the maximum working week, there is a formula for calculating a night worker's average normal hours for each 24-hour period as follows:

$$\frac{a}{b - c}$$

where:

a   is the normal (not actual) working hours during the reference period;

b   is the number of 24-hour periods during the applicable reference period; and

c   is the number of hours during that period which comprise or are included in weekly rest periods under *Regulation 11*, which is then divided by 24.

If the night work involves 'special hazards or heavy physical or mental strain', then a strict eight-hour time limit is imposed on working time in each 24-hour period and no averaging is allowed over a reference period. The identification of night work with such characteristics is by means of either a collective or workforce agreement which takes account of the specific effects and hazards of night work, or by the risk assessment which all employers are required to carry out under the *Management of Health and Safety at Work Regulations 1992* (as to which, see RISK ASSESSMENT).

The derogations in *Regulation 21* (special categories of workers) apply to the provisions on length of night work. Workers whose working time is unmeasured or cannot be predetermined are also excluded (*Reg 20*). Other exemptions may be made by means of collective or workforce agreement (*Reg 23*).

Health assessment and transfer of night workers to day work

W10021   An employer must, before assigning a worker to night work, provide him with the opportunity to have a free health assessment (*Reg 7*). The purpose of the assessment is to determine whether the worker is fit to undertake the night work. While there is no reliable evidence as to any specific health factor which rules out night work, a number of medical conditions could arise or could be made worse by working at night, such as diabetes, cardiovascular conditions or gastric intestinal disorders.

Employers are under a further duty to ensure that each night worker has the opportunity to have such health assessments 'at regular intervals of whatever duration may be appropriate in his case' (*Reg 7(1)(b)*).

The Regulations do not specify the way in which the health assessment must be carried out, nor is there specific reference to medical assessments, so that strictly speaking, such assessments could be carried out by qualified health professionals rather than by a medical practitioner.

Contrast this with the position as regards the transfer from night to day work. If a night worker is found to be suffering from health problems that are recognised as being connected with night work, he or she is entitled to be transferred to suitable day work 'where it is possible'. In such a situation, the Regulations provide that a 'registered medical practitioner' must have advised the employer that the worker is suffering from health problems which the practitioner considers to be connected with the performance by that night worker of night work.

Annual leave

Entitlement to annual leave

W10022   By virtue of *Regulation 13*, workers will for the first time under English law have a statutory right to paid holiday. The right is available to all workers within the scope of the Regulations, providing that they have been continuously employed for 13 weeks. This requirement is satisfied if the worker's relations with his employer have been governed by a contract during the whole or part of each of those weeks.

All qualifying workers will be entitled to at least three weeks annual leave, rising to four weeks on 23 November 1999 in each 'leave year'. The phasing in of four weeks' leave in 1999 is subject to transitional provisions which provide as follows.

(*a*)   In any leave year beginning on or before 23 November 1998, the entitlement is three weeks.

(*b*)   In any leave year beginning after 23 November 1998 but before 23 November 1999, the entitlement is three weeks plus a proportion of a fourth week equivalent to the proportion of the year beginning on 23 November 1998 which has elapsed at the start of that leave year. This provision is logical if somewhat confusing. It is best demonstrated by means of an example. If an employee's leave year commences on 1 January 1999, he will be entitled to three weeks plus one day. If it commences on 24 May 1999, he will be entitled to three weeks and four days' annual leave. This is because holiday entitlement including a fraction of any day will be rounded up to a whole day (*Reg 13(6)*).

(*c*)   Where the leave year begins after 23 November 1999, the entitlement to annual leave is four weeks.

For the purposes of *Regulation 13*, a worker's leave year begins on any day provided for in a relevant agreement, or, where there is no such provision in a relevant agreement, 1 October 1998 or the anniversary of the date on which the worker began employment (whichever is the later). In the majority of cases, written statements of terms and conditions contain a reference to the holiday or leave year. If they do not, employers are recommended to ensure that they do so. Failure in this regard could result in administrative confusion as each employee could have a different holiday year for the purposes of calculations under the Regulations.

The statutory leave entitlement may be taken in instalments, but it can only be taken in the leave year to which it relates and a payment in lieu of the statutory entitlement cannot be made except where the worker's employment is terminated. It should be noted that this relates only to the entitlement under the Regulations, so that if an employer provides for annual leave over and above the statutory entitlement, the enhanced element of the holiday can be carried forward or paid for in lieu as agreed between the parties.

Compensation related to entitlement to annual leave

W10023   Where an employee has outstanding leave due to him when the employment relationship ends, Regulation 14 specifically provides that an allowance is payable in lieu. It states that in the absence of any relevant agreement to the contrary, the amount of such allowance will be determined by the formula

$$(a \times b) - c$$

where:

a   is the period of leave to which the worker is entitled under the calculations;

b   is the proportion of the worker's leave year which expired before the effective date of termination;

c   is the period of leave taken by the worker between the start of the leave year and the effective date of termination (*Reg 14(3)*).

Regulation 14(4) provides that where there is a relevant agreement which so provides, an employee shall compensate his employer – whether by way of payment, additional work or otherwise – in relation to any holiday entitlement taken in excess of the statutory entitlement.

Payment, and notice requirements, for annual leave

W10024   *Regulation 16* specifies the way in which a worker is paid in respect of any period of annual leave: this is at the rate of a week's pay in respect of each week of leave.

Regulation 15 deals with the dates on which leave entitlement can be taken, and sets out detailed requirements as to notice. This Regulation is extremely complicated and before going into the details, it should be noted that alternative provisions concerning the notice requirements can be contained in a relevant agreement. Bearing in mind the detailed nature of the provisions, it is recommended that employers consider specifying such notice requirements in their contracts of employment, thereby avoiding the need for confusion at a later stage.

Regulation 15 provides that a worker must give his employer notice equivalent to twice the amount of leave he is proposing to take. An employer can then prevent the worker from taking the leave on a particular date by giving notice equivalent to the number of days' leave which the employer wishes to prohibit. An employer can also, by giving notice equivalent to twice the number of days' leave in question, require an employee to take all or part of his leave on certain dates. This would, of course, be useful with regard to seasonal shutdowns over summer and Christmas holidays etc.

Records

W10025   The publicity and controversy surrounding the introduction of the Regulations related primarily to the maximum working week and the annual leave entitlement. However, it may well be that the provisions relating to record keeping could prove, in practice, most significant for employers. *Regulation 9* introduces an obligation on employers to keep specific records of working hours. All employers (except in relation to workers serving in the armed forces – *Reg 25(1)*) are under a duty to keep records which are adequate to show that certain specified limits are being complied with in the case of each entitled worker employed by him. These limits are:

(*a*)   the maximum working week (see W10010 above);

(*b*)   the length of night work (including night work which is hazardous or subject to heavy mental strain) (see W10020 above); and

(*c*)   the requirement to provide health assessments for night workers (see W10021 above).

These records are required to be maintained for two years from the date on which they were made.

In addition, where a worker has agreed to exclude the maximum working week under *Regulation 5* (see W10013 above), an employer is required to maintain further records which:

(i)   identify each of the workers with whom the employer has agreed that the 48-hour working week will not apply;

(ii)   set out any terms on which the worker agreed that the limit should not apply; and

(iii)   specify the number of hours worked by that worker for the employer during each week since the agreement came into effect.

Again, such records must be kept for two years.

Excluded sectors

Total exclusions

W10026   By virtue of *Regulation 18*, the sectors of activities listed below are totally excluded from the terms of the Regulations:

(*a*)   air, rail, road, sea, inland waterway and lake transport;

(*b*)   sea fishing;

(*c*)   other work at sea;

(*d*)   the activities of doctors in training;

(*e*)   specified services, e.g. armed forces, the police, civil protection services, where the characteristics of these services inevitably conflict with the provisions of the Regulations.

It remains to be seen to what extent related activities will fall within this exemption; for example, the work of baggage handlers at airports. The DTI's Guidance to the Working Time Regulations seeks to clarify this issue, but the position is ultimately, at present, unclear.

Partial exemptions

Domestic service

W10027   The following provisions of the Regulations do not apply in relation to workers employed as domestic servants in private households:

(*a*)   the 48-hour working week (see W10010 above);

(*b*)   length of night work (see W10020 above);

(*c*)   health assessments for night workers (see W10021 above);

(*d*)   monotonous work (see W10018 above).

Unmeasured working time

W10028   The requirements of the Regulations listed below are, by virtue of *Regulation 20*, not applicable to workers where, on account of the specific characteristics of the activity in which they are engaged, the duration of their working time is not measured or pre-determined or can be determined by the workers themselves. The provisions excluded are:

(*a*)   the 48 hour working week (see W10010 above);

(*b*)   minimum daily and weekly rest periods and rest breaks (see W10014 *et seq.* above);

(*c*)   length of night work (see W10020 above).

This would leave such workers with requirements relating to monotonous work, the requirement for health assessments for night workers, the requirement to keep records and annual leave. It should also be noted that there is no requirement to provide such workers with compensatory rest where the requirements of the Regulations are not complied with.

This provision is often thought to exclude the Regulations in relation to 'managing executives or other persons with autonomous decision-making powers'. However, it should be noted that this is simply *one* of the three examples given in *Regulation 20*, as regards the type of worker with unmeasured working time. *The application of the Regulation could be much wider than this*, and will depend on whether the worker in question is genuinely able to control his work, to the extent of being able to determine how many hours he works.

As is inevitable with new legislation, it remains to be seen how the tribunals will interpret this particular provision.

Special categories of workers

W10029   *Regulation 21* provides that in the case of certain categories of employees, the following Regulations do not apply:

(*a*)   length of night work (see W10020 above);

(*b*)   minimum daily rest and weekly rest periods and rest breaks (see W10014 *et seq.* above).

This leaves the 48-hour working week, requirements relating to monotonous work, the requirement for health assessments for night workers, the requirement to keep records and annual leave. However, it should be noted that where any of the allowable derogations are utilised, an employer will have to provide compensatory rest periods (see W10032 below).

Further, for these categories of workers, the reference period over which the 48-hour working week is averaged is 26 weeks and not 17 (*Reg 4(5)*).

The special categories of worker are as follows:

(i)   where the worker's activities mean that his place of work and place of residence are distant from one another, or the worker has different places of work which are distant from one another;

(ii)   workers engaged in security or surveillance activities, which require a permanent presence in order to protect property and persons – examples given are security guards and caretakers;

(iii)   where the worker's activities involve the need for continuity of service or production – specific examples are:

(A)   services relating to the reception, treatment or care provided by hospitals or similar establishments, residential institutions and prisons;

(B)   workers at docks or airports;

(C)   press, radio, television, cinematographic production, postal and telecommunications services, and civil protection services;

(D)   gas, water and electricity production, transmission and distribution, household refuse collection and incineration;

(E)   industries in which work cannot be interrupted on technical grounds;

(F)   research and development activities;

(G)   agriculture;

(iv)   any industry where there is a foreseeable surge of activity – specific cases suggested are:

(A)   agriculture;

(B)   tourism;

(C)   postal services;

(v)   where the worker's activities are affected by:

(A)   unusual and unforeseeable circumstances beyond the control of the employer;

(B)   exceptional events which could not be avoided even with the exercise of all due care by the employer;

(C)   an accident or the imminent risk of an accident.

Shift workers

W10030   Shift workers are defined by *Regulation 22* as workers who work in a system whereby they succeed each other at the same work station according to a certain pattern, including a rotating pattern which may be continuous or discontinuous, entailing the need for workers to work at different times over a given period of days or weeks.

In the case of shift workers the provisions for daily rest periods (see W10014 above) and weekly rest periods (see W10016 above) can be excluded in order to facilitate the changing of shifts, on the understanding that compensatory rest must be provided (see W10032 below). In addition, those provisions also do not apply to workers engaged in activities involving periods of work split up over the day – the example given is that of cleaning staff.

Collective and workforce agreements

W10031   By virtue of *Regulation 23(a)*, employers and employees have the power to exclude or modify the following provisions:

(*a*)   length of night work (see W10020 above);

(*b*)   minimum daily rest and weekly rest periods and rest breaks (see W10014 *et seq.* above),

by way of collective or workforce agreements. Compensatory rest must be provided (see W10032 below).

In addition, *Regulation 23(b)* allows the reference period for calculating the maximum working week to be extended to up to 52 weeks, if there are objective or technical reasons concerning the organisation of work to justify this.

This Regulation gives the parties a good deal of flexibility (on the understanding that they are prepared to consent with each other) to opt out of significant provisions contained in the Regulations.

Compensatory rest

W10032   *Regulation 24* provides that where a worker is not strictly governed by the working time rules because of:

(*a*)   a derogation under *Regulation 21* (see W10029 above); or

(*b*)   the application of a collective or workforce agreement under *Regulation 23(a)* (see W10031 above); or

(*c*)   the special shift work rules under *Regulation 22* (see W10030 above);

and as a result, the worker is required by his employer to work during what would otherwise be a rest period or rest break, then the employer must wherever possible allow him to take an equivalent period of compensatory rest. In exceptional cases, in which it is not possible for objective reasons to grant such a rest period, the employer must afford the employee such protection as may be appropriate in order to safeguard his health and safety.

Enforcement

W10033   The Regulations divide the enforcement responsibilities between the Health and Safety Executive and the employment tribunals.

Health and safety offences

W10034   *Regulation 28* provides that certain provisions of the Regulations (referred to as 'the relevant requirements') will be enforced by the Health and Safety Executive (except to the extent that a local authority may be responsible for their enforcement by virtue of *Regulation 28(3)*). The relevant requirements are:

(*a*)   the 48 hour working week;

(*b*)   length of night work;

(*c*)   health assessment and transfers from night work;

(*d*)   monotonous work;

(*e*)   record keeping; and

(*f*)   failure to provide compensatory rest, where the provision concerning the length of night work is modified or excluded.

Any employer who fails to comply with any of the relevant requirements will be guilty of an offence and shall be liable on summary conviction (in the magistrates' court) to a fine not exceeding the statutory maximum and on conviction on indictment (in the Crown Court) to a fine.

In addition, the Health and Safety Executive can take enforcement proceedings utilising certain provisions of the *Health and Safety at Work etc. Act 1974*, as set out in *Regulations 28 and 29*. Employers may face criminal liability under these provisions, the sanctions for which range, according to the offence, from a fine to two years' imprisonment. (For enforcement of health and safety legislation generally, see ENFORCEMENT.)

Employment tribunals

Enforcement of the Regulations

W10035   By virtue of *Regulation 30*, certain provisions of the Regulations may be enforced by a worker presenting a claim to an employment tribunal where an employer has refused to permit him to exercise such rights. These are:

(*a*)   daily rest period;

(*b*)   weekly rest period;

(*c*)   rest break;

(*d*)   annual leave;

(*e*)   failure to provide compensatory rest, insofar as it relates to situations where daily or weekly rest breaks are modified or excluded;

(*f*)   the failure to pay the whole or any part of the amount relating to paid annual leave, or payment on termination in lieu of accrued but untaken holiday.

A complaint must be made within (i) three months (other than in the case of members of the armed forces – see below) of the act or omission complained of (or in the case of a rest period or leave extending over more than one day, of the date on which it should have been permitted to begin) or (ii) such further period as the tribunal considers reasonable, where it is satisfied that it was not reasonably practicable for the complaint to be presented within that time. (The time limit in respect of members of the armed forces is six months.)

Where an employment tribunal decides that a complaint is well-founded, it must make a declaration to that effect and can award compensation to be paid by the employer to the worker. This shall·be such amount as the employment tribunal considers just and equitable in all the circumstances, having regard to (i) the employer's default in refusing to permit the worker to exercise his right and (ii) any loss sustained by the worker which is attributable to the matters complained of. With regard to complaints relating to holiday pay or payment in lieu of accrued holiday on termination, the tribunal can also order the employer to pay the worker the amount which it finds properly due.

There is no qualifying service period with regard to such complaints being presented to a tribunal.

Protection against detriment, and against unfair dismissal

W10036   *Regulation 31* inserts a new *section 45A* into the *Employment Rights Act 1996*, so as to provide protection for a worker against being subjected to any detriment, where the worker has:

(a)   refused (or proposed to refuse) to comply with a requirement which the employer imposed (or proposed to impose) in contravention of the Regulations;

(b)   refused (or proposed to refuse) to forgo a right conferred on him by the Regulations;

(c)   failed to sign a workforce agreement or make any other agreement provided for under the Regulations, such as an individual opt-out from the maximum weekly working time limit;

(d)   being a candidate in an election of work place representatives or having been elected, carries out any activities as such a representative or candidate; or

(e)   in good faith, (i) made an allegation that the employer has contravened a right under the Regulations, or (ii) brought proceedings under the Regulations.

The right to bring these claims would (as with discrimination claims) allow an individual to pursue a claim relating to a breach of the Regulations whilst continuing in employment.

By virtue of the inserted *section 101A* of the *Employment Rights Act 1996*, the dismissal of an employee on all but ground (e) above is automatically unfair, although this will only apply to employees and not to the wider definition of worker (for the position of workers who are not employees, see below). The compensation available would be subject to any cap on unfair dismissal compensation, which is currently £12,000. Employees whose contracts were terminated on ground (e) above would be protected from dismissal for assertion of a statutory right, by virtue of *section 104* of the 1996 Act which has been amended accordingly.

An employee would also be protected if selected for redundancy on any of the grounds listed above. This would be automatically unfair selection, by virtue of the amended *section 105* of the 1996 Act.

Workers (i.e. those who are not employees) whose contracts are terminated for any of the grounds set out above can claim that they have suffered a detriment, and they may claim compensation, which would be capped in the same way as an award for unfair dismissal.

Contracting out of the Regulations

W10037   An agreement to contract out of the provisions of the Regulations can be made via a conciliation officer or by means of a compromise agreement, and the provisions are similar and consistent with the current provisions in *section 203* of the *Employment Rights Act 1996* (as amended by the *Employment Rights (Dispute Resolution) Act 1998*).

Conclusion

W10038   The Regulations break new ground in English law and it remains to be seen whether their introduction will substantially change current industrial practice.

Workplaces – Health, Safety and Welfare

Introduction

Five key elements are endemic to workplace integrity, namely, (*a*) structure (based on function), (*b*) health, (*c*) safety, (*d*) welfare and (*e*) hygiene. Originally legislation only insisted on these basic requirements in factories and offices and shops. With the introduction of the *Health and Safety at Work etc. Act 1974* (*HSWA*), however, emphasis shifted notionally to workplaces generally. What matters now is the contract of employment rather than the place of work. As long as a person is at work, permanently or temporarily, sedentary or otherwise, in a managerial capacity or on the shopfloor, indoors or outside, mobile, peripatetic or otherwise, he or she is entitled to the protection of *HSWA*, and any subsequent regulations. More particularly, most workplaces (excluding construction sites (which are governed by the *Construction (Health, Safety and Welfare) Regulations 1996*, see C8030 CONSTRUCTION AND BUILDING OPERATIONS)), must conform to minimum standards which are contained in the *Workplace (Health, Safety and Welfare) Regulations 1992* – see W11002–W11028 below). The *Workplace (Health, Safety and Welfare) Regulations 1992* consolidate the health, safety and welfare requirements formerly contained in the *Factories Act 1961* and the *Offices, Shops and Railway Premises Act 1963*, thus concentrating these requirements in a single piece of legislation applicable to virtually all workplaces. The following is a summary of the principal provisions of the *Workplace (Health, Safety and Welfare) Regulations 1992*:

(*a*)   maintenance [*Reg 5*] (see W11003);

(*b*)   ventilation [*Reg 6*] (see VENTILATION);

(*c*)   temperature [*Reg 7*] (see W11005);

(*d*)   lighting [*Reg 8*] (see LIGHTING);

(*e*)   cleanliness and waste storage [*Reg 9*] (see W11006);

(*f*)   room dimensions and space [*Reg 10*] (see W11007);

(*g*)   workstations and seating [*Reg 11*] (see W11008);

(*h*)   conditions of floors and traffic routes [*Reg 12*] (see W11009);

(*j*)   freedom from falls and falling objects [*Reg 13*] (see WORK AT HEIGHTS);

(*k*)   windows and transparent or translucent doors, gates and walls (see W11011);

(*l*)   windows, skylights and ventilators [*Reg 18*] (see W11012);

(*m*)   window cleaning [*Regs 14–16*] (see WORK AT HEIGHTS);

(*n*)   organisation of traffic routes [*Reg 17*] (see W11014);

(*o*)   doors and gates [*Reg 18*] (see W11015);

(*p*)   escalators and travelators [*Reg 19*] (see W11016);

(*q*)   sanitary conveniences/washing facilities [*Regs 20, 21*] (see W11018–W11022);

(*r*)   drinking water [*Reg 22*] (see W11023);

(*s*)   clothing accommodation and facilities for changing clothing [*Reg 23*] (see W11025–W11026); and

(*t*)   rest/meal facilities [*Reg 25*] (see W11026).

In addition, since 1 April 1996, all workplaces have had to conform with the requirements of the *Health and Safety (Safety Signs and Signals) Regulations 1996 (SI 1996 No 341)*, which standardised safety signs and signals throughout all places of work.

This section (W11002–W11028 below) deals specifically with the requirements of the *Workplace (Health, Safety and Welfare) Regulations 1992*, although those dealing with ventilation, lighting and work at heights are dealt with in more detail in other chapters, as referenced. It also looks at the *Health and Safety (Safety Signs and Signals) Regulations 1996 (SI 1996 No 341)* and the relevant parts of the *Building Regulations 1991 (SI 1991 No 2768)*, together with the section of the *Disability Discrimination Act 1995* that sets out duties concerning adjustments to premises. (For typical hazards in offices and shops, see further OFFICES AND SHOPS.)

Workplace (Health, Safety and Welfare) Regulations 1992 (SI 1992 No 3004)

Definition of 'workplace'

W11002   A workplace is any non-domestic premises available to any person as a place of work, including:

(*a*)   canteens, toilets;

(*b*)   parts of a workroom or workplace (e.g. corridor, staircase, or other means of access/egress other than a public road);

(*c*)   a completed modification, extension, or conversion of an original workplace;

but excluding

(i)   boats, ships, hovercrafts, trains and road vehicles (although the requirements in *regulation 13*, which deal with falls and falling objects, apply when aircraft, trains and road vehicles are stationary inside a workplace);

(ii)   building operations/works of engineering construction;

(iii)   mining activities.

[*Workplace (Health, Safety and Welfare) Regulations 1992, Regs 2, 3 and 4*].

Regulations 20 to 25 (which deal with toilets, washing and changing facilities, clothing accommodation, drinking water and eating and rest facilities) apply to temporary work sites, but only so far as is reasonably practicable.

General maintenance of the workplace

W11003   All workplaces, equipment and devices should be maintained

(*a*)   in an efficient state,

(*b*)   in an efficient working order, and

(*c*)   in a good state of repair.

[*Workplace (Health, Safety and Welfare) Regulations 1992, Reg 5*].

Dangerous defects should be reported and acted on as a matter of good housekeeping (and to avoid possible subsequent civil liability). Defects resulting in equipment/plant becoming unsuitable for use, though not necessarily dangerous, should lead to decommissioning of plant until repaired – or, if this might lead to the number of facilities being less than required by statute, repaired forthwith (e.g. defective toilet).

To this end, a suitable maintenance programme must be instituted, including:

(*a*)   regular maintenance (inspection, testing, adjustment, lubrication, cleaning);

(*b*)   rectification of potentially dangerous defects and the prevention of access to defective equipment;

(*c*)   record of maintenance/servicing.

Ventilation

W11004   *Regulation 6* deals with the provision of sufficient ventilation in enclosed workplaces. This is dealt with in detail in VENTILATION.

Temperature

W11005   The temperature in all workplaces inside buildings should be reasonable during working hours (*Reg 7*). Workroom temperature should enable people to work (and visit sanitary conveniences) in reasonable comfort, without the need for extra or special clothing. The approved code of practice (ACoP) sets out that the minimum acceptable temperature is 16°C at the workstation, except where work involves considerable physical effort, when it reduces to 13°C (dry bulb thermometer reading). Space heating of the average workplace should be 16°C, which should be maintained throughout the remainder of the working day. However, this temperature is a minimum temperature.

The following temperatures for different types of work are recommended by the Chartered Institute of Building Services Engineers (CIBSE):

(*a*)   heavy work in factories 13°C;

(*b*)   light work in factories 16°C;

(*c*)   hospital wards and shops 18°C; and

(*d*)   office and dining rooms 20°C.

Maintenance of such temperatures may not always be feasible, as, for instance, where hot/cold production/storage processes are involved, or where food has to be stored. In such cases, an approximate temperature should be maintained. With cold storage, this may be achievable by keeping a small chilling area separate or by product insulation; whereas, in the case of hot processes, insulation of hot plant or pipes, provision of cooling plant, window shading and positioning of workstations away from radiant heat should be considered in order to achieve a reasonably comfortable temperature. Moreover, where it is necessary from time to time to work in rooms normally unoccupied (e.g. storerooms), temporary heating should be installed. Thermometers must be provided so that workers can periodically check the temperatures.

Where, despite the provision of local heating or cooling, temperatures are still not reasonably comfortable, suitable protective clothing or rest facilities should be provided, or there should be systems of work in place, such as job rotation, to minimise the length of time workers are exposed to uncomfortable temperatures.

The method of heating or cooling should not result in dangerous or offensive gases or fumes entering the workplace.

General cleanliness

W11006   All furniture and fittings of every workplace must be kept sufficiently clean. Surfaces of floors, walls and ceilings must be capable of being kept sufficiently clean and waste materials must not accumulate otherwise than in waste receptacles. [*Workplace (Health, Safety and Welfare) Regulations 1992, Reg 9*].

The level and frequency of cleanliness will vary according to workplace use and purpose. Obviously a factory canteen should be cleaner than a factory floor. Floors and indoor traffic routes should be cleaned at least once a week, though dirt and refuse not in suitable receptacles should be removed at least daily, particularly in hot atmospheres or hot weather. Interior walls, ceilings and work surfaces should be cleaned at suitable intervals and ceilings and interior walls painted and/or tiled so that they can be kept clean. Surface treatment should be renewed when it can no longer be cleaned properly. In addition, cleaning will be necessary to remove spillages and waste matter from drains or sanitary conveniences. Methods of cleaning, however, should not expose anyone to substantial amounts of dust, and absorbent floors likely to be contaminated by oil or other substances difficult to remove, should be sealed or coated, say, with non-slip floor paint (not covered with carpet!).

Workroom dimensions/space

W11007   Every room in which people work should have sufficient

(*a*)   floor area,

(*b*)   height, and

(*c*)   unoccupied space

for health, safety and welfare purposes. [*Workplace (Health, Safety and Welfare) Regulations 1992, Reg 10*].

Workrooms should have enough uncluttered space to allow people to go to and from workstations with relative ease. The number of people who may work in any particular room at any time will depend not only on the size of the room but also on the space given over to furniture, fittings, equipment and general room layout. Workrooms should be of sufficient height to afford staff safe access to workstations. If, however, the workroom is in an old building, say, with low beams or other possible obstructions, this should be clearly marked, e.g. 'Low beams, mind your head'.

The total volume of the room (when empty), divided by the number of people normally working there, should be 11 cubic metres (minimum) per person, although this does not apply to:

(i)   retail sales kiosks, attendants' shelters etc.,

(ii)   lecture/meeting rooms etc.

[*Sch 1*].

In making this calculation, any part of a room which is higher than 3 metres is counted as being 3 metres high.

Where furniture occupies a considerable part of the room, 11 metres may not be sufficient space per person. Here more careful planning and general room layout is required. Similarly, rooms may need to be larger or have fewer people working in them depending on the contents and layout of the room and the nature of the work.

Workstations and seating

W11008   *(a) Workstations*

Every workstation must be so arranged that:

(i)   it is suitable for

    (a)   any person at work who is likely to work at the workstation, and

    (b)   any work likely to be done there;

(ii)   so far as reasonably practicable, it provides protection from adverse weather;

(iii)   it enables a person to leave it swiftly or to be assisted in an emergency; and

(iv)   it ensures any person is not likely to slip or fall.

[*Workplace (Health, Safety and Welfare) Regulations 1992, Reg 11(1)(2)*].

(b) Workstation seating

A suitable seat must be provided for each person at work whose work (or a substantial part of it) can or must be done seated. The seat should be suitable for

(i)   the person doing the work, and

(ii)   the work to be done.

Where necessary, a suitable footrest should be provided.

[*Workplace (Health, Safety and Welfare) Regulations 1992, Reg 11(3)(4)*].

It should be possible to carry out work safely and comfortably. Work materials and equipment in frequent use (or controls) should always be within easy reach, so that people do not have to bend or stretch unduly, and the worker should be at a suitable height in relation to the work surface. Workstations, including seating and access, should be suitable for special needs, for instance, those of disabled workers. The workstation should allow people likely to have to do work there adequate freedom of movement and ability to stand upright, thereby avoiding the need to work in cramped conditions. More particularly, seating should be suitable, providing adequate support for the lower back and a footrest provided, if feet cannot be put comfortably flat on the floor.

Workstations with visual display units (VDUs) are subject to the *Health and Safety (Display Screen Equipment) Regulations 1992 (SI 1992 No 2792)* (see OFFICES AND SHOPS).

The Health and Safety Executive (HSE) revised its guidance on seating in 1998, and advises employers to use risk assessments in order to ensure that safe seating is provided. *Seating at Work*, HS(G)57 is available, price £5.95, from HSE Books, PO Box 1999, Sudbury, Suffolk CO10 6FS (tel: 01787 313995).

Condition of floors and traffic routes

W11009   The principal dangers connected with industrial and commercial floors are slipping, tripping and falling. Slip, trip and fall resistance are a combination of the right floor surface and the appropriate type of footwear. Manufacturers of such floors and footwear should design and produce floors and footwear with slip resistance uppermost in mind. For their part, employers should ensure that level changes, multiple changes of floor surfaces, steps and ramps etc. are clearly indicated. Safety underfoot is at bottom a trade-off between slip resistance and ease of cleaning. Floors with rough surfaces tend to be more slip-resistant than floors with smooth surfaces, especially when wet; by contrast, smooth surfaces are much easier to clean but less slip-resistant. Use of vinyl flooring in public areas – basically slip-resistant – is on the increase. Vinyl floors should be periodically stripped, degreased and resealed with slip-resistant finish; linoleum floors similarly.

Apart from being safe, floors must also be hygienically clean. In this connection, quarry tiles have long been 'firm favourites' in commercial kitchens, hospital kitchens etc. but can be hygienically deceptive. In particular, grouted joints can trap bacteria as well as presenting endless practical cleaning problems. Hence the gradual transition to seamless floors in hygiene-critical areas. Whichever floor surface is appropriate and whichever treatment is suitable, underfoot safety depends on workplace activity (office or factory), variety of spillages (food, water, oil, chemicals), nature of traffic (pedestrian, cars, trucks).

Thus, floors in workplaces must:

(*a*)   be constructed so as to be suitable for use. [*Workplace (Health, Safety and Welfare) Regulations 1992, Reg 12(1)*].

They should always be of sound construction and adequate strength and stability to sustain loads and passing internal traffic; they should never be overloaded (see *Greaves v Baynham Meikle [1975] 3 AER 99* for possible consequences in civil law).

(*b*)   (i)   not have holes or slopes, and

(ii)   not be uneven or slippery

so as to expose a person to risk of injury. [*Workplace (Health, Safety and Welfare) Regulations 1992, Reg 12(2)(a)*].

The surfaces of floors and traffic routes should be even and free from holes, bumps and slipping hazards that could cause a person to slip, trip or fall, or drop or lose control of something being lifted or carried; or cause instability or loss of control of a vehicle.

Holes, bumps or uneven surfaces or areas resulting from damage or wear and tear should be made good and, pending this, barriers should be erected or locations conspicuously marked. Temporary holes, following, say, removal of floorboards, should be adequately guarded. Special needs should be catered for, for instance, disabled workers or those with impaired sight. (Deep holes are governed by *Reg 13* (see W9003 WORK AT HEIGHTS).) Where possible, steep slopes should be avoided, and otherwise provided with a secure handrail. Ramps used by disabled persons should also have handrails.

(*c*)   be kept free from

(i)   obstructions, and

(ii)   articles/substances likely to cause persons to slip, trip or fall so far as reasonably practicable. [*Workplace (Health, Safety and Welfare) Regulations 1992, Reg 12(3)*].

Floors should be kept free of obstructions impeding access or presenting hazards, particularly near or on steps, stairs, escalators and moving walkways, on emergency routes or outlets, in or near doorways or gangways or by corners or junctions. Where temporary obstructions are unavoidable, access should be prevented and people warned of the possible hazard. Furniture being moved should not be left in a place where it can cause a hazard.

(*d*)   have effective drainage. [*Workplace (Health, Safety and Welfare) Regulations 1992, Reg 12(2)(b)*].

Where floors are likely to get wet, effective drainage (without drains becoming contaminated with toxic, corrosive substances) should drain it away, e.g. in laundries, potteries and food processing plants. Drains and channels should be situated so as to reduce the area of wet floor and the floor should slope slightly towards the drain and ideally have covers flush with the floor surface. Processes and plant which cause discharges or leaks of liquids should be enclosed and leaks from taps caught and drained away. In food processing and preparation plants, work surfaces should be arranged so as to minimise the likelihood of spillage. Where a leak or spillage occurs, it should be fenced off or mopped up immediately.

Staircases should be provided with a handrail. Any open side of a staircase should have minimum fencing of an upper rail at 900mm or higher, and a lower rail.

It is important also to consider the dangers posed by snow and ice upon, for example, external fire escapes.

Falls and falling objects

W11010   *Regulation 13* deals with falls and falling objects, which are covered in detail in WORK AT HEIGHTS.

It also requires that tanks, pits and other structures containing dangerous substances are securely covered or fenced where there is a risk of a person falling. Traffic routes over such open structures should also be securely fenced.

Windows and transparent or translucent doors, gates and walls

W11011   Transparent or translucent surfaces in windows, doors, gates, walls and partitions should be constructed of safety material or be adequately protected against breakage, where necessary for health and safety reasons, where:

(*a*)   any part is at shoulder level or below in doors and gates; or

(*b*)   any part is at waist level or below in windows, walls and partitions, with the exception of glass houses.

Screens or barriers can be used as an alternative to the use of safety materials. Narrow panels of up to 250mm width are excluded from the requirement.

Transparent or translucent surfaces should be marked to make them apparent where this is necessary for health and safety reasons.

[*Workplace (Health, Safety and Welfare) Regulations 1992, Reg 14*].

Windows, skylights and ventilators

W11012   Openable windows, skylights and ventilators must be capable of being opened, closed and adjusted safely. They must not be positioned so as to pose a risk when open.

They should be capable of being reached and operated safely, with window poles or similar equipment, or stable platforms, made available where necessary. Where there is the danger of falling from a height, devices should be provided to prevent this by ensuring the window cannot open too far. They should not cause a hazard by projecting into an area where people are likely to collide with them when open. The bottom edge of opening windows should normally be at least 800mm above floor level, unless there is a barrier to prevent falls.

[*Workplace (Health, Safety and Welfare) Regulations 1992, Reg 15*].

Ability to clean windows etc. safely

W11013   *Regulation 16* deals with the safe cleaning of windows and skylights where these cannot be cleaned from the ground or other suitable surface. This is dealt with in detail in WORK AT HEIGHTS.

Organisation of traffic routes

W11014   Traffic routes in workplaces should allow pedestrians and vehicles to circulate safely, be safely constructed, be suitably indicated where necessary for health and safety reasons, and be kept clear of obstructions.

They should be planned to give the safest route, wide enough for the safe movement of the largest vehicle permitted to use them, and they should avoid vulnerable items like fuel or chemical plants or pipes, and open and unprotected edges.

There should be safe areas for loading and unloading. Sharp or blind bends should be avoided where possible, and if they cannot be avoided, one-way systems or mirrors to improve visibility should be used. Sensible speed limits should be set and enforced. There should be prominent warning of any limited headroom or potentially dangerous obstructions such as overhead electric cables. Routes should be marked where necessary and there should be suitable and sufficient parking areas in safe locations.

Traffic routes should keep vehicles and pedestrians apart and there should be pedestrian crossing points on vehicle routes. Traffic routes and parking and loading areas should be soundly constructed on level ground. Health and Safety Executive (HSE) guidance in this area can be found in the publication, *Workplace transport safety – guidance for employers*, HS(G)136, price £7.50, available from HSE Books.

[*Workplace (Health, Safety and Welfare) Regulations 1992, Reg 17*].

Doors and gates

W11015   Doors and gates must be suitably constructed and fitted with safety devices. In particular,

(i)   a sliding door/gate must have a device to prevent it coming off its track during use;

(ii)   an upward opening door/gate must have a device to prevent its falling back;

(iii)   a powered door/gate must

      (*a*)   have features preventing it causing injury by trapping a person (e.g. accessible emergency stop controls),

      (*b*)   be able to be operated manually unless it opens automatically if the power fails;

(iv)   a door/gate capable of opening, by being pushed from either side, must provide a clear view of the space close to both sides.

[*Workplace (Health, Safety and Welfare) Regulations 1992, Reg 18*].

Doors and gates that swing in both directions should have a transparent panel, unless they are low enough to see over.

Escalators and travelators

W11016   Escalators and travelators must:

(*a*)   function safely;

(*b*)   be equipped with safety devices;

(*c*)   be fitted with emergency stop controls.

[*Workplace (Health, Safety and Welfare) Regulations 1992, Reg 19*].

Welfare facilities

W11017   'Welfare facilities' is a wide term, embracing both sanitary and washing accommodation at workplaces, provision of drinking water, clothing accommodation (including facilities for changing clothes) and facilities for rest and eating meals (see W11023–W11026 below). In the past, breach of welfare duties, being public health-oriented, has tended not to give rise to additional civil liability, though breach of current welfare requirements would probably, if injury ensued, be actionable as a breach of statutory duty (see E11015 EMPLOYERS' DUTIES TO THEIR EMPLOYEES).

The need for sufficient suitable hygienic lavatory and washing facilities in all workplaces is obvious. Sufficient facilities must be provided to enable everyone at work to use them without undue delay. They do not have to be in the actual workplace but ideally should be situated in the building(s) containing them and they should provide protection from the weather, be well-ventilated, well-lit and enjoy a reasonable temperature. Where disabled workers are employed, special provision should be made for their sanitary and washing requirements. Wash basins should allow washing of hands, face and forearms and, where work is particularly strenuous, dirty, or results in skin contamination (e.g. molten metal work), showers or baths should be provided. In the case of showers, they should be fed by hot and cold water and fitted with a thermostatic mixer valve. Washing facilities should ensure privacy for the user and be separate from the water closet, with a door that can be secured from the inside; nor should it be possible to see urinals or the communal shower from outside the facilities when the entrance/exit door opens. Entrance/exit doors should be fitted to both washing and sanitary facilities (unless there are other means of ensuring privacy). Windows to sanitary accommodation, showers/bathrooms should be obscured either by being frosted, or by blinds or curtains (unless it is impossible to see into them from outside).

This section examines current statutory requirements in all workplaces. For requirements relating to sanitary conveniences and washing facilities on construction sites see C8045 CONSTRUCTION AND BUILDING OPERATIONS.

Sanitary conveniences in all workplaces

W11018 Suitable and sufficient sanitary conveniences must be provided at readily accessible places. In particular,

(*a*) the rooms containing them must be adequately ventilated and lit;

(*b*) they (and the rooms in which they are situate) must be kept clean and in an orderly condition;

(*c*) separate rooms containing conveniences must be provided for men and women except where the convenience is in a separate room which can be locked from the inside.

[*Workplace (Health, Safety and Welfare) Regulations 1992, Reg 20*].

Washing facilities in all workplaces

W11019 Suitable and sufficient washing facilities (including showers where necessary (see W11017 above)), must be provided at readily accessible places or points. In particular, facilities must:

(*a*) be provided in the immediate vicinity of every sanitary convenience (whether or not provided elsewhere);

(*b*) be provided in the vicinity of any changing rooms – whether or not provided elsewhere;

(*c*) include a supply of clean hot and cold or warm water (if possible, running water);

(*d*) include soap (or something similar);

(*e*) include towels (or the equivalent);

(*f*) be in rooms sufficiently well-ventilated and well-lit;

(*g*) be kept clean and in an orderly condition (including rooms in which they are situate);

(*h*) be separate for men and women, except where they are provided in a lockable room intended to be used by one person at a time, or where they are provided for the purposes of washing hands, forearms and face only, where separate provision is not necessary.

[*Workplace (Health, Safety and Welfare) Regulations 1992, Reg 21*].

Minimum number of facilities – sanitary conveniences and washing facilities

(a) People at work

W11020

Number of people at work	Number of WCs	Number of wash stations
1 to 5	1	1
6 to 25	2	2
26 to 50	3	3
51 to 75	4	4
76 to 100	5	5

(*b*) *Men at work*

Number of men at work	Number of WCs	Number of urinals
1 to 15	1	1
16 to 30	2	1
31 to 45	2	2
46 to 60	3	2
61 to 75	3	3
76 to 90	4	3
91 to 100	4	4

For every 25 people above 100 an additional WC and wash station should be provided; in the case of WCs used only by *men*, an additional WC per every 50 men above 100 is sufficient (provided that at least an equal number of additional urinals is provided). [*Sch 1, Part II*].

Particularly dirty work etc.

W11021 Where work results in heavy soiling of hands, arms and forearms, there should be one wash station for every 10 people at work up to 50 people; and one extra for every additional 20 people. And where sanitary and wash facilities are also used by members of the public, the number of conveniences and facilities should be increased so that workers can use them without undue delay.

Temporary work sites

W11022 At temporary work sites suitable and sufficient sanitary conveniences and washing facilities should be provided so far as is reasonably practicable (see E15017 ENFORCEMENT for meaning). If possible, these should incorporate flushing sanitary conveniences and washing facilities with running water.

Drinking water

W11023 An adequate supply of wholesome drinking water must be provided for all persons at work in the workplace. It must be readily accessible at suitable places and conspicuously marked, unless non-drinkable cold water supplies are clearly marked. In addition, there must be provided a sufficient number of suitable cups (or other drinking vessels), unless the water supply is in a jet. [*Workplace (Health, Safety and Welfare) Regulations 1992, Reg 22*].

Where water cannot be obtained from the mains supply, it should only be provided in refillable containers. The containers should be enclosed to prevent contamination and refilled at least daily. So far as reasonably practicable, drinking water taps should not be installed in sanitary accommodation, or in places where contamination is likely, for instance, in a workshop containing lead processes.

Clothing accommodation

W11024 Suitable and sufficient accommodation must be provided for:

(*a*)   any person at work's own clothing which is not worn during working hours; and (*b*)   special clothing which is worn by any person at work but which is not taken home, for example, overalls, uniforms and thermal clothing.

[*Workplace (Health, Safety and Welfare) Regulations 1992, Reg 23(1)*].

Accommodation is not suitable unless it:

(i)   provides suitable security for the person's own clothing where changing facilities are required;

(ii)   includes separate accommodation for clothing worn at work and for other clothing, where necessary to avoid risks to health or damage to clothing; and

(iii)   is in a suitable location.

[*Workplace (Health, Safety and Welfare) Regulations 1992, Reg 23(2)*].

Work clothing is overalls, uniforms, thermal clothing and hats worn for hygiene purposes. Workers' own clothing should be able to hang in a clean, warm, dry, well-ventilated place. If this is not possible in the workroom, then it should be put elsewhere. Accommodation should take the form of a separate hook or peg. Clothing which is dirty, damp or contaminated owing to work should be accommodated separately from the worker's own clothes.

Facilities for changing clothing

W11025   Suitable and sufficient facilities must be provided for any person at work in the workplace to change clothing where:

(*a*)   the person has to wear special clothing for work, and

(*b*)   the person cannot be expected to change in another room.

Facilities are not suitable unless they include:

(i)   separate facilities for men and women, or

(ii)   separate use of facilities by men and women.

[*Workplace (Health, Safety and Welfare) Regulations 1992, Reg 24*].

Changing rooms (or room) should be provided for workers who change into special work clothing and where they remove more than outer clothing; also where it is necessary to prevent workers' own clothes being contaminated by a harmful substance. Changing facilities should be easily accessible from workrooms and eating places. They should contain adequate seating and clothing accommodation, and showers or baths if these are provided (see W11017 above). Privacy of user should be ensured. The facilities should be large enough to cater for the maximum number of persons at work expected to use them at any one time without overcrowding or undue delay.

Rest and eating facilities

W11026   Suitable and sufficient rest facilities must be provided at readily accessible places. [*Workplace (Health, Safety and Welfare) Regulations 1992, Reg 25(1)*].

(*a*) *Rest facilities*

A rest facility is:

(i)   in the case of a new workplace, extension or conversion – a rest room (or rooms);

(ii)   in other cases, a rest room (or rooms) or rest area; including

(iii)   (in both cases):

—   appropriate facilities for eating meals where food eaten in the workplace would otherwise be likely to become contaminated;

—   suitable arrangements for protecting non-smokers from tobacco smoke;

—   a facility for a pregnant or nursing mother to rest in.

Canteens or restaurants may be used as rest rooms provided that there is no obligation to buy food there (ACoP). [*Workplace (Health, Safety and Welfare) Regulations 1992, Regs 25(2)-(4)*].

(b) Eating facilities

Where workers regularly eat meals at work, facilities must be provided for them to eat meals. [*Workplace (Health, Safety and Welfare) Regulations 1992, Reg 25(5)*].

In offices and other workplaces where there is no risk of contamination, seats in the work area are sufficient, although workers should not be interrupted excessively during breaks, for example, by the public. In other cases, rest areas or rooms should be provided and in the case of new workplaces, this should be a separate rest room. Rest facilities should be large enough, and have enough seats with backrests and tables, for the number of workers likely to use them at one time.

Where workers regularly eat meals at work, there should be suitable and sufficient facilities. These should be provided where food would otherwise be contaminated, by dust or water for example. Seats in work areas can be suitable eating facilities, provided the work area is clean. There should be a means to prepare or obtain a hot drink, and where persons work during hours or at places where hot food cannot be obtained readily obtained, there should be the means for heating their own food. Eating facilities should be kept clean.

Smoking

W11027   Although providing protection to non-smokers from tobacco smoke is the only specific legal requirement concerning smoking at work, there have been a number of legal cases, and compensation awards have been made to employees who have claimed their health has been affected by breathing in tobacco smoke at work.

Stockport Metropolitan Council has made two out of court settlements of £25,000 and £15,000 to employees who claimed that their health was damaged as a result of passive smoking. In addition, an Employment Appeal Tribunal (EAT) case, *Dryden v Greater Glasgow Health Board* [*1992*] *IRLR 469*, held that a change to a complete smoking ban, which meant an employee who smoked had to leave her job, did not amount to constructive dismissal. In this case, the employer had consulted workers about the introduction of the ban.

In another EAT case, *Walton and Morse v Dorrington* [*1997*], a tribunal decision that an employee had been constructively dismissed when her employer failed to provide her with a smoke free environment or deal with her problems relating to passive smoking, was upheld.

In the first passive smoking case to reach the courts, in May 1998, a nurse lost her action for damages against her employer. Silvia Sparrow claimed that she had developed asthma as a result of exposure to environmental tobacco smoke in a residential care home for elderly people. But the court said she had failed to prove that her former employers, St Andrew's Homes Ltd, were negligent so as to cause injury to her.

The Health and Safety Executive (HSE) publication, *Passive smoking at work*, IND(G)63(L), recommends that all employers should introduce a policy to control smoking in the workplace in full consultation with employees. This should give priority to protecting non-smokers from tobacco smoke. It also recommends that employers take special care of people who have a health condition, such as asthma, which could be made worse by tobacco smoke.

Civil liability

W11028   There is no specific reference to civil liability in the Regulations. However, safety regulations are actionable, even if silent (as here), and, if a person suffered injury/damage as a result of breach by an employer, he could sue. Certainly, there is civil liability for breach of the *Building Regulations* (W11042 below).

Safety signs at work – Health and Safety (Safety Signs and Signals) Regulations 1996 (SI 1996 No 341)

W11029   Traditionally, safety signs, communications and warnings have played a residual role in reducing the risk of injury or damage at work, the need for them generally having been engineered out or accommodated in the system of work – a situation unaffected by the current regulations.

Types of signs

W11030   Safety signs and signals can be of the following types:

(*a*)   permanent (e.g. signboards);

(*b*)   occasional (e.g. acoustic signals or verbal communications – acoustic signals should be avoided where there is considerable ambient noise).

Interchanging and combining signs

W11031   Examples of interchanging and combining signs are:

(*a*)   a safety colour (see W11032 below) or signboard to mark places where there is an obstacle;

(*b*)   illuminated signs, acoustic signals or verbal communication; and

(*c*)   hand signals or verbal communication.

[*Sch 1, Part I, para 3*].

Safety colours

W11032

Colour	Meaning or purpose	Instructions and information
Red	Prohibition sign	Dangerous behaviour
	Danger	Stop, shutdown, emergency cut-out services
		Evacuate
	Fire-fighting equipment	Identification and location
Yellow or Amber	Warning sign	Be careful, take precautions
		Examine
Blue	Mandatory sign	Specific behaviour or action
		Wear personal protective equipment
Green	Emergency escape, first-aid sign	Doors, exits, routes, equipment and facilities
	No danger	Return to normal

[*Sch 1, Part I, para 4*].

Varieties of safety signs and signals

W11033   Safety signs and signals include, comprehensively:

(*a*)   safety signs – providing information about health and safety at work by means of a signboard, safety colour, illuminated sign, acoustic signal, hand signal or verbal communication;

(*b*)   signboards – signs giving information by way of a simple pictogram, lighting intensity providing visibility (these should be weather-resistant and easily seen);

(*c*)   mandatory signs – signs prescribing behaviour (e.g. safety boots must be worn);

(*d*)   prohibition signs – signs prohibiting behaviour likely to cause a health and safety risk (e.g. no smoking);

(*e*)   hand signals – movement or position of arms/hands for guiding persons carrying out operations that could endanger employees;

(*f*)   verbal communications – predetermined spoken messages communicated by human or artificial voice, preferably short, simple and as clear as possible.

[*Reg 2*].

Duty of employer

W11034   It is only where a risk assessment carried out under the *Management of Health and Safety at Work Regulations 1992 (SI 1992 No 2051)* (see EMPLOYERS' DUTIES TO THEIR EMPLOYEES) indicates that a risk cannot be avoided, engineered out or reduced significantly by way of a system of work that resort to signs and signals becomes necessary. In these circumstances, all employers (including offshore employers) must:

(*a*)   provide and maintain any appropriate safety sign(s) (see W11036–W11040 below) (including fire safety signals) but not a hand signal or verbal communication;

(*b*)   so far as is reasonably practicable, ensure that correct hand signals or verbal communications are used;

(*c*)   provide and maintain any necessary road traffic sign (where there is a risk to employees in connection with traffic); and

(*d*)   provide employees with comprehensible and relevant information, training and instruction and measures to be taken in connection with safety signs.

[*Regs 4, 5*].

Schedule 1 to the Regulations sets out the minimum requirements concerning safety signs and signals with regard to the type of signs to be used in particular circumstances, interchanging and combining signs, signboards, signs on containers and pipes, the identification and location of fire-fighting equipment, signs used for obstacles and dangerous locations, and for marking traffic routes, illuminated signs, acoustic signals, verbal communication and hand signals.

Exclusions

W11035   Excluded from the operation of these Regulations are:

(*a*)   the supply of dangerous substances or products;

(*b*)   the transportation of dangerous goods;

(*c*)   road traffic signs (except where there is a particular risk to employees. Where there is a risk arising from the movement of traffic and the risk is addressed by a sign stipulated in the *Road Traffic Regulations Act 1984* (e.g. speed restriction sign), these signs must be used, whether or not the Act applies to that place of work. In effect this means that where road speed and other signs are needed on a company's road, these must replicate the signs used for the purpose on public roads; and

(*d*)   activities on board ship.

[*Reg 3(1)*].

Examples of safety signs

Prohibitory signs

W11036   Intrinsic features:

—   round shape

—   black pictogram on white background, red edging and diagonal line (the red part to take up at least 35% of the sign area).

No smoking   Smoking and naked   No access for
                    flames forbidden   pedestrians

Do not extinguish   Not drinkable   No access for
with water   unauthorised persons

No access for industrial   Do not touch
vehicles

fig. 1 Safety signs (prohibitory)

Warning signs

W11037   Intrinsic features:

—   triangular shape

—   black pictogram on a yellow background with black edging (the yellow part to
     take up at least 50% of the area of the sign).

Flammable material   Explosive material   Toxic material
or high temperature

fig. 2 Safety signs (warning)

Mandatory signs

W11038   Intrinsic features:

—   round shape

—   white pictogram on a blue background (the blue part to take up at least 50% of the area of the sign).

Eye protection
must be worn

Safety helmet
must be worn

Ear protection
must be worn

Respiratory equipment
must be worn

Safety boots
must be worn

Safety gloves
must be worn

Safety overalls
must be worn

Face protection
must be worn

Safety harness
must be worn

Pedestrians must
use this route

General mandatory sign
(to be accompanied where
necessary by another sign)

fig. 3 Safety signs (mandatory)

Emergency escape or first-aid signs

W11039   Intrinsic features:

—   rectangular or square shape

—   white pictogram on a green background (the green part to take up at least
50% of the area of the sign).

Emergency exit/escape route

This way
(supplementary information sign)

First-aid post   Stretcher   Safety shower   Eyewash

Emergency telephone for first-aid or escape

fig. 4 Safety signs (emergency escape or first-aid)

Fire-fighting signs

W11040   Intrinsic features:

—   rectangular or square shape

—   white pictogram on a red background (the red part to take up at least 50% of the area of the sign).

| Fire hose | Ladder | Fire extinguisher | Emergency fire telephone |

This way
(supplementary information sign)

fig. 5 Safety signs (fire-fighting)

Examples of hand signals

W11041   *Meaning*   *Description*   *Illustration*

A. General signals

Meaning	Description	Illustration
START Attention Start of Command	both arms are extended horizontally with the palms facing forwards.	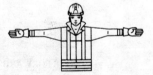
STOP Interruption End of movement	the right arm points upwards with the palm facing forwards.	
END of the operation	both hands are clasped at chest height.	

B. Vertical movements

RAISE the right arm points upwards with the palm facing forward and slowly makes a circle.

LOWER the right arm points downwards with the palm facing inwards and slowly makes a circle.

VERTICAL DISTANCE the hands indicate the relevant distance.

C. Horizontal movements

MOVE FORWARDS both arms are bent with the palms facing upwards, and the forearms make slow movements towards the body.

MOVE BACKWARDS both arms are bent with the palms facing downwards, and the forearms make slow movements away from the body.

RIGHT
to the signalman's the right arm is extended more or less horizontally with the palm facing downwards and slowly makes small movements to the right.

LEFT to the signalman's	the left arm is extended more or less horizontally with the palm facing downwards and slowly makes small movements to the left.	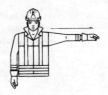
HORIZONTAL DISTANCE	the hands indicate the relevant distance.	

D. Danger

DANGER Emergency stop	both arms point upwards with the palms facing forwards.	

QUICK	all movements faster.
SLOW	all movements slower.

fig. 6 Hand signals

Controls over building work – Building Regulations 1991 (SI 1991 No 2768)

W11042 Certain requirements, in the interests of the health, safety, hygiene and welfare, of occupants of buildings (including industrial and commercial premises), are specified in the *Building Regulations 1991*. These deal with the minimum standards of design and building work for the construction of domestic, commercial and industrial buildings.

The Regulations deal with structure, fire safety, site preparation and resistance to moisture, toxic substances, resistance to the passage of sound, ventilation, hygiene, drainage and waste disposal, heat producing appliances, protection from falling, collision and impact, conservation of fuel and power, access and facilities for disabled people, glazing – safety in relation to impact, opening and cleaning, and materials and workmanship.

The building must be:

(*a*)   (if it has five or more storeys) constructed so that, in the event of an accident, it will not suffer collapse disproportionate to its cause;

(*b*)   constructed so that, in the event of failure of any part of a roof (if the roof is in a part of a public building, shop or shopping mall with a roof with a clear span exceeding 9 metres between supports), it will not suffer collapse disproportionate to its cause;

(*c*)   designed and constructed so that there are means of escape in case of fire to a place of safety outside, and to inhibit the spread of fire internally and externally (see further FIRE AND FIRE PRECAUTIONS);

(*d*)   designed and constructed to provide facilities to assist fire-fighters.

Also,

(i)   precautions should be taken to avoid danger to health and safety caused by dangerous toxic substances on or in ground on which the building is to stand;

(ii)   reasonable precautions should be taken to prevent cavity wall insulating material from giving off toxic fumes;

(iii)   there must be

— adequate means of ventilation for occupants, and

— adequate sanitary conveniences;

(iv)   stairs, ramps, floors, balconies and roofs must be guarded with barriers to protect users from the risk of falling.

[*Building Regulations 1991, Sch 1*].

Access for disabled persons

W11043   As part and parcel of compliance with the *Building Regulations 1991*, access and certain other facilities to both industrial, commercial (and domestic) buildings, in the case of non-domestic buildings, should be made available to disabled persons (though, arguably, compliance can be achieved in other ways), that is, persons who have

(*a*)   difficulty in walking or use a wheelchair, or

(*b*)   impaired hearing or sight.

The provisions apply to:

(i)   newly erected buildings,

(ii)   substantially reconstructed buildings, and

(iii)   extensions to a building with a ground floor.

[*Building Regulations 1991, Sch 1*].

To achieve adequate access and use of the premises for the disabled, it is suggested that the following should be provided:

(1)   grippable handrails (to a height of 900 mm above the surface of a ramp or the pitch line of a flight of steps and 1,000 mm above the surface of a landing);

(2)   stairs with neither sharply tapered treads nor open risers;

(3)   wheelchair stairlifts (as an alternative to passenger lifts);

(4)   platform lifts (as an alternative to a ramp) to enable wheelchair users to move to different levels within a storey;

(5)   sanitary conveniences located so that a wheelchair user does not have to travel more than one storey to reach a suitable WC (i.e. one which is wheelchair manoeuvrable); as far as ambulant disabled people are concerned, at least one WC compartment should be provided within each range of WCs in storeys not designed to be accessible to the disabled.

Civil liability for breach of the Building Regulations 1991

W11044   There is civil liability for breach of the *Building Regulations 1991*, which is strict, though common law actions for negligence for personal injury, arising from occupation of defective premises and caused by breach of the *Building Regulations*, are also possible. [*Building Act 1984, s 38(3)*]. In this connection (i.e. action for negligence at common law), local authorities do not owe a duty of care to a building owner to see that he complies with the *Building Regulations* (*Richardson v West Lindsey District Council and others [1990] 1 AER 296*).

Buildings primarily affected are: shops, offices, factories, warehouses, schools and other educational establishments (including student residential accommodation), institutions and premises to which the public is admitted on payment or otherwise.

Disability Discrimination Act 1995

W11045   The *Disability Discrimination Act 1995 (DDA)* makes it unlawful for employers of 15 or more employees to treat a disabled person less favourably, without a justifiable reason. *Section 6* of the Act requires employers to make reasonable adjustments to any physical feature of their premises to avoid putting disabled workers at a substantial disadvantage. The Act covers contract and self-employed workers as well as employees. The duty comes into operation when a disabled person is employed, or applies, or considers applying, for a job.

Disability is defined as being where a person has a physical or mental impairment (to mobility, dexterity, co-ordination, continence or memory) which causes substantial and long-term (more than twelve months) effects on their ability to carry out a normal day-to-day activities.

There is a provision in the Act to enable employers who lease their premises to obtain their landlord's permission to make alterations in order to make any necessary reasonable adjustments to the workplace. Enforcement of the Act is carried out through the employment tribunals.

The *Disability Discrimination (Employment Relations) Regulations 1996 (SI 1996 No 1456)* set out the duty to make adjustments in more detail. These specify that physical features of the employer's premises are:

(*a*)   any feature arising from the design or construction of a building on the premises or any approach to, exit from or access to such a building;

(*b*)   any fixtures, fittings, furniture, equipment or materials in or on the premises; and

(*c*)   any other physical element or quality of land included in the premises.

Transport activities

W11046   A proposal for a directive which would mean that workplaces on board means of transport (i.e. air, road, rail and water) would have to meet similar minimal requirements as other workplaces was adopted in 1992 and was due to come into force in 1994. However, progress has been slow and although the 1994 date is no longer valid, no alternative date has been put forward.

Factories Act 1961

W11047   Although large parts of the *Factories Act 1961* have now been repealed and replaced by more recent legislation, some provisions are still in force, although the Health and Safety Commission (HSC) is considering complete repeal. Additionally, civil actions for injury, relating to breach of health and safety provisions of the *Factories Act* (though not welfare) may well continue for some time, since actions for personal injury can be initiated for up to three years after injury/disease has occurred. [*Limitation Act 1980, s 11*].

Residual application of the Factories Act 1961

W11048   The *Factories Act 1961* applies to factories, as defined in *s 175*, including 'factories belonging to or in the occupation of the Crown, to building operations and works of engineering construction undertaken by or on behalf of the Crown, and to employment by or under the Crown of persons in painting buildings', e.g. hospital painters. [*Factories Act 1961, s 173(1)*].

Enforcement of the Factories Act 1961 and regulations

W11049   Offences under the Act are normally committed by occupiers rather than owners of factories. Unless they happen to occupy a factory as well, the owners of a factory would not normally be charged. Offences therefore relate to physical occupation or control of a factory (for an extended meaning of 'occupier', see OCCUPIERS' LIABILITY). Hence the person or persons or body corporate having managerial responsibility in respect of a factory are those who commit an offence under *s 155(1)*. This will generally be the managing director and board of directors and/or individual executive directors. Moreover, if a company is in liquidation and the receiver is in control, he is the person who will be prosecuted and this has in fact happened (*Meigh v Wickenden [1942] 2 KB 160; Lord Advocate v Aero Technologies 1991 SLT 134* where the receiver was 'in occupation' and so under a duty to prevent 'accidents by fire or explosion', for the purposes of the *Explosives Act 1875, s 23*).

Defence of factory occupier

W11050   The main defence open to a factory occupier charged with breach of the *Factories Act 1961* is that the Act itself, or more likely regulations made under it, placed the statutory duty on some person other than the occupier. Thus, where there is a contravention by any person of any regulation or order under the *Factories Act 1961*, 'that person shall be guilty of an offence and the occupier or owner . . . shall not be guilty of an offence, by reason only of the contravention of the provision . . . unless it is proved that he failed to take all reasonable steps to prevent the contravention . . .'. [*Factories Act 1961, s 155(2)*].

Before this defence can be invoked by a factory occupier or company, it is necessary to show that:

(*a*)   a statutory duty had been laid on someone other than the factory occupier by a regulation or order passed under the Act;

(*b*)   the factory occupier took all reasonable steps to prevent the contravention (a difficult test to satisfy).

NB. This statutory defence is not open to a building contractor (in his capacity as a notional factory occupier).

Effect on possible civil liability

W11051   Whether conviction of an employee under *s 155(2)* would prejudice a subsequent claim for damages by him against a factory occupier, must be regarded as an open question. Thus, in *Potts v Reid [1942] 2 AER 161* the court said 'Criminal and civil liability are two separate things . . . The legislation (the *Factories Act 1937*) might well be unwilling to convict an owner who failed to carry out a statutory duty of a crime with which he was not himself directly concerned, but still be ready to leave the civil liability untouched'. Similarly in *Boyle v Kodak Ltd [1969] 2 AER 439* it was said, 'When considering the civil liability engrafted by judicial decision upon the criminal liability which has been imposed by statute, it is no good looking to the statute and seeing from it where the criminal liability would lie, for we are concerned only with civil liability. We must look to the cases' (per Lord Diplock). Moreover, a breach of general duties of *HSWA* gives rise only to civil liability at common law and not under statute. (Though this is not the position where there is a breach of a specific regulation under *HSWA*.) On the other hand, there is at least one isolated instance of an employee being denied damages where he was in breach of specific regulations (*ICI Ltd v Shatwell [1964] 2 AER 999*). It is thought, however, that this decision would not apply in the case of breach of a *general* statutory duty, such as *s 155(2)*.

Appendix 1

Associations, organisations and departments connected with health and safety

Advisory, Conciliation and Arbitration Service (ACAS)
Brandon House
180 Borough High Street
London
SE1 1LW
Telephone: (0171) 210 3613

Association of British Insurers (ABI)
Head Office
51 Gresham Street
London
EC2V 7HQ
Telephone: (0171) 600 3333

Association of Industrial Truck Trainers
Independent Training Standards Scheme and Register
Scammell House
High Street
Ascot
Berkshire
SL5 7JF
Telephone: (01530) 417 234

British Chiropractic Association (BCA)
Blagrave House
17 Blagrave Street
Reading
Berkshire
RG1 1QB
Telephone: (0118) 950 5950

British Industrial Truck Association (BITA)
Scammell House
High Street
Ascot
Berkshire
SL5 7JF
Telephone: (01344) 623 800

British Occupational Hygiene Society
Suite 2
Georgian House
Great Northern Road
Derby
DE1 1LT
Telephone: (01332) 298 101

British Safety Council (BSC)
National Safety Centre
70 Chancellors Road
London
W6 9RS
Telephone: (0181) 741 1231

British Standards Institution (BSI)
389 Chiswick High Road
London
W4 4AL
Telephone: (0181) 996 9000

Chartered Institute of Environmental Health (CIEH)
Chadwick Court
15 Hatfields
London
SE1 8DJ
Telephone: (0171) 928 6006

Construction Industry Training Board (CITB)
Bircham Newton
Kings Lynn
Norfolk
PE31 6RH
Telephone: (01485) 577 577

Department for Education and Employment (DfEE)
Public Enquiries
Century Buildings
Great Smith Street
London
SW1P 3BT
Telephone: (0845) 609 9960

Department of the Environment, Transport and the Regions (DETR)
Public Enquiries
Ashdown House
123 Victoria Street
London
SW1E 6DE
Telephone: (0171) 890 3000

Department of Health (DoH)
Public Enquiries
Richmond House
79 Whitehall
London
SW1A 2NS
Telephone: (0171) 210 4850

Department of Social Security (DSS)
Richmond House
79 Whitehall
London
SW1A 2NS
Telephone: (0171) 712 2171

Department of Trade and Industry (DTI)
Public Enquiries
10-18 Victoria Street
London
SW1H 0NN
Telephone: (0171) 215 5000

Environment Agency
Apollo Court
2 Bishops Square Business Park
St Albans Road West
Hatfield
Hertfordshire
AL10 9EX
Telephone: (01707) 632 300

Fire Protection Association (FPA) Loss Prevention Council
Melrose Avenue
Borehamwood
Herts
WD6 2BJ
Telephone: (0181) 207 2345

Health and Safety Commission (HSC)
Rose Court
2 Southwark Bridge
London
SE1 9HS
Telephone: (0171) 717 6000

Health and Safety Executive (HSE)
Information Centre & Public Enquiry Point
Broad Lane
Sheffield
S3 7HQ
Telephone: (0541) 545 500

Health and Safety Publications
HSE Books
PO Box 1999
Sudbury
Suffolk
CO10 6FS
Telephone: (01787) 881 165

Institute of Occupational Hygienists
Suite 2
Georgian House
Great Northern Road
Derby
DE1 1LT
Telephone: (01332) 298 087

Institution of Occupational Safety and Health (IOSH)
The Grange
Highfield Drive
Wigston
Leicester
LE18 1NN
Telephone: (0116) 257 3100

Lantra National Training
National Agricultural Centre
Stoneleigh
Near Kenilworth
Warwickshire
CV8 2LG
Telephone: (01203) 696 996

Loss Prevention Council
(*see* Fire Protection Association above)

Qualifications and Curriculum Authority (QCA)
29 Bolton Street
London
W1Y 7PD
Telephone: (0171) 509 5555

Road Haulage and Distribution Training Council
14 Warren Yard
Warren Farm Office Village
Stratford Road
Milton Keynes
MK12 5NW
Telephone: (01908) 313 360

RTITB Ltd
Ercall House
8 Pearson Road
Central Park
Telford
TF2 9TX
Telephone: (01952) 777 777

Royal Society for the Prevention of Accidents (RoSPA)
Edgbaston Park
35 Bristol Road
Birmingham
B5 7ST
Telephone: (0121) 248 2000

Society for the Prevention of Asbestosis and Industrial Diseases (SPAID)
39 Drapers Road
Enfield
Middlesex
EN2 8LU
Telephone: (0181) 388 1640

Storage Equipment Manufacturers' Association (SEMA)
MacLaren Buildings
35 Dale End
Birmingham
B4 7LN
Telephone: (0121) 200 2100

Appendix 2

Current HSE Publications

Guidance Notes

There are 6 principal series of guidance notes available. These are: Chemical Sa (CS); Environmental Hygiene (EH); General Series (GS); Medical Series (M Plant and Machinery (PM), and Legal Series (L).

The following list indicates publications currently in print available from F Books.

Chemical safety

CS 3	Storage and use of sodium chlorate and other similar strong oxidants. 1998
CS 4	The keeping of LPG in cylinders and similar containers. 1986
CS 8	Small scale storage and display of LPG at retail premises. 1985
CS 9	Bulk storage and use of liquid carbon dioxide: hazards and procedures. 1985
CS 11	Storage and use of LPG on metered estates. 1987
CS 15	The cleaning and gas freeing of tanks containing flammable residues. 1985
CS 18	Storage and handling of ammonium nitrate. 1986
CS 21	Storage and handling of organic peroxides. 1991
CS 22	Fumigation. 1996
CS 23	Disposal of waste explosives. 1999

Environmental hygiene

EH 1	Cadmium: health and safety precautions. 1995
EH 2	Chromium and its inorganic compounds: health and safety precautions. 1998
EH 10	Asbestos: exposure limits and measurement of airborne dust concentrations. 1995
EH 13	Beryllium: health and safety precautions. 1995
EH 16	Isocyanates: health hazards and precautionary measures. 1997
EH 17	Mercury and its inorganic divalent compounds. 1996
EH 19	Antimony and its compounds: health hazards and precautionar measures. 1997
EH 20	Phosphine: health and safety precautions. 1979
EH 38	Ozone: health hazards and precautionary measures. 1996
EH 40/98	Occupational exposure limits. 1998
EH 43	Carbon monoxide. 1998
EH 44	Dust: general principles of protection. 1997
EH 46	Man-made mineral fibres. 1990
EH 47	Provision, use and maintenance of hygiene facilities for work w asbestos insulation and coatings. 1990
EH 50	Training operatives and supervisors for work with asbestos insulation and coatings. 1988
EH 51	Enclosures provided for work with asbestos insulation, coating and insulating board. 1989

EH 53	Respiratory protective equipment for use against airborne radioactivity. 1989
EH 54	Assessment of exposure to fume from welding and allied processes. 1990
EH 55	The control of exposure to fume from welding, brazing and similar processes. 1990
EH 57	The problems of asbestos removal at high temperatures. 1993
EH 58	Carcinogenicity of mineral oils. 1990
EH 59	Respirable crystalline silica. 1997
EH 60	Nickel and its inorganic compounds: health hazards and precautionary measures. 1997
EH 63	Vinyl chloride: toxic hazards and precautions. 1992
EH 64	Summary criteria for occupational exposure limits 1996. 1996
EH 64	Criteria documents summaries – 1998 supplement. 1998
EH 65/1	Trimethylbenzenes – criteria document for an OEL. 1992
EH 65/2	Pulverised fuel ash – criteria document for an OEL. 1992
EH 65/3	N,N-Dimethylacetamide – criteria document for an OEL. 1992
EH 65/4	1,2-dichloroethane – criteria document for an OEL. 1993
EH 65/5	4,4'-Methylene dianiline – criteria document for an OEL. 1993
EH 65/6	Epichlorohydrin – criteria document for an OEL. 1993
EH 65/7	Chlorodifluoromethane – criteria document for an OEL. 1994
EH 65/8	Cumene – criteria document for an OEL. 1994
EH 65/9	1,4-dichlorobenzene – criteria document for an OEL. 1994
EH 65/10	Carbon tetrachloride – criteria document for an OEL. 1994
EH 65/11	Chloroform – criteria document for an OEL. 1994
EH 65/12	Portland cement dust – criteria document for an OEL. 1994
EH 65/13	Kaolin – criteria document for an OEL. 1994
EH 65/14	Paracetamol – criteria document for an OEL. 1994
EH 65/15	1,1,1,2-Tetrafluoroethane HFC 134a – criteria document for an OEL. 1995
EH 65/16	Methyl methacrylate – criteria document for an OEL. 1995
EH 65/17	p-Aramid respirable fibres – criteria document for an OEL. 1995
EH 65/18	Propranolol – criteria document for an OEL. 1995
EH 65/19	Mercury and its inorganic divalent compounds – criteria document for an OEL. 1995
EH 65/20	Ortho-toluidine – criteria document for an OEL. 1996
EH 65/21	Propylene oxide – criteria document for an OEL. 1996
EH 65/22	Softwood dust – criteria document for an OEL. 1996
EH 65/23	Antimony and its compounds – criteria document for an OEL. 1996
EH 65/24	Platinum metal and soluble platinum salts – criteria document for an OEL. 1996
EH 65/25	Iodomethane – criteria document for an OEL. 1996
EH 65/26	Azodicarbonamide – criteria document for an OEL. 1996
EH 65/27	Dimethyl and diethyl sulphates – criteria document for an OEL. 1996
EH 65/28	Hydrazine – criteria document for an OEL. 1996
EH 65/29	Acid anhydrides – criteria document for an OEL. 1996
EH 65/30	Review of fibre toxicology – criteria document for an OEL. 1996
EH 65/31	Rosin-based solder flux fume – criteria document for an OEL. 1997
EH 65/32	Glutaraldehyde. 1997
EH 66	Grain dust. 1998
EH 67	Grain dust in maltings (maximum exposure limits). 1993
EH 68	Cobalt: health and safety precautions. 1995

EH 69	How to handle PCBs without harming yourself or the environment. 1995
EH 70	Control of fire-water run-off from CIMAH sites to prevent environmental damage. 1995
EH 72/1	Phenylhydrazine – risk assessment document. 1997
EH 72/2	Dimethylaminoethanol – risk assessment document. 1997
EH 72/3	Bromoethane – risk assessment document. 1997
EH 72/4	3-Chloropropene – risk assessment document. 1997
EH 72/5	Chlorotoluene. 1997
EH 72/6	2-Furaldehyde. 1997
EH 72/7	1,2-Diaminoethane (Ethylenediamine (EDA)). 1997
EH 72/8	Aniline _risk assessment document. 1998
EH 72/9	Barium sulphate – risk assessment document. 1998
EH 72/10	N-Methyl-2-Pyrrolidone – risk assessment document. 1998
EH 73	Arsenic and its compounds: Health hazards and precautionary measures. 1997
EH 74/1	Exposure assessment: dichloromethane. 1998

General series

GS 4	Safety in pressure testing. 1998
GS 6	Avoidance of danger from overhead electrical lines. 1997
GS 28/2	Safe erection of structures: Part 2. Site management and procedures. 1985
GS 28/3	Safe erection of structures: Part 3. Working places and access. 1986
GS 32	Health and safety in shoe repair premises. 1984
GS 38	Electrical test equipment for use by electricians. 1995
GS 46	In situ timber treatment using timber preservatives: health, safety and environmental precautions. 1989
GS 48	Training and standards of competence for people working with chainsaws. 1997
GS 50	Electrical safety at places of entertainment. 1997
GS 53	Single-flue steel industrial chimneys: inspection and maintenance. 1997

Medical series

MS 7	Colour vision. 1987
MS 12	Mercury: medical guidance notes. 1996
MS 17	Biological monitoring of workers exposed to organo–phosphorus pesticides. 1987
MS 24	Health surveillance of occupational skin disease. 1998
MS 25	Medical aspects of occupational asthma. 1998
MS 26	A guide to audiometric testing programmes. 1995

Plant and machinery

PM 4	High temperature textile dyeing machines. 1997
PM 5	Automatically controlled steam and hot water boilers. 1989
PM 15	Safety in the use of pallets. 1998
PM 16	Eyebolts. 1978
PM 17	Pneumatic nailing and stapling guns. 1979
PM 24	Safety at rack and pinion hoists. 1981
PM 29	Electrical risks from steam/water pressure cleaners. 1995

PM 35	Safety in the use of reversing dough brakes. 1983
PM 38	Selection and use of electric handlamps. 1992
PM 39	Hydrogen cracking of grade T(8) chain and components. 1998
PM 40	Protection of workers at welded steel tube mills. 1984
PM 48	Safe operation of passenger carrying amusement devices: the octopus. 1985
PM 55	Safe working with overhead travelling cranes. 1985
PM 56	Noise from pneumatic systems. 1985
PM 57	Safe operation of passenger carrying amusement devices: the big wheel. 1986
PM 59	Safe operation of passenger carrying amusement devices: the paratrooper. 1986
PM 60	Steam boiler blowdown systems. 1998
PM 61	Safe operation of passenger carrying amusement devices: the chair-o-plane. 1986
PM 63	Inclined hoists used in building and construction work. 1987
PM 65	Worker protection at crocodile (alligator) shears. 1986
PM 66	Scrap baling machines. 1986
PM 68	Safe operation of passenger carrying amusement devices: rollercoaster. 1987
PM 69	Safety in the use of freight containers. 1987
PM 70	Safe operation of passenger carrying amusement devices: ark/speedways. 1988
PM 71	Safe operation of passenger carrying amusement devices: water chutes. 1989
PM 72	Safe operation of passenger carrying amusement devices: the trabant. 1990
PM 73	Safety at autoclaves. 1998
PM 75	Glass reinforced plastic vessels and tanks: advice to users. 1991
PM 76	Safe operation of passenger carrying amusement devices: inflatable bouncing devices. 1991
PM 77	Fitness of equipment used for medical exposure to ionising radiation. 1998
PM 78	Passenger carrying aerial ropeways. 1994
PM 79	Power presses: thorough examination and testing. 1995
PM 81	Safe management of ammonia refrigeration systems: food and other workplaces. 1995
PM 82	The selection, installation and maintenance of electrical apparatus for use in and around buildings containing explosives. 1997
PM 83	Drilling machines: guarding of spindles and attachments. 1998

Health and Safety: Guidance Booklets

The purpose of this series is to provide guidance for those who have duties under *HSWA* and other relevant legislation. It gives guidance on the practical application of regulations made under *HSWA*, but should not be regarded as an authoritative interpretation of the law.

HS(G) 6	Safety in working with lift trucks. 1993
HS(G) 16	Evaporating and other ovens. 1981
HS(G) 17	Safety in the use of abrasive wheels. 1992
HS(G) 25	Control of Industrial Major Accident Hazards Regulations 1984 (CIMAH): further guidance on emergency plans. 1985
HS(G) 28	Safety advice for bulk chlorine installations. 1999
HS(G) 29	Locomotive boilers. 1986

HS(G) 31	Pie and tart machines. 1986.
HS(G) 32	Safety in falsework for in situ beams and slabs. 1987
HS(G) 37	An introduction to local exhaust ventilation. 1993
HS(G) 38	Lighting at work. 1997
HS(G) 39	Compressed air safety. 1998
HS(G) 40	Chlorine from drums and cylinders. 1999
HS(G) 41	Petrol filling stations: construction and operation. 1990
HS(G) 42	Safety in the use of metal cutting guillotines and shears. 1988
HS(G) 43	Industrial robot safety. 1988
HS(G) 45	Safety in meat preparation: guidance for butchers. 1995
HS(G) 47	Avoiding danger from underground services. 1989
HS(G) 48	Human factors in industrial safety. 1989
HS(G) 49	The examination and testing of portable radiation instruments for external radiations. 1990
HS(G) 51	The storage of flammable liquids in containers. 1998
HS(G) 53	The selection, use and maintenance of respiratory protective equipment: a practical guide. 1998
HS(G) 54	The maintenance, examination and testing of local exhaust ventilation. 1998
HS(G) 55	Health and safety in kitchens and food preparation areas. 1990
HS(G) 57	Seating at work. 1997
HS(G) 60	Work related upper limb disorders: a guide to prevention. 1990
HS(G) 62	Health and safety in tyre and exhaust fitting premises. 1991
HS(G) 63	Radiation protection off site for emergency services in the event of a nuclear accident. 1991
HS(G) 64	Assessment of fire hazards from solid materials and the precautions required for their safe storage and use: a guide for manufacturers, suppliers, storekeepers and users. 1991
HS(G) 65	Successful health and safety management. 1997
HS(G) 66	Protection of workers and the general public during the development of contaminated land. 1991
HS(G) 67	Health and safety in motor vehicle repair. 1997
HS(G) 70	The control of legionellosis including legionnaire's disease. 1993
HS(G) 71	Chemical warehousing: storage of packaged dangerous substances. 1998
HS(G) 72	Control of respirable silica dust in heavy clay and refractory processes. 1992
HS(G) 73	Control of respirable crystalline silica in quarries. 1992
HS(G) 76	Health and safety in retail and wholesale warehouses. 1992
HS(G) 77	COSHH and peripatetic workers. 1992
HS(G) 78	Dangerous goods in cargo transport units: packing and carriage for transport by sea. 1998
HS(G) 79	Health and safety in golf course management and maintenance. 1994
HS(G) 85	Electricity at work: safe working practices. 1993
HS(G) 87	Safety in the remote diagnosis of manufacturing plant and equipment. 1995
HS(G) 88	Hand-arm vibration. 1994
HS(G) 89	Safeguarding agricultural machinery. 1998
HS(G) 90	VDUs: an easy guide to the Regulations: how to comply with the Health and safety (Display Screen Equipment) Regulations 1992. 1994
HS(G) 91	A framework for the restriction of occupational exposure to ionising radiation. 1992
HS(G) 92	Safe use and storage of cellular plastics. 1996

HS(G) 93	The assessment of pressure vessels operating at low temperature. 1993
HS(G) 94	Safety in the use of gamma and electron irradiation facilities. 1998
HS(G) 95	The radiation safety of lasers used for display purposes. 1996
HS(G) 96	The costs of accidents at work. 1997
HS(G) 97	A step by step guide to COSHH assessment. 1993
HS(G) 100	Prevention of violence to staff in banks and building societies. 1993
HS(G) 101	The costs to the British economy of work accidents and work related ill health. 1995
HS(G) 103	Safe handling of combustible dusts: precautions against explosions. 1994
HS(G) 104	Health and safety in residential care homes. 1993
HS(G) 105	Health and safety in horse riding establishments. 1993
HS(G) 107	Maintaining portable and transportable electrical equipment. 1994
HS(G) 109	Control of noise in quarries. 1993
HS(G) 110	Seven steps to successful substitution of hazardous substances. 1994
HS(G) 110W	Seven steps to successful substitution of hazardous substances. (Welsh version) 1994
HS(G) 112	Health and safety at motor sports events: a guide for employers and organisers. 1999
HS(G) 113	Lift trucks in potentially flammable atmospheres. 1996
HS(G) 114	Conditions for the authorisation of explosives in Great Britain. 1994
HS(G) 115	Manual handling: solutions you can handle. 1994
HS(G) 116	Stress at work: a guide for employers. 1995
HS(G) 117	Making sense of NONS: a guide to the Notification of New Substances Regulations 1993. 1994
HS(G) 118	Electrical safety in arc welding. 1994
HS(G) 119	Manual handling for drinks delivery. 1994
HS(G) 120	Nuclear site licences under the Nuclear Installations Act 1965: notes for applicants. 1994
HS(G) 121	A pain in your workplace? Ergonomic problems and solutions. 1994
HS(G) 122	New and expectant mothers at work: a guide for employers. 1994
HS(G) 123	Working together on firework displays: a guide to safety for firework display organisers and operators. 1995
HS(G) 124	Giving your own firework display: how to run and fire it safely. 1995
HS(G) 125	A brief guide on COSHH for the offshore oil and gas industry. 1994
HS(G) 126	CHIP 2 for everyone. 1995
HS(G) 129	Health and safety in engineering workshops. 1995
HS(G) 131	Energetic and spontaneously combustible substances: identification and safe handling. 1995
HS(G) 132	How to deal with sick building syndrome: guidance for employers, building owners and building managers. 1995
HS(G) 133	Preventing violence to retail staff. 1995
HS(G) 135	Storage and handling of industrial nitrocellulose. 1995
HS(G) 136	Workplace transport safety: guidance for employers. 1995
HS(G) 137	Health risk management: a practical guide for managers in small and medium-sized enterprises. 1995
HS(G) 137W	Health risk management: a practical guide for managers in small and medium-sized enterprises. (Welsh version) 1996

HS(G) 138	Sound solutions: techniques to reduce noise at work. 1995
HS(G) 139	The safe use of compressed gases in welding, flame cutting and allied processes. 1997
HS(G) 140	Safe use and handling of flammable liquids. 1996
HS(G) 141	Electrical safety on construction sites. 1995
HS(G) 142	Dealing with offshore emergencies. 1996
HS(G) 144	Safe use of vehicles on construction sites. 1998
HS(G) 146	Dispensing petrol: assessing and controlling the risk of fire and explosion at sites where petrol is stored and dispensed as a fuel. 1996
HS(G) 148	Sheeting and unsheeting of tipper lorries: guidance for the road haulage industry. 1996
HS(G) 150	Health and safety in construction. 1996
HS(G) 151	Protecting the public – your next move. 1997
HS(G) 153/1	Railway safety principles and guidance: part 1. 1996
HS(G) 153/2	Railway safety principles and guidance: part 2 section A. Guidance on the infrastructure. 1996
HS(G) 153/3	Railway safety principles and guidance: part 2 section B. Guidance on stations. 1996
HS(G) 153/4	Railway safety principles and guidance: part 2 section C. Guidance on electric traction systems. 1996
HS(G) 153/5	Railway safety principles and guidance: part 2 section D. Guidance on signalling. 1996
HS(G) 153/6	Railway safety principles and guidance: part 2 section E. Guidance on level crossings. 1996
HS(G) 153/7	Railway safety principles and guidance: part 2 section F. Guidance on trains. 1996
HS(G) 153/8	Railway safety principles and guidance: part 2 section G. Guidance on tramways. 1997
HS(G) 154	Managing crowds safely. 1996
HS(G) 155	Slips and trips: guidance for employers on identifying hazards and controlling risks. 1996
HS(G) 156	Slips and trips: guidance for the food processing industry. 1996
HS(G) 158	Flame arresters: preventing the spread of fires and explosions in equipment that contains flammable gases and vapours. 1996
HS(G) 160	The carriage of dangerous goods explained: Part 1. Guidance for consignors of dangerous goods by road and rail (classification, packaging, labelling and provision of information). 1996
HS(G) 161	The carriage of dangerous goods explained: Part 2. Guidance for road vehicle operators and others involved in the carriage of dangerous goods by road. 1996
HS(G) 162	The carriage of dangerous goods explained: Part 4. Guidance for operators, drivers and others involved in the carriage of explosives by road. 1996
HS(G) 163	The carriage of dangerous goods explained: Part 3. Guidance for rail operators and others involved in the carriage of dangerous goods by rail. 1996
HS(G) 164	The carriage of dangerous goods explained: Part 5. Guidance for consignors, rail operators and others involved in the packaging, labelling and carriage of radioactive material by rail. 1996
HS(G) 165	Young people at work: a guide for employers. 1997
HS(G) 166	Formula for health and safety: guidance for small to medium-sized firms in the chemical manufacturing industry. 1996

HS(G) 167	Biological monitoring in the workplace: a guide to its practical application to chemical exposure. 1997
HS(G) 168	Fire safety in construction: guidance for clients, designers and those managing and carrying out construction work involving significant fire risks. 1997
HS(G) 169	Camera operations on location: guidance for managers and camera crews for work in news gathering, current affairs and factual programming. 1997
HS(G) 170	Vibration solutions: practical ways to reduce hand-arm vibration injury. 1997
HS(G) 171	Well handled: offshore manual handling solutions. 1997
HS(G) 172	Health and safety in sawmilling: a run-of-the-mill-business?. 1997
HS(G) 173	Monitoring strategies for toxic substances. 1997
HS(G) 174	Anthrax: health hazards. 1997
HS(G) 175	Fairgrounds and amusement parks: guidance on safe practice. 1997
HS(G) 176	The storage of flammable liquids in tanks. 1998
HS(G) 178	The spraying of flammable liquids. 1998
HS(G) 180	Application of electro-sensitive protective equipment using light curtains and light beam devices in machinery. 1999'
HS(G) 181	Assessment principles for offshore safety cases. 1998
HS(G) 182	Sound solutions offshore: practical examples of noise reduction. 1998
HS(G) 183	Five steps to risk assessment: case studies. 1998
HS(G) 184	Guidance on the handling, storage and transport of airbags and seat pretensioners. 1998
HS(G) 185	Health and safety in excavations: be safe and shore. 1999
HS(G) 186	The bulk transfer of dangerous liquids and gasses between ship and shore. 1999
HS(G) 187	Control of diesel engine exhaust emissions in the workplace. 1999
HS(G) 188	Health risk management: a guide to working with solvents. 1999
HS(G) 189/1	Controlled asbestos stripping techniques for work requiring a licence. 1999
HS(G) 189/2	Working with asbestos cement. 1999

Legal – Approved Codes of Practice (COP series), HS(R) series and new L series

Code numbers in the HS(R) series and the COP series are gradually being superseded by the L series. Publications in the L series contain guidance on Regulations and Approved Codes of Practice.

Approved Codes of Practice

COP 2	Control of lead at work (in support of SI 1980 No 1248) – approved code of practice. 1998
COP 6	Plastic containers with nominal capacities up to 5 litres for petroleum spirit: requirements for testing and marking or labelling (in support of SI 1982 No 830) – approved code of practice. 1982
COP 14	Road tanker testing: examination, testing and certification of the carrying tanks of road tankers and of tank containers used for the conveyance of dangerous substances by road (in support of SI 1981 No 1059) – approved code of practice. 1985

COP 15	Zoos: safety, health and welfare standards for employers and persons at work – approved code of practice and guidance notes. 1985
COP 20	Standards of training in safe gas installation – approved code of practice. 1987
COP 23	Exposure to radon: the Ionising Radiations Regulations 1985 – approved code of practice. 1988
COP 24	Preventing accidents to children in agriculture – approved code of practice and guidance notes. 1988
COP 25	Safety in docks: Docks Regulations 1988 – approved code of practice with regulations and guidance. 1988
COP 26	Rider operated lift trucks: operator training – approved code of practice and supplementary guidance. 1988
COP 27	Explosives at quarries: Quarries (Explosives) Regulations 1988 – approved code of practice. 1989
COP 28	Safety of exit from mines underground workings: Mines (Safety of Exit) Regulations 1988 – approved code of practice. 1988
COP 32	First-aid on offshore installations and pipeline works: Offshore Installations and Pipeline Works (First-Aid) Regulations 1989 – approved code of practice with regulations and guidance. 1990
COP 34	Use of electricity in mines: Electricity at Work Regulations 1989 – approved code of practice. 1989
COP 37	Safety of pressure systems: Pressure Systems and Transportable Gas Containers Regulations 1989 – approved code of practice. 1990
COP 38	Safety of transportable gas containers: Pressure Systems and Transportable Gas Containers Regulations 1989 – approved code of practice. 1990

HS(R) series

HS(R) 4	A guide to the Offices Shops and Railway Premises Act 1963. 1989
HS(R) 17	A guide to the Classification and Labelling of Explosives Regulations 1983. 1983
HS(R) 21	A guide to the Control of Industrial Major Accident Hazards (CIMAH) Regulations 1984. 1990
HS(R) 25	Memorandum of guidance on the Electricity at Work Regulations 1989. 1989
HS(R) 27	A guide to the Dangerous Substances in Harbour Areas Regulations 1987. 1988
HS(R) 28	Guide to the Loading and Unloading of Fishing Vessels Regulations 1988. 1988
HS(R) 29	Guide to the notification and marking of sites in accordance with the Dangerous Substances (Notification and Marking of Sites) Regulations. 1990

L series

L 1	A guide to the Health and Safety at Work etc Act 1974. 1992
L 5	General COSHH ACOP, Carcinogens ACOP and Biological Agents ACOP. Control of Substances Hazardous to Health Regulations 1994 – approved code of practice. 1997

L7   Dose limitation-restriction of exposure: additional guidance on regulation 6 of the Ionising Radiations Regulations 1985 – approved code of practice, part 4. 1991 (see also COP 23)

L 8   The prevention or control of legionellosis (including legionnaire's disease) – approved code of practice. 1995

L 9   Safe use of pesticides for non-agricultural purposes. Control of Substances Hazardous to Health Regulations 1994 – approved code of practice. 1991

L 10   A guide to the Control of Explosives Regulations 1991. 1991

L 11   A guide to the Asbestos (Licensing) Regulations 1983. 1991

L 13   A guide to the Packaging of Explosives for Carriage Regulations 1991. 1991

L 16   Design and construction of vented, non-pressure road tankers used for the carriage of flammable liquids. Road Traffic (Carriage of Dangerous Substances in Road Tankers and Tank Containers) Regulations 1992 – approved code of practice. 1993

L 19   Design and construction of vacuum operated road tankers used for the carriage of hazardous wastes. Road Traffic (Carriage of Dangerous Substances in Road Tankers and Tank Containers) Regulations 1992 – approved code of practice. 1993

L 21   Management of health and safety at work. Management of Health and Safety at Work Regulations 1992 – approved code of practice. 1992

L 22   Work equipment. Provision and Use of Work Equipment Regulations 1992 – guidance on regulations. 1992

L 23   Manual handling. Manual Handling Operations Regulations 1992 – guidance on regulations. 1992

L 24   Workplace health, safety and welfare. Workplace (Health, Safety and Welfare) Regulations 1992 – approved code of practice and guidance. 1992

L 25   Personal protective equipment at work. Personal Protective Equipment at Work Regulations 1992 – guidance on regulations. 1992

L 26   Display screen equipment work. Health and Safety (Display Screen Equipment) Regulations 1992 – guidance on regulations. 1992

L 27   The control of asbestos at work. Control of Asbestos at Work Regulations 1987 – approved code of practice. 1999

L 28   Work with asbestos insulation, asbestos coating and asbestos insulating board. Control of Asbestos at Work Regulations 1987 – approved code of practice. 1999

L 29   A guide to the Genetically Modified Organisms (Contained Use) Regulations 1992 as amended in 1996. 1996

L 31   A guide to the Public Information for Radiation Emergencies Regulations 1992. 1993

L 42   Shafts and winding in mines – approved code of practice on the Mines (Shafts and Winding) Regulations 1993. 1993

L 43   First-aid at mines. Health and Safety (First-Aid) Regulations 1981 – approved code of practice. 1993

L 44   The management and administration of safety and health at mines. Management and Administration of Safety and Health at Mines Regulations 1993 – approved code of practice. 1993

L 45   Explosives at coal and other safety-lamp mines. Coal and Other Safety-lamp Mines (Explosives) Regulations 1993 – approved code of practice. 1993

L 46	Prevention of inrushes in mines – approved code of practice. 1993
L 47	The Coal Mines (Owners' Operating Rules) Regulations 1993 – guidance on the regulations. 1993
L 49	Protection of outside workers against ionising radiations. Ionising Radiations (Outside Workers) Regulations 1993 – approved code of practice. 1993
L 50	Railways safety critical work. Railways (Safety Critical Work) Regulations 1994 – approved code of practice and guidance. 1996
L 51	Carriage of Dangerous Goods by Rail. Carriage of Dangerous Goods by Rail Regulations 1994. 1994
L 52	Railway safety cases. Railways (Safety Case) Regulations 1994 – guidance on regulations. 1994
L 54	Managing construction for health and safety. The Construction (Design and Management) Regulations 1994 – approved code of practice. 1995
L 55	Preventing asthma at work. How to control respiratory sensitisers. 1994
L 56	Safety in the installation and use of gas systems and appliances. The Gas Safety (Installation and Use) Regulations 1994 – approved code of practice. 1994
L 58	The protection of persons against ionising radiation arising from any work activity. 1994
L 59	A guide to the approval of railway works, plant and equipment. 1994
L 60	Control of substances hazardous to health in the production of pottery. The Control of Substances Hazardous to Health Regulations 1994. The Control of Lead at Work Regulations 1980 – approved code of practice. 1995
L 62	Safety datasheets for substances and preparations dangerous for supply. Guidance on Regulation 6 of the CHIP Regulations 1994 – approved code of practice. 1995
L 64	Safety signs and signals. The Health and Safety (Safety Signs and Signals) Regulations 1996 – guidance on regulations. 1997
L 65	Prevention of fire and explosion, and emergency response on offshore installations. Offshore Installations Regulations 1995 – approved code of practice and guidance. 1997
L 66	Guide to the Placing on the Market and Supervision of Transfers of Explosives Regulations 1993 (POMSTER). 1995
L 67	Control of vinyl chloride at work. Control of Substances Hazardous to Health Regulations 1994 – approved code of practice. 1995
L 70	A guide to the Offshore Installations and Pipeline Works (Management and Administration) Regulations 1995. 1995
L 71	Escape and rescue from mines. Escape and Rescue from Mines Regulations 1995 – approved code of practice. 1995
L 72	A guide to Borehole Sites and Operations Regulations 1995. 1995
L 73	A guide to the Reporting of Injuries, Diseases and Dangerous Occurrences Regulations 1995. 1996
	A guide to the Reporting of Injuries, Diseases and Dangerous Occurrences Regulations 1995 and electronic copies of report forms F2508, F2508A, F2508G and OIR/9B. 1999
L 74	First aid at work. The Health and Safety (First-Aid) Regulations 1981 – approved code of practice and guidance. 1997

L 75	Guidance for railways, tramways, trolley vehicle systems and other guided transport systems on RIDDOR 95. 1996
L 77	Guidance to the licensing authority on the Adventure Activities Licensing Regulations 1996. The Activity Centres (Young Persons' Safety) Act 1995 – guidance on regulations. 1996
L 79	A guide to the Quarries Miscellaneous Health and Safety Provisions Regulations 1995 – guidance on the regulations. 1996
L 80	A guide to the Gas Safety (Management) Regulations 1996. 1996
L 81	The design, construction and installation of gas service pipes. The Pipelines Safety Regulations 1996 – approved code of practice and guidance. 1996
L 82	A guide to the Pipelines Safety Regulations 1996. 1996
L 84	A guide to the well aspects of amendments of the Offshore Installations and Wells (Design and Construction etc.) Regulations 1996. 1996
L 85	A guide to the integrity, workplace environment and miscellaneous aspects of the Offshore Installations and Wells (Design and Construction etc.) Regulations 1996 – guidance on regulations. 1996
L86	Control of substances hazardous to health in fumigation operations. Control of Substances Hazardous to Health Regulations 1994 – approved code of practice. 1996
L87	Safety representatives and safety committees (the brown book) – approved code of practice and guidance on the regulations. 1996
L 88	Approved requirements and test methods for the classification and packaging of dangerous goods for carriage. Carriage of Dangerous Goods (Classification, Packaging and Labelling) and Use of Transportable Pressure Receptacles Regulations 1996. 1996
L 89	Approved vehicle requirements. Carriage of Dangerous Goods by Road Regulations 1996. 1999
L 90	Approved Carriage List: information approved for the carriage of dangerous goods by road and rail other than explosives and radioactive material. 1999
L91	Suitability of vehicles and containers and limits on quantities for the carriage of explosives. Carriage of Explosives by Road Regulations 1996 – approved code of practice. 1996
L 92	Approved requirements for the construction of vehicles intended for the carriage of explosives by road. Carriage of Explosives by Road Regulations 1996. 1999
L 93	Approved tank requirements: the provisions for bottom loading and vapour recovery systems of mobile containers carrying petrol. Carriage of Dangerous Goods by Road Regulations 1996. Carriage of Dangerous Goods by Rail Regulations 1996. 1996
L 94	Approved requirements for the packaging, labelling and carriage of radioactive material by rail. Packaging, Labelling and Carriage of Radioactive Material by Rail Regulations 1996. 1996
L95	A guide to the Health and Safety (Consultation with Employees) Regulations 1996. 1996
L96	A guide to the Work in Compressed Air Regulations 1996. 1996
L 97	A guide to the Level Crossings Regulations 1997. 1997
L 98	Railway safety miscellaneous provisions. Railway Safety (Miscellaneous Provisions) Regulations 1997 – guidance on regulations. 1997

L 100	Approved guide to the classification and labelling of substances dangerous for supply. CHIP 97 – regulations and guidance. 1997
L 101	Safe work in confined spaces. Confined Spaces Regulations 1997 – approved code of practice. 1997
L 103	Commercial diving projects offshore. Diving at Work Regulations 1997 – approved code of practice. 1998
L 104	Commercial diving projects inland/inshore. Diving at Work Regulations 1997 – approved code of practice. 1998
L 105	Recreational diving projects. Diving at Work Regulations 1997 – approved code of practice. 1998
L 106	Media diving projects. Diving at Work Regulations 1997 – approved code of practice. 1998
L 107	Scientific and archaeological diving projects. Diving at Work Regulations 1997 – approved code of practice. 1998
L 108	Guidance on the Noise at Work Regulations 1989. 1998
L 112	Safe use of power presses. 1998
L 113	Safe use of lifting equipment. Lifting Operations and Lifting Equipment Regulations 1998. 1998
L 114	Safe use of woodworking machinery. 1998
L 115	CHIP approved supply list. 1998

Free Publications

Catalogues

CAT34	1999 price list for general etc. HSC/E publications.
CAT35	1998 price list for research and technical HSE publications.
MISC1	10 List of videos available from HSE Videos.

Legislation and enforcement policy

HSC13	Health and safety regulations – a short guide. (Also available in Welsh)
HSC14	What to expect when a health and safety inspector calls.
HSE4	Short guide to the Employers' Liability (Compulsory Insurance) Regulations. Revised 1998
HSE31	Everyone's guide to RIDDOR. (Also available in Welsh)
HSE32	RIDDOR – information for doctors.
HSE33	RIDDOR – offshore.
HSE36	Employers' Liability (Compulsory Insurance) Regulations: a guide for employees.
INDG184	Signpost to the Safety Signs Regulations 1996: guidance on the Regulations.
INDG244	Workplace health safety and welfare – a short guide.
MISC030	HSC: enforcement policy statement. (Also available in Welsh)

General guidance for employers

HSC6	Writing a safety policy: advice for employers.
HSE27	Your health and safety: a guide for workers. (Available in Bengali; Gujarati; Hindi; Punjabi; Urdu, accompanied by an English translation)
HSE34	HSE and you – citizens charter. 1996/1997 (Also available in Welsh; Bengali; Gujarati; Hindi; Punjabi; Urdu)
HSE 35	Working with employers. 1996/1997 (Also available in Welsh)

INDG133	Selecting a health and safety consultant.
INDG179REV	Policy statement on open government. Revised 1998
INDG229	Using work equipment safely.
INDG232	Consulting employees on health and safety: a guide to the law.
INDG235	A guide to information, instruction and training: common provisions in health and safety law.
INDG259	An introduction to health and safety. (Also available in Welsh)
INDG267	Health and safety and the year 2000 problem. 1998
INDG268	Working together: guidance on health and safety of contractors and suppliers. 1998
INDG283	Contingency planning for a safe year 2000. 1998
INDG287	Year 2000 risk assessment: will you come through the millennium safely? 1999
MISC069	An employers' guide to 'good health is good business'. (Phase 2)
MISC071	Health and safety in small firms. (Also available in Welsh)
MISC130	Good health is good business. (Phase 3)

General guidance for employees and the self-employed

HSE34	HSE and you – citizens charter. 1996/1997 (Also available in Welsh; Bengali; Gujarati; Hindi; Punjabi; Urdu)
HSE36	Employers' Liability (Compulsory Insurance) Regulations: a guide for employees.
INDG62	Protecting your health at work. (Also available in Welsh)
INDG116	What your doctor needs to know if you think you have a work-related health problem. (Also available in Welsh)
INDG179REV	Policy statement on open government. Revised
INDG232	Consulting employees on health and safety: a guide to the law.
INDG235	A guide to information, instruction and training: common provisions in health and safety law.

Breathing

INDG36REV	Passive smoking at work. Revised (Also available in Welsh)
INDG95	Respiratory sensitisers and COSHH: an employer's guide.
INDG137	Grin and wear it: respiratory protective equipment.
INDG172	Breathe easy: a worker's pocket card on respiratory sensitisers.
INDG188	Asbestos alert (pocket card) for building maintenance, repair and refurbishment workers. (Also available in Welsh)
INDG223REV	Managing asbestos in workplace buildings. Revised
INDG248	Solder fume and you.

Chemicals

CHIS1	Lessons to be learnt from recent major accidents. 1997
INDG98	Permit to work systems. Revised 1997
INDG161L	Emergency action for burns. 1997
INDG186	Read the label: how to find out if chemicals are dangerous.
INDG243	Computer control – a question of safety.
INDG245	Biological monitoring for chemicals in the workplace. 1997
INDG246	Prepared for emergency.
INDG254	Chemical reaction hazards. 1997

Construction

CIS8REV	Safety in excavations. Revised 1997
CIS17	Construction health and safety checklist. Revised 1996
CIS18	Provision of welfare facilities at fixed construction sites. Revised 1996
CIS24	Chemical cleaners. Revised 1998
CIS27	Solvents. Revised 1998
CIS39	CDM Regulations 1994: the role of the client.
CIS40	CDM Regulations 1994: the role of the planning supervisor.
CIS41	CDM Regulations 1994: the role of the designer.
CIS42	CDM Regulations 1994: the pre-tender stage health and safety plan.
CIS43	CDM Regulations 1994: the health and safety plan during the construction phase.
CIS45	Establishing exclusion zones when using explosives in demolition.
CIS46	Provision of welfare facilities at transient construction sites. 1997
CIS47	Inspections and reports. 1997
CIS49	General access to scaffolds and ladders.
CIS50	PPE: safety helmets. 1997
CIS51	Construction fire safety. 1997
INDG127L	Noise in construction. Revised
INDG212	Glazing and workplace health and safety.
INDG220	A guide to the Construction (Health, Safety and Welfare) Regulations 1996.
INDG258	Work in confined spaces.
INDG262	Head protection for Sikhs wearing turbans. 1998 (Available from Sikh Community and Youth Service, Birmingham *Tel:* 0121 523 0417)

Dangerous substances – general

INDG86L	Contained use of genetically modified organisms.
INDG91REV	Drug misuse at work: a guide for employers. Revised 1997
INDG115REV	An introduction to the Control of Explosives Regulations. Revised
INDG136	COSHH: the new brief guide for employers. Revised (Also available in Welsh)
INDG181D	The complete idiot's guide to CHIP2: a guide to the Chemicals (Hazard Information and Packaging) Regulations.
INDG182	Why do I need a safety data sheet?: for those who use or supply dangerous chemicals.
INDG227	Safe working with flammable substances.
INDG231	Electrical safety and you.
INDG238REV	Gas appliances: get them checked; keep them safe! Revised 1999 (Available in Welsh; Bengali; Gujarati; Hindi; Punjabi; Urdu)
INDG240	Don't mix it: a guide for employers on alcohol at work.
INDG273	Working safely with solvents: a guide to safe working practices. 1998
INDG276	Feral honey bees: points to consider when asked to treat a honey bee nest. 1998
INDG285	Landlords: a guide to landlords' duties – Gas Safety (Installation and Use) Regulations 1998. 1999
L99(F)	General COSHH ACOP (1996 edition): a brief guide to the changes.
PML52	7 steps to successful substitution of hazardous substances.

Dangerous substances – by type

HSE8	Misuse of oxygen: fire and explosion in the use and misuse of oxygen.
INDG66	VCM and you.
INDG197	Working with sewage: the health hazards – a pocket card for employees.
INDG198	Working with sewage: the health hazards – a pocket card for employers.
INDG230	Storage and safe handling of ammonium nitrate.
INDG248	Solder fume and you.
INDG249	Controlling health risks from Rosin (Colophony) based solder fluxes.
INDG257	Pesticides: use them safely.
MISC076	Cyanide poisoning.
MSA1REV	Lead and you. Revised 1998
MSA7	Cadmium and you.
MSA8	Arsenic and you.
MSA13REV	Benzene and you. Revised
MSA14REV	Nickel and you. Revised
MSA15	Silica dust and you.
MSA16	Chromium and you.
MSA17	Cobalt and you.
MSA18	Berylium and you.
MSA19	PCBs and you.
MSA21	MbOCA and you.
MSB4	Skin cancer by pitch and tar.
MSB5	Skin cancer by oil.

Diving

DVIS1	General hazards. 1998
DVIS2	Diving system winches. 1998
DVIS3	Breathing gas management. 1998
DVIS4	Compression chambers. 1998
DVIS5	Exposure limits for air diving operations. 1998
DVIS6	Maintenance of diving bell hoists. 1998
DVIS7	Bell run and bell lock-out times in relation to habitats. 1998
INDG266	Are you involved in a diving project? 1998

Engineering

EIS1	Hot work on vehicle wheels. 1997
EIS2	Accidents at metalworking lathes using emery cloth. 1997
EIS3	Monitoring requirements in the electroplating industry including electrolytic chromium processes. 1998
EIS4	Workplace welfare in the electroplating industry. 1998
EIS5	Health surveillance requirements in the electroplating industry. 1998
EIS6	Electrical systems in the electroplating industry. 1998
EIS7	Safeguarding 3-roll bending machines. Revised 1998
EIS12	Metal-cutting saws. 1998
EIS13	Safeguarding of combination metalworking machines.
EIS14	Skin creams and skin protection in the engineering sector. 1996
EIS15	Control of exposure to triglycidyl isocyanurate (TGIC) in powder coatings. Revised 1998

EIS16	Preventing injuries from the manual handling of sharp edges in the engineering industry.
EIS17	Assessing exposure to Rosin (Colophony) based solder flux fume. 1997
EIS18	Isocyanates: health surveillance in motor vehicle repair. 1997
EIS19	Engineering machine tools: retrofitting CNC. 1997
EIS20	Maintenance and cleaning of solvent degreasing tanks. 1998
EIS21	Immersion and cold cleaning of engineering components. 1998
EIS22	Health and safety at degreasing operations: sources of guidance. 1998
EIS26	Noise in engineering. 1998
EIS27	Control of noise at metal cutting saws. 1998
EIS28	Safeguarding at horizontal boring machines. 1998
EIS29	Control of noise at power presses. 1998
INDG165	Health surveillance and metalworking fluids: a guide for the responsible person.
INDG167	Health risks from metalworking fluids: aspects of good machine design.
INDG168	Metalworking fluids: a guide to good management and practice for minimising risks to health.
INDG169	Metalworking fluids and you.

First aid at work

INDG214	First aid at work – your questions answered.
INDG215	Basic advice on first aid at work.
INDG281	Help on work-related stress. 1998

Foundries

FNIS1	Foundry moulding machines: noise hazards.
FNIS2	Foundry machine guarding: introductory sheet.
FNIS3	Foundry machine guarding: mould and core-making machinery.
FNIS4	Foundry machine guarding: sand handling equipment.
FNIS5	Foundry machine guarding: shakeouts, sand mixer and shotblasts.
FNIS6	Fettling: noise hazards.
FNIS7	Hazards associated with foundry processes: rumbling – noise hazard. 1996
FNIS8	Hazards associated with foundry processes: hand-arm vibration – the current picture. 1996
FNIS9	Hazards associated with foundry processes: hand-arm vibration – symptoms and solutions.
IACL83	Hearing protection on foundries: advice for employees.
IACL104	Health surveillance in foundries. 1998

Health service

| IACL64 | Glutaraldehyde and you. Revised 1998 |
| HSIS1 | RIDDOR 1995: guidance for health services. 1998 |

Homeworking

| INDG226 | Homeworking: guidance for employers and employees on health and safety. |

Ionising radiation

INDG159	A summary of the Gardner study into leukaemia and other cancers in the children of male workers at Sellafield.
INDG206	Wear your dosemeter: poster.
INDG207C	Wear your dosemeter: a pocket card for employees.
INDG210	Radon in the workplace.
INDG224	Controlling the radiation safety of display laser installations.
IRIS1	Industrial radiography: ionising radiation protection.
IRIS2	Radiation doses: assessment and recording.
IRIS3	Portable nuclear moisture density gauges in the construction industry.
MISC05	Radiation safety.
MISC035	Radon – guidance from HSE and BRE.

Machinery

INDG68	Do you use a steam/water pressure cleaner? You could be in for a shock! Revised
INDG139	Electric storage batteries: safe charging and use.
INDG178	Written schemes of examination: pressure systems.
INDG270	Supplying new machinery. 1998
INDG271	Buying new machinery. 1998

Major hazards

INDG196	Safety reports: how HSE assesses these in connection with the Control of Industrial Major Accident Hazards Regulations.

Mining and quarrying

QIS1	A manager's guide to safe coal cleaning and the control of pedestrians at opencast coal sites.
TOP07	Improving cab design and driver vision on free-steered vehicles used underground in mining.

Noise

INDG75	Introducing the Noise at Work Regulations: a brief guide to the requirements for controlling noise at work. (Also available in Welsh)
INDG99	Noise at work: advice to employees.
INDG193	Health surveillance in noisy industries.
INDG200	Ear protection in noisy firms: employers' duties explained.
INDG201	Hear this: a pocket card for employees in noisy working environments.
INDG263	Keep the noise down: advice for purchasers of workplace machinery. 1997

Offices and other buildings

IACL27	Legionnaire's disease
INDG36REV1	Working with VDUs. Revised 1998 (Also available in Welsh)
INDG173	Officewise. (Also available in Welsh)
INDG236	Maintaining portable electrical equipment in offices and other low risk environments.

INDG253   Controlling legionella in nursing and residential care homes. 1997
OSR1   Office, shop and railway premises. (Also available in Welsh)

Offshore oil and gas

INDG94   Offshore first-aid.
INDG119REV   Safety representatives and safety committees on offshore
     installations. Revised 1999
INDG219   How offshore helicopter travel is regulated.
INDG239   Play your part!
INDG250   How HSE assesses Offshore Safety Cases. 1997
INDG274   Offshore health and safety legislation: some questions answered.
     1998

Risk assessment and the prevention of accidents

INDG69REV   Violence to staff. Revised
INDG73REV   Working alone in safety. Revised
INDG163REV   5 steps to risk assessment. Revised 1998
INDG208   Be safe – save money: the cost of accidents – a guide for small
     firms.
INDG213   5 steps to information, instruction and training – meeting risk
     assessment requirements.
INDG218   Guide to risk assessment requirements: common provisions in
     health and safety law.
INDG225   Preventing trips, slips and falls at work.
INDG275   Management of health and safety: 5 steps to success. Revised 1998
MISC038   The use of risk assessment in government departments.
MISC154   Improving the assessment and management of risk within
     government departments. 1998

The Body

INDG84   Leptopirosis: are you at risk?
INDG90   If the task fits – ergonomics at work.
INDG126REV   Vibration white finger: general advice for employees. Revised 1998
INDG143   Getting to grips with manual handling: a short guide for
     employers.
INDG147RV1   Keep your top on: hazards of the sun. (Also available in Welsh)
INDG171L   Upper limb disorders: assessing the risks.
INDG174   A short guide to the Personal Protective Equipment at Work
     Regulations 1992.
INDG175REV   Hand-arm vibration: advice for employers. Revised
INDG233   Preventing dermatitis at work: advice for employers and
     employees.
INDG242   In the driving seat: advice to employers on reducing back pain in
     drivers and machinery operators.
MISC112   Reducing the risk of hand-arm vibration injury among
     stonemasons. 1998

Woodworking

WIS6REV   COSHH and the woodworking industries. Revised 1997
WIS7   Accidents at woodworking machines. 1996
WIS13   Noise at woodworking machines. 1997
WIS15   Safe working at woodworking machines. 1997

Appendix 3

Relevant British Standards

Access equipment	BS 6037
Acoustic measurement/machine tools	BS 4813
Agricultural machinery: combine and forage harvesters	BS EN 632
Agricultural machinery: silage cutters	BS EN 703
Airborne noise emission	
earth-moving machinery	BS 6812
hydraulic transmission systems	BS 5944
portable chain saws	BS 6916–6
Ambient air: determination of asbestos fibres – direct-transfer transmission electron microscopy method	BS ISO 10312
Anchorages	
industrial safety harnesses	BS EN 795
self-locking, industrial	BS EN 353, 355, 360, 362, 365
Arc welding equipment	BS 638
Artificial daylight lamps	
colour assessment	BS 950
for sensitometry	BS 1380–4
Artificial lighting	BS 8206
Barriers, in and about buildings	BS 6180
Bromochlorodifluoromethane	
fire extinguishing systems	BS 5306
fire extinguishers	BS EN 27201
Carbon steel welded horizontal cylindrical storage tanks	BS 2594
Carpet cleaners, electric, industrial use	BS 5415
Cellulose fibres	BS 1771–2
Chain lever hoists	BS 4898
Chain pulley blocks, hand-operated	BS 3243
Chain slings	
alloy steel	BS 3458
high tensile steel	BS 2902
steel use and maintenance	BS 6968
welded	BS 6304
Chairs	
adjustable office furniture	BS 5459
office furniture, design/dimensions	BS 5940
office furniture, ergonomic design	BS 3044
Chemical protective clothing	
against gases and vapours	pr EN 464
liquid chemicals	pr EN 463, 465, 466, 467, 468
Circular saws	
hand-held electric	BS 2769
safeguarding	BS 6854–2
woodworking	BS 411
Cleaning and surface repair of buildings	BS 6270
Closed circuit escape breathing apparatus	BS EN 400
Clothing for protection against intense heat	BS EN 366, 367

Concrete cladding	BS 8297
Construction equipment	
hoists	BS 7212
suspended safety chairs, cradles	BS 2830
Control of noise (construction and open sites)	BS 5228
Cranes, safe use	BS 5744, 7121
Disabled people, means of escape	BS 5588
Drill Rigs	BS EN 791
Dust	
high efficiency respirators	BS EN 136, 143
particulate emission	BS 3405
particulate emission, high accuracy	BS 893
Ear protectors, sound attenuation measurement	BS EN 24689–1
Earphones	
audiometry, calibration, acoustic couplers	BS 4668
audiometry, calibration ears	BS 4669
Earthing	BS 7430
Earth moving equipment	BS 6912
Electrical equipment	
explosive atmospheres	BS 4683, 5501, 5345, 6941
fire hazard testing	BS 6458
guidance to wiring regulations	BS 7671
impedance measurement	BS 6161–6
Electrical resistance materials	
bare fine resistance wires	BS 1117
conductor sizes, low-voltage industrial switchgear and controlgear	BS EN 60947–1
double electrical insulation	BS 2754
earth-leakage circuit-breakers	
— AC voltage operated	BS 842
— current-operated	BS 4293
— portable RCDs	BS 7071
electric shock protection, construction of electrical equipment	BS 2754
enclosures for high-voltage cable terminations, transformers and reactors	BS 6435
fans, industrial	BS 848
industrial electric plugs	BS EN 60309
industrial machines	BS 2771
marking for low-voltage industrial switchgear/controlgear	BS 6272
metallic	BS 115
resistivity measurement	BS 5714
static electricity	BS 5958
switchgear	BS 5486, 7354, BS EN 60298
test for resistance per unit length	BS 3466
Emergency exits	BS 1125
Emergency lighting	BS 5266
Environmental management systems	BS EN 14001
Ergonomics of the thermal environment	BS ISO 9920
Ergonomic requirements for office work with VDUs	BS EN 29241

protective clothing for users of hand-held chain saws	pr EN 381
PVC moulded safety footwear	BS EN 345, 346
requirements/test methods for safety protective and occupational footwear for professional use	pr EN 344
specification for safety footwear for professional use	pr EN 347
women's protective footwear	BS EN 346
Freight containers	BS 3951
Gaiters and footwear for protection against burns and impact risks in foundries	BS 4676
Gas detector tubes	BS 5343, BS EN 1231
Gas fired hot water boilers	BS 6798
Gas welding equipment	BS EN 731
Glazing	BS 6262
Gloves: medical gloves for single use	BS EN 455
Gloves: rubber gloves for electrical purposes	BS 697
Goggles, industrial/non-industrial use	BS EN 166, 167, 168
Grinding machines	
hand-held electric	BS 2769
pneumatic, portable	BS 4390
spindle noses	BS 1089
Head protection — fire fighters	BS EN 443
Headforms for use in testing protective helmets	BS EN 960
Hearing protectors	BS EN 352
Part 1 Ear Muffs	
Part 2 Ear Plugs	
High visibility warning clothing	pr EN 471
Hoisting slings	BS 6166
alloy steel, chain	BS 3458
chain, welded	BS 6304
high tensile, steel chain	BS 2902
textile	BS 6668
wire rope	BS 1290
Hoists	
construction, safe use	BS 7212
electric, passenger/materials	BS 4465
working platforms	BS 7171
Hose reels with semi-rigid hose	BS EN 671-1
Hose systems with lay-flat hose cloth for fixed fire fighting systems	BS EN 671-2
Hot environments	
estimation of heat stress on the working man	BS EN 27243
Household and similar electrical appliances	BS EN 60335
Industrial gloves	BS EN 374, 388, 407, 420
Industrial safety helmets, firemen's	BS EN 443
Industrial trucks	
hand-operated stillage trucks, dimensions	BS 4337
pallet trucks, dimensions	BS ISO 509
pedals, construction/layout	BS 7178

Insulating material	BS 7737, BS 7831, BS 5626, BS EN 26874, BS EN 60383-2, BS 7822, BS 2844, BS 5691
Ionising radiation	
exposure rate calculation	BS 4094
units of measurement	BS 5775
Jib cranes	
high pedestal and portal	BS 2452
power-driven, mobile	BS 1757
Ladders	
code of practice	BS 5395
permanent for chimneys, high structures	BS 4211
portable aluminium	BS 2037
portable timber	BS 1129
Lamps, artificial daylight, for colour assessment	BS 950
Life jackets	BS EN 394, 396
Lifting chains	
alloy, steel	BS 3113
high tensile steel	BS 1663
safe working on lifts	BS 7255
Lighting systems: automatic change-over contractors for emergency lighting	BS 764
Machine guards	
chain saws	BS 6916
conveyors and elevators	BS 5667
earth-moving equipment	BS EN ISO 3457
woodworking machines	BS 6854
Machine tools	
emergency stop equipment, functional aspects	BS EN 418
noise measurement methods	BS 4813
safeguarding	BS 5304
Machinery, safety of	
drafting and presentation	BS EN 414
ergonomic design principles	BS EN 614-1
hazardous substances emitted by machines	BS EN 626
indication, marking and actuation, requirements for visual, auditory and tactile signals	BS EN 61310-1
indication, marking and actuation, requirements for marking	BS EN 61310-2
minimum gaps to avoid crushing parts of body	BS EN 349
principles and specifications for machinery manufacturers	BS EN 626-1
Machines, vibration	BS 4675–2, 7854
Materials handling	
conveyor belts	BS 5767
freight containers	BS 3951
Mobile cranes	BS 1757
Mobile road construction machinery	BS EN 500
Mortising machines, single chain	BS 4361
Natural fibre ropes	BS EN 698, 701, 1261
cords, lines, twines	BS 6125

Nets, safety	BS EN 1263
code of practice for use of safety nets, containment nets and sheets on construction sites	BS EN 1263
Noise	
airborne, chain saws	BS 6916–6
airborne, earth-moving equipment	BS 6812
airborne, hydraulic transmission systems	BS 5944
effects on hearing handicap	BS 5330
industrial noise, method for rating	BS 4142
industrial premises, measurement	BS 4142
machine tools, measurement methods	BS 4813
sound exposure meters	BS EN 61252
Noise induced hearing loss	
effects of noise exposure	BS 5330
pure tone air conduction threshold audiometry	BS 6655
Occupational safety and health management systems	BS 8800
Office buildings, fire precautions	BS 5588
Office furniture, design/dimensions	BS 5940
Office machines	
electrically energised, safety	BS EN 60950, BS 7002
keyboards, control keys	BS ISO/IEC 9995 (1–8)
noise measurement	BS 7135
Oil burning equipment	BS 799
Oil firing	BS 5410
Open bar gratings – specification	BS 4592–1
Overhead travelling cranes	
power-driven	BS 466
safe use	BS 5744
Packaging	
pictorial marking for handling of goods	BS EN 20780
Particulate air pollutants	
in effluent gases, measurement	BS 3405
in effluent gases, measurement, high accuracy	BS 893
Passenger hoists	
electric, building sites	BS 4465
vehicular	BS 6109
working platforms, mobile, elevating	BS 7171
Patent glazing	BS 5516
Pedestrian guardrails (metal)	BS 7818
Performance of windows	BS 6375
Personal eye protection	
filters for welding and related techniques	BS EN 169
infrared filters	BS EN 171
non-optical test methods	pr EN 168
optical test methods	pr EN 167
specifications	pr EN 166
ultraviolet filters	BS EN 170
vocabulary	pr EN 165
Pipelines, identification marking	BS 1710
Pneumatic tools	
portable grinding machines	BS 4390
Portable fire extinguishers	BS EN 3, BS 7863

Sampling methods
      airborne radioactive materials   BS 5243
      particulate emissions   BS 3405
Scaffolds, code of practice   BS 5973, 5974
Scalp protectors   BS EN 812
Shaft construction and descent   BS 8008
Sound insulation in buildings   BS EN ISO 140
Staging
      lightweight portable timber   BS 1129
      portable aluminium alloy   BS 2037
Stairs, ladders, walkways   BS 5395
Steam boilers
      electric boilers   BS 1894
      safety valves for   BS 6759–1
      welded steel low pressure boilers   BS 855
Step ladders
      portable aluminium alloy   BS 2037
      portable timber   BS 1129
Storage tanks
      carbon steel welded horizontal cylindrical   BS 2594
      vertical steel welded non-refrigerated   BS 2654
      butt-welded shells
Suspended access equipment, permanently installed   BS 6037
Suspended safety chairs   BS 2830
Suspended scaffolds, temporarily installed   BS 5974
Tables, office furniture, ergonomic design   BS 3044
Textile floor coverings   BS 5287
Textile machinery, safety requirements   BS EN ISO 11111
Transportable gas containers
      acetylene containers   BS 6071
      periodic inspection, testing and maintenance   BS 5430
      welded steel tanks for road transport of   BS 7122
      liquefiable gases
Travelling cranes, power-driven jib   BS 357, 5744
Vertical steel welded non-refrigerated storage tanks, BS 2654
  manufacture of
Vibration measurement
      chain saws   BS 6916
      rotating shafts   BS ISO 7919–1
Visual display terminals, ergonomics and design   BS 7179
Water absorption and translucency of china or porcelain BS 5416
Water services, installation, testing and maintenance   BS 6700
Welders, protective clothing   BS EN 470
Window cleaning   BS 8213
Windows, performance of   BS 6375
Woodworking machines   BS 6854
Woodworking noise   BS 7140
Wool and wool blends   BS 1771–1
Working platforms
      mobile, elevating   BS 7171
      permanent, suspended access   BS 6037

Workplace atmospheres
  performance of procedures for measurement of   BS EN 482
  chemical agents
  size definitions for measurement of airborne   BS EN 481
  particulates
Workwear and career wear   BS 5426

Appendix 4

A Summary of Risk Assessment Requirements

Regulations / Features	Management of Health and Safety at Work Regulations 1992 (as amended)	Manual Handling Operations Regulations 1992	Personal Protective Equipment at Work Regulations 1992 (as amended by SI 1998 No 860)	Health and Safety (Display Screen Equipment) Regulations 1992
On whom duties placed	1. Employers 2. Self-employed persons	1. Employers 2. Self-employed persons	1. Employers 2. Self-employed persons	Employers
Identity of those Assessed and Geographical Location	1. Employees (at Work) 2. Persons not in the employer's employment who may face risks arising out of or in connection with the conduct by him of his undertaking 3. New and expectant mothers. The MHSW Regulations ACoP recommends that employers should identify groups of workers particularly at risk such as young and inexperienced workers, new and expectant mothers, night workers, homeworkers, those who work alone and disabled staff.	Employees (at Work) The HSE's Manual Handling Regulations Guidance emphasises that employers must make allowance for those who might be pregnant or have a disability or health problem.	Employees (at Work)	1. Users (Employees who habitually use display screen equipment as a significant part of their normal work) 2. Operators (Self-Employed persons who habitually use display screen equipment as a significant part of their normal work)
Hazards or Risks to be Assessed	All Risks Physical, biological and chemical agents	All manual handling operations (with regard to factors – task, load, working environment, individual capability, other factors – listed in Schedule 1)	Any risks which have not been adequately controlled by other means	Workstations
Purpose of Assessment	To identify measures needed to be taken to comply with the requirements and prohibitions imposed by or under the relevant statutory provisions	To consider the questions set out in column 2 of Schedule 1 pertaining to the factors listed in that Schedule (see above)	To assess risks to health and safety which have not been avoided by other means	To assess workstations for health and safety risks to which users/operators are exposed

Regulations Features	Management of Health and Safety at Work Regulations 1992 (as amended)	Manual Handling Operations Regulations 1992	Personal Protective Equipment at Work Regulations 1992 (as amended by SI 1998 No 860)	Health and Safety (Display Screen Equipment) Regulations 1992
Qualification of Duty	Suitable and Sufficient	Suitable and Sufficient		Suitable and Sufficient
When assessment has to be made		Make assessment where it is not reasonably practicable to avoid the need for employees to undertake any manual handling operations which involve risk of injury	Assessment to be made *before* choosing any personal protective equipment	
Record Provision (a) Threshold (b) Contents (c) How long to be kept?	(a) Five or more employees (b) Significant findings and any group of employees especially at risk			
Review Provision	Review assessment if: – reason to suspect it is no longer valid – there has been a significant change	Review assessment if: – reason to suspect it is no longer valid – there has been a significant change	Review assessment if: – reason to suspect it is no longer valid – there has been a significant change	Review assessment if: – reason to suspect it is no longer valid – there has been a significant change
Action on Review	Changes to assessment to be made where required	Changes to assessment to be made where required	Changes to assessment to be made where required	Changes to assessment to be made where required
Details		Employers shall – take steps to reduce risk of injury to lowest level reasonably practicable – take steps to provide (to employees) general indications, and, where reasonably practicable, precise information on: – weight of load – heaviest side of load where centre of gravity is not central	Assessment to include: – definition of the characteristics which PPE must have in order to be effective against the risks (taking into account any risks which the equipment itself may create) – comparison of the characteristics of the PPE available to the required characteristics	Employers shall reduce risks identified by assessment to lowest extent reasonably practicable

Regulations / Features	Noise at Work Regulations 1989	Control of Substances Hazardous to Health Regulations 1999	Control of Asbestos at Work Regulations 1987 (as amended by SI 1992 No 3068 and SI 1998 No 3235)	Control of Lead at Work Regulations 1998
On whom duties placed	Employers and self-employed persons to ensure competent person makes assessment	1. Employers 2. Self-employed persons 3. Employees	1. Employers 2. Self-employed persons	1. Employers 2. Self-employed persons 3. Employees
Identity of those Assessed and Geographical Location	Employees (at Work)	Employees liable to be exposed to substances hazardous to health by any work. Other persons who may be affected by the employer's work	1. Employees (at Work) 2. Other Persons	1. Employees 2. Other persons likely to be affected by the work. The HSC's ACoP on the Regulations states as well as an employer's own employees these include: – other workers, including another employer's employees/other employees not working/working with lead, i.e. maintenance staff, cleaners etc. – visitors to the work site – families of those exposed to lead at work and who may be affected by lead carried home unintentionally on clothing and footwear
Hazards or Risks to be Assessed	Noise	Any substance hazardous to health	Asbestos	Exposure to lead
Purpose of Assessment	1. To identify which employees are exposed 2. To provide such information, with regard to the noise, as will facilitate compliance with Regs 7,8,9 and 11	To identify risk to enable a decision to be made on the measures to take to prevent or adequately control exposure	1. To identify type of asbestos. The 1998 Amendment Regulations extend the ambit of the 1987 Regulations to include *all* types of asbestos work that may lead to exposure 2. To determine nature and degree of exposure 3. To set out steps to reduce exposure to lowest level reasonably practicable	To allow employer to make a valid decision about whether the work concerned is likely to result in any employees being 'significantly' exposed to lead and to identify the measures needed to prevent or control exposure

Regulations / Features	Noise at Work Regulations 1989	Control of Substances Hazardous to Health Regulations 1999	Control of Asbestos at Work Regulations 1987 (as amended by SI 1992 No 3068 and SI 1998 No 3235)	Control of Lead at Work Regulations 1998
Qualification of Duty	Adequate	Suitable and Sufficient SFAIRP for other persons (whether at work or not) who may be affected by the employer's work 'Due diligence' defence	Adequate	Suitable and Sufficient
When assessment has to be made	Assessment to be made when any employee is likely to be exposed to the first action level or above or to the peak action level or above.	Assessment to be made *before* work is commenced	Assessment to be made *before* work is commenced	Assessment to be made *before* work is commenced
Record Provision	Record to be kept until a further assessment is made	No specific recording requirement *but certain records related to assessment to be kept.*	No specific recording requirement *but certain records related to assessment to be kept.*	No specific recording requirement *but certain records related to assessment to be kept.*
(a) Threshold		*(a)* Health record to be made relating to each employee exposed	(a) Health record to be made relating to each employee exposed	(a) The MHSW Regulations require employers to record the 'significant' finding of the assessment if five or more employees.
(b) Contents		*(b)* At least the information specified in the Appendix to the 1999 General COSHH ACoP	(b) The health record must contain at least the following information: (i) name, sex, date of birth, address and NI No (ii) types of work carried out with asbestos, its location, end and start dates and average duration in hours per week (iii) any work with asbestos prior to present employment, and	(b) The HSC's ACoP and Guidance on the Lead Regulations states that the recorded findings of the assessment should include: (i) the significant hazards identified by the assessment arising from exposure to lead (ii) the existing control measures in place and the extent to which they control the risks (iii) the people who may be affected by these significant risks and hazards, and

Regulations / Features	Noise at Work Regulations 1989	Control of Substances Hazardous to Health Regulations 1999	Control of Asbestos at Work Regulations 1987 (as amended by SI 1992 No 3068 and SI 1998 No 3235)	Control of Lead at Work Regulations 1998
			(iv) dates of medical examination	(iv) where appropriate, the type of protective clothing and respiratory equipment to be issued to employees
(c) How long to be kept?		*(c) To be kept for at least 40 years from last entry*	(c) To be kept for at least 40 years from last entry	(c) The MHSW Regulations do not set a period for retaining recorded assessments, but the ACoP and Guidance (see above) says that they should be kept for a minimum of five years
Review Provision	Review assessment if: – reason to suspect that it is no longer valid – there has been a significant change	Review assessment: – regularly; and forthwith if, – reason to suspect assessment is no longer valid, and/or – there has been a significant change	Review assessment: – regularly; and if, – reason to suspect it is no longer valid – there has been a significant change	The ACoP and Guidance (see above) says assessment should be reviewed if: – evidence to suggest it is no longer valid – significant change in the work
Action on Review	Changes to assessment to be made where required	Changes to assessment to be made where required		Changes to assessment to be made where required
Details		Assessment should include the steps that need to be taken to comply with other requirements of the Regulations		Employer must take steps that need to be taken to comply with other requirements of the Regulations

Appendix 5

A Summary of Requirements for the Provision of Information

Legislation Duties On	The Management of Health and Safety at Work Regulations 1992	The Manual Handling Operations Regulations 1992	Personal Protective Equipment at Work Regulations 1992	Health and Safety (Display Screen Equipment) Regulations 1992
Employer to provide for: own employees	(a) Risks identified by the assessment (b) Preventive and protective measures (c) Procedures in event of serious and imminent danger (d) Competent persons re evacuation (e) Risks notified by other employers	Those undertaking m/h ops (a) General indications, and where reasonably practicable, precise information on: (i) Weight of each load, (ii) Heaviest side	Such information as is adequate and appropriate on: (i) Risks PPE will avoid/limit (ii) Purpose/manner of use, (iii) Action to be taken by employee	For his employees who are 'users' employer must provide information on: – All aspects of health and safety relating to their workstation; – Measures taken to comply with Regulations 2 (risk assessment), 3 (workstations), 4 (breaks), 5 (eyes and eyesight) and 6 (training)
Employer/ self-employed person to provide for other workers	(f) Risks to health and safety arising from undertaking (g) To enable them to identify competent persons re evacuation (h) Any special occ. qualifications or skills needed to work safely (i) Any health surveillance required			For 'users' employed by other employers, and 'operators', at work in his undertaking the employer must provide information on: – All aspects of health and safety relating to their workstation; – Measures taken to comply with Regulations 2 and 3 for 'users' only Regulations 4 and 6(2) (training when workstation modified)
Employer/ self-employed person to provide for other employers, self-employed persons/others	(j) Risks to health and safety arising from undertaking (k) Measures taken in compliance (l) To enable them to identify competent persons re evacuation (m) Any special occ. qualifications or skills needed to work safely (n) Specific features of jobs in relation to health and safety			

Legislation	The Provision and Use of Work Equipment Regulations 1998 (new provisions replacing the revoked Power Press Regulations are incorporated in Part IV of these Regulations)	The Noise at Work Regulations 1992	The Control of Substances Hazardous to Health Regulations 1999	The Control of Asbestos at Work Regulations 1987
Duties On				
Employer to provide for: own employees	Every employer must ensure that all employees using work equipment are provided with adequate health and safety information and, where appropriate, written instructions about the use of such equipment. The employer must also ensure that any employee supervising or managing the use of work equipment has available adequate health and safety information and, as above, where appropriate, written instructions. The information and instructions required above must include information and, where appropriate, written instructions on:	Every employer shall provide any of his employees, who are likely to be exposed to the first action level or above, information on:	(a) Such information, instruction and training as is suitable and sufficient about the risks and precautions including:	Adequate information, instruction and training for:
	(i) All health and safety aspects arising from the use of the work equipment including conditions in which and methods by which it can be used	(i) Risk of damage to hearing	(i) Results of monitoring of exposure and in particular, in the case of any substance hazardous to health for which a maximum exposure limit has been approved, the provision of that information to the employee or his representative	(a) Employees liable to be exposed so they are aware of risks/precautions
	(ii) Any limitations on these uses	(ii) What steps can be taken to minimise risk	(ii) Health surveillance information	
	(iii) Any foreseeable difficulties that could arise	(iii) Steps that the employee must take in order to obtain personal ear protection	(b) Necessary information, instruction and training for person carrying out any work in connection with employer's duties	(b) Employees who carry out work in connection with employer's duties
	(iv) The methods to deal with them	(iv) Employees' obligations		
	(v) Any conclusions to be drawn from experience in using the work equipment			

Legislation	The Provision and Use of Work Equipment Regulations 1998 (new provisions replacing the revoked Power Press Regulations are incorporated in Part IV of these Regulations)	The Noise at Work Regulations 1992	The Control of Substances Hazardous to Health Regulations 1999	The Control of Asbestos at Work Regulations 1987
Duties On				
Employer/self-employed person to provide for other workers	Employers and the self-employed are under a duty to provide information etc. to other workers only in so far as they have control, to *any* extent, of (i) Work equipment (ii) A person at work who uses or supervises or manages the use of work equipment (iii) The way in which such equipment is used at work to the extent of that control. *Note:* the Regulations do *not* apply to a person who has supplied work equipment by way of sale, agreement for sale, or hire purchase agreement		(c) Necessary information, instruction and training for person (whether or not an employee) carrying out any work in connection with employer's duties and information on risks and precautions SFAIRP. These obligations do *not* extend to non-employees unless they are on the premises where the work is being carried out	
Employer/self-employed person to provide for other employers, self-employed persons/others	See above		(d) Necessary information, instruction and training for person carrying out any work in connection with employer's duties and information on risks and precautions SFAIRP, subject to above	

Legislation	The Provision and Use of Work Equipment Regulations 1998 (new provisions replacing the revoked Power Press Regulations are incorporated in Part IV of these Regulations)	The Noise at Work Regulations 1992	The Control of Substances Hazardous to Health Regulations 1999	The Control of Asbestos at Work Regulations 1987
Duties On				
Employer to provide for: own employees	Employer undertaking work liable to expose any employee to lead must provide such information, instruction and training as is suitable and sufficient to enable the employee to know: (a) The risks to health created by such exposure, and (b) The precautions which must be taken That information must include: (i) The results of any monitoring of exposure to lead carried out in accordance with the Regulations (ii) Information on the collective results of any medical surveillance carried out in accordance with the Regulations (iii) An explanation of the significance of (i) and (ii) above	Employer to provide information necessary to ensure his health and enable him to perform any operations in which he is involved with due regard to the health and safety of others	Employer to ensure that the approved poster is kept displayed in a readable condition at an accessible place to the employee while he is at work and must provide the employee with the approved leaflet. Employer has to have information of EMAS office and enforcing authority on poster	
Employer/self-employed person to provide for other workers	An employer/self-employed person is under no duty to provide information etc. to a person other than an employee unless that person is on the premises where the work is being carried out	Self-employed person to ensure that he has information to ensure his and others' health and safety		

Legislation Duties On	Control of Lead at Work Regulations 1998	Dangerous Substances in Harbour Areas Regulations 1987	Health and Safety Information for Employees Regulations 1989 (as amended by SI 1995 No 2923)	Carriage of Dangerous Goods by Road Regulations 1996 (as amended by SI 1999 No 303)
Employer/ self-employed person to provide for other employers, self-employed persons/others	See above	Operator to provide persons present on the berth with information to ensure their and others' health and safety.		Consignor of dangerous substances to supply sufficient accurate written information to enable the operator to: (a) comply with his duties under these Regs; and (b) be aware of the hazards created by the substance to health and safety (c) adequate information about identity, quantity and nature of hazards created by substance information to operator. This must be accurate, sufficient and so far as possible in writing. Operator to keep information for at least three months after completion of journey and must have information before carriage

| Legislation

Duties On	Carriage of Dangerous Goods by Road (Driver Training) Regulations 1996	Safety Representatives and Safety Committees Regulations 1977 (as amended by SI 1999 No 860) and Health and Safety (Consultation with Employees) Regulations 1996	The Health and Safety (First-aid) Regulations 1981	The Pressure Systems and Transportable Gas Containers Regulations 1989
Employer to provide for: own employees		To allow safety reps to carry out inspections to allow access to relevant documents to make available all the information necessary to allow fulfilment of functions	Inform his employees of the arrangements that have been made in connection with the provision of first-aid, including the location of equipment, facilities and personnel	
Employer/ self-employed person to provide for other workers				
Employer/ self-employed person to provide for other employers, self-employed persons/others		Safety representatives to receive information from inspectors		(a) Written information concerning modification or repair – for user of system immediately after modification or repair (b) Any person who designs, or supplies, pressure system or components thereof – sufficient written information concerning design, construction, examination, operation and maintenance with the design, or with the pressure system/article

Legislation / Duties On	The Work in Compressed Air Regulations 1996	The Chemicals (Hazard Information and Packaging for Supply) Regulations 1994 (as amended)	Carriage of Dangerous Goods by Road Regulations 1996 (as amended by SI 1999 No 303)	Carriage of Explosives by Road Regulations 1996
Employer to provide for: own employees	The 'compressed air contractor', as defined, is to ensure that adequate information etc. is given to *all* persons working in compressed air on the risks arising from such work and the precautions to be taken. The HSE Guidance to the 1996 Regulations stresses that the provision of information etc. in such circumstances may be carried out by anyone competent to do so, but the compressed air contractor is responsible for ensuring that it is carried out to standard		Sufficient accurate written information to enable the operator to: (a) comply with his duties under these Regs; and (b) be aware of the hazards created by the substance to health and safety Adequate information about identity, quantity and nature of hazards created by substance	The following information in writing at the start of the journey: (a) in the case of classified explosives the Division and Compatibility Group of each type of explosive carried; (b) the net mass of each type of explosive carried (c) whether, in the case of explosives in Compatibility Group C, D or G, the explosives carried are explosive substances or explosive articles (d) name and address of consignor, operator and consignee (e) information to enable driver and attendant to know nature of danger and action to be taken in an emergency
Employer/ self-employed person to provide for other workers	See above			
Employer/ self-employed person to provide for other employers, self-employed persons/others	See above	Supplier of dangerous chemicals to communicate with recipients information on the hazards presented		

Legislation	The Packaging of Explosives for Carriage Regulations 1991		
Duties On			
Employer to provide for: own employees			
Employer / self-employed person to provide for other workers			
Employer / self-employed person to provide for other employers, self-employed persons/others	All packages of explosives of net mass not exceeding 400kg shall be marked with the UN mark allocated by the competent authority for that design type of packaging		

Summary of the Requirements for Training/Instruction and Consultation

Legislation Duties On	Management of Health and Safety at Work Regulations 1992	Manual Handling Operations Regulations 1992	Personal Protective Equipment at Work Regulations 1992	Health and Safety (Display Screen Equipment) Regulations 1992
Employer provides training/instruction for employees	Adequate health and safety training: on recruitment on being exposed to new/increased risks e.g. on transfer/change of responsibilities; new work equipment; new technology; new system of work		Adequate and appropriate training about risks the ppe will avoid/limit; purposes of ppe; action to be taken by employee	Employer shall provide adequate health and safety training in use of workstation to: – his employees who are 'users' on date of coming into force of the regulations – his employees about to become users employers also shall provide such training to employee 'users' when the organisation of their workstation is substantially modified Current users of DSE. Adequate health and safety training in the use of workstation, and whenever organisation of workstation modified
Employer provides training/instruction for specified employees/others	Employees who have access to any area (where such access is subject to restriction): adequate instruction for evacuation procedures			

Legislation Duties On	The Provision and Use of Work Equipment Regulations 1998	The Noise at Work Regulations 1989	The Control of Substances Hazardous to Health Regulations 1999	The Control of Asbestos at Work Regulations 1987
Employer provides training/ instruction for employees	All persons who use work equipment: – adequate training for purposes of health and safety inc. training in the methods of use, risks and precautions. For employers' obligations regarding instruction see Provision of Information above	Every employer shall provide each of his employees, who is likely to be exposed to the first action level or above, instruction and training on: (i) risk of damage to hearing (ii) what steps can be taken to minimise risk (iii) steps that employee must take in order to obtain personal ear protectors (iv) employees' obligations	Employer to provide – (a) such information, instruction and training as is suitable and sufficient about the risks to health created by exposure to substances hazardous to health and the precautions which should be taken. Without prejudice to the above the information must include: (i) information on the results of any monitoring of exposure at the workplace in accordance with the Regulations, and (ii) in the case of any substance hazardous to health and for which a maximum exposure limit has been approved, the employee or his representative must be informed if the results of that monitoring show that the maximum exposure limit has been exceeded (iii) information on the collective results of any health surveillance undertaken in accordance with the Regulations (b) Necessary information, instruction and training for persons carrying out any work in accordance with the employer's duties (c) Necessary information, instruction and training for person (whether or not an employee) carrying out any work in connection with employer's duties, subject to the proviso that the obligation does not extend to non-employees unless those persons are on the premises where the work is being carried out	
Employer provides training/ instruction for specified employees/ others	Obligations as above. The HSC's ACoP and Guidance on the Regulations emphasises that 'training and proper supervision of "young people" is particularly important because of their relative immaturity and unfamiliarity with the working environment'			Adequate information, instruction and training for – (a) employees liable to be exposed so they are aware of risks/precautions (b) who carry out work in connection with employer's duties

Legislation Duties On	The Control of Lead at Work Regulations 1998	The Dangerous Substances in Harbour Areas Regulations 1987	The Health and Safety Information for Employees Regulations 1989	Health and Safety (Consultation with Employees) Regulations 1996
Employer provides training/ instruction for employees	Employer undertaking work liable to expose employee to lead must provide employee with such information, instruction and training as is suitable and sufficient for the employee to know: (i) the risk to health created by such exposure, and (ii) the precautions that must be taken	Employer and self-employed person to provide instruction, training and supervision necessary to ensure his health and safety and to enable him to perform any operations in which he is involved with due regard to the health and safety of others.		Employer to consult either: (a) with employees directly, or (b) with representatives of employee safety in non-unionised workforces, and to allow time-off for training.
Employer provides training/ instruction for specified employees/ others	The above obligation subsists so long as the other persons are on the premises where the work is being carried out	Operator to provide instruction, as necessary, to persons present on the berth to ensure their health and safety.		

Legislation	Carriage of Dangerous Goods by Road (Driver Training) Regulations 1996	The Safety Representatives and Safety Committees Regulations 1977 and Health and Safety (Consultation with Employees) Regulations 1996	The Work in Compressed Air Regulations 1996	Construction (Health, Safety and Welfare) Regulations 1996
Duties On				
Employer provides training/ instruction for employees			The 'compressed air contractor', as defined, to provide adequate training on risks and precautions. See entry for Regulations under Provision of Information	Adequate training of employees to avoid acts causing injury or damage
Employer provides training/ instruction for specified employees/ others	Operator must ensure driver of vehicle has received adequate instruction and training. This includes understanding his duties under other relevant h & s legislation	Allow time off with pay for training of safety reps (as may be reasonable); consult with safety reps and with other trade unions reps over establishment of safety committees; consult safety reps on: instruction of measures which may affect h & s of employees – arrangements for appointing those who give health and safety assistance – health and safety information provided to workforce – planning and organisation of health and safety training for employee – health and safety implications of new technologies		

Legislation	Packaging of Explosives for Carriage Regulations 1991		
Duties On			
Employer provides training/ instruction for employees			
Employer provides training/ instruction for specified employees/ others			

Table of Cases

This table is referenced to paragraph numbers in the work.

Table of Statutes

Table of Statutory Instruments

Index

References are to sections and paragraph numbers of this book.